20-95

Strateg

Y

McGraw-Hill Series in Management

CONSULTING EDITORS

Fred Luthans
Keith Davis

Arnold and Feldman: Organizational Behavior
Bartol and Martin: Management
Bernardin and Russell: Human Resource Management: An Experiential Approach
Boone and Bowen: Great Writings in Management and Organizational Behavior
Boone and Kurtz: Management
Bovée, Thill, Wood, and Dovel: Management
Cascio: Managing Human Resources: Productivity, Quality of Work Life, Profits
Certo and Peter: Selected Cases in Strategic Management
Certo and Peter: Strategic Management: A Focus on Process
Certo and Peter: Strategic Management: Concepts and Applications
Daughtrey and Ricks: Contemporary Supervision: Managing People and Technology
Davidson and de la Torre: Managing the Global Corporation: Case Studies in Strategy and Management
Dess and Miller: Strategic Management
Dilworth: Operations Management: Design, Planning, and Control for Manufacturing and Services
Dilworth: Production and Operations Management
Dobler, Burt, and Lee: Purchasing and Materials Management: Text and Cases
Feldman and Arnold: Managing Individual and Group Behavior in Organizations
Frederick, Post, and Davis: Business and Society: Management, Public Policy, Ethics
Hodgetts and Luthans: International Management
Hoffman and Moore: Business Ethics: Readings and Cases in Corporate Morality
Jauch and Glueck: Business Policy and Strategic Management
Jauch and Glueck: Strategic Management and Business Policy
Jauch and Townsend: Cases in Strategic Management and Business Policy
Katz and Kochan: An Introduction to Collective Bargaining and Industrial Relations
Koontz and Weihrich: Essentials of Management
Kopelman: Managing Productivity in Organizations: A Practical, People-Oriented Perspective
Kuriloff, Hemphill, and Cloud: Starting and Managing the Small Business
Levin, Rubin, Stinson, and Gardner: Quantitative Approaches to Management
Luthans: Organizational Behavior
Luthans and Thompson: Contemporary Readings in Organizational Behavior
Miles: Theories of Management: Implications for Organizational Behavior and Development

Miles and Snow: Organizational Strategy, Structure, and Process
Mills: Labor-Management Relations
Mitchell and Larson: People in Organizations: An Introduction to Organizational Behavior
Molander: Responsive Capitalism: Case Studies in Corporate Social Conduct
Monks: Operations Management: Theory and Problems
Newstrom and Davis: Organizational Behavior: Human Behavior at Work
Newstrom and Davis: Organizational Behavior: Readings and Exercises
Pearce and Robinson: Corporate Strategies: Readings from *Business Week*
Porter and McKibbin: Management Education and Development: Drift or Thrust into the 21st Century?
Prasow and Peters: Arbitration and Collective Bargaining: Conflict Resolution in Labor Relations
Quick and Quick: Organizational Stress and Preventive Management
Rue and Holland: Strategic Management: Concepts and Experiences
Rugman, Lecraw, and Booth: International Business: Firm and Environment
Sayles: Leadership: Managing in Real Organizations
Schlesinger, Eccles, and Gabarro: Managing Behavior in Organizations: Text, Cases and Readings
Schroeder: Operations Management: Decision Making in the Operations Function
Steers and Porter: Motivation and Work Behavior
Steiner: Industry, Society, and Change: A Casebook
Steiner and Steiner: Business, Government, and Society: A Managerial Perspective, Text and Cases
Steinhoff and Burgess: Small Business Management Fundamentals
Sutermeister: People and Productivity
Walker: Human Resource Strategy
Weihrich: Management Excellence: Productivity through MBO
Weihrich and Koontz: Management: A Global Perspective
Werther and Davis: Human Resources and Personnel Management
Wofford, Gerloff, and Cummins: Organizational Communications: The Keystone to Managerial Effectiveness
Yoffie: International Trade and Competition

Strategic Management

Gregory G. Dess
University of Texas at Arlington

Alex Miller
University of Tennessee

McGRAW-HILL, INC.

New York St. Louis San Francisco Auckland Bogotá Caracas
Lisbon London Madrid Mexico Milan Montreal New Delhi
Paris San Juan Singapore Sydney Tokyo Toronto

STRATEGIC MANAGEMENT
International Editions 1993

1 2 3 4 5 6 7 8 9 0 KKP KKP 9 8 7 6 5 4 3

This book was set in Stempel Garamond by Progressive Typographers, Inc.
The editors were Lynn Richardson, Dan Alpert, Cecilia Gardner, and Curt Berkowitz;
the design was done by Circa 86, Inc.; the production supervisor was Al Rihner.

Library of Congress Cataloging-in-Publication Data

Dess, Gregory G.
Strategic management / Gregory G. Dess, Alex Miller.
p. cm. - (McGraw-Hill series in management)
Includes bibliographical references and index.
ISBN 0-07-016569-6
1. Strategic planning. 2. Strategic planning - Case studies.
I. Miller, Alex, (date). II. Title. III. Series.
HD30.28.D474 1993
658.4'012-dc20 92-17467

When ordering this title, use ISBN 0-07-112594-9

Printed in Singapore

CONTENTS IN BRIEF

CONTENTS

Cases

PREFACE

With the fundamental changes now taking place in business competition, a firm's success in the coming century will depend on equally fundamental changes in its managers. Today's business environment is one of global competition, scarce resources, rapid technological changes, constantly changing markets, increasing demands for social responsibility, and shrinking organizations. In such a world, traditional concepts of strategic planning are still necessary, but no longer sufficient, for success. Today's competitive environment requires new concepts for strategic management, as well as broad-based, organization-wide participation in the strategic management process. Given the new challenges that organizations are facing, they are finding it essential for every manager to adopt a strategic perspective. In short, today's environment requires that strategic management be viewed as a basic skill for *all* managers rather than the specialty of a particular function or organizational level. This book is a response to the new business environment and the requirements it places on organizations and on those who manage them.

THE CHALLENGES OF TEACHING STRATEGIC MANAGEMENT

A successful strategic management text will help the instructor meet the challenges of three sets of conflicting student expectations:

1. *Although students expect this upper-level capstone course to be founded on solid theoretical principles, they also expect material in a business policy course to be relevant.* The textbook should draw upon a broad range of rigorous academic research. However, it must consistently translate this research into practical information for students. Relevance should be constantly reinforced throughout the text with richly detailed examples, input from managers who have proven their skills as strategists, and cases that illustrate the concepts in practice. More than any other, the strategic management course demands that rigor be married to relevance, and the textbook used must reflect this combination of virtues.

2. *Although students expect this course to be integrative and fairly complex, the material must still be accessible.* A strategic management text should not be watered down, but the material must be presented in a style that students find engaging. Difficult concepts must be clearly and carefully explained. The content must flow in a straightforward and logical sequence. Simple examples should accompany all central points. The material should stretch students' thinking without being out of their reach.

3. *Although a course in strategic management is expected to address the issues facing general managers at the top of the organization, students must understand that the material it presents will apply to their very first job.* Strategic management is not a set of procedures for top managers, nor is it a specialized function for high-level staff. It is a set of skills and a way of thinking that must be developed and applied by all managers, regardless of their positions in the organization. The text and cases must explain this central idea and show in detail what it implies for the practice of management.

FEATURES OF THIS TEXT

To address these challenges, *Strategic Management* offers the following specific features:

- *Sound treatment of all the basics.* The text offers thorough coverage of all the elements of strategic management that have proven their value through academic research and managerial experience.

- *Integrated coverage of the most topical subjects.* In addition to the standard topics, we have integrated material on several current topics that students should understand, including cross-functional teams, competing on speed, downsizing, flattened organization structures, empowerment, total quality management, customer-driven strategies, self-directed work groups, corporate entrepreneurship, and environmental management.

- *In-depth coverage of content areas encouraged by the AACSB.* On the basis of input from industry, the accrediting board encourages greater coverage of the following topics:

  1. *Global competition and international management.* Chapter 7 is devoted to these subjects. Beyond this chapter-length treatment, strategy formulation at the international level is tightly integrated throughout the text with other formulation material and with material on strategy implementation. Application boxes numbered 5.1, 7.1, 7.2, 7.3, 7.4, 9.5, 11.2, and 11.4, as well as thirteen of the cases, either feature foreign firms or stress international management and global competition.

  2. *Ethics and social responsibility.* These topics represent a major portion of Chapter 11, and additional treatment is found in examples throughout the text. Application boxes 3.5, 6.1, 7.3, 8.3, 10.1, 11.5, and 11.6, and nine of the cases, are either focused on ethics and social responsibility or include significant material on these topics.

  3. *Entrepreneurship and small business.* Throughout the text we provide extensive consideration of how strategic management is applicable in small businesses. Application boxes 1.1, 1.2, 2.1, 3.2, 6.4, 8.2, and twelve of the cases, either focus directly on small businesses or illustrate principles in entrepreneurship or new corporate ventures.

- *More examples than any other book on the market.* We present fifty-eight Application boxes (about five per chapter), each describing a real-world situation. In addition, every major point made in the text is illustrated by at least one example.

- *Exclusive interviews with leading executives.* We interviewed some of the strongest managers at premier firms so that student readers could hear from people who actually apply the concepts of strategic management to their own work in the real world. Each chapter opens with one of these interviews—a voice of experience speaking on the relevance and portent of the material we cover in that chapter.

- *Case selection.* We offer thirty-six class-tested cases, ten of which we ourselves wrote. Students will find here a rich mixture of classic and contemporary cases involving small and large businesses, formulation and implementation issues, manufacturing and service examples, and domestic and international firms.

- *Industry series.* Fourteen of the cases are grouped into five industry-specific series, which provide a richer understanding of issues than is possible from a normal grouping of stand-alone cases. These industry series allow students to revisit industries throughout the course so that they can relate what they first learned about strategic analysis to what they have studied in strategy formulation to what they are learning about strategy implementation.

AN INTEGRATED FRAMEWORK

The text and cases as a whole are aimed at providing students with a consistent framework across strategic analysis, strategy formulation, and strategy implementation. Students can tie various concepts together into a whole, instead of just wandering through a loose series of topics. One integrating concept we use is value. We begin with a treatment of the value chain in Part I, on strategic analysis. In Part II, on strategy formulation, we present competitive advantages based on delivering superior customer value as the foundation for all superior strategies; the students see how the value chain can explain the establishment of such competitive advantages. We also stress how strategy formulation at all four levels (business, functional, corporate, and international) should be focused on customer value in order to build the strongest possible competitive advantages for the firm. In Part III, on strategy implementation, we describe how businesses can be organized in order to facilitate the pursuit of competitive advantages based on customer value and management of the value chain. Numerous cases illustrate these concepts, documenting the importance of value in the practice of management.

Other integrative themes include stakeholders, global competition, combining different forms of competitive advantage, empowerment, ethics, and strategic management in smaller businesses. Again, our goal in emphasizing such themes throughout the text and cases is to provide students with an integrated framework for strategic thinking rather than a laundry list of disconnected issues.

THE STRONGEST INSTRUCTOR'S PACKAGE AVAILABLE

Our goal was to set new standards of excellence in the development of the ancillary package, which consists of:

- A two-volume instructor's manual, including teaching notes for each chapter and case, a comprehensive test bank, experiential exercises, and transparency masters
- Overhead transparencies
- Computerized test bank
- Supplementary videos
- Multiple software options

ACKNOWLEDGMENTS

This book is a result of contributions from one of the strongest teams of individuals with whom we have ever had the pleasure of working. We wish to acknowledge the especially important contributions made by the many individuals who reviewed earlier drafts of our chapters:

Gaber Abou El Enein, Mankato State University
Cliff Barbee, Houston Baptist University
George B. Davis, Cleveland State University
Peter S. Davis, Memphis State University
Alex DeNoble, San Diego State University
Marc J. Dollinger, Indiana State University
William B. Gartner, Georgetown University
Jerry L. Geisler, California State University, Stanislaus
Dawn Harris, Loyola University of Chicago
Frank Hoy, University of Texas at El Paso
Donald Huffmire, University of Connecticut
John Kilpatrick, Idaho State University
Bruce Kogut, University of Pennsylvania, The Wharton School
Paul Larson, University of Montana
Pamela S. Lewis, University of Central Florida
William Litzinger, University of Texas
Dan Lockhardt, University of Kentucky
Martin K. Marsh, California State University, Bakersfield
Tom Morris, University of San Diego
Ernest Nordtvedt, Loyola University
Hugh M. O'Neill, University of Connecticut
Joseph G. P. Paolillo, University of Mississippi
Michael W. Pitts, Virginia Commonwealth University
Jesus A. Ponce de Leon, Southern Illinois University
John E. Prescott, University of Pittsburgh
Richard Reed, Washington State University
William W. Sandberg, University of South Carolina
Marshall Schminke, Creighton University
James C. Spee, California State University, Fullerton
Ken G. Smith, University of Maryland at College Park
Harriet Stephenson, Seattle University
Arus Tajul, Kent State University
Marilyn Taylor, University of Kansas
Arieh A. Ullmann, State University of New York at Binghamton
Michael C. White, University of Tulsa
Carolyn Woo, Purdue University

We are also very grateful to the following executives, who were gracious enough to provide us with their time for the interviews that begin all of our chapters:

Nolan D. Archibald, Chairman, President, and Chief Executive Officer, Black & Decker Corporation
Deborah A. Coleman, Vice President for Information Systems and Technology, Apple Computer, Inc.
Robert L. Crandall, Chairman and Chief Executive Officer, American Airlines
R. Michael Franz, President and Chief Executive Officer, Murata Business Systems
Major General Jeffery D. Kahla, U.S. Air Force
Charles F. Knight, Chief Executive Officer, Emerson Electric Company
Bobbie A. Koehler, Merchandising Manager, Ford Division, Ford Motor Company
Ralph S. Larsen, Chairman and Chief Executive Officer, Johnson & Johnson
Judy C. Lewent, Vice President for Finance and Chief Financial Officer, Merck & Co., Inc.
B. Joseph Messner, President, Bushnell Division, Bausch & Lomb
Anthony J. F. O'Reilly, President and Chief Executive Officer, H. J. Heinz Company
Addison Barry Rand, Corporate Vice President and President of Marketing, Xerox Corporation

The support from McGraw-Hill has been absolutely outstanding throughout the long process of converting our first concepts for a book into the finished product. Special thanks go to Dan Alpert, Curt Berkowitz, Cecilia Gardner, Becky Kohn, Kathy Loy, Margaret Metz, Josh Pincus, Valerie Raymond, Lynn Richardson, and Alan Sachs.

Our colleagues and students deserve much credit for exercising our minds, sharpening our reasoning, and forcing us to clarify our presentation of complex material. Special thanks to Cliff Bowman and Gerry Johnson for lunchtime debates at The Cock. Other groups and colleagues include the Strategic Management faculty and doctoral students at the University of Texas at Arlington (Dave Arnott, Andy Kotulic, Tom Lumpkin, Stephanie Newport [now at Creighton University], Joe Picken, Richard Priem, Abdul Rasheed, and Joe Rosenstein), the Strategic Management Group at Tennessee, the Strategy Group at the Cranfield Institute of Technology, and the M.B.A. Core Team at Tennessee.

One colleague who must be singled out because of our extraordinarily high debt of gratitude is Abdul Rasheed. Abdul not only coauthored Chapters 2 and 3 and two cases but also devoted countless hours to providing valued input on the other chapters and instructor materials. How he maintained a cheerful and enthusiastic demeanor through all the many revisions and constant interruptions we'll never know, but we're afraid to ask! He's truly an exemplary colleague and wonderful friend.

Finally, our greatest debt of gratitude goes to our families for their patience and support. We dedicate this work to Greg's wife, Margie, and parents, William and Mary Dess, and the Lick Skillet Gang in Tennessee: Gus, Brando, Eagl'Eye, Wyndow, and Bubba 3.

Gregory G. Dess
Alex Miller

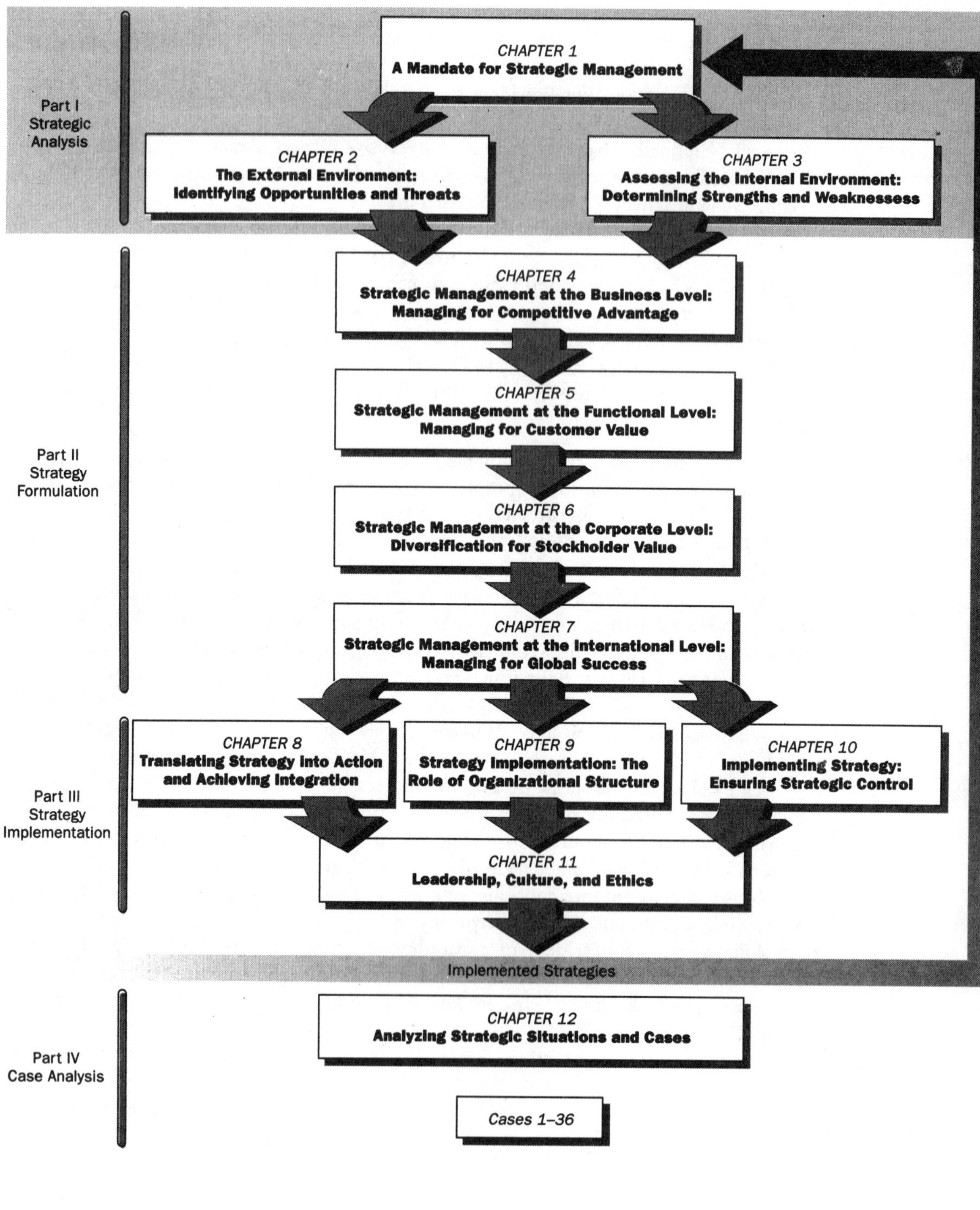
Part I
Strategic
Analysis
CHAPTER 1
A Mandate for Strategic Management
CHAPTER 2
The External Environment:
Identifying Opportunities and Threats
CHAPTER 3
Assessing the Internal Environment:
Determining Strengths and Weaknessess
Part II
Strategy
Formulation
CHAPTER 4
Strategic Management at the Business Level:
Managing for Competitive Advantage
CHAPTER 5
Strategic Management at the Functional Level:
Managing for Customer Value
CHAPTER 6
Strategic Management at the Corporate Level:
Diversification for Stockholder Value
CHAPTER 7
Strategic Management at the International Level:
Managing for Global Success
Part III
Strategy
Implementation
CHAPTER 8
Translating Strategy into Action
and Achieving Integration
CHAPTER 9
Strategy Implementation: The
Role of Organizational Structure
CHAPTER 10
Implementing Strategy:
Ensuring Strategic Control
CHAPTER 11
Leadership, Culture, and Ethics
Implemented Strategies
Part IV
Case Analysis
CHAPTER 12
Analyzing Strategic Situations and Cases
Cases 1–36

PART I

Strategic Analysis

CHAPTER 1

A Mandate for Strategic Management

Anyone who expects to be a successful manager in the future must study strategic management today. The world has become such a complex and fast-moving marketplace that firms can no longer succeed when only a few managers or staff experts are involved in formulating and implementing strategies. In leading firms throughout a wide range of industries, managers and other employees across all the traditional functional areas and organizational levels are taking on new strategic responsibilities. Their involvement may require that they contribute their expertise to what we will describe as the formal strategic planning processes. Or, it may involve them less formally in the day-to-day process of continually evolving a strategy. In either case, managers in any functional specialty must understand basic strategic management concepts.

This first chapter consists of three parts. First, we will define some fundamental concepts, such as strategy and strategic management. Then we will describe the major components of the strategic management process through a detailed overview of the remaining chapters of the text. In the final section we will describe a hierarchy of strategic goals (vision, mission, and objectives) which is the first, and perhaps most critical, component of the strategic management process.

After reading this chapter, you will understand:

- Why broad, organizationwide involvement in the strategic management process is necessary
- Basic terms used to discuss strategic management
- The major components of strategic management and where they are covered in this text
- The role of formal strategic planning and the incremental nature of strategic management
- The need for the "constancy of purpose" best achieved through a widely understood and accepted vision, mission statement, and set of strategic objectives

EXECUTIVE INTERVIEW

Robert L. Crandall
Chairman and Chief Executive Officer
American Airlines

Robert L. Crandall became chairman and chief executive officer of both AMR Corporation and American Airlines in 1985. He has been president since 1980 and a member of American's board of directors since 1976. Under his leadership, American has more than doubled in size to become the largest airline outside the former Soviet Union. American is the nation's most profitable airline and one of the most innovative. Crandall's accomplishments have won him wide recognition, including commendations from publications such as *Business Week, Financial World, Wall Street Transcript*, and *Aviation Week & Space Technology*.

What is the role of strategic management at American Airlines?

Strategic planning—at American and every other well-run corporation—determines the acquisition and allocation of assets. By itself, it is nothing. It must be carefully integrated with tactical management—that is, the excellent execution of day-to-day responsibilities—to achieve our strategic goals.

At American, long-term planning is extremely important because the assets we use are both long lived and very expensive. Airplanes, other equipment, airport terminals, maintenance bases, and other facilities are all expensive assets with extremely long life cycles; hence, it is important that their acquisition and development be carefully planned. The same can be said of the scarce resource of international routes, which are hard won when acquired through governmental channels, and costly when purchased from other airlines.

American's management process assigns probable economic values to alternative long-term courses of action—one aircraft versus another, one route opportunity versus another. From the possible combinations, we then construct a long-term plan likely to yield a satisfactory return on investment. Subsequently, the process assigns responsibility for execution of the strategic plan and for the effective use—the tactical management—of the assets that strategic planning has provided.

What is the role of middle- and lower-level managers in the strategic management process of American Airlines?

Airlines are highly centralized businesses. Because the company's principal assets (airplanes) are highly mobile and because the company, as a worldwide retailer, wishes to present a common face to consumers everywhere, strategic planning is highly centralized. The principal function of lower- and middle-level management, both line and staff, is the best possible execution of policies planned by senior management.

Although middle- and lower-level managers have a very limited role in strategic planning, we work hard at encouraging them—along with all frontline employees—to find ways to improve the quality of the execution of the tactics agreed upon to achieve our strategic goals.

What is the importance of managers throughout the organization having a shared vision of American Airlines' mission and objectives?

It is extremely important that managers throughout the corporation have a shared vision of American's mission and objectives.

While planning at American is highly centralized, execution is, necessarily, highly decentralized. Moreover, the airline is extraordinarily labor intensive. The customer's primary impression of the corporation is created by the frontline employee who must, in turn, receive consistent training and guidance from middle- and first-level management. Thus, we can appropriately represent the company to the customer only if lower and intermediate levels of management have a clear understanding of the company's goals and objectives, and a real commitment to perfect execution of the tactical steps required to realize those goals and objectives.

How can a CEO shape the corporate vision?

The CEO's role is to synthesize, from internal and external sources, the company's long-term goals and objectives, which become, in their composite form, the company's vision. The CEO must also play a major role in supporting that vision both by example and by internally communicating its nature and importance.

WHY IS STRATEGIC MANAGEMENT IMPORTANT?

If you are like most of the students who use this text, you have already had a fair amount of training in a functional specialty, such as operations, human resource management, marketing, accounting, finance, and so forth. There is an important distinction between strategic management and these functions. Strategic management is not a single function or task, limited to a single staff group known as "strategic planners." Rather, it is a set of managerial skills that must be used *throughout* the organization. Strategic management orchestrates the contributions of the various functions: it provides a guiding force that integrates the efforts of specialists throughout the organization. The following points explain how developing a strategic management perspective helps one to capitalize on expertise in an individual function.

Strategic Management Is Aimed toward Achieving Organizationwide Goals

Effective managers have a clear understanding of their organization's goals. Functional specialists who limit their outlooks to individual functional areas run the risk of achieving a local maximum while avoiding a global optimum. In other words, they may do what is best for their particular specialty, rather than what is best for the entire business.[1] To understand how the needs of the firm differ from the needs of the single functional area, a manager must become involved in the organization's overall strategic management process.

Strategic Management Considers a Broad Range of Stakeholders

Organizations must meet the needs of various constituencies, such as customers, suppliers, employees, owners, and the public at large. We call these groups *stakeholders,* because they each have something at stake in the success or failure of the organization. Firms and stakeholders can impact each other in various ways, as illustrated in Exhibit 1.1. Functional

EXHIBIT 1.1
Some Relationships between a Firm and Its Stakeholders

Stakeholder Group	*Firm Impacts Stakeholders*	*Stakeholders Impact Firm*
Customers	Quality of products and/or services, warranty service, pricing, consumer education, product safety	Comparison shopping, consumer boycotts, product liability, lawsuits, word-of-mouth advertising
Employees	On-the-job safety, quality of work life, compensation, benefits	Strikes, productivity, vandalism, theft, work force commitment
Community	Creation of jobs, contribution to local tax revenues, pollution, funding for local charities, community projects	Education of work force, municipal services, zoning for expansion, right of way to highways and rail lines
Stockholders	Stock-price appreciation, dividend yields, risk of investment, nonfinancial returns to investing	Stock-price effects on average cost of capital, stockholders' votes on major issues facing corporation

specialists tend to focus on serving individual stakeholders, rather than balancing the needs of all stakeholders. For example, human resource managers may focus on employees, purchasing managers on suppliers, and sales managers on customers. But, for an organization to flourish, management, throughout its ranks, must understand how managers' decisions affect the various stakeholders involved.[2] The strategic perspective entails simultaneous consideration of all stakeholder groups so that reasoned tradeoffs are possible. We will return to a discussion of the importance of stakeholders later in this chapter.

Strategic Management Entails Multiple Time Horizons

Managers cannot ignore the need to maintain the long-run viability of their organization, though they must also be aware of the short-run ramifications of anything they do. Consequently, strategic management requires constant shifting back and forth between long-run and short-run thinking.[3] Managers of functional areas tend to focus on short-term issues alone, but if they can broaden their time frame perspectives, they will understand how to position their functional discipline to make the best contribution both today and tomorrow.

Strategic Management Is Concerned with Both Efficiency and Effectiveness

The difference between these two concepts is sometimes explained as "doing things right" (efficiency) versus "doing the right things" (effectiveness).[4] Managers who take a narrow view of their responsibilities often concentrate the majority of their efforts on improving the efficiency of their own functional area, while neglecting the organization's overall operations. By working so hard at doing things right, they may not consider whether they are working on the right thing. The strategic perspective encourages a balanced emphasis on both dimensions.

WHAT IS A STRATEGY?

To understand strategic management, one must first understand what a strategy is. We will distinguish between two types of strategies. Strategies that managers propose, design, and expect are *intended strategies,* and those that actually materialize in time are *realized strategies.*[5]

Intended Strategies

As illustrated in Application 1.1 and in Exhibit 1.2, intended strategies consist of three major components: goals, policies, and plans.

Goals

A typical organization has some goals that are very broad, and some that are very narrow.[6] For example, at the broadest level, your personal goals may include leading a happy, fulfilling, and long life, but you may also have a much narrower goal of making an A in this course. In order to reach your broad goal, you must first achieve a long series of narrower

Application 1.1

Goals, Policies, and Plans in a Small Business

In 1984, John Hillidge became managing director of Export Packaging Services, Ltd. EPS was a 30-year-old English company which specialized in packing unassembled automobiles for shipping and assembly in countries outside the United Kingdom. (Exporting unassembled cars entails lower duties and trade tariffs.) When Hillidge took over the company, the British automobile was suffering from weak worldwide demand, and EPS, solely dependent upon U.K. auto international sales, was losing over £250,000 per year and facing bankruptcy. Hillidge led the company in formulating a strategic plan that included the following three major elements.

Goals

Managers determined a range of goals extending from the very broad to the very specific. In developing a mission statement for the business, managers concluded that they were not really in the car-packing business, but the logistics management business. They defined logistics management as "taking responsibility on behalf of a customer for the dedicated management and control of a customer's material flow to agreed performance standards." More focused goals dealt with specific performance targets like "increase the annual level of contributions to overhead by £500,000 over three years."

Policies

In determining how they could best meet the goals they had established, managers formulated a number of policies to set limits and establish guidelines for important practices. For instance, one policy stated that "direct incentive schemes are not favoured because of their potential effect on the quality of service." Another stated that "we do not have a standard product or service, but rather seek to provide precisely what each individual customer requires."

Plans

Managers also developed a number of plans that helped identify the means to achieve their goals. One plan was "to establish over the next three years a broad base in terms of both market segment and type of service." Another was "to increase dependence of current customers on EPS services." These fairly general statements were supported by a number of more detailed plans, such as what specific customers to target in their market expansion. Seven specific customer attributes were identified, including membership in a growth industry, willingness to sign contracts for 3 to 5 years, and warehousing needs of 15,000 to 30,000 square feet.

The goals, policies, and plans the managers formulated combined to create a successful basis for turning the company around. The company was able to identify a number of customers, primarily in high-tech industries, that valued a complete logistics management service. Thus, the strategic planning process had redefined both what the company did and who it served. These changes were, in turn, responsible for greatly improving the firm's profitability. From a loss of £276,000 in 1987, the company improved to a £450,000 profit in 1990.

Source

Hillidge, J. (1990, June). Planning for growth in a small company. *Long Range Planning, 23,* 76–81.

ones. If you are not careful, you may invest time, energy, and other resources in reaching narrow goals that do not move you closer to achieving your broader goals.

In the same way, it is essential that organizations have a consistent set of narrow goals, each of which will move them toward their broader goals. Think of this as a hierarchy, ranging from (1) a broad *vision* of what the organization should be, to (2) more defined goals describing the organization's *mission,* to (3) specific detailed goals we shall call strategic *objectives.* This hierarchy of goals is the foundation of the entire strategic management process; we discuss it in more detail later in this chapter.

EXHIBIT 1.2
The Elements of an Intended Strategy

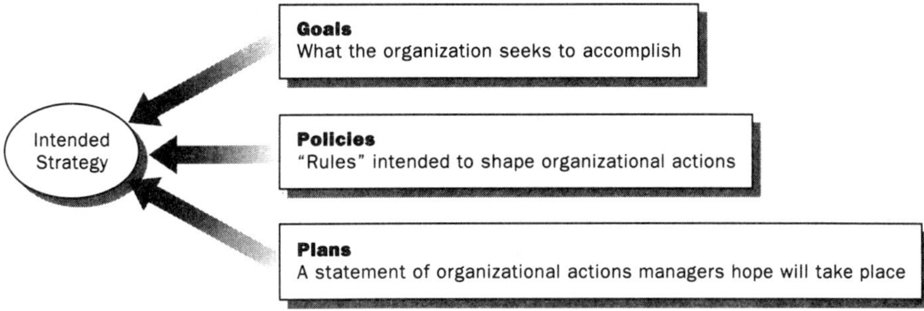

Policies
In addition to information regarding what an organization hopes to accomplish, intended strategies must also provide guidelines for how an organization will work toward its goals. These guidelines take the form of either policies or plans. Policies are rules that are explicitly stated or implicitly understood. Here are some hypothetical examples:

- We will not be undersold.
- We will not operate east of the Mississippi.
- We will not question why an item is returned.
- We will make, rather than purchase, the most critical components for assembly of our products.
- We will fund future growth through retained earnings.

Like most rules, policies can usually be stated in negative terms. For instance, the last two examples above could easily be rewritten to read, "We will *not* depend upon outside suppliers for the most critical components for the assembly of our products" and "We will *not* take on long-term debt." In short, policies are general guidelines that indicate limits or constraints on what is to be attempted.

Plans
Plans deal with the means we use to pursue certain ends:

- To maintain our desired rate of growth, we will open four new stores in the next 2 years.
- To expand our market, we will create consumer versions of our industrial products in the upcoming decade.
- To become more cost competitive, we will restructure the organization, cutting overhead costs by one-third in the upcoming fiscal year.
- To increase demand for our products, we will spend heavily on advertising to establish brand recognition.

Timing is often a critical element of plans, and is therefore explicitly stated, as in the first example above. Timing may also be implied, as in the last example above; we assume that once the brand is established, advertising spending will probably be reduced.

Realized Strategies

In contrast to intended strategies, which focus on the future, realized strategies reference the past. The goals, policies, and plans constituting an organization's intended strategy may be quite different from what actually happened, its realized strategy. Theoretically, an intended strategy could be successfully implemented and realized in its entirety. This possibility is portrayed by the top arrow in Exhibit 1.3, connecting the intended, deliberate, and realized elements of a strategy in a straight line. In practice, however, an original strategy almost always changes several times throughout implementation. Unexpected obstacles may force quick-thinking managers to alter an intended strategy. The original strategy might also change to take advantage of unforeseen opportunities. The change may be purely unintentional, as in the case of a firm that planned to diversify into a new market, but did not succeed in developing the proposed new product, and thus remained undiversified. Regardless of the causes for change, an intended strategy seldom ever survives in its original form. Plans that never materialize are labeled the "unrealized" element of a strategy in Exhibit 1.3. The new developments form an "emergent" strategy, one that emerges over time. The final realized strategy is a combination of deliberate and emergent elements.

To see how realized strategies are a combination of intended and emergent components, consider this example from the public sector. A state agency was given funds to rent shelters for housing homeless people in the state's major cities. (This was an intended strategy.) However, lack of adequate space left room for fewer homeless than planned, causing the intended strategy to be unrealized. On the other hand, because fewer buildings were rented, money was available for alternative types of support, and providing meals three nights a week became part of the agency's emergent strategy. In the end, the services provided by the agency were both more and less than what was originally expected. This is usually the case with realized strategies.

Exhibit 1.4 outlines a few of the changes that occurred in Saturn's strategy from the time initial plans for the new General Motors division were first drawn up until the cars

EXHIBIT 1.3
The Realized Strategy Is Usually Both More and Less than the Strategy That Was Intended

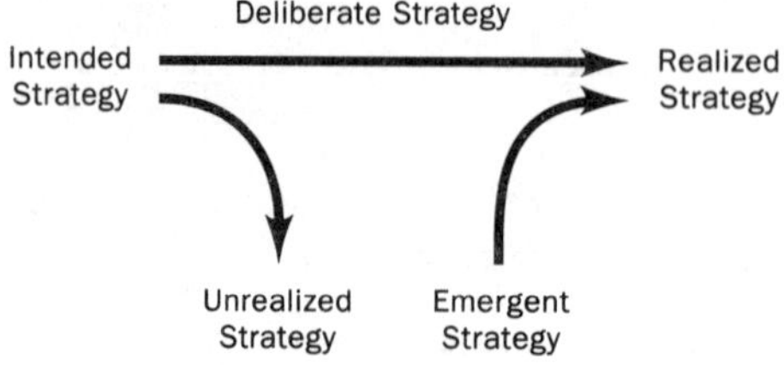

Source: Mintzberg, H., & Waters, J. A. (1985). Of strategies, deliberate and emergent. *Strategic Management Journal, 6,* 257–272.

EXHIBIT 1.4
Elements of Saturn's Intended and Realized Strategies

Elements of Intended Saturn Strategy	*Developments Requiring Strategic Response*	*Resulting Elements of Realized Saturn Strategy*
Economy vehicle (priced around $6,000). Fuel efficient subcompact offering a product-line extension for General Motors.	Concern for fuel efficiency diminishes after the energy crisis of the seventies. GM loses 11% market share in the U.S. and becomes more concerned about targeting sporty imports.	Sporty compact with $8,000 to $12,000 price range designed to have the "look and feel of an import."
Heavy automation and emphasis on robots.	Experience in other GM divisions leads to better understanding of the limitations of automation and the importance of "human factors" and work force involvement.	Balanced mix of advanced and traditional manufacturing technologies, and greater emphasis on employee training.
Scale. A $5 billion investment from GM for a plant with annual output of 500,000 cars per year.	More global competitors enter U.S. market, resulting in deteriorating GM, corporate performance. GM sees diminished cash flows and develops concerns about sales potential for new Saturn line.	$3 billion investment in a plant with annual output of 240,000 cars.

Source: Author's correspondence with Saturn management.

began rolling off the line. From this experience we see how an intended strategy can change for the better. Given the situation in the automobile industry during the eighties, it is doubtful that Saturn's intended strategy (conceived in the seventies) would have been appropriate. The realized strategy, however, appeared to be very successful by the early 1990s. Reviews of the car were quite positive, consumer demand was strong, and Saturn won numerous industry awards for excellence.[7]

WHAT IS STRATEGIC MANAGEMENT?

Strategic management is a process that combines three major interrelated activities: strategic analysis, strategy formulation, and strategy implementation. Basically, *strategic analysis* is the "homework" required to develop an appropriate strategy. *Strategy formulation* is the process that transforms this homework into a plan—the intended strategy. *Strategy implementation* is the process of putting the plan into action—seeing that as much as possible of the intended strategy becomes the realized strategy. The remainder of this book concentrates on refining and illustrating these basic concepts. Exhibit 1.5 shows how the chapters are organized around these three components of strategic management.

Strategic Analysis

Strategic analysis is the foundation for the strategic management process. It consists of three parts (covered in Chapters 1 to 3). The first is a consideration of an organization's goals. The second is an exploration of the opportunities and threats present in the external environment. The third is a study of the organization's internal strengths and weaknesses.

Strategic Goals

The hierarchy of vision, mission, and objectives channels the efforts of an organization's various managers and employees in a common direction. Strategic goals play two inseparable roles; they exist as a target and they become a unifying element that allows the organization to move toward this target. Although strategic goals are vital to shaping a strategy, they should not be treated separately from the other elements of strategic analysis: goals are *not* established independently from the situation facing the organization and its managers.[8] Rather, goals develop through a cycle in which managers consider what they hope to achieve, in relation to the opportunities and threats in the environment and the organization's capabilities. The interaction of goals and context is depicted as two-way arrows within the strategy analysis component of Exhibit 1.5.

SWOT Analysis

Successful strategic management depends on matching internal strengths and weaknesses to external opportunities and threats.[9] Chapter 2 covers external opportunities and threats, and Chapter 3 covers internal strengths and weaknesses. Together, these factors comprise SWOT (strengths, weaknesses, opportunities, and threats) analysis.

EXHIBIT 1.5
The Components of Strategic Management

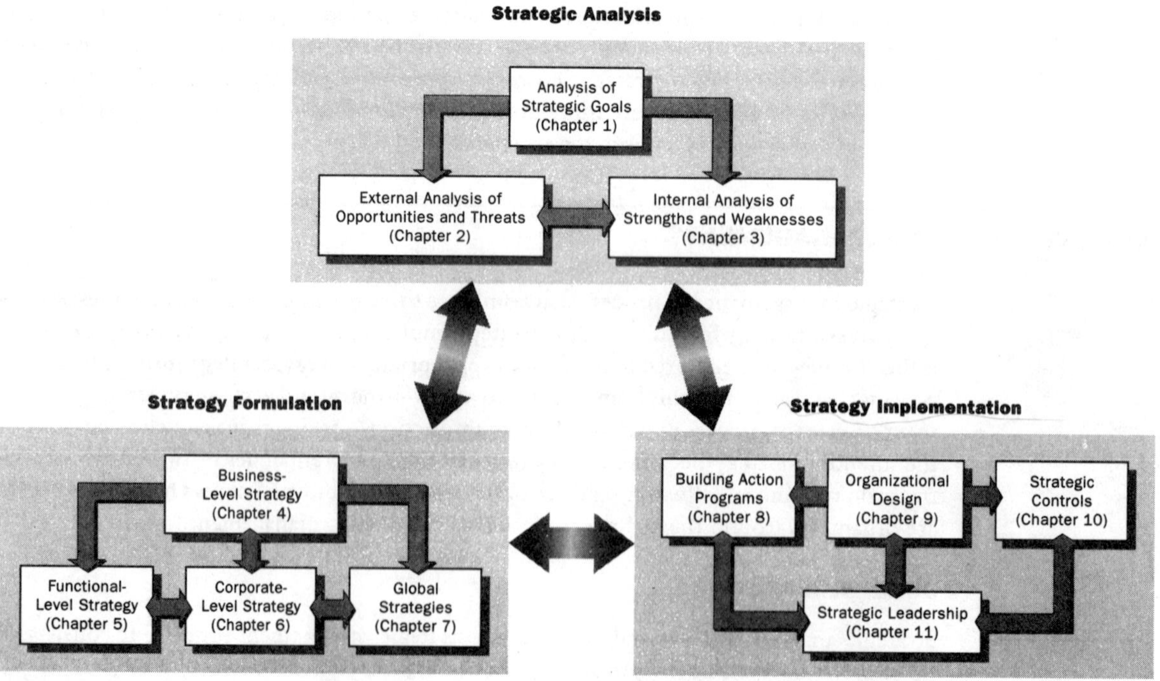

The resources outside an organization which could contribute to its continued success and growth are considered the opportunities of its external environment. Examples are new customers, emerging technology, available financing, and labor market for future employees. However, the environment also holds threats for the organization: competitors, regulations that change required ways of doing business, shifts in consumer demands away from current products, and the creation of substitute products. Managers must integrate information covering a broad range of these and other considerations, and select some part of the overall environment within which they will focus their own energies in competition. We will provide frameworks for analyzing both the general and the competitive environments in Chapter 2.

To formulate sound strategies, a manager must know the capabilities and limits constraining the organization's options. These are the organization's internal strengths and weaknesses. Examples of organizational strengths include a highly skilled work force, strong patent protection, readily available lines of financial credit, and strong brand awareness. Offsetting weaknesses might be overhead costs above the industry average, exceedingly long product development lead times, outdated management information systems, and slow logistical networks. Chapter 3 provides a framework for exploring this topic.

Strategic Analysis Illustrated

The Timex watch company provides a good example of interaction among goals, internal strengths and weaknesses, and external opportunities and threats. After World War II, during which the company produced timing devices for explosives, Timex began to search for new opportunities to employ its strength in designing and producing simple, cheap, and rugged mechanical timers. Wristwatches by leading designers were expensive, delicate objects sold through jewelry stores. Timex saw an opportunity to change this and established the goal of becoming a dominant competitor in the low end of the watch market. The firm successfully used its strengths to take advantage of the opportunity and soon reached its goal. At the height of the firm's success, one of every three watches sold in the world was a Timex.

However, the advent of digital electronic watches presented a threat. Initially, Timex ignored this threat, believing that digital technology would never be competitive with mechanical watches. Because of this, Timex failed to address its weakness in digital and electronics design and production. (The company employed virtually no electrical engineers.) When the cost of digital technology fell to the point that highly reliable electronic watches were less expensive than an old-fashioned looking Timex, the company's position weakened. Electronics firms stormed the market, and Timex spent years struggling to build comparable strengths in digital technology just to survive. Based on a new analysis of the strategic situation, Timex realized that it would never again enjoy the industry domination that it once claimed, and the firm developed new goals that took it into a number of new markets such as personal computers. However, the firm has never repeated the near-perfect alignment among strategic goals, internal strengths, and external opportunities it once had in the wristwatch market.

Strategy Formulation

A sound strategic analysis provides the basis for formulating strategy on each of four possible levels: functional, business, corporate, and international. Briefly, *corporations* are composed of *businesses,* which are in turn composed of *functions.* Strategies are formulated within each of these levels. Furthermore, if the corporation has businesses in more than one country, strategy formulation also takes on an *international* dimension.[10]

Business Level

Although strategy formulation takes place on a number of levels, emphasis should be centered squarely on the business level.[11] At this level, firms face one another as competitors for customers and sales. Corporations compete with other corporations only when they each own businesses that offer similar products to similar markets. For example, Ford and Boeing are not generally considered to be competitors; Ford is best known for automobiles and Boeing is best known for commercial aircraft. But both corporations own aerospace businesses and share customers in that market, thereby competing with one another at the business level.

We identify a business as a portion of an organization that provides a cohesive bundle of goods and/or services to an identifiable market. This definition is necessarily fuzzy; the borders dividing corporations into businesses are almost always somewhat fluid. For instance, a corporation specializing in electronics might have one business that provides light bulbs to automobile manufacturers and another that produces televisions for home use. The distinctions between these are obvious, but what if the same company expands its light bulb operation into the production of lighting fixtures for the home market? Does that create a new business? What if they begin producing video recording equipment to complement their televisions? Should televisions and recording products be combined to form an overall video business?

The answers to these questions hinge upon the need for separate strategic plans. If a single strategy will cover a combination of two or more products and markets, then they may be combined to form a single strategic business unit (SBU).[12] If they cannot be well served by a single strategic plan, the operations should be divided across two or more SBUs. In this way, individual businesses are the focus of much of the entire strategic management process.

In competing with one another, businesses search for an advantage that will attract customers to them and away from competitors. These *competitive advantages* may take a variety of forms, but most can be categorized as either high differentiation, low cost, or quick response. Success at the business level largely depends on gaining and maintaining an advantage over the competition along one or more of these three dimensions. Chapter 4 is devoted to defining each dimension and explaining how organizations go about capturing these competitive advantages.

Function Level

The competitive advantages that cause a business to flourish depend on the value that the organization creates for its customers. The work of creating value takes place within and across the various functional areas that compose the business. These various functions can be linked conceptually by a framework called the *value chain.* This framework assumes that every function within the business is capable of producing value for customers. Some functions, like production, marketing, sales, and service, contribute to overall customer value directly. We call these *primary functions. Secondary functions,* like management information systems and human resource management, also provide value for the external customer, but their contribution is usually more indirect. They most often contribute to external customer value by working through the primary functions, sometimes called the secondary function's *internal customers.* Chapter 5 discusses the link between customer value and competitive advantage.

Corporate Level

A corporation expands to include additional businesses through diversification. There are several commonly observed reasons managers choose to diversify, not all equally sound from a strategic standpoint. The soundest diversification strategies are those in which the corporation capitalizes upon its unique expertise in critical functions. Such hard-to-duplicate forms of expertise are called *distinctive core competencies.* If a corporation can identify a business whose competitive advantage can be strengthened by employing the corporation's distinctive core competence, that business is an ideal target for diversification. Chapter 6 covers diversification.

This diversification process is one that stresses the central importance of customer value and competitive advantage within the new business unit. In other words, corporate-level strategies for diversification are best built upon an appreciation of the requirements for success at the business level. Recall also that success at the business level is dependent upon creating customer value at the function level. The process of strategy formulation must be linked at all three levels in order to be maximally effective. Later in the chapter, we will discuss how the formal strategic planning process is designed to achieve this sort of integration.

International Level

The most complex organizations integrate strategy formulation across national borders, as well as across corporate, business, and function levels. While facing all the challenges of strictly domestic businesses, these organizations must also contend with differences in social, political, cultural, and economic systems of different nations. Chapter 7 explores the conflicts arising from attempts to be flexible in meeting the local market's demands while using tightly structured management to capitalize upon corporate strengths around the world. To gain flexibility for the local market, some corporations have granted their business units around the world almost complete autonomy. Such decentralization is called a *multidomestic strategy,* because each business unit is only responsible for its own isolated *domestic* market. The other approach seeks to take maximum advantage of corporate strengths through centralization of operations. This option is called a *global strategy,* because it treats the entire world as one market. In the past, organizations have used only one approach or the other. More recently, pioneering firms have begun to develop "hybrid" strategies in which they attempt to combine the best elements of both global and multidomestic approaches. Successful development of such strategies requires a thorough understanding of individual businesses, as well as an understanding of the capabilities of the corporation. Exhibit 1.5 shows how international, corporate, business, and functional strategies are linked.

Strategy Formulation Illustrated

The recent experience of a leading competitor in the disposable diaper market provides a good example of how the four levels of strategy formulation are linked. National retailers wanted diaper packaging that reflected the numerous options available (labels for extra large or extra small packages, special promotions, etc.). Managers within the *business* level of a much larger consumer products corporation concluded that their competitive position in this market could be significantly strengthened by overcoming delays in supplying these key accounts with preferred packaging. Working at the *function level,* managers in logistics and operations traced the factors limiting flexibility to the need for customized printing. These function-level managers were sent around the world in search of printing equipment that would allow the business to adjust its packaging quickly and thereby enhance its competitive advantage.

They discovered a printing specialist in Germany with the required technology, and returned to the United States to take a crash course in German, while managers at the *corporate level* worked out the details of a joint venture at the *international level* between the U.S. diaper business and the German printing specialist. Eighteen months after the problem was first identified, the German-based joint venture was offering the U.S. diaper business the greatest packaging flexibility of any competitor in the market. By linking the contributions of managers at all four levels (business, function, corporate, and international), the firm was able to further fine-tune its strategy and stay ahead of its competition.

Strategy Implementation

Formulating a strategy is no guarantee that it will actually materialize. The process of transforming intended strategies into realized strategies is called *strategy implementation.* We shall consider its four most critical elements: integration, organization structure, controls, and leadership.

Integration

As we will see in Chapter 8, for a strategy to be fully realized, several forms of integration must take place. One form is integration of elements *within* a single organizational entity. For example, the organization must be staffed in such a way that it commands the skills required to carry out the intended strategy. Organizational systems must be in place to capitalize on and support these skills. Another form of integration links various organizational entities. This can include linking functions within businesses, businesses within corporations, and international operations within a multinational corporation. Finally, we discuss integrating short-term objectives and action plans with the longer-term and broader goals described by the organization's vision and mission statement.

Organization Structure

Strategy implementation requires that channels of communication be opened across the organization, that responsibilities be defined, and that authority be delegated. Through these requirements, managers establish the organization's structure. In this pursuit, managers face an almost limitless set of options for combining varying degrees of centralization, formalization, and complexity. Each option holds its advantages and disadvantages, which we describe in Chapter 9.

Strategic Controls

In implementing strategies, managers use strategic controls for two very different purposes. One purpose is to keep implementation efforts "on track." The other is to adjust preconceived plans to unexpected external and internal developments. In Chapter 10, we explain that regardless of the purpose behind strategic controls, managers depend on quality information. Managers can also use more direct controls, such as rewards, rules, and the organization's culture to affect the behavior of individuals.

Strategic Leadership

Exhibit 1.5 shows leadership as a factor influencing each of the other three elements of strategy implementation. Leadership, the topic of Chapter 11, is the means by which these factors are integrated within and across organizational entities. Leaders are the architects of organizational structure, the engineers of an organization's control systems, and the driving force behind strategy implementation. Leaders use organizational culture to carry out their visions and shape the ideas and ideals that influence behavior throughout the organization. Ethics is one element of culture especially important to the long-run success of the firm, and is therefore a critical responsibility of leadership.

Strategy Implementation Illustrated

CMP Publications Inc., a family-owned business headquartered in Manhasset, New York, provides an interesting example of how strategy implementation can influence an organization's effectiveness.[13] Founded in 1971 by Gerry and Lila Leeds, the firm produced business newspapers and magazines. All were leaders in rapidly growing markets, such as computers and health care. Although the firm had an enviable growth record, by 1986 CMP was experiencing serious problems. The Leeds became harder to contact. The publishers (executives responsible for the individual newspapers or magazines) found it more difficult to move requests through corporate departments. Answers to day-to-day questions seemed almost out of reach, and it took longer to get action on new ideas. Such problems could have caused the firm's market share to erode.

Fortunately, the Leeds took quick action after they recognized the root of these problems. CMP had outgrown its antiquated, highly centralized organization structure. It was time to decentralize authority. The first step was to break the company into separate autonomous divisions—"companies within a company." A group publisher, who could operate and help the division grow, was put in charge of each "company." A publications committee, consisting of the firm's top-level executives and all the group publishers, made decisions formerly left to the Leeds alone. Group publishers, though acting individually, were responsible for staying within the guidelines of strategic objectives they helped to formulate.

These changes created an organizational culture characterized by greater risk taking, creativity, and innovation. Furthermore, by meeting at regular intervals, the publications committee enhanced the integration and coordination of all activities across the entire firm. From the perspective of the firm's top management, the changes also proved to be very timely. Because the Leeds were planning to retire, it eased the transition of CMP's leadership to their son, Michael, a group publisher. With much less experience, he would have found it quite difficult to tackle all the decision-making responsibility his parents had handled for so long under the former organizational structure. After this successful strategy implementation, CMP Publications could manage its growth more competently. In a 3-year period, the number of publications increased from ten to fourteen, and in the fourth year, sales jumped to $174 million—an 11 percent increase over the previous year's sales.

WHERE CAN STRATEGIC MANAGEMENT BE APPLIED?

The nature of strategic management is changing in such a way that all managers, regardless of organizational level or functional specialty, are becoming more involved in helping formulate and implement strategies for the entire business. Given the broad and integrative nature of strategic management, it is sometimes viewed as the exclusive responsibility of top managers, or perhaps that of their specialized strategic planning staffs. But, we take the position that such views are nearsighted. Throughout the organization, *every* manager should expect to use or contribute to the strategic management process. Top managers are, and should be, deeply involved; as well, there must be staff support, particularly in large complex organizations. However, as strategic management evolves, even lower-level managers and employees are coming to have new responsibilities and more important roles to play in the strategic management process.[14]

For example, at Johnsonville Foods, employees on the factory floor play a key role in shaping and carrying out the firm's strategies.[15] Johnsonville's CEO, Ralph Stayer, was approached by a major food retailer about producing sausages the retailer would market under a private label. Stayer initially thought that the extra work would overload his plant and his workers. But before actually turning down the contract, he discussed the matter with the firm's 200 production workers, a routine practice at Johnsonville.

In teams of twenty, all the workers were asked to weigh the potential benefits and drawbacks to the proposed contract. The most important potential benefit was that the added production would result in economies of scale that would lower costs. This, coupled with the higher volume, would raise company profits. Because every worker at Johnsonville was on a bonus system linked to company profits, all employees stood to gain. The drawbacks and risks to the new contract centered on the argument that the tremendous increase in volume would overstress the factory and the work force, and overall quality would slip. If this happened, not only would the company lose the new contract, but it would also have jeopardized its relationship with its existing customers.

After 10 days of deliberation, the teams reported back, "We can do it." Their analysis showed that after working 7-day weeks in the short run, they could eventually expand their hourly production output, and the work load would level off. The teams then divided up to address specific challenges, such as new machinery, production scheduling, and the hiring of additional workers. One team discovered how volume could be increased by 40 percent while holding cost increases to only 20 percent. Another group designed new equipment and performed the discounted cash flow analysis to back up their requests for capital. Traditionally, issues such as these would have been assigned to managers far away from a factory floor.

The Johnsonville employees' strategic plans for expansion were successful. Productivity rose 50 percent after the firm took on the new contract. Since then, sales have continued to rise at twice the rate of payroll expenses as employees continue to find more efficient ways of doing things. CEO Stayer is sold on the ability of his work force to help in making strategic decisions and then make those decisions work: "If I had tried to implement this from above, we would have lost the whole business."

Hundreds of organizations ranging from small firms like Johnsonville to large organizations like General Motors' Saturn Division have found they no longer need as many layers of managers as responsibility for strategic issues is reapportioned. The result has been a widespread trend to "flatten" organizations by removing layers of managers, a change further discussed in Chapter 9. Flattening organizations is a practice which has clear implications for employees; lower-level managers and hourly employees have been "empowered" to take over responsibilities that have traditionally belonged to managers.[16] But flattened organizations offer implications for top managers as well.

Without armies of specialized middle managers to oversee the details of operations, upper managers are finding it necessary to adopt a more hands-on approach in their work. In other words, while recent trends have increased the roles of lower-level managers and employees in the strategic management process, top management's involvement remains critical. Today more than ever before, activities must be integrated across the width and breadth of the entire organization. Two complementary approaches to achieving this integration are formal planning and incremental management.

Formal Planning and Incremental Management

We have seen that strategic management is a complex process consisting of analysis, formulation, and implementation. Managers and workers throughout the entire organization have individual roles to play, all of which must somehow be integrated. The complexity of the issues coupled with the diversity and sheer number of individuals involved pose a serious challenge to any attempt at strategic management. How do organizations face the challenge? What can be done to ensure that efforts across the organization remain part of some larger, orchestrated whole, instead of just a staggering series of disconnected decisions and isolated actions?

There are two different but complementary methods for dealing with this issue. *Formal strategic planning* attempts to lay out the shortest path possible for the organization to travel when moving from one point to another. Because the shortest path between two points is a straight line, we have depicted this type of organizational movement as a linear process (see Exhibit 1.6).

On the other hand, experienced managers realize that organizations seldom travel straight down the path laid out in formal plans. They move in the same direction as described in the plan, but they do so in small, incremental steps, testing the feasibility of the plan and adjusting it as they go. We call this method *incremental management* (see Exhibit 1.7). Each approach can make contributions, and each has limitations. The best managers know how to combine them to achieve the most effective strategic management process.

EXHIBIT 1.6
Formal Planning Systems Attempt to Move an Organization to a New Strategic Position (and Maintain That Position) As Efficiently and Directly As Possible

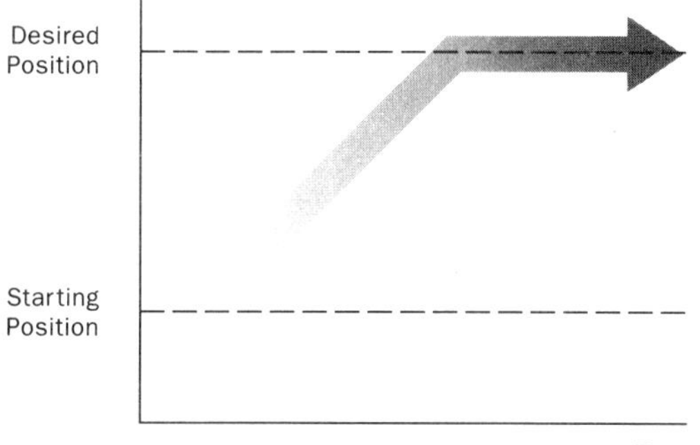

EXHIBIT 1.7
Organizations Typically Move to New Strategic Positions (and Maintain Those Positions) by Making More or Less Continuous Incremental Adjustments

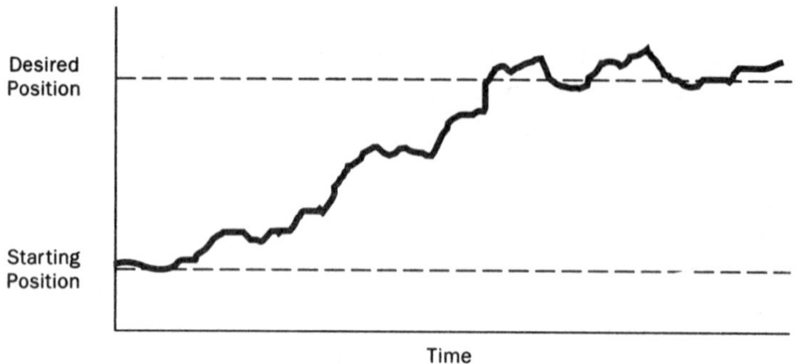

Formal Strategic Planning

The trend toward decentralizing power has brought with it an increased emphasis on formal strategic planning. The formal plan becomes a way to communicate overall organizational goals to independent members, and thereby help them understand how they can best contribute through their individual initiatives.

Peter Drucker, one of the most respected observers of management issues in the last 30 years, compares the executive and his or her plan to a symphony conductor with a complex musical score to direct.[17] The conductor cannot play each instrument as well as the specialized symphony members; those experts are expected to perfect their individual contributions on their own. The conductor interprets the score and communicates an overall vision for how the piece should sound. Without the conductor and this understanding of the overall score, symphony becomes cacophony. Similarly, executive leadership and direction must be provided through an overall strategic plan if decentralization and self-direction are to function effectively.

A typical formal planning process is a cycle of activities that takes a year to complete. Exhibit 1.8 illustrates such a formal planning process. It consists of four parts:

1. Identifying and understanding gaps between previously established goals and past performance
2. Identifying resources needed to close the gap between current performance and future goals
3. Distributing those resources
4. Monitoring their use in moving the organization closer to reaching its goals

These four phases all require cooperation among managers working at the corporate, business, and functional levels.* Consider, for instance, the need to incorporate information on the context within which plans are developed ("Strategic Context" in Exhibit 1.8).

---

* In more complex multinational corporations, the cycles must be expanded to include international-level operations within the overall process, but the fundamental ideas remain the same.

EXHIBIT 1.8
A Typical Formal Strategic Planning Process

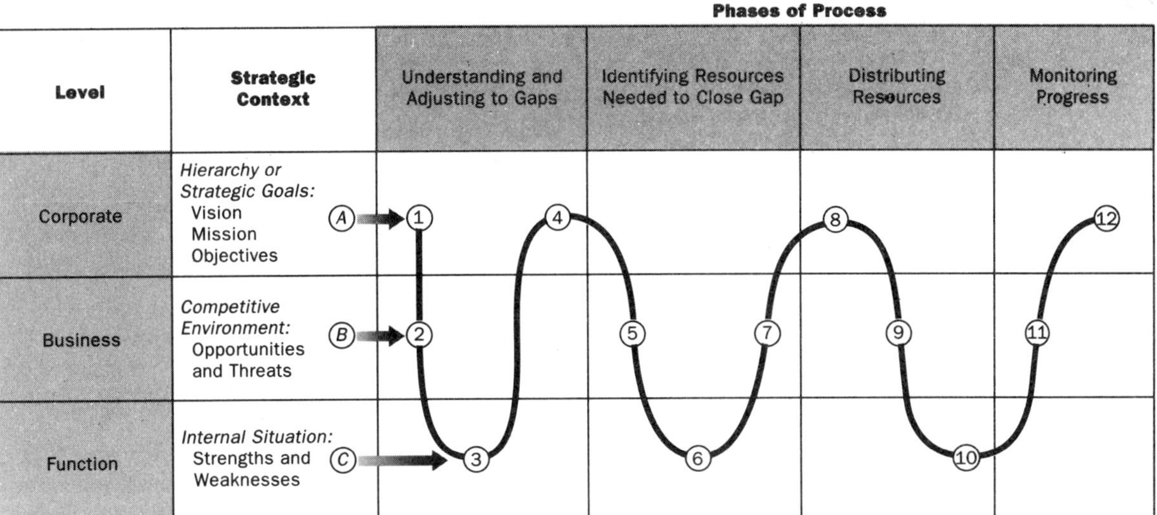

1. Evaluate performance in light of goals and identify gaps.
2. Relate gaps to environmental conditions.
3. Relate gaps to organizational capabilities.
4. Identify future goals, given understanding of gaps.
5. Describe broad action plans aimed at meeting goals.
6. Identify resources required by each function to implement plans.
7. Aggregate needs by function into overall needs of business.
8. Allocate resources across multiple business units.
9. Reallocate resources across multiple functions.
10. Deploy resources within functions.
11. Monitor use of resources within functions.
12. Monitor use of resources across businesses.

The breadth of knowledge required to appreciate the various goals that guide the planning efforts throughout the organization is most likely to be found at the corporate level (see *A*). However, information about the specific competitive environment facing a particular business within the corporation is most likely to be found within the individual business units (see *B*). Finally, the details of current organizational capabilities are probably found within the various functions (see *C*). A strategic planning process, such as the one depicted in Exhibit 1.8, serves to integrate the wide range of decisions and actions strategic management requires. By laying out a rational process that has each organizational level feeding information and resources to other levels, the formal planning process serves as a useful integrating device. The power of such a process is described in Application 1.2, which looks at successful planning in a small company.

Properly done, formal planning provides the organization with a road map that facilitates personal individual initiative. Carter Fox, CEO of Chesapeake Corporation, a $600 million paper products company, puts it this way: "We control the operating units through a system of profit plans and strategic plans. They are rigorously debated and analyzed, but once we have an approved plan, I want people to take the initiative and let me know what is

Application 1.2

A Small Firm's Use of Formal Strategic Planning

Liberty Industries, a firm founded in 1964, specialized in wooden packaging products, such as pallets, and was only a tiny three-person organization for nearly a decade. By 1987, however, the firm's sales grew by a factor of 20, approaching $20 million a year. The planning system that had always been effective was no longer adequate to meet the challenges facing the organization.

With the help of a consultant, the firm developed a nine-step planning process:

1. Define the organization's purpose and reason for being.
2. Monitor the environment in which the organization operates.
3. Make a realistic assessment of strengths and weaknesses.
4. Make assumptions about unpredictable future events.
5. Develop specific and measurable objectives in areas contributing to the organization's purpose.
6. Formulate strategies on how to use available organizational resources in addressing environmental conditions and to meeting strategic objectives.
7. Develop long- and short-range plans to meet objectives.
8. Constantly appraise performance and evaluate gaps between performance and objectives and purpose.
9. Reevaluate purpose, environment, strengths, and weaknesses before setting objectives for next year.

In identifying Liberty's purpose, managers developed a mission statement that included the following: "Liberty is in the business of marketing industrial packaging products and services worldwide in order to realize a profit for the benefit of stockholders, employees, customers, and suppliers. Any industry that transports and/or warehouses its products is a potential recipient of Liberty Industries services." With this short statement, managers identified the firm's product/market domain and its obligations to key stakeholders.

In their environmental analysis of opportunities and threats, the managers identified the following key issues:

- Annual growth in demand for wood pallets was expected to be only 3 to 5 percent per year.
- Plastic packaging was expected to grow at a slightly higher rate than wood in the short run, and to represent substantially greater growth opportunities in the future.

Analysis of internal strengths and weaknesses revealed that:

- The firm had a strong reputation for providing quality products and services.
- New manufacturing capabilities were opening up in the plastics market thanks to a joint venture with a leading German packaging firm.
- In-house design and engineering capabilities were inadequate for continued high level of service, given the recent growth.
- Operating efficiencies related to weak information transfers between the corporate and regional offices were limiting profits.

Based on this three-part strategic analysis, the firm formulated a strategy that included plans to complete product/market research on plastic packaging and begin marketing/manufacturing programs, further diversify out of wood packaging through additional joint ventures, hire a new engineering coordinator, and computerize its facilities to improve information flow. Although the planning process involved was simple, managers felt the firm was better positioned for the future than it had ever been.

Source

Based on information found in Migliore, Henry R., & Ringness, Ronald C. (1987, May–June). Nailing down a future for a small wood-products business. *Planning Review*, pp. 30–37.

done later."[18] Through a formal planning process, managers like Carter Fox coordinate the actions of the diverse set of individuals required to address many strategic issues.

Research suggests that formal strategic planning will improve firm performance, but it is no panacea, and we must acknowledge its limitations.[19] Planning is by definition a future-oriented activity, and unfortunately, our forecasts are often inaccurate; sometimes even laughably wrong. In the 1950s, experts agreed that the entire world would never need more than about nine computers at any one time. Today, there are some models of automobiles with that many "computers on a chip" in each individual car! Sometimes poor predictions have devastating consequences for a business. In the eighties, scores of microcomputer manufacturers went out of business because they mistakenly predicted that their operating system would become the industry standard.

A second limitation to formal strategic planning is that managers usually lack the power needed to enforce organizational adherence to plans as they were originally conceived. Even if one could foresee the future and build perfect plans accordingly, strict adherence is difficult to enforce.[20] At one time executives might have been in a position to manage by coercion, but that is no longer the typical case. Through the process of empowerment discussed earlier, many organizations have been flattened to the point that the "generals" no longer have sufficient numbers of "lieutenants" to enforce their orders. With the information revolution brought on by computerization, middle managers can no longer be denied access to the data they need to make their own informed judgments and act accordingly.[21] Factory floor workers are becoming experts at operating increasingly complicated and valuable machines, and in many cases only they know enough to properly manage their work.

As Ralph Stayer, CEO of Johnsonville Foods, explains:

> The debacle of ordering change and watching it fail to occur showed me my limitation. I had come to realize that I didn't really control the performance of people at Johnsonville, that as a manager, I really didn't manage people. They managed themselves. But I did manage the context . . . contextual factors with the ability to shape the way people think and what they expect.[22]

Executives are coming to realize their power consists of the ability to get diverse organization members to support the same goals, and then allow them freedom to determine how best to accomplish those shared goals. The idea is that everyone need not march in lockstep in order to move in the same direction.

Managing Incrementally

Given the future's uncertainty, and the difficulty of enforcing plans, most strategic plans are only general guidelines for self-directed work. Detailed sets of instructions for each individual are not feasible. Too much is unknown at any one time to write such instructions, and today's information will soon change. In this situation, strategic management cannot be viewed merely as the process of designing a plan and carrying out its implementation. In fact, much of management is a process of continually rethinking and adjusting an organization's plans and activities.[23] Managers may concede that they lack the ability to foresee the future as well as the power to enforce adherence to their plans; still they refuse to allow their organizations to wander about aimlessly. Such executives manage incrementally, but with a definite purpose. This approach to strategic management, called *logical incrementalism,* has the following attributes:[24]

- Managers have a vision of what they want the organization to be in years to come, but they try to move toward this position in an evolutionary way.
- They do this by attempting to build a strong but flexible core business, while continually experimenting with a number of "side bet" ventures.
- These ventures are accepted as gambles because managers realize that the future is unknown and unknowable.
- Rather than trying to predict the future, managers seek to become highly sensitive to environmental developments, constantly scanning the world around them for new trends.
- When these new trends are observed, managers respond by carrying out small-scale experiments to see how the organization as a whole might best adapt.
- Realizing they cannot hope to spot all important trends and run all the needed organizational experiments, managers encourage similar testing throughout the organization.
- Managers assume that no single point of view dominates decision making, and important decisions are made at all levels of the business.

Contrary to appearances, research has shown incremental management to be far from random.[25] Decision makers throughout the organization are linked by a common understanding of what the overall strategy is and how they can help see it accomplished. Some decisions may seem unrelated on the surface, but when taken as a whole, they may actually be moving the organization toward its goals.

A detailed example of the incremental dimension of management is given in Application 1.3 on Motorola's development of its training programs, a key component of the corporation's strategy. The image that comes to mind in looking at the incremental two-steps-forward-one-step-back process of strategic management in examples like Motorola is that of a pinball. The steel ball in an arcade game follows a convoluted path, being bounced from bumper to bumper to flipper and back again. Yet, somehow, the ball eventually makes it back to the hole at the bottom of the table. Gravity is the hidden force that draws the pinball to its final destination. What is the comparable force that can drive a strategic movement, slowly but surely overcoming obstacles and setbacks? Edward Deming, the American management consultant who pioneered many of the concepts now known collectively as *Japanese management,* calls this driving force *constancy of purpose.*

CONSTANCY OF PURPOSE THROUGH STRATEGIC GOALS

Constancy of purpose is the result of employing an action-shaping set of values that are long lived and widely held throughout the organization. This is what formal planning systems are intended to convey as they weave organizational levels together with their flows of information and resources. Constancy of purpose is also the "logic" behind logical

Application 1.3

Incremental Management and Motorola University

Motorola's experience in establishing better training programs for its workers is a good example of the incremental nature of management. When Motorola flattened its organization and placed greater responsibility for planning in lower organizational ranks, it discovered that many of its workers and managers lacked the education to handle such responsibilities successfully. As a result, the corporation's training program took on new importance. Bob Galvin, the corporation's CEO, asked the human resource department to create a 5-year strategic plan that would convert its current training into the educational program the company needed. (Here we see an individual function's being asked to think strategically, a theme sounded throughout this chapter and again in Chapter 5, which is devoted exclusively to strategic management at the functional level.)

This request sounded straightforward enough, but it became quite challenging. The center developed sequences of courses, and the typical Motorola plant with 2,500 workers spent 50,000 worker-hours per year in these courses, apparently to little avail. Frustrated, Galvin had two universities evaluate Motorola's training efforts. The results showed that if Galvin's vision was to be realized, everyone in a plant, from the top official to the junior line workers, should be trained in a similar way of thinking. This was much bigger than the human resource department's original task. Over the next several years, with Galvin's continued encouragement, the group identified a number of stumbling blocks:

- Top managers were focusing their training on refinement of their individual specialties, instead of planning courses aimed at helping defend Motorola from the onslaught of cheaper and better-made imports. A specialized 17-day program for the corporation's 200 top managers covered global competition, manufacturing management, and cycle-time reduction.
- Math tests revealed that in one high-tech facility, 40 percent of the workers who were supposed to be self-directed could not pass a simple math test. A new math course uncovered yet another problem: many people were failing math tests not because of their math deficiencies, but because they could not read. Appropriate reading courses were established.
- Two scientists were assigned to create an educational electronics kit for high school teachers that cost only $10 per student. They then discovered that the typical high school physics teacher has only $2 per year per student to spend on all classroom supplies. So, the corporation identified its most important feeder schools and began donating the kits to these schools and training teachers in their use.

In the end, Motorola's training budget grew from a respectable $7 million per year to a totally unexpected $120 million per year, as efforts continue to build "Motorola University" into a global institution, offering courses around the world. At the same time, the corporation is devising programs to attract the best high school and college graduates to Motorola. None of these programs were part of the original plan, but all serve to move the corporation ever closer to its CEO's steadfast vision. Motorola moves toward its goal incrementally, overcoming setbacks and avoiding getting sidetracked from its plans by maintaining its constancy of purpose.

Sources

Wiggenhorn, W. (1990, July–August). Motorola U: When training becomes an education. *Harvard Business Review*, pp. 71–83.

Cheng, A. F. (1990, October). Hands-on learning at Motorola. *Training and Development Journal, 44*, 34–35.

incrementalism, converting what might otherwise be aimless organizational wandering into deliberate movement in a chosen direction. Regardless of whether one is considering linear planning or incremental management, constancy of purpose is a critical ingredient of the strategic management process.

But how is it created? To understand what gives an organization constancy of purpose, we must return to a concept first introduced much earlier in the chapter: a hierarchy of strategic goals spanning across a *vision* that results in widespread commitment to an organizational *mission* as demonstrated by working toward strategic *objectives.*[26] We explained that vision, mission, and objectives set forth ideas that unify the energy and the forces scattered throughout an organization. They are a beginning point for any formal strategic planning process, and they provide the energy and sense of direction necessary to ensure that incremental behavior culminates in overall progress.[27]

Vision

In strategic management, a vision refers to the goals that are broadest, most general, and all-inclusive. A vision describes aspirations for the future, without specifying the means necessary to achieve those desired ends.[28] The most effective visions are those that inspire, and this inspiration often takes the form of asking for the best, the most, or the greatest. It may be the best service, the most rugged product, or the greatest sense of achievement, but it must be inspirational.[29] As one observer puts it, "A vision must have 'mojo,' an appeal to the emotions and aspirations of the troops that goes beyond the usual carrots and sticks."[30] Reuben Mark, Colgate's fiery CEO, emphasizes the need for a vision to excite the human imagination: "You're never going to get anyone to charge the machine guns only for financial objectives. It's got to make them feel better, feel part of something."[31]

If they are to inspire, visions must be communicated; often, to very large numbers of people.[32] Communicating a vision takes place in two ways. The most obvious is the mission statement (discussed below). A less obvious, but perhaps an even better means of communicating a vision is through persuasive leadership. For instance, the behavior of the leaders espousing any particular vision will define what is meant by the terms used in a mission statement.

As an example, consider how leaders at Saturn convinced skeptics that quality really was a top priority for the company. Historically, when production on a new car model began, no one expected quality to be the best. Typically, it took several months for quality levels to improve, as the countless small wrinkles associated with such a complicated endeavor were ironed out. Meanwhile, production would continue, and the resulting cars would not be as good as they might have been. So, when Saturn's managers halted production and lost millions in sales while the firm worked out minor quality problems, the vision became clear: this organization was truly committed to quality.

It is clear from experiences like Saturn's that actions really do speak louder than words. But words are also important. Especially those spoken by the leader trying to encourage belief in a vision. Management experts call such messages "stump speeches," referring to the days when campaigning politicians would travel rural America and deliver their speeches wherever they could find a handful of people and a stump to use as a stage.[33] Experience suggests that the most useful stump speeches are 3 to 5 minutes long and communicate two or three key ideas. They also concentrate on explaining what the vision implies about the future for the organization. Bruce Merrifield, former deputy secretary of commerce, was convinced that small businesses, especially entrepreneurial high-tech firms, were important to the U.S. economy and that the Department of Commerce should actively seek to encourage their development.[34] To explain his idea, Merrifield prepared three simple charts documenting the contribution of small technology firms to the U.S. economy. Merrifield made it a point to lead all visitors to his office, regardless of the purpose of their visit, into a discussion of these charts, which were on an easel in the middle of the room. In case he had an opportunity to talk about these points away from the office, he carried a smaller version of the same charts with him when he traveled. Managers like Merrifield see that a critical part of their role is personal involvement in communicating their visions.

Mission

A vision becomes tangible as a mission statement. Writing such a statement specifies a leader's beliefs about an organization and the directions in which it should move. It can also identify what is unique about the character of the organization.[35] In Application 1.4, we have presented mission statements from three firms, representing different industries and different organizational sizes.

Although they are still personal statements, not subject to any particular rules regarding what they must include, mission statements usually attempt to answer several of the following questions:[36]

- What is our reason for being? What is our basic purpose?[37]
- What is unique or distinctive about our organization?

Application 1.4

Three Examples of Mission Statements

Ford Motor Company

Ford Motor Company is a worldwide leader in automotive and automotive-related products and services as well as in newer industries, such as aerospace, communications, and financial services. Our mission is to improve continually our products and services to meet our customers' needs, allowing us to prosper as a business and to provide a reasonable return for our stockholders, the owners of our business.

Audio Animation, Inc.

We will develop solution-oriented digital signal processing technologies for the benefit of our customers, and deliver the finest products and services to our industries. We will build a profitable company known for its integrity, based on the goals of long-term growth and profitability for the benefit of our customers, stockholders, employees, and community.

We will create a positive working environment for our employees, which promotes job satisfaction, personal growth, and an opportunity to share in the prosperity of the company.

American Airlines

We will be the global market leader in air transportation and related information services. That leadership will be attained by:

- Setting the industry standard for safety and security
- Providing world-class customer service
- Creating an open and participative work environment which seeks positive changes, rewards innovation, and provides growth, security, and opportunity to all employees
- Providing consistently superior financial returns for shareholders

Source

Authors' personal correspondence with companies.

- What is likely to be different about our business 3 to 5 years in the future?
- Who are, or who should be, our principal customers, clients, or key market segments?
- What are our principal products and services, present and future?
- What are, or what should be, our principal economic concerns?
- What are the basic beliefs, values, aspirations, and philosophical priorities of the firm?[38]

Addressing such questions explicitly by writing a formal mission statement for the organization can have three major benefits, as discussed in the following sections.

Mission Statements Establish Boundaries to Guide Strategy Formulation

By providing a sense of strategic direction, mission statements focus attention toward certain goals and away from other possibilities. Overly restrictive mission statements run the risk of inducing shortsightedness however, and, without some degree of focus, the organization may not be effective.[39] Such organizations may wander from one opportunity to another and their managers can spend inordinate amounts of time analyzing what *could* be done without ever actually *doing* much of anything. The authors know of a small, entrepreneurial technology-based business that exhibited just such behavior. For the first decade of the firm's life, its managers could not resist considering the dozens of potential applications for their new technological discovery. Their reasoning was that each of the applications could conceivably develop into a multimillion dollar market, so they could not afford to overlook any of them. It was only after the more attractive of these markets became dominated by focused competitors that the managers finally made the crucial strategic decision regarding which markets to pursue and which to ignore. This decision became the foundation of their mission statement.

In using the mission statement to identify boundaries and provide focus for the organization, managers must reach a difficult balance between being too restrictive and providing guidelines that are unclear. Managers refer to these shortcomings as writing a mission statement which is either too broad or too narrow. The ideal mission statement is relatively stable and seeks to identify the broader goals that are least likely to ever become inappropriate. However, this mission statement is also flexible enough so that the organization can be a dynamic entity capable of responding to changes as they occur. A classic example of this sort of balancing is the effort involved in defining what business a given organization is in. Consider the examples below illustrating the range of broad and narrow options:

Broad Definition	*Narrow Definition*
Transportation	Intracity light delivery
Clothing	Casual fashions for teenage girls
Engine repair	In-shop repair of foreign cars
Furniture	Waterbeds
Health care	Physical therapy for the aged[40]

Managers who carefully consider what business they are in often reach important new insights about their organization—insights that can change the strategic management of the firm. For instance, MCI was one of several telecommunications startups to enter the long-distance telephone market once the Bell system was dismantled. Although MCI managers saw themselves as being in the telephone business, they grew to realize that this perspective did not make them unique, nor did it help to explain the tremendous success the firm enjoyed. After all, there were several new startups in the telephone business, and they were not all successful.

After closer inspection, managers observed that they spent a tremendous amount of time working with government regulators trying to change the telecommunications industry from a regulated monopoly to a less regulated and more competitive market. Much of their success was due to the excellence of this work, and managers came to think of MCI as being not just in the telephone business, but in the government relations business as well. Based on this new understanding, government relations was given more consideration in the strategic planning process of the firm.[41]

Mission Statements Establish Standards for Organizational Performance along Multiple Dimensions

Exhibit 1.9 lists eight dimensions of performance illustrating expectations found in mission statements. Note that profitability, though clearly important, is only one of these eight dimensions. Research on the details of sixty-one mission statements from Fortune 500 firms found that 90 percent mention financial soundness, profitability, or growth of the firm.[42] Without profit, the business cannot support itself or continue to attract outside support. Without profit, it will eventually cease to exist, failing to meet all of its performance standards, financial and nonfinancial alike. In fact, research shows profitability to be a good predictor of a firm's ability to invest significant funds in social programs.[43] Because profit is so fundamental, its inclusion in a mission statement seldom helps distinguish what is unique about a particular firm. In other words, knowing that McDonald's and IBM are both interested in making a profit offers little insight about the unique mission of either organization. In order to discern what makes such organizations unique, we generally look at their nonfinancial standards of performance.

While the firm's standards for financial performance are likely to be stated in terms of obligations to its stockholders, nonfinancial dimensions of performance are more likely to be discussed in terms of the firm's obligations to a number of diverse stakeholders.[44] These stakeholders can include any parties that have an interest in the success or performance of the firm. Obligations to the firm's stockholders are referred to as its *fiscal responsibility,*

EXHIBIT 1.9
Eight Dimensions of Strategic Goals

Market Standing: Desired market share and competitive niche

Innovation: Efforts toward development of new methods and new products

Productivity: Aiming at specific levels of production efficiency

Physical and Financial Resources: Capital and equipment required to meet other strategic goals

Profitability: The level of profit and other indicators of financial performance

Managerial Performance and Development: Rates and levels of managerial productivity and growth

Worker Performance and Attitude: Expected rates of workers' productivity and positive attitudes

Public responsibility: The company's responsibilities to its customers and society

Source: Based on Drucker, P. F. (1954). *The practice of management* (pp. 65–83). New York: Harper & Row.

EXHIBIT 1.10
Recognition of Multiple Stakeholders in Mission Statements

Company	Stakeholder Group	Relevant Portion of Mission
Du Pont	Stockholders	Each of our businesses must deliver financial results superior to those of its leading competitors . . . for we consider ourselves successful only if we return to our shareholders a long-term financial reward comparable to the better-performing, large industrial companies.
Reynolds	Customers	In our relationship with customers, our objectives are: ■ Offer our products for sale on the basis of competitive price, quality, service, and reliability. ■ Furnish dependable products through continuing emphasis on product design, product development, quality standards, and manufacturing performance. ■ Provide innovative leadership in product development and marketing.
Dow	Employees	Employees are the source of Dow's success. We treat them with respect, promote teamwork, and encourage personal freedom and growth. Excellence in performance is sought and rewarded.
3M	Community at large	3M management recognizes that 3M's business operations have broad societal impact. It will endeavor to be sensitive to public attitudes and social concerns in the workplace, the community, the environment, and within the different political and economic systems where 3M conducts business. It will strive to keep the public, employees, and investors well informed about 3M business operations.

Source: Author's correspondence with companies.

while obligations to its stakeholders are referred to as its *social responsibility.* The mission statement's consideration of social responsibility may include discussion of the firm's relationship with customers, employees, the community, society at large, and so forth. Examples of these obligations are given in Exhibit 1.10.

Describing the firm's relationship with a broad range of stakeholders helps legitimize concern for issues other than financial returns. Broad-based understanding of such ideals translated into more explicit action-shaping statements is the cornerstone upon which effective strategic management is built, a point emphasized by Charles E. Exley, Jr., former chairman and CEO of NCR Corporation, in Application 1.5.

Mission Statements Suggest Standards for Individual Ethical Behavior

Ethics are the principles concerning an individual's duty to do what is morally right.[45] These duties often go well beyond the minimal requirements for legal behavior set forth in laws.[46] Carrying out these duties often requires making difficult judgments requiring decisions on how to balance the needs of one stakeholder group against those of other groups. Suppose you discover that your firm's sole supplier of a vital chemical ingredient has for years been improperly disposing of chemicals. You are not sure how extensive the problem is, but you suspect that some of the chemicals being dumped are capable of serious environmental damage. You are inclined to report what you know to the Environmental Protection Agency, but you realize that such an action could have serious ramifications. A multimillion dollar cleanup may force your supplier (who is, after all, one of your stake-

Application 1.5

The Role of Corporate Values

The following is excerpted from a statement entitled "Stressing Corporate Values" by Charles E. Exley, Jr., former chairman and CEO of NCR Corporation.

> How big a role do corporate values play in the continuing success of a corporation? . . . I believe that the key to our survival and success during this long period has been our focus on enduring values. These enduring values are the quality of the people who are the company and the institutional beliefs which these people share.
>
> . . . Among the most important of these beliefs is that the primary mission in any company should be to create value for its *stakeholders*—that is, *all* of the constituencies with a stake in the fortunes of the company. These include customers, NCR people, suppliers, communities, and investors.
>
> A growing company dedicated to achieving superior results needs to ensure that its actions are aligned with the legitimate expectations of its stakeholders. It is necessary, therefore, to try to anticipate the needs of the various stakeholder groups, and determine a course that will enable the company to achieve its management objectives while fulfilling responsibilities to the stakeholders.
>
> . . . NCR's present characterization of its mission simply gives expression to what we have been doing for some time—creating value for our stakeholders—and serves as a useful reminder of key principles which must be translated into actions fundamental to our success.
>
> The argument has been made that with this approach shareholders receive diminished status as merely one of the stakeholder groups and that the corporation's only direct obligation is to corporate owners. Yet we see no conflict in making a commitment to build mutually beneficial relationships with all of the stakeholders of a company. While it may appear that the various stakeholders will always have conflicting demands, in practice, the points of conflict are few, and the points of common interest are many.
>
> . . . We at NCR are convinced that in today's competitive environment, strong corporate values are the key to success. Although we take our obligation to shareholders very seriously, we feel that this group is in no way downgraded as a result of being identified as a primary part of a larger stakeholder group. Each constituency plays a critical role that should never be overshadowed or ignored.

Source

Authors' correspondence with the firm.

holders) out of business. That would be bad, but even worse, your business would also be shut down since the key ingredient would no longer be supplied.

Clearly, forcing your business to halt operations (even if just temporarily until an alternative solution is found) would have serious negative implications for several other stakeholder groups: stockholders, customers, and employees, in particular. If top managers in your organization have not made clear their opinion on such matters, uncertainty regarding how they might respond to your actions further complicates your reasoning. What risk do you have of being labeled a "whistle blower" by disapproving superiors? What duty do you have to serve one stakeholder group (the community being affected by the dumping) versus all the other stakeholder groups and yourself? The longer you wait to act, the longer you may be guilty of condoning something that is illegal. On the other hand, the issues involved do not lend themselves to making snap judgments.

Obviously, the worst time to start thinking about how to best respond to such a crisis is *after* its eruption. Your options and your duty would be much clearer, and your response to this growing problem could take place much faster, if you had a well-reasoned and clearly articulated statement of how individuals in your organization are expected to behave in such situations. The mission statement is an ideal means of providing just such guidelines. In Chapter 11, we will provide detailed discussion of the role that mission statements can play in establishing clear guidelines for shaping individual behavior *before* an ethical dilemma arises.

Objectives

As suggested from the examples given in Exhibit 1.10, most mission statements are more specific than anyone's visionary thinking, but they are still hardly concrete directions for action. Therefore, just as mission statements try to make a vision more specific, objectives are attempts to make mission statements more concrete. (Short-term targets, called *action plans,* are still more specific, but we need not consider their role until Chapter 9.) The strategic objectives identified by most organizations share several features, discussed in the following sections.

They Address Both Financial and Nonfinancial Issues

Given the diverse interests of the stakeholders mentioned in most mission statements, it should not be surprising that most organizations have objectives that are both financial and nonfinancial in nature. Exhibit 1.11 gives examples of both.

They Can Be Reached with a Stretch

The best objectives appear to be those which require that an organization "stretch" in order to reach them. As Edwin Land, founder of Polaroid, described it, the sorts of objectives which draw the greatest strengths out of people are those they see as "manifestly important and nearly impossible."[47] By constantly setting goals that demand more effort, an organization is more likely to reach its fullest potential. However, this is not meant to suggest that goals should be set arbitrarily high. Unrealistically high objectives can actually harm an

EXHIBIT 1.11
Examples of Strategic Objectives

Financial Objectives

Reynolds Aluminum: To be an industry leader in profitability and growth and to achieve an average return on equity of 20%.

Boeing: Profitability as measured against our ability to achieve and then maintain a 20% average annual return on stockholder's equity.

Boeing: Growth over the plan period as measured against a goal to achieve: greater than 5% average annual real sales growth from 1988 base.

General Electric: We will run only businesses that are number 1 or number 2 in their global markets.

Nonfinancial Objectives

Boeing: Integrity, in the broadest sense, must pervade our actions in all relationships, including those with our customers, suppliers, and each other. This is a commitment to uncompromising values and conduct. It includes compliance with all laws and regulations.

General Electric: We will be a more contemporary, more accessible, more responsive company, in touch with our customers, firmly in control of our own destiny, driven by more fulfilled people in control of theirs.

Source: Authors' correspondence with companies.

organization; knowing that the objective cannot be attained, the organization ignores it and finds itself operating without the guidance an objective is meant to offer.

They Incorporate the Dimension of Time

Virtually all objectives require consideration of the time dimension if they are to be useful. A business that has moved up from number 6 to number 2 in market share in 2 years faces a far greater challenge than a similar firm that allows itself 10 years. Measurement is usually next to meaningless without some time limitation.

They Facilitate Reasoned Tradeoffs

Most businesses will have a range of objectives, as suggested by Exhibit 1.11, and often these can contradict each other. For instance, a firm may have low-cost leadership and low-employee turnover as simultaneous objectives. When a recession occurs, managers are faced with a dilemma. With orders down, maintaining the work force will incur an expense that may destroy the firm's cost competitiveness. But laying off employees means the lives of loyal and valued workers will be thrown into turmoil. Management's task is to make the tradeoffs required in such situations, and carefully established objectives help with such difficult decisions.

They Reduce Conflict

Clearly stated objectives reduce misunderstandings and rivalry among organizational members. Such internal competition is often a manifestation of uncertainty regarding the overall direction of the firm. Objectives form the basis for cooperative managerial behavior. Focusing on overall firm progress, not divisional or departmental success, can facilitate beneficial intraorganizational relationships, such as resource and information sharing.

They Can Be Measured

Not every objective can be easily measured, but it is still important to monitor and measure progress toward the most important objectives. For many firms, improved quality is a strategically important objective. Yet, quality is a very difficult concept to measure. So instead, most firms use proxies for quality, such as warranty claims, defect rates, or customer satisfaction surveys. In groping with the issue of quantifying hard-to-measure objectives, many firms use a simple rule of thumb stated in the form of a question: "Using this measurement, will we know when we have reached our objective?"

They Avoid Unintended Consequences

There is potential danger involved in setting objectives and establishing measurements without considering the ramifications of the behavior they might motivate. There is an axiom: "Organizations produce whatever is measured." This warns against setting objectives casually and without regard to what will happen if the organization aggressively pursues improving performance along the resulting measure. If managers are not careful, they will establish performance measures that generate far different behavior from that intended. The authors know of several manufacturing facilities that have fallen prey to such situations.

One such case is a foundry, a manufacturing process in which the smelting furnace (1) represents a huge portion of the total investment in the plant, (2) generates the largest single category of operating expenses, (3) is largely a fixed cost, and (4) acts as a production bottleneck which creates the limit on production capacity for the entire operation. In light of these facts, it is reasonable to identify minimizing furnace expenses per ton of output as an important goal for this plant. And if this is a legitimate goal, then why wouldn't tons of furnace output per week be a good measure of progress toward meeting this goal? The problems with this practice did not become apparent until well after the goal and measurement were established.

The plant manager, aware that his performance was being measured in large part by tons of furnace output per week, sought to maximize production volume. One of the means of maximizing output was to produce sheets of metal in only the largest possible dimensions. But not all orders required the largest sizes, so much of the output had to be cut down to size after leaving the foundry. This, of course, added additional costs to the finished goods, but this additional cost was not reflected in the tons of output-per-week measure. In fact, since the trimmings could be melted down more quickly than the original raw ore, having lots of trimmings to add to future production helped raise efficiency as measured by the tons of furnace output per week. In other words, while the goal was to improve efficiency, progress toward the goal was being measured to actually encourage waste. As one seasoned veteran at this foundry explained, "The biggest problem with some of our objectives is that we meet them!" Given measurements' ability to shape behavior, they require careful consideration as a critical part of establishing strategic goals and laying the foundation for the rest of the strategic management process.

Summary

Strategies consist of goals, policies, and plans. We can discuss strategies for the future, or intended strategies, and we can also identify historical strategic developments, called realized strategies. Strategic management involves strategic analysis, strategy formulation, and strategy implementation.

Strategic management is evolving to include a much broader mix of managers from throughout the organization. Historically, only managers at the top of the organization were involved in strategic decisions. However, there is an obvious trend for today's organizations to draw upon and integrate the managerial resources in their middle- and lower-level managers as well. This means that those preparing to manage at any organizational level should be well versed in the fundamentals of strategic management.

Because strategic management is expanding to encompass managers at so many different levels, there is greater need today for an organization to have a unifying sense of common purpose. The formal strategic planning process is one way to communicate that purpose, but it is not enough by itself. Organizations do not (and cannot) strictly adhere to the details of formal plans. Rather, they move toward goals in a series of small steps, occasionally readjusting their direction.

To keep an organization on track, there must be a sense of constancy in its overall purpose. Constancy of purpose requires that managers have a common vision, an accepted mission, and clear objectives. Experience shows that to be most effective, the hierarchy of vision/mission/objectives must include both financial as well as nonfinancial considerations. The stakeholder perspective explicitly acknowledges the multiple contingencies which organizations must serve, and helps balance the needs of each against the others.

Notes

1. Shapiro, B. P. (1988, November–December). What the hell is market-oriented? *Harvard Business Review, 66*, 119–125.
2. Vincent, D. R. (1988, March–April). Understanding organizational power. *Journal of Business Strategy, 9*, 40–44.
3. Carlson, F. P. (1990, May–June). The long and short of strategic planning. *Journal of Business Strategy, 11*, 15–19.
4. Drucker, P. F. (1988, January–February). The coming of the new organization. *Harvard Business Review, 66*, 45–53.
5. See Mintzberg, H. (1989). *Mintzberg on management* (esp. chap. 2). New York: Free Press.
6. Some theorists have attempted to distinguish carefully among the different types of goals according to their level of specificity or breadth. See, for example, Richards, M. D. (1987). *Setting strategic goals and objectives* (3d ed.). St. Paul, MN: West. Unfortunately, there is little agreement in management literature on whose set of definitions is correct, and considering all the options in detail creates a semantic hurdle we will not attempt to clear. To avoid complicating matters further, we will simply describe our terminology without discussing options we could have chosen or justifying our particular selections. We have used goals to refer to desired future states, regardless of the level of specificity. Where the level of specificity is important to note, we use vision, mission, and objective to refer to increasingly detailed and specific types of goals. In Chapter 8, we refer even more specifically to action plans.
7. Stovicek, D. (1991, January). Manufacturing excellence awards: The five winners. *Automation, 38*, 18–28; Treece, J. B. (1990, April 9). Here comes GM's Saturn. *Business Week*, pp. 56–62.
8. In fact, it is fair to say that goals are linked not only to the other elements of strategic analysis, but to strategy formulation and implementation as well. But saying that goals are linked to everything involved in strategic management is not very enlightening. Therefore, we have chosen to maintain a distinction between goals and strategies as separate ends and means considerations. See Dess, G. G. (1987, May–June). Consensus on strategy formulation and organizational performance: Competitors in a fragmented industry. *Strategic Management Journal*, pp. 259–260.
9. Andrews, K. R. (1987). *The concept of corporate strategy* (3d ed.). Homewood, IL: Irwin; Ansoff, H. I. (1965). *Corporate strategy.* New York: McGraw-Hill; Hofer, C. W., & Schendel, D. (1978). *Strategy formulation: Analytical concepts.* St. Paul, MN: West.
10. Traditionally, strategy formulation has focused on the three levels of corporate, business, and function, with international issues treated as a subset of corporate-level management. While we agree that expansion into international competition is a decision that is best handled at the corporate level, the complexities involved in such a decision warrant coverage in a separate chapter. Therefore, we first introduce international management in Chapter 6 on corporate-level management, but then we greatly expand coverage of the important topic in Chapter 7. For a discussion of the diverse and complex topics involved in international management, see Porter, M. E. (Ed.). (1986). *Competition in global industries.* Boston: Harvard Business School Press.
11. Hall, G. E. (1987, January–February). Reflections on running a diversified company. *Harvard Business Review, 65*, 84–92.
12. The SBU's analog in the public sector is the Strategic Public Planning Unit (SPPU). For dis-

cussion of its central role in strategic planning in public organizations, see Montanari, J. R., & Bracker, J. S. (1986, May–June). The strategic management process at the public planning unit level. *Strategic Management Journal, 7*, 251–265.

13. Richman, T. (1990, January). Reorganizing for growth. *Inc.*, pp. 110–111.
14. For discussion of the potential benefits of such broad-based involvement, see Versteeg, A. (1990, November–December). Self-directed work teams yield long-term benefits. *Journal of Business Strategy, 11*, 9–12; Wooldridge, B., & Floyd, S. W. (1990). The strategy process, middle management involvement, and organizational performance. *Strategic Management Journal, 11*, 231–241; and Westley, F. R. (1990). Middle managers and strategy: Microdynamics of inclusion. *Strategic Management Journal, 11*, 337–351.
15. Dumaine, B. (1990, May 7). Who needs a boss? *Fortune, 121*, 52–60; and Stewart, T. A. (1989, November 6). New ways to exercise power. *Fortune, 120*, 52–64.
16. Schuler, R. S., & Jackson, S. E. (1987). Linking competitive strategies with human resource management practices. *The Academy of Management Executive, 1*, 207–219; and Lawler, E. E. (1988). Choosing an involvement strategy. *The Academy of Management Executive, 2*, 197–204.
17. Drucker (Ref. 4), loc. cit.
18. Stewart, T. A. (1989, November 6). New ways to exercise power. *Fortune, 120*, 52–64.
19. Gray, Daniel. (1986, January–February). Uses and misuses of strategic planning. *Harvard Business Review, 64*, 89–97; Greenley, G. E. (1986, April). Does strategic planning improve company performance? *Long Range Planning*, pp. 101–109.
20. Research documents that attempt to force compliance to plans is generally unsuccessful. See Nutt, P. C. (1987, January–February). Identifying and appraising how managers install strategy. *Strategic Management Journal, 8*, 1–14.
21. Goddard, R. W. (1990). The rise of the new organization—doing business in the 1990s: It was never like this before. *Management World, 19*, 3–5.
22. Stayer, R. (1990, November–December). How I learned to let my workers lead. *Harvard Business Review, 68*, 72.
23. Lindblom, C. (1959, June). The science of muddling through. *Public Administration Review*, pp. 79–88.
24. Quinn, J. B. (1980). *Strategies for change: Logical incrementalism.* Homewood, IL: Irwin.
25. Johnson, G. (1988, January–February). Rethinking incrementalism. *Strategic Management Journal, 9*, 75–91.
26. For a discussion of eight "rules" for converting broad-based understanding of strategic goals into action throughout the organization, see Tregoe, B. B. (1990, January–February). An action-oriented approach to strategy. *Journal of Business Strategy, 11*, 16–21.
27. For a discussion of how this works within Levi Strauss & Co., see Howard, R. (1990, September–October). Values make the company: An interview with Robert Haas. *Harvard Business Review, 68*, 132–144.
28. Tregoe, B. B. (1990, January–February). Implementing the vision: The lessons learned. *Planning Review, 18*, 39–44, 48.
29. BankAmerica Corporation provides a good example. See Beck, R. N. (1987). Visions, values, and strategies: Changing attitudes and culture. *Academy of Management Executive, 1*, 33–41.
30. Kiechel, W. (1989, October 23). A hard look at executive vision. *Fortune, 120*, 207–211.
31. Dumaine, B. (1989, July 3). What the leaders of tomorrow see. *Fortune, 120*, 49–62.

32. Matejka, K., & Federouch, A. G. (1990, September). Uniting employees around a mission. *Supervisory Management, 35*, 3.
33. Peters, T. (1987). *Thriving on chaos* (p. 406). New York: Knopf.
34. Merrifield, D. B. (1991). A modern Marshall plan for evolving economies. *Journal of Business Venturing, 6*, 231–236.
35. Want, J. H. (1986, August). Corporate mission: The intangible contributor to performance. *Management Review*, pp. 50–54.
36. For additional guidelines in preparing mission statements, see Pearce, J. A. II, & David, F. (1987). Corporate mission statements: The bottom line. *Academy of Management Executive, 1*, 109–115.
37. In general, nonprofit organizations appeared to have considered these particular issues more thoroughly than profit firms. See discussion in Drucker, P. F. (1989, July–August). What business can learn from non-profits. *Harvard Business Review, 67*, 88–93.
38. See McGinnis, V. (1981, July). The mission statement: A key step in strategic planning. *Business*, pp. 39–43; Nash, L. (1988, March–April). Mission statements: Mirrors and windows. *Harvard Business Review, 66*, 155–156; and Want, J. H. (1988, July). Corporate mission. *Management Review*, pp. 46–50.
39. Levitt, T. (1975, September–October). Marketing myopia. *Harvard Business Review*, p. 26.
40. Richman, T. (1983, August). What business are you really in? *Inc.*, pp. 77–86; Abell, D. F. (1980). *Defining the business: The starting point of strategic planning.* Englewood Cliffs, NJ: Prentice-Hall.
41. McGowan, W. G. (1986, Fall). What business are we really in? The question revisited. *Sloan Management Review*, pp. 59–62.
42. Pearce & David (Ref. 36), loc. cit.
43. McGuire, J. B., Sundgren, A., & Schneeweis, T. (1988). Corporate social responsibility and firm financial performance. *Academy of Management Journal, 31*, 854–872.
44. For a discussion of the critical importance of these nonfinancial considerations, see Griesinger, D. W. (1990). The human side of economic organization. *Academy of Management Review, 15*, 478–499.
45. To learn more about how this general definition is stated more specifically in practice, see Nel, D., Pitt, L., & Watson, R. (1989). Business ethics: Defining the twilight zone. *Journal of Business Ethics, 8*, 781–791; and The business roundtable. (1988, February). *Corporate Ethics: A Prime Business Asset.*
46. Laws generally reflect society's belief in what is morally right and wrong. However, an issue's legality usually does *not* reflect the totality of its perceived morality. This distinction suggests that the letter of the law (a matter of what is legal) is not always the same as the spirit of the law (a matter of what is ethical). See Raiborn, C. A., & Payne, D. (1990). Corporate codes of conduct: A collective conscience and continuum. *Journal of Business Ethics, 9*, 879–889.
47. Peters (Ref. 33), op. cit., p. 402.

CHAPTER 2

The External Environment: Identifying Opportunities and Threats

Many of the challenges facing managers today originate outside their firms. A careful analysis of the external environment can identify major opportunities and threats. Environmental analysis provides managers with important information for strategic decision making and encourages strategic thinking in organizations. Successful firms follow broad environmental trends and continually assess changes taking place in their industry.

Our discussion of the external environment is divided into four major sections. The first section describes how firms collect information about important environmental trends and detailed intelligence on major competitors. This information, in turn, provides important input for making useful forecasts. The next two sections of the chapter address the two parts of the external environment: general environment and competitive environment. Here we will include political, legal, and macroeconomic issues as part of the general environment. The competitive environment includes industry-related factors, such as potential entry by new competitors and rivalry among existing competitors. These factors generally affect the profitability of the firm more than do factors in the general environment. However, the general and competitive environments have a high degree of interdependence. The fourth section discusses how the two environments interact and the implications for managers.

After reading this chapter, you will understand:

- The concept of environmental analysis and its importance in strategy formulation
- The external environment as a source of both opportunities and threats
- Why environmental scanning and competitor intelligence are important inputs in developing forecasts
- Various segments of the general environment and their interrelationships
- How the competitive environment affects competition and profitability within an industry
- The concept of strategic groups and how the nature of competition differs among strategic groups
- How the general and competitive environments interact

EXECUTIVE INTERVIEW

Major General Jeffery D. Kahla
The United States Air Force

Major General Jeffery D. Kahla is the commander of the worldwide Army and Air Force Exchange Service (AAFES). The Exchange Service provides merchandise and services in over 16,000 facilities to military people and families throughout the United States and in twenty-six overseas locations. These operations include 6,125 retail and military clothing stores, 2,200 food facilities, 5,500 personal services concessions, 600 automotive facilities, 100,000 vending machines, 360 movie theaters, and catalog services. In fiscal year 1989, AAFES ranked tenth among retail organizations in the nation, employing more than 82,000 people, with sales over $6.8 billion.

General Kahla has a bachelor's degree in business administration from the University of Washington and a master of science degree from the Graduate School of Business at Stanford University. The general has held a variety of high-level command and staff positions in his twenty-nine-year Air Force career.

During the late 1980s, there were proposed major reductions in military installations and spending. How has this affected the strategic planning and operations at AAFES?

We view these changes as challenges to our strategic planning function. The political realities of the 1990s will require us to anticipate and take actions to minimize the impact of installation closures and a smaller customer base. These challenges are being addressed by a restructured organization to reduce layering and overhead, the use of new technology to maximize productivity, and improved distribution systems to ensure better merchandise availability.

With a flattened organization, we are getting closer to our customer. We will focus on the customer's perception of what value is in their shopping experience. We have identified customer shopping preferences through surveys and management input. AAFES is undergoing a "debureaucratizing" so customers are comfortable in their dealings with their exchanges.

Our plans for the future will be flexible, imaginative, and positive, and always with an eye to our customers. We will be committed to improving service and support for the changing needs of the military family wherever they serve.

Given the importance of environmental business trends and events for AAFES, how do its managers monitor external influences?

Although we are a government entity, our retailing businesses must reflect external business influences and offerings for a clientele very much aware of what is happening outside the military installation. Our managers are tasked with keeping abreast of market changes and trends through a variety of methods.

We, like other major retailers, acquaint ourselves with the competition and attend trade shows to identify trends and outside shopping behaviors. We avail ourselves of the expertise and advice of industry and academic consultants. We read trade publications and attend marketing conferences. Most importantly, though, we listen to our customers.

AAFES customers are sophisticated ones. They have lived in several locations. Most have lived in foreign countries. Their experience with international markets makes it our responsibility to blend goods for a multitude of tastes and cultures. So, we ask their opinion through surveys and comment forms. Then, armed with this information plus our research of the outside, we are better able to establish services or provide goods desirable to our particular customers. This is oftentimes quite a balancing act. It is certainly challenging.

What environmental trends (e.g., demographic, sociopolitical, macroeconomic, sociocultural) beyond congressional and Department of Defense budgeting are important for AAFES?

Everything is important. We're a business with business cycles sensitive to fluctuations in politics, demographics, and finances.

The political vagaries challenging the outside business community also challenge us. We aren't much different in that respect. Trade issues affect our stock assortment. Changes to interstate transportation laws affect distribution and prices. Environmental control concerns affect our service stations, fast food and retail businesses. The involvement in the Middle East affects gasoline availability and prices. We are subject to change much more than our private counterparts due to international political concerns.

Continued

Technology has had a tremendous impact on us and our industry. Every aspect of our businesses can be enhanced because of technology, and we are in the process of doing so. Improved communications keep our entire organization informed and focused on important issues. Industry changes can be adopted more easily, making products and services more timely and more readily available—and making us more efficient. One goal is to make it look easy to our customers. What goes on behind the scenes should never affect the customer, and technology helps us do that.

As the demographics of the military family changes, so do our marketing responses. The two-income family has created shopping behavior changes. Time-restrained families demand quality and convenience for their money. Our response has changed from providing goods and services to creating a relationship empathetic to the needs of the customer. In this respect, we broaden the customer's use of our stores.

The shrinking labor pool affects AAFES in that our normal military family reservoir of employees is no longer readily available. We compete for employees with better benefits and career progression, and importance of family issues has created a more flexible working environment.

What types of people will be most critical to carry out your plans for the future?

The people who will carry out the plans of the organization will be those interested in a diverse, global company, and who are dedicated to serving its customers. We will require people who are analytical or visionary in order to steer our company in the future, but the most critical will be people who ascribe to outstanding customer service standards. In an age of sameness, customer service will differentiate the retailing winners from losers in the nineties.

Also, as competition increases, our management, particularly at the exchange level, will have to be more entrepreneurial than ever before. With the flattened organization, it will be possible for our people to bring needs and concerns directly to the headquarters for action. Quick responses through improved communications will result in better customer service. Fortunately, AAFES has people with dedication and entrepreneurial spirit.

OBTAINING AND USING ENVIRONMENTAL INFORMATION

To make effective decisions managers must understand the external environment in which their firms operate.[1] Firms must continually monitor the events and general trends in their environments, as well as the actions and intentions of their competitors. The first two parts of this section cover environmental scanning and competitor intelligence. Exhibit 2.1 shows that these activities provide the inputs for forecasting, which is discussed later in the chapter. We will conclude the section by addressing some of the major limitations of forecasting.

Scanning

Scanning activities involve monitoring and evaluating information from the external environment and disseminating it to key people within the organization. Because scanning is an expensive and time-consuming process, businesses must direct their efforts to evaluating those trends that have a significant impact on their present and future product-market activities. A popular method of scanning involves being aware of general trends and events while closely monitoring specific factors that directly influence the firm. Companies in the baby food industry, for example, are likely to scan broadly general demographic informa-

EXHIBIT 2.1
Key Inputs to Forecasting

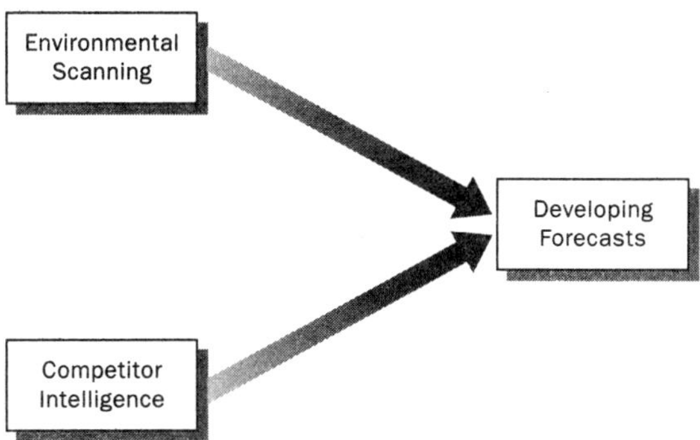

tion, such as income levels, population migration, and birth rates. However, they would closely monitor specific information related to the number of births occurring in different geographic areas.

Environmental scanning is done by designated units in the organization or by managers in a variety of line and staff positions. In many organizations, these tend to be nontechnical personnel who prepare summaries of relevant articles. Corporations also often spend considerable sums on data provided by various organizations. For example, the *Economist* intelligence unit periodically produces country and industry reports to which many international banks subscribe. Firms also retain the services of consultants who prepare reports analyzing and interpreting the impact a specific development has on the industry and the firm.[2]

To remain competitive, firms must also scan important global trends and events.[3] American firms, however, are often slow in becoming aware of significant technological advances, such as important inventions, improvements in manufacturing processes, and innovations in fabricating or assembling products. Compared to their international competitors, U.S. firms are less likely to

- Send their researchers, engineers, and technicians to international conferences and trade shows
- Visit their global competitors
- Systematically gather data on the results of government-funded research in other nations
- Carefully review technical or scientific journals and newspapers published in other countries

By contrast, many Japanese firms consider global scanning for technological insights to be a critical means for improving their technological expertise. In Japanese firms, global scanning takes a variety of forms:

- Organizing study teams to visit research laboratories in the United States and Europe

Attending pertinent conferences and trade shows, and carefully scanning publications from many countries

Financing research and development activities in American universities and corporate laboratories and closely monitoring the results

- Gathering technological information around the world through government agencies, and making it available to industry through such agencies as Japan's Ministry of Trade and Industry (MITI)

While approximately 5,000 Japanese scientists worked in U.S. laboratories in 1988, only about 150 U.S. scientists worked in Japanese laboratories. Perhaps part of Japan's success in international markets may be attributed to their commitment and ability to collect and analyze vast amounts of environmental information from throughout the world.

Many firms are practicing a type of environmental scanning that is becoming increasingly popular—monitoring other firms either inside or outside of their industry with the purpose of learning from their experience. An example of a small firm that has greatly benefited from this practice is Manco, Inc., a Westlake, Ohio-based firm with annual sales of $60 million. Application 2.1 describes how Manco, Inc. monitors other firms for purposes of learning.

Gathering Intelligence about Competitors

Continuous scanning of changes in the external environment enables managers to determine how the firm should be positioned in the long run to exploit new opportunities. However, in the short-to-medium term, it is equally important for the firm to anticipate the actions of its current competitors and be aware of potential new entrants. Information about the competition helps managers develop strategies to counteract or preempt their competitors. Firms gather information about competitors by systematically looking at a large number of factors, including planned new-product introductions, capacity increases, cost structures, executive incentive and compensation plans, and financial position.

An increasing number of firms are recognizing the need for competitive intelligence activities. For example:[4]

- In the late 1970s, Xerox's hold on the photocopier market was challenged when Canon introduced a copier that retailed for less than Xerox's manufacturing cost on a comparable machine. To learn from its competitor's success, Xerox engineers disassembled their rival's copier. Xerox then strived to beat Canon's 300 components on both cost and quality. Xerox has since regained its dominance in this industry.
- Coors's wine cooler failed soon after its introduction in 1985. However, the company remained interested in this segment of the industry. A five-person task force was charged with determining what level of profits Gallo, the leading competitor, was making on its wine coolers. After subjecting Gallo's product to chemical analysis to determine its ingredients, Coors went to suppliers to determine the prices of these ingredients. Realizing they could not compete with Gallo on the basis of price, Coors decided to not reenter the market.
- During 1986, Marriott Corporation assembled a team of six employees to collect information on competitors in the economy segment of the hotel industry. This team

Application 2.1

Manco, Inc.: How a Small Business Learns from Larger Role Models

Manco, Inc., has come a long way from its days as a small ($4 million) distributor of industrial tape in the late 1970s. Under Jack Kahl, president and CEO, it has grown into a $60 million distributor of tapes, weather stripping, and mailing supplies. Jack Kahl attributes this rapid growth to his willingness and ability to learn from other firms, especially firms that he views as role models. Manco has learned a great deal about merchandising and marketing from Walt Disney, about communication and leadership from Wal-Mart, and about recruitment and hiring from Pepsico.

Where did Kahl find his role models? How did he choose them? Sometimes his system for learning from big companies seems more like art than science, but here are some guidelines he follows:

1. *Finding role model candidates.* Kahl looks just about everywhere: in magazines, in books, and among customers, competitors, and suppliers. Federal Express Corp. came under greater scrutiny after Kahl heard a speech by Fred Smith, its founder and chief executive. He hooked up with another CEO when they were buying boats at the same time. He also studies *Fortune*'s annual most-admired-company poll and sends away for the best annual reports, as ranked by *Chief Executive* magazine. Any smart company—though its problems and circumstances may be very different from your own—probably has something to impart, he says.
2. *Choosing which companies to follow.* Almost all of Kahl's top teachers are well-known and well-established companies. "We follow the absolute best," says Kahl. It makes sense; after all, he wants to find ideas that he knows have worked. There is, of course, an element of subjectivity. He admires Merck & Co., the prescription-drug giant, but says, "For whatever reason, I just haven't kept up with them." He does tend to stick with companies that face some of the same broad challenges that Manco does, such as selling consumer products or working through retail channels.
3. *Studying them.* Don't stop with annual reports, 10-Ks, speeches, and articles. Mingle at trade shows, use a clipping service, ask customers what they know. Kahl has been known to call up Wall Street retailing analysts and pump them with queries: Who's doing well and why? Is what I hear about K-Mart true? To keep abreast of many of their role models, the Manco folks have cultivated often-overlooked contacts, such as retail flow supervisors.
4. *Bringing the ideas inside your company.* Nothing you learn from role models will affect your business, of course, if you don't create forums where ideas can spread. At Manco, top executives meet on Thursday afternoon; that evening, the entire company is invited to get together. Individual departments, such as marketing, hold their own idea-swapping sessions. Manco also churns out newsletters: *Duck Tales* goes to everyone, *Duck Calls* targets the sales staff, and *Food Facts* is sent to food brokers. Kahl constantly shares articles and offers classes at Manco U., a giant conference room in the company's headquarters. "This is how we compete," he says. "The fun for us is learning fast."

Source

Excerpted from Hyatt, J. (1991, February). Steal this strategy. *Inc.*, pp. 49–57 (with permission).

traveled the country and stayed at a variety of competitors' motels, gathering information on several issues including room decor; services provided; brands of soap, shampoo, and towels; and quality of soundproofing. Such detailed data about their rivals' strengths and weaknesses encouraged Marriott to allocate $500 million to launch the highly successful Fairfield Inn chain of economy-priced motels.

In each of these cases, a thorough knowledge of the competition's strengths, weaknesses, and cost structures enabled Xerox, Coors, and Marriott either to avoid costly mistakes or to improve their competitive position.

Competitive intelligence generally involves the gathering of information about competitors in the public domain.[5] For example, it is possible to get information about a competitor's proposed construction or extension of a facility from the tax assessor, or the local builders' council, which files building plans for use by companies bidding on plant construction. Plants and production are monitored by the Occupational Safety and Health Administration and the Environmental Protection Agency, as well as by various state-level offices. These offices can be valuable sources of information regarding competitors' technology, production capacity and utilization rates, and plant layouts. In regulated industries, such as communications, banking, and trucking, useful information about competitors can be obtained from the Federal Communications Commission, Federal Deposit Insurance Corporation, and Interstate Commerce Commission, respectively. Very often, closely watching a competitor's employment advertisements can provide extremely valuable information about current problems or future plans. Local newspapers and specialized trade journals also offer a great deal of information about competitors.[6] When searching beyond information that is available in the public domain, managers must make sure they do not misrepresent themselves or violate accepted standards of ethical corporate behavior.[7] For example, in its attempt to thwart an unfriendly takeover attempt by its chief rival, Mary Kay, Avon hired detectives to rifle Mary Kay's trash dumpster.[8] Avon's investigators claim that they did not do anything illegal and even have videotapes to prove that the dumpster was in a public parking lot. Mary Kay, however, wants its garbage back and is suing for damages. In addition to legal issues, this incident has also raised a considerable ethical controversy.

From Information Acquisition to Forecasting

Once information is gathered by scanning the external environment and by collecting intelligence on competitors, managers are able to make forecasts about the future. Forecasting involves the prediction of future events or trends which can range from broad issues such as a nation's gross national product (GNP) for the next year to narrow issues such as the sales for a firm's product in a specific geographic market. As part of environmental forecasting, managers need to anticipate long-term changes in the national and international economies, as well as broad social changes. These changes often have profound implications for the formulation and implementation of their firms' strategies. Application 2.2 summarizes predictions for trends in the 1990s. Many companies have already taken into account such predictions in their strategies. For example, U.S. firms, such as Nike and Coca-Cola, anticipated China's emergence as a major economic power and had already established a presence in that country by the mid-1980s.

Managers also need to make forecasts about more specific issues, such as customer preferences, demand for the firm's existing and proposed products and services, availability and prices of input materials, and the impact of technological innovations. This environmental forecasting provides valuable information for understanding the current and potential changes in the environment that are relevant from the firm's point of view.[9]

Limitations of Forecasting

Despite advances in forecasting techniques, forecasting still remains as much an art as a science. Even the most sophisticated methods are of little benefit when the model on which

Application 2.2

What's Next? A Spectrum of Possibilities

The predictions below from *Fortune* cover up to the year 2000 and are presented in order of *decreasing probability* ranging from almost certain to possible.

- The Hispanic population will grow by one-third, while the non-Hispanic U.S. population will grow by less than one-tenth.
- Catastrophic health insurance will be mandated by federal law.
- U.S.-born white males will make up only about 15 percent of the net increase in the labor force.
- Major business schools will require proficiency in at least one foreign language.
- China will emerge as a major economic power.
- Tuition plus room and board at an Ivy League university will rise to $40,000 a year.
- Inflation will stay between 4 percent and 5 percent.
- A lot of leveraged buyouts taken privately in the eighties will go public.
- In assembly-line operations, shape-recognizing robots will remove defective parts, then manufacture and install replacements.
- Employees will directly own more than half the stock in half of the Fortune 500 companies.

The following predictions for the year 2000 are from *Megatrends 2000* by John Naisbitt and Patricia Aburdene:

- A single optic fiber will be able to transmit 10 million conversations simultaneously. This compares with only 3,000 conversations per fiber in 1988.
- Eighty million more people will be added to the wealthiest Asian countries (compared to about 10 million in Europe).
- The average age of the U.S. population will be significantly less than the average in both Europe and Japan.
- There will be 2 billion airline passengers annually—twice the 1990 level.
- The Pacific Rim's GNP will exceed that of western Europe and equal that of North America. (In 1960, its GNP was approximately one-half of North America's and one-third of Europe's.)
- California will have the world's fourth largest economy—behind the rest of the United States, Japan, and Germany.
- The United States labor supply will increase less than 1 percent a year—the slowest growth since the 1930s. The 1990s will be the tightest labor market in decades.

Sources

Kupfer, A. (1988, September 26). Managing new for the 1990's. *Fortune*, pp. 44–47.

Naisbitt, J., & Aburdene, P. (1990). *Megatrends 2000*. New York: William Morrow.

the forecasts are based is itself inaccurate (for example, inadequate understanding of key variables and their relationships) or when data are incomplete or unreliable.

Several factors may lead to less than ideal forecasts. Application 2.3 identifies some of the basic reasons why forecasts miss their mark.

Beyond basic judgment errors that result in inaccurate forecasts, there are factors related to the actual environmental analysis process in the corporation that may cause problems. One of the major causes of incorrect forecasts is what is sometimes referred to as the *safe forecast* problem. In this situation, planners, fearful of adverse reactions, tend to become too conservative in their forecasting in order to avoid risk. For example, managers may deliberately underestimate sales projections in order to attain targets easily and receive

Application 2.3

Failures in Growth Market Forecasting

Basing their work on published forecasts, Steven Schnarrs and Conrad Berenson identified eight major causes of failure in growth-market forecasting. Their study covered forecasts made between 1960 and 1979 and included every fifth issue of *Business Week* and *Fortune*, as well as the entire record of *The Wall Street Journal.*

Source

Copyright 1986 by the Regents of the University of California. Reprinted from Schnarrs, S. P., & Berenson, C. (1986). Growth market forecasting. *California Management Review, 28*(4), 71–88. By permission of the regents.

Cause of Failure	*Example*
1. Overvaluation of technological wonders	3-D color TV Robot soldiers Nuclear-powered, underwater recreation centers
2. No relative advantage for the consumer	Quadraphonic stereo systems Freeze-dried meats
3. Too expensive for the benefit provided	Foam-filled tires Moving sidewalks Graphite fibers
4. Shift in the relative advantage demanded by the consumer	Steam-powered cars
5. Changes in social and demographic variables	"Roll-your-own" cigarettes Nuclear earth excavation
6. Technical problems	Electric cars
7. Undue pessimism	Demise of big-budget/big-profit films
8. Political factors	National Health Insurance to be enacted in 1985 Marine mining

rewards associated with them. This may prevent the organization from taking advantage of new opportunities. A related problem is the urge to gather excessive amounts of information rather than to think critically about key information. For example, Texas Instruments used to predict fifteen variables in its 10-year forecast. When they cut the number of variables from fifteen to four, they were able to focus on the key variables that have the greatest impact on performance. Thus, they found their planning process to be much more effective.[10]

A survey of forecasting practices in 127 corporations identified four major stumbling blocks to the successful application of forecasting.[11] These were:

- A lack of effective communication between forecast preparers and managers who used the forecasts for decision making

- A lack of effective forecasting skills
- A disparity between forecast preparers and users in perceptions of the company's forecasting requirements
- A failure to plan a set of actions that realizes the full benefit of the forecasting activities

Forecasting procedures that are not adequately integrated into the company's strategic planning process may remain a fruitless exercise. While environmental forecasts are a necessary input in planning for the future, managers must recognize that they can neither foretell the future nor eliminate uncertainty for the organization through the use of these techniques.[12] However, effective forecasting does reduce the frequency and magnitude of surprises that may confront the firm.

THE GENERAL ENVIRONMENT

The general environment consists of factors external to the industry that may have a significant impact on the firm's strategies. A firm cannot typically control its general environment. Also, many developments in the general environment are difficult to predict with any degree of accuracy. For example, macroeconomic developments, such as interest rates, the rate of inflation, and exchange rates, are extremely difficult to predict on a medium and long-term basis. However, some trends in the general environment, such as population distribution by age, ethnicity, and income levels, can be forecast with a high degree of accuracy.

The general environment consists of many diverse but interrelated parts. Here we will look at six broad segments: *demographic, sociocultural, political/legal, technological, macroeconomic,* and *global.* Exhibit 2.2 lists some major issues in each segment. These issues often overlap and developments in one area may influence those in another. The development of high-definition television by Japanese and European companies, for example, has forced the U.S. government to reevaluate provisions of the antitrust laws that could prevent U.S. companies from engaging in collective research and development activities. In this case, a technological development prompted a change in the political/legal environment.

Developments in the general environment often provide a firm with opportunities for expansion in terms of both products and markets. For example, the emergence of Hispanics as an increasingly important consumer group provides many firms with an opportunity to cater to their specific needs. Changes and trends in the general environment may also pose serious threats to entire industries. For example, high interest rates always have a very detrimental effect on the demand for "big ticket" items such as homes and automobiles. The competitive environment, on the other hand, largely determines the nature of competition among firms within an industry. A firm's managers typically have more influence over the competitive environment. Developments and trends in the competitive environment can usually be predicted with a relatively high degree of accuracy. However, in industries characterized by extremely high rates of technological change, such as prescription drugs, predicting future developments is quite difficult.

General environmental changes may alter the boundaries of an industry, as has been the case with deregulation in the financial services, telecommunications, and airlines industries.[13] An environmental trend that presents new opportunities for one industry may have

EXHIBIT 2.2
Some Important Factors in the General Environment

Demographic Environment
- Aging of the population
- Ethnic composition
- Maturing of the baby boom generation
- Regional changes in population growth and decline

Sociocultural Environment
- Women in the work force
- Health and fitness awareness
- Erosion of educational standards
- Spread of addictive drugs
- Concern for the environment

Political/Legal Environment
- Deregulation
- Relaxed antitrust enforcement
- Environmental protection laws

Technological Environment
- Biotechnology
- Consumer electronics
- Superconductivity
- High-definition television technology
- Process innovations (e.g., robotics and minimills)
- Industrial disasters

Macroeconomic Environment
- Interest rates
- Exchange rates
- Inflation rates
- Savings rates
- Trade deficit/surplus
- Budget deficit/surplus

Global Environment
- Similarity in consumer tastes and preferences
- Powerful economic alliances
- Opening of eastern bloc countries
- Third world debt problems

the opposite effect on another industry. Even within the same industry, an environmental development that one firm perceives as an opportunity, may seem to be a threat to another. For example, the predicted decrease in the population of 18-year-olds to 24-year-olds is a threat to colleges and universities that only see their traditional market diminishing. However, institutions have turned this threat into an opportunity by successfully offering programs such as adult continuing education classes and degree programs to older students.

Demographic Changes

As we approach the 21st century, dramatic changes are taking place in the demographic profile of the United States. Some of these major changes pose significant challenges for many businesses. These include the aging of the population, population shifts among regions, changes in ethnic composition, and continuing effects of the baby boom generation (i.e., individuals born between 1946 and 1962). Let's now look at each of these changes.

Over the past few decades, stagnant or declining birth rates combined with increasing life expectancy have led to an increase in the average age of the population. This has resulted in increased demand for services and facilities appropriate for the elderly, such as convalescent homes and health services. Estimates project a decline of 17 percent in the 18-year-old to 24-year-old age group by 1995.[14] This will further aggravate the labor shortages currently experienced in some sectors of the economy.

The geographic distribution of the U.S. population is also changing continuously. Over the past few decades, more people have migrated to the south and west than to the northeast and midwest.[15] This trend has influenced relocation decisions for many firms.

Changes in the ethnic composition of the United States provide many challenges and opportunities for U.S. firms. The Census Bureau reported that the Hispanic population has increased by roughly 30 percent from 1980 to 1987 (14.5 million to 18.5 million)—five times the growth rate of the non-Hispanic population. By the year 2000, it is estimated that 25.2 million Hispanics will live in the United States.[16] Some organizations have started specifically targeting Hispanics in their advertising campaigns.

By the late 1980s, roughly one-third of the U.S. population belonged to the baby boom generation. Baby boomers are now in their peak earning and consumption years and therefore represent a very important market segment for products and services such as automobiles, specialty foods, financial services, travel, and clothing. Recognizing the importance of this demographic trend, automobile manufacturers, such as Toyota, Nissan, Honda, and Mercedes Benz, have introduced medium-priced luxury cars in the $25,000 to $40,000 price range.

Sociocultural Changes

Social attitudes and cultural values constantly evolve and can have a significant impact on U.S. businesses. Some of these, which we will briefly discuss below, include more women in the work force, a greater concern about health and fitness, an erosion of U.S. secondary educational standards relative to other developed countries, the pervasive influence of addictive drugs, and the increasing militancy of consumer activists.

Since the 1970s, increasing numbers of women have joined the work force at all levels; approximately 80 percent of women aged 20 to 30 are currently employed outside of the home.[17] This trend has led to greater disposable incomes for families with two working members, thus increasing demand for "big ticket" items such as cars, homes, and leisure travel. It has also led to increased demand for childcare services, convenience foods, restaurants, and other products and services for working couples.

The current fitness boom has been responsible for the success of a wide variety of firms in businesses such as athletic shoes and equipment, health foods, and fitness clubs and spas. Increasing numbers of restaurants and hotels are offering low-calorie menus and exercise facilities to attract health-conscious customers.

Several sociocultural changes may pose major threats to many businesses. According to recent estimates, approximately a quarter of the U.S. labor force—20 to 27 million adults—lack basic reading, writing, and math skills. Consequently, more than half of the Fortune 500 companies have assumed an important role in educating the work force.[18] Application 2.4 describes efforts of some U.S. corporations to address the problem of decreasing skill levels in the work force.

Application 2.4

U.S. Business: Playing an Increasing Role in Education

Maintaining a skilled and trained work force is an increasingly difficult challenge for U.S. businesses. Thirty percent of all high school students drop out before graduation. Many who do graduate do not have basic problem-solving skills. The challenge of American business is intensified by the decreasing number of available new workers.

William Wiggenhorn, Motorola's director of training, dramatizes America's comparative educational standing vis-à-vis the Japanese. He calculates it costs U.S. businesses $200 (on average) to train a worker in statistical quality control versus $0.47 for a worker in Japan. Unless the educational system dramatically improves, U.S. companies may be fighting a losing battle to regain their competitive edge over their foreign rivals.

Many U.S. corporations are playing an active role in employee education, spending approximately $30 billion each year to upgrade employee skills. General Motors spends more than 15 percent of its $170 million job training budget for remedial education. American Express devotes $10 million a year to basic English and social skills for its entry-level employees. Since 1982, 8,500 of Ford's 106,000 blue-collar workers have enrolled in the company's fifty learning centers located in its U.S. plants.

Developing close alliances with the public school system has also been a common practice for U.S. corporations. Chemical Bank finds that it must interview forty high school students to find one who is capable of completing its training program. In response, the firm has become involved in many educational activities in two high schools and has formed a high school debating league. General Electric spends $50,000 per year to work with top students at the Manhattan Center for Science and Mathematics, a new public school in New York's Spanish Harlem, to prepare students for careers in science and engineering. In 2 years, 95 percent of the seniors have graduated. One thousand Dallas businesses have adopted the city's 200 public schools—providing volunteers, funds, and equipment.

Sources

Perry, N. J. (1988, July 9). The education crisis: What business can do. *Fortune*, pp. 71–81.

Gorman, C. (1988, December 19). The literacy gap. *Time*, pp. 56–58.

Ehrlich, E. (1988, September 19). Business is becoming a substitute teacher. *Business Week*, pp. 134–135.

Reich, R. B. (1990, November). Metamorphosis of the American worker. *Business Month*, pp. 58–61, 64–66.

Farrell, C. (1990, December 17). Why we should invest in human capital. *Business Week*, pp. 88–90.

Loss of productivity as a result of drug and alcohol abuse and cigarette smoking continues to represent a major expense to businesses and U.S. society. During the late 1980s, the abuse of drugs and alcohol cost the United States more than $140 billion annually, including $100 billion in lost productivity.[19] Such lost productivity further erodes U.S. competitiveness in comparison to firms from relatively drug-free societies, such as Japan, and has forced many companies to institute drug education and testing programs to stem these productivity losses.

Finally, lobbying by consumer activist groups, along with the surgeon general's reports, have had a very negative impact on tobacco companies. In response, many companies, such as Phillip Morris, have diversified into nontobacco businesses.

The Political and Legal Environment

Political and legal developments can expand or limit a company's freedom of action and make the environment more hostile or more supportive of its activities. Major developments in recent years include greater deregulation in some industries and a more lenient interpretation of antitrust laws, greater environmental protection legislation, growing power of political action committees, and decreased spending for national defense. We will now look at an example from each of these developments.

Deregulation in industries such as airlines, trucking, banking, and utilities has led to new entries and increased competitive intensity. Firms that realized the trend early were able to complete large mergers and acquisitions in the 1980s. For example, Phillip Morris acquired Kraft for $13 billion, Chevron bought Gulf Oil Corporation for $13.3 billion, and Kohlberg, Kravis, Roberts (KKR) acquired RJR Nabisco for $25 billion. The enormous size of these deals suggests that very few companies are invulnerable to takeover attempts. Currently, there appears to be a renewed appreciation for the role governments need to play even in free markets. Deregulation is often cited as the major cause of the collapse of the savings and loan industry in the late 1980s. The expected cost to the government is estimated to be between $140 billion and $500 billion.[20]

Sometimes, government regulations foster the development of new industries. The increasing number of government regulations and stronger penalties for illegally dumping toxic waste caused additional expenses to several industries. But this also created a large demand for the services of waste disposal firms. Clean Harbors, Inc., located in Braintree, Massachusetts, had revenues exceeding $100 million annually within 8 years of inception. Chemical Waste Management, located in Oakbrook, Illinois, saw a profit growth from $25 million in 1985 to over $100 million by the end of the decade.[21]

There is a growing debate about the influence exerted by political action committees (PACs) in public policy making. PACs are formed by interest groups to influence public policy making to their advantage. This is very often done by raising and contributing large amounts of funds to candidates for political office who are in a position to promote or defeat legislation. Application 2.5 discusses the growth of political action committees (PACs) in response to federal regulations regarding campaign contributions.

A political development of far-reaching significance is the end of the cold war. This is expected to bring about fundamental changes in the defense spending of the United States. Some estimates suggest that defense spending will fall by 13.6 percent to $261 billion by 1995, and to perhaps $225 billion by the year 2000. This may lead to the reduction of as many as one million defense-related jobs between 1989 and 1995, including 830,000 in the private sector. This represents approximately 20 percent of all jobs in defense-related industries.[22]

Technological Developments

Technological developments affect most products and services as well as the processes by which they are created and delivered. Such advances create new products, shorten the life cycle of existing products, and change the level of capital investment and production costs of individual products.

Recent advances in biotechnology have created a variety of new products ranging from new life-saving drugs to corn that produces its own pesticides. Companies like Genentech and Biosource Genetics Corporation have been successful in bringing to the marketplace several products based on advances in biotechnology. In the area of consumer electronics, the development of high-definition television may have applications in areas such as mili-

Application 2.5

Political Action Committees (PACs): Access or Corruption?

The 1974 amendments to the Campaign Reform Act restrict the amount of money individuals may contribute to a single candidate to $1,000 and to multiple candidates in a federal election to $25,000 per year. Although companies, unions, or other organizations may not contribute *directly* to political campaigns, they may form and contribute to PACs, which give money to politicians. A PAC cannot donate more than $10,000 to a single campaign, but it may contribute to as many different campaigns as it wishes.

Overall, total PAC contributions to political campaigns skyrocketed from $25 million during the 1980 elections to more than $80 million during the 1988 elections. Not surprisingly, firms and industries most heavily regulated or influenced by legislation form the wealthiest PACs:

- AT&T ranks first with a PAC fund of $1.45 million (as of 1987), which was used to support 398 congressional candidates.
- United Parcel Service gave $616,000 in 1986 to more than 300 members of Congress through its corporate PAC.

During the 1988 congressional elections, PACs *increased* the amount of funds directed toward incumbents by 29.4 percent, while the money spent on challengers was relatively constant. Overall, for every dollar spent on challengers, approximately $19 goes to incumbents. Some argue that PAC money may freeze the balance of power between the two parties, giving many incumbents what can amount to a lifetime appointment to Congress.

Two extreme positions have emerged: Do PACs merely ensure that interest groups are given a fair hearing in the corridors of power? Or is it the case, as Fred Wertheimer, president of Washington-based Common Cause, has argued: "House members are shielded by a wall of political money that makes them nearly invincible"?

Sources

Harbrecht, D. A., & Fly, R. (1987, June 1). Is Congress ready to bite the hands that feed it? *Business Week*, pp. 102–103.

Gorman, C. (1988, October 31). The price of power. *Time*, pp. 44–45.

Bonfante, J., Gorey, H., & Woodbury, R. (1990, November 19). Keep the bums in. *Time*, pp. 32–34, 39–42.

Dwyer, P. (1990, August 20). The campaign reform bill was born to be vetoed. *Business Week*, p. 45.

tary surveillance, production of semiconductor chips, and medical diagnosis.[23] Another exciting technological development of recent years has been advances in superconductivity. This is expected to lead to more efficient power plants and underwater propulsion systems.

The history of compact discs (CDs) illustrates how technological developments can abruptly shorten the life cycle of an existing product. The introduction of CDs has led to a significant decline in demand for long-playing (LP) records. As of 1988, CDs outsold LP records by 3 to 1.[24] By 1990, CDs had established complete market dominance and were outselling LPs by 24 to 1.[25] Another example is the advent of fax machines, which rendered telex equipment obsolete.[26] Similarly, major process improvements, such as minimill technology in steel manufacturing and the use of robotics in automobile assembly plants, have radically changed the economics of production. Minimills require only a fraction of the capital necessary to build an integrated steel mill. On the other hand, the use of robotics and other process changes have greatly increased the capital investment necessary for a modern automobile plant.

Although technological innovations play a key role in industrial growth, they may also lead to problems. Major industrial disasters such as Chernobyl and Three Mile Island in the nuclear power industry, the chemical leakage in the Union Carbide Plant in Bhopal, India, and controversies regarding the possible impact of pesticides in the food chain have raised major concerns about the potential damage that technological developments can do to the environment. Policy makers need to consider issues such as the depletion of the ozone layer, acid rain, and the overall deterioration of the environment when assessing the full impact of technology.

The Macroeconomic Environment

The overall state of the economy greatly influences the strategies and performance of various industries and competitors within each industry. Some of the more prominent indicators by which the health of an economy can be judged are growth in GNP, interest rates, inflation rates, savings rates, and trade and budget deficits/surpluses.

These indicators are highly interrelated. The GNP represents the dollar measure of the value of all goods and services produced within an economy. As such, an increase in the GNP is generally associated with higher levels of consumer and industrial demand for products and services. Demand for many goods and services, such as automobiles and entertainment, rises and falls according to fluctuations in interest rates; the higher the interest rate, the lower the demand. The cost of capital also goes up during periods of higher interest rates, thus depressing capital investment. Because interest rates are such an important factor in decisions involving major expenditures for plant and equipment, managers need to monitor them closely.

The fluctuating price of oil was a major cause of changes in inflation rates during most of the 1980s. Early in the decade, soaring oil prices fueled inflation to double-digit levels. When prices fell in the mid-1980s, the inflation rate dropped to below 2 percent. There is widespread concern about the low savings rate in the United States compared to other industrialized countries such as Japan, because the level of savings represents a pool of capital that can be used for industrial expansion.

Two important issues that continue to play a major role in the macroeconomic environment are the trade and budget deficits. The annual trade deficit during the latter half of the 1980s has ranged between $100 and $150 billion. Oil imports alone have fluctuated from a high of $80 billion early in the decade to a low of $35 billion in 1986.[27] Trade deficits are ultimately financed by increasing debt or by the sale of national assets. The continuing federal budget deficit during the late 1980s has been a cause for alarm since it negatively affects national savings. In other words, it diminishes U.S. capacity to make domestic and foreign investments. Further, debt servicing begins to claim a larger part of the national budgets, diverting funds from investment in much needed areas such as infrastructure and education. From its earlier position as the world's biggest creditor nation, the United States has become a major debtor nation. Some of the major factors that contributed to substantial deficits include the aggressive export growth strategies pursued by many newly industrialized countries such as Korea and Taiwan, a gradual decline in the competitiveness of U.S. manufacturers, and the propensity of the U.S. consumer to save less and spend more. From a deficit of around $50 billion a year in the early 1980s, the deficit reached a peak of $170 billion by 1987, and then declined to approximately $125 billion per year for the rest of the 1980s.[28]

The Global Environment

Today, most successful large business organizations have expanded the scope of their operations into the international arena. Both production and marketing efforts of large corporations have become increasingly globalized. This trend has been accelerated by factors such as cheaper and faster means of transportation, more powerful communication, and more similarity in tastes and consumption patterns across nations. Also, worldwide markets have made it easier for companies to recoup large investments in new technologies. In global markets, managers must be aware of potential competition from national and international competitors. Let's look at some of the trends that might affect organizations in the international arena.

One trend that has influenced the world economy is the emergence of powerful economic alliances among countries. Some of these are the European Community (EC), Organization of Petroleum Exporting Countries (OPEC), Organization of American States (OAS), and Association of South East Asian Nations (ASEAN). The creation of a "truly common market" in Europe by 1992, which greatly diminishes trade barriers among the twelve-member countries, presents major opportunities and threats.[29] For example, U.S. auto makers already present in Europe would greatly benefit from the common manufacturing standards that are being implemented. On the other hand, the rise of giant European corporations through the consolidation of several firms in member countries would pose a greater competitive threat to U.S. companies doing business in Europe.

In recent years, strategic alliances have become increasingly popular among multinational companies as a means to gain access to markets in other countries as well as to acquire state-of-the-art technologies.[30] Prominent examples of alliances include Texas Instruments and Kobe Steel to make logic semiconductors in Japan; Boeing and Fuji, Mitsubishi, and Kawasaki to produce the new Boeing 777; and Corning and Ciba-Geigy to produce a variety of medical equipment. However, not all alliances are successful. For example, AT&T's joint venture with Olivetti of Italy was a failure. The marriage between AT&T's communications equipment and Olivetti's personal computing equipment failed because of problems in merging the two technologies. Further, cultural differences between the two companies also contributed to the failure.

Developments in the global environment may have both positive and negative implications for today's managers. Industries such as automobiles, ship building, and personal computers are faced with a new competitor in Hyundai of South Korea. On the other hand, the large populations of the U.S.S.R., Eastern Europe, and China provide a lucrative market for many consumer goods firms. Companies such as Coca-Cola, Pepsi, and McDonald's have been among the first to make use of the opportunities provided by the move toward economic liberalization in these countries. Similarly, a united and prosperous Germany could prove to be a lucrative market for a variety of consumer goods. The reunification of Germany is expected to result in the creation of an economic superpower with a combined population of 78 million. Some experts estimate that the rate of GNP growth of a united Germany will be 50 percent higher than what the West German growth rate would have been without the unification.[31]

A problem that could have serious consequences for a variety of U.S. businesses is the international debt crisis. The inability on the part of many debtor nations to meet their credit obligations severely restricts capital inflows into these countries, which stifles their

EXHIBIT 2.3
Interrelationships among Different Segments of the General Environment

Example 1: High-Definition Television (HDTV)

The development of HDTV by Japanese electronics firms is indicative of Japan's supremacy in consumer electronics (global and technological). This could worsen the U.S. trade deficit with Japan (macroeconomic). U.S. electronics firms are trying to persuade the U.S. government to change antitrust laws in order to allow joint research and development (political/legal).

Example 2: The U.S. Trade Deficit

The persistence of large U.S. trade deficits (macroeconomic) has led to greater demand for protectionist measures, such as trade barriers and quotas (political/legal). These measures lead to higher prices for U.S. consumers and fuel inflation (macroeconomic). Also, in the long run, the protected U.S. industry may become less competitive internationally (global).

Example 3: Erosion of U.S. Educational Standards

As U.S. educational standards decline, American industry is confronted with the problem of a less-skilled work force (sociocultural). Such declining skill levels may especially have negative consequences for the high-technology sector of the U.S. economy (technological). This may lead to a decline in U.S. productivity (macroeconomic) and render U.S. industries less competitive in global markets (global).

Note: This exhibit does not attempt to represent all cause-and-effect relationships. Our intent is to illustrate some of the probable interrelationships among various environmental segments.

industrial development and their purchasing power. It also threatens financial institutions in creditor nations since any default by debtors could seriously jeopardize their creditors' liquidity and solvency.

Interrelationships among Segments of the General Environment

As we have already noted, events and trends in any one segment of the general environment will often influence other segments as well. Managers must recognize that the segments do not operate independently of each other.

Exhibit 2.3 provides three examples of interrelationships among segments of the general environment: high-definition television, the U.S. trade deficit, and the erosion of U.S. educational standards.

The Impact of the General Environment on Industries

The systematic analysis of the external environment should lead to the identification of major trends in various segments. This information becomes useful only if the firm also evaluates the impact of each of the trends on its future profitability and growth, and responds appropriately. Exhibit 2.4 provides several examples of how an environmental trend can influence various industries in very different ways.

There are three important issues to consider when assessing the impact of an environmental trend.

EXHIBIT 2.4
Impact of General Environmental Trends on Different Industries

Segment/Trend	*Industry*	*Very Positive*	*Somewhat Positive*	*Neither Positive nor Negative*	*Somewhat Negative*	*Very Negative*
Demographic						
Aging population	Medical services	✓				
	Colleges and universities				✓	
Increased purchasing power of baby boomers	Luxury automobiles	✓				
	Financial services		✓			
Sociocultural						
More women in the work force	Convenience foods	✓				
	Clothing		✓			
Greater health and fitness awareness	Exercise equipment	✓				
	Meat products					✓
Political/Legal						
Deregulation	Banking				✓	
	Airline*	✓				
Increased environmental legislation	Waste management	✓				
	Automobile				✓	
Technological						
Advances in laser technology	Compact disc	✓				
	Long-playing records					✓
Progress in biotechnology	Ethical drugs	✓				
	Breakfast cereal			✓		
Macroeconomic						
Declining interest rates	Housing construction	✓				
	Prescription drugs			✓		
Global						
Growing competitive strength of newly industrialized countries (NICs)	Domestic shoe manufacturing					✓
	Book publishing			✓		
Opening of communist countries	Fast food		✓			
	Defense					✓

* In general, airline deregulation has had a negative effect on the established airlines and a positive effect on the new entrants.

1. *The same environmental trend may have very different effects on various industries.* For example, growing awareness about health and fitness has greatly helped industries such as exercise equipment, athletic shoes, and frozen yogurt. However, fast foods as well as dairy and meat products have suffered as a result of this trend. For example, between 1987 and 1989, per capita consumption of beef declined 6.5 percent to 68.6 pounds while that of poultry—recognized as a healthier food—increased 8.0 percent to 84 pounds.[32]

2. *The impact of an environmental trend often differs significantly for different firms within the same industry.* For example, deregulation in the airline industry has brought on increased competition. As a result, many of the older, established airlines have experienced declines in profitability. However, many smaller airlines, as well as newer entrants, were able to aggressively enter new markets.

3. *All environmental trends may not necessarily have much impact on a specific industry.* For example, even though advances in biotechnology have had a significant impact on the pharmaceutical industry, they are unlikely to have any serious impact on industries such as breakfast cereals and infant formulas in the near future.

THE COMPETITIVE ENVIRONMENT

In addition to the general environment, managers must also consider the competitive environment (also referred to as the *task* or *industry environment*). The profitability of the firm and the nature of competition in the industry are more directly influenced by developments in the competitive environment.

The competitive environment consists of factors particularly relevant to a firm's strategy, including competitors (existing and potential), customers, and suppliers. Potential competitors, for example, may include a supplier thinking of integrating forward, such as a U.S. automobile manufacturer acquiring a car rental company, or a firm in an entirely different industry introducing a similar product that uses a more efficient technology.

In the following sections we discuss key concepts and analytical techniques that managers should use in order to assess their competitive environments. First, we examine the five forces model and provide an integrative example to illustrate how the forces can be used to explain the low profitability of the metal container industry. We will then introduce the concept of strategic groups, showing that even within an industry it is often very useful to group firms on the basis of similarities of their strategies. In fact, competition tends to be more intense among firms *within* a strategic group than *between* strategic groups.

The Five Forces Model of Industry Competition

The "five forces model," developed by Michael E. Porter, has been the most commonly utilized analytical tool for examining the competitive environment. It describes the competitive environment in terms of five basic competitive forces:

1. The threat of new entrants to the market
2. The bargaining power of the firm's suppliers
3. The bargaining power of the firm's customers
4. The threat of substitute products
5. The intensity of rivalry among competing firms

Together, these forces determine the nature and extent of competition, as well as the profit potential of an industry. Exhibit 2.5 presents the five forces model. Managers should understand how each of these five forces affects the competitive environment of the industry in which their firm competes. Such an understanding will ultimately allow the manager to determine the most appropriate and defensible strategic position within the industry.[33]

The Threat of New Entrants

A new entrant into an industry represents a competitive threat to existing firms; it adds new production capacity and the potential to erode the market share of existing competitors.

EXHIBIT 2.5
The Five Forces Model of Competition

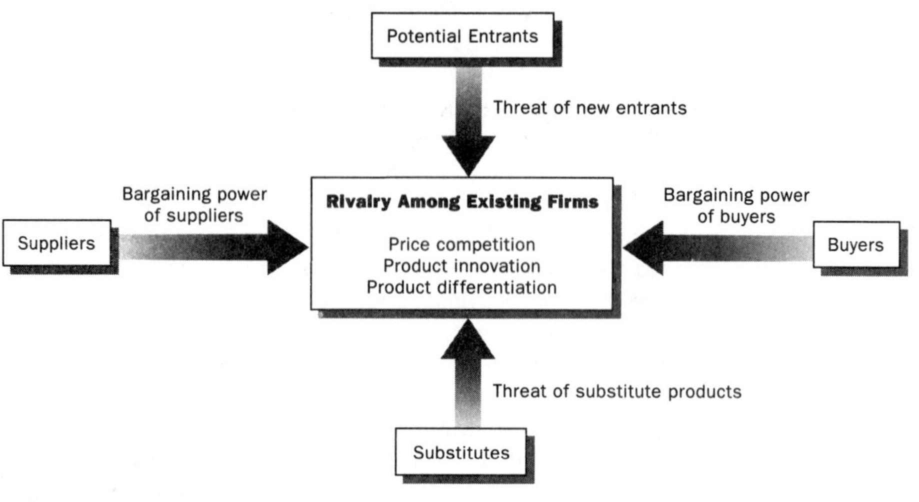

Source: Adapted with permission of The Free Press, a Division of Macmillan, Inc., from Porter, Michael E. (1980). *Competitive strategy: Techniques for analyzing industries and competitors.* New York: Free Press. Copyright © 1980 by The Free Press.

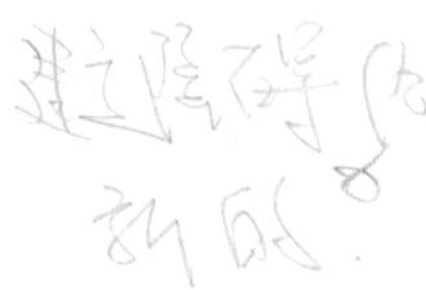

The new entrant may also bring substantial resources (such as a large advertising or R&D budget) which were not previously required for success in the industry. To reduce the threat of entry, managers may erect substantial barriers to entry or signal their intention to retaliate aggressively. Some major barriers to entry include:

- **Economies of scale**
  Reduction in cost due to production in large volume.
- **Product differentiation**
  Differences in physical or perceptual characteristics which make a product unique in the eyes of the consumer.
- **Capital requirements**
  Amount of investment required to enter an industry, including plant and equipment as well as working capital.
- **Switching costs**
  Costs incurred by a user in changing from one supplier to another. These may include psychological costs in addition to financial costs.
- **Access to distribution channels**
  Costs associated with developing a means to distribute a product or service.
- **Cost disadvantages independent of scale**
  Factors that provide an advantage to existing competitors even when the new entrant has comparable economies of scale. These may include proprietary product knowledge, favorable access to raw materials, favorable locations, and government subsidies.

The factors that deter new entry depend on the specific characteristics of an industry. For example, in the automobile industry, *product differentiation* and *economies of scale* are major deterrents to new entry. In manufacturing industries, entry is deterred by substantial *capital requirements.* Similarly, many U.S. manufacturers have been frustrated by their failure to gain *access to distribution channels* in Japan and other countries. In the software industry, *switching costs* involved in retraining employees have made customers continue to use existing packages even when better products may be available.

The motion picture industry has traditionally had very high entry barriers for several reasons. Major productions, on average, take 18 months to produce and require approximately a $60 million investment before they reach movie theaters.[34] (Exhibit 2.6 provides a detailed breakdown of costs and revenues.) The probability of failure is very high with few means of recovering the investment if the movie flops. An additional barrier new entrants face is the difficulty involved in obtaining outlets for exhibition. However, the lure of enormous profits if a movie achieves blockbuster status, as did *Batman, Dances with Wolves,* and *Home Alone,* remains a strong inducement to the industry's players.

Clorox's entry in late 1988 into the $4 billion-a-year laundry detergent market is an example of both the threat of entry and the danger of sharp retaliation from an entrenched competitor.[35] Clorox's new entry, called Clorox Super Detergent, triggered a double retaliation from the industry leader, Procter & Gamble, which held a 50 percent market share. P&G's double-barreled response included a new laundry product of its own, Tide with Bleach, as well as a new entry into the $660 million-a-year bleach market in which Clorox had a 50 percent market share and from which Clorox earned about half of its net profits. By sharply retaliating to Clorox's product entry, P&G not only eroded Clorox's competitive position, but also signaled that any future entry by potential competitors would be aggressively challenged. Not many were surprised when Clorox announced its withdrawal from the detergent industry in May 1991.[36]

EXHIBIT 2.6
Hollywood's Breakeven Scenario

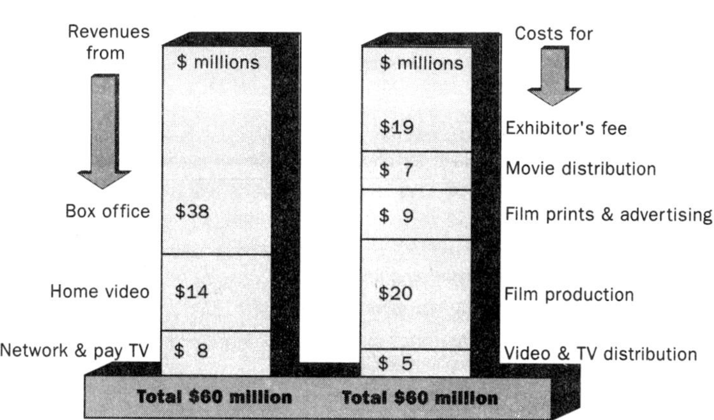

Source: Knowlton, C. (1988, August 29). Lessons from Hollywood hit men. *Fortune*, p. 81.

The Bargaining Power of Suppliers

There are many ways in which suppliers can affect an industry's profit potential; they may either increase their prices or reduce the quality of goods and services they provide to the industry. Conditions under which a supplier group would be powerful include:

- **Dominance by a few suppliers**
- **Greater concentration than the buyer industry**
  An industry's concentration, usually referred to as its concentration ratio, is the proportion of the industry's total output accounted for by the largest firms in the industry.
- **Nonavailability of substitute products**
- **Relative lack of importance of the buyer to the supplier group**
- **Importance of the supplier's product or service to the buyer**
- **High differentiation by the supplier**
- **High switching costs for the buyer**
- **Credible threat of forward integration by suppliers**
  Forward integration would involve a supplier moving into a later stage of the manufacturing process or distribution.

Suppliers traditionally have been powerful in industries such as soft drink concentrates, large-scale sophisticated weapons systems, and mainframe computers. In each of these markets, the suppliers are few in number, their products are vital to the buyers, and switching from one supplier to another is quite problematic and costly.

Producers of memory chips provide a clear example of supplier power. Toward the late 1980s the profit margins of computer manufacturers were significantly eroded by a shortage in the supply of 256K and 1M bit DRAM (dynamic random access memory) chips. As indicated in Exhibit 2.7, suppliers were clearly able to extract higher prices from their smaller customers than their larger, high-volume customers, such as IBM, Apple, and DEC.

EXHIBIT 2.7
DRAM Prices by Customer Segment, 1988

A dynamic random access memory chip, or DRAM, is a silicon chip the size of a fingernail. The computer industry is facing a short supply of the DRAMs that has caused delays in deliveries and hoarding within the industry. Thefts have also been reported, and the demand has driven up the price of the chips. Below are the costs of the chips within different markets (top prices reported).

Market Segment	***256K***	***1Mbit***
Major customers such as IBM, Apple, and DEC	$2.70–$3.00	$15–$20
Smaller companies buying directly from manufacturers	$3.50–$4.50	$25–$30
Companies that must buy from franchised distributors and brokers (they are unable to buy directly from the chip manufacturers)	$7–$12	$35–$50
Customers circumventing official distribution channels	$15	$90

Source: Adapted from Malone, M. S. (1988, May 28). Saying thanks for the memories. *Dallas Morning News,* pp. 1F, 4F. (Reprinted with permission of the *Dallas Morning News.*)

The formation of Delta Pride Catfish in 1981 is an example of the power that a group of suppliers can achieve if they exercise the threat of forward integration.[37] Catfish farmers in Mississippi historically supplied their harvest to processing plants run by large agribusiness firms like ConAgra and Farm Fresh. When the farmers increased their production of catfish in response to growing demand in the late 1970s, they found that the processors were holding back on their plans to increase their processing capabilities in hopes of higher retail prices for catfish. The farmers responded by forming a cooperative, raising $4.5 million, and constructing their own processing plant, which they supplied themselves. Within 2 years, ConAgra's market share had dropped from 35 to 11 percent, and Farm Fresh's market share fell by over 20 percent. By the late 1980s, Delta Pride controlled over 40 percent of the 280-million-pounds-per-year U.S. catfish market.

The Bargaining Power of Customers

Buyers of an industry's product can exert bargaining power over that industry by forcing prices down, by reducing the amount of goods they purchase from the industry, or by demanding better quality for the same price. Factors that lead to greater buyer power include:

- **Greater concentration than the supplier group**
- **Large volume purchases**
- **Undifferentiated or standard products or services of the supplier**
- **Credible threat of backward integration by buyers**

  Backward integration would involve a buyer moving into an earlier stage of manufacturing or distribution.
- **Accurate information about the cost structure of the supplier**

Also, the greater the price sensitivity of the buyer, the lower the profit potential of the supplier industry. A buyer industry is likely to be more price sensitive if the following apply:

- The products represent a significant fraction of the buyer's total cost
- It earns low profits
- The supplier's product is unimportant to the quality of the buyer's final product
- The supplier's product may lead to only marginal savings for the buyer

The "big three" U.S. automobile manufacturers traditionally have been able to extract significant price concessions from their suppliers because of *high volume purchases, a credible threat of backward integration, and high buyer concentration.* Similarly, many large residential construction companies have considerable bargaining power over the suppliers of commodity-type products, such as lumber and other wood products. Contractors are likely to exercise their power over suppliers when the items they buy from them represent a significant part of their overall cost of construction. A growing trend among small businesses is to augment their bargaining power over suppliers through joining or forming buying groups. Approximately 8,000 small businesses in the Cleveland, Ohio, area have enjoyed significantly lower health care costs through their membership in the Council of Smaller Enterprises (COSE).[38] Between 1984 and 1990, COSE's health insurance costs rose a total of only 34.5 percent—substantially less than an average 154 percent increase experienced by other small firms in the area. A major part of COSE's success in containing health care costs can be attributed to its enormous bargaining power with insurance companies. COSE's members have a total of approximately 145,000 employees and dependents, which makes them bigger than most larger companies in the United States. This emerging trend may enable managers to alter the relative bargaining power of buyers and suppliers in many industries.

The Threat of Substitute Products

The availability of substitute products places an upper price limit on the products of an industry. When prices of existing products rise above that of the substitute product, customers tend to switch to the substitute. A firm competing against a substitute product can attempt to differentiate its product. Alternatively, the firm can attempt to increase the buyer's costs of switching between its product and a substitute product. Substitute products which must be closely monitored include those that are showing improvements in terms of performance and declines in price.

Nutrasweet and teleconferencing are examples of the power of substitute products and services. The widespread use of Nutrasweet has placed a ceiling on the prices that sugar manufacturers can charge soft drink and juice concentrate producers. Many analysts feel that teleconferencing technology poses a major potential threat for business-related airline travel.

The threat posed to the overnight letter-carrier business by office facsimile machines provides an interesting example of how the introduction of a substitute product can adversely affect an industry's growth and profit potential. Federal Express, the nation's largest overnight letter carrier (with 45 percent of the U.S. market), has seen its annual growth rate in domestic shipment volume decline in recent years. This is attributed to the increasing usage of office fax machines. Zapmail, Federal's attempt to enter the office fax business, was unsuccessful. Analysts have estimated that facsimile machines alone could replace almost 30 percent of Federal's overnight letter shipments.[39] Shipment volume growth has slowed down and competition has intensified within the industry. Federal Express's net profit margin, which averaged around 10 percent in the early 1980s, declined to less than 2 percent by 1990 and is not expected to exceed 3 percent through 1995.[40]

The Intensity of Rivalry among Competitors

Many industries in free market economies have high levels of competition among existing firms. Such competition is usually characterized by intense price competition, product differentiation, or product innovation. Managers must realize that these forms of competition may not always be mutually exclusive and may occur at the same time. For example, the soft drink industry in recent years has been characterized by frequent price discounts, high advertising intensity, and proliferation of new products. Intense rivalry usually results from the interaction of the following factors:

- **Numerous or equally balanced competitors**
- **Slow industry growth**
- **High fixed or storage cost**
- **Lack of differentiation or switching costs**

- **Manufacturing capacity increases possible only in large increments**
  The minimum efficient scale requirements in many industries are such that increases in production capacity are possible only in very large increments. This may lead to excess supply and lower prices, at least in the short run.
- **Competitors with diverse strategies, origins, and personalities**
- **High strategic stakes**
  Success in certain highly visible markets may be necessary before a product can achieve acceptance in other markets.
- **High exit barriers for economic, strategic, or emotional reasons**

The automobile, paper, and paint industries provide examples of how the above factors often lead to intense competition. The entry of several foreign manufacturers, relatively low growth of the market, and increasing capital investment needs have caused competition in the auto industry to intensify during the last two decades. Most foreign auto manufacturers continue to target the U.S. market aggressively because of the high strategic stakes involved. In the paper industry, rivalry, traditionally, has been intense because capacity can be increased only in large amounts; the cost of the minimum efficient size of most new paper plants is more than several hundred million dollars. Also, most paper products are not easily differentiated. The exit barriers are very high because manufacturing facilities, once established, cannot be put to alternate uses. In the paint industry, the presence of relatively large numbers of small firms is a major cause of rivalry. Many small owner-operated paint companies are willing to accept low levels of profitability in order to stay in business.

Intense rivalry among competitors in an industry can take three specific forms: price competition, product innovation, and product differentiation. (These strategies will be discussed in greater detail in Chapter 4.) A checklist of some of the major factors to consider while conducting a competitive analysis is presented in Exhibit 2.8.

Combining the Five Forces: The Case of the Metal Container Industry

In the previous sections, we have discussed each of the five forces individually with examples of their application in a variety of industries. Application 2.6 provides an example of how the five forces, in combination, can be used to explain the nature of competition within an industry. The metal container industry has traditionally been an industry characterized by low profitability. Further, major improvements in profitability are not expected in the near future. The application of the five forces model helps to explain why this is the case.

Strategic Groups within Industries

When formulating strategies, managers must remember that competitors in an industry can be quite dissimilar. Companies within an industry differ along several important dimensions, such as product quality, technological leadership, pricing policy, and customer service.[41] It is often possible to classify firms in an industry into a small number of strategic groups on the basis of similarities in their strategies. As shown in Exhibit 2.9, the department store industry may be classified into at least four strategic groups on the basis of two dimensions: perceived quality and retail price.[42]

EXHIBIT 2.8
Competitive Analysis Checklist

Threat of new entrants is high when:	high	low
Economies of scale are		XX
Product differentiation is		XX
Capital requirements are		XX
Switching costs are		XX
Incumbent's control of distribution channels is		XX
Incumbent's proprietary knowledge is		XX
Incumbent's access to raw materials is		XX
Incumbent's access to government subsidies is		XX

Power of buyers is high when:	high	low
Concentration of buyers relative to suppliers is	XX	
Volume of purchase is	XX	
Product differentiation of suppliers is		XX
Threat of backward integration by buyers is	XX	
Buyer's knowledge about supplier's cost structure is	XX	
Extent of buyer's profits is		XX
Cost savings from the supplier's product are		XX
Importance of the supplier's input to quality of buyer's final product is		XX
Percentage of total buyer's cost spent on the supplier's input is	XX	

Power of suppliers is high when:	high	low
Concentration relative to buyer industry is	XX	
Availability of substitute products is		XX
Importance of customer to the supplier is		XX
Differentiation of the supplier's products and services is	XX	
Switching costs of the buyer are	XX	
Threat of forward integration by the supplier is	XX	

Intensity of competitive rivalry is high when:	high	low
Number of competitors is	XX	
Industry growth rate is		XX
Fixed costs are	XX	
Storage costs are	XX	
Product differentiation is		XX
Switching costs are		XX
Exit barriers are	XX	
Strategic stakes are	XX	

Threat of substitute products is high when:	high	low
Profitability of industry producing substitute is	XX	
Rate of improvement in price-performance relationship of substitute product is	XX	

These four groups are *upscale department stores, national chain department stores, full-line discount department stores,* and *warehouse stores:*

- The upscale department stores usually cater to local markets; they are flexible and are able to respond quickly to environmental changes. Customer service and credit, as well as brand name merchandise, are their primary means of competition.

Application 2.6

Applying Porter's Five Forces Model: The Metal Container Industry

The metal container industry historically has been characterized by relatively low growth, intense competition, and unattractive levels of profitability. During the 1980s, this industry was negatively affected by such factors as further consolidation of soft drink bottlers and a strong trend toward substitution by many types of plastic packaging. The underlying reasons for the slow growth and low profitability of the metal container industry can be best understood if we apply Porter's five forces model. Many of the factors that depress the level of profitability in the metal container industry have persisted without major changes since the mid-1960s. Therefore, we will first provide a brief historical overview of the metal container industry as of 1976, followed by an analysis of this industry using Porter's five forces model.

The Industry

With sales of $7.6 billion, metal containers made up almost a third of all packaging products used in the United States in 1976. Metal cans, made either from aluminum or tin-plated steel, represent the major segment within metal containers. Between 1967 and 1976 the number of metal cans shipped grew with GNP. The greatest gains were in the beverage segment (soft drink and beer cans), while shipments of motor oil, paint, and other general packaging cans actually declined.

Though there are about 100 firms in the metal container industry, it is dominated by four major manufacturers. Two giants, American Can and Continental Can, together make up 35 percent of all domestic production. National Can and Crown Cork and Seal are also major forces with market shares of 8.7 percent and 8.3 percent, respectively.

Because of the large number of competitors, the can industry is very price competitive. Since variable costs, (material, 64 percent; labor, 15 percent; and freight, 8 percent) account for 87 percent of total cost, on average, there is very little operating leverage from extra sales volume. A new two-piece can plant costs only $10 to $15 million per line and the minimum efficient plant size is two to three lines. There are few financial or "scale" barriers to entry.

Through the 1960s, American steel companies were the sole suppliers of the metal used by the industry. Can companies, in turn, were the fourth largest consumer of steel. During the 1970s, aluminum came to dominate the traditional tin-plated steel markets. Also, of the four large aluminum producers, two had already integrated forward into manufacturing aluminum cans.

On the customer side, over 80 percent of output is purchased by major food and beverage companies. The can constitutes about 45 percent of total cost to beverage companies. Because can plants are often set up to supply a single customer, the loss of a large order from that customer greatly reduces efficiency and profits. Several food and beverage companies have already integrated backward into can production. Campbell Soup is a major producer of three-piece steel cans. The proportion of "captive" production increased from 18 to 26 percent between 1970 and 1976. This backward integration has taken place primarily in three-piece cans, because buyers do not possess the technical skills to develop their own two-piece lines.

Five Forces Analysis

The profit potential of the metal container industry is analyzed using the five forces framework.

Bargaining Power of Suppliers

A. Aluminum companies
   1. There are only four suppliers of aluminum (Alcoa, Alcan, Reynolds, and Kaiser); further, these companies are much more concentrated than the metal container industry.
   2. These suppliers have vast resources and pose credible threat of forward integration (in fact, Alcoa and Reynolds have already integrated forward into can manufacture).
   3. Can manufacturers do not pose any threat of backward integration.

Net conclusion: Aluminum companies can exert considerable amounts of bargaining power over metal can manufacturers in negotiating raw material prices.

B. Steel companies
   1. There are few suppliers of tin-plated steel.
   2. Steel companies pose a credible threat of forward integration, but have not yet actually done so.
   3. Can companies do not pose any threat of backward integration.

Net conclusion: Steel companies can exert a good deal of bargaining power over metal can manufacturers.

Application 2.6 (cont.)

Bargaining Power of Customers

Eighty percent of metal containers are purchased by food and beverage companies.

1. Buyers of cans are very large and powerful.
2. The cost of the can is a significant fraction of the buyer's costs.
3. Customers buy in large quantities.
4. Customers buy an essentially undifferentiated product and face no switching costs.
5. Can manufacturers typically locate a plant to serve a single customer so that the loss of a large order from that customer could greatly cut into profits.
6. There is low customer loyalty.
7. Buyers pose a credible threat of backward integration. In fact, several food and beverage companies already make their own cans (e.g., Campbell Soup is a major producer of three-piece steel cans).
8. Can manufacturers have no ability to integrate forward into the food and beverages industry.

Net conclusion: Buyers can exert a great deal of power over metal can producers.

The Threat of Substitute Products

A. Plastic
   1. It is lighter.
   2. It is resistant to breakage.
   3. It has versatility, thereby lowering shelf-space requirements.

Net conclusion: Plastics pose a significant threat to tin-plated steel in many user segments.

B. Fiber-foil
   1. It is 20 percent lighter than steel cans.
   2. It is 15 percent cheaper than steel cans.

Net conclusion: In certain user segments (particularly for motor oil and frozen juices), fiber-foil is a significant threat to tin-plated steel.

Overall conclusion: With the exception of food cans, metal containers face a significant threat from substitute materials such as plastic and fiber-foil.

The Threat of New Entrants

1. Economics of scale in this industry are quite low and, as such, cannot be used as an entry barrier; for example, the minimum efficient size for two-piece can lines is two to three lines.
2. Capital investments are certainly not an entry barrier (especially for suppliers and buyers); for example, for two-piece can lines the per-line cost is $10 to $15 million.
3. Technology is not an entry barrier for three-piece containers. However, the canning technology for the two-piece lines is not available with buyers such as Campbell Soup.
4. Brand loyalty is absent and is not available as an entry barrier.

Net conclusion: Metal container industry has very low entry barriers, as evident from the fact that this industry is characterized by a large number of small players.

The Intensity of Rivalry

Notwithstanding the fact that there are only four major players in this industry (Continental Can, American Can, National Can, and CC&S), price rivalry is intense, for the following reasons:

1. This is a slow-growth, mature industry (3 percent annual growth rate).
2. Metal containers are largely undifferentiated products, forcing customers to choose on the basis of price, if service is comparable.
3. The existence of close substitutes keeps the lid on prices.
4. Low-entry barrier puts a cap on selling prices.
5. Presence of very powerful buyers and very powerful suppliers keeps the container prices down (as otherwise they will enter the industry).

Net conclusion: Price competition is quite intense.

Overall conclusion: Given the very high supplier power and buyer power, low barriers to entry, availability of close substitutes, and intense price competition among existing players, the profit potential in the metal container industry is expected to be low. In fact, in 1986, *Forbes* magazine ranked this industry at twenty-four out of the total of thirty-one industries in the United States on the criterion of return on equity.

Source

Govindarajan, V., & Shank, J. K. (1989). Strategic cost analysis: The Crown Cork and Seal case. *Journal of Cost Management, 2*(4), 5–16. Reprinted with permission from the *Journal of Cost Management.*

EXHIBIT 2.9
Strategic Groups in the Department Store Industry

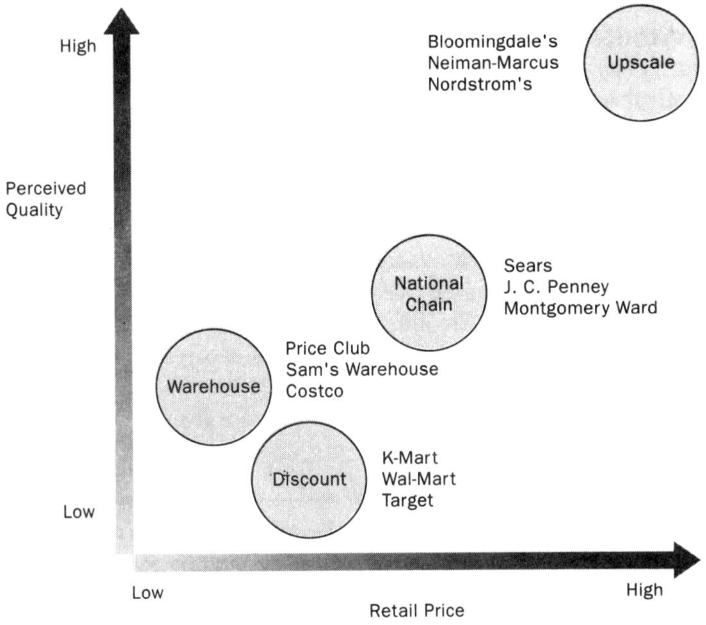

Source: Adapted from Sami, C. (1989). *Retail marketing strategy.* New York: Quorum.

- The national chain department stores have much higher levels of centralized control, which lead to less flexibility in local markets. Store brands are heavily promoted and the use of the national media is extensive.
- Discount department stores must be designed to facilitate self-service. The stores are usually free-standing buildings, located in lower rent areas. Customer service is low and merchandise normally consists of national brands.
- Warehouse stores, a relatively recent development in the merchandising industry, offer a wide variety of brand name merchandise to cost-conscious customers who prefer to buy in large volume. To maintain low costs, displays are kept very modest, customers bag their own purchases, merchandise is stacked high on metal racks, and the stores are typically located in lower rent areas. Further, warehouse stores spend very little on advertising and other promotional activities.

The intensity of rivalry is generally much stronger *within* each of the four strategic groups than *between* them. Each of the competitors within a strategic group follows similar strategies and tries to attract similar types of customers. Not surprisingly, K-Mart's annual increases in sales volume have been more adversely affected by Wal-Mart's meteoric rise than by competitors in other strategic groups such as Macy's and Marshall Field's. However, Sears's change in pricing strategy to "everyday low pricing" has put them in more direct competition with K-Mart and Wal-Mart. Sears hopes to make up for the erosion in gross margins through increased volume, lower selling expenses, and lower distribution costs. Similarly, in recent years, J. C. Penney has been moving upscale into more direct competition with stores such as Dillard's and Macy's.

As with the department store industry, the strategic groups within the automobile industry have also been changing. The number of strategic groups in an industry, as well as the membership within a group, does not typically remain constant over long periods of time. For example, the Japanese manufacturers who primarily catered to the low end of the market in the 1970s are now emerging as serious rivals to the European luxury car makers. Toyota's Lexus, Nissan's Infiniti, and Honda's Acura are taking market share away from prestigious European names like BMW, Porsche, and Jaguar.

Managers have many reasons to pay careful attention to the existence of strategic groups and mobility among them. First, the overall profitability levels vary significantly across strategic groups. Second, the threat of new entry is most serious from members of the nearest strategic groups since they have reasonable knowledge of the industry and incremental capital requirements are relatively low. Third, the relative strengths of the "five forces" may differ considerably across strategic groups.

INTERRELATIONSHIPS BETWEEN THE GENERAL AND COMPETITIVE ENVIRONMENTS

The general and competitive environments are strongly interrelated and change over time. Exhibit 2.10 depicts the interrelated nature of the general environment and the competitive environment. Typically, the influence of the general environment on the competitive environment is greater than that of the competitive environment on the general environment. For example, macroeconomic developments, such as changes in interest rates and currency fluctuations, may have a significant impact on the nature of demand and the profitability of many industries. But, individual or collective actions by firms within an industry rarely have a significant impact on macroeconomic indicators. The relative thickness of the arrows in Exhibit 2.10 indicates the magnitude of the interaction between the general and competitive environments.

Each segment of the general environment can have a strong impact on one or more of the five forces that determine the nature of industry competition. For example:

- Because fewer teenagers are currently entering the work force, businesses such as amusement parks and fast food restaurants are facing labor shortages. Thus, teenagers and young adults are often able to bargain for more attractive jobs and higher wages.
- Technological developments outside an industry can greatly affect its growth potential. The improving performance and declining costs associated with teleconferencing technologies pose a credible threat to travel and hotel industries in the long run. That is, teleconferencing may increasingly become a viable substitute for business-related travel.
- Global developments such as the Iraqi invasion of Kuwait in August, 1990, have a significant impact on the relative bargaining power between oil producers and users.

EXHIBIT 2.10
The General and Competitive Environment

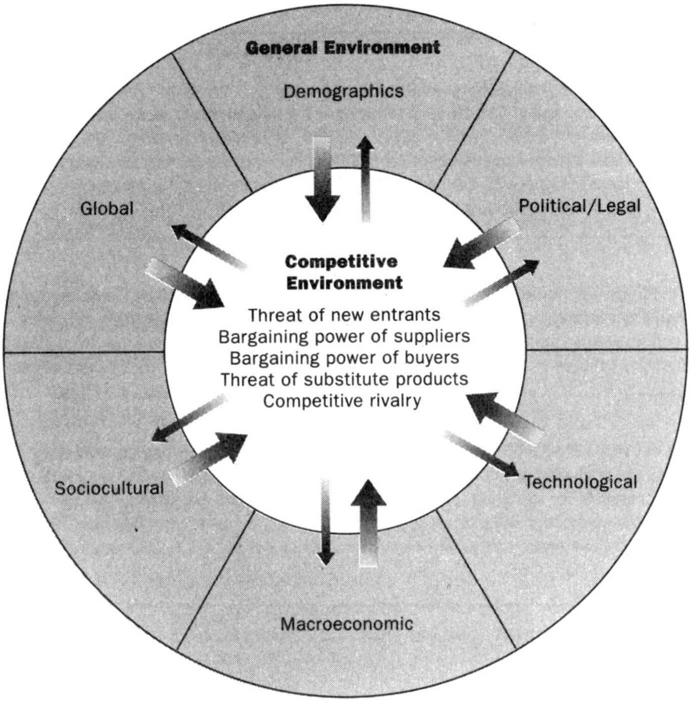

Clearly, when the supply of a scarce resource is restricted, the sellers become more powerful. The U.S. airline industry was adversely affected; every 1 cent per gallon increase in fuel prices costs the industry $150 to $160 million in annual operating profits.[43]

The relationship between the general environment and the competitive environment can be further illustrated by building on our earlier application of the five forces model to the metal container industry. While there have been some changes in products, markets, and technologies, the overall profitability level and nature of competition hasn't changed much in this industry over the past several years. Many of these changes have their origin in the general environment. A few of these developments and their impact on the competitive environment of the metal container industry are shown in Exhibit 2.11.

Summary

Analyzing the external environment is critical in identifying various opportunities and threats for the business organization. Environmental analysis begins with collecting information through carefully scanning the environment and the systematic gathering of competitor intelligence. These two activities provide important inputs for the development of

EXHIBIT 2.11
Interrelationships between the General and Competitive Environments: The Case of the Metal Container Industry

Example 1

Increasing concern about health and fitness (sociocultural) in the United States has resulted in stagnant demand for many alcoholic beverages. This trend is reflected in the shipments of metal containers to the beer industry, which have only increased from 36.0 billion units in 1986 to 36.6 billion units in 1990. Conversely, demand for metal cans by the soft drink industry has increased from 36.8 billion units to 52.6 billion units during the same period. Therefore, one would expect that the soft drink producers would have improved their bargaining power relative to the brewers since they would likely make larger volume purchases.

Example 2

As of 1990, 67 percent of all women with children were employed outside the home (demographic). This trend has resulted in a dramatic increase in demand for convenience in food preparation. Currently, 75 percent of both households and businesses own microwave ovens, which increases the demand for microwavable food containers. This has benefited the producers of plastic containers (a substitute product) at the expense of metal container manufacturers.

Example 3

Growing environmental awareness (sociocultural) is leading to increasing legislation (political-legal) regarding disposable products such as plastic containers. Connecticut has already passed a law which regulates packaging to increase its recyclability. Similarly, governors of nine northeastern states are working in partnership with the industry and the public to develop a regionally coordinated strategy on waste management. Such developments may prove to be favorable for the metal container industry, since its products are much more recyclable than plastic cans and containers.

Sources: Copperthite, K. G. (1990). Cans and containers. *U.S. Industrial Outlook 1990* (pp. 11–2 to 11–4). Washington, DC: U.S. Government Printing Ofice; and Ferguson, W.B., III. (1990, April 27). Packaging and container industry. *Valueline investment survey* (p. 949). New York: Value Line Publishing.

useful forecasts. However, forecasts can suffer from many limitations, including an overestimation of technological potential and unforeseen shifts in customer preferences.

The external environment consists of the general and the competitive environments. The general environment consists of broad trends or factors outside the industry that may have a significant impact on the organization. The important segments of the general environment are demographic, sociocultural, political and legal, technological, macroeconomic, and global. Changes in the external environment do not affect all firms or industries the same way; an environmental development may mean a major opportunity for one firm or industry while it may pose a threat to another firm or industry.

The competitive environment consists of factors within an industry that have a direct and often immediate impact on firms. A systematic and widely used approach to understanding the competitive environment is industry analysis and the application of the five forces model. These forces are (1) threat of new entrants to the market, (2) the bargaining power of the firm's customers, (3) the bargaining power of the firm's suppliers, (4) the threat of substitute products, and (5) rivalry among competing firms. Together, these forces largely determine the level of profitability in an industry. Even within an industry, firms may be viewed as belonging to different strategic groups. Competition is particularly intense among firms within a given strategic group.

The general and the competitive environments are characterized by a high level of interdependence. Many developments in the general environment may have a significant effect on any or all of the five forces that depict the intensity of competition within an industry.

Notes

1. For a discussion of important environmental changes see Day, G. S. (1984). *Strategic market planning: The pursuit of competitive advantage.* St. Paul, MN: West; and for a detailed treatment of the need, as well as techniques, for environmental analysis, see Fahey, L., & Narayanan, V. K. (1986). *Macroenvironmental analysis for strategic management.* St. Paul, MN: West.
2. For a further discussion of environmental scanning practices of U.S. leading corporations, see Lenz, R. T., & Engledow, J. L. (1986). Environmental analysis units and strategic decision-making: Field study of selected leading edge firms. *Strategic Management Journal, 7*, 69–89; Engledow, J. L., & Lenz, R. T. (1985). Whatever happened to environmental analysis? *Long Range Planning, 18*, 93–106; Stroup, M. A. (1988, July–August). Environmental scanning at Monsanto. *Planning Review, 16*(4), 24–27.
3. Reich, R. B., (1989, October). The quiet path to technological preeminence. *Scientific American, 261*(4), 4–47.
4. Dumaine, B. (1988, November 7). Corporate spies snoop to conquer. *Fortune,* pp. 68–69, 72, 76.
5. The following discussion draws from Kight, L. K. (1989). The search for intelligence in divisions and subsidiaries. *Planning Review, 3*, 40–42.
6. A more comprehensive understanding of the techniques to use in competitor intelligence gathering can be obtained from Fuld, L. M. (1988). *Monitoring the competition.* London: Wiley.
7. Beltramini, R. F. (1986, August). Ethics and the use of competitive information acquisition strategies. *Journal of Business Ethics, 5*(4), 307–311.
8. Zellner, W. (1991, April 1). Dumpster raids? That's not very ladylike, Avon. *Business Week,* p. 32.
9. For a more detailed understanding of forecasting techniques, refer to Keating, B. (1985). Business forecasting. *Creative Computing, 11*, 120–135; Wheelwright, S. C., & Clark, D. G. (1976). Corporate forecasting: Promise and reality. *Harvard Business Review, 54*, 40–42, 47–48, 52, 60, 64, 198; Chambers, J. C., Mullick, S. K., & Smith, D. D. (1971). How to choose the right forecasting technique. *Harvard Business Review, 49*, 45–74; Makridakis, S., & Wheelwright, S. C. (1987). *Handbook of forecasting.* New York: Wiley.
10. An interesting update on the performance of the companies that were considered excellent by Peters and Waterman in their 1982 best-selling book *In Search of Excellence* is provided in "Who's excellent now?" (1984, November 5). *Business Week,* pp. 76–88.
11. Wheelwright, S. C., & Clarke, D. G. (1976). Corporate forecasting: Promise and reality. *Harvard Business Review, 54*(6), 40–64.
12. Fahey, L., & Narayanan, V. K. (1984). *Macroenvironmental analysis for strategic management.* St. Paul, MN: West.
13. Narayanan, V. K. (1989). How a broader environment can shape industry events. In Liam Fahey (Ed.), *Strategic planning management reader* (pp. 47–51). Englewood Cliffs, NJ: Prentice-Hall.
14. Reich, R. B. (1990, November). Metamorphosis of the American worker. *Business Month,* pp. 58–61, 64–66.

15. Dodge, R. (1988, July 14). Stats show U.S. shrinks as it ages. *Dallas Morning News,* p. 1D.
16. For interesting perspectives on the impact of the growing Hispanic population on U.S. businesses, refer to Garcia, C. E. (1988, January 4). Hispanic market is accessible if research is designed correctly. *Marketing News,* pp. 46–47; de Cordoba, J. (1988, February 19). More firms court Hispanic customers—but find them a tough market to market. *The Wall Street Journal,* p. 25; Schwartz, J. (1988, January). Hispanics in the eighties. *American Demographics,* pp. 43–45.
17. The changing nature of the work force: An interview with John Elkins. (1987). *Journal of Business Strategy, 8*(2), 5–8; and Castro, J. (1990, Fall). Get set: Here they come. *Time,* pp. 50–52.
18. Gorman, C. (1988, December 19). The literacy gap. *Time,* p. 56.
19. Wrich, J. T. (1988). Beyond testing: Coping with drugs at work. *Harvard Business Review, 66*(1), 120–130.
20. Farnham, A. (1990, November 5). The S&L felons. *Fortune,* pp. 90, 94, 96–102, 104, 106, 108; Hector, G. (1990, September 10). S&Ls: Where did all those billions go? *Fortune,* pp. 84–85, 88. For an interesting historical perspective on the savings and loan crisis, see Mayer, M. 1990. *The greatest-ever bank robbery: The collapse of the savings and loan industry.* New York: Scribner's.
21. Hammer, J. (1988, October 3). The big haul in toxic waste. *Newsweek,* pp. 38–39.
22. Ellis, J. E., Schine, E., Griffiths, D., & Carlson, B. W. (1990, July 2). Who pays for peace? *Business Week,* pp. 64–67, 69–70.
23. Andrews, E. L. (1990, June). Translated, HDTV means "Beat Japan." *Business Month,* pp. 67–68.
24. Koretz, G. (1989, April 3). Higher oil prices are casting an ominous shadow. *Business Week,* p. 24.
25. Zachary, G. P. (1991, May 9). Many record fans say vinyl LPs are groovier than CDs. *The Wall Street Journal,* p. 1.
26. Lewin, R., & Sookdoo, R. (1991, January 17). The most fascinating ideas for 1991. *Fortune,* p. 32.
27. Koretz (Ref. 24), loc cit.
28. The issue of the U.S. trade deficit and the associated policy alternatives are discussed in Lawrence, R. Z., & Litan, R. E. (1987). Why protectionism doesn't pay. *Harvard Business Review, 65,* 60–67; Magnusson, P. (1989, February 27). Will we ever close the trade gap? *Business Week,* pp. 86–88, 92; Baig, E. C. (1988, July 18). 50 leading U.S. exporters. *Fortune,* pp. 70–71; Holstein, W. J. (1990, May 14). The stateless corporation. *Business Week,* pp. 98–105.
29. See, for example, Kirkland, R. I., Jr. (1988, October 24). Outsider's guide to Europe in 1992. *Fortune,* pp. 121–127; Demarce, A. T. (1990, December 3). The new Germany's glowing future. *Fortune,* p. 147; and Weihrich, H. (1991). Europe 1992 and a United Germany: Opportunities and threats for United States firms. *Academy of Management Executive,* 5(1), 93–96.
30. The following examples are based on Wysocki, B., Jr. (1990, March 26). Cross-border alliances become favorite way to crack new markets. *The Wall Street Journal,* pp. A1, A5; Main, Jeremy. (1990, December 17). Making global alliances work. *Fortune,* pp. 121–124, 126.
31. Dumaree, A. T. (1990, December 3). The new Germany's glowing future. *Fortune,* pp. 146–148, 150, 152, 154.
32. Whitaker, D. R. (1990). Meat and poultry products. *1990 U.S. industrial outlook* (pp. 34-2 to 34-7). Washington, DC: U.S. Government Printing Office.
33. Michael E. Porter has made seminal contributions to the study of competitor and industry analysis. This chapter draws heavily from his works, particularly, *Competitive strategy: techniques for analyzing industries and competitors.* (1980). New York: Free Press; and How competitive forces shape strategy. (1979). *Harvard Business Review, 57*(2), 137–145.

34. Knowlton, C. (1988, August 29). Lessons from Hollywood hit men. *Fortune,* pp. 78–82.
35. Lappen, A. A. (1988, November 28). Battling for a bleachhead. *Forbes,* p. 138.
36. Shao, M. (1991, June 24). A bright idea that Clorox wishes it never had. *Business Week,* pp. 118–119.
37. Fritz, M. (1988, December 12). Agribusiness: Catfish story. *Forbes,* p. 37.
38. Mangelsdorf, M. E. (1991, May). Safety in numbers. *Inc.,* pp. 24–25.
39. King, R. W. (1989, February 13). Mr. Smith goes global. *Business Week,* pp. 66–69.
40. Royce, M. M. (1990, December 28). Federal Express. *Value Line,* p. 261.
41. There have been numerous empirical studies of the formation and performance implications of strategic groups within industries. The following two articles provide an excellent summary and critique of this literature: McGee, J., & Thomas, H. (1986). Strategic groups: Theory, research, and taxonomy. *Strategic Management Journal, 7,* 141–160; and Thomas, H., & Venkatraman, N. (1988). Research on strategic groups: Progress and prognosis. *Journal of Management Studies, 25,* 537–555.
42. These strategic groups for the department stores and much of the brief description of each strategic group are based on discussions with Professor Roger Dickinson at The University of Texas at Arlington; Sami, C. (1989). *Retail marketing strategy.* New York: Quorum.
43. Collins, B. A. (1990, December 28). *Air Transport Industry: Value Line Investment Survey,* pp. 251–252.

CHAPTER 3

Assessing the Internal Environment: Determining Strengths and Weaknesses

The most effective strategies are based on a thorough understanding of an organization's internal environment. However, the process of internal analysis is often subjective because of the difficulties in quantifying a firm's strengths and weaknesses. This chapter looks at several ways of achieving greater rigor and objectivity in assessing the internal environment. The major analytical tool for assessing a company's strengths and weaknesses is the value chain analysis, which divides the activities of a firm into separate primary and support activities. Each activity is then evaluated to determine whether it is a source of strength or weakness.

This chapter is divided into four major sections. First, we will explore value chain analysis as a means of evaluating a firm's strengths and weaknesses. Then, we will discuss how examining a firm's financial position, culture and leadership, and legitimacy and reputation are vital to conducting an effective internal analysis. In the third section, we present three key approaches to making the analysis of a firm's strengths and weaknesses more meaningful: (1) assessing an organization's competitive position with respect to the industry's critical success factors, (2) comparing the performance of the firm during different time periods, and (3) comparing the firm with industry norms and key competitors. Finally, we will address the importance of converting a firm's strengths into competitive advantages.

After reading this chapter, you will understand:

- The importance of the value chain and the primary and support activities that comprise it in conducting a firm's internal analysis
- Key issues outside the value chain: financial analysis, organizational culture and leadership, and legitimacy and reputation
- The importance of comparing a firm's strengths and weaknesses to historical performance, industry norms, and critical success factors
- The central role of the value chain in formulating a firm's strategy

EXECUTIVE INTERVIEW

Deborah A. Coleman
Vice President, Information Systems and Technology Apple Computer, Inc.

Deborah A. Coleman is vice president, information systems and technology, of Apple Computer, Inc. Coleman joined Apple in 1981. She helped plan, and later manage, the Macintosh computer manufacturing plant in Fremont, California. From 1985 to 1987 she was vice president of operations, responsible for manufacturing in the United States, the Far East, and Europe. In this position, Coleman helped build Macintosh operations by adapting manufacturing techniques developed by the Japanese. After this, Coleman served as chief financial officer from 1987 to 1989.

Coleman was appointed to her current position in 1990. She is responsible for overseeing eighteen data centers around the world, telecommunications, networks, databases, and information systems that support Apple worldwide. Coleman holds a B.A. in English from Brown University and an M.B.A. from Stanford University. She is an active member of many charitable and professional organizations.

How does information systems and technology at Apple create value for your customers?

Information systems and technology (IS&T) at Apple Computer provides systems and services that directly and indirectly affect Apple's end customers. IS&T works in partnership with its internal customers—Apple's operations, marketing, customer service, and other business and administrative functions—in selecting and applying information technology to the business. By providing global support for these internal customers, IS&T helps streamline the company's operations, aiming to automate all aspects of fundamental business operations and to bridge gaps in existing transaction processes. IS&T operations reduce the cost of doing business at Apple, employing a companywide approach to addressing business needs. Performance is measured and reported, and IS&T is accountable for producing results for its customers. By continually striving for improvement in processes, practices, capabilities, vendor partnerships, and services, IS&T seeks best practice approaches and incorporates them quickly into the business.

IS&T systems and services also enable Apple to provide direct, electronic customer support and to implement systems which link Apple's product resellers and software developers with the customer. Channel and customer support systems improve Apple's ability to deliver high-quality customer support and use information technology to enhance Apple's ability to communicate with and manage its channel relationships. For example, Apple has developed a strategy for electronic data interchange, the automation of data transfer between Apple and selected resellers and suppliers. Customer support helplines are another means by which information technology is used to directly service Apple's customers. Apple's business needs are central to every decision made in IS&T.

How has the use of information technology responded to a dynamic industry and to Apple Computer's rapidly growing business?

Apple has enjoyed one of the biggest business success stories of all times; the business has grown to over $6 billion in revenues in only 13 years. Building the foundation, including the people, organizations, processes, and philosophies in order to get business done effectively has been a real challenge—especially in the face of 30 to 70 percent annual growth. From 1982 to 1990, the information systems function at Apple grew from only 50 people, mainly located in Cupertino, California, to over 1,000, located around the world. The function has been centralized and decentralized a number of times.

In 1988, a cross-company focus on IS&T processes and infrastructure commenced—the Project Effectiveness Program (PEP). PEP team members were selected from organizations throughout IS&T—chartered to improve the applications development process by implementing development policies, tools, training, and staff support. At the same time, IS&T has worked toward implementing effective processes for software development and continual improvement of the processes for effective data access, capture, storage, and management, emphasizing managing data in an integrated way across the company. Apple has also increased investment in asset protection, disaster

Continued

recovery, improved data center operations, and in a telecommunications network infrastructure.

How does Apple evaluate the effectiveness of its information systems and technology?

Apple's vision is to exemplify how best to utilize information technology in running a business. Therefore, information technology must (1) effectively and efficiently support the day-to-day operation of the business, (2) support easy and timely access to management information, (3) improve individual and work group productivity and communication, (4) improve customer service and support, (5) integrate Apple's supplier and reseller channels, and (6) integrate Apple with its business partners. All major IS&T projects are analyzed for business needs, scope, costs and benefits, and business and technical risk.

During the business planning process, a business sponsor (customer organization or individual group funding the project) and executive sponsor (a specific high-level manager in the customer or IS&T organization who assumes full project responsibility) are assigned for each major project. Therefore, an internal system of checks and balances is in place. In addition, several executive and management-level review boards periodically review the strategic, economic, and technological implications for individual and collective information technology efforts. Finally, an audit of information technology operations and services occurs each year as a part of the corporatewide audit process. Apple has also initiated a total quality management process across all aspects of its business. Beginning this fiscal year, the Apple IS&T quality council will develop and implement a system of customer metrics for use in evaluating the effectiveness of IS&T projects.

THE VALUE CHAIN: A FRAMEWORK FOR STUDYING A FIRM'S STRENGTHS AND WEAKNESSES

To exploit opportunities and minimize threats in the external environment, managers must carefully analyze a firm's internal strengths and weaknesses. *Value chain analysis* is a useful framework for systematically identifying these strengths and weaknesses.[1] Value chain analysis assumes that a firm's basic economic purpose is to create value (measured by a firm's total revenue). In value chain analysis, managers divide the activities of the firm into a set of separate activities that add value. By assessing a firm's strengths and weaknesses with respect to each of these activities, managers achieve an in-depth understanding of their firm's capabilities.

We can view a firm as a collection of activities necessary to design, produce, market, deliver, and support its products. Each of these activities could add value to a product or a service. Each of them can also be a source of competitive advantage for a firm.

Value activities can be divided into two major categories, primary activities and support activities, as indicated in Exhibit 3.1. *Primary activities* contribute to the physical creation of the product, its sale and transfer to the buyer, and after-sale service. *Support activities* assist the primary activities and each other.

Primary Activities

The five categories of primary activities are inbound logistics, operations, outbound logistics, marketing and sales, and service. Each of these activities can be further divided for conducting a thorough internal analysis. In the following sections we will discuss the five primary activities in greater detail. Exhibit 3.2 provides a summary of some of the important factors that managers should consider when analyzing primary activities.

EXHIBIT 3.1
The Value Chain: Primary and Support Activities

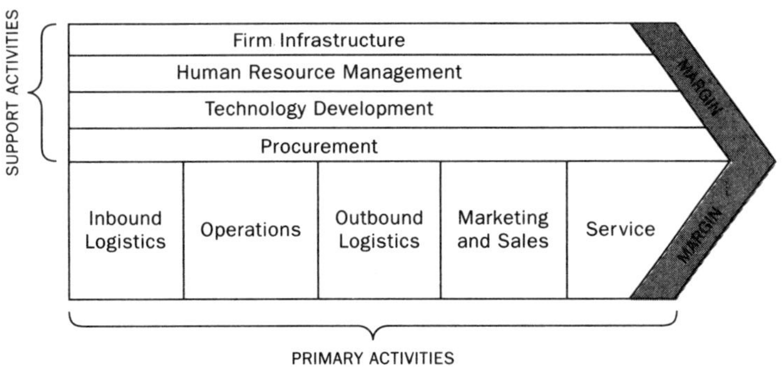

Source: Adapted with permission of The Free Press, a Division of Macmillan, Inc., from Porter, Michael E. (1985). *Competitive advantage: Creating and sustaining superior performance.* New York: Free Press. Copyright © 1985 by Michael E. Porter.

EXHIBIT 3.2
Evaluating a Firm's Value Chain: Primary Activities

Inbound Logistics
- Soundness of material and inventory control systems
- Efficiency of raw material warehousing activities

Operations
- Productivity of equipment compared to that of key competitors
- Appropriate automation of production processes
- Effectiveness of production control systems to improve quality and reduce costs
- Efficiency of plant layout and work-flow design

Outbound Logistics
- Timeliness and efficiency of delivery of finished goods and services
- Efficiency of finished goods warehousing activities

Marketing and Sales
- Effectiveness of market research to identify customer segments and needs
- Innovation in sales promotion and advertising
- Evaluation of alternate distribution channels
- Motivation and competence of sales force
- Development of an image of quality and a favorable reputation
- Extent of brand loyalty among consumers
- Extent of market dominance within the market segment or overall market

Customer Service
- Means to solicit customer inputs for product improvements
- Promptness of attention to customer complaints
- Appropriateness of warranty and guarantee policies
- Quality of customer education and training
- Ability to provide replacement parts and repair services

Note: Each item should be rated as poor, average, or excellent.

Inbound Logistics

Inbound logistics encompasses the activities of receiving, storing, and managing inputs, and includes such functions as materials handling, warehousing, inventory control, vehicle scheduling, and returns to suppliers. Improvements in any one of these activities typically result in cost reductions and increased productivity.

General Motors, the world's largest automobile manufacturer, has undertaken several measures to improve the efficiency of its inbound logistics. One example is their arrangement with Robin Transports, a Lansing, Michigan-based company, for parts delivery to automobile assembly plants.[2] Robin's trailers were designed with fabric walls which enable them to be unloaded from the sides as well as from the rear. These trailers can load and unload in places where standard trailers cannot go, and are able to unload near GM's assembly lines. Robin loads the trailers in sequence for ease of handling and delivers at specified times when GM is ready to receive the shipments. In order to justify its investment in special handling equipment for the trailers, Robin obtained status from GM as a preferred carrier with a premium rate. GM set up its production assembly to benefit from this different mode of materials handling. GM realized productivity improvements from this through inventory reduction, just-in-time (JIT) delivery, and more efficient materials handling.

Operations

Operations involves the activities required to convert inputs into final products. This includes activities such as machining, packaging, assembly, equipment maintenance, and testing. Improvements in these activities often lead to higher-quality products, greater efficiency, and quicker response to market conditions.

International Paper's (IP) strategy during the 1980s illustrates the value of effective operations activities. When John Georges became chief operating officer in 1981, he recognized the pressing need for greater manufacturing efficiency.[3] During the next several years, IP invested over $7 billion in capital improvements to rebuild its neglected and inefficient pulp and paper mills. Now, IP is generally credited with having the most efficient production lines in the industry. Also, rebuilding existing mills instead of constructing new mills has significantly cut IP's lead times. The investments in plant and equipment enabled IP to shift production at some plants from low-margin cyclical products (e.g., brown linerboard used in the shipping business) to higher-margin stable products (e.g., white paper products for schools and offices). IP's return on equity (ROE) averaged 8 percent (compared to an industry norm of 10 percent) before 1981. By 1988, their ROE had increased to 17 percent, along with an 82 percent earnings growth over the previous year.

Outbound Logistics

Once the finished goods are produced, they need to be distributed to the firm's customers. This involves such outbound logistics as warehousing, materials handling, delivery vehicle operation, and order processing. Improvements in these activities often result in greater efficiency and higher levels of service to the firm's customers.

Seagate Technology, the world's leading manufacturer of hard disk drives for personal computers, determined that one way to compete successfully against Japanese rivals was to guarantee 4-day deliveries.[4] For outbound logistics from its U.S. distribution center in California, the firm developed a partnership with Skyway Freight Systems to be Seagate's sole vendor serving the entire United States. The payments to Skyway were less than 1 percent of each disk drive's total cost. However, the service was so good that in 6 months—in which thousands of shipments were handled—the program experienced only three customer complaints. Moreover, these complaints were the result of a misunderstanding of what "4 business days" meant rather than actual failures in delivering the product.

Marketing and Sales

A firm's marketing and sales activities revolve around four key issues: product mix, price, promotion, and channels of distribution. Depending upon the market segment that a firm is attempting to target, as well as the complexities of the production process, a firm may decide to have either a narrow or a broad product mix. The price that a firm is able to charge for its products provides a measure of the value that it has created for the customer. For any product or service to be successful, it must be promoted with carefully planned packaging, advertising, and other creative uses of the media. Finally, there are many important issues in determining how a product is to be distributed to its targeted customers. These include assessing the relative importance of distributors as opposed to a direct sales force, and determining the location of retail outlets.

Although firms such as Johnson & Johnson, McDonald's, and Coca-Cola have enjoyed success as market leaders in their respective industries, many other firms have successfully exploited a smaller segment or niche within their industries. Examples include A&W Root Beer and White Castle. It is doubtful whether A&W could have achieved such success if it had developed a cola drink to compete directly with Coca-Cola and Pepsi, which have a combined 70 percent market share in the soft drink industry.[5] Although White Castle was a pioneer in the fast food industry, it no longer has the resources required to compete with industry giants like McDonald's and Burger King. Instead, it has started selling microwavable hamburgers through grocery stores. The change in product offering and distribution channels was possible because of White Castle's steam process, which adds a high moisture content to the hamburgers, a necessary condition for microwave heating.[6] In this case, a change in the means of distribution enables White Castle to survive in an intensely competitive industry populated by much larger dominant players.

Service

Managers are increasingly recognizing customer service as one of their firm's most important value activities. Customer service includes activities such as installation, repair, customer training, parts supply, and product adjustment, as well as courtesy and prompt response to customer inquiries and complaints. In industries where initial product purchase requires substantial capital outlay and specialized customer training, the need for superior customer service can erect substantial entry barriers.

Many very successful companies are devoted to customer service to the point of obsession.[7] IBM measures customer satisfaction on a monthly basis, and a large share of the incentive compensation of top management is based on this monthly measure. Frito-Lay is another company that goes to great lengths to achieve what they call a "99.5 percent service level." The company is willing to spend several hundred dollars sending a truck to restock a store with a few cartons of potato chips, even though such trips do not make any short-term economic sense. The entire executive staff of Apple Computer spends time on a regular basis listening to the toll-free customer call-in number. Senior executives of Levi-Strauss spend one Saturday a month selling jeans at retail outlets. Campbell Soup chairman Gordon McGovern regularly dispatches company executives to the kitchens of some 300 households across the country to see how meals are prepared.

The Hartford Steam Boiler Inspection and Insurance Company demonstrates how outstanding service can be a means of achieving competitive advantage. This company enjoys 37 percent of the U.S. market for boiler and machinery insurance. It has developed a sophisticated database on its customers' boilers, which enables its engineers to provide advice and improve utilization, in addition to inspection of installations. This successful service delivery system is the result of a 123-year-old marriage between insurance and engineering. In 1989, the company earned $78 million on revenues of $485 million and growth in earnings per share averaged an impressive 21 percent during the 1980s.[8]

As these examples suggest, service-oriented companies have three principal characteristics. These are (1) intensive, active involvement on the part of senior management; (2) a remarkable people orientation; and (3) a high level of measurement and feedback.

Support Activities

Human resource management, technology development, procurement, and firm infrastructure are the four major categories of support activities that will be discussed in this section. As with primary activities, each of these support activities may be further divided into a number of distinct activities. For example, a firm's infrastructure consists of its general management, finance, accounting, information systems, and legal and governmental relations. In addition to providing support for primary activities, these activities provide support to each other. For example, a firm must have an effective human resource management strategy if it is to recruit, reward, and retain the kind of research and development (R&D) professionals necessary for technology development activities. Exhibit 3.3 summarizes some of the important factors to consider.

Human Resource Management

Human resource management includes activities required to recruit, train, develop, and compensate all levels of employees. The influence of human resource management permeates every activity in the value chain. The overall costs of human resource management activities are not easily quantified. They include such complex issues as the cost of employee turnover and executive compensation packages. Many costs associated with human resource management are increasing dramatically. For example, most managers are feeling an increasing burden in providing health care insurance to active and retired employees. These expenses have adversely affected their firm's competitive position in foreign markets.

Improving the skill levels of employees and maintaining good employee relations are vital to creating value and lowering costs. By training employees in several jobs, managers can help their companies respond to the market faster through increased efficiency, quality, productivity, and job satisfaction. For example, Motorola has revised its compensation system to reward employees who learn a variety of skills. National Steel has improved its efficiency by consolidating seventy-eight job classifications into sixteen and broadening worker responsibilities.[9] Maintaining good employee relations can also prevent labor-management confrontations. Ingersoll Milling Machine of Rockford, Illinois, takes pride in the fact that during its more than 100 years in business, it hasn't lost even a single day's work because of labor problems.[10] Human beings are the corporation's most valuable and

EXHIBIT 3.3
Evaluating a Firm's Value Chain: Support Activities

Human Resource Management

- Effectiveness of procedures for recruiting, training, and promoting all levels of employees
- Appropriateness of reward systems for motivating and challenging employees
- A work environment that minimizes absenteeism and keeps turnover at desirable levels
- Relations with trade unions
- Active participation by managers and technical personnel in professional organizations
- Levels of employee motivation and job satisfaction

Technology Development

- Success of research and development activities (in leading to product and process innovations)
- Quality of working relationships between R&D personnel and other departments
- Timeliness of technology development activities in meeting critical deadlines
- Quality of laboratories and other facilities
- Qualification and experience of laboratory technicians and scientists
- Ability of work environment to encourage creativity and innovation

Procurement

- Development of alternate sources for inputs to minimize dependence on a single supplier
- Procurement of raw materials:
  On a timely basis
  At lowest possible cost
  At acceptable levels of quality
- Procedures for procurement of plant, machinery, and buildings
- Development of criteria for lease versus purchase decisions
- Good, long-term relationships with reliable suppliers

Firm Infrastructure

- Capability to identify new-product market opportunities and potential environmental threats
- Quality of the strategic planning system to achieve corporate objectives
- Coordination and integration of all activities associated with the value chain among organizational subunits
- Ability to obtain relatively low-cost funds for capital expenditures and working capital
- Level of information systems support in making strategic and routine decisions
- Timely and accurate information for management on general and competitive environments
- Relationships with public policy makers and interest groups
- Public image and corporate citizenship

Note: Each item should be rated as poor, average, or excellent.

flexible form of capital, and in an environment of unpredictable and rapid changes it is necessary to develop a work force that can adapt quickly.

Technology Development

Technology pervades every value activity in an organization. It affects activities ranging from product and process developments to order entry and the distribution of goods and services to the customer. This means that technology development goes beyond the narrower traditional research and development. In other words, technology development extends beyond technologies applied only to the product itself. Major U.S. industries, such as automobiles and steel, have seen the need to invest in technology development to achieve long-term, sustainable competitive advantage. The decline of these industries during the 1970s is often partly attributed to their short-term orientation, including an overemphasis on quarterly profit and loss statements and a neglect of technology development activities.

Apple Computer is an example of a company that has greatly improved the efficiency of its manufacturing operation by successfully implementing robotics technology. Apple opted for soft, or flexible, automation that could be quickly changed to accommodate a variety of tasks. By selecting simple and single robot arms and by using robots that performed simple, repetitive tasks which could be easily modified, Apple improved its ability to respond to the rapidly changing market.[11] On the other hand, despite substantial capital investments, General Motors has encountered numerous difficulties in implementing robotics technology because of a relative lack of flexibility in its systems. Investing significant resources in modern technologies may help a firm attain a competitive advantage.

However, managers need to realize that investment in technology is also a potential source of risk for the business. Not only are large investments involved but there are uncertainties associated with many factors, such as changes in consumer demand, rapid imitation by competitors, and changes in the technology itself.

Procurement

Procurement refers to the function of purchasing inputs used in the firm's value chain. These include raw materials, supplies, and other inputs directly used in the production process, as well as equipment, machinery, and buildings. Purchased inputs are important for support activities as well as primary activities. For example, the decision to select a particular advertising agency to promote a firm involves considerable financial commitment and may have a major impact on a firm's sales and profitability. The cost of purchased inputs is roughly 60 percent of the total sales revenues of most U.S. corporations. Thus, managers should recognize that even a small percentage saving on these costs can have a dramatic impact on the firm's profitability.[12] Improved procurement practices, such as close monitoring for defects, can lead to better quality inputs at reduced costs. Also, other activities associated with receiving and using the inputs can be improved.

The JIT system has gained increased popularity in recent years among corporations in Japan, Europe, and North America.[13] JIT achieves the objective of obtaining low-cost, high-quality, on-time production by eliminating accumulations of stock between successive processes and by minimizing idleness in facilities and workers. This approach reduces setup times and costs, and a firm's suppliers become extended storage facilities of the company itself. Application 3.1 provides examples of how applications of JIT have benefited many corporations such as Hewlett-Packard, General Electric, and Honeywell. Because of factors such as distant suppliers, poor quality of parts, unreliable freight systems, and resistance from workers not all applications of JIT have been successful in the United States.

Firm Infrastructure

Firm infrastucture includes activities such as finance and accounting, legal and governmental affairs, information systems, and general management. These activities generally support the entire value chain and may originate at various levels within an organization. Expenses associated with a firm's infrastructure activities are sometimes viewed as overhead. However, such activities can be a source of competitive advantage. For example, firms in highly regulated industries devote significant time and money to legal and governmental affairs to bring about a favorable legislative environment. To achieve such a goal, many firms form political action committees, hire lobbyists, and encourage the interaction of top

Application 3.1

Examples of Successful Applications of JIT

Hewlett-Packard, Boise, Idaho (dot-matrix printers):

- Lead time cut from 5 days to 1 day
- Work in progress (WIP) cut from 7 days to less than 1 day
- Raw material cut from 1 month to 10 days maximum

General Electric, Louisville (dishwashers):

- Lead time cut from 6 days to 18 hours
- Raw and in-process stock cut by more than half
- Scrap and rework cut 51 percent
- Field service calls cut 53 percent

Intel, Singapore (printed circuit board assembly and test):

- Lead time cut from 25 to 6 days
- Raw material inventory cut by two-thirds to three-quarters

Honeywell, Minneapolis (electronic air cleaners):

- Work in progress (WIP) cut 80 percent in subassemblies and component parts
- Scrap and salvage costs cut 54 percent
- Productivity up 15 percent

Rockwell, Richardson, Texas (telecommunications):

- Lead time in fabrication cut from 8.2 to 1.5 weeks
- Lead time for wave-guide parts cut from 17.3 to 2.2 weeks
- Lead time in sheet metal cut from 6 to 1.2 weeks

Texas Instruments, Sherman, Texas (defense weapons systems):

- In metal fabrication, cut WIP from 18,000 to under 1,000 pieces
- Cut production lead time from 14 to about 2 days
- Cut scrap and rework by 75 to 80 percent

Digital Equipment Corporation, Colorado Springs (computer disk drives and controllers):

- In Winchester disk drive final assembly, lead time cut from 2.0 to 0.25 days, WIP cut from $5 million to $900,000
- In diversified disk product subassembly, WIP cut from $119,000 to $18,000, rework cut from 300 to 0 units, productivity up 63 percent.

Source

Adapted with permission of The Free Press, a Division of Macmillan, Inc., from *World class manufacturing: The lessons of simplicity applied,* by Richard J. Schonberger. Copyright © 1986 by Richard J. Schonberger.

executives with powerful policymakers. We will now discuss the various aspects of a firm's infrastructure.

Finance and Accounting. Finance and accounting functions play a critical role in the effective management of the firm. Competitive advantage can be achieved through the ability to raise capital from equity markets and lending sources, establishment of sophisticated capital budgeting practices, and understanding and effective implementation of appropriate cost accounting systems. In managing the portfolio of a firm that competes in many different product markets, cost accounting procedures and capital budgeting practices are used to make corporate-level resource allocation decisions. These systems allow managers to make meaningful comparisons of the performances of different divisions.

Legal Issues and Governmental Relations. Legal issues and governmental relations claim a large amount of top management's time. Handling such issues effectively can have a significant impact on a corporation's long-term viability. In the late 1980s, the number of companies maintaining offices in Washington, D.C., was close to 7,090, up from fewer than 150 in the 1960s. In addition, approximately 2,500 companies have other forms of Washington representation, such as the more than 15,000 lobbyists who represent their interests to Congress and regulatory agencies.[14] Legal liabilities caused by defective products and environmental disasters lead to economic and noneconomic burdens to corporations in terms of compensation paid to victims and the loss of goodwill. Examples include Exxon's huge oil spill off the Alaskan coast, Johns Manville Corporation's liability for asbestos poisoning, and Union Carbide's chemical accident in Bhopal, India. Such incidents can have a substantial negative impact, not only on a company's reputation, but also on its financial position. Therefore, managers must constantly seek to minimize the potential liabilities their firms face from the political and legal environment.

Information Systems. Every value activity has both a physical and an information-processing component.[15] The physical component includes all the physical tasks necessary to perform the activity. The information-processing component consists of the activities necessary to collect, process, and channel the data required to perform the activity. Therefore, all value activities are influenced by information systems. Today, firms are using increasing amounts of information throughout the organization. By relying on a sophisticated information system, Wal-Mart has greatly reduced inventory carrying costs, as well as customer response time.[16] Sales and stock at each store are constantly monitored. Stores beam orders by way of satellite to the central computer at headquarters, and suppliers schedule shipments accordingly to satisfy Wal-Mart's needs. This information system enables Wal-Mart to fill a store's order within 36 hours, much faster than its competitors.

Information systems can be used to enhance a firm's competitive advantage.[17] The bargaining power of buyers can be reduced by introducing switching costs that make it more costly for a buyer to go to a competitor. For example, a large medical supply company has provided on-line order entry terminals and inventory management software to its customers. Profitability in the banking industry is largely determined by the ability to manage its single largest cost—the cost of funds. By using sophisticated information systems for portfolio management, many banks have attained a lower average cost of funds. This, in turn, has reduced the power of the suppliers of funds.

Merrill Lynch's superior information system capabilities made possible the introduction of cash management accounts (CMA) in 1978. CMAs combined a variety of products, such as money market accounts, credit lines, and brokerage services, previously available only separately. They became a far more efficient substitute for a large group of conventional financial products.

Information systems also provide a means to deter entry into an industry. For example, many life insurance companies have enhanced their competitive position by building and maintaining large on-line information systems accessible to their customers at all times. But the costs involved in developing such systems are so high, they discourage new entry. The nature and intensity of competition in an industry can also be affected by the use of information systems. Many smaller banks are collectively improving their competitive positions against their larger competitors by sharing a common group of automated teller machines (ATMs).

Application 3.2

How Small Firms Use Information Systems to Achieve Competitive Advantage

Greater Houston Transportation Company, which owns Austin's American Cab, spent more than 2 years testing computerized dispatching in the 137 cabs that operate under the name "American" in Austin, Texas. Here's how the system works: When a customer calls for a cab, the order taker punches the order into a central computer system. The computer determines which of forty-two Austin zones contains the address. (It also checks the address for accuracy, thus screening out crank calls.) The call is then sent electronically to the closest driver. The address and customer name are spelled out on the cab's computer monitor. If the driver rejects the call, it automatically goes to the next driver. The results were so good that Greater Houston put the system in its 1,400-plus Houston cabs—which include Yellow Cab, Town Car, and Fiesta.

Yellow Cab of Dallas, Inc. (which is separate from Yellow Cab in Houston), switched to computerized dispatching, using a system by Motorola. The system is in 200 of Yellow's 300 cabs. Drivers have responded so well that Karl Kuhlman, company president, expects to add more cabs. Drivers like it because other drivers can't skim their calls. "There are approximately 13 or 14 cab companies operating in Dallas. They can all carry scanners. They can scan our calls and go get those passengers. This eliminates all that," says Mr. Kuhlman.

Rudy Bruhns, executive vice president of Greater Houston, points to the service advantage of being able to handle peak periods with ease. "If it's raining or there's a special event in town, we can handle that. We're finding between 75 and 90 percent of our orders are dispatched within two minutes." The response time has improved, Mr. Bruhns says, because the dispatcher never falls behind. "The maximum a voice dispatcher can do is 200 (calls) per hour." With computerized dispatching, the company has tripled that number.

The use of computerized dispatching with in-cab monitors is beginning to spread across the country, but it is still a relatively new and expensive technology. Yellow Cab of Dallas, whose system is only the fifth Motorola system installed in the United States, will cost about $2.5 million when it's fully installed. "This technology will improve service not only for passengers, but the people who drive our cabs," says Kuhlman. The competitive advantage is clearly worth it.

Source

Adapted from Kunde, D. (1989, May 23). Computers help speed the way for Austin Cab. *The Dallas Morning News*, p. 1D. (Adapted with permission of *The Dallas Morning News*.)

The importance of information systems as a competitive resource may be assessed by identifying activities in which information systems can be used to achieve competitive advantage. Application 3.2 illustrates that this kind of advantage can be attained in smaller businesses as well—taxicab companies.

General Management. General management encompasses both the structure and systems that support all of an organization's activities. Prompted by such factors as intensified international competition and possible attacks by corporate raiders, many large U.S. corporations have undergone major reorganizations resulting in leaner corporate staffs, a thinning of middle management, and divestment of many marginally profitable operations. As noted by Andrall Pearson, former president of Pepsico, Inc., excessive layers of management may prevent senior managers from considering new ideas and elaborate approval systems can delay decisions until it is too late for effective action.[18]

Most turnarounds are brought about by a change in top management, clearly indicating the value of top management skills. When Richard Miller was appointed CEO of the troubled Wang Laboratories in the summer of 1989, he brought with him an impressive record of turning around declining operations: Penn Central and General Electric's consumer electronics division.[19] Upon joining Wang, he immediately assembled a turnaround team of approximately seventy middle-level managers from all parts of the company. Within 40 days, this team was able to identify $800 million in relatively unproductive assets. Within a year the firm managed to sell $600 million of these assets. This dramatically reduced its debt and strengthened its focus on the core business. Despite Wang's precarious financial position, Miller remains committed to a long-term orientation: "I have not laid off a single development engineer, and I won't sacrifice R&D, which is the future of this company."

Value Chain Analysis: An Application

Identifying a firm's costs in terms of the value activities can provide several meaningful insights to the managers in making important decisions. Application 3.3 provides the example of a firm which, with the help of Ernst and Young, a leading accounting and consulting firm, replaced its traditional cost accounting system with an activity-based costing system. The firm discovered that its profits from individual products were very different from what they were believed to be under the traditional costing system. This led to a new set of resource allocation decisions that would enhance the firm's competitive advantage and improve its overall profitability.

Application 3.3

Applying Activity-Based Costing to a Manufacturing Firm

Ernst & Young, one of the world's largest accounting and professional services firms, is actively involved in helping corporations adopt activity-based costing methods.* One client, a $300 million division of a leading tool manufacturer, was concerned with high manufacturing overhead, as well as high sales, general, and administrative (SG&A) expenses, but was not able to determine how to properly allocate their costs to individual product lines.

This firm's traditional cost accounting system used direct labor as a basis for allocating manufacturing overhead. For every dollar of direct labor expense required to manufacture a product, on average, $5 of manufacturing overhead expense was allocated. In addition, operating expenses such as commissions, corporate allocations and other SG&A, which accounted for 33 percent of total product cost, were not assigned to specific product lines. These operating expenses were applied evenly across product lines based on a fixed percent (29 percent) of each product's selling price. These allocation methods resulted in a distorted picture of product costs.

Ernst & Young was engaged to construct a model that would provide more meaningful product cost information. Three products were selected and analyzed to develop a cost flow model that related costs to the specific value chain activities associated with each product. Some costs could be directly assigned to products, such as labor, material, and setup costs. Other costs were aggregated and allocated to products based on appropriate output measures. For example, costs associated with development of a new catalog were allocated to the products based on number of pages for each product.

The output of the cost model was new product costs for the three products selected. The "Traditional" column in Exhibit 3.4 shows product cost components under the traditional cost system. The "Activity-Based" column reflects the new product cost. Under the new cost structure, sales discounts are directly assigned to products, and manufacturing overhead and operating expenses are allocated to the products based on relevant operational costs. Based on the new calculations, it becomes evident that product #1 is contributing negatively to the division's profits. Also, product #2 is significantly less profitable than previously represented, and product #3 is much more profitable.

The company used the revised product cost information to make decisions regarding investment in plant and

Application 3.3 (cont.)

facilities, target inventory levels, selling price, advertising expenditures, distribution channels, and investment in R&D. The previous inaccurate product costs had led to promotion and investment in unprofitable products, and underinvestment in profitable ones. By clearly understanding what value chain activities were associated with each product and assigning costs accordingly, management was able to focus company resources on reducing or eliminating activities which did not add value. Thus, accurate product cost information helped the division enhance its competitive advantage in its industry.

* We would like to thank J. Neil Smiley, senior manager, Ernst & Young, for providing us with this example. Given its proprietary nature, the names of the firm and division are not revealed.

EXHIBIT 3.4
A Comparison of Product Costing under Traditional and Activity-Based Costing Systems

	Product #1		*Product #2*		*Product #3*	
	Traditional	*Activity-Based*	*Traditional*	*Activity-Based*	*Traditional*	*Activity-Based*
Selling price	$3.84	$3.84	$4.92	$4.92	$9.57	$9.57
Sales discounts		0.10		0.13		0.25
Net selling price	$3.84	$3.74	$4.92	$4.79	$9.57	$9.32
Cost of sales (COS)						
Material	$0.17	$0.17	$0.20	$0.20	$0.15	$0.15
Labor	0.21	0.29	0.33	0.48	0.63	0.96
Setup	*	0.11	*	0.15	*	0.11
Overhead	1.54	1.43	2.57	2.32	3.20	2.63
Other COS	†	0.62	†	0.22	†	0.18
Total COS	$1.92	$2.62	$3.10	$3.37	$3.98	$4.03
Gross profit	$1.92	$1.12	$1.82	$1.42	$5.59	$5.29
Operating expenses						
Commissions		$0.22		$0.28		$0.54
Corp. allocations		0.04		0.05		0.09
Other SG&A		0.76		0.76		0.76
Other inc. expenses		0.15		0.29		0.15
Total opr. expenses	$1.11‡	$1.17	$1.43‡	$1.38	$2.78‡	$1.54
Division pretax profit	$0.81	($0.05)	$0.39	$0.04	$2.81	$3.75

* Included in overhead.
† Not assigned.
‡ 29% of selling price.

BEYOND THE VALUE CHAIN: OTHER ISSUES IN INTERNAL ANALYSIS

Value chain analysis allows us to assess the strengths and weaknesses of a firm's primary and support activities. To make a more complete internal assessment of an organization, we must look at five other considerations: financial analysis, culture, leadership, legitimacy, and reputation.

Financial Analysis

A starting point in assessing the financial position of a firm is the computation and analysis of four basic categories of financial ratios: *liquidity, leverage, activity,* and *profitability.*

- *Liquidity* ratios provide measures of a firm's capacity to meet its short-term financial obligations.
- *Leverage* ratios provide an indication of a firm's financial risk, that is, the relative proportion of its debt to its equity.
- *Activity* ratios reflect whether or not a firm is using its resources efficiently.
- *Profitability* ratios provide information regarding a firm's overall economic performance.

A detailed ratio analysis provides managers with important insights regarding such issues as overhead cost structure, ability to raise capital, adequacy of working capital and contingency reserves, and efficient use of assets. Ratio analysis relies on judgment and sound interpretation. For example, industry norms, comparison of a firm's ratios with those of key competitors, and improvements or deterioration in key ratios over time are critical inputs when assessing a firm's relative competitive position.

Managers may gain insights into a firm's overall financial position by analyzing its cash flow position. In fact, profits do not always lead to a simultaneous improvement in a firm's cash position. For example, a liberal credit policy may result in increased profits from sales. However, delay or default in the collection of receivables may severely affect a firm's ability to meet its current and long-term liabilities. A general rule of thumb is that all long-term financial commitments and at least a part of the short-term commitments should be met with long-term funds, that is, equity or long-term debt, to avoid serious cash flow problems from time to time. Alternatively, it is generally unwise to use short-term borrowing to fund long-term capital requirements. An appendix to this chapter provides more detailed coverage of the computation and use of financial ratios.

EXHIBIT 3.5
Evaluating a Firm's Financial Position

- Cost of funds compared to industry norms and key competitors
- Ability to raise additional funds for present operations, as well as for growth and acquisitions
- Liquidity ratios compared to industry norms and key competitors
- Leverage ratios compared to industry norms and key competitors
- Activity ratios compared to industry norms and key competitors
- Profitability ratios compared to industry norms and key competitors
- Relationships with all creditors and stockholders
- Dividend policy
- Appropriateness of match between sources and uses of funds

Note: Each item should be rated as poor, average, or excellent.

In many cases, a firm's financial strategy is determined to a large extent by its overall corporate strategy. Often companies repurchase a large portion of their outstanding stock to avoid the possibility of a hostile takeover. Such repurchases may require the firm to slash operating budgets, slow research and development activities, delay capital investment, and resort to excessive borrowing. This situation illustrates the necessity of interpreting financial information and ratios in the overall context of a firm.

Some important issues in evaluating the financial strengths of a firm are given in Exhibit 3.5.

Organizational Culture and Leadership

Managers have increasingly recognized the importance of an organization's culture in achieving competitive advantage. Organizational culture can be viewed as a complex set of values, beliefs, assumptions, and symbols that define the way in which a firm conducts its business.[20] Organizational culture has a major influence on goals, strategies, and policies; it also facilitates or inhibits the implementation of a chosen strategy. The problems AT&T encountered in its less than successful entry into the personal computer market are generally attributed to a culture that emphasized technological leadership and service rather than a response to market needs.

The quality of leadership which top management provides has a critical influence on the formation and evolution of an organization's culture and the overall strategic direction of the company. John Kotter, a noted expert on leadership, considers leadership to be the ability to induce organizationwide change through sharing a vision with a large number of others throughout the organization.[21] The values and beliefs of the founder and/or chief executive often form the culture of an organization. For example, it is difficult to separate the culture of an organization such as Federal Express from its charismatic founder, Fred Smith. Mr. Smith's infectious enthusiasm and aggressive personality have played a critical role in Federal Express's dominant position in the express mail industry.

McDonald's Corporation is an example of an organization whose success can be greatly attributed to the quality of its leadership and culture. McDonald's philosophy of assembly-line cooking and preparation, fast service, a wholesome atmosphere, and a near-religious devotion to the hamburger are all core values instilled by its founder, Ray Kroc, who died in 1984. New employees still gather in the Oak Brook, Illinois, headquarters to listen to his videotaped inspirational messages. On Founder's Day, every October 9th, 10,000 executives and suppliers, including the chief executive officer, cook and clean in restaurants throughout the chain.[22]

Although an organization's culture and leadership are important influences on a firm's performance, they are very difficult to quantify, analyze, and understand.* Different types of culture and styles of leadership are appropriate for different organizations and industries. Application 3.4 highlights Southwest Airlines' chief executive officer, Herb Kelleher, and the important role he has played in developing and maintaining the unique culture of that organization.

Some general issues to bear in mind when assessing an organization's quality of leadership and culture are included in Exhibit 3.6.

---

* The topics of organizational culture and leadership will be addressed in detail in Chapter 11.

Application 3.4

Herb Kelleher: A Boy and His Airline

At 57, Herb Kelleher looks and acts like a first-generation astronaut, hard-driving, hard-drinking, fast-living sort of guy whose swept-back hair frames a prominent widow's peak and madcap blue eyes. His office is filled with small porcelain statues of wild turkeys, a tribute to his drink of choice. He smokes five packs of cigarettes a day, rarely drawing a clean breath of air, but so far he is in proud and happy defiance of the laws of health.

Herb Kelleher is the current president, chief executive officer, and chief financial officer of Southwest Airlines. As of 1989, Southwest is the eleventh-largest airline in the country and one of the strongest carriers in the nation. In 1988, with Texas still in a slump and the airline industry in upheaval, Southwest made $57 million in profits, its best year ever, and it reported $860.4 million in revenues. Kelleher's $20,000 investment in the fledgling airline made him a founding shareholder. He raised Southwest's first $543,000 using the same list of power brokers he contacted to help finance John Connally's 1962 gubernatorial campaign. Kelleher the competitor is always looking for new conquests. His plan is to have the airline double its size—in revenues and number of planes—by the mid-1990s.

More than being just a business, Southwest Airlines approaches being a cult, with 6,500 employees for members. The employees own 10 percent of the airline and ownership begets loyalty. Each new employee is shown the *Southwest Shuffle* videotape, which describes the workings of each department—from baggage handlers to the pilots to the secretarial pool—in rap. (This one is sung by the mechanics: "When you need spare parts to put on the plane/We get the right ones/And we order it again.") Every Friday at noon, the employees in Dallas gather in the headquarters parking lot for a cookout.

Kelleher's list of employees is updated constantly, and he tries to know the names of all of them. They call him Herb or Herbie, but never Mr. Kelleher. On Black Wednesday—the day before Thanksgiving and traditionally the busiest day of the year for airlines—Herb works in the baggage department at Love Field, loading and unloading customer bags.

Southwest Airlines is an extension of Kelleher and he is not prepared to imagine it without him. "The history of Southwest Airlines is still unfolding," says Kelleher. "I'm not finished yet." The board of directors is concerned that a man who smokes five packs of cigarettes a day has not identified a clear successor. Employees wander the halls of the headquarters, wondering what would happen to them and their airline if Kelleher dropped dead of a heart attack. When Roy Spence, the president of Southwest's advertising agency, was asked what would happen to the airline if Herb died today, Spence became slack-jawed. He took a few seconds to think about it and then said, with a straight face, "Herb ain't never going to die."

Source

Excerpted from Jarboe, Jan. (1989). A boy and his airline. *Texas Monthly, 17,* 98–103, 140–144, 153–155 (with permission).

Legitimacy and Reputation

A firm's product-market strategies are essentially activities directed toward the goal of positioning itself within an industry and earning sustained economic profits. Political strategies to enhance an organization's legitimacy and reputation are aimed at producing favorable legislation and public opinion. At times, the public may perceive that a firm's or industry's products or activities are harmful to the environment or to consumers. This can lead to legislation or public outcry that severely affects growth and profit potential. Industries that have declined in legitimacy and reputation include the nuclear power industry after the Three Mile Island accident, the tobacco industry as a result of unfavorable medical findings linking its product to cancer and other diseases, and the oil industry after Exxon's

EXHIBIT 3.6
Assessing an Organization's Culture and Leadership

- The sense of identity and affiliation the firm provides to organizational members
- Consistency of the cultures of subunits with each other and with the overall corporate culture
- Ability of the culture to foster innovation, creativity, and openness to new ideas
- Capacity to adapt and evolve, consistent with the demands of changes in environment and strategy
- Executive, managerial, and employee motivation (based on both monetary and nonmonetary rewards)

Note: Each item should be rated as poor, average, or excellent.

Alaskan oil spill in early 1989. Most other industries are subject to various forms of societal control as well. For example, the legitimacy of the automobile industry was negatively affected by the public perception that its products had poor fuel efficiency and pollution control. This led to legislated standards for emission control and fuel economy.

A firm's advertising often reflects its ethical standards. Advertisements that are proven to be deliberately false or misleading can have serious repercussions on a firm's reputation and legitimacy. Application 3.5 describes some of the deceptions practiced by food companies and the actions taken against them.

Many firms perceived to have social legitimacy and reputation—because they either provide essential services or are critical to the national security—benefit substantially from favorable government policies. For example, the aircraft industry and other high-tech industries such as electronics and biotechnology regularly receive extensive government funding for new product development. It is increasingly important for firms individually or collectively (e.g., through industry associations) to develop and maintain a good reputation and a perception of legitimacy with key environmental stakeholders.

A firm's relative position with regard to legitimacy and reputation is more difficult to assess than most primary and support activities. However, the items included in Exhibit 3.7 can help in making a broad assessment.

MAKING MEANINGFUL COMPARISONS

We have looked at the various value chain activities and other areas which need to be evaluated when conducting an internal analysis for a firm. However, there is always the possibility that unless appropriate standards of comparison are used, the evaluations managers make may prove to be biased. Three approaches that managers commonly use to minimize subjectivity are

1. Comparison of the firm's performance across various time periods
2. Comparison of the firm's performance with industry norms and key competitors

Application 3.5

Ethics and Advertising: The Case of Misleading or False Food Labels

About half of all consumers say they depend on labels to determine which food to buy . . . A casual stroll down the aisles of a supermarket reveals just how often . . . shoppers are being shamelessly deceived.

- Budget Gourmet Light and Healthy Salisbury Steak, which is labeled "low fat," derives 45 percent of its total calories from fat.
- Diet Coke contains more than the one heavily advertised calorie per can (so does Diet Pepsi).
- There is no real fruit—just fruit flavors—in Post Fruity Pebbles.
- Honey Nut Cheerios provides less honey than sugar and more salt than nuts.
- Mrs. Smith's Natural Juice Apple Pie contains artificial preservatives. The word "natural" refers to the fruit juice used to make the pie.

Throughout the past decade, federal food watchdogs napped to the sounds of this cacophony of false claims. The Food and Drug Administration virtually invited abuse by lifting its own long-standing ban against health promotions on food labels. But the deregulatory winds have shifted and the sleeping sentry has awakened. In a blaze of whistle-blowing the FDA, headed by tough new commissioner David Kessler, is cracking down. The agency has begun seizing products with misleading labels, developing new guidelines for nutritional information and exposing hollow health claims.

Already Kessler has fired several salvos at deceivers. First hit was Procter & Gamble. The conglomerate had received numerous letters from the FDA complaining about the labeling of its Citrus Hill Fresh Choice orange juice, which is made from concentrate. In April, Kessler instructed his inspectors to publicly seize 2,000 cases of the juice. Two days and many headlines later, the company, based in Cincinnati, agreed to remove the term "fresh" from its label. Soon after, executives at Ragu' Foods of Trumbull, Connecticut, consented to drop the offending word from their Ragu' Fresh Italian pasta sauces, which, like many other prepared sauces, are heat processed. In May, the FDA ordered that the "no-cholesterol" claim be removed from Best Foods' Mazola Corn Oil and HeartBeat Canola Oil, made by Great Foods of America. Like all plant oils, these products never contained cholesterol.

Just last week, Kessler's FDA took aim at juice producers by proposing new regulations that would force them to disclose for the first time exactly how much and what kinds of juice are in their fruit juice drinks. Such a rule would reveal, for instance, that Veryfine drinks contain only 10 percent fruit juice. It would also inform consumers that even the claims made by many cranberry and raspberry drinks to be "100 percent juice" are somewhat misleading: they are filled with deflavored apple or grape extracts that are little more than natural sugar water. . . .

The relabeling effort may cost food manufacturers $600 million during the next two decades. They will pass on the tab to consumers, but fortunately it is very low: only about 11 cents for every $100 worth of groceries, according to government estimates. Even the most conservative projections place the potential benefit from reduced medical costs and increased productivity at $3.6 billion. If everyone who reads labels were to adopt a healthier diet, the savings could jump to more than $100 billion.

Source

Excerpted from Gorman, C. (1991, July 15). The fight over food labels. *Time*, pp. 51–52, 54–56 (with permission).

3. Assessment of how well the firm is doing with respect to the critical success factors of the industry or industries in which it competes

In addition, managers often use "rules of thumb" which come from an intuitive understanding of the industry, consultants' suggestions, and perceptions of present and desired performance levels.

EXHIBIT 3.7
Assessing an Organization's Legitimacy and Reputation

- Effectiveness in coping with restrictive regulations (i.e., environmental, antitrust, and product liability)
- Relationship with consumer activist groups
- Relationship with the media
- Relationship with policy makers and government officials
- Ability to obtain government grants and funding
- Extent of trade-tariff protection

Note: Each item should be rated as poor, average, or excellent.

Historical Comparisons

Viewing a company's performance in its proper historical context means asking if the firm's performance is improving or declining in comparison to previous years. Historical comparisons are useful for two reasons. First, during periods of normal economic growth, year-to-year comparisons provide information to managers about changes in a firm's competitive position in its industry. Second, historical comparisons help form a sound basis for setting realistic objectives and fair performance evaluation standards. The information used to perform such comparisons is usually readily available. Competitor information, on the other hand, may be difficult and/or costly to obtain, particularly when many firms in the industry are privately held.

Managers must exercise care when interpreting the results of historical comparisons. Year-to-year comparisons may be highly misleading in periods of recession or economic boom. For example, an increase of 2 percent in sales during a recessionary period may be quite acceptable, whereas a 10 percent increase in sales during a boom period may actually reflect an erosion of market share. Also, historical comparisons may be misleading if the overall strategy of the firm has changed. For example, firms pursuing a strategy of increasing market share may experience lower levels of profitability but higher market penetration than normally expected. Finally, year-to-year comparisons expressed in percentages might be misleading. Firms such as Compaq Computer Corporation, which experienced phenomenal growth in the early 1980s, cannot sustain such performance because of the inherent limits to growth in any industry. Also, historical comparisons can be misleading when baseline figures are not properly taken into account. Thus, at first glance, an American automobile manufacturer may seem to be quite successful if it increases its exports to Japan by 80 percent in a single year. However, if this represents a volume increase from 2,000 to 3,600 units, it is still not achieving a meaningful level of market penetration.

Comparisons with Industry Norms

Some of the limitations of historical comparisons can be overcome by comparing a firm's position to industry norms and to its key competitors. Three advantages of such a comparative analysis are as follows:

1. The insight it may provide into what activities or strategies lead to improving or declining performance
2. The ability to detect or anticipate changes in competitors' strategies
3. The ability to assess a firm's relative competitive position in an industry

Generally speaking, industry norms are most useful as a standard of comparison if the sizes and strategies of firms within an industry are relatively similar, such as in the case of regional banking and public utilities. When the sizes and strategies of competitors are quite different, it may be necessary to confine comparisons within the firm's strategic group. For example, in the retailing industry, firms follow a wide variety of strategies in terms of pricing, geographic scope, and breadth of product mix. So, in analyzing K-Mart's competitive position, it is more useful to use Wal-Mart as a key competitor instead of the entire industry.

Industries vary significantly in terms of their structures, critical success factors, and the relative strength of their competitive forces. Exhibit 3.8 illustrates how important financial ratios differ among the aircraft manufacturing, advertising, and variety store industries. Here, the difference between the current ratio and the quick (acid test) ratio is very small for advertising agencies but is quite large for aircraft manufacturers and variety stores. This is primarily because advertising agencies maintain very little inventory whereas aircraft manufacturers maintain substantial work-in-process and raw materials inventories. Variety stores also carry large amounts of finished goods inventory. Similarly, the collection period for variety stores is very short because most sales are for cash. Also, the asset-to-sales ratio for the aircraft industry is very high because of the industry's investments in machinery, plant, and equipment. Clearly, when managers evaluate the performance of their firm, they should make comparisons among firms within their industry.

Exhibit 3.9 presents a brief comparison of some of the key competitors in the toy industry for the years 1987 to 1990. Although sales have been growing each year, there have been wide fluctuations in the net profit margins in the industry. For the most part, the profitability of the major players, Hasbro, Mattel, and Tonka, have not paralleled the industry pattern. Hasbro has been able to maintain relatively consistent levels of profitability, while Mattel and Tonka have had rather large fluctuations—especially in terms of profitability. Hasbro, once derided as "has-been" for not entering the electronics and video

EXHIBIT 3.8
Differences in Industry Ratios across Industries, 1987

	Aircraft Manufacturer	*Advertising Agency*	*Variety Store*
Quick ratio	0.5	1.3	0.5
Current ratio	1.5	1.5	3.5
Collection period (days)	33.1	42.3	3.3
Assets/sales	58.8%	22.4%	44.7%
Return on sales	2.6%	3.9%	3.2%
Return on assets	3.5%	7.7%	6.3%

Source: *Industry norms and key business ratios (1987–1988)* (pp. 120, 146, 176). New York: Dun and Bradstreet Credit Services.

EXHIBIT 3.9
The Toy Industry: Comparison of Key Competitors (Sales in Billions of Dollars)

	1987		1988		1989		1990 (Est.)	
	Sales	*Net Profit Margin (%)*	*Sales*	*Net Profit Margin (%)*	*Sales*	*Net Profit Margin (%)*	*Sales*	*Net Profit Margin (%)*
Industry	3.753	(Negative)	4.447	4.5	5.073	6.2	5.300	4.4
Hasbro	1.345	3.6	1.358	5.3	1.410	6.5	1.450	6.0
Mattel	1.020	−9.0	0.990	3.6	1.237	7.2	1.475	7.1
Tonka	0.383	−0.02	0.908	−0.88	.871	0.9	.785	−4.3

Source: Mattson, S. R. (1990, November 23). *Value line*, pp. 1552, 1555, 1557, 1558.

segment of the industry, was able to avoid the very costly effects of a shakeout in this segment.

Identifying Critical Success Factors and Key Competitors

Critical success factors (CSFs) are those few but important areas in which good results will ensure successful competitive performance for the organization.[23] Poor results in these areas lead to declining performance for the firm. CSFs are areas of activity that managers must continuously monitor. The CSFs for a particular company are determined by a variety of environmental and firm-specific factors. Application 3.6 discusses major sources of CSFs.

One of the most important CSFs for the pharmaceutical industry is an R&D strategy that leads to the timely introduction of new products. This industry is characterized by intense competition, short product life cycles, and long lead times between basic research, product development, FDA approval, and commercialization. Firms in this industry must commit vast resources to R&D activities in order to develop new products and ensure their long-term profitability and cash flow. The relatively poor performance of Pfizer in the early 1980s could be largely attributed to their R&D budget, which was well below the industry average. Recognizing this problem, Pfizer doubled its R&D expenditures in the late 1980s, resulting in the development and commercialization of new products, including Procardia XL and Cardura, medications for angina and hypertension, respectively.[24] These products have significantly contributed to Pfizer's total revenues. Procardia XL's sales of $460 million in 1989 represented a 26 percent increase over the product's 1988 sales. Cardura was introduced in fifteen new countries, bringing the total to twenty-four countries.[25]

As in the case of Pfizer, identifying an industry's critical success factors plays a key role in determining a firm's competitive position. However, competitor analysis becomes more meaningful if it includes an identification of key competitors and a comparison with these competitors across the critical success factors.

Application 3.7 identifies the critical success factors for the discount department store segment (or strategic group) of the department store industry and compares three leading

Application 3.6

Prime Sources of Critical Success Factors (CSFs)

A research team at M.I.T. has identified four major sources of CSFs for an organization.

1. *Structure of the particular industry.* Each industry by its very nature has a set of critical success factors that are determined by the characteristics of the industry itself. Each company in the industry must pay attention to these factors. For example, for supermarket chains, product mix, inventory turnover, sales promotion, and pricing are the most important CSFs. For the airline industry, fuel efficiency, load factors, and an excellent reservation system are considered to be the most important CSFs.
2. *Competitive strategy, industry position, and geographic location.* Each company in an industry is in a unique situation that is determined by its history and current competitive strategy. For smaller organizations within an industry dominated by one or two large companies, the actions of the major companies will often produce new and significant problems. A competitive strategy for the smaller firm may mean establishing a new market niche, discontinuing a product line completely, or redistributing resources among various product lines. For example, in the personal computer industry, the survival of many smaller companies depends on the compatibility of their products with IBM. Just as differences in a firm's position within an industry dictate CSFs, differences in geographic location can lead to differing CSFs from one company to another.
3. *Environmental factors.* Changes in the gross national product, the economy, political factors, and demographics lead to changes in the critical success factors of various industries and firms. At the beginning of 1973, virtually no chief executive in the United States would have listed "energy supply availability" as a critical success factor. Following the oil embargo, however, this factor suddenly became very important.
4. *Temporal factors.* Internal organizational considerations often become temporal critical success factors. These are areas of activity that are significant for the success of an organization for a particular period of time because the activities are below the threshold of acceptability. For example, if several key executives of an investment banking firm quit to form a competing "spinoff firm," rebuilding of the executive group would become a critical success factor for the organization.

Source

Rockart, J. F. (1979). Chief executives define their own data needs. *Harvard Business Review, 57*(2), 81–93.

Application 3.7

Competitor Analysis in the Discount Department Store Industry*

The late 1980s witnessed the sudden emergence of the Bentonville, Arkansas-based Wal-Mart Stores as the nation's largest retailer, edging past both Sears and K-Mart. By 1990, Wal-Mart had total sales of $32.6 billion, growing at an annual rate of 26 percent between 1988 and 1990. During the same period, the sales of their major rivals, K-Mart and Sears, were substantially lower, showing annual growth rates of 9.9 percent and 1.2 percent, respectively. Wal-Mart's astounding growth rate was also accompanied by an equally phenomenal net profit margin of 4.1 percent, nearly twice that of its two largest competitors. The performance of Wal-Mart's stock also made its founder, Sam Walton, one of the richest men in the United States.

As indicated in Exhibit 3.10, Wal-Mart compares very favorably with its rivals on each of the industry's six critical success factors. Careful attention to every aspect of sales and administrative costs, such as office and retailing facilities as well as shrinkage (defined as the loss in retail dollars due to employee theft, customer theft, and bookkeeping errors), minimizes expenses. During the first half of the 1980s, Wal-Mart's sales and administrative expenses as a percentage of sales averaged approximately 16 percent. This compares extremely favorably to Sears

Application 3.7 (cont.)

and K-Mart, which averaged approximately 29 percent and 23 percent, respectively. Also, Wal-Mart's shrinkage rate averages only 1 percent of sales compared to approximately 2 percent for its rivals. By constructing its retail facilities within less than 1 day's driving from its distribution centers, Wal-Mart is able to serve its customers more efficiently. Wal-Mart avoids sales and keeps prices low, cultivating a reputation for value in small-town America. In contrast, Sears has suffered due to its inability to project a consistent image since it introduced its everyday low pricing strategy on March 1, 1989. According to Leonard Barry, director of the center for retailing studies at Texas A&M University, "Sears is still not competitive in the mind of the consumer, and it doesn't have the prestige of upscale specialty shops. Everyday low pricing is not going to get it out of the middle."

Wal-Mart has developed and maintained a distinctive organization culture which has greatly helped it to achieve dominance in the industry. Employees are referred to as "associates" and are beneficiaries of an innovative profit-sharing program. Until recently, the founder, Sam Walton, took pride in personally visiting each store at least once every year. Sears, on the other hand, suffers from low employee morale, a result of frequent large layoffs during the latter part of the 1980s. Wal-Mart has been characterized by low turnover in its top-management ranks, leading to stability and continuity in its strategies. Wal-Mart has also been more successful than its rivals in converting its significant buyer power into lower prices and more reliable supplies.

Sources

Huey, J. (1989, January 30). Wal-Mart. Will it take over the world? *Fortune*, pp. 52–56, 58, 61.

Schwadel, F. (1989, March 1). The "sale" is fading as a retailing tactic. *The Wall Street Journal*, pp. B1 and B6.

Baldwin, P. (1991, February 14). Wal-Mart ranks no. 1 in '90 with $32.6 billion in sales. *The Dallas Morning News*, pp. 1D and 5D.

Kahn, R. (1990, November 6). Comparison of expense rate of big 3 retailers. Consultant report (with permission).

* We wish to thank Professors Roger Dickinson and Roger Gates of the Department of Marketing at the University of Texas at Arlington for their assistance in preparing this example.

EXHIBIT 3.10
Evaluating Wal-Mart, K-Mart, and Sears across Critical Success Factors*

	Ratings		
Critical Success Factor	***Wal-Mart***	***K-Mart***	***Sears***
1. Low sales and administrative expense	5	3	1
2. Efficient distribution systems	5	4	4
3. Reputation for value	5	3	2
4. Organization culture	4	2	1
5. Top-management turnover	5	3	4
6. Supplier relationships	4	4	3

* 5 = very favorable; 1 = very unfavorable.
Note: The CSFs and ratings of key competitors above are only for illustrative purposes. Both involve judgment and there may be differences across evaluators. Also, both are subject to change because of changes in the industry environment and the strategies followe[illegible] individual firms.

competitors across these critical success factors. It is evident that Wal-Mar[illegible] largely attributed to its superior strength with respect to these critic[illegible] comparison to its rivals. In contrast, Sears has been quite unsuc[illegible] enter this segment (or strategic group) of this industry throu[illegible] strategy. The reasons for Sears's failure can be understood [illegible] the critical success factors compared to Wal-Mart an[illegible]

THE CENTRAL PLACE OF THE VALUE CHAIN IN STRATEGY FORMULATION

In this chapter, we have addressed the analysis of the strengths and weaknesses of a firm based on its value chain activities and related issues. In the next section of the book, we will look at how strategies are formulated on four levels: *business, functional, corporate,* and *global.* Before going on to these topics, it is important to understand the relationship among these four levels and the activities depicted in the value chain.

- *The Business Level.* Firms compete with one another for customers at what is known as the business level. Success in this competition is dependent upon sustaining competitive advantage. *Cost advantages* relative to competitors can arise from more efficient manufacturing processes, lower labor and material costs, or a cost-effective distribution system. A firm can *differentiate* its products on the basis of such factors as product features, price, service, or quality. Advantages derived from *faster response times* may reflect a firm's ability to innovate rapidly, quickly adjust to market conditions, or offer faster delivery of products and services. However, advantages based on cost, differentiation, or response time are not always mutually exclusive. For example, Wal-Mart has an extremely efficient ordering system, far superior to that of the competition. This competitive advantage enables Wal-Mart to provide better customer service because it can ensure that merchandise is available at all times. It also helps the company attain cost advantages by reducing ordering costs and avoiding errors. Finally, the ordering system permits quick inventory adjustments that can respond to changes in consumer preferences.

- *The Functional Level.* The ordering system used at Wal-Mart is managed by its purchasing department, only one of many functions within the company that contribute to its overall competitive advantage. Every department or function has some effect on the goods or services provided customers. So, every function must be managed to create value for the customer which will, in turn, be translated into a competitive advantage for the firm.

- ... *te Level.* Managers at the corporate level have the final responsibility for ... for the firm's owners. Stockholder value is not the same thing as cus... ut the two are closely linked. Stockholder value refers to wealth that ... creates for its owners through either stock price appreciation or ... to owners in the form of dividends. Creating wealth in either fashion ... success of the various business units that comprise the corpora... ting stockholder value depends upon first creating customer value, ... nagers need to understand how their decisions affect the ability of ... yees to carry out the activities of the value chain at a much

... hen managers formulate strategies at the global level, they con... ly into various businesses, but also into various countries. ... tions of what is and isn't of value may differ markedly, ... tomers share the common trait of seeking out whatever it is they value. Success in any country is based on creating the sort of superior customer value which can be translated into a competitive advantage. A carefully constructed global strategy can work to greatly strengthen a firm's entire value chain in any one country.

Summary

Internal analysis involves identifying and evaluating various functional areas and related issues. The concept of the value chain helps managers to analyze the various activities that a firm must perform. These can be broadly divided into primary activities and support activities. Primary activities are concerned with the physical creation of the product, its delivery to the customer, and after-sale service. Primary activities include inbound logistics, operations, outbound logistics, marketing and sales, and customer service. Support activities include information systems, human resource management, technology development, procurement, and a firm's infrastructure. To fully understand the internal environment, managers must also consider the financial position of the firm, its culture and leadership, as well as its legitimacy and reputation.

Interpretations and judgments make the results of an internal analysis more meaningful. To gain additional insight when determining a firm's strengths and weaknesses, managers should use comparisons of their financial ratios against industry standards and key competitors, as well as a comparison of their firm's performance over time. It is also important to evaluate a firm's performance with regard to the critical success factors of the industry (or industries) in which it competes compared to important competitors.

Notes

1. This section draws heavily from Porter, M. E. (1985). *Competitive advantage: Creating and sustaining superior performance* (chap. 2). New York: Free Press.
2. Bowersox, D. J. (1990). The strategic benefits of logistic alliances. *Harvard Business Review, 68*(4), 36–45.
3. Lowffelholz, S. (1989, July 25). Putting it on paper. *Financial World,* pp. 26–29.
4. Quinn, J. B., Doorley, T. L., & Paquette, P. C. (1990). Technology in services: Rethinking strategic focus. *Sloan Management Review, 32,* 79–87.
5. Winters, P. (1988, August 15). Cream of the smaller crop. *Advertising Age,* p. 510.
6. Hume, S. (1987, November 2). White Castle builds savvy in marketing. *Advertising Age,* pp. 6, 108.
7. The following examples of outstanding customer service are drawn from Peters, Thomas J., & Waterman, Robert H., Jr. (1982). *In search of excellence.* New York: Harper & Row; and Peters, Thomas J., & Austin, Nancy K. (1985). *A passion for excellence.* New York: Random House.
8. Hartford Steam Boiler. (1991, January 11). *Value line investment survey* (Pt. 3, Ed. 4, p. 634). New York: Value Line Publishing.
9. Alster, N. (1989, February 13). What flexible workers can do. *Fortune,* p. 62.
10. Martin, R. L. (1988). Private ownership, people, and experience. . . . *Manufacturing Engineering, 7,* 41–42.

11. Martin, R. L. (1988). Apple gets an "A." *Manufacturing Engineering, 7,* 44–45.
12. Porter, M. E. (1985). *Competitive advantage: Creating and sustaining superior performance.* New York: Free Press.
13. Aggarwal, S. C. (1985). MRP, JIT, OPT, FMS? *Harvard Business Review, 63*(5), 8–16; and Taylor, A., III. (1990, November 19). Why Toyota keeps getting better and better and better. *Fortune,* pp. 66–72, 74–76, 79.
14. Yoffie, D. B. (1988). How an industry builds competitive advantage. *Harvard Business Review, 66*(3), 82–89.
15. Why information is important in each stage of the value chain is discussed in Porter, Michael, & Millar, Victor E. (1985). How information gives you competitive advantage. *Harvard Business Review, 63*(4), 149–160.
16. Huey, J. (1989, January 30). Wal-Mart: Will it take over the world? *Fortune,* pp. 52–61.
17. Konsynski, B. R., & McFarlan, F. W. (1990). Information partnerships: Shared data, shared scale. *Harvard Business Review, 68*(5), 114–120.
18. Pearson, A. E. (1988). Tough-minded ways to get innovative. *Harvard Business Review, 66*(3), 99–106.
19. Dumaine, B. (1990, July 16). The new turnaround champs. *Fortune,* pp. 36–40, 42, 44.
20. An interesting perspective on organizational culture, in which it can be viewed as a means to reduce monitoring, control costs, and obtain individual compliance, is advanced in Barney, J. B. (1986). Organizational culture: Can it be a source of sustained competitive advantage? *Academy of Management Review, 11,* 656–665. For two detailed studies of individual company cultures, refer to Webber, A. M. (1990). Consensus, continuity, and common sense: An interview with Compaq's Rod Canion. *Harvard Business Review, 68*(7), 114–123; and Ishizuna, Y. (1990). The transformation of Nissan: The reform of corporate culture. *Long Range Planning, 23*(3), 9–15.
21. Kotter, J. P. (1988). *The leadership factor.* New York: Free Press.
22. Johnson, R. (1987, December 18). McDonald's combines a dead man's advice with a lively strategy. *The Wall Street Journal,* pp. 1, 13.
23. Rockart, J. F. (1979). Chief executives define their own data needs. *Harvard Business Review, 57*(2), 81–93; and Leidecker, J. K., & Bruno, A. V. (1984). Identifying and using critical success factors. *Long Range Planning, 17*(2), 23–32.
24. Curran, J. J. (1988, July 4). Companies that rob the future. *Fortune,* pp. 84–89.
25. Pfizer, Inc. (1990). *Moody's industrial manual 1990* (Vol. 2, p. 3288). New York: Moody's Investor Service; and Waldholz, M. (1991, January 25). Pfizer's board raises dividend, sets 2-for-1 split. *The New York Times,* p. C12.

Appendix to Chapter 3
Understanding and Analyzing Financial Statements*

Introduction

Evaluating a company involves a multitude of judgmental factors, such as quality of management, the extent of new product development, and marketing acumen. No evaluation can be complete, however, without a thorough financial analysis.

---

* Adapted from Cordell, D. M., & Crary, D. T. *Understanding and analyzing financial statements,* published manuscript (with permission).

In what follows we briefly explain some of the basic tools of financial analysis. We begin by describing the major financial statements: the balance sheet, the income statement, and the statement of retained earnings. We will show how various items from these statements can be utilized in ratio analysis to further our understanding of the firm's financial situation.

Balance Sheet

Financial analysis of a company begins with a review of its current financial condition. A balance sheet, which is also called a statement of condition or a statement of financial position, provides a snapshot of the firm's financial situation on a particular date.

The balance sheet in Exhibit 3.11 contains three major sections: (1) assets—everything the company owns (even if purchased by credit) or owed to the company; (2) liabilities (debt)—everything the company owes; and (3) stockholders' equity—the difference between the company's assets and its liabilities. The basic accounting identity can be expressed as

$$\text{Assets} = \text{liabilities} + \text{stockholders' equity}$$

This equation must always hold; any change in the total of one side must equal the change in the total of the other side.

As an example, consider a company that wants to purchase a $100 machine (a fixed asset). It may purchase the machine with $100 in cash (another asset), leaving the asset total unchanged. However, it may instead ask the seller to send a bill for the machine. In this case cash does not leave the firm immediately; and the asset total increases by $100. However,

EXHIBIT 3.11
DC Widgets, Inc.: Balance Sheet
(in Thousands of Dollars)

	December 31, 1991	*December 31, 1990*
Assets		
Current assets		
Cash	$ 187.6	$ 183.6
Marketable securities (note A)	385.5	377.7
Accounts receivable (net of allowance for doubtful accounts of $14.0 in 1991 and $11.25 in 1990)	668.0	575.5
Inventories (note A)	894.6	997.9
Prepayments and deferred charges	21.3	17.3
Total current assets	$2157.0	$2152.0
Property, plant, and equipment		
Land	$1338.0	$1338.0
Buildings and leasehold improvements	2000.0	1750.0
Equipment	5500.0	5312.3
Gross property, plant, and equipment	8838.0	8400.3
Less accumulated depreciation and amortization	− 5324.5	− 4882.6
Net property, plant, and equipment	$3513.5	$3517.7
Other assets (note B)	142.3	117.3
Total assets	$5812.8	$5787.0

Continued

EXHIBIT 3.11 (cont.)
DC Widgets, Inc.: Balance Sheet
(in Thousands of Dollars)

	December 31, 1991	December 31, 1990
Liabilities and Stockholders' Equity		
Current liabilities		
Accounts payable	$ 536.9	$ 697.5
Wages payable	112.5	197.5
Accrued expenses	30.0	22.5
Accrued income taxes	289.5	287.6
Current maturities of long-term debt	41.7	36.9
Notes payable	7.5	6.0
Total current liabilities	$1018.1	$1248.0
Deferred income taxes	124.1	123.3
Long-term debt		
Mortgage bonds (12% interest, due 1998; net of current maturities; annual sinking fund payment of $25)	$ 409.1	$ 438.9
Debentures (14% interest, due 2004; net of current maturities; annual sinking fund payment of $12)	272.7	292.6
Total long-term debt	$ 681.8	$ 731.5
Total liabilities	$1824.0	$2102.8
Stockholders' equity		
Preferred stock (8% cumulative, $50 par; 10810 share authorized, issued and outstanding)	540.5	540.5
Common equity	300.0	300.0
Capital stock ($1 par value, 300,000 shares issued and outstanding; 500,000 shares authorized)		
Paid in capital	508.5	508.5
Retained earnings	2639.8	2335.2
Total common equity	3448.3	3143.7
Total stockholders' equity	3988.8	3684.2
Total liabilities and stockholders' equity	$5812.8	$5787.0

Note A: Significant accounting policies
Marketable securities: Recorded at cost which was the lower of cost or market value in both 1991 and 1990. Market value was $390,000 for 1991 and $410,000 for 1990.
Inventories: Valued according to the FIFO (first-in, first-out) method.

Note B: Other assets
Other assets include investment at market value in Western Widget Corporation, an unconsolidated subsidiary. Valued at cost, the Western Widget stock would be worth $115,000.

the bill from the seller represents a liability, causing the right-hand side of the equation to go up by an equal amount. A more complex example might show the owners of the company infusing $100 cash into the company for purchase of the machine. In this case stockholders' equity is increased concurrently with the cash account; both sides of the equation increase equivalently. Subsequently, the cash account is drawn down for purchase of the machine, changing both the cash and fixed asset accounts but leaving the asset total unchanged.

Income Statement

Traditionally, the income statement has been considered the primary evidence of company performance. As Exhibit 3.12 shows, it presents sales revenue and then subtracts associated expenses and taxes. The income statement is rarely equivalent to a summary of cash flow. An example of why they may differ is that the revenue figures reflect sales for which cash collections have not been received and do not reflect cash collections for previous sales. Another example is that some items, such as depreciation, are deductible expenses on the

EXHIBIT 3.12
DC Widgets, Inc.: Income Statement (in Thousands of Dollars)

	December 31, 1991	*December 31, 1990*
Sales (net of returns and discounts)	$5931.6	$5157.9
Cost of goods sold	− 3690.5	− 3209.1
Gross profit	$2241.1	$1948.8
Operating expenses		
Selling	$ 155.5	$ 150.1
Administrative	103.7	100.1
Advertising	78.3	62.4
Lease	37.0	37.0
Repairs and maintenance	41.3	25.4
Depreciation	441.9	397.3
Operating profit	$1383.4	$1176.5
Other income	34.7	34.0
Earnings before interest and taxes	1418.1	1210.5
Interest expense		
Note	1.1	0.7
Mortgage bonds	49.1	52.7
Debentures	38.2	41.0
Total interest expense	88.4	94.4
Earnings before taxes	1329.7	1116.1
Provision for income taxes 40%	531.9	446.5
Net income	797.8	669.6
Preferred stock dividends	43.2	43.2
Earnings available to common shareholders	$754.6	$626.4
Average number of shares outstanding	300,000	300,000
Primary earnings per share	$2.52	$2.09
Fully diluted earnings per share	$2.52	$2.09
Dividends per common share	$1.50	$1.40

income statement even though they do not involve a cash flow. Other cash flows, such as repayment of principal on debt and investment in fixed assets, are not reflected on the income statement.

Statement of Retained Earnings

Often attached to the end of the income statement, this simplest of the financial statements is shown in Exhibit 3.13. It examines the change in retained earnings from one year to the next. The statement starts with the retained earnings balance at the beginning of the year. Because that portion of net income not paid in dividends becomes part of retained earnings, the statement adds net income and then subtracts preferred and common dividends. The resultant figure coincides with the retained earnings line on the balance sheet.

Ratio Analysis

A ratio analysis is an important tool to evaluate the financial condition and performance of the firm. Ratio analysis involves evaluating a set of financial ratios, looking at trends in those ratios, and comparing them to the average values for other companies in the industry. Management uses it to maintain efficient operational control, but it is also invaluable in analyzing a firm for potential debt or equity investment. Four categories of ratios are especially important: liquidity, activity, leverage, and profitability. Below, we define and calculate many representative ratios for DC Widgets, Inc., for 1991.

Liquidity Ratios. A company's ability to meet imminent financial obligations is known as liquidity. If the firm is very liquid, it is protected from technical insolvency which could occur if it were unable to meet an obligation. However, too much liquidity unnecessarily retards profitability. Two widely used liquidity ratios are

$$\text{Current} = \frac{\text{current assets}}{\text{current liabilities}} = \frac{\$2157}{\$1018.1} = 2.12$$

$$\text{Quick ratio} = \frac{\text{current assets} - \text{inventory}}{\text{current liabilities}} = \frac{\$1262.4}{\$1018.1} = 1.24$$

While both the current and quick ratios include current liabilities in the denominator, the quick ratio recognizes that inventory is usually less liquid than other current assets. In the

EXHIBIT 3.13
DC Widgets, Inc.: Statement of Retained Earnings (in Thousands of Dollars)

	December 31, 1991	***December 31, 1990***
Retained earnings at beginning of year	$2335.2	$2128.8
Net income	797.8	669.6
Total	$3133.0	$2798.4
Less: Dividends on preferred stock	43.2	43.2
Dividends on common stock	450.0	420.0
Retained earnings at end of year	$2639.8	$2335.2

case of a long production process or obsolescence, inventory may not provide much liquidity at all because it could not be turned quickly into cash.

Activity Ratios. In general, activity ratios measure the firm's efficiency in generating sales and making collections.

$$\text{Inventory turnover} = \frac{\text{sales}}{\text{inventory}} = \frac{\$5931.6}{\$894.6} = 6.63$$

$$\text{Average collection period} = \frac{\text{accounts receivable}}{\text{sales per day}} = \frac{\$668}{\$16.25} = 41.1$$

$$\text{Total asset turnover} = \frac{\text{sales}}{\text{total assets}} = \frac{\$5931.6}{\$5812.8} = 1.02$$

$$\text{Fixed asset turnover} = \frac{\text{sales}}{\text{net fixed assets}} = \frac{\$5931.6}{\$5812.8} = 1.02$$

Other things being equal, a high inventory turnover is more efficient because the firm does not have many assets tied up in inventory. However, very low levels of inventory can lead to stock outs and lost profits. Similarly, a short average collection period, while suggesting success in collecting receivables, may also be the result of a credit policy which stifles profitable sales.

Total asset turnover and fixed asset turnover measure the company's ability to generate sales for a given level of assets. A higher ratio indicates a more efficient firm, but again one must recognize that an excessively high ratio may suggest that a reduced level of assets may be impeding sales.

Leverage Ratios. This group concentrates on the amount of financing provided by creditors relative to the amount provided by the owners. Leverage ratios evaluate default risk in that debt payments must be made for the company to remain solvent. Closely related is the concept of financial risk, or variability in earnings per share.

$$\text{Debt ratio} = \frac{\text{total liabilities}}{\text{total assets}} = \frac{\$1824.0}{\$5812.8} = 0.31$$

$$\text{Debt on equity} = \frac{\text{total liabilities}}{\text{total common equity}} = \frac{\$1824.0}{\$3988.8} = 0.46$$

$$\text{Times interest earned} = \frac{\text{EBIT}}{\text{interest expense}} = \frac{\$1418.1}{\$88.4} = 16$$

$$\text{Fixed charge coverage} = \frac{\text{earnings before taxes + interest expense + lease obligations}}{\text{interest expense + lease obligations}}$$

$$= \frac{1329.7 + 88.4 + 37.0}{88.4 + 37.0} = 11.60$$

For each of the first two ratios, a relatively high value suggests that a relatively high proportion of financing is supplied by debt. In the short run, leverage benefits the firm if it is able to invest borrowed funds at a rate in excess of the after-tax borrowing rate. However, if the investment rate turns out to be lower than the borrowing rate, the firm suffers because of the leverage. In general, additional leverage increases earnings per share, but it also makes the earnings per share more variable, or risky, since the investment rate is not known with certainty before the fact.

Times interest earned gives an idea of how annual earning capacity compares to the amount of interest payments which must be covered. Naturally, a higher number suggests greater ability to meet projected interest payments. Fixed charge coverage is a similar concept which also considers long-term lease obligations that must be met.

Profitability Ratios. The ability to generate profits is a key measure of managerial success. Some important profit ratios are

$$\text{Profit margin} = \frac{\text{net income}}{\text{sales}} = \frac{\$797.8}{\$5931.6} = 0.13$$

$$\text{Return on assets} = \frac{\text{net income}}{\text{total assets}} = \frac{\$797.8}{\$5812.8} = 0.14$$

$$\text{Return on equity} = \frac{\text{net income}}{\text{total common equity}} = \frac{\$797.8}{\$3988.8} = 0.20$$

For profit margin and return on assets, high ratios are clearly superior to low ratios. They indicate an ability to generate high profits for a given level of sales or assets. With return on equity, though, one must be cognizant that a high value may be more the result of the level of financial leverage than of managerial efficiency. Thus a high degree of financial risk may accompany a high return on equity.

Conclusion

Financial analysis is not a standardized or mechanical process, but rather it is a means of analysis that must be directed toward the needs of a specific situation. It is much more important to select the appropriate tools in a given circumstance than to be able to calculate countless ratios.

Financial analysis must be part of a thoughtful consideration of the significant factors, trends, or relationships that are appropriate to helping solve the problem at hand. If approached in this manner, financial analysis can be a productive starting point for assessing financial strengths and weaknesses, creditworthiness, and other attributes of a firm based on past performance.

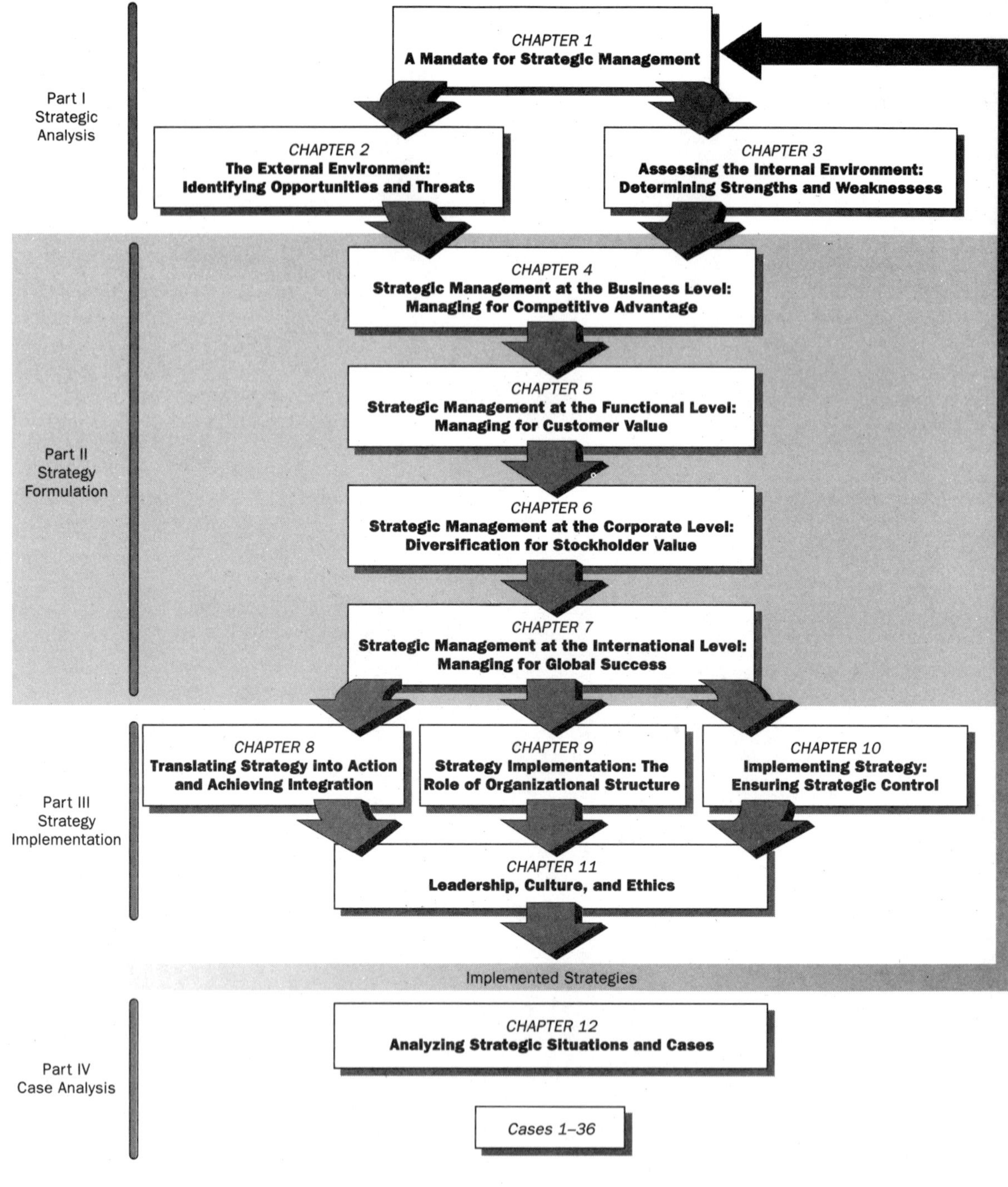

Part I
Strategic Analysis
CHAPTER 1
A Mandate for Strategic Management
CHAPTER 2
The External Environment: Identifying Opportunities and Threats
CHAPTER 3
Assessing the Internal Environment: Determining Strengths and Weaknessess
Part II
Strategy Formulation
CHAPTER 4
Strategic Management at the Business Level: Managing for Competitive Advantage
CHAPTER 5
Strategic Management at the Functional Level: Managing for Customer Value
CHAPTER 6
Strategic Management at the Corporate Level: Diversification for Stockholder Value
CHAPTER 7
Strategic Management at the International Level: Managing for Global Success
Part III
Strategy Implementation
CHAPTER 8
Translating Strategy into Action and Achieving Integration
CHAPTER 9
Strategy Implementation: The Role of Organizational Structure
CHAPTER 10
Implementing Strategy: Ensuring Strategic Control
CHAPTER 11
Leadership, Culture, and Ethics
Implemented Strategies
Part IV
Case Analysis
CHAPTER 12
Analyzing Strategic Situations and Cases
Cases 1–36

PART II

Strategy Formulation

CHAPTER 4

Strategic Management at the Business Level: Managing for Competitive Advantage

Firms compete directly with one another for markets at what is called the business level of strategic management. Competitors may be individual business units of a large diversified corporation, or they may be stand-alone businesses, undiversified, perhaps even unincorporated. Competition takes place at the business level, so strategic management here is crucial to the overall success of the firm. Accordingly, the concept of competitive advantage is the cornerstone of this chapter.

In the first of its three sections, the chapter discusses the three most important categories of competitive advantage: differentiation, cost leadership, and quick response. The second section describes the relationship between market focus, the pursuit of a niche strategy, and the three forms of competitive advantage. The third explains the stages of the market life cycle model and considers how managing for competitive advantage differs in each of these stages.

After reading this chapter, you will understand:

- The concept of competitive advantage and its importance
- The benefits and risks of each basic form of competitive advantage
- The effect of market focus on competitive advantage
- The concept of the market life cycle and its application to formulating strategies
- The process of achieving and maintaining a competitive advantage during the course of the market life cycle

EXECUTIVE INTERVIEW

Addison Barry Rand
Corporate Vice President and President of Marketing Xerox Corporation

Addison Barry Rand is a corporate vice president and president of Xerox Corporation's United States Marketing Group. His group is responsible for over $6 billion of revenue, approximately half of the worldwide revenue for Xerox from its business products and systems division.

Rand joined Xerox in 1968 as a trainee and has held a variety of positions in sales, marketing, and general management. He was elected a corporate officer in 1985 and appointed to his current position in 1986. He earned a bachelor's degree in marketing from American University and master's degrees in business administration and management sciences from Stanford University.

What do you see as the most important forms of competitive advantage for firms in the photocopier business?

Like customers everywhere, ours are looking for a superior value which amounts to a combination of quality and cost. They also want this superior value delivered to them quickly. The competitors that have the best mix of these three customer requirements will be the ones with the strongest competitive advantage.

How does Xerox attempt to differentiate its products from those of the competition's?

We do not want to compete with what our customer would view as a commodity product. We work hard to find the broadest possible range of methods for adding value to our products and services from a customer's perspective. In other words, we differentiate our products on the basis of not only their ability to make superior copies, but on machine reliability, billing accuracy, on service quality, and so on. In short, we try to differentiate ourselves in everything we do.

Do you take as broad a view of cost?

We have to. Our customer is interested in price, but to be competitive and on price, we have to control a very wide range of costs. Clearly, there are important cost savings to be gained through increasing production efficiency, but a dollar saved by reducing marketing costs is just as valuable as one saved through reductions in manufacturing expenses.

Why has speed become such an important source of competitive advantage in your industry?

It has become more important today because the customer has learned to value it more. Consider the thousands of small businesses that depend on copiers to keep their offices moving. Often, businesses like these do not have a second machine, so if they encounter problems, they need service immediately. We compete against hundreds of local dealers who each offer same day response to customer calls. If we are going to compete effectively, we have to stress speed. That is just one example, but customers value speed in virtually everything we do, from answering the phone to introducing new products.

How does Xerox manage the tradeoff between differentiation, cost, and speed?

There are a surprising number of cases where having all three does not require a tradeoff. If the organization can be managed as a whole, as a system that cuts across functions rather than just as a series of independent functions, the means of simultaneously achieving all three advantages become more evident. Clearly, the most successful firms in any industry will be those with managers who understand how to combine quality, cost, and speed to build the strongest possible blend of competitive advantages.

COMPETITIVE ADVANTAGES

To be successful, a business must hold some advantage relative to its competition. This advantage may take the form of greater differentiation, in which case the customer finds the firm's products or services unique in some way that makes them more attractive and therefore worth a premium price, as in the case of Rolls Royce automobiles. Alternatively, the firm may have a lower cost position, which allows it to charge similar (or even lower) prices while realizing better-than-average margins. The Wal-Mart chain of retail stores enjoys a low-cost position. These two forms of competitive advantage provide the basis for much of the thinking about business-level strategy in the past decade.[1] Recently, however, the importance of another form of competitive advantage has emerged: the ability to respond to the customer faster than competitors do. Here, Domino's Pizza, with its guarantee of pizza delivery in 30 minutes or less, is a good example. A firm that holds more than one of these advantages is in a particularly strong competitive position.

In the long run, a business without one or more of these competitive advantages is probably destined to earn no more than what economists call "normal profits"[2] (see Application 4.1). Normal profits allow investors to earn a return equal to the average return

Application 4.1

The Impact of Competitive Advantage on Business Performance

Research shows that a competitive advantage is clearly instrumental in achieving higher-than-normal levels of profitability. Exhibit 4.1 shows the importance of two forms of competitive advantage (differentiation and cost) in seven different industrial sectors. The data reported in this table are taken from the PIMS (profit impact of market strategy) database, which measures differentiation and cost, providing data from over 2,500 business units within some 200, mostly large, United States-based corporations.

Differentiation is measured as any nonprice attribute identified by customers' evaluation of competing goods and/or services. Cost advantages are measured as the direct costs of the reporting firm, expressed in percentage terms, relative to the estimated average of its leading competitors. (No comparable data are available to measure superior response time as a competitive advantage.)

The businesses within seven industrial sectors were divided into equal thirds, in terms of their differentiation and cost positions relative to the competitors in their particular markets. Data on the middle thirds were dropped, and the four combinations of high and low differentiation and cost were compared on the basis of average return on investment (ROI), perhaps the most common measure of profitability. The value of data such as this is not in pinpointing performance targets. Rather, the data are useful primarily as a general description of what businesses in a wide range of industrial settings have done. The data are too general for use as the basis of strategy formulation, but they do indicate at least three general points:

- *Firms that hold neither form of competitive advantage (low/low) generally perform poorly in terms of their average profitability.* There was considerable variation around the overall average of 9.5 percent, but, considering that these measures of profitability are calculated before corporate overhead and taxes, not even the best of these could be expected to exceed typical costs of capital. In one industrial sector (raw or semi-finished goods), profitability for this group was less than one-tenth what it was for a high-flying counterpart in the "hybrid" category, described below. Other analyses also indicated that this group performed very poorly in terms of growth, with an overall market share loss of nearly a quarter of a point per year.
- *Holding one form of competitive advantage (high/low) can lead to higher levels of profitability.* These firms

Application 4.1 (cont.)

typically enjoyed levels of profitability at least twice that of low/low firms in the same industrial sector. There was no consistent pattern in the kind of advantage that was most profitable, and we would advise against reading too much into any differences in the profitability levels between the two.

- *Holding both forms of competitive advantage (high/high) most often leads to the highest possible levels of profitability.* Firms in this "hybrid" category enjoy returns on investment ranging from the mid- to high 30s, in percentage terms. With the average ROI for all business units in the database near 22 percent, such performance must be considered outstanding. Again, this stellar performance was mirrored in terms of data on growth, with the average hybrid gaining nearly six-tenths of a point of market share per year.

In the past, managers were often advised to concentrate on a single competitive advantage, rather than run the risk of having strategic positions which were "stuck in the middle," being "neither fish nor fowl." This thinking seems especially plausible, considering the clear importance the data show for having some form of competitive advantage, and the inconclusive differences among the benefits of either individual advantage. However, as the exhibit points out, in every industrial sector, the highest performance levels are those seen by firms holding both types of competitive advantage simultaneously.

EXHIBIT 4.1
Competitive Advantage Increases Profitability

	Average ROI (%)			
Differentiation Advantage:	***Low***	***Low***	***High***	***High***
Industry Sector / ***Cost Advantage:***	***Low***	***High***	***Low***	***High***
Manufacturing				
Consumer Products				
Durable goods	14.2	20.2	21.0	38.7
Nondurable goods	9.7	27.0	15.0	33.2
Industrial products:				
Capital goods	8.1	19.7	28.5	35.2
Raw or semifinished goods	2.9	28.8	15.1	34.9
Components for finished goods	10.5	22.8	29.0	38.8
Supplies of consumable goods	14.1	33.3	31.0	38.4
Services	10.0	22.8	26.8	31.5
Overall	9.5	26.2	22.0	34.7

Source: Authors' analysis of the PIMS database.

they would expect to receive from any other similarly risky investment. Over the long run, firms that perform below this normal profits level will fail to attract or maintain the investments necessary to continue to operate. Performance that yields only normal profits is not particularly noteworthy because normal profits are only average. Businesses usually strive to achieve performance above the level of normal profits, and therefore, the pursuit of competitive advantage has become the central theme of strategic management at the business level. The director of planning at Clark Equipment Company, the leading U.S. firm in the highly competitive forklift industry, explains:

> The process of strategic management is coming to be defined, in fact, as the management of competitive advantage—that is, as a process of identifying, developing, and taking advantage of enclaves in which a tangible and preservable business advantage can be achieved.[3]

Differentiation

In pursuing a competitive advantage based on *differentiation,* firms attempt to create unique bundles of products and/or services that will be highly valued by customers. The value chain in Exhibit 4.2 presents some examples of competitive advantage that differentiation can provide. Here are some of the attributes firms use to differentiate their products:

- *Product features:* The physical characteristics and capabilities of a product may be an important form of differentiation. For example, Philips developed a television that can display two channels on the same screen.
- *After-sales service:* Convenience and quality of service may be a critical factor in deciding among alternative products. Sears attracts customers who value an efficient nationwide network of repair services.

EXHIBIT 4.2
Examples of How Firms Achieve *Differentiation* as a Competitive Advantage

Support activity		
FIRM INFRASTRUCTURE	Extensive database on consumers suggests more effective advertising.	"Celebrity" CEO reinforces company image.
HUMAN RESOURCE MANAGEMENT	Incentive programs encourage high-quality production.	Training programs produce better service representatives.
TECHNOLOGY DEVELOPMENT	Cutting-edge product features outperform competitions'.	Patented production technology produces superior quality product.
PROCUREMENT	Purchase of name brand components raises image of finished product.	Most effective media space is purchased for advertising.

INBOUND LOGISTICS	OPERATIONS	OUTBOUND LOGISTICS	MARKETING AND SALES	SERVICE
Superior incoming materials raise quality of finished products.	Low defect rates improve customer satisfaction.	Just-in-time delivery to suppliers minimizes their down time.	Effective advertising builds image.	Courteous repair and service technicians build rapport with customers.
	Conformance to product specifications improves product performance.	Better shipping procedures minimize damages.	Superior technical product sales data aid customer in selection.	Replacing with high-quality parts assures product's ability to perform.

MARGIN

MARGIN

Source: Adapted with permission of The Free Press, a Division of Macmillan, Inc., from Porter, Michael E. (1985). *Competitive advantage: Creating and sustaining superior performance.* New York: Free Press. Copyright © 1985 by Michael E. Porter.

- *Desirable image:* This is the obvious basis of virtually all fashion products, ranging from designer blue jeans to furs.
- *Technological innovation:* Technical advances provide the basis of competitive advantage in a broad range of firms. Cambridge Speakerworks patented a stereo speaker system that gives sound quality comparable to giant loudspeakers, but is small enough to fit in any apartment.
- *Reputation of the firm:* A distinguished reputation may be an important source of sales. The saying in the computer industry in reference to IBM's reputation is "nobody ever got fired for buying from Big Blue."
- *Manufacturing consistency:* This is especially important in making components that must mesh with others to produce a finished good. This need has given rise to greater emphasis on statistical process control (SPC) and a broad range of quality control techniques aimed at manufacturing.
- *Status symbol:* Cars that cost more than some houses are obviously purchased for reasons other than transportation.

A differentiation strategy can be based on any combination of nonprice attributes such as these. If it is successful in creating some unique and desirable product or service attribute, the firm builds brand loyalty in customers, decreases the number of alternative products the customers are willing to consider, and reduces the customers' sensitivity to prices. These results produce higher profit margins without requiring lower costs. Pursuit of this strategy often involves accepting lower market shares, because mass marketing is usually incompatible with the image of exclusivity associated with premium-priced products. High differentiation may also limit the feasibility of competing on the basis of cost or price, because extra R&D, higher-quality materials, more advertising, and so forth, are often the basis of differentiation.

A successful differentiation strategy allows a business to address the five competitive forces (introduced in Chapter 2) in such a way that the firm enjoys higher-than-typical returns:

Competitive rivalry may be lessened as firms successfully distinguish themselves. In this way, firms in the same industry may avoid head-to-head confrontations. Jaguar's differentiated products do not compete directly with Hyundai's even though both firms produce automobiles.

Brand-loyal customers are less sensitive to prices. As a result, if a firm's suppliers raise prices, the firm can more easily pass along the resulting cost hike to its customers. In fact, many firms that are successful differentiators are also premium pricers—that is, their customers pay the highest prices in the industry.

New entrants or firms offering product substitutes must overcome this brand loyalty. The customer may feel strongly about a successfully differentiated product. It has proven to be difficult to introduce a new cola-flavored soft drink in the United States, because the existing market leaders have so effectively established the loyalty in their customers. It has been equally difficult to establish a substitute product that would entice customers away from colas.

Though the advantages are clear, there are also risks to following a strategy based on differentiation:

If several competitors pursue similar differentiation tactics, they may all be perceived as equals. At one time, for example, autofocusing was an unusual product feature that differentiated the cameras of the first firms to offer it. Today, every major camera producer offers autofocusing, so it no longer serves to differentiate. If this "me too" behavior goes far enough, the competitors will become virtually indistinguishable and competition may be reduced to price wars. This is a form of competition for which firms built around a differentiation strategy are particularly ill suited.

Specialists operating in niche markets may offer insurmountable levels of differentiation. Firms that attempt to offer differentiated products to large segments of the market may discover that they cannot tailor their products and services to specific customer needs as well as specialized competitors. Tandem Computers built a tremendously successful company by following a classic niche strategy. Rather than design a general-purpose computer system intended for a variety of applications, Tandem targeted interaction-intense on-line systems, in which the cost of downtime was monumental. (Banking operations, credit card validations, and hotel reservations are all examples of such applications.) Tandem designed a system in which individual components could fail while the system as a whole remained in operation. By producing superior products for the market segment in need of a fail-safe technology, Tandem achieved a level of differentiation other computer companies could not reach with their general-purpose machines. Tandem became famous for its sustained 100 percent plus annual growth rate and some of the highest price/earnings ratios ever seen on Wall Street.

Attempts to stay a step ahead of the competition may result in expensive "gold plating." This refers to the addition of features that are not valued by the customer. When this tactic is pursued, competitors can counter by taking a wait-and-see position, monitoring customer responses to newly introduced changes, and then moving quickly to replicate successes and avoid failures. An example would be the addition of wipers for the headlights of cars. This option was first offered on luxury cars, while the rest of the industry monitored customers' reactions. When it became apparent that the wipers were of little value to most consumers, wait-and-see competitors avoided the expense of developing their own versions.

Cost Leadership

Success with the competitive advantage we call *cost leadership* requires achieving a low-cost position relative to one's competition. Pursuit of this advantage often involves offering a no-frills product aimed at the most typical customer in a large target market. Exhibit 4.3 offers some examples of how a competitive advantage can be gained through cost leadership. Because costs can usually be lowered as a product becomes more standardized, low-cost manufacturing firms strive for long production runs, and low-cost service firms tend to offer uniform packages. By targeting broadly defined markets with standard products, such firms hope to gain the greatest possible benefits from economies of scale and experience curve effects. A firm aiming for low-cost production will typically spend less on

EXHIBIT 4.3
Examples of How Firms Achieve *Cost Leadership* as a Competitive Advantage

FIRM INFRASTRUCTURE	Flatter organization structure cuts corporate overhead.	Simplified information system reduces costs of accounting department.	MARGIN
HUMAN RESOURCE MANAGEMENT	Employee policies minimize turnover.	Training production employees reduces waste and scrap.	
TECHNOLOGY DEVELOPMENT	Process breakthrough lowers production costs.	Product reformulation allows use of cheaper ingredients.	
PROCUREMENT	Global purchasing delivers low-cost components from offshore.	Real estate purchases in rural areas significantly lower cost of building new plant.	

INBOUND LOGISTICS	OPERATIONS	OUTBOUND LOGISTICS	MARKETING AND SALES	SERVICE	
Long-term "win-win" relationship results in supplier's passing through cost savings.	Economy of scale in plant reduces manufacturing costs. Experience effects raise efficiency over time.	Computerized routing lowers transportation expenses. Shipping in bulk lowers transportation cost per ton.	National advertising campaign creates economies of scale in buying media space/time.	Expert service technicians repair product right the first time, avoiding the expense of follow-up calls.	MARGIN

Source: Adapted with permission of The Free Press, a Division of Macmillan, Inc., from Porter, Michael E. (1985). *Competitive advantage: Creating and sustaining superior performance*. New York: Free Press. Copyright © 1985 by Michael E. Porter.

R&D than competitors following a differentiation strategy. This is especially true of product-related R&D, although a larger portion of the total R&D budget might be directed toward process-oriented R&D intended to make the product easier and cheaper to produce. Advertising will probably be minimal, with promotional efforts stressing price comparisons.

If successful, a low-cost strategy allows a firm to address the five forces in their competitive environment so it can realize higher-than-normal profits:

Holding the low-cost position may convince rivals not to enter a price war. Price wars can be ruinous to all the competitors involved. Thus, a cost advantage great enough to serve as a deterrent may be an important "peacekeeping" weapon.

Low-cost producers are protected from customer pressure to lower prices. Competitors cannot consistently price below what is known as their survival price. (The survival price allows profit margins just adequate to maintain a business.) By definition, the low-cost leader has a lower survival price than any competitor, so customers will not be able to play one competing supplier against the other to force prices down below a level at which the cost leader can still make profits. To do so would force less efficient suppliers out of business, leaving the low-cost supplier with a monopoly.

Because of their higher margins, low-cost producers are better able to withstand increases in their costs from suppliers. In some industries, the costs of key supplies are volatile. (For example, a bad crop year can raise coffee production costs dramatically for all competitors in the industry.) In this case, the lowest-cost producer may be the only one that comes near to making a profit.

New entrants competing on the basis of price must face the cost leader without having the experience necessary to become efficient. As the cumulative volume of production increases, production costs tend to decrease—the "experience curve" effect. It is likely that the low-cost leader has already moved far down whatever experience curve is operating in the industry. New entrants lacking this experience are not likely to enjoy comparable efficiency and may be forced to enter the market using some competitive advantage not related to low pricing.

Low-cost producers are in the best position to use pricing to compete with substitute products. As new composite materials continue to chip away at demand for structural steel, the most efficient mills, the minimills discussed later in the chapter, will be the least-threatened competitors in the industry. The low profit margin usually associated with minimills are the least likely to attract competition from the new substitutes. Furthermore, because of their low-cost position, minimills can remain price competitive with composite materials longer than other less efficient steel producers.

The merits of a cost leadership strategy must be compared to its various risks:

Cost leadership is likely to be an "all or nothing" strategy. In competitive markets for commodity-like products (those offering little differentiation), the number 1 competitor in terms of low cost may be able to price its products at a level that will not allow less efficient producers to remain in operation. Where product differentiation is not a consideration, customers will naturally seek the lowest price, leaving even the second most cost-efficient producer in an undesirable position.

Cost cutting that leads to loss of desirable product attributes can be ruinous. Watney's Red, a controversial British beer, illustrates this point. The U.K. beer industry has historically been dominated by ales and bitters, but starting in the 1950s, lagers have taken an increasing share of the market. The makers of Watney's Red mistook this willingness to buy these very different tasting brews to mean that taste was not an important consideration for the customer. Cheaper raw materials, brewing methods, and handling procedures were used to lower the cost of Watney's Red. Not only was the product strongly resisted by the British marketplace, it did much to motivate the creation of CAMRA (the CAMpaign for Real Ales), one of the most vocal consumer advocate groups in Britain today.

Many cost-saving tactics are easily duplicated by competitors. Even competitors pursuing high-differentiation positions for their flagship product line may choose to offer a low-cost line of products, often producing them with the same facilities as their top-of-the-line products. In fact, some generic goods are identical to branded products, but are simply sold with a different label. Such goods are virtual by-products in terms of the minimal incremental investment required to produce them. Therefore, they can provide serious price competition for firms depending on a low-cost position to secure all their sales.

Cost differences among competitors often decline as the market matures. As a product ages, the absolute amount of production required to achieve any given percentage increase in its cumulative volume rises, and consequently, the strength of experience effects declines. When a business begins operation, it may double its cumulative volume in each of the first 2 months, but eventually it will take 3 months to double its cumulative volume, then 1 year, then 2 years, and so on. Once volume reaches high enough levels, further movement along the cost curve is almost imperceptible, because it may take decades to double cumulative volume again. Thus, as the product ages, competitors that once lagged behind are able to catch up.

Dedication to cost cutting often limits a firm's abilities to remain competitive in other ways. In particular, an emphasis on cost control frequently precludes investment in innovation. This leaves the firm vulnerable to technical advances that might make the product obsolete, regardless of any price cuts the firm can offer. An example of this, discussed in detail in the following chapter, was Ford's single-minded pursuit of production efficiencies in producing the Model T. Ford was able to dramatically reduce costs, in part, by refusing to introduce new product features. Meanwhile, GM responded to growing demand for new-product designs and was able to capture a much larger portion of the market.[4]

Quick Response

For the past decade, much attention has been focused on the competitive advantages of cost leadership and product differentiation. However, in today's business environment, firms are discovering a new form of competitive advantage: moving faster than their competitors.[5] Exhibit 4.4 provides examples of this form of competitive advantage, known as *quick response.*

Quick response, in all its various forms, is more than just another sort of differentiation, although the two are obviously complementary. Quick response refers to the *availability* of a response to the customer, whether a new product, a product improvement, or even a managerial decision.[6] Managers in many of today's businesses know that it is not always enough to be the cost leader or to offer a unique product or service; it is also important to be able to respond quickly to customer needs.[7] Just as high costs or unattractive features can diminish the desirability of a product or service, responses that are not readily available may also force a customer to choose other alternatives.

Quick response advantages can take several forms:[8]

Developing new products. Perhaps the most obvious type of quick response is the time it takes a firm to develop a new product. At AT&T, the time to design a new phone has decreased from 2 years to 1 year, giving the company a definite advantage over slower firms.

EXHIBIT 4.4

Examples of How Firms Achieve *Quick Response* as a Competitive Advantage

Support activity	Examples
FIRM INFRASTRUCTURE	Top management team's knowledge of industry means faster adjustment to developing trends. Management information systems provide necessary data in "real time."
HUMAN RESOURCE MANAGEMENT	Well-executed training programs make production workers effective from day 1.
TECHNOLOGY DEVELOPMENT	Product development process yields new models in half the time required by competition. New process invention reduces required manufacturing time.
PROCUREMENT	Work with suppliers ensures that they are incorporating the latest technological advances.

INBOUND LOGISTICS	OPERATIONS	OUTBOUND LOGISTICS	MARKETING AND SALES	SERVICE
Location and operation of warehouses minimizes shipping delays.	Single minute exchange of dies means quick adjustment to new orders.	Just-in-time deliveries to suppliers minimizes their down time.	Technically knowledgeable sales staff answers more questions without needing an engineer.	Location of service technicians allows guarantee of 24-hour response time with needed repair parts.
Long-term "vendor partnership" results in supplier's locating new plant to allow "over-the-fence" deliveries.	New production line layout reduces wasted traffic inside plant.	Same day shipping option attracts customers with last minute orders.	Field representatives FAX orders immediately—production begins earlier.	

MARGIN

MARGIN

Source: Adapted with permission of The Free Press, a Division of Macmillan, Inc., from Porter, Michael E. (1985). *Competitive advantage: Creating and sustaining superior performance.* New York: Free Press. Copyright © 1985 by Michael E. Porter.

Customizing products. The speed with which firms can offer custom-built products has increased rapidly with advances in new production technology. At General Electric, it now takes 3 days to build a custom-made industrial circuit box that previously required 3 weeks.

Improving existing products. One of the many factors accounting for Japanese consumer electronics firms' success is the speed with which they continually upgrade their products.

Delivery of ordered products. The importance of speed applies to off-the-shelf products as well. Benetton, the Italian sportswear company, owes much of its success to its sophisticated handling procedures, which provide an unparalleled ability to fill customer orders around the world in as little as 7 days. This speed allows Benetton's customers to adjust to unexpected trends as each fashion season unfolds, a valuable option in the unpredictable world of fashion retailing.

Adjusting marketing efforts. Anheuser-Busch, the leading U.S. beer producer, entered the English market at about the same time as Elder's, the leading Australian company. However, Elder's was much quicker in adjusting to the new market, and outstripped Anheuser-Busch's Budweiser brand as a result. Years after entering the market, Budweiser's advertising campaigns still look very American, while at the outset, Elder's ads shifted away from a purely Australian look to a more genteel English look.

Answering customer questions. Simply getting an answer for a customer can be the basis for a real competitive advantage. Consider the customer's perspective of a bank that is able to reduce the time needed to approve a car loan from the typical 3 days to just 30 minutes.

How does availability, the product of superior response time, affect a firm's ability to face the five forces from its environment?

The firms with the lowest response time in a market can avoid head-to-head rivalry. To the extent that firms can develop or improve new products more quickly than their competitors, their lagging competitors will not have comparable products. Motorola rushed its pocket-sized cellular telephone to market months before any competitor had a comparable product. This allowed Motorola to enjoy something of a monopoly position in miniature telephones while competitors scrambled to catch up.

The fastest firms can charge customers premium prices. Motorola's speed in bringing its innovations to market means its products are often a generation ahead of what the competition has on the market. The company reasonably expects to charge customers a premium price for its "new and improved" generation of products. In other markets, faster firms earn the right to charge premium prices, not by introducing new types of products, but by simply delivering comparable products faster than competitors.

Firms who resolve to respond quickly may encourage quick responses from suppliers. Supplier-producer coordination is essential for producing new products quickly, and a quick response strategy might appear to place more bargaining power in the hands of suppliers. (A firm can be no faster than its suppliers will allow it to be.) However, in practice, aggressive suppliers realize that by working with innovative quick-response companies, they can remain more innovative themselves. As these quick-response customers create new business opportunities for themselves, they indirectly create more demand for their suppliers.

Quick responders deal with the threats of new entrants and substitute products by leading in innovations themselves. The fastest competitors in a given market are usually the most capable of making timely advances in products or services. By remaining leaders in innovation, these firms stay a step ahead of new entrants and substitute products.

While quick response is emerging as a source of competitive advantage in its own right, it does not require that firms ignore the competitive advantages of high differentiation or low cost. In fact, speed can actually improve performance on these other dimensions of competition.[9] To understand how, we must first consider the concept of value-added time.

Adding value to a product consists of any activity that increases the product's worth to the customer, such as the design of a product, its manufacturing, its packaging, its delivery, and so forth. Generally, value is being added to a product only .05 to 5 percent of the time between the customer's order and actual delivery of goods and services. Meanwhile, costs are being incurred more or less continuously.

In other words, if it takes 6 weeks (240 hours) for a factory to fill an order, the product may well have been actively worked on for only about 6 hours, or 2.5 percent of the time. The other 234 hours involved idle time, paper processing, scheduling, inventory, finding missing components, rework due to poor quality, shipping, and so forth—activities which do not add value but which do incur costs. In fact, during these 234 hours of increasing costs, the product's value may have been, in fact, decreasing, and offsetting any attempts to successfully differentiate the product. With a few exceptions, such as wines, most products suffer from being inventoried: parts rust or get damaged, designs become obsolete, and items are lost. Besides this, any delay forces the customer to wait, and this effectively decreases the value of the product. By taking 240 hours to respond to the customer, this slow firm is driving its costs up and its differentiation down.

Atlas Door provides a counter example as a firm able to use quick response to improve cost leadership and differentiation.[10] Atlas produces industrial doors, a product with an almost infinite variety of specifications regarding size, material, and construction. Historically, firms in this industry have taken 4 months to respond to an order. Atlas entered the market determined to drastically reduce the time required to fill an order. It set up a just-in-time factory and greatly improved standard delivery logistics. Atlas also developed computer-assisted design capabilities so customers could describe a door to an Atlas engineer, who would then draw up the order while the customer answered questions on the phone. Atlas soon became the only competitor in the industry that could consistently fill orders in weeks instead of months. With contract deadlines to meet, customers in the construction business found such availability hard to resist. The new ordering and design systems at Atlas greatly reduced mistakes, and this differentiation allowed it to charge a premium price, while its faster overall production process lowered costs.

As one would expect, the results were spectacular. In its first 10 years of operation, Atlas's pretax earnings were 20 percent of sales, about five times greater than the industry average. In just 10 years, it was able to establish itself as the number 1 company in the industry, replacing the former leading door suppliers in 80 percent of the distributors in the nation. Such benefits of quick response extend to many industries. Research has shown that high-tech products that reach the market 6 months late but within the limits of their expense budgets will earn an average of 33 percent less than their expected profit over their first 5 years. For comparison, products that come to market on time but 50 percent over expense budget show an average expected profits loss of only 4 percent.[11]

Although quick response is often advantageous, it is not always the best strategy for an organization to pursue. The organization may not have the systems available that make competition on the basis of response times feasible. The technological and human systems required to produce fast responses are different from those required to produce, say, low-cost, mass-produced items. Attempts to force speed out of an organization not designed to deliver it will probably result in damaging the business rather than improving it. Also, speed is not equally important to all markets or customers. In stable markets, where the way of operating businesses has not changed for years, there may be little hope of competing successfully on the basis of response times. Customers in such unchanging markets will probably be able to forecast their requirements sufficiently far in advance that virtually any competitor can meet their needs. Finally, speed creates stress. The pace of life inside organizations that compete on the basis of speed is likely to be hectic, and managers may not have the luxury of unhurried decision making. Although some businesses seem to thrive on a culture that stresses speed, this stressful environment may take a heavy toll on key employees.

MARKET FOCUS AND COMPETITIVE ADVANTAGE

The extent to which a firm concentrates on a narrowly defined or niche segment of the market is referred to as its *focus.* Focus alone does not constitute a competitive advantage, but it may fundamentally affect a firm's ability to achieve a competitive advantage.

A differentiation strategy is often associated with focusing on a narrowly defined market niche. A broad, mass-market emphasis may be incongruous with some sorts of differentiation, especially those based on status and image. A status symbol loses its effectiveness if shared by all. Additionally, firms that focus on specific segments of the overall market may be in a better position to deliver the forms of differentiation with the most appeal to that segment. We have already seen how Tandem successfully used this tactic by focusing on the fail-safe niche within the mainframe computer market.

A cost leadership strategy is often associated with a broadly defined target market. Broadly defined markets typically yield the largest possible volume for any given product line, and this volume results in lower costs through economies of scale and experience curve effects. *Economies of scale* refers to amortizing a given expense or investment over a greater production base. For example, any airline must set up a computer system to handle reservations and flight schedules, but it costs less to do so on a per customer basis for a large airline than a small one. *Experience effects* occur when a task becomes easier as it is repeated until the process is routinized.

We can measure practice as the cumulative production volume, that is, the total number of units it has produced over the years. In many industries, this cumulative experience has allowed firms to lower their costs by significant fractions. According to the theory of experience effects, if a business is selling more units than its competition, it should also be improving production faster (getting more efficient in terms of unit costs), because it is getting more practice (greater experience). With lower costs, the business can price more competitively, and with lower prices it can attract more customers, and increase sales volume, which will further lower costs (see Exhibit 4.5). Obviously, this is a cycle that feeds on itself, and, on the basis of this reasoning, the firms with the largest share in a given market were also expected to be the most profitable. There was a time when it was very popular to build strategies to capitalize on this self-perpetuating cycle; this was sometimes called *riding the experience curve.*[12] To gain maximum benefits from economies of scale and experience effects, firms often concentrate on high-volume mass markets.

However, specialization is an alternative route to low cost. By concentrating on a narrowly defined mix of customers and products, some firms are able to compete effectively on the basis of costs against much larger "all-purpose" competitors, as illustrated in Exhibit 4.6, on mini steel mills.

EXHIBIT 4.5
The Cycle of Experience Effects

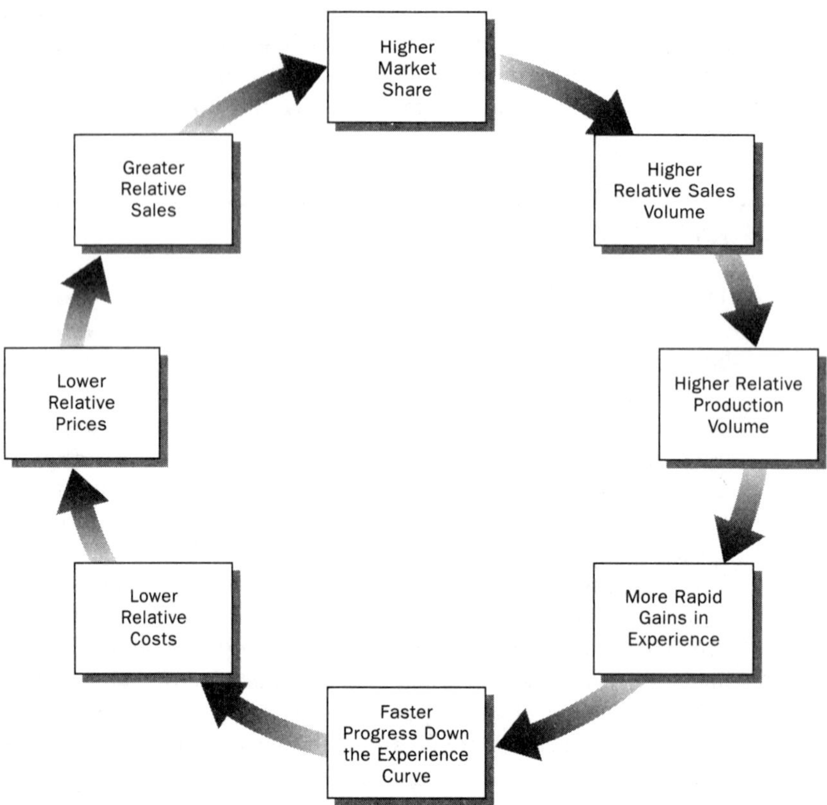

Minimills concentrate on a narrow line of simple-to-manufacture products, relatively small items made from scrap metal melted in electric arc furnaces. Scrap metal is the lowest-cost raw material for steel production, and the minimill's electric arc furnaces are cost efficient at low volumes, compared to traditional oxygen furnaces. Furthermore, conventional mills have had trouble filling their capacity with sufficient volumes in the face of stiff international competition. In spite of the benefits one might expect from the traditional producers' greater economies of scale and experience curve effects, leading minimills have been able to obtain levels of profitability roughly three times that of traditional integrated steel producers.

Market focus also affects a firm's ability to compete on the basis of response times. In some markets, narrowly focused competitors are more able to react to changing customer needs. However, much of the technology spurring competition on the basis of response times generally has a flexibility that serves a broad mix of customer needs even more rapidly than narrowly focused, "dedicated" producers can.

There are also risks associated with focusing on a specific segment of the market. For example, a firm may miss opportunities or find itself unable to adjust to changes in the

EXHIBIT 4.6
Minimills Can Achieve Lower Costs than Traditional Mills, Even at Lower Volume

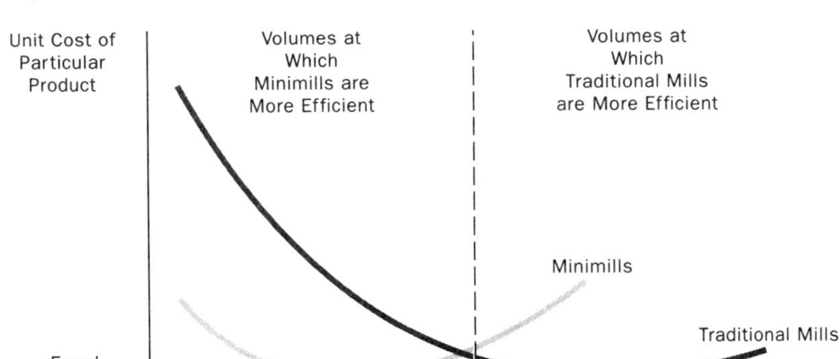

target market. Niche players often become targets for takeover by firms wishing to fill out their own capabilities. There is also the danger of forgetting that focus alone is not the basis for a viable competitive advantage. Unless focusing improves the firm's ability to provide greater differentiation, lower costs, or shorter response times, it will not improve the competitive position of the firm.

STRATEGIC MANAGEMENT IN DIFFERENT STAGES OF THE MARKET LIFE CYCLE

Here we study how managing for competitive advantage differs across the stages of the market life cycle.[13] The market life cycle is a conceptual model which suggests that markets can evolve through stages typically labeled introduction, growth, maturity, and decline. (As discussed below, we also consider turnaround as a possible stage, but since it is not part of the natural market evolutionary process, it is in a somewhat special category.) As markets move from one life cycle stage to another, strategic considerations change.[14] The changes range from rates of innovation to customer price sensitivity to intensity of competitive rivalry and beyond.[15] Exhibit 4.7 shows how some important characteristics of markets change over time. As you might expect, strategy must be adjusted to meet the new market conditions from one stage to the next.

In other words, the market life cycle provides a useful framework for studying business-level strategy formulation, because it provides a "shorthand" for the numerous differences in strategic situations and the behavior appropriate to each. The product life cycles and technological life cycles are well known and important concepts that we have at-

EXHIBIT 4.7
Some Common Characteristics of Market Life Cycle Stages

	Life Cycle Stage			
Characteristic	***Introduction***	***Growth***	***Maturity***	***Decline***
Overall market growth	Building rapidly, but on a small base	Faster than GNP	Equal or less than GNP	Decreasing
Product technology	High level of major product innovation, dominant designs not yet established	Dominant design emerges, emphasis placed on product variety	Small incremental innovations, many based on cost savings vs. performance improvements	Little or no change in product
Production technology	Emphasis placed on flexibility, process not fixed until dominant design emerges	As dominant design emerges, production process can become more specialized	Emphasis on efficiency, most likely stage for automation	Little or no change in process
Pricing patterns	Prices are high but volatile	Prices decline rapidly as costs fall and competition rises	Prices decline slowly as productivity allows costs to fall	Prices stable
Promotional efforts	Target innovators and try to build awareness of product	Build brand awareness	Tailor promotion to a variety of market segments	Limit market, largely depend on inertia to maintain viable level of sales
Entry and exit	A few pioneers begin to explore the market	Many firms scramble to enter what appears to be a promising market	As market is saturated, growth slows and shakeout begins	A few survivors remain to serve the market
Nature of competition	Limited, focus is often inward, looking toward product rather than toward competitors	Growth may mask success of competitors	Competitive rivalry peaks as competitors try to survive the shakeout	As shakeout is completed, survivors seek to deescalate competition
Capital investment requirements	Substantial, needed to support initial creation of business and/or product	Peak period, needed to fund growth	Reinvestment as needed to maintain viability	Minimal, may in fact "disinvest" by selling off assets
Profitability and cash flow	Unprofitable, substantial negative cash flow	Profitable, but cash flow may still be negative	Profits declining, but larger investment level may mean cash flow is strong	Profits are low, cash flow is small (either negative or positive)

tempted to build into our consideration of an overall market life cycle. Du Pont's use of a "competitive life cycle," similar to the market life cycle, is described in Application 4.2.

While it is clearly a useful concept, there are two caveats to bear in mind when considering the market life cycle. First, the market life cycle is not intended to be used as a short-run forecasting device. Strategists find it more useful to consider the market life cycle as a conceptual framework for understanding what changes might occur over time rather than when they are likely to occur. Second, industry life cycles are reversible and repeatable. For example, Tide, a synthetic laundry detergent produced by Procter & Gamble, was introduced in 1947, but continues to see strong growth today. The product was significantly modified fifty-five times during its first 30 years.[16] Demand continues to grow as

Application 4.2

Du Pont's Use of Life Cycles in Strategic Management

E. I. du Pont de Nemours & Company, the giant diversified chemicals company, is a leader in using life cycle models. The company's use of a life cycle model to direct its strategic analysis and its strategic behavior is instructive; it illustrates how managers can adapt the life cycle concept to their particular market's situation.

Managers at Du Pont use what they call the "competitive life cycle" as a framework for their strategic planning process. This model describes the most typical evolutionary path that competitors within the chemical products industry follow. It is an attempt to capture information in the product life cycle, combining with it predictions about how the nature of competition is expected to change. The result is similar to the market life cycle model we have been looking at.

The initial stage of the evolutionary process consists of a market occupied by a single innovative firm, the sole supplier. This firm is the first to offer a new product that almost always has "functional" competition from substitute products, but not head-to-head competition from "in-kind" products. At some point, in-kind competitors do enter the market, and this begins the competitive penetration phase of Du Pont's model. Entrants to the market during this phase are forced to offer lower prices to overcome gains made by the first entrant, and there is a widespread struggle among competitors to establish levels of market share that will ensure long-run viability. In Du Pont's experience, as market growth slows the competitors' relative market shares stabilize, and they label the next evolutionary phase share stability. During this time, price and value differences are expected to continually erode, until at some point, the product is considered to be an undifferentiated product in the commodity competition phase. Du Pont expects this to be the last phase, except, possibly, withdrawal.

While evolution along this path will clearly affect several types of strategic considerations, Du Pont is especially aware of the impact these changes will have on the sort of strategic analysis that is useful in the competitive market's development (see Exhibit 4.8). From the beginning of the sole supplier stage and continuing throughout the life cycle, the importance of understanding the customer is stressed.

"Value in use" analysis, aimed at providing this understanding, is considered a cornerstone of Du Pont's strategic planning. In this analysis, managers perform an economic assessment of a given Du Pont product in several of its most important uses. The goal is to estimate the price at which the product would be equal to the value of a customer's most logical alternative. Because this analysis depends upon the economics facing the customer, Du Pont has found it to be a good means of ensuring that managers clearly understand customer needs. These needs are expected to change over time, so value in use analysis will be repeated as the competitive life cycle unfolds.

EXHIBIT 4.8
Du Pont's Use of the Life Cycle Concept Emphasizes Changes in Competition

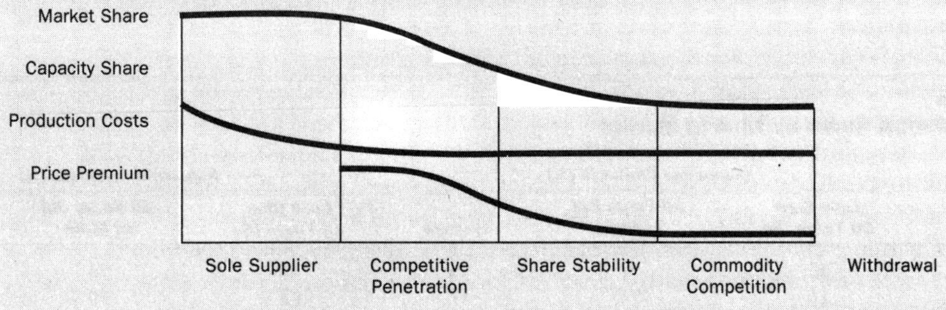

Source: Frey, John B. (1985, January). Pricing and product life cycles. *CHEMTECH*, p. 16.

Continued

Application 4.2 (cont.)

In trying to maintain or establish viable market portions during the competitive penetration phase, value in use analysis is supplemented with "competitor reaction" analysis. Du Pont is interested in maintaining a strong competitive position relative to its competition, to prepare for an eventual industry shakeout. For this reason, managers track both Du Pont's behavior and the competition's.

In the final stages of the competitive life cycle, managers use "profitability analysis" as they consider the relative merits of staying in the market or withdrawing. Du Pont has found that the relative stability of the later stages of the life cycle makes it easier to forecast financial performance accurately and to determine the scenarios in which the company will successfully compete.

Source

Frey, J. B., Jr. (1985, January). Pricing and product life cycles. *CHEMTECH*, pp. 15–21.

Procter & Gamble makes improvements—offering a liquid form, packaging innovations, and so on. Products such as Tide suggest that a turnaround phase is an appropriate supplement to the traditional life cycle model.

We now look at different strategic management practices within each stage of the market life cycle: introduction, growth, maturity, and decline.

Introduction

The early stages of a market's development establish the climate for much of what is to follow. While firms may enter a market during any stage of its life cycle, studies show that the entrepreneurial pioneers who enter the market first typically gain important advantages.[17] Competitive advantages that are gained because the pioneer was one of the first to enter a market are sometimes called "first-mover advantages."[18] First movers are notable for their tendency to hold on to the competitive advantages and market shares they gain as the market matures.[19]

Although market shares tend to become more balanced as markets mature, Exhibit 4.9 documents the finding that market share gained by successful pioneers during the market's introduction stage are often sustained for many years.[20] One of the reasons pioneers can hold their market share is that they also tend to gain advantages over their competition by being the first to enter a new market.[21] In their early stages, markets begin to establish the

EXHIBIT 4.9
Average Market Share by Time in Market

	Consumer Products (%)			*Industrial Products (%)*		
	Less than 20 Years Old	***20 Years Old or More***	***Average***	***Less than 20 Years Old***	***20 Years Old or More***	***Average***
Pioneer	35	27	29	32	28	29
Early follower	17	17	17	22	20	21
Late entrant	11	16	13	15	16	15

Source: Robinson, W. T., & Fornell, C. (1986). Market pioneering and sustainable market share advantages. *The PIMSletter on business strategy* (No. 39). Cambridge, MA: Strategic Planning Institute.

"rules of the game" that often translate into important competitive advantages.[22] For instance, IBM's success in establishing MS-DOS as an industry standard meant that later entrants in the personal computer market were forced to develop expertise in that operating system or fight the battle of establishing and supporting an alternative one.

There are numerous other means by which pioneers may gain important competitive advantages.[23] By being the first to offer a particular good or service, pioneers often benefit from establishing strong brand recognition. Kleenex and Xerox, both pioneers, were able to establish such strong name recognition that the entire facial tissue and photocopier markets are often identified by their names. Such strong brand recognition may serve as an important switching cost.[24] Pioneers may also be able to differentiate their products or services by marketing their products when there are no countering advertisements being run by competitors.[25] Finally, products and services offered by pioneers may be considered differentiated simply because their products are new.[26]

But the competitive advantages gained by pioneers are not always sustained. Texas Instruments had the expertise in semiconductor design and manufacturing that allowed it to succeed in gaining an impressive market share as a pioneer in the early stages of the digital watch market, while Timex, lacking any competence in the new technology, floundered. However, as the market matured, the basis of competition shifted from electronics design and manufacturing (TI's core competence) to consumer marketing (Timex's core competence). In the end, TI was forced to drop out of the market entirely, taking large writeoffs, while Timex remains a strong competitor. The key to maintaining competitive advantages gained by pioneering a market is to adjust the strategy as required by developments during subsequent market life cycle stages.

Growth

The growth stage of a market's life cycle is often associated with glamour and success. At this stage of the life cycle, demand for the product or service may be growing faster than the industry is able to supply it. There is less price pressure, exciting advances are being made in new technologies, and sales volume (if not profits) soars. Consequently, we often make basic assumptions about the benefits of growth that turn out to be untrue.[27] Consider three of the most common of these assumptions and how each one can be misleading:

One might think it is easier to gain share in growth markets. In the growth stage, customers are less likely to have established strong brand loyalties, making it easier for them to switch suppliers. Because the market as a whole is growing rapidly, competitors are often less likely to retaliate (or, in fact, even notice) when customers are "stolen."[28] This reason might be appropriate if the market being considered is for a product or service so radically new that it faces no substitutes from more established industries. Usually, even if new products do not face as much "in-kind" competition (from the same kind of product), they often face "functional" competition (from a different product that is used for a similar purpose). For instance, during much of its growth stage, producers in the digital watch market competed with more established mechanical watch manufacturers, which could offer a product that was often more reliable and less expensive. Given this inferiority, gaining share was not merely a process of convincing shoppers to purchase one digital model over another; it involved getting them to shop for a digital watch instead of a mechanical one.

We often assume that there is less price pressure in growth markets. Because products in growth markets often enjoy a demand in excess of supply, many growth markets can support premium pricing. During this stage, young firms are often tempted to price their goods unusually high in order to recoup as much as possible of the heavy investment from their initial startup. However, to the extent that premium pricing at this stage attracts more competitors, the long-run attractiveness of the market to any particular competitor is decreased. Having more competitors is likely to reduce the average profits of all competitors in the industry, create a more traumatic eventual market shakeout, and generally make the market more rivalrous. Thus, managers in this situation must balance the need for short-term returns with the need for long-term viability.

We expect developing critical technical expertise to be easier in the growth phase. During the earliest stages of a market's development, technology generally evolves toward a "dominant design"—a fairly standard form of the basic product. For example, anyone developing a mass-production car today will design an internal combustion engine fueled with gasoline, because that is the dominant design incorporated into the plans of mechanics, service stations, and so on.[29] But in the earliest days of the automobile industry, many designs called for a steam-powered vehicle that burned wood or coal. Participation in the evolutionary process of defining the dominant design is often viewed as essential to achieving and maintaining a competitive position in terms of technological expertise. However, many followers have outperformed "cutting-edge" firms whose technology they mimic. By avoiding the expense of pioneering R&D work, these firms are able to invest more in developing efficient manufacturing facilities or strong marketing programs. IBM's entry into personal computers was neither the earliest nor the most technologically sophisticated. In fact, in making its computers, the company largely depended upon components pioneered and produced elsewhere. But IBM's marketing investment far exceeded that of any competitor, and it was able to establish its operating software as a dominant design.

Maturity

More American businesses compete in mature markets than in any other stage of the life cycle. Markets in the mature stage of their life cycle have four characteristics in common. First, a lack of continued growth, which means that not all the firms that entered the market in the growth stage can be supported. Second, most of the key technology no longer benefits from patent protection. Third, cumulative experience can no longer provide an important advantage to any one competitor, since experience has reduced costs to the point that further reductions are difficult. Finally, there are few obvious forms of differentiation that are not already being pursued, so there is a growing trend to compete on the basis of price.

As it enters this phase, the market is beginning to stagnate, and a shakeout looms as a likely possibility.[30] This situation does not allow much opportunity for establishing a strong competitive advantage relative to the competition. It is difficult to gain an advantage that other competitors cannot copy, and the size of any particular competitive advantage is likely to be small relative to differences seen in other stages. As markets mature, the size of

EXHIBIT 4.10
Firms with Leadership Positions in Terms of Competitive Advantage Can Perform Well, Even if They Compete in a Market with Low Average Performance

	Return on Equity	Return on Capital	Revenue Growth
A. Average of eight industries with "hostile environments"	12.9%	9.4%	11.5%
B. Fortune "1,000" average	15.1%	11.0%	13.1%
C. Average of eight leaders in competitive advantages	20.2%	16.3%	14.7%

Source: Hall, William K. Survival strategies in a hostile environment. *Harvard Business Review,* 1980, September–October pp. 75–85.

pricing and differentiation advantages among competitors typically decreases. Still, there is strong evidence to support the case that if an advantage can be realized, the returns to the competitor in this market can be impressive.

A study of sixty-four businesses scattered across eight such mature "hostile environments" supports this point.[31] The majority of competitors in these markets were unable to achieve and maintain any important competitive advantage. The return on investment in many of these firms was far below the cost of capital, meaning that they could not economically continue to invest in their future. Exhibit 4.10 (line A) shows the poor overall showing of these markets. As a group, they compare quite unfavorably to the performance average of the largest 1,000 U.S. firms in terms of profitability and growth (line B). However, in these same industries, firms that were able to achieve leadership positions in terms of costs and/or differentiation (line C) compare quite favorably to overall U.S. industry averages. In fact, these leaders have the sort of performance many competitors in more glamorous growth industries would be proud to claim.

How do firms thrive in such hostile mature markets? As described earlier in the discussion of Du Pont's use of life cycle theories, as markets mature and decline, there is a tendency for the basis of competition to drift away from product differentiation and premium pricing, and toward price competition and commodity-like products. However, moving toward competition on the basis of pricing may not be the best strategy. Research in both the United States and Europe indicates that as markets mature, competition on the basis of differentiation is preferable to price competition.

For instance, a study of survivors and nonsurvivors in the U.S. television market shakeout found that nonsurvivors were notable for placing their primary marketing emphasis on price even though they had no cost or price advantage.[32] Meanwhile, the survivors avoided price competition and instead offered products of superior quality at prices equivalent to the competition's. Studies of the corrugated cardboard and stainless steel industries in Europe produced similar results, leading the researchers to conclude that "a 'total quality' strategy seems to be the best differentiation strategy in stalemate industries."[33]

Of course, the strongest competitive position is a combination of advantages. But, as data from research on these mature markets indicates, competing on the basis of differentiation achieved by quality alone can lead to good performance levels. It also has the advantage of minimizing the threat of a price war in the market.

Decline

Most markets will eventually be threatened by the development of substitute products, satiated demand, or changing customer needs. Consequently, they will face a period of decline. Often the market virtually disappears, as was the case with wooden power boats, horse-drawn farm implements, and mechanical adding machines. Others survive with a reduced demand, such as the market for home sewing notions or typewriters. In either case, the decline of the market means that the majority of competitors will face curtailed operations and possible shutdown. Yet, there are firms that survive and even thrive against these odds.[34] For example, Jostens, Inc., the maker of school rings, uses a greatly increased diversity of models and features and improved sales training to keep demand for its product growing. As a result, even though the number of high school graduates has been declining since 1976, both Jostens' sales and its profits have increased for 28 consecutive years. James B. Beam Distilling Co. has seen demand for its straight bourbon products fall sharply as the market moved toward white wines and other pale alcoholic beverages, such as gin and vodka. Yet its profits have reached record levels since it responded to this change in the market with the introduction of ZZZingers, a line of canned bourbon mixers.

Such examples are not meant to suggest that it is easy for firms to succeed when the overall market trend is one of decline.[35] In fact, it is rare for more than one or two competitors to survive severe market declines. Strategic management in the decline stage of the market life cycle must accurately assess an individual firm's viability, and this again reduces to an examination of what competitive advantage the firm can maintain. Where that advantage is not capable of supporting a business, the only rational response is to develop a strategy for "milking" as much as possible from the business before terminating its operations. Where the firm's competitive advantage is sufficiently strong, the appropriate strategy may be one that positions the business as a long-term survivor of an otherwise disappearing market. In considering this range of strategies, four distinct alternatives emerge: divestment, harvesting, niche, and leadership.[36]

Divestment

The natural response for many managers facing a declining market is to sell out. This is an appropriate response if it allows them to recover more of the investment than would be available from holding on to the business and implementing one of the other three strategies described below. The decision to divest is complicated by the importance and difficulty of moving quickly. Selling businesses late in a market's decline stage is understandably more difficult, and occasionally corporations will avoid this by selling businesses in mature markets before the "fire sale" mentality that sometimes comes with the onset of market decline. However, because the market life cycle is notoriously poor at suggesting accurate short-run forecasts, managers run the risk of selling out a business which has a long and profitable life still ahead.

Though it may seem a "clean" solution, sometimes divestment is not a practical option.[37] Often the present management team is the most knowledgeable available, and savvy new investors may not be attracted to competing in a declining market with an uninitiated management team. Interested buyers for firms in declining markets may already have some sort of association with the business being sold before it is offered for sale. Such buyers would include customers who wish to ensure supplies of key ingredients, employees who think they can save the company, and competitors who wish to consolidate the industry's capacity.

Harvest

Unlike divestment, a harvesting strategy is a process of gradually letting a business wither, in a carefully controlled and calculated fashion. Typically, businesses being harvested are managed in such a way that they produce cash flows that can be diverted to businesses elsewhere in the corporation that have more promising futures. This process typically includes a combination of tactics, such as curtailing any further investment, cutting maintenance expenditures, reducing marketing efforts, halting all R&D, and reducing the size of the managerial work force.

The side effects of this strategy are often problematic. Morale suffers as employees realize that their jobs may not be secure. Suppliers become leery of continued sales to a customer nearing shutdown, and customers become concerned about after-the-sale service. Managing a business through this phase can generate important cash flows, but it is sometimes difficult to get managers to implement a harvest strategy. Few management teams are willing to stake their careers on proving that they can excel at "killing off" businesses.

Niche

As a market declines, there often remain pockets of demand capable of supporting one or more businesses. For instance, long after the development of integrated circuits brought on the general demise of the vacuum-tube market, there remained a market for replacement parts to service equipment with the older technology. Suppliers of these replacement parts enjoy a strong market position, because they have little competition and the demand for replacement parts is seldom price sensitive. Unfortunately, the low levels of demand typical of these residual markets are usually incapable of supporting more than one business, so it cannot be considered a solution for all competitors.

Leadership

The aim in pursuing this strategic option is to establish a firm in a dominant position so that it will essentially have the declining market to itself. This strategy requires lowering the "exit barriers" that might keep competitors in the market. The concept of entry barriers was introduced in Chapter 3; they are structural characteristics of a market that obstruct competitors from freely entering a market. Exit barriers are the mirror image of this concept, applied instead to competitors' leaving a market.

Sometimes a firm simply cannot afford to exit a market. For instance, if a firm has invested in specialized equipment for which there is no other use, it may be better off maintaining a marginal operation than taking a complete write-off of the assets. A diversified corporation may also have reasons to maintain a business in a market, even though the business is incapable of supporting itself. For example, the individual business provides an important link in the corporation's overall chain of vertical integration. These are economical barriers to exit, but there are also social and behavioral costs, such as large-scale worker layoffs and resistance from managers whose careers have long been tied to success in a given market.

The firm pursuing the leadership position can often help its competitors overcome their exit barriers and thereby move to ensure its emergence as the last survivor. For instance, Proctor-Silex contracts to provide its competitors with private-labeled goods so that the competitors' corporate parents can maintain full product lines without actually competing in Proctor-Silex's particular market. Similarly, General Electric produces spare parts for the product lines of former competitors, thus freeing its competitors to exit particular markets without losing after-sales service capability, or the goodwill and image that is important to them in their remaining markets.

A firm pursuing a leadership position may also make use of "market signaling" to convey to its competitors that the competitors' continued participation in the market will be costly. Aggressive pricing, promotion, and product and/or process improvements can warn competitors that the signaling firm wili not relinquish the market without a fight that will raise the costs for everyone involved. A competitor not already committed to pursuing a leadership position itself may see enough in these signals to concede without a fight.

Implications of Competitive Advantage

Regardless of the strategy pursued, it is important for managers in a declining market to bear certain guidelines in mind. First, they must overcome the tendency to deny the market's decline. Only by recognizing the decline will they be able to favorably position their firms for the transition. Second, they should attempt to avoid wars of attrition where competitors facing high exit barriers battle it out to see who has the greatest staying power. Finally, they should not attempt to maintain a business (even if for harvesting) unless the business has some real competitive advantage. Without an advantage, customers will quickly take their business elsewhere and the struggling firm will be left in an even more undesirable position, its value and future prospects further dissipated.

Business Strategies for Turnaround

Each year, thousands of firms face a desperate situation: They must turn around their businesses or face bankruptcy. In considering turnaround strategies, we must recognize that the market life cycle of growth and decline is avoidable. Numerous firms pride themselves on having "beaten" the cycle and reversed their fortunes through a process of business turnaround. In this section, we will consider three phases in such a turnaround process: the evaluation phase, the cutting phase, and the building phase.

The Evaluation Phase

In hindsight, the need for a turnaround is often painfully obvious. Unfortunately, and perhaps surprisingly, this is not always the case as firms slip toward impending doom. Managers are often surprised to discover that things have gone awry, and that a once healthy business is now in trouble.[38] There are two general approaches for evaluating a firm's health in hopes of avoiding such unpleasant surprises. One approach emphasizes financial health and the other emphasizes organizational health. Both are useful for managers facing a turnaround situation.

In assessing the organizational health of a business, managers can monitor its "vital signs" for evidence of problems.[39] Organizational trends that typically precede a decline in performance include:

- *Excess Personnel:* An especially telling trend is one in which managerial ranks are increasing even while the number of low-level jobs is not. Similarly, an increasing ratio of staff-to-line positions is often a precursor of declining business performance.

- *Cumbersome Administrative Procedures:* A consultant was contracted to study how to make a troubled federal research facility more efficient. The project turned out to be bigger than originally anticipated, and a no-cost time extension to the contract was requested. Although no money was involved, fourteen signatures were required for approval. Obviously, here was one area in which the organization could improve efficiency!
- *Fear of Conflict:* In organizations where the consensus is that there is more to lose from rocking the boat than there is to gain from potentially controversial projects, decline is probably not too far away. In contrast, organizations like 3M and Hewlett Packard, trying to stay young, encourage managers to take new risks, and the inevitable mistakes that result are not viewed as the end of a manager's career. Such risk taking is a critical component of intrapreneurship, as described in Chapter 6.
- *Other Warning Signals:* These include developing tolerance for incompetence, losing sight of any clear goals or decision benchmarks, and decreasing communication effectiveness.

The financial health of a business, and the likelihood of its failure (bankruptcy), has been the subject of considerable research. The result is a number of models that allow managers to predict the likelihood of bankruptcy on the basis of traditional accounting ratios. One such model, available commercially, is based on data from 2,600 public companies listed in Standard and Poor's Compustat database.[40] Such models are quite accurate in spotting firms that are likely to have trouble meeting their financial obligations, but cannot explain why a business is failing. Therefore, we recommend that they be used in conjunction with the organizational analysis described above. By tracking both financial trends and organizational developments, managers may get a warning early enough to adjust before the need for an actual turnaround develops, and possibly avoid more draconian measures in the cutting phase of turnarounds, to which we now turn.

The Cutting Phase

Once it becomes obvious that a firm must either turn around its performance or risk bankruptcy, the process typically begins with a cutting phase aimed at survival and focuses on stopping the hemorrhaging cash flows which are often involved in turnaround situations. As Application 4.3 on Chrysler's famous turnaround reveals, the cuts can be sweeping, taking in large portions of the work force, entire managerial levels, and even whole operating divisions. Certainly, attempts are made to wring cash out of operations through reducing accounts receivable and all forms of inventories, leasing or selling underutilized assets, and reducing all discretionary expenses, at least temporarily. Often, measures appear to be taken as much for their "shock value" as their cash value. For example, one faltering family business was purchased by a large public firm, a takeover specialist committed to turning around the operations of smaller firms. The acquiring firm began its efforts by selling the art collection and silverware in the executive dining room in the name of increasing cash flows. However, the cash generated was probably less important than the symbolism of the act.

Handled improperly, such measures can have a demoralizing effect on managers and workers. It is also essential that the businesses not be pared down so much that no basis for long-term viability remains. One company president, a turnaround veteran himself, warns

Application 4.3

Turnaround at the Chrysler Corporation

In 1977 Chrysler Corporation, the third largest automobile producer in the United States, was facing a difficult situation. Serious safety hazards had forced it to recall more than 1 million vehicles for retrofitting, and new federal fuel-economy and emissions regulations were forcing a $7.5 billion retooling effort. The debt required to finance these tasks, in addition to the company's normal operating debt, placed the corporation in grave danger; anything that threatened cash flows and the firm's ability to service its huge debt could force it to declare bankruptcy.

First quarter sales in 1978 slumped; the company reported quarterly losses of $120 million. The next quarter saw an improvement, but the corporation had quarterly earnings of only $30 million—not nearly enough to finance the efforts it was legally bound to undertake. When third quarter results were reported, it seemed to many that a disaster was inevitable; the company had lost another $160 million. On the same day that this information was released, the board announced that the company had hired a new CEO, Lee Iacocca. His efforts to save the company illustrate the three processes involved in most successful turnarounds.

The evaluation phase. Iacocca immediately set out to understand what factors would be most important in saving the company. He undertook a complete review of all Chrysler operations. This analysis indicated that in many key operating areas, the company was floundering, out of control. The sales dealerships were poorly managed, and company-owned dealerships often competed directly against independent dealerships. Inventories were bloated far beyond need. Production operations were exceedingly complex because of the proliferation of countless unique components. Product quality was unsatisfactory; cars regularly came off the assembly line with multiple serious defects. Warranty costs ran at $350 million a year, but no one in management knew the causes of the top ten most frequent warranty claims. Tens of thousands of unsold cars were rusting unsheltered in the Michigan State Fairground.

The analysis also indicated that to correct these and other problems, the company needed a lot of cash, and quickly. Banks refused to extend any more loans to the company, and it was obvious that operations could not provide the necessary cash flow. (In 1979–1980, the company lost over $1.3 billion.) The only alternative was to obtain a government guarantee to back the loans, and thus reduce the risk to the point that a consortium of banks would finance the company. In late 1979, Congress passed a bill providing up to $1.5 billion in loan guarantees for the company, an unprecedented act on the part of the federal government.

The cutting phase. Based on information gathered in the evaluation process, Chrysler made many deep cuts. Thirty-three of the thirty-five highest-ranking managers were fired. Nearly 8,500 financial staff positions were eliminated; the total white-collar work force was reduced from 40,000 to 21,000. The blue-collar work force was halved from 160,000 to 80,000. Union and nonunion workers took drastic wage and benefit reductions, saving $1.2 billion. The company closed or consolidated 20 plants. The number of different parts used in production was reduced from 75,000 to 40,000, and inventories were reduced by $1 billion. Within 3 years, the company was able to cut its breakeven point to half of what it had been. The company became, in Iacocca's words, "half the size but twice the company."

The building phase. A key to rebuilding Chrysler was the success of its K-Car concept. Beginning in 1980, all of Chrysler's new models were built over a single engine and drive train, known as the K-Car platform. This method has allowed the company to secure a stronger position in all three forms of competitive advantage we have discussed. For example, multiple use of the same components on different models allowed the company to order supplies in large quantities. This enabled it to bargain with suppliers more effectively. Simplified production processes, consisting of thousands fewer component parts, were easier to manage and automate; as a result, product quality rapidly improved. Chrysler's "5–50" warranty, covering the engine and power train on all its models, became the strongest in the industry, and an important source of differentiation. Finally, by using "off-the-shelf" K-Car designs, the company could rapidly introduce new products, and even new categories of products, like its pioneering work in the minivan product category. The efforts to build on the K-Car concept represented only one part of what amounted to a $6.6 billion, 5-year building program designed to secure the company's long-term health.

As Exhibit 4.11 indicates, these three processes

Application 4.3 (cont.)

were effective in turning around the Chrysler Corporation. The company was able to repay its government-backed loans far ahead of schedule, as its revenues and profits rose steadily. What is especially remarkable is that much of this turnaround was carried out during the worldwide recession of 1982, which seriously affected the automobile industry as a whole. Backed by sound analysis, decisive cutting, and a rebuilding program aimed at gaining a mix of competitive advantages, Chrysler was able to succeed against formidable odds.

Sources

Iacocca, L. (1983). The rescue and resuscitation of Chrysler. *The Journal of Business Strategy, 4*, 67–69.

Iacocca, L. (1984). *Iacocca: An autobiography*. Toronto: Bantam.

Reich, R. B., & Donahue, J. D. (1985). *New deals: The Chrysler revival and the American system*. New York: Times Books.

Taylor, A., III. (1987, June 22). Lee Iacocca's production whiz. *Fortune*, pp. 26–31.

EXHIBIT 4.11
Chrysler's Turnaround as Shown by Operating Income

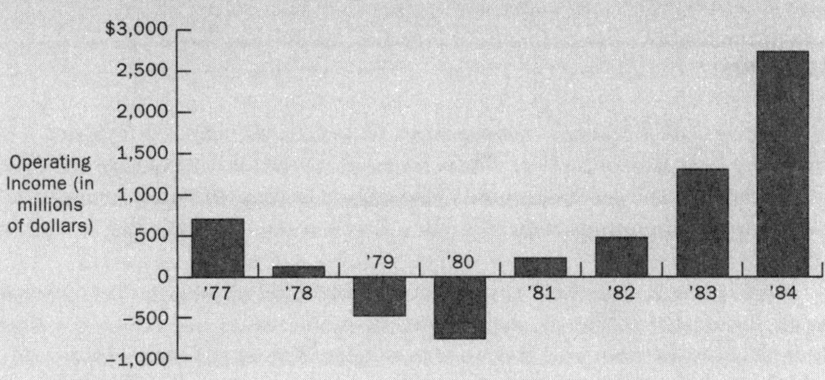

Source: Chrysler Annual Reports.

sarcastically, "Short-term bottom-line effects are easy to achieve. Usually, all that is necessary is to decimate the business." [41] This brings up the question of what to build the firm's future on after all the cutting is done.

The Building Phase

After the slide toward failure has been halted, an upturn must be started and sustained if the turnaround is to be successful. The building phase most often requires focusing on a segment of a market where the company has some chance for maintaining a competitive advantage. The process involved is the one which has been the theme for much of this chapter: Find that overlap of customer needs and company strengths in which the firm can compare favorably to its competition and build upon that to achieve a sustainable competitive advantage.[42]

In a study of 260 mature industrial strategic business units, each with a history that indicated the need for a turnaround, researchers found that the only clearly successful tactics were those identified as "asset and cost surgery" and "selective product/market pruning."[43] The cost-cutting strategy entailed cuts in overhead and administration, marketing, accounts receivable, and inventories, along with declines in plant and equipment newness and (at least short-term) increases in employee productivity and capacity utilization. The market focus tactics included concentrating on less price-sensitive markets, where the firms could compete on the basis of product quality rather than production costs. As a result of this focusing, they were able to reduce marketing expenses and inventories. Interestingly, firms following this approach actually reported decreased capacity utilization (in sharp contrast to the turnarounds following cost-cutting tactics), probably due to focusing on high-profit market segments, rather than volume.

These tactics might seem familiar to you from our previous discussion. The "asset/cost surgery" strategy emphasizes restoring cost competitiveness to the troubled firm. Likewise, the "selective product/market pruning" strategy emphasizes searching out a market in which the firm can compete by offering customers a differentiated product.

Summary

In the long run, a business continues to be successful only if it sustains a competitive advantage over its competitors. Three forms of competitive advantage are differentiation, cost leadership, and quick response. (Though not a competitive advantage in its own right, market focus often impacts heavily on a firm's success in achieving competitive advantages.)

Differentiation, in which firms create products and/or services that customers value, is based on nonprice attributes, such as reputation, innovation, consistency, and service. Cost leadership results from practices, such as standardization and mass production, to operate at lower costs so the firm can realize higher-than-normal profits. The ability to provide a quick response to customer needs is a powerful competitive advantage. From filling an order to answering customer questions, to applying the latest innovations, quick response can deliver a competitive advantage that compares with that of the most differentiated or lowest-cost competitors. Besides offering its own potential for competitive advantage, quick response can help make differentiation and cost leadership more effective. A firm that maintains more than one of these competitive advantages simultaneously will enjoy even greater measures of success.

Every business is different, as is the competitive environment it faces and the strategy it pursues. We can effectively capture many of these differences with the market life cycle model. While not a forecasting device, this framework helps to organize our thinking about the competitive environment through the use of chronological stages: introduction, growth, maturity, decline, and turnaround. Appropriate strategies vary according to the current phase of the market life cycle.

In the introduction stage, competitive advantages and market shares are being established that can impact competitors for years to come. In growth markets, shares are easily gained, prices are not under pressure, and foundations for long-term competitive advantages are being formed. In mature markets, patents lose protection, individual firms attempt their own workable forms of differentiation, and prices become more important to the customer. Declining markets are characterized by satiated consumer demand, obsolescence of technologies, and falling total market sales. However, the decline of a market need not signal disaster to a firm. Profitable alternatives including divestment, harvesting, locating a safe niche, and leadership as the sole survivor in the industry are all possible, if the business has the appropriate competitive positioning.

Perhaps the most dramatic of strategies is the turnaround. Determination and careful consideration can lead to comprehensive evaluation of a firm's problems, precise and purposeful cuts in facilities and personnel, and discovery of the appropriate grounds upon which to build a phoenix business. The key to success in formulating a winning turnaround strategy, like any other business-level strategy, rests on understanding, achieving, and maintaining a competitive advantage.

Notes

1. By far, the most influential writer on the topic of competitive advantage, and perhaps business-level strategies in general, is Michael Porter. Throughout this chapter, we draw heavily upon his work, especially in considering the competitive advantages of differentiation and cost leadership. Porter has written two books on the subject of business-level strategy: Porter, M. E. (1980). *Competitive strategy.* New York: Free Press (in which chaps. 2, 8, and 10 to 12 present thinking particularly relevant to this chapter); and Porter, M. E. (1985). *Competitive advantage.* New York: Free Press (in which chaps. 1, 3, and 4 are most relevant).
2. Historically, competitive advantages, such as differentiation and cost leadership, were viewed as incompatible, either-or options. But research has shown that this is not the case. See, for example, Phillips, L. W., Chang, D., & Buzzell, R. D. (1983, Spring). Product quality, cost position, and business performance: A test of some key hypotheses. *Journal of Marketing, 47,* 26–43; White, R. E. (1986). Generic business strategies, organizational context and performance: An empirical investigation. *Strategic Management Journal, 7,* 217–231; Dess, G. G., & Davis, P. S. (1984). Porter's generic strategies as determinants of strategic group membership and organizational performance. *Academy of Management Journal, 27,* 465–488; and Kim, L., & Lim, Y. (1988). Environment, generic strategies, and performance in a rapidly developing country: A taxonomic approach. *Academy of Management Journal, 31,* 802–827. For three important theoretical contributions which support the viability of combining business-level strategies, refer to Murray, A. I. (1988). A contingency view of Porter's generic strategies. *Academy of Management Review, 13,* 627–638; Hill, C. W. L. (1988). Differentiation versus low cost or differentiation and low cost: A contingency framework. *Academy of Management Review, 13,* 401–412; and Jones, G. R., & Butler, J. E. (1988). Costs, revenue and business-level strategy. *Academy of Management Review, 13,* 307–321.
3. South, S. E. (1981, Spring). Competitive advantage: The cornerstone of strategic thinking. *The Journal of Business Strategy, 1,* 16.
4. Abernathy, W. J., & Wayne, K. (1974, September–October). Limits of the learning curve. *Harvard Business Review, 52,* 109–119.
5. Bhide, A. (1986, September). Hustle as strategy. *Harvard Business Review, 64,* 59–65.
6. To learn how to speed managerial decisions, see Eisenhardt, K. M. (1989). Making fast strategic decisions in high-velocity environments. *Academy of Management Journal,* pp. 543–576; and Judge, W. Q., & Miller, A. (1991). Antecedents and outcomes of decision speed in different environmental contexts. *Academy of Management Journal, 34,* 449–463.

7. Thomas, P. R. (1990). *Competitiveness through total cycle time: An overview for CEOs.* New York: McGraw-Hill.
8. There is emerging a useful body of literature which addresses the role of response time as a competitive advantage. This section draws heavily upon Dumaine, B. (1989, February 13). How managers can succeed through speed. *Fortune,* pp. 30–35; Bower, J. L., & Hout, T. M. (1988, November–December). Fast-cycle capability for competitive power. *Harvard Business Review,* pp. 110–118; Stalk, G., Jr. (1988, July–August). Time—the next source of competitive advantage. *Harvard Business Review,* pp. 41–51; and Meredith, J. R. (1987, Spring). The strategic advantages of the factory of the future. *California Management Review, 29,* 27–41.
9. Thomas, P. R. (1991). *Getting competitive: Middle managers and the cycle time ethic.* New York: McGraw-Hill.
10. Stalk (Ref. 8), loc. cit.
11. Nevens, T. M., Summe, G. L., & Uttal, B. (1990, May–June). Commercializing technology: What the best companies do. *Harvard Business Review,* pp. 154–163.
12. Ghemawat, P. (1985, March–April). Building strategy on the experience curve. *Harvard Business Review, 63,* 143–149.
13. Anderson, C. R., & Zeithaml, C. P. (1984). Stage of the product life cycle, business strategy, and business performance. *Academy of Management Journal, 27,* 5–24.
14. Hambrick, D. C., & Lei, D. (1985). Toward an empirical prioritization of contingency variables for business strategy. *Academy of Management Journal, 28,* 763–788.
15. Hofer, C. W. (1975). Toward a contingency theory of business strategy. *Academy of Management Journal, 18,* 784–810.
16. Day, G. (1981). The product life cycle: Analysis and applications issues. *Journal of Marketing, 45*(4), 60–67.
17. Strategic implications of entry during other stages of the market life cycle are discussed in Covin, J. G., & Slevin, D. P. (1990). New venture strategic posture, structure, and performance: An industry life cycle analysis. *Journal of Business Venturing, 5,* 123–135.
18. Lieberman, M. B., & Montgomery, D. B. (1988, Summer). First mover advantages. *Strategic Management Journal, 9,* 41–58.
19. Mitchell, W. (1991, February). Dual clocks: Entry order influence on incumbent and newcomer market share and survival when specialized assets retain their value. *Strategic Management Journal, 12,* 85–100.
20. Lambkin, M. (1988). Order of entry and performance in new markets [Special issue]. *Strategic Management Journal, 9,* 127–140; Urban, G. L., Carter, T., Gaskin, S., & Muchia, Z. (1986). Market share rewards to pioneering brands: An empirical analysis and strategic implications. *Management Science, 32*(6), 645–659.
21. Miller, A., Gartner, W., & Wilson, R. (1989). Entry order, market share, and competitive advantage: A study of their relationships in new corporate ventures. *Journal of Business Venturing, 4,* 197–209.
22. Robinson, W. T., & Fornell, C. (1985). Sources of market pioneer advantages in consumer goods industries. *Journal of Marketing Research, 22*(3), 305–317.
23. Whitten, I. T. (1979). *Brand performance in the cigarette industry and the importance of early entry,* 1913–1973. Washington, DC: Federal Trade Commission.
24. Porter, M. (1980). *Competitive strategy.* New York: Free Press.
25. Schmalensee, R. (1982). Product differentiation advantages of pioneering brands. *American Economic Review, 72,* 159–180.

26. Utterback, J. M. A., & William, J. (1975). A dynamic model of process and product innovation. *Omega, 3,* 631.
27. This section is based on work found in Aaker, D. A. (1986, September–October). The perils of high-growth markets. *Strategic Management Journal, 7,* 409–421.
28. Miller, A., & Dewhirst, H. D. (1992). Technological intensity as a predictor vs. a moderator of the competitive responses to new entrants. *Journal of High Technology Management Research, 3*(1), 39–63.
29. Abernathy, W. J., & Utterback, J. M. (1978). Patterns of industrial innovation. *Technology Review, 80*(7), 41–47.
30. Calori, R., & Ardisson, J. M. (1988, May–June). Differentiation strategies in "Stalemate Industries." *Strategic Management Journal, 9,* 255–269.
31. Hall, W. K. (1980, September–October). Survival strategies in a hostile environment. *Harvard Business Review,* pp. 75–85.
32. Willard, G. E., & Cooper, A. C. (1985, November–December). Survivors of industry shakeouts: The case of the U.S. color television set industry. *Strategic Management Journal, 6,* 299–318.
33. Calori and Ardisson (Ref. 30), loc. cit.
34. The examples given, as well as several others, are discussed in greater detail in Fierman, J. (1985). How to make money in mature markets. *Fortune, 112*(12), 40–47.
35. Cameron, K. S., Dutton, R. I., & Whetten, D. A. (1988). *Readings in organizational decline.* Cambridge, MA: Ballinger.
36. Discussion of these four types of strategies draws heavily upon Harrigan, K. R., & Porter, M. E. (1983, July–August). End-game strategies for declining industries. *Harvard Business Review,* pp. 111–121.
37. Harrigan, K. R. (1984, Winter). Managing declining businesses. *The Journal of Business Strategy,* pp. 74–78.
38. D'Aveni, R. A. (1989, September). The aftermath of organizational decline: A longitudinal study of the strategic and managerial characteristics of declining firms. *Academy of Management Journal,* pp. 577–605.
39. A more complete discussion of these and other "vital signs" is available in Lorange, P., & Nelson, R. T. (1987, Spring). How to recognize—and avoid—organizational decline. *Sloan Management Review,* pp. 41–48.
40. For guidelines on how to fit use of such models into an overall turnaround process, see Dolan, P. F. (1983, Summer). A four-phase rescue plan for today's troubled companies. *The Journal of Business Strategy, 4,* 22–31.
41. Shostack, G. L. (1988, March–April). A turnaround is a delicate operation. *The Journal of Business Strategy,* pp. 59–61.
42. For further discussion of the importance of competitive advantage in achieving a turnaround, see Hofer, C. W. (1980, Summer). Turnaround strategies. *The Journal of Business Strategy, 1,* 19–31.
43. Hambrick, D. C., & Schecter, S. M. (1983). Turnaround strategies for mature industrial-product business units. *Academy of Management Journal, 26,* 231–248.

CHAPTER 5

Strategic Management at the Functional Level: Managing for Customer Value

In Chapter 4, we considered the importance of competitive advantage to the success of the firm. But recall from Chapter 3 that competitive advantages are built within the functions that make up the various links of the firm's value chain. Strategy formulation depends on understanding how functions can be managed to create the best customer value and, in turn, the strongest competitive advantages.

This chapter has three sections. In the first, we look at how every function has its role to play in contributing to customer value. In the second section, we consider the need for continuous improvement in the performance of individual functions. The last section discusses developing trends that may affect the strategic management of six specific business functions: marketing, operations, research and development, accounting, purchasing, and human resource management.

After reading this chapter, you will understand:

- Why managing at the functional level is of strategic importance
- That every function has a potential role to play in creating value for the customer and competitive advantages for the firm
- That every function should strive for superior quality, efficiency, and delivery
- That every function both has customers and is a customer
- The need for continual improvement and efforts from each function toward becoming the "best in its class"
- The latest developments that are of critical strategic importance in some specific business functions

EXECUTIVE INTERVIEW

Bobbie A. Koehler
Merchandising Manager, Ford Division Ford Motor Company

Bobbie A. Koehler is merchandising manager for the Ford division of Ford Motor Company. Koehler joined Ford Motor Company in 1972 in the Ford Division's Pittsburgh district sales office. In 1979 she moved to the Lincoln-Mercury division. Her assignments included positions as district sales manager in Cleveland and Detroit, assistant district sales manager in Washington, D.C., and general field manager in Chicago. Koehler returned to the Ford Division in 1986 as an executive assistant for dealer affairs. In September 1987 she was named western regional sales manager. She was appointed to her present position in 1989.

Koehler graduated from the University of Pittsburgh with a bachelor's degree in business administration. She has also completed Stanford University's senior executive program.

Does it really make sense to talk about strategic management for an individual function like merchandising?

It makes no sense to manage a merchandising function without serious consideration of strategic issues, including fit. In my experience, when a function is managed purely "functionally," it operates reactively, inefficiently, and creates a nonenriching, nonchallenging environment for all employees.

Without a healthy balance between strategic and functional responsibilities, an organization often creates programs which not only conflict, but can subvert a company's strategic goals. For instance, a strategy for many companies today is creating a level of customer satisfaction that builds intensely loyal customers. A merchandising department that is managed functionally can easily create "programs" which seriously conflict in that the focus of such programs is "one sale at a time," without regard for the long-term relationship (which happens to be one of the company's strategic goals).

This conflict creates frustration for the company, leading to criticism of the function, resulting in demoralization of the organization.

Consideration of strategic management within a functional responsibility not only makes sense, but is imperative!

Does your department have both internal and external customers?

The merchandising department is responsible for many diverse activities:

- Owner satisfaction and loyalty
- Contests and incentives (retail customers, dealers, employees)
- Retail promotion strategies and execution (retail customers)
- Regional marketing
- Communications (all divisional meetings with dealers and salespersons)
- Display and exhibits
- Motor sports
- Retail leasing
- Recreational vehicle sales and marketing
- New product launches including training (share with marketing plans)

While our responsibilities are many and diverse, our primary internal and external customer sets are few. Internally, our primary customers are our field organization; employees throughout the company who participate in Ford division communication processes/programs. Our external sets of customers are dealers, pool/conversion companies, Ford owners and prospective customers.

You obviously have a well-developed strategy for merchandising. How important is coordination with other functions or departments?

In today's world, a strategy for any function can be well developed (and executed, I might add) only if it is coordinated with other related (or potentially impacted) functions or departments. Therefore, in direct response to your question, interrelationships are critically important.

An example would be the launch of a new product, such as Escort. The objective was to convince the entire dealer organization and the Ford field organization that the CT20 Escort could compete head-on with the Honda Accord and Toyota Corolla models in every respect . . . and therefore required a BIG selling and ownership experience.

Continued

This effort actively involved seventeen operations or components of the company, including the UAW as well as our advertising agencies.

By the way, 6 months after launch, the 1991 Escort has achieved the highest customer satisfaction ratings of any Ford car line introduced or in service today.

In reflecting on this question, I was unable to think of any program, process, or project which merchandising has undertaken or is responsible for that has not or would not have benefited from a cross-functional relationship.

MANAGING STRATEGICALLY AT THE FUNCTIONAL LEVEL

Strategic management is often equated with top management, implying that the strategic perspective is applicable only to managing entire businesses. Historically, the tendency has been to pay little more than lip service to the idea of adopting a strategic perspective in managing individual functional areas. Yet, there are two important reasons to approach functional-level management strategically.

First, several tasks face managers at the functional level that are directly analogous to tasks facing business-level managers. For instance, we portray functions and departments as having customers and suppliers—analogous to a business organization in microcosm. Second, as organizations today are becoming flatter, there are fewer positions for top managers and more opportunities to practice strategic management in lower levels. The tools, techniques, and perspectives of strategic management are now of vital importance to functional-level managers.

All Functions Can Create Customer Value

While high differentiation, low cost, and quick response are competitive advantages of an entire business, their counterparts in individual functions exist as carrying out a departmental activity with high quality, great efficiency, and rapid delivery. Exhibit 5.1 illustrates how the definitions of quality, efficiency, and delivery differ across functional areas. Efficiency in an advertising department is obviously very different from efficiency in a manufacturing department. Yet, *all* departments must share responsibility for the firm's overall competitive position.[1]

To understand why creating customer value is everybody's business, briefly consider the alternative.[2] That is, consider what happens when managers divide up responsibility for quality, cost, and delivery across different functional departments. Begin with quality because businesses regularly single out an individual quality control department. This practice is not an effective means of managing quality. After all, the personnel in a quality control department do not actually perform any of the activities that determine the quality of the firm's goods or services. For instance, they don't design products (that is the responsibility of the R&D department) and they don't produce things (the operations department does). In most organizations, the quality control department can only police the activities of other departments as they actually design and produce goods and services. This is done

EXHIBIT 5.1
Examples of Quality, Efficiency, and Delivery in Several Functions

	Quality	*Efficiency*	*Delivery*
Marketing	Provides accurate assessment of customer's product preferences to R&D	Targets advertising campaign at customers, using cost-effective medium	Quickly uncovers and reacts to changing market trends
Operations	Consistently produces goods matching engineering design	Minimizes scrap and rework through high-production yield	Quickly adapts to latest demands with production flexibility
Research and development	Designs products that combine customer demand and production capabilities	Uses computers to test feasibility of idea before going to more expensive full-scale prototype	Carries out parallel product/process designs to speed up overall innovation
Accounting	Provides the information that managers in other functions need to make decisions	Simplifies and computerizes to decrease the cost of gathering information	Provides information in "real time" (as the events described are still happening)
Purchasing	Selects vendors for their ability to join in an effective "partnership"	Given the required vendor quality, negotiates prices to provide good value	Schedules inbound deliveries efficiently, avoiding both extensive inventories and stock outs
Personnel	Trains work force to perform required tasks	Minimizes employee turnover, reducing hiring and training expenses	In response to strong growth in sales, finds large numbers of employees and quickly teaches needed skills

through an inspection process which is designed not so much to elicit high quality as to catch poor quality.

Catching poor quality through inspection is much less desirable than simply designing and building quality products in the first place. Inspection can never be perfect, and when poor quality products make it past the inspectors, the firm's overall reputation suffers. Reworking the mistakes that do get caught often nearly doubles a product's cost, thereby drastically reducing efficiency, and the whole inspect-and-rework cycle slows down the delivery process. (Note the relationship: when quality suffers, so do efficiency and delivery.)

Furthermore, the concerns of quality control inspectors seldom reflect the totality of quality issues that concern customers.[3] Inspection focuses on "quality of conformance," which refers to catching products with attributes not matching (or conforming to) those specified in the product's design. But if the design itself is inferior, quality inspection cannot address the problem, and may even make it worse. Imagine the consequences of designing a car door with a handle that tends to pinch fingers. If the quality control department can ensure good level of conformance to this design through a rigorous inspection process, the resulting "quality" will cause even more fingers to be pinched! High-conformance quality is obviously of little value unless the quality of design is also high,[4] a factor over which quality control departments have little influence, because that is the domain of R&D.

Finally, some elements that influence the customer's perception of overall quality are not even part of the product per se.[5] Consistently high-quality goods in a firm's retail outlet will not increase sales if the sales staff mistreats customers. In some cases, improvements from U.S. automobile manufacturers have been negated by continued shoddy behavior of dealers and service departments.[6] In contrast, excellent dealer service can have a dramatic impact on the customers' overall perception of value.[7]

Clearly, R&D, sales, and service functions can do much to influence the customer's perception of overall quality. If a business hopes to have the highest perceived quality overall, then that must be the goal of all these functions, and not just that of quality control. The same need for widespread cooperation applies to the goals of efficiency and delivery. Historically, firms have focused cost-control efforts on reducing direct labor expenses. Yet, in most businesses, labor now amounts to less than 25 percent of the total cost of goods sold. The remaining 75 percent or more of expenses is spread across literally dozens of categories, so a firm's cost-cutting efforts must be widespread if they are to be very effective. Similarly, for a logistics or distribution department to carry out speedy deliveries, every department involved in the value chain, from inbound logistics of raw materials to outbound shipment of finshed goods, must move quickly.

Every Function Is a Supplier as Well as a Customer

By looking at every function as both having customers and being a customer, the central importance of maximizing customer value becomes clear. Each department or function can be seen as the center of a conceptual model like the one shown in Exhibit 5.2. The model shows a generic function receiving inputs from suppliers and offering output to customers. Organizations can be viewed as a series of these input-output sequences, with each function

EXHIBIT 5.2
Every Function Can Be Viewed as the Middle Link in Internal and External Supplier-to-Customer Chains

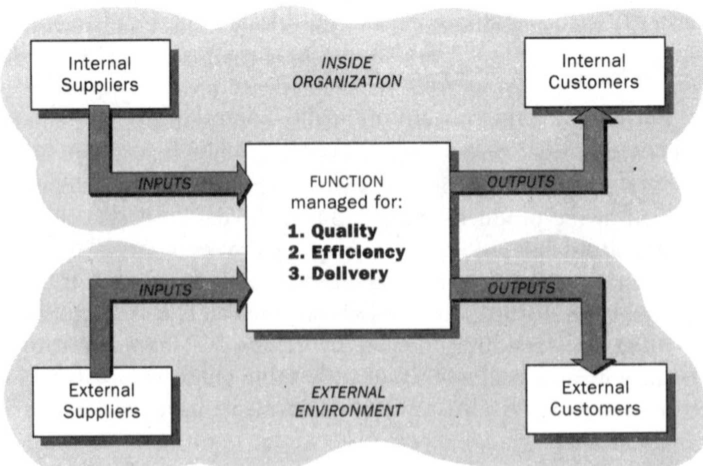

taking something from one set of departments and offering something to another. Note also that both suppliers and customers may be either external or internal.

You may find it unusual to think of some departments in this way. Consider, for instance, an accounting department. Who are its suppliers and customers? Obviously, they are not those normally identified in thinking about the business, but they do exist. This department's *external suppliers* would include the hardware and software vendors providing the purchased computer facilities. *Internal suppliers* would include all the departments that collect the data which the accounting department assimilates. *External customers* would include all federal and state agencies with which the business must file tax forms, while *internal customers* would include all the departments that depend upon the accounting department for financial data and reports.

This perspective can have a fundamental effect on how managers view their responsibilities. By identifying themselves as the center of a series of linked input-output (supplier-customer) relationships, functional-level managers can more readily identify the role they play in strengthening the firm's overall value chain and its competitive advantage. Even functions, such as accounting, that appear to have no direct impact on the firm's external customers, can see that, through their impact on their own internal customers, they are linked to these external customers. A function's effectiveness at serving its own internal customers greatly affects the ability of the entire firm to serve its external customers.

KAIZEN: CONTINUALLY IMPROVING CUSTOMER VALUE

In Japan, many firms excel at continuous improvement, a process called *kaizen*.[8] The standard of performance in the kaizen philosophy is not simply to improve, but to keep on improving, always with the goal of becoming *dantotsu*, Japanese for "the best of the best".[9] (Other Japanese concepts important to functional-level management are defined in Application 5.1.)

To reach the standard of dantotsu, the most aggressive competitors around the world believe that *every* function must try to be distinguishable as the "best in class." In order to reach this goal, they use benchmarking (comparing themselves to and learning from the best practices of other firms) and experimentation (progress by trial and error). Where these techniques fail to produce the desired high-performance levels, firms may decide to "outsource" (find an outside supplier) and assign the work to a firm that does a better job.

Benchmarking

This involves studying how other firms carry out a function to determine what level of performance is required to be competitive, or possibly to see just how high a level of performance is possible.[10] For instance, the chief of the fire brigade at a large chemical plant knew that his department was already quite good; their response time in drills had improved noticeably over what it had been under his predecessor. However, as part of a plantwide continuous improvement effort, he visited what were widely considered to be the best small fire fighting groups anywhere. One of these, at a large airport, was responsible for an airfield many times the size of his chemical plant. These airport firefighters had a

Application 5.1

A Sampler of Japanese Terms for Operations Management

The tremendous success the Japanese have enjoyed in a number of markets has managers around the world interested in learning more about their ideas for managing. Consequently, the Japanese have been quite influential in shaping the language used everywhere in discussing management issues, especially in regard to operations management. The Japanese managerial terms listed below, along with *kaizen* (discussed elsewhere in the text), are the ones most commonly heard outside Japan.

Kanban: Translates roughly as "instruction card," sometimes called the Toyota production system or the just-in-time inventory system. Kanban was first developed at Toyota and was based on the U.S. supermarket, where customers go to pick up only the items they need on a given shopping trip. In adapting this inventory method to manufacturing, cards (called kanban) are used to track which items are used and which need replenishing.

Jidoka: Translates roughly as "autonomation." Jidoka is an extension of the idea of automation. An automated machine automatically performs a specific task, but it requires an operator to make any judgments or adjustments. Autonomation gives the machine the "intelligence" and the "autonomy" to make judgments and adjustments by itself. In some applications, jidoka can greatly reduce the labor intensiveness of a production process.

Poka-yoke: Translates roughly as "foolproof." An example would be two parts designed so that they could be combined in assembly only one way—the *right* way. The idea of poka-yoke is to avoid making mistakes in assembly in the first place, thus removing the need for inspection or reworking later on.

Andon: Translates roughly as "lantern" or "trouble light." An andon light panel is used to communicate problems with a given machine or workstation to all personnel within eyesight. A severe enough problem can shut an entire assembly line down, so any able person is expected to respond to an andon light and help resolve the problem. This type of troubleshooting is sometimes called "management by sight." It is especially useful in combination with highly automated facilities where there may be many more machines than people.

Muda: Translates roughly as "waste." Muda refers to any kind of scrap or useless activity. Obviously, the most efficient processes are those that minimize muda. Much of kaizen is directed toward eliminating muda.

response time considerably better than his. One reason was that firefighters at airports are usually notified about where a troubled plane will land, so they can station a crew close by. The chief realized that in his chemical plant, some spots were much more likely than others to have a fire. By scattering pairs of firefighters closer to these "hot spots," he could have a team on the spot much more quickly than would be possible from their current centralized location, and they could begin fighting fires sooner.

Effective benchmarking does not always require this much similarity between functions. For instance, when Chaparral Steel was contemplating the creation of a micromill, a steel mill operated by approximately forty employees, they wanted to see just how well small teams could be employed to carry out standardized tasks. They used a McDonald's restaurant as their basis of comparison. By comparing each function to the "best in class" standard—even if that means going far outside their own industries—firms like Chaparral remind themselves that there is always room for continued improvement.

Experimentation

This is an essential part of kaizen because only trivial processes can be perfectly planned in advance. Anything more significant requires constant tinkering; in a continually changing world, no process can ever be perfected, only improved. For many organizations, this represents a novel set of expectations for managers and employees; it implies that people are *expected* to make some mistakes.

In fact, adopting experimentation and accepting failures are changes so great that managers often have trouble accepting them. Why should they try new things when experimentation might lead to eventual failure? To overcome such hesitancy, experimentation must be legitimated as an acceptable way of managing. Typically, this legitimation involves endorsing companywide procedures for experimentation. Some companies have found it especially useful to put in writing how experimentation is to be carried out. Given the companywide endorsement of a set procedure, experiments are judged not on their outcome, but on how well managers followed the approved procedure for experimentation. Most such guidelines are some adaptation of a simple planning cycle that Edward Deming developed for helping Japanese functional-level managers rebuild their businesses after World War II.

Sent to war-ravaged Japan by the U.S. government to help rebuild the country's economy, Deming quickly realized that the monumental task of rebuilding would require the efforts of hundreds of thousands of individuals, each working on a relatively small part of the whole problem. Yet, to coordinate their activities, these individuals needed to share a common language of problem solving. Therefore, Deming proposed his simple four-part planning cycle that could be used by virtually anyone, facing virtually any sort of problem.[11] Shown in Exhibit 5.3, it became known as the plan, do, check, act (PDCA) planning cycle.

When using the PDCA cycle, a problem is systematically addressed by first developing a plan. The plan is then carried out, and assessments are made to check its effectiveness. The last step in the cycle requires doing whatever is necessary to correct any problems. Because the plan is so basic, PDCA can be used in virtually any function and at any level within an organization. In an organization committed to the philosophy of kaizen, there will be hundreds, perhaps even thousands, of PDCA-like loops in motion at any one time.

Companies have customized many variations on this simple idea, and many, such as Procter & Gamble, have taken the practice a step further. P & G has printed its own more complex version on pocket-sized cards for employees to use as guidelines in tackling various managerial problems. At firms where they have been most successful, such procedures have become part of the employees' language, helping to facilitate better communication across functions. In such organizations, PDCA (or derivatives of this same idea) may serve as a set of guidelines for running meetings, a set of standards for evaluating problem-solving efforts, or perhaps as a means of depersonalizing the delicate process of criticizing colleagues. Although the generic structure of this process of problem solving may not be optimal for any particular problem, managers find its ability to unify the thinking of diverse parties and direct them toward a common goal will more than offset this limitation.

EXHIBIT 5.3
Deming's PDCA Cycle

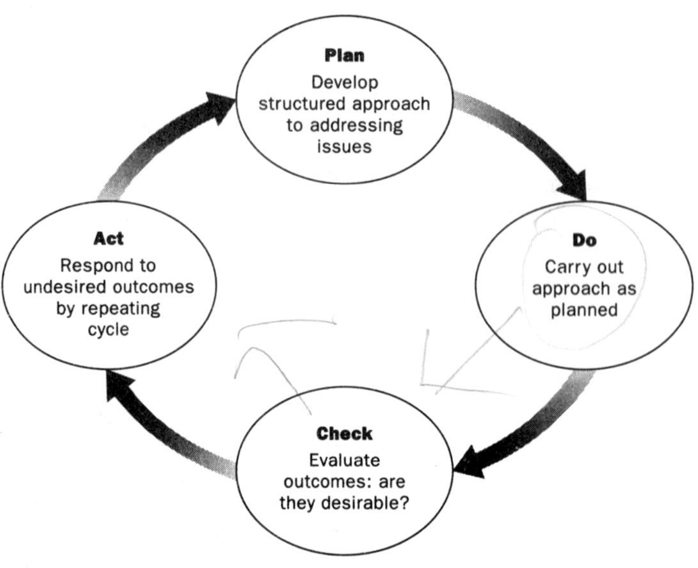

Source: Adapted and reprinted with permission from THE MEMORY JOGGER PLUS+, copyright 1989, GOAL/QPC, Methuen, MA 01844.

Outsourcing

It is impossible for a firm to excel in *all* areas. Where the firm itself cannot excel at a particular function, it may choose to outsource the function to a firm that does. Outsourcing traditionally referred to the practice of purchasing material from an external supplier. Today, this practice is regularly applied not just to materials, but to entire functions.[12] For instance, Westinghouse excels at *making* appliances, but it discovered that transportation companies had more expertise and such huge economies of scale that Westinghouse could never be more than a second-best alternative for *delivering* appliances. In order to improve the overall value offered to its customers, Westinghouse found it wise to outsource the entire delivery function, entering into a long-term agreement with transportation specialists for deliveries of Westinghouse's products.

The list of functions firms are willing to outsource has grown to include virtually any business activity. This includes functions that have historically been viewed as part of the very heart of most businesses. For instance, NeXT, a leading innovator in the microcomputer industry, relied upon the German company, FrogDesigns, for design of the physical appearance of its computer. Nike outsources virtually all the production of its athletic shoes and sportswear. Outsourcing leaves NeXT and Nike free to concentrate their efforts on the tasks at which they can excel.

It is increasingly common for the most competitive organizations to apply the "best in class" criteria to deciding where to turn for every function: if a given department is not the best in its class in terms of its quality, efficiency, and delivery, they will outsource the function to whomever is. Application 5.2 gives an example of this practice.

Application 5.2

Outsourcing to Get the "Best in Class"

It may be surprising to think that companies can afford to outsource when they have similar items or services provided by departments within their organizations. However, in a competitive marketplace, there is no room to settle for second best. This attitude is well illustrated by the history of one electronic instruments firm that outsourced several key items, all various models of the same integrated circuits the company made in-house in several of its own divisions.

A particular division began "shopping" for integrated circuit (IC) suppliers internally, where it had fourteen sister divisions, each of which could have conceivably supplied at least some of the various items needed. However, when the division making the purchases evaluated the sample parts these in-house sources supplied, they found the quality of parts from four of the suppliers to be unacceptable. Five other suppliers offered parts of marginal quality, inferior to ICs from outside sources, and the remaining five suppliers could not supply all of the different models needed.

The quality of the ICs would, in large part, determine the overall quality of the finished product, so the division decided it had no alternative but to use the best available suppliers, even though it obviously meant using outsiders. But historically, this division had been one of the top five customers of the sister divisions it was now refusing to do business with. The five marginal suppliers were especially incensed, because on average, they had improved their yield (the percent of acceptable parts) by a factor of nearly 100 (not 100 percent better, but 100 *times* better) in just the last 4 years. The purchasing division countered by explaining that during the same 4 years, the best competition had improved their yields by 120 times.

So much was at stake that the issue became a conflict, and high-level managers were called in to mediate. In light of the competition the business faced, they concluded that they could not afford the luxury of using anything but the best possible sources of supply, and they agreed to outsource the needed items. Each of the divisions whose parts were rejected set to work with massive efforts to outpace the competition, and in 3 years, they became the "best in class" supplier of the ICs they produced.

STRATEGIC DEVELOPMENTS IN SIX CRITICAL FUNCTIONS

What changes are occurring because of the drive for continuous improvement of customer value? We shall explore this question by looking at six of the many functional areas in a firm: marketing, operations, research and development, accounting, purchasing, and human resource management. This sample will show us how changes in the approach to functional-level management are giving it greater strategic importance.

Marketing: Adapting to the "Age of Diversity"

In industry after industry, what was once correctly viewed as a single, homogeneous mass market is splintering into a diverse set of smaller specialty markets.[13] For instance, the trend toward greater product diversity became obvious in the automobile industry in the early 1980s, when the number of categories of trucks and vans more than doubled.[14] In the last decade, the same trend has reshaped the publishing industry, with the number of magazines for sale in the United States nearly tripling (to 3,000), and the number of special-interest newsletters doubling (to 4,000).[15] This type of industry evolution is creating the "age of

Application 5.3

Montgomery Ward Adapts to the "Age of Diversity"

When Bernard Brennan became CEO of Montgomery Ward & Co. in 1985, he took over a retailing business that was struggling to compete with low costs in various segments of the industry. Operations included a department store, a catalog, and a discount chain; all were losing market share to increasingly aggressive and successful specialty stores. These specialty stores focused on a diverse set of market niches—a reflection of the emerging "age of diversity." Brennan realized that he had to adapt his firm to the changing marketplace. He set about establishing what he considered to be the key requirements of a specialty retailing strategy: brand names, compelling assortments, value pricing, and excellent service.

Brennan began the transformation by shutting down the catalog and discount businesses, raising $1.5 billion in working capital. This he used to reduce debt and invest in specialty stores. To test his concept, he gutted a 40,000-square-foot full-line department store, and refurbished it as two specialty stores, Home Ideas and Electric Avenue. An immediate success, the two stores quickly generated more sales than the full-line operation ever had. Furthermore, the margins in the specialty stores were better. Based on this experiment, Brennan eventually replaced the traditional businesses with six specialty stores in "power categories."

Brennan also wanted Montgomery Ward to be much faster about moving its products from the manufacturer to the customer. To support its new marketing strategy, the company completely revamped its logistics function. A $50 million investment in an electronic ordering and inventory control system allowed the company to establish what is called the "fast flow" system. Four million square feet of warehouse space was replaced by just two small warehouses serving the entire corporation's needs. More than 70 percent of all items were never warehoused—they moved directly from the manufacturer to the store shelf. The amount of storage space in retail outlets was reduced from one-third of the total building space to only 15 percent. Total savings from the new logistics program amounted to over $100 million in just the first 3 years.

Montgomery Ward is proving that traditional mass marketers can adapt to the age of diversity, but it requires more than just changing marketing—it demands a rethinking of the entire business.

Source

Johnson, J. L. (1989, September). The remaking of Montgomery Ward. *DM, 17,* 25.

diversity," a development with profound strategic implications.[16] Application 5.3 discusses an example of the impact of increasing customer diversity on mass merchandising.

To capitalize on the specialized needs of a splintered market, more firms are willing to serve a narrow market niche:

- Carport, Inc., thrives in the fiercely competitive parking lot business by offering customers ultra-deluxe service. Focusing strictly on airport customers, Carport drives them to and from their appropriate gates, checks their luggage, and takes care of having their car serviced, washed, and waxed while they are out of town.
- McGraw-Hill (publisher of this book) has pioneered the process of customizing textbooks. Faculty can order the specific materials they want included in their own unique edition of a book, and a computerized production system will have it in the campus bookstore within days.
- Recent growth in the mail order merchandising industry is largely due to the proliferation of specialty firms providing unparalleled service to extremely narrow market

segments. The Right Start, Inc., targets its catalog strictly toward the parents of newborns and toddlers. This company unconditionally guarantees the quality of every item it sells, offers 24-hour toll-free ordering 365 days a year, and provides next day delivery and free delivery on orders of five or more items. This level of service is hard to surpass, but the company tops it all by guaranteeing that its prices are the lowest.

The implications of the age of diversity affect not just marketing departments, but virtually every business function.[17] As Regis McKenna, the marketing genius behind many of the most successful companies to come out of Silicon Valley, explains: "Whatever method a company may use, the purpose is the same: to get the entire company to focus on the fragmented, ever-evolving customer base." McKenna emphasizes that a *companywide* marketing orientation is increasingly important because markets are being segmented on so many different bases: customer types, product niches, customer services, and so forth. With changes taking place on so many different fronts, firms cannot assume that any one department, such as marketing, can keep up. Other departments might be the key to defining a major new market opportunity. The R&D department might introduce the next generation of computer chips, or the distribution department might discover that people will buy fresh flowers in grocery stores.

Because customers will have more options and can be more fickle, flexible manufacturing has become more important as a means of customizing products to suit individual customer requirements. Within marketing, intensified promotional efforts targeted to broadly defined traditional markets now run the danger of becoming "white noise," as they offer less perceived differentiation for similar products.

Perhaps the single most important change is the role market share (your sales volume relative to the competition's) plays in marketing strategy. At one time, many considered market share to be *the* key to success, and many firms held being number 1 or number 2 in terms of market share as one of their most important goals.[18] Their reasoning was based on market share's link to cost. In many industries, economies of scale and experience effects, both associated with large-volume production, were considered vital in lowering costs. Because volume was seen as critical to cost, market share became a critical goal for marketing.

However, in the age of diversity, firms cannot rely on cost control through high volume as the foundation of their strategy for two reasons.[19] First, there are many market segments in which cost is not the primary consideration in purchasing decisions. Second, there are numerous cases in which some of the lowest-volume niche firms also have the lowest costs.

In such markets, there are fewer chances for dominating a mass market, and there are more opportunities for healthy profits in smaller market segments. Consider the case of IBM in the personal computer market. As shown in Exhibit 5.4*a*, IBM was the clear market leader in 1984, with a 31 percent market share. Apple (with 16 percent) and half a dozen smaller competitors (with shares of 3 to 7 percent) accounted for another 43 percent of the market. The remaining 26 percent of the market was held by "other," a category of competitors too small to identify individually. According to theories of economies of scale and experience effects, IBM's advantage should have been unbeatable, because no one could compete with IBM on costs and price.

But in today's diverse markets, the advantages of size are minimized. The firms that actually competed successfully on the basis of costs and price were the so-called clone

EXHIBIT 5.4
The PC Market in 1984 and 1990

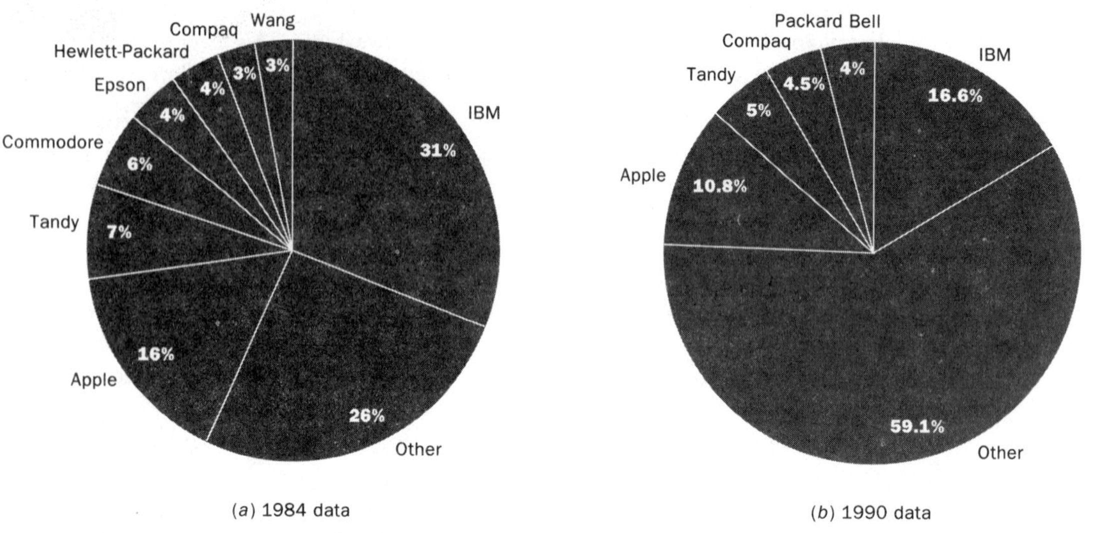

Sources: *(a)* McKenna, R. (1988, September–October). Marketing in an age of diversity. *Harvard Business Review*, pp. 88–95. *(b)* Breannan, L. (1991). Big blue's traditional customers may be taking a walk. *P.C. Week*, *8* (25), 163.

makers, smaller firms mimicking IBM's hardware. Meanwhile, other niche players chose not to compete on costs and price and instead appealed to customer segments with specialized computing needs. The result was that by 1986, rather suddenly, IBM found itself in second place behind "other." By then, IBM held only 26 percent of the market, while "other" held 31 percent, thanks to the hundreds of small, specialty manufacturers that had entered the market offering either lower-priced, or more specialized machines. IBM could not hope to counterattack on scores of different fronts simultaneously, and it found itself serving a narrowing middle-of-the road market. As shown in Exhibit 5.4*b*, by 1990 "other's" share had doubled while IBM's had fallen by nearly half. Similar cases are found in many other industries, suggesting that providing customer value must shift away from a pure cost/price orientation to one that considers all the customer's needs.

Operations: More than Just Making Products

In the last decade, U.S. firms have begun to utilize operations, sometimes known as production, as a strategic tool.[20] In the past, operations departments in the United States have emphasized efficiency, at the expense of product quality and the flexibility required to quickly deliver on changing customer needs.[21] Efficiency in an operations department is typically measured as throughput.[22] In a steel mill, for example, this would be the tons of steel produced per week. In order to maximize such throughput measures, managers did not place a priority on product quality. They were more intent on producing as much as they could as cheaply as they could. They built plants efficient at producing a specific product, but lacking the flexibility to deliver anything else, thereby crippling the firm when it came to adjusting to changing customer needs.

Henry Ford's famous remark, "They can have any color of car they want as long as it is

Application 5.4

Henry Ford, the Model T, and the Experience Curve

In 1909, when the lowest-priced car his company sold cost $850 and a set of tires alone cost $60, Henry Ford announced that he would soon be selling a new car, the Model T, for just $400. At the time of this announcement, he could not *make* a car for $400, let alone profitably *sell* one for that price. However, he believed that he might eventually do so, given enough experience. Low price gave him the volume necessary to gain the experience that would lead to the low costs, and this would make his low price profitable—the classic "riding the experience curve" strategy. (Note the implicit assumption in this circular reasoning: Successful competition is based primarily on low price.)

Ford was spectacularly successful at cutting costs. The corporation was vertically integrated backward into all the raw materials required to produce a car at that time. This included operations in coal and iron for steel production, rubber plantations for tires, forestry for the many wooden car parts, weaving mills for upholstery, and sand for glass production. Ford's River Rouge plant has seldom been matched in terms of production efficiency.

Eventually, the plant grew so efficient that iron ore arriving at one end of the plant left the other end 4 days later as a finished car. Inventories were cut by half and labor expenses were reduced by 60 percent, even though wages increased by more than a factor of 3. By 1925, the price of a Model T in real dollars was less than one-fifth what it had been in 1909 and Ford's market share had increased from 10 to 40 percent.

Meanwhile, annual profits rose from $15 million to more than $200 million. The cost reductions that were the foundation of this success were not the automatic results of volume production. Ford and his managers hammered relentlessly at costs in order to reduce them. One example, illustrative of the countless ways in which costs were reduced, is Ford's clever use of something other companies would call scrap. Car motors were crated to facilitate handling between the time they were produced and the time they were fitted to a chassis. Standard practice was to scrap the crate once the motor was removed. However, someone at Ford designed the crates so that they could be disassembled after being used as motor crates and reassembled for use as the frames attached to the backs of the trucklike Model T.

Ford's success in focusing on cost savings came at the expense of manufacturing flexibility. The plant, so efficient at producing one model, was incapable of producing anything else. In the mid 1920s, people began to prefer more enclosed, comfortable automobiles. As the market evolved, Ford's single-minded dedication to the Model T became a liability. General Motors and Chrysler were quick to respond to these changes, promptly introducing several new models each. Adapting to this new marketplace was traumatic for Ford. The plant had to be shut down for a year of retooling. Sixty thousand employees were laid off while 15,000 machine tools were replaced and another 25,000 were rebuilt. Meanwhile, the company lost $200 million. More importantly, the competition had a head start, a disadvantage that Ford has never completely overcome.

Source

Abernathy, W. J., & Wayne, K (1974, September–October). The limits of the learning curve. *Harvard Business Review, 52,* 109–119.

black," is an example of such efficiency-dominated thinking. Cars with black paint absorbed heat faster, dried more quickly, and therefore cost less to produce than cars of any other color. Although many customers would have paid handsomely for other colors, serving the complete set of customer needs was ignored and meeting the need for cheap automobiles was stressed above all else. (Application 5.4 discusses Ford's infamous emphasis on cost.)

Today, successful firms have come to realize that the operations function is responsible for a lot more than just efficiency.[23] Many firms are discovering that greater product quality and increased operating flexibility go hand in hand with reduced costs, resulting in greater speed in meeting customer needs.[24] Today we see a number of increasingly popular practices in operations (most have had their greatest acceptance in the production departments of manufacturing firms) that simultaneously improve quality, efficiency, and delivery capabilities. These include statistical process control (SPC), just-in-time (JIT) inventory control, and flexible manufacturing systems (FMS).

Statistical Process Control

SPC consists of a series of quantitatively based managerial practices originally designed to improve the quality of conformance.[25] Statistical analysis is used to monitor production processes to ensure that they are "in control"—operating in a way that yields predictable outcomes. In addition to improving quality, systems that operate predictably can help improve production efficiency through decreased rework, scrap, warranty expenses, and customer returns.[26] Predictability is also a key requirement of efficient delivery processes. If production systems are not predictable (in control), then it is necessary to maintain inventories to protect against unforeseen fluctuations in output anywhere in the production system. This approach to inventory control is sometimes called "just in case," and the higher inventory levels required to ensure on-time delivery increase costs. Having systems that are in control is a prerequisite of implementing a more efficient just-in-time inventory system.

Just-in-Time

JIT was originally developed to improve efficiency by reducing the cost of carrying inventory, but it also helps improve quality and delivery.[27] Where inventories are built up "just in case," they usually grow large enough to mask quality control problems. Good and bad quality output get mixed in inventory and the trail grows too cold to track down the source of quality problems. Producing inventory just in time means that so few items are in an inventory that quality is easily monitored. Delivery is improved because items are available to customers (either internal or external) just when they are needed and just in the quantities desired, without the added cost of carrying large inventories.[28]

Flexible Manufacturing Systems

FMS refers to highly computerized and automated production systems that are not limited to producing only a few products. These systems were originally designed to improve delivery capabilities by adjusting immediately to shifting demand.[29] But besides improving delivery, an FMS can increase efficiency through decreased labor costs and increased throughput.[30] In Japan, where managers have had the greatest success with FMS, it is now common for machines to shift from production of one product to another in less than a minute, whereas elsewhere, the same change might require hours of downtime. The great precision and reliability of the computer-controlled machines used in FMS can also increase quality. By utilizing tools and techniques like SPC, JIT, and FMS, the operations function is no longer limited to increasing efficiency, but plays a critical role in influencing overall customer value.

Research and Development: Integrating Technology for Greater Competitiveness

We live in an age dominated by technology.[31] It is estimated that 85 percent of all the scientists who have ever lived are now at work. Technological breakthroughs occur so rapidly that scientific training is quickly obsolete. For engineers trained in certain fields, the applicability of their college training is believed to decrease by 50 percent every 5 years. Technical advances in countless fields have altered what we produce, the way our businesses operate, and the way we manage. It is impossible to imagine a future in which technological advances are not a crucial part of business competition and success.[32]

In managing technology, we refer to developments that provide an entirely different way of doing something as *scientific advances*. Incremental improvements of a given technology are called *engineering advances*. So the electric light bulb's replacement of the kerosene lamp would be considered a scientific advance, but the fact that today's light bulbs are fifteen times more efficient than Thomas Edison's best model is the result of countless engineering advances.[33] Engineering advances are not limited to product improvements. They may also be aimed at improving the manufacturability of a product, the ease with which it can be repaired, its costs, and so on. In short, engineering is involved in virtually every aspect of successfully commercializing a given scientific breakthrough.[34]

Historically, firms have succeeded on the basis of either scientific breakthroughs or engineering advances. Today, it appears increasingly important to have *both*.[35] Texas Instruments became a highly profitable multibillion dollar corporation primarily on the basis of scientific advances. During its early years, much of TI's technology was so advanced that customers had few alternative sources for it and the company thrived on breakthroughs. However, this is no longer true. Many companies around the world have mastered the technological requirements of competing in the markets that made TI so successful. With knowledge of the technology so widespread, TI has found it impossible to compete solely on the basis of scientific advances.[36] During the 1980s, the firm suffered greatly reduced sales, and was profitable only 1 year in 5. It has become apparent to companies like TI that science must be integrated, through effective engineering, into an overall business effort that provides the customer with superior value.

But in other companies, the importance of integrating technology with the rest of the business has been overlooked, and a gap has developed between those responsible for scientific advances and those responsible for the rest of the business.[37] Effective engineering can close this gap by transforming the basic scientific advance into a product of value to customers, that operations can build, that field representatives can service, and so on. Effective engineering allows a company to build a business around a scientific breakthrough.[38]

Perhaps the most critical gap engineering must focus on is the one between the designers of new products and the makers of those products. It is not uncommon for R&D departments to design products without giving much thought to what it will cost to actually produce their design. Too often, the relationship between design and manufacturing is one in which designs are "thrown over the wall" and manufacturing is told "we designed one and got it to work—now you must build millions, and build them cheaply." IBM's development of the Proprinter is a good example of how the design-manufacture gap can be closed.[39]

When IBM first introduced its personal computer, its least expensive printer cost \$5,500—more than twice the cost of the computer itself! This printer was the result of many scientific advances, but was far too expensive to manufacture for success in the home PC market. A small cross-functional design team (combining product design specialists and experts in manufacturing) was assigned to design a printer that IBM could profitably produce for the PC market. At the time, the typical PC printer contained about 150 parts.

Because more parts means higher costs (associated with design, assembly, inventory, accounting, etc.), the team's goal was to greatly reduce the number of parts in their printer. They also were determined to eliminate all screws, pulleys, or springs requiring human adjustment in order to provide a printer that robots could easily assemble. The result was a printer that had only sixty-two parts, and that was so well-designed to facilitate manufacturing that both robotic and hand assembly were extremely easy and inexpensive.

This example highlights the necessary connections between R&D and operations,[40] but integrating technology into an overall business requires strong ties between R&D and other key functions, especially marketing.[41] In most organizations, the marketing department serves as R&D's link to the customer, and without this link, the R&D department runs the risk of designing products that it wants rather than those that meet customer needs. The point is clear: The science component of R&D must be well integrated with the other functions through engineering if the overall R&D effort is to achieve its greatest impact on customer value.[42]

Accounting: Better Information for Strategic Management

Accounting can be broadly categorized as either financial or managerial. Although financial accounting practices are still largely controlled by financial reporting requirements and an extensive body of tax laws, managerial accounting practices are more flexible. Changes in managerial accounting appear to be of great strategic importance.[43] To understand why this is true, it is important to first consider how most managerial accounting practices were developed.[44]

The managerial accounting systems found in most of today's businesses look very similar to those developed at the beginning of the industrial revolution, when the United States had a very different economy than it now has. At the turn of the century, roughly 75 percent of the economy was based on manufacturing, and within this sector, about 75 percent of all expenses were for direct labor. Accounting practices were explicitly designed for this environment. For instance, because overhead expenses were so small relative to labor expenses, rather than develop elaborate systems for precisely allocating overhead to particular products or production facilities, accountants simply prorated overhead according to direct labor. In today's business environment, it is services—not manufacturing—that account for about 75 percent of the economy in the United States. Moreover, within manufacturing, direct labor now may account for less than 25 percent of the total cost of goods sold. Overhead is much more likely than labor to be the largest single expense category in today's business world. Given such changes in the nature of business, it comes as no surprise that firms have found they must revamp their internal accounting practices as well. Failure to make such changes can mean that strategically important decisions are made using misleading accounting information.

Consider the experience of a firm that did not adapt its accounting practices to its business environment. The business, a small part of a larger corporation, produced a sophisticated electronic instrument in facilities near Chicago. Corporate overhead, which typically amounted to around 60 percent of its total expenses, was allocated on the basis of direct labor costs using a complicated computerized system. To avoid all possible labor expenses (and the corresponding overhead allocations), the business partially assembled the instrument in Mexico before shipping it to Chicago for testing and calibration. After initial calibration, the product was shipped back to Mexico for final assembly; then it was returned to headquarters for a second calibration, before shipment to distributors.

This system minimized overhead allocations by using cheaper labor for assembly, but it had several drawbacks. Product quality suffered as the delicate and finely tuned instruments were shipped back and forth to Mexico. Although a single unit could conceivably be built in less than 4 uninterrupted hours, delivery times were generally 7 months or longer. Real costs were unnecessarily high, even though the business was actually minimizing the costs on its books.

The corporation brought in a new management team to see if they could salvage the failing business. This new team found that direct labor accounted for only 3 percent of the total cost of producing the product, but the complex accounting system designed to measure direct labor amounted to 4 percent of the cost of goods sold! The company scrapped the labor-tracking system and allocated overhead on the basis of the amount of time it took to fill a customer's order.

This simple change made it prohibitively expensive to ship items to Mexico for assembly. Doing so increased the time required to produce the item, which raised overhead allocations by a similar amount. Now it made more sense to both assemble and test the instruments in Chicago. Within 6 months of making this change, delivery times were reduced to 14 days and product failures were reduced to a fraction of what they had been. The firm paid more for labor, but it remained one of the smallest expense categories with other savings more than making up for it.

This firm recognized that if the overall business is to be competitive, then its accounting function must be designed around today's business environment and must reflect today's concern for competitiveness.[45] This usually entails supplementing or replacing traditional accounting practices with new practices that match the current environment and support strategies for competitiveness.[46]

Purchasing: Toward Partnerships with Vendors

It is not unusual for the cost of purchased goods and materials to exceed 60 percent of a manufacturing firm's total cost of goods sold. A category of expenses this large is obviously of strategic importance, and firms are finding it useful to adopt new approaches toward purchasing.[47] As a result, what was once purchasing is now more akin to "vendor relations."[48] Traditional purchasing emphasized multiple sources and contracting for supplies on the basis of price bids as a means of encouraging competition between suppliers. Today, leading purchasing departments are relying on single vendors for even their most important supplies, and rather than selecting their suppliers through price competition alone, these firms seek out a small number of suppliers with which they hope to build lasting business relationships.

Plus, a leading manufacturer of memory devices for microcomputers, provides a specific example of these changes.[49] Plus managers decided that they could not manage the manufacturing part of their business as well as they felt was necessary in order to complement the other key functions. They decided to outsource the manufacturing and began looking for firms that specialized in supplying the sort of electromechanical devices Plus wanted built. They evaluated potential suppliers on the basis of trust and the potential for a strong partnership, quality, delivery capability and timing, and finally, aggressive pricing.

Once they found the most promising supplier, Plus set about developing a long-term relationship with that firm, treating it as other firms might treat a partner in a joint venture. Plus explicitly avoided the sort of cutthroat bargaining sessions which characterize some negotiations with suppliers, arguing that such practices were demeaning to everyone involved as well as damaging toward efforts to create a partner-to-partner working relationship. The emphasis of most negotiations was to have both parties understand what the other needed in order to hold up its end of the partnership while making a profit. In approaching this and other suppliers, Plus usually went into negotiations with a price request 20 to 30 percent less than the standard street price for the items they were seeking. Vendors were often put off by this request, until they realized that they were guaranteed to be a sole source. Plus managers then showed the vendor enough of the Plus business plan to convince them that the company would have a large volume of business. Finally, Plus offered to help suppliers figure how to make the item profitably at the price Plus had budgeted. All the while, the idea of the partnership was treated as if it were "kind of holy," to quote one Plus manager.

With this effort, Plus effectively extended its organizational boundaries to include its suppliers. Relationships between Plus managers and the managers of its suppliers were stronger than those typical of many departments within the same company. This effort to recruit managers within other organizations to be part of the Plus team went to extremes that other companies might consider unreasonable. For example, managers actually went three layers deep in the supply chain, visiting vendors of their vendors to get everyone critically involved in their project on board. For Plus, the effort clearly paid off. Plus was the first firm to put its new memory device on the market. Although the market was soon flooded with dozens of similar devices, the efficiency and quality of its suppliers allowed Plus to hold 65 to 70 percent of the market against these later entrants. In developing such strong cross-organizational relationships with vendors, purchasing departments in firms like Plus are taking on added strategic significance.

Human Resource Management: Building Organizational Capabilities

Nowhere are recent changes in functional-level management practices more dramatic than those in managing personnel, sometimes called human resource management (HRM).[50] These changes are both facilitated and required by changes occurring in many of the other functions.[51] In the past, many businesses, and in some cases entire industries, were well known for their hard-nosed, adversarial approach to managing labor. HRM's function was to hire the required laborers and to negotiate with the unions to hold wages and benefits as low as possible. The attitude at many factories was once typified by statements such as "Check your brain at the door" and "We hired you for your muscle, not your mind." In short, the work force was treated as if it had little to contribute to the business other than physical labor. Today, the work force is more likely to be viewed as a crucial source of competitive advantage.[52] Consider the exemplary human resource management described in Exhibit 5.5 and the following examples:[53]

- Northern Telecom now considers labor expenses to be a fixed investment, rather than a variable expense. The company believes that so much is invested in training its work force, and that workers have become so skilled, that they are far too valuable for the company to consider laying off workers in response to a decline in volume. Labor is now treated as a component of overhead.

EXHIBIT 5.5
Traditional and Emerging Ideas of Human Resource Management

Traditional	Emerging
Emphasis solely on physical skills	Emphasis on total contribution to the firm
Expectation of predictable, repetitious behavior	Expectation of innovative and creative behavior
Comfort with stability and conformity	Tolerance of ambiguity and change
Avoidance of responsibility and decision making	Accepting responsibility for making decisions
Training covering only specific tasks	Open-ended commitment: broad continuous development
Emphasis placed on outcomes and results	Emphasis placed on processes and means
High concern for quantity and throughput	High concern for total customer value
Concern for individual efficiency	Concern for overall effectiveness
Functional and subfunctional specialization	Cross-functional integration
Labor force seen as unnecessary expense	Labor force seen as critical investment
Work force is management's adversary	Management and work force are partners

- Saturn completely rewrote the automobile industry's typical labor-management agreement in establishing itself as a new General Motors division. The new agreement specifies that labor and management will share responsibility for many of the tasks they held individually in the past. For instance, both groups have input as to how work is to be scheduled. In fact, the list of shared responsibilities of Saturn managers and United Auto Workers union officials is much longer than the list of either group's individual responsibilities.
- Texas Instruments has implemented a plan calling for 100 percent involvement of its employees as part of a companywide quality improvement effort. Results to date show impressive returns, indicative of the contributions employees can make if given the right opportunities. At one of the plants leading in this movement, over 60 percent of all hourly workers implemented ten or more of their own ideas for better performance. While only half of the more than 7,000 total ideas had their impact on profitability quantified (employees are not required to quantify cost savings in order for their ideas to be implemented) those that were quantified provided more than $7 million of additional profits. Note the significance here: TI has over fifty plants, and the improvements mentioned here were for just one plant in just one year.
- Realizing the need to develop the potential of both their labor force and their managerial teams, corporations are investing millions of dollars in continuing education and management development programs. Motorola's programs have become a "university" with a multimillion dollar annual budget. Xerox invested $125 million in one corporationwide development program aimed at educating *all* its employees, management and labor alike, in using an identical set of problem-solving tools.[54]

These examples clearly show that some American managers have come to see their employees as important sources of expertise.[55] As a result of this change, these firms, and others like them, now have an entirely different set of expectations for employees. If employees are to have increasingly vital roles to play in determining the competitiveness of our firms, then managing our human resources will obviously be of greater strategic importance.

Summary

Management at the functional level is critically important to the successful strategic management of the firm because it is at this level that the organization's work is actually accomplished. The numerous functions, or departments, comprising a firm's value chain determine its ability to gain and hold an overall competitive advantage. Each function has a potentially vital role to play in contributing to overall customer value by managing the quality, efficiency, and delivery of its own output. The combination of these various capabilities within functional departments determines the firm's overall competitive position in terms of its differentiation, cost, and response time.

The importance of each function in creating customer value can best be seen in the idea that every department both *is* a customer and *has* customers. Furthermore, virtually every function has both *internal* and *external* customers and suppliers. This is a challenging situation that makes adoption of a strategic perspective particularly appropriate to managing individual functions.

The appropriate standard of performance for functions is one of continuous improvement, always trying to be "best in class." Striving to remain the best in class requires continuous improvement, a process sometimes called kaizen. Benchmarking and experimentation are important practices for facilitating continuous improvement. However, when firms realize that they cannot hope to be best in class in every possible department, they may decide to outsource the function to a firm that specializes in it.

Ideas about what practices constitute best in class performance are changing dramatically for several key business functions. Marketing is adapting to greater diversity and increasingly fragmented markets. Operations is focusing on more than just making low-cost products in high volume. Accounting is developing new systems for providing strategists with better financial information. Purchasing is placing much greater emphasis on establishing effective partnership arrangements with key suppliers. Research and development is placing greater emphasis on integrating a full range of technological skills into the overall business operation. Personnel is increasingly concerned with tapping the full range of expertise resident in the work force, rather than just concentrating on performance of physical labor.

Notes

1. Dertouzos, M. L., Lester, R. K., & Solow, R. M. (1989). *Made in America: Regaining the productive edge.* Cambridge, MA: MIT Press; also Band, W. A. (1991). *Creating value for customers: Designing and implementing a total corporate strategy.* New York: Wiley.
2. Shapiro, B. P. (1988, November–December). What the hell is market-oriented? *Harvard Business Review, 66,* 119. Writing much earlier, C. E. Summer identified the "law of subdisciplinization." See Summer, C. E. (1959, January). The managerial mind. *Harvard Business Review,* pp. 25–31.

3. Garvin, D. A. (1988). *Managing quality: The strategic and competitive edge.* New York: Free Press.
4. For further discussion of the critical importance of the quality of design, see Noori, H. (1989, November). The Taguchi methods: Achieving design and output quality. *Academy of Management Executive, 3,* 322–326.
5. Takeuchi, H., & Quelch, J. A. (1983, July–August). Quality is more than making a good product. *Harvard Business Review, 61,* 139–149.
6. Melcher, R. A. (1990, October 22). A new era for auto quality. *Business Week,* pp. 84–96.
7. Treece, J. B. (1991, May 27). Getting mileage from a recall. *Business Week,* pp. 38–39.
8. For an in-depth look at Japanese management techniques, look at Schonberger, R. J. (1982). *Japanese manufacturing techniques.* New York: Free Press, and Suzaki, K. (1987). *The manufacturing challenge: Techniques for continuous improvements.* New York: Free Press. A specific example of the Japanese approach to management is given in Manji, J. F. (1989, October). The Toyota touch. *Automation,* pp. 42–44.
9. Imai, M. (1986). *Kaizen—the key to Japan's competitive success.* New York: Random House.
10. Pryor, L. S. (1989, November–December). Benchmarking: A self-improvement strategy. *The Journal of Business Strategy, 10,* 28–32.
11. Deming, W. E. (1985, Spring). The roots of quality control in Japan. *Pacific Basin Quarterly,* pp. 3–4.
12. Quinn, J. B., Doorley, T. L., & Paquette, P. C. (1990, Winter). Technology in services: rethinking strategic focus. *Sloan Management Review,* pp. 79–87. For insightful discussions of the strategic implications of outsourcing, see Bettis, R. A., Bradley, S. P., & Hamel, G. (1992, February). Outsourcing and industrial decline. *The Executive, 6,* 7–22; Welch, J. A., & Nayak, P. R. (1992, February). Strategic sourcing: A progressive approach to the make-or-buy decision. *The Executive, 6,* 23–31.
13. Swenson, C. A. (1988, January–February). How to sell to a segmented market. *The Journal of Business Strategy,* pp. 18–22.
14. Nevens, T. M., Summe, G. L., & Uttal, B. (1990, May–June). Commercializing technology: What the best companies do. *Harvard Business Review,* pp. 154–163.
15. Hapoienu, S. L. (1990, November–December). The rise of micromarketing. *The Journal of Business Strategy,* pp. 37–42; Ivy, M. (1991, September 16). Be a media mogul—start a newsletter. *Business Week,* pp. 120–121.
16. McKenna, R. (1988, September–October). Marketing in an age of diversity. *Harvard Business Review, 66,* 88–92.
17. For a more in-depth coverage of the strategic issues involved in marketing, see Cravens, D. W. (1987). *Strategic marketing.* Homewood, IL: Richard D. Irwin; and Day, G. S. (1984). *Strategic market planning.* St. Paul, MN: West.
18. Gale, B. T., & Sultan, R. G. M. (1975, January–February). Market share—a key to profitability. *Harvard Business Review, 53,* 97.
19. Lieberman, M. B. (1989, September–October). The learning curve, technology barriers to entry, and competitive survival in the chemical processing industry. *Strategic Management Journal, 10,* 431–447.
20. For more information about recent developments in manufacturing management, especially as they relate to strategic issues, see Gunn, T. G. (1987). *Manufacturing for competitive advantage: Becoming a world class manufacturer.* Cambridge, MA: Ballinger; Kotha, S., & Orne, D. (1989, May–June). Generic manufacturing strategies. *Strategic Management Journal, 10,* 211–

231; and King, R. A. (1988, September–October). Overcoming manufacturing myopia. *The Journal of Business Strategy,* pp. 60–62; Main, J. (1990, May 21). Manufacturing the right way. *Fortune, 121,* 54–64.

21. Hayes, R. H., & Jaikumar, R. (1988, September–October). Manufacturing's crisis: New technologies, obsolete organizations. *Harvard Business Review,* pp. 77–85; also De Meyer, A., Nakane, J., Miller, J. G., & Ferdows, K. (1989, March–April). Flexibility: The next competitive battle—the manufacturing futures survey. *Strategic Management Journal, 10,* 135–144.
22. For a discussion of the similarities and differences of operations in service firms versus manufacturing firms see Chase, R. B., & Erikson, W. J. (1988, August). The service factory. *The Academy of Management Executive, 2,* 191–196; as well as Chase, R. B., & Garvin, D. A. (1989, July–August). The service factory. *Harvard Business Review, 67,* 61–69.
23. Hayes, R. H., Wheelwright, S. C., & Clark, K. B. (1988). *Dynamic manufacturing: Creating the learning organization.* New York: Free Press.
24. Blackburn, J. D. (1991). *Time-based competition: The next battle ground in American manufacturing.* Homewood, IL: Richard D. Irwin.
25. Ishikawa, K. (1985). *What is total quality control? The Japanese way.* Englewood Cliffs, NJ: Prentice-Hall.
26. Groocock, J. M. (1986). *The chain of quality: Market dominance through product superiority.* New York: Wiley.
27. Schmenner, R. H. (1988, Fall). The merit of making things fast. *Sloan Management Review,* pp. 11–17.
28. Hall, E. (1989, November). Just-in-time management: A critical assessment. *The Academy of Management Executive, 3,* 315–318; Karmarkar, U. (1989, September–October). Getting control of just-in-time. *Harvard Business Review, 67,* 122–131.
29. Witt, C. E. (1989, October). Flexibility: Sun's shining example. *Material Handling Engineering, 44,* 42–46.
30. Jaikumar, R. (1986, November–December). Postindustrial manufacturing. *Harvard Business Review, 64,* 69–76.
31. More on the impact of technology, especially on its strategic impact, can be found in Burgelman, R. A., & Maidique, M. A. (1988). *Strategic management of technology and innovation,* Homewood, IL: Richard D. Irwin; Horwitch, M. (Ed.). (1986). *Technology in the modern corporation: A strategic perspective.* New York: Pergamon Press.
32. Franko, L. G. (1989, September–October). Global corporate competition: Who's winning, who's losing, and the R&D factor as one reason why. *Strategic Management Journal, 10,* 449–474.
33. Other examples of evolutionary and revolutionary advances are given in Foster, R. N. (1986). *Innovation: The attacker's advantage.* New York: Summit Books.
34. Baba, Y. (1989, January–February). The dynamics of continuous innovation in scale-intensive industries. *Strategic Management Journal,* pp. 89–100.
35. Gomory, R. E., & Scmitt, R. W. (1988). Science and product. *Policy Forum,* pp. 1131–1203.
36. Clark, K. B. (1989, November–December). What strategy can do for technology. *Harvard Business Review, 67,* 94–98.
37. Kuwahara, Y., Okada, O., & Horikoshi, H. (1989, June). Planning research and development at Hitachi. *Long Range Planning, 22,* 54–63.
38. Nevens, Summe, & Uttal (Ref. 14), loc. cit.
39. This example is taken from Gomory, R. E. (1989, November). From the "ladder of science" to the product development cycle. *Harvard Business Review, 67,* 99–105.

40. For similar examples, see Whitney, D. E. (1988, July–August). Manufacturing by design. *Harvard Business Review, 66,* 83–91.
41. Erickson, T. J., Magee, J. F., Roussel, P. A., & Saad, K. N. (1990, Spring). Managing technology as a business strategy. *Sloan Management Review,* pp. 73–78.
42. Hauser, J. B., & Clausing, D. (1988, May–June). The house of quality. *Harvard Business Review,* pp. 63–73.
43. Shank, J. K. (1989, Spring). Strategic cost management: New wine, or just new bottles? *Journal of Management Accounting Research, 1,* 47–65.
44. Johnson, H. T., & Kaplan, R. S. (1987). *Relevance lost: The rise and fall of management accounting.* Boston: Harvard Business School Press.
45. See other developments in Hergert, M., & Morris, D. (1989, March–April). Accounting data for value chain analysis. *Strategic Management Journal, 10,* 175–188.
46. Cooper, R. (1989, January–February). You need a new cost system when. . . . *Harvard Business Review, 67,* 77–82; also Kaplan, R. S. (1988). One cost system isn't enough. *Harvard Business Review, 66,* 61–66; Cooper, R., & Kaplan, R. S. (1988, September–October). Measure costs right: Make the right decisions. *Harvard Business Review, 66,* 96–103.
47. Kraljic, P. (1983, September–October). Purchasing must become supply management. *Harvard Business Review,* pp. 109–117.
48. See Heinritz, S. F. (1986). *Purchasing: Principles and applications* (7th ed.). Englewood Cliffs, NJ: Prentice-Hall; also Lyons, T. F., Krachenberg, A. R., & Henke, J. W., Jr. (1990, Spring). Mixed motive marriages: What's next for buyer-supplier relations? *Sloan Management Review,* pp. 29–36; and Finkin, E. F. (1988, January–February). Developing profitable purchasing strategies. *The Journal of Business Strategy,* pp. 48–51, for in-depth discussion of current purchasing practices.
49. Wheelwright, S. C., & Langowitz, N. S. (1989, July–August). Plus development corporation: Joint venturing a breakthrough product. *Planning Review, 17,* 6–20.
50. For detailed discussion of how modern personnel management is linked to strategy, see Lengnick-Hall, C. A., & Lengnick-Hall, M. L. (1988, July). Strategic human resource management: A review of the literature and a proposed typology. *Academy of Management Review,* pp. 454–470; Baird, L., & Meshoulam, I. (1988, January). Managing two fits of strategic human resource management. *Academy of Management Review,* pp. 116–128; Schuler, R. S., & Jackson, S. E. (1987, August). Linking competitive strategies with human resource management practices. *Academy of Management Executive,* pp. 207–219; and Boyett, J. H., & Conn, H. B. (1991). *Workplace 2000: The revolution reshaping American business.* New York: Dutton, The Penguin Group.
51. For a discussion of the interrelated nature of organizational change, see Kilmann, R. H. (1984). *Beyond the quick fix: Managing five tracks to organizational success.* San Francisco & London: Jossey-Bass.
52. Ulrich, D., & Lake, D. (1991). Organizational capability: Creating competitive advantage. *Academy of Management Executive, 5,* 77–92.
53. The examples given in the text are based on the authors' firsthand experience. Other examples are given in Smith, A. (1989, February). The "people factor" in competitiveness. *Executive Speeches, 3,* 13–17.
54. Kerr, J. L., & Jackofsky, E. F. (1989, Summer). Aligning managers with strategies: Management development versus selection. *Strategic Management Journal,* pp. 157–170.
55. Semler, R. (1989, September–October). Managing without managers. *Harvard Business Review, 67,* 76–84.

CHAPTER 6

Strategic Management at the Corporate Level: Diversification for Stockholder Value

In our framework of strategy formulation, a corporation is a firm that consists of more than one business. The General Electric corporation, for instance, is comprised of several businesses including consumer electronics, heavy locomotives, and aerospace contracting. Firms that operate more than one business are referred to as being *diversified.* In this chapter, we will consider the role of diversification in the overall strategic management of the firm, why corporations diversify, and how diversification is best managed.

The chapter has five sections. The first considers the role of diversification in creating various benefits for the firm and its owners. The second explores how managerial behavior can limit the benefits stockholders receive from diversification. In the third and fourth sections we review the most common forms of diversification and cover the means by which firms diversify, respectively. The final section discusses divestments, an element of diversification often overlooked.

After reading this chapter, you will understand:

- The role of corporate diversification in creating value for stockholders that they cannot obtain for themselves
- How corporate managers increase stockholders' wealth by building on the organization's core competences
- How the benefits that managers and stockholders receive from diversification may conflict
- The various forms that diversification can take: vertical, horizontal, and global
- The most common means of diversifying: acquisitions, strategic alliances, and internal development

EXECUTIVE INTERVIEW

Ralph S. Larsen
Chairman and CEO
Johnson & Johnson

Ralph S. Larsen is chairman and chief executive officer of Johnson & Johnson, the largest health care products company in the world. Larsen began his career with Johnson & Johnson in 1962 as a manufacturing trainee. After holding a series of positions in both manufacturing and distribution, he became vice president for marketing in the subsidiary that makes Tylenol products. Before assuming his current position in 1989, Larsen was division president and chairman of Johnson & Johnson's consumer sector. Under Larsen's leadership, Johnson & Johnson's worldwide sales reached a record $11.2 billion in 1990.

Johnson & Johnson competes in many different health care product areas including consumer, professional, and pharmaceutical products. What do you see as Johnson & Johnson's core competences and how does the firm build on them?

We are a leader in consumer markets with a variety of baby products, adhesive bandages, dental care products, analgesics, and pharmaceuticals ranging from oral contraceptives to antifungals to psychiatric compounds. The company serves the health care industry with such products as sutures, surgical instruments and dressings, eye care products, and blood pressure monitors. In order to keep serving this fast-changing market with innovative products, we invest steadily in new science and technology that can generate new products. Spending on R&D now totals more than $900 million annually. In recent years it has resulted in the first disposable contact lens, the first once-a-day nonsedating antihistamine, the first oral therapy for childhood lead poisoning and the first noncaloric sweetener created from sugar.

What is the role of the corporate office in creating stockholder value beyond what the business units could do themselves?

Johnson & Johnson is a highly decentralized family of companies that operates worldwide in a relatively autonomous way. The principal function of the corporate office is to provide oversight and coordination for these companies and their products, to ensure that the operating companies benefit from the resources and experiences of their sister companies, and to allow constituencies outside the company to better understand corporate policies and strategies. Ultimately, the corporate office is responsible for ensuring that the company is represented in all of the promising growth areas of health care and taking steps to fill in any gaps in strategic thinking or actions that might occur.

How does Johnson & Johnson encourage and reward entrepreneurship in its business units?

Each operating company is a highly specialized unit. Its job is to know its customer best and to understand, anticipate, and serve customer needs better than competitors. Management of our individual companies is charged with the responsibility of assessing the changing product technology, distribution, market dynamics, and customer needs, and making sure that the strategic plan of their company meets those needs. The people in individual operating companies have a stake in the success of their companies as well as Johnson & Johnson as a whole. They are encouraged and rewarded based on their ability to create new ways of meeting the needs of the market in which they specialize.

Are strategic alliances—the combination of two or more corporations to form a cooperative partnership—important for Johnson & Johnson? If so, what must be done to ensure their success?

We rely primarily on internal research and development to generate the new products required for future growth. But we recognize that no one company—and no one country—has a monopoly on innovative ideas and products. Accordingly, we have successfully made a number of strategic alliances with other companies to avail ourselves of their expertise. A good example is the joint venture we created with Merck & Co. to bring new nonprescription drugs to the market. It combines the consumer products marketing expertise of Johnson & Johnson with the pharmaceutical research ability of Merck. Another is the

Continued

relationship with the biotechnology firm, Chiron Corporation, which resulted in our bringing to market worldwide the first diagnostic test for hepatitis C. For strategic alliances to work, there must be a commonality of interest and we must provide something the other organization values—manufacturing know-how, marketing or sales skills, research and regulatory affairs knowledge, and so on.

THE ROLE OF DIVERSIFICATION

Corporate diversification is everywhere. The overwhelming majority of the Fortune 1,000 (the largest 1,000 corporations in the United States) are diversified—many of them to a very great extent. Companies like Johnson & Johnson, Time Warner, and Textron consist of dozens—even hundreds—of different businesses. Besides these corporate giants, many smaller firms, some with only a handful of employees, are also diversified. For example, the authors know of one relatively small family business which includes car washes, used car sales, an auto parts store, and a wrecker service—clearly a diversified corporation. Exhibit 6.1 gives a breakdown of the number and value of acquisitions by industry in 1990. These industries cover the map, making it clear that diversification is a pervasive phenomenon of modern business.

What is the strategic role of diversification? To some extent, stockholders do not need corporate-level managers in order to diversify their holdings. When corporate managers diversify the corporation, they are essentially investing stockholders' funds in an additional business. When Coca Cola bought Columbia Pictures, Coke stockholders found themselves owning both a soft drink producer and a movie production firm. Were the investors better off having Coke make the investment than they would have been had they invested

EXHIBIT 6.1
1990 Merger and Acquisition Activity by Industry

	Value (In Millions of Dollars)	***Number of Acquisitions***
Apparel and footwear	$ 669.8	49
Banking	9,523.1	407
Building materials	6,316.5	77
Business, professional, and social services	7,783.1	317
Chemicals	3,757.0	67
Communications	10,476.5	73
Computer and data processing	3,185.8	173
Computer and office equipment	3,398.6	83
Construction and real estate	753.7	65
Consumer products	4,240.3	77
Electrical and electronic equipment	4,420.5	146
Energy	9,290.9	146
Entertainment	15,631.5	48
Fabricated metals	1,222.0	63
Food and tobacco	9,068.7	94
Health care	10,661.5	191

Source: *Mergers & Acquisitions*, Philadelphia (1991, May–June).

equivalent funds in Columbia themselves? If corporate managers are not doing something for their stockholders that the stockholders cannot do for themselves, then the corporate managers are not adding much value to the stockholders' investments.

Imagine, for example, that 10,000 investors had $400 each to invest in stock. They each considered investing half in Superior, Inc., a strong, well-managed company, and half in Underdog, Ltd., a weak, poorly managed company. An alternative would be to invest everything in Superior and then have its corporate managers buy Underdog on their behalf. In the first case, where the investors each buy shares in both companies, the managers from Superior cannot contribute their talents to Underdog because they are still separate entities, although they do happen to be owned by the same people. In the latter case, the same people again own both companies, but because they have been combined into one corporation, it is now possible to have Superior managers go to work on Underdog. Corporate managers can now add value in a way that the individual investors cannot arrange through their individual efforts.

The corporation's value is ultimately determined by how well its various business units perform. Because high business-level performance depends on a sustained competitive advantage, corporate managers seek diversification moves that add businesses with competitive advantages or that improve the competitive advantages of their existing businesses.[1] Diversification that strengthens the value chain and increases competitive advantages is the best possible example of investing stockholders' funds in a way that individual investors cannot.[2] This is the standard we will use to evaluate the benefits of diversification.

EVALUATING THE BENEFITS OF DIVERSIFICATION

In this section, we will consider the five reasons most commonly given for diversifying. We will evaluate these reasons in light of our standard for good corporate management: creating value for stockholders that they cannot create for themselves. We will begin with the most powerful reasons for diversifying and then move on to those least defensible, but still commonly cited.

Capitalizing on Core Competences

Core competences are the most significant value-creating skills within a corporation. These skills can often be extended to products or markets beyond those in which they were originally developed.[3] This extension represents an excellent opportunity for diversification. Philip Morris is an example of a company that uses this tactic successfully. When considering diversification targets, Philip Morris realized that the core competence it had developed in marketing cigarettes could be applied in similar markets. Based on this idea, the company purchased Miller Brewing and then used the Philip Morris marketing muscle to move the Miller brand from seventh place to second in the market.

Any core competence that meets the following three requirements is a viable basis for the corporation to strengthen a new business unit:[4]

The core competence must translate into a meaningful competitive advantage. In other words, the competence must help the business establish some strength relative to its competition. Every link of the value chain (every key business function) is a viable basis for building on a core competence. For instance, Black & Decker has a core competence in small electrical motors and rechargeable batteries. On this basis, the firm has successfully diversified out of small power tools for woodworking into higher-margin items like electrical kitchen appliances, miniaturized vacuum cleaners, and rechargeable flashlights.

The new business must have enough similarity to existing businesses to benefit from the corporation's core competence. This does not necessarily mean that the products themselves must be similar. However, at least one element of their value chains must require similar skills in creating competitive advantage, in order for the corporation to capitalize on its core competences. An example is Coca-Cola's move into leisure clothing. At first glance, one might think that soft drinks and sweatshirts have little in common, but in an important strategic sense, they are in fact closely related; the marketing of both types of products can be based upon selling a trademark and an image as much as selling the product itself. In soft drinks, its core business, Coca-Cola emphasizes marketing as a key component of its value chain by building demand through strong customer awareness. Coke used this same expertise in marketing an image to successfully introduce a line of clothing bearing various Coca-Cola trademarks. In its first full year of business, Coca-Cola Clothes generated $100 million in wholesale revenues—impressive growth in any industry and by far the best growth in the clothing industry.[5]

The bundle of competences should be difficult for competition to imitate. If the skills being transferred are commonly available or easily replicated, they are unlikely to provide the basis of a sustainable competitive advantage.[6] An individual core competence need not be unique; rather, it is the *collection* of competences that should be unique, or at least difficult to replicate. For example, Canon, the Japanese diversified manufacturer, has demonstrated an unmatched ability to enter and dominate markets ranging from photocopiers and cameras to laser printers. Its dominance in these varied markets is based on mastery of technologies that are crucial to successful engineering and design in all these products. Canon is a world leader in its core competences of optics, imaging, and microprocessor controls. Other companies are good at each of these technologies, but Canon is arguably the best overall. This provides the company with a basis for diversification that competitors cannot easily match.

A corporation that builds on core competences utilizes skills that can be combined to strengthen value chains and build greater competitive advantages. This leads to *synergies* among business units whereby they are more productive together than they would be if functioning independently. The collection of skills used in this situation is largely intangible, but, as we discuss in the next section, corporations can also build synergies by sharing tangible resources.

Sharing Infrastructures

Infrastructures are tangible resources, such as production facilities, marketing programs, purchasing procedures, and delivery routes.[7] These are the basic "nuts and bolts" of any business, and the ability to share these resources can be an important benefit of diversification. An example of this is Procter & Gamble's sharing of delivery systems. P&G sells a wide range of products that are made in manufacturing facilities spread over an equally wide geographic range. Yet, many of these items share two characteristics: They are destined for the same retail outlets and they are fairly expensive to ship. Because of this, it is more efficient for P&G's various businesses to share delivery systems. Rather than send an entire truckload of cookies to a single retail outlet, P&G mixes its truckloads to provide the product blend that each customer desires. In this way, P&G can use one truck with a mix of items to do what otherwise might require a dozen trucks. In addition, because it is inefficient to ship "pure" loads of very light but bulky items (such as potato chips) or very dense goods (such as liquid detergent), P&G also saves on fuel bills and road taxes.

Note the two features that allow P&G to benefit from sharing infrastructures. First, the businesses have similar needs, that is, they use the same retail outlets. (Of course, without similar needs, businesses have no opportunity for sharing infrastructures.) Second, delivery expenses represent a significant part of the value chain for these products, so they help determine the competitiveness of P&G's products. Resource sharing must improve competitiveness if it is to be useful.

Balancing Financial Resources

Different businesses (even within the same corporation) are capable of generating dramatically different levels of cash. Some businesses produce much more cash than they need to continue operating, while others need much more than they can produce. Historically, much of the emphasis in managing diversified corporations has been placed upon efficiently balancing cash flows among the corporation's business units. By combining cash producers and cash users in the same corporation, managers can meet the needs of both.

In such a corporation, the sibling businesses are treated as a portfolio of investments, and cash flows are managed and balanced across the family of businesses, rather than merely within each individual business. This approach, called *portfolio management,* first became popular in the 1970s, when a number of leading corporations and consulting firms offered several similar frameworks to guide managers in allocating cash among diverse business units.[8] We will briefly consider three popular variations of portfolio management and then look at general benefits and limitations of this approach.[9] The various versions of the portfolio approach are commonly referred to by the labels of their grid's two axes: market growth and market share.

The Growth-Share Matrix

According to the growth-share matrix, developed during the 1970s by the Boston Consulting Group (BCG), two relatively simple factors predict whether an individual business will be a cash producer or a cash user: (1) the growth rate of the market within which the business competes and (2) its share of that market. Businesses in fast-growing markets probably have greater needs for cash to scale up production, open new facilities, advertise, develop new products, and so on. On the other hand, businesses in declining markets may have already lived through their peak periods of product demands, and are more likely to have sufficient assets for serving the present dwindling demand. Businesses in this situation generally produce considerable cash, but do not have a ready place to invest it. Thus, businesses in growing markets may need more cash than they have, while businesses in mature or declining markets may have more cash than they need.

Additionally, businesses with large market shares are more likely to enjoy economies of scale and greater experience curve benefits. Lower costs would mean higher profits and higher profits would mean greater cash flows. In short, the BCG framework suggests that higher market shares are associated with greater cash flows.

Exhibit 6.2 shows the combined effects of market growth and market share. The four cells of the matrix indicate different strategies.

Cash cows are expected to produce far more cash than they can usefully employ in-house. Such businesses are often "milked" to finance other businesses upon which the future of the corporation may depend. *Dogs* are businesses holding small shares of slow-growing (or even declining) markets. They are unlikely ever to become important sources of cash, and they may in fact be great users of cash for which there is little likely return. A strategy often suggested for such businesses is to "harvest" them by not investing in them and instead shifting cash flows to more promising businesses. *Problem children* have low market shares of rapidly growing markets. They represent a potential opportunity; if their market shares can be increased, they may become cash cows. However, if their market shares cannot be increased before market growth slows, they will in effect become dogs. Developing a strategy for problem children means either investing large sums in hopes of gaining a viable market share, or not investing and possibly missing a growth market. *Stars* are often the hope of the future. They currently hold large market shares in a rapidly growing market, so their cash flows may be minimal or even negative. The recommended strategy is to nurture them, maintaining their health and waiting for market growth to slow so that cash flows will increase. Theoretically, the cash-hungry stars will be transformed into cash-rich cows, which can be milked to nurture still another generation of businesses.

EXHIBIT 6.2
The Growth-Share Matrix

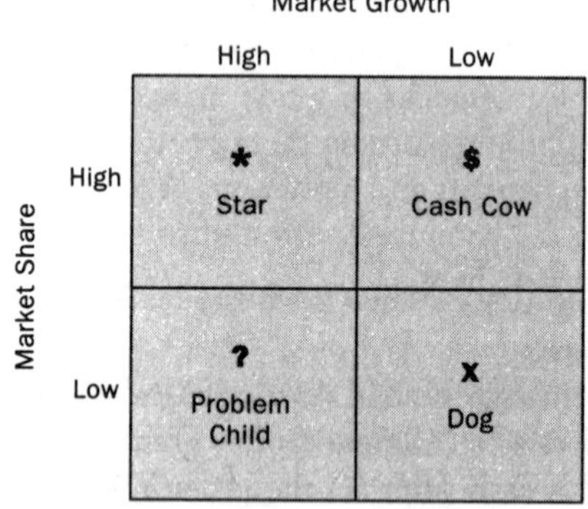

Description of Dimensions

Market Growth: Industry growth rate in constant dollars (dividing point is typically the GNP's growth rate)

Market Share: Sales relative to those of other competitors in the market (dividing point is usually selected to have only the two–three largest competitors in any market fall into the high market share region)

Source: The growth-share matrix was originally developed by the Boston Consulting Group.

The Market Life Cycle–Competitive Strength Matrix

Critics of the growth-share matrix contend that it fails to consider the wide range of factors affecting cash flow beyond market growth and market share. A somewhat more involved picture of the situation facing a business can be depicted by adding a judgmental assessment of the strategic business unit's overall competitive strength. A second refinement is to utilize the richer concept of the market life cycle as a replacement for market growth. Recall from Chapter 4 that growth rates tend to vary predictably across the stages of the market life cycle, but that the life cycle model depicts numerous strategic issues beyond just growth. The explicit consideration of the market life cycle found in this portfolio management framework provides a useful bridge between strategy formulation at the business level and strategy formulation at the corporate level. Exhibit 6.3 shows the cash flows and investment requirements implied by various combinations of competitive strength and market life cycle stages.

While the market life cycle–competitive strength framework is obviously richer than the growth-share matrix, its central message is the same. To see the relationship between

EXHIBIT 6.3
The Market Life Cycle–Competitive Strength Matrix

Stage of Market Life Cycle
Introduction Growth Maturity Decline

Competitive Strength
High
Moderate
Low

PUSH: Invest Aggressively
CAUTION: Invest Selectively
DANGER: Harvest

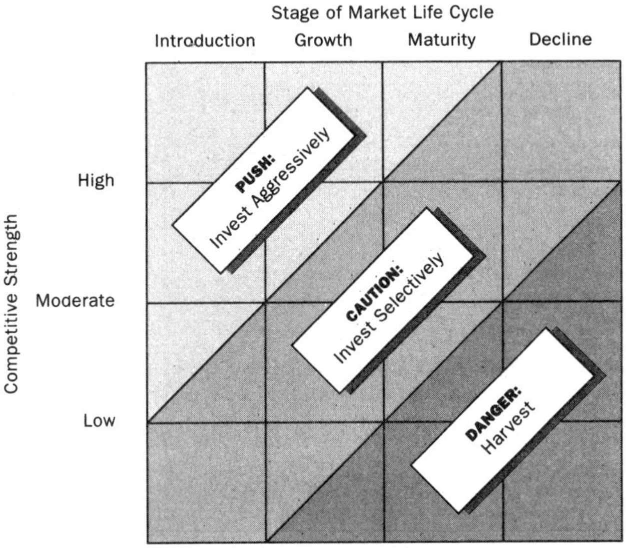

Description of Dimensions

Stage of Market Life Cycle: See Chapter 4

Competitive Strength: Overall subjective rating, based on a wide range of factors regarding the likelihood of gaining and maintaining a competitive advantage

Source: This type of matrix was originally developed by Arthur D. Little, a consulting firm that coupled the matrix to a comprehensive methodology for developing strategic plans.

these two frameworks, redraw the market life cycle–competitive strength matrix with the growth-share matrix superimposed. This will reveal the similarities of strategies suggested by the corresponding positions on the two grids. Cash cows will still be in the upper right quadrant, dogs in the lower right quadrant, and so on. The reason for this similarity is clear if you remember that market growth is closely linked to the market life cycle and market share is at once both a cause and an effect of competitive strength.

The Industry Attractiveness–Business Position Matrix

While the market life cycle–competitive strength matrix is more refined than the growth-share matrix, some have found that it still is limited in its coverage of important issues. An

EXHIBIT 6.4

Examples of Factors Considered in Constructing an Industry Attractiveness–Business Position Matrix

Industry Attractiveness

Bargaining power of suppliers/customers
- Relative size of typical players
- Numbers of each
- Importance of purchases from or sales to
- Ability to vertically integrate

Threat of substitute products/new entrants
- Technological maturity/stability
- Diversity of the market
- Barriers to entry
- Flexibility of distribution system

Nature of competitive rivalry
- Number of competitors
- Size of competitors
- Strength of competitors' corporate parents
- Price wars
- Competition on multiple dimensions

Economic factors
- Sales volatility
- Cyclicality of demand
- Market growth
- Capital intensity

Financial norms
- Average profitability
- Typical leverage
- Credit practices

Sociopolitical considerations
- Government regulation
- Community support
- Ethical standards

Business Position

Level of differentiation
- Advertising effectiveness
- Product quality
- Company image
- Patented products
- Brand awareness

Cost position
- Economies of scale
- Manufacturing costs
- Overhead
- Scrap/waste/rework
- Experience effects
- Labor rates
- Patented processes

Response time
- Manufacturing flexibility
- Time needed to introduce new products
- Delivery times
- Organizational flexibility

Financial strength
- Solvency
- Liquidity
- Breakeven point
- Cash flows
- Profitability
- Growth in revenues

Human assets
- Turnover
- Skill level
- Relative wage/salary
- Morale
- Managerial commitment
- Unionization

Public approval
- Goodwill
- Reputation
- Image

alternative, the broadest portfolio management framework we will consider, is the industry attractiveness–business position matrix. This approach considers the matters raised in the other two frameworks, and incorporates the wide range of other considerations, such as those shown in Exhibit 6.4.

Information about these factors are typically combined to reach a subjective evaluation of overall industry attractiveness and business position. The strategic implications suggested by combining the resulting evaluation of industry attractiveness and business position in a matrix are identified in Exhibit 6.5. It should be clear that while this framework entails the broadest possible set of considerations, it is fundamentally similar to the simpler frameworks described above.

These frameworks share three characteristics: (1) They consider some dimension(s) of both the external environment and internal capabilities of a business. (2) They simplify information about environmental conditions and business strengths by locating business units graphically on a two-dimensional matrix or grid. (3) A business unit's position in the matrix suggests its likely need for, or ability to provide, financial resources (cash). Given those commonalities, we can evaluate the usefulness of these portfolio management techniques as a group.

EXHIBIT 6.5
The Industry Attractiveness–Business Position Matrix

Business Position \ Industry Attractiveness	High	Medium	Low
High	Invest	Selective Growth	Up or Out
Medium	Selective Growth	Up or Out	Harvest
Low	Up or Out	Harvest	Divest

Description of Dimensions

Industry Attractiveness: Subjective assessment based on broadest possible range of external opportunities and threats beyond the strict control of management

Business Position: Subjective assessment of how strong a competitive advantage is created by a broad range of the firm's internal strengths and weaknesses

Source: This type of matrix was conceived by consultants at McKinsey and Company and managers at General Electric.

Benefits and Limits of Portfolio Management

Portfolio matrices offer a useful framework for considering potential differences among businesses in the same corporation, and experience shows that they offer several important benefits:[10] (1) They are good for communicating large amounts of information about individual business units and overall corporate plans. (2) They bring to focus important differences among businesses, and help illustrate the rationale behind corporate plans to invest funds in business A that have been obtained from business B. (3) They provide simple but useful guidelines for checking for consistency among business requests for resources and the likely opportunity for the business to use those resources effectively. (4) They suggest reasonable performance levels for business units facing the various strategic situations. (Obviously, the growth and profitability expected of a "star" is quite different from that expected of a "dog.")

While these benefits are important, portfolio management should not be considered the sole, or even the primary, basis for formulating corporate-level plans.[11] They are more appropriately used as tools that can help initiate a complete corporate strategy. Some of the most commonly cited problems follow:

- The simple matrices tend to trivialize strategic thinking. To be fair, this criticism should probably be laid at the feet of those who have misused them; they were never intended to replace careful thought, though in practice they sometimes have done so.
- It can be difficult to identify individual businesses.[12] There are no exact principles for deciding what constitutes a separate market or an individual product line. Should a beverage company treat its coffee and tea operations as two businesses or one?
- There is not enough time in the yearly planning cycle to allow detailed analysis of every business in many large diversified firms. Therefore, even the most ardent supporters of portfolio approaches to corporate management "fudge" a little. Firms usually have around thirty entities in their portfolios, regardless of how many businesses have to be combined to reach this manageable number.[13]
- Simple models are generally not very accurate. After two decades of use, it is now obvious that models such as the BCG matrix have occasionally led to inappropriate strategic moves because of this inaccuracy. For instance, one study reported that over half of all businesses that should have been cash users according to the BCG matrix were, in fact, cash providers.[14] On the other hand, roughly one-fourth of all businesses expected to be cash providers were, in fact, cash users. While similar studies have not been carried out for the other portfolio frameworks described here, it is unreasonable to expect that any framework that reduces a strategic situation to two dimensions will be highly accurate in its prescriptions.

Maintaining Growth

Another benefit of diversification is continued growth. Especially among larger firms, diversification is undoubtedly one of the most common sources of corporate growth. Using diversification, BASF, the giant German chemical company, was able to maintain a level of growth through the 1980s more typical of rapidly growing start-up businesses, even

EXHIBIT 6.6
Typical Tradeoff between Corporate Growth Rate and Corporate Profitability

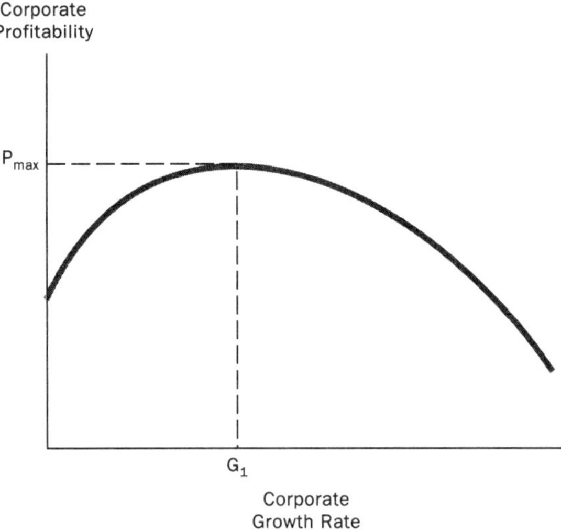

though it was a mature multibillion dollar multinational corporation. In the last half of that decade, BASF was growing at an average of 36 percent per year—roughly doubling in size every 2 years—from a base that was already huge.[15]

Is growth always desirable? There is considerable argument over the idea that to generate the best return on stockholder investments, corporations should pursue only moderate levels of growth, as depicted in Exhibit 6.6. Beyond this level, profitability is likely to decline as the pursuit of high growth levels drives the corporation into more marginal businesses, and the cost of operating the increasingly large corporation outstrips the growth in profits additional businesses might provide.

Reducing Risk

Corporate managers have sometimes tried to justify diversification on the basis of risk reduction.[16] To understand how diversification is related to risk, first note that different businesses respond differently to particular economic cycles: Demand for pleasure boats typically declines during a recession while demand for public transportation typically increases. We call businesses such as these two "countercyclical." By mixing such countercyclical businesses within the same diversified corporation, a bad year for one business can be offset by a better year for another business. In this way, the variability of the overall corporation's earnings would be reduced, and stockholder investment would be less risky.[17]

However, investors do not need corporate managers to achieve the risk-reducing effect. They can simply invest their individual funds in the different businesses (boat and bus manufacturers in this example) to achieve the same risk-reducing effect: A bad year for one of their investments will be offset by the improved performance of their other investment, and the risk associated with their overall portfolio of investments will be reduced. In fact, as we shall explain later in the chapter, individual investors can usually achieve this sort of risk reduction through diversification at a lower cost than corporate managers can. This being the case, diversification for the sake of risk reduction alone hardly meets the goal of having corporate managers create value for the investor in some way that the investor cannot accomplish alone.

MANAGERIAL BEHAVIOR THAT LIMITS THE BENEFITS OF DIVERSIFICATION

Diversification is complicated by the fact that the managers carrying it out do not always benefit in the same way that the corporation's owners do.[18] To appreciate this important point, it is necessary to understand the relationship between corporate managers and the corporation's stockholders. Theoretically, corporate managers are meant to act as the agents for the stockholders whose interests they are hired to represent.[19] However, an area of research known as *agency theory* leads us to ask whether managers are always able to act in the stockholders' best interests.[20]

Agency theory suggests that managers will not always place stockholders' interests above their own.[21] In fact, stockholders have been dubbed the "least important constituency" by some who have researched the way that corporate executives manage the diversification process.[22] In managing diversification, corporate managers face an ethical dilemma as they attempt to balance their own interests against those of stockholders.[23] For instance, stockholders often enjoy high profits from the sale of their stock when their firm is taken over. On the other hand, managers of firms that have been taken over often lose their jobs. Critics contend that corporate managers sometimes protect their jobs by using an antitakeover tactic called "greenmail." Here, the managers offer to have the company buy back a shark's stock at highly inflated prices in return for a promise that the shark will stop trying to take over the firm. Critics question the ethics of a tactic that uses corporate assets to secure managerial positions by buying off raiders at a price the average stockholder cannot get. Other controversial antitakeover tactics are described in Application 6.1.

Consider how the potential benefits of diversification are affected by conflicts between the interests of managers and those of stockholders.

Capitalizing on Core Competences

Managers in newly acquired businesses often resent and oppose transferring skills from the core business. Managers good enough at their work to make their business an attractive acquisition may wonder why the new corporate parent presumes to know better. In the case of Philip Morris and the Miller Brewing acquisition, Philip Morris ended up replacing several key executives at Miller after they resisted the transfer of marketing skills from Philip Morris, even though Philip Morris was undoubtedly one of the best marketers in the world. Philip Morris was eventually able to overcome this obstacle, but other corporations are less fortunate and face continued resistance from their acquisitions. The story of Electronic Data Systems and General Motors, told in Application 6.2, is a good example of the problems this can entail.

Application 6.1

Antitakeover Tactics and the Ethical Issues They Raise

Stockholders can often benefit dramatically from an acquisition; the purchase usually entails a takeover premium that increases the price of the stock they own (see Application 6.2). But many takeovers involve wholesale dismissal of the management team. Because fighting takeovers is sometimes in management's best interest, the use of antitakeover tactics raises controversial ethical issues. Managers claim that to take a long-term perspective toward managing the business they must feel secure in their jobs. Critics claim that these tactics, sometimes collectively called "shark repellant," insulate managers from market forces which would otherwise require them to do a better job. They argue that the real purpose of shark repellant is self-serving. These critics also point out that the tactics favor certain classes of stockholders (specifically, sharks) above all others. Here is a sampler of antitakeover tactics that are controversial because they appear to serve the needs of managers more often than they benefit the firm's owners:

- **Scorched Earth.** Selling off key assets in an effort to purposely make the business unattractive to sharks. The assets sold are referred to as the *crown jewels* because they are often those which make the company most attractive in the first place. When sharks threaten, crown jewels may be offered at greatly reduced prices to ensure a quick sale. Obviously, this defense could result in mortally wounding the corporation.
- **White Knight:** In order to avoid being acquired in a hostile (unwanted) takeover, managers approach a third firm about acquisition. In order to induce this "white knight" to rescue the corporation, it is often offered the targeted firm's stock on very favorable terms —sometimes much less than the price the shark was offering or the price other stockholders must pay. When the friendly acquiring firm buys only a portion of the corporation, it is known as a *white squire.*
- **Greenmail:** Financial inducements offered by the threatened firm to stop a shark from acquiring it. The inducement is commonly an offer to buy back (usually at an attractive premium) any of the corporation's stock the shark has already purchased in exchange for the shark's guarantee that it will not threaten the defending firm. Again, this is special treatment offered only to selected stockholders.
- **Golden Parachutes:** High-pay packages, often running three times normal annual compensation, promised to executives fired as a result of a takeover. Sharks are repelled by the idea of having the management team of the acquired corporation leave *en masse*—especially if they leave with so much cash.
- **Poison Pills:** Any of a number of devices aimed at reducing the worth of a company once it has been taken over. For instance, a clause requiring that huge dividend payments be made upon takeover would raise the effective cost of the acquisition, because the shark would have to allow for the cost of meeting the payments. Because there are so many ways to sabotage the future operations of a business, poison pills remain the most popular form of shark repellent.
- **Pac-Man:** A defense based on trying to consume the hunting shark before it attacks. In this situation, offense becomes defense and the hunter becomes the hunted. The risk of using this tactic is that it sometimes sets up a cycle of bid and counterbid in which the price of both firms escalates. When this happens, the "winner" of the bidding war may be saddled with more debt than it can hope to service.

Sharing Infrastructures

Managers may feel threatened when a corporation attempts to have businesses share resources. A corporation may decide to have one set of managers or one set of facilities serve two businesses; in this case, the other managers or facilities will no longer be needed. Generally, when a corporation pursues a strategy of sharing infrastructures, it asks manag-

Application 6.2

General Motors' Acquisition of Electronic Data Systems

For years information processing had been growing more important at General Motors until, by the mid-1980s, the company had more than 100 major computer networks, few of which were capable of communicating with one another. The cost of such unmanaged growth was astronomical, and GM was well on its way to being the highest-cost producer of U.S. automobiles. After making two attempts, Roger Smith, GM's CEO, admitted that the company could not get its data processing under control.

Then in 1984, Smith oversaw the $2.5 billion acquisition of Electronic Data Systems (EDS), one of the leading companies in the field of computer systems integration. The purchase was financed by issuing a special class of stock, GM-E. The GM-E stock sold well, because EDS had a history of 35 percent compound annual profits growth rate. The plan was for EDS to remain a largely independent subsidiary, directed by Ross Perot, who had built EDS on a $1,000 investment. GM would transfer its 7,000-person data processing staff to EDS, and would negotiate contracts for EDS to integrate its massive information processing systems. Smith also expressed hope that some of the entrepreneurial EDS style would rub off on GM.

A series of unanticipated developments turned the acquisition sour, however, and Perot began a public crusade to "nuke the GM management system." What went wrong? We can learn something of the difficulty of managing diversification by observing several problems with the EDS acquisition:

- *Neither company really understood the needs or capabilities of the other.* Smith thought EDS could facilitate GM's move to automate and computerize its factories. But when initially purchased, EDS did not employ a single programmer with expertise in writing code for machine control. Meanwhile, Perot believed that Smith had the same managerial style as he. However, GM had 800,000 employees, many of them United Auto Workers union members, and Perot was responsible for only 17,000 fiercely loyal employees in a corporate culture that was very different.

- *The deal was inadvertently structured to place managers from the two organizations in adversarial roles.* When the GM-E stock was created, the contract stipulated that dividends would be based on performance of the EDS subsidiary—not GM overall. Executive compensation at EDS had long depended heavily upon stock options to motivate superior managerial performance. Because top EDS managers owned a lot of stock, they had a natural interest in seeing that EDS made the highest possible levels of profit. But their customers inside GM felt EDS would charge higher prices that would drive GM's costs up. Many GM managers were angry to see their operations incurring costs that would improve EDS profits and in turn make EDS managers richer. The result was that 4 years after the acquisition, many of GM's largest divisions still had not negotiated long-term contracts with EDS for their data processing needs.

- *Some key relationships were never adequately specified before the acquisition.* In the discussions which took place before the actual acquisition, many issues that would eventually become points of conflict were never broached. Perot was a self-made multibillionaire, described by one acquaintance as "a great team player as long as he got to be captain." Yet, the contract specified in only the most general of terms how he was to work for, and report to, Smith. When Smith began to send teams of inspectors to oversee operations at EDS, Perot simply refused to allow them access to "his" company. Meanwhile, Perot insisted that any suggestion for change coming from GM be cleared with him personally before EDS managers carried it out. The result was a managerial gridlock that prevented EDS from being integrated into GM operations.

- *The cultural difference between the two companies was extreme.* Managerial activity at GM was controlled by a bureaucracy designed to monitor it. Activity at EDS was a function of the cultlike following that had built up around Perot. Ex-military (a graduate of Annapolis), Perot insisted upon conservative dress and patriotic politics. GM people who were transferred to EDS were amazed to learn that beards, long hair, suede shoes, and alcohol at lunch were all strictly forbidden. GM had a decades-long history of adversarial relations with its blue-collar, unionized work force. Perot had made history when he hired a retired Green Beret officer to help him lead a covert operation into Iran to free two EDS workers being held hostage. EDS recruit-

Application 6.2 (cont.)

ing was aimed at people just coming out of the military, and Perot liked to brag in public that EDS workers were trained to kill a snake when they saw one. He complained that GM managers were trained to form a committee to study snakes when they saw one.

As Perot became ever more publicly vocal in his criticisms, GM decided it had to do something to remedy the deteriorating situation. Smith offered Perot and his top three executives $750 million for their shares of EDS stock, more than twice the stock's market value. In return, they resigned, and agreed not to set up companies that would compete with EDS. Perot lost his seat on GM's board, and agreed to incur a fine of $7.5 million if he continued to publicly criticize Smith or GM. The settlement was so spectacular that it gave rise to a new term for one of the less attractive aspects of the acquisition game: "hush-mail."

Sources

Schwartz, J. (1987, September). Can EDS prosper without its charismatic founder? *Internal Management*, pp. 59–62.

Moore, T. (1988, February 15). Make or break time for General Motors. *Fortune*, pp. 32–50.

O'Reilly, B. (1988, October 24). EDS after Perot: How tough is it? *Fortune*, pp. 72–76.

ers to reduce their numbers, and some managers lose their jobs. Clearly, managers have reason to resist this sort of effort at making the corporation more efficient.

Balancing Financial Resources

While balancing cash flows across businesses sounds logical, consider how managers might respond to having their business labeled a "dog." How often are careers advanced by killing off a business efficiently, even if it is done for the good of the corporation? Individual managers often believe that their success probably depends more on the performance of their particular businesses than on the performance of the corporation. In such circumstances, it is difficult for managers to sacrifice their business for the good of other businesses in the corporation's portfolio, even if the corporation as a whole would benefit.

Maintaining Growth

Corporate growth seems to have at least as much to do with improving the welfare of managers as the welfare of stockholders. Managers may be in favor of growth because they expect personal benefits from increasing the size of the corporation. For example, managers in larger corporations typically get paid more than their counterparts in smaller corporations.[24] One study found that, other things being equal, for every 10 percent increase in company size, U.S. CEOs could expect a 2 percent increase in annual pay.[25] This is true even though larger corporations are not necessarily more profitable.

Larger corporations offer managers more prestige and perks. Every year the popular business press celebrates corporate size with listings like the Fortune 500, the 500 largest corporations in the United States. Whether appropriate or not, being a top-ranking executive at a large corporation is considered more prestigious than holding a similar rank in a smaller firm. Corporate jets, executive townhouses, lavish corporate headquarters, and so on, are all expensive executive perquisites, or perks, as they are commonly known. Larger corporations are more likely to be able to afford such perks, because they represent a smaller percentage of overall corporate assets and expenses.

Managers may also perceive that larger corporations offer greater job security. Larger corporations have traditionally been more difficult to acquire in a takeover. Increasing the size of their corporation may help managers feel that they have reduced a threat to their personal job security. With the ever-increasing size of takeover targets, this tactic may no longer be effective. However, it is probably one of the factors managers consider when they review plans for increasing the size of their corporations.

There are ways in which corporations *and* stockholders can benefit from growth. However, the relationship between corporate size and corporate financial performance is quite tenuous, and the benefits to growth appear to accrue more directly to managers than to the stockholders they are presumably hired to serve.[26] This suggests that growth alone is not a strong argument for diversifying. It is probably more appropriate to consider growth as the by-product of diversification, rather than as a reason for diversifying.

Reducing Risk

As we have seen, because individual investors can diversify their portfolios of stock, using countercyclical stocks to reduce their overall risks, corporate diversification for the sake of risk reduction is not a good strategy. However, some corporate managers may pursue this tactic because it effectively reduces the risks they face.[27] When a corporation is in a variety of industries, the corporation itself faces less risk of volatile earnings. Less volatility means that downsizing is less likely to be a threat to managerial positions. Clearly, managers do not benefit from diversification in the same way that owners do, and this difference often limits the benefits owners derive from corporate diversification.

THE FORMS OF DIVERSIFICATION

How is diversification carried out? The various forms and means of diversification can be mixed and matched to create a wide range of options. We will consider three forms of diversification: vertical, horizontal, and global. We will also discuss the three most important means of diversifying: acquisitions, strategic alliances, and internal development. In Exhibit 6.7, we have identified one example of each of the nine possible combinations of means and forms of diversifying.

Vertical Integration

When a corporation performs more than one step of the process involved in converting raw materials into a product delivered and ready for consumption, it is considered to be vertically diversified. In Exhibit 6.8, Vertico is a hypothetical vertically diversified corporation consisting of a fishing fleet, which could be managed as one business, and a wholesaling operation, which could be managed separately as a second business. A corporation that has diversified vertically usually tries to integrate its businesses so that one efficiently "feeds" the other. Coordinating upstream operations (those closer to the raw materials) with downstream operations (those closer to the customer) is called *vertical integration.*

Advantages of Vertical Integration

1. *Lower transaction costs.* The most commonly expected advantage of vertical integration is the elimination, or at least the reduction, of the costs of buying and selling

EXHIBIT 6.7
Examples of Different Combinations of Means and Forms of Diversification

	Forms of Diversification		
Means of Diversification	**Vertical**	**Horizontal**	**Global**
Acquisitions	Time, Inc. acquires Warner Communications, creating a vertically integrated entertainment business.	Philip Morris buys Miller Brewing and Seven-Up in an effort to diversify out of the cigarette business.	BASF, a German chemical producer, buys Inmont, a U.S. chemicals company, to overcome limited growth opportunities at home.
Strategic alliances	Cetus, a leading firm in the biotechnology field, teams up with Kodak, which provides the capital and marketing needed to introduce new Cetus technology.	Dow Chemical and Corning Glass join forces to create a joint venture more profitable than either of its parents.	Fuji Photo Films and Xerox, Inc., form a simple import sales operation, which later grows to become one of the world's leading producers of photocopiers.
Internal development	Humana develops a full line of health care services, vertically integrating across insurance, hospitals, and follow-up treatment services.	3M consistently gets more than 25% of its revenues from products it has developed within the last 5 years.	Anheuser Busch attempts to open up new markets by taking Budweiser, its flagship product, into the United Kingdom.

EXHIBIT 6.8
Vertico and Horizinc, Hypothetical Examples of Vertically and Horizontally Diversified Corporations

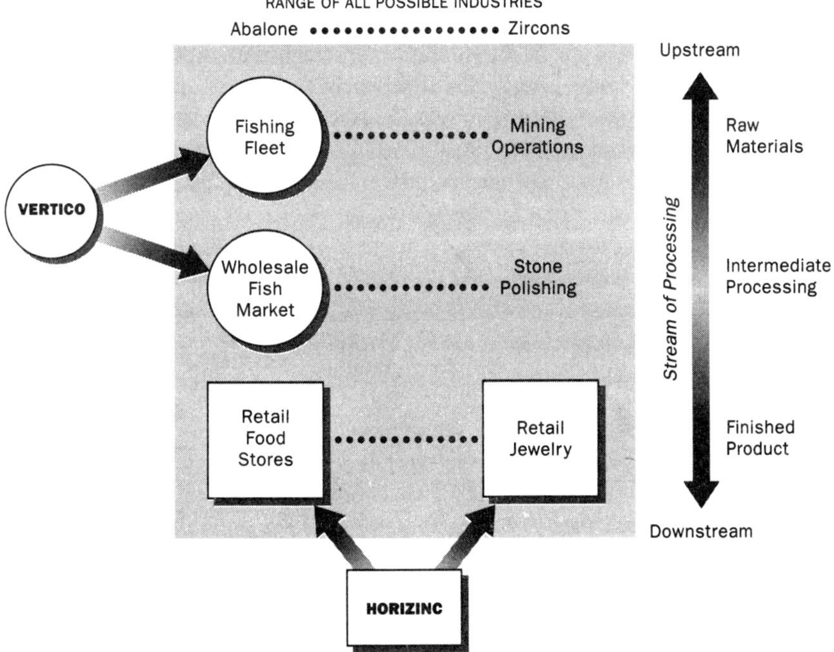

(called transaction costs) that are incurred when separate firms carry out the various steps of converting raw materials to finished goods.[28] When two such steps are integrated, the marketing and sales efforts formerly carried out in the upstream business can be eliminated, because the downstream customer is now part of the same corporation. For instance, Eastman Chemical, a division of Eastman Kodak, supplies many of the raw materials needed to produce and develop film, photographs, and slides. Because the chemical division and the photography business are both parts of the same corporation, the former is able to supply the latter while incurring less cost than an outside vendor would.

2. *Improved coordination.* Corporations may also wish to vertically integrate in order to have smoother, better coordinated operations. For instance, movies have grown increasingly expensive to produce. Today, a big production can easily cost $60 million. However, vertically integrated studios are less dependent upon the movie itself as their sole means of recouping the investment. If carefully coordinated, a bundle of products building upon the foundation provided by the film can dramatically increase the total returns of a movie venture. The sort of coordination required is probably most easily achieved within a single corporate entity. This was the justification given for combining Time, Inc. (publishing and cable TV), and Warner Communications (film studios and recording). The result was a vertically integrated corporation with the ability to produce and market soundtracks, books, videos, and pay television showings, all spun off what would have been stand-alone films in a less vertically integrated corporation.[29]

Disadvantages of Vertical Integration

1. *Unbalanced capacities may limit transaction cost savings.* The minimum size that a plant can be while still remaining reasonably cost efficient is known as its *minimum efficient scale.* If the minimum efficient scale of one link in a vertically integrated corporation is radically different from that of another, then some means must be found to employ the excess capacity of the larger operation. This usually means that the excess capacity must be sold to other firms, which, unfortunately, incurs the transaction costs vertical integration is designed to avoid. For example, tube production has a much higher minimum efficient scale than any other component of a television. North American Philips (NAP), producer of Magnavox and Sylvania consumer electronics, sells about half of its television picture tubes to firms producing competing brands. It is inefficient for NAP to produce just enough tubes for its own consumption. But it avoids marketing and selling costs only on those tubes it sells in-house.

2. *Flexibility is reduced.* By committing to a corporate strategy of vertical integration, firms may anchor themselves to products or technologies that may become outdated and noncompetitive.[30] Firms choosing to vertically integrate accept a responsibility for more than just a wider portion of the production process—they also accept responsibility for remaining innovative in all these business segments. For the end product to remain up to date and competitive, the entire chain of vertically integrated subunits must remain innovative. The task of keeping up on so many fronts

may be overwhelming, and the corporation may fall behind its more focused competitors.

3. *Difficulties arise in integrating different specializations.* The managerial skills and corporate cultures that best serve upstream operations may be incompatible with those required downstream. For example, the authors are familiar with a vertically integrated high-technology company in which the specializations comprise an informal, but well-defined, caste system. Product design engineers rank much higher than production engineers in this caste system, and both groups generally consider themselves to be superior to service technicians. Because of the communication difficulties this attitude causes, a generation of new products failed. Production engineers were ignored when they complained to design engineers that the new products were needlessly difficult to manufacture. When poorly assembled parts began to break down in the field, service technicians were not given the documentation and supplies required to make the repairs; sometimes, they were forced to go to a local hardware store to buy parts with which to improvise a repair on a machine. Clearly, if a vertically diversified firm is to become truly vertically integrated, it must overcome anything that segregates the various specialists.

When to Vertically Integrate

Many corporations balance the advantages and disadvantages of vertical integration by pursuing a strategy of *tapered* or *hybrid* vertical integration. In these strategies, some elements of the corporation may be fully integrated, while others have little vertical integration. The level of integration is best adjusted in light of three questions:[31]

1. *Are our existing suppliers or customers meeting the final consumer's needs?* If the firms in the production and distribution chain are doing an adequate job, it is probably unwise to consider taking over their functions by vertically integrating. In this case, it makes more sense to concentrate managerial resources on problem areas.

2. *How volatile is the competitive situation?* Highly volatile situations, in which technologies are changing, customer needs are evolving, and competitors have still not agreed on the "rules of the game" are poor candidates for vertical integration. Such situations require a flexibility that vertically integrated corporations do not have. Once vertically integrated, a company cannot easily move into and out of the businesses.

3. *Is it possible to "own" a business without actually buying it?* Many of the benefits of vertical integration can be reached when upstream and downstream firms are willing to work closely with one another, even though both remain independent businesses. Motorola was one of the first firms to be awarded the Malcolm Baldrige National Quality Award, an award given annually to leaders in total quality management. Motorola feels so strongly about quality that it decided to require all its hundreds of suppliers to be entered in the Malcolm Baldrige quality competition and to use the competition as an impetus to upgrade their quality dramatically. Because Motorola represented a major account for many of its suppliers, they had little option but to comply. In other words, Motorola was able to significantly influence the behavior of its suppliers without actually owning them.

Diversity and Relatedness in Horizontal Diversification

Horizontal diversification entails moving into more than one industry. Returning to Exhibit 6.8, Horizinc, another hypothetical corporation, serves two distinct markets with two very different products. It competes in the seafood industry as a retailer of abalone, and it competes in the jewelry business as a retailer of zircons (a semiprecious gem). It is not vertically integrated in either case. Although Horizinc operates in two industries, it performs only one function (retailing) in the raw-materials-to-finished-goods transformation process of both.

Abalone and zircons represent very different markets; this arrangement is a strategic decision with a mix of advantages and disadvantages. In fact, the central issue in managing horizontal diversification is to determine how closely related the new business should be to the old business. Most corporations seek out opportunities to diversify into businesses which somehow relate to those they already have, although a few *conglomerates* make no such effort, and pursue a strategy of unrelated diversification.

The Case for Conglomerates

At one time, building conglomerates of unrelated businesses was widely considered to be an ideal corporate strategy.[32] In the 1960s, firms like Textron, ITT, Gulf & Western, and Teledyne led the way in building vast corporate holdings consisting of every imaginable sort of business. For instance, Textron owned Bell Helicopters, Gorham Silver, Homelite Chainsaws, Talon Zippers, and Sheaffer Pens, and was involved in spacecraft propulsion, staplers, chemicals, and air-cushion vehicles.[33] Building conglomerates with such diversity was based on the assumption that corporate managers have the expertise to recognize undervalued stocks that many individual investors would miss. Furthermore, they argued, when it comes to financing acquisitions, corporations have economies of scale that are unavailable to individuals purchasing limited numbers of shares. For example, a corporation may be able to borrow the money at a lower rate of interest, or it may be able to lower the brokerage commissions from purchasing stock on a per share basis by trading very large numbers of shares at once.

The Case against Conglomerates

Looking at the past 30 years of building and managing conglomerates, many managers and researchers today seriously question the wisdom of this corporate strategy.[34] The most important historical evidence against conglomerates falls into two categories: conglomerate discounts and takeover premiums.

1. *Conglomerate Discounts.* Since their initial popularity in the sixties, stocks for conglomerates have typically sold at what is known as a *conglomerate discount.* A conglomerate discount exists when the stock of a conglomerate sells for less than the total of the individual stocks would if each business in the corporation sold its stock separately. Conglomerate discounts are evidence that the market perceives "negative synergy," meaning that the pieces are worth more than the whole. This perception might be based on a fear that managing a corporation as diverse and complex as many conglomerates entails excessively high overhead. Or, it might reflect concern that association with a large corporation is somehow limiting the flexibility of the individual business units. In either of these cases, investors might be willing to pay more for the corporation dismantled than they are willing to pay for it whole.

We can measure conglomerate discounts using *price-earnings (P/E) ratios.* A P/E ratio is simply the price of a share of stock divided by the corporation's annual earnings per share. P/Es indicate investor expectations about the future success of a given corporation; a high P/E means that investors have high expectations for that corporation and they are willing to pay relatively more for its stock. In the sixties, when unrelated diversification was considered to be an ideal corporate strategy, the stock of conglomerates traded at a premium relative to the rest of the market. In fact, at the peak of their popularity, conglomerates often sold for over 50 percent more per their dollar of earnings than the average corporation. In other words, the average P/E ratio of conglomerates was about 50 percent greater than the average P/E for other stocks.

This began to change in the 1970s, when the conglomerates consistently traded at an average P/E lower than the rest of the market's. When the stocks of conglomerates trade at average P/Es less than the average P/Es of undiversified firms, the stock market would probably value all of the businesses making up the conglomerate more as individual companies than bundled together in one corporation. This is a very volatile situation for corporations and investors alike, a situation which gave rise to the tremendous volume of acquisitions and takeovers seen in the late 1980s (see Exhibit 6.9). Investors realized that they could acquire a corporation and then sell off its individual parts for more than they had paid for the original corporation as a whole. Without ever having to operate any of the businesses, those involved in such a takeover could make millions. Firms or individuals specializing in this process have come to be called *corporate raiders.*

To avoid having their corporations dismantled in such "raids," many corporate managers moved to "deconglomerize" first. For instance, in the early and mid-1980s, Gulf & Western sold off businesses producing cement, cigars, video games, apparel, automotive

EXHIBIT 6.9
Trends in U.S. Acquisitions (> $1 Million)

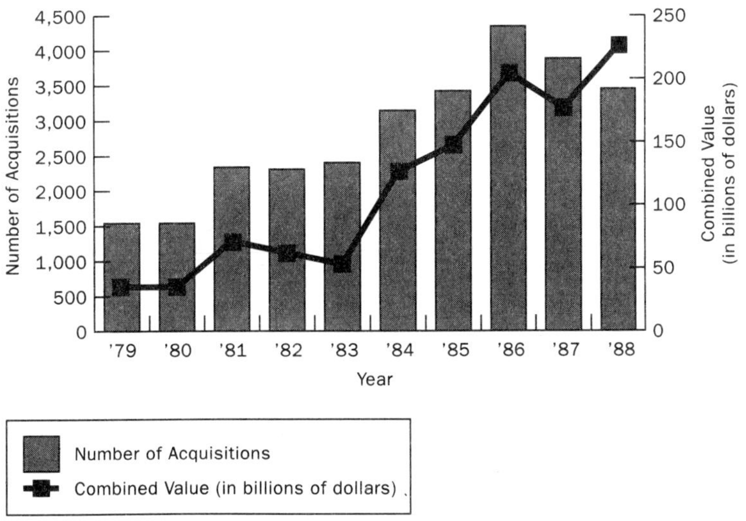

Number of Acquisitions
Combined Value (in billions of dollars)

Source: *Mergers & Acquisitions,* Philadelphia (1991, May–June).

parts, bedding, heavy industrial equipment, wallpaper, horse racing, and sugar. With a much more focused corporation, and a simpler mix of businesses, Gulf & Western began trading at a P/E very near the average for the market in general, making it an unlikely target for any takeover attempts based on plans to further dismantle the corporation. Reflecting on this metamorphosis, Marvin Davis, Gulf & Western's CEO, commented, "Rhyme must follow reason. There must be some kind of fit among diverse operations. A degree of stretching may be acceptable, [but] stretch too far and the result is greater strain than strength."[35]

2. *Takeover Premiums.* If one corporation wishes to buy another, it must expect to pay some sort of *takeover premium.* This is the difference in the normal trading price of the takeover target's stock and the price required to entice stockholders to sell enough stock to give the acquiring firm a controlling interest. It is typical to pay premiums of 50 percent or more to acquire controlling interest of a corporation.

For example, before word leaked out that a corporate raider was interested in acquiring United Airlines, stock in the airline was selling for about $150. In order to be able to quickly buy a controlling interest in UAL, the raider offered to pay about $240 a share for the stock. The $90 difference represents the takeover premium that managers in the raiding corporation felt they would need to pay in order to obtain a controlling interest in UAL. If, like most individual investors, the raider had decided to buy only a small number of shares in UAL, it would not have had to pay any takeover premium. The smaller number of shares could have been bought at the going market price, but fewer shares would not offer the raider a controlling interest. Therefore, in some ways, buying stocks in large blocks is less efficient than individuals' buying stock in smaller blocks.

Takeover premiums and conglomerate discounts create challenges for corporate managers. If not careful, managers may pay more for an acquisition than individual investors would and have the stock later trade for less because of the conglomerate discount. Because this danger exists, corporate managers should be confident that they can create value for stockholders sufficient to overcome takeover premiums and conglomerate discounts.

Global Diversification

The importance of the international aspects of diversification has risen sharply in the past decade. As Exhibit 6.10 indicates, a rapidly growing percentage of all U.S. mergers and acquisitions involve a foreign firm. In 1990, nearly 27 percent of the dollar value of all U.S. mergers and acquisitions were comprised of deals in which foreign firms acquired U.S. firms. Another 10 percent involved U.S. firms diversifying globally by buying foreign firms. In other words, more than one-third of the U.S. merger and acquisition activity involves global diversification.

The next chapter is devoted to a discussion of international management and global diversification. Here, we simply point out that this form of diversification is an alternative to those already considered. Exhibit 6.7 provides some examples of global diversification, but the challenges of international competition are great enough that they merit the separate coverage found in Chapter 7.

EXHIBIT 6.10
International Acquisition Activity

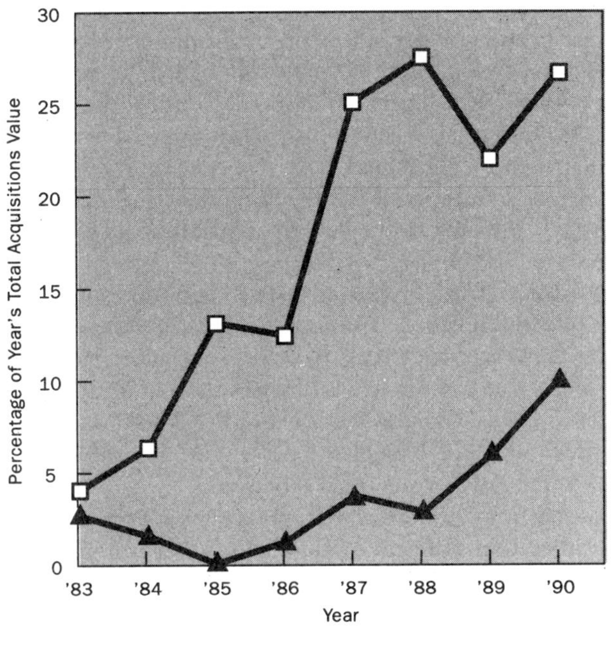

Foreign Acquisitions of U.S. Businesses
U.S. Acquisitions of Foreign Businesses

Source: *Mergers & Acquisitions*, Philadelphia (1991, May–June).

THE MEANS OF DIVERSIFICATION

Each of the three forms of diversification discussed in the preceding section can be achieved in several ways. We will focus on the three most commonly employed: (1) acquisitions, (2) strategic alliances, and (3) internal development.

Acquisitions

Acquisition refers to the purchase of a company that is already in operation.[36] In the late 1980s, approximately $200 billion of corporate assets traded hands annually in corporate acquisitions, as corporations saw acquisitions as an attractive means of generating profits on Wall Street. The sharp decline of acquisition activity in the early 1990s indicates that managers were encountering significant problems in managing such a high level of activity as the limitations of this corporate strategy became evident.[37] In this section we shall use examples from the publishing industry to illustrate why acquisitions have been the most popular means of diversifying, and also to expose some of the potential problems in managing diversification by acquisitions.

One of the primary advantages of diversification by acquisition is its speed. While it may take years to develop a new business from scratch, it may take only months (or even just days) to acquire one and get it up to speed. Consider the case of Murdoch Magazines' purchase of a trade journals business (magazines targeted to specific industries or professions) from Ziff-Davis Publishing Co. In reporting on the acquisition, Murdoch's president said, "We were in business within 20 minutes and we were completely organized within 30 days."[38] It would have taken years for Murdoch to build the business from the ground up.

Another advantage of purchasing an existing business is that it has a track record to review prior to the acquisition. Murdoch bought the trade journal business even though most industry observers felt that Ziff-Davis's consumer magazines business was more attractive. Careful study of the two businesses showed Murdoch's managers that the unglamorous trade journal business was a better fit with Murdoch's no-nonsense corporate culture. Murdoch was able to build a 35 percent increase in advertising revenues from the new business within just 3 years of its acquisition.

Not all acquisitions turn out as well as Murdoch's. Perhaps the most common problem is that of melding two different cultures into one corporation.[39] While Murdoch was buying the trade journals business from Ziff-Davis, CBS, Inc., bought their consumer magazine business. At CBS, broadcasting has always maintained a position as the most important part of the corporation, while publishing took a back seat. In the wave of takeovers that occurred during the mid-1980s, CBS began to feel threatened as a potential acquisition target and began selling off its weakest businesses to raise cash for its defense in a takeover fight. As something of a second-class citizen in the corporation, the publishing division at CBS realized that if it did not quickly move to strengthen itself, CBS might sell it as part of this cash-raising campaign. When the head of the division heard that the Ziff-Davis consumer magazines business, with its fat 25 percent margins, was up for sale, his command was: "Make a preemptive bid, overpay, I don't give a damn what you do. But get them."[40] Managers at CBS then spent $326 million to purchase the business, $100 million more than the next highest bid.

Shortly after the takeover, a mass exodus of the magazine group's top management began. They objected to what they viewed as CBS's efforts to force a different corporate culture on them. Ziff-Davis had been an entrepreneurial firm, pioneering new techniques for selling advertising. Its managers found CBS to be bureaucratic and slow. Said one: "The corporate motto should have been 'we'll get back to you on that.' Everyone was a conduit to the next guy, and no one ever gave you a straight answer."[41] As a result of such difficulties, the margins on the consumer magazine business quickly fell by more than half to a mediocre 11.6 percent.

Along with difficulties in combining businesses with different cultures, another disadvantage to acquisitions is that they can be very expensive. As shown by the case of CBS's paying $100 million more than the next highest bid, it does not make sense to be too rushed or unthinking when buying a business. But, even the expenses of an acquisition carried out cooly and deliberately can be startlingly high. An example is given in Application 6.3.

Application 6.3

An Example of the Costs of Acquisitions

During the first 6 months of 1989, common stock in UAL, the holding company of United Airlines, traded for approximately $100 to $150. Then in late summer, rumors began to circulate that the stock might be "in play," meaning that someone might be trying to take over the company. Prices began to rise in anticipation of a takeover, and by August, when a takeover offer was indeed announced, the stock was regularly trading for more than $200.

When Marvin Davis, a corporate raider from the west coast, announced his plans for acquiring UAL, they included an offer to buy shares at $240. But the UAL board of directors used greenmail (see Application 6.1) to negotiate a settlement with Davis that restricted him from making any attempts to acquire a controlling interest in the corporation. By that time, the idea of buying the company had spread to UAL's managers and pilots. Fearing the worst if the next corporate raider should be successful, these UAL employees decided to try to put together their own takeover deal.

The deal they put together required more than $7 billion to buy up all outstanding UAL shares at a price of $300. All the data suggest that this represented a takeover premium of approximately 100 percent; the "normal" price of the stock, the price it traded for before rumors of a takeover began to spread, was somewhere below $150. Furthermore, analysts studying the earnings potential of the airline widely agreed that a fair price for the stock was $135 to $150. Finally, when the employee takeover fell through, the stock plummeted in just a few days back to a trading price as low as $145. In other words, all the evidence suggests that the managers and pilots were faced with paying about twice as much per share to buy the whole company as they would otherwise have had to pay to buy shares individually.

Even though the deal fell through, it still cost $53.7 million. The investment bankers and their lawyers, the two groups chiefly responsible for structuring the unsuccessful deal, got a total of $26.7 million for their effort. Another $16 million was required to repay a fund created by the pilot's union for the employee stock-ownership plan. The two banks that took the lead in trying to put together the $6 billion in bank loans were paid $8 million for their work. The final $3 million fee went to another bank for merely promising to make a loan which it never actually had to make.

When takeover costs such as these are incurred, it places a tremendous burden on the new owners to perform. Unless the newly acquired corporation's performance is dramatically improved, these expenses cannot be justified.

Sources

Smith, R., & Hilder, D. B. (1989, October 23). Just how much is UAL's stock worth? *The Wall Street Journal,* p. C1.

Smith, R., & Valente, J. (1989, October 25). Shares in UAL take wild ride on bid rumors. *The Wall Street Journal,* p. A3.

Smith, R. (1989, October 31). UAL is being billed for $53.7 million in expenses from failed buy-out bid. *The Wall Street Journal,* p. A6.

Strategic Alliances: Joint Ventures

Diversification by strategic alliance refers to arrangements in which two corporations combine forces to form a cooperative partnership. Typically, neither company owns the other, though they often create a third commercial entity, typically referred to as a *joint venture,* which they co-own.[42] Strategic alliances make the most sense in cases where both parties have strengths that offset the other's weaknesses.[43] A good example is Dow Corning, an extremely successful joint venture which regularly boasts performance levels higher than either of its parents, Dow Chemical and Corning Glass.

Sharing offsetting strengths through such a joint venture has several benefits. Neither partner must invest in developing the full range of capabilities required by the new venture.

Financing should be easier to attract, since the new business has two backers instead of just one and the partners can share in the risks of development. All these factors help explain why joint ventures are so common between large corporations and small businesses, especially in the emerging field of biotechnology.[44] Most of the advances in this field are being made by small entrepreneurial firms that lack the financial strength to produce goods in this very capital-intensive industry and the sales forces capable of reaching the broad range of potential customers. Because of this and the risks involved in developing such new products, numerous small biotech firms have teamed up with large corporations. Cetus, one of the leading biotech firms, has a number of such strategic alliances, including one with Kodak to produce and market some of the first diagnostic instruments based on the new biotechnology. Cetus provides the bulk of the research, and Kodak provides financing and marketing capabilities.

Perhaps the most serious disadvantage of joint ventures is the difficulty of achieving close coordination between two companies that almost certainly have different goals, strategies, procedures, and cultures. Nothing can harm a joint venture's chances of success faster than such incompatibilities. One study revealed that nearly half of all joint ventures that failed experienced conflict between the partners.[45] In order to avoid such conflicts, it is helpful to consider the following guidelines for the strategic management of joint ventures:[46]

Establish clear understanding between partners. At a minimum, potential partners in a joint venture should discuss in some detail (1) the mission of the new business, (2) the market(s) it will serve, (3) the product(s) it will offer, (4) the obligations of each partner, and (5) how the joint venture will be dissolved if necessary.

Do not depend upon a contract to make a joint venture work. Though contracts are essential, if the partners take an adversarial, legalistic approach to managing the joint venture, it will almost surely fail. Joint ventures succeed because managers work to make them successful, not because of legal agreements. Dow Corning was created with a handshake and was already a promising venture before the lawyers eventually drew up the contracts.

Do not try to shortchange your partner. Strategic alliances should be collaborative efforts in which all parties contribute willingly for the good of the partnership. While each partner must look after its own interests, there is no room for greed in such an arrangement.[47]

Internal Development: Corporate Entrepreneurship

Diversification through internal development refers to building new businesses more or less from the ground up, a process sometimes referred to as corporate entrepreneurship.[48] To create new businesses, corporations have developed four types of programs.[49] The first type consists of the corporation's acting simply as a venture capitalist. *Venture capitalists* provide the funds, sometimes called risk capital, required to start a new business. Exxon Enterprises found that this was its most successful type of corporate entrepreneurship program.[50] Over a 10-year period, the company invested in eighteen new ventures. Six of these became attractive enough that the corporation eventually bought them. The remaining twelve were never brought into the corporation, but overall, they still represented a sound financial investment. Exxon invested $12 million in them, and over a 10-year period, they returned $218 million in cash or marketable securities.[51]

A second tactic for fostering corporate entrepreneurship is the *new-venture incubator.* Here, the corporation provides funding, low-cost space and equipment, and limited managerial oversight. The ventures supported may have started inside the corporate sponsor, or they may be independent start-ups the corporation is assisting. Corporations often use incubator programs in an effort to take advantage of excess resources, such as extra space, idle equipment, and unused managerial talent.[52] But in trying to coordinate the new venture's use of these resources with those of the established businesses, corporations often encounter difficulties.[53] Kodak encountered difficulties in integrating mainstream businesses with the "new-stream" businesses in its incubator program, and eventually closed the program, though it had been modestly successful in creating profitable new lines of business.[54]

A third option is the *idea generation and transfer program.* This program attempts to birth new business ideas that are then transferred to established operations for further development and ongoing management. Firms have generally had more success with these types of programs than the first two described. Even though the amounts of corporate resources invested in these idea generation and transfer programs are usually much less than the investment in a corporation's venture capital or incubator programs, the results from idea generation and transfer programs have often been much more significant. For example, Raytheon's New Product Development Center, an idea generation and transfer program, has often produced fifty or more patentable innovations a year.[55] Many of these were important new-product enhancements, such as ovens which combined conventional and microwave capabilities and laundries that operated using plastic "credit cards" rather than coins. These accomplishments lead to important new sources of revenue, but idea generation and transfer programs are limited in that they seldom foster innovations leading to the development of entirely new businesses. More typically, they lead to new products or product refinements for an existing business, as in the Raytheon example.

The last category of corporate entrepreneurship programs is called *intrapreneurship,* because it involves individuals or small teams working within the corporation that develop their ideas into businesses.[56] Perhaps the corporation best known for pursuing this means of diversification is Minnesota Mining and Manufacturing (3M). This corporation consistently beats its goal of having 25 percent of its revenues generated by products no more than 5 years old. This is accomplished by adherence to a number of practices aimed at spreading an entrepreneurial spirit among its employees. For an example, see the story of Post-its in Application 6.4. Such stories have made 3M's culture of entrepreneurship legendary.

Unfortunately, not all attempts at fostering intrapreneurship are nearly as successful as 3M's. Internal development is often risky.[57] Of the nineteen new internal ventures that Exxon Enterprises tried, not one produced a business with significant profits.[58] The risks associated with developing new businesses vary widely, depending on whether or not a market for the product already exists and whether or not the technology is new. The experiences of numerous companies suggest that almost all new businesses offering familiar product technology to existing markets will be successes, while probably fewer than one in eight new businesses offering new products to an undeveloped market will succeed. Internal development is also very slow. One study found that it takes about 8 years, on average,

Application 6.4

Intrapreneurship at 3M

Post-its, the quintessential intrapreneurial success story, began when Art Fry, a researcher at Minnesota Mining and Manufacturing, became annoyed with the scraps of paper he used to mark places in his church choir hymnal. As he moved from song to song, his markers fell out and he found himself fumbling for his place instead of singing. In looking for a solution to his problem, Fry discovered that, years earlier, someone at 3M had developed an adhesive that was considered a failure: It was strong enough to hold a strip of paper, but only temporarily.

Fry reasoned that further development might prove this "failure" to be a solution to his problem. Fry could have left the company and attempted to start his own business, in classic entrepreneurial fashion. But, in hindsight, he figures that without 3M, success would have been impossible. From the outset, 3M facilitated Fry's work with its policies designed to encourage innovation. For instance, every 3M employee is guaranteed 15 percent of his time on the job to set aside for personal projects. In the early days, Fry used this personal time to work on his new idea. Later, when the product was stumbling in the marketplace, 3M proved that it could not only encourage innovations, but it could also help to turn those innovations into successful businesses.

After a year's work, Fry finally thought he had developed a superior "temporarily permanent" adhesive for his note pads, and his marketing rollout began. The product was test marketed in four U.S. cities using normal advertising and promotional methods. Few people bought it, and initially, the product seemed doomed. However, 3M's market research showed that virtually everyone who tried the product became a dedicated customer. Lew Lehr, 3M's CEO, heard about the problem with the product's introduction and stepped in. If people needed to test the product themselves to appreciate it, free samples would facilitate the process.

It was not something the corporation had ever tried before, but Lehr had his secretary send out 1,000 sample pads—one to the CEO of every Fortune 500 company and one to every CEO's secretary. Once Lehr had shown his personal interest in the project and his approval of the use of free samples, both were legitimated within 3M. The new marketing approach, featuring free ten-page trial-sized pads, was a tremendous success. Six years after its introduction, the product had thoroughly saturated the market, becoming as common in any office as paper clips and rubber bands. Reflecting on the tremendous success of his modest innovation, Fry concluded, "Of course, the strength of the organization is what made it possible for the development of the Post-it Note. I couldn't have developed it on the outside. Developing it on the inside means that 80 percent of what is needed is already there—in systems, equipment, people."

Source

Lessons from a successful intrapreneur: An interview with Post-it Notes' inventor Art Fry. (1988, March–April). *The Journal of Business Strategy*, pp. 18–24.

for new businesses developed internally to break even, and another 4 years for them to reach levels of profitability that match those of typical mature businesses in the United States.[59]

Each of the four types of corporate entrepreneurship programs can be as important for their impact on corporate culture as for their impact on diversification or financial performance. Following deregulation of the telephone industry, Ohio Bell's Enter-Prize program was created to transform the firm's culture from that of a heavily dependent subsidiary of a highly successful monopoly to an entrepreneurial market leader, capable of fending for itself in a highly competitive market.[60] During years of operating in a heavily regulated environment, Ohio Bell had developed a culture in which employees were excellent at carrying out orders, but unable to direct themselves, and in which there was widespread resistance to any new ideas or management techniques. Under the Enter-Prize program, employees were paid anywhere from $50 to $50,000 for their entrepreneurial ideas on how to make Ohio Bell more competitive. Employees with ideas for a potential new business were given or loaned resources to test the feasibility of their ideas. While managers estimated that Enter-Prize returned $5 to the corporation for every $1 invested, they insist that the greatest gains have come from fostering a more entrepreneurial culture that now pervades the organization and impacts businesses throughout the corporation.

DIVESTMENTS: THE NEGLECTED SIDE OF DIVERSIFICATION

Corporate management must not only decide what businesses the corporation will enter; it must also decide what businesses the corporation will exit. Although the subject receives much less media attention, divesting businesses is an integral part of corporate management. In fact, research shows that corporations will eventually exit many of the markets they enter through diversification long before the markets disappear. One study revealed that corporations divested themselves of approximately one-half of all the business units they ever owned.[61] The top ten industries for divestments in 1990 are listed in Exhibit 6.11.

Why do businesses divest? While poor performance is the most obvious reason for selling a business, others are important:

- *Better alternatives are available.* Corporations may decide to sell off businesses because their assets have more value in some other application. Greyhound sold a number of its downtown bus terminals because the real estate had much more value as building sites than as bus stations.
- *Other acquisitions need financing.* Some businesses are sold to help finance the corporation's other acquisitions. U.S. Steel (now USX) sold off $3 billion worth of businesses and other assets to finance its purchase of Marathon Oil.
- *Ongoing operations must be financed.* Leveraged buyouts (acquisitions financed with heavy use of debt) regularly include plans to sell off parts of the new acquisition in

EXHIBIT 6.11
The Top Ten Industries for Divestments in 1990

	Value (In Millions of Dollars)	Number of Divestments
Banking	$ 582.9	83
Media	1,784.8	82
Business, professional, and social services	2,208.9	80
Wholesaling	1,182.3	66
Electrical and electronic equipment	1,295.6	61
Energy	4,542.0	60
Health care	810.6	60
Nonbank financial	5,234.4	56
Machinery	1,234.1	54
Retail trade	4,244.2	51

Source: *Mergers & Acquisitions*, Philadelphia (1991, May–June).

order to help generate cash quickly. For instance, when Hanson Trust, one of Britain's largest corporations (built almost entirely through acquisitions), purchased Imperial Group for £2.1 billion, it immediately recouped £1.4 billion by divesting the new acquisition's brewing business.

Because divestments represent an important part of corporate management's responsibilities, they should be managed strategically.[62] Unfortunately, this is seldom done. Divesting corporations have been described as more interested in minimizing trauma than maximizing profits. Divestments still symbolize failure to many managers, and the result is that they often jump at a chance to get rid of the "loser" and to distance themselves from the whole affair, as described in Application 6.5.

Application 6.5

Mismanaging Divestments

Corporate managers are not always the cool-headed profit maximizers their stockholders might like them to be. This is most apparent when considering the outcomes of some spectacular deals corporate managers have made in divesting businesses:

- In 1987, the chemical industry was suffering from its fourth year of continued poor performance. Industry giants Dow, PPG, Corpus Christi Petrochemicals, and ICI all sold petrochemical businesses to an investor group led by Gordon Cain. With $23 million of their own money (and another $1 billion in debt) the Cain Chemical Company purchased the businesses, held them for 9 months, and then sold the group to Occidental Petroleum for a profit of $1.2 billion.
- As part of the "deconglomerizing" U.S. industries went through in the 1980s, RCA corporation sold Gibson Greetings, Inc., to a group of investors known as Wesray Capital Corp. RCA sold the business for $80 million, but only 16 months later the investor group took Gibson public with a market value of around $290 million.
- Merck & Co. sold its Calgon Carbon Corp., a producer of filtering agents used in pollution controls, in a deal masterminded by Calgon's general manager, Thomas McConomy. McConomy put up just $325,000 to purchase 13.4 percent of the company as part of a $110 million total purchase price. Five years later, when he took the company public, his stake was worth $80 million.
- In 1983, Atlantic Richfield had lost $100 million in the previous 6 years of operating its 100-year-old Anaconda copper mine. It shut down the mine completely and 2 years later, began to look for a purchaser. Dennis Washington, a Montana construction magnate, considered buying the business for scrap, but Anaconda managers convinced him that the mine could once again be operated profitably.

  Washington offered $13.5 million for the mine, 38,000 acres of wilderness, another 12,000 acres of mining land, and the $4.1 million (in revenues) Butte Water Co. Within months, he had already recouped $8 million of his investment from selling a fraction of the land. Meanwhile, the price of copper more than doubled to a level almost three times the mine's new breakeven price. Washington's comment? "Once the pencil pushers at big companies decide it's time to sell, you can negotiate a helluva deal."

Obviously, not all divestments turn out to be such apparently poor decisions. Many are made for sound reasons and at a nice profit. The important point to note is that corporate managers are capable of making grievous blunders if they do not work diligently to ensure that a sound, carefully reasoned approach to divestments is followed.

Source

Excerpted by permission of *Forbes* magazine, May 15, 1989.

Divestments should be considered a part of the overall corporate strategy, not just an isolated quick fix. The business in question should be carefully evaluated, not in terms of its potential in the current setting, but in an ideal situation. Then, a systematic search should be made for potential buyers, which could offer this ideal setting. Once they are identified, a sales plan should be created to highlight the fit between the particular business and each of the potential buyers. Selling a business involves the same sort of analysis as buying one, with the focus shifting from how the business fits into your corporation to how it fits into their corporation. Because of the impact divestment can have on employees and the local community in general, corporate managers should also consider their ethical and social responsibility to manage divestments carefully.[63]

Summary

The managers most obviously held accountable to stockholders are those at the corporate level. One of their key responsibilities is to see that stockholders' funds are invested in such a way that they generate more value for the stockholders than stockholders could generate for themselves. Corporate managers can continue to invest in their present businesses or they can invest in different businesses, an option that entails some form of diversification. The benefits corporate managers personally receive from diversification are often different from, and sometimes in conflict with, those realized by stockholders.

Perhaps the best justification for diversification is to further capitalize on core competences the corporation has already developed. Other good reasons are to utilize corporate infrastructures more fully, and to facilitate shifting of cash flows from businesses generating excess cash to those needing additional cash. Other reasons sometimes given for diversification are maintenance of growth and reduction of risk, but often managers benefit from these factors more than stockholders do.

The most common forms of diversification are vertical integration, horizontal diversification, and global diversification. Diversification is usually carried out through acquisitions, strategic alliances, or internal development. The forms and means of diversification can be combined to create a wide range of strategic options for corporate managers. Another option, one that is an important, if sometimes neglected, part of corporate strategies, is divestment. In looking at these options, managers must consider how reshaping the corporation's portfolio of businesses will affect the value of stockholders' investments.

Notes

1. Rappaport, A. (1987, Spring). Linking competitive strategy and shareholder value analysis. *The Journal of Business Strategy,* pp. 58–67; Day, G. S., & Fahey, L. (1990, March–April). Putting strategy into shareholder value analysis. *Harvard Business Review,* pp. 156–162.
2. Lubatkin, M. (1988). Value-creating mergers: Fact or folklore? *Academy of Management Executive, 2,* 295–302; Oviatt, B. M. (1988). Agency and transaction cost perspectives on the manager-shareholder relationship: Incentives for congruent interests. *Academy of Management Review, 13,* 214–225.

3. Prahalad, C. K., & Hamel, G. (1990, May–June). The core competence of the corporation. *Harvard Business Review,* pp. 79–91.
4. Porter, M. (1987, May–June). From competitive advantage to corporate strategy. *Harvard Business Review, 65,* 43–59; and Prahalad & Hamel (Ref. 3), loc. cit.
5. Sloan, P. (1986, April 28). Brand names seek new wrinkle with clothes. *Advertising Age,* p. 28.
6. Reed, R., & DeFillippi, R. J. (1990). Casual ambiguity, barriers to imitation, and sustainable competitive advantage. *Academy of Management Review, 15,* 88–102.
7. Porter (Ref. 4), loc. cit.
8. Hedley, B. (1977, February). Strategy and the business portfolio. *Long Range Planning, 10,* 9–15.
9. For a thorough comparison of these various portfolio management techniques, see Abell, D. F., & Hammond, J. S. (1979). *Strategic market planning.* Englewood Cliffs, NJ: Prentice-Hall.
10. Haspeslagh, P. (1983, January–February). Portfolio planning: Uses and limits. *Harvard Business Review, 60,* 58–73.
11. Hax, A. C., & Majluf, N. S. (1991). *The strategic concept and process.* Englewood Cliffs, NJ: Prentice-Hall.
12. For an in-depth discussion of the problems of identifying individual businesses within larger diversified corporations, see Abell, D. F. (1980). *Defining the business: The starting point of strategic planning.* Englewood Cliffs, NJ: Prentice-Hall.
13. Proctor, R. A. (1990). Strategic planning: An overview of product portfolio models. *Marketing Intelligence and Planning, 8*(7), 4–10.
14. Buzzell, R. D., & Gale, B. T. (1987). *The PIMS principles: Linking strategy to performance.* New York: Free Press.
15. Capital cargo—more German marks for U.S. chemical operations (1985, June 25). *Chemical Week,* pp. 24–27.
16. There are several forms of corporate risk. The risk to which we refer here is technically called business risk. Those interested in other forms of strategic risk are referred to Miller, K. D. (1990). Strategic risk and corporate performance: An analysis of alternative risk measures. *Academy of Management Journal, 33,* 756–779.
17. There is research that suggests that reducing variability in this way improves cash flow and allows corporations to acquire factors of production (e.g., capital equipment) at lower costs. See Amit, R., & Wernerfelt, B. (1990). Why do firms reduce business risk? *Academy of Management Journal, 33,* 520–533.
18. Lubatkin, M. (1988, November). Value-creating mergers: Fact or folklore? *Academy of Management Executive,* pp. 295–302; Oviatt, B. M. (1988, April). Agency and transaction cost perspectives on the manager-shareholder relationship: Incentives for congruent interests. *Academy of Management Review,* pp. 214–225.
19. We are using "agent" here in the legal sense of one authorized to transact business, including executing contracts, for another. Davidson, S., Stickney, C., & Weil, R. (1984). *The language of business.* Englewood Cliffs, NJ: Prentice-Hall.
20. Eisenhardt, K. M. (1989). Agency theory: An assessment and review. *Academy of Management Review, 14,* 57–74.
21. Jensen, M. C., & Meckling, W. H. (1976). Theory of the firm: Managerial behavior, agency costs, and ownership structure. *Journal of Financial Economics, 3*(4), 305–360.
22. Haspeslagh, P. C., & Jemison, D. B. (1987, Winter). Acquisitions: Myths and reality. *Sloan Management Review, 28,* 53–58.

23. McGee, R. W. (1989, March). Ethical issues in acquisitions and mergers. *Mid-Atlantic Journal of Business*, pp. 19–39; Werhane, P. H. (1988, January–February). Two ethical issues in mergers and acquisitions. *Journal of Business Ethics, 7*, 41–45.
24. Lambert, R. A., Larcker, D. F., & Weigelt, K. (1991, July). How sensitive is executive compensation to organizational size? *Strategic Management Journal, 12*, 395–402.
25. Crystal, G. S. (1989, June 5). Seeking the sense in CEO pay. *Fortune, 119*, 88–104.
26. For further discussion of how corporations and managers benefit from growth through diversification, see Dalton, D. R., & Kesner, I. F. (1985, Summer). Organizational growth: Big is beautiful. *The Journal of Business Strategy, 6*, 38–48.
27. Walter, G. A., & Barney, J. B. (1990, January). Management objectives in mergers and acquisitions. *Strategic Management Journal*, pp. 79–86.
28. Williamson, O. (1975). *Markets and hierarchies: Analysis and antitrust implications.* New York: Free Press.
29. Saporito, B. (1989, November 20). The inside story of Time Warner. *Fortune, 120*, 164–210.
30. This point is discussed in some detail in Hayes, R. H., & Abernathy, W. J. (1980, July–August). Managing our way to economic decline. *Harvard Business Review*, p. 67.
31. These questions are adapted from Kathryn Harrigan's research presented in Harrigan, K. (1986, November–December). Matching vertical integration strategies to competitive conditions. *Strategic Management Journal, 7*, 535–555. These and additional criteria are discussed in Ewaldz, D. B. (1991, July–August). How integrated should your company be? *The Journal of Business Strategy*, pp. 52–55.
32. Leontiades, M. (1986, Spring). The rewards of diversifying into unrelated businesses. *The Journal of Business Strategy, 6*, 81–87.
33. To learn the fascinating story of how such a corporation was built, read the entertaining book, Little, R. (1979). *How to lose $1,000,000,000 and other valuable advice.* Boston & Toronto: Little, Brown.
34. For example, research indicates the best way to protect shareholder value against economic downturns is to diversify only to the extent that "all of one's eggs are in similar baskets." See Lubatkin, M., & Chatterjee, S. (1991, May). The strategy-shareholder value relationship: Testing temporal stability across market cycles. *Strategic Management Journal, 12*, 251–270.
35. Davis, M. S. (1985, June 25). Two plus two doesn't equal five. *Fortune*, p. 177.
36. *Mergers* refers to the act of combining two corporations, but this usually entails that one corporation acquire the other. Therefore, to simplify this material, we do not make a distinction between acquisitions and mergers. For a discussion of the shared strategic goals of mergers and acquisitions, see Walter, G. A., & Barney, J. B. (1990, January). Management objectives in mergers and acquisitions. *Strategic Management Journal, 11*, 79–86.
37. Foust, D., & Smart, T. (1990, June 25). The merger parade runs into a brick wall. *Business Week*, p. 38.
38. The Murdoch/Ziff-Davis/CBS story, used as an example throughout this section, is found in Behar, R. (1987, April 6). We'll get back to you on that. *Forbes*, pp. 42–44.
39. Other difficulties associated with diversification through acquisition are described in Davidson, K. (1991, May–June). Why acquisitions may not be the best route to innovation. *The Journal of Business Strategy*, pp. 50–52. Additionally, for an insightful discussion on how an acquisition strategy may lead to a reduction in R&D spending, refer to Hitt, M. A., Hoskisson, R. E., Ireland, R. D., & Harrison, J. S. (1991, November). Are acquisitions a poison pill for innovation? *The Executive, 5*, 22–34.

40. Ibid.
41. Ibid.
42. Harrigan, K. R. (1988, March–April). Joint ventures and competitive strategy. *Strategic Management Journal, 9,* 141–158.
43. Schillaci, C. E. (1987, Fall). Designing successful joint ventures. *The Journal of Business Strategy,* pp. 59–63.
44. Niederkofler, M. (1991). The evolution of strategic alliances: Opportunities for managerial influence. *Journal of Business Venturing, 6,* 237–257.
45. Scanlon, P. R. (1990, July–August). Collaborative ventures. *The Journal of Business Strategy,* pp. 81–83.
46. These and other important considerations are discussed in Harrigan, K. R. (1986). *Managing for joint venture success.* Lexington, MA: D. C. Heath.
47. Lorange, P., & Roos, J. (1991, January–February). Why some strategic alliances succeed and others fail. *The Journal of Business Strategy,* pp. 25–30.
48. For discussion of the determinants of success in corporate entrepreneurship, see Zahra, S. A. (1991). Predictors and financial outcomes of corporate entrepreneurship: An exploratory study. *Journal of Business Venturing, 6,* 259–285; Miller, A., & Camp, B. (1985). Exploring determinants of success in corporate ventures. *Journal of Business Venturing, 1,* 87–105; Burgelman, R. A. (1985, January–February). Managing the new venture division: Research findings and implications for strategic management. *Strategic Management Journal, 6,* 39–54.
49. This typology of new venture programs was developed in a Harvard Business School research program on corporate entrepreneurship headed by Rosabeth Moss Kanter. See MacMillan, I. (1990). Introduction of Kanter's case series. *Journal of Business Venturing, 5,* 413.
50. Sykes, H. (1986, May–June). Lessons from a new ventures program. *Harvard Business Review,* pp. 69–74.
51. Other corporations have been far less successful in acting as venture capitalists. See Kanter, R. M., North, J., Bernstein, A. P., & Williamson, A. (1990). Engines of progress: Designing and running entrepreneurial vehicles in established companies. *Journal of Business Venturing, 5,* 415–430.
52. An often overlooked resource that can be highly valuable to a new corporate venture is the corporation's image. See Williams, M. L., Tsai, M., & Day, D. (1991). Intangible assets, entry strategies, and venture success in industrial markets. *Journal of Business Venturing, 6,* 315–333.
53. Miller, A., Spann, M. S., & Lerner, L. (1991). Competitive advantages in new corporate ventures: The impact of resource sharing and reporting level. *Journal of Business Venturing, 6,* 335–350.
54. Kanter, R. M., Richardson, L., North, J., & Morgan, E. (1991). Engines of progress: Designing and running entrepreneurial vehicles in established companies. The new venture process at Eastman Kodak, 1983–1989. *Journal of Business Venturing, 6,* 63–82.
55. Kanter, R. M., North, J., Richardson, L., & Zolner, J. (1991). Engines of progress: Designing and running entrepreneurial vehicles in established companies. Raytheon's new product center, 1969–1989. *Journal of Business Venturing, 6,* 145–163.
56. Pinchot, G. (1985). *Intrapreneuring.* New York: Harper & Row.
57. Cosgrove, M. (1991, May–June). Roadblocks to new business development. *The Journal of Business Strategy,* pp. 53–57.
58. Statistical analysis indicates that 45 percent of the variability in new venture performance in

Exxon Enterprises can be explained by just two factors: Market risk and technological risk. Sykes (Ref. 50), loc. cit.

59. Biggadike, H. R. (1979, May–June). The risky business of diversification. *Harvard Business Review, 57,* 103–111.
60. Kanter, R. M., & Richardson, L. (1991). Engines of progress: Designing and running entrepreneurial vehicles in established companies. The enter-prize program at Ohio Bell, 1985–1990. *Journal of Business Venturing, 6,* 209–229.
61. Porter, M. E. (1987, May–June). From competitive advantage to corporate strategy. *Harvard Business Review, 65,* 43–59.
62. See discussion in Harowitz, H., & Halliday, D. (1984, Fall). The new alchemy: Divestment for profit. *The Journal of Business Strategy, 5,* 112–116.
63. Hennessy, E. L., Jr. (1988, Fall). The ethics of corporate restructuring. *Directors & Boards, 13,* 8–12.

CHAPTER 7

Strategic Management at the International Level: Managing for Global Success

The internationalization of competition is inevitable. Future managers in every industry will be either directly involved in or affected by international competition. Tomorrow's winners will be those firms with managers who are comfortable in the international arena. These managers will design strategies for their multinational corporations (MNCs), which establish competitive advantages in specific markets by tapping corporate resources worldwide.

This chapter has five major sections. The first discusses the importance of adopting a global perspective and the advantages and disadvantages of international diversification. The second reviews the most important options for entering international markets. The third discusses the forms of competitive advantage important to international competition, and introduces governmental relations in a critical role. The fourth explains how organizations must respond to local markets while tapping global resources if they are to have the strongest possible international strategies. The final section details how this combination results in greater competitive advantages.

After reading this chapter, you will understand:

- The necessity for enthusiastically participating in global competition
- The most common strategies for entering the international market and how firms progress from one entry strategy to the next
- How government support becomes a fourth source of competitive advantage in the international arena
- How concern for economic efficiency drives international firms toward a global strategy of tightly integrating their operations around the world
- How dealing with the unique cultures of foreign markets encourages a multidomestic strategy in which individual units freely adjust operations to local needs
- That the most powerful combination of competitive advantages can only be obtained by mixing elements of both global and multidomestic strategies

EXECUTIVE INTERVIEW

R. Michael Franz
President and Chief Executive Officer
Murata Business Systems

R. Michael Franz has been president and chief executive officer of Murata Business Systems since the firm's creation in 1982. Before joining Murata, Franz was director of marketing for the Imaging Systems Division of the Burroughs Corporation Office Systems Group.

During the first 4 years of operation, Murata has tripled its revenues annually, to more than $260 million. Franz has led the way in broadening the company's domestic and international network of distribution. Murata entered the cellular industry with a new line of portable cellular telephones and has established itself as a leader in the $2 billion fax market. The company currently markets its products in Canada, Europe, Latin America, Oceania, and the United States.

Franz received a bachelor's degree in general humanities and a master's degree in business administration from the University of Santa Clara. He also serves as an adjunct professor at the University of Texas, Arlington.

How important is the worldwide market outside of Japan for Murata?

International business is a key part of Murata's business. Our territory includes the United States, Canada, Latin America, and Oceania. These markets are a major part of our company's past successes and will no doubt play an even greater role in the future.

We recognize that the competitive companies of the 1990s will be global-oriented, and therefore must have a global mentality. Businesses can no longer afford to view markets simply city by city or country by country. Instead, they must develop a regional outlook as countries coalesce into regional markets. It is an absolute requirement that businesses understand the needs of the specific markets in which they wish to compete.

It has been said many times that the 90s is the decade for multinational companies. At Murata, we are positioning ourselves to be a major global player by the end of the decade.

Some say that the most successful multinational corporations "think global but act local." What aspects of Murata's strategy are global and apply equally to virtually all operations around the world?

The one aspect of Murata's strategy that applies throughout our international markets is first-class customer service. Banners hang throughout our headquarters building with "Responsiveness" and "Satisfied Customers—Our Greatest Strength" adorning them. We've worked hard to earn our reputation for quick, efficient, and courteous service in the United States and abroad.

Murata's Service Operations Department is the largest department in the company, reflecting our belief that customer satisfaction is a top priority. For our customers in the United States, Canada, and Mexico, we offer two separate "800" numbers. We receive close to 20,000 calls per month, and 90 percent of the time we're able to solve the customer's problems on the spot through on-line diagnostic testing. This saves the customer the hassle of unhooking his [her] fax, boxing it up, sending it to the shop, and losing his [her] fax capability during the interim.

And for customers with machines in need of a repair, we can send a service technician to the customer's business or home via a third-party repair service. We guarantee to have someone on site in less than one day anywhere in the United States. Or, if the customer prefers, we will ship the machine to our Dallas headquarters and work on it there. We'll do whatever is most convenient for the customer.

For our other international customers, we fully supply our international distributors with spare parts for every unit we sell. And, when necessary, these distributors dispatch service technicians to repair the machines on site. Our international service is comparable to our domestic service, and a chief requirement for becoming a Murata distributor is a strong customer service orientation.

So quality customer service is a common goal of Murata and its business partners worldwide.

What elements of Murata's strategy are most often adjusted to individual countries' demands?

My primary response has to be product design. We have to tailor individual products to individual markets, or we won't be competitive. In particular, cosmetic, technical, and production issues come to mind.

Continued

Cosmetic designs are modified to meet the demands and to take advantage of each specific market. For example, we sell products in Sweden under the FACIT name because the Murata name is unknown. We also do not sell the "M" series machines because most of Europe does not yet have a retail fax market.

Each country has unique telephone system requirements. Some countries also have very strict product safety testing requirements. In general, for a single model of machine our factory may actually produce over twenty-five unique machines to meet the technical requirements of all markets.

The functional operation of the machines must be modified for a specific country's requirements. For instance, the number of redial attempts is regulated in Sweden and Germany. Many other variations exist.

The mix of products offered will vary by market. The very low end sells well in the United Kingdom, which has a channel selling products directly to end users similar to our retail channels in the United States. In Germany, on the other hand, dealers are legally required to install a machine, meaning the very low-end, low-profit machines are not in demand.

Also, some markets require products to be manufactured in that particular country, for example, France and Brazil.

THE IMPORTANCE OF A WORLDWIDE PERSPECTIVE ON STRATEGY

Today's increasingly global marketplace calls for an international outlook on business in general and in formulating competitive strategies in particular.[1] Yet many managers, especially those of U.S. firms, attempt to deny it. With the world's single largest market at home, too many U.S. managers are tempted to duck what they view as the unnecessary complexities of international competition. Research reveals that U.S. managers are far less internationally oriented than the managers of their foreign competitors. In one survey, only 35 percent of American managers responding felt that work experience abroad was important, compared to 74 percent in the non-American sample. While 67 percent of all Americans saw maintaining an international outlook and perspective as critical to their success, the number is still low compared to managers from other regions. The comparable number for European managers was 81 percent, Latin Americans, 87 percent, and 100 percent for the Japanese responding.[2] Surveys in 1985 revealed that only 5 percent of all U.S. manufacturers faced a foreign company among their top five competitors. By 1990, the situation had changed dramatically: more than 30 percent reported that at least three of their top five competitors were foreign. In fact, nearly half predicted that, by 1992, their firms would fall into this category.

Discounting the importance of worldwide competition is a serious mistake, for several reasons. As shown in Exhibit 7.1, the fastest growing economies are not in North America, but in Europe and Japan. Most industries have been affected by the onslaught of international competition in recent years. In the past two decades, industry after industry has changed from serving a simple domestic marketplace to a complex world market. Some firms have tried to avoid the "globalization" of their industries by concentrating narrowly on their domestic operations.[3] Unfortunately, the results have left them even more vulnerable to the international competition relentlessly hounding them. RCA decided it could best defend itself against the threat of Japanese television manufacturers by concentrating its efforts on the United States market. A decade later, RCA was forced to sell its manufac-

EXHIBIT 7.1
The Relative Size of Regional Stock Markets in 1980 and 1990

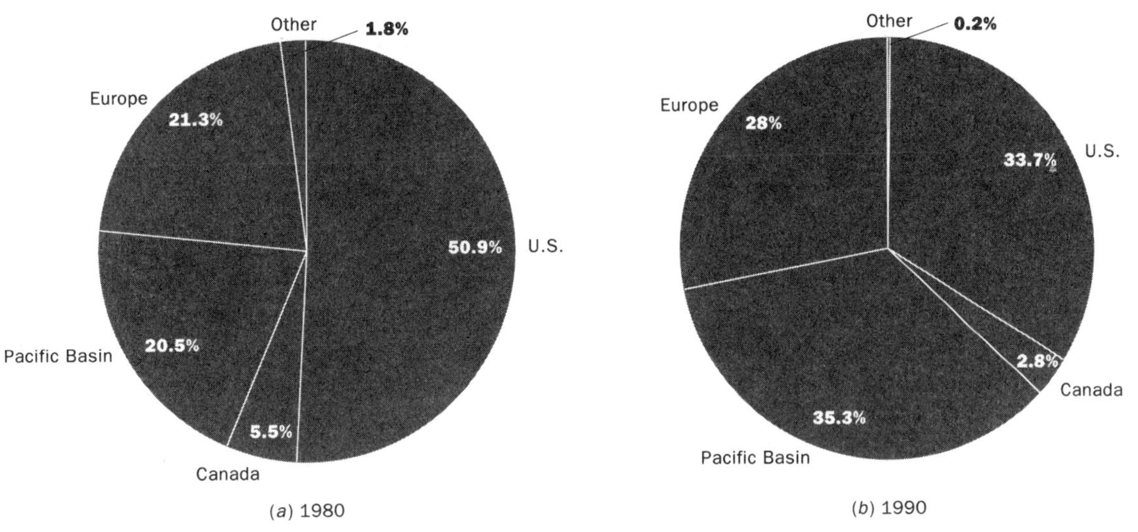

Source: *The Fidelity Guide to International Investing,* available from Fidelity Investments, Inc.

turing operation to a French firm, Thomson, that was willing to compete internationally against rising Japanese firms.[4]

The trend toward worldwide markets makes it difficult to predict where competitors will spring up. A decade ago, few would have predicted that one of the strongest competitors in the software programming industry, Tata Consultancy Services, would be based in Bombay, India.[5] But, since 1950, India has granted 190,000 science and engineering degrees, third after the United States and the Soviet Union. A work force with this training is likely to excel internationally at programming. Furthermore, because programming requires relatively little capital investment and can be exported electronically, it is well-suited for the resources available to Indian firms.

Managers must also recognize that foreign investment in the United States is increasing, bringing an international dimension to what were once purely domestic businesses. Exhibit 7.2 identifies the nations most active in international investing involving the United States. In the last half of the 1980s, foreign investors spent billions of dollars annually, taking advantage of the weak dollar to purchase U.S. assets. Today, these investors own 6 percent of all the stock and corporate debt and 2 percent of all the commercial real estate in the United States.[6]

In recent years, foreign investment in U.S. assets has regularly expanded faster than domestic investment.[7] Exhibit 7.3 compares the growth of U.S. acquisitions of foreign businesses to foreign acquisitions of U.S. firms. In the early 1990s, nearly 30 percent (by dollar value) of all acquisitions of U.S. firms were made by foreign firms.[8] As a result, many businesses considered to be American are, in fact, foreign owned. For instance, Bruce

EXHIBIT 7.2
International Acquisition Activity in 1990

Nationalities of Foreign Acquisitions Made by U.S. Firms			Nationalities of Foreign Firms Making U.S. Acquisitions		
Target Country	**No. of Deals**	**Value (In Millions of Dollars)**	**Acquiring Country**	**No. of Deals**	**Value (In Millions of Dollars)**
Canada	72	723.6	United Kingdom	141	9,731.6
United Kingdom	69	4,628.9	Japan	85	6,540.3
Germany	25	189.7	Canada	61	1,696.2
France	22	662.6	France	47	9,315.0
Australia	20	727.3	Germany	29	438.2
The Netherlands	10	457.2	Switzerland	23	5,421.7

Source: *Mergers & Acquisitions*, Philadelphia (1991, May–June).

EXHIBIT 7.3
International Acquisition Activity

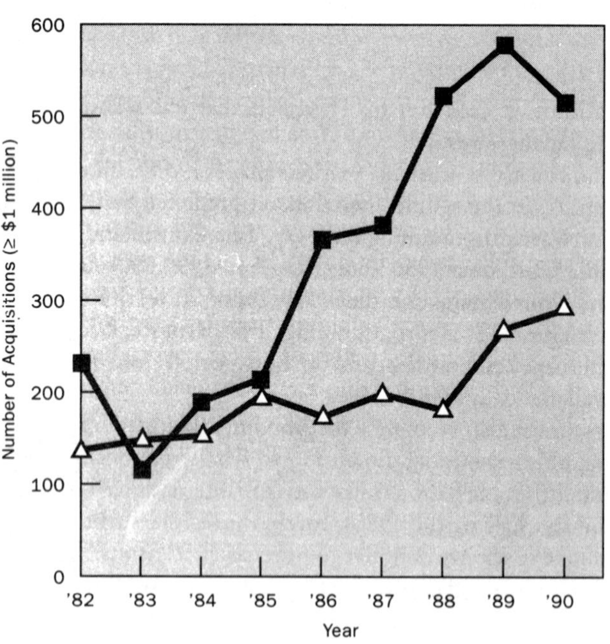

Source: *Mergers & Acquisitions*, Philadelphia (1991, May–June).

Application 7.1

Managing in a Changing Europe: 1992 and Beyond

Although historians remind us that Europe has often been the site of important social and economic change, the changes currently underway are of an unprecedented magnitude. Just as the Project EC 92 initiative portends the unification of major economies in western Europe, several nations in eastern Europe are making dramatic shifts from centrally planned economies toward free market economies.

In western Europe, Project EC 92 is an initiative to facilitate trade between the twelve nations of the European Community (EC). The focus of the effort consists of hundreds of new agreements among member nations regarding everything from check clearing procedures, to immigration laws, to design specifications for electric appliances. By reducing barriers to cross-border commerce, European industries will most likely undergo considerable restructuring and consolidation. The resulting firms will be formidable global competitors. A Pan-European market of 312 million will become the wealthiest consumer group in the world.

Meanwhile, nations in eastern Europe are also undergoing profound shifts in their economies. A unified Germany will eventually dwarf the other economies on the continent. Soviet bloc countries will continue to evolve toward free market economies as countless state-owned industries are privatized. These evolving economies will be a source of new competitors and customers. MNCs with a strong presence in western Europe have already begun their expansion into eastern Europe.

As U.S. managers plan to enter Europe's new markets, they must recognize that success at home is no guarantee of success abroad. One major hurdle is European and American perceptions of each other. One manager, experienced in both cultures, says that European executives characterize their U.S. counterparts using the "four I's": Innocent, Insensitive, Imperialistic, and Impatient. At the same time, U.S. executives speak of the Europeans using the "four B's": Bounded by tradition, Behind the times, Balky, and Broken up into small, idiosyncratic countries. Obviously, before trade between Europe and America flows seamlessly, attitudes must begin changing as dramatically as regulations are.

Sources

Weihrich, H. (1991, February). Europe 1992 and a unified Germany: Opportunities and threats for United States firms. *The Executive*, pp. 93–96.

Cerruti, J. L., & Holtzman, J. (1990, November–December). Business strategy in the new European landscape. *The Journal of Business Strategy*, pp. 18–23.

Arnold, M. R. (1990, July–August). European and U.S. managers: Breaking down the wall. *The Journal of Business Strategy*, pp. 28–31.

Springsteen has worked for a Japanese firm ever since Sony purchased CBS records, and an increasing number of "American" ski resorts and golf courses are owned by Japanese firms. Because of the heavy investments foreign firms have made in U.S. companies, many managers who once thought they worked in a strictly domestic business have become part of the international scene almost overnight.

Crucial growth opportunities exist overseas, both in developed and in developing nations. In 1992, the twelve nations making up the European Community will begin replacing hundreds of regulations, which previously divided their countries into separate markets, with regulations that will unite the countries economically.[9] To the extent that "Project EC 92" is effective, the European Community will become the world's single wealthiest market, larger than the United States, the Soviet Union, or southeast Asia (see Application 7.1). In the late eighties, large portions of the Soviet bloc began opening borders to international trade in what will surely be recorded as one of the greatest economic revolutions in history.[10] Firms that fail to adapt to such changes by moving toward a worldwide perspective will miss opportunities to be major contenders in the upcoming century.

While changes in developed nations offer exciting growth opportunities, the greatest growth potential undoubtedly lies in developing nations. One MNC, Coca Cola, has taken advantage of this. The firm's soft drinks are consumed at an annual rate of 274 eight-ounce servings per capita in the United States. This may be the greatest market penetration in the history of consumer retailing. In other developed nations consumption is not nearly so high (89 servings per year in Japan and 63 per year in Britain), but competitive substitutes are already well entrenched in these markets. The growth potential in the U.S. domestic market or in developed markets around the world is small compared to Indonesia, where 180 million people consume only 3.2 servings per year, or China, where 1.1 billion people consume only 0.2 serving per year.[11] Recognizing this, Coke is already one of the most fully internationalized firms in the world, with operations in 155 countries, many of which are developing nations. Clearly, there is tremendous growth potential offered by developing markets to firms that until now have considered only developed nations.

Smaller firms can also benefit from expanding globally. Industrial giants, like the firms that make up the Fortune 500 (all with at least half a billion dollars in annual sales), get much of the media coverage given to world competition. However, their actions should not overshadow the international activity of medium-sized firms.[12] For instance, in the United States, roughly 7,500 firms not on the Fortune 500 still have sales of more than $100 million. Through the eighties, the *foreign* sales of these firms grew at an annual rate of 20 percent—five times the domestic growth rate of U.S. firms overall. Many other small businesses with sales less than $100 million exist almost entirely as suppliers to foreign markets. Clearly, the potential for worldwide competition is not limited by organizational size.[13]

The Advantages and Disadvantages of Global Diversification

As managers pursue competition in the international arena, they must consider the potential advantages and disadvantages.

Advantages

Expansion into international operation can provide lower costs of operation.[14] Costs of production vary dramatically around the world, making it profitable to open up global operations even when the primary market remains at home. For instance, Nike produces shoes in China, where the cost of labor is far below that in the United States, even though most of the Chinese-produced shoes are sold back in the United States.

International expansion can also supplement limited domestic opportunities. Purely domestic firms are dependent on their home countries for sales and growth. But if a firm wishes to grow faster than its home country's economy, it can achieve economies of scale and greater volume by seeking international sales opportunities. In the 1980s, a number of corporations from countries with stronger currencies acquired U.S. businesses at "bargain" rates. For example, BASF AG, a giant West German chemical products company, and a number of other like-minded German corporations bought several billion dollars worth of U.S. chemical businesses in the eighties in order to overcome limited growth opportunities at home.[15]

A global competitor with limited competition at home may use high profits from its home markets to subsidize its operations in other countries.[16] Because of this, many corporations have found that to be effective competitors domestically, they must be willing to fight international competitors on their home turf.[17] For example, a U.S. firm may wish to enter the Japanese market in order to drive down the margins its Japanese competitors would otherwise enjoy at home. By doing so, the United States firm would hope to limit the ability of the Japanese firm to use high profits from home to support price competition in the United States.

A joint venture between Fuji Photo Film and Xerox is a classic example of how global diversification can aid a corporation by taking the fight to international competitors.[18] In the mid-sixties, Xerox established a strategic alliance with Fuji to help overcome difficulties it was having in exporting copiers to the Japanese market. Within two decades, what had started out as a simple sales operation had grown into the third largest producer of its own line of photocopiers—in Japan. Although Fuji Xerox became a freestanding corporation (with sales in the $1.5 billion range), its success in opening up the Japanese market and in leading the global fight against other Japanese competitors was vital to Xerox, one of its corporate parents. Xerox managers freely admitted that they learned much from their Japanese offspring on how to win in international competition for photocopier sales.

Disadvantages

There are several disadvantages of international operations that managers should keep in mind. First, it often entails greater and more complex risks: all those faced in domestic operations and more. For instance, corporations operating in two countries must be concerned with exchange rates for two currencies. In the early eighties, the British carmaker, Jaguar, went through a radical turnaround process, avoiding bankruptcy and establishing itself as a legitimate competitor in the international luxury car market. However, the United States was the largest market for Jaguars, and the effects of all the company's hard work and advances were wiped out in the last half of the eighties, when the purchasing power of the U.S. dollar tumbled.

International operations also face greater social and political risks than domestic operations. For instance, Iranian businesses with bank accounts in U.S. banks found their funds confiscated by the United States government as part of a retaliation over Iran's taking American citizens as hostages. In such cases, politics directly affects the commercial activities of international firms.

A second disadvantage is that even relatively similar countries have vastly different ways of competing, which creates new managerial hurdles. An example is Anheuser Busch, the leading beer producer in the United States.[19] Because beer is consumed around the world, one might think it would be a good candidate for Anheuser Busch to take global, especially to a country whose culture is similar to that of the United States. Yet, when the company tried to enter the British market, it stumbled, making a number of mistakes in its marketing rollout. Budweiser, its primary product, has a higher alcohol content than most British beers. This was a disadvantage because U.K. import duties are based on alcoholic content. As well, the company's marketing campaign could not convince the British that Budweiser was as strong as their own traditional brands, which were noticeably stronger in flavor than Budweiser's. Ironically, Anheuser Busch was paying stiffer import duties for its higher alcohol content, but suffering from a widespread British opinion that all American beers are weak. The marketing expertise that served Anheuser Busch so well in the United States was almost totally ineffective in Britain.

ENTRY STRATEGIES FOR INTERNATIONAL EXPANSION

Because of the complexities involved, when firms first enter the international arena they generally start on a smaller scale and hope to expand later.[20] Exhibit 7.4 outlines strategies for entering foreign markets. It shows a number of different forms of foreign involvement. These are often called entry strategies, and can be categorized under the headings of exporting (foreign sales), licensing and franchising (contractual arrangements), and joint ventures and wholly owned subsidiaries (foreign investment). Each entails different levels of risk and control. Typically, firms start with the low-risk/low-control options and then advance to higher levels of risk and control as they gain experience and build confidence.[21] We can look at each in turn.

Exporting

It is fair to say that most MNCs got their start in international business through exporting. In an export operation, the firm maintains its production facilities at home and transfers its products abroad. Exporting offers the advantage of not requiring a very substantial presence abroad; usually the firm hires foreign agents to act on the exporter's behalf in arranging contracts. Foreign investment is minimal because the factory is at home and the products can often be shipped directly to the foreign customer's warehouse. Offsetting these advantages are high transportation costs associated with exporting, and the difficulty of dealing with problems like government regulation, cultural differences, and currency exchange from a distance.

EXHIBIT 7.4
Strategies for Entering Foreign Markets

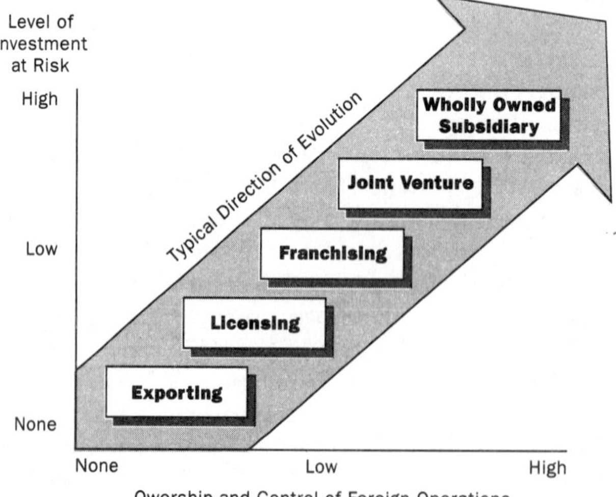

Licensing and Franchising

Two major forms of contractual arrangements are commonly used in international expansion: licensing and franchising. Both involve a contract between parties in different countries. Franchise contracts cover more aspects of the operation and are typically of a longer duration than licensing contracts. A licensor in one country makes limited rights and/or resources available to the licensee in a second country. The rights and/or resources may include patents, trademarks, technology, managerial skills, and so on. These allow the licensee to produce and market a product similar to that the licensor has already been producing in its home country, without requiring the licensor to actually create a new operation abroad. For example, licensors around the world have contracts to produce and sell clothing bearing pictures of Mickey Mouse and other Walt Disney characters.

A franchise usually covers a broader "package" of rights and resources such as trademarks, production equipment, proven managerial systems, standardized operating procedures, access to advertising and promotional materials, loans and financing, product ingredients, and general management assistance. McDonald's is an obvious example of a corporation with franchise contracts around the world.

This type of arrangement can lead to the creation of a new business, in which case the franchise is designed to stand in perpetuity. On the other hand, licenses are more often granted to businesses that existed before the license was arranged and the business serving as the licensee is expected to outlive the license contract.

Joint Ventures and Wholly Owned Subsidiaries

The most significant form of foreign involvement entails direct investment in another country. This means that the firm owns assets based in the foreign country, which provides it with a greater level of control than in the other modes of international expansion. But foreign investment is the riskiest of the global-entry strategies.

To avoid facing all this risk alone, many international firms enter into joint ventures in which companies in two different countries join forces to build a third business entity. As with domestic joint ventures, discussed in Chapter 6, both firms contribute to the cost of creating the third business and both share in its returns. The world automobile industry includes numerous international joint ventures. One of the most successful is New United Motor Manufacturing, Inc., or NUMMI, formed by the Toyota Motor Corporation and General Motors to produce 250,000 subcompacts a year for the Toyota and Chevrolet line.

Another alternative is the wholly owned foreign business over which one company has complete control. This arrangement has the advantages of shortening distribution channels and somewhat simplifying logistics. In addition, managers actually located on site will more quickly perceive changing cultural, economic, and political conditions. However, the company must make financial and managerial investments to acquire or create a business in the foreign country, and this investment is subject to a wide range of political and economic risks. This strategy may be most successful for companies with experience in the other forms of international involvement.

Leads and additional practical advice for those interested in pursuing international options are given in Application 7.2. Once a firm has determined how it will enter a foreign market, it must decide how the international operations should be managed and operated.[22]

Application 7.2

Practical Tips for "Going International"

There are several practical suggestions we can offer to those contemplating involvement in international competition.

Do your homework We hope it is clear from the many examples given in this chapter that there are important differences between international and domestic competition. Your chances of succeeding in this different arena will be greatly increased by investing time in learning more about these differences in general, and also about differences which apply to your specific industry. A good way to start this research is reviewing the vast amount of excellent written material on the subject, for instance:

Exportise, Small Business Foundation of America, 20 Park Plaza, Boston, MA 02116

The Ernst & Young Guide to Expanding in the Global Market. John Wiley & Sons, 605 Third Avenue, New York, NY 10158-0012

S. Woolley. Going Global? Here's How. *Business Week*, July 2, 1990, pp. 88–89.

Analyze the foreign opportunity Given the lack of demographics or other important data in some countries, it may not be feasible to do elaborate formal analysis before entering a given market. For example, McDonald's often begins its analysis of market potential by simply touring grocery stores to look for indications that hamburgers are popular locally.

Utilize host-country contacts Because formal studies are so difficult, local contacts with firsthand knowledge are often critical. These contacts can provide invaluable expertise concerning the local business environment, customs, and market potential. Additionally, host-government officials are often more willing to work with their own citizenry.

Balance your needs for competitiveness against what is fair MNCs are more often than not guests in another nation's homeland. As such, they cannot afford to single-mindedly follow their own narrow interests. They must consider what is fair to their local contacts as well as their host country in general. In the late sixties, Northern Telecom, Ltd., of Canada began establishing a relationship with the national telephone company in Turkey. Today, that joint venture employs over 2,000 people, and cumulative export sales to date are measured in the billions of dollars. Even though NTL's equity position has gradually declined from 51 percent to just 30 percent, in formulating its plans the company can hardly afford to ignore the needs of such a valuable partner.

Be patient Because they present a different set of strategic challenges, international operations normally require more time to develop similar levels of efficiency as domestic operations. For instance, even though McDonald's startup process is virtually perfected as far as domestic operations go (after all, they open a new restaurant every day in the United States), it does not expect to break even for 6 to 10 years after it first moves into a new country. Clearly, a move into international operations has to be a long-term strategic commitment.

Source

Woolley, S. (1990, July 2). Going global? Here's how. *Business Week*, pp. 88–89.

In the remainder of this chapter, we consider the process of formulating strategies for operating businesses in a worldwide context.

A FRAMEWORK FOR FORMULATING WORLDWIDE OPERATING STRATEGIES

As shown in Exhibit 7.5, there are two dimensions within our framework for formulating international strategies.[23] The first of these is competitive advantage. Businesses that oper-

EXHIBIT 7.5
A Framework with Examples of How MNC Strategy Affects Competitive Advantage

	MNC Strategy	
Sources of Competitive Advantage	***Multidomestic Attributes***	***Global Attributes***
High differentiation	Tailor marketing efforts to fit each individual country.	Market "world" products with standardized advertising copy.
Low cost	Avoid transportation costs and trade tariffs by producing locally.	Use high-volume centralized production facilities to maximize economies of scale.
Quick response	Form joint ventures with local partners to avoid delays in entering new markets.	Combine technology from throughout worldwide operations to innovate faster than individuals can.
Government relations	Build goodwill by working with local governmental agencies to address problems facing host nations.	Circumvent trade restrictions limiting success of one country's operations by funneling its business through other countries in global network.

ate across national borders face many of the same competitive challenges as their domestic counterparts. In particular, as described in Chapter 4, they must strive to achieve a sustainable competitive advantage through high differentiation, low cost, quick response, or a combination of these. However, international businesses present additional challenges. In operating across national borders, political and governmental issues take on such importance that they provide the basis for a fourth type of competitive advantage—one we shall call governmental relations.

The second dimension of our framework concerns the extent to which a corporation with operating units scattered around the world has these operations integrated and/or standardized. Corporations with multiple foreign operations that act independently of one another follow a strategy referred to as *multidomestic;* each individual operation treats itself as an independent business. In a multidomestic strategy, the country of each operation becomes its domestic market. As far as the on-site managers of such an operation are concerned, they are more or less an independent business focused solely on their local market.

Corporations with businesses whose operations are standardized or tightly integrated from country to country follow a *global* strategy. These corporations operate all units under a single unifying strategy regardless of location. Under such a strategy, on-site managers scattered across the various countries see themselves as serving a portion of a single, homogeneous worldwide market. When following a strict global strategy, adaptations to market needs are handled centrally, because the corporation views the entire world as a single market.

In order for firms to achieve the strongest possible competitive advantage, they must combine the elements of both global and multidomestic strategies. As Ira Herbert, Coca-Cola's chief marketing officer, explained: "Think globally, but act locally."[24] The usefulness of this idea is not limited to U.S. firms. For example, Asea Brown Boveri, the $25 billion worldwide giant that produces such products as robots, high-speed trains, turbines, and transformers uses this same strategy.[25] The company is headquartered in Europe, has heavy manufacturing operations around the world, keeps the books in dollars, and is considered by many to be the role model for any European firm wishing to capitalize on the changes that are part of the EC 92 initiative. Percy Barnevik, the man most responsible for creating this far-flung empire, says that ABB's goal is to make their products more efficiently, uniting a network of manufacturing facilities and technical expertise it has created around the world (which sounds like a global strategy). But, at the same time, ABB strives to meet each country's needs so that its products seem to come from a domestic producer (seemingly a multidomestic orientation). This is a classic example of thinking globally and acting locally. Barnevik sums up his opinion of the power of such a strategy:

> You want to be able to optimize a business globally—to specialize in the production of components, to drive economies of scale as far as you can. . . . But you also want to have deep local roots everywhere you operate. . . . If you build such an organization, you create a business advantage that's damn difficult to copy.[26]

Governmental Relations as a Competitive Advantage

Even strictly domestic firms must be concerned about relationships with the government.[27] However, when a business operates under the jurisdiction of two or more nations, the problems are compounded, and governmental relations can become either an invaluable advantage or an overwhelming disadvantage.[28] Governmental authorities can play many roles, all with potential benefits and costs to international competitors:[29]

Regulators: The legality of business practices often depends on a local government's disposition on a given issue. This disposition can vary greatly among countries and even within one country over time, and the success of an international operation often hinges upon this one point. Monsanto, one of the world's largest suppliers of agricultural chemicals, had for many years shipped herbicides in bulk to Brazil, where they were then packaged for the South American market. Concerned about its balance of trade, the Brazilian government began to pressure Monsanto to build a factory that would handle the entire production operation, not just packaging. When Monsanto resisted, the government allowed a local company to produce a line of herbicides that Monsanto claims violated its patents. Faced with the resulting local competition, Monsanto was forced to defend itself in the local market by building the plant after all, while defending its patent rights in the Brazilian courts. The company's director of international operations admits, "If we had to do it over, we'd have made our investment earlier and avoided all this."[30]

Conegotiators: Global competition can make for some strange bedfellows, as international firms cultivate a coalition of governmental support often ranging far outside their home country. U.S. lawmakers in Washington have recently begun to negotiate against regulators in Europe for the right of Japanese carmakers operating in the United States to export more cars to Europe. Normally, these same U.S. legislators are concerned about regulating the flow of Japanese imports to the United States, but in this case, they are allies, working as conegotiators in support of the Japanese firms' rights in Europe.[31]

Suppliers: In many nations, the state owns key natural resources. In such situations, the government may act as a supplier of these resources to foreign firms. This is true for some crucial resources, such as energy, as many oil and coal reserves are controlled by national governments.

Competitors: The public service sector of any nation provides at least some goods and services that are substitutes for those private enterprise provides in other nations. In such cases, these public service organizations constitute a form of competition with actual or potential suppliers from the private sector. Private airlines often compete abroad with government-owned airlines.

Customers: Depending on the industry, foreign governments may be vital customers whose support is critical for sales volume. Boeing, a leading supplier of commercial aircraft around the world, often sells its planes to, or through, a local government. The power and importance of governments as customers means that Boeing must be open and receptive to unusual business deals that the firm would probably not consider otherwise. In a process known as countertrade,[32] the company has bartered planes for oil, tin, copper, and in one case, even feathers! Although the feathers deal fell through, Boeing's director of international sales says, "You can't close the door on anything."[33]

Before moving on, we should point out that the firm's home government can also have a strong influence on its success abroad. Again, consider Boeing's international experiences. Given Boeing's willingness to adapt its practices to local customs, the firm has been able to do well in selling aircraft to wealthy nations in the Middle East. However, Boeing claims that when the United States government moved to block the sale of Boeing aircraft to Libya, it angered other Arab nations, which then began to buy aircraft from other countries. So, an international competitor must contend with its own relationship with a host country, and also cope with poor relationships among the nations themselves.

Global versus Multidomestic Strategies

Social and economic pressures drive international competitors in two opposing directions. On the one hand, there are economic pressures that encourage managers to treat operations in different countries only as a part of some greater whole which must be managed for overall efficiency. On the other hand, there are social pressures that encourage managers within each country to be responsive to the unique cultural and political circumstances in their narrow slice of the overall world market. These economic and social forces are so great that they are commonly referred to as the two *imperatives* facing MNC managers.[34] The former creates pressure to operate with a global strategy, and the latter encourages firms to operate under a multidomestic strategy. The following two sections discuss the differences in these two strategies. We will explore how responding to conflicting social and economic pressures with a combination of both a multidomestic and a global strategy helps achieve the strongest mix of competitive advantages. A summary of some important differences among the multidomestic, global, and hybrid strategic options facing MNCs is provided in Exhibit 7.6.

The Economic Imperative and Global Strategies

In some industries, the volume necessary for the greatest economies of scale and learning curve effects (originally described in Chapters 4 and 5) is not obtainable within a single country. In this case, it makes sense to combine operations in different countries to increase throughput and gain economies of scale. A corporation with global integration can use its network of operating sites to achieve greater overall efficiency than any single site could achieve individually.

For example, Caterpillar, the world's leading producer of heavy earth-moving equipment, utilizes this sort of integration in its worldwide operations. The factories that build

EXHIBIT 7.6
Three Forms of Strategy for International Operations

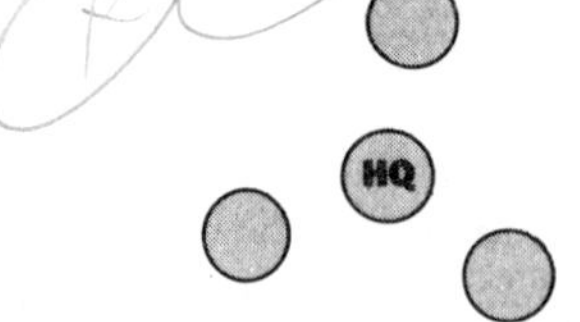

The Multidomestic Strategy

- Units in various countries are independent
- Each unit treats its markets as distinct from all others
- Corporate headquarters is not much more than just another unit

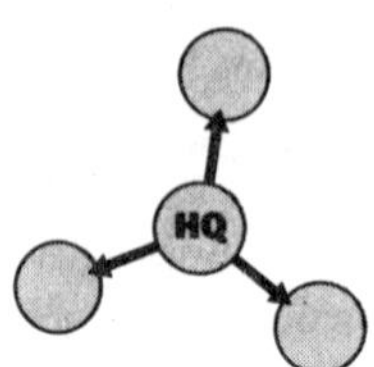

The Global Strategy

- Units in various countries are under centralized control from corporate headquarters
- Headquarters seek out standardized products suitable for a variety of markets
- Production is coordinated centrally to create economies of scale

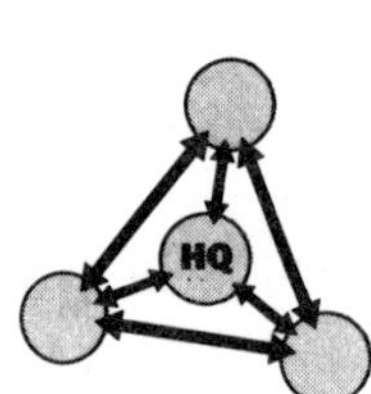

The Hybrid Strategy

- Units coordinate their activities with headquarters and with one another
- Units in various countries may adapt to special circumstances only they face
- Entire organization draws upon relevant corporate resources, wherever they are

Caterpillar products require heavy capital investment, best absorbed with high-volume production of a fairly standardized product line. Furthermore, while the company's customers around the world require access to a broad range of earth-moving equipment, specific needs do not vary much by nation. In other words, a particular customer may need a particular combination of bulldozers, highlifts, and backhoes, but the equipment required to move dirt is basically the same within any country. Therefore, Caterpillar has its factories within a given country focus on volume production of a relatively narrow range of products, resulting in maximum economies of scale and learning curve effects within each factory. As a result of this focus, no single factory can produce the broad line of equipment that customers need, so each factory cooperates with others in Caterpillar's worldwide system to provide the overall range of products required. When the same parts are manufactured in more than one nation, central control of designs assures that these parts are interchangeable and that they will fit on any appropriate Caterpillar, regardless of its country of origin. This is a global strategy, because each country's operation is viewed as a part of a single worldwide plan.

Use of such strategies and the globalization of industries is on the rise because of several trends. The emergence of products with worldwide acceptance like Nikon cameras and German engineering services has facilitated worldwide integration. Development of cheaper, more reliable transportation and worldwide communication networks has also encouraged globalization. Observers of today's international competition refer to a "global village" in which we all live in the same neighborhood and trade in the same shops. Success

Application 7.3

Bribery: An Ethical Dilemma of International Management

Bribery, the practice of giving cash, gifts, or favors in order to receive favorable treatment, is one of the most common ethical dilemmas facing international managers. In many places, bribery has long been an accepted part of daily commerce, with no stigma attached to it. Managers competing in such an environment may correctly feel themselves to be at a disadvantage if they refuse to offer bribes while their competitors exhibit no such qualms.

Cultural practices, including bribery, are often confusing to foreign managers. Norms vary widely from country to country. The Foreign Corrupt Practices Act makes it illegal for U.S. managers to give or take bribes, regardless of the country within which they are operating. On the other hand, the German government treats most bribes made in other countries as tax deductible business expenses.

Even within a single country, norms appear to be changing rapidly as the level of international commerce continues to increase. For example, Nigeria has a long tradition of accepting bribes as daily business. However, with more foreign managers operating in Nigeria, an important distinction is being made today between bribes made by Nigerians and bribes made by outsiders. One study summed up the distinction by explaining that "When in Rome, the Romans do not want you doing as the Romans do."

Laws such as the Foreign Corrupt Practices Act are intended to resolve the ambiguity regarding when bribes are and are not acceptable by making all such behavior illegal. The act's defenders see it as a symbol of high U.S. ethical standards, while its critics see it as a naive and impractical barrier to U.S. competitiveness and fair trade around the world. Both sides agree that it is very difficult to unambiguously delineate ethical and unethical behavior. When asked to evaluate a managerial scenario involving bribery, about half of the U.S. managers responding considered the behavior unethical, while the other half were either neutral or found it to be acceptable.

Rather than depend upon laws to guide managerial behavior in such ambiguous situations, many firms have developed their own approaches to dealing with bribery. Some of the simplest of these procedures are the most effective. For instance, Cadbury Schweppes PLC uses just two questions in helping its international managers determine whether or not a questionable payment is acceptable from the company's point of view: Does the payment appear on the face of the invoice? Would it embarrass the company or the recipient if the payment were noted by the press? The first question is aimed at ensuring that all business payments go on the firm's books. The second is an acknowledgment that, ultimately, the best person to decide on the acceptability of a given payment is the manager on the scene.

Sources

Longenecker, J. G., McKinney, J. A., & Moore, C. W. (1988). The ethical issue of international bribery: A study of attitudes among U.S. business professionals. *Journal of Business Ethics, 7,* 341–346.

Tsalikis, J., & Nwachukwu, O. (1991). A comparison of Nigerian to American views of bribery and extortion in international commerce. *Journal of Business Ethics, 10,* 85–98.

Cadbury, A., Sir (1987, September–October). Ethical managers make their own rules. *Harvard Business Review,* pp. 69–73.

as a merchant in the global village requires MNCs to understand how to build global strategies.

The Social Imperative and Multidomestic Strategies

Concurrent with the trend toward greater globalization has been a somewhat opposing trend that encourages MNCs to adapt far-flung operations to specific situations. Several factors can make this desirable. For instance, social and cultural differences necessitate changes in tactics for dealing with stakeholders. For example, see Application 7.3 on how social norms regarding bribery impact international management. Governments in countries around the world also frequently insist that the actions of the MNC are consonant with the interests of the host nation. As industrialization spreads, local competitors scramble to serve narrowing market segments, forcing MNCs to be equally adaptable. With a local supplier capable of producing a tailored product, customers are no longer forced to accept products designed for the middle of the road or for another country.

Differences such as these cause most businesses to adjust the way they do business from one country to the next. Firms must often adapt their products and the way those products are marketed to suit particular circumstances. Some of these adaptations are fairly minor, as in the case of Hewlett-Packard's changing its keyboard layouts to reflect different typing requirements and changing its business software to match different accounting practices. Others are more substantive, as in the case of Avon in Japan.

Avon markets its line of cosmetics using a sales technique that has been successful nearly everywhere in the world: women sell the products door to door. However, during its first years in Japan, the company had little success using this approach. After careful study of the problem, the managers at Avon finally discovered that Japanese women are often too reserved to make a forceful sales pitch to strangers. The company adjusted its approach to selling in Japan, emphasizing sales to women who were not strangers and an advertising campaign featuring a soft-sell approach with poetic images. Since this adjustment, the firm has enlisted more than 350,000 saleswomen in Japan and its sales have grown more than 25 percent per year.

COMBINING GLOBAL AND MULTIDOMESTIC STRATEGIES

Within a worldwide market, the best strategies are neither purely multidomestic nor purely global, but a combination of both.[35] This becomes readily apparent when we see the shortcomings of single-mindedly pursuing an international strategy based on either global integration alone or multidomestic adaptation alone.[36]

Faulty Assumptions Supporting a "Pure" Global Strategy

What are the assumptions that would make pursuit of a "pure" global strategy sensible? According to Theodore Levitt, considered by many to be the father of the concept of global strategies, there are three.[37] Although these assumptions appear to be perfectly reasonable, critics have been quick to point out numerous cases where one or more of them do not hold.[38] Here, we present the three assumptions, along with some counterexamples:

1. *Customer needs, interests, and tastes are becoming increasingly homogenized.* While there are undoubtedly many industries where substantial similarities exist among customers in different countries (earth-moving equipment, cameras, and soft drinks are just a few of the examples already mentioned in this chapter), there are probably many more where substantial differences exist.[39] For instance, Findus, the frozen foods division of Nestlé, the giant Swiss food company, does well marketing fish fingers in the United Kingdom, but in France, its successful products are beef bourguignon and coq au vin, and in Italy, they are vitello con funghi and braciole. Even Findus products that ostensibly have an international appeal actually differ substantially from country to country. For example, the pizzas Findus sells in the United

Kingdom include cheese with ham and pineapple toppings on a French bread crust, hardly an internationally accepted recipe for pizza.

2. *Consumers around the world are willing to trade off idiosyncratic preferences in product features for lower price.* This assumption encourages MNCs to compete with aggressive pricing on low-cost products which meet the common needs of customers around the world. This implies a global orientation, with low cost achieved through the high volume offered by standardized products produced in centralized facilities. The problem with such an orientation is that it may lead firms to focus on the least desirable customers. Price-sensitive customers are notorious for their lack of brand loyalty, while many premium goods, such as Cartier watches and Godiva chocolates, command a loyal following around the world. Furthermore, in international competition, there are several means by which any one competitor's cost position may be eroded so severely as to make price competition impractical. Host governments may subsidize local competitors, trade tariffs may add costs to exporting, and transportation and distribution costs may favor local suppliers. All these suggest that there are many instances where a focus on price/cost competition will be misguided, and the link between the economic imperative and global strategies is therefore weakened.

3. *Substantial economies of scale in production and marketing can be achieved by treating the world's markets as homogeneous.*[40] Note that there are actually two types of economies of scale mentioned in this statement: those related to production and others related to marketing. The economic imperative discussed above implies pressure to build large centralized production facilities which supply a wide geographic region covering several countries. However, there are counterpressures that might lead managers of MNCs to adopt a more decentralized strategy for their operations, featuring smaller plants which serve local markets. Recent developments in flexible manufacturing have allowed for a decline in the minimum volume required to reach acceptable levels of production efficiency.[41] In addition, such a localized multiplant strategy provides a sort of insurance against instability from sources such as fluctuating exchange rates or government regulations.

In regard to economies of scale in marketing, one might argue that worldwide marketing campaigns offer the potential of important economies of scale in product development and advertising.[42] Some MNCs have made ambitious attempts at having uniform products and marketing efforts throughout the world to gain such economies of scale. Gillette's Sensor razor is one example.

Gillette invested $200 million in developing its Sensor razor. Because the razor retails at only $4, the firm was interested in generating the widest possible distribution in order to have the volume required to amortize the R&D investment.[43] The firm developed a successful single advertising campaign to sell its Atra razor throughout Europe, which saved millions in packaging and advertising. Confident from this experience, Gillette launched the new Sensor razor with a single advertising campaign for nineteen markets scattered around the world. Results were excellent, and demand from retailers ran ahead of Gillette's ability to supply the product. Based on this success, the Sensor's global marketing effort may serve as the model Gillette uses in rolling out an entire line of "world" cosmetic products for men.[44]

For every example like Gillette's Sensor, however, there are counterexamples, firms that failed to develop a product or marketing program with universal appeal. Kellogg's experience in marketing breakfast cereals around the world is just one. Kellogg has found it must make major adjustments to its marketing efforts depending upon the eating habits of a given country.[45] In Brazil, where the traditional breakfast is coffee and a roll, emphasis is placed on teaching the consumer to view cereal as a breakfast food to be eaten with milk, rather than a snack food to be eaten alone. But, in France, the emphasis is placed on convincing the consumer that cold cereals can be nutritious and taste good. Overcoming language differences provides still another reason to adjust marketing efforts. In Japan, consumers have trouble pronouncing "snap, crackle, and pop," the sounds Kellogg attributes to its Rice Krispies cereal. So in Japan, Rice Krispies go "patchy, pitchy, putchy." And because the name Bran Buds translates roughly into "burned farmer" in Sweden, Kellogg found it beneficial to alter that name for the Swedish market.

Convergence of Global and Multidomestic Strategies

As a result of the forces and counterforces driving MNCs to adopt elements of both global and multidomestic strategies, we are now observing a pervasive convergence of these strategies in the most successful MNCs. Industries that were once cited as examples of pure multidomestic operations are becoming globalized, and vice versa. The consumer electronics industry and the laundry detergent industry provide classic examples of each trend.

Consumer Electronics: From Global toward Multidomestic

Until 10 years ago, the consumer electronics industry was marked by its increasing economies of scale in R&D, manufacturing, and marketing, all forces encouraging more global strategies in this industry. For example, the minimum efficient scale for a television set in the late seventies was around 2.5 million sets per year—forty to fifty times the minimum efficient scale of a plant 20 years earlier. Such tremendous economies of scale assured that only a handful of very-high-volume worldwide suppliers would ultimately survive the shakeout that followed the industry's reaching the maturity stage in its market life cycle. Matsushita, the Japanese electronics giant producing the Panasonic and Quasar lines, among others, is representative of the survivors. The firm emphasized worldwide sales of a standardized product line and production in huge centralized plants. This is a classic global strategy designed to produce maximum volume of homogeneous products.

Ironically, the success of global strategies such as Matsushita's led some competitors toward a more multidomestic approach. Host governments began to resist what was viewed as a flood of Japanese imports upsetting their trade balances, and political action, including antidumping lawsuits (against importing goods at unrealistically low prices in order to drive out local competition), and limited trade agreements followed. The cumulative effect of these moves was to encourage foreign firms to set up smaller local production facilities scattered around the world. By placing a plant inside a number of host nations, such foreign-owned corporations built up governmental support in a wide range of countries, not just in their native home country.

Meanwhile, niche players attacked the market global players once held. The competitors succeeded in customizing products to local consumer tastes more precisely. So, for instance, the British firm Amstrad introduced a fast-growing line of consumer electronics featuring wood cabinetry and specific types of control panels that British consumers desired. Eventually, the success of firms like Amstrad forced Matsushita to reverse itself on its strategy of offering limited, standardized products for markets around the world. In several product categories, the firm has recently more than doubled the number of models available around the world. While its sales per individual model have declined sharply, overall sales have risen.

Laundry Detergents: From Multidomestic toward Global

While Matsushita continues to add elements of a multidomestic orientation to its generally global strategy, MNCs that were once strictly multidomestic are becoming more global. For instance, laundry detergents have, until recently, been produced primarily by firms pursuing a multidomestic operation, a situation created by several factors acting in combination. As recently as 1980, the use of washing machines varied from less than 30 percent penetration in Britain to over 85 percent penetration in Germany. Habits and standard practices for washing clothes varied widely too. In northern Europe, "boil washing" had long been the standard, while in the Mediterranean countries, most washing was done in cold water. Differences in water hardness, fabric mixes, perfume preferences, legislation governing phosphate effluents, and marketing practices (in Holland, each brand is limited to a certain number of minutes of television advertising per year) also did their part to ensure that a multidomestic orientation prevailed in the industry.

However, this trend has been reversed in the past 10 years. Sharply increased sales of washing machines have greatly standardized laundry practices, as has the widespread use of synthetic fibers. Coupled with these changes was cost pressure brought on by the oil crisis of the mid-seventies: raw materials for producing detergents rose sharply, just as a worldwide recession made passing along increased costs to the consumer impossible. As a result of this dilemma, manufacturers were forced to actively seek out new means of economizing. The result was a more global perspective. Although they had previously left R&D up to the chemical companies that supplied their raw materials, some detergent manufacturers found that by standardizing products, they could efficiently do the R&D themselves, and thereby hope to achieve a competitive advantage not easily copied by rivals.

For example, Procter & Gamble benefited from treating research and development on laundry detergent as part of an integrated global strategy. P&G has a detergent, sold with only minor modifications around the world, under the label of Tide in the United States, Ariel in Europe, and Cheer in southeast Asia. The product combines major technical advances from the company's research laboratories in Japan, Germany, and the United States. Without global coordination, the technologies resident in the regional laboratories would have never been combined to provide P&G with a product versatile enough to sell in so many different markets.

Both these examples indicate that MNCs are moving toward a blend of attributes, some relating to a multidomestic orientation, and others to a global perspective. In Application 7.4, we see that McDonald's, the world's leading restaurant chain, also benefits from a combination of multidomestic and global attributes. In the following section, we discuss how such combinations allow MNCs to achieve the strongest possible mix of competitive advantages.

Application 7.4

McDonald's Combines Global and Multidomestic Strategies

McDonald's, the world's most successful fast food restaurant chain, provides a classic example of a MNC which successfully combines elements of both global and multidomestic approaches to international competition. The company, which operates in more than forty countries with over 2,000 outlets outside the United States, realizes more than 40 percent of its growth in sales through international expansion.

One reason for McDonald's success in moving into new countries is its willingness to adapt its operations to the needs of the local partners that it typically uses in its foreign operations. One such partner in Singapore says, "The message that comes out of Chicago [site of the corporation's headquarters] is 'What can we do for you?' rather than 'What did you do and why?'" McDonald's corporate managers regularly depend upon their operators for advice on such matters as menu changes. For instance, beverage selections available on McDonald's menus differ considerably around the world. In Germany, McDonald's sells beer; in Brazil, it serves soft drinks made from the guarana, a berry native only to the Amazon; and in Malaysia it offers milkshakes flavored with durian, a fruit popular locally because of its reported effectiveness as an aphrodisiac.

But the role of local partners and the multidomestic orientation that their involvement implies goes far beyond menus. McDonald's is well known in the United States for its cutting-edge work in the area of site selection. However, the company does not automatically presume that this expertise is transferable to every new country it enters. For instance, when McDonald's entered Japan, its local partner steered it away from the suburban locations typical in the United States, toward urban sites that customers could get to without cars. Den Fujita, president of McDonald's Co. (Japan) Ltd., says, "We don't just sit here and take everything from the United States. We have to make improvements to get better operations."

Ironically, even with this heavy emphasis on local operations, McDonald's provides an excellent example of a MNC with a high level of global integration. For example, on products popular the world over, like its french fries, McDonald's works unceasingly to ensure conformity in all locations. This includes teaching farmers in eighteen selected countries around the world to grow russet potatoes just like those from Idaho.

The company is even more stringent in its requirements for global uniformity in "production" management. Detailed descriptions of standard operating procedures determining product and service consistency fill telephone directory-sized "shop manuals." The firm now operates "Hamburger Universities" in several countries around the world, and because professors are rotated from country to country, and every store sends students to a "Hamburger U" somewhere, the corporation can make sure that the "McDonald's experience" is the same for consumers the world over. So, while elements of each country's operations are uniquely tailored to what that country needs, this customization takes place within the context of an overall global strategy that emphasizes uniformity.

Sources

Deveny, K., Pluenneke, J. E., Yang, D. J., Maremont, M., & Black, R. (1986). McWorld. *Business Week*, pp. 63–68.

Tully, S. (1990, July 2). Doing business in one Germany. *Fortune*, pp. 80–83.

Renshaw, J. (1987, Summer). Cultural savvy—the essential factor. *Multinational Business*, pp. 33–36.

INTERNATIONAL STRATEGY AND COMPETITIVE ADVANTAGE

Like their domestic counterparts, maintaining a competitive advantage is critical to the success of international businesses. How do attributes of multidomestic and global international strategies relate to each of the forms of competitive advantage?

Differentiation

Thanks in large part to the power of the Marlboro Man advertising campaign, Marlboro cigarettes has achieved greater worldwide acceptance than virtually any other product in history. This success has been based in large part on differentiating the brand by use of a global marketing campaign. Historically, a single set of advertisements, created in the United States, has been used all over the world, wherever cigarette commercials are allowed. This was as pure an approach to global marketing as possible, and it worked well for years. Some have estimated that, at times, the Marlboro brand alone accounted for 60 percent of Philip Morris's total corporate profits. However, there is recent evidence that even this prime example of pure global marketing is being adjusted for regional differences in what amounts to at least a small step toward a multidomestic orientation.[46]

Recently, the advertising agency that handled the account divided the world into twenty-five primary markets for cigarettes, and its creative people from each of these regions submitted ideas for the year's advertising campaign. In its first year, this approach brought in sixty-nine suggestions, and the ad agency's top creative directors from around the world selected nine storyboards, which were then submitted to Philip Morris for review. Philip Morris approved five of the commercials, from which local managers operating independently in individual countries were free to make their selections. Obviously, this is still an approach very much aligned with the notion of worldwide differentiation through global marketing, yet, it is increasingly tempered with recognition of the need for flexibility regarding cultural differences.

Other companies have found that global marketing did not work successfully for them, and have been much more aggressive than Philip Morris in moving toward a multidomestic approach to achieving differentiation for their products. For instance, when Parker Pen tried to standardize marketing for its line of ink pens to 154 markets around the world, it encountered severe problems. Under the new global strategy, the local authority of some managers was sharply reduced, and they resisted the plan. The new centralized, high-volume plant could not produce adequate numbers of good pens, and the company began losing money. The business was eventually sold for only $100 million to a group of managers who had opposed the global strategy from the outset.[47] Once these managers took over, they quickly restored local-manager autonomy, particularly emphasizing decentralized, country-specific advertising. Soon, Parker had become the number 1 selling line of pens in many of its markets, and from a half million dollar loss in the year of the takeover, the company rebounded the next year with $23 million in profits.[48] Exhibit 7.7 presents other ways in which both multidomestic and global strategies can contribute to the competitive advantage of differentiation.

EXHIBIT 7.7
The Competitive Advantage of DIFFERENTIATION May Be . . .

Facilitated by the Elements of a Multidomestic Strategy, Such As . . .	*Facilitated by the Elements of a Global Strategy, Such As . . .*
. . . increased freedom of individual business units to adjust promotion and advertising to local tastes	. . . economies of scale in advertising and promotion of images with a worldwide appeal
. . . flexibility in applying local research and development to developing tailored products meeting country-specific needs	. . . the ability to draw upon the resources of a coordinated network of R&D laboratories in developing world products
. . . the ability to adapt after-the-sale service to the specific cultural norms of a particular market	. . . the creation of a worldwide network offering consistent levels of service, regardless of location

Cost Leadership

As we have noted, the justification for a global strategy is often the assumption that it will provide greater economies of scale and learning curve effects, thereby providing the competitive advantage of cost leadership. However, firms with low-cost positions have also successfully followed a multidomestic strategy (see Exhibit 7.8). Both can work, and the key to understanding which is more likely to be cost effective in a given situation is understanding what accounts for most of the costs entailed in the industry's value chain. Industries in which proportionally more value is added in upstream activities are more likely to benefit from a global strategy than those industries in which more value is added downstream.[49]

For example, industries such as chemicals, commercial aircraft, computers, and heavy construction equipment all have much of their value added in R&D, product design, and manufacturing activities (all relatively upstream), and each of these industries is dominated by firms that have a strong global orientation to their strategies. By centralizing these upstream activities, these firms can lower their costs and gain efficiencies that the multidomestic approach of many smaller efforts scattered among a number of nations cannot provide.

On the other hand, industries such as insurance, prepared foods, and security services all have much of their value added by downstream activities such as marketing, sales, and services. These industries tend toward strategies based on a multidomestic orientation because the important activities of their value chains do not lend themselves to mass production at centralized locations. In fact, attempts to centralize such activities would probably induce *dis*economies of scale because of the complexity of coordinating such diversity. For example, Findus' would have difficulty making pizzas to fit all the world's tastes in just one centralized kitchen.

It is worth noting that the decision to adopt a global or a multidomestic perspective is not nearly as simple as these examples might lead one to think; there are exceptions to every generalization. The best competitors do not concentrate on just one form of competitive advantage, but struggle to excel on multiple dimensions. Because of this, a firm inclined to adopt a global strategy to lower costs might end up pursuing a more multidomestic strategy because of what it offers in the way of differentiation, quick response, or governmental support.

Also, it is important to note that the decision is not made by managers of the MNC alone. Quite often, the government of the host country plays a strong role in determining

EXHIBIT 7.8
The Competitive Advantage of COST LEADERSHIP May Be . . .

Facilitated by the Elements of a Multidomestic Strategy, Such As . . .	***Facilitated by the Elements of a Global Strategy, Such As . . .***
. . . decreased shipping and transportation costs inherent in local production	. . . economies of scale gained through centralized production of standardized products
. . . avoidance of trade duties and tariffs by manufacturing within the country that would otherwise be taxing imports	. . . decreased duplication of inventories which are often involved in having multiple plants producing similar products

what the MNC's strategy will look like. For example, several Latin American countries will not let foreigners hold a majority of the stock in a local business, while other countries refuse to allow a MNC to operate within their borders without sharing their technology with local manufacturers. In such cases, MNCs either adapt to the situation of the individual nation—a multidomestic response—or choose not to operate in that country at all.

General Electric provides a good example of how these other matters may take precedence over concern for cost alone in deciding between a multidomestic and a global strategy.[50] To secure a $450-million contract to build locomotives in China, General Electric had to agree to simultaneously work on transferring its locomotive technology to local Chinese manufacturers over the contract's 10-year life. Production of locomotives has tremendous economies of scale, and normally, concern for economic efficiency and cost competitiveness would lead GE to produce the 420 units it required in a centralized factory outside of China. However, by taking a less than economically optimal opportunity in building locomotives with local firms, the company gained valuable experience in working with the Chinese and improved its competitive advantage in terms of its governmental relations. GE obviously felt that the potential gain in governmental relations was worth the loss of efficiency in locomotive production. Government support will be a useful long-term asset in selling GE's broad range of products in the world's most populous country.

Quick Response

In the GE example, the MNC is essentially entering into a joint venture with local firms in China. This is a tactic often used to increase the speed with which a MNC enters and penetrates a given national market. Having a local partner can facilitate processes such as obtaining government permits and securing lines of credit from local banks. Local partners are also valuable sources of information about local business practices and essential practical information like which of the local law firms are the best. This means that by adopting a country-by-country approach to international expansion, the MNC is able to respond more quickly to the unique situation each country offers.

However, at times, a multidomestic approach can actually slow down the response time of a MNC, resulting in a lost competitive advantage. For instance, Hewlett-Packard traditionally produced versions of its computer software and manuals in local languages for countries outside the United States only after an initial rollout at home. In this multidomestic approach, each country was considered as a separate step toward worldwide distribution. But the incremental procedure allowed foreign competitors to learn of what was coming to their market long enough before it arrived, and so had time to adjust their own products accordingly. HP had adopted a more global approach to the rollout of its new line of highly successful graphic terminals, simultaneously introducing the product and supporting documentation in fifteen languages.[51]

Otis Elevator also responds more quickly to market opportunities as a result of its global approach to managing innovation. It latest line of "smart" elevators is the product of R&D at six different research centers in five different countries: France, Germany, Japan, Spain, and the United States. Otis estimates that this global approach cut the development time for the new line of elevators from 4 years to 2 years and saved the company more than $10 million in design costs. Exhibit 7.9 summarizes some of the ways that multidomestic and global strategies support the competitive advantage of quick response.

EXHIBIT 7.9
The Competitive Advantage of QUICK RESPONSE May Be . . .

Facilitated by the Elements of a Multidomestic Strategy, Such As . . .	*Facilitated by the Elements of a Global Strategy, Such As . . .*
. . . joint ventures with local businesses provide faster startups, as local partners "know the ropes"	. . . a centrally coordinated effort can bring greater corporate resources to bear on problems of establishing an operation in a new market
. . . local independence allows better responsiveness to local developments	. . . R&D laboratories cooperating with one another on innovations progress faster than a single independent laboratory could

Government Support

As with the other forms of competitive advantage, there are means by which a combination of multidomestic and global approaches can also help a MNC obtain governmental support (see Exhibit 7.10). While it adopts a strong global perspective overall, IBM provides many good examples of what a MNC can do within an individual country to achieve local governmental support by operating in a multidomestic mode. For instance, IBM built support for itself in several Latin American countries by sponsoring nutritional programs for children, while it advised Mexico on agricultural priorities.[52] Meanwhile, halfway around the world, Polaroid, another politically savvy MNC, is helping the Italian government restore Leonardo da Vinci's *Last Supper.* Obviously, such actions are not done strictly as ends in themselves; they help the MNC establish its legitimacy with the country's government, creating a comfortable environment for business with the support of the local authorities.

But, a multidomestic approach is not always the most effective means of dealing with government agencies. In fact, some MNCs deal with governmental/political pressure by taking advantage of their unified global network of operations. When Germany's BASF's research on biotechnology came under fire from the "Greens," a collection of environmentally conscious and politically powerful interest groups, the company decided to shift the research being protested in Germany to its facilities in Cambridge, Massachusetts.[53] BASF's experience indicated that the move offered them a climate where the community

EXHIBIT 7.10
The Competitive Advantage of GOVERNMENTAL SUPPORT May Be . . .

Facilitated by the Elements of a Multidomestic Strategy, Such As . . .	*Facilitated by the Elements of a Global Strategy, Such As . . .*
. . . greater goodwill resulting from employing local work forces, rather than simply importing finished goods made elsewhere	. . . greater bargaining power associated with the corporation as a whole, rather than a local operation acting individually
. . . flexibility in adjusting to local laws and customs	. . . flexibility in shifting operations throughout a coordinated network as conditions vary in specific locales

had, to a relatively greater extent, resolved controversies concerning safety, animal rights, and the environment. Rather than fight isolated political movements in any particular country, such globally oriented MNCs can shift sensitive work to the location within their worldwide operation where it will best fit the values of the local citizens.[54]

Northern Telecom, Ltd., the leading Canadian telecommunications firm, made a somewhat similar use of its global operations to overcome trade barriers that were preventing it from penetrating the Japanese market. The Japanese government was under severe pressure from the United States, its largest nation customer, to address the growing imbalance of trade between the two countries. Much of this political pressure was aimed at making it easier for U.S. operations to export products to Japan. Japan responded to the pressure by lifting some key restrictions on U.S. imports, although these restrictions remained in effect against other nations. As a result, it became much easier to export telecommunications devices into Japan from a base in the United States rather than Canada. Therefore, Northern Telecom operates its Japanese business out of its U.S. subsidiary's headquarters, rather than the corporate headquarters in Canada. Again, the global integration of the firm allows it to better adjust its operation to fit the political realities it encounters, and governmental support serves as a competitive advantage rather than a disadvantage.

Summary

Our world is advancing rapidly and inexorably toward a global marketplace. The most successful firms of the future will be those that embrace this change and center their strategies around it. These multinational corporations will be in the best position to build strategies which employ corporate resources to strengthen the competitive advantages of their foreign operations.

The competitive advantages important to a foreign operation overlap with those important to domestic businesses. Differentiation, cost leadership, and quick response are powerful weapons, regardless of geography. But, in international competition, where different governments are involved, a fourth form of competitive advantage—governmental support—becomes equally important.

In pursuit of these four forms of competitive advantage, MNCs have historically followed either of two very different strategies. One is called multidomestic, because MNCs using it treated their various foreign markets as if they were really just a collection of locally managed domestic markets. In this arrangement, the managers in each country were more or less independent, responding to local developments on their own, as they saw fit. In sharp contrast, other MNCs attempted to develop a single global strategy, in which all foreign operations were integrated under one centralized plan.

After years of experience with both of these strategies, it is now clear to many corporations that in order to have the very strongest combination of competitive advantages, MNCs should blend elements of both global and multidomestic strategies into their worldwide operations. The essence of such a combination is "thinking globally, but acting locally."

Notes

1. Chakravarthy, B. S., & Perlmutter, H. V. (1985). Strategic planning for a global business. *Columbia Journal of World Business,* pp. 3–10; Bolt, J. F. (1988, January–February). Global competitors: Some criteria for success. *Business Horizons,* pp. 34–41.
2. Steingraber, F. G. (1990, January–February). Managing in the 1990s. *Business Horizons,* pp. 50–61.
3. O'Reilly, B. (1989, November 6). America's place in world competition. *Fortune, 120,* 83–96.
4. England, R. S. (1989, May 30). A lost opportunity. *Financial World, 158,* 18–20.
5. Kirkland, R. I., Jr. (1988, March 4). Entering a new age of boundless competition. *Fortune, 117,* 40–48.
6. Shilton, L., & Sablosky, T. (1990, Winter). A look at foreign investment in U.S. real estate. *Real Estate Finance Journal, 5,* 32–37.
7. Hemmerick, S. (1989, October 2). Assets swell by 20%—but Japanese outspend U.S. investors. *Pensions and Investment Age, 17,* 33.
8. Cross border mergers and acquisitions during 1990. (1991, May–June). *Mergers & Acquisitions,* p. 47.
9. Goette, E. E. (1990, March–April). Europe 1992: Update for business planners. *The Journal of Business Strategy,* pp. 10–13.
10. Tully, S. (1990, March 12). What eastern Europe offers. *Fortune,* pp. 52–55.
11. Herbert, I. C. (1988, September–October). How Coke markets to the world. *The Journal of Business Strategy,* pp. 4–7.
12. Gilbert, N. (1988, October). How middle-sized corporations manage global operations. *Management Review, 77,* 46–50.
13. See, for example, Hardy, M. J. (1989, November–December). Going global: One company's road to international management. *The Journal of Business Strategy,* pp. 24–27.
14. Porter, M. E. (1990, March–April). The competitive advantage of nations. *Harvard Business Review,* pp. 73–93.
15. Capital cargo—more German marks for U.S. chemical operations. (1985, June 25). *Chemical Week,* pp. 24–27.
16. Flanigan, J. (1985, August 26). "Multinational," as we know it, is obsolete. *Forbes,* pp. 30–32.
17. Kim, W. C., & Mauborgne, R. A. (1988, January–February). Becoming an effective global competitor. *The Journal of Business Strategy,* pp. 33–37.
18. For details on the important role that Fuji Xerox played in helping to improve the competitiveness of Xerox in the United States, see Jacobson, G., & Hillkirk, J. (1986). *Xerox—American samurai.* New York: Macmillan.
19. Hemp, P. (1988, June 9). King of beers in a bitter battle in Britain. *The Wall Street Journal,* p. 24.
20. Van Horn, M. (1990, March–April). Market-entry approaches for the Pacific rim. *The Journal of Business Strategy,* pp. 14–19.
21. Kirkconnell, P. K. (1988, Autumn). Practical thinking about going international. *Business Quarterly, 53,* 40–45.
22. Clearly, entry mode cannot be easily separated from the type of operation and form of management which arises post-entry. See Hill, C. W. L., Hwang, P., & Kim, W. C. (1990, February). An eclectic theory of the choice of international entry mode. *Strategic Management Journal,* pp. 117–128.

23. Alternative, but complementary frameworks for international strategies are found in Ghoshal, S. (1987, September–October). Global strategy: An organizing framework. *Strategic Management Journal, 8,* 425–440; and Yip, G. S., Loewe, P. M., & Yoshino, M. Y. (1988, Winter). How to take your company to the global market. *Columbia Journal of World Business,* pp. 37–48.
24. Herbert (Ref. 11), loc. cit.
25. Kapstein, J., & Reed, S. (1990, July 23). The Euro-gospel according to Percy Barnevik. *Business Week,* pp. 64–66.
26. Taylor, W. (1991, March–April). The logic of global business: An interview with ABB's Percy Barnevik. *Harvard Business Review,* pp. 91–105.
27. Prager, A. J., & Cala, J. J. (1990, January–February). Coexisting with regulators. *The Journal of Business Strategy,* pp. 22–25.
28. Ring, P. S., Lenway, S. A., & Govekar, M. (1990, February). Management of the political imperative in international business. *Strategic Management Journal,* pp. 141–151; Choate, P. (1990, September–October). Political advantage: Japan's campaign for America. *Harvard Business Review,* pp. 87–103; Sethi, S. P., & Luther, K. A. N. (1986, Winter). Political risk analysis and direct foreign investment: Some problems of definition and measurement. *California Management Review,* p. 57.
29. Doz, Y. L. (1985). *Strategic management in multinational companies.* Oxford: Pergamon Press.
30. Labich, K. (1986, April 14). America's international winners. *Fortune,* p. 40.
31. Holstein, W. J., Reed, S., Kapstein, J., Vogel, T., & Weber, J. (1990, May 14). The stateless corporation. *Business Week,* pp. 98–105.
32. For guidelines on the important role that countertrade plays in international operations, see Carter, J. R., & Gagne, J. (1988, Spring). The dos and don'ts of international countertrade. *Sloan Management Review,* pp. 31–37; and Schaffer, M. (1990, May–June). Countertrade as an export strategy. *The Journal of Business Strategy,* pp. 33–38.
33. Labich (Ref. 30), op. cit., pp. 34–46.
34. Doz (Ref. 29), loc. cit.
35. This point has been heavily researched and greatly refined by the research team of Christopher Bartlett and Sumantra Ghoshal. See Bartlett, C. A., & Ghoshal, S. (1989). *Managing across borders: The transnational solution.* Boston: Harvard Business School Press; and Ghoshal, S., & Bartlett, C. A. (1990). The multinational corporation as an interorganizational network. *Academy of Management Review, 15,* 603–625.
36. Quelch, J. A., & Hoff, E. J. (1986, May–June). Customizing global marketing. *Harvard Business Review,* pp. 59–68.
37. Hammonds, K. H. (1990, January 29). Ted Levitt is back in the trenches. *Business Week,* pp. 82–84; Levitt, T. (1983, May–June). The globalization of markets. *Harvard Business Review,* pp. 92–102.
38. Douglas, S. P., & Wind, Y. (1987, Winter). The myth of globalization. *Columbia Journal of World Business, 22,* 19–29.
39. Douglas, S. P., & Craig, C. S. (1989, Fall). Evolution of global marketing strategy: Scale, scope, and synergy. *Columbia Journal of World Business, 24,* 47–59.
40. Hout, T., Porter, M. E., & Rudden, E. (1982, September–October). How global companies win out. *Harvard Business Review,* pp. 98–108.
41. Kogut, B. (1985, Fall). Designing global strategies: Profiting from operational flexibility. *Sloan Management Review,* pp. 27–38.

42. Friedmann, R. (1986, Summer). Psychological meaning of products: A simplification of the standardization vs. adaptation debate. *Columbia Journal of World Business,* pp. 97–103.
43. Hammonds, K. H. (1990, January 29). How a $4 razor ends up costing $300 million. *Business Week,* pp. 62–63.
44. Levine, J. (1990, February 5). Global lather. *Forbes, 145,* 146, 148.
45. Labich (Ref. 30), loc. cit.
46. Hill, J. S., & Winski, J. M. (1987, November 16). Goodbye global ads. *Advertising Age, 58,* 22.
47. Winski, J. M., & Wentz, L. (1986, January 1). Parker pen: What went wrong? *Advertising Age, 1,* 60–61, 71.
48. Cote, K., Hill, J. S., & Winski, J. M. (1987, July 13). World brands: Parker pen finds black ink. *Advertising Age, 58,* 49.
49. Kogut, B. (1985, Summer). Designing global strategies: Comparative and competitive value-added chains. *Sloan Management Review,* pp. 15–28.
50. Labich (Ref. 30), loc. cit.
51. Holstein et al. (Ref. 31), loc. cit.
52. Labich (Ref. 30), loc. cit.
53. Holstein et al. (Ref. 31), loc. cit.
54. Holstein et al. (Ref. 31), loc. cit.

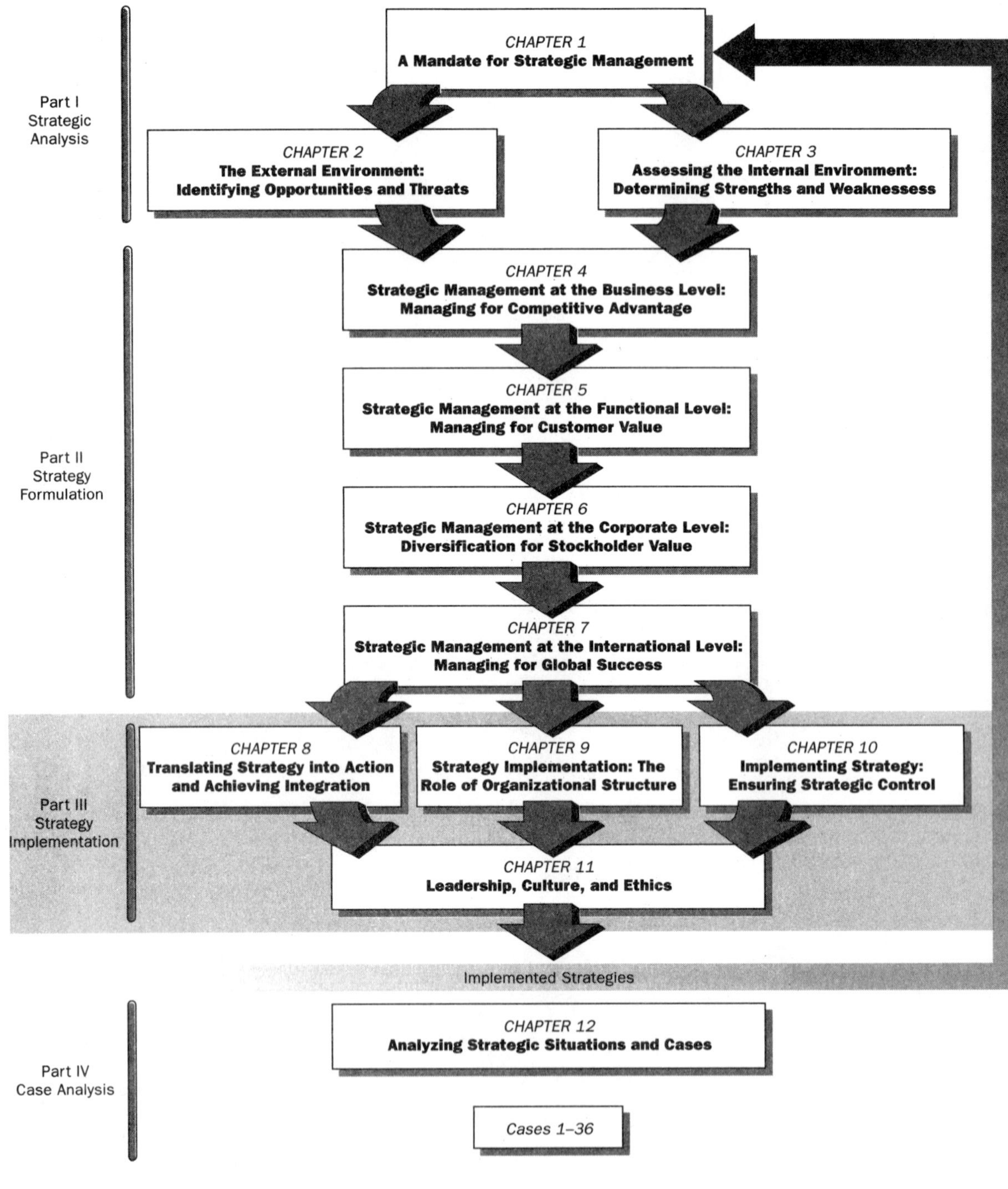

Part I
Strategic
Analysis
CHAPTER 1
A Mandate for Strategic Management
CHAPTER 2
The External Environment:
Identifying Opportunities and Threats
CHAPTER 3
Assessing the Internal Environment:
Determining Strengths and Weaknessess
Part II
Strategy
Formulation
CHAPTER 4
Strategic Management at the Business Level:
Managing for Competitive Advantage
CHAPTER 5
Strategic Management at the Functional Level:
Managing for Customer Value
CHAPTER 6
Strategic Management at the Corporate Level:
Diversification for Stockholder Value
CHAPTER 7
Strategic Management at the International Level:
Managing for Global Success
Part III
Strategy
Implementation
CHAPTER 8
Translating Strategy into Action
and Achieving Integration
CHAPTER 9
Strategy Implementation: The
Role of Organizational Structure
CHAPTER 10
Implementing Strategy:
Ensuring Strategic Control
CHAPTER 11
Leadership, Culture, and Ethics
Implemented Strategies
Part IV
Case Analysis
CHAPTER 12
Analyzing Strategic Situations and Cases
Cases 1–36

PART III

Strategy Implementation

CHAPTER 8

Translating Strategy into Action and Achieving Integration

Successful firms pay as much attention to planning the implementation of their strategies as they give to formulating them. After all, mission statements must be translated into specific actions. Also, managers must ensure that the diverse activities within an organization are integrated to help the firm achieve sustainable competitive advantage.

This chapter is divided into three major sections. The first section emphasizes the need to ensure consistency among the various organizational elements. The second section discusses various means used to translate an organization's broad intent and mission into specific actions. These include the development of appropriate short-term objectives as well as the judicious use of policies. The third section discusses the need to achieve coordination and integration among various functional areas, diverse business units, and different geographical areas within an organization. Such integration leads to the development and exploitation of the core competencies of the organization on a worldwide scale in the most efficient fashion.

After reading this chapter, you will understand:

- How successful strategy implementation depends on a fit among several interrelated elements of the organization
- The critical relationships between a firm's long-term strategy and short-term plans
- The role of policies and procedures in implementing strategies
- The need for coordination across functional areas
- The importance of integration among different business units
- How global competitiveness can be enhanced by coordinating a firm's international operations

EXECUTIVE INTERVIEW

Judy C. Lewent
Vice President for Finance and Chief Financial Officer
Merck & Co., Inc.

Judy C. Lewent is vice president for finance and chief financial officer of Merck & Co., Inc. She joined Merck in 1980 as director of acquisitions and capital and was promoted to assistant controller of the Merck Sharp & Dohme Research Laboratories in 1983. From there, Lewent became executive director of financial evaluation and analysis in 1985 and vice president and treasurer in 1987. Lewent assumed her current position in 1990.

A graduate of MIT's Sloan School of Management, Lewent is a member of the Government Policies and Pharmaceutical R&D Advisory Panel of the Office of Technology Assessment.

As CFO, how do you use strategy implementation to attain overall coordination and integration?

We carry out the company's dual strategy in addressing a rapidly changing global pharmaceutical industry. One strategy is to invest heavily in research ($1 billion in 1991 alone) to discover and develop innovative medicines. This has resulted in the introduction of nineteen new drugs in seven therapeutic classes in the past decade. Because we expend huge sums of money in this effort, we use financial models to measure how well research programs are contributing to the long-term growth objectives of the company. These models have also helped to assess the economic feasibility of future research projects.

Our second strategy is growth through strategic alliances. Today, no single company can conduct research projects for all therapies. We have helped structure many alliances with other companies over the last decade—joint ventures, codevelopment, and licensing arrangements—with the goal of having the strongest research program in the industry for every major disease category.

What approaches or techniques does Merck use to ensure integration across its functional areas?

The financial planning process begins with Merck's Operating Review Committee, a body of the company's top line and staff officers, who serve as an advisory group to the chief executive officer. The committee sets the priorities in profit planning for all areas of the company. The finance area uses financial models to support senior-level decision making and provide the computer technology to track the processes as the financial plan is implemented throughout the organization.

Our system of performance grids further ensures that all functions are working toward the same objectives. Each operating division and corporate staff area has a grid that clearly defines its key financial and strategic objectives, and establishes performance ratings corresponding to various levels of progress toward those objectives. This system provides a strong incentive to each of our divisions and staff areas to work together to help the company achieve both its short- and long-term objectives. We believe the organizational lines between finance and other areas of the business are becoming more and more blurred as financial tools, methods, and technology are integrated within the business units. Such integration reinforces the overall "top down" and "bottom up" philosophy of Merck's top management.

How do policies, rules, and procedures contribute to the successful implementation of strategy at Merck?

Incorporated in the overall business strategy are systems, procedures, and policies to assure that assets are yielding strong returns; financial information and reporting are timely, accurate, and reliable; and an effective system of internal controls that is operative.

Merck has a strong measurement-oriented culture, including the management of its substantial research and development (R&D) investment process. A few years ago, the finance area used an economic model to measure the profitability of the research enterprise. This was a very different approach from the old accounting model that treated research as a straight-line expense and not as an asset. In the economic model, R&D is capitalized and amortized because these investments are part of the company's economic asset base. The model provides a measurement of how well research projects are contributing to the long-term growth objectives of the company.

Continued

The focus on asset management spills over to other operating and staff groups who periodically review assets in terms of returns, redirecting those assets that are not making their cost of capital. Consequently, Merck's divisional managers are full resource managers held accountable to a comprehensive ROA-based measurement and performance evaluation system. These efforts have resulted in moving Merck from the bottom half into the upper quartile of the twelve leading pharmaceutical companies in terms of ROA.

The finance area uses "state-of-the-art" computer techniques, taking advantage of the best in the technical environment, including the quantitative power of software and hardware. The area constantly looks for new ways to leverage Merck's position during the "normal course of business." For example, models are used to hedge foreign exchange exposure to evaluate capital, licensing, and strategic alliances contributing to our long-term growth objectives, and to understand the dynamics of the pharmaceutical business.

To ensure that the system of internal controls and policies are understood by employees, the company conducts a Management's Stewardship Program and an Ethical Business Practice Program. These programs reinforce the importance and understanding of key corporate policies, procedures, systems, and internal controls.

A FRAMEWORK FOR UNDERSTANDING IMPLEMENTATION ISSUES

A well-conceived strategy is one that can be implemented. Issues of implementation must be taken into account *during* the strategy formulation process.[1] Imagine how worthless a brilliant military invasion plan would be if it overlooked the fact that the logistics chain cannot supply the troops.[2] Similarly, in the business world, many strategies fail because of a lack of consistency among the chosen strategy and many other important factors such as the organization's structure, reward systems, and capabilities.

Early in 1977, McKinsey and Company, a prominent consulting firm, assembled a task force to investigate how firms should organize themselves to implement strategies and to achieve greater organizational effectiveness. In addition to visiting business schools in the United States and Europe and many successful companies, the task force discussed the issue extensively with consultants and client executives around the world who were well known for their skill and experience. The result of McKinsey and Company's efforts was the development of what they called the 7-S framework. The underlying thesis of this framework is that successful managers must recognize that effective implementation involves a consistent relationship with many factors—the S's in their framework. Exhibit 8.1 provides a brief description of the seven S's—structure, style, staff, systems, skills, strategy, superordinate goals—and a diagram that reflects their interactive relationship.

The 7-S framework was developed to simplify the study of an inherently complex and challenging process. This framework conveys four important ideas:

1. A multiplicity of factors influence an organization's ability to change and its proper mode of change. Beyond structure and strategy, there are the five other factors. The 7-S framework acknowledges the complexity involved in analyzing organizations and segmenting them into manageable parts.

2. The seven variables are interconnected and it is difficult, perhaps impossible, to make significant progress in one factor without also making progress in the others as well.

3. Many carefully planned strategies fail because of a manager's lack of attention to many of the S's. Just as a logistics bottleneck can destroy a well-developed military

EXHIBIT 8.1
The McKinsey 7-S Framework

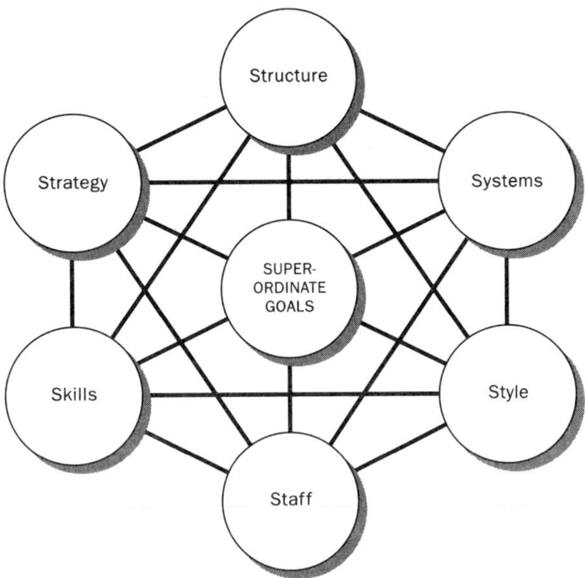

Strategy:	A set of actions aimed at gaining a sustainable advantage over the competition.
Structure:	The organization chart and associated information that shows who reports to whom and how tasks are both divided up and integrated.
Systems:	The processes and flows that show how an organization operates on a daily basis (e.g., information systems, capital budgeting systems, manufacturing processes, quality control systems, and performance measurement systems).
Style:	What managers consider to be important by the way they collectively spend their time and attention and how they use symbolic behavior. It is more important how management behaves than what management says.
Staff:	What companies do to foster the process of developing managers and shaping the basic values of the management team.
Superordinate goals:	The values that go beyond, but usually include, statement of goals and objectives in determining a firm's destiny. These values are shared by most of the people in the organization.
Skills:	Those dominant attributes or capabilities that are possesed by an organization.

Source: Adapted from Waterman, R. H., Jr. (1982). The seven elements of strategic fit. *The Journal of Business Strategy, 2*(3), 69–73. Reprinted with permission from *The Journal of Business Strategy*.

strategy, inappropriate systems or a lack of well-trained staff can render ineffective the best-laid plans.

4. It isn't obvious which of the seven factors will be most important in changing a particular organization at a particular point in time. At times, the critical factor might be strategy. At other times, the critical factor could be systems or structure. (This is reflected by the shape of the diagram.)

To illustrate the importance of consistency among factors other than strategy and structure, consider the case of a firm deciding to change its strategy from focusing on a single product-market area to growth through the aggressive acquisitions of unrelated businesses. Successfully implementing this strategy would involve more than just structural changes. That is, there would be more than moving from a highly centralized functional structure to a decentralized divisional structure. Other changes include:

- A less authoritarian management style (assuming that an authoritative style exists) at the corporate level in order to ensure greater autonomy of the diverse operations
- Greater skill and support staff to analyze and evaluate the financial and operational aspects of managing a broader corporate portfolio of businesses
- Changes in the reward system to motivate and make managers responsible and accountable for the bottom-line performance of the individual businesses

Let's examine a firm that did not succeed in this (Revco) and a success story (Nucor). The fortunes of the latter firm may be traced to its alignment of the McKinsey 7 S's.

The decline of the Revco Drug Company in the mid-1980s illustrates how an improper alignment can lead to failure. In 1986, Revco went private through a $1.3 billion leveraged buyout (LBO). This strategy was justified on the basis of an overly optimistic prediction that in 1987 the firm would experience a 13 percent increase in sales and a 42 percent increase in profits. Revco adopted an aggressive marketing strategy of broadened product lines, intensive advertising, and emphasis on cut-rate store brands. However, the competition was becoming intense in many markets as grocery stores expanded pharmacy operations and deep discount pharmacies entered the market. At the same time, Revco cut middle-management positions. This increased the number of stores that the district managers supervised from ten to forty. A lack of funding led to poor training for store managers whose skills were not adequately developed. A new bonus system rewarded store managers on the basis of overall sales increases. In attempting to maximize compensation, managers loaded their stores with low-margin, fast-moving goods and ignored the many everyday pharmacy inventory items. Further, many pharmacies did not have state-of-the-art computer systems and none of the stores had optical scanners at the checkout stations. This made information on merchandise movement slow, poor in quality, and expensive to obtain. Third-party prescription plans started dropping Revco as a source because Revco's information systems could not provide usage and other necessary data. These problems led to a severe erosion in profitability, which fell from $90 million in 1984 to a loss of $60 million in 1987. Revco's problems led to a Chapter 11 filing in 1988 when it failed to make the first interest payment on their junk bonds.

Revco's failure illustrates the adverse effects of a poor "match" among many of McKinsey's S's. Undergoing a leveraged buyout placed heavy demands on the firm to generate cash to meet their large debt payments. However, such severe financial constraints, in part, precluded Revco from updating its information systems. This area of weakness clearly placed it at a competitive disadvantage. Further, the drastic increase in the span of control—an important element of structure—of the district managers severely limited its ability to train store managers. The poorly designed reward system encouraged managers to focus exclusively on sales volume. This made them ignore critical pharmacy inventory items, which in turn caused them to lose customers. Clearly, many factors—the external environment, overall strategy, and poorly run operations—led to Revco's demise.

Application 8.1

Consistency Across the S's in McKinsey's Framework

Nucor, one of the most consistently profitable steel companies, owes its success to its minimill technology- and performance-based compensation system. The latter is a particularly good example of how management developed a creative approach to another old concept—pay for performance.

At Nucor, a significant part of all employee wages is based directly on productivity. Incentive systems are designed around groups. Base salaries are low, but productivity bonuses can add between 50 and 100 percent to total compensation—with no upper limit. When plants are running at full capacity, workers can make more than $35,000 a year in a region in which half of that might be the norm. Most important, these guidelines apply to everyone in the company, from production workers to senior executives.

In the production incentive program, the groups range from twenty-five to thirty-five people working on a task. In the melting and casting group, for example, the employees begin by assuming a base production of twelve tons of good billets per hour; above this base, each person in the group receives a 4 percent bonus for every ton produced per hour. If, over a week, they average thirty tons per hour—which is considered low—they earn a 72 percent bonus [4 × (30 − 12)] for that week. This bonus multiplier affects all pay, overtime as well as regular.

Nucor's program is easy to understand, works with group operation goals that are both definable and measurable, and distributes rewards rapidly. Bonuses are paid promptly, along with the regular checks. If employees work hard and produce well, they get their money—not at the end of the year, but at the end of the week. Employees can tie increased effort and productivity directly to increased reward and compensation. Nucor assumes that each bonus group is, in a real sense, a business unto itself. The company provides the building, equipment, technology, and direction—but what each group earns is entirely dependent on how much it produces.

Source

Kuhn, R. L. (1988). Creative strategic management. *The Journal of Business Strategy, 9,* 62–64. Reprinted with permission from *The Journal of Business Strategy.* Copyright © by Warren, Gorham & Lamont, Inc., 210 South Street, Boston, MA 02111. All rights reserved.

Many firms may attribute much of their success to an effective integration of the "S's" in McKinsey's framework. Application 8.1 provides the example of Nucor, a highly successful steel manufacturer. Nucor's consistency in strategy (minimill technology) and incentive systems includes an excellent alignment with structure (small work groups or teams), and a resultant improvement in employee skills fostered by the small-group work environment.

TACTICAL ASPECTS OF STRATEGY IMPLEMENTATION

In the following sections, we will discuss the means by which the broad intent of the organization can be translated into a series of specific actions that are consistent with each other. We will then address the nature of short-term objectives and the criteria for establishing them. Finally, we will discuss the role of policies and procedures in effective strategy implementation.

Translating a Firm's Mission into Actions

Although the implementation process varies considerably across firms, the underlying commonality in many of them can be seen by looking at an overview of the planning processes of successful major U.S. corporations.[3] Exhibit 8.2 shows these processes for the Ford Motor Company and the Boeing Company.*

Ford Motor Company's "strategic plan" parallels Boeing's "long-range plan." Similarly, Ford's "business plan" is analogous to Boeing's "division plan" and Ford's "budget" is like Boeing's "operating plan." While the labels may differ, the commonalities are evident in the time horizons associated with each level as well as in the specificity of the activities implied in each.

Ford's depiction of the overall planning process as a pyramid conveys three important considerations.[4]

1. The pyramid grows from the general vision base to a specific, 1-year budget.
2. As one ascends the pyramid, the amount of complexity and detail increases.
3. The likelihood of short-term change is greatest at the apex of the pyramid.

In all activities throughout the pyramid, the focus is on Ford's three-core strategies: being low-cost producer, achieving highest quality, and maximizing customer value. Ford strives to ensure that all activities in the firm are founded on and consistent with their core strategies. This logical and progressive development of specific actions from broad statements of intent can be found in many successful companies. MSA Aircraft Interior Products, Inc., a manufacturer located in San Antonio, Texas, illustrates how a consistent mission statement and set of objectives and action plans can help even smaller firms become more successful. Application 8.2 provides details of how MSA is implementing its growth strategy through well-defined action plans.

As the process moves from a firm's mission statement to the development of objectives and action plans, it becomes increasingly specific. The specificity of action plans is critical to the implementation of the selected strategies. Unless action plans are specific, there may be little assurance that managers have thought out all of the resource requirements for implementing the plans. Similarly, unless the plans are specific, managers may not fully understand what needs to be implemented. Action plans must also have a clear time frame for completion. This is essential for the scheduling of key activities and the allocation of required resources. Last, individual managers must be held accountable for the implementation of action plans. This often helps to provide the necessary motivation to effectively implement action plans on a timely basis.

Action plans, though specific, still permit a degree of autonomy for managers in selecting and modifying activities provided each culminates in the desired outcome. For example, action plans which relate to product development (as in Application 8.2) provide managers with a great deal of flexibility in making decisions about raw materials, design specifications, and warranty terms. However, such decisions must typically be made within the overall constraints imposed by the operating budget and targeted manufacturing costs.

---

* At first glance, these planning processes may appear to depict only strategy formulation. The distinction, in practice, between formulation and implementation is somewhat subjective. Business-level strategies may be viewed as part of the implementation of corporate-level strategies and functional-level strategies as part of the implementation of business-level strategies. The major issue here is that the planning process is an integrated, hierarchical process. For clarity of presentation, this text follows the accepted approach that formulation precedes implementation. However, we recognize the highly interactive nature of the overall planning-implementation process.

EXHIBIT 8.2
Examples of Overall Planning Processes

FORD MOTOR COMPANY

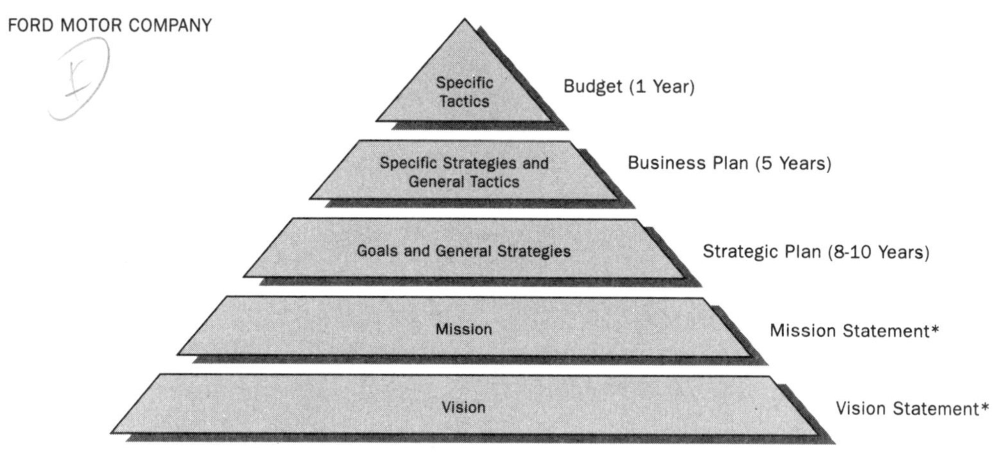

* Ford's "Vision Statement" applies to entire company; the various "Mission Statements" apply to each major business.

BOEING COMPANY

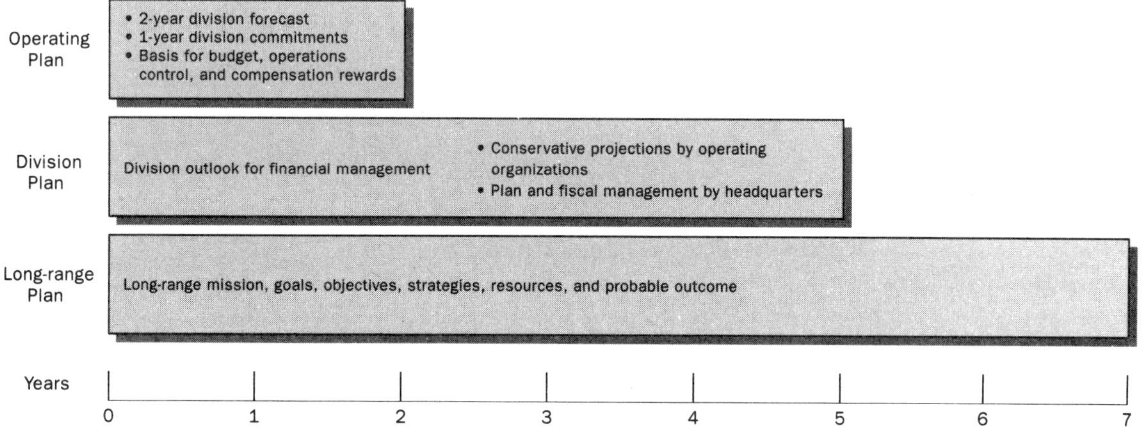

Sources: Company records.

Developing Meaningful Short-Term Objectives

Developing meaningful short-term objectives is critical in determining the success or failure of an organization's strategy. Short-term objectives may be viewed as the foundation, or building blocks, from which long-term objectives are eventually achieved. Effective short-term objectives have many common properties. They should

- Be *specific* and *measurable*
- Include a *specific time horizon* for their accomplishment

Application 8.2

Developing Meaningful Action Plans: MSA Aircraft Interior Products, Inc.

MSA Aircraft Interior Products, Inc., is a San Antonio, Texas-based manufacturing firm founded in 1983 by Mike Spraggins and Robert Plenge. The firm fulfills a small but highly profitable niche in the aviation industry with two key products. The Accordia line consists of patented, lightweight, self-contained window-shade assemblies. MSA's interior cabin shells are state-of-the-art assemblies which include window panels, side panels, headliners, and suspension-system structures. MSA's products have been installed on a variety of aircraft such as the Gulfstream series, Cessna Citation aircraft, and Boeing's 727, 737, 757, and 707 series aircraft.

Much of MSA's success can be attributed to carefully articulated action plans that are consistent with the firm's mission and objectives. During the past 5 years, the firm has increased its sales and profits at an annual rate of 15 to 18 percent. It has also been successful in adding many prestigious companies to its customer base. Below are excerpts from MSA's mission statement and objectives as well as the action plans to achieve its objective of a 20-percent annual increase in total sales.

Mission Statement (Excerpted)

- Be recognized as an innovative and reliable supplier of quality interior products for the high-end, personalized transportation segments of the aviation, marine, and automotive industries.
- Design, develop, and manufacture interior fixtures and components which provide exceptional value to the customer through the development of innovative designs in a manner which permits decorative design flexibility while retaining the superior functionality, reliability, and maintainability of well-engineered factory-produced products.
- Grow, be profitable, and provide a fair return, commensurate with the degree of risk, for owners and stockholders.

Objectives (Excerpted)

1. Achieve sustained and profitable growth:
   20 percent annual growth in revenues
   12 percent pretax profit margins
   18 percent return on shareholders' equity
2. Expand the company's revenues through the development and introduction of two or more new products capable of generating revenues in excess of $8,000,000 per year by 1995.
3. Continue to aggressively expand market opportunities and applications for the Accordia line of window-shade assemblies, with the objective of sustaining or exceeding a 20 percent annual growth rate for at least the next 3 years.

Action Plan for Objective #3

Description	*Primary Responsibility*	*Target Date*
1. Develop and implement 1992 marketing plan, including specific plans for addressing Falcon 20 retrofit programs, and expanded sales of cabin shells.	R. H. Plenge (V.P. Marketing)	December 15, 1991
2. Negotiate new supplier agreement with Gulfstream Aerospace.	M. Spraggins (President)	March 1, 1992
3. Continue and complete the development of the UltraSlim window and have a fully tested and documented design ready for production at a manufacturing cost of less than $900 per unit.	D. R. Pearson (V.P. Operations)	June 15, 1992
4. Develop a window design suitable for L-1011 and similar wide-body aircraft and have a fully tested and documented design ready for production at a manufacturing cost comparable to the current Boeing window.	D. R. Pearson (V.P. Operations)	September 15, 1992

MSA's action plans are supported by detailed month-by-month budgets as well as strong financial incentives for their executives. Budgets are prepared by each individual department and include all revenue and cost items. Managers are motivated by their participation in a profit-sharing program and the firm's two founders each receive a bonus equal to 3 percent of total sales.

Source

For purposes of confidentiality, some of the information presented in this application has been disguised. We would like to thank company management and Mr. Joseph Picken, consultant, for providing us with the information used in this application.

- Be *achievable*, yet *challenging* enough to interest and motivate managers who must strive to attain them

Performance is enhanced when individuals are encouraged to attain specific, difficult, but achievable goals (as opposed to vague "do your best" goals).[5]

Short-term objectives must provide proper direction, but they should allow enough flexibility for the firm to keep pace with and anticipate important changes in the external environment. These might include a competitor introducing a substitute product, new governmental regulations, and changes in consumer tastes. Unexpected events that occur within a firm might include the resignation or death of key executives, wildcat strikes, or a major accident at a production facility. Such changes often mean the firm must adjust both short- and long-term objectives. Aggressive fare cutting by People's Express in the early 1980s had an adverse effect on the load factors and profitability of the more established airlines that shared common routes. Short-term performance objectives had to be revised downward. The emergence of new competitors can also have long-term consequences for the overall structure of an industry. A preeminent example is Wal-Mart's rise to prominence in the retailing industry during the 1980s. Wal-Mart's success has changed the structure of the industry by forcing its competitors (such as Sears) to reevaluate their strategies.

Regardless of how well a firm's short-term objectives are thought out and articulated, there will always be unanticipated changes in the business environment. However, routine and easily recognizable issues often occupy a disproportionate amount of managerial attention and may "skew thinking in the direction of what is noticed, not what is noteworthy."[6] Managers must, therefore, allocate a part of their time and effort on recognizing and responding to unanticipated events which may have an important impact on their business.

Short-term objectives must be beneficial to the overall strategic plan and *effectively integrated* into the organization's overall strategy and long-term objectives. Thus, managers must keep short-term perspectives in the forefront of their activities and within the framework of their firm's overall strategy and long-term objectives. The ongoing integration of overall strategy, long-term objectives, and short-term objectives is indispensable. Achieving such integration requires close awareness of many issues. Among the most important is logical consistency and organizational rationality.[7]

Logical Consistency

Logical consistency refers to the ability of short-term objectives to contribute to accomplishment of an organization's long-term objectives. The need for logical consistency is twofold: (1) to partition, reduce, or translate long-term objectives into specific short-term indicators of performance; and (2) to ensure that these short-term measures are consistent with the overall long-term health of the organization.

An example of translating long-term objectives into short-term objectives would be the relationship between long-term strategic ends and short-term financial requirements. To achieve long-term goals of expansion and market penetration, investments in plant and equipment are necessary. Funding for such expenditures may require the use of debt or equity financing. However, the availability or cost of capital would be strongly influenced by short-term performance results. Earnings-per-share ratios in the short term, for example, could affect the outside valuation of a firm's potential and subsequent success in the equity markets. Also, a firm's debt-to-equity ratio compared to industry standards would be an indicator of its solvency and may affect the amount that the firm can borrow and the cost at which it may borrow. Thus, the pursuit of its long-term growth goals would require the firm to formulate short-term objectives aimed at increasing earnings per share or decreasing debt-to-equity ratios.

The integration of short- and long-term objectives and activities is not always so logical and straightforward. Short-term planning activities are often complicated by an important feature of organizational life: the rationality and desires of those involved in the strategy formulation and implementation process.

Organizational versus Individual Rationality

Generally, people in organizations tend to act rationally. That is, the actions of each organizational member is guided by his or her best interests with regard to rewards and career advancement.[8] However, the sum total of individual behaviors which may be perfectly logical and rational from individual points of view may often lead to a collective organizational action that is undesirable. Thus, individual rationality does not necessarily guarantee organizational rationality.

Managers in different functional areas may aggressively pursue their short-term objectives with such fervor that the overall organization may suffer.[9] For example, the sales and marketing department may promise customized orders with unrealistically fast delivery in order to attract customers and to meet challenging sales and market penetration targets. The production and operations department, on the other hand, may want to have long production runs of a standardized product to attain their short-term productivity objectives. Because customized sales orders slow the production process and lower overall productivity, production managers may refuse to schedule or may delay the production of special orders. Clearly, the organization would suffer adverse consequences from this conflict and lose customers.

Dysfunctional conflict may also occur across product lines when managers pursue their own short-term performance objectives. For example, several product-line managers may have responsibility for their own products, but little authority to get things done.[10] The intent of top executives may be to test the mettle of the product managers to assess their potential for promotion into positions of higher responsibility and reward. All of the product-line managers will work very hard to influence other managers to obtain scarce resources. Some managers will excel and others will have relatively low performance or various product-related measures of success. However, they may not attain an optimal product mix for the entire organization. In this situation, positive intentions and desired short-term performance at the individual level may not translate into optimal performance for the organization.

The Role of Policies in Strategy Implementation

Many situations that an organization encounters do not have regular, identifiable patterns. The most appropriate way for managers to handle routine events is to establish a policy that can be applied to each occurrence. Policies, rules, and procedures are terms often used interchangeably, to denote activities that organizations have adopted for dealing with routine events. Typically,

- Rules are viewed as specific statements of what is or is not to be done in specific situations

- Procedures are generally considered to be ordered sets of tasks that are designed to achieve a goal
- Policies are often seen as general guidelines that indicate limits or constraints on how goals should be achieved

Just as short-term objectives are designed to maximize contribution to overall corporate goals, policies are developed to support and reinforce the long-term objectives that the firm has designated.

Policies are the most specific and least flexible of the implementation activities that we have discussed so far. This is because they are intended to reduce uncertainty about appropriate responses to routine questions and to promote uniformity and speed in responses among different managers. They establish an indirect control over managerial activity.

Policies are used in many ways including:

- Interpreting the implications of various laws and regulations for individual firms
- Addressing social customs
- Establishing guidelines for conducting regular operations
- Reinforcing the intent of the firm to comply with legislation such as equal employment opportunities, occupational health and safety, sexual harassment, or protection of the environment

In the context of strategic management, policies address routine business decisions that affect achievement of overall organizational goals. The number of such decisions is potentially infinite, and making individual assessments of each possible set of contingencies is impossible for managers. Policies simplify the process of arriving at a conclusion. A few examples might include:

- Issuing credit only if a customer's income is above a specified level
- Evaluating employee performance annually
- Having new employees serve a 90-day probationary period
- Requiring approval from more than one person for all expenses above a certain level
- Establishing a procedure for handling refunds, replacements, or repairs of faulty merchandise

Effective policy statements should summarize and integrate rules into a coherent set of behavioral guidelines that contribute to achieving overall strategic goals. On the other hand, excessive rules and regulations may stifle creativity and lead to blind "follower" behavior. The result may be a work force that spends time and effort on trivial activities rather than getting the job done.

3M Corporation's corporate branding policy is an excellent example of the effective use of policies. Clearly, brand image is very important to a consumer products firm such as 3M. Before any of 3M's identifying trademarks or servicemarks may be attached to a new product, a representative sample of the target market is identified and approved. Their response to the proposed use of a 3M logo becomes the decision rule. Two of the policy

EXHIBIT 8.3
3M Corporation: Two Policy Statements and Implementation Guidelines

Policy Statement: 3M as a brand or endorsement will be used on every 3M product or service worldwide unless market research indicates that the use of 3M would be detrimental to purchase intent.

Implementation Guidelines:

1. Marketing research must demonstrate that 25 percent or more of the sample indicate that they "definitely would not try" or "probably would not try" the new 3M brand in order to consider the use of the brand as detrimental.
2. To show that an endorsement by 3M is detrimental to the company's brand image, the market sample is split, with one-half receiving a sample product without the 3M endorsement, the other half receiving a product with the 3M endorsement. If the likelihood of purchase is significantly lower for the endorsed sample, then the 3M endorsement would be considered detrimental.

Policy Statement: The extension of existing primary brands (Scotch, Scotch-Brite, Post-it, etc.) into product categories that are outside the existing brand definition will be governed by customer-response market research.

Implementation Guidelines:
Marketing research must indicate a significantly higher score for new products using existing primary brands on combined responses of "definitely will purchase" and "probably will purchase" (on a five-point scale). The new product using the brand must also score higher when tested against at least two other potential names, scored individually.

Source: Company documents.

statements and the associated implementation guidelines that govern product branding are shown in Exhibit 8.3.

It is very difficult to ascertain how "good" is a good reputation, or if placing a company logo on a product that has not been properly tested can, in fact, interfere with sales of the new product or damage the company's overall image. The policies are intended to simplify some of these rather complex questions.

Formulating and adhering to policies and procedures are necessary not only to implement strategies but also to ensure that the conduct of the organization and its members conforms to acceptable ethical standards. Standards of ethical behavior must be continually emphasized through such mechanisms as policy manuals, ethical codes, and company newsletters. Application 8.3 discusses policies and procedures implemented by St. Paul Companies and Chemical Bank.

ACHIEVING INTEGRATION: A KEY CHALLENGE IN STRATEGY IMPLEMENTATION

As organizations become more complex (in terms of functional area diversity, product-market scope, and geographic domain), there is a corresponding need to develop structures, systems, and mechanisms to achieve integration.[11] As we saw in Chapter 3, activities and organizational units are typically characterized by a considerable degree of interdependence. Recognizing such interdependencies and achieving effective coordination and integration is vital to attaining a sustainable competitive advantage.

The three major types of interdependencies that managers should consider are those

Application 8.3

Ensuring Ethical Conduct: The Role of Policies and Procedures

Several companies have developed exemplary ethical codes. In 1986, the St. Paul Companies (a provider of commercial and personal insurance and related products) revised their extensive corporate code, entitled "In Good Conscience." In each of its five sections, the code offers specific guidance and examples for all employees to follow. Below are a few examples of the issues and level of specificity the codes contain.

- *Insider Information.* If an employee has any information that would affect the price of the company's stock, including information about changes in the company's quarterly profits, he or she cannot buy or sell stock until the announcement has been made and published.
- *Gifts and Entertainment.* Common gifts such as an inexpensive ball-point pen or an appointment diary are generally acceptable. But liquor, lavish entertainment, clothing, or travel should not be accepted.
- *Contact with Legislators.* Employees should refer to the company's governmental affairs or legal department if they are contacted by legislators on matters relating to the company.

At Chemical Bank, in addition to formal standards and training, policies and procedures are also used to ensure that the bank maintains high ethical standards.

- The Purchasing Department has procedures to ensure fair and equitable treatment of the bank's suppliers. In order to avoid even the appearance of reciprocity, there is no review to determine which suppliers are Chemical customers before the bank awards contracts. Chemical's own printing subsidiary is expected to compete against other companies for most of the bank's printing orders. Every December the Purchasing Department sends a letter to all the bank's suppliers instructing them not to give gifts to Chemical employees.
- Under Chemical's Job Security Program, if an employee's position is eliminated, he or she has priority for other open jobs in the bank. As a result, about 75 percent of redundant employees find work elsewhere at Chemical. Those who do not are provided with help from outplacement counselors. Finally, Chemical's affirmative action program entails reductions in bonuses for managers who fail to meet goals in hiring and promoting minorities.

Sources

Murphy, P. E. (1989). Creating ethical corporate cultures. *Sloan Management Review, 31,* 81–87.

The Ethics Resource Center, Inc. (1988, February). Chemical Bank programs in business ethics and corporate responsibility. *Corporate Ethics: A Prime Business Asset,* pp. 31–40. The Ethics Resource Center, Inc., Washington, DC.

among functional areas, business units, and different geographical areas. These three categories of interrelationships and how they can be effectively managed to attain competitive advantage are discussed in the following three sections.

Cross-Functional Coordination

Tasks and responsibilities within all but the smallest organizations must be divided between relatively specialized managers and departments. Without the clear assignment of responsibilities, managers may duplicate some tasks and ignore others. By organizing a firm into departments based on functional specialization, tasks are completed without duplication. This is a very obvious solution, but it often may lead to some unintended consequences. For example, in many organizations, it may bring a pattern of decision making that serves the needs of an individual department rather than the needs of the business as a whole.[12]

There are several reasons departments become self-centered in this way. For example, a marketing manager's performance is evaluated most often and most closely by other managers in the marketing department. These marketing managers share related expertise, relatively similar values, and a common interest in seeing the marketing department achieve its objectives. These similarities may often lead to a "we versus them" attitude. Thus, the members of a department often feel the competition is not so much from another firm as it is from other departments within the same firm. The following three real-life examples are indicative of the types of interdepartmental conflicts that frequently occur.

Sales versus Logistics. The logistics department of an industrial electronics firm discovered that even though it had dramatically reduced the time it took to fill and ship orders, customer complaints of late arrivals had not similarly decreased. After looking into the matter, the managers realized that as the firm's delivery capability had improved, sales people had made increasingly unrealistic promises for even better delivery dates, allowing them to gain more orders. Of course, these promises could not be kept, and as a result, some customers perceived that the firm's on-time delivery performance had actually declined!

R&D versus Manufacturing. For years, R&D engineers in an electronics office equipment business designed new models with little regard for whether or not the manufacturing department could actually build the product. When manufacturing finally responded by creating its own "design for manufacturability" research center that R&D saw as a threat to its "turf," R&D's designs began to improve remarkably. Items that had formerly required dozens of parts, countless assembly steps, complicated wiring procedures, and various types of fasteners, were totally redesigned. The resulting models performed as well or better than their predecessors. They required only a fraction of the parts, they could be snapped together in minutes by one person, and they often had the wiring built into components themselves. In addition, these more "manufacturable" designs had better quality, cost less, and could be produced much more quickly.

Marketing versus Quality Control. The marketing department of a company selling baking mixes has a major sales campaign early each fall in anticipation of increased demand for their products over the upcoming holiday season. The campaigns are usually great successes in terms of short-term sales gains, and the firm regularly sells more mix than consumers actually use during the holiday season. As a result, mixes are shelved in consumer's homes for an excessive period of time. When they are finally used, they often fail to perform as well as they would have when they were fresh. Consequently, customers complain of poor-quality products. Sales volume was increased temporarily, but only at the cost of considerable damage to the firm's reputation for quality.

In each of these examples, managers viewed their own departments as the most important in determining firm performance. During World War II, General George Marshall observed similar behavior in overseeing military divisions fighting in various theaters. He described a condition he labeled as "localitis":

> . . . the conviction, ardently held by every theater commander, that the war was being won or lost in his own zone of responsibility, and that the withholding of whatever was necessary for local success was evidence of blindness, if not imbecility, in the high command.[13]

No department (or functional area) should act as if it were solely responsible for improving the firm's performance. Rather, each function should view itself as part of a

Application 8.4

The Pervasive Need for Cross-Functional Management

Implementing the just-in-time (JIT) inventory system at General Motors' new Saturn assembly plant is a good demonstration of the fact that the need for interdepartmental cooperation goes far beyond the more traditional functional areas.

When Saturn, General Motors' first new car division in over 70 years, decided to adopt a just-in-time inventory system, it was obvious to the Production Scheduling Department that this meant unusually heavy truck traffic into and out of the new plant. Suppliers would be asked to make many small shipments, some more than once a day, rather than the more traditional high-volume shipments. In fact, they estimated that on a typical day, more than 700 trucks would arrive, unload, and leave, making it busy even for a truck depot.

But the Saturn plant was not a truck depot, it was an assembly plant that employed over 1,800 workers per shift, who also had to come and go. The Plant Safety Department realized that the traffic congestion and the chance for serious automobile accidents created by this mixture of traffic would be serious. Both truckers and employees would be happier and safer if they could be segregated.

The Grounds Department offered a solution. Miles outside the plant, while they were still on the highway approach, trucks were routed down one road and employees down another. An outer roadway encircling the plant carried workers to parking lots that were connected to the plant by way of covered walkways. These walkways crossed over an inner route that brought supply trucks to the building's doors. Both sets of roads were tailored to the specific traffic they carried. Thus, the problem was solved through cross-functional management.

team, responsible for offering the highest possible value to the customer. The barriers that commonly separate departments and set them against each other as competitors within the same firm can be effectively removed by forming cross-functional teams. An interesting example of this approach is Ford Motor Company's revision of its procedures for developing and building cars.[14]

Alex Trotman, executive vice president of North American Operations, believes that product development can be made much more effective by breaking down the barriers among Ford's immense functional organizations: design, product engineering, factory engineering, and sales and marketing. To rework the entire process, he has assembled a single team consisting of fifty line executives who represent all of the functional groups. They have been meeting several times a week for nearly a year in a large room filled with wall-sized flow charts. In part, their goal is to make the thinking that went into Ford's product developmental success of the 1980s, the Taurus and Sable, more like standard operating procedure. Oscar "Bud" Marx, vice president of Ford's $9-billion-a-year components manufacturing business explains: "We have to control the process better, especially cost and weight." To date, Trotman has cut a year out of development time. Ford can now get a new model like the 1990 Lincoln Town Car out in 41 months, close to the standards achieved by their Japanese rivals. Clearly, Ford's effective cross-functional coordination enabled the firm to achieve the three forms of competitive advantage simultaneously—differentiation, overall low cost, quick response.

Application 8.4 illustrates a unique example of the need to integrate activities across departments.

Integrating Activities across Business Units

Any corporation that operates multiple types of businesses is considered to be diversified. Diversification efforts require effective integration among the firm's business units if the firm is to enjoy synergistic benefits—a combined performance greater than the sum of the individual parts.[15] As we discussed in Chapter 6, there are two major sources of synergy:

- *Utilization of common infrastructures,* including resources that are more or less tangible such as production facilities, marketing programs, legal and accounting activities
- *Capitalizing on core competencies* such as marketing skills, production techniques, and R&D process and product technologies

The promise of synergistic benefits is not always realized in practice. Managers must be aware that the challenge of achieving internal coordination and integration among various business units, as well as responding to the demands of diverse product-market areas, may exceed the organization's capabilities. This situation is often referred to as "negative synergy" (i.e., 2 + 2 = 3). For example, Times-Mirror, a media corporation whose primary businesses include magazines, newspapers, and broadcasting, purchased timberland in order to control the source of a key raw material: newsprint. Clearly, the skills required to manage this purchase successfully were very different from those needed to operate their core businesses. Times-Mirror eventually divested the timberland operations, acknowledging their failure to realize the hoped-for synergies.

Even in cases where the potential for synergy is very high, many organizations fail to exploit such potential for a variety of structural and cultural reasons. Also, there are problems caused by inappropriate control systems which are neither designed to reward joint efforts nor to measure joint performance. Hence, interrelationships among different organizational subunits must be carefully recognized, developed, and nurtured. Organizations adopt a variety of means to facilitate interrelationships and establish interdependencies among their different subunits. These practices, generally referred to as horizontal organization, serve to link business units together within the broad organization structure.[16] Some broad types of horizontal organization and their general characteristics are briefly introduced below. (These will be discussed in greater detail in Chapter 9.)

- *Horizontal structure.* This involves dividing the firm into a small number of groups, each of which consists of similar or related businesses. This enables each group to share resources and exploit synergies. The coordination among businesses is achieved through mechanisms such as interdivisional task forces and committees. Such mechanisms help to integrate activities both within a group as well as across two or more groups in an organization.
- *Horizontal systems.* The interrelationships that exist across business units are explicitly recognized and built into the planning and control process. The open communication resulting from planning and review sessions, which include managers from business units, lead to the sharing of resources as well as concerns.
- *Horizontal human resource practices.* The extent of cooperation among business units increases when they develop an understanding of the problems others face. Means to cultivate an understanding include job rotation of managers among business units,

Application 8.5

Achieving Integrated Diversity at General Electric Company

When John F. Welch, Jr., became chairman and CEO of General Electric in 1981, the firm consisted of 350 strategic business units. Welch believed that this was too many businesses to manage effectively and that many weaker businesses (and managers) were sheltered from critical analysis and evaluation. Welch promptly subjected all of the businesses to a strategic test: ". . . the businesses we kept . . . had to rank first or second in their industry. . . . If you rank third, fourth, or fifth in your market, you can't profit as much during the good times, and you are far more vulnerable in hard times." Accordingly, during the 1980s, GE closed or sold businesses which represented 25 percent of corporate sales and generated $10 billion in annual sales. The remaining operations were consolidated into thirteen core businesses—augmented by $17 billion in acquisitions and $20 billion in capital spending.

GE's successful restructuring program is clearly reflected in its recent financial performance. During the second half of the 1980s alone, GE's payroll was reduced from 410,000 to 291,000; its revenue and net income doubled to $55 billion and $4 billion, respectively; and its return on equity increased from 17 to 20 percent. Also, perhaps most impressive, during the 1980s, GE increased its stock market value from $12 billion to $58 billion—the highest valuation among United States corporations.

After GE's consolidation, all thirteen of its core businesses are ranked either number 1 or number 2 in their global markets. The leaders of these businesses are GE's chief operating officers (COOs)—charged with running their enterprises with little day-to-day interference from corporate headquarters. Each of these COOs, in turn, report directly to either John Welch or one of his two vice chairmen. The NBC, medical systems, and major appliance businesses report directly to Welch. Three of GE's businesses—aircraft engines, aerospace, locomotives—report directly to Vice Chairman Edward Hood. Lawrence Bossidy, the other vice chairman, is responsible for seven businesses: plastics, power systems, lighting, motors, electrical distribution, communications, and financial services.

GE's top management strongly believes that diversity, even when based on strong individual businesses making significant individual contributions, is not enough. In order to maximize the strength of their businesses, they felt they must achieve what they termed "integrated diversity"—by putting in place a management system that integrates their diversity more simply, allows the effective allocation of technical, financial, and human resources, and enables GE to respond quickly to market conditions. Central to managing GE's integrated diversity was the importance of sharing management practices across businesses—that is, the best techniques and the best generic management principles that will produce rapid growth and profitability.

In addition to grouping similar businesses into GE's thirteen core businesses, three types of top management meetings developed by Welch are vital in achieving integrated diversity. These meetings are designed to foster cross-fertilization of ideas among GE's top managers.

- First, each January, GE's top 500 managers meet for 2½ days at Boca Raton, Florida. There, the cross-pollination begins, not only in formal presentations, but in hotel rooms, cocktail lounges, and on the tennis courts and golf courses. Here, a marketing manager from appliances may learn about how to deal with hospital and nursing home purchase agents from a colleague in medical systems. Also, a general manager of lighting's Salisbury, North Carolina, operation may explain productivity gains from his radically designed lighting panel plant to manufacturing managers from locomotives, motors, and electrical distribution.

- Second, every October, a more select group of GE's top 100 executives attend a 2½-day session at the Arizona Biltmore Hotel in Phoenix. Here, the discussions are more strategic in nature. The financial head at communications may ask his or her counterparts at plastics and NBC for assistance in evaluating acquisition opportunities. Also, executives at aircraft engines can share information about upcoming aircraft purchasing decisions with the head of financial services' large aircraft leasing businesses. Such meetings tend to foster close and supportive working relationships across businesses. For example, according to Welch: "When appliances had their compressor problem, guys from the other businesses saw that Roger Schipke was a victim of bad luck and began volunteering to help—chipping in $20 million here, $10 million there, and so on."

Application 8.5 (cont.)

- Third, each quarter the Corporate Executive Committee (CEC)—an elite group of the top thirty to forty senior executives—meets at GE's hotel-style conference center near the corporate headquarters. At these 2-day meetings, Welch presides at the curved end of a large U-shaped table. The sessions proceed at a brisk, businesslike, but always congenial pace. Here, as he did in December 1989, Welch may state that economic conditions dictate a $200-million reduction in 1990 capital spending and ask for volunteer contributions from his executive's spending programs. He believes, "It's better that they do it themselves." At these meetings, business unit COOs often share experiences and provide valuable insights for their counterparts.

  For example, John Opie of lighting, after successfully acquiring Tungsram, a Hungarian firm, may relate what he has learned firsthand about currency valuations and international deal making. Or, Gary Wendt, COO of financial services, may report on the disappointing post-Thanksgiving reports from his business's credit card customers. This would suggest a poor Christmas season—unless retailers start aggressive price discounting. Such intelligence is vital for the heads of consumer-linked businesses, such as appliances or NBC.

Sources

Benson, T. E. (1989, December 4). America's best CEOs. *Industry Week*, pp. 16–22.

Quickel, S. W. (1990, April 3). Welch on Welch. *Financial World*, pp. 62–67.

Sherman S. P. (1989, March 27). The mind of Jack Welch. *Fortune*, pp. 39–42, 46, 50.

Tichy, N., & Charan, R. (1989). Speed, simplicity, and self confidence. *Harvard Business Review, 67*(5), 112–120.

1989 GE annual report.

common training programs, and management forums in which managers from different business units share ideas or educate each other on developments in their businesses.

In practice, no single type of horizontal organization is usually adequate to realize the full synergistic potential within an organization. An array of practices which mutually reinforce each other is essential. Application 8.5 explains how General Electric Company has successfully used a wide variety of means to achieve coordination and integration across its business units.

Integrating a Firm's International Operations

The central argument throughout Chapter 7 was that the most successful strategies for MNCs are those combining the benefits of both a multidomestic and a global perspective. This combination places great demands upon an organization.[17] Peter Drucker points out some of the difficulties with combining multidomestic and global perspectives within the same organization. Based upon his broad experiences with MNC's, he describes a hypothetical company that is based in the United States, but has operations around the world. The fictitious MNC's German subsidiary has been in existence for 70 years, it is managed entirely by German managers, and it is accepted as a German company. If the MNC attempts to shift some of the production that has historically been done in Germany to a centralized facility (moving toward a global strategy for operations), Drucker believes that the German managers will contest the move.

> What you are basically doing is subordinating them to an alien strategy. . . . the union will fight you, the state government will fight you, and you will be attacked in the German newspapers. You will be the ugly American.[18]

Drucker's point is that an organization may find it difficult to combine global and multidomestic ways of doing business. Other writers make the same point. One study involving an in-depth look at nine MNCs found that almost every manager interviewed failed to consider the possibility of combining a multidomestic and a global approach to running an operation, opting instead to view them as separate alternatives.[19] Another study concluded that organizational problems in responding to pressures toward both multidomestic and global orientations were the "Achilles heel" of most MNCs.[20]

Both these studies concluded that there was evidence that MNCs tend to be too inflexible in their application of any given organizational structure or practice. The implication of these studies is that there is enough variation in the situations faced by MNCs that any attempt to have worldwide consistency in the "look" of the corporation's organization is probably misdirected. This is often based upon one or more of three implicit assumptions that MNC managers often make, resulting in an overly simplified view of the organizational challenges they face:

1. *A widespread assumption that different organizational units should be managed in a way that is both uniform and consistent.* Yet, evidence suggests that the most successful MNCs are those that have unique combinations of different responses for different problems. For instance, it may be needlessly cumbersome to impose a matrix organization on all businesses. Instead, reporting lines could differ from country to country, depending upon the role of the operation or market it contains. For instance, as Europe consolidates through the European Community 1992 initiative, there will undoubtedly be a greater need for previously independent operations to begin coordinating their activities. However, this probably will not substantially alter their interactions with sister operations in southeast Asia.

   MNCs have found a broad range of reasons like this for organizing their various international operations in different ways. Philips, the Dutch consumer electronics producer, distinguishes among businesses on the basis of the life-cycle stage of their dominant product: compact disc businesses (growth stage) are organized and managed differently than portable radio businesses (mature/declining stage). Procter & Gamble establishes differences among its operations in different parts of the world depending upon whether or not the country in question is a "lead country" charged with new-product development. L. M. Ericsson, a Swedish firm leading in the development of digital switching devices for the telecommunications industry, centralizes all of its basic research, but then decentralizes developmental work on applications. These MNCs have realized that there are no simple solutions to the organizational challenges they face and have responded by adapting parts of their organizations to facilitate global integration while other elements encourage multidomestic specialization.

2. *A widespread tendency for MNCs to establish clear interunit relationships which stress either dependence or independence.* Yet, there is evidence which suggests a more appropriate response is one which stresses the *inter*dependence of these organizational units. Kao, a Japanese soap and detergent company historically known for its centralized approach to international management, had an experience in introducing shampoo into Thailand which illustrates this concept.

   By providing centralized R&D, Kao supplied technology to its operations throughout the world. So, for instance, in Thailand, the shampoo introduced by the local Kao operation was far superior to anything it could have developed on its own. However, the managers at the Thailand operation were, in fact, not only dependent upon corporate headquarters for R&D, but for virtually all decisions, reflecting the tendency for MNCs to treat local operations as wholly dependent or wholly independent. The Thailand business failed to adapt the packaging, promotion, and distribution from what the corporate headquarters had developed for the Japanese market. Therefore, the product, despite its technological superiority, flopped in Thailand. Clearly, the needed relationship between the Japanese headquarters and the Thailand office was not one of simple dependence or independence. Both should have realized an interdependence.

MNCs with operations around the world are becoming aware of their subunits' interdependence upon one another for (1) goods, (2) resources, and (3) information. First, the most fundamental justification for a globally integrated operation is that by coordinating the flow of goods through a smaller number of centralized facilities, the MNC can be more efficient. Second, global integration allows MNCs to shift resources, using successes in one area to offset weaknesses in another. The resources transferred may be capital, equipment, or skills. Finally, as we have seen in a number of examples presented in this chapter, MNCs can benefit from the transfer of intelligence, ideas, and knowledge garnered from operations around the world. This is increasingly true as more and more countries develop important technological capabilities with implications for global operations and product development. The next section and Application 8.6 on Texas Instruments illustrate how these three types of interdependence hold important implications for coordination of the MNC's diverse activities.

3. *A widespread belief that the MNC's corporate management should implement simple, clearly understood, corporatewide mechanisms for decision making and control.* Yet, there is experience to indicate that a variety of coordination mechanisms is probably more valuable than a clear-cut set of control mechanisms. Philips, selling consumer electronics worldwide with a headquarters in the Netherlands, has developed very different mechanisms for coordinating the flow of goods, resources, and information among its subunits around the world.

The flow of goods is coordinated by standardizing product specifications and rationalizing the process of sourcing materials to operations around the world. By making these flows reasonably predictable, the company can manage the flow of goods through its production facilities using fairly formalized standard operating procedures.

However, the company has not found coordinating the flow of financial, technical, and human resources to be so easily routinized. Many decisions are handled in a strictly centralized fashion. Here, issues such as capital budgeting decisions are decided by the board of directors, and the corporate staff is influential in making personnel assignments and transfers.

The most difficult flow for Philips to manage has been the flow of information. Of course, routine information can be handled by conventional information systems, but the sheer diversity and complexity of information of strategic importance means that no one system can hope to capture all that is useful to the MNC. To deal with

Application 8.6

Texas Instruments Organizes for Worldwide Operations

Texas Instruments provides an ideal example of the organizational procedures MNCs use to coordinate the flows of products, resources, and information around the world. The company, a leader in microchips, has been involved in international operations for 30 years. However, it still continues to discover new ways to better adjust to new global developments. In particular, under the direction of CEO Jerry Junkins, TI is moving away from an almost complete devotion to a multidomestic strategy, toward one that includes several elements of global integration. In making such a move, the company has realized a much greater need for organizational coordination.

Flow of Products

For instance, in coordinating the flow of products from country to country, TI's managers have had to adopt entirely new relationships with one another. For example, Akira Ishikawa is the TI manager in charge of operations in Japan, but in order to encourage global coordination, he is also the manager in charge of worldwide production of memory chips. Recently, Japan was running a chronic shortage of memory chips. In the past, Ishikawa would have been tempted to build production capacity for his operation in Japan, even though there was already worldwide excess capacity in chip production. But, given his new responsibility for worldwide production of these chips, he struck a deal with a plant in Lubbock, Texas, during a time when its plant was running far below capacity. In return, the Lubbock plant agreed to continue to give Ishikawa's order in Japan first priority, even if demand picks up in the United States.

Flow of Resources

Currently, TI's more established businesses are subsidizing the development of what it considers the key markets for success in the international marketplace of the future. For instance, the company hopes to use profits earned from memory chips to fund a worldwide leadership position in customized chips. These are specialized, lower-volume products that the customers design for themselves. This emerging growth sector requires careful monitoring of global trends to avoid investing in production equipment that will be incapable of producing the types of chips that may be in demand. This need for information has caused TI to place what is perhaps its greatest emphasis in international management on the coordination of information flows.

Flow of Information

In order to keep his top managers with global responsibilities informed on worldwide trends, Junkins insists that they all attend quarterly meetings with their overseas counterparts in order to set international strategies. As a symbol of their individual commitment to the detailed plans they hammer out, each manager must stand before the group and sign his or her name on a blackboard while the event is recorded with a snapshot. Between these quarterly sessions, TI managers stay in touch with one another using the firm's in-house network of 40,000 computer terminals in fifty countries.

Source

Kupfer, Andrew. (1988, March 14). The long arm of Jerry Junkins. *Fortune*, p. 48.

this problem, Philips has found it necessary to encourage communication by a blend of techniques for facilitating social interaction among its managers around the world. These include frequent transfers, the creation of a series of forums for interunit learning, and the active encouragement of the use of informal communication channels among far-flung operations.

Many MNCs have not successfully coped with organizational challenges. Organizational responses appear to be as mixed and complex as the global arena itself. Perhaps the best summary of the situation is provided by Theodore Levitt, in his comments on the difficulty of crafting a straightforward response to the problems organizations face in international operations:

> There is no one reliably right answer—there isn't even a satisfactory contingent answer. What works well for one company or one place may fail for another in precisely the same place, depending on the capabilities, histories, reputations, resources, and even the cultures of both.[21]

Summary

This chapter begins our discussion of strategy implementation. Strategy formulation and implementation are integrally related. The 7S framework provides a means of understanding the nature of interrelationships among various organizational factors that is necessary for superior organizational performance. These factors are systems, style, strategy, structure, skills, staff, and superordinate goals. Each of these factors is equally important and many organizational failures can be attributed to the inability to achieve or maintain a balance among them.

An organization must translate its mission into long-term and short-term objectives. Objectives provide a means for ensuring that all of an organization's actions are consistent and are directed toward the successful accomplishment of its strategy. Clearly articulated objectives impose a clear time frame within which goals are to be accomplished. Such objectives also must be specific, measurable, achievable, and challenging. Objectives are a vital motivational tool for the organization's managers and employees. Policies also play an important role in fulfilling an organization's mission. However, excessive reliance on rules may prove to be very dysfunctional because they may stifle creativity and lead to rigid and inflexible behavior.

As organizations grow, the internal and external complexity they have to deal with increases significantly. The increase of the number and diversity of functional areas, the creation of a diverse number of products and services, and the management of operations in a variety of nations, are all factors that necessitate the implementation of various integration and coordination mechanisms within an organization. At the functional level, managers must recognize the inherent potential for conflict that exists among a firm's functional areas. The effective use of cross-functional teams can greatly reduce conflicts among various functional areas within a firm. Multibusiness organizations can attain significant superior performance by exploiting the potential for synergies that exist among different businesses. Three forms of horizontal organization that can help firms to tap their synergistic potential are horizontal structure, horizontal systems, and horizontal human resource practices. Finally, as the nature of a firm's competition becomes increasingly global in nature, there is a compelling necessity to coordinate activities across national boundaries. By pursuing a judicious combination of multidomestic and global strategies, a firm can hope to attain greater international competitiveness.

Notes

1. For a recent discussion of issues to consider in implementing strategies, refer to Hambrick, D. C., & Cannella, A. A., Jr. (1989). Strategy implementation as substance and selling. *Academy of Management Executive, 3*(4), 278–385.

2. This section draws heavily on Waterman, R. H., Peters, T. J., & Phillips, J. R. (1980). Structure is not organization. *Business Horizons, 23*(3), 14–26.
3. Much of this section's discussion is drawn from correspondence and documents received from corporate executives at Ford Motor Company, Boeing Company, Merck and Co., Inc., and 3M Company. The information was received in response to a letter of request. We gratefully acknowledge their willingness to share this information with us.
4. Letter, dated March 8, 1990, addressed to first author of text from Mr. Morgan H. Edwards, a corporate strategy executive at the Ford Motor Company.
5. For a recent, extensive review, refer to Mento, A. J., Steel, R. P., & Karren, R. J. (1987). A meta-analytic study of the effects of goal-setting on task performance: 1966–1984. *Organizational Behavior and Decision Processes, 39,* 52–83.
6. Isenberg, D. J. (1987). The tactics of strategic opportunism. *Harvard Business Review, 65,* 92–97.
7. A portion of the discussion in the following two sections will be based on Hrebiniak, L. G., & Joyce, W. F. (1986). The strategic importance of managing myopia. *Sloan Management Review, 28*(1), 5–14.
8. Ibid., p. 8.
9. For a seminal discussion of organizational bases of conflict and the attendant dysfunctional outcomes, see Katz, D. (1964). Approaches to managing conflict. In Robert L. Kahn and Elise Boulding (Eds.), *Power and conflict in organizations.* New York: Basic Books.
10. Hrebiniak, L. G., & Joyce, W. F. (1986). *Implementing strategy* (p. 8). New York: Macmillan.
11. For a seminal work on this issue, refer to Lawrence, P. R., & Lorsch, J. W. (1967). *Organization and environment.* Cambridge, MA: Harvard University Press. For a discussion and examples of how to achieve integration at both the functional level and across businesses, see Newport, S., Dess, G. G., & Rasheed, A. (1991, November–December). Nurturing strategic coherency. *Planning Review, 19,* 18–22, 26–27, 47.
12. Shapiro, B. P. (1988). What the hell is "market oriented"? *Harvard Business Review, 66*(6), 119–125.
13. Schlesinger, A. M. (1958). *The coming of the New Deal.* Boston. Houghton Mifflin.
14. Taylor, Alex, III. (1991, February 11). The odd eclipse of a star CEO. *Fortune,* pp. 86–88, 90, 92, 94, 96.
15. One of the earliest and most recognized explanations of synergy is provided in Ansoff, H. I. (1965). *Corporate strategy.* New York: McGraw-Hill.
16. The following types of horizontal structure draw from Porter, M. E. (1985). *Competitive advantage* (chap. 1) New York: Free Press; and Hax, A. C., & Majluf, N. S. (1991). *The strategy concept and process: A pragmatic approach* (chap. 11). Englewood Cliffs, NJ: Prentice-Hall.
17. Bartlett, C. A. (1986). Building and managing the transnational: The new organizational challenge. In M. E. Porter (Ed.). *Competition in global industries* (pp. 367–401). Boston: Harvard Business School Press.
18. Flanigan, J. (1985, August 26). "Multinational," as we know it, is obsolete. *Forbes,* p. 30.
19. Bartlett, C. A., & Ghoshal, S. (1987). Managing across borders: New strategic requirements. *Sloan Management Review, 29*(3), 7–17.
20. Hout, T., Porter, M. E., & Rudden, E. (1982). How global companies win out. *Harvard Business Review, 60*(5), 98–108.
21. Levitt, T. (1983). The globalization of markets. *Harvard Business Review, 61*(3), 100.

CHAPTER 9

Strategy Implementation: The Role of Organizational Structure

To implement an organization's strategy, managers must define responsibility, delegate authority, and clearly specify channels of communication. Tasks must be organized into meaningful groups, such as products, markets, or functional areas. This activity should create a structure that is best suited to a firm's strategy.

We will begin the chapter by discussing the three most important dimensions of an organization's structure: complexity, formalization, and centralization. These three dimensions greatly influence an organization's strategy and provide important insights into how an organization actually functions. The next section of the chapter describes several alternate types of structure, such as the simple, functional, divisional, and matrix forms. The growing trend toward internationalization presents many challenges in determining an appropriate structure. Here, we address conditions under which each type of structure is most appropriate, as well as the advantages and disadvantages of each type. Finally, we will look at some of the more common growth patterns of large U.S. corporations and how changes in a firm's strategy can be associated with changes in its structure.

After reading this chapter, you will understand:

- The dimensions of organization structures and their relationship to strategy
- The advantages and disadvantages of alternate types of organization structure
- The relationship between a firm's international strategy and its structure
- How combinations of various types of organizational structures can fulfill specific strategic requirements
- The dominant patterns of change in a firm's structure in response to changes in strategy

EXECUTIVE INTERVIEW

B. Joseph Messner
President, Bushnell Division
Bausch & Lomb

Joe Messner is president of the Bushnell Division of Bausch & Lomb. After holding several financial management positions in the Soft Lens Division and Corporate Staff areas, he became corporate director of finance for the Healthcare and Consumer Products Group. In 1984 he was promoted to vice president and controller of the Ray Ban Sunglass Division. He assumed his current position in 1988.

As president of Bushnell, Messner has worldwide responsibility for Bausch & Lomb's sports optics business. Under Messner's leadership, Bushnell has benefited from the introduction of several innovative products and tremendous success with Bausch & Lomb's Elites binoculars.

Messner has a degree in accounting from Stonehill College and an M.B.A. from Suffolk University.

How does Bausch & Lomb control and monitor the performance of its divisions such as Bushnell?

Each division president is responsible for obtaining the executive committee's approval of his or her division's strategic plan. The division must operate within the approved strategic charter. The operating plan is the division's annual financial commitment; as such, any anticipated variances to plan need to be communicated to corporate in advance. An executive narrative and financial summary is submitted to the board monthly, highlighting the division's performance and key operating issues. Business reviews are held with corporate on a quarterly basis.

Can you briefly describe the process that your division must undertake to obtain funds from the corporate headquarters for major capital expenditures?

The vast majority of capital expenditures are planned and managed within the division. Significant expenditures for acquisitions, manufacturing expansion, etc., require corporate approval. The approval process for a multimillion-dollar manufacturing expansion project, for example, would begin with the division capital expenditure request submittal. This submission would clearly state the purpose, a review of alternatives, and a detailed financial analysis. The project could require presentation to the Management Executive Committee (the CEO and chairman of the board, and his staff), depending on the overall size of the project and its strategic importance. Final corporate approvals can normally be obtained within 30 to 60 days. Acquisitions can be responded to even more quickly. All expenditures need to be strategically and/or financially justified. Key financial criteria include discounted cash flows, internal rate of return, payback, and earnings per share impact.

How are marketing and R&D activities at Bushnell coordinated with the corporate headquarters?

Bausch & Lomb's operating divisions are fully integrated business units; marketing and R&D staffs are totally decentralized at the division level. Technological competencies are recognized and shared among divisions. In our optics-related businesses, for example, each division has particular strengths in different technologies. In the design of a new binocular at Bushnell, we might incorporate an optical coating developed by our Thin Film Coating Division or an aspheric lens design from our Contact Lens Division. In recent years, the divisions have also worked closely on joint marketing and sales promotions. Corporate's role is to foster cooperation between division marketing and R&D staffs, but not to direct. The successful sharing of ideas and technologies is based solely on each division's willingness to participate.

What specific mechanisms are in place at Bausch & Lomb to minimize conflicts among divisions as well as between the divisions and corporate offices?

We resolve conflicts the old fashioned way, one on one, person to person. A committee of division heads and corporate staff is a last resort to resolve disputes between divisions. Well-understood business imperatives, at the corporate and operating division levels, help to prevent conflicts from arising. These strategic imperatives or critical success factors are updated annually, and experience has shown that they are highly successful at maintaining management focus and avoiding misunderstanding of strategic direction.

Continued

Does the overall relationship between Bushnell and its parent company support and enhance the attainment of the division's business objectives?

There are two key aspects of the relationship which need to be recognized. First, the corporate culture is very much results-oriented. This is rewarded in above-average delivery of performance incentives (bonuses, stock grants, and stock options). Operating objectives normally target sales, operating earnings, asset management or a comparable return on investment ratio, and the attainment of other specific strategic goals (market share, new business development). Furthermore, attention to the individual division businesses is primarily on an exception-only basis. Poor operating results or variances to plan will precipitate corporate involvement.

The second aspect worth noting is the organizational structure. The individual divisions are fully integrated businesses which operate with a great deal of autonomy. This decentralized environment is generally viewed as one of the key corporatewide contributors to the overall success of Bausch & Lomb. Each business unit is focused, responsive to its markets and customers, and fully accountable for its own success.

DIMENSIONS OF STRUCTURE

Organizational structure refers to the formalized pattern of interactions that link the tasks, technologies, and people of a firm. Organizational structures are designed to ensure that these resources are used most effectively toward accomplishing the organization's mission.[1] Structure provides managers with a way to balance two conflicting forces: a need for the division of tasks into meaningful groups, and the need to integrate these groups to ensure organizational efficiency and effectiveness.[2] Structure identifies the executive, managerial, and administrative organization of a firm, indicating responsibility and hierarchy. It influences the flow of information as well as the context and nature of human interactions. An organization's structure is often described in terms of its dimensions: centralization, formalization, and complexity.[3] Alternatively, organizations may be classified into broad types of structure: simple, functional, divisional, or matrix.

As we will see, structural dimensions and structural types are strongly related to each other. Also, we will briefly address the issue of how a firm's structure can strongly influence its strategy.*

Complexity

The complexity of an organization's structure has three components.[4]

1. *Horizontal differentiation* indicates the extent to which the tasks required of the firm have been divided into homogeneous groups. The bases for these groups may be

* Relationships exist among the *dimensions* of structure and both the forms of competitive advantage and corporate-level strategies that are often only implied in discussions of linkages among forms of competitive advantage, corporate-level strategies, and structural *types.* In the interest of clarity, this section will discuss only those salient relationships that exist among structural dimensions and forms of competitive advantage. The relationships discussed in the following sections become more complicated, of course, if a firm is successfully pursuing multiple forms of competitive advantage. Later sections deal more extensively with the more complicated linkages among forms of competitive advantage and corporate-level strategies and structures.

functional areas (management, marketing, finance, etc.), stages of production (assembly, inspection, shipping, etc.), or client served (commercial, residential, professional, etc.).

2. *Vertical differentiation* refers to the number of levels in the organization's hierarchy. A tall structure would have many levels and a flat organization would have relatively few levels in the hierarchy.
3. *Spatial dispersion* reflects the extent to which an organization has few or many locations as well as its overall geographic scope.

As any one or all of these three components increase, the organization's need for control and coordination mechanisms also grows. For example, all other things being equal, a large, national grocery chain such as Kroger would have greater structural complexity because of their more numerous store locations and large geographic scope than a smaller, regional chain. One of the challenges executives face is to match coordination and control mechanisms as organizations grow in sales volume, expand geographically, and enter new product-market areas.

The relationship among the dimension of complexity and forms of competitive advantage is rather complicated.* Many factors, such as the firm's size and the industry within which it competes, may make this relationship tenuous. Still, we can identify some basic relationships that hold in most cases.

With an *overall low-cost* competitive advantage, a key concern is establishing an optimal level of efficiency. Efficiency in this case hinges on achieving economies of scale which are best realized by establishing a limited number of optimum-capacity manufacturing sites. Thus, a low level of spatial dispersion is necessary. In order to maintain tight control, the span of control of individual managers must be restricted. This requires a relatively tall organizational structure with many levels in the hierarchy (high vertical differentiation). Finally, to use resources effectively, organizational tasks must be divided into many specialized sets of activities (functional areas). Therefore, a high level of horizontal differentiation should be expected when overall low-cost advantages are implemented successfully.

When the competitive advantage chosen is *differentiation,* the firm engages in major product changes and increased product variety, depending on the preferences expressed by target-market segments. The need to capitalize on emerging trends in key markets requires that the firm be able to exchange information rapidly, a capability enhanced by a relatively flat organization structure. A low level of vertical differentiation allows decisions to be made quickly because there are fewer levels of approval through which problem solutions must be filtered. Secondly, with numerous locations of operations, firms pursuing this strategy can rely on expertise developed in local markets to offer insights into regional differences in tastes and preferences. Clearly, a high degree of spatial dispersion enhances market responsiveness. As the product offerings become more numerous, various managers are designated to oversee operations specific to each new product line, project, or target market. Because of this, a high level of horizontal differentiation among product managers is often a characteristic of firms engaging in differentiation.

* We would like to acknowledge the helpful comments of Anil Gupta of the University of Maryland in suggesting linkages among forms of competitive advantage and dimensions of organization structure.

Application 9.1

The Trend toward Flatter Organization Structures

The 1950s and 1960s were the golden age of the middle managers. During this period, their numbers grew fivefold. By 1980, managers (at all levels) made up 10 percent of the U.S. industrial work force—compared to 4.4 percent in Japan.

Times have changed. Major corporate restructuring caused approximately a million U.S. managers and staff professionals to lose their jobs during the 1980s. Similarly, one-third of all middle-management jobs were eliminated. By the latter part of 1988, for example, Mobil Corporation had slashed its white-collar payroll by 17 percent, Du Pont by 15 percent; Ford Motor Company had reduced its worldwide salaried work force in thirty-five of the most recent thirty-six quarters; and General Electric Company's Medical Systems Group had cut its management ranks by 35 percent within the past 18 months.

In order to build competitive, flexible, and responsive organizations, structural changes are often necessary. By reducing layers of management, increasing spans of control, and delegating decision-making responsibility to lower levels (e.g., business units), an organization increases its ability to respond to changing, and often unpredictable, environments. Management writer and consultant Peter Drucker contends that many levels of organizational hierarchy neither make decisions nor lead. They primarily relay information from one level of the hierarchy to the next. In a large U.S. defense contractor, for example, as many as six out of the fourteen levels of management did not play an important part in gathering information for either the top corporate level or operating personnel. Tom Peters, author of *Thriving on Chaos*, has described the organization of the 1990s as one in which boundaries are more permeable, positions and roles are more flexible, and the values of customers are central to all employees.

Many companies have cut the layers of management between the chief executive and frontline supervisors from a dozen to six or fewer. Most at risk are middle managers who lack operating responsibility—those who advise, counsel, or coordinate. "Generally speaking," says an Owens-Corning Fiberglass Corporation manager, "you want to make a product or sell a product. Everything else is peripheral." Only recently, thirteen levels of management separated William Fowble, Eastman Kodak Company senior vice president and general manager, from the factory floor. Now, he is just four levels from production.

Fewer levels of management typically mean a broader span of control—an increase in the number of people reporting to each manager. How can managers successfully cope with this? Mike Walsh, CEO of Union Pacific, provides an interesting perspective. His firm controls 23,000 miles of railroad in nineteen states, 2,800 locomotives, 84,000 freight cars, and has 30,000 employees. Using state-of-the-art technology, Walsh is consolidating ten dispatching centers into a central one in Omaha that will schedule and track trains on a giant electronic map. However, Walsh believes that technology is not enough—CEOs must also have a thorough understanding of the many facets of their business. "I don't think the CEO of the 1990s will get away with being a hothouse plant," says Walsh. "A CEO will have to know how to work the valves and switches in the middle of the night."

Sources

Bryne, J. A. (1988, September 12). Caught in the middle: Six managers speak out on corporate life. *Business Week*, pp. 80–85, 88.

Drucker, P. F. (1988). The coming of the new organization. *Harvard Business Review, 66*, 45–53.

McClenahen, J. S. (1988, April 18). Flexible structures to absorb the shocks. *Industry Week*, pp. 41–44.

Peters, T. (1987). *Thriving on chaos: Handbook for a management revolution.* New York: Harper & Row.

Ulrich, D., & Wiersema, M. F. (1989). Gaining a strategic and organizational capability in a turbulent business environment. *Academy of Management Executive, 3*(2), 115–122.

Application 9.1 describes an important trend in large corporations—major reductions among the ranks of middle managers—and the flatter organization structures that result.

Formalization

Formalization reflects the extent to which rules and procedures govern activities in an organization. Formalization can be a double-edged sword. While it may minimize uncertainty and confusion over authority and responsibility, it may also limit individual discretion, risk taking, and innovation.[5] The extent of formalization usually varies substantially across functional areas and among hierarchical levels in an organization. For example, to promote creativity, an apparel manufacturer would impose relatively few rules on its fashion designers. However, its manufacturing operations would require procedures targeted at maximizing efficient use of fabric and notions (thread, buttons, etc.). Similarly, top-level executives, regardless of their functional responsibility, would typically be subject to fewer restrictions on their activities than lower-level managers.

The competitive advantage a business chooses to follow influences the level of formalization that is appropriate for the organization. Businesses stressing *overall low cost* require relatively standardized products, manufactured in large quantities. The economies of scale achieved in this way enable the business to market output at competitive prices. In this situation, costs must be closely monitored, necessitating highly detailed and formalized cost and financial control procedures. Adherence to rules and regulations promotes tight control of all phases of the operation.

Implementation of a *differentiation* competitive advantage may suffer from the use of

Application 9.2

Eliminating Excessive Rules and Procedures

Rules and procedures may often provide an effective means of dealing with situations that are relatively routine. However, when they become excessive, they may increase expenses, slow reaction times, and stifle creativity. They may also lead to feelings of frustration among managers throughout the organization. For example, an 18-year veteran with General Electric's Medical Systems Group said of his firm's approval process:

> Even though we've cut back, one of my pet peeves is the approval process. Not long ago I had to get my boss's boss to reimburse someone to board a dog for $300—because one of my guys is going on assignment for us for about 29 days, including several days in Japan. It was a waste of my time. The company has formed a task force to eliminate just that kind of approval problem.

Many firms, such as Oryx and Square D, have improved their performance, in part, by reducing the number of rules and policies. Between 1984 and 1990, Oryx, the largest independent oil and gas producer in the world in 1990, cut its cost of oil exploration in half and doubled the rate at which depleted reserves are replaced. Some of its success was due to alterations in its internal policies. Reports, reviews, procedures, and rules that did not address its core business—finding more oil—were eliminated. Thus, 25 percent of internal reports were no longer required. The number of signatures required for capital expenditure requests was cut from twenty to four. The time required to complete the annual budget subsequently decreased from 7 months to 6 weeks. Fifteen hundred jobs were eliminated as well, many of them in middle-management areas where there was no longer any work to be done.

A similar "policy consolidation" occurred at Square D, a leading electrical equipment manufacturer. When Jerre Stead joined the firm from Honeywell in 1987, he found 760 official corporate policies and procedures, printed in four thick manuals. There were rules about who could speak to whom within the company, and the circumstances under which designated employees could speak to customers. He threw out all four manuals and replaced them with eleven policy statements that stressed the primacy of quality and customer service. During the last half of the 1980s, Square D increased its sales from continuing operations by 37 percent and reduced its work force by 17 percent.

Sources

Henkoff, R. (1990, April 9). Cost cutting: How to do it right. *Fortune*, pp. 40, 41, 43.

Byrne, J. A. (1988, September 12). Caught in the middle: Six managers speak out on corporate life. *Business Week*, pp. 80–85, 88.

extensive formalization. A key feature of differentiation is the development of a variety of products and services designed to appeal to specific target groups. Individual creativity and latitude are necessary for the experimentation and innovation sought in a differentiation strategy. Creativity would be impeded by large numbers of rules and regulations. As international competition intensifies, U.S. businesses are finding that high levels of formalization may prevent them from responding quickly to market and technological changes. So, in addition to reducing the number of levels in the hierarchy, there has also been a trend toward eliminating restrictive rules and procedures.[6] Application 9.2 describes some of the advantages of eliminating excessive rules, regulations, and procedures.

Centralization

Centralization is the extent to which the authority for decision making is retained at higher managerial levels in an organization. Although it provides an important means for coordinating decisions, it may place excessive demands on top-level executives.[7] As organizations grow in size and scope, their decision-making activities must be decentralized.[8] Decentralization does not necessarily mean that top managers materially reduce their control; rules and procedures may guide the decision-making processes of lower-level managers, placing constraints on their discretion.* Often decentralization provides the firm with the ability to adapt more quickly to rapid changes in the environment because the responsibility for decision making is placed on lower-level managers who are closer to the action. Despite the apparent advantages of decentralization, during times of crisis, a forceful and centralized approach is essential. Lee Iacocca's decisive and timely leadership in the late 1970s was one of the key factors that kept Chrysler from bankruptcy. In general, executives must decentralize decision making so that they are able to attend to those decisions they should be a direct part of, and so that sufficient time remains for them to attend to the pressing issues associated with the strategic direction of the firm.

Just as there are important relationships between the complexity and formalization dimensions and types of competitive advantage, there are implications for the appropriate degree of centralization embodied in any given strategy. When a firm pursues *overall low cost,* there is a need for tight integration and coordination among functional areas to achieve the requisite level of production efficiency. Such integration is enhanced by consolidating decision-making authority at the top level of the organization.

Differentiation requires a firm to maintain a high level of awareness of customer preferences. This enables quick response to changes in demand and incorporates up-to-date market information into its strategic plans. By decentralizing decision-making authority, critical issues can be addressed by managers who are most frequently and closely in contact with key market segments.[9]

Recently, there has been an increasing popularity of self-managed teams, composed of production, clerical, or professional employees as a means of achieving a high level of decentralization. When used effectively, self-managed teams lead to increases in productivity, and improvements in morale, creativity, and innovation. Application 9.3 provides examples of this recent development.

---

* This use of rules and procedures to direct the activities and decision processes of lower-level managers is also called *bureaucratic control.*

Application 9.3

The Emerging Trend toward Self-Managed Teams

They have been called by some the productivity breakthrough of the 1990s: the still-controversial self-managed teams, cross-functional teams, high-performance teams, or, to coin a phrase, superteams. According to Jerry Junkins, CEO of Texas Instruments, "No matter what your business, these teams are the wave of the future." And Corning CEO, Jamie Houghton—whose firm has 3,000 teams—agrees: "If you really believe in quality, when you cut through everything, it's empowering your people that leads to teams."

Teams go beyond the quality circles that were so popular in the 1980s where, in many cases, workers would meet once a week to discuss relatively minor issues. Teams are controversial because they ultimately force managers to do what they often resist: give up control. If teams are working effectively, they essentially manage themselves. Teams arrange schedules, set profit targets, order materials, and interact with customers. They may also play a role in hiring and firing team members as well as managers.

Teams typically consist of between three and thirty employees. They may include blue-collar and white-collar employees as well as professionals. Companies that use them often reap significant gains in productivity and innovation. This is because teams are composed of people with different skills, from different parts of the company, who can provide a broader view of problems and cross functional barriers easily to get the job done rapidly.

Teams are a relatively recent phenomenon. In the early 1980s, only a few progressive companies such as Procter & Gamble, Digital Equipment, and TRW were experimenting with them. By the end of the 1980s, a survey indicated that while only 7 percent of the 476 Fortune 1000 companies which were surveyed were organized into self-management teams, half of these firms said that they would be relying on them significantly more in the future.

Below are examples of how teams have been successfully implemented with production, clerical, and professional personnel, respectively.

- General Mills has found the productivity of its plants that use self-managed teams to be 40 percent higher than its traditional factories. A major reason is the decreased need for middle managers. At its cereal plant in Lodi, California, the workers take care of everything from scheduling to maintenance. Also, the firm has found that teams may often set higher goals than management. At the Carlisle, Pennsylvania, plant, which makes Squeezit juice, teams changed some equipment and increased production by 5 percent—even though plant management had thought the plant was running at full capacity.
- In 1988, Federal Express organized the 1,000 clerical workers in its office operations in Memphis, Tennessee into teams of five to ten people, and gave them a high level of autonomy. The teams played a key role in cutting service problems—such as incorrect bills and lost packages—by 13 percent.
- The Ford Motor Company used teams to develop the Taurus and Sable product lines. In the initial stages, teams composed of planners, designers, engineers, and manufacturers were put together. The teams played a key role in reducing delays in transferring technology from the R&D laboratories to production and getting products to the dealerships. Taurus and Sable have become major product successes.

For teams to be effective, many issues must be addressed. Among these: How do you make sure a team stays on track? How should a team be rewarded for cost savings or innovations? How much spending authority should a team have? If the corporate hierarchy flattens, how should the company respond to decreased opportunities for the advancement of team members? How can (or should) outstanding individual efforts be recognized? How should disputes among team members be resolved?

Clearly, teams aren't appropriate for all operations. They should be used only if there is a high level of interaction among three or more people. Although simple manufacturing jobs may not be appropriate, more complex jobs in a wide variety of industries, such as manufacturing, insurance, banking, and telecommunications, are good candidates.

Sources

Dumaine, B. (1990, May 7). Who needs a boss? *Fortune*, pp. 52–60.

Henkoff, R. (1990, April 9). Cost cutting: How to do it right. *Fortune*, pp. 40, 41, 43.

Peters, T. (1988, April 18). Creating the fleet-footed organization. *Industry Week*, pp. 35–39.

Ulrich, D. & Wiersema, M. (1989). Gaining strategic and organizational capacity in a turbulent environment. *Academy of Management Executive*, *3*(2), 115–122.

EXHIBIT 9.1
Dimensions of Structure: Links to Competitive Advantage

		Relationships to Forms of Competitive Advantage		
Dimension	***Definition***	***Differentiation***	***Overall Low Cost***	***Quick Response***
Complexity				
Horizontal differentiation	Degree to which tasks have been divided into homogeneous groups	High	High	Mixed
Vertical differentiation	Number of levels in the organization's hierarchy	Low	High	Mixed
Spatial dispersion	Extent to which firm has few or many locations, overall geographic scope	High	Low	Mixed
Formalization	Extent to which rules and regulations govern organizational activities	Low	High	Mixed
Centralization	Extent to which authority for decision making is concentrated at top managerial level	Low	High	Mixed

Exhibit 9.1 summarizes key definitions and characteristics of the dimensions of structure in relation to the forms of competitive advantage. Note that the relationships between the third form of competitive advantage—quick response—and the dimensions of strategy are difficult to characterize in a consistent manner. For example, the successful implementation of a quick-response strategy may require highly centralized manufacturing operations in order to ensure the required integration. However, the *marketing activities* should be highly decentralized in order to react quickly to changes in market conditions and consumer preferences. Similarly, highly formalized manufacturing operations would likely be necessary to ensure the coordination of production activities. Informal marketing activities would be necessary to adapt quickly to local market conditions, respectively. Therefore, the relationships between this form of competitive advantage and the dimensions of structure can most appropriately be described as "mixed."

How Dimensions of Structure Influence Strategy Formulation

Generally speaking, discussions of the relationship between strategy and structure strongly imply that structure follows strategy. That is, the strategy a firm chooses dictates the division of tasks, the appropriate patterns of information flow, and authority relationships within the organization. However, we must also acknowledge the role an existing structure might play in strategy formulation. For example, once a firm's structure is in place, it is very difficult and expensive to change.[10] Executives may not be able to adjust to major modifications in their duties and responsibilities, or may not welcome the disruption associated with a transfer to a new location. Also, there are many costs associated with hiring, training, and outplacing executive, managerial, and operating personnel. Thus, strategy cannot be formulated without considering structural elements.

The dimensions of an organization's structure can also strongly influence a firm's performance, strategy formulation process, and day-to-day operations.[11] As we have seen, a firm's structure can play a key role in its strategy and its ability to compete successfully in the marketplace. For example, in Application 9.1, many firms such as Union Pacific attained several benefits, such as greater flexibility and quicker response to customer demands, when the number of levels (or the extent of vertical differentiation) of their hierarchy was reduced. Also, as noted in Application 9.2, Square D was better able to focus on the salience of quality and customer service by reducing the number of corporate policies and procedures (a measure of formalization). This helped them to increase sales while reducing the size of their work force. Finally, as discussed in Application 9.3, self-managed teams (a means of increasing the extent of decentralization) have increased productivity for General Mills, cut errors in service operations for Federal Express, and reduced the amount of time to develop and market products for the Ford Motor Company.

TYPES OF STRUCTURE: LINKAGES TO STRATEGY

Most organizations begin very small and either die or remain small.[12] Those few that survive and prosper embark on strategies designed to increase their overall scope of operations and allow entrance into other product-market areas. Organizational growth places additional pressure on executives to control and coordinate the firm's increasing size and diversity. The most appropriate type of organization structure depends upon the nature and magnitude of growth in a firm. In this section we discuss alternate types of structural forms, their advantages and disadvantages, as well as their relationships to the strategies that organizations undertake.[13]

Only small firms with very narrow product-market scope will adopt and maintain a *simple structure.* When a firm grows in overall revenue or engages in vertical integration, a *functional structure* becomes more suitable. If a firm expands its product-market scope into unrelated areas, it will generally need to decentralize its operations and adopt a *divisional structure.* Two well-known variants of divisional structures are the *strategic business unit* (SBU) structure and the *holding company* structure. The *matrix* type of structure is designed to address unique sets of organizational contingencies involving the need for both functional-area expertise and coordination across product lines.

As firms enter foreign markets, they will use one of several types of structural arrangements, such as an *international division, worldwide product division,* or a *worldwide matrix structure.* Finally, many firms rely on *combination structures*—in which the aforementioned types of organization structures are blended to match their particular strategic direction.

Simple Structure

The simple structure is one of the oldest organizational forms. Owner-managed companies, which were predominant during the 1800s, often used the simple structure. These organizations were often limited to a single, or very narrow, product line and a type of structure in which the owner-manager made all major decisions directly. The owner-manager attempted to monitor all activities, and the staff merely served as an extension of the top executive's personality.[14]

A simple structure usually evolves as a new business is founded. The structure is highly informal with the coordination of tasks accomplished by direct supervision. Decision-making authority is highly centralized. There is little specialization of tasks (low complexity); few rules and regulations yield a low degree of formalization; and information systems are unsophisticated. Although the chief executive officer or owner-manager is generally heavily involved in all phases of the enterprise, a manager is usually employed to assist in directing day-to-day operations.

Firms with simple structures typically compete in fragmented industries that consist of many highly competitive firms. Intense rivalry often restricts profit potential and increases vulnerability. Relatively low investment in research and development, as well as plant and equipment, make entry and exit barriers low. Thus, firms enter and leave the market with relative ease—often creating intense price-based competitive pressure and market-share instability. For example, important demographic changes in the United States during the past few decades have led to a proliferation of fast food establishments. Typically, many of the smaller, weaker competitors have very little control over buyers (customers) or suppliers. Thus, intense price competition and unstable demand often force them out of business.

A major advantage of simple structure is flexibility. Because of small size and high centralization, a firm with a simple structure can move quickly to take advantage of market opportunities. Also, with a flat structure, communication is fast and direct and new product strategies can be implemented quickly. Further, low complexity precludes many of the coordination problems that exist in larger organizations. Small firms are often able to outmaneuver much larger, formalized, complex organizations.

A small firm with a simple structure may foster creativity and individualism because of its low level of formalization. However, the lack of rules and regulations may also lead to problems. Individuals may not clearly understand their responsibilities, which can lead to conflict and confusion. Others may use the lack of regulations to act in their own self-interest. This can lead to an overall decrease in motivation and satisfaction as well as the possible misuse of organizational resources. Further, the small organization's flat structure provides little opportunity for upward mobility, and without some promise of future advancement, recruiting and retaining quality personnel can be a problem.

Functional Structure

When an organization is small (ten to fifteen people), a formal arrangement for defining and grouping activities is usually not necessary. However, growth may place excessive demands and pressure on the owner-manager to acquire and process the information necessary to run the organization. It is unlikely that an individual would be sufficiently skilled in the number of specialties (accounting, marketing, finance, etc.) required to manage a prospering business. In this case, the manager must hire specialists in various functional areas. This leads to a functional structure in which the major functions of the organization are grouped internally and led by a functional specialist on whom the owner-manager relies for technical competence in the area. Coordination of the functional subunits is one of the most important responsibilities of the chief executive.

Functional structures are usually found in organizations where there is high production volume, single or closely related lines of products or services, or some vertical integration. Initially, organizations tend to expand their overall scope of operations either by further penetration of existing markets, by introducing similar products in additional markets, or by engaging in vertical integration. Although such expansion activities increase the overall complexity of the organization, the functional form of structure still provides a high level of centralization. Centralization helps maintain tight integration and control necessary for linking related product-market activities or the multiple stages of the value chain. An example of an effective use of a functional organizational structure is Parkdale Mills, located in North Carolina, the largest yarn mill in the United States.[15] Yarn making is a commodity business, and Parkdale is generally considered to be the industry's low-cost producer. The company invests heavily to equip the mill with the latest technology. It maintains a narrow product line, a common attribute of functionally organized firms. Tasks are highly standardized and the company refuses to change the twist or blend of a yarn for specific customers. Centralized authority rests with Duke Kimbrell, the current owner, who operates with a bare bones staff of ten top executives. He is considered shrewd about the cotton market, technology, customer loyalty, and incentive pay.

Clearly, the functional structure works well for Parkdale. But it is not always so effective. Exhibit 9.2 presents a diagram of a functional structure and lists some of its advantages and disadvantages. Let's look at both sides in more detail.

EXHIBIT 9.2
Advantages and Disadvantages of a Functional Structure

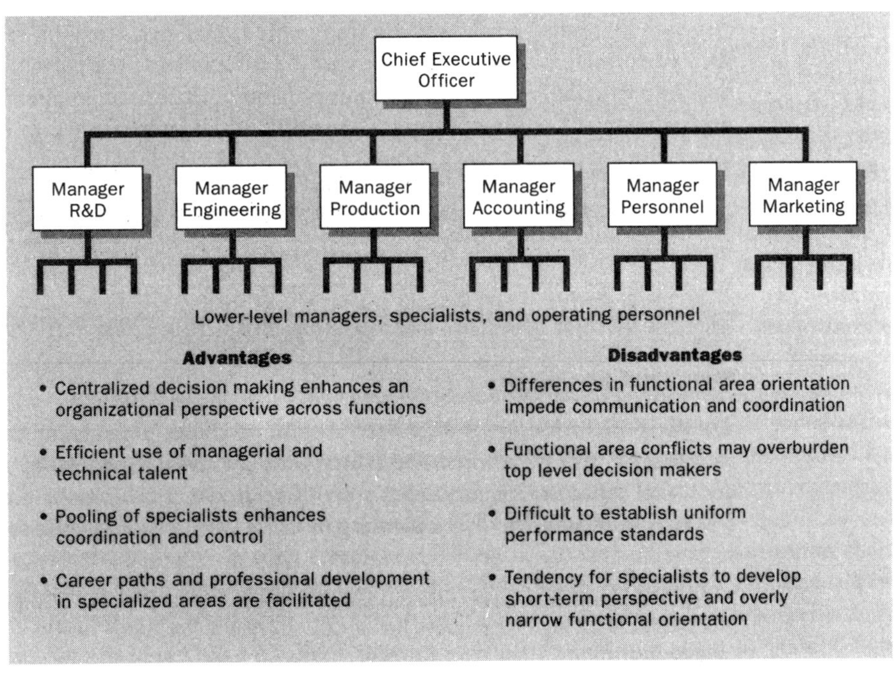

Functional Structure: Advantages

A functional structure offers several advantages that contribute to a firm's effectiveness. Centralized decision making helps to ensure that an organizational perspective is retained across all functional areas. The high level of centralization enables the chief executive to address both operating and strategic issues.

The grouping of activities by functions is particularly advantageous to organizations operating in relatively similar product and market areas. When technical expertise is critical, costly, and scarce, it is appropriate to pool available experts together within a single functional department. This may help to maximize their contribution across the entire organization. This increases the efficient use of managerial talent within the functional areas and also makes it easier to coordinate the efforts of the functional-area specialists. A functional structure provides clearly marked career paths for specialists and thus makes it easier to hire and retain their services. They also may benefit from working with colleagues who share similar interests.[16]

Functional Structure: Disadvantages

Executives in functionally organized firms must be aware of many potential disadvantages. Coordination and communication may become difficult because each functional area has its own value system, time orientation, and vocabulary.* Research and development personnel, for example, may use sophisticated and technical jargon and may not react favorably to time pressure when production managers need immediate assistance to solve process design problems. Problems stemming from functional-area conflicts may be frequently referred to the chief executive. In this situation, a chief executive may become inundated with time-consuming problems that distract from more important issues.

Control and evaluation may become more difficult because of the lack of a standard measure of performance for functional-area managers. Because it is very difficult to separate each functional area's contribution to the overall performance, managers may feel that their performance evaluation and reward does not reflect their particular contribution. This may be particularly true when a major portion of their total compensation is based on the profitability of the organization. Given difficulties in performance evaluation, perceived uncertainty regarding one's promotion potential may lead to motivational problems.

Functional organizational structures may inadvertently encourage a limited point of view that focuses on a narrow set of tasks. Functional-area managers may become isolated from centralized strategic decision processes and lose sight of the organization's mission and objectives. Accordingly, they may be more concerned with the short-term performance within their specialties and fail to develop a long-range point of view.

Divisional Structure

The divisional structure is organized around products, projects, or markets. Each division includes its own functional specialists who are usually organized into departments. A divisional structure encompasses a set of relatively autonomous entities governed by a central administration. The operating divisions are relatively independent. Each division

* One of the challenges facing organizations is to achieve integration and coordination across functional departments through the effective use of various types of horizontal structure, systems, and human resource practices. These were discussed in Chapter 8 and Application 9.3.

has products, services, or markets that are different from those of other divisions. Also, divisional executives play a key role—in conjunction with corporate-level executives—in determining product-market and financial objectives for the division as well as their contribution to overall corporate performance. Divisional objectives have specific product emphases and rewards are based on measures of financial performance.

General Motors was among the earliest firms to adopt the divisional type of organization structure. In the 1920s they formed five major product divisions (Cadillac, Pontiac, Chevrolet, Buick, and Oldsmobile) and several industrial divisions. Since then, many firms have discovered that as they diversified into new product-market activities, single functional departments are unable to manage the increased complexity of the overall business. Operational decision making in a large business places excessive demands on the firm's top management. If top-level managers are to attend to broader, longer-term organizational issues, they must delegate decision making to lower-level managers. The percentage of diversified firms in the Fortune 500 has increased from only 30 percent in 1950 to approximately 75 percent by the late 1980s. During the same period, the percentage of Fortune 500 firms adopting the divisional form of organization structure increased from under 20 percent to approximately 90 percent.[17]

When is a divisional structure so beneficial? A divisional structure improves efficiency (as measured by rate of return) in firms pursuing unrelated diversification strategies. However, vertically integrated firms actually decrease in efficiency when using a divisional structure.[18] One reason for this might be that the interdependence associated with vertical integration inhibits maximizing resource utilization in divisions. Vertical integration requires a high level of interdependence among the various stages in the value chain: raw material procurement to distribution to final customers. This makes centralized control and coordination of activities critical. The decentralization of a divisional structure would clearly be dysfunctional for a vertically integrated firm. Exhibit 9.3 depicts a typical divisionally structured organization and lists some of the advantages and disadvantages of such a structure.

Divisionalization does not necessarily mean decentralization. Ordinarily, the corporate headquarters will establish performance standards—often in terms of sales growth and return on investment (ROI)—and leave the operating controls to the discretion of the divisional managers. But, sometimes, they will closely monitor strategy implementation. The challenge is to create an optimal balance between control and autonomy. The relative level of autonomy generally depends upon a firm's diversification strategy and the performance of its divisions. The extent of corporate control of operating divisions is typically greater for firms pursuing related diversification, and will increase during times of performance decline.

A somewhat related issue is the amount and type of resources, skills, and activities to be centralized at the corporate headquarters. In addition to acting as a low-cost source of capital, corporate headquarters may provide their divisions or business units with three other primary types of resources: executives, corporate R&D, and centralized marketing.[19] As discussed in Chapter 6, firms undertaking a strategy of related diversification will be much more likely to try to achieve synergistic effects and scale economies than firms pursuing a strategy of unrelated diversification. Related diversifiers will tend to centralize important activities associated with functional areas such as marketing and research and development.[20] Application 9.4 provides an example of two large, diversified firms that

EXHIBIT 9.3
Advantages and Disadvantages of a Divisional Structure

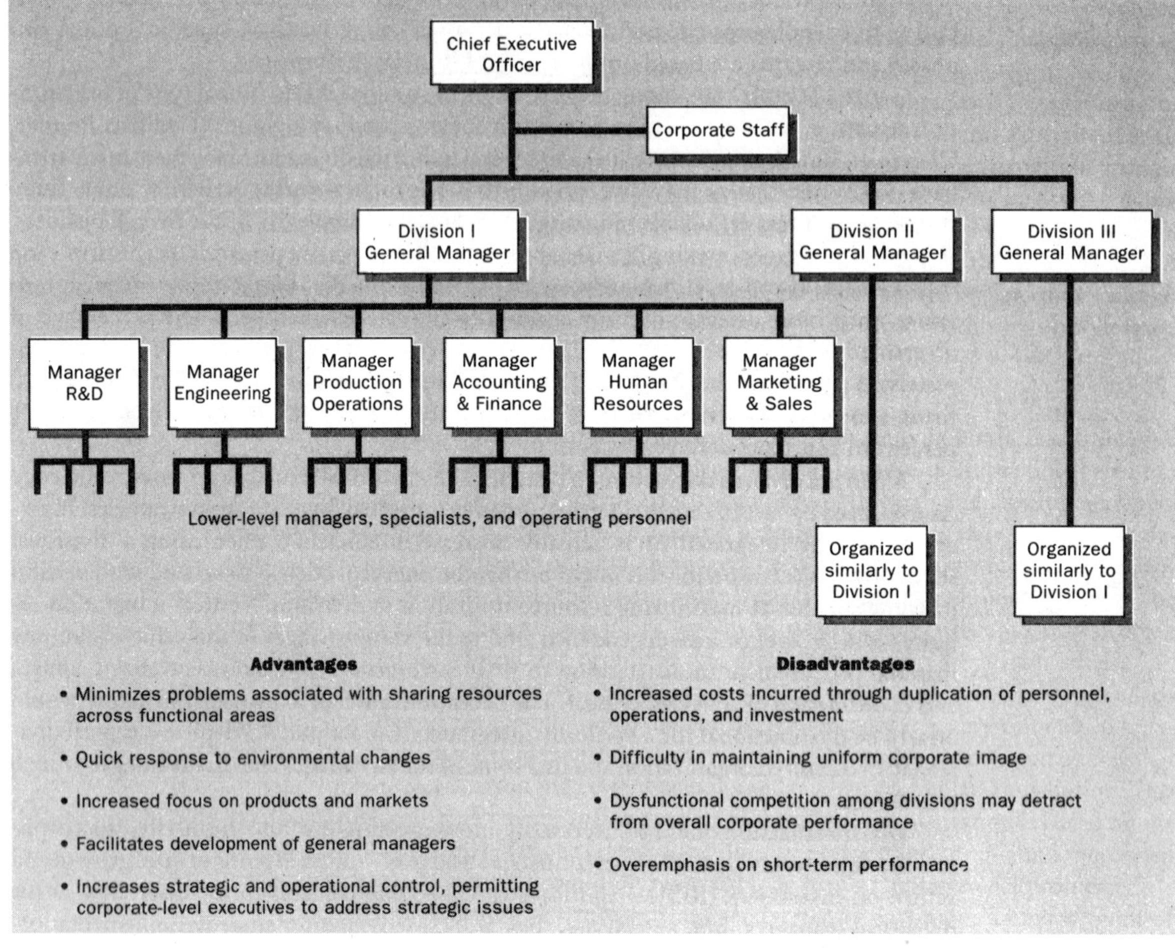

dramatically improved their performance by taking distinctly different approaches to the issue of centralizing functional activities at the corporate level.

Divisional Structure: Advantages

In a divisional organization, managers are able to concentrate on their particular product lines or markets. Managers have access to resources and to staff functional specialists to carry out required activities. Although there is usually strong competition for corporate resources, a divisional structure avoids many typical problems found in functional structure organizations that share resources.

A divisional structure improves a firm's ability to adapt during rapid environmental change. Delegating decision making to lower managerial levels moves the decisions closer to the products and markets. This facilitates faster decisions from those who are more

Application 9.4

Centralization and Corporate Strategies: The Case of Brun

Brunswick Corporation is an international, diversified firm consisting of four industry divisions. In 1982, Brunswick survived a hostile takeover attempt but had to pay a high price: selling its crown jewel, the medical division. This division had accounted for about one-fifth of Brunswick's total sales and approximately one-third of its net earnings. Jack Riechert, CEO, instituted an aggressive retrenchment strategy. Unprofitable areas were sold off, and the corporate staff was cut from 550 to 180. Brunswick saved $20 million from reductions in corporate staff and $5 million from cutbacks at the operating division level. Why? According to Reichert, "When nobody at the corporate level asks questions, you don't need people in the divisions to answer them." Response time has improved dramatically and the accounting, finance, and human resources functions are performed much more effectively at the divisional levels. Sales have increased from $1 billion in 1982 to $3 billion in 1987 and net profits have increased from $19.2 million to $175.4 million over the same period.

At H. J. Heinz Company's management meeting in Pittsburgh in 1987, Chairman Anthony O'Reilly warned his top 100 executives of the continuing erosion of the market position of some of their key products. Although sales had been recently showing 6 to 8 percent annual increases and profit margins were among the highest in the industry, the market share of many key brands such as Ore-Ida frozen fried potatoes and 9 Lives cat food had eroded. Heinz decided to change its emphasis from cost cutting to quality and spent $500 million to acquire new food companies. To d

further diversification

tralized many market

sharing resources ar

purchasing activities, Hei

million annually. This should help the compan

its profitability as it expands its global share in its most dominant products—ketchup and Weight Watchers diet meals. Such changes did not come about easily. By tradition, European units seldom shared information—even when they made the same products. And, divisions even competed with each other for acquisitions and raw materials! Insists O'Reilly, "The petty privilege of individual managers is no longer tolerable."

The changes in organizational structure implemented at Brunswick and Heinz illustrate many interesting points. First, changes in a firm's strategy should be accompanied by appropriate changes in structure. Second, when a firm's divisions have little in common, as in the case of Brunswick, decentralization seems to yield better results. On the other hand, when a firm, such as Heinz, is operating in related product market areas, centralization of some activities can increase coordination and efficiency.

Sources

Brunswick's dramatic turnaround: Interview with Jack F. Reichert. (1988). *The Journal of Business Strategy, 9*, 4–7.

Miles, G. L. (1989, December 11). Heinz ain't broke, but it's doing a lot of fixing. *Business Week*, pp. 86–88.

specialized and knowledgeable in the product area. Another strength of the divisional-structure type is the high degree of emphasis on products and markets.

As organizations increase their product-market diversity, there is an increasing demand for general managers—those individuals with the ability to comprehend and integrate the activities of diverse functional areas. Divisional structures facilitate the training and development of general managers, because divisional managers are given the authority for formulating and implementing strategy and are held accountable for the results. Westinghouse used this management development effectively by grooming the general manager of its industrial division to succeed the chairman.[21]

Internal controls are generally better with a divisional structure.[22] By delegating operating responsibilities to the semiautonomous divisions, there is less need for the corporate-level executives to be involved in operating activities. The chief executive officer can spend more time identifying strategic or long-term opportunities and threats, and therefore more effectively allocate resources among the divisions.

Divisional Structure: Disadvantages

There are several disadvantages associated with divisional structures. Increased costs incurred in initiating and maintaining the structure can be significant. There will be duplication of administrative functions and the attendant operating and capital expenditures.

Maintaining a consistent corporate image may be more difficult in a divisional organization. In some instances, sharing a single company trademark or brand can enhance the performance of new or poorly performing products by borrowing the identifiability and customer loyalty of stronger products. In other cases, a single defective product that becomes associated with customer dissatisfaction can damage the reputation of all of a company's products. Companies such as General Motors and Procter & Gamble have developed multiple brand names for their products. However, 3M has consistently used its name on a multitude of products. You may recall from Chapter 8, that the 3M Corporation conducts extensive analysis before deciding to give products the company brand. In this way the company maintains its outstanding image as a producer of high-quality products.

One major disadvantage of a divisional structure has traditionally been its overemphasis on short-term profitability. Intense pressures placed on divisional managers to meet short-term ROI targets and contribution to corporate earnings per share have often fostered a lack of concern for expenditures, such as investments in research and development and marketing research. The pressures often cause divisions to focus more energy on competing with each other for corporate resources and rewards rather than on competing with their rivals in the marketplace. This may eventually lead to an erosion of overall corporate performance. Some writers believe that the short-term focus played a major part in the decline of the international competitiveness of U.S. industry during the past few decades.[23]

American Home, a drug and household products firm, provides a good example of overemphasis on short-term profitability.[24] American Home is a decentralized firm with a divisional structure. Although the firm's pretax income increased at double-digit rates for the prior 10-year period, by 1983 its profitability began to erode. Between 1984 and 1986, its annual profits increased only 3 percent. The company's primary symptom was a lack of competitive products. However, it appears the underlying causes were an overemphasis on tight cost control and short-term profitability. To achieve challenging short-term ROI targets, divisional managers cut research and development budgets severely to the point where their research and development spending was only 3 percent of sales, compared to the industry average of 6.1 percent.

Variations of the Divisional Structure

Corporations often diversify their product-market activities to such a large extent that new types of structures become necessary. Two such structures are the strategic business unit (SBU) structure and the holding company structure. Both of these structures are considered to be variations of the divisional structure and they share many of the advantages and disadvantages with the divisional form. We will discuss each of these two types of structures in the following two sections.

SBU (Strategic Business Unit) Structure

Widely diversified corporations such as Westinghouse may consist of dozens of different divisions. If Westinghouse were to use a purely divisional structure (i.e., without SBUs), it would likely be impossible for the corporate staff to plan for and control such tremendously diverse activity. The span of control would be too large and the corporate office would become overloaded. With an SBU structure, divisions with similar products, markets, and/or technologies are combined into homogenous groups in order to achieve synergies. Generally speaking, the more related the individual businesses within a corporation, the fewer the number of SBUs that will be required. Each of the SBUs in the organization becomes a profit center. Also, each division (or business) within a given SBU is a profit center and is controlled by SBU headquarters. The SBU structure is shown in Exhibit 9.4.

A major benefit of the SBU structure is that it makes the task of planning and control by corporate headquarters staff more manageable. For example, if a corporation consists of ninety divisions that can be grouped into ten SBUs, the span of control for the corporate officers would be ten instead of ninety.[25] Because the SBU form of organization allows greater decentralization of authority, individual firms can react more quickly to important environmental changes. Finally, an SBU structure enables divisions within the SBU to achieve greater control and coordination than if all the divisions reported directly to corporate headquarters—as in the case of a divisional structure. This may enhance synergistic effects among the individual divisions.

On the negative side, it may prove difficult to exploit these inter-SBU synergies (or synergies across SBUs). The additional level of management increases the number of personnel and overhead expense. With the additional hierarchical level, corporate management

EXHIBIT 9.4
The Strategic Business Unit (SBU) Structure*

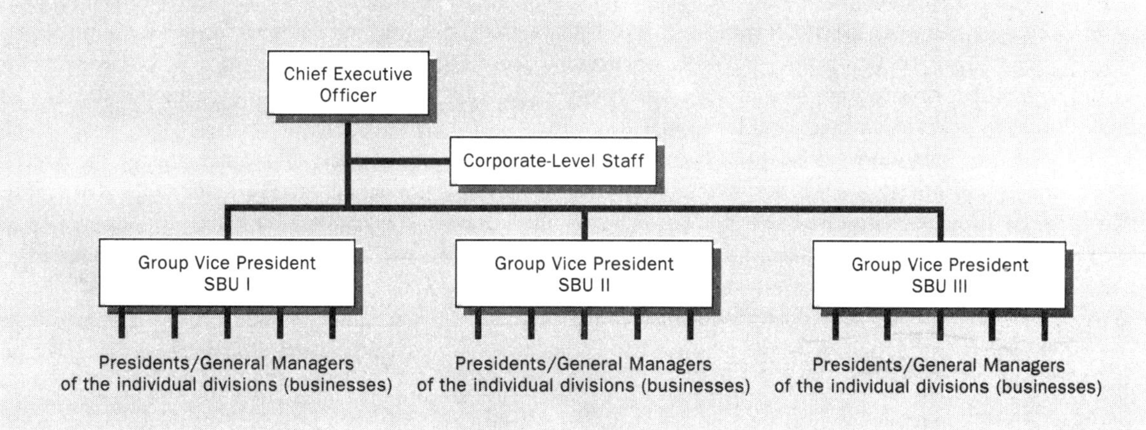

* For very large corporations with a large number of divisions (or businesses), an additional level may be added to the hierarchy. Top-level executives (often called executive vice presidents or group vice presidents) are charged with the responsibility of controlling and coordinating the activities of *groups* of SBUs.

is farther removed from the individual divisions and may become unaware of significant developments that could have a major impact on the overall corporation. Similarly, the added level in the hierarchy may lead to distortion of information and slower communication for the entire company because information must pass up and down one more level in the hierarchy.

Another disadvantage of the SBU structure is associated with how the corporation groups the individual businesses into SBUs.[26] Often, corporate headquarters use portfolio models, such as the Boston Consulting Group (BCG) matrix discussed in Chapter 6, to guide the allocation of capital and other resources to the various SBUs within the corporation. If the corporate office were to label an SBU a "cash cow," the primary purpose of that SBU would be to generate cash to improve the competitive position of the other SBUs in the firm's overall portfolio. Access to capital for developmental purposes would probably be denied even if the same SBU also contained a "star" or "question mark" business. These businesses would then suffer from lack of the necessary funds to maintain or enhance its competitive position. In this way, the overall competitive position of the SBU could be eroded and attractive opportunities forgone. For example, an SBU which manufactures and distributes toiletry products may consist primarily of businesses that are in the mature stage of the product life cycle but have strong competitive positions. The SBU may also consist of a business which manufactures a relatively new product, such as a skin care product that regenerates facial cells. Although this product may have a relatively small market share, it may have the potential to benefit handsomely from substantial future demand. This business should be viewed as a "question mark." But if corporate headquarters has categorized the entire SBU as a "cash cow," it may be unwilling to infuse the capital necessary for R&D and marketing in the growth area. In this way, the company may lose an excellent opportunity.

Holding Company Structure

The holding company (also referred to as *conglomerate*) structure is also a variation of the divisional structure. Whereas the SBU structure is most appropriate when similarities exist among the individual divisions (or businesses), the holding company structure is appropriate when a corporation's portfolio of businesses do not have much in common. This structure is most appropriate for firms like ITT and Textron which follow a strategy of unrelated (or conglomerate) diversification. Each division (or business) is viewed as an autonomous profit center and the purpose of the corporate office is to manage the overall portfolio—maximizing profitability by determining which businesses to acquire or divest. Corporate staffs tend to be very small because their involvement in the overall operation of the businesses is minimal.

The major advantage of a holding company structure is the small corporate office and the associated savings in personnel expense and overhead. In many cases, the corporate office serves as an in-house consultant to existing businesses and helps them turn around newly acquired businesses that are not performing well. Also, the high level of autonomy associated with the holding company structure serves to enhance the motivational level of divisional executives and enables them to respond quickly to market changes. The primary disadvantage is the inherent lack of control and dependence that corporate-level executives have on the divisional executives. The corporation is particularly vulnerable if a division experiences major problems or competitive threats, or if talented divisional executives resign. The corporation is also vulnerable to mistakes in man the corporate office does not have adequate knowledge of t does it maintain sufficient levels of staff support to turn arou

Although the number of corporations following strategies cation has declined, there are still many success stories. A goo Group, a conglomerate with $3.24 billion in sales. It consists products ranging from screws to railroad cars.[27] Return on equ percent and profits increased 25 percent in 1987 to $145 million, whi ent to $2.3 billion. A key to CEO Robert Pritzker's success is maintai omy in the operating divisions. Controllers of the individual businesses are requi to report both to their general managers and to the corporate controller; this mechanism ensures financial control and monitoring. Planning is informal and 5-year plans are avoided because Pritzker believes one cannot anticipate events that far in advance. To retain financial flexibility necessary to respond to emergencies the Marmon Group avoids highly leveraged acquisitions.

Matrix Structure

Managers typically have two fundamental structural choices: functional or divisional. In a functional structure, people and activities are grouped together by function: marketing, finance, research and development, etc. In the divisional structure, people and activities are organized according to products, product groups, services, regions, or markets. In some cases, however, a firm may face a situation in which departments need both technological expertise within functions and coordination across product lines. The matrix structure offers a solution to this dilemma by increasing the capacity for information handling and decision making within organizations and by establishing formal, lateral channels of communication that complement existing hierarchical channels.[28] Thus, the matrix structure attempts to combine the advantages of both functional and product-oriented structures.

The matrix form of organization is designed to cope with the varying activity requirements that are associated with complex, project-oriented businesses. Aerospace firms were among the first to organize in a matrix structure, in the early 1960s, when technology was developing rapidly. Aerospace projects occur in many phases, each requiring a different mix of resources. Different types of engineers and support personnel are needed at various stages in any project: innovative designers who are good at conceptualizing are used in the initial phase, persistent and detail-oriented people are necessary in the design and development phase, and technically skilled customer service personnel are required for the field service phase. These projects also need some participants who are flexible enough to stay with a project from beginning to end.[29] The matrix structure provides management the flexibility required to ensure that a proper combination of organizational resources is always available.

The matrix structure combines two lines of authority: a vertical line from functional managers, and a horizontal line from the project, program, or geographical area director. Functional departments provide specialist groupings and the development of expertise in functional areas. Project departments provide the direction for scheduling, budgeting, and general administration for various projects.[30] Support functions (e.g., personnel, security, and purchasing) are generally outside the matrix. They are structured in the more tradi-

...es and Disadvantages of a Matrix Structure

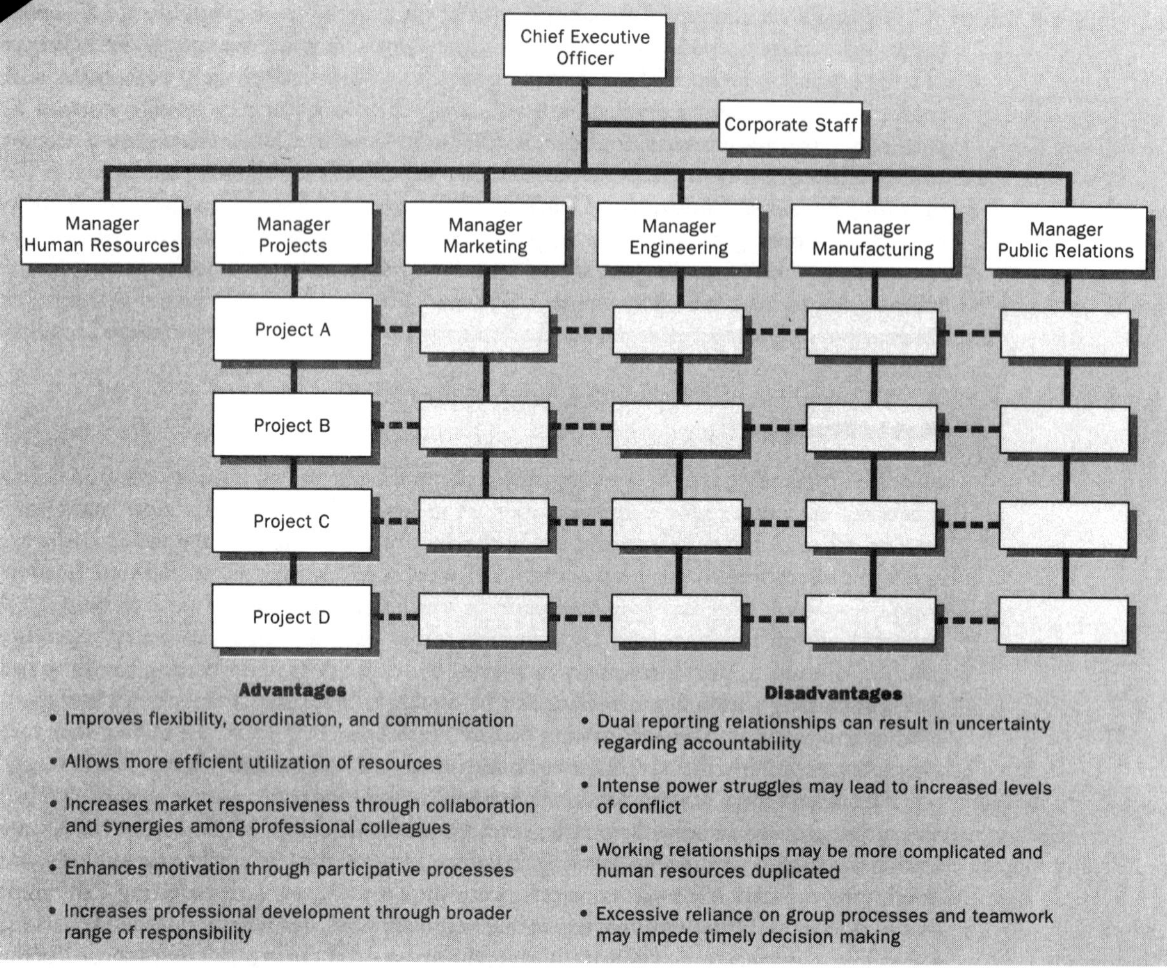

tional line and staff design. Top management is also outside the matrix. Top management performs the usual managerial functions, but also has tasks associated with coordinating the efforts of functional and project units. For the matrix to contribute to organizational performance, top management must be strongly committed to the concept and be flexible enough to deal with its unique properties and challenges.

Exhibit 9.5 presents a diagram of a matrix organization and lists some of its advantages and disadvantages.

Matrix Structure: Advantages

The dual authority structure of the matrix provides its users a great many advantages, such as flexibility, better coordination, enhanced communication, and a faster response time.

Matrix structures tend to emphasize close working relationships among departments rather than the boundaries between them, thereby increasing the opportunity for people at lower levels in the hierarchy.

An important aspect of the matrix is the potential for efficient utilization of resources. Individuals or groups of technical specialists, as well as equipment, can be shared across a number of projects or products. This avoids one of the major disadvantages of divisional structures: duplication of resources to provide independent support for each product or market.

Another advantage of matrix structures is increased responsiveness to the market. For example, if engineers assigned to a single product group are unable to implement changes to satisfy customer requirements, they are linked to engineering groups in other product areas and can collaborate with professional colleagues. This structure also provides the advantage of bringing together the diverse viewpoints and perspectives of different specialties and departments in interdisciplinary project teams.

Enhanced employee motivation is another advantage of organizations that incorporate the matrix structure. Because project teams are used extensively, such firms tend to be more participatory and democratic than those with functional organization structures. A matrix organization structure facilitates professional development by providing more opportunities to expand employee experience and perspective. Placed in situations where they must take account of a wider range of issues than those particular to their own specialties, professionals can demonstrate their capabilities and enhance promotional prospects.[31]

Matrix Structure: Disadvantages

During the 1970s, the popularity of the matrix system spread to health care organizations, construction companies, electronic firms, banks, and other industries.[32] These firms believed that a new approach was needed to adapt to changing markets, more rapid product obsolescence, intensifying international competition, heightened social consciousness, and increasing government regulations. However, by the late 1980s, several firms had become disenchanted with the matrix structure and had abandoned it, reverting to more traditional organizational forms.

The potential advantages of adopting a matrix structure are often never fully realized. In fact, many promising aspects, such as dual-authority arrangements, teamwork, and resource sharing can backfire.[33] If the dual-authority structure is not carefully and explicitly documented, informal mechanisms may develop to coordinate critical tasks. This will leave employees uncertain about their accountability to various supervisors. Similarly, disagreements among project and functional supervisors over how various resources should be shared may lead to power struggles. Managers may frequently escalate conflict by referring decisions up the chain of command rather than solving problems among each other. When project managers and functional managers agree on project goals and how to use available technology, they can achieve a workable balance o

Another frequent problem with matrix structures is that effi
if the dual-command structure leads to an excessive number of r
does not necessarily require doubling the work force at the n
necessary for small divisions to have a full complement of top m
managers, and full-time functional-area managers if some proje
similar enough to be directed by a single manager.

The synergies expected from collaboration among professionals cannot be realized if matrix management is assumed to be equivalent to group management. All team members do not have to be involved in all decisions. Too much democracy or too many required levels of approval can indefinitely delay decisions.

International Operations: Implications for Organization Structure

Up to this point, we have not explicitly addressed the implications of a firm's international operations on its structure. As discussed throughout the text, and particularly in Chapter 7, managers today must have an international outlook on their firm's business(es) and competitive strategies. To be successful in the global marketplace, managers must ensure consistency between their competitive strategies and the structure of their organizations. As organizations expand into foreign markets, they typically follow a pattern of change in structure that closely parallels the changes in their strategy. Three major contingencies which seem to influence the structural type adopted by firms with foreign operations are (1) product diversity, (2) the extent to which a firm is dependent on foreign sales, and (3) the type of strategy that is driving a firm's international operations.[34]

As international operations become an important part of the firm's overall operations, managers must make corresponding changes in their firm's structure. Among the types of structures that are used to manage a firm's international operations are international division, geographic-area division, worldwide functional, worldwide product division, worldwide matrix, and worldwide mixed.[35]

Recall that multidomestic strategies are driven by political and cultural imperatives and encourage managers within each country or geographic area to be responsive to local conditions. The type of structures that would be consistent with such an orientation are the *international division* and *geographic-area division* structures. In both cases, local managers are provided with a high level of autonomy to operate their product divisions within the constraints and demands of their geographic market. As a firm's foreign sales increase as a percentage of its total sales, it will likely move from an international division structure to a geographic-area division structure. Also, as a firm's product diversity becomes large, it is more likely to benefit from a worldwide matrix structure. On the other hand, global strategies are driven by economic pressures that require managers to view operations in different geographic areas as only a component of an overall operation that must be managed for overall efficiency. The type of structures that are consistent with the efficiency perspective are the *worldwide functional* and *worldwide product division* structures. Here, division managers view the marketplace as homogenous and devote relatively little attention to local market, political, and economic factors. The choice between these two types of structures is guided largely by the extent of product diversity. Firms with low levels of product diversity may find the worldwide functional structure appropriate and firms with higher levels of product diversity may opt for a worldwide product division structure. However, when a firm has significant product-market diversity resulting from a series of highly unrelated international acquisitions, we are likely to see a worldwide holding company structure. Such firms are characterized by very little commonality among products, markets, or technologies, and have little need for integration.

Exhibit 9.6 presents the structural alternatives we have mentioned for firms with

EXHIBIT 9.6
Choice of International Structures: Key Contingencies

Type of International Strategy

Product Diversity	Multidomestic: Low	Multidomestic: High	Global: Low	Global: High
High	Worldwide Product Division	Geographic Area	Worldwide Product Division	Worldwide Matrix
Low	International Division	Geographic Area	Worldwide Functional	Worldwide Functional

Foreign Sales as a Percentage of Total Firm Sales

varying levels of product diversity, foreign sales, and different strategies underlying their international operations.*

International Division Structure

Under the *international division structure,* a firm's international operations report to a division which is separated from its domestic operations. This is the structure that an organization typically uses when it first begins foreign operations or when a firm has relatively low levels of product diversity and foreign sales. The Baby Bells, formed by the break up of AT&T, are beginning to move into foreign markets, building on their domestic experience.[36] Bell Atlantic Corporation, for example, formed an international division when it began overseas operations. One of its major international ventures is a consortium with Ameritech of Chicago (another Baby Bell) and two New Zealand firms to acquire that country's state-owned telecommunications company.

The international division structure has a number of advantages. It provides a high degree of flexibility for foreign subsidiaries to develop strategies in accordance with local market conditions. The structure also concentrates the responsibility for, and control of, foreign operations with one person (and his or her staff) who usually has broad international experience. This leads to greater expertise in all facets of international operations.

The disadvantages of the international division structure are rooted in the relationship between the firm's domestic and foreign operations. Typically, the head of the international division is at the same hierarchical level as the product managers for the domestic opera-

* For purposes of simplicity, we have divided the degree of product diversity and percentage of foreign sales to total firm sales into two broad categories. Clearly, such distinctions are considerably more complex. There are also many other factors which exert a strong influence on the choice of structures. These include the extent of vertical integration and the sophistication of technology used by the firm. Also, as discussed later, firms may elect to adopt a worldwide mixed structure to derive the benefits of combining the structures in Exhibit 9.6. This becomes particularly likely when firms, in pursuit of the efficiencies of global coordination and the need to be responsive to varying local market conditions, adopt various forms of mixed structures. The need to combine the benefits of global and multidomestic strategies was discussed in detail in Chapter 7.

tions. Because the manager of the international division is responsible for a number of different products, he or she must secure the cooperation of multiple product managers. Often, however, these product managers are evaluated and rewarded solely on the basis of their domestic operations. Therefore, they may tend to give top priority to their own operations in terms of allocating funds, filling sales orders, and assigning personnel. This, of course, may prevent the firm from fully exploiting opportunities if foreign markets are becoming comparatively more attractive than domestic operations.

Geographic-Area Division Structure

As a firm expands its foreign operations as a percentage of its total sales, it will likely change from an international division structure to a *geographic-area division structure.* The firm divides the world into geographic areas, and each area has its own headquarters. All operations and products in a region become the responsibility of the area division manager. This structure enables the firm to achieve greater coordination among operations within regions. This structure also enables a firm to respond more quickly to local market conditions and is often found in organizations with mature, standardized product lines for which marketing, rather than production or technology, is the critical factor. For example, some packaged goods, such as soap products, have little to gain from manufacturing economies of scale and must be marketed differently in different geographic areas. Unfortunately, better coordination within regions often comes at the expense of worldwide product-line coordination; overall, there will generally be a loss in the efficient utilization of resources.

Worldwide Functional Structure

Firms with a relatively low level of product diversity often use a *worldwide functional structure.* Here, executives have global responsibility for individual functional areas. A recent study found that organizations that adopted a worldwide functional structure were *raw material extractors*—characterized by high levels of vertical integration and capital intensity.[37] These firms deal largely with very similar raw materials which do not impose differing requirements from one country to another. Their key strategic focus therefore is close coordination and integration among functional areas (e.g., exploration, production, and sales), not new-product introduction or marketing.

The worldwide functional structure, as one would expect, is vulnerable to the same potential weaknesses as the functional structure. That is, there may be too much emphasis on the functional areas to the detriment of the firm as a whole. Similarly, many issues may have to be resolved by top-level managers because the functional-level managers may lack a broader perspective.

Worldwide Product Division Structure

Under a *worldwide product division structure,* division managers are responsible for their products on a worldwide basis. This type of structure is often appropriate when there is a high product diversity and relatively little need to adapt products to local markets. Strategic decision making tends to be highly centralized and integrated because each product division has global responsibility for a product line's performance. This structure also enables a firm to achieve global specialization and economies of scale in marketing, R&D, and manufacturing. However, the structure is generally not sensitive to local marketing, political, and economic conditions, because it stresses strategic performance on a global basis.

The responsibility for product lines is centralized into profit centers, reducing the

Application 9.5

Imperial Chemical Industries Move to a Worldwide Product Division Structure

Imperial Chemical Industries' (ICI) name is entirely appropriate: the sun never sets on ICI's far-flung empire. The world's 38th-largest industrial corporation, British-based ICI sells $21 billion a year of pharmaceuticals, film, polymers, agricultural chemicals, explosives, and other products. The firm now has business-unit headquarters in twenty-five countries, manufacturing plants in twenty countries, and R&D centers in four countries.

In 1983, ICI began a move from a multidomestic strategy and geographic-area structure to establish worldwide business units. The company focused its resources on its strongest business units. Four of nine new business units are headquartered outside Britain. Two are in Wilmington, Delaware (ICI is growing 20 percent a year in the United States but only 2 to 3 percent at home). Factories in Britain and Brazil producing advanced materials or specialty chemicals, respectively, answer to an executive in Wilmington.

To avoid overlapping research in different locations, laboratories were given lead roles near their most important markets. Advanced materials research moved to Phoenix, Arizona, in order to be near clients in defense industries, while leather dye research went to the south of France, the heart of the market.

"It's a major change," says Hugh Miller, an American who heads the advanced materials and electronics group. "It's hard on people who have built national empires and now don't have such freedom. We are asking people to be less nationalistic and more concerned with what happens outside their country." The payoff, says Miller, is better decision making. "Before, each territory would work up projects and you'd have warring factions competing in London for the same money. Now with one responsible for a global product line, it becomes immaterial where a project is located. His profits will be the same. When you start operating in this manner, it takes a lot of steam out of the defense of fiefdoms." In pharmaceuticals, for example, better—and quicker—decision making has helped ICI reduce the time lag in introducing new drugs to different markets from half a dozen years to 1 or 2 years. ICI hopes eventually to make the introductions simultaneous.

Source

Main, J. (1989, August 28). How to go global and why. *Fortune*, pp. 70–73, 76 (with permission).

potential for conflicts. Application 9.5 gives an example of how one company found this to be the case when it reorganized from a geographic-area structure to a worldwide product structure.

Worldwide Matrix Structure

A *worldwide matrix structure* overlays two of the structures already discussed. Reporting relationships occur along two different channels to two different kinds of headquarters.[38] For example, in a product division by area division matrix structure, a plastics business in France would report to both the worldwide plastics division headquarters (the produce channel) and the European area headquarters (the geographic-area channel). This structure simultaneously achieves formulation and implementation along two different dimensions. The product divisions will tend to optimize their product line's performance by coordinating manufacturing and R&D, as well as certain aspects of marketing on a global basis. The area division hierarchies, on the other hand, will be responsible for sales and market share for their regions. They will be responsible for responding to local government, union, and societal conditions. However, the added flexibility from a worldwide matrix structure is not without its costs. Dual hierarchies involve more managers and staffs. Also, because each hierarchy may compete for the same resources, conflicts that arise require considerable managerial effort.

Dow Chemical is an example of a company that has successfully implemented a worldwide matrix structure. Dow has plants in thirty-two countries and a leading market position with many of its 1,800 different products such as ethylene, polyethylene, and polystyrene. The worldwide market structure has enabled Dow to be flexible enough to cope with different businesses and priorities within a single management system. Dow's matrix is based on three overlapping components: function, business, and geographic area. A small team of senior executives at headquarters set the performance goals for each business.[39]

Worldwide Mixed Structure

A *worldwide mixed structure* involves various foreign operations reporting to different types of headquarters. For example, in a product division and geographic-area division mixed structure, French plastics operations may report to the worldwide plastics division headquarters, while French cosmetics operations may report to the European division headquarters. Mixed structures are most appropriate when one product line requires a global strategy while another requires a multidomestic strategy.

Combination Structures: Mixing "Pure" Types

In practice, most organizations have structures that do not strictly conform to one of the broad types we have discussed. Organizations frequently operate with a combination of structures; they combine characteristics of more than one structural type as they grow and their strategies change. Often, this is necessary because a firm is changing its strategic direction. Also, a *combination structure* may actually be the most appropriate structure to meet challenges posed by expanding international operations as well as by such factors as diversity in technologies, products, and markets.

For example, Lotus Development Corporation has undergone a major structural reorganization to reflect its growing dependence on international operations.* In 1986, Lotus was organized primarily by functional-area departments: finance and operations, sales and service, international and information services, marketing and business development, and research and development. At that point in time, the functional structure was well suited to Lotus' narrow product-market diversity and relatively low level of international sales.

However, by 1990, the company had dramatically expanded its international operations and increased its product-market diversity. Although their international sales were based primarily on the Lotus 1-2-3 spreadsheet software, their domestic sales were becoming more diverse. The 1989 release of their technologically advanced 3.0 version of the 1-2-3 software created opportunities to enter many new markets such as spreadsheets for work stations and integrated software systems. These developments led to the creation of four business groups, including a separate division for international operations, which were to operate in conjunction with finance and operations and corporate communication depart-

---

* The authors would like to acknowledge and thank Paul Gerber, a 1990 M.B.A. graduate at the University of Texas at Arlington, for his assistance in preparing the material on the Lotus Development Corporation.

EXHIBIT 9.7
Lotus Development Corporation Organizational Structure, 1990

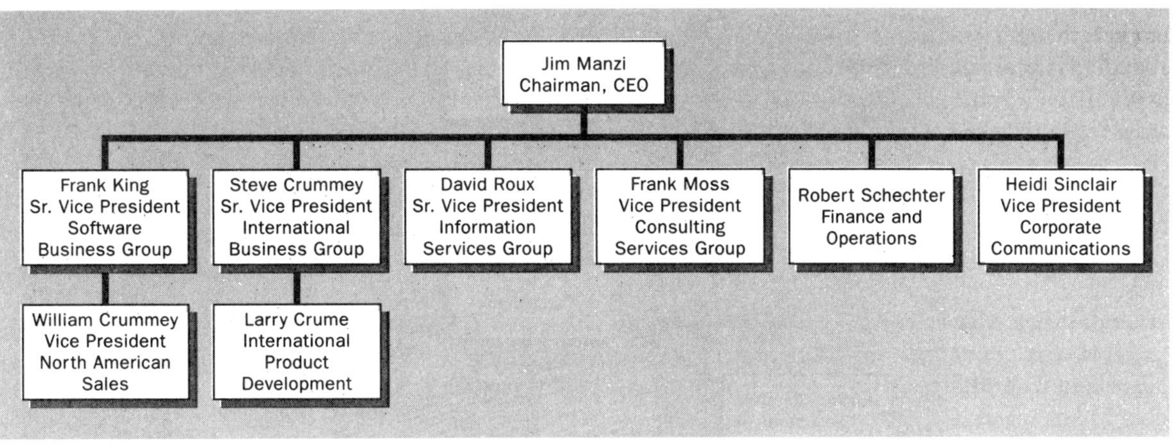

Sources: Harrington, M. J. (1990, March 26). Lotus juggles company structure. *Computerworld*, p. 6; Lotus set to become software consultant, revamps its business. *The Wall Street Journal* (1990, March 21), p. B4; and Lotus Development Corporation announces reorganization to decentralize company operations. *Business Wire* (1990, March 20), Cambridge, MA.

ments (see Exhibit 9.7). Although Lotus adopted primarily a divisional structure, it still retained two functional-area departments.

Firms vary in the type of combination structures they adopt in response to environmental challenges and strategic requirements. For example, some corporations with extensive international operations may adopt a worldwide mixed structure. This enables them to have different divisions operating under different types of structures. A division which pursues a global strategy would likely adopt a worldwide product division or worldwide functional division structure, whereas, a division that follows a multidomestic strategy would probably implement a geographic-area division structure. Another combination would be the addition of separate divisions to a matrix structure. In this case, the related businesses may be organized into a matrix structure and unrelated businesses maintained as autonomous divisions. The number of different combination structures is quite large.

GROWTH PATTERNS IN U.S. CORPORATIONS

Throughout this chapter, we have discussed how strategies and structures change as a firm grows in size, product diversity, and geographic scope. Exhibit 9.8 depicts possible growth patterns that firms may follow. The dominant pattern of change experienced by many large U.S. firms is indicated by the bold arrows. Young firms with simple structures begin to increase in output and sales, and become vertically integrated in an effort to secure sources of supply and channels of distribution. A functional structure is adopted in order to concentrate efforts on achieving maximum efficiency and improving their operations and product. As their initial markets mature, businesses look for similar products to manufac-

EXHIBIT 9.8
Common Growth Patterns of Large U.S. Corporations

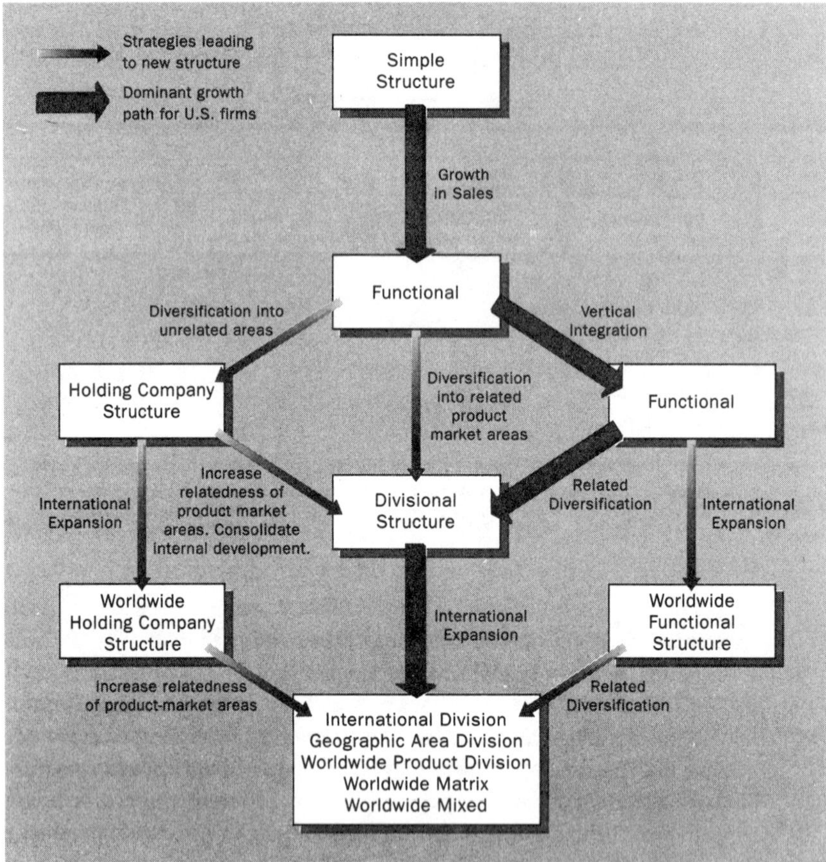

Source: Adapted by permission from Galbraith, J. R., & Kazanjian, R. K. (1986). *Strategy implementation: The role of structure and process* (2nd ed.) (p. 139).

ture and market. This new strategy of related diversification may indicate a need to reorganize around product lines or geographic markets, leading to a divisional structure. With growing profits, it becomes feasible to expand into more diverse areas. Depending on the extent of international expansion, type of strategy (global or multidomestic), and degree of product diversity, the firm may choose from international division, geographic-area division, worldwide functional, worldwide product division, worldwide matrix, or worldwide mixed structures.

Other relatively common variations in the growth pattern of U.S. corporations are indicated by fine-lined arrows. For example, some firms find it most desirable, perhaps because of a flexible manufacturing technology, to expand into several product lines. Rather than concern themselves with solidifying distributor and supplier relationships through vertical integration, they organize themselves divisionally along product lines. Some firms elect to branch out into unrelated products by acquiring already operational businesses. These firms reason that buying product expertise is often more economical than developing it internally. This conglomerate strategy is based on extreme differences in the products and markets these firms enter as well as the maturity of the businesses acquired. It frequently indicates the appropriateness of a holding company structure. Clearly, these growth patterns do not represent an exhaustive list, but only offer a suggestion of what combinations of strategy and structure are possible.

Summary

Dimensions of organizational structure include complexity, formalization, and centralization. The major types of structure are simple, functional, divisional, and matrix. Holding company and multinational structures can be considered as variants of the divisional form. Dimensions and types of structure are related to an organization's strategy, and to each other.

Each structural type is most appropriate under different conditions and offers certain advantages and disadvantages. Typically, a small organization will have a simple structure which provides it with such advantages as a high level of flexibility as well as rapid and relatively problem-free communication. However, the simple structure may lead to numerous problems, such as unclear boundaries of authority and few career-advancement opportunities. A functional type of organization structure becomes appropriate when a firm increases its scope of product-market activities or engages in vertical integration. This type of structure helps to increase the efficient allocation, coordination, and control of an organization's resources—particularly managerial and technical talent. A major disadvantage of the functional structure is the inherent conflict among functional-area managers because of their highly specialized points of view.

As a firm diversifies into unrelated product-market areas, adopting a divisional structure enables it to form relatively autonomous groups of business activities, such as product lines, customer types, or geographic regions. Such decentralization has many advantages. For example, corporate-level managers are able to concentrate more on the firm's overall strategy and divisional-level executives are responsible for operating activities. This usually allows quicker responses to changes in the external environment. On the other hand, divisional structures have higher costs because of additional personnel and capital investment. Also, divisional executives tend to overemphasize short-term performance results.

As firms further diversify their product-market scopes, two types of structures often evolve—strategic business unit (SBU) and holding company structures. These structures are considered to be variants of the divisional form of structure. Under the SBU structure, divisions with similar products, markets, and technologies are combined into homogeneous groupings (SBUs). This helps to achieve potential synergies. Holding company structures, on the other hand, are most appropriate when there are few similarities among a firm's portfolio of businesses.

The matrix structure may provide the advantages of both functional and divisional structures. It is most appropriate when a firm requires both technical expertise within its functional areas and coordination across its products or projects. There are many potential advantages of matrix structures, such as improved communication, resource utilization, and market response. Disadvantages include power struggles over personnel and resources, and problems of coordination.

When organizations expand into foreign markets, the type of structural form which is adopted is usually determined by two important contingencies: product diversity and the extent to which a firm is dependent on foreign sales. When a firm's international operations are small, the organization may simply incorporate the international aspects of its operations into its existing structure. However, as a firm's dependence on foreign sales increases and the firm's product diversity increases, the organization will likely form an international division which may be subsequently subdivided into several regions or areas as geographic expansion continues. The primary determinants of structural changes are a firm's size, extent of product diversity, and geographic scope.

Notes

1. Duncan, R. E. (1979). What is the right organization structure? Decision tree analysis provides the right answer. *Organizational Dynamics, 7*(3), 59–80.
2. Lawrence, P., & Lorsch, J. (1967). *Organizations and environment.* Homewood, IL: Irwin.
3. See, for example, Fredrickson, J. W. (1986). The strategic decision process and organization structure. *Academy of Management Review, 11,* 280–297.
4. These three components have been suggested by Hall, Richard H. (1987). *Organizations: Structure, processes, and outcomes* (4th ed.) (pp. 60–64). Englewood Cliffs, NJ: Prentice-Hall.
5. Many sociologists have made some pioneering contributions to our understanding of the dysfunctional personal and organizational consequences of excessive formalization in organizations. See, for example, Thompson, Victor. (1961). *Modern organizations.* New York: McGraw-Hill; and Merton, Robert K. (1957). *Social theory and social structure.* Glenco, IL: Free Press.
6. Henkoff, R. (1990, April 9). Cost cutting: How to do it right. *Fortune,* pp. 40–49.
7. Fredrickson, J. W. (1986). The strategic decision process and organizational structure. *Academy of Management Review, 11,* 280–297; Galbraith, J. R. (1973). *Designing complex organizations.* Reading, MA: Addison-Wesley.
8. Pugh, D. S., Hickson, D. J., Hinings, C. R., & Turner, C. (1968). Dimensions of organization structure. *Administrative Science Quarterly, 13,* 65–91.
9. Kiechel, W. (1988, February). Corporate strategy for the 1990s. *Fortune,* pp. 34–42.
10. Miller, D., & Friesen, P. H. (1980). Momentum and revolution in organizational adaptation. *Academy of Management Journal, 23,* 591–614.
11. Several writers have provided cogent arguments as to how dimensions of a firm's structure can exert a strong influence on the strategy formulation process and the firm's ability to compete successfully. Among these are Fredrickson, J. W. (1986). The strategic decision process and organization structure. *Academy of Management Review, 11,* 280–297; Hall, D. J., & Saias, M. A. (1980). Strategy follows structure! *Strategic Management Journal, 1,* 149–163; and Burgleman, R. A. (1983). A model of the interaction of strategic behavior, corporate context, and the concept of strategy. *Academy of Management Review, 8,* 61–70.
12. From 1952 through 1985, up to 60 percent of all businesses failed within their first 5 years of operation according to Goldstick, G. (1988). *Business Rx: How to get in the black and stay there.* New York: Wiley.

13. The pioneering work regarding the evolution of a firm's strategy and its relationship to structure (i.e., simple, functional, divisional) is known as the Scott Stages Model. It is discussed in Galbraith, J. R., & Kazanjian, R. K. (1986). *Strategy implementation: The role of structure and process* (2nd ed.). St. Paul, MN: West.
14. Miles, R. E. (1989). Adaptations to technology and competition: A new industrial relations system for the 21st century. *California Management Review, 31*(2), 9–27.
15. Berman, P. (1987, November 2). The fast track isn't always the best track. *Forbes,* pp. 60–64.
16. Jelinek, M. (1986). *Organizations by design: Theory and practice.* Plano, TX: Business Publications, Inc.
17. The seminal works relating strategy to structure are Chandler, A. D. (1962). *Strategy and structure.* Cambridge, MA: MIT Press; Rumelt, R. P. (1974). *Strategy, structure, and economic performance.* Boston: Division of Research, Harvard Business School. This trend was also observed in other industrial countries such as England, Spain, and Germany. Refer to Channon, D. (1973). *The strategy and structure of British enterprise.* London: Macmillan; Franco, L. (1976). *The European multinationals.* Greenwich, CT: Greylock Press; and Thanheiser, H. (1972). *Strategy and structure of German firms.* Unpublished doctoral dissertation. Harvard Business School, Cambridge, MA. Evidence of the increasing popularity of the divisional form of organization structure and some of the dysfunctions associated with it are provided by Hill, C. W. L., Hitt, M. A., & Hoskisson, R. E. (1988). Declining U.S. competitiveness: Reflections on a crisis. *Academy of Management Executive,* 2(1), 51–60.
18. Hoskisson, R. E. (1987). Multidivisional structure and performance: The contingency of diversification strategy. *Academy of Management Journal, 30,* 625–644.
19. Yavitz, B., & Newman, W. H. (1982). What the corporation should provide its business units. *Journal of Business Strategy, 3,* 14–19.
20. Robert Pitts also found that related diversifiers tended to have higher levels of interdivisional transfers of executives than unrelated firms. Refer to his article, Strategies and structure for diversification. (1977). *Academy of Management Journal, 20,* 197–208.
21. Stewart, T. A. (1989, July 3). Westinghouse gets respect at last. *Fortune,* pp. 92–94, 96, 98.
22. An interesting perspective on the advantages of a divisional type of organization structure is provided by Williamson, Oliver. (1975). *Markets and hierarchies: Analysis and antitrust implications.* New York: Free Press. He argued that the divisional form of organizational structure (also referred to as a multidivisional, or M-form, structure) helps to overcome problems relating to both internal and strategic control that are generally faced by diversified firms. Diversified firms that retained a functional organizational structure, he advised, would not only have lower efficiency because of a loss of internal control, but also a weaker long-term perspective because of a loss of strategic control. Information overload for the CEO would result because of the demand to process too much information. With the formation of relatively autonomous divisions and the delegation of operating responsibilities implicit in a divisional form, the role of top corporate executives becomes one of allocating resources as well as evaluating opportunities and threats for the entire organization.
23. Perhaps the seminal article on the issue of overemphasis on a short-term orientation by U.S. corporations is Hayes, R. H., & Abernathy, W. J. (1980). Managing our way to economic decline. *Harvard Business Review, 58*(4), 67–77.
24. Hill, C. W. L., Hitt, M. A., & Hoskisson, R. E. (1988). Declining U.S. competitiveness: Reflections on a crisis. *Academy of Management Executive,* 2(1), 51–60.
25. It has been suggested that forty-five may be the upper limit for the number of SBUs within a corporation. Beyond this number, the overload of information at the corporate level is felt.

Refer to Bettis, R. A., & Hall, W. K. (1983). The business portfolio approach: Where it falls down in practice. *Long Range Planning, 16,* 95–104.

26. Ibid.
27. Weiner, S. B. (1988, May 2). Making money the Pritzker way. *Forbes,* p. 73.
28. Joyce, W. F. (1986). Matrix organization: A social experiment. *Academy of Management Journal, 29,* 536–561.
29. Kelley, K. L. (1984, January 12). Are two bosses better than one? *Machine Design,* pp. 73–76.
30. Ibid.
31. Larson, E. W., & Gobeli, D. H. (1987). Matrix management: Contradictions and insights. *California Management Review, 29*(3), 126–138.
32. Kur, C. E. (1982). Making matrix management work. *Supervisory Management, 27,* 37–43.
33. This section draws heavily on the work of Davis, S. M., & Lawrence, P. R. (1978). Problems of matrix organizations. *Harvard Business Review, 56*(3), 131–142; and Larson, E. W., & Gobeli, D. H. (1987). Matrix management: Contradictions and insights. *California Management Review, 29*(4), 126–138.
34. Stopford, J. M., & Wells, L. T., Jr. (1972). *Managing in the multinational enterprise.* New York: Basic Books; Daniels, J. D., Pitts, R. A., & Tretter, M. J. (1984). Strategy and structure of U.S. multinationals: An exploratory study. *Academy of Management Journal, 27*(2), 292–307.
35. For an overview of the relationships between types of international strategy and organization structure, refer to Galbraith, J. R., & Kazanjian, R. K. (1986). *Strategy implementation: The role of structure and process* (2nd ed.). St. Paul, MN: West (especially Chaps. 2 and 9). An excellent recent study of the relationships between international strategy, structure, and economic performance is Habib, M. M., & Victor, B. (1991). Strategy, structure and performance of U.S. manufacturing and service MNCs: A comparative analysis. *Strategic Management Journal, 12*(8), 589–606.
36. McClenahen, J. S. (1990, September 17). The bells are ringing. *Industry Week,* pp. 56, 58.
37. Daniels, J. D., Pitts, R. A., & Tretter, M. J. (1984). Strategy and structure of U.S. multinationals: An exploratory study. *Academy of Management Journal, 27*(2), 292–307.
38. Our discussion of the worldwide matrix structure and worldwide mixed structure is drawn from Engelhoff, W. G. (1988). Strategy and structure in multinational corporations: A revision of the Stopford and Wells model. *Strategic Management Journal, 9*(1), 1–14.
39. Staff. (1989, August 5). Dow draws its matrix again—and again, and again. *The Economist,* pp. 55–56.

CHAPTER 10

Strategies are not always implemented as planned. Strategic control plays two roles: It helps to ensure that the firm's strategy is on track, and it enables top management to respond to unforeseen external and internal developments with changes in strategy.

We have divided this chapter into two major sections. The first section discusses the components of strategic control. It also addresses the importance of executive information systems (EIS) and many types of barriers that managers face in establishing and maintaining an effective strategic control system. The second section describes the three fundamental control approaches: rewards, rules, and culture. When appropriately used, either singly or in combination, they lead to higher organizational performance at all levels. This section also describes how reward systems, when appropriately designed, can be a powerful tool in achieving strategic control by motivating managers to ensure that strategies are effectively implemented.

After reading this chapter, you will understand:

- The difference between strategic control and operational control
- How executive information systems (EIS) help maintain effective strategic control
- Barriers that a manager faces in developing and using a strategic control system
- The three fundamental approaches to controlling behavior—reward, rules, and culture—when each is appropriate, and how they can be used in combination
- The critical role reward systems play in achieving the intended strategies of the organization

EXECUTIVE INTERVIEW

Charles F. Knight
Chief Executive Officer
Emerson Electric Company

Charles F. Knight is CEO of Emerson Electric Company. Emerson manufactures a broad range of electronic, electrical, and other products for industrial, commercial, and consumer markets. Before joining Emerson as vice chairman in 1972, Knight was president and chief executive officer of Lester B. Knight and Associates, a multinational consulting firm.

Since Knight became CEO of Emerson in 1973, sales have increased approximately sevenfold, to $7.6 billion in fiscal 1990. That year marked the company's 33d consecutive year of increased earnings and earnings per share, and its 34th consecutive year of increased dividends per share.

Knight received a bachelor's degree in mechanical engineering and an M.B.A. from Cornell University.

How does Emerson Electric assure that its overall corporate objectives are integrated and consistent with those of its individual businesses?

Fundamental to the management process at Emerson is setting tough targets at all levels of the company, and sticking to them. This is accomplished through a commitment to detailed planning and regular follow-up. Each year, top management meets with the leadership of each operating division at their planning conference. The division's management reviews, and we challenge, their assessment of market dynamics, competitive position, sources of growth, planned operational improvements, cost reductions, etc. Each division comes away from that conference with an "agreed to" strategic plan, including specific goals in several areas which are consistent with corporate objectives. Division managements operate with a great deal of autonomy in running their businesses, so long as they meet or are on plan to meet their targets. We monitor key division financial indicators monthly, and meet with each division president and chief financial officer quarterly to review progress and to help with problems, if any arise. This system is effective in part because division management compensation is tied to division performance, including meeting agreed upon targets.

What types of information must Emerson obtain about its competitors to maintain its overall low-cost position?

It is important to note that Emerson strives to be the *best cost producer*, which may or may not be the lowest cost position. There is a significant difference; a best cost producer manufactures products at the lowest relevant global cost for similar high levels of quality. The elements of Emerson's best cost producer strategy start with an unyielding commitment to quality, emphasize a detailed knowledge of competitors' cost and quality, and then include a focused manufacturing strategy, effective employee communication, formalized cost-reduction programs, and a commitment to capital expenditures.

To understand a competitor's relative cost requires detailed analysis of functional performance, parts count, weight, methods, and location of manufacture for labor and freight cost analysis, etc. Because of the international nature of manufacturing competition today, the cost of data collection is high and the process is time-consuming. However, this requirement is essential to understanding worldwide competitive product/service achievements, which become the floor of our required targets.

How does Emerson monitor the external environment to determine if changes need to be made in the strategy that is being implemented?

There are several external environments for which the dynamics must be constantly monitored: economic conditions, customer requirements, and competitive technological or design changes. All of these are addressed annually through the planning conference process, and more frequently in many ways. Close business relationships with customers may be the most important.

Regarding changes in economic conditions, we prepare annually, by requiring each operating division to establish A, B, and C budgets. The A budget scenario assumes spending and revenue at levels consistent with their best estimate of the economy and market conditions for the coming year. If conditions deteriorate, the division can quickly adjust to a B or, if necessary, a C budget. Developing these alternatives in advance is crucial to quick implementation, and protects the overall profitability of the company.

STRATEGIC CONTROL AND EVALUATION

Effectiveness in strategy formulation does not necessarily lead to high organizational performance. The failure to achieve objectives may be the result of implementation problems. Such problems often reflect shortcomings of a firm's control system.[1] The traditional approach to strategic control relies primarily on *feedback* control. A more contemporary approach stresses the importance of *feedforward* control.

The Traditional Approach to Strategic Control

Traditional approaches to control stress review and feedback of performance to determine if plans and objectives are being achieved.[2] This information is used to solve problems or take corrective actions. This approach sees strategic management as a sequential process of strategy formulation, strategy implementation, and strategy evaluation, with little interaction among the major phases or steps. This process is depicted in Exhibit 10.1.

This feedback approach to control may be appropriate for operational, day-to-day activities, or for firms competing in highly stable industries. However, when managers must control and evaluate long-term strategies, the limitations of relying primarily on feedback control become quite evident. Feedback control requires waiting for a strategy to be implemented before obtaining information on how well it is performing. Long-term strategies typically require the commitment of substantial human and financial resources and have long-term time horizons. This delays the possibility of corrective action and changing strategic direction for as much as several years. During this time, a firm may experience the loss of a key customer, a competitor may introduce a new product that targets the same customer group, or key executives and technical personnel may leave the firm. But many situations require a rapid response. In Chapter 2 we mentioned Procter & Gamble's forceful and effective retaliation to Clorox's entry into the detergent business. P&G added bleach to its Tide product line and offered a bleach of its own. In contrast, a few large firms in the agribusiness industry, such as ConAgra, apparently failed to respond to the demands of a key supplier group—small, independent catfish farmers. As a result, Delta Pride Catfish formed in 1981 and severely eroded ConAgra's market share.

Clearly, organizations must remain flexible and adapt to important changes both inside the firm and in its external environment. Increasingly, overly sophisticated, formalized planning processes may become dysfunctional. For example, Jack Welch, chairman and CEO of General Electric, contends that GE's strategic plans became "less and less

EXHIBIT 10.1
Traditional Strategic Management Process

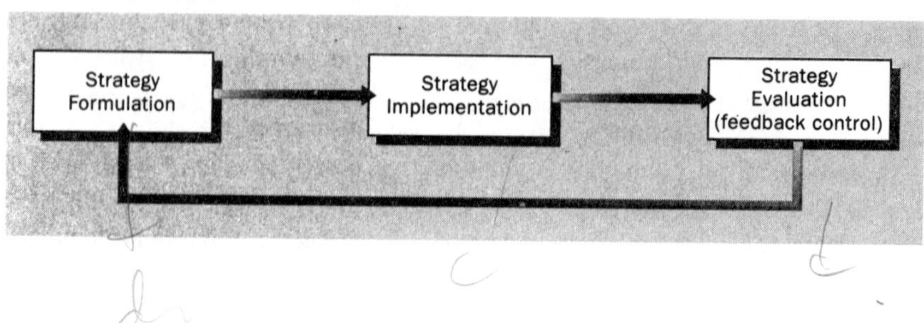

useful as they got bigger and bigger, as more and more hours went into preparing them, and as planners embellished them with increasingly sophisticated graphics and fancy covers."[3] Similarly, William Bricker, CEO of Diamond Shamrock, provides an interesting analogy.[4] He prefers to view strategies as a compass instead of as a road map. He believes that a simple compass provides an indication of what general direction should be taken and permits a good deal of ingenuity in overcoming unanticipated difficulties. A road map, on the other hand, explicitly details every turn that must be taken.

A Contemporary Approach to Strategic Control

Today, managers must anticipate change. This involves a proactive approach to strategic control that is more future-directed, utilizes state-of-the-art technology and executive information systems (EIS), and recognizes and overcomes inherent barriers to control.

The limitations of feedback control in traditional control systems may be corrected through use of a *feedforward* approach. This future-oriented approach helps anticipate important changes and trends.

There are three forms of feedforward control: premise control, strategic surveillance, and implementation control.[5] Exhibit 10.2 shows a strategic control system that incorporates the principles of feedforward control. We will now look at this system in more detail.

EXHIBIT 10.2
A Model of the Strategic Control Process

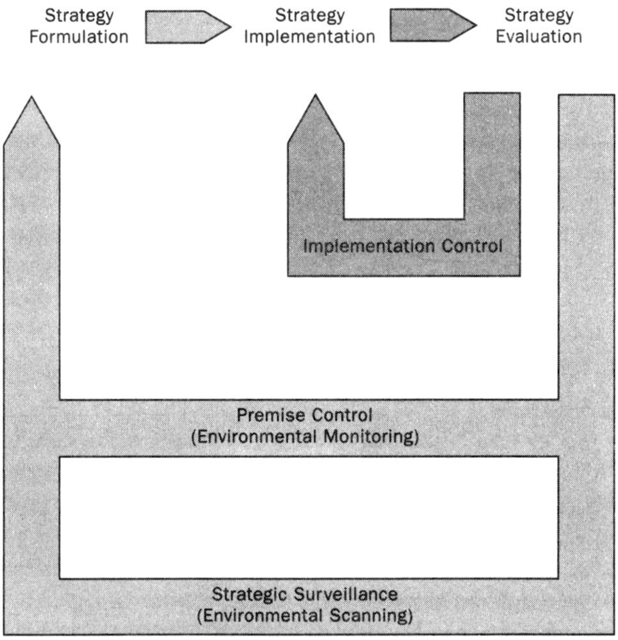

Source: Adapted from Schreyogg, G., & Steinmann, H. (1987). Strategic control: A new perspective. *Academy of Management Review, 12,* 91–103; and Preble, J. (1990). *Towards a comprehensive system of strategic control.* Working paper. University of Delaware, Newark, DE.

Premise Control

In the strategy formulation process, the development of premises (or assumptions) is an important early step; they provide a basis for developing strategies. Premises may include any number of factors that are deemed important in both the industry environment and the general environment. Premise control requires systematic and continuous monitoring of important environmental factors to determine if previously agreed-upon planning premises remain valid. Major changes may call for a change in strategy. Du Pont's acquisition of Conoco for $7.6 billion in 1981 was largely motivated by a desire to have a captive supplier of petroleum products. On the basis of expectations about increasing oil prices and diminishing supply, management felt the purchase price was reasonable. However, the premises they made about the market proved to be wrong, and during the late 1980s, estimated earnings had to be revised downward. Similarly, many of the LBOs of the 1980s were based on overly optimistic premises about growth and resultant cash flows. In many cases these premises proved to be incorrect, resulting in a number of bankruptcies. Examples of well-known firms whose LBOs failed include Revco Drug Stores, Federated Department Stores, and Sealy Mattress Company.

Premise control is conducted by specialists within the organization (trained in political science, economics, industry analysis, etc.) or by outside consultants.[6] Premise control must avoid accumulation of excessive amounts of data which would lead to a case of information overload and sabotage the value of the process. Efforts must be directed at key success premises—those that would have a major impact on the firm if they were to change. So, premise control is a focused and highly selective type of control. A representative list of key premises that a hypothetical U.S. manufacturing firm may use in developing their long-term plans is provided in Exhibit 10.3.

Emerson Electric's growth from basically a manufacturer of electric motors to a $7.6 billion diversified electronics technology firm illustrates the benefits of premise control. Emerson competes successfully as the industry's low-cost producer and provides high-quality products. Careful monitoring of competitors is a vital ingredient of their winning strategy. Emerson's intelligence-gathering process is very thorough and includes activities such as continually reexamining their assumptions regarding the costs of their competitors' plants. Chuck Knight, Emerson's CEO, contends, "We knew what Makita's and Bosch's and Black and Decker's costs were. We never would have built the plants we did without knowing."[7] For Emerson Electric, which has steadfastly followed a strategy of cost leadership, it is absolutely essential to monitor their competitors' costs, since each new plant they build must be even more cost effective.

Strategic Surveillance

Not all changes or trends that may have a potentially significant impact on the firm are necessarily identified by managers during the formulation of its strategy. Strategic surveillance is less focused and more flexible than premise control. Instead of continually monitoring a few key predetermined indicators as in premise control, strategic surveillance is much broader. Its goal is to identify previously undetected critical events before they become either missed opportunities or serious threats.

Strategic surveillance is designed to monitor internal and external events that not only may threaten the course of a firm's strategy but also may provide opportunities. An approach that may be useful for systematically assessing *internal* factors is the use of

EXHIBIT 10.3
Key Premises of a Hypothetical Manufacturing Firm

- Economic growth
  - 3% growth in GNP
  - 5% increase in net disposable income
- Demand growth for our products and services
  - 6% growth in the domestic market
  - 8% growth in overseas market
- Competitor behavior
  - Major rival likely to cut prices by 5%
  - Foreign competitor likely to introduce a new product
- Cost and availability of inputs
  - Prime interest rate to range between 9.5 and 10.5%
  - Work force to remain nonunionized
  - Raw material prices except for petroleum-derived materials to increase by 5% (petroleum-derived raw materials to increase by 8%)
- Technological change
  - Research and development expenditures in the industry to remain below 2% of sales revenue
- Regulatory changes
  - Restrictive legislation on pollution control
  - Free trade policies of government to continue without major changes
- Consumer behavior
  - Consumers willing to pay significantly more for upgraded products
  - Consumer expectations about warranties, product safety, etc., will continue to increase

strengths and weaknesses analysis. In Chapter 4, we discussed the value chain as a useful framework for assessing a firm's strengths and weaknesses and as a means of achieving competitive advantage. To conduct strategic surveillance, a team of managers from various functional areas within the firm might be charged with the task of determining brief lists of key strengths (or critical success factors) upon which the company should base its future, and weaknesses that must be avoided. Such lists should be continually assessed, not only to determine how a firm measures on the key factors, but also to determine if the list needs to be modified as competitive conditions change.

A representative list of trends that could have an important effect on critical success factors of a firm would include:

Positive Effect

- Development of process engineering techniques leading to significant reductions in unit variable costs
- Unanticipated success in hiring key research and development personnel
- Defects per unit of output below anticipated levels
- Application of a technological innovation across multiple divisions within the company

Negative Effect

- Turnover/resignation of key executive or technical personnel
- Decline in morale
- Unanticipated delays in major plant completion
- Decline in customer perceptions of product quality

The strategic surveillance of external factors can be accomplished through environmental scanning. This type of surveillance is analogous to a radar screen continually scanning the environment for new images or "blips" in the screen.[8] As with the process of premise control, the environment may be broken down into segments of both the general environment and the industry environment. Selected environmental sectors are further subdivided into clusters of variables which represent various aspects of that particular dimension. For example, the economic segment of the general environment may include interest rates, inflation rates, business cycles, income trends, employment trends, money supply, and so on.*

Below is a list of important *external environmental trends* that may need to be scanned in the course of strategic surveillance:

- Growth of the government as a customer
- Development of the European Community (EC)
- Business with eastern European countries
- Growth of the service sector
- Societal concerns about ecology issues
- Competition from developing countries
- Shortages of strategic resources (e.g., oil, titanium)

The use of leading-edge technology is vital to General Electric (GE) Company's quest for global leadership in many areas such as its $7 billion jet engine business, $1.5 billion medical systems business, and $5 billion aerospace business. Dr. Walter Robb, GE's senior vice president for corporate R&D, believes that to ensure success, strategic surveillance is vital. Decisions regarding technological issues depend in large part on what the competition is doing. Keeping up with publications, patents, presentations at technical meetings, and news about hirings are all means by which Dr. Robb stays abreast of R&D activities. He has also used many ideas that he has learned from observing Japanese businesses. Among these are how teamwork can shorten design cycles through the close coordination of personnel from marketing, engineering, and design.[9]

Implementation Control

Two important components of implementation control are *operations control* and *strategic implementation control.* After looking at each, we will discuss the importance of budget and reward systems in achieving effective implementation control.

---

* There is typically some overlap among the variables considered in premise control and strategic surveillance. The latter is, of course, much more extensive, unstructured, and unfocused.

Operations Control. Operations control is concerned with whether or not a firm's strategy is being implemented as planned. It addresses such questions as:

- Are short-term profit, growth, and efficiency objectives being attained?
- Are resources being allocated properly?
- Is the firm within budget and on schedule?

Data for operations control, such as productivity, cash flow, budget variances, and so on, are generally derived from typical accounting and financial reports.

Strategic Implementation Control. Strategic implementation control is concerned with a much broader question: Should the firm's overall strategy be changed in light of unfolding events and trends? If deviations from plans are observed, it does not automatically signal a crisis or failure.[10] Implementation control involves more than the determination of whether or not short-term objectives are obtained—it looks at results within the broader context of ongoing events and trends in both the internal and external environment. This evaluation and assessment may reveal that a strategy continues to be successful.

At Borg-Warner, the strategy implementation for a selected number of business units is monitored by the CEO through a strategic issues system.[11] During the annual budgeting process corporate-level planners identify approximately twenty or thirty critical strategic business units (SBUs) out of the 100 SBU plans that are submitted and evaluated. Of these, top management at the corporate level selects ten or twelve SBUs whose plans represent "strategic issues." These critical SBUs are those whose impact—positive or negative—on Borg-Warner's overall performance is considered vital. For these SBUs, budget allocation decisions are withheld until further analysis and presentations by SBU-level management. The chief operating officer at corporate headquarters is provided with a "strategy response" by the corporate planning staff and a set of questions to raise at his or her quarterly operating reviews. These questions help to determine whether or not the strategy is being implemented in accordance with directives from corporate headquarters. Depending on deviations from plans and an evaluation of changes in the external and internal environment, top management may permit the deviation, change the budget allocation, or require a new strategy by SBU management. The quarterly review process continues until the new strategy is completely implemented. Clearly, top-level management at Borg-Warner is not content with waiting for the annual budgeting process to make corrective changes in strategy. Rather, strategic control is viewed as an ongoing process involving many hierarchical levels of line and staff executives and specialists.

Some of the more important issues involved in effective implementation control are shown below:

- Reviewing the suitability of strategies and objectives, given important changes in the external environment
- Ensuring that efforts to attain targeted levels of performance do not lead to dysfunctional managerial behavior
- Monitoring the achievement of desired levels of performance in financial and nonfinancial terms
- Preparing action plans to deal with deviations of actual performance from targeted levels

- Installing and maintaining appropriate reward and information systems that best support strategy implementation

Effective implementation control also requires that appropriate mechanisms are in place to ensure compliance with the company's ethical standards. Application 10.1 explains how Dow Chemical uses "ethical audits" as a means to promote ethical behavior.

Exhibit 10.4 summarizes some of the important characteristics of the three forms of strategic control: premise control, strategic surveillance, and implementation control.

Appropriate budgets and well-designed reward systems are essential for implementation control to be effective. Poor allocation of resources and inadequate managerial incentives for achieving desired objectives often prevent firms from addressing the issues adequately.

Effective Implementation Control: The Importance of Budget Systems. A firm's budget is often viewed as a road map against which a company's actual revenues and expenditures are assessed. This map allows firms a certain degree of control by focusing attention on areas of concern so that necessary corrective actions can be undertaken. There are compelling reasons for predicting future levels of income, expenses, and cash flows. When used effectively, budgets should reduce unnecessary spending and lead to profits.

A firm's budget is an important tool in implementing its strategy. Managers must develop their budgets in a manner that is consistent with the company's overall strategy.

Application 10.1

Monitoring the Ethical Environment: The Use of Ethical Audits at Dow Corning

Dow Corning has a long-standing ethics program. Its general code, which includes a seven-point values statement, has been revised four times since its inception in 1976. The company started using face-to-face "ethical audits" at its plants worldwide over a decade ago. The number of participants attending these 4- to 6-hour audits ranges from five to forty. Auditors meet with the manager in charge on the evening before to determine the most pressing issues. The actual questions are based on relevant sections in the corporate code and are tailored for the audit location. At sales offices, for example, the auditors concentrate on issues such as kickbacks, unusual requests from customers, and special pricing terms. At manufacturing plants, the focus is on conservation and environmental issues. An ethical audit may include the following questions:

- Are there any examples of business that Dow Corning has lost because of the refusal to provide "gifts" or other incentives to government officials?
- Do any employees have ownership or financial interest in any of our distributors?
- Has Dow Corning been compelled to terminate any distributors because of their business practices?
- Do any Dow Corning policies conflict with local practices?

John Swanson, manager of Corporate Internal and Management Communications, coordinates this effort. He believes the audit makes it "virtually impossible for employees to consciously make an unethical decision." Approximately twenty meetings occur every year. The Business Conduct Committee members, who act as session leaders, then prepare a report for the Audit Committee of the Board of Directors, which stresses the fact that there are no shortcuts to implementing this program: It requires time and extensive interaction with the people involved.

Source

Murphy, P. E. (1989). Creating ethical corporate cultures. *Sloan Management Review, 31,* 81–87.

EXHIBIT 10.4
Characteristics of Strategic Control Elements

	Elements of Strategic Control		
Characteristics	**Premise Control**	**Strategic Surveillance**	**Implementation Control**
Purpose	Keep premises current and strategies valid	Early detection of environmental changes or shifts that could affect strategic direction	Monitor the effects of actions as they impact strategy
Mechanism	Environmental monitoring	Environmental scanning	Implementation process
Procedure	List premises Track assumption development Update premises Modify strategies	External environment: Determine sectors and variables Continously scan Collect, analyze, and disseminate environmental data Internal environment: Strengths and weaknesses analysis Comparisons with competitors on critical success factors	Establish standards Determine intermediate goals Periodically collect control data Evaluate results relative to strategic objectives

Source: Adapted from Preble, J. (1990). *Towards a comprehensive system of strategic control.* Working paper. University of Delaware, Newark, DE.

Budgets provide managers with the coordination and control necessary to attain their goals. Additionally, the budget provides a benchmark against which a company's performance can be evaluated when variations between actual performance and budgeted performance arise. Managers may remedy the situation by addressing the issues responsible for the lower-than-expected performance, or in some cases, by changing the budget itself to reflect unanticipated changes in the internal or external environment.

As discussed earlier in the chapter, one of the challenges of top executives is to create a proper balance between the attainment of both long-term strategic objectives and short-term operating objectives. Allocating resources solely on the basis of short-term goals (for example, quarterly or annual profitability) may lead to the neglect of important maintenance, R&D, and other activities whose payoff may be reflected primarily in a later time period.[12] Often there may be an overemphasis on keeping spending within the budget. Application 10.2 discusses some of the detrimental effects of overly rigid budgeting systems. On the other hand, excessive attention to long-term strategic goals may lead to insufficient attention directed toward the control of operating expenses and other ongoing, day-to-day activities.

To strike a proper balance between strategic and operating objectives, it is necessary to develop separate budgets for each type of activity.[13] Without a clear distinction, managers may view resources allocated for strategic activities as a "gift" in addition to the operating budget, either viewing them as "fat" and "frills" or using them for attaining operating objectives. A firm's *strategic budget* is based on two elements. First, it includes an allocation of resources necessary to change the direction of a particular business, that is, those resources necessary to implement a major change in business strategy. Second, the resources

Application 10.2

Budgets: Overcoming the Potential Downside

Many experts contend that budgets often emphasize things such as departmental spending limits and head counts and overlook important values such as quality and customer service—as well as profits. Budgets may also create barriers between the various functional and product-market areas of a firm and between a firm and its customers. Robert Gunn, a consultant with AT&T, claims, "When you're controlled by a budget, you're not controlling your business."

Budgeting is often an annual ritual not connected to the firm's overall strategy. Although budgets are useful for tracking expenditures, when used inappropriately they can become harmful. Budgets may become management's main tool for assessing performance, and may distort long-term planning or prevent managers from shifting resources. A budget may become an end in itself, with managers believing that "making the numbers" is their primary goal. Budgets may be used primarily to control negative behavior, like spending too much, instead of reinforcing positive behavior, like growing the business.

Successful companies do not base their control system strictly on budgets. Rather, they rely on financial measures such as return on invested capital and on nonfinancial measures such as market share, and indicators of customer satisfaction and product quality.

Below are some examples of how the budget process can be used effectively and well-managed firms that have done so.

- *Measure both output and input.* Ineffective budgets rely exclusively on cost targets. Thus, managers focus on controlling how much their operations spend—not how much they earn. Managers become oriented inward, emphasize rules instead of initiative, and question every small variance in a department's budget.

  At Emerson Electric, however, the key measure is profit, not spending, and this orientation is found at all operations—as far down the organization chart as possible. Al Suter, president, says, "If a division president has an opportunity to gain market share, he can go out and buy all the steel he needs. No one has to ask."

- *Design against turf wars.* When divisions are primarily oriented toward "making their budgets," they may attempt to transfer work and costs to other divisions. This becomes an excellent formula for alienating customers. Donald Curtis, a senior partner at DeLoitte and Touche, says, "An excuse like, 'It's not my fault, it's the credit department's fault' is a non-answer to the customer." Thus, organizations need to find ways to link budgets together horizontally, not vertically.

  At Xerox, field operations have been restructured to combine sales, service, and order entry into geographic units—rather than organize them into separate hierarchies that may constantly fight over funding allocations. Also, at Emerson Electric, the reward structure provides a good reason for all operations in a division to collaborate. The separate operations must account for profits—not costs—and the manager's incentive pay is based on the division's performance as a whole.

- *Build budget busting into the system.* Simply revising an annual budget every few months may serve only to tighten budgetary constraints. Such an approach does little to encourage managers to think or act strategically.

  At 3M, the chief financial officer asks his operating managers to include a line in their strategic forecasts labeled NIGOs—"nonincremental growth opportunities." These include either new products that may be developed within the coming year or potential product entries into new markets. The revenues and costs associated with such items are difficult to predict.

Clearly, flexibility in the budgeting process has its benefits. Allen Jacobsen, CEO of 3M, has told his division general managers, "I never want to hear anyone put down a project because it isn't in the budget." Managers should feel safe to act on the knowledge that their business is not based strictly on a fiscal year. Robert Hershock, a group vice president at 3M, who was recently promoted to his position, reflects the perspective of his chairman: "I've overrun budgets—overrun them pretty good sometimes. I was never criticized if I could justify it."

Source

Stewart, T. A. (1990, June 4). Why budgets are bad for business. *Fortune*, pp. 179, 182, 186, 190 (with permission).

EXHIBIT 10.5
Strategic and Operational Budgets for a Hypothetical Food Products Company: Allocations for Five Functional Departments

	Research and Development	*Engineering*	*Production and Operations*	*Marketing and Sales*	*Accounting and Finance*
Strategic budgets for project I* (funds required for major changes in business strategy or for major projects)	$0.2 million	$0.1 million	$1.0 million	$6.0 million	$2.0 million
Strategic budget for project II† (funds for major changes in business strategy or for major projects)	$1.2 million	$0.3 million	$2.0 million	$4.0 million	$0.5 million
Operational budget (funds necessary to maintain current operations)	$4.0 million	$5.0 million	$10.0 million	$8.0 million	$3.0 million

* Project I: Enter European market with a line of frozen dinner entrees.
† Project II: Develop a low-calorie frozen dessert.
Source: Modified from P. Lorange. (1984). Strategic control: Some issues in making it operationally more useful. In R. Lamb (ed.), *Competitive Strategic Management.* Englewood Cliffs, NJ: Prentice-Hall.

should be identified with specific strategic projects or programs. Strategic resources may be classified into four basic types:*

1. Human resources to carry out strategic activities (e.g., person-months, salary)
2. Nonpersonnel costs associated with R&D (e.g., product testing, market research)
3. Investments in land, plant, equipment, and so forth
4. Working capital (e.g., inventory changes, credit volume)

The primary justification for a particular allocation of strategic resources is that it should enhance the firm or business unit's long-term competitive position and financial results.

The *operational budget,* on the other hand, should include those resources necessary to maintain current operations at a successful level. The level of resources should be consistent with the anticipated operating level for the firm or business unit and include the incremental changes necessary to meet next year's target. Thus, it should facilitate attaining the following year's objectives. Exhibit 10.5 illustrates the interrelationships between strategic and operational budgets for a hypothetical food products firm.

All five functional departments are allocated resources for conducting ongoing operational activities. In addition, for strategic projects, additional allocations of funds must be made to each of the departments. The level of funding for strategic projects varies rather significantly across projects. For example, R&D is much less important for project I (entering a new market) than for project II (developing a new product). By separating the

* Although all strategic resources may be classified into one of these four categories, it does *not* follow that all of these types of expenditures are necessarily strategic. For example, research and development expenditures, such as routine process engineering development, may be necessary to attain short-term objectives or simply to maintain day-to-day operations.

total budget allocated to a department into both an operational budget and a strategic budget, top executives endeavor to achieve greater accountability. Further, appropriate levels of resources and effort are directed toward both strategic and short-term objectives.

Strategic Control: The Role of Executive Information Systems

A strategic control system cannot be effective unless it is supported by an information system which provides timely and accurate information. An executive information system (EIS) is a structured, computer-based planning and control system for top management.* It provides executives with the data and information of their choice and in the desired form.[14] It is primarily a system that executives may directly access through their personal computers to monitor what is going on within the company and in its external environment. With the availability of such information, the executive may then work to resolve problems or take advantage of opportunities that he or she has uncovered. EIS should deliver only information critical to executives and it is most useful when used to address specific business objectives or critical success factors. This valuable resource provides new data-monitoring techniques and timely information through computer terminals or personal computers without the burden of large amounts of paper reports. EIS should change and evolve in response to the competitive concerns of the executives it supports, growing with the executive and the organization.

Executive information systems are based on concepts with which executives are usually already familiar. Typically, executives already receive or would like to receive most of the information an EIS provides. With EIS, the executive receives it quicker, more efficiently, and in a more convenient form. EIS pulls information together that previously had to be viewed separately and uses graphics to aid in comprehension. EIS generally provides not only decision support, but also human communications support. The coordination and scheduling of meetings, follow-up, and other interpersonal aids are all components of information systems. Also, EIS should improve time management and enhance team coordination.

A key objective in building an EIS is to start with a system that helps an executive gain further insight into the business and its critical success factors. Three conditions that often determine the success of executive information systems are:

- *A committed and informed executive sponsor.* The desire for an EIS must come from top management. A system is rarely used effectively by executives if it is initiated largely by the information systems department.
- *An operating sponsor.* The development of an EIS is often delegated to a trusted and informed senior executive. This person must be able to communicate both with the other executives and with the development staff.
- A clear link to critical success factors and to business objectives.

* For our purposes, EIS and executive support systems (ESS) are considered to be synonymous. Whereas EIS and ESS are relatively new tools designed to provide top management with immediate access to information in an appropriate format for executive decision making, decision support systems (DSS) are much broader in scope. They are typically used to assist managers in problem solving through models, data management, creating forecasts, and graphics.

Currently, there is a growing trend in the use of executive information systems.[15] While only about 2 percent of top executives used these systems in 1983, the figure rose to 13 percent by 1988. This figure is expected to rise to 25 percent by 1993.[16]

Phillips 66 Company (a division of Phillips Petroleum Company) illustrates how executive information systems can lead to improved strategic control and increased performance.[17] In 1985, after eliminating 40 percent of its management jobs, President Robert G. Wallace needed a more efficient means of obtaining and processing information relating

Application 10.3

Frito-Lay's Effective Executive Information System

Frito-Lay is the $4.5 billion snack food division of Pepsico, Inc. In early 1990, Frito-Lay's sales were slumping in the San Antonio and Houston markets. To investigate the problem, Robert H. Beeby, CEO, retrieved relevant data from his executive information system for south Texas and isolated the cause of the declining sales. A regional competitor had recently introduced El Galindo, a white-corn tortilla chip that was capturing more shelf space than Frito-Lay's traditional Tostitos tortilla chips. Two years ago it would have taken Frito-Lay months just to isolate the problem. However, within 3 months, Beeby had Frito producing a white-corn version of Tostitos and the firm quickly won back its lost market.

The EIS that allowed Mr. Beeby to respond quickly is part of an extensive information system that gathers data from two primary sources: scanners at supermarket checkout counters, and handheld computers operated by Frito-Lay's 10,000 sales representatives. The handheld computers make daily updates possible. These updates provide information about real-time trends for over 100 product lines in over 400,000 stores. At the end of each workday, the handheld computer is connected to a minicomputer at a Frito-Lay distribution center so the results can be sent to headquarters. The central computer sends information back to the handheld computers on pricing changes and promotions for use the next day. Also, each week the system provides the sales representatives with a review of the previous week's results on their routes.

The system, which required an initial investment of $40 million, involves everyone from the front-line sales representatives to the CEO. It collects sales data, scans the data for trends, and flags problems and opportunities for executive attention. This system enables managers to monitor the following:

- Competitor sales by product and store location
- Competitor share of display space
- The success of marketing promotions
- Brands, products, and food categories that contribute most to a store's bottom line (return-on-inventory investment)
- Daily and weekly analysis of performance of all 10,000 route salespeople

The sophisticated EIS at Frito-Lay has played a key role in fulfilling an important sales goal set in 1985: a 6 percent annual sales growth (twice the industry average) and double-digit earnings growth. Other important benefits follow:

- The handheld computers have saved sales representatives an average of 5 hours a week in record keeping. The extra time is spent making new sales calls.
- The company has realized a savings of $39 million a year on returned products or "stales" because of better inventory management.
- The analysis of sales data has enabled sales representatives to spend less time preparing proposed layouts of grocery products (diagrams indicating the placement of items on shelves in a store) to store managers. This has enabled the layouts to be run off the computer within 15 minutes versus several days under the previous manual system.

Sources

Feder, B. J. (1990, November 8). Frito-Lay's speedy data network. *The New York Times*, pp. C1 and C7.

Rothfeder, J., & Bartimo, J. (1990, July 2). How software is making food sales a piece of cake. *Business Week*, pp. 54–55.

Kunde, D. (1990, July 29). In the chips. *The Dallas Morning News*, pp. 1H and 2H.

to important internal and external factors. His staff then developed an EIS that tracked data such as trends in oil pricing, refinery operating results, and chemical plant product statistics.

Wallace explains that the system saves him about an hour each day and is much more efficient than plowing through reams of paper reports. He estimates that the system is directly responsible for increasing profits by approximately $100 million in 1988 because managers not only receive information faster, they understand it better. For example, because Phillips 66 buys and sells oil futures, tracking market trends is critical. "If the price of oil moves by just one penny a day," says Wallace, "that could be worth a sales volume of about $60 million a year." Wallace feels there are similarities between his use of the executive information systems and his experience as a Navy antiaircraft gunner during World War II. As a gunner, he was able to scan vast areas of the sky and quickly identify enemy planes when they were specks on the horizon. Looking at his screen, he says, "I can see trends in seconds. I can't do that if I'm scanning a lot of tables on paper."[18] Application 10.3 discusses the executive information system at Frito-Lay—a division of Pepsico, Inc.

Barriers to Strategic Control

Effective strategic control systems play an important role in ensuring the long-term viability of a business enterprise. However, to be effective, the systems must overcome potential problems, or barriers, which may be classified as systemic, behavioral, or political.[19]

Systemic Barriers

Systemic barriers originate from limitations in the design of the control system or a firm's inability to manage the system once it is implemented. One major systemic barrier is the difficulty of comparing performance results across businesses. It is difficult to isolate a standard against which to control. For example, against what standard can the ROI achieved in a particular business be judged? How can one know if a specific ROI is good or bad? Such problems may be lessened if top management has a fundamental knowledge of each of the firm's businesses. However, as a firm's product-market scope becomes diverse, the corporate office may become too far removed from the individual businesses to exercise effective control.

Another systemic barrier is excessive amounts of paperwork that may actually slow down the firm's ability to react quickly to important environmental changes. In this situation, the information provided to operating executives and the corporate office may lose relevance and lead to unreliable forecasts. Excessive amounts of information may lead to information overload and misinterpretation.

A final systemic problem is the conflict between strategic objectives passed down from the corporate office and short-term objectives at the business level. For example, when an oil company shut down one of its European refineries, it needed a larger crew for its other European refinery. However, this was inconsistent with the corporate office's goal of reducing manpower for both.

Such inconsistencies may reflect insufficient coordination among the multiple hierarchical levels within the firm. More formal mechanisms may be necessary to review objectives and goals to ensure needed integration. This problem may be exacerbated within highly diversified firms where the corporate office is far removed from the individual businesses.

Behavioral Barriers

Behavioral barriers often have their underlying cause in a manager's tendency to address issues from a limited or biased perspective because of background, education, and training. For example, executives may have invested a great deal of time into a particular product and are therefore unable to examine critically its life cycle position. For example, executives who have managed a cash cow for 15 years might still prefer to think of it as a growth business. This attitude is sometimes seen in managers who want to revive a business that should gradually die. Such vested interests may restrict a clear, objective perspective and adversely affect the usefulness of strategic control.

A related issue is the fear of losing face or of being proven wrong. For example, an executive who has sponsored a particular strategy or project may screen out negative performance information, unintentionally sabotaging the control system. Such executives are usually *not* deliberately trying to recast the data. Rather, they simply cannot see the information signals objectively. Such entrapment makes it difficult for the executives to respond, or even comprehend, the information signals that the strategic control system is providing.

Difficulties associated with abandoning familiar thought patterns and acquired behaviors are another important behavioral barrier. In the oil industry, for example, the external environment is critical and difficult to assess. There is frequently a strong tendency to gain confidence by studying past successes instead of looking forward. The future may appear to be too uncertain. Although such familiar patterns of thought may be quite reassuring, they serve to restrict one's ability to critically reassess current events and new trends.

A first step in reducing behavioral barriers is instilling a greater awareness of such problems. Career planning, seminars, executive development, and job reassignment may be helpful. Additional steps involve making the overall strategic control process more explicit. Issues to be addressed include the following questions:

- What environmental variables need to be monitored?
- What are our critical assumptions?
- Who is to monitor what and how often?
- How should the information be reported?
- How can line and staff personnel effectively interact in a timely manner?

Political Barriers

A primary goal of the strategic management process is to generate a sufficiently broad agreement on the organization's overall strategy. The strategy must be politically acceptable to the various power groups and coalitions within the organization. Conflicts may arise when there are changes in the relative power among the coalitions or groups within an organization. This can lead to a reluctance to share information or collaborate in a constructive manner. For example, if a planning unit's influence or power within an organization increases, the controller's office may feel that some of the planning unit's gain has come at its expense. This feeling is accentuated when the planning unit is relatively new. Planners often focus on making sure that accountants in the controller's office don't produce any wrong numbers and the accountants resent the power of the new planning group. Further, controllers may perceive their planning colleagues as poor quantitative analysts. On the other hand, planners may complain that the controllers are too quantitatively oriented and, therefore, fail to take a longer-term strategic perspective.

A clear delineation of responsibilities may help reduce conflicts. The roles and responsibilities of the planning and control units must be defined on the basis of how they relate to the long-term success of the firm. This often involves a good deal of negotiation and discussion. A common approach is to have both the planning and control functions report to the same senior staff executive.

Another key political barrier to effective strategic control systems is the unwillingness of lower-level managers to pass unfavorable information up the hierarchy to top management.* Trust throughout an organization is an indispensable feature of effective control systems. Job insecurity, scapegoating, or the categorization of line executives as "winners" or "losers" are all factors that can undermine control systems.

ALTERNATE APPROACHES TO CONTROL IN ORGANIZATIONS

Until now we have focused on specific tools, techniques, and systems useful for planning, monitoring, and assessing the implementation of a firm's strategy. We will now turn to the behavioral dimension of control. Here, the thrust is on ensuring that the behavior of individuals at all levels in an organization is directed toward achieving organizational goals and objectives. The three fundamental types of control are rules, rewards, and culture. Based on a variety of internal and external factors, an organization may pursue any one or a combination of them.

As discussed in Chapter 3, organizational culture can be used as a means, through unwritten norms and values, to obtain desired behavior in the organization. An alternate way is through establishing rules and regulations. A third approach is granting or withholding of rewards that organization members value.[20] Rules may be considered external to an individual and intended to *constrain* behavior. Culture, on the other hand, can be viewed as values and norms that are internalized and therefore *influence* behavior. In either case, rewards can be effective in reinforcing the desired effects of culture and rules among an organization's members at all levels. Sustained individual contributions to an organization's performance must be supported by monetary and/or nonmonetary rewards. After all, even charitable organizations must provide nonmonetary rewards for volunteers. These rewards are often as simple as a certificate, lapel pin, or even a warm handshake!

Not all organizations place the same emphasis on each type of control.[21] For example, in professional organizations, such as high-technology firms engaged in basic research, members typically work under high levels of autonomy. Here, an individual's performance is usually very difficult to measure accurately because of the long lead times involved in

* In reporting information upward, distortion as well as filtering can occur because of both behavioral and political reasons. The key distinction, however, is that in the former case it is unintentional and due to their inherent biases resulting from professional background and functional area orientation. In the latter case, it is done intentionally with the purpose of maintaining or increasing the power of one organizational unit over another.

research and development activities. Thus, internalized norms and values become very important.

Control in bureaucratic organizations has long been recognized as dependent on members observing a highly formalized set of rules and regulations. Here, most activities are quite routine and the desired behavior can be specified in a very detailed manner because there is generally little need for innovative or creative activity. In the private sector, for example, managing an assembly plant requires close adherence to many rules as well as exacting sequences of assembly operations. Similarly, in the public sector, the Department of Motor Vehicles in most states must follow clearly presented procedures when issuing or renewing driver licences.

In organizations where the measurement of an individual's output or performance is quite straightforward, control is primarily dependent on granting or withholding rewards. Frequently, a sales manager's compensation is in the form of a commission and bonus directly tied to his or her sales volume, which is relatively easy to assess. In this situation, behavior is more strongly influenced by the attractiveness of compensation than by the norms and values implicit in the organization's culture. Furthermore, the measurability of output precludes the need for an elaborate system of rules to control behavior.

The use of rewards as a means of control is also applicable at the corporate or business level of a firm. For a corporation following a strategy of unrelated diversification, each unit may be sufficiently independent to allow for the relatively easy assessment of its sales volume and resulting profit contribution. There is little need for resource sharing or other means for achieving synergistic benefits for the corporation. The need for a corporatewide culture is reduced. Also, the diversity inherent in such firms precludes the use of extensive corporationwide rules and regulations. Under such circumstances, rewards become the most effective means of assuring organizational control.[22] Exhibit 10.6 provides an over-

EXHIBIT 10.6
Organizational Control: Alternate Approaches

Approach	***Some Situational Factors***
Culture: A system of unwritten rules which forms an internalized influence over behavior	■ Often found in professional organizations ■ Associated with high autonomy ■ Norms are the basis for behavior
Rules: Written and explicit guidelines which provide external constraints on behavior	■ Associated with standardized output ■ Tasks are generally repetitive and routine ■ Little need for innovation or creative activity
Rewards: The use of performance-based incentive systems to motivate	■ Measurement of output and performance is rather straightforward ■ Most appropriate in organizations pursuing unrelated diversification strategies ■ Rewards may be used to reinforce other means of control

view of alternate approaches to organizational control and a few situational factors associated with them.

Combining the Three Types of Control

Some organizations may effectively emphasize two or all three major types of organizational control. At H. J. Heinz Co., Inc., for example, CEO Anthony O'Reilly depends on both attractive financial rewards and a strong culture to motivate and develop executive talent.[23] Heinz executives enjoy generous stock options and other incentives such as bonuses based on both short- and long-term performance. Because all employees at the same level receive the same incentives based on overall company performance, they are encouraged to focus on the entire company, not just their particular operation. Thus, although O'Reilly strongly advocates managerial autonomy, he believes that such a reward system has effectively "banished the notion of territorial privilege." O'Reilly also strengthens and reinforces the company's culture in many ways. He develops camaraderie through weekend house parties at his Irish estate, Castlemartin, or through working retreats. Heinz executives refer to the latter as "Rolling Rock sessions"—named after the Pittsburgh country club at which they take place. Such gatherings serve not only to address important strategic issues, but also to reinforce the company's culture. For example, according to O'Reilly, "When senior executives come in from the volleyball court to divvy up the marketing budget or capital funds, our decisions are virtually always unanimous." Application 10.4 profiles a firm that uses all three: United Parcel Service (UPS). UPS has prospered by insisting on adherence to rigid procedures, by instilling a strong corporate culture, and by developing a very attractive reward system.

The Critical Role of Reward Systems in Achieving Results

The appropriate use of reward systems plays a critical role in motivating managers to conform to organizational strategies, achieve performance targets, and reduce the gap between organizational and individual goals. In contrast, reward systems, if improperly designed, can lead to behaviors that are either detrimental to organizational performance or lead to lower morale and dissatisfaction.

Increasing numbers of organizations are using reward (or compensation) systems in which employees share in the risks and benefits of their firm's performance. According to a national survey, 26 percent of the companies that provided incentive compensation offered it to a wider range of employees in 1988 and 1989 than in the past.[24] Often, such incentives enable organizations to become more competitive and successful.[25] For example, Wal-Mart, a dominant discount retailer, attributes some of its success to its incentive systems for store managers. Through profit sharing and stock purchase plans, many store managers earn over $100,000 per year. Au Bon Pain, a specialty bakery, initiated profit sharing of up to 50 percent of store profits. Some store managers were able to earn up to $100,000—when the industry norm was about $25,000. Also, entry-level workers were paid up to $25,000 a year. Shortly after this program was initiated, performance improved dramatically and turnover among entry-level workers was only around 75 percent versus over 200 percent for the industry as a whole. Also, Lincoln Electric—with over 25 years of extensive profit sharing at all levels of the company—has withstood severe global competition and

Application 10.4

United Parcel Service: An Emphasis on Organization Culture, Procedures, and Rewards

Originally named the American Messenger Company, United Parcel Service (UPS) was founded by James Casey in 1907. Casey started the firm with $100, two bicycles, one telephone, and six employees who delivered packages and telegrams. By 1989, UPS had profits of $693 million on $12.4 billion in sales and was frequently ranked first in its industry in *Fortune's* reputations survey. What are the keys to UPS's success?

First, its culture has been called a unique mix of egalitarianism and slavish dedication to efficiency. UPS's policy is to promote from within, and most managers begin their careers by driving a truck or by sorting and loading packages. During busy periods, executives help sort packages and the headquarters in Greenwich, Connecticut, has very few amenities. There are no reserved parking places, no executive has a private secretary, and all executives make their own photocopies and travel arrangements. At all levels, employees have an intense commitment to hard work and a strong identification with the company. Often managers have to encourage their subordinates to work *fewer* hours. Approximately 80 percent of the full-time work force attend voluntary, after-hours workshops which address the firm's competitive challenges. Such dedication does not occur by chance, but rather through selective recruitment and extensive socialization. UPS employs approximately 40,000 college students as part-time workers and offers the most promising individuals full-time positions (usually as van drivers) upon graduation. Joseph R. Moderow, a UPS senior vice president, claims: "It is the greatest recruiting ground imaginable." Top managers, most of whom have come up through the ranks, instill a spirit of winning so pervasive that individuals who fail are ranked not as losers, but as "least best." Workers develop a Japanese-style identification with the company.

A second reason for UPS's success is consistent with its culture, which stresses efficiency: intense dedication to developing detailed procedures. As early as the 1920s, Casey hired pioneers of time-and-motion studies, such as Frank Gilbreth and Frederick Taylor, to measure the time that each driver spent on his or her specific tasks. The tradition of tight cost control has continued. More than 1,000 industrial engineers use time-and-motion studies to set standards for many routine tasks. For example, sorters at the large Addison, Illinois, hub are expected to load delivery vans at the rate of 500 to 650 packages per hour. And studies have determined how fast delivery people should walk (3 feet a second), which finger to hold key rings on (the middle finger), and how delivery people should fold their money (face up, sequentially ordered). Gene Hughes, a strategic planner, sums it up well: "They do it like clockwork: nothing deviates."

The reward system is also an integral component of UPS's successful strategy. James Casey believed that the company must be "owned by its managers and managed by its owners." Today, the company's 20,000 managers control the stock through a generous annual bonus plan. In 1988, for example, the average midlevel manager with 10 years of service received not only a salary of $54,000 but also approximately $14,000 in stock and a $7,500 dividend check. All employees must sell their stock when they leave or retire.

UPS faces many challenges from both strong domestic rivals, such as Federal Express and Roadway Package Systems, as well as many viable international competitors. Also, its integration of new technologies, such as electronic scanners to track packages and demands for volume discounts, could place pressures on UPS's margins and competitive position. However, Jeffrey Sonnenfeld, an Emory University professor who has written an in-depth case on UPS, believes that the firm's performance and culture should remain strong. "You've got to remember there is an enormous reservoir of internal goodwill to be tapped," he claims. "People will make sure things work out because they want *their* company to succeed."

Sources

Nulty, P. (1991, March 11). The national business hall of fame. *Fortune*, pp. 98–103.

Labich, K. (1988, January 18). Big changes at Big Brown. *Fortune*, pp. 56–64.

Schuler, R. S., & Jackson, S. E. (1987). Linking competitive strategies with human resource management practices. *The Academy of Management Executive, 1*, 207–219.

Vogel, T. (1990, June 4). Can UPS deliver the goods in a new world? *Business Week*, pp. 80–82.

Application 10.5

Successful and Unsuccessful Reward Systems

A Successful Reward System

A unique reward system devised by Larry Phillips, CEO of Phillips-Van Heusen (a manufacturer of shirts, sweaters, and casual shoes) illustrates some of the important principles of effective reward (or compensation) systems. In 1987, Mr. Phillips decided to award his eleven top executives $1 million each if the firms earnings per share (EPS) increased at a 35 percent compounded annual rate over a 4-year period. This generous incentive was structured so that the first $500,000 could be earned incrementally if EPS goals were met each year and the other $500,000 would be awarded if the firm achieved the overall goal. As one would probably expect, Phillips-Van Heusen's sales and earnings have dramatically increased in the first 2 years of the program (1988 and 1989). The goal was attained the first year, but narrowly missed the second year. Still, the chief financial officer, Irwin Winter, is optimistic that the overall goal will be attained. These financial results are all the more impressive, given the extensive debt that the firm had taken on in mid-1987 to repel a corporate raider and its continuing large investments necessary to build new businesses.

Although Phillips' incentive program is unique, it is clearly consistent with his overall corporate growth objective. Also, by linking the incentive to overall corporate performance, cooperation among the business units has been tremendous. Mr. Phillips believes that the plan "put everybody in his own confessional. Now each of these guys is terribly supportive of every other division of this company. You don't find that very often in corporate America." By providing incremental annual incentives, the top executive team also had a built-in motivation to focus on not only the 4-year objective, but the annual objectives as well.

An Unsuccessful Reward System

The Evans Products Company, with headquarters in Portland, Oregon, was a large conglomerate competing in the housing, railcar, forest products, retail home center, and industrial products businesses. Its organization structure was highly centralized, with clearly delineated profit centers. A McKinsey executive compensation plan set bonuses as a direct correlate of earnings so that financial incentives were directed toward meeting ambitious sales goals. However, the company sought protection under Chapter 11 of the Federal Bankruptcy Code in 1985 and was liquidated in 1987.

Why did Evans fail? Not because of the lack of an explicit reward system or dysfunctional culture. Rather, its reward system was inconsistent with deteriorating competitive and economic conditions. The housing and railcar businesses were in a cyclical downturn which is typical of these industries. Unwilling to let sales and profits decline as a result of scaling down operations in response to the business cycles, Mr. Orloff and two of his group presidents elected to continue operations and encourage sales by providing liberal financing to customers. The company put railcars out on lease and sold houses to customers in order to buttress a negative cash flow for the entire corporation. The company continued to "borrow short and lend long" until it finally ran out of cash and exhausted all its credit lines.

Sources

Knowlton, C. (1990, April 9). 11 men's million-dollar motivator. *Fortune*, pp. 65–66, 68.

Zaleznik, A. (1990). The leadership gap. *The Academy of Management Executive*, *4*, 7–22.

of incentive systems and their contrasting effects on organizational performance.

The example of Evans Business Products serves to illustrate the notion that not all incentive systems serve the best interests of all organizational members as well as their stockholders. For example, many performance plans pose greater risks for lower-level employees than higher-level executives.[26] At General Motors, former chairman Roger B. Smith's annual bonus fell 7 percent to $1.4 million in response to a 13 percent decrease in profits in 1989. However, the profit sharing paid to hourly and lower-level salaried workers fell 81 percent to only $50 per person! Issues of fairness, contribution to corporate well-being, and so on, are, of course, open to debate. Nonetheless, most would agree that such compensation discrepancies hardly help union-management relationships in GM's fight for market share and earnings in an extremely competitive, global industry.

The widening gap between the compensation of top-level executives and lower-level managers has resulted in efforts by some companies to increase the benchmarks or targets that must be attained before a bonus is paid. Also, some other corporations have increased the stock price at which stock options may be exercised. At Itel Containers International, for example, stock options are exercisable at a price that rises 50 percent per year. Phillip Kantz, president and CEO, states, "They want us to be running against the same dilution from inflation that stockholders are." Such efforts may serve to increase perceptions of equity and provide a closer linkage between the compensation of top-level management and corporate performance.

Several new approaches to rewarding senior management have emerged in recent years.[27] First, many firms have adopted plans to compensate top management for achieving certain *performance levels over several years* (usually 3 to 5 years) rather than just 1 year. This change is in response to the dysfunctional effects of rewarding solely on the basis of short-term performance that was addressed earlier in Chapters 8 and 9. By using deferred stock options as rewards—often called "golden handcuffs"—both corporate and divisional-level executives are able to build a personal financial base that increases with time.

Second, the *weighted strategic factors approach* recognizes the lack of uniformity among the strategic positions within a diversified firm. This method permits the identification of various factors related to future profitability which are incorporated into incentive packages and against which performance is evaluated. For example, a firm may identify four strategic factors: return on assets, cash flow, progress against plan on identified strategic projects, and market share. The manager of a high-growth business may be rewarded with a bonus on these four factors according to a weighting of 10, 0, 45, and 45 percent respectively, whereas a manager of a low-growth business would receive a bonus weighted 50, 50, 0, and 0 percent.

Third, *strategic funds deferral* is used to encourage managers to view developmental expenses differently from expenses necessary to sustain current operations. Here, return on assets is calculated for current operations only. Investments associated with strategic projects, which are usually included in such calculations, are separated out. This approach permits the separation of the evaluation of performance for both funds spent for the generation of current revenues *and* those invested for the future of the business. This approach also provides additional incentives for managers to take a longer-term perspective toward their business and *not* overemphasize short-term goals and objectives.

Summary

Successful implementation of strategies requires a well-designed control system. Operational control is restricted to monitoring performance and providing important feedback to top management as to whether implementation is progressing according to plan. Strategic control, on the other hand, is concerned with important changes that may occur inside and outside the organization that necessitate changes in a firm's strategic direction. There are three important elements of the strategic control process: premise control, strategic surveillance, and implementation control. An organization's ability to exercise strategic control may be greatly enhanced by the use of executive information systems which focus on an organization's critical success factors and business objectives. Also, in many organizations, there are barriers to effective strategic control. The general types of barriers are systemic, behavioral, and political. Overcoming such barriers is critical for the successful implementation of an organization's strategy.

An organization can pursue different approaches to control in order to ensure that the behavior of individuals is directed toward the achievement of organizational goals and objectives. The three basic approaches to control adopted by organizations are rules, rewards, and culture. Most often, based on the specific environmental and internal conditions faced by an organization, it may adopt an appropriate combination of all three approaches. The design and implementation of reward systems play a crucial role in motivating individuals at all levels throughout an organization. Reward systems, depending on their specific characteristics, cannot only play a positive role but also may lead to dysfunctional behavior and erode organizational performance. Several recent innovative approaches to rewarding senior managers include (1) compensating managers for achieving certain performance levels over several years, (2) a weighted strategic factors approach, and (3) a strategic funds deferral.

Notes

1. For a seminal discussion on the importance of strategic control systems, see Lorange, P. (1980). *Corporate planning: An executive viewpoint.* Englewood Cliffs, NJ: Prentice-Hall.
2. See, for example, Schendel, D., & Hofer, D. (1979). *Strategic management.* Boston: Little, Brown. Preble, John. (1990). *Towards a comprehensive system of strategic control.* Working paper. University of Delaware, Newark, DE; and Schreyogg, Georg, & Steinmann, Horst. (1987). Strategic control: A new perspective. *Academy of Management Review, 12,* 91–103 are thought-provoking works on important differences between traditional and contemporary approaches to strategic control. This section draws rather liberally from these three sources.
3. Hayes, R. H. (1985). Strategic planning. Forward in reverse. *Harvard Business Review, 63*(6), 111–119.
4. Ibid., p. 114.
5. A similar type of feedforward control system that has received attention in both the academic- and practitioner-oriented literature is strategic issue management. See Ansoff, H. I. (1984). *Implanting strategic management.* Englewood Cliffs, NJ: Prentice-Hall (especially pp. 337–350) for an insightful perspective.
6. The authors would like to thank Professor John Preble of the University of Delaware for sharing his ideas on how to implement premise control and strategic surveillance in organizations.
7. Saporito, B. (1989, May 22). Shades of Geneen at Emerson Electric. *Fortune,* p. 39.
8. Wilson, I. H. (1983). The benefits of environmental analysis. In K. J. Albert (Ed.), *The strategic management handbook* (pp. 9.1–9.17). New York: McGraw-Hill.

9. Koerner, E. (1989). GE's high-tech strategy. *Long Range Planning, 22*(4), 11–19.
10. Schreyogg and Steinmann (Ref. 2), op. cit., p. 97.
11. Collier, D. (1984). How to implement strategy. *The Journal of Business Strategy, 5,* 92–96.
12. For an interesting discussion of some of the dysfunctional behavior by managers in the budgeting process in six organizations, refer to Bart, C. K. (1988). Budgeting gamesmanship. *Academy of Management Executive, 2*(4), 285–294.
13. The material in this section draws on the work of Lorange, Peter. (1984). Strategic control: Some issues in making it more operationally useful. In R. Lamb (Ed.). *Competitive strategic management* (pp. 247–271). Englewood Cliffs, NJ: Prentice-Hall; and Lorange, P., Morton, M. F. S., & Ghoshal, S. (1986). *Strategic control.* St. Paul, MN: West.
14. For additional insight into executive information systems, refer to Eisen, J. (1988, September 26). How to grab an exec's attention. *Computerworld, 22,* 19; McLeod, R., Jr., & Jones, J. W. (1986). Making executive information systems more effective. *Business Horizons,* pp. 29–37; Reck, R. H., & Hall, J. R. (1986). Executive information systems: An overview of development. *Journal of Information Systems Management, 3*(4), 25–30; and Rinaldi, D., & Jastrzembski, T. (1986, October 27). Executive information systems put strategic data at your CEO's fingertips. *Computerworld,* p. 39.
15. A study by John Rockart and David DeLong investigated the linkage between executive support systems and business objectives for a sample of thirty firms. They found that the eighteen systems judged to be most valuable addressed specific business needs or problems. On the other hand, the seven systems judged moderately successful were only vaguely linked to business objectives and the five systems considered ineffective were, for the most part, not linked to business needs. This study is addressed in their book *Executive support systems: The emergence of top management computer use.* (1988). Homewood, IL: Irwin. (For our purposes, executive information systems [EIS] and executive support systems [ESS] are treated synonymously.)
16. The estimates of usage and expenditures for executive support systems are based on Gelford, S. M. (1988, June 27). The computer age dawns in the corner office. *Business Week,* p. 84.
17. Ibid., p. 84; and Main, J. (1989, March 13). At last, a software CEOs can use. *Fortune,* p. 77.
18. Main, J. (1989, March 13). At last, a software CEOs can use. *Fortune,* p. 77.
19. This discussion draws from Lorange, P., & Murphy, D. (1984). Considerations in implementing strategic control. *The Journal of Business Strategy, 5,* 27–35. Their study was based on telephone interviews with a corporate-level planner and a corporate-level controller in each of eighteen *Fortune 500* firms. There are several important distinctions between the roles of planners and controllers which may, in turn, lead to conflict. Planners are typically future-oriented, externally focused, and comfortable with nonfinancial and qualitative indicators of performance. Controllers, on the other hand, typically rely on data relating to the past more for evaluation than planning, are very internally oriented, and prefer quantitative data originating from accounting records. For a recent discussion of some of the difficulties in establishing an effective strategic control system, see Goold, M., & Quinn, J. J. (1990). The paradox of strategic controls. *Strategic Management Journal, 11,* 43–57.
20. For a seminal discussion of alternate approaches to organizational control, refer to Ouchi, William G. (1980). Markets, bureaucracies, and clans. *Administrative Science Quarterly, 25,* 129–141. Although our discussion is somewhat parallel to his argument, there are some important differences. For example, our discussion of rewards is somewhat broader than Ouchi's concept of markets.

21. Hall, R. H. (1987). *Organizations: Structures, processes and outcomes* (4th ed.). Englewood Cliffs, NJ: Prentice-Hall.
22. For interesting perspectives of the relationship between a firm's strategy and reward systems, refer to Kerr, J., & Slocum, J. W., Jr. (1987). Managing corporate culture through reward systems. *The Academy of Management Executive, 1,* 99–110; and Lei, D., Slocum, J. W., Jr., & Slater, R. W. (1990, Autumn). Global strategy and reward systems: The key roles of management development and corporate culture. *Organizational Dynamics,* pp. 27–41.
23. Stewart, T. A. (1989, November 6). New ways to exercise power. *Fortune,* pp. 52–54, 58, 62, 64.
24. Bannett, A. (1990, April 18). Executive pay. *The Wall Street Journal,* p. R8.
25. The Wal-Mart, Au Bon Pain, and Lincoln Electric examples are discussed in Ulrich, D., & Wiersema, M. (1989). Gaining strategic and organizational capability in a turbulent business environment. *The Academy of Management Executive, 3,* 115–122. Au Bon Pain is also discussed in Sellers, Patricia (1990, June 4). What customers really want. *Fortune,* p. 60.
26. The examples of General Motors and ITEL Containers International, as well as the discussion in the next paragraph, draw on Bennett, A. (1990, April 18). Executive pay. *The Wall Street Journal,* p. R7.
27. These approaches are discussed in Galbraith, J. R., & Kazanjian, R. K. (1986). *Strategy implementation: Structure, systems, and process* (2nd ed.) (pp. 96–97). St. Paul, MN: West.

CHAPTER 11

Leadership, Culture, and Ethics

Leadership plays a vital role in creating and implementing a firm's strategic vision. Successful leaders also shape their organization's culture by instilling a commitment to excellence and ethical behavior. As firms expand globally, leaders must also be aware of the crucial role that foreign cultures play in either facilitating or hindering strategy implementation.

We have divided this chapter into two major sections. The first section describes the concept of leadership and the three critical activities that all leaders must perform if they are to be effective. In the second section, we discuss the importance of culture in recognizing and reinforcing an organization's dominant values. We also discuss how the extremely difficult and time-consuming process of changing an organization's culture can be effectively managed. The increasing globalization of businesses presents managers with the challenge of managing their organizations in multiple cultural settings. The chapter concludes with a discussion of issues involved in the development of an organization culture based on ethical behavior.

After reading this chapter, you will understand:

- The three critical activities that are essential for successful executive leadership
- The role of transformational leadership in attaining a successful strategic redirection
- How an organization's dominant values can strongly influence organizational behavior
- The difficulty involved in changing an organization's culture
- The importance of an awareness and sensitivity to important aspects of a foreign nation's culture when conducting international operations
- How managers can create an ethical organizational culture
- Effective management of ethical crises

EXECUTIVE INTERVIEW

Anthony J. F. O'Reilly
President and Chief Executive Officer
H. J. Heinz Company

Elected president and chief executive officer of H. J. Heinz Company in June 1979, and chairman in 1987 upon the death of Henry J. Heinz II, Anthony O'Reilly is responsible for a global food-processing organization whose products are made in 15 countries and marketed in over 200 countries and territories. Powerful brand names such as Heinz, Weight Watchers, StarKist, Ore-Ida, and 9-Lives ensure that 55 percent of sales come from number 1 brands. Sales in 1990 were $6 billion, with 60 percent in the United States and 40 percent abroad. When O'Reilly became CEO 10 years ago, the market capitalization was $908 million, compared with a market capitalization of nearly $9 billion at the end of 1989, with the same number of shares in issue. A Heinz shareholder who reinvested dividends realized an impressive total return of 1,396.9 percent for the decade, equivalent to a 31 percent annual compounded return.

O'Reilly was born in Dublin in 1936 and was educated at that city's Belvedere College, at University College Dublin, and at the Incorporated Law Society of Ireland. An honors graduate in civil law and a solicitor, he also earned a Ph.D. in agricultural marketing from the University of Bradford, England.

What skills do you think are most critical for successful top executives at Heinz?

The most critical skills for senior Heinz executives are alertness, adaptability, and entrepreneurial spirit. This is partly a reflection of our corporate culture and partly a response to the nature of the food and nutrition industry. As a global enterprise, Heinz penetrates many markets and many cultures. We have more than 3,000 varieties of products, which we market in more than 200 nations and territories worldwide. Our success as a global corporation depends on our capacity for innovation and our ability to meet and even anticipate local tastes and trends.

Consumers have an insatiable appetite for variety. This is particularly true in the weight-loss and wellness market, where inventiveness has been the key to the long-standing success of our Weight Watchers brand products and services. It also applies to our sensitivity to social issues, such as the environment. Innovations like Heinz Italy's "Environmental Oasis," StarKist's dolphin-safe tuna, and Heinz U.S.A.'s recyclable plastic ketchup bottle have sprung from our constant attention to changing public attitudes.

How would you describe the corporate culture at H. J. Heinz Company?

The heart of corporate culture at H. J. Heinz Company is total quality management (TQM). We strive in every department of every affiliate to do each job right the first time through a quality process that stresses communication and creative problem solving. We emphasize cooperation among disciplines and train our employees in TQM methodologies. Though still determined to be the low-cost operator, we give quality precedence over cost. We have found that by spending a bit more up front for quality, we ultimately reap considerable savings by eliminating rework, waste, and duplication.

Our management culture stresses collegiality, rather than political intrigue. We have very short lines of communication and minimal corporate staffing. (There are only 150 people in our world headquarters office, including managers, accountants, lawyers, and all support and secretarial staff.) When I wish to speak to a president of an affiliate, I will do so directly. If one of our senior vice presidents wishes to discuss an issue with me or one of his colleagues, he will do it in person whenever possible. We avoid a proliferation of memos and reported speech.

What role do you play, as CEO, in building and maintaining a strong corporate culture?

The CEO has a vital role to play in promulgating and inspiring corporate culture at Heinz, particularly with regard to total quality management. We have found that the quality process penetrates deepest when it is endorsed directly by the CEO and all senior management. TQM starts at my office. Managers need to know that TQM is not just another set of initials. The fact that Heinz's senior management has undergone TQM training is a clear and credible sign to all employees that we take this new quality culture seriously and that we expect it to reinvigorate our company.

Continued

The CEO also sets the tone for corporate management style. I do not surround myself with courtiers and ambassadors, nor do my executive colleagues. If the CEO insists on regular, informal, and direct communication, then other managers soon realize they can derive no benefit from insulating themselves with large staffs.

How important are reward and compensation systems in improving an organization's performance?

We subscribe to the axiom that there is nothing like the prospect of a public hanging to focus the mind. As shareholders themselves, Heinz managers are motivated by strong self-interest and a direct financial stake in the company's performance. Fifteen percent of the company's equity is employee-owned. We do pay our managers an average amount to come to the office each day. We do reward them handsomely if the company's consolidated performance continues to improve. This form of compensation imparts an acute sensitivity to shareholder interests.

Its incentive system reinforces Heinz's collegial corporate culture. Affiliate managers do not derive financial benefit from the misfortune of their colleagues. We are collectively enriched by our consolidated performance. This dampens the desire for empire building and greatly encourages cooperative thought and action.

What role do middle managers play in formulating and implementing strategy at H. J. Heinz Company?

We rely heavily on the skill and judgment of our middle managers. Heinz is a diverse enterprise whose products must appeal to a wide range of cultures and tastes. Accordingly, the company is decentralized, entrusting major decisions on marketing, sales, and product formulation to its affiliates. As chief executive in his own domain, the affiliate president must plan and execute strategy in concert with middle management.

Unambiguous corporate goals and policies are set at world headquarters in connection with affiliates. Frequently, they are informed by the work of interaffiliate task forces. Their implementation is a function of the ingenuity and dogged drive of our affiliate managers. Likewise, curious and impatient middle managers are the predominant source of the new products and new ideas that are the lifeblood of our company.

LEADERSHIP: A STRATEGIC PERSPECTIVE

Management and leadership are two different but complementary skills necessary to ensure an organization's success. John P. Kotter, a noted expert on leadership, makes the following distinction between management and leadership:[1]

> Management is about coping with complexity. Its practices and procedures are largely a response to one of the most significant developments of the 20th century: the emergence of large organizations. Without good management, complex enterprises tend to become chaotic in ways that threaten their very existence. Good management brings a degree of order and consistency to key dimensions like the quality and profitability of products.
>
> Leadership, by contrast, is about coping with change. Part of the reason it has become so important in recent years is that the business world has become more competitive and more volatile. . . . The net result is that doing what was done yesterday, or doing it 5 percent better, is no longer a formula for success. Major changes are more and more necessary to survive and compete effectively in this new environment. More change always demands more leadership.

Application 11.1

Leadership: An Iconoclastic Perspective

By the time four or five books have been published on a topic, you're tempted to think of it as yesterday's news, a wrap, case closed. But just as I was beginning to dismiss the subject of leadership in precisely this manner, *Fortune* magazine arrived on my desk.

Corporate America, *Fortune* informed me, is searching for leaders. *Real* leaders, not just managers. Men and women who have *vision*, who seek *change*, who can *transform* their organizations. Looking to instill these traits in their executives, big firms have sent them on all sorts of nutty training programs. In one such, teams from General Foods Corporation found themselves trying to build rafts and sail down a river, first under nitpicking managerial inspection and then on their own. Which rafts sank and which ones floated? No—you tell me.

Maybe executives in big companies need all the help they can get (anyway, being picked for a sexy new leadership training program sure beats working). But what cooled the cockles of my heart about the new search for leadership was precisely what had turned me off about the aforementioned books. Both treat leadership as something like painting by the numbers. Learn the rules, and you too can be a corporate Rembrandt.

If the world were only so simple, we could all be leaders, even without building a raft. Trouble is, the qualities that seem so important in one context are irrelevant (or downright harmful) in another. Look again at a few of the qualities often suggested for effective leaders.

Leaders have a vision. Who could disagree? Show me an entrepreneur without a vision and I'll show you an entrepreneur who needs a new PR firm. Just don't try to put your vision in the bank. Nolan Bushnell, creator of Chuck E. Cheese and Pizza Time Theatres, was long on vision. Unfortunately he was short on customers.

Leaders strengthen others: Sharing power and information. Jan Carlzon, president and chief executive officer of Scandinavian Airlines System (SAS) and by all accounts one of the most imaginative executives in his industry, tells, in his book *Moments of Truth* (Ballinger, 1987), how he "flattened" his organization's pyramid, giving "more responsibility to the frontline personnel." He even began calling first-line employees "managers"—a reminder, he writes, "that their roles had undergone a fundamental change." Great stuff—and exactly what Donald Burr, founder of People Express Airlines, Inc., did with his company. One succeeded. The other didn't.

Leaders experiment and take risks. Remember a few years back, when Amdahl Corporation founder Gene M. Amdahl left to form a new company called Trilogy Systems Corporation? Trilogy would engineer a great leap forward in computers based on developing an advanced new chip. Alas, the company has vanished and Amdahl has embarked on yet another venture. Maybe people are acclaimed as leaders when the risks they take pay off.

Right there, of course, is one reason leadership can't be reduced to a set of skills or personality traits to be acquired on weekend retreats or learned from reading books. Plenty of people have possessed all the attributes the books ascribe to leaders, but they were sorely lacking in judgment. In business, an executive's judgments about the marketplace, people, and a myriad of other variables are more important in determining a company's success or failure than abstract "leadership" qualities. What undermined Burr wasn't his innovative approach to managing people, it was the fact that he tried to expand his company too quickly.

Artists know their work is good if it sells, or if other knowledgeable people respect it. Business leadership—not quite so rarefied a commodity as artistic talent, thank goodness—is even easier to judge. If you want to know how you're doing as a leader, don't ask yourself whether you have 20-20 vision or whether you're taking enough risks. Instead, just ask yourself how your company is doing—and how you're viewed by the people who work for, and with, you. Where leadership is concerned, a little time spent investigating those questions, in their many facets, is worth a lot of trips down the river on a raft.

Source

Excerpted from Case, J. (1987, December). Desperately seeking leadership. *Inc.*, pp. 20, 22 (adapted with permission).

In order to succeed and prosper, organizations must not only meet their current commitments to various stakeholder groups, but also identify and adapt to changing demands of these groups over time.[2] Without both strong management and strong leadership, an organization's performance is likely to decline. That is, strong management without strong leadership can result in a bureaucratic and stifling organization. On the other hand, strong leadership without strong management can become virtually cultlike where an organization follows a leader uncritically without careful planning and budgeting.

Clearly, leadership is a complex and multifaceted subject. While a good deal of the writing on the topic of leadership has centered on a leader's style and personality tributes, ultimately, effective leadership must result in a firm's long-term viability. Application 11.1 provides an irreverent but insightful perspective on this issue.

We will address leadership in the next two sections. The first section will discuss the three interdependent activities that are vital to effective leadership. The second section addresses the many factors that may be largely beyond the leader's control but which can influence an organization's performance. Such factors—called constraints on leadership—clearly influence the overall leadership process. This section concludes with a discussion of transformational leadership, suggested as a means of revitalizing organizations and overcoming constraints.

Successful Leadership: Excelling at Three Interdependent Activities

Throughout the text, we have seen how important it is for a leader to be involved in both formulating and implementing strategy. One business school professor and consultant frequently asks groups of managers to imagine that their organization is an ocean liner and that they are the leader of the crew.[3] They are then asked what they consider their role to be. Among the most common answers are "the captain," "the navigator," "the helmsman, actually controlling the direction," "the engineer down there stoking the fire, providing energy," and "the social director, making sure everyone's enrolled, involved, and communicating." Perhaps the most neglected (and possibly most important) role is that of the *designer* of the ship. In essence, no role has more influence than the designer. Imagine how meaningless it would be, for example, for the captain to order "Turn starboard 30 degrees," if the designer had built the ship with a rudder that would only turn to port, or which takes several hours to turn starboard. It's fruitless to be the leader in an organization that is poorly designed. A leader's visions or strategies are of little value to the organization if they do not direct sufficient consideration and effort toward implementation. Effective leaders recognize that to be successful, they must continually be involved in three interdependent activities.[4] First, they must play a vital role in *setting a direction* for the firm—both in terms of a broad vision and strategies.[5] Second, leaders need to be continually involved with *designing the organization,* that is, evaluating and, when necessary, changing structures, systems, and processes necessary to ensure successful implementation and results. Third, leaders must be committed to *instilling a culture* commited to excellence and ethical behavior. People throughout the organization must be encouraged to share the vision and strategies and to exert maximum effort and behave in an ethical manner.[6] Exhibit 11.1 shows the relationship among these three key activities. Let's look more closely at each.

EXHIBIT 11.1
Three Key Interrelated Strategic Leadership Activities

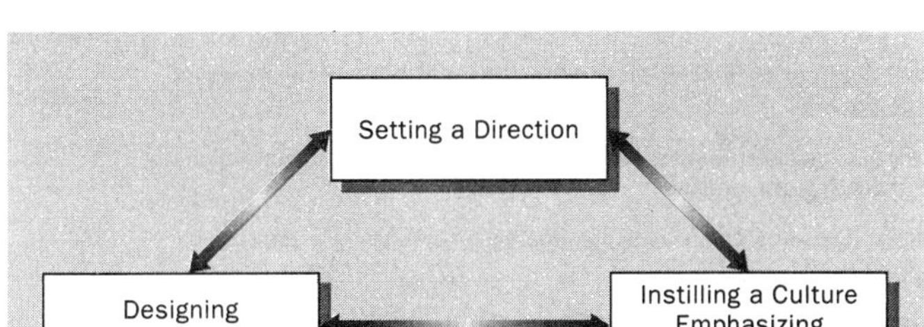

Setting a Direction

Setting the direction of change is fundamental to leadership and goes well beyond even long-term planning.[7] Planning is a management process—often designed to produce orderly results, not change. Setting a direction requires a leader to gather a broad range of data from both formal and informal sources and look for patterns, relationships, and linkages. In essence, the direction-setting aspect of leadership does not produce plans, it creates clearly articulated and easily understandable visions and strategies which describe a business, technology, or corporation culture in terms of what it should become over the long term.

In today's highly complex and uncertain environment, leaders need a holistic understanding of an organization's stakeholders, or *strategic vision.*[8] Strategic vision requires the ability to scan the environment to develop a knowledge of all of the company's stakeholders and integrate this knowledge into a concept or vision of what the organization could be. It involves the ability to solve increasingly complex problems and become proactive in perspective and approach, and the capacity to develop strategic options—that is, practice contingency planning. Leaders who develop a strategic vision, in turn, provide many benefits for their organizations: a clear future direction; a framework for the organization's mission and goals; and enhanced employee communication, participation, and commitment. Exhibit 11.2 presents some of the qualities of visionary leadership.

For a leader's vision and strategies to be communicated and understood through the organization, he or she must focus on the essentials. Jack Welch, CEO of General Electric, is one such leader. He reorganized GE by keeping only those businesses which had, or were capable of achieving, an outstanding competitive position—first or second in worldwide market shares—in their industry. During the 1980s, he reduced the company's businesses from 100 marginal performers to 14 outstanding performers which range from aircraft engines to light bulbs to major appliances. Welch also eliminated over 100,000 jobs and acquired companies worth $16 billion. The simplification at GE has dramatically increased productivity, profits, and earnings per share.[9]

Recently, the concept of *strategic intent* has been developed to explain why a few select companies have been able to rise to positions of global leadership.[10] The goal of strategic intent is to create an obsession with winning at all levels of the organization and then to sustain that obsession over a 10- to 20-year quest for global leadership. Strategic intent calls

EXHIBIT 11.2
Qualities of Visionary Leadership

- *Holistic:* Comprehends all environmental factors that have an impact on an organization.
- *Interactive:* Sees the organization and environment as acting on, adapting to, and altering one another.
- *Insightful:* Discerns differences, isolates key elements, and makes thoughtful decisions.
- *Speculative:* Deals with uncertainty, contradictory data, and incomplete information.
- *Imaginative:* Fills spaces between what actually is and what could and should be.
- *Contingency thinking:* Deals with complexity of environment, entertains new, alternative assumptions about future environments, and engages in more complex problem solving.

Source: Morris, E. (1987). Vision and strategy: A focus for the future. *Journal of Business Strategy, 8,* 51–58 (with permission.)

for creating a simple and succinct criterion that is understandable by everyone in the organization and that leaders use to chart their firms' progress. For example, Komatsu set out to "encircle Caterpillar," Cannon sought to "beat Xerox," and Honda strove to become a second Ford—an automobile pioneer. In the turbulent information technology industry, it was hard to pick a single competitor as a target. Thus, NEC's strategic intent, set in the early 1970s, was to acquire the technologies that would put it in the best position to exploit the convergence of computing and telecommunications. Other industry observers foresaw this convergence, but only NEC made convergence the guiding theme for subsequent strategic decisions by adopting "computing and communications" as its intent. NEC now has a dominant global position in its industry.

Designing the Organization

Even effective leaders often experience difficulties in successfully implementing their vision and strategies. Such problems may stem from many sources, including:

- Lack of understanding of responsibility and accountability among managers
- Reward systems that do not motivate individuals toward desired goals
- Inadequate or inappropriate budgeting and control systems
- Insufficient mechanisms to coordinate and integrate activities across the organization

Leaders must be actively involved in building structures, teams, systems, and organizational processes that facilitate the implementation of their vision and strategies. For example, we have seen the necessity for consistency between the desired form of competitive advantage and how the organization is structured. Clearly, a firm would generally be unable to achieve an overall low-cost advantage without closely monitoring its costs through detailed and formalized cost and financial control procedures. Similarly, attaining a differentiation advantage would necessitate encouraging innovation, creativity, and sensitivity to market conditions. Such efforts would typically be impeded by the use of a large number of rules and regulations, as well as by highly centralized decision making.

Changes in structure initiated by John Young, CEO of Hewlett-Packard (HP), provide an example of the importance of the role of top-level executives in designing (or redesigning) their organization.[11] Although HP had traditionally been recognized as one of America's best-managed companies, by the late 1980s an unwieldy bureaucracy had bogged down decision making throughout the company. A key source of the problem was the organization's cumbersome committee structure, which was a dysfunctional outcome of HP's culture of egalitarianism, mutual respect, and consensus decision making. Designed initially to foster communication among HP's many diverse operating groups, the committee structure resulted in increased costs and slowed development of innovative products. For example, in early 1990, a key manager informed Young that the development of a series of products vital to HP's strategy (such as high-speed workstations) were a year behind schedule. Also, both earnings and the market value of HP stock had decreased precipitously. Young, realizing that many changes had to be made, acted promptly. First, he removed 200 engineers working on the high-speed workstations from HP's management structure so that they could devote all their time to this important project. Second, Young eliminated the committee structure and drastically reduced the number of hierarchical levels in HP's structure. Third, he divided the computer business—which accounted for 70 percent of HP's $13.2 billion in annual sales—into two main groups. One group handles personal computers, printers, and other products sold through dealers. The other group oversees the sales of workstations and minicomputers to big customers. Last, in place of HP's single corporate sales force established in the mid-1980s, each of the two computer groups formed its own sales and marketing teams. The streamlining of HP's structure helped the firm to operate more efficiently, quickened product development, and increased its ability to react to market changes. Within 4 months of Young's announced changes, product development had accelerated, earnings were up 18 percent, the work force was cut from 95,000 to 91,000, and HP's stock price nearly doubled from 26 to 46.

Instilling a Culture Committed to Excellence and Ethical Behavior

All organizations have their own cultures, that is, the values and beliefs shared by its members, which determine to a considerable degree how its managers respond to problems and opportunities.[12] But whatever culture a leader inherits from the organization's past, shaping—or reshaping—it is a critically important activity. This is true in small- and medium-sized firms as well as in giants such as Eastman Kodak.

Chuck Trowbridge was able to dramatically reverse the sagging performance of Eastman Kodak's copy products group by instilling his organization with a culture dedicated to excellence—making the organization a world-class manufacturing organization. However, implementing such a culture did not come easy. When Trowbridge became general manager of the newly formed group, sales had recently grown to nearly $1 billion. However, costs were high, profits were negligible, and problems were nearly everywhere. Changing the culture required several mechanisms designed to enhance face-to-face communication as well as many forms of written communication. Central to Trowbridge's efforts was the vital role played by Bob Crandall, head of the group's engineering and manufacturing organization. To stress the new direction and align people, Crandall set up several mechanisms. For example, he organized *weekly* meetings with the twelve managers reporting directly to him; *monthly* "copy product forums" which included a different employee from each of his departments; *quarterly* meetings with all 100 of his supervisors to discuss recent improvements and new projects to achieve higher performance; and *quarterly* "state of the department" meetings in which his managers met with all of the employees in their departments. In addition, Crandall held a meeting each week with his managers and his organization's largest supplier, the Kodak Apparatus Division. This division supplied one-third of the parts used in the design and manufacture of his products. Trowbridge and Crandall also used many forms of written communications in implementing the new culture. For example, a newsletter titled *Copy Products Journal* was sent to employees once a month and a program called "Dialog Letters" allowed employees to anonymously ask top executives questions and be guaranteed a reply. Perhaps the most powerful form of written communication was the use of charts that vividly reported measures of quality, cost, and delivery for each product, against different targets. A prominent chart reporting quality levels and costs for the different work groups was displayed in a main hallway near the cafeteria and a hundred smaller versions were displayed throughout the manufacturing area.

Performance improvements associated with the new organization culture began to appear within 6 months and continued to increase. These favorable results helped to make the efforts more credible and increased commitment to the changes. Viewed over an extended period, the improvements were striking. Between 1984 and 1988, defects per unit declined from 30 to 0.3—a hundredfold improvement. Also, over a 3-year period, costs on another product line decreased 24 percent, deliveries on schedule increased from 82 percent in 1985 to 95 percent in 1987, and productivity measured in units per manufacturing employee doubled between 1985 and 1988.[13]

In addition to striving for excellence, leaders must also instill a culture that promotes exemplary ethical behavior. An organization's ethical standards, in large part, determine how it treats its customers and how it relates to its employees, suppliers, and other stakeholder groups. Leaders not only provide direction through codes, policies, procedures, and programs, they must also consistently embrace these ethical standards and provide an example for employees to follow through their own actions.

Unethical behavior often catches up with people and causes serious problems for both managers and their organization. Consider the Manville Corporation, at one time a giant of American industry. This firm was nearly destroyed by a scandal that many still find incomprehensible. In the mid-forties, information began to reach the top executives of Manville Corporation that asbestos, one of the firm's chief products, was linked to debilitating, even fatal, lung diseases. Court testimony has since revealed a 40-year coverup that involved collusion between top management and company health officials on a policy of concealing chest x-rays from affected employees. The court found that the company purposely hid from employees the health risks of producing asbestos, and failed to look for safer ways of handling the product, because replacing workers and paying worker's compensation claims was considered a more cost-effective alternative. In testimony, a former prosecuting lawyer recalled how he once asked one of Manville's defendants: "You mean you would just let them work until they dropped dead?" and received the chilling answer, "Yes, we save a lot of money that way."[14]

Application 11.2 demonstrates the importance and interdependent nature of the three central activities of effective leadership that we have discussed in this section.

Application 11.2

Ricardo Semler: An Unorthodox and Highly Successful Leader

Ricardo Semler joined Semco in 1980, 27 years after his father had founded the firm which manufactured hydraulic pumps for ships. At that time, Semco had annual sales of $4 million, employed approximately 100 people, and was on the brink of bankruptcy. By 1988, Semco had become one of Brazil's fastest-growing firms. It enjoyed a profit margin of 10 percent on sales of $37 million and its 800 employees produced a wide range of sophisticated products such as marine pumps, digital scanners, commercial dishwashers, and truck filters. Additionally, the firm boasted nearly 300 applicants for each job opening and was considered by management associations, labor unions, and the press as the best company to work for in Brazil. Much of Semco's dramatic success may be attributed to Ricardo Semler's creative, aggressive, and unorthodox leadership. Shortly after assuming his position, his management team agreed on two fundamental and immediate needs: a strategic redirection toward diversification and the professionalization of the entire work force.

Initially, Semco pursued licenses to produce other companies' products at its own manufacturing facilities. By 1982, Semco had signed seven license agreements. The marine division—once the entire company—now accounted for only 60 percent of total sales.

Semler then led the firm on an acquisition phase which involved the expenditure of millions of dollars. Because Brazil did not have long-term debt financing at the time, this growth was funded by short-term borrowing at rates 30 percent above the rate of inflation, which ranged from an annual rate of 40 to 900 percent.

Central to Semco's success in implementing such an aggressive diversification strategy are three components that underlie Semler's business philosophy: democracy, profit sharing, and information. According to Semler, "If we eliminated one, the others would be meaningless."

Democracy, or employee involvement, refers to the belief that companies benefit more from the enterprising participation of its employees than from their grudging compliance. Prior to 1980, workers had virtually no input in Semco's company matters. Managers, protective of their power and privilege, typically refused to let their subordinates make any decisions for themselves. Not surprisingly, workers cared little about their productivity or company profits. To enhance employee participation, the workers were allowed to vote on important company decisions, such as the location of new production plants, and have a voice in the selection of superiors. Employee morale and productivity were increased through a reduction in rules and regulations, more flexible work hours, and an emphasis on job rotation. Management accountability was increased through the use of twice-yearly anonymous questionnaires completed by all employees. The questionnaires were designed to gauge the company's credibility and top management's competence.

To enhance worker involvement, Semler also initiated many changes in organizational structure. Primary among these were the use of smaller work groups and a reduction in the number of levels in the organization hierarchy to only three—one at the corporate level and two at the operating levels of the manufacturing units. Such structural changes played a major role in increasing sales, reducing inventories, accelerating the pace of product introductions and deliveries, and improving quality. The commercial food service equipment unit is one example of how dramatically performance improved. Within a 1-year period, sales doubled, inventories fell from 136 days to 46 days, eight new products were introduced (they had been delayed in R&D for 2 years), and rejection rates on federally inspected scales were reduced from 33 percent to less than 1 percent. Increased productivity in this unit led to a work force reduction of 32 percent carried out through attrition and retirement incentives. Semco was, in effect, able to achieve all three forms of competitive advantage simultaneously—overall low cost, differentiation, and quick response.

Semler's business philosophy also includes profit sharing. At Semco, each division has its own profit-sharing plan. Twice each year, employees of each division are entitled to a share of 23 percent of the division's after-tax profits. Each division elects three employees who invest the funds until the division meets to decide—by simple majority vote—what to do with the money.

Communication of key company information is a vital component of Semler's business philosophy. Profit sharing is of little use unless all employees understand how profits are generated in the first place. All employees have monthly access to the vital statistics of the business. These include costs, overhead, sales, payroll, taxes, and

Application 11.2 (cont.)

profits. Further, all employees are required to attend training classes—conducted by the union—to understand the firm's income statement and balance sheet. This sharing of company information, coupled with the direct participation of the employees in profit sharing, facilitates a better understanding of the company's competitive position. Such understanding inevitably leads to improved employee productivity and higher morale.

Source

Semler, R. (1989). Managing without managers. *Harvard Business Review, 67*(5), 76–84.

Leadership: The Importance of Internal and External Constraints

In many societies, leadership is often accorded a heroic or lofty status. Whether evaluating political elections, athletic teams, or business enterprises, leadership is often viewed as the most important factor that determines an organization's success or failure. Such a perspective has been termed a "romanticized view" of leadership which "implies a strong faith in the importance of leadership factors to the functioning and dysfunctioning of organized systems."[15] This orientation is reinforced by many factors:

- Intense media attention directed at high-level executives
- High levels of compensation paid to top executives[16]
- Stock market reaction to the announcement of CEO changes[17]

The romanticized view suggests that business leaders are viewed either positively or negatively on the basis of firm performance. It ignores the many constraints that affect leadership decisions and outcomes. In studying fluctuations in the performance of organizations, researchers have examined the relative importance of external pressures, internal constraints, and leadership on organizational performance.[18] Such studies have led to an external control model—in which leadership is not automatically assumed to be the most important factor determining organizational actions and performance outcomes. The model investigates many factors that may severely constrain a leader's influence. Recall that top executives must not only satisfy stockholder demand for a reasonable return on investment, but also other "parties at interest," such as governments, the local community, suppliers, and so on. Stakeholder demands constrain an executive's decision making, autonomy, and firm performance. A study by *Business Week* indicated that executives strongly agree that the influence of most stakeholders has increased in recent years.[19] The results of this study are shown in Exhibit 11.3.

Recognizing Constraints on Leadership

The implications of these trends in stakeholder influence are dramatic. Although a CEO may be running his or her firm successfully, if investment bankers believe the firm is worth more broken up than intact, corporate raiders may attempt to dismantle it. If shareholders

EXHIBIT 11.3

Changing Levels of Influence among Significant Stakeholders

Response to *Business Week* /Harris Executive Poll Question:

Compared with 5 years ago, would you say that the following individuals or institutions have gained, lost, or kept their influence over decisions in companies such as yours?

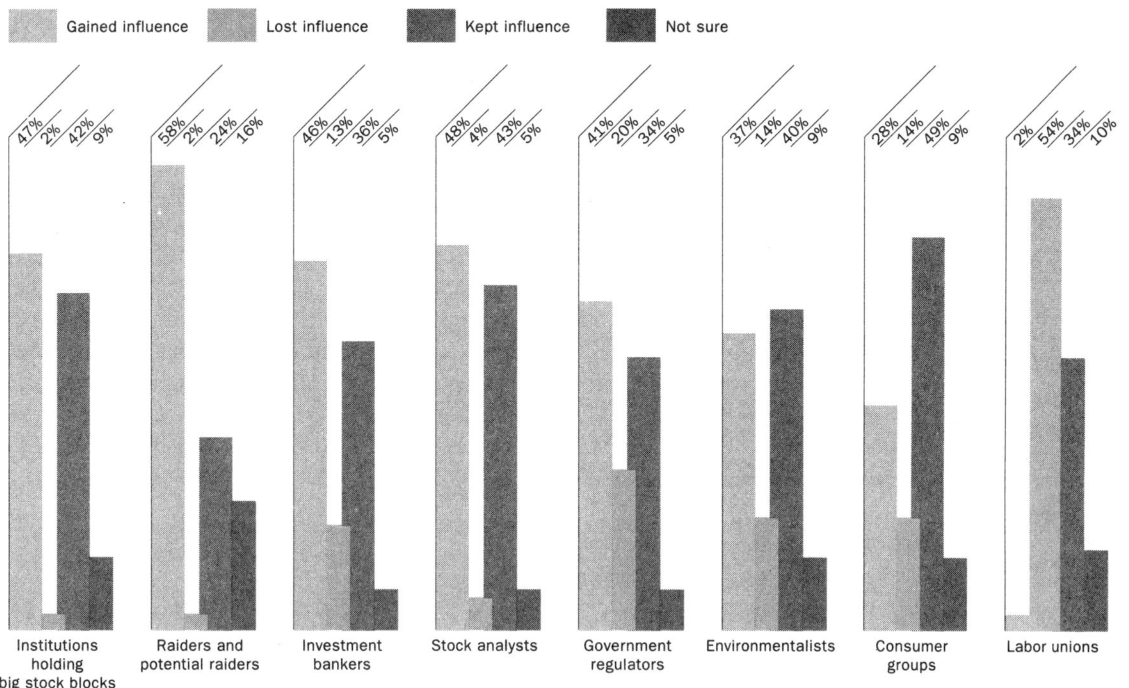

Source: These are results of a survey of 400 chief executives of companies drawn from *Business Week's* top 1000; Nussbaum, B. (1987, October 23). The changing role of the CEO. *Business Week*, p. 28 (with permission).

or the board of directors believe the CEO is not implementing change or improving performance fast enough, his or her job may be in jeopardy. Let's discuss examples of the constraints imposed by two important stakeholder groups—corporate raiders and boards of directors—on leadership.*

Serious threats from corporate raiders have forced many CEOs to make major decisions quickly—often detrimental to the long-term viability of the firm.[20] Firms such as USX, Union Carbide, Heinz, Westinghouse, and Marriott have undergone major restructuring to avoid becoming takeover targets.† Also, some CEOs, such as Robert E. Mercer of

* These groups can also be important stockholders, of course, if they control large amounts of common stock.

† Many of the commonly used antitakeover tactics, such as greenmail and poison pills, were discussed in Chapter 6.

the Goodyear Tire and Rubber Company, have had to abandon their diversification strategies because of the large amount of debt that was incurred to repel a hostile takeover attempt.[21]

The board of directors may also oust a CEO with whom they have become dissatisfied. At Pillsbury Corporation, John Stafford succeeded William Spoor as CEO in 1985 when Spoor stepped down to pursue other interests.[22] By 1987, Spoor, who had remained a director, was chosen by a group of directors to resume some of his former authority and replace Stafford as chairman of the executive committee of the board. This change was deemed necessary because of Stafford's failure to improve the performance of Pillsbury's restaurant division. The "culprit," Burger King, had suffered from management problems, poor advertising, and flat sales. In 1988, Spoor also replaced Stafford as CEO.

In addition to important stakeholder groups, the influence of a CEO's leadership as well as his or her effect on the "bottom line" can also be dramatically, often adversely, affected by employee errors or poor judgment. William Schreyer, CEO of Merrill Lynch, received an ominous telephone call at 6:30 A.M. on April 28, 1987, from Daniel Tulley, president and chief operations officer.[23] He was informed that a trader at Merrill Lynch, who dealt with mortgage-backed securities, had "taken an enormous hit" which would cost the firm hundreds of millions of dollars. After his feelings of anger and betrayal subsided, Schreyer felt a sense of total frustration. He thought, "How can you control 50,000 employees? . . . I thought of Gorbachev and the call he got on the meltdown at Chernobyl. This was my Chernobyl."

Overcoming Leadership Constraints: The Role of Transformational Leadership

Leadership plays a particularly critical role during an organization's early, formative years and during its major changes in strategic direction.[24] While all organizations face pressure to adapt to ongoing changes in their environments, there comes a time when the environment changes so rapidly or so dramatically, that a major realignment of the company's strategy is required. In such challenging times, a specific kind of leader is required: one who is capable of transforming the organization. Transformational leaders focus their energy on the urgency of reestablishing a company's competitive edge and building strategic flexibility. When a company's survival depends on transformation, a leader must be capable of communicating his or her vision in a compelling way, and willing to take decisive action, often in new directions.[25] There are many such examples. Under Gerald Tsai's direction, Primerica sold its core packaging business and became a financial service company. Greyhound, long identified with transportation, was transformed into a retailing business by John Teets who was named CEO in 1982.[26] Lee Iacocca formulated a visionary solution to Chrysler's impending bankruptcy in the late 1970s and then generated a tremendous amount of support for it—both inside and outside the corporation.[27]

When called for, transformational leadership must be exercised at all levels of the organization. At times, all managers must transform their business units or departments in order to bring them into alignment with the new direction of the corporation. For example, when Westinghouse demanded improved performance from its Thermo King European division, the director of its operations in the Republic of Ireland focused his efforts on quality customer service and communicated his vision through problem-solving teams, high participation, and increased performance standards. In 2 years, the plant became one

The Role of Dominant Values

Successful leaders typically instill distinctive cultures that permeate all aspects of their organization. The basic set of values which a firm develops is influenced by a number of factors such as its products, the nature of competition, type of customers, and its technology.[33] Most successful organizations are strongly oriented toward a dominant value such as service, product quality, innovation, speed, or efficiency. This typically enables a firm to attain a competitive advantage. We will now briefly discuss the role that dominant cultures play in some of today's highly successful organizations.

Service

Alaska Airlines attributes much of its success in a fiercely competitive industry to its dominant organizational value, customer service.[34] Its emphasis on customer service has enabled the airline to compete successfully with rivals ten times its size in attracting a prized customer segment: business fliers who pay full fare. For starters, Alaska Airlines spends $7.80 per passenger on each meal—twice the average of United States-based carriers. Entrees include fresh salmon on coach and venison on flights to and from Alaska. The airline also offers more legroom than its competitors, providing only 135 seats on its Boeing 727-200 aircraft, compared to its rivals' 155 seats. At Alaska Airlines, prompt departures are a top priority. The firm's chief operating officer personally looks into all flight delays in order to minimize recurrences. To increase on-time arrivals and departures, the carrier recently spent $12 million to install guidance equipment and to train its pilots to use it. This equipment often enables pilots to fly when competitors are grounded by fog—a frequent phenomenon in the northwest. Alaska Airlines considers maintaining excellent customer service an ongoing challenge. The airline frequently trains its personnel, conducts focus groups, and surveys frequent fliers.

Not surprisingly, Alaska Airlines' performance over the past two decades has been outstanding. Since 1971, the airline has enjoyed an average annual revenue growth of 24 percent to $1.05 billion in 1990, and it has achieved an unbroken string of profitable years during this period. Further, in 1991, *Consumer Reports* ranked Alaska Airlines as number 1 in virtually all aspects of its operations, from check-in to baggage handling, and *Air Transport World* named it "Airline of the Year."

Product Quality

When it comes to product quality, there are no shortcuts at Rubbermaid, which placed very high in that category in a 1990 *Fortune* survey.[35] Rubbermaid's culture places a strong emphasis on product quality and customer needs. Stanley Gault, Rubbermaid's CEO, is considered the company's top quality controller. Once he overheard a Manhattan doorman swearing while using a Rubbermaid dustpan. When Gault discovered that the lip of the dustpan was too thick and left a line of dirt on the floor, he instructed Rubbermaid's engineers to redesign the dustpan.

Hewlett-Packard's culture is also dominated by product quality, which enhances its strategy of staying ahead of the competition.[36] In 1979, a companywide challenge was made to all division managers to improve product quality tenfold by 1989. To meet this challenge, just-in-time (JIT) manufacturing was implemented in many divisions. The effective implementation of a JIT system required close coordination with a small number of reliable suppliers. Vendors therefore had to become more competitive and offer better quality supplies to gain Hewlett-Packard's business. By 1984, the division which manufactures computer circuit boards reported a defect rate of only four per one million connections and, by 1989, all fifty-five divisions of Hewlett-Packard had some form of JIT manufacturing. Another technique used at Hewlett-Packard is a computer system which analyzes each product's design and suggests alterations that simplify production. This expert system has reduced failure rates by 84 percent and manufacturing time by 80 percent.[37]

Innovation

Innovation and a creative spirit are at the core of the 3M Company's culture. 3M has successfully diversified into forty-five product lines in fifteen different technologies.[38] 3M's culture of innovation is promoted by several policies that help 3M to regularly achieve their corporatewide "25 percent," which requires that 25 percent of sales from each of their forty-two divisions come from products developed within the most recent 5-year period.[39] *First,* anyone in the company may spend up to 15 percent of the workweek on any activity as long as it is product-related. *Second,* a panel of technical experts and scientists may award up to ninety $50,000 grants to help support the development of new products. *Third,* salaries and promotion are closely linked to successful "championing" of new products from the early stages of development to commercialization. Accordingly, innovators who create successful products get to manage them autonomously.

Speed

Honda is one firm that has reaped substantial benefits by instilling speed as a dominant organizational value. The company entered Formula One auto racing in 1983, and by 1989 it had already won the demanding annual circuit three times. By rotating its young engineers through the Formula One team, Honda teaches its people the racing spirit, which involves thinking in minutes, not hours. Shoichiro Irimajiri, a managing director at Honda, draws the important linkages between the race track and the factory: "When a problem arises, you have to find the solution now. And if it is a problem you have never seen before, you have to have the flexibility to create a new solution on the spot." Clearly, such an orientation should help Honda's managers and engineers quickly respond to change in the marketplace.

Tom Monaghan, CEO of Domino's Pizza, has proven that putting speed in an organization's culture can be fun. Monaghan, who owns the Detroit Tigers, a professional baseball team, and jogs 6½ miles a day, models his firm on a professional sports league. His regional divisions compete to (1) make the best pizza, (2) deliver it quicker, and (3) sell more than the other regions. Similar to professional quarterbacks on Monday mornings, Domino's pizzamakers watch films of the fastest pizzamakers in the country. Delivery personnel are directed to run from the truck to the house and take stairs two at a time (elevators take too long). The Domino's franchisee in Washington, D.C., takes his managers out every Monday on a 6-mile run. Monaghan explains: "Our whole business is built on speed."

Efficiency

Food Lion, Inc., based in Salisbury, North Carolina, is one of the top performers in the highly competitive supermarket industry.[40] This success is largely attributed to their strong culture of efficiency and control which permeates the entire organization. This orientation

Application 11.3

Conrail: From Government Subsidy to Private Enterprise

Born out of an act of Congress in April 1976, Conrail (Consolidated Rail Company) was expected to form a profitable rail carrier from the bankrupt railroads it inherited. But each of the firms it inherited had its own corporate culture. The only factor they had in common was that their strategies and cultures had resulted in bankruptcy. Conrail management had to create a new culture for the new corporation.

Marketing-oriented strategies were developed but senior management realized that if they were to succeed they had to build a top-to-bottom commitment to those strategies. Senior managers attended executive programs in long-term planning and middle managers attended a 2-week general management program that was designed to enhance their strategic and financial management skills as well as to strengthen their ability to understand, communicate, and implement company strategies. An internal program was implemented for first-line managers to help them develop a "know why versus know how" management style. This style was intended to communicate the corporate vision of the future throughout the entire organization and build employee commitment to that vision. Conrail built its culture by increasing the interaction between staff people and the operations people. This helped ensure that they would get to understand each other's problems and learn to work together as a team. In this way, solutions would benefit the company as a whole and not just one faction over the other.

The turnaround at Conrail has been most impressive. After a few years in which Conrail lost money, its net income increased from $39 million in 1981 to an average of approximately $300 million per year for the rest of the decade. Consistent with its long-range plan, the government sold its interest in Conrail through a public stock offering on March 26, 1987.

Sources

MacQueen, C. R., & Vicere, A. A. (1987, December). Conrail's development program: On track toward the company's vision. *Personnel*, pp. 10–15.

Eisthen, R. A. (1990, March 30). Conrail. *Value Line Investment Service*, p. 290.

tempted blending of the two cultures failed. The entrepreneurs could not tolerate the slow pace of Exxon's bureaucratic processes and resigned. Eventually, Exxon's executives, whose expertise was in oil, not office systems, decided to take a heavy loss and get out of this line of business.[49] Application 11.3 describes how one company formed a viable, unifying culture.

Managing Diverse Cultures in the Global Marketplace

A manager's success in the worldwide marketplace depends not only on job-related expertise but also on sensitivity and responsiveness to a new cultural environment.[50] The assumption that a person successful in the home environment will be equally successful in a foreign country that has a completely new set of cultural conditions is one of the often-d factors contributing to failure in international business assignments.[51] Today's man-d skills in cross-cultural management and the ability to work in organizations and client populations from several countries.[52] Awareness and sensitivity to ... es is vital in understanding and improving the interaction of coworkers, clients, ... nd alliance partners from different countries and cultures.

Four ... ant dimensions upon which many cultures vary are social relationships, values and attitudes, education, and religion. These are particularly relevant for effective management in the international context.[53]

Social Relationships

People in different societies organize their social relationships and activities in a manner that is consistent with their society's values, religions, and economies. One example of how important this is occurred when a U.S. firm found that a manager it hired to operate a plant in Taiwan continually deferred his decision making to a subordinate. Apparently, the subordinate had outranked the manager during his military career and the U.S. managers had failed to take this social relationship into account.

Multinational corporations can minimize such mistakes by closely observing and organizing knowledge about the norms and forms of social organization relevant to their international operations. Also, managers need to assess the extent to which outside values and organizational forms can be successfully introduced into the host culture. Du Pont, for example, employs researchers to identify key stakeholder groups, such as political parties and consumer activist organizations, in each country of operation. Researchers then assess the groups according to their "latent influence" and "group cohesiveness." This helps Du Pont determine how it should react to the peculiarities of social forces in foreign environments.

Values and Attitudes

The values and attitudes of the people in a foreign culture are important considerations for the multinational corporation. Attitudes toward time, for example, can have important implications for a firm. According to a Honeywell executive with international experience: "Time as a cultural value is something we don't understand until we are in another culture. It took me six months to accept the fact that my staff meetings would start thirty minutes late, and nobody would be bothered but me!"

Employee attitudes toward material rewards and promotions can also affect productivity and morale. For example, an American executive promoted the most outstanding member of a Japanese marketing team to the head of the group.[54] However, instead of feeling proud, the man seemed deeply ashamed, the others uncomfortable and demoralized. Performance rapidly declined. What happened? One of the group members explained that the Japanese felt most comfortable working as a team, with all being equally involved in decision making. The American's attempt at motivation only served to undermine the harmonious cooperation that the Japanese workers valued.

Clearly, managers should not rely solely on their own culture's norms when developing human resource management programs. They should carefully consider a society's different values.

Education

Effective training increases people's productivity. Thus, corporations need to develop educational programs, such as classroom training, apprenticeships, demonstration laboratories, and test shops, that are consistent with the nature of the local work force.

The education level of native employees determines the amount and type of job training that is most appropriate. In Indonesia, where illiteracy is high, education is typically the responsibility of one's family. Here, company training programs emphasizing visual demonstrations where learning takes place through observation and imitation would be preferred to classroom and textbook approaches.

Workers will also be more receptive to training that is consistent with their cultural orientation. Kentucky Fried Chicken was very successful, for example, in implementing a training program in Japan that promoted the firm as a family for which the employees were educated to become important members. This technique used the Japanese belief in strong family ties and close loyalty to one's place of work.

Religion

Religion is another important consideration in conducting business in foreign countries. Once, an American chief engineer at a petroleum plant in Bangladesh insisted that, because of an emergency, a subordinate had to report to work the next day, which happened to be an important Muslim holiday. Upon hearing the demand placed on their colleague, the Muslim employees charged the American engineer with insulting their religion. Within an hour, there was a walkout and the plant shut down.

To minimize the potential for such disruptions and poor relations with host countries, managers should be sensitive to the religious heterogeneity that exists in multinational corporations. Managers must be aware of religious holidays, respect the religious beliefs of others, and adapt business practices to the religious constraints of foreign cultures.

Application 11.4

Honeywell's Cross-Cultural Training Program

Honeywell, a large Minnesota-based high-technology firm, receives more than one-third of its $5 billion sales revenue from foreign operations. The firm recognized the need to develop intercultural training for its managers who live and travel abroad. The president of Honeywell Control Systems, Jim Renier, working with the corporate human resource development staff, initiated a program in 1981 to advance both international managerial skills and intercultural awareness. This included a needs analysis and training program.

A needs analysis surveyed most of the employees who traveled extensively, lived abroad, or interacted regularly with people in other companies. This survey was designed to determine cultural barriers as well as the strengths and weaknesses of Honeywell's management practices in worldwide operations. Its goal was to design an effective program that could assist employees to prepare to live abroad, as well as to reenter the home country when their assignments were completed. The results of the survey were analyzed by using standard statistical procedures and by collecting anecdotal data that respondents provided. The survey also kept top executives informed of the changing economic and market conditions, exchange rates, and ethical practices found in the countries in which Honeywell had international operations.

After the survey, a seminar was developed for top executives and management to discuss issues such as matrix management, international marketing, foreign currency and risk management, and cultural values. To raise cross-cultural awareness, a training program was designed to focus on three specific areas:

1. *Culture-specific information.* Data covering other countries and particularly a country one would be entering
2. *Cultural general information.* Values, practices, and assumptions of countries other than the United States
3. *Self-specific information.* Identifying one's own cultural paradigm including values, assumptions, and perceptions about others

In addition to seminars and training programs, videotapes and other information about specific countries and cultures are provided for self-study to those going overseas. This cross-cultural program has lessened the cultural gap between expatriate and native personnel, and increased the employees' efficiency and productivity on a worldwide basis.

Source

Adapted from Kim, W. E., & Mauborgne, R. A. (1987). Cross-cultural strategies. *Journal of Business Strategy, 8*(1), 28–35.

Many organizations, recognizing the need to bridge the cultural gap between expatriate and native personnel, have developed seminars and training programs to train and educate managers. Application 11.4 is an example of how Honeywell, Inc., a large high-technology firm, has addressed this need.

The Leader's Role in Building an Ethical Culture

One survey revealed that 63 percent of Fortune 500 CEOs maintain that a strong culture of ethical behavior results in a strategic advantage.[55] It does so by encouraging decision making that inspires customer trust and helps the organization avoid the negative results of unethical behavior including lawsuits, fines, and lost consumer confidence.

To display ethical behavior consistently, managers and top executives must accept personal responsibility for building such a culture. A leader must demonstrate that such behavior is central to his or her vision and to the organization's mission. Organizational cultures, structures, and processes must all foster ethical responses to managerial challenges. In the following sections we offer suggestions for shaping an organizational culture that avoids ethical crises but also provides a mechanism for response should an ethical crisis occur.[56]

Avoiding Ethical Crises

Managers should take a proactive stance in accepting their responsibilities to society, and should work to ensure that ethical issues are resolved long before they progress to the crisis stage. Perhaps the greatest value in studying ethics and social responsibility is to help managers recognize a potential crisis, and deal with it before it develops. There is much that managers can do to avoid having their organizations slip into the sort of moral and ethical crises given in the examples of the Manville Corporation earlier in this chapter. Four factors are especially important in the avoidance of ethical crises: corporate credos, role models, reward structures, and control systems.

Corporate Credos. Strategic management has been described as the process of answering three deceptively simple questions: Where are we now? Where do we want to be? How are we going to get there? According to Edward Freeman, a leading scholar in the field, strategists must instill a sense of ethics or social responsibility by adding to this list, as the first question, "What do we stand for?"[57]

If the leaders of a firm can answer this question adequately, they will have gone far toward shaping the moral dimension of the organization. One way leaders attempt to answer the question "What do we stand for?" is by writing a corporate credo, which should be incorporated into their own management decisions. A credo is a statement describing the corporation's commitment to certain standards of behavior. It may be part of the firm's overall mission statement (see Chapter 1), or it may be a separate document focused more on ethics and social responsibility than on the mission statement. An example of a credo, Security Pacific's, that combines elements of a mission statement is presented in Application 11.5.

Johnson & Johnson's credo, reprinted as Exhibit 11.5, stresses honesty, integrity, superior products, and putting people before profits—phrases that are common to many such corporate documents.[58] What distinguishes the J&J credo from those of other compa-

Application 11.5

Security Pacific's Corporate Credo

In 1987, more than seventy senior managers from Security Pacific, a Los Angeles-based national bank, set out to explicitly state its corporate position on ethics. The process grew to include over 250 employees and the result was a collection of six missionlike statements addressing the bank's commitment to its most critical stakeholders. Experts have identified this as a role model for other firms to follow.

Commitment to Customer

The first commitment is to provide our customers with quality products and services that are innovative and technologically responsible to their current requirements, at appropriate prices. To perform these tasks with integrity requires that we maintain confidentiality and protect customer privacy, promote customer satisfaction, and serve customer needs. We strive to serve qualified customers and industries that are socially responsible according to broadly accepted community and company standards.

Commitment to Employee

The second commitment is to establish an environment for our employees that promotes professional growth, encourages each person to achieve his or her highest potential, and promotes individual creativity and responsibility. Security Pacific acknowledges our responsibility to employees, including providing for open and honest communication, state expectations, fair and timely assessment of performance, and equitable compensation, which rewards employee contributions to company objectives within a framework of equal opportunity and affirmative action.

Commitment of Employee to Security Pacific

The third commitment is that of the employee to Security Pacific. As employees, we strive to understand and adhere to the corporation's policies and objectives, act in a professional manner, and give our best effort to improve Security Pacific. We recognize the trust and confidence placed in us by our customers and community and act with integrity and honesty in all situations to preserve that trust and confidence. We act responsibly to avoid conflicts of interest and other situations that are potentially harmful to the corporation.

Commitment of Employee to Employee

The fourth commitment is that of employees to their fellow employees. We must be committed to promote a climate of mutual respect, integrity, and professional relationships, characterized by open and honest communication within and across all levels of the organization. Such a climate will promote attainment of the corporation's goals and objectives, while leaving room for individual initiative within a competitive environment.

Commitment to Communities

The fifth commitment is that of Security Pacific to the communities we serve. We must constantly strive to improve the quality of life through our support of community organizations and projects, through encouraging service to the community by our employees, and by promoting participation in community services. By the appropriate use of our resources, we work to support, or further advance, the interests of the community, particularly in times of crisis or social need. The corporation and its employees are committed to complying fully with each community's laws and regulations.

Commitment to Stockholder

The sixth commitment of Security Pacific is to its stockholders. We will strive to provide consistent growth and superior rate of return on their investment, to maintain a position and reputation as a leading financial institution, to protect stockholder investments, and to provide full and timely information. Achievement of these goals for Security Pacific is dependent upon the successful development of the five previous sets of relationships.

Source

Murphy, P. E. (1989). Creating ethical structures. *Sloan Management Review, 28,* 81–87.

EXHIBIT 11.5
Johnson & Johnson's Credo

We believe our first responsibility is to the doctors, nurses, and patients, to mothers, and all others who use our products and services. In meeting their needs, everything we do must be high quality. We must constantly strive to reduce our costs in order to maintain reasonable prices. Customer's orders must be serviced promptly and accurately. Our suppliers and distributors must have an opportunity to make a fair profit.

We are responsible to our employees—the men and women who work with us throughout the world. Everyone must be considered as an individual. We must respect their dignity and recognize their merit. They must have a sense of security in their jobs. Compensation must be fair and adequate, and working conditions must be clean, orderly, and safe. Employees must feel free to make suggestions and complaints. There must be equal opportunity for employment, development, and advancement for those qualified. We must provide competent management, and their actions must be just and ethical.

We are responsible to the communities in which we live and work and to the world community as well.

We must be good citizens—support good works and charities and bear our fair share of taxes. We must encourage civic improvements and better health and education.

We must maintain in good order the property we are privileged to use, protecting the environment and natural resources.

Our final responsibility is to stockholders. Business must make a sound profit. We must experiment with new ideas. Research must be carried on, innovative programs developed, and mistakes paid for. New equipment must be purchased, new facilities provided, and new products launched. Reserves must be created to provide for adverse times.

When we operate according to these principles, the stockholders should realize a fair return.

Source: Company documents.

nies is the amount of energy the company's highest officials devote to ensuring that employees live by its precepts.

In 1975, many companies began to write or rewrite codes of ethics in the wake of Watergate and other public scandals. The public's consensus was that big business suffered from a failure of ethics. J&J undertook a massive effort to assure that its original credo, already decades old, was still valid. Over a 3-year period, more than 1,200 managers attended 2-day seminars in groups of 25, with the explicit instructions to challenge the credo. Either the CEO or the president of the corporation personally presided over each session. In the end, the company came out of the process believing that its original document was still valid. But the questioning continues. The "challenge meetings" are still replicated every other year for all new top managers. This tremendous effort to have the organization question, internalize, and then implement its corporate credo paid off handsomely for J&J in 1982, when eight people died from swallowing capsules of Tylenol, one of its flagship products, that someone had laced with cyanide.

Role Models. Beyond credos, leaders can act as role models of the sort of ethical behavior they hope the rest of the organization will imitate. Without this personal commitment to ethics, a manager's credos and other such statements soon appear hypocritical. When managers don't support their statements with consistent action, frustrated subordinates may, in effect, think, "I cannot hear what you are saying because I'm too busy watching what you are doing." Leaders who wish their organizations to be moral must themselves be beyond reproach.

To return to Johnson & Johnson, Ralph Larsen, the corporation's CEO, says he did not personally learn what ethical behavior at J&J meant from a document or in a training session. Rather, he observed ethics in action when, as a management trainee, he attended a morning meeting in which managers agreed not to ship a very large run of children's shampoo. The product was perfectly safe and effective, but it failed to meet the company's advertised claim of "no more tears." This decision left Larsen with an important model of responsible management he could use when making future decisions.

Today, as he travels to the corporation's 200-plus business units scattered all over the world, Larsen never fails to mention the corporation's commitment to the ideals set forth in its credo. Leaders, such as Larsen, who unhesitatingly make an across-the-board recall of a product because of a problem which affects a limited number of untraceable units (as in the case of the Tylenol crisis), send a certain message throughout their organizations. Leaders who condone the suppression of information about actual or potential ill effects of a product (as in the Manville example presented earlier) send an entirely different message.

Reward Structures. Providing role models is only part of what it takes to implement the practices set forth in a code of ethics. It is entirely possible for a highly moral CEO to preside over an amoral organization. The failure to instill morality may be due not to the leader's personal actions, but may instead result from an organizational structure and system that moral leadership should challenge. The same factors, which can either aid or hinder in implementation of strategy in general, can be applied to the implementation of a standard of ethics in particular.

For instance, individuals who see rewards being distributed on the basis of outcomes alone will naturally be less concerned about the means by which they achieve outcomes. This is often a problem in rewarding sales personnel. Most commission-incentive systems are based purely on sales volume: the more you sell, the more you earn. This emphasis on results without concern for the manner in which they are attained, has often led to kickbacks, bribes, and other unethical behavior on the part of sales staff. Executives who wish to avoid such problems must make it clear that they expect results, but that they also care about the means employed to reach them. Therefore, the rewards system must be carefully linked to the organization's control systems.

Control Systems. Information systems should serve not only to inform, but to control. For instance, in attempting to control the means by which sales are accomplished, many companies wrestle with the issue of what does and does not constitute a bribe. The answer is made difficult by the fact that standard industry practices differ dramatically from country to country. Payments that would be uniformly interpreted as bribes in the United States are just as uniformly seen as appropriate means of doing business in other countries.

Cadbury Schweppes, the British-based multinational, has found that one simple but effective step in controlling the use of bribes is to require that all payments, no matter how unusual, are recorded on the firm's books. Sir Adrian Cadbury, the corporation's chairman, reports that this practice causes managers to pause and consider whether a payment is a necessary and standard cost of doing business, or simply a bribe.[59]

Responding to an Ethical Crisis

No organization is immune to situations which allow, even promote, unethical behavior. Modern organizations are large and complex. Organizations that are generally very well-respected for their strong commitment to ethical behavior have been surprised by isolated incidents of bad behavior.

For instance, General Electric has an enviable reputation as a company with a long and deep commitment to ethical management. However, one of its divisions, involved in contract work for the defense department, was found guilty of transferring expenses among projects in order to increase its revenues. When some defense projects ran up costs greater than those the Pentagon had agreed to pay, managers shifted costs from that project to others still operating under budget. GE was forced to pay more than $16 million in fines, but even more important, the company's reputation suffered: It was tarred with the same brush as companies much more heavily involved with widespread corruption in government contracting. Interestingly, those involved in this crime were well aware of the corporation's ethical standards and its code of conduct.[60]

As the GE example illustrates, no organization, however great its efforts, can guarantee complete avoidance of all questionable actions. It is impossible to guard against every conceivable crisis that tests the moral fiber of a given organization. Therefore, managers should anticipate, and be prepared to deal with, ethical crises when they occur. In these cases, it is important for leaders to manage not only issues internal to the organization, but those external as well. Application 11.6, on the efforts of General Dynamics to recover from defense scandals, illustrates the measures taken to address internal issues for avoiding a crisis in the first place.

Once a crisis actually occurs, the public is often affected, and this involves an entirely new set of external issues to manage. When the public learns of a situation in which a business has failed to live up to its social responsibilities, it is interested in seeing the full story revealed and justice served. However, managers must make a distinction between justice offered by a legitimate jury and "justice" advocated by a lynch mob. Too often in situations dealing with business and the public, a sort of mob hysteria threatens justice, and management must deal with this threat as though it were any other environmental threat. We can offer the following advice for managers who face such a situation.[61]

Do Not Attempt a Cover-Up. Disguising wrongdoing is not mere cowardice, it is morally reprehensible. The public is not as easily fooled, nor as unreasonable in its expectations as many managers seem to think. Experience shows that most attempted cover-ups will be seen by the public for what they are. The tobacco companies have argued for years that tobacco smoking has never been positively linked to lung cancer, but opinion polls reveal that the vast majority of the public sees this as a ruse on the part of management in that industry.

On the other hand, experience also shows that the public is not naive enough to expect perfection from business managers. Treated honestly, by managers who are obviously making a sincere effort to correct a wrong, the public has proven to be remarkably fair-minded. For instance, opinion polls have shown that a sizable percentage of the public believes that smokers have no right to sue tobacco companies for damages stemming from smoking, because the smokers knew of the danger when they chose to smoke. In this case, the public is not duped by the tobacco companies, nor is the public purely antibusiness in its stand on smokers' rights.

Take the Initiative. In the typical crisis of social responsibility, the situation involves a confusing mixture of the news media, representatives from various stakeholder groups, politicians, outside experts, and, of course, managers representing the business itself. The statements elicited and their underlying sentiments can feed on themselves, often resulting in the sort of mob hysteria mentioned earlier.

Application 11.6

General Dynamics Acts to Restore an Ethical Culture

For years, General Dynamics, the second largest defense contractor in the United States, was America's symbol of waste and corruption. The company supplies the Army's M1 tanks, the Navy's Trident submarines, and the Air Force's F-16 fighters. In these enterprises, it has been involved in such widespread bribery and fraud that the total amount for which it bilked taxpayers will never be known. A few examples include:

- The Navy's top officer overseeing the Trident submarine program, Admiral Hyman Rickover, received $67,000 in gifts from GD, including diamond earrings for his wife.
- The government was billed for an $18,000 country club initiation fee as part of GD's fulfillment of one of its defense contracts.
- GD charged the government $9,609 for a single wrench.
- GD's CEO charged the government for travel between his country home in Georgia and his company's headquarters in St. Louis by corporate jet.

The result of such unethical behavior has been years of court battles and a ruined corporate reputation. Stanley Pace was hired to restore the corporation's reputation, and the approach he has taken mirrors many of the lessons discussed in this chapter:

Establish a Code of Ethics Which Explains What the Company Stands For

One of Pace's first actions was to replace GD's dusty old brochure on ethics with a new twenty-page book of standards. The new book combined general guidelines, like "Be honest and trustworthy," with more specific guidelines for actions, like "All cash and bank transactions must be handled so as to avoid any question of bribery, kickbacks, or any suspicion of impropriety whatsoever." To drive the importance of such guidelines home, Pace had the booklet sent to all 103,000 employees, and asked each of them to return a signed form after reading it.

Offer a Role Model

Pace has a reputation that is so good he has been nicknamed "Mr. Clean." He is a West Point graduate, was shot down over Germany on his 39th mission during World War II, spent 9 months as a prisoner of war, and followed with a 30-year career in corporate America, where his record has been spotless.

Reward Ends, but Monitor Means

GD is still an aggressive competitor for government contracts, but now it places great emphasis on ensuring that it does not cheat in order to win. Standards are so tight that employees with neighbors who happen to work for suppliers or customers are instructed not to exchange Christmas gifts, and military visitors to corporate headquarters are expected to pay for their own coffee.

Establish a Control System That Encourages Ethical Decision Making

Formerly, one of the most common crimes at GD was shifting labor expenses from one contract to another in order to increase overall profits. A sloppy control system facilitated this, but it has since been replaced. Now, an electronic system automatically records who does what on which machine for how long and then compares this actual behavior to what was planned.

Facilitate Whistle Blowing

An "ethics hotline" that workers could use to make anonymous reports of misconduct was established. The first 2 months the system was in place, 400 such calls were made.

Stress the Role of Individual Responsibility

As the company's ethics director explained, "We are not trying to teach them to be honest. We have to assume that employees are honest. But, it is important to reaffirm and heighten an awareness of the company's values."

Source

Worthy, G. (1986, April 28). Mr. Clean charts a new course at General Dynamics. *Fortune*, pp. 70–76.

Such a threat must be proactively managed, but too often managers who face this sort of situation only react to the actions of others. Rather than merely responding to what develops, good crisis managers move to make things happen. For a good example of what this can entail, we can return to Johnson & Johnson, and study its response to the news that eight people had died from taking Tylenol capsules adulterated with cyanide. The public reaction was fear: A product they had trusted was a killer. Experts immediately predicted that the Tylenol brand name was ruined forever. People speculated about the safety of other J&J products. Friends and families of the victims expressed their anger and resentment to the press. During the first 8 days after the deaths, 20 percent of all national news was devoted to coverage of this one story. The situation was growing out of control.

J&J's management was convinced that the tampering had occurred after the product was on the store shelves, and therefore occurred over a limited geographic area. But the company chose to take no chances. With absolute minimum delay, it quickly removed all Tylenol from store shelves and supply channels in the United States, destroying 31 million bottles of pills. Such quick action, based on widespread understanding and belief in the J&J credo, was crucial to the firm's ability to cope successfully with this crisis. Additionally, the company sent mailgrams to 450,000 members of the health community worldwide, warning them of what had happened. Six weeks after the first deaths, J&J had already spent $100 million to deal with the crisis. It then held a news conference to announce a new triple-sealed package. The conference reached 600 reporters in thirty cities through satellite transmission. Subsequently, the president and the chairman of the company began a nationwide tour of television news shows, on which they described the problem and J&J's response more than fifty times. Meanwhile, lower-ranking officials made a combined total of more than 2,500 additional media contacts delivering the same message. Altogether, the effort cost J&J an estimated $250 million, but within 6 months of the deaths, Tylenol had already regained 85 percent of its original market share, and it remains the market leader.

Focus on Shared Objectives. Rather than let a crisis become an "us versus them" situation, good crisis managers turn the attention toward the common interests of concerned parties. By finding a shared concern to build upon, an equitable solution is more likely. Lumber companies and environmentalists often appear to have diametrically opposed positions. Yet both share an interest in seeing that forestry lands are well-managed. Both groups seem to be best served working together to manage forests wisely, rather than simply opposing one another.

Recently, residents in Brooklyn, New York, had their suspicions officially confirmed when community health officers reported that nearby underground oil tanks had been leaking for 40 years. Drip by drip, an oil "spill" even larger than the Valdez disaster had accumulated 10 to 50 feet below the surface. Fumes in the crowded community above the escaped oil presented health problems and ruined property values. Numerous corporations owned oil tanks in the area, so absolute responsibility was uncertain. When questioned about the extent of their part in contributing to the environmental nightmare, Mobil representatives replied that there was no way of knowing, but that their company had a policy of acting on any such crisis for which they might be even partially responsible. Mobil focused its energies on cleaning up the mess. Both Mobil's actions and its work redirected attention away from crippling finger pointing and toward more constructive consideration of shared objectives.

Use a Wide-Angle Lens. When a business is in a crisis involving its stakeholders, the various stakeholder groups naturally tend to focus on the issues most relevant to themselves. However, if they are to successfully meet the needs of a broad range of stockholders, managers must view the crisis through a "wide-angle lens." In fact, many situations call for managers to go beyond consideration of the specific interest groups who have a stake in the business, and consider the needs of society in general.

For instance, consider the dilemma facing a power company that plans to construct some type of power plant. A nuclear plant is viewed by the public near the site to be a personal threat to their safety. A hydroelectric plant is viewed by owners of lands bordering the river to be dammed as a threat to their property. Environmentalists point out that a coal-fired plant will create pollution problems downwind. The power company is legally obliged to supply the needed electricity, but regardless of the alternative, at least one stakeholder group is likely to object. In dealing with this dilemma, the managers must ensure that the ensuing debate addresses the problem as a whole, and does not turn into a series of doomed attempts to address each stakeholder's demands individually. This requires that managers view the picture as a whole, and avoid focusing on a subset of stakeholder interests.

Summary

Two critical elements of the strategic management process are leadership and organization culture. Leadership has three important interdependent activities. These include setting a direction, designing the organization, and instilling a culture committed to excellence and ethical behavior. Although leadership is undeniably a key facet in high-performing organizations, there are also many internal and external factors which constrain the extent of influence that a leader may have on the actions his or her organization may take, as well as the firm's performance. Important internal factors would include actions taken by the board of directors and by individual employees. Some of the external factors that may constrain leader influence are institutions holding large blocks of stock, investment bankers, government regulators, consumer groups, and labor unions. When a firm faces dramatic changes in its environment, often its only means of maintaining a competitive position is to undertake a complete strategic redirection. Transformational leadership stressing vision, urgency, and flexibility is required to effect such a redirection.

Organizational culture is a system of shared values and beliefs that interact with a company's people, organizational structure, and control systems to produce behavioral norms. Most successful organizations have dominant values such as services, product quality, innovation, speed, and efficiency. Such dominant values promote and reinforce distinct cultures that influence all aspects of an organization's activity. However, since an organization's culture is often deeply rooted in the manager's and employee's beliefs and values, attempts to change it are difficult and usually met with resistance. Often, a change of leadership becomes necessary. Also, mergers and acquisitions often fail because of the clash among dissimilar cultures.

As international markets become increasingly important to a firm's viability, the need for managers to be aware and sensitive to important aspects of the foreign nations in which their firms conduct business also becomes more critical. Key aspects of a nation's culture include social relationships, values and attitudes, education, and religion. Many firms have developed seminars and training programs designed to help their managers become more effective when they deal with cultural diversity.

Leaders must play a central role in building an organizational culture committed to high standards of ethical conduct. Leaders need to take a proactive orientation to help ensure that ethical crises will be avoided. These include developing and reinforcing corporate credos, serving as role models for exemplary ethical behavior, and developing and maintaining reward structures and control systems that elicit and reinforce ethical behavior. However, no organization is immune to situations in which unethical behavior may occur. When it does, managers may minimize adverse consequences by taking the initiative, focusing on shared objectives, and by involving a broad range of shareholders.

Notes

1. Kotter, John P. (1990). What leaders really do. *Harvard Business Review, 68*(3), 104.
2. Kotter, J. P. (1990). *A force for change.* New York: Free Press.
3. Senge, P. M. (1990). The leader's new work: Building learning organizations. *Sloan Management Review, 31*(4), 7–23.
4. These three activities are salient in much of the normative strategic management literature such as Uyterhoeven, H. E. R., Ackerman, R. W., & Rosenblum, J. W. (1972). *Strategy and organization: Text and cases in general management* (rev. ed.). Homewood, IL: Irwin; and Andrews, K. R. (1980). *The concept of corporate strategy* (2nd ed.). Homewood, IL: Irwin. These three activities and our discussion draw from Kotter, J. P. (1990). What leaders really do. *Harvard Business Review, 68*(3), 103–111; and Pearson, A. E. (1990). Six basics for general managers. *Harvard Business Review, 67*(4), 94–101.
5. Many authors have noted the importance of obtaining inputs from many sources as a key component of the strategy formulation process. This typically helps not only improve the quality of the strategy but also its political feasibility. See, for example, Wrapp, E. (1967). Good managers don't make policy decisions. *Harvard Business Review, 45*(5), 91–99; and Hambrick, D. C., & Cannella, A. A., Jr. (1988). Strategy implementation as substance and selling. *The Academy of Management Executive, 3*(4), 278–285. For an interesting and seminal perspective on the relationship between strategy formulation and implementation, as well as the political considerations for public sector organizations, refer to Lindblom, C. E. (1959). The science of muddling through. *Public Administration Review, 19*(1), 79–88.
6. As discussed in Chapter 1, in practice, chief executive officers exhibit a wide range of differences in how they actually participate in strategy formulation and implementation. For example, Bourgeois, L. J., III, & Brodwin, D. R. (1984). Strategic implementation: Five approaches to an elusive phenomenon. *Strategic Management Journal, 5,* 241–264 suggest five different models of CEO involvement ranging from a "top-down approach" wherein the CEO plays the central role in formulating a firm's strategy to a "bottom-up approach." Here, the CEO "encourages managers to come forward as champions of sound strategies." Other insightful discussions of how the roles of top executives may differ across organizations and the associated performance implications include Mintzberg, H., & Walters, J. A. (1985). Of strategies, deliberate and emergent. *Strategic Management Journal, 6,* 257–272; and Nutt, P. C. (1987).

Identifying and appraising how managers install strategies. *Strategic Management Journal, 8,* 1–14.

7. The introductory material in this section draws on Kotter, J. P. (1990). What leaders really do. *Harvard Business Review, 68*(3), 103–111.
8. The discussion of strategic vision draws on Morris, E. (1987). Vision and strategy: A focus for the future. *The Journal of Business Strategy, 8,* 51–58.
9. Tichy, N., & Charan, R. (1989). Speed, simplicity, self-confidence: An interview with Jack Welch. *Harvard Business Review, 67*(5), 112–120.
10. Hamel, G., & Prahalad, C. K. (1989). Strategic intent. *Harvard Business Review, 67*(3), 63–76.
11. Buell, B. (1991, April 1). Hewlett-Packard rethinks itself. *Business Week,* pp. 76–79.
12. Pearson, A. E. (1989). Six basics for general managers. *Harvard Business Review, 67*(4), 94–101. Andrall Pearson's ideas regarding an organization's "work environment" are similar to many writers' perspectives on organization culture. For an insightful discussion of how leadership affects an organization's culture, see Trice, H. M., & Beyer, J. M. (1991). Cultural leadership in organizations. *Organization Science, 2* (2), 149–169.
13. Kotter, J. P. (1990). *A force for change* (pp. 52–55). New York: Free Press.
14. Gellerman, S. W. (1986). Why "good" managers make bad ethical choices. *Harvard Business Review, 64,* 85–90.
15. Meindl, J. R., & Ehrlich, S. B. (1987). The romance of leadership and the evaluation of organizational performance. *Academy of Management Journal, 30,* 92–109.
16. For interesting perspectives on CEO compensation such as how their compensation is determined and the central question of "Are they worth it?" refer to Crystal, G. S. (1991). *In search of excess: The overcompensation of American executives.* New York: W. W. Norton; and Fierman, J. (1990, March 12). The people who set the CEO's pay. *Fortune,* pp. 58–59, 62, 66.
17. For an interesting review of studies which have investigated the impact of the announcements of CEO changes on the value of a firm's stock, refer to Chung, K. H., Rogers, R. C., Lubatkin, M. L., & Owers, J. E. (1987). Do insiders make better CEOs than outsiders. *The Academy of Management Executive, 1*(3), 323–329.
18. There have been many studies directed toward exploring the effect of leadership on organizational performance. The more important studies which examined corporations include Lieberson, S., & O'Connor, J. F. (1972). Leadership and organizational performance: A study of large corporations. *American Sociological Review, 37,* 117–130; Weiner, N., & Mahoney, T. A. (1981). A model of corporate performance as a function of environmental, organizational, and leadership influences. *Academy of Management Journal, 24,* 453–470; Day, D. V., & Lord, R. G. (1988). Executive leadership and organizational performance: Suggestions for a new theory and methodology. *Journal of Management, 14,* 453–464; Beatty, R. P., & Zajac, E. J. (1987). CEO change and firm performance in large corporations: Succession effects and manager effects. *Strategic Management Journal, 8,* 305–317; and Thomas, A. B. (1988). Does leadership make a difference to organizational performance? *Administrative Science Quarterly, 33,* 388–400. Most of these studies have viewed performance as a function of external influences and organizational characteristics as well as leadership influences. As argued by Weiner and Mahoney (1981): "At any point in time corporate leaders must operate within a set of fixed organizational constraints . . . leaders must make strategic choices within these external and internal influences that may make the difference between organizational success or failure" (p. 456). The relative importance of leadership compared to internal constraints (e.g., company size) and external constraints (e.g., industry concentration) has varied widely

across these studies and has depended on such factors as research methodologies and analysis of data as well as the definition and measurement of key variables.

19. Nussbaum, B. (1987, October 23). The changing role of the CEO. *Business Week,* pp. 13–17, 20–21, 24, 28. For an interesting discussion of stakeholder management, refer to Savage, G. T., Nix, T. W., & Blair, J. D. (1991). Strategies for assessing and managing organizational stakeholders. *The Executive, 5*(2), 61–75.
20. For an interesting discussion of the threats of corporate raiders to major corporations, refer to Keichel, W., III. (1988, February 29). Corporate strategy for the 1990s. *Fortune,* pp. 34–38, 42.
21. Bryne, J. A., & Baum, L. (1987, October 23). The limits of power. *Business Week,* pp. 33–35.
22. Dumaine, B. A. (1987, November 23). A CEO bake-off at Pillsbury. *Fortune,* pp. 109–116.
23. Nussbaum (Ref. 19), op. cit., p. 14.
24. See, for example, Tushman, M. L., & Romanelli, E. (1985). Organizational evolution: A metamorphosis model of convergence and reorientation. *Research in Organizational Behavior, 7,* 171–222; and Brenner, B., Ivey, M., & Grover, G. (1991, November 25). Tough times, tough bosses. *Business Week,* pp. 174–179.
25. Mann, C. P. (1988). Transformational leadership in the executive office. *Public Relations Quarterly, 33,* 19–23; Wiersema, M., & Ulrich, D. (1989). Strategic redirection and the role of top management. In William D. Guth (Ed.), *Handbook of business strategy* (pp. 14–1 to 14–15). Boston, MA: Warren, Gorham, and Lamont, Inc.
26. Ulrich, D., & Wiersema, M. (1989). Gaining strategic and organizational capability in a turbulent business environment. *The Academy of Management Executive, 3,* 115–122; Wiersema, M., & Ulrich, D. (1989). Strategic redirection and the role of top management. In William D. Guth (Ed.), *Handbook of business strategy* (pp. 14–1 to 14–15). Boston, MA: Warren, Gorham, and Lamont, Inc.; Mann, C. (1988). Transformational leadership in the executive office. *Public Relations Quarterly, 33,* 19–23; and Tichy, N. M., & Devanna, M. A. (1986). New York: Wiley.
27. Mann, C. (1988). Transformational leadership in the executive office. *Public Relations Quarterly, 33,* 19–23.
28. Ibid.
29. These primary activities are suggested by Tichy, N. M., & Ulrich, D. O. (1984). The leadership challenge: A call for the transformational leader. *Sloan Management Review, 4*(26), 59–67.
30. Ouichi, W. (1981). *Theory Z.* Reading, MA: Addison-Wesley; Deal, T. E., & Kennedy, A. A. (1982). *Corporate cultures.* Reading, MA: Addison-Wesley; Peters, T. J., & Waterman, R. H. (1982). *In search of excellence,* New York: Harper & Row; Peters, T., & Austin, A. (1985). *A passion for excellence,* New York: Random House. For an insightful critique of *In Search of Excellence,* see Hitt, M. A., & Ireland, R. D. (1987, May). Peters and Waterman revisited: The unended quest for excellence. *Academy of Management Executive, 1,* 91–98.
31. Uttal, B. (1983, October 17). The corporate culture vultures. *Fortune,* pp. 66, 68–72.
32. Dumaine, B. (1990, January 15). Creating a new company culture. *Fortune,* pp. 127–131.
33. Deal, T. E., & Kennedy, A. A. (1982). *Corporate cultures: The rites and rituals of corporate life.* Reading, MA: Addison-Wesley.
34. Yang, D. J. (1991, October 25). Northern hospitality. *Business Week,* p. 118.
35. O'Reilly, B. (1990, January 29). Leaders of the most admired: Quality of products. *Fortune,* pp. 42–43.

36. Kaufman, S. (1989, May). Quest for quality. *Business Month,* pp. 60–62, 64–65.
37. Dumaine, B. (1989, January 29). How managers can succeed through speed. *Fortune,* pp. 54–59; and Kaufman, S. (1989, May). Quest for quality. *Business Month,* pp. 60–62, 64–65.
38. Dumaine, B. (1990, January 29). Leaders of the most admired: Ability to innovate. *Fortune,* pp. 43–44.
39. Mitchell, R. (1989, April 10). Masters of innovation: How 3M keeps its new products coming. *Business Week,* pp. 58–61.
40. Food Lion, Inc., 1990 Annual Report; and Smith, D. (1991, February 25). Food Lion to leap into Texas. *The Charlotte Observor,* pp. 1D, 10D.
41. Sathe, V. (1983). Implications of corporate culture: A manager's guide to action. *Organizational Dynamics, 12*(4), 4–23.
42. Wilkins, A. (1983). The culture audit: A tool for understanding organizations. *Organizational Dynamics, 12*(4), 24–38.
43. Bennett, A. (1990, April 18). Pay for performance. *The Wall Street Journal,* p. R7; and Crystal, G. S. (1989, June 5). Seeking sense in CEO pay. *Fortune,* pp. 88, 90, 92, 96, 100, and 104.
44. Deal, T. E., & Kennedy, A. A. (1982). *Corporate cultures* (p. 163). Reading, MA: Addison-Wesley.
45. Deal, T. E., & Kennedy, A. A. (1982). *Corporate cultures.* Reading, MA: Addison-Wesley; Gordon, G. C. (1985). Five key issues in understanding and changing culture. In R. H. Kilmann, M. J. Saxton, & R. Serpa (Eds.), *Gaining Control of the Corporate Culture* (pp. 1–16). San Francisco: Jossey-Bass; Nixon, B. (1987, July). Strategy and culture—bridging the gap. *Accountancy,* pp. 90–92; and Dumaine, B. (1990, January 15). Creating a new company culture. *Fortune,* pp. 127–131.
46. Schein, E. H. (1989). Corporate culture is the real key to creativity. *Business Month,* pp. 73–75.
47. Lefkoe, M. (1987, July 20). Why so many mergers fail. *Fortune,* pp. 113–114.
48. Silk, L. (1989). Marrying two company cultures is not easy. *Business Month,* pp. 8–9.
49. Donelly, R. M. (1987). Exxon's "office of the future" fiasco. *Planning Review, 15,* 12–15.
50. Ferraro, G. P. (1990). *The cultural dimension of international business.* Englewood Cliffs, NJ: Prentice-Hall. For a discussion of the potential benefits and costs of culturally diverse organizations (in terms of gender, race, ethnicity, and nationality) refer to Cox, T., Jr. (1991). The multicultural organization. *The Executive, 5*(2), 34–47.
51. See, for example, Hays, R. D. (1974). Expatriate selection: Insuring success and avoiding failure. *Journal of International Business Studies, 5,* 25–37; and Tung, R. L. (1981). Selection and training for overseas assignments. *Columbia Journal of World Business, 16*(1), 68–78.
52. For a recent and integrative discussion of cross-cultural management, see Adler, N. J. (1991). *International dimensions of organizational behavior.* Boston, MA: PWS-Kent.
53. This discussion draws upon Kim, W. C., & Mauborgne, R. A. (1987). Cross-cultural strategies. *The Journal of Business Strategy, 8*(2), 28–35. Other dimensions upon which cultures may vary are presented in Ferraro, G. P. (1990). *The cultural dimension of international business.* Englewood Cliffs, NJ: Prentice-Hall.
54. Anderson, D. C. (1985, June). How to offend a Mexican businessman. *Across the Board,* pp. 53–56.
55. Harrington, S. J. (1991). What corporate America is teaching about ethics. *The Academy of Management Executive, 5*(1), 21–29.
56. Murphy, P. E. (1989, Winter). Creating ethical corporate structures. *Sloan Management Re-*

view, pp. 81–97. For a discussion of the current state of ethics training in American corporations, see Harrington, S. J. (1991). What corporate America is teaching about ethics. *The Executive,* 5(1), 21–30.

57. Freeman, R. E., & Gilbert, D. R. J. (1988). *Corporate strategy and the search for ethics,* Englewood Cliffs, NJ: Prentice-Hall.
58. Material in this section on Johnson & Johnson's credo and its role in addressing the Tylenol crisis was derived from Dumaine, B. (1990, January 29). Leaders of the most admired: Corporate citizenship. *Fortune,* pp. 50–54; and Byrne, J. A. (1988, February 15). Businesses are signing up for Ethics 101. *Business Week,* pp. 56–57.
59. Cadbury, S. A. (1987). Ethical managers make their own rules. *Harvard Business Review, 65,* 69–73.
60. Pollack, A. (1990, May 25). Whose fault are scandals? *The New York Times,* pp. C1–C2.
61. The points below were developed from Kuechle, D. (1985). Crisis management, and executive quagmire. *Business Quarterly,* pp. 53–70.

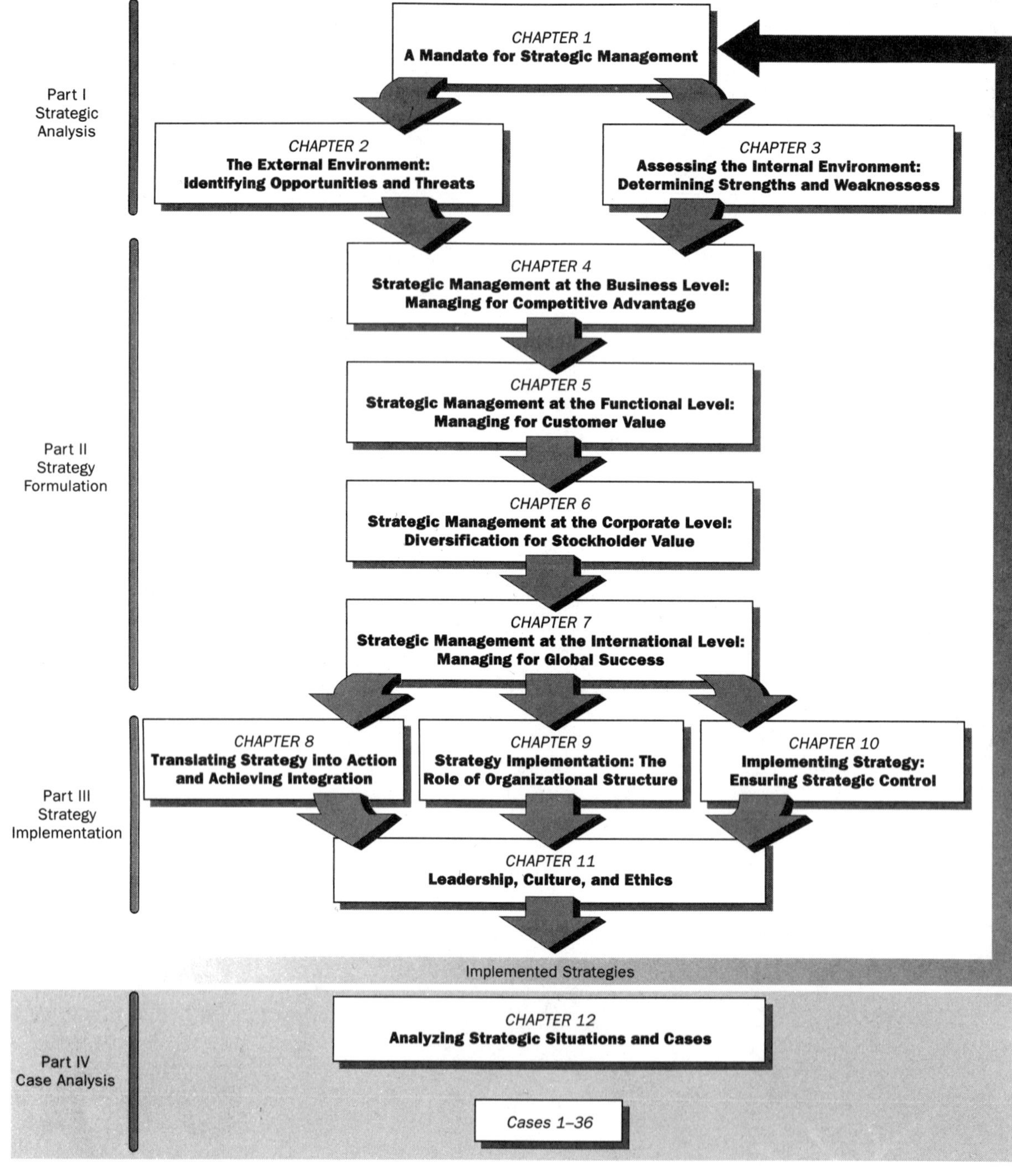
Part I
Strategic
Analysis
CHAPTER 1
A Mandate for Strategic Management
CHAPTER 2
The External Environment:
Identifying Opportunities and Threats
CHAPTER 3
Assessing the Internal Environment:
Determining Strengths and Weaknessess
Part II
Strategy
Formulation
CHAPTER 4
Strategic Management at the Business Level:
Managing for Competitive Advantage
CHAPTER 5
Strategic Management at the Functional Level:
Managing for Customer Value
CHAPTER 6
Strategic Management at the Corporate Level:
Diversification for Stockholder Value
CHAPTER 7
Strategic Management at the International Level:
Managing for Global Success
Part III
Strategy
Implementation
CHAPTER 8
Translating Strategy into Action
and Achieving Integration
CHAPTER 9
Strategy Implementation: The
Role of Organizational Structure
CHAPTER 10
Implementing Strategy:
Ensuring Strategic Control
CHAPTER 11
Leadership, Culture, and Ethics
Implemented Strategies
Part IV
Case Analysis
CHAPTER 12
Analyzing Strategic Situations and Cases
Cases 1–36

PART IV

Case Analysis

CHAPTER 12

Analyzing Strategic Situations and Cases

Strategic management courses are characterized by extensive reliance on the case method as an instructional tool. The cases that you will be studying describe situations that real companies face which often present problems that are difficult to define and resolve. This chapter focuses on how to conduct an in-depth strategic analysis of an organization, as well as the important contribution that the case method makes in developing vital managerial skills.

This chapter is divided into three major sections. First, we describe the basic differences between the case method and other methods of instruction. We also discuss four key skills that result from the use of the case method and serve to enhance managerial success. Second, we explain how to perform a strategic analysis of an organization. Finally, we offer suggestions for how students may derive the maximum benefit from class discussion of cases as well as from writing in-depth case analyses.

After reading this chapter, you will understand:

- The importance of the case method and how it differs from more conventional classroom techniques
- Four skills that are critical for managerial success which the case method helps to develop
- The basic steps in performing a strategic analysis
- How to improve the quality of one's participation in classroom discussion and in the preparation of written case analyses

EXECUTIVE INTERVIEW

Nolan D. Archibald
Chairman, President and Chief Executive Officer
Black & Decker Corporation

Nolan D. Archibald is chairman, president, and chief executive officer of the Black & Decker Corporation, a leading global marketer and manufacturer of power tools, home improvement, household, and commercial products, and professional systems services. He joined Black & Decker as president, chief operating officer, and director in 1985, and was appointed president and chief executive officer in March 1986 and Chairman, President, and CEO in December 1986.

Under Mr. Archibald's leadership, Black & Decker has been revitalized as a market-driven, global competitor in the consumer and commercial products field. At 48 years of age, Mr. Archibald is one of the youngest CEOs of a publicly held Fortune 100 company. He was selected by *Fortune* in 1986 as one of America's "10 Most Wanted Managers" and was cited by *Business Week* as one of the best managers of 1987.

Prior to joining Black & Decker, Mr. Archibald held various management positions at Beatrice Companies, Inc., from 1977 to 1985. An All-American basketball player in college, Mr. Archibald is a graduate of Weber State College in Utah and holds an M.B.A. degree from the Harvard Graduate School of Business.

How has strategic analysis contributed to Black & Decker's success?

Black & Decker is a global operating company, not a portfolio of diversified financial assets. Therefore, the keys to success are to compete aggressively in our specific product markets and to capitalize on synergies and linkages across our businesses. Maintaining an external focus through strategic analysis is the foundation for both success factors.

For example, it is our formal objective to be the market leader or a strong second in all of our business. Accomplishing this sometimes heroic goal requires rigorous strategic analysis along several dimensions. We invest heavily in getting to know the end users of our products, through both formal market research and traditional "hands on" observation. We use fact-based knowledge to help shape our product development plans and marketing programs. Similarly, we work closely with our suppliers and our trade customers to understand their ways of doing business in order to forge working partnerships that improve the overall efficiency of our supply chain. Finally, we maintain constant vigilance of the competitive environment. We "benchmark" our performance in core competencies against the best of our competitors to ensure that our quality, costs, and service levels provide a basis for sustainable competitive advantage.

Why is it important for business students to develop a generalist's perspective to supplement their functional-area specialties?

In the past, many companies tended to attack business problems through functional specialization and sequential processing. Each functional organization performed a well-defined role, often in isolation, and then passed "work in process" along to the next function. For example, product development would flow from product definition in Marketing to product design in Engineering to production methods development in Manufacturing. The results were typically workable, but rarely optimal. Product designs that met functional specifications were often inefficient and sometimes not producible.

Now, enlightened companies attack problems with concurrent multifunctional participation. All of the relevant functions work in parallel as an integrated team. The process is heavily "front-end loaded" for precise definition of requirements and approaches. Solutions are derived through constant iterative interaction.

Effective multifunctional teams require highly competent specialists who have a generalist's perspective. To make the concurrent multifunctional approach work, each team member must have a basic understanding of the others' functions in order to facilitate communications and to make critical trade-offs. All team members must operate with a sensitivity to the whole business system, not just to narrowly defined specialties.

What developments are increasing the need for managers at Black & Decker to have a broader, organization-wide focus or perspective?

Three driving forces are exerting a profound influence on the Black & Decker organization: globalization,

Continued

total quality management, and quick response. Each is forcing our managers to look beyond their individual businesses or narrowly defined specialties to adopt a broader, corporate perspective or an even broader, business-system perspective.

For example, we clearly recognize that we are competing in a global economy. To be successful, we must synchronize our efforts worldwide to eliminate any redundant or duplicated activities, to leverage our bases of unique competencies, and to exploit scale economies. Isolated business units cannot be as effective and as efficient as a well-coordinated worldwide network of related businesses sharing their expertise and resources.

Similarly, like most other U.S. companies, we previously operated with a very narrow definition of quality that focused on statistical process controls and product failures. We now recognize that total quality is an all-encompassing objective geared to providing complete customer satisfaction through excellence in all aspects of the operation. Achieving total quality requires close functional cooperation and a corporate-wide attitude that the customer really is king.

Finally, quick response is a recently emerging strategic imperative that recognizes the urgent need for the efficient management of time and assets. Our trade customers are developing sophisticated information and management systems that allow them to operate their businesses under tighter controls. Part of their efficiency gain is derived by requiring more service from suppliers: shorter lead times, smaller orders, more shipments direct to stores. Responding to the escalating customer requirements can be accomplished only through an integrated logistics approach. Our managers must look beyond their functions and beyond our corporate boundaries. Quick response requires mutually beneficial partnerships with our trade customers and suppliers that forge new ways of doing business.

The bottom line is that all of our managers must adopt a perspective that is corporate-wide, worldwide, and spans the entire business system.

What do you see as being the key analytical skills for managers involved in strategy at Black & Decker?

First and foremost, we are a market-driven company, so our managers must have a sensitivity to customers and end users. They must be comfortable with traditional market research techniques and also have an intuitive sense of the "soft" factors that underlie how a market really works and how an end user really thinks and feels.

Similarly, since we are externally focused, our managers are expected to have a keen sense of competitive analysis. They must be able to isolate key factors for success and objectively benchmark our relative performance against the best competitors.

Finally, we are in business to increase shareholder values. So our managers must be profit-oriented and appropriately skilled in financial and economic analysis. We expect decisions and actions that are both strategically and financially sound.

WHY ANALYZE STRATEGIC MANAGEMENT CASES?

Case analysis is a vital instructional method in strategic management courses.[1] Cases form the basis for detailed analysis, open discussion, and recommendations as to the type of action that an organization should take. In contrast to more traditional forms of instruction, such as lecture presentations, the case method requires you to become much more actively involved in the learning process. It has been said that "in the case method, birds learn to fly; with other techniques they are often given an airline pass."[2] You will be expected to step into the organization and feel the excitement, responsibilities, and tension of a real management situation. Such an attitude has been aptly described by Malcolm P. McNair, for many years a distinguished case teacher at the Harvard Business School, as "the willing suspension of disbelief," that is, temporarily forgetting that one is a student in a class.[3]

A strategic management case is typically a detailed record of managerial challenges top executives of an organization face. It generally includes a chronology of major events in the organizations's history; important sales, cost, and financial data; as well as opinions and perspectives provided by key executives. Firms in the public and private sector do not, of course, exist in isolation. Thus, a very important aspect of strategic management cases is the variety of information about external factors such as key competitors, the nature of industry competition, and important environmental events and trends.

As you read cases and begin to analyze them, you will see that the critical issues are not usually explicitly identified. Information is somewhat ambiguous and irrelevant. Most important, there is no correct answer to the problems or challenges facing the organization.[4] While these characteristics of cases may be frustrating, they make your role as a strategic manager more realistic. These attributes, discussed in Exhibit 12.1, also characterize the challenges that today's executives must face on a daily basis.

Given this realism, cases are useful to students for four reasons:

1. Case analysis will help you develop analytical and judgment skills.

Case analysis requires you to observe, diagnose, synthesize, theorize, and apply concepts to real world situations.[5] Such learning helps students develop what has been called "complicated understanding," that is, complex thinking skills as well as an awareness that multiple perspectives to a problem exist and that there is no "one right answer."[6] Complicated understanding helps students avoid seeking simplistic solutions to organizational

EXHIBIT 12.1
Attributes of Strategic Management Cases

1. *The critical issues are not explicitly identified.*
Throughout most of your educational experience, you were required to solve problems that were generally explicitly stated. However, the case method, like the "real world," assumes that problems are seldom clearly defined. Therefore, one of the critical skills that the case method helps students to develop is the ability to identify, from the description of the situation, the underlying issues and problems.

2. *The information is ambiguous and contradictory.*
A case typically depicts an unstructured problem situation. It includes different points of view expressed by key executives as well as the case writer! Often, there will be many contradictions and some of the information may even appear to be ambiguous. Thus, with the case method, students must rely on and further develop their judgment skills in evaluating a wide variety of information and sources.

3. *Some information may be redundant or irrelevant.*
Typically, cases are several pages long and contain information on a number of aspects including the firm's history, key personnel, financial performance, and products and markets. All of this information may not be necessary to identify and solve the major problems facing the organization. Today's manager is inundated with a tremendous amount of information from both inside and outside the company. Thus, a critical skill for managerial success is the ability to decide what is relevant and what is not. The case method helps to develop this vital skill.

4. *Typically, there is no unique answer.*
One of the frustrations that students often experience with the case method is the absence of neat, clear, and unique solutions. However, this is true of the problems faced by practicing managers. Depending upon the assumptions that one may make, there may be multiple acceptable solutions to a business problem. When proposing recommendations, students, therefore, must make explicit the critical assumptions upon which their recommendations are based.

Source: Adapted from Edge, A. E., & Coleman, D. R. (1986). *The guide to case analysis and reporting* (3rd ed.). Honolulu: Systems Logistics, Inc.

problems and issues. Also, individuals who are able to develop such skills should be better able to generate more effective action alternatives because they become more fully aware of key organizational and environmental issues. Thus, students' ability to understand complex problems is enhanced.

2. Case analysis will help you learn how to ask the right questions.

A successful executive once commented: "Ninety percent of the task of a top manager is to ask useful questions. Answers are relatively easy to find, but asking good questions, that is the most critical skill."[7] Even if your instructor assigns discussion questions for each case, he or she is not preempting your task of identifying the problems in the case. You must ask: "What are the problems which this manager has to resolve?" Students and managers alike must avoid the tendency to analyze and evaluate facts and figures before carefully determining what problems need to be addressed.

Case analysis enables aspiring managers to improve their ability to resolve underlying *problems* instead of focusing on the more superficial *symptoms.* To identify and ask the right questions, managers must go beyond symptoms and uncover problems. For example, as discussed in Chapter 3, Pfizer, a large multinational pharmaceutical company, experienced relatively poor financial performance in the early 1980s. One of the *symptoms* of this problem was a lack of new products. Upon further analysis, it was found that the underlying *problem* was top management's decision to reduce research and development spending in order to improve short-term financial performance.

Application 12.1 provides an example of the effective identification of key problems and issues facing a firm. Here, the issues are comprehensive and include elements of both strategy formulation (e.g., what diversification strategy to undertake, in what market segments to compete) as well as strategy implementation (e.g., the organization of the marketing function, the relative amount of centralization versus decentralization in the organization structure, the staffing of the accounting and data processing functions).

3. Cases will expose you to a wide variety of organizations and managerial situations.

The variety of real-life situations, depicted in the cases in this section of the text, provide you with a broad base of experiences. From this, you are able to develop insights into the nature of many types of managerial tasks and responsibilities. You can use such learning activities to help assess your strengths, limitations, and interests. Therefore, you should be able to make more informed career decisions.

4. Experience in analyzing cases enhances your oral and written communication skills.

The ability to articulate one's perspectives and insights, listen carefully to others, and incorporate their insights into one's perspective are vital skills for all managers. Consider the example of an engineer, a former colleague of one of the authors, who spent several intense months (including many unpaid overtime hours) working on a project that involved rearranging the repair operations at a large telecommunications facility. He did an outstanding job coordinating the project which was completed on schedule and within budget. The annual savings generated were substantial—much greater than the original projections. However, because the engineer's formal presentation to top management was very poorly organized, the project was not well-received.

Managers must also be able to express themselves effectively in written form. Devel-

Application 12.1

Issue Identification at a Liquified Petroleum (Propane) Marketing Business

Mega Corporation* is a large marketer of liquified petroleum (propane) in the United States. Mega's parent company had recently undergone a leveraged buyout (LBO) in order to avoid a possible takeover. The LBO resulted in the assumption of a massive amount of debt which placed intense pressure on its subsidiaries, including Mega Corporation, to improve earnings and generate cash.

To turn around Mega Corporation's sagging performance, a new CEO was hired. After noting the poor morale and teamwork among the senior executives, the CEO hired a consultant to help perform a strategic analysis. The consultant conducted interviews with the senior executives and suggested many issues that needed to be resolved. These included the following:

The Top Management Team

How do we structure the group better? Do we need two groups—one composed of the new CEO and the senior vice presidents (SVPs) to drive strategy, and a larger group to review and set policy? How often should various groups meet, and what should be their character? How do we improve the level of trust, and reduce turf protecting? How can we increase accountability?

Corporate Strategy

What short-term (1 to 2 years) strategies should be set for ourselves? How do we improve inaccuracies in market forecasting? Should we keep the wholesale business? How do we go about capturing greater market share against sleepy competitors? Should we concentrate our focus on certain market segments? What do we do about terminals and gas processing? What long-term (3 to 5 years) strategies should we adopt? What kind of diversification strategy, if any, should we have? Should we develop a supply business for other LPG firms? What R&D should we undertake?

Product Flow or Distribution Process

Should we perform an in-depth study to determine the real costs of moving propane through the system, and the best ways to manage the flow? Can we better articulate how customer problems and inquiries get handled so that our response is better? How can the SVPs of marketing, supply, and transportation work more closely together to improve the efficiency of the process?

Organization Structure

Do we have the right balance in our structure? Should we divide marketing into two departments—east and west? Should the transportation and supply departments be combined? Should the data processing and personnel departments report to the CEO? Should training and safety personnel continue to report to the legal department? What should our overall position on centralization versus decentralization be?

Corporate Staff

Do we have too many people in the accounting and data processing department? How do we improve the response of data processing to our information needs? What do we do about the staff culture, which seems to be slow and still attuned to the regulation era? Do we have enough high-powered talent below the top level? Do we have enough people in the legal department to handle lobbying?

The identification of the above issues served to form the basis for numerous subsequent planning meetings and retreats attended by Mega's top executives. Soon, action plans for implementing a carefully thought-out strategy, which emphasized aggressive financial goals and growth through market development and acquisitions, was in place.

The new strategy was very successful. At the end of the first year, the company had significantly exceeded its profit plan and its return on assets was up 40 percent. Also, Mega's new CEO confidently predicted that the subsidiary's profits would double within 3 years of his appointment.

Source

Adapted from Greiner, L., & Bhambri, A. (1990, March/April). The dynamics of strategic change at Mega Corporation. *Planning Review*, pp. 18–26. (With permission.)

* The actual name of the firm is withheld for reasons of confidentiality.

oping the ability to clearly and persuasively articulate one's views and write succinctly and forcefully serves to strengthen one's credibility. Such skills require extensive practice. The written case assignments that are typically required in the strategic management course help to develop this valuable skill.

HOW TO PERFORM A STRATEGIC ANALYSIS

Every case is unique. In this section we will look at guidelines on how to complete a detailed and thorough analysis. First, we will suggest a general approach to keep in mind regarding the overall process of a strategic analysis and then we will outline nine steps that provide a framework for conducting a strategic analysis.

The Overall Process of Strategic Analysis

In strategic analysis, many alternate paths may reach the same goal. Different individuals may have alternate, and equally effective, approaches to solving problems. However, there is strong agreement on a few of the important, sequential phases that one should follow when conducting a strategic analysis.[8]

Phase 1. Read the case quickly in order to develop a general understanding of its major issues. Ask yourself such questions as "What is the case about?" and "What types of information am I being given to analyze?"

Phase 2. Reread the case carefully. Underline key facts and identify important information. Ask yourself, "What are the important issues?" and "What are the basic problems that this manager must resolve?" Strive to put yourself in the position of the key decision maker. That is, develop a sense of involvement.

Phase 3. Decide what issues must be resolved and provide answers to them. Use and analyze the data and information in the case. Ensure that the assumptions you are making are reasonable (e.g., approximately 10 percent annual increase in demand for a product line over the next 2 years, no major change in the value of the dollar for the next year).

Phase 4. Develop a set of recommendations that your analysis supports. Explicitly evaluate and reject alternate courses of action based upon your analysis. Carefully address implementation considerations—that is, how can the company attain the recommended actions? Be sure to take personnel, financial, and other resources and constraints into account.

A Framework for Strategic Analysis

A detailed strategic analysis will deal with each of the nine points described below. However, not all of these will be equally important in every case, and one part of doing a good strategic analysis is determining what issues are most critical. The nine points roughly correspond to the sequential ordering of the chapters in the text. The purpose of the discussion here is to summarize these ideas and show how they fit together to form the basis for understanding the strategic situation facing a firm.

1. Mission and Objectives. Successful analysis depends upon understanding what the organization is attempting to accomplish. This requires more than just the consideration of a profit motive. Normally, companies must be concerned about maintaining some level of profitability if they are to remain in business. However, beyond a profit objective, virtually all organizations have other missions which they hope to accomplish. (Obviously, in nonprofit organizations nonfinancial objectives are preeminently important.) Companies typically have a wide range of constituencies, or stakeholders. While all of these stakeholders may benefit from the firm's being profitable enough to remain in business, they may not all benefit from the firm's narrowly focused pursuit of maximum profits. Usually, managers pursue profits as one of several objectives. The only proper strategic analysis of such a firm is one that considers *all* the most important objectives being sought. A useful way to understand a firm's total set of objectives is to consider its history. In most firms, current objectives have grown out of yesterday's corporate experiences, much like an individual's background shapes his or her aspirations for the future. To understand this background, it may be helpful to construct a chronology of important, "character shaping" events in the history of a firm. In constructing such a chronology, seek to answer questions like the following: Who were the founders of the firm? What led to their initial success? What obstacles has the firm overcome? Who are its managerial "folk heroes" ? This information will help you understand the nature and importance of a corporate mission and managerial objectives that go beyond mere profit targets.

2. External Analysis. Understanding a firm's strengths and weaknesses is useful only when looked at in conjunction with information about the opportunities and threats that the environment holds for the business. For purposes of analysis, the environment of a firm can be broadly classified into two categories. First, the competitive environment, which consists of forces such as the power of substitute products and the height of entry barriers which determine the nature of competition in an industry. Second, the general environment, which includes changes in factors such as technology, regulation, general economic indicators, and so on, can have a dramatic effect on a firm as well as the industry in which it competes. Both of these environments typically have a significant impact on important decisions which managers must make. Moreover, these two types of environments are interrelated and one cannot be studied independently of the other.

Analyzing the threats and opportunities which the environment holds for a business —the subject of Chapter 2—is a vital part of what is commonly referred to as a SWOT analysis (*s*trengths, *w*eaknesses, *o*pportunities, *t*hreats). What good is expertise in buggy whip production (an internal strength) if automobiles are looming on the horizon (an external threat)? How serious a weakness is a public utility's poor advertising skills (an internal factor) if the public service commission (an external factor) plans to continue to grant it a monopoly? It is only by considering external opportunities and threats that internal strengths and weaknesses take on their full meaning. Such external factors cover a broad spectrum of considerations. To help tap information sources covering this wide range of environmental factors, the appendix to this chapter identifies a number of reference sources to help you research businesses and industries.

Environmental analysis is vital for organizations in both the private and public sectors. Application 12.2 lists some of the important trends in the general environment which were

Application 12.2

Trends in the General Environment, According to the Internal Revenue Service

To provide a sense of overall direction and to improve the efficiency, effectiveness, and productivity of a staff that is geographically dispersed, the IRS has developed a sophisticated management system. A strategic business plan is at the heart of this system. The plan encompasses the next 5 years and is regularly updated to recognize new environmental developments and to ensure that it is in conformity with the mission of the IRS. The strategic business plan is an evolving source of guidance to the IRS and all of its management processes are based on the plan. It provides the IRS with an enhanced ability to anticipate and manage environmental challenges.

Below are some of the major technological, demographic, socioeconomic, and regulatory trends that the IRS takes into consideration while developing the strategic business plan for the period through fiscal year 1996.

Technology

- Information technology will continue making practical, fast-paced advances which will impact on our systems modernization efforts and tax administration in general.
- Database technology will continue to be the most sophisticated way to organize complex groups of information and distribute that information to diverse user functions. The entire tax system will eventually migrate to a DBMS/data management environment.
- Telecommunications networks will provide for transmission of voice, data, and video information.
- Information will be electronically captured, images of returns will be electronically stored and retrieved, and information and funds will be electronically transmitted.
- Use of artificial intelligence and expert systems will enable workers to give more accurate responses to taxpayers and will assist in work-load prioritization.
- The organizational impact of information technology must be planned for and managed. New technology and systems will shape our organization, procedures, and workplace culture in ways beyond how they affect individual programs.
- Training requirements for both new and experienced employees will increase substantially because of impending technological change and lower skill levels of new employees.

Demographic Trends

- Individual returns are projected to increase by 7.5 percent between 1989 and 1996. The trend toward smaller households—more childless couples, single-parent families, and unrelated persons living together—translates into more tax returns and increased work load. Two-paycheck families continue to increase the filing of multiple schedules and more complex returns.
- Return work load will be increasingly complex because older Americans are the wealthiest segment of the population and large numbers of "baby boomers" are starting their own businesses. Noncompliance is generally high among small businesses.
- The mobility of the taxpaying public is increasing.
- Demands on taxpayer service and compliance activities for educating taxpayers and ensuring compliance will increase because of new immigrants who will account for a large portion of U.S. population growth.

Socioeconomic Trends

- Internationalization of trade, communications, financial transactions, and corporate organization structure requires new approaches to international returns processing and compliance efforts.
- With federal employment perceived as a less attractive alternative to private industry, retention of our best employees is an increasingly serious problem.
- Recruitment efforts will be impacted by the declining population among college-age persons, growth in families headed by single parents, and by competition for qualified workers in the rapidly growing information and services industries.
- The age of the average worker will increase from 36 to 39 by the year 2000. By 1994, 25 percent of IRS professional/technical employees will be eligible to retire.
- Technological advances mean employers are requiring higher skill levels, while the U.S. education system is

Application 12.2 (cont.)

producing workers who have lower capabilities in math, problem solving, and communications.

- Increasing pressure will continue to be placed on the IRS to provide high-quality service in a time of changing tax law, increasing work load and expectations, and strong fiscal conservatism.
- Public demand for return-preparation assistance and account-status information is increasing.
- There is an increasing need to structure jobs around worker requirements (e.g., job sharing, part-time positions, telecommuting, etc.) because of the decreasing numbers of available workers.

Regulatory Trends

- Regulatory changes continue to add complexity and increase administrative costs for major support services.
- Trends toward decentralization of certain operational aspects of administrative support functions, such as building management, employment screening, and so forth, require new skills for the IRS.
- Tax laws have changed at an increasing pace for more than a decade and continued change is inevitable.

Source

Strategic business plan thru fiscal year 1996. (revised 8/90). Document 7382. Washington, DC: Internal Revenue Service, Department of the Treasury.

identified as part of the strategic business plan (through fiscal year 1996) prepared by the United States Internal Revenue Service.

Exhibit 12.2 suggests a number of items which may be useful starting places for conducting a SWOT analysis.

3. Internal Analysis. In this part of the SWOT analysis, one examines what *internal* factors create competitive muscle for the firms, and also identify those which serve to limit its power. (These issues are addressed in Chapter 3.) The value chain concept is a very powerful tool in analyzing a firm's strengths and weaknesses. The value chain views a firm as a collection of activities necessary to design, produce, market, deliver, and support its products. Analyzing each of these activities in detail enables managers to understand the behavior of costs as well as the potential sources of differentiation.

Conducting a firm's SWOT analysis also typically entails a thorough analysis of the firm's financial situation since financial standing is so often a key strength or weakness. (An appendix to Chapter 3 offers detailed guidelines for carrying out such a financial analysis.) Beyond financial considerations, there are numerous other issues which may be appropriately raised in assessing the company's strengths and weaknesses.

4. Business-Level Strategy. A company's strategy can be analyzed on four complementary levels. The most fundamental level of strategy formulation concerns the development of strategy for a single business (Chapter 4). The business may be a stand alone or it may be a strategic business unit (SBU) within a larger corporation. Because a corporation may consist of several different businesses, it follows that it may also be involved with several different business-level strategies. One would not expect a business producing heavy industrial turbines to have a strategy identical to another business producing consumer light bulbs—even if they are in the same corporation—as at the General Electric Corporation.

Business-level strategies are designed to help the business compete more effectively against others in its marketplace. More specifically, these strategies are designed to give the

EXHIBIT 12.2
SWOT Analysis: An Illustrative Framework

Strengths	*Weaknesses*	*Opportunities*	*Threats*
Effective material and inventory control systems	Outdated equipment compared to that of key competitors	Diversification into related product-market areas	Market penetration by foreign competitors
Innovative sales promotion and advertising	Inadequate market research to identify customer segments and needs	Forward or backward integration to enhance competitive position	Intensifying domestic competition
Promptness of attention to customer complaints	Delays in providing replacement parts and repair services	Increase in the height of entry barriers	Decreasing entry barriers
Timely and accurate information to management on general and competitive environments	Inadequate information support in making strategic and routine decisions	Decreasing labor costs	Better and cheaper substitute products
Effective procedures for recruiting, training, and promoting employees	Unfavorable relations with trade unions	Appeal to additional customer segments	Increasing material costs
Success of research and development activities (in leading to product and process innovations)	Ineffective working relationships between R&D personnel and other departments	Demographic changes leading to increased market demand	Increasing concentration among buyer groups
Good, long-term relationships with reliable suppliers	Excessive dependence on a single supplier	Unfavorable sociocultural changes	Adverse demographic changes
Favorable relationships with the public	Inadequate strategic planning systems	Deregulation providing new market opportunities	Sociocultural changes that depress demand
Liquidity, leverage, activity, and profitability ratios superior to industry norms and key competitors	Inability to raise additional funds	Technological developments that help extend the growth plan of the product life cycle	Increased environmental legislation
Capacity to adapt and evolve, consistent with demands of changes in environment and strategy	Inability of the culture to foster innovation, creativity, and openness to new ideas	Decreasing cost of funds	Potential product obsolescence because of technological developments
Good relationships with policy makers and government officials	Poor relationships with the media	Declining trade barriers in foreign countries	Rising interest rates
Thorough understanding of overall strategy by functional-area managers	A lack of effective integration of activities across functional areas		Political instability in countries where foreign operations are located

business some advantage in terms of its differentiation, cost, or response time. Such competitive advantages are again based on understanding the match between the firm's strengths and weaknesses, and the environment's opportunities and threats. If the firm has to face international competitors that have an advantage of lower-cost labor, does this represent a threat in terms of the relative costs of its products? If so, what strengths can the firm draw upon to overcome this cost disadvantage? If such an offsetting strength is not there, what would need to be done to develop one? By answering such questions, SWOT becomes the basis for analyzing and formulating strategies at the business level.

5. Functional-Level Strategy. The most "fine-grained" strategic analysis takes place at what is known as the functional level (Chapter 5). Businesses usually consist of various functions, each with its own strategy. Some of the key functions in typical businesses are marketing, research and development, engineering, purchasing, manufacturing, quality control, sales, accounting, and personnel. Each of these functions has its own unique role to play in adding value to the overall business and each function has its own customers too, be they internal (e.g., the purchasing department supplying material to its customers in manufacturing) or external (e.g., the sales department shipping finished goods to retail outlets). In serving these customers, managers of the various functions try to achieve the most favorable blend of quality, cost, and speed possible. Hopefully, by this point it is clear that achieving the best possible blend of these attributes is dependent on matching internal strengths and weaknesses to external opportunities and threats.

6. Corporate-Level Strategy. Analyzing a corporate strategy involves understanding what business or businesses the company is in or should be in (Chapter 6). Some corporations are single-business entities, while others consist of several virtually unrelated businesses. However, most corporations lie somewhere between these two extremes, often having several businesses which are similar enough to one another that they may share or exchange resources with one another or with the corporate parent. Determining the mix of businesses, and the manner in which they will interact with one another, are the two essential elements of a corporate strategy. The evaluation of such a corporate strategy can best be made in light of the SWOT analysis described above. Is the mix of businesses appropriate, given the opportunities and threats present in the environment? If the corporation is to alter its mix of businesses, should it build upon strengths already existing in its core businesses or should it move in new directions to avoid environmental threats looming ahead?

7. International-Level Strategy. When a corporation expands to cover more than its home country, an extension of its corporate-level strategy is required. Strategy formulation at the international level must overcome several potentially conflicting forces (Chapter 7). One set of forces drives managers to develop individualized strategies for each country in which the corporation operates. Such strategies are called multidomestic strategies because they treat the multiple national markets being served as if they were individual domestic markets. A second set of forces encourages the firm to develop a single highly integrated strategy that will be applied to all markets served worldwide. This is called a global strategy. (Details on the forces driving a strategy to be multidomestic or global are given in Chapter 7.) Research and experience suggest that the most successful international strategies are those that combine elements of multidomestic and global strategies.

8. Strategy Implementation. The first seven points that we have addressed primarily deal with how effectively a firm has formulated its strategy. Now, the focus turns to how well a firm implements its strategy through its structure, processes, and systems. (These issues are addressed in Chapters 8, 9, 10, and 11.) Without careful attention to such issues, even well-articulated and sound strategies may go astray, failing to achieve their intended performance outcomes. Managers must constantly endeavor to ensure that the desired strategy is consistent with many other important organizational elements. For example, to achieve ambitious revenue targets, a firm must have a reward system that motivates its sales force, and an effective strategic control system which detects important changes in customer tastes and preferences and provides meaningful up-to-date information on product sales by key market segments. Successful firms also achieve consistency between their strategy and their organization structure. Firms following a strategy of diversification into unrelated product-market areas, for example, should adopt a decentralized organization structure to enable it to react quickly to changing market trends.

Two of the most difficult issues to analyze that play a vital role in strategy implementation are the quality of an organization's leadership and culture. These vital factors strongly influence a firm's performance. Among the questions that must be considered: Do the top executives have a clear vision for the organization? Do managers motivate and inspire employees at all levels of the organization? Does the organization's culture serve to establish and reinforce its dominant values of excellence and ethical behavior?

9. Developing Recommendations. You are now ready to begin what is perhaps the most creative and exciting aspect of strategic analysis—developing recommendations. In a sense, the recommendations that you develop constitute the solutions to the problems and issues that you have identified and analyzed. To a large extent, the quality of your recommendations is highly dependent on how skillfully and thoroughly you have analyzed the organization.

Like the issues that have been suggested and the problems that have been identified, your recommendations must be as comprehensive as possible. They must address important factors related to both the formulation and implementation of the firm's strategy. Furthermore, recommendations must include clear action plans with explicit time frames.

In evaluating recommendations, the following criteria should be carefully considered:[9]

- *Goal consistency:* Are the recommendations consistent with the organization's mission, goals, and objectives? Are the recommendations consistent with each other?
- *Strategic relevance:* Do the recommendations address the basic problems identified? Do the recommendations lead to a sustainable competitive advantage?
- *Organizational capability:* Does the organization possess the financial, human, and technical capabilities necessary to implement the recommendations?
- *Political feasibility:* Will the recommendations encounter excessive resistance from either the CEO or other powerful interest groups in the organization?

GETTING THE MOST OUT OF CASE ANALYSIS

This chapter has discussed many potential benefits of the case method which are vital for successful managerial careers. We will now propose some suggestions on how to maximize your learning experience in class discussions and in written case analyses, respectively.

Class Discussion of Strategic Management Cases

The value of the case method is strongly determined by the value of in-class discussions. Fast-moving and insightful discussions enhance learning and spark enthusiasm for future class sessions. Below are several tips to facilitate the learning process.

- *Take a stand on issues.* Although one should not be closed-minded, it is important to defend ideas in which you strongly believe. Not only does this enable you to enhance your skills of persuasion, but it also contributes to a more thorough and meaningful class discussion.

- *Keep an open mind.* An interesting and thorough class discussion will inevitably bring out many different perspectives on a problem—generally a more complete analysis than that possible by any single individual. If you dismiss the views of others on emotional or intuitive grounds without carefully evaluating them, you may miss much of the benefit from discussions. Critical analysis and a willingness to consider alternate perspectives are hallmarks of good management.
- *Bring in your outside experience.* You may have already had a good deal of work experience in public or private sector organizations. Many valuable insights and perspectives can be brought to bear on strategic management cases by relating them to other organizational situations. Such contributions generally enhance the overall quality of case discussions.
- *Incorporate previous cases into class discussion.* Learning can be enhanced and further reinforced by including similar or relevant issues from previous cases which were analyzed during the term. Such insights provide additional frames of reference for analyzing a case and help to broaden everyone's perspectives on key issues.
- *Bring in outside research.* If you are particularly interested in a case, you can provide additional insights by conducting some library research. This may include obtaining financial and product-market information on other firms in the industry, investigating overall industry trends, and so on. Such information may spur additional discussion and provide new perspectives on key issues in a given case. (However, since such information may unintentionally interfere with the instructor's learning objectives for a case, you should inquire in advance if such research is encouraged.)
- *Be concise and to the point.* In case discussions, you must try to be succinct and to the point. Brevity and hard-hitting arguments naturally improve the strength or punch of your position on an issue. It also helps increase the overall flow of class discussion and make better use of class time. Recall the adage: "Many rise to the occasion, but few know when to sit down."[10]
- *Get off to a fast start.* Don't be shy. The course will be more enjoyable and meaningful if you regularly volunteer.
- *Critically evaluate your own performance.* Many successful executives find it useful to periodically evaluate their performance in meetings, important decisions, interactions with fellow managers, and so on. Such questions as "Where was I particularly effective?" and "What issues did I not handle well and how can I improve?" help managers learn from their experience. Such an approach should also be taken by students when evaluating their class performance. Be a hard "self-grader."
- *Learn from other students.* Every case discussion will invariably result in a wide variety of contributions—insightful, witty, absurd, creative, irrelevant, mediocre, and so on. You should observe your fellow students' approach to addressing key issues, problem solving, and other important skills. Such observations may provide new insights and strengthen your analytical and communication skills.

Written Case Analyses

Many of the guidelines we have suggested for preparing cases for class discussion also apply to developing written analyses. Similar to the preparation for class discussions, it is difficult to prescribe an explicit and detailed framework to follow for all written case assignments. The nature and objectives of written assignments may vary considerably. For example, some written assignments may be structured. Your instructor may prepare a few questions that focus on a specific issue or problem. Other assignments may be more unstructured, as when you are asked to identify and resolve a broad range of issues a company faces at a particular point in time.

Below are some general tips for improving the overall quality of your written case assignments.

- *Achieve careful coordination among group members on group assignments.* Written case assignments are often completed in small groups. For groups to be effective, it is essential to maintain an effective level of collaboration and interaction among members. This increases the potential for building on everyone's strengths and improves the natural flow of the written analysis. Be sure to allow sufficient time to coordinate the activities and subprojects completed by the individual group members and implement constructive suggestions.

- *Avoid extensive restatement of the case material.* Written case analyses require more than an excellent writing style, superb organization, and a professional appearance. You must also be rigorous, insightful, and minimize the tendency to restate facts in the case. Go well beyond mere description and routine analysis. For example, don't simply calculate and report financial ratios. Rather, address such issues as:

  How have the ratios changed over time?

  How do the ratios compare to key competitors and industry standards?

  What insights can be gained by viewing financial ratios in relation to each other instead of only in isolation?

- *Make judicious use of tables and graphs.* Tables and graphs are very useful for presenting factual information which supports your arguments and recommendations. Tables and graphs also help present a large amount of qualitative (e.g., types of products a firm produces) and quantitative (e.g., annual sales and financial ratios) data in a concise and easy-to-read manner without detracting from the natural flow of your analysis. All tables and graphs should be carefully referenced in the text of the report and clearly labeled.

  To be effective, tables and graphs must provide information that is very pertinent to the key issues in a case. Excessive use may weaken the overall impact of the report and dilute some of the more substantive issues.

- *Eliminate spelling errors and use proper grammar.* Your completed manuscript must have a professional appearance. Typos and errors in spelling, punctuation, and grammar can obscure or undermine some of the substantive issues in your case analysis. Be sure to plan for sufficient time to proofread your written analysis prior to the due date. Also, refer to a dictionary and thesaurus to improve your spelling and word usage.

Summary

This chapter addresses the importance of analyzing strategic situations and cases in a strategic management course. There are many attributes of the case method which contribute to its relevance to aspiring managers. Among these are critical issues are not explicitly identified, information is ambiguous and sometimes contradictory, some information may be redundant and irrelevant, and there is typically no one right answer. Case analysis is a useful pedagogy for four major reasons. First, it serves to develop analytical skills. Second, cases help aspiring managers learn how to ask the right questions. Third, it enables students to gain exposure to a wide variety of organizations and managerial situations. Fourth, it improves one's oral and written communication skills.

There are several important guidelines for conducting a detailed and thorough case analysis. A general approach is proposed for conducting strategic analysis. This consists of four phases: a rapid reading of the case to gain a general understanding of the central issues, a more careful reading to identify key issues and problems, the determination of what issues must be resolved, and the provision of a set of recommendations. In addition to the four phases suggested for a general analysis, a more detailed framework for strategic analysis was suggested which corresponds to the first eleven chapters of the text. The proposed nine steps include mission and objectives, external analysis, internal analysis, business-level strategy, functional-level strategy, corporate-level strategy, international-level strategy, strategy implementation, and recommendations.

Improving one's performance in the class discussion of strategic management cases involves taking a stand on issues, keeping an open mind, being concise, and critically evaluating your performance. Written analyses of strategic management cases should utilize careful coordination among group members, avoid extensive restatement of case material, and make judicious use of tables and graphs.

Notes

1. Among the sources that this chapter draws on are Bonoma, T. V. (1981). *Questions and answers about case learning.* Harvard Business School Case 9-582-059; Edge, A. E., & Coleman, D. R. (1986). *The guide to case analysis and reporting* (3rd ed.). Honolulu: Systems Logistics, Inc. Gragg, C. I. (1940). *Because wisdom can't be told.* Harvard Business School Case 451-005; Hammond, J. S., Corey, E. R., & Marshall, M. (1980). *Learning by the case method.* Harvard Business School Case 9-376-241; and Masoner, M. (1988). *An audit of the case study method.* New York: Praeger; Ronstadt, R. (1980). *The art of case analysis: A guide to the diagnosis of business situations.* Dover, MA: Lord Publishing.
2. Bonoma (Ref. 1), op. cit., p. 8.
3. Edge & Coleman (Ref. 1), op. cit., p. 7.
4. Edge & Coleman (Ref. 1), op. cit., p. 9.
5. Lockwood, C. A., Keats, B. W., & Dess, G. G. (1989–1990). Bridging the strategy research and practice "gap." *The Organizational Behavior and Teaching Review, 14*(1), 82–96.
6. Weick, K. (1979). *The social psychology of organizing.* Reading, MA: Addison-Wesley.
7. Hammond, Corey, & Marshall (Ref. 1), op. cit., p. 2.

8. The following phases are a synthesis of Hammond, J. S., Corey, E. R., & Marshall, M. (1980). *Learning by the case method.* Harvard Business School Case 9-376-241, and Bonoma, T. V. (1981). *Questions and answers about case learning.* Harvard Business School Case 9-582-059.
9. Adapted from Rumelt, R. P. (1979). Strategy evaluation. In D. E. Schendel & C. W. Hofer (Eds.). *Strategic management: A new view of business policy and planning.* Boston: Little, Brown.
10. Edge, & Coleman (Ref. 1), op. cit., p. 14.

Appendix to Chapter 12
Sources of Company and Industry Information*

This appendix provides a brief overview of important sources of information that may be useful while conducting company and industry analyses. Most university libraries and some public libraries carry these reference materials. In addition, there are numerous computer databases available, many of which are available at modest fees to academic users.

We have organized these references into eight categories: Industry Surveys and Rankings, Industry Ratios, Industry Forecasts, National and Industry Statistics, Industry Trade Publications, Magazine/Newspaper Indexes, Databases, and Information on Publicly-held Corporations.

I. Industry Surveys and Rankings

"Annual Report on American Industry" in FORBES. New York: Forbes, Inc. (first January issue each year)
Covers 1,177 of the largest public companies in 20 major industry groups and 70 subgroups. Compares them in terms of profitability, growth, and marketing performance. Corporations are ranked against their immediate competitors, firms in related industry groups, and against all other companies.
HG 5001. F6[1]

CORPORATE AND INDUSTRY RESEARCH REPORTS (CIRR). Eastchester, NY: JA Micropublishing. 1982–1989. Continued by Bowker Business Research, 1990–1991.
Reports prepared by analysts from investment firms and brokerage houses give analysis, projections, forecasts, market strategies, economic trends, and product developments on over 5,000 companies and 300 industries. Includes comparative data on companies within industries. Full-text reports are in microfiche format. Publication has ceased. See Investext entry below.
HG4001.C531

INTERNATIONAL DIRECTORY OF COMPANY HISTORIES (in five volumes). Chicago: St. James Press.
Narrative histories of 1,250 of the world's largest and most influential companies in 36 industries assembled from magazines, books, annual reports, and material supplied by the

* This appendix is largely based on materials prepared by Ruthie Brock and Tommie Wingfield, Business Librarians at the University of Texas at Arlington. We gratefully acknowledge their contribution.

[1] Library of Congress and Superintendent of Documents call numbers are provided. Some libraries may use other classifications or variations of these call numbers.

companies themselves. Indicates whether the company is public or private.
HD2721. I68 1988

INVESTEXT (CD-ROM). Belmont, CA: Information Access Co. 1990– (monthly)
Similar to CIRR, this source contains full-text reports prepared by analysts from investment firms and brokerage houses which give analysis, projections, forecasts, market strategies, economic trends, and product developments on over 8,000 companies, 2,000 of which are publicly held, and 53 high-tech industries. Includes comparative data on companies within industries. Reports can be printed or down-loaded to disk.

MANUFACTURING USA: INDUSTRY ANALYSES, STATISTICS, AND LEADING COMPANIES. First Edition. Detroit: Gale Research.
A comprehensive guide to economic activity in 448 manufacturing industries. Provides unique analysis and synthesis of federal statistics.
HD9721. M364

MOODY'S INVESTORS FACT SHEETS: INDUSTRY REVIEW. New York: Moody's Investors Service. (looseleaf)
Contains key financial information, comparative statistics, operating data, and ratios on over 4,000 companies. Information is arranged into 140 industry groups.
HG4907. M662

STANDARD & POOR'S INDUSTRY SURVEYS. New York: Standard & Poor's Corp. (annual with updates)
Compiling basic data on over 20 leading U.S. industries, the "Basic Analysis" for each industry gives commentary, analysis, projections, and comparisons of leading companies. The "Current Analysis" is a supplement for reporting recent developments in the industry.
HG4902. S82

U.S. Office of Management and Budget, Executive Office of the President. STANDARD INDUSTRIAL CLASSIFICATION MANUAL. Washington, DC: U.S. Government Printing Office, 1987.
The standard industrial classification (SIC) is a numerical system utilized by the U.S. government to facilitate the collection and dissemination of statistics on industries. This manual contains the latest revision of SIC codes and cross reference tables to previous codes.
PrEx 2.6/2: In 27/987

VALUE LINE INVESTMENT SURVEY. New York: A. Bernhard & Co. (loose-leaf with weekly additions)
Analyzes and reports on over 1,700 companies in 90+ industries. Includes a 10-year statistical history of 23 investment factors for each company and an overview for each of the covered industries. Company and industry reports are published quarterly with interim weekly updates.
HG4501. V26

WARD'S BUSINESS DIRECTORY OF U.S. PRIVATE AND PUBLIC COMPANIES. Detroit: Gale Research. (annual)
In addition to the standard alphabetical listing, companies are ranked by sales within four

digit industry (SIC) categories. A special feature section provides totals (sales, employees, number of companies) per industry and revenue per employee of the top 1,000 companies. No minimum sales for inclusion permits some coverage of smaller, private firms.
HG4057. A458

II. Industry Ratios

Dun & Bradstreet Credit Services. INDUSTRY NORMS AND KEY BUSINESS RATIOS. New York: Dun & Bradstreet Credit Services. (annual)
Provides industry norms and key business ratios on 800 lines of business as defined by SIC codes. Ratios for single year only.
HF5681. R25 I52

Robert Morris Associates. ANNUAL STATEMENT STUDIES. Philadelphia: Robert Morris Associates. (annual)
Contains industry norms and financial and operating ratios for about 300 lines of business including manufacturers, wholesalers, retailers, services, and contractors. Includes historical data for 5 years.
HF5681. B2 R6

Troy, Leo. ALMANAC OF BUSINESS AND INDUSTRIAL FINANCIAL RATIOS. Englewood Cliffs, NJ: Prentice-Hall. (annual)
Financial and operating ratios for about 160 industries including banks and financial industries, as well as the usual manufacturing, wholesaling, and retailing industries. Derived from Internal Revenue Service data.
HF5681. R25 A45

III. Industry Forecasts

International Trade Administration, U.S. Department of Commerce. U.S. INDUSTRIAL OUTLOOK. Washington, DC: U.S. Government Printing Office. (annual)
Useful volume for information on recent trends and outlook for 3 to 5 years in over 350 industries. The brief narrative with statistics contains discussions of change in supply and demand for each industry, developments in domestic and overseas markets, price changes, employment trends, and capital investment.
C61.34

PREDICASTS FORECASTS. Cleveland, OH: Predicasts, Inc. (quarterly with annual cumulations)
Gives short- and long-range forecast statistics for basic economic indicators and for individual products by seven-digit SIC number. Accompanying each forecast is a reference to the source from which the statistics were taken.
HC101. P71

IV. National and Industry Statistics

AMERICAN STATISTICS INDEX (ASI). Washington, DC: Congressional Information Service. (monthly with annual cumulations)
Complements Statistical Reference Index by leading to statistical information published in U.S. government publications. Contains an "Index by Category" which identifies sources

of statistics reported in specific ways, such as by city or state or by age or sex.
HA195. Z926

Bureau of the Census. U.S. Department of Commerce. ECONOMIC CENSUS PUBLICATIONS (listed below). Washington, DC: U.S. Government Printing Office. (at five year intervals)
Economic censuses are all taken in the years ending with the numbers 2 and 7. They typically give number of establishments, employment, payrolls, and hours worked. Depending on the census, information is provided on the quantity and value of products shipped and materials consumed, value of retail products sold, value of minerals mined, number of vehicles, vehicle miles, and ton miles transporting freight, etc. In the years between the Census of Manufacturers, the bureau publishes the ANNUAL SURVEY OF MANUFACTURERS which gives statistics for broad industry groups and selected products. These censuses are:

Census of Construction Industries
Census of Manufacturers
Census of Mineral Industries
Census of Retail Trade
Census of Service Industries
Census of Transportation
Census of Wholesale Trade

C3.24/4 thru C3.257/5

Bureau of the Census, U.S. Department of Commerce. STATISTICAL ABSTRACT OF THE UNITED STATES. Washington, DC: U.S. Government Printing Office. (annual)
Very important statistical reference work because it serves as the primary source for U.S. industrial, social, political, and economic statistics and as a bibliographical guide. Source notes at the foot of each table credit the agency issuing the original data.
C3.134

Bureau of Economic Analysis, U.S. Department of Commerce. SURVEY OF CURRENT BUSINESS. Washington, DC: U.S. Government Printing Office. (monthly)
Important source for up-to-date information on the U.S. economy. Includes GNP, personal income, leading economic indicators, U.S. balance of payments, and corporate profits. Beginning April 1990 "Business Cycle Indicators" are also included following the discontinuation of Business Conditions Digest. A historical record of the statistical series (about 1,900) that appear in the SURVEY OF CURRENT BUSINESS is reported in BUSINESS STATISTICS.
C59.11

Internal Revenue Service, U.S. Treasury Department. STATISTICS OF INCOME: CORPORATION INCOME TAX RETURNS. Washington, DC: U.S. Government Printing Office. (annual)
Balance sheet and income statement statistics derived from a sample of corporate income tax returns. Includes tables by industry, with breakdown by asset size, etc.
T22.35/5

STATISTICAL REFERENCE INDEX (SRI). Washington, DC: Congressional Information Service. (monthly with annual cumulations)
Indexes significant statistical information published by industry trade associations, independent research organizations, universities, and state governments. Excellent leads to sources with comparative data. Accompanying microfiche collection includes the full text of many of the publications indexed.
HA214. S73

V. Industry Trade Publications

Trade journals and tabloids are useful sources of information regarding the industries they cover. They frequently publish detailed articles on trends, alert readers to changes in government regulations, announce personnel changes in major companies, cover new products, and can be excellent sources of industry statistics. The following titles are illustrative examples. Many others exist.

Air Transport World
American Banker
Aviation Week and Space Technology
Best's Review—Life/Health
Best's Review—Property/Casualty
Beverage Industry
Beverage World
Computerworld
DM: Discount Merchandiser
DNR: Daily News Record
Data Communications
Editor and Publisher
Electronic Business
Food and Beverage Marketing
Food Processing
Frozen Food Digest
Hotel and Motel Management
Hotels
Infoworld
Nation's Restaurant News
Oil and Gas Journal
PC Week
Packaging
Progressive Grocer
Publisher's Weekly
Restaurant Business
Supermarket Business
Supermarket News
Telephony
Travel Weekly
Vending Times
WWD: Women's Wear Daily

VI. Magazine/Newspaper Indexes

ABI/INFORM. Louisville: UMI/Data Courier (online only, no print version) Frequent updates.
Abstracts of articles covering management, law, taxation, finance, data processing, advertising, human resources, and other areas of vital interest to decision makers in business.

BUSINESS PERIODICALS INDEX (BPI). New York: H. W. Wilson Co. (monthly with quarterly and annual cumulations)
Articles from over 300 key business periodicals covering all aspects of business including management, marketing, economics, finance, accounting, banking, insurance, investments, computers, specific industries, businesses, trades, and topics of current interest. Has a book review section.
HF5001. B8

INFOTRAC (General Periodicals-Academic CD-ROM). Belmont, CA: Information Access Co. 1982– (backfile disk plus monthly updates)
Selected coverage of over 1000 predominantly business magazines plus 60 days of THE WALL STREET JOURNAL and the business section of THE NEW YORK TIMES.

PAIS INTERNATIONAL IN PRINT. New York: Public Affairs Information Service. (monthly with quarterly and annual cumulations)
Economic and business information, especially related to regulated or recently deregulated industries, and geopolitical, international or interdisciplinary aspects of business topics. Includes selected books and government publications as well as business periodicals. The title changed in 1991 to include the word "International" to reflect the added emphasis on international coverage and the addition of more foreign language articles.
H83. Z968

PREDICASTS F & S INDEX UNITED STATES. Cleveland, OH: Predicasts, Inc. (weekly with monthly, quarterly, and annual cumulations)
Covers company, product, and industry information from over 750 financial publications, business-oriented newspapers, trade magazines, and special reports. Corporate acquisitions and mergers, new products, market information, technological developments, and social and political factors affecting business are among topics indexed.
HF1040.8. P74

PREDICASTS F & S INDEX EUROPE. Cleveland, OH: Predicasts, Inc. (monthly with quarterly and annual cumulations)
HF1040.9. E8 P72

PREDICASTS F & S INDEX INTERNATIONAL. Cleveland, OH: Predicasts, Inc. (monthly with quarterly and annual cumulations)
HF54. U5 P7

WALL STREET JOURNAL INDEX. Ann Arbor, MI: University Microfilms International. (monthly with quarterly and annual cumulations)
An index to THE WALL STREET JOURNAL in two volumes; the "Corporate" volume is arranged by company and the "General News" is arranged by subject/industry. Includes a separate index for BARRON'S.
HG1. W26

VII. Databases

Academic libraries have access to many of the databases on the Dow Jones News Retrieval System at a special rate. On the "Text" portion, full text articles from the Wall Street Journal and many business magazines are available. Full text versions of many cities' newspapers (which often give excellent business coverage) are also available on Datatimes. BRS Information Technologies, ORBIT Search Service, and DIALOG Information Retrieval Service are examples of additional vendors which provide business-related databases, some of which are industry specific.

VIII. Information on Publicly-Held Companies

ANNUAL REPORTS AND 10-K REPORTS

Publicly-owned companies must issue annual financial statements to stockholders and file more detailed reports of various kinds with the Securities and Exchange Commission. Two vendors which make these reports available on microfiche or other formats are:

DISCLOSURE (Corporate reports). Bethesda: Disclosure, Incorporated. Also available as a CD-Rom product and accessible through Dow Jones News Retrieval System, Dialog Information Retrieval Services, and BRS Information Technologies.

Q-FILE (Corporate reports on microfiche: annual reports, 10-K's, 8-K's, Proxy reports). St. Petersburg, FL: Q-Data Corporation.

Moody's Investors Service. MOODY'S MANUALS (listed below). New York: Moody's Investors Service. (annual with updates)
Each of these important manuals covers U.S., Canadian, and other foreign companies listed on U.S. exchanges and includes a brief corporate history, a list of subsidiaries, principal plants and properties; business lines and products; officers and directors; comparative income statements and balance sheet statistics. The blue center sections in each manual provide various industry statistics. Each set also has a looseleaf binder for updates.

MOODY'S BANK AND FINANCE MANUAL
HG4961. M65
MOODY'S INDUSTRIAL MANUAL
HG4961. M67
MOODY'S INTERNATIONAL MANUAL
HG4009. M66
MOODY'S MUNICIPAL & GOVERNMENT MANUAL
HG4931. M6
MOODY'S OTC INDUSTRIAL MANUAL
HG4915. M68
MOODY'S OTC UNLISTED MANUAL
HG4907. M68
MOODY'S PUBLIC UTILITY MANUAL
HG4961. M7245
MOODY'S TRANSPORTATION MANUAL
HG4971. M74

Standard & Poor's Corp. STANDARD CORPORATION DESCRIPTIONS. New York: Standard & Poor's Corp. (looseleaf)
An excellent financial service, similar to Moody's above, but in looseleaf binders format. Separate volume for DAILY NEWS updates.
HG4501. S7663

SMALL-BUSINESS CASES

CASE 1

United Products, Inc.*

Having just returned from lunch, George Brown, president of United Products, Inc., was sitting in his office thinking about his upcoming winter vacation—in a few days he and his family would be leaving from Boston to spend three weeks skiing on Europe's finest slopes. His daydreaming was interrupted by a telephone call from Hank Stevens, UPI's general manager. Mr. Stevens wanted to know if their two o'clock meeting was still on. The meeting had been scheduled to review actions UPI could take in light of the company's sluggish sales and the currently depressed national economy. In addition, Brown and Stevens were to go over the financial results for the company's recently completed fiscal year—they had just been received from UPI's auditors. Although it had not been a bad year, results were not as good as expected and this, in conjunction with the economic situation, had prompted Mr. Brown to reappraise the plans he had for the company during the upcoming year.

COMPANY HISTORY

United Products, Inc., established in 1941, was engaged in the sales and service of basic supply items for shipping and receiving, production and packaging, research and development, and office and warehouse departments. Mr. Brown's father, the founder of the company, recognized the tax advantages in establishing separate businesses rather than trying to consolidate all of his operations in one large organization. Accordingly, over the years the elder Mr. Brown had created new companies and either closed down or sold off older companies as business conditions seemed to warrant. As of the mid-1960s, his holdings consisted of a chain of four related sales distribution companies covering the geographic area from Chicago eastward.

In 1967, feeling it was time to step aside and turn over active control of the business to his sons, the elder Mr. Brown recapitalized and restructured his companies, merging some and disposing of others. When the restructuring process was completed, he had set up two major companies. United Products, Inc., was to be run by his youngest son, George Brown, with its headquarters in Massachusetts, while his other son, Richard Brown, was to operate United Products Southeast, Inc., headquartered in Florida.

Although the Brown brothers occasionally worked together and were on each other's board of directors, the two companies operated on their own. As George Brown explained,

* Prepared by Jeffrey C. Shuman, Associate Professor of Management, Bentley College.

"Since we are brothers, we often get together and discuss business, but the two are separate companies and each files its own tax return."

During 1972, United Products moved into new facilities in Woburn, Massachusetts. From this location it was thought that the company would be able to serve its entire New England market area effectively. "Our abilities and our desires to expand and improve our overall operation will be enhanced in the new specially designed structure containing our offices, repair facilities, and warehouse," is how George Brown viewed the role of the new facilities. Concurrent with the move, the company segmented the more than 3,500 different items it carried into eight major product categories:

1. *Stapling machines.* Manual and powered wire stitchers, carton stitchers, nailers, hammers, and tackers
2. *Staples.* All sizes and types (steel, bronze, monel, stainless steel, aluminum, brass, etc.) to fit almost all makes of equipment
3. *Stenciling equipment and supplies.* Featuring Marsh hand and electric machines, stencil brushes, boards, and inks
4. *Gummed tape machines.* Hand and electric, featuring Marsh, Derby, and Counter-boy equipment
5. *Industrial tapes.* Specializing in strapping, masking, cellophane, electrical, cloth, nylon, and waterproof tapes made by 3M, Mystik, Behr Manning, and Dymo
6. *Gluing machines.* Hand and electric
7. *Work gloves.* All sizes and types (cotton, leather, neoprene, nylon, rubber, asbestos, and so on)
8. *Marking and labeling equipment*

In a flyer mailed to United Products' 6,000 accounts announcing the move to its new facilities, the company talked about its growth in this fashion:

Here we grow again—thanks to you—our many long-time valued customers . . .

Time and circumstances have decreed another United Products transPLANT—this time, to an unpolluted garden-type industrial area, ideally located for an ever-increasing list of our customers.

Now, in the new 28,000-sq. ft. plant with enlarged offices and warehouse, we at UNITED PRODUCTS reach the peak of efficiency in offering our customers the combined benefits of maximum inventories, accelerated deliveries, and better repair services.

By 1974, the company had grown to a point where sales were $3.5 million (double that of four years earlier) and 34 people were employed. Results for 1973 compared to 1972 showed a sales increase of 22 percent and a 40 percent gain in profits. Exhibit 1 contains selected financial figures for 1971, 1972, and 1973, in addition to the fiscal 1973 balance sheet.

EXHIBIT 1
Selected Financial Information, United Products, Inc.

	11/30/71	11/30/72	11/30/73
Current assets	$ 862,783	$ 689,024	$ 937,793
Other assets	204,566	774,571	750,646
Current liabilities	381,465	223,004	342,939
Net worth	685,884	750,446	873,954
Sales	n.a.*	2,830,000	3,450,000

Statement of financial condition, November 30, 1973:

Cash on hand	$ 46,961	Accounts payable	$ 321,885
Accounts receivable	535,714	Notes payable	20,993
Merchandise in inventory	352,136		
Prepaid insurance, interest, taxes	2,980		
Current assets	$ 937,791	Current liabilities	$ 342,878
Fixtures and equipment	$ 42,891	Retained earnings	$ 471,655
Motor vehicles	49,037	Capital stock	519,800
Land and buildings	658,768	Surplus	354,154
Total assets	$1,688,487	Total liabilities	$1,688,487

* n.a.: Not available.

COMPETITION

George Brown indicated that UPI does not have clearly defined rivals against whom it competes head-on with respect to all of its 3,500-plus items:

> It is hard to get figures on competition since we compete with no one company directly. Different distributors carry lines which compete with various of our product lines, but there is no one company which competes against us across our full range of products.

On a regular basis, Mr. Brown receives Dun & Bradstreet's *Business Information Reports* on specific firms with which he competes. Mr. Brown feels that since the rival firms are, like his own firm, privately held, the financial figures reported are easily manipulated and, therefore, are not a sound basis on which to devise strategies and plans. Exhibit 2 contains comparative financial figures for two competing companies, and Exhibit 3 contains D&B's description of their operations, along with D&B's comments about two other firms operating in UPI's New England market area.

MANAGEMENT PHILOSOPHY

When Mr. Brown took over UPI in 1967 at the age of 24, he set a personal goal of becoming financially secure and developing a highly profitable business. With the rapid growth of the company, he soon realized his goal of financial independence and in so doing began to lose interest in the company. "I became a rich person at age 28 and had few friends with equal

EXHIBIT 2
Financial Information on Rival Firms

East Coast Supply Co., Inc.—Sales $1 Million

	Fiscal December 31, 1971	Fiscal December 31, 1972	Fiscal December 31, 1973
Current assets	$ 88,555	$ 132,354	$ 163,953
Other assets	16,082	18,045	27,422
Current liabilities	41,472	47,606	74,582
Net worth	63,165	102,793	116,793

Statement of financial condition, December 31, 1973:

Cash	$ 42,948	Accounts payable	$ 39,195
Accounts receivable	86,123	Notes payable	27,588
Merchandise in inventory	34,882	Taxes	7,799
Current assets	$163,953	Current liabilities	$ 74,582
Fixtures and equipment	$ 15,211	Capital stock	$ 10,000
Deposits	12,211	Retained earnings	106,793
Total assets	$191,375	Total liabilities and net worth	191,375

Atlantic Paper Products, Inc.—Sales $6 Million

	June 30, 1970	June 30, 1971	June 30, 1972
Current assets	$884,746	$1,243,259	$1,484,450
Other assets	93,755	101,974	107,001
Current liabilities	574,855	520,572	1,120,036
Net worth	403,646	439,677	471,415
Long-term debt	0	384,984	

wealth that were my age. The business no longer presented a challenge and I was unhappy with the way things were going."

After taking a ten-month "mental vacation" from the business, George Brown felt he was ready to return to work. He had concluded that one way of proving himself to himself and satisfying his ego would be to make the company as profitable as possible. However, according to Mr. Brown, "The company can only grow at approximately 20 percent per year, since this is the amount of energy I am willing to commit to the business."

In 1974, at age 31, Mr. Brown described his philosophical outlook as "very conservative" and surmised that he ran UPI in much the same way as his 65-year-old father would. In describing his managerial philosophy and some of the operating policies he had established, he said:

> I am very concerned about making UPI a nice place to work. I have to enjoy what I'm doing and have fun at it at the same time. I cannot make any more money, since I'm putting away as much money as I can. The government won't allow me to make more money, since I already take the maximum amount.
>
> I like to feel comfortable, and if we grew too quickly it could get out of hand. I realize the business doesn't grow to its potential but why should I put more into

EXHIBIT 3
Descriptions of Major Competitors

East Coast Supply Co., Inc.

Manufactures and distributes pressure sensitive tapes to industrial users throughout New England area on 1/10 net 30-day terms. Thirty-four employed including the officers, 33 here. Location: Rents 15,000 square feet on first floor of two-story building in good repair. Premises are orderly. Nonseasonal business. Branches are located at 80 Olife Street, New Haven, Connecticut, and 86 Weybosset Street, Providence, Rhode Island.

Atlantic Paper Products, Inc.

Wholesales paper products, pressure sensitive tapes, paper specialties, twines and other merchandise of this type. Sales to industrial accounts and commercial users on 1/10 net 30-day terms. There are about 1,000 accounts in eastern Massachusetts and sales are fairly steady throughout the year. Employs 60, including officers. Location: Rents 130,000 square feet of floor space in a six-story brick, mill-type building in a commercial area on a principal street. Premises orderly.

The Johnson Sales Co.

Wholesales shipping room supplies, including staplings and packing devices, marking and stencil equipment. Sells to industrial and commercial accounts throughout the New England area. Seasons are steady. Terms are 1/10 net 30 days. Number of accounts not learned, 15 are employed including the owner. Location: Rents the first floor of a two-story yellow brick building in good condition. Housekeeping is good.

Big City Staple Corp.

Wholesales industrial staples, with sales to 2,000 industrial and commercial firms, sold on 1/10 net 30-day terms. Territory mainly New Jersey. Employs ten including the officers. Seasons steady and competition active. Location: Rents 5,000 square feet in one-story cinder block and brick structure in good condition, premises in neat order. Located on well-traveled street in a commercial area.

it. . . . The company could grow, but why grow? Why is progress good? You have to pay for everything in life and I'm not willing to work harder. . . .

Another thing, I am a scrupulously honest businessman and it is very hard to grow large if you're honest. There are many deals that I could get into that would make UPI a lot of money, but I'm too moral of a person to get involved. . . .

To me, happiness is being satisfied with what you have, I've got my wife, children and health: why risk these for something I don't need? I don't have the desire to make money because I didn't come from a poor family; I'm not hungry.

I have never liked the feeling of owing anything to anyone. If you can't afford to buy something, then don't. I don't like to borrow any money and I don't like the company to borrow any. All of our bills are paid within 15 days. I suppose I've constrained the business as a result of this feeling, but it's my business. The company can only afford to pay for a 20-percent growth rate so that's all we'll grow.

ORGANIZATIONAL STRUCTURE

Upon returning to the company from his "mental vacation" in 1971 George Brown realigned UPI's organizational structure as shown in Exhibit 4 (the company does not have a

EXHIBIT 4
UPI Organization Chart, December 1974

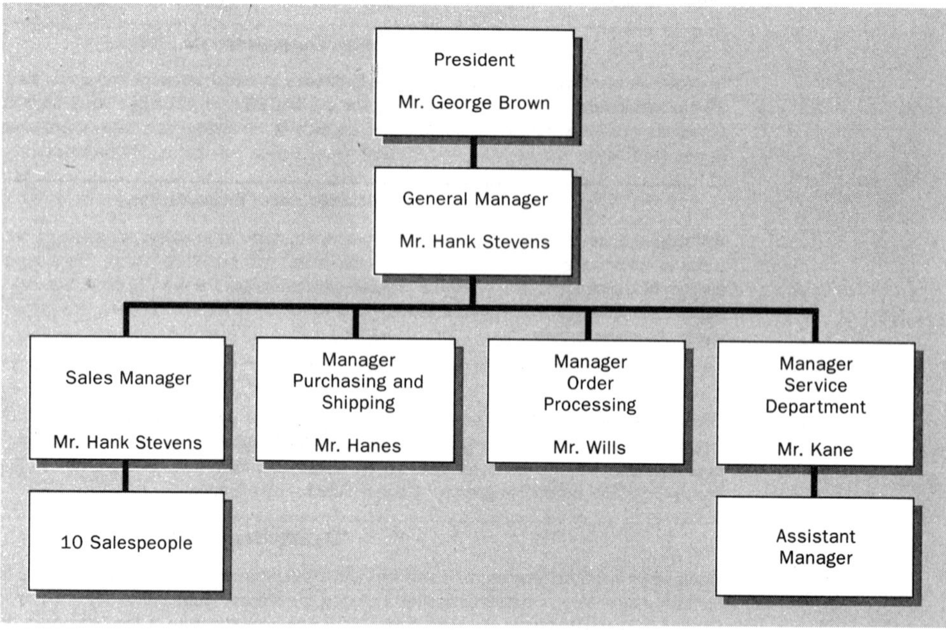

formal organizational chart; this one is drawn from the case researcher's notes). With respect to the way his company was organized, he remarked:

> We have to have it on a functional basis now. We are also trying something new for us by moving to the general manager concept. In the past when I was away, there was no one with complete authority; now my general manager is in charge in my absence.

In discussing the new structuring of the organization, Mr. Brown was quick to point out that the company has not established formalized job descriptions. "Job descriptions are not worth anything. My people wear too many hats, and besides, we're too small to put it in writing." At present the company employs 34 people, including Mr. Brown.

Mr. Brown is quick to point out that he has never had a personnel problem. "All my people enjoy working here." He believes that "nobody should work for nothing" and has, therefore, established a personal goal of seeing to it that no one employed by UPI makes less than $10,000 per year. Mr. Brown commented on his attitude toward his employees as follows:

> The men might complain about the amount of responsibility placed on them, but I think it's good for them. It helps them develop to their potential. I'm a nice guy who is interested in all of my people. I feel a strong social obligation to my employees and have developed very close relationships with all of them. My door is always open to them no matter what the problem may be.
>
> I make it a policy never to yell at anyone in public; it's not good for morale.

Maybe it's part of my conservative philosophy but I want everyone to call me Mr. Brown, not George. I think it's good for people to have a Mr. Brown. Although I want to run a nice friendly business, I have learned that it's hard to be real friends with an employee. You can only go so far. Employers and employees cannot mix socially; it just doesn't work out over the long run.

This is not your normal business. I am very approachable; I don't demand much and I allow an easy open dialogue with my employees. Seldom do I take any punitive action. I'm just not a hard driving, tough guy . . . I'm an easygoing guy.

It would take much of the enjoyment out of the business for me to come in here and run this place like a machine.[1]

I find it hard to motivate the company's salesmen. Since we have so much trouble finding good capable men, I'm not likely to fire any that I have. This situation makes it hard for me to put pressure on them to produce.

The bonus system, if you want to call it that, is I guess what you'd call very arbitrary. I have not set up specific sales quotas, or targeted goals for my inside people so, as a result, I base my bonus decisions on my assessment of how well I feel an employee performed during the past year.

Recently, I've given some thought to selling the company. I could probably get around \$3 to \$4 million for it. If I did that, I'm not sure what I would do with my time. Besides my family and UPI there is not much that I am interested in. A couple of years ago when I took my extended vacation I got bored and couldn't wait to get back to the company.

UPI'S PLANNING PROCESS

George Brown claims to be a firm believer in planning. "I find myself spending more and more time planning for the company. Currently, I'm averaging about 50 percent of my time and I see this increasing." As he described it, the planning process at United Products is really a very loose system:

> We have no set way as to how we do the planning. Basically, the process is directed at ways of increasing the profitability of the company. I look at the salesmen's performance on a weekly and monthly basis, and use this information in the development of the plans.
>
> Since we have a very informal planning process, we only forecast out one year at most. The company's plans are reevaluated each month and, if necessary, new plans are set. Only on rare occasions have we ever planned beyond one year. However, I think the current economic and political situation may force us into developing plans that cover a two-year period.
>
> I am familiar with commonly accepted theory about planning systems, but I do not feel it is necessary for UPI to institute, in a formal manner, any of those I've read about. We perform many of the activities advocated in the planning models, but we

[1] When the case researcher arrived at the plant one afternoon, he observed Mr. Brown running around the office deeply involved in a water fight with one of his office girls. By the way, he lost.

> do them in a relaxed, casual fashion. For example, I am a member of many organizations connected with my business and receive industry newsletters on a regular basis. In addition, I receive input from friends and business associates both inside and outside my line of business. Since we do not have a formal process, planning tends to be a continuous process at UPI.

Although goals are not formally developed and written down, Mr. Brown said he established targets for the company to achieve in the areas of sales, profits, and organizational climate:

1. Increase sales volume of business by 20 percent per year.
2. Increase gross profit margin 0.5 to 1 percent per year.
3. Make UPI a friendly place to work.

Mr. Brown feels that the company has been able to grow at about 20 percent a year in the past and should be able to realize that level in the future. In addition, he believes that sales growth is a necessary evil: "Those companies that don't grow are swallowed up by the competition, and besides, given the level of energy I'm willing to exert, I think 20 percent is a reasonable level of growth."

In the area of profits, the company actually sets no specific targeted figures other than simply an increase in the gross profit margin (as stated above). Mr. Brown observed:

> We do not set a goal because we would not have a way of measuring it. I have no way of knowing how much money I am making until the end of the year, without considerable time and effort.

When asked about UPI's strengths and weaknesses, Mr. Brown indicated that the company had four areas of strength:

1. The number of different products carried.
2. The quality of its employees, particularly salesmen.
3. The absence of any debt.
4. Purchasing capabilities.

The major weakness he viewed as an inability to get and train new personnel—primarily in the area of sales.

SALES FORCE

UPI's salesmen are not assigned a sales quota for the year, but rather are evaluated based on Mr. Brown's assessment of the particular salesman's territory and initiative. He feels his salesmen make more than the salesmen of his competitors. Several of UPI's ten salesmen have earned as much as $40,000 in a single year. All salesmen are compensated on a straight, sliding-scale commission basis calculated as follows:

8 percent for first $180,000 in sales

7 percent for next $60,000

6 percent for next $60,000

5 percent for all sales over $300,000

Mr. Brown is pleased with the sales success of his company and feels that United Products' greatest strength is its ability to "sell anything to anybody." Still, he perceives UPI's main problem as finding good salesmen. "There just aren't good salesmen around and this is a problem because salesmen are the lifeblood of our business."

UPI'S MANAGEMENT TEAM

At the time of the company's reorganization, Hank Stevens was brought in as general manager and assistant to the president. Over the past several years, Mr. Stevens' areas of responsibility have grown to an extent where they now comprise approximately 80 percent of the activities that were formerly done by Mr. Brown. As a result of this, George Brown sometimes finds himself with little to do and often works only five hours per day. As he described it:

> Hank's management discretionary power has increased steadily since he has been here—partly as a result of the extent of responsibility I've placed on him and partly due to his aggressiveness. As it now stands, he makes almost all of the daily operating decisions for the company, leaving me with only the top-management decisions. Let's be realistic, there just aren't that many top-management decisions that have to be made here in the course of a day. A lot of the time, I walk around the plant checking on what other people are doing and, I guess, acting as a morale booster.

When asked about the management capabilities of Hank Stevens, Mr. Brown responded by saying, "Hank probably feels that he is working at a very fast pace, but when you evaluate the effectiveness of his actions, he is actually moving forward at what I would consider to be a very slow pace. However, everything else considered, Hank is the best of what is around. I guess if I could find a really good sales manager, I would add him to the company and relieve Hank of that area of responsibility."

Hank Stevens

Hank Stevens, 32, joined UPI at the time of the reorganization in 1970 after having graduated from a local university with a B.S. in economics. As general manager, Mr. Stevens' responsibilities included planning, purchasing, and sales management, as well as involvement in other decisions that affected UPI's policies. Mr. Stevens feels that he has been fortunate in that "Ever since I came to UPI, I've reported to the president and in essence have had everyone else reporting to me."

When asked about the goals of UPI, Mr. Stevens responded that, "As I see it, we have goals in three major areas: profitability, sales level and personal relationships." In discussing his own personal goals, Hank explained that he hoped that the organization would grow and as a result he would be able to grow along with it. Since Mr. Stevens works so closely with Mr. Brown, he has given considerable thought to his boss's business philosophy:

> I feel that George's business philosophy is unique. I guess the best way to describe it is to say that above all he is a businessman. Also, he has very high moral values and as a result of that he is extremely honest and would never cheat anybody. Actually, the company would probably look better financially if it was run by someone who didn't operate with the same values as George.

When asked about the sales force at UPI, Mr. Stevens commented that "when a new salesman starts with the company, he does so with full salary. After a period of about two years, we change him over to a commission basis." As has always been the case, UPI concentrated its sales efforts on large customers. Mr. Stevens noted that "on the average the company processes approximately 105 orders per day, with an average dollar value per order of roughly $132. It's not that we won't write small orders, we just don't solicit business from small accounts. It just makes more sense to concentrate on the larger accounts."

Jim Hanes

Jim Hanes, 24, has been with UPI for over six years and during that time has worked his way up from assistant service manager to his current position as the number-three man in the company—manager of purchasing and shipping. Jim is responsible for the front office, repair work, and the warehouse. He feels that his reporting responsibility is approximately 60 percent to Mr. Stevens and 40 percent to Mr. Brown. "Since I have responsibility for all merchandise entering and leaving the company, I get involved with both Hank and George, and, therefore, I guess I report to both of them."

In talking about where he would go from his present position, he explained that:

> I guess the next step is for me to become a salesman so that I can broaden my background and move up in the company. However, I am a little worried; I don't think the salesmen in our company are given the right sales training. As the system works now, a new man is assigned to work with an experienced salesman for about six weeks—after which time he is given his own territory. Perhaps if our sales manager had more experience as a salesman, then he would handle the training differently.

In commenting on his understanding of Mr. Brown's philosophy, Jim summed up his position thusly, "George is a very open person. I think he is too honest for a businessman. He certainly gives his people responsibility. He gives you the ball and lets you run with it. I don't think enough planning is done at UPI. At most, it appears that we look ahead one year, and even then what plans are developed are kept very flexible."

UPI'S CORPORATE STRATEGY

When asked about UPI's current strategy, Mr. Brown responded that "the company is presently a distributor in the industrial packaging equipment, shipping supplies, and heavy duty stapling equipment business. In the past when we've wanted to grow, we have done one or both of the following: either add new lines of merchandise or additional salesmen. For example, this past year I got the idea of what I call a contract sales department. It is a simple concept. I took one man, put him in an office with a telephone and a listing of the *Fortune* top 1,000 companies, and told him to call and get new business. You would be surprised at how easy it was to pick up new accounts."

Mr. Stevens looks at UPI as being in the distribution and shipping of packaging supplies business. "In order for UPI to reach the goals that have been set we have to sell more products. That is, we can grow by adding new salesmen, adding more product lines, purchasing more effectively, and undertaking more aggressive sales promotion."

Mr. Brown believes that UPI should try to maximize the profit on every item sold. To do this the company tries to set its prices at a level which is approximately 10 percent above the competition. Mr. Brown explained his pricing philosophy:

> I don't understand why people are afraid to raise prices. If you increase the price, you will pick up more business and make more money. That allows you to keep the volume low and still make more money. In addition, although the customer may pay more, he gets more. The higher price allows me to provide top notch service to all my customers.

In his view, UPI is an innovative company. "Until very recently we were always innovating with new products and new applications. Now I think it's again time that we started to look for additional new and exciting products."

Brown was aware that UPI's strategic emphasis on service, together with his business philosophy, had resulted in UPI's organization being larger than it had to be, given the level of business. Mr. Brown explained the reasoning behind this condition. "I know the organization is bigger than it has to be. We could probably handle three times the present volume of business with our present staff and facility. I think it's because of my conservative attitude: I've always wanted the organization to stay a step ahead of what is really needed. I feel comfortable with a built-in backup system and, therefore, I am willing to pay for it."

In December 1974, Mr. Brown talked optimistically about the future. He felt that sales should reach the $6–$7 million range by 1978. "Looked at in another way, we should be able to grow at 20–25 percent per year without any particular effort." He went on to say:

> I want to grow and, therefore, I am making a concerted effort. I am constantly looking for possible merger avenues or expansion possibilities. I do not want to expand geographically. I would rather control that market area we are now in.
>
> I recently sent a letter to all competitors in New England offering to buy them out. Believe it or not, no one responded.
>
> I do not see any problems in the future. The history has been good, therefore, why won't it continue to happen?
>
> Growth is easy. All I have to do is pick up a new line and I've automatically increased sales and profits. Basically we are distributors, and we operate as middlemen between the manufacturers and users.
>
> In light of what has been happening in the market, I feel that supply and demand will continue to be a problem. Therefore, I am giving serious thought to integrating vertically and becoming a manufacturer. This will guarantee our supply.[2]

---

[2] Refer to Exhibit 5 which contains minutes of a United Products sales meeting held at the end of 1973.

EXHIBIT 5
Minutes of UPI's Sales Meeting, December 5, 1973

Mr. Brown presided at the meeting. His opening remarks highlighted the extraordinary times our country and our company are going through as far as the general economy and the energy crisis are concerned, and the extraordinary effects of these unusual crises on people and businesses, including our company and our sources of supply.

He thanked all present for the many thoughtful, considered and excellent suggestions which they had offered in writing as to how best the salesmen and their company might handle the gasoline crisis without incurring an undue loss of sales and profits, and still maintaining the high standards of service to which UNITED PRODUCTS' thousands of satisfied customers are accustomed.

The whole situation, according to Mr. Brown, boils down to a question of supply and prices. Mr. Brown reported that on his recent trip to the Orient, there were very few companies who wanted to sell their merchandise to us—rather, THEY WANTED TO BUY FROM US MANY OF THE ITEMS WE NORMALLY BUY FROM FOREIGN COMPANIES, i.e., carton-closing staples, tape, gloves, et cetera . . . and at inflated prices!!! The Tokyo, Japan, market is so great that they are using up everything they can produce—and the steel companies would rather make flat steel than the steel rods which are used for making staples. A very serious problem exists, as a result, in the carton-closing staple field not only in Japan, but also in Europe and America.

Mr. Brown advised that every year the company's costs of operating increase just as each individual's cost of living goes up and up yearly. Additional personnel, increased group and auto insurance premiums, increased Social Security payments, new office equipment and supplies, new catalogues, "Beeper system" for more salesmen—all of these costs accumulate and result in large expenditures of money. Manufacturers cover their increased operating costs by pricing their products higher—but to date, UNITED PRODUCTS has never put into their prices the increased costs resulting from increased operating expenses. Last year, the 3 percent increase which the company needed then was put into effect by many of you. HOWEVER, in order for the company to realize that additional profit, this 3 percent price increase had to be put into effect ACROSS THE BOARD . . . all customers . . . all items!

That Did Not Happen!!!

Mr. Brown advised that UNITED PRODUCTS got LAMBASTED when all of the sources of supply started to increase their prices. When SPOTNAILS, for example, went up 10 percent, the salesmen only increased their prices 7 percent, et cetera. We did *not get the 3 percent price increase above the manufacturers' price increase*—and we needed it then and need it even more NOW.

Eliminating the possibility of cutting commissions, there are three possible solutions for the problem of how to get this much needed and ABSOLUTELY IMPERATIVE additional 3 percent PRICE INCREASE ACROSS THE BOARD to cover the constantly growing operating costs for running a successful, progressive-minded and growing business whose high standards of service and performance are highly regarded by customers and sources of supply alike, namely:

a. A 3 percent increase on all items to all customers across the board.

b. A surcharge on all invoices or decrease in discounts allowed off LIST.

c. A GCI charge (government cost increase) on all invoices.

Considerable discussion regarding these three possibilities resulted in the following conclusions concerning the best method for obtaining this special 3 percent ACROSS THE BOARD PRICE INCREASE, as follows:

a. A new PRICE BOOK should be issued with all new prices to reflect not only the manufacturers' new increased prices, but in addition the 3 percent UNITED PRODUCTS PRICE INCREASE. All of the salesmen agreed that it would be easier to effect the additional 3 percent price increase if the 3 percent was "built in" on their price book sheets.

b. This new PRICE BOOK will be set up in such a way that prices will be stipulated according to quantity of item purchased . . . with no variances allowed. WITH NO EXCEPTIONS, the price of any item will depend on the quantity a customer buys.

c. Some items will continue to be handled on a discount basis—but lower discounts in order to ascertain that UNITED PRODUCTS is getting its 3 percent price increase.

d. Until these new PRICE BOOKS are issued, all salesmen were instructed to proceed IMMEDIATELY to effect these 3 percent price increases.

Ten New Accounts Contest

Seven of our ten salesmen won a calculator as a result of opening up 10 new accounts each . . . a total of 70 NEW ACCOUNTS for our company!!! However, both Mr. Brown and Mr. Stevens confessed that the dollar volume amount

EXHIBIT 5 (cont.)
Minutes of UPI's Sales Meeting, December 5, 1973

stipulated in the contest had been set ridiculously low, as a "feeler" to determine the success and effectiveness of such a contest. All the salesmen voiced their approval of all of the contests offered to them—and agreed that they had enjoyed many excellent opportunities of increasing their personal exchequers.

New Customer Letters

Mr. Brown again reminded all present that we have an excellent printed letter, which is available for sending to every new customer—and urged all to take advantage of this service by the office personnel by clearly indicating on their sales and order slips "NEW CUSTOMER." The procedure is but another step towards our goal of becoming more and more professional in our approach with our customers.

New Catalogs

Mr. Brown advised that by the first of the new year, hopefully, all our hard-cover catalogs with their new divider breakdowns will be ready for hand-delivering to large accounts. These catalogs cost the company over $5 and should only be distributed by hand to those customers who can and will make intelligent and effective use of them.

Excessive Issuance of Credits

As a result of a detailed study made by Mr. Brown of the nature and reasons for the ever-increasing number of credits being issued, he instructed all of the salesmen to follow these procedures when requesting the issuing of CREDITS:

a. Issue the CREDIT at the right time.

b. Do not sell an item where it is not needed.

c. NEVER PUT "NO COMMENT" for the reason why merchandise is being returned. EVERY CREDIT MUST HAVE A REASON FOR ITS ISSUANCE.

The ever-increasing number of CREDITS being issued is extremely costly to the company: (1) new merchandise comes back 90-plus days after it has been billed, and frequently, if not always, is returned by the customer FREIGHT COLLECT; (2) CREDIT 9-part forms, postage for mailing, and extra work for both the Bookkeeping and Billing and Order Processing Departments mean higher expenses for the Company. More intelligent, considered and selective selling, plus greater care on the part of the Order Processing personnel, according to Mr. Brown, could easily eliminate a large percentage of these CREDITS.

> Actually, I don't want to do the manufacturing. I think it would be better if I bought the manufacturing equipment and then had someone else use it to make my products.

THE FUTURE

Nevertheless, after reviewing with his accountant the results for the just-completed fiscal year, Mr. Brown was concerned about UPI's future course. "I know changes have to be made for next year as a result of this year, but I'm not sure what they should be." Mr. Brown continued:

> I think this next year is going to be a real bad year. Prices will probably fall like a rock from the levels they reached during 1974 and as a result those items that would have been profitable for the company aren't going to be, and we have much too large of an inventory as it is. It isn't easy to take away customers from the competition. As a

> result of this, I feel we have to step up our efforts to get new lines and new accounts. Recently, I've given some thought to laying off one or two people for economic reasons, but I'm not sure. I will probably give raises to all employees even though it's not a good business decision, but it's an ingrained part of my business philosophy.

When asked if he had informed his employees of his concern about the future, Mr. Brown referred to the minutes of a sales meeting that had been held in November 1974:

> . . . Mr. Brown then presided at the meeting, and announced that Al King had won the coveted award of "Salesman of the Month." This was a "first" for our Al, and well deserved for his outstanding sales results in October. Congratulations and applause were extended him by all present. The balance of the meeting was then spent in a lengthy, detailed discussion, led by Mr. George Brown, of the general, overall picture of what the future portends in the sales area as a result of the current inflationary, recessionary and complex competitive conditions prevailing in the economy.
>
> The gist of the entire discussion can be best summarized as follows:
>
> 1. Everyone present must recognize the very real difficulties that lie ahead in these precarious economic times.
> 2. The only steps available to the salesmen and to the company for survival during the rough period ahead are as follows:
>   A. Minimize the contacts with existing accounts.
>   B. Spend the *majority* of time *developing new accounts* on the less competitive products, and *selling new products to established accounts.*
> 3. *Concentrate on and promote our new items.*
> 4. Mr. Brown and inside management are making and will continue to make every concentrated effort to find new products and new lines for the coming year.

In preparation for his meeting with Hank Stevens, Mr. Brown had drawn up a list of activities to which Hank should address himself while running UPI during George's upcoming vacation. Mr. Brown believed that upon his return from Europe his activities at UPI would be increasing as a result of the problems caused by the uncertain economic conditions. The first item on the list was a possible redefinition of UPI's marketing strategy. Mr. Brown now believed that UPI would have to be much more liberal with respect to new products considered for sale. "I'm not saying we are going to get into the consumer goods business, but I think we need to give consideration to handling consumer products which require no service and which carry a high-profit-margin factor for the company."

As he sat at his desk thinking about possible changes which he could make in UPI's planning process, Mr. Brown was convinced that if he hadn't done some planning in the past, the situation would be more drastic than it was. Yet at the same time, he wasn't sure that a more structured and formalized planning process would put UPI in any better position to face the more difficult times that he saw ahead.

CASE 2

Brithinee Electric, Inc.*

Wallace, Jr., and Don Brithinee are identical twin brothers in their early forties. Wallace, Jr. (also known as Wally), holds the title of president while Don is the company's vice president and controller. As teenagers, they started Brithinee Electric Company with their parents. The senior Wallace Brithinee was the firm's first president and major stockholder. The Brithinee twins worked for the company while they entered U.C. Riverside at the age of 16. They graduated with highest honors at 19, and by the age of 23, both had earned Ph.D.s in mathematics from U.C. Riverside. By 1988, Brithinee Electric had twenty-three employees, and was commemorating 25 years in business. A celebration called for an elaborate dinner to be held upon a chartered boat with important Brithinee Electric customers and friends.

The company appears to be financially successful both from appearance of physical facilities and from remarks made by employees. A 16,750 square-foot Mediterranean-style structure houses the firm. Constructed primarily during the years of 1971 and 1972, the building was expanded later in 1979. The Brithinee facility is located in an industrial area of Colton, California, a region of southern California expected to have high population growth. Outside on the lawn rests an industrial motor on a small pedestal surrounded by a bed of petunias. Inside, the facility is attractive with original oil paintings hung in the office sections of the building. Some pictures depict European settings. On the walls are displayed various awards given to the Brithinees for outstanding service or distribution. One is from Toshiba, another from Baldor.

The company has been changing, especially in the eighties. The core business of Brithinee is directed fundamentally toward large industrial electric motors, both as a distributor and as a firm which undertakes the rewinding of the motors. When insulation breaks down in a motor and the bearings need service or replacement, this company offers its service to rewind and rebuild the motor. Part of the service includes free pickup and delivery of motors for their customers.

The company's primary industry (large-scale motors) declined significantly up through 1984. Wally felt this decline could not be attributed only to the imports of competitive products, but rather on the fact that U.S. businesses require fewer large motors than before. The increased usage of smaller motors has been an important industry trend and Brithinee watched a number of their competitors go out of business. Even though the overall industry has "shrunk," Brithinee Electric still grew in sales and revenues throughout the eighties.

The most pressing issue facing this company at the initial write-up of the case is one of employee development and job rotation. With the desire to have the company flexible to opportunities, Wally expressed the need to have employees with a broad range of talents and skills, but this need for job rotation was not universal at their company. Wally wondered about the employees of Brithinee: What are their personal goals? Is there room for

* Prepared by Sue Greenfeld, California State University at San Bernardino.

them to be fulfilled at Brithinee Electric? Don wondered: How can we get our employees to be more independent so that the firm is not totally dependent upon the 100% involvement of the Brithinee "boys"?

COMPANY HISTORY

Zora and Wallace Brithinee, Sr., came to the southern California area from Detroit shortly after WWII. Wallace Brithinee, Sr., was primarily a "motorman," an individual who specializes in the repair and maintenance of electrical motors. He received his training primarily through vocational programs while in high school and by fixing motors during his service in the U.S. Navy prior to his relocation to California.

The Brithinees' first business began in 1946 but lasted only about nine years. It was never considered very successful. Wally, Jr., described these lean days as "a form of starvation." Wallace Brithinee, Sr., abandoned his business, took the equipment home, and began working for someone else. However, this early experience would prove helpful in the later development of the current business. In the interim, the senior Brithinee helped set up another shop for a man in Ontario, California.

Then in about 1961 or 1962, Wallace Brithinee, Sr., formed another organization, called Brithinee and Coleman, with a local contractor named Bill Coleman. At that time, the Brithinee twins started working in the business. However, after a year, there was a falling out of the partners. In October of 1963, Brithinee, Sr., initiated the current business with his family. The twins were 15 at the time.

In the early days, everything was done "the hard way." The work was backbreaking. Electric motors are heavy, and the business had no cranes to facilitate the moving of equipment. Customers have critical needs and frequently their motors need fixing immediately. Wally, Jr., described the situation as "working around the clock." Back in the sixties, the entire business consisted of repair work. Don elaborated that one major element contributing to Brithinee Electric's survival in those days was the "sweat and muscle" of him and his brother to get the emergency repair work out. This he viewed as a contribution to capital because their work was performed mostly without financial compensation.

Then around 1970, Lincoln Electric came out with an appealing low-price motor. This made Brithinee consider that rather than get involved in one of "these midnight rushes" to repair an old motor, they might be able to sell their customers a new motor instead. They then instigated the stocking of new motors which represented the first major change in the direction of the company.

Next came the construction of 10,000 square feet of the current facility taking about one and a half years to build. Primarily this was the responsibility of Wallace Brithinee, Sr., but after completion of the building, Wallace, Sr., became less involved with the business. His two sons increasingly took over. At this time, the company began hiring more people. The mid-seventies witnessed a growth spurt. The number of employees increased from seven or eight in the early seventies to twenty-three by 1980. Wally described the construction of the current facility as a very bold step in Brithinee's history, but in 1972 they were very optimistic about the future of the company.

In the late seventies, problems arose on the home front. In 1978 Zora Brithinee was diagnosed as having multiple cancer starting as hip pain. This meant that Wallace Brith-

EXHIBIT 1
Floor Plan of Brithinee Electric

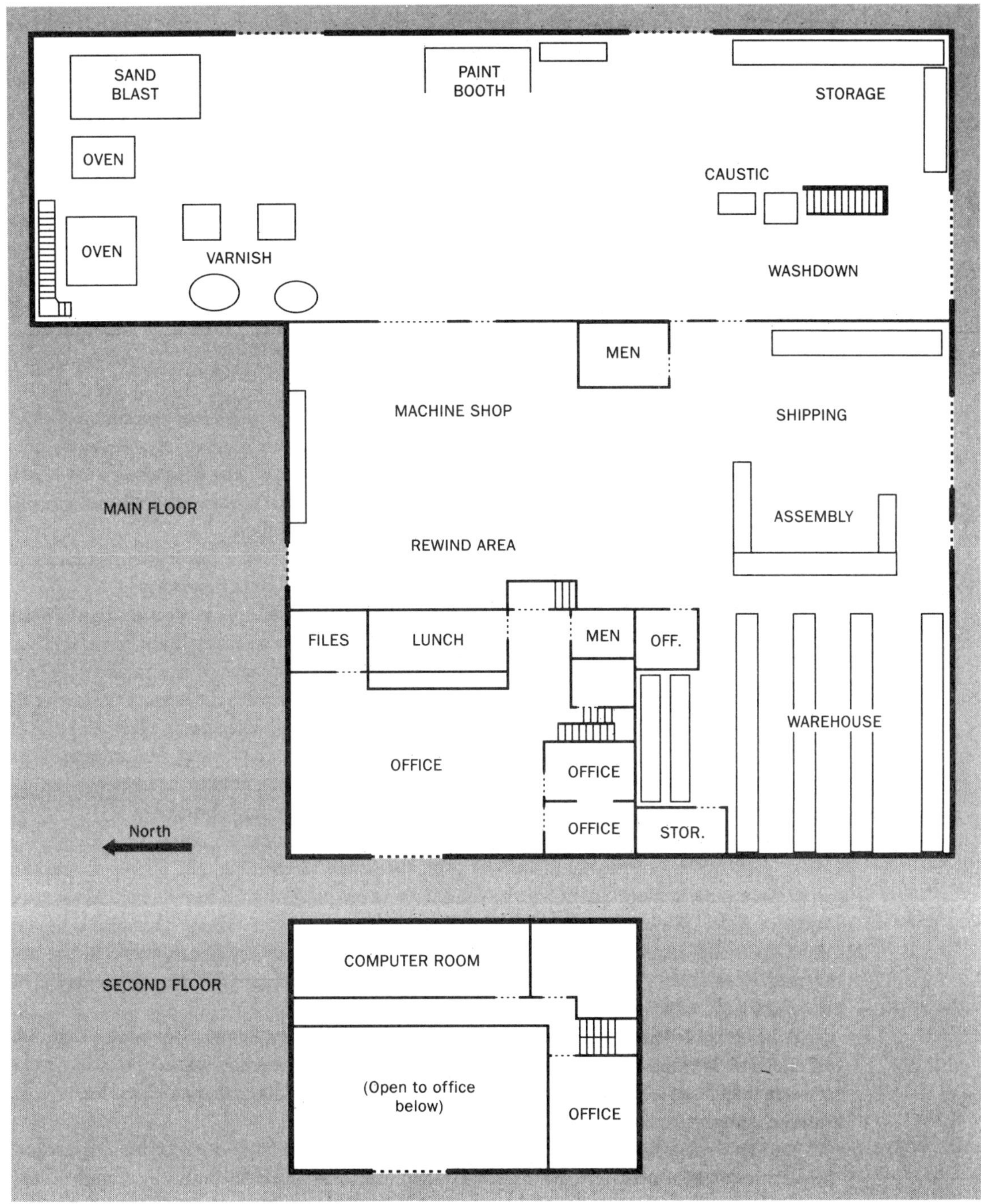

inee's time and attention was devoted to her care and he was quite distraught over her death briefly afterwards. A short time later he suffered a heart attack. Luckily he recovered quite well, but this created transitional problems. There was no real place for the senior Brithinee after he returned to the business in 1980. He eventually "retired" from the business.

In the eighties, the firm started to get into "big ticket" items where an order might call for a single piece of equipment selling for $40,000 or $100,000. This strategy replaced relying on repairs and the sales of smaller items. By 1987, the shop did approximately $1 million in repairs, a figure that has been relatively flat since 1980. Sales, on the other hand, showed constant upward growth and were approximately $4 million in 1987. The latter also included development of custom-made equipment, one of Brithinee's newer areas.

COMPANY FACILITY

The front part of the facility is devoted to offices where proposal development and engineering design are conducted. One project includes a graphic display of a water system which they were developing for the Eisenhower Medical Center. The firm also does its own in-house brochures. The office staff wears many different hats, answering the telephone, taking an order, making a purchase or doing research and design.

The coffee room is small but serves multiple purposes as a combination conference and lunch center. A white board lists the day's assignment for the shop workers.

The back of the facility is large. Here motors are repaired and rewound. In 1979 the facility's back area was expanded by 6,750 square feet. At the entry door is a panel for testing equipment as a motor enters or leaves. On the north end of the facility are two industrial ovens: one for bonding the wiring in the motor, another for "cleaning" a motor. In the latter case, the 700°F temperatures burn off the bonding material to allow the motor to be rebuilt and rewound. Other shop areas are used to create the wiring, "impregnate" the wiring, perform vibration analysis, and rebuild old motors or build new customized equipment for their customers. The entire shop area appears clean and orderly.

Throughout the ceiling is an elaborate set of cranes and steel frames. This allows for ease of moving large equipment and motors. Brithinee Electric has the ability to move a piece of equipment from one corner to another without expending a tremendous amount of energy or time. "Swamp coolers" also have been installed in the ceiling. This draws hot air out of the shop area and keeps this part of the facility relatively comfortable in the hot summers of southern California where temperatures often reach 100° during the day. The office areas are air-conditioned.

A foreman's office is located near the entrance to the shop floor as one enters from the coffee room. A time clock is attached to the outside of the foreman's office. Inside, on the foreman's desk sits a Macintosh computer. This permits the foreman, Rod Samples, to keep a record on each customer job.

Due to a security problem and a desire to not construct high-density fencing around the perimeter of the property, Brithinee parks ten vehicles inside the building at night. They have been doing this since the mid-seventies. Their rationale for not building a fence was their desire to keep the outside of the firm looking aesthetically pleasing.

CHANGING INDUSTRY CHARACTERISTICS

The motor repair industry is one of shrinkage. In the sixties, many larger firms such as Siemens A.G. of Germany and General Electric bought up repair and service shops. Exxon, for one, wanted to diversify strategically out of oil when they purchased Reliance Electric. Yet realized profits throughout the industry were lower than expected and many organizations floundered during that time period. Exxon also left this industry by selling off Reliance Electric.

This industry shrinkage was one reason Brithinee Electric made the decision to enter the market of state-of-the-art electronic motor controls. They also made the decision to investigate artificial turf systems and have done some work in this area. They want to stay flexible in case opportunities develop where they have some expertise. They consider their primary customers to be the food industry, water pump facilities, sand and gravel industry, and grass turf businesses. Customers are located throughout California, but are primarily focused in the high desert (up through the middle of California), low desert (Coachella and Imperial Valley), San Diego, San Bernardino, Riverside, and Ontario.

In terms of forecasting sales or repairs, their industry is unpredictable. The summer months tend to be a little slower than other times, but not always. The weather is a big factor. Rain causes high levels of demand as motors fail or need servicing. Many sales and repairs are "one-of-a-kind." A repair job can take anywhere from 6 to 120 hours. Inside their casing, motors differ significantly from manufacturer to manufacturer.

Dick Marino, the outside salesman, indicated that in the area of repairing motors, Brithinee has about 75 competitors, many of them "mom and pop" operations. Another employee noted that some customers were becoming more price conscious in the recent economy. Brithinee's prices are considered above the industry norm. According to Don, Brithinee Electric works to distinguish itself by providing high-quality service, and most of Brithinee's customers are not that price sensitive.

COMPUTERIZATION

The early 1980s was the time that Brithinee's major supplier of electrical hardware (Toshiba International Corporation of Houston, Texas) first introduced a line of microprocessor-based motor control hardware and later a line of small-scale programmable controllers. Although Brithinee Electric had occasionally sold electric drive hardware from other manufacturers, there was a reluctance on the part of Wally and Don to sell this more complex hardware until they felt it could be offered with the "great reliability and support they were accustomed to give" their customers.

Yet these new systems could be a promising sales opportunity if the firm could master the complexities of this new "smart" machinery. According to Wally, the underlying philosophy of "smart" machinery implies more complete control of a piece of machinery. The machine, for example, uses only as much energy as is needed to produce the desired outcome. Since the machine uses only as much power as is absolutely necessary, the machine's components can be reduced in size, helping to conserve materials as well as energy.

While "smart machinery" is relatively new for industrial motors in the United States, the Brithinees discovered this philosophy in place for some time by their European suppliers. In particular, their German gear motor suppliers have produced for a long time what are, in appearance, "undersized" gear motors for their power ratings. Yet these same products are among the most reliable products the Brithinees offer.

By providing the combination of hardware, application engineering, and software needed, Wally stated that an overall systematic application is required. This means being familiar with how the customer uses motors in a total systems approach. In some cases, this includes working with the customer's engineering staff to find solutions.

This also suggests how essential a knowledge of programming and electrical controls is to Brithinee Electric. Wally mentioned that the main issue is providing both system reliability and the complete service backup necessary to maintain the software and the systems that customers had come to expect from Brithinee Electric. Customers had told Don and Wally a great many horror stories of equipment that never worked correctly, and for which the service was sadly lacking. Wally affirmed that the Brithinee company is "determined not to enter a market where they could not properly support their product."

Wally and Don very much want to be in the business of "smart machinery," but finding talented help continues to be a problem. One employee, George Rainey, had been very instrumental in building the control-panel assembly operation at Brithinee, but he recently retired. In his place, Brithinee Electric hired a young electronics technician familiar with Toshiba electronic drive products. Like everyone else, this person wears many hats: He makes presentations to customers, he develops prices on systems hardware, and he services equipment built by Brithinee Electric and by some of its competitors.

Still, Wally Brithinee expressed concern that the firm is too thinly staffed in the area of high-technology products. Furthermore, Wally has been unable to motivate his programmer/technician, or to make him sense the team spirit that Wally feels the others have. Consequently, Wally feels the need to develop a backup for the programmer/technician should he decide to leave.

INVENTORY AND THE OFFICE STAFF

Brithinee Electric has an inventory philosophy of "completeness," where they attempt to maintain at least one of every part they might need to help a customer out of a "midnight jam." They also have a contract with a friendly customer in Coachella Valley, California, to carry certain items of their inventory. Coachella Valley is in the low desert approximately 75 miles away from their main facility. A separate record is maintained for that stock. Thus Brithinee carries one of the largest inventories of motor equipment in southern California.

They also have a philosophy for the office staff where all ten people including Wally and Don sell to customers, and buy parts to service their customers. This means no separate sales or purchasing department exists. For example, if a customer needs a certain type of part and Brithinee Electric does not have it in stock, the person will then call the manufacturer directly and order the part. The part will then be invoiced and reshipped to the customer.

One employee wondered whether eventually this would have to be changed, but for the time being, she seemed to think it was working. Don disagrees. He wants to develop a better system. He feels there is a definite lack of control and this is bothersome. It causes a duplication of paperwork with so many people capable of producing forms on their own desk computers. According to Don, the main culprit of this process is Wally. Don said, "I haven't been able to reach him on that point yet." Purchasing worries Don because the "process is too disseminated" over different individuals. The only office person not selling to customers is Kathy. She buys bearings, windings, and parts for the shop.

FINANCES AT BRITHINEE

Finances are tightly watched by Don. Before any invoices are paid, Don's red stamp of approval has to appear. All checks bear his signature, but Don laughingly stated that

EXHIBIT 2
Brithinee Electric (1969 through 1987)

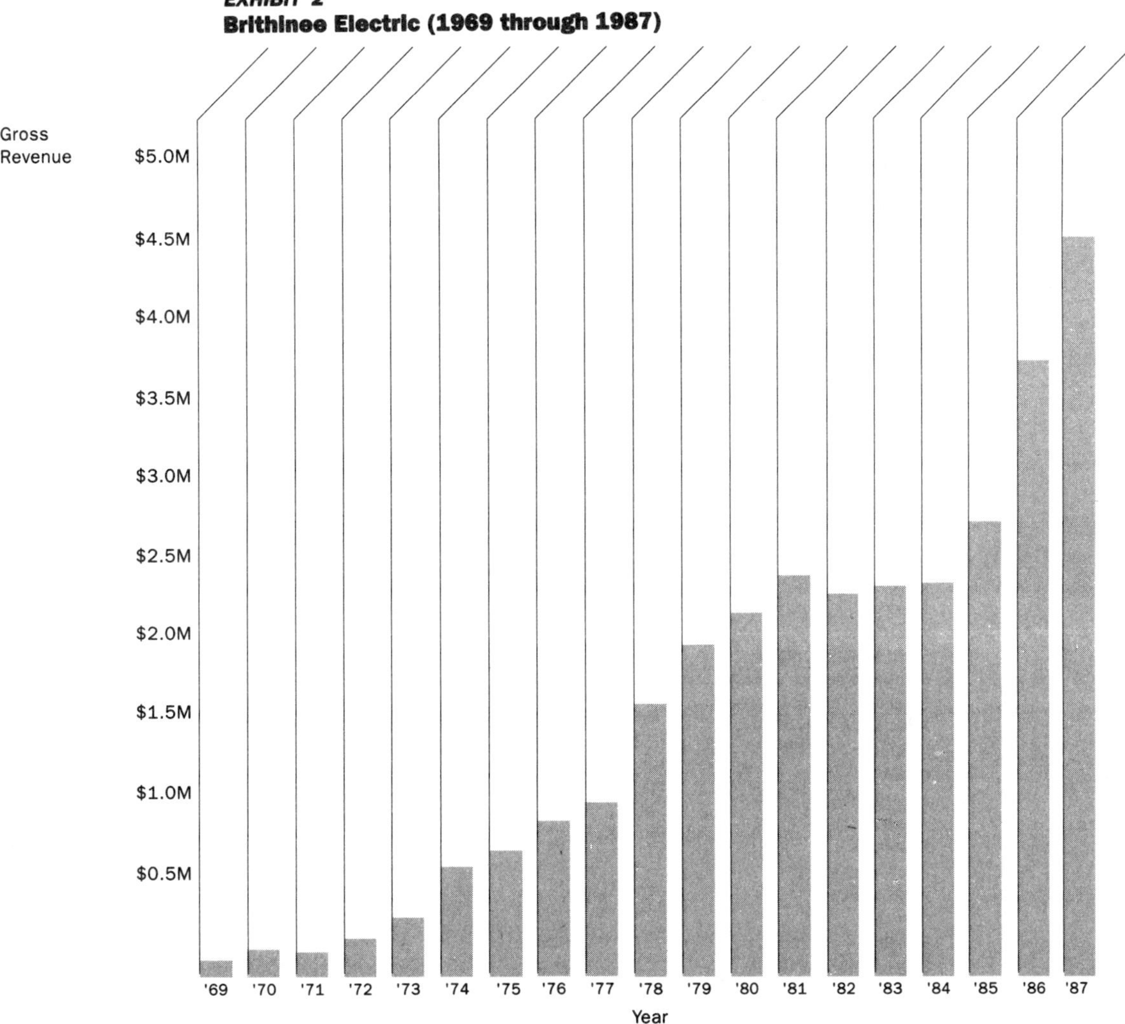

EXHIBIT 3a
Brithinee Electric, Inc.
Statement of Income—Repairs

	1986	***1987***
Income:		
Rewinds	$ 210,340.21	$ 224,095.95
Rewind labor	210,340.10	223,095.91
Parts	221,033.78	247,770.66
Labor	267,436.34	297,213.64
Machine repair	80,307.50	105,603.83
Balancing	43,255.39	50,481.24
Restack	4,274.00	1,944.00
Repair disc. stator	(1,539.98)	(2,277.02)
Repair disc. resale	(430.79)	(549.90)
Misc. income—repairs	5,479.86	5,059.54
Mfg. investment—repairs	384.95	120.42
Interest income—repairs	2,882.19	4,057.57
Total income	$1,043,763.55	$1,156,615.84
Cost of repairs:		
Repair materials	$ 95,646.98	$ 103,306.38
Parts	109,458.20	99,955.25
Outside services	14,370.43	22,168.25
Office vacation	3,052.88	0.00
Shop salaries	408,845.43	463,869.98
Total cost of repairs	$ 631,373.92	$ 689,299.86
Gross profit	$ 412,389.63	$ 467,315.98
Operating expenses:		
Accounting & legal	$ 737.50	$ 1,169.13
Advertising	1,599.74	2,318.77
Auto—gas & parking	4,805.56	6,509.71
Auto lease & truck rental	303.71	488.01
Auto repair/maint.—parts	19,520.61	16,205.34
Bank charges	4.97	250.00
Business promotion	6,103.08	5,452.30
Over/shorts	0.08	21.89
Coffee room supplies	1,636.60	1,776.35
Computer supplies	5,398.75	15,467.34
Depreciation—repairs	27,502.13	32,866.72
Donations	880.48	1,261.97
Dues & subscriptions	1,848.41	1,138.74
Employee welfare—repairs	1,500.87	1,812.36
Equipment rental—repairs	589.50	1,148.75
Meetings & conventions	3,473.37	4,052.74
Insurance	43,906.86	51,729.39
Interest	353.58	0.22
Maintenance supplies	2,033.17	2,755.60
Office supplies	5,809.04	7,475.03
Postage	1,698.16	1,769.09
Outside services	6,541.82	7,379.56
Profit sharing	43,139.49	48,343.37
Rent	31,020.00	43,458.00
Repair & maint. shop	11,084.61	23,178.69
Salaries, clerical	41,981.74	44,619.52
Officers' salaries	83,060.00	74,914.00
Salaries, sales	28,366.95	29,325.77

EXHIBIT 3a (cont.)
Brithinee Electric, Inc.
Statement of Income—Repairs

	1986	1987
Shop expense—repairs	13,709.10	2,052.65
Uniforms	3,162.54	3,310.75
Taxes—licenses	10,406.70	7,016.96
Taxes—payroll	48,034.37	53,919.57
Accrued payroll taxes	- -	1,364.06
Telephone	15,461.60	17,044.21
Travel	2,337.79	1,504.02
Utilities	35,296.98	43,228.50
Total operating expenses	$ 503,309.86	$ 556,329.08
Net income (loss)	($90,920.23)	($89,013.10)

EXHIBIT 3b
Brithinee Electric, Inc.
Statement of Income—Sales

	1986	1987
Income:		
3-phase/1-phase motors	$1,063,876.95	$1,186,831.37
Gear motors	212,124.79	177,569.48
DC motors	39,938.09	24,892.96
Controls	427,822.49	366,251.16
Inverters	970,344.74	1,654,893.67
Programmable controllers	14,605.47	14,265.15
Parts	80,874.30	62,180.63
Labor, sales	5,671.01	3,165.00
Labor, inverter service	16,162.08	16,106.66
Restock	407.85	50.00
Freight	13,748.99	14,050.44
Customer purchases (other)	2,127.44	840.75
Interest income—sales	3,204.92	4,057.63
Misc. Income	7,554.61	5,059.58
MFG investment	384.94	120.44
Total Income	$2,858,848.67	$3,530,334.92
Cost of sales:		
Purchases	$ 350.45	$ 33.60
Accounts payable—discount	(25,053.35)	(25,192.42)
3-phase motors	778,354.25	827,859.34
DC & gear motors	182,018.16	139,098.20
Controls	271,061.28	299,136.39
Inverters	823,397.63	1,336,496.44
Programmable controllers	15,151.22	25,553.84
Parts	66,201.84	47,004.86
Sales—commissions	1,602.65	1,048.66
Inventory variance	(90,073.32)	(88,766.10)
Total cost of sales	$2,023,010.81	$2,562,272.81
Gross profit	$ 835,837.86	$ 968,062.11

EXHIBIT 3b (cont.)
Brithinee Electric, Inc.
Statement of Income—Sales

	1986	1987
Operating expenses:		
Accounting & legal	$ 737.50	$ 1,530.11
Advertising	1,599.74	2,318.78
Auto—gas & parking	4,805.51	6,511.00
Auto lease & truck rental	303.72	487.99
Auto repair/maint.—parts	19,522.18	16,207.00
Bank charges	9.28	250.00
Business promotion	6,142.50	5,469.59
Cash discounts	26,711.32	27,477.85
Over/shorts	0.49	20.64
Coffee room supplies	1,636.63	1,776.47
Depreciation—sales	27,502.13	32,866.73
Computer supplies	6,043.74	15,467.42
Donations	880.47	1,261.98
Dues and subscriptions	1,880.19	1,138.75
Employee welfare—sales	1,500.88	1,812.38
Equipment rental—sales	589.50	714.14
Meetings & conventions	3,473.38	4,052.78
Freight	41,977.78	40,832.11
Insurance	40,788.75	49,351.73
Interest	353.60	0.23
Maintenance supplies	2,033.20	2,884.22
Office supplies	5,807.03	7,349.74
Postage	1,682.49	1,757.41
Outside services	6,479.29	8,167.57
Profit sharing	43,139.50	48,343.38
Rent	31,020.00	43,458.00
Repair & maint. shop	2,320.93	135.79
Salaries, clerical	59,217.33	85,582.40
Officers' salaries	114,140.00	139,126.00
Salaries, sales	29,942.19	40,291.35
Shop expense—sales	6,573.31	528.94
Taxes—licenses	9,673.71	7,092.62
Taxes—payroll	318.82	1,303.23
Accrued payroll taxes	0.00	1,364.06
Telephone	15,455.75	17,044.29
Travel	2,337.80	1,428.42
Utilities		
Total operating expenses	$ 516,600.64	$ 615,405.10
Net income (loss)	$ 319,237.22	$ 352,657.01

signing all the checks "doesn't mean you know the numbers." Don said Brithinee Electric is on sound financial footing. Recently the company has been able to line up a $200,000 unsecured credit line. This will relieve pressure on cash flow if for some reason a major customer is unreasonably slow in paying the account to Brithinee or if the company needs additional working capital for expansion or equipment. To illustrate, one major customer in North Hollywood purchases approximately $80,000 of product per month from Brithinee. Thus, Brithinee is highly dependent upon that customer to pay its bills on time. Prior

EXHIBIT 4
Brithinee Electric, Inc.
Balance Sheet
As of December 31

	1986	***1987***
Current assets:		
Petty cash fund	$ 645.28	$ 1,654.19
Cash in bank—SPNB	23,146.60	14,290.72
Intercapital liquid fund	1.36	1.36
U.S. Securities Trust (ILAF)	22,348.19	23,156.57
SPNB—money market account	110,966.26	121,372.03
Accounts receivable	391,910.94	414,851.06
Inventory	479,193.19	567,959.29
Prepaid income taxes	42,000.00	94,186.00
Total current assets	$1,070,211.82	$1,237,471.22
Fixed assets:		
Shop equipment	$ 268,921.58	$ 299,423.08
Auto & trucks	214,148.14	229,492.76
Office equipment	76,140.39	100,986.04
Leasehold improvement	32,221.74	32,221.74
Total fixed assets at cost	$ 591,431.85	$ 662,123.62
Accum. deprec.—schedule 1	($477,014.10)	($542,747.55)
Net depreciable fixed assets	$ 114,417.75	$ 119,376.07
Other assets:		
Sales tax deposit	$ 2,150.00	$ 2,150.00
Deposits—schedule 2—note 5	7,820.00	7,820.00
Oil & tax investment	4,746.10	4,746.10
Organizational cost	920.90	920.90
Amortization	(920.90)	(920.90)
Total other assets	$ 14,716.10	$ 14,716.10
Total assets	$1,199,345.67	$1,371,563.39
Current liabilities:		
Accounts payable	$ 360,403.12	$ 385,913.07
SUI payable	(4.20)	10.23
FUI payable	38.69	11.29
Sales tax payable	8,320.12	11,253.90
Accured payroll liability	0.00	27,281.15
Accured payroll taxes	0.00	2,728.12
Total current liabilities	$ 368,757.73	$ 427,197.76
Long-term liabilities:		
Total long-term liabilities	0.00	0.00
Shareholder's equity:		
Capital stock note 4	$ 13,000.00	$ 13,000.00
Treasury stock	(80,072.30)	(123,748.10)
Retained earnings	669,342.95	791,469.82
Net income (loss)	228,317.29	263,643.91
Total shareholders' equity	$ 830,587.94	$ 944,365.63
Total liab. & shareholders' eqty.	$1,199,345,67	$1,371,563.39

to 1984, Brithinee had some cash flow problems but Don worked very hard to correct this area. Brithinee keeps three sets of records: one for repairs, one for sales, and one consolidated for both repairs and sales.

According to Don, the firm has a good credit rating. Each year they replace two or three of their vehicles. The company pays cash for such purchases. Don feels this is cheaper than borrowing. Brithinee Electric's philosophy regarding long-term debt is to have none. Don realized that some in business school might advocate leverage, but for them, he feels more "comfortable" having zero debt. Don calls the company financially conservative.

In this industry, average terms are net 30 days meaning that customers have 30 days to pay. Don thought most competitors have an average collection period of 60 days. Brithinee Electric's ranges from 31 to 33 days. Don stated "that is no accident. That has been planned." Some accounts earn cash discounts such as 1/10, n/30. If an account seriously abuses the credit extended to them, then Brithinee just changes the terms.

According to Madeleine, who is in charge of accounts receivable, Brithinee Electric gives credit very cautiously. A new customer might get only 10 days before the bill is due. For new customers or those who changed their paying habits (e.g., one who stopped taking cash discounts), Madeleine might have them checked through Dun & Bradstreet's credit service. For very large account receivables, she might call a customer's accounts payable personnel to find out when Brithinee Electric was scheduled to be paid and/or to verify that the invoice had been received.

Each month a certain amount of excess cash accumulates. Don stated that he likes to keep a cash cushion in the bank, but wondered if the company could turn some cash into a more productive asset.

SAFETY ISSUES

One challenge is to keep the facility clean. Another is to avoid physical injuries, especially those to one's back. For this reason, Brithinee Electric emphasizes keeping the work areas clutter free and stresses the correct use of cranes. Proper lifting and proper handling is top priority. One person, Linda Butek, had been assigned as an assistant to top management to oversee safety-related issues. Her position had been created 2 years previously. If someone on the shop floor sees anything needing safety attention, he or she fills out a form. This would be submitted to Linda. The company has also been spending time on earthquake preparedness. This includes securing and bracing shelving. In an earthquake, shelving could shake and fall over. Earthquake preparedness is a recurring issue for California. Scientists have been predicting a 50-50 chance that a major quake will occur in California within the next 50 years. In 1988 many Californians panicked when reminded that Nostradamus, a 16th century astrologer, predicted a city in the new world would rupture and fall into the sea. Some believed he was referring to either San Francisco or Los Angeles.

For other safety questions, one unresolved matter deals with the health of Brithinee's employees. One motor rewinder had acquired carpal tunnel syndrome. This is a numbness or pain of the thumb and first two fingers which occurs from their overuse. This is a common problem for people who use their hands for extended periods of time, such as workers in textile manufacturing, upholstering, and assembly-line work. In the motor rewinder's hands, the pain and numbness lasted nearly 5 months. During that time she could not work for the company. Brithinee Electric held the position open for the individual, but the firm does not appear active in educating their employees about this type of occupational illness.

However, the company was taking very positive steps in the area of waste disposal. Virtually anything coming into the shop might be considered a hazardous material. Customers' motors are dirty. They have to be washed off so they are clean for repair. That water needs treatment and/or disposal. Brithinee Electric then is considered a "hazardous waste generator." Linda Butek attends seminars all the time to help reduce the company's waste. Keeping up is a constant challenge. New legislation in hazardous waste disposal recently passed, but is not yet really enforced. New legislation is also in the making in the state of California. In 1988, California had greater restrictions concerning hazardous waste than did the federal government. For example, one bill calls for counties to develop a hazardous waste management plan and reduce or minimize hazardous waste in their area. Another bill mandates that each company in an area must have a hazardous waste reduction plan as well. Neither bill had passed at the time this case was written, but there existed an expectation that these bills might be voted into law in the near future.

Brithinee is very interested in reducing the amount of water they need for their operation. This means they would become a "hazardous waste treatment" facility and this raises an entirely new set of regulations that need attention. Linda presented this question: Is it better for Brithinee to have more waste lower in hazardous content, or is it better to have a smaller, but more concentrated hazardous waste? Brithinee Electric has already taken a position on this question, but they are still concerned about whether their decision was the right one. As of 1988, Linda felt guidance from San Bernardino County and other government agencies had been inadequate in this regard. This is an area of major future expense.

In addition, Brithinee Electric has other hazardous products on the premises: propane to run the fork-lifts, grease for motors, plus paints and varnishes. The paint area and the ovens generate fumes. There is a sandblast area to clean off certain types of motors as well. Therefore, Brithinee is also considered a "hazardous material handler." All areas must have permits and this means annual site visitations at different times from different government agencies: the city of Colton, the county of San Bernardino, the state of California and the Air Quality Management District (AQMD).

To illustrate, both the paint booth and the ovens are required to have permits from the AQMD. This agency wants to see the type of equipment used, how the area is being ventilated, and make sure that not too much smoke or pollutants are being released into the air. The fire department has increasing responsibility as related to hazard materials and makes frequent checks. The fire department wants to know the exact location of hazard products in order to protect their fire personnel and to use the appropriate fire extinguishing techniques when necessary. The Department of Health Services of San Bernardino County has the responsibility for overseeing the hazardous waste generators. The Environmental Protection Agency from the state of California is also interested in looking over the permits of Brithinee Electric. In none of the site visitation cases will Brithinee be notified prior to the agency's visit. Inspection agencies have the right to turn up on any day in order to see the operation.

QUALITY CIRCLES AT BRITHINEE AND JOB ROTATION

In the late 1970s and 1980s, many U.S. firms experimented with quality circles where ten to twelve people meet once a week. In these circles, people discuss how they can do the job better and attain more quality in the product or service. Westinghouse and Lockheed both used quality circles extensively during that time for certain major projects. Brithinee Electric also attempted to institute quality circles in the early eighties, but their experiment lasted only 2 or 3 months. One employee thought the idea was good and questioned why the circles were abandoned, but two other employees complained that the circles degenerated into gripe sessions.

Contrary to the expressed hopes of Wally, many shop personnel do not feel job rotation or job enrichment exists at Brithinee. Only the office staff expressed a sense that enough job variety prevails. On the other hand, almost universally the shop personnel said they wanted more variety in their jobs. They feel "bored" at times, but these statements were followed by the same people saying "there is too much work to allow for job rotation."

Many shop personnel attribute the lack of job rotation to the shop foreman, Rod Samples, who makes all the work assignments for the shop and posts them on the coffee room board. Rod is characterized as "a bright guy," "sharp," "knows his stuff," "intuitive," but also as "moody," "abrasive," "aloof" and "does not communicate" with everyone as he should. At the encouragement of Wally and Don, Rod has participated in various supervisory training programs, but no employee interviewed referenced any improvement in Rod's interpersonal skills. Wally expressed both his appreciation and frustration in Rod's behavior. One problem is the lack of a suitable alternative. Rod is methodical; he does the paperwork correctly and gets the work done, but he at times seems to demean the contributions of the shop workers. For example, when Wally would ask a shop worker a question, Rod would sometimes intercede and answer for the worker. Wally wanted the worker to answer for himself or herself. Wally identifies Rod as a "bottleneck" to the implementation of his and his brother's philosophy concerning job rotation. Wally wondered: How should the company handle Rod?

Although many shop personnel indicated that they are very happy to be working at Brithinee, a constant thread emerged throughout the interviews. Many feel that they somehow want more recognition and/or feedback for the job they do. They need to hear they are doing a good job. Some feel positive feedback through the handsome bonuses they receive in their paychecks, but, even so, they also want the verbal praise as well.

ORGANIZATIONAL CULTURE

There appears to be a high degree of family sentiment within the organization. Yet, this opinion was more frequently vocalized by Wally, Don, and by members of the office staff than by individuals from the shop. Employees in the shop tend to have less overall formal education and to be less self-motivated in attending seminars and learning than the office personnel. Although not apparent in the first round of interviews, this pattern began to emerge as more individuals were questioned. Members of the office staff mention the company in terms of "we," the company, more often than did the thirteen members of the shop. Office staff expressed the notion that Brithinee is very good about allowing their employees to grow into different jobs (i.e., permitting the person's job to change as the person gains new or different skills).

However, this is not a universal sentiment even in the office. A few mentioned that a slight friction exists between the personalities of the office versus those in the shop. One individual said that the office personnel think they are "la-dee-da" (or better than the shop employees). Another employee revealed that he was surprised to see so many "cliques" in such a small organization. He indicated five "cliques" at Brithinee exist. Don responded that Brithinee has some groups of people who are more comfortable with each other than outside the group, but he did not consider this abnormal. No one in the organization felt that these groupings harm the productivity of the organization. Overall the morale of the shop personnel appears lower than the morale of the office staff.

PERSONNEL PRACTICES

According to Don and Wally, people hired after 1972 tended to have no background in building motors. Instead people were hired who exhibited a "good work" attitude. Rod Samples, the production manager, stated that people were trained for their job at Brithinee Electric. Turnover was low. Few employees ever left Brithinee. Reasons cited include: good benefits, nice atmosphere, clean organization. One employee who had worked in another shop prior to Brithinee Electric described the experience as "going from the dungeon to Disneyland." Yet, a fair number of employees in the shop were disgruntled. One major issue for some is lack of job rotation.

In addition, Don and Wally were known for not firing anyone. Only one employee was ever mentioned as "being fired" and this individual had been caught stealing copper wire and reselling it. A couple of employees did point out instances where some employees had been "encouraged" to leave. Don indicated only three individuals had ever been "fired" from Brithinee. He had been responsible for firing two of them. In the latter cases, a lack of personality agreement was cited as the cause. With turnover so low, this means, in the past 3 years, only five new people had been hired. Of these five individuals, the jobs had been essentially created for three of them.

The following comments by Wally highlight the personnel policies at Brithinee:

> We are not anxious to hire and fire people. We aren't one to say we have a job so let's go out and hire five more people. We just don't believe in it. We add people slowly. We try to bring them into the culture (not so easy to do sometimes), and [we] try to make them feel that they are part of the family so to speak. People don't accept new people very easily. Depends. Very hard to fit people in without creating friction, without creating hard feelings from the older folk who are already there. It's tough to find people who are non-threatening to others. It's a tough situation and that's a problem. We haven't figured out how to solve all of that just yet. . . . We don't want prima donnas here. . . . Our customers view us as having high quality people throughout.

All employees except Wally and Don Brithinee are paid on an hourly basis. This even includes the outside salesman, Dick Merino, who stated that he prefers it that way. Almost all the employees like being paid hourly because they frequently can earn more money by working overtime. To illustrate, the production manager, Rod Samples, often works from 7:00 A.M. to 5:00 P.M., 6 days a week. He does this by choice, but he appreciates being well-compensated for his time. Overtime is frequent, but according to Don, not enough to justify hiring more people.

Most of the employees feel that they are well-paid. However, there are exceptions. Two employees indicated that individuals are not paid fairly. (The lowest paid made approximately four times the minimum wage or approximately the average starting salary of a college graduate in accounting. The highest paid shop person made about twice that.) Although the casewriter pursued the issue of pay equity, the individuals who complained could not actually explain their rationale for why they perceived this pay inequity. It just exists in their eyes. In a different instance, one employee thought most people for what they do are overpaid at Brithinee. Others thought pay at Brithinee is a mystery. Don said individuals are rewarded on the basis of "effort" to the extent that pay increases are based 85% to 90% on effort in meeting the needs of the customer, and 10% to 15% on skill.

Ideally Don and Wally would like to stagger the evaluations so that two employees would be evaluated every month; but in actuality, half the employees are evaluated at a time. Don asserted "trying to put a dollar sign on a human being . . . that's the toughest job an employer has—to put a value on another person's time and effort."

Many of the employees complimented Don and Wally Brithinee for being "first-class" guys. If an employee wants a new piece of equipment because (1) the old piece of equipment is old or dangerous, or (2) a new piece of equipment would allow the person to do his or her job better, Don and Wally would buy the equipment regardless of the price. The only question asked: Would this help to do the job better with higher quality?

PROFIT SHARING

Profits are pooled from all areas and shared by the employees regardless of how the profits are generated, either by repairs or sales. To encourage a philosophy of meeting the customer needs, the company does not pay more to repair people if they fit more motors nor do they pay salespeople on commission. The Brithinee profit sharing program was described by many employees as "generous." Employees of the company are unaware, however, that new changes in the tax reform package might have an impact on how Brithinee handles their profit sharing in the future.

BENEFITS

New employees receive a 1-week vacation after 1 year, 2 weeks after 2 years, 3 weeks after 5 years, and 4 weeks plus 1 day after 10 years. There is no allotment for sick leave. Don feels strongly that their system eliminates sick leave abuse, which has been problematic for other companies. Brithinee's industry, typically, does not have widespread use of sick leave. Don stated, "the goal is to reward people for being here." He also added that employees could accumulate vacation allotment and then use it for other occasions, such as illness or personal leave.

FUTURE CHALLENGES FOR BRITHINEE

Almost universally Brithinee employees responded favorably about Brithinee's future, but there are concerns. One person asked: How can Brithinee compete in a very price conscious environment? There was also an acknowledgment that the industry is very competitive and has become even more competitive in the past few years. Customer loyalty to Brithinee is not as strong as it had once been because so many people are very price conscious. One of the persons involved in inside sales plainly stated: "[I]t is just harder to make a sale than it was before."

Employees appear to have a strong sense of what the company stands for, i.e., quality service; but no one remembered the company having a formal written mission statement. Don said the following:

> We never crystallized our mission . . . but I guess it would be to provide first class or highest quality service for industrial clients to their rotating electrical apparatus and to provide very dependable service in the distribution of electrical motor controls and electronic control devices.

Don added that Brithinee Electric wants to be known for their good service. They would not just take any job. They would turn down jobs which they felt unequipped to handle. Don stated they want to give the highest value to their customers.

By the year 1993, Don wants to see a Brithinee Electric expansion beyond the current location. Plus he wants to see a more independent work force (one less dependent on his brother and himself). He feels this would make the business more valuable and "more tolerable." This would be a "great accomplishment." He also hopes to see a better developed sales effort with a broadening of the sales products. He wants to achieve more sophisticated systems than they now sell. Don admitted they do not have a formal planning system at the current time to help them achieve these objectives. However, he seemed confident that taking these items slowly one step at a time would be the way to accomplish them.

Don expressed the sentiment that he works day-in and day-out to create an independent work force. He attempts to push decisions on to other people, force them to be less dependent on him and his brother, train people so they have the tools to make decisions. Then day-in and day-out, he stresses the philosophy of Brithinee Electric, which is "service to the customer first over quick profits or any other short-term goals." He stated that "devotion to the customers adds to the permanence of our business." Later, he commented, "our motor business was built up on—if it was in our grasp to do the job, we said 'yes, we will do it' and we made ourselves available even if that meant canceling our plans to do something else . . . but we did it and that's how we built up this business . . . we have always been willing to put ourselves out. Even at three in the morning."

In terms of broadening beyond the local location, Don and Wally have been in discussion with other businesses. In the past couple of months, another business in Oxnard, California, had been offered to them as a possible purchase, but no steps have been taken in this area. They were still evaluating it. The most likely type of purchase would be another business similar to their own, but possibly in the San Diego area where they already have a few customers. They want to be able to clone most of their business but cover another area. Don wondered: Is it more cost effective to set up a location in San Diego which is 100 miles south or is it better to attempt to handle those customers from the current location, using their own trucks and delivery service? Could they handle all their work from Colton and still be properly represented in San Diego?

PLAN FOR SUCCESSION

They have no plan for eventual succession of the company. Wally is single and has no children. Don has one child, a daughter 5 months old. In 1980, they already experienced one crisis over transition which occurred when the twins' father returned to the business after his wife's death. After the senior Brithinee recovered from his heart attack, he positioned himself out of the company. Currently, Wally reflected that Brithinee Electric has no plans to sell out. Personally he is having "too much fun."

CASE 3

Wall Drug Store: Facing the 90's*

SIZZLING STEAK: WALL DRUG

WESTERN ART: WALL DRUG

BEAUTIFUL WESTERN ART: WALL DRUG

FREE COFFEE AND DO-NUTS FOR VIETNAM VETERANS: WALL DRUG

FREE COFFEE AND DO-NUTS FOR HONEYMOONERS: WALL DRUG

MAKE YOUR DAY: WALL DRUG

W'ALL MAKE YOU HAPPY: WALL DRUG

FREE ICE WATER: WALL DRUG

Travelers driving across the rolling prairie of western South Dakota on Interstate Highway 90 are amused, irritated, and beguiled by scores of roadside signs and billboards advertising the attractions of something called Wall Drug. There are signs promising 5 cent coffee, homemade rolls, and roast beef dinners; signs intended to amuse (HAVE YOU DUG WALL DRUG?; W-A-A-L I'LL BE DRUGGED); signs publicizing publicity (FEATURED ON TODAY SHOW: WALL DRUG; WALL DRUG FEATURED IN PEOPLE; WALL DRUG AS TOLD BY WALL ST. JOURNAL; WALL DRUG AS TOLD BY TIME); and signs advertising Black Hills gold jewelry, cowboy boots, and camping supplies. By the time travelers reach the little (pop. 770) town of Wall, more than half of them are curious enough to exit under the friendly stare of an 80 foot, bright green, concrete brontosaurus which towers over the Wall Auto Livery, a Sinclair station. Two blocks to the left they find main street and a block long business district with a hardware store, a grocery store, a dozen gift shops, restaurants, museums, and Wall Drug, the self-proclaimed "World's Largest Drug Store."

The Wall Drug Store occupies half of the east side of this block. Behind the iron hitching posts lining the curb and the pine board store front are a restaurant and twenty odd small shops selling souvenirs, western clothing, moccasins and boots, Indian pottery, western jewelry, western books, stuffed jackalopes,[1] fudge, posters, oil paintings and, of course, prescription drugs. Life-sized concrete or fiberglass old West characters lounge on benches in an enclosed mall giving tourists opportunities for photos of themselves sitting on a cowboy's lap or with an arm around a dance hall girl. Two animated, life-sized, mannequin cowboy orchestras play and sing for the crowds, and nearby a more menacing

* Prepared by Professor Phil Fisher and Professors Emeritus Robert Johnson and James Taylor of the University of South Dakota. It was presented at the North American Case Research Meeting, 1990.

[1] Jackalopes are stuffed jackrabbits with antelope or deer antlers. Flying jackalopes have pheasant wings. These creations of taxidermy were priced from $99 to $129.

mannequin shouts out challenges to passers to try and match his quick draw in a gun fight for only fifty cents.

In back of the store is an open yard ringed with buildings featuring more animated displays, including a piano playing gorilla, and a singing family on a Sunday drive in a restored 1908 Hupmobile. This area, termed the "backyard," includes a six foot stuffed rabbit, a stuffed buffalo, a stuffed bucking horse, and a large, saddled fiberglass jackalope all providing more photo opportunities for visiting tourists. An old fashioned covered well dispenses free ice water for coolers and thermos bottles from a modern faucet.

A private collection of over 300 original paintings portraying the American West is displayed on the walls of the restaurant dining rooms. Throughout the store, those walls not covered with shelves of merchandise are covered with photographs. There are old photographs of Sioux chiefs, and western characters such as Calamity Jane, General Custer, and Wild Bill Hickock. There are hundreds of photographs of less famous cowboys and homesteaders. There are photographs showing people standing in front of signs giving the mileage to Wall Drug from such places as Paris, Amsterdam, Cairo, London, New Delhi, and Tokyo. And there are pictures of the generations of the Hustead family who created, own, and manage this unique drug store which is visited each year by approximately 2 million people.

As the tourist season opened in the Spring of 1990, Bill Hustead, the CEO of Wall Drug, his parents, Ted and Dorothy, his wife, Marjorie, and his sons, Rick and Ted, made last minute preparations for the flood of expected customers. At the same time they continued to consider the pros and cons of plans for the most ambitious expansion in the company's history.

WALL DRUG HISTORY

Ted Hustead graduated from the University of Nebraska with a degree in pharmacy in 1929. In December of 1931, in the depths of the depression, Ted and his wife, Dorothy, bought the drugstore in Wall, South Dakota, for $2,500. Dorothy, Ted, and their four-year-old son, Bill, moved into living quarters in the back twenty feet of the store. Business was not good (the first month's receipts were $350) and prospects in Wall did not seem bright. Wall, South Dakota, in 1931 is described in the following selection from a book about the Wall Drug Store.

> Wall, then, a huddle of poor wooden buildings, many unpainted, housing some 300 desperate souls; a 19th century depot and wooden water tank; dirt (or mud) streets; few trees; a stop on the railroad, it wasn't even on the highway. U.S. 16 and 14 went right on by, as did the tourists speeding between the Badlands and the Black Hills. There was nothing in Wall to stop for.[2]

Neither the drugstore nor the town of Wall prospered until Dorothy Hustead conceived the idea of placing a sign promising free ice water to anyone who would stop at their

---

[2] Jennings, Dana Close. (1969). *Free ice water: The story of Wall Drug* (p. 26). Aberdeen, SD: North Plains Press.

store. The first sign was a series of small signs along the highway that read "GET A SODA/GET A BEER/TURN NEXT CORNER/JUST AS NEAR/TO HIGHWAY 16 AND 14/FREE ICE WATER/WALL DRUG." On a blazing hot Sunday afternoon in the summer of 1936, Ted put the signs up and travelers were turning off the highway to stop at the drugstore before he got back. Located at the western edge of the Badlands National Monument, and near the major highway between the Monument and the Black Hills 50 miles further to the west, they began to draw a stream of weary, thirsty tourists into the store.

Ted began putting signs up all along the highways leading to Wall. One series read "SLOW DOWN THE OLD HACK/WALL DRUG CORNER/JUST ACROSS THE RAILROAD TRACK." The attention-catching signs were a boon to Wall Drug Store and the town of Wall prospered too. In an article in *Good Housekeeping* in 1951, the Hustead's signs were called "the most ingenious and irresistible system of signs ever devised."

Just after World War II, a friend of the Husteads, traveling across Europe for the Red Cross got the idea of putting up Wall Drug signs overseas. The idea caught on and soon South Dakota servicemen who were familiar with the signs back home began to carry small Wall Drug signs all over the world. Many wrote the store requesting signs. For example, a sign was placed in Paris, "WALL DRUG STORE, 4278 MILES." Wall Drug signs were placed all over the world including areas near the North and South Poles, the 38th parallel in Korea and on jungle trails in Vietnam. The Husteads sent more than 200 signs to servicemen requesting them from Vietnam. These signs led to news stories and publicity which further increased the reputation of the store.

Articles about Ted Hustead and the Wall Drug Store began appearing in newspapers and magazines. In August 1950, *Redbook* magazine carried a story which was later condensed in *Readers' Digest.* The number of newspapers and magazines carrying feature stories or referring to Wall Drug increased over the years. As of May 1990, Wall Drug Store files contained over 700 clippings of stories about the store. The store had also been featured on several network and cable television shows.

The store and its sales grew steadily. From 1931 to 1941, the store was in a rented building on the west side of Wall's Main Street. In 1941, the Husteads bought an old lodge hall in Wasta, South Dakota (15 miles west of Wall), and moved it to a lot on the east side of the street. This building became the core around which the current store was built.

Tourist travel greatly increased after World War II, and the signs brought increasing numbers of people to the store. Bill Hustead recalls that he was embarrassed because the facilities were not large enough to service the crowds of customers. The store did not even have modern rest rooms, but sales during this period grew to $200,000 annually by 1950.

In 1951, Bill Hustead, now a pharmacy graduate of South Dakota State University, joined his parents in the store. In 1953, they expanded the store into a former store room to the south. This became the Western Clothing Room. In 1954, they built an outside store on the south side of the Western Clothing Room. This resulted in a 30% increase in sales. In 1956, a self-service cafe was added on the north side of the store. The cafe expansion was built around a large cottonwood tree which remained, its trunk rising out of the center of the dining area up through the roof.

By 1958, the Wall Drug Store had two men in a truck working full time to maintain 600 signs displayed along highways throughout the Midwest. The store also gave away thousands of small signs each year to people who requested them.

In the early 1960's, Highway 16, the main east-west route across South Dakota to the Black Hills, was replaced by Interstate Highway 90. The new highway was routed near the south edge of Wall. The Husteads, who had been considering building an all new Wall Drug Store along with a gasoline service station near the old highway, did build the station, the Wall Auto Livery, at the new highway interchange.

In 1963, they added a new fireproof construction coffee shop. A new kitchen, also of fireproof construction, was added to the back of the coffee shop the following year. Also in 1964 and 1965, new administrative offices and a new pharmacy were opened on a second floor over the kitchen. Another dining room and the backyard area were added in 1968. This was followed in 1971 with the Art Gallery Dining Room. By the early 70's annual sales volume had reached $1,000,000.

In 1971, the Husteads bought a theater that bordered their store on the south. The next year they demolished it and constructed a new addition, called the Wall Drug Mall. All previous expansions had been financed from profits of the business or short-term loans. Ted and Bill broke with this by borrowing $250,000 for 10 years to finance the Mall.

The Mall was designed as a miniature western town within a large enclosure. The strolling mall was designed as a street between shops fashioned like two-story frontier stores. The store fronts and interiors were made of various kinds of American wood—pine, black walnut, gumwood, cedar, hackberry, maple, and oak. The store fronts were recreated from photographs of Western towns in the 1880's. These shops stocked products which were more expensive than the souvenir merchandise of the older shops. In 1983, the Mall was extended to include a half dozen more shops, a travelers' chapel modeled after one built by Trappist Monks in Dubuque, Iowa, in 1850, and a replica of the original 1931 drugstore called Hustead's Apothecary, which serves as a museum of Hustead family and Wall Drug artifacts.

EXHIBIT 1
Wall Drug Store Sales and Net Income (in Thousands of Dollars)

Year	*Sales*	*Net Income*
1975	$2,679	$118
1976	3,464	165
1977	3,777	155
1978	4,125	206
1979	3,552	33
1980	3,970	185
1981	4,821	224
1982	4,733	203
1983	4,851	257
1984	5,055	285
1985	5,273	161
1986	5,611	233
1987	6,142	249
1988	6,504	204
1989	7,419	242

Source: Company records.

EXHIBIT 2
Wall Drug Store Map, 1990

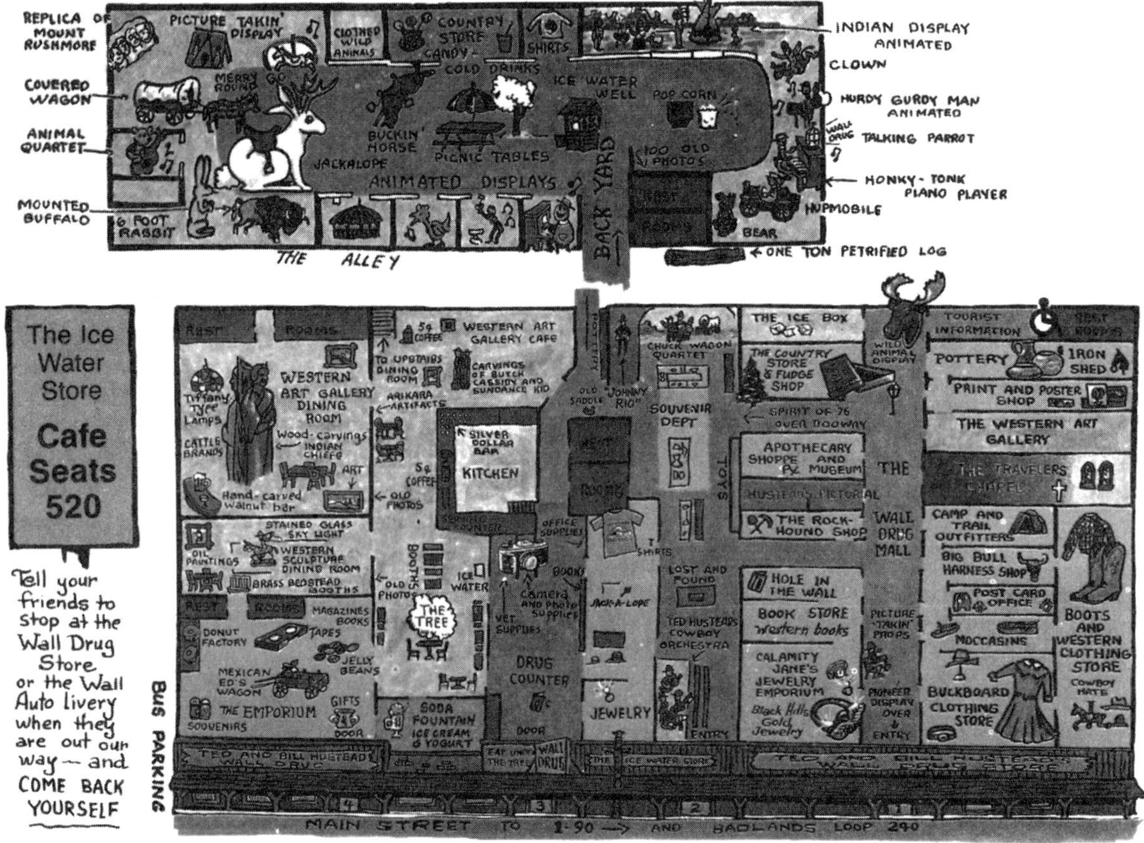

Source: Company document.

The store was also expanded on the north end in 1975 and 1976 and on the south of the original Mall in 1978. Wall Drug continued to have increased sales every year until 1979. That year, a revolution in Iran started a chain of events which resulted in a doubling of the price of crude oil and temporary shortages of gasoline in the United States. This caused many service stations to experience periods of time that summer when they were out of gasoline. Travel by automobile decreased, and the Wall Drug Store was one of many businesses hit by a decrease in sales. By 1981, however, sales had recovered. Exhibit 1 gives sales and net income after taxes for 1975 through 1989. In 1990, the store and its backyard covered 48,000 square feet and sales were $7.4 million. A map of the Wall Drug Store as it was in 1990 is shown in Exhibit 2.

THE HIGHWAY BEAUTIFICATION ACT AND WALL DRUG SIGNS

In 1965, Congress passed the Highway Beautification Act, which was designed to reduce the number of roadside signs. Anticipating the removal of many Wall Drug signs, the Husteads invested in new signs that were allowed under the initial legislation. Since these signs could be no closer than 660 feet from the highway, they had to be very large and cost around $9,000 each. By the time they were installed, the laws had been amended to exclude them.

In the late 1960's, concerned about the effects of losing their roadside signs, the Husteads began advertising in unusual and unlikely places. They began taking small advertisements in the European *International Herald Tribune* and Greenwich Village's *Village Voice.* They advertised 5 cent coffee, 49 cent breakfasts, and veterinary supplies. They put advertisements on double-decker busses in London, on the walls in the Paris Metro (subway), along the canals in Amsterdam, and in rail stations in Kenya. These ads brought letters and telephone calls and then news articles. First, *The Village Voice* carried an article, and in 1971, the Sunday *New York Times.* Bill Hustead appeared on the network television show "To Tell the Truth." In all, 260 articles about the store were printed in the 1970's and approximately the same number during the 1980's.

Passage of the Highway Beautification Act did not mean an end to roadside signs. Compliance with this legislation was slow in many states. Disputes over whether sign owners should be compensated for removed signs and a lack of local support for the law meant that some signs remained.

Bill Hustead served in the South Dakota state legislature during the 1960's and was chairman of the state joint senate-house Committee on Transportation when the Highway Beautification Act was passed. He and his committee wrote South Dakota's compliance law which resulted in the removal of 22,000 of the 28,000 roadside signs in the state. The federal government then fined the state for noncompliance, objecting to the establishment of commercial zones in which signs were permitted. The owners of roadside businesses challenged this federal enforcement and were successful. The federal government finally accepted a plan which allowed county governments to establish zones where signs were permitted. In South Dakota, this zoning resulted in an additional 1,000 signs being erected bringing the total to 7,000. Bill also testified at federal and state legislative hearings on laws to comply with the federal law. In 1981, Bill Hustead was appointed to the South Dakota Highway Commission, a position he still held in 1990.

By 1990, most remaining Wall Drug roadside signs were located in South Dakota, and there were fewer than 300. Existing signs were being permitted, but no new signs could be erected. Existing signs could be maintained and repainted, but could not be moved or enlarged. Federal legislation proposed in 1989 would have removed these signs without compensation, but the proposed bill was not passed; and the Husteads were more optimistic about the future of roadside advertising than they had been in many years.

Wall Drug sign coverage was still fairly intensive along Interstate 90. In 1990, a count of signs over a 250 mile stretch of I-90 east of Wall identified 86 Wall Drug signs. No two signs were alike, although about half had a characteristic design. These contained a short message, HAND MADE JEWELRY, for example, in dark green letters on a white background, and the logo, WALL DRUG, below in yellow letters on a dark green background. Other signs had a variety of colors and formats. A crew still serviced the signs twice a year, and all signs observed in 1990 were in excellent condition.

BUSINESS ENVIRONMENT

Wall is located at the northwest edge of The Badlands National Park (see Exhibit 3). The Badlands National Park is an area of 244,000 acres of barren ridges and peaks formed by centuries of erosion which exposed colorful layers of different minerals and fossil remains of prehistoric animals. Approximately one million people visit the Monument each year.

Rapid City, South Dakota (population, 44,000), is 50 miles to the west of Wall. Rapid City is on the eastern rim of the Black Hills, a forested mountain region and the site of several active gold mines. The Black Hills is also the site of the Mount Rushmore Memorial, which attracts about 2 million visitors each year. Forest Service visitation figures for the Badlands and Mount Rushmore are given in Exhibit 4.

Interstate Highway 90 is the only east-west interstate highway in South Dakota. It passes near The Badlands National Monument and through the Black Hills carrying most of the tourists which visit these areas. Exhibit 5 gives the traffic count on I-90 by month for 1988 and 1989. According to Ted Hustead, counts of traffic in the area of Wall showed that 78% of all cars which left Interstate 90 to drive a parallel road through the Badlands also entered Wall. For westbound I-90 traffic, 55% exited at Wall, and 45% of eastbound traffic turned off at the Wall exit. These counts were made during the summer months.

There were seven other gift shops in Wall, and an old West wax museum, a wild life

EXHIBIT 3
South Dakota: Location of Wall Drug Store

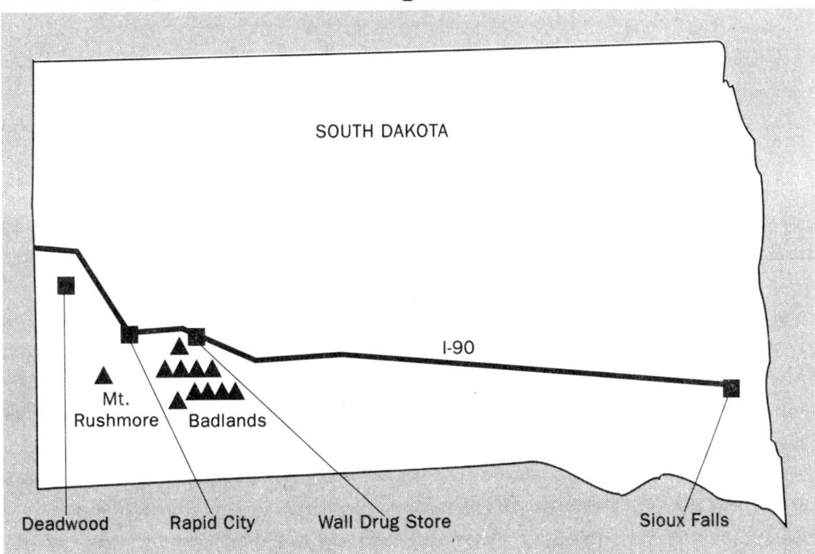

EXHIBIT 4
Annual Visitors

	Badlands National Monument	Mount Rushmore Memorial
1971	1,293,011	2,314,522
1973	1,400,000	n.a.*
1975	1,165,161	1,994,314
1977	1,303,471	2,271,838
1979	870,000	1,642,757
1981	1,187,970	2,054,567
1983	1,038,981	1,983,710
1985	962,242	2,112,281
1987	1,186,398	1,949,902
1988	1,122,040	2,013,749
1989	1,249,956	2,075,190

* n.a.: Not available.
Source: U.S. Forest Service.

museum, a taffy shop, and a Cactus Saloon and a Badlands Bar on Wall's Main Street. All depended primarily upon tourist business during the summer months. In the Spring of 1990, the Hustead family was preparing two new gift shops for June 1 openings. These shops were across the street from the main store. They were called Dakota Mercantile and The Tumbleweed.

Voters in South Dakota approved a referendum in 1988 to permit limited betting ($5) casino gambling to be licensed in the city of Deadwood, South Dakota (pop. 2409). Situated in the Black Hills 90 miles west of Wall and 11 miles off Interstate Highway 90, Deadwood was founded by gold miners and is near to several still active gold mines. During the 1880's it was home to well known western characters such as Calamity Jane and Wild Bill Hick-

EXHIBIT 5
Automatic Traffic Recorder Data
Average Daily Traffic on I-90 near Wall, S.D.

	1988	1989
January	1,674	1,975
February	1,867	1,954
March	2,184	2,353
April	2,567	2,606
May	3,361	3,420
June	4,919	5,160
July	5,615	5,847
August	5,629	6,086
September	3,875	4,233
October	3,401	3,609
November	2,675	3,141
December	2,372	2,374
Annual daily average	3,345	3,563

Source: South Dakota Department of Transportation.

EXHIBIT 6
Sales Receipts (in Thousands of Dollars)
Eating and Lodging Establishments

	Wall, S.D.		Deadwood, S.D.	
	Eating	Lodging	Eating	Lodging
1988:				
Jan.–Feb.	$106	$ 16	$275	$172
Mar.–Apr.	118	37	285	145
May–Jun.	358	366	502	318
Jul.–Aug.	550	740	823	613
Sep.–Oct.	270	204	372	434
Nov.–Dec.	115	32	296	158
1989:				
Jan.–Feb.	83	13	277	201
Mar.–Apr.	124	45	295	141
May–Jun.	385	414	538	344
Jul.–Aug.	641	911	883	724
Sep.–Oct.	328	300	434	243
Nov.–Dec.	134	54	495	265
1990:				
Jan.–Feb.	103	28	715	363

Source: South Dakota Department of Revenue.

ock. Hickock, in fact, was shot in the back and killed while playing poker in Deadwood. Legal gambling began again in November of 1989. While the full impact of the Deadwood gambling casinos on tourism in South Dakota could not yet be measured in early 1990, it was expected to result in an increase in traffic on Interstate 90, the most direct highway from the East. Exhibit 6 shows sales for all eating establishments and hotels and motels in Wall and Deadwood by two month periods from January 1988 through February 1990.

MANAGEMENT

Bill Hustead, 63, was the President and Chief Executive Officer of the Wall Drug Store. Bill and his wife, Marjorie, owned 60 percent of the stock in the company. Marjorie was the corporation Secretary and was active in the business and in charge of merchandise buying. Ted and Dorothy Hustead owned the remaining 40 percent of the stock. Both were in their late 80's and still participated in the store management. Ted was Chairman of the Board and was involved primarily in public and employee relations. Dorothy was also an officer of the corporation and managed the store's cash receipts accounting and banking.

Two of Bill and Marjorie's sons, Rick, 40, and Teddy, 39, were also active in store management. Rick had a Master's degree in guidance and counseling and had worked as a high school guidance counselor before joining the store in 1980. His primary responsibility was managing restaurant operations. Teddy had a degree in business and had worked for several years in the Alaskan oil fields before Rick persuaded him to join the store in 1988.

He was responsible for day-to-day management of the shops. Both brothers participated in strategic planning and policy making for the overall business.

While neither Rick or Teddy were pharmacists, Rick's wife, Kathy, was a registered pharmacist and worked three days a week managing the store's prescription drug business. In 1990, Teddy married and his wife, Karen, was to become the newest member of the Hustead family management team. Karen was the Executive Vice President of the Badlands and Black Hills Association. This was an organization of tourism related businesses in the region. It was expected that she would start as a floating troubleshooter involved in day-to-day store operations to learn the business, and that she would also have a role in public and governmental relations for the store.

Bill spoke about the significant roles of his mother and wife in the success of the Wall Drug Store.

> It's known as Ted and Bill Hustead's Wall Drug, but for years Dorothy was the backbone of the store. A few years ago, Dad and I were honored at a banquet and as I sat there and listened to the speeches a voice deep within me cried, Dorothy, Dorothy. She was the one with the idea to put up the signs. She was the one who worked behind the counter and in the restaurant.
>
> My wife, Marjorie, is the most valuable asset we have. After she took over the buying, we raised our net from the jewelry store by $50,000. She has a wide sphere of influence and is a stabilizing force.

If the Wall Drug Store was a family institution, it was also seen as an institution of great importance to the town of Wall and to the store's full-time employees. Bill Hustead's conversations about the Wall Drug Store frequently emphasized the importance of the business to the economy of the town of Wall, its importance as the only source of income in Wall for most of its full-time employees, and of the need to secure its continued success for the sake of the town and the store's employees. He also spoke of the business in terms of personal and family pride.

> The priest here in Wall thought I might have a calling for the priesthood, so my folks sent me to Trinity High School in Sioux City, Iowa. . . . One time I had a date with a girl who took me to her home. Some relatives, a married sister, I think, and her husband were there, and they made some slighting remarks about that "little store with all the signs." I was embarrassed. Gosh, Mom had the idea about the signs but then did Dad have to put them up all the way from Wisconsin to Montana?
>
> Then, when I worked in the store during the summer, I was embarrassed sometimes at some of the things customers would say about the store. Our facilities were so poor. We didn't even have indoor rest rooms.

There were two key managers who were not family members. Mike Huether worked with Rick in managing restaurant operations. The two were about the same age and had the same level of responsibility, but Bill noted that, "Mike isn't as likely to go to the mat with me." Huether was a long time employee who had worked at the Wall Drug Store since he was 18. Karen Poppe with 16 years' experience was the personnel manager. As the store grew and the competition for seasonal employees increased this function had become critical to the store's ability to grow or even function at the current level of operations.

The Wall Drug Store had no organization chart or written job descriptions, but all the managers believed that they had clear understandings as to their responsibilities and authority. Rick explained, "There is overlap. Ted (Teddy) and I have specific and joint responsibility. Ted's focus is more in retail. My focus is more in the restaurant. There is no organizational chart, but we spend enough time talking to each other so that our roles are defined."

Rick thought the store needed a more complete management staff but that they had made progress toward that in his ten years there. "Bill is a builder and a brilliant businessman. What I wanted to do is run the business more efficiently. It's paid off with more profits."

MANAGEMENT SUCCESSION

Asked about the difficulties of having three generations of the family active in the store management, Bill spoke of his own plans. "I went to a religious retreat earlier this month, then attended my cousin's funeral in the East and a funeral of a high school friend and I'm ten days behind in my work. Sometimes I think this darn job is killing me. I can't work ten or twelve hour days anymore."

The aspirations of his sons were a factor also. "My forty-year-old sons will have to have independence. The boys in the store (a brother and three sisters were not involved with the store) will get as much of the store as I can give them, but it's not that good a business. There's too much pressure." Asked about the fact that his father at 87 was still active in the business, he said, "I love my father. He's the best P.R. man anybody ever had."

He elaborated more on his past contributions to the business. "My plan was to work for awhile and then buy a drugstore in Jackson Hole, Wyoming, but Dad and Mom encouraged me to come here. They needed me desperately. Dad was never a floor man and they really needed someone on the floor."

Rick discussed the issue of management succession from his perspective. "We have a clear understanding with some documentation but no time table. Teddy came in with the understanding that we'd be partners. I'd like to see my Dad stay on as long as he wants. He is politically influential. He's a tremendous businessman. He's an asset to the business and to us. I hope he'll keep involved to the point he enjoys it. Control is not a major issue. If anyone is concerned about succession it's Bill." Rick also pointed out that the family had life insurance protection to assure that the business would not be crippled by inheritance taxes should anyone in the family die.

Ted, Sr., made it clear that he no longer expected to take an active role in making policy decisions. The 1989 South Dakota legislature had approved the licensing of video poker and keno machines which would accept bets up to two dollars. The Husteads had installed a few in the Western Art Gallery Dining Room where they had a liquor license and bar. Their intent was to evaluate the results and either remove them or install more depending on their profitability and their perceived contribution or detraction from the atmosphere. Asked about his attitude toward the decision to install video lottery machines, Ted said, "They don't need to ask me, and I don't want them to ask me, but if they had, I'd have said I didn't think much of them" (the video lottery machines).

Speaking of Bill's contribution to the store, Ted, Sr., commented, "My son Bill is an idea man. The Mall was his. He called in an architect and gave him the plans. Bill has built the art collection. He has a great appreciation for art. I bought the first few paintings, Bill bought the rest."

STORE OPERATIONS

The Wall Drug Store had approximately 30 permanent employees. Peak summer employment would reach 225. About 100 people from the local area were employed to do seasonal work and 120 college students were recruited to complete the work force. Ninety-five percent of the local seasonal employees would be people who had worked at Wall Drug in previous years. Many were housewives and senior citizens who could begin work in May and work during September and October when the college students were not available. About forty percent of the college students each year were repeat employees from previous years, but Wall Drug had to recruit about 70 new employees each year.

Student recruiting was handled by Karen Poppe. Each year 200 colleges and universities were sent recruitment information just prior to the Christmas break. She also made recruiting trips to about six colleges and attended several "job fairs." Recruitment of seasonal employees was becoming increasingly difficult and was seen by the Wall Drug management as a potential limit to their growth.

Mrs. Poppe and the Husteads thought that Wall's remoteness was a major obstacle to recruitment of summer employees from college campuses. The nationwide increase in the tourism industry meant that there were more companies recruiting from the same source. At the job fairs, Mrs. Poppe found herself competing with such major attractions as Disney World and other theme parks, and better known vacation areas such as Yellowstone Park. This made persuading students to choose the little town of Wall on the treeless plains of South Dakota more difficult each year.

Summer employees were housed in small dormitories and houses owned by the store. The store owned a swimming pool for employees and would have social gatherings such as picnics or volleyball games. Summer employees were paid $4.00 an hour and worked 40 hours plus 8 hours of overtime for which they were paid time-and-a-half. They paid $25 per week for their rooms. Students who stayed through the Labor Day weekend also got a 5 percent bonus and a rent reduction of $17 per week for the entire summer.

While the gambling casinos in Deadwood, South Dakota, 90 miles to the West were expected to result in increased traffic on I-90, they also competed for seasonal employees. In 1990, unskilled casino employees in Deadwood were being paid $7.00 an hour.

Wall Drug had formerly hired 1 of every 5 applicants for summer jobs. By 1990, they were having difficulty filling their positions. The labor scarcity had also had an effect on their personnel policies. As Bill explained, "We would exercise discipline. We expected to send a few people home just to let everyone know that we were serious. Now we get them out here and try to make it work. If they can't make change, we try to find a place for them. And it works better. We have a better atmosphere now."

New employees were trained to be courteous and informed about the Badlands, Black Hills, and other sites of interest in the area. Karen Poppe coordinated new employee orientation, but most of the members of the Hustead family participated. Ted, Sr., studied the applications and pictures of all summer employees so that he could greet them by name when they arrived and whenever he saw them working in the store.

The Wall Drug Store and restaurant had a total area of 48,000 square feet. By comparison, the average Wal-Mart store covered a little more than 56,000 square feet. In 1989, Wall Drug merchandise sales were $5.6 million. The restaurant was a self-service restaurant with seating for 500; it had sales of $1.8 million. In 1989, the average McDonald's had $1.6 million in sales. The opening of the two new stores, Dakota Mercantile and The Tumbleweed, would add another 6,000 square feet.

Wall Drug visitors frequently asked about purchasing items by mail. For several years the store had about $50,000 in mail order sales without catalogs or order forms. In 1989, Teddy designed a simple order form with the title, "Order By Mail Year Around From WALL DRUG." It listed a few items under the categories of jewelry, western art, boots and moccasins, western wear, western books and "Etc., Etc., Etc." Items listed under this last category were jackalopes, flying jackalopes, steer skulls, rattlesnake ashtrays, horse twitches, and souvenirs galore. This one page sheet also included a map of the store but listed no prices. It was available at cash registers for customers to take with them. Mail order sales increased to over $87,000 in 1989 and sales for the first three months of 1990 were up 47 percent over 1989. Most mail order sales were for bigger ticket items such as jewelry. The store also sold over 60 jackalopes by mail in 1989.

Commenting on Teddy's success with increasing mail order sales, Rick said, "A catalog would be the next step. We talk about building a model for this business, but we need to hire the talent to run it."

The Husteads were also trying to expand their tour bus business. Bus tours were an increasingly important factor in tourism. They were especially popular with senior citizens and foreign visitors. The Husteads believed that the ability to provide fast food service from their 500 seat, self-service restaurant would be a reason for bus tours to include them as a stop. They were also interested in persuading tour operators now running busses from Denver to the Black Hills to include the 100 mile round trip from Rapid City to the Badlands as part of the tour. This would also include a stop at Wall Drug. Attracting more of this business was assigned to Teddy who had increased the store's promotional efforts at bus tour operator conventions and trade shows. This had resulted in some increase in business, and about 90 busses were expected to include Wall Drug as a stop in 1990.

FINANCE

Exhibits 7 and 8 present income statements and balance sheets from 1983 through 1989. Historically, the store's growth and expansion projects had been financed through retained earnings and loans of up to ten year's duration. The long-term debt of $151,000 outstanding in 1989 consisted of approximately $82,000 owed on a stock repurchase agreement and a $69,000 interest bearing note. These debts were held by Hustead family members not active in the business and were being paid in monthly installments.

Wall Drug had a profit sharing plan for all employees who worked more than 1,000 hours during any year. At the discretion of the four senior Husteads who were the corporate officers, the plan paid up to 15% of employees' salaries into a retirement trust fund managed by an independent financial institution. Profits had always been sufficient to pay the full 15 percent. The store terminated a smaller noncontributory defined benefit plan in

EXHIBIT 7
Wall Drug Store: Income Statement
(in Thousands of Dollars)

	1983	*1984*	*1985*	*1986*	*1987*	*1988*	*1989*
Net sales	$4,851	$5,055	$5,273	$5,611	$6,142	$6,504	$7,419
Cost of goods sold	2,586	2,553	2,793	2,854	3,338	3,579	4,164
Gross profit	$2,265	$2,502	$2,480	$2,757	$2,804	$2,925	$3,255
General and administrative:							
Wages and salaries	$1,006	$1,129	$1,233	$1,274	$1,305	$1,443	$1,541
Officers' salaries	143	154	135	151	164	155	178
Depreciation	123	136	148	149	170	168	200
Profit sharing contribution	100	113	119	135	126	146	157
Advertising	93	82	99	122	107	123	44
Utilities	84	111	106	124	120	129	141
Conventions and conferences	1	1	3	3	16	14	21
Other	356	424	465	501	505	534	655
Total G & A expenses	$1,906	$2,150	$2,308	$2,459	$2,513	$2,712	$2,937
Income from operations	$ 359	$ 352	$ 172	$ 298	$ 291	$ 213	$ 318
Dividend and interest income	48	57	52	68	71	69	63
Interest (Expense)	(40)	(46)	(46)	(41)	(57)	(67)	(69)
Other income and (Expenses)	53	64	52	56	59	61	62
Pre tax income	$ 420	$ 427	$ 230	$ 381	$ 364	$ 276	$ 374
Income tax	162	143	69	148	115	72	132
Net income	$ 258	$ 284	$ 161	$ 233	$ 249	$ 204	$ 242
Preferred stock dividend	1	1	0	2	1	1	1
Add to retained earnings	$ 257	$ 283	$ 161	$ 231	$ 248	$ 203	$ 241

Numbers may not add due to rounding.
Source: Company records.

1988. All participating employees were fully vested in their earned benefits under the old plan.

Inventory levels are shown as of December 31. Orders for the coming season began arriving in December, but most would arrive from January through April. Peak inventory levels would reach $2.5 million. Many suppliers would postdate invoices for July and August, which eased the cash flow burden of financing this seasonal inventory.

The art collection was used primarily to attract customers and repeat customers. Prices for the paintings were not established. When paintings were sold the prices were negotiated. The collection was carried in the accounts as merchandise inventory and valued at cost.

A small part of the inventory consisted of gold bullion which would be sold periodically to the store's main jewelry supplier in Rapid City. This practice provided a hedge against rising gold prices. In 1990, because of the need to finance the new stores, the stocks of bullion were low.

The $300,000 reserve for self insurance was established in 1982. The store was a self insurer for collision and comprehensive coverage of its motor vehicles, of the deductible

EXHIBIT 8
Wall Drug Store: Balance Sheets
Years Ended December 31
(in Thousands of Dollars)

	1983	1984	1985	1986	1987	1988	1989
		Assets					
Assets							
Current assets:							
Cash	$ 40	$ 12	$ 18	$ 29	$ 70	$ 59	$ 267
Current marketable securities	205	0	0	1	1	2	0
Accounts receivable	13	25	24	25	36	48	41
Merchandise inventory	405	616	718	968	1,322	1,429	1,330
Prepaid taxes and other	33	32	114	57	68	112	52
Total current assets	$ 696	$ 685	$ 874	$1,080	$1,497	$1,650	$1,690
Investments and other assets:							
Noncurrent marketable securities	402	489	600	785	739	646	487
Life insurance and other	7	7	7	8	14	13	79
Total other assets	$ 409	$ 496	$ 607	$ 793	$ 753	$ 659	$ 566
Property and equipment:							
Land	$ 174	$ 177	$ 187	$ 186	$ 171	$ 181	$ 181
Building and improvements	1,935	2,057	2,112	2,160	2,434	2,495	2,567
Equipment, furniture and fixture	1,065	1,232	1,278	1,372	1,492	1,628	1,795
Construction in progress	0	0	0	55	0	0	148
Total property and equipment	$3,174	$3,466	$3,577	$3,774*	$4,097	$4,304	$4,691
Less accumulated depreciation	1,475	1,609	1,732	1,869	2,032	2,182	2,385
Net property and equipment	$1,669	$1,857	$1,845	$1,905*	$2,065	$2,122	$2,306
Goodwill at cost less accumulated amortization	16	14	12	10	9	7	5
Total assets	$2,820	$3,052	$3,338	$3,788	$4,324	4,438	$4,567
		Liabilities and Equity					
Liabilities							
Current liabilities:							
Current maturities of long-term debt	$ 40	$ 10	$ 2	$ 2	$ 2	$ 2	$ 2
Notes payable	50	85	175	310	598	500	275
Accounts payable	61	40	41	54	60	44	77
Taxes payable	93	67	75	95	81	75	128
Accrued profit sharing contribution	100	113	119	135	127	146	157
Accrued pension plan payable	0	0	29	25	31	15	0
Accrued payroll and bonuses	65	50	34	48	56	56	73
Accrued interest payable	4	2	4	1	7	5	2
Total current liabilities	$ 413	$ 367	$ 479	$ 670	$ 962	$ 843	$ 714
Long-term debt	182	173	173	172	156	154	152
Deferred income taxes	10	25	27	56	68	101	121
Stockholders' equity:							
Preferred stock	$ 30	$ 30	$ 30	$ 30	$ 30	$ 30	$ 30
Class A common stock	48	48	48	48	48	48	48
Class B common stock (nonvoting)	53	53	53	53	53	53	53
Capital in excess of par	52	52	52	52	52	52	52
Reserve for self insurance	300	300	300	300	300	300	300
Retained earnings	1,732	2,004	2,176	2,407	2,654	2,857	3,097
Total stockholders' equity	$2,215	$2,487	$2,659	$2,890	$3,137	$3,340	$3,580
Total liabilities and equity	$2,820	$3,052	$3,338	$3,788	$4,322	$4,438	$4,567

* These numbers may be slightly off due to rounding.
Source: Company records.

portion of its employees' medical coverage and a portion of the casualty coverage of some buildings and their contents. A portion of the store's marketable securities funded this reserve.

EXPANSION PLANS FOR THE 1990'S

As he prepared for the 1990 tourist season, Bill Hustead, CEO of Wall Drug, was making plans for the store's most ambitious expansion. This expansion would include a large open mall ringed with shops to be built to the rear of the existing backyard area. Houses along the street to the rear of the store, already owned by the Husteads, would be moved or razed to make room for this expansion.

New shops with a combined floor space of nearly 15,000 square feet would include a shop selling Indian handicraft items, a poster store, a yogurt shop, a fast food hamburger shop, and a store for motorcyclists. (Sturgis, South Dakota, in the Black Hills is the site of an annual summer motorcycle rally which attracts thousands of motorcyclists from all over North America.) A major feature of the new addition would be a free gallery displaying a recently acquired collection of over 700 old photographs of cattle drives, rodeos, Indians, cowboys, and other early settlers of South Dakota and Montana. The Husteads estimated that approximately twelve to fourteen additional employees would be required to staff this expansion during the peak season.

Bill planned to build this expansion over a period of three to five years. As with previous expansions, he planned to act as his own general contractor and direct the actual construction. When the project was finished, the existing backyard would be removed. This was constructed of metal buildings and had about 3,000 square feet of floor space.

The last project being planned was to build the Wall Drug Western Art Gallery and guest house. This would be a three story mansion, a replica of an old Southern plantation house, to display the best of the Wall Drug Store's western art collection. It would also display beautiful furnishings, elegant table settings, crystal, and other accoutrements of graceful living. The Hustead art collection included 30 paintings portraying Christmas in the West. Bill planned to have a Christmas room in the mansion to display these paintings and a permanent Christmas trees with antique ornaments. The third floor was planned as a theater which would show films or videotapes about some of the artists and a film or a videotape about the Wall Drug Store. Some rooms in the mansion were to be set aside as guest quarters.

Bill planned to charge a small admission fee to the mansion. This income would be used to purchase new paintings for the art collection. Bill explained:

> There is more to business than just profit. We are aiming at sophisticated people who will get a kick out of this. Forty percent of our business is from repeat customers so we've got to keep moving in such a way as to impress people. We've got to keep forward momentum.

Bill believed that the very survival of the business and the jobs and aspirations of his full time employees depended on the Wall Drug Store's continued development.

> We are not Wal-Mart. We are in the entertainment business. We can't just sit here with what we've got and expect people to keep coming.

Bill Hustead was aware that his two sons had serious reservations about his expansion plans. Commenting on the proposed expansion, Rick said,

> Dad is more oriented to seeing the business as a real attraction—a "must stop" attraction. I'm more concerned with the nuts and bolts. I want to be profitable. I want a better handle on our inventory and labor. My concern is always that we are profitable and don't overextend or build things that won't be profitable. What he plans to do is interesting, but I have real questions about the mansion. Are we going to realize a profit? This could cost one and a half or two million dollars. Fortunately it is the farthest down the road. We should expand the food service first.
>
> I'm conservative. I resisted the new shops (Dakota Mercantile and The Tumbleweed) at first. The building estimates were $210,000. They cost $300,000. They are nice shops but getting personnel to run them is an issue.

The Husteads did not use a formal system of evaluating return on investment in making decisions about expansion. Rick noted, however, that these decisions were subjected to analysis. "Dad knows his expenses and his volumes. We know that we have to gross $200,000 or better in the new shops to be successful."

Bill estimated that the new stores would have a payback of approximately five years. He reported that their cost had actually been about $240,000. As to the expense of the proposed expansion plans, he said, "There is no way we are going to spend one and a half to two million dollars. The total cost of the backyard expansion and the art gallery will be between eight to nine hundred thousand and one and a half million dollars."

Teddy felt that he was somewhere in the middle on the expansion plans.

> We have got to replace the backyard and make the store more interesting, but the mansion never has made too much sense to me. I have a lot of respect for my father, but he got this idea from homes in the South. I don't know if it applies to the West. On the other hand, we are getting to have a world class collection of western art. I don't ever want to underestimate him.

Teddy also pointed out that the existing building needed extensive repairs. "The roof around the tree needs to be replaced. A few years ago the tree was trimmed back, and it died so now it has to go." Teddy estimated that these repairs would cost $200,000. He noted further that the store's administrative offices had been built in 1964 for a much smaller staff and were inadequate for current operations.

Bill commented on the objection his sons had raised to the mansion style art gallery. "People from the South settled in South Dakota and some houses of this type were built here, but it wouldn't have to be a southern style mansion. It could be another type of building."

In May, the 1990 season began on a promising note. The first two weeks of sales in the Dakota Mercantile and Tumbleweed stores were very good. "It's now or never," Bill commented, reflecting on the seasonal character of their business. Sales in the main store were also running ahead of 1989's, and bus loads of travelers bound for Deadwood were stopping to eat and shop.

CASE 4

Brooktrout Technology, Inc.*

> It's violent out there, and people in violent industries sometimes get killed. It's violent because it's changing rapidly. There are bodies all over the place in the voice mail segment. Computerm, for example, had $14 million invested and sold out for a pittance.
>
> There are some very big companies, like AT&T, that are our potential customers—but they can also produce their *own* electronic messaging products. When you go to these big companies it's like walking underneath elephants: you just hope the elephant doesn't step on you. But they don't move real fast, so you can watch out for them.

It was June of 1989, and Eric Giler, president of Brooktrout Technology, Inc., knew his company was at a crossroads. What strategy would best bring the high growth he wanted, while minimizing risk? Giler faced tough choices in marketing and finance as he wondered how to capitalize on his firm's technical skills.

Brooktrout designed and built electronic messaging systems—the equipment which automatically answers a business telephone and accepts a message for a specific individual. Some products were full systems in their own cabinets; others were separate electronic cards to be plugged into computers. Brooktrout sold mainly to original equipment manufacturers (OEMs) in the telecommunications industry. Its customers included some of the world's largest builders of telephone equipment.

Brooktrout Technology was founded in 1984 by Eric Giler, David Duehren, and Patrick Hynes; all had worked together previously at Teradyne, Inc. The new company lost money in each of its first five years, but Eric expected 1989 to be profitable, with sales approaching $5 million (Exhibit 1 shows financial data on the company). Eric commented,

> It's high risk, but also high reward. We can build a $100 million company in this business; after all, it's a multi-billion dollar industry. The expertise we have is our technology. We understand what makes it possible to do electronic messaging and our goal in life is to sell it on an OEM basis to companies that need it. We will make a product that is cheaper, or faster.

TELECOMMUNICATIONS INDUSTRY: HISTORY

On January 8, 1982, American Telephone and Telegraph Company agreed to end its 48-year history as a regulated monopoly. In its total lifespan of 106 years, the company had

* Prepared by Raymond M. Kinnunen and Wendy Vittori, Northeastern University, and John A. Seeger, Bentley College, as a basis for class discussion. Financial statements have been disguised. Distributed by the North American Case Research Association. Videotapes of Eric Giler discussing this case with Executive MBA students are available from Northeastern University, College of Business Administration, Boston, MA 02115.

created the telecommunications system which served as a world model. AT&T provided local phone service through its wholly owned geographic subsidiaries (e.g., New England Telephone and Telegraph) to 80% of American homes. Through its Western Electric manufacturing arm, it made virtually all of the nation's telephone equipment. Through its Bell Laboratories—renowned as the leading electronics R&D center of the world—it developed new technologies (including, for example, the first transistors). Unfettered by competition, AT&T devoted itself to providing superb quality and service. By regulation, it was assured a profit based on its investment. AT&T's asset base thus grew phenomenally; by 1984, when the company was divided, its total of $150 billion in assets dwarfed the size of most nations' economies. In assets and profits, AT&T was the largest company in the world.

For most of its history, to preserve the quality of its lines, AT&T absolutely prohibited any other company's equipment from being attached to its network. The historic Carterfone decision in 1968 made it legal for non-Bell equipment to be attached to public lines; the first privately owned telephone answering machine, barred by AT&T for years, now had to be admitted to the network and the market for terminal equipment was opened.

As a monopoly, AT&T had been restrained from competing in the open marketplace; at the same time it was often criticized for commercial practices which made market penetration difficult for makers of specialized terminal equipment. In the industry, it was widely thought that AT&T saw itself as the major potential competitor to IBM in the computer industry. In the 1982 agreement, settling an antitrust suit by the government, the

EXHIBIT 1
Brooktrout Technology, Inc.
Statement of Operations
(in Thousands of Dollars)

					Projected	
	1985	***1986***	***1987***	***1988***	***1989***	***1990***
Revenues:						
Voice					3,490	6,396
Facsimile					1,231	3,444
Total revenues	$271	$510	$1,378	$2,418	$4,721	$9,840
Cost of sales:						
Voice					1,920	3,518
Facsimile					391	1,722
Total cost of sales	114	191	566	1,076	2,311	5,240
Gross profit	157	319	812	1,342	2,410	4,600
Operating expenses:						
Sales & mktg.	79	134	425	682	685	1,118
Research & devel.	214	553	354	568	726	1,332
General & admin.	289	622	474	422	568	925
Total expenses	582	1,309	1,253	1,672	1,979	3,375
Net interest exp.	(5)	(175)	(391)	(120)	(110)	(198)
Net income/(loss)	($430)	($1,165)	($832)	($450)	$321	$1,027

EXHIBIT 1 (cont.)
Brooktrout Technology, Inc.
Financial Statements—Balance Sheet
(in Thousands of Dollars)

	1985	*1986*	*1987*	*1988*
Assets				
Current assets:				
Cash	$ 96	$ 82	$274	$122
Accounts receivable	115	74	318	402
Inventory	62	44	124	236
Other current assets	0	26	5	24
Total current assets	273	226	721	784
Property & equipment (net of accumulated depreciation)	86	81	101	119
Other assets	26	16	13	8
Total assets	$385	$323	$835	$911
Liabilities and shareholders' equity				
Current liabilities:				
Accounts payable	$110	$126	$254	$440
Notes payable	72	160	102	90
Current portion of long-term debt	12	28	85	84
Other liabilities	70	71	86	140
Total current liabilities	264	385	527	754
Notes payable to stockholders	88	416	578	548
Other long-term debt	6	340	300	331
Total liabilities	358	1,141	1,405	1,633
Net stockholders' equity	28	(818)	(571)	(722)
Total liabilities and stockholders' equity	$386	$ 323	$ 834	$ 911

company officially acceded to being dismantled. Its local telephone operating companies, still working as regulated monopolies, were spun off into seven regional holding companies. The breakup—the largest financial transaction in world history—was completed in late 1983. AT&T was now free to compete. (See Exhibits 2 and 3 for comparative sizes of the units, before and after the breakup.)

TELECOMMUNICATIONS INDUSTRY: STRUCTURE

The telecommunications industry consisted of three major segments—local telephone companies, long distance carriers, and telephone equipment manufacturers—and one relatively small segment, information products and services, where Brooktrout Technology competed. (Exhibit 4 gives examples of leading entrants in all four segments.)

The information products and services segment resulted from the combination of computer and telecommunications technologies during the 1980s. These combined technologies made it possible for data to be processed as well as transmitted by the communica-

EXHIBIT 2
Brooktrout Technology, Inc.
Values and Operating Results of Leading Telephone Companies
(in Millions of Dollars)

	Assets	Sales	Market Value	Net Profit
AT&T (1983)	149,530	69,403	59,392	5,747
AT&T (1988)	35,152	35,210	30,868	− 1,669
Bell operating companies, 1988:				
Ameritech	19,163	9,903	12,888	1,237
Bell Atlantic	24,729	10,880	14,013	1,317
BellSouth	28,472	13,597	18,504	1,666
Nynex	25,378	12,661	12,997	1,315
Pacific Telesis	21,191	9,483	12,934	1,188
Southwestern Bell	20,985	8,453	12,129	1,060
U.S. West	22,416	9,221	10,548	1,132
Other firms, 1988:				
GTE	31,104	16,460	14,520	1,225
MCI Communications	5,843	5,137	5,498	356

Source: The Forbes 500s (1984, April 30; 1989, May 1). *Forbes.*

tions networks, thus creating "intelligent communications" (new products combining hardware innovations, computer technology, and software). By 1989, this segment of the telecommunications industry was a hotbed of competitive marketing activity, with contenders ranging from heavyweights like AT&T's own Bell Laboratories, to entrepreneurial newcomers such as Brooktrout Technology, Inc.

EXHIBIT 3
Brooktrout Technology, Inc.
Rankings of Leading Telephone Companies

	Assets	Sales	Market Value	Net Profit
AT&T (1983)	1	3	2	1
AT&T (1988)	36	9	4	n/m*
Bell operating companies, 1988:				
Ameritech	85	66	28	19
Bell Atlantic	63	51	22	16
BellSouth	52	38	12	13
Nynex	60	41	26	17
Pacific Telesis	75	72	27	24
Southwestern Bell	79	83	32	30
U.S. West	69	73	38	27
Other firms, 1988:				
GTE	41	32	20	20
MCI Communications	271	154	81	142

* n/m = Not meaningful.
Note: Figures give rank among the top 500 American businesses, including banks and financial services firms.
Source: The Forbes 500s (1984, April 30; 1989, May 1). *Forbes.*

EXHIBIT 4
Brooktrout Technology, Inc.
Segments of the Industry (and Examples of Active Competitors)

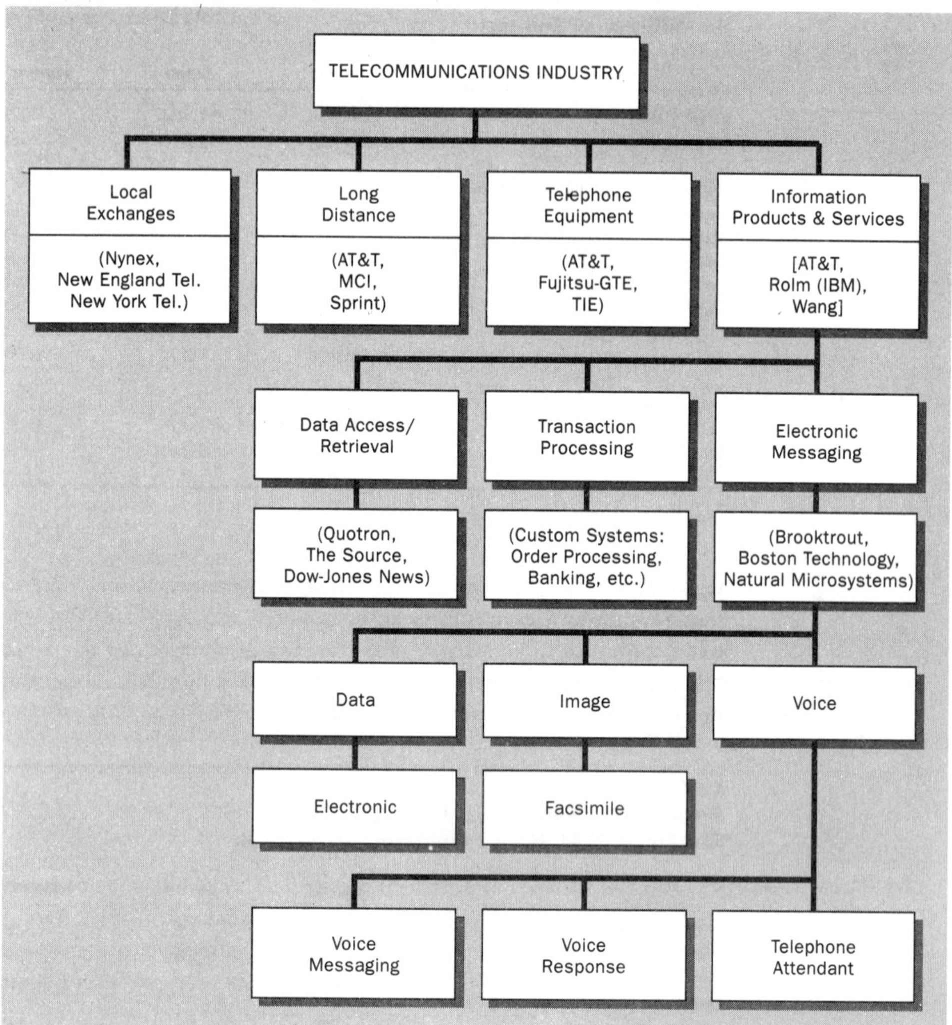

Local Exchange Operators

Before deregulation, local telephone companies were the only source for all telephone equipment and services. After deregulation, many vendors began to supply the market. Businesses began to purchase and install their own private branch exchanges (PBXs), which performed all the telephone functions that were internal to a given business. PBXs were sold based on lower costs, more features, and greater control for a business over its phone usage than the telephone company's standard service could offer.

With competition increasing, local telephone companies enhanced the level of service they provided beyond simple transmission. Since pricing on local phone calls was regulated, their principal competitive weapons were additional services. The telephone companies turned to the private sector for equipment they could sell in competition with the industry newcomers. Thus the new manufacturers of telecommunications equipment had two markets—one to businesses, and another to the telephone companies who in turn sold to businesses.

New opportunities for products and services continued to grow. In 1988, a court decision permitted local telephone companies to transmit information services. Options such as call-forwarding and call-waiting could now be offered to even single-line subscribers. In the future lay provision of services such as stock quotations and transactions, and merchandise selection and purchase, all through the telephone company. A recent advance allowed multiple phone numbers to be channeled to a single line, a cost-effective solution for home businesses with only one phone line. Publishing and computer/telecommunications integration were major new business thrusts.

Long Distance Carriers

Long distance transmission continued to be dominated by AT&T following deregulation, with 87% of the long distance customers handled by AT&T in 1988. The only major competitors to AT&T were MCI and US Sprint, each with 5–6% of the customer base. Both of these new firms were pursuing high-growth strategies in 1989 based on the lower cost and higher quality of fiber optic, microwave, and satellite transmission technologies.

Low costs were vital in selling telecommunications services to business. Dedicated long distance services, where a corporation owned its own satellite network, were also attracting a share of the total long distance transmissions in the United States. Long distance carriers were beginning to install these end-to-end transmission services for large customers. This connected long distance service directly to a PBX, eliminating the need to connect via the local exchange.

Telephone Equipment Manufacturers

After deregulation, the decision on what equipment to buy and where to install it was made by the customer, who could lease or purchase as much or as little equipment as desired, from a vendor of its choice. Private branch exchange (PBX) equipment sales grew tremendously, breaking $3 billion per year in 1988.

Twenty years after the Carterfone decision, the market for "customer premise" equipment had grown to $8 billion per year, but the growth rate was expected to slow from 8.7% in 1988 to 4.8% by 1992. Several larger firms (AT&T, Northern Telecom, Siemens) together controlled more than 50% of the market. However, smaller manufacturers, like TIE Communications, had made inroads by offering lower prices, enhanced features (least-cost routing, voice messaging, and other advanced exchange and information services), quality of service, testing, and maintenance. Under this kind of competitive pressure, prices of electronic components fell by half every two to three years.

Small entrepreneurial manufacturers and software houses (like Brooktrout Technology) provided many of the innovations behind new services. These small firms might sell to the larger equipment firms, to the regional Bell operating companies, and/or to the end

EXHIBIT 5
Brooktrout Technology, Inc.
Merger and Acquisition Activity in Consumer Premises Equipment Firms
Representative Activity, 1987–1988

	CPE Sales (In Millions of Dollars)			
CPE Manufacturer	**1986**	**1987**	**1988(a)**	**Acquired by**
Contel/Executone	$268	$305	$335*	Isotek/Vodavi
Tel Plus Comm., Inc.	255	283*	320	Siemens
RCA Telephone Systems	120	130	140*	Mitel
Universal Comm. Systems	87	106*	n/a	BellSouth
Jarvis Corp.	36	38*	40	Isotec
All American Businessphones	25	28	30*	TIE (b)
Gray Communications	25	22	25*	AIM Tel
Henkel & McCoy/Telecom	19	21*	25	Star Datacom
Interconnect Comm. Corp.	7	22*	38	Inter-Tel
	$842	$955	$953	

* = Year of acquisition.
a = Estimated sales following acquisition.
b = Acquisition proposed.
Source: *Telephony* (1988, April 11).

users themselves. Acquisition and merger activity was high (see Exhibit 5), as larger firms brought these high-technology skills in-house.

Information Products and Services

The compound annual growth rate for the information products and services segment was forecast to be approximately 25% from 1988 to 1992.[1] Some of the major subsegments (examples are given in Exhibit 4) were Data Access and Retrieval, Transaction Processing, and Electronic Messaging (the segment where Brooktrout Technology competed).

Electronic Messaging products allowed users to send and receive messages from other users, by voice, data, or image transmission. The messaging product either replaced or augmented a person-to-person phone conversation. Specific examples included electronic mail, facsimile, and voice messaging.

Principal "Voice Store and Forward" (VSF) products were telephone attendant systems, voice messaging, and voice response systems. Telephone attendant systems replaced a switchboard operator with an automated system—a "silicon Sally" computerized voice which prompted the caller to enter codes in order to route a call to the proper extension. Voice messaging provided for recording, storing, and playing back messages, as with a simple telephone answering machine but using a much more flexible computer storage and retrieval technology. Voice response systems could carry on a dialogue with the caller in order to perform functions such as order-taking and account inquiry.

Although VSF was a small subsegment within the overall telecommunications in-

[1] *Telephony*, May 16, 1988.

EXHIBIT 6
Brooktrout Technology, Inc.
The Market for Telecommunications, 1988
(in Millions of Dollars)

	1988 Revenues	Projected Compound Annual Growth Rate (Percent)*
Public network services:		
Local services	$ 87,558	
Long distance services	52,400	
Cellular/public data nets	2,842	
Total network services	$142,800	
Business communications equipment market—voice:		
Private branch exchanges (PBXs)	$3,182	2.6
Key systems	2,316	0.9
Facsimile	1,041	17.8
Voice messaging	426	23.6
Automated call distribution	284	7.1
Call accounting	281	4.4
Video teleconferencing	264	26.5
Phones	125	6.9
Integrated voice-data terminals	73	2.9
Total voice equipment market	$7,992	
Business communications equipment market—data:		
Local area networks	$2,400	22.4
Modems	1,200	−6.2
Front-end processors	625	6.7
Network management systems	457	13.8
Private packet switching	432	17.0
T-1 multiplexors	403	12.9
Statistical multiplexors	299	−5.5
Circuit/data switching units	122	12.7
Data PBXs	85	−4.7
Total data equipment market	$6,023	

* Estimated annual growth rates for the period 1988–1992.
Source: *Forecast '88,* Dataquest Inc.

dustry, in 1989 it was growing very rapidly (see Exhibit 6). From revenues of $200 million in 1986 and $426 million in 1988, the VSF segment was expected to reach $1 billion in 1990.[2]

Voice Store and Forward

Brooktrout Technology in 1989 competed in the Voice Store and Forward segment, with products in both voice messaging and facsimile messaging. A VSF system was based on a technology known as "digital signal processing," used to capture voice signals and convert them into a string of digital "bits" which could be computer processed. Only a few VSF manufacturers, such as Brooktrout, had developed in-house expertise in this basic technology.

[2] "Voice Mail Matures: Sales Boom as Applications Explode." *Teleconnect,* September, 1988.

EXHIBIT 7
Brooktrout Technology, Inc.
VSF Equipment Market

System Size	Number of Ports*	System Size as Percent of Total Market	Percent Market Share for Segment Size	
Large systems (mainframe)	32–1500	52	Rolm	45
			AT&T	13
Medium systems (minicomputer)	8–32	47	Centigram	17
			Opcom	17
			Rolm	14
			Wang	13
			Digital Sound	11
			Genesis	11
			AT&T	3
Small systems (personal computer)	1–8	1	Natural Microsystems	30
			Brooktrout	20
			AT&T	15

* Ports are the number of telephone lines a system is capable of accommodating simultaneously. System capacities here are estimates by Eric Giler.
Source: Frost & Sullivan (1988). Report Number A1867 (quoted with permission).

Traditionally, voice processing applications had required the processing power of a host mini-computer, and products based on these large systems still represented the vast majority of the market in 1989 (see Exhibit 7). However, the new generation of more powerful personal computers was creating an increasingly strong alternative for low-end VSF host computers. In fact, the market researcher, Dataquest, had predicted:

> The low-end segment [of VSF] brings to the voice messaging market what PCs brought to the computer industry—cost-effective, flexible, powerful applications processors for small to medium-size businesses or organizations.[3]

Others had forecast that PC-based systems were not likely to achieve significant market share, because telephone answering machines and service bureaus could provide the services needed by a small user at a lower cost (almost no cost with a telephone answering machine). Service bureaus used large-scale VSF systems based on mini or mainframe computer hosts, and rented voice messaging services to companies without their own on-site VSF systems. This could be a cost-effective alternative to PC-based systems for small users who needed the sophisticated capabilities of VSF. Even larger firms were contracting service bureaus for voice services. Probe Research, Inc., forecast VSF service bureau revenues to be $271 million by 1990.

Local telephone companies were also looking at the opportunities that voice messaging might offer. Ameritech, one of the regional Bell companies, had acquired Tigon Corp.,

[3] *Telephony,* November 14, 1988.

the nation's largest voice messaging service bureau (with corporate clients like Ford Motor Co.), in late 1988. Bell Atlantic had recently contracted with Boston Technology, a small voice messaging company founded in 1986, for its newly introduced central-office-based voice processing system. Although Boston Technology had first developed small, stand-alone systems, "from the beginning, we believed that there was a need for a huge voice processing system," said Greg Carr, the firm's president. "Their proposal got our attention immediately," commented Kathy Maier, Bell Atlantic's product manager for enhanced voice services. "Its size—1536 ports, 7000 hours of voice storage capacity, support of 104,000 voice mailboxes—is a major factor."

Facsimile machines were the most recent addition to the electronic messaging segment. These machines, which were priced as low as $600 in 1989, used digital signal processing technology similar to that used in VSF to transmit images via telephone lines. Sales of facsimile machines in 1988 of $2.2 billion were projected to reach $6.6 billion by 1992.[4]

Electronic mail involved computer-to-computer communication of data (rather than voice) messages. Although more expensive and not so easy to use as VSF or facsimile (because it required specialized training for each user), electronic mail had the great advantage of transmitting both messages and data in a format that could be understood and further manipulated by computer programs.

Distribution

The distribution system for Information Products and Services was complex. For example, all of the following were being used to distribute Voice Store and Forward systems.

Local Exchange Operators. Telephone companies purchased VSF equipment on an OEM basis, to build into the equipment they sold for their own telephone services, such as Centrex. GTE, for example, offered many services including Telemessager (voice mail) and Telemail (electronic mail).

Telephone Equipment Manufacturers (OEMs). These firms purchased and incorporated VSF products into their own devices, such as PBXs. In some cases, they would simply license the VSF technology and manufacture the actual products themselves. Many of these manufacturers would customize their VSF systems in order to differentiate their end products in the mind of the end user, even though the components might have a common origin. The identity of the VSF manufacturer was generally not revealed in the end product. Prominent among these original equipment manufacturers were AT&T, Rolm, TIE, and Iwatsu. The largest suppliers of VSF products to OEMs were Brooktrout, Genesis, and AT&T.

Telephone System Dealers. Dealers were either independent or affiliated with an equipment manufacturer. Independent dealers generally carried multiple brands of business telephone systems, PBXs, and other telecommunications equipment. There had been an increasing trend for equipment manufacturers to integrate forward by purchasing independent dealers. As a result, some of the dealers sold only one brand of equipment (e.g.,

---

[4] *Communications Week,* February 20, 1989.

Rolm or GTE), while others still represented multiple brands. Dealers generally provided complete installation and maintenance service.

Service Bureaus. Purchased large VSF systems to be time-shared by both small and large businesses.

Computer Stores. Low-end VSF systems could be sold as add-on circuit boards for personal computers, through computer stores.

Direct Sales. Some firms, most notably Natural Microsystems, had promoted and sold their products directly to end users, using methods such as direct mail or advertising directed to the personal computer owner.

Historically, PC-based VSF systems had been sold principally on an OEM basis to the telephone equipment manufacturers. Some two-thirds of VSF manufacturers' revenues were derived from OEMs. The remaining third was split between direct sales and computer and telephone system dealers.

Industry Trends

Several key trends were apparent in the telecommunications equipment industry at the end of the 1980s. Competition seemed likely to intensify. Worldwide markets were likely to appear as multinational firms spread their use of electronic messaging and overseas telephone companies upgraded their services. Prices were expected to decline as Asian manufacturers and new entrants brought lower costs into mainstream products. Continued reduction of the regulations on the Bell Operating Companies could translate to faster market expansion and larger shares for their OEM purchases. Rapid acceptance of new technologies, as exemplified by the history of the facsimile machine, could make any new product an overnight phenomenon. The appearance of new applications for electronic messaging products was likely, but what they would be was unknown.

In technology, customers and suppliers alike were pushing for adoption of industry-wide communications standards, rather than vendor-specific codes. This trend influenced the entire computer/software industry; it would eliminate the many difficulties that existed in 1989 in transferring information across networks containing hardware from many different makers. Information service providers stood to benefit directly from standardization, as their products could be used on a wider array of equipment.

In 1989, the information products and services industry was dynamic, complex, and highly unpredictable. A key phrase for the future of the telecommunications industry appeared to be system integration. One industry analyst stated:

> Computers can switch phone calls, and PBXs can do computing. [We can] predict a day, perhaps five or ten years away, when system integration for the business customer will include not only telephone service but word processing, commercial data processing, and facsimile data transmission.[5]

---

[5] Gerald R. Faulhaber, *Telecommunications in Turmoil: Technology and Public Policy.* Cambridge, MA, Ballinger, 1987, pp. 129–130.

BROOKTROUT TECHNOLOGY, INC.

History

In 1984, Eric Giler, Dave Duehren, and Pat Hynes—a technical marketer and two design engineers—founded Brooktrout Technology to take advantage of the technical ideas they had begun to think about at their previous jobs. With their expertise in digital signal processing, they felt they could integrate voice messaging with text, graphics, image processing, and data communications—putting all the functions into a single piece of hardware.

Armed with a business plan projecting $3 million in sales the first year, they began to seek financing. Eric Giler reflected on the early efforts:

> We thought at first that raising capital would be easy. But when we tried, we found doors closing on us for two reasons. One, we were young. Second, the venture capitalists couldn't believe that people would talk to machines, even if the systems worked perfectly. So for the first six months we operated the company out of an apartment.

Eric and his partners decided to seek money privately, and in several private placements in the first two years raised $1.5 million from approximately 50 investors. In 1987, a major telephone equipment manufacturer injected $1 million in cash for a minority equity position. By 1989 Brooktrout had raised a total of $2.5 million to finance its growth, and was anticipating its first profitable year (Exhibit 1 shows financial data and projections). The founders, equal owners from the beginning, still retained a 30% ownership stake in Brooktrout.

Eric Giler, Brooktrout's president, had received an undergraduate degree in management science from Carnegie-Mellon and an M.B.A. from Harvard (in 1982). Pat Hynes (V.P. of Engineering) and Dave Duehren (V.P. of R&D) were electrical engineers. Both had bachelors degrees from M.I.T.; Duehren's M.S. was also from M.I.T., while Hynes's was from Columbia. Hynes, an avid trout fisherman, chose the name for the new company.

In 1987 Eric hired Stephen Ide, a twenty-year veteran in telecommunications and a former consultant to Brooktrout, as Vice President of Sales and Marketing. Ide had founded and served as president of Computer Telephone Corp., a publicly held company with $14 million in sales. In 1988, Bob Leahy, former Controller and Treasurer of Cambridge Robotic Systems, was hired as Treasurer. Leahy, holder of a B.S. in Accounting from Bentley College, brought a diverse background in high-technology finance. Eric was comfortable with the progress they had made building the top management team as well as the technical organization; by mid-1989, six additional engineers—hired directly out of local colleges—supplemented the efforts of Hynes and Duehren. Another five worked in production and seven in marketing. "We have the team in place; now we have to figure out how to grow it," said Eric.

Brooktrout Products

The first products to be made by Brooktrout were for voice messaging. At the time, Eric Giler said, this seemed the most logical segment to enter: the technology was just beginning

EXHIBIT 8
Brooktrout Technology, Inc.
Brooktrout Projects, as of Mid-1989

Voice Messaging
Operator Plus:

- Advanced call processing systems for small- and medium-sized companies
- Automated attendant, voice messaging, and voice response capabilities
- Digital signal processing technology to record, store, and play back digitized human voice
- Up to six ports capacity
- Up to 24 hours of stored messages

V-mail 210/DID:

- Allows outside callers to leave messages for individuals without dialing extensions, mailbox numbers, etc.
- Each user assigned an individual direct inward dial number
- Ideal for answering services, voice mail service bureaus, and cellular telephone sites

Phoneware 470:

- Development system
- Speeds creation of telephone-based speech-processing applications software
- Ideal for voice-prompted order entry, voice bulletin boards, and information dissemination

Fax Messaging
Fax-Mail Systems:

- Complete hardware/software systems
- Allows personal computers and fax machines to communicate worldwide over standard telephone lines
- Plugs into any IBM PC/XT/AT or compatible computer
- Permits PCs to receive transmissions from fax machines, store files on disk, display them on PC monitors, or print them out
- Compatible with CCITT Group III fax (machines transmitting a letter-sized page in less than one minute)

to take off, while the facsimile machine as an image communication device was not that far along. They then moved into the imaging segment with a circuit board facsimile messaging system ("Fax-Mail"), which enabled computer data to be translated electronically into facsimile images. With Fax-Mail, a PC user could send a computer file straight to the facsimile transmitter, without printing out the image first. (See Exhibit 8 for a description of Brooktrout's voice and fax products in mid-1989.)

In mid-1989, Fax-Mail was sold at retail to end users for installation in their own personal computers, at a price of $499. The voice messaging products ranged in price from $5,000 to $20,000 retail. Most were sold to OEMs, at discounts up to 50 percent.

Brooktrout also did some design work under contract to specific customers. (Even AT&T had made inquiries about Brooktrout's capabilities.) A current contract with a major manufacturer was developing data transfer between modems and facsimile machines. A major advantage of designing under contract was avoiding the need to raise additional capital for the research effort. However, in the end Brooktrout might not have full rights to the products they developed.

Brooktrout Strategy

Traditionally, individual companies specialized in either voice, data, or image communication. Brooktrout believed these three modes of communication would become integrated in the near future, as the technology of digital signal processing became cheaper and better. Eric commented:

> Nobody does all three. Our goal over the long term is to provide solutions in all three areas, for all the major telecommunications and computer manufacturers. We want to do something different from what other people are doing, based on our expertise in technology and our understanding of what makes electronic messaging possible.

Brooktrout estimated it had 5 to 10% of the voice segment market, selling against 30 to 40 competitors. Several of those were achieving success by selling further down the distribution channel, directly to dealers. Brooktrout, on the other hand, still sold its voice mail products mainly to OEMs. An advantage to selling to the OEMs, Eric said, was the ready access gained to certain segments of the industry. For instance, TIE Communications had developed a product using Brooktrout's technology that they sold to the Bell Operating Companies. TIE had access to the people in Nynex, Ameritech, etc., where Brooktrout did not.

Occasionally Brooktrout was called upon by their OEMs to assist in developing end-user applications for their products. Although this required additional effort, successful applications translated directly into more demand for Brooktrout's products.

Brooktrout had major OEM agreements for its voice and fax products with TIE, the second largest Customer Premise Equipment (CPE) supplier of small business phone systems behind AT&T, and with the American division of Iwatsu, a major Japanese equipment manufacturer. Both TIE and Iwatsu built Brooktrout products into their own offerings; both also labeled the Brooktrout equipment with their own name and sold it separately. TIE's dealers sold only TIE products, where Iwatsu dealers also sold products made by other manufacturers.

Although Eric felt that selling to OEMs was the best bet for the future, his sales department saw things differently. They believed the company could grow more rapidly by promoting and selling through dealers. Eric reported:

> What the salespeople are saying is, "Here we have stuff we can sell now. We can make money. We can sell lots of them." The problem I have is that our organization is not set up to deal directly with dealers.

All the sales department employees had either worked for dealers or owned their own dealerships. Eric felt, however, that the Brooktrout organization was not prepared to meet the needs of dealers or the dealers' customers. For example, operating manuals and instruction books would be required, along with 24 hour telephone and technical support. He said:

> We can sell to dealers to the extent it furthers our OEM goals. To the extent it isn't supporting those goals, I'm not sure it's worth it. Recently a potential investor complained about our selling to OEMs. He said, "Oh, that's the wrong way to do it. What you do is sell to users, then the users like it and they tell the dealers; the dealers like it and they tell the manufacturers, and the manufacturers have to have it."
>
> I never thought of it that way. The reason I never thought of it is simple: that's what you do when you have money!

Although distribution was an important consideration, many industry experts felt that market timing was also a critical success factor. The major task was to build a competitive product. Once the product was sold to an OEM and incorporated in its products, it became very difficult for competitors to dislodge it. Eric commented:

> The biggest competitive advantage I've seen in this business is what I call the first mover advantage. The guy who's first to do something kicks ass. It doesn't matter what anyone else does. Over the long haul, that's our best bet. And it probably doesn't matter where in the channel you sell as long as you're the first mover.
>
> Anyone can do anything—that's my premise. I have never seen anything in technology that is totally proprietary. You have to be careful though. There are also the pioneers with arrows in their backs; I've seen a bit of that also.

Sometimes being first was not that easy. The facsimile circuit board for personal computers was first introduced by a small California firm, Gamma Fax, while Brooktrout's similar product—fully designed and ready for production—sat on the shelf. Eric had felt the market wasn't ready: "naw, fax for personal computers? Who understands that stuff?" Now Brooktrout had to make up for the first-to-market advantage that Gamma Fax had captured.

The Future

Eric and his partners aimed to be the first company to fully integrate voice, data, and image messaging—"tying all these things together; that's the long-term vision." Brooktrout would soon have the key technology they needed for that integrated product, as a result of one of their current development contracts. To exploit the new opportunity, however, would take more capital and other resources than Brooktrout had available in mid-1989.

> I have the product idea: a voice machine that will let a company handle requests for literature with no human intervention at all. The customers call in and the machine asks what they want. When it defines what literature they want, the machine faxes the stuff to them instantly. The customer should love it: he doesn't even have to wait for the mail, much less for some clerk to fill the request. There isn't any other product like that, anywhere.
>
> If I had the money I would pursue it right now. I know it's going to hit. But I have to consider the effects of more stock dilution. I'd really prefer not to sell any stock.
>
> But people don't operate strategically on a day-to-day basis. If a venture capitalist called me right now and made the right kind of deal I would take the dilution.

Eric was at a crossroads. He knew that the capital structure of Brooktrout, with fifty shareholders, was not very attractive to venture capitalists. It had actually scared some away. And he had other products, too, which had not been brought to market because of capital needs.

He wanted to bet on the new product where literature could be requested over the phone. That concept was very different. It would allow Brooktrout to diversify its customer base and, if successful, could possibly get them to the point of going public or being acquired by a larger company. But, he asked, what market channel would best reach all the potential users of such a product?

Eric also knew that there was some merit in selling directly to dealers as the salespeople wanted, and that being first was the "best possible thing to do."

> Say we go out and raise more money and get diluted. Does the stock's value get pumped up? Some of the investors want out now. We have fifty investors and there's not a day that goes by that I don't talk to one of them.
>
> If I had the capital resources right now I would just be the best voice and fax company around. There is nobody there yet. We know it's going to be a big market; it doesn't take a rocket scientist to figure that out. It does take some thinking about how you want to position yourself, because it's a very fragmented set of business opportunities. Do you want a turnkey setup? Do you want to sell to OEMs? Do you want to build a system or do you want to just sell components?
>
> This is a very complex industry. There are people who spend their lives trying to figure this stuff out; they get paid a lot of money for being wrong. I've never seen so many consultants in all my life.

When asked where he thought Brooktrout would be in five years, Eric replied:

> Five years is too long to project in a violent industry. I would probably like to see the harvest point before that. If your business is really hot, it's very hard to maintain your independence, because the thing grows and you get assimilated into something whether you want to or not. Ultimately, you go public or you get acquired. We just want to keep playing the game—growing the beast as big as we can.
>
> From a personal perspective, it will be fun at $10 million [in sales]. That's when it starts to get fun. You're not playing around as much, and you have enough mass to expect the bottom line to hit about 15%. That's what I'd like to see.

CASE 5

The Battle of the Superpremium Ice Creams*

THE MEETING

"OK, we're getting nowhere. Let's take a thirty minute break to clear our brains" said Ben Cohen, president of Ben & Jerry's Homemade. He leaned back, closed his eyes and stretched his tired muscles. The meeting had been going for 6 hours. He and the company's general manager, Chico Lager, had driven to Ithaca, New York, from Burlington, Vermont, that evening for an emergency meeting of the board of directors. Topic: battle plans to fight Haagen-Dazs' attempt to squeeze Ben & Jerry's out of the Boston market for super premium ice cream. It was 3 A.M. already and they hadn't decided on a plan of action. What was it the antitrust lawyer had said? "Essentially, a simple case of market foreclosure." Reuben Mattus, president of Haagen-Dazs, had declared war on his upstart competitor and it was up to Ben to come up with a strategy to ward him off. Ben could visualize Reuben Mattus gloating over what he thought was a fait accompli.

True, the Pillsbury Company had bought Haagen-Dazs, but Ben was willing to bet his beard that it was Reuben calling the shots on his venture. It was just the sort of hard ball business that he knew best.

If only Jerry Greenfield were here. Together they could overcome this problem the same way they had overcome problems since becoming pals in high school on Long Island.

THE EARLY YEARS

Things were easier in the old days when he and Jerry were starting out. All they had wanted to do was move to a quiet college town and start some more or less entertaining business. Two ex-hippies from Long Island starting a small business in rural Vermont. Who would have ever thought it would lead to a battle with one of the world's largest corporations! Originally they had leaned toward a bagel-making operation, with an ice cream store as a backup possibility. The choice was made for them when they found out how much bagel-making machines cost. No loss, because both Ben and Jerry already had experience in the ice cream industry; Ben had worked on an ice cream truck and Jerry had scooped ice cream in college.

Whatever business they went into had to be better than what they had been doing. Greenfield, who had been unable to get into medical school, was working in North Carolina as a lab technician. Cohen was teaching pottery making to emotionally disturbed children near Lake Champlain in upstate New York. So, being the true big-time capitalists that they were, they moved to Burlington, Vermont, to have some independence, live in a

---

* Prepared by Arieh A. Ullmann, State University of New York at Binghamton. Distributed by the North American Case Research Association.

pleasant college town, and maybe even have some fun. Armed with $8,000 in capital they bought an old fashioned rock-salt ice cream maker and rented an abandoned garage about a half mile from the University of Vermont. While they worked at renovating the garage, they read several books about making homemade ice cream. They completed their formal education by sending to the Pennsylvania State University for a $5 correspondence course. Only much later did they inform themselves about some key characteristics of the industry (Appendix).

Jerry made the ice cream, which was popular from the start, and Ben handled the hot food, which wasn't. In the summer they showed free movies on the wall of the building next door. On cold winter days they had a special called POPCDBZWE (Penny Off Per Celsius Degree Below Zero Winter Extravaganza). Don Rose would come in and play his honky-tonk piano to entertain the customers as they stood in what seemed like never-ending lines. Rose earned the distinction of being named a "Ben & Jerry's Lifer" entitling him to free ice cream for the rest of his life.

The most fun of all was the autumnal "Fall Down" that Ben and Jerry staged on the lawn of the First Congregational Church in Burlington. A typical Fall Down included an apple-peeling contest, entertainment by Don Rose on his piano, a lip-sync contest, and a Ben & Jerry's look-alike contest. The highlight of the event was what Ben and Jerry advertised as "the Dramatic Sledgehammer Smashing of a cinder block on the bare stomach of the noted Indian mystic Habeeni Ben Coheeni." Ben learned the Dramatic Sledgehammer Smashing trick in a half-credit course called "Carnival Techniques" at Oberlin.

They got into the wholesale ice cream business by accident. Ben was getting bored being stuck behind a stove in a former gas station. Local restaurants had been asking about being supplied with ice cream and Ben had been persuaded that traveling around Vermont selling ice cream might be a pleasant life. Ben & Jerry's started producing ice cream by the pint with Jerry as production manager and Ben as open-portfolioed ice cream ambassador. They called their wares simply Ben & Jerry's Homemade—although some consideration was given to putting an umlaut over the "e" in Ben to match the ersatz European-sounding name concocted by Reuben Mattus.

When it came to marketing, Ben & Jerry's had nothing in common with Haagen-Dazs. On top of the container was a photograph of the two, looking pretty much like Vermont hippies from the sixties generation. No map of Denmark for them. The list of ingredients on the container was done in the sort of printing often found on menus in health food restaurants. Not only natural ingredients, but natural owners with pride in their product.

When asked to compare his ice cream with brands like Haagen-Dazs, Alpen Zauber, and Frusen Gladje, Ben liked to say his "is the only superpremium ice cream you can pronounce." Their sixties sense of limitations was reflected in the motto, "Vermont's Finest All-Natural Ice Cream." This was rather modest considering that John Skow, in a cover story for *Time* magazine on ice cream, stated that "What you must understand at the outset is that Ben & Jerry's, in Burlington, Vt., makes the best ice cream in the world."

Everything had to be in their style. It was their style to be amazed, if not slightly embarrassed, by their success. It was their style to give back part of the profits to the community. It was their style to be in business to have fun, not to get rich. Even the promotions were in their style. The "Lick Winter" promotion not only included airfare and accommodations in Florida, but dinner with Jerry's parents, who retired down there, and a day at Walt Disney World with Ben's uncle.

From the beginning they set out to produce a high-butterfat, low-air-content ice cream. Not to copy the ice cream that Reuben Mattus had pioneered, but because that was the type of ice cream they would want as consumers. They used natural flavors, and plenty of it. Jerry said that it took a strong dose of flavor to get any response from Ben, the sampler, who "doesn't have a real acute sense of taste." Even the flavors were different. From the beginning, Ben & Jerry's specialized in flavors with names like Heath Bar Crunch, White Russian, and Dastardly Mash.

It wasn't all fun and games though. Not everything came easily. They had their share of problems. Take the chilling Heath Bar Crunch crisis, for instance. Along with Dastardly Mash (rich chocolate ice cream with pecans, almonds, chocolate chips, and raisins), Heath Bar Crunch was Ben's personal favorite. When they first started out, Ben and Jerry would pound a pile of Heath Bars with a hammer and pour the smashed pieces into a fruit feeder hooked up to their ice maker. As the ice cream worked its way through the machine, the fruit feeder was supposed to distribute bits of Heath Bar evenly throughout the ice cream. It never worked that way. Some of the pieces were too big and clogged the feeder line. Who knows how many pints got by without a single piece of Heath Bar! To make matters worse, when Ben and Jerry smacked the feeder line, Heath Bar pieces caved into the ice cream so that some pints wound up packed with Heath Bar bits and no ice cream. The problem was eventually solved by freezing the Heath bars to minus twenty degrees and dropping them from a height of exactly 6 feet so they shattered just right.

GROWTH AND CHANGE

By 1983, Ben & Jerry's was selling over $1 million of wholesale ice cream annually in Vermont, New Hampshire, Maine, and upstate New York. Ben & Jerry's manufacturing operation consisted of a small group of young people in a tiny tin hut formerly used to repair trucks.

It was around this time that Jerry decided to move to Arizona. "It got to the point where it was too big for me," he said. "It wasn't as personally rewarding. I was more comfortable in the filling station." Besides, as chief production officer, Jerry had found that quality control had added about 50 pounds on him.

So alone, the remaining partner had to decide whether or not to test the Boston market, and if successful, how to finance additional capacity. Once it was clear that the Boston market bode well, raising capital became a problem. In typical Ben & Jerry's fashion, an intrastate stock issue was floated. It was open only to bona fide Vermont residents. Ben, Jerry, and the new general manager, Fred (Chico) Lager, traveled from town to town talking to potential stockholders in meetings which included a sample of the "Real Thing." This initial stock offering raised $750,000. An urban-development grant and industrial revenue bonds were obtained to complete the financial package.

Compared to most zoning hearings, the one to discuss Ben & Jerry's proposed $3 million ice cream manufacturing and retail facility was an ice cream social. No one at the meeting came to argue about it and permits were quickly issued. At the conclusion of deliberations, Ben passed around several pints of Ben & Jerry's Homemade. In August 1984, ground was broken for the 25,000 square foot manufacturing plant.

HAAGEN-DAZS

Reuben Mattus, in complete contrast to both Ben and Jerry, fit easily into the stereotypical immigrant-entrepreneur mold. He overcame his lack of education, background, and capital with shrewdness, guile, and sheer hard work. Graciousness toward competitors was not within the type of ice cream business he had known for half a century. When he tried to be gracious toward Ben and Jerry he would say, "They're very unconventional."

In early 1980, Reuben Mattus, in his seventies, was still chairman of Haagen-Dazs. Having emigrated from Poland shortly after World War I, Reuben dropped out of high school to help support his family in Brooklyn. His uncle, Nathan, was already in the ice cream business in partnership with an Italian. He peddled Italian lemon ice from a horse cart.

The rules of competition that Reuben learned as a child were pretty straightforward. For instance, since his mother was a widow with a family to support, it was fair for his uncle to become partners with her in a noncompeting ice cream business in the Bronx. However, one of his brothers set up an ice cream business across the street from uncle Nathan and the two of them spent the rest of their lives ruthlessly trying to steal each other's customers. There were dozens of little ice cream companies in Brooklyn and the Bronx back then. Most were run by immigrants who competed with the tenacity of those whose livelihoods depended on it.

Mattus could tell stories of one crisis after another. There were times during World War II when supplies were nearly impossible to come by. When they could be obtained they were sometimes spoiled. He learned a lesson from this that would stick with him for the rest of his life. One time he had bought a large supply of milk powder which was usable but had a slightly stale taste. Once better ingredients were available, he replaced the milk powder only to find that his customers complained that the taste of the ice cream had changed. Ahh, quality; consistency!

At another time, just after the war, large corporations began paying supermarket chains thousand of dollars in "advance rebates." They seemed unstoppable in their efforts to purge the freezer cases of the small independent local brands.

Mattus felt he survived by application of brute labor and the ability to stay one jump ahead of the others through innovation. "All my life people copied me," he said. "I would start something: they would copy it and undermine me."

In the late fifties, Americans seemed to judge foodstuffs strictly on their costs and convenience. The whole ice cream business was focused on producing the cheapest ice cream in the biggest container. Because of the small size of his operation, Mattus knew that he was unprepared to compete on a price basis. He feared that the big companies were about to drive him out of business—mostly by economic muscle, but partly by using marketing techniques that he had developed.

Mattus' solution to this threat was to produce the best possible ice cream instead of the cheapest. In that undertaking, the small size of his operation was an advantage: He could control quality and consistency to a degree impossible in a large corporation. Instead of whipping as much air into his product as the law allowed, he would use very little. Instead of skimping on butterfat, he would produce an ice cream with 16 percent butterfat. Instead of artificial flavor, color, and sweetener, he would use only natural ingredients. Thus was born the market with the appropriately excessive name of "superpremium ice cream."

"At the time, European products were held in high esteem," he recalled. "They were the 'in' thing. So I wanted a European sounding name." Mattus' mentor, Simon Levowitz, often spoke of the quality and consistency maintained by an ice cream company in Copenhagen called "Premier Is." As an immigrant who had grown up in a Brooklyn neighborhood, Denmark had another advantage. "I figured there were people who hated the Irish, there were people who hated the Italians, there were people who hated the Poles, there were people who hated the Jews," he said. "But nobody hated the Danes." So, Mattus put a map of Denmark on his containers and invented the Danish-sounding name "Haagen-Dazs." "When shoppers saw the name Haagen-Dazs, in that extra quarter of a second that the name caught their eye, they stopped and looked at the package. They picked it up and felt it was very heavy. They saw the price and thought, 'Maybe I'm gonna get ripped off.' But they had to see what this was all about, so they took it home, tasted it, and they were hooked." What did a Danish map marking Oslo and Copenhagen on the top have to do with the ice cream made in Woodbridge, New Jersey? Absolutely nothing.

The big companies could have crushed Reuben's new enterprise in an instant. They weren't paying any attention. At first, Reuben had trouble getting distribution for Haagen-Dazs, not because anyone was trying to squeeze him out of the market, but because the distributors didn't believe anyone would buy such extraordinarily expensive ice cream. Eventually, however, the taste of the American public caught up with his ice cream.

THE CRISIS

It was in early 1984, at the time when Ben & Jerry's Homemade began gaining popularity in the Boston market that the current problems erupted. Two major ice cream wholesalers told Ben that the sales manager for Haagen-Dazs had told them that if they continued to carry Ben & Jerry's, Haagen-Dazs would no longer sell them its product. Contracts detailing all aspects of this exclusivity arrangement were being written and would soon be sent out.

The distributors needed to offer a complete line of ice cream brands in order to secure supermarket accounts. No supermarket could do without Haagen-Dazs, which was the best-selling gourmet ice cream nationwide. Haagen-Dazs was threatening to cripple any distributor who carried Ben & Jerry's Homemade. Haagen-Dazs could bring great pressures to bear on the distributors. It could take the form of limiting the selection of flavors available to the distributors or failing to ship timely or complete orders. The distributors simply could not do business with the supermarket chains and other outlets without that product, and would be easy prey to competitors who could offer Haagen-Dazs as part of a complete line.

Ben could not understand why Haagen-Dazs was so worried. It was so much bigger than Ben & Jerry's Homemade (Exhibits 1 and 2). The two distributors in question sold the two brands at a four-to-one ratio in Haagen-Dazs' favor. It was flattering, in a way, that Haagen-Dazs felt it had to take such drastic action against a newcomer in the market. "We must be doing something right," Ben chuckled. Not only was the relative size of the two ice cream competitors so lopsided, but Haagen-Dazs' parent was Pillsbury, the multibillion

EXHIBIT 1
Ben & Jerry's Homemade, Inc.
Selected Financial Data
(in Thousands of Dollars, Except per Share Amounts)

	Year Ended December 31			
	1980 (Unaudited)	***1981 (Unaudited)***	***1982***	***1983***
Summary of operations:				
Net sales	$374	$615	$968	$1,815
Cost of sales	267	309	586	1,239
Gross profit	$107	$306	$382	$576
Selling, delivery and administrative expenses	$67	$273	$366	$479
Operating Income	$40	$33	$16	$97
Other income (expense)—net	$(4)	$(4)	$(11)	$(26)
Income before income taxes and extraordinary items	$36	$29	$ 5	$71
Federal and state income taxes	3	--	--	14
Income before extraordinary items	$33	$29	$ 5	$57
Extraordinary item	--	--	61	--
Net income (loss)	$33	$29	$(59)	$57
Net income (loss) per common share	$0.03	$0.02	$(0.04)	$0.05
Average common shares outstanding	1,260	1,260	1,260	1,074
Balance sheet data:				
Working capital	$12	$ 24	$(43)	$ 57
Total assets	$92	$193	$295	$509
Long-term debt (less current maturities)	$22	$ 69	$ 80	$157
Stockholders' equity	$48	$ 77	$ 21	$154

dollar conglomerate. They had unlimited amounts of capital available to throw into a pitched battle for ice cream supremacy. Why were they resorting to such tactics?

One thing is for sure, Ben thought as the others were entering the room, we aren't just going to let the Doughboy walk right over us.

Appendix to Case 5
The Ice Cream Industry

History of Ice Cream

Ice cream probably evolved from chilled wines and other iced beverages. Alexander the Great was reputed to be fond of iced beverages. In 62 A.D., the Roman Emperor, Nero, sent fleets of slaves to the mountains of the Apennines to fetch snow and ice which were flavored with nectar, fruit pulp, and honey.

When Marco Polo, the 13th century adventurer, returned to Europe he brought with him recipes for water ices used in Asia for thousands of years. These water ices became popular in Venice and throughout Italy. In 1660 the Cafe Procope was founded in Paris by an Italian named Coltelli; water ices and possibly cream ices were manufactured and dispensed there. This delicacy found its way to the American Colonies in 1700 when

Governor Blanden of Maryland served ice cream to his guests. Dolly Madison created a sensation when she served ice cream for dessert in the White House during the second inaugural ball in 1812.

The first hand-cranked freezer was invented by Nancy Johnson in 1846. She failed to patent it and a similar type was patented by a Mr. Young in 1848. The first commercial ice cream plant was established in Baltimore in 1851 by Jacob Fussell. With the coming of mechanical refrigeration, the first batch freezer was invented by H. H. Miller of Canton, Ohio. Around 1926, the first continuous freezer was commercially perfected by Clarence Vogt of Louisville, Kentucky.

The first ice cream cone was made at the St. Louis World's Fair in 1904. Since then, billions of cones have been consumed each year. Other products, such as ice cream-on-a-stick, ice cream bars, and other forms of ice cream such as ice milk and sherbet, known in the industry as "novelties," had their beginning in the 1920s.

Definitions

Ice cream is a frozen food made from a mixture of dairy products, such as milk, cream, and nonfat milk, combined with sugars, flavorings, fruits, nuts, and so on. Ice cream which contains at least 1.4 percent egg yolk is called French ice cream or frozen custard. Ice cream and French ice cream contain a minimum of 10 percent milkfat and weigh not less than 4.5 pounds per gallon.

Ice milk is a frozen dessert which is similar to ice cream except that it contains between 2 and 7 percent milkfat.

Sherbet, both fruit sherbet and those flavored with flavors other than fruit, contains between 1 and 2 percent milkfat and weighs not less than 6 pounds per gallon.

EXHIBIT 2
Pillsbury Company
Consolidated Income Statement and Balance Sheet Data
(in Millions of Dollars, Except per Share Data)

	1983	*1982*	*1981*
Operations:			
Net sales	$3,685.9	$3,385.1	$3,301.7
Earnings before taxes	230.2	228.0	201.9
Net earnings	138.9	136.3	119.6
Net earnings per common share	3.2	3.14	2.98
Financial position:			
Current assets	$1,021.6	$1,133.0	$989.9
Current liabilities	704.9	816.5	687.6
Working capital	316.7	316.5	302.3
Property, plant & equipment	1,053.2	1,009.0	950.6
Long-term debt	572.4	597.1	631.0
Stockholders' equity	956.4	890.0	747.2
Invested capital	1,661.7	1,611.8	1,486.9
Total assets	2,366.6	2,428.3	2,174.5
Employees	56,200	55,200	60,000

EXHIBIT 2 (cont.)
Pillsbury Company
Segment Data
Years Ended May 31
(in Millions of Dollars)

	1983	1982
Net sales		
Consumer foods	$1,652.1	$1,635.7
Restaurants	1,494.6	1,279.3
Agri products	627.5	568.6
less agri-products intersegment sales	(88.3)	(98.5)
Total net sales	$3,685.9	$3,385.1
Operating profit		
Consumer foods	$139.4	$134.8
Restaurants	135.3	116.3
Agri-products	16.4	28.6
Total operating profit	$291.1	$279.7
General corporate expense, net	(21.5)	(12.4)
Interest expense, net	(39.4)	(39.3)
Earnings before taxes on income	$230.2	$228.0
Identifiable assets		
Consumer foods	$ 725.4	$ 747.9
Restaurants	1,025.7	993.3
Agri-products	486.1	536.6
Corporate	129.4	150.5
Total identifiable assets	$2,366.6	$2,428.3
Capital expenditures		
Consumer foods	$ 48.7	$ 50.0
Restaurants	164.0	126.8
Agri-products	20.9	15.8
Corporate	10.3	15.9
Total capital expenditures	$243.9	$208.5
Depreciation—expense		
Consumer foods	$ 33.0	$30.3
Restaurants	54.7	48.6
Agri-products	13.6	11.5
Corporate	4.2	2.4
Total depreciation—expenses	$105.5	$92.8

Water ices, both fruit ices and those flavored with flavors other than fruit, contain no dairy ingredients, and weigh not less than 6 pounds per gallon.

Mellorine is a frozen dessert similar to ice milk in which the milkfat is replaced, in whole or in part, with vegetable fat of at least 6 percent.

Manufacturing Process

The basic mix for ice cream is largely cream, other milk ingredients (like dairy solids), and sweeteners. Small amounts of functional ingredients, such as stabilizers which prevent the formation of ice crystals in the ice cream, are added. The manufacturer then blends the ingredients for the mix in proper proportions in a mixing tank.

The mix is then pasteurized. The most common type of pasteurization is the high-temperature–short-time method in which the mix is heated to 175°F and held for 25 seconds. The hot mix then goes to the homogenizer where the milkfat globules are broken into still smaller particles to help make the ice cream smooth. This is accomplished by subjecting the mix to a pressure of about 2,500 pounds per square inch. The hot mix is then quickly cooled to a temperature of about 40°F.

Next, the mix is frozen using one of two methods. A batch freezer processes a single quantity of ice cream at a time. The continuous freezer operates on a steady flow of mix. With either method, blades in the freezer, or "dashers" as they are called, whip and aerate the mix. Without this aeration, the finished product would be an inedible, solid, frozen mass of cream, milk, sugar, and flavoring. This aeration, called *overrun,* is controlled by laws which require the finished ice cream to weigh no less than 4.5 pounds per gallon and contain at least 1.6 pounds of total food solids.

Ingredients such as fruits and nuts are added after the freezing by a mechanical flavor feeder. Liquid flavors are added to the mix prior to freezing.

After the freezing and filling operations, the ice cream goes to the "hardening room" where subzero temperatures further harden the ice cream. From the hardening room, it is loaded into refrigerated trucks for delivery to distributors or retailers.

Consumption

The United States has the world's biggest ice cream consumers with a production[1] of 44.13 pints per capita, followed by the Australians (37.21), the New Zealanders (35.87), the Canadians (31.88), the Swedes (28.57), and the Norwegians (20.47).

Geographically, the people in the W.N. central region of the United States are the biggest ice cream eaters with a production of 33.24 quarts per capita in 1984, followed by the New Englanders (29.20), the Pacific region (23.64), whereas the south central region is at the bottom with 17.96 quarts.

Since 1970, production of ice cream and related products has increased only 9.2 percent. Measured in per capita figures, production has, in fact, declined. Also, the shares of the various products have remained quite stable, except for the decline in the production in mellorine products at the expense of other frozen dairy products, especially ice creams (Exhibit 3).

Consumption is seasonal with a peak during the warm summer weather (Exhibit 4). Eighty-three percent of U.S. households purchase ice cream for home consumption.

Studies of male and female eating patterns have shown that males eat more ice cream than females. Teenage boys, on average, eat 4.93 ounces of ice cream per day while teenage girls eat 3.43 ounces.

Industry Structure

Given the characteristics of the product, the industry had historically been composed of a multitude of regional and local producers, primarily local dairies which viewed ice cream as a sideline of selling milk. Improvements in refrigeration and distribution technology in

---

[1] Assuming insignificant imports and exports production equals consumption.

EXHIBIT 3

Total and per Capita Production (Hard and Soft) Ice Cream and Related Products, 1950–1984

	All Products Reported		Ice Cream		Ice Milk†		Sherbet		Water Ices		Other Frozen Dairy Products‡		Mellorine-Type Products	
Year	Total* 1,000 Gallons	Per Capita Quarts	Total 1,000 Gallons	Per Capita Quarts	Total 1,000 Gallons	Per Capita Quarts	Total 1,000 Gallons	Per Capita Quarts	Total 1,000 Gallons	Per Capita Quarts	Total 1,000 Gallons	Per Capita Quarts	Total 1,000 Gallons	Per Capita Quarts
1950	634,768	16.79	554,351	14.66	36,870	0.98	17,018	0.45	18,299	0.48	8,230	0.22		
1955	819,934	19.96	628,525	15.30	90,185	2.20	37,365	0.91	28,158	0.69	3,440	0.08	32,261	0.78
1960	969,004	21.54	699,605	15.55	145,177	3.23	40,734	0.91	33,361	0.74	4,913	0.11	45,214	1.00
1965	1,130,215	23.36	757,000	15.65	230,992	4.77	45,449	0.94	37,119	0.77	6,486	0.13	53,169	1.10
1970	1,193,144	23.42	761,732	14.95	286,663	5.63	48,887	0.96	37,265	0.73	6,719	0.13	51,878	1.02
1975	1,263,213	23.45	836,552	15.53	298,789	5.55	48,542	0.90	38,230	0.71	11,062	0.20	30,038	0.56
1980	1,225,223	21.58	829,798	14.61	293,384	5.17	45,187	0.80	33,386	0.59	10,278	0.18	13,190	0.23
1981	1,238,712	21.61	832,450	14.52	290,992	5.08	45,732	0.80	34,344	0.60	24,003	0.42	11,191	0.19
1982	1,248,552	21.54	852,072	14.70	280,559	4.84	45,575	0.79	35,158	0.61	25,058	0.43	10,130	0.17
1983	1,295,294	22.14	881,543	15.07	294,913	5.04	47,732	0.82	39,425	0.67	21,595	0.37	10,086	0.17
1984	1,303,031	22.07	883.525	14.96	299,624	5.08	47,292	0.80	41,613	0.70	22,741	0.39	8,236	0.14

* Data from 1859 to 1919 indicate only the estimated trend of production.
† Includes freezer-made milkshake beginning 1954.
‡ For 1940–1953 includes frozen custard and frosted or frozen malted milk.
Source: Prepared by the International Association of Ice Cream Manufacturers from data published by the U.S. Department of Agriculture

recent decades allowed transportation over longer distances. As a consequence, smaller producers have been either squeezed out of the market or absorbed by larger corporations. Thus, employment and the number of plants producing ice cream and related products decreased significantly, while new plant and capital expenditures followed a different pattern (Exhibits 5 and 6).

In the early 1980s the industry was dominated by a few large corporations with

EXHIBIT 4

Monthly Production of Ice Cream and Related Products as a Percent of Annual Average, 1963–1983

Month	1963	1983
January	71.2	72.1
February	72.1	79.6
March	90.2	106.2
April	104.8	96.9
May	117.8	111.7
June	126.8	130.6
July	141.7	123.5
August	134.5	127.6
September	102.1	110.6
October	95.7	88.4
November	75.0	78.8
December	68.1	73.9

EXHIBIT 5
Number of Plants Producing Ice Cream and Related Products, 1970–1984

Year	Ice Cream	Ice Milk	Sherbert	Water Ices	Mellorine-Type Products
1970	1,628	1,088	1,122	377	203
1971	1,520	1,008	1,065	335	177
1972	1,451	984	1,022	363	180
1973	1,330	902	976	321	146
1974	1,239	824	904	299	146
1975	1,167	746	850	281	124
1976	1,124	718	812	281	119
1977	1,095	702	782	273	110
1978	1,062	670	744	263	101
1979	990	604	690	234	89
1980	949	576	654	220	76
1981	895	548	614	212	74
1982	884	524	608	212	67
1983	862	495	594	201	71
1984	853	477	570	199	57

Source: Prepared by the International Association of Ice Cream Manufacturers from data published by the U.S. Department of Agriculture.

multiple brands enjoying sales strength in different regions (Exhibit 7). In addition, many large grocery chains carried their private-label brands. Despite those large diversified companies, no brand had achieved market-share dominance; regional producers continued to represent a prominent factor.

The strategies of these companies differed. Some relied on regional brands, while

EXHIBIT 6
Employees, Wages, Value of Shipments, and Capital Expenditures Frozen Desserts Industry, 1970–1982

	All Employees*			
Year	Number (In Thousands)	Payroll (In Millions of Dollars)	Value of Product Shipments† (In Millions of Dollars)	Capital Expenditures Total (In Millions of Dollars)
1970	24.1	$166.8	$1,343.2	$43.7
1971	22.6	173.5	1,389.0	28.0
1972	21.1	184.7	1,519.4	35.8
1973	21.3	195.9	1,639.5	29.2
1974	21.3	196.5	1,787.9	27.8
1975	20.2	208.5	2,012.9	37.2
1976	20.3	223.6	2,063.3	43.2
1977	19.1	247.0	2,229.4	56.8
1978	18.5	252.5	2,397.2	56.4
1979	19.9	277.4	2,733.2	46.3
1980	19.6	288.6	3,041.5	46.8
1981	20.1	325.6	3,322.1	41.8
1982	17.8	313.5	3,281.1	79.9

* Data for plants with ice cream and other frozen desserts as the leading product group in value of shipments.
† Includes value of shipments of ice cream and other frozen desserts by plants classified in other industries, such as fluid milk.
Source: Bureau of the Census, U.S. Department of Commerce.

EXHIBIT 7
Major Ice Cream Manufacturers in the Northeast

Company	Brands
Baskin-Robbins	Baskin-Robbins
Bassett's Ice Cream Company	Bassett's
Borden	Borden
Friendly Restaurants	Friendly's
Kraft	Breyer's, Sealtest, Frusen Gladje
Pillsbury	Haagen-Dazs
Schrafft's Ice Cream Company	Schrafft's

Baskin-Robbins established a national brand. Some producers operated relatively small plants in the vicinity of major consumption centers, others preferred large facilities.

According to the International Association of Ice Cream Manufacturers, the industry's trade association, a processor's sales dollar included raw material costs 52.5 cents, processing and packaging 30.9 cents, distribution expense 9.4 cents, administrative expense 2.8 cents, income taxes 2.2 cents, and net profit 2.2 cents.

EXHIBIT 8
Supermarket Frozen Food Department Gross Profit Margin, Contribution by Product Category, 1983–1984, Weekly Average

Product Category	Gross Margin, %	Gross Margin Sales, %
Ice cream	27.6	7.7
Specialty ice cream	29.0	6.7
Novelties	30.1	3.3
Juices	26.8	11.8
Fruits	31.1	1.0
Vegetables—reg.	30.8	8.5
Vegetables—spec.	29.6	3.8
Potatoes	29.6	3.4
Meat/poultry	30.0	5.0
Fish/seafood	30.2	5.1
Pot pies	27.3	1.2
Dinners	29.5	5.0
Special prep. foods	29.5	15.0
Dough/rolls	29.8	1.9
Breakfast items	29.1	2.2
Pies	27.5	2.6
Cakes	30.2	3.4
Pizza	28.5	5.6
Nationality foods	30.0	2.9
Miscellaneous	29.2	3.7
Total/Average	29.3	99.8*

* Does not add to 100% because of rounding.

Source: Ice Cream Performance and Profitability in U.S. Supermarket. International Association of Ice Cream Manufacturers.

Distribution

While numerous ice cream parlors, parlor franchise outlets, and dipping stores covered the entire country, the bulk of the annual ice cream production was sold in supermarkets. Ice cream and related products comprised 18 percent of the average supermarket's frozen food department sales (Exhibit 8).

Some ice cream companies contracted out the manufacture of their brands to local dairies, which also distributed the products to the supermarkets and kept the freezers stocked with the most popular flavors. Other companies not only produced their own ice cream but also maintained their own distributors to service the supermarkets.

INDUSTRY-SPECIFIC CASES: THE U.S. ATHLETIC SHOE INDUSTRY

CASE 6

The U.S. Athletic Shoe Industry*

In 1839, Charles Goodyear mixed rubber with sulfur to make a product that remained elastic at any temperature. "Vulcanized rubber" revolutionized many established industries, and created entirely new ones. Forty years after Goodyear's invention, the corporation he started began producing canvas-topped sneakers, and the athletic shoe industry was born. In 1895, Goodyear was selling enough shoes that the company decided to name the product line. They settled on Keds because K was considered by experts to be the strongest letter in the alphabet. By 1915, several brands of sneakers were on the market, including a top-selling model by Converse; sneakers were firmly established as essential footwear for the well-dressed active boy.

The combination of a canvas top on a rubber compound sole remained the dominant design for nearly 100 years. Then in the 1960s, came the harbingers of change: an offbeat duo on the west coast, Philip Knight and Bill Bowerman. Knight was a shy college student who ran under Bowerman's coaching on the University of Oregon track team. After graduation, Knight went to Stanford for his M.B.A., while back in Portland, Bowerman experimented with constructing better track shoes. The leading track shoes of that time were produced by Adidas and Puma, two giant manufacturers who supplied the world from their factories in Europe. These shoes were all leather, had little cushioning, and used steel spikes for traction. Bowerman began constructing shoes that were lighter, better padded, and featured wafflelike patterns in their rubber soles. (The prototypes were actually produced on a waffle iron.) Soon, athletes were setting records in the new shoes. After Knight graduated from business school, he and Bowerman set up a company, the precursor to Nike, to specialize in designing and selling high-performance shoes made in Japan.

In 1966, Nike introduced the Tiger Cortez, a lightweight nylon and suede leather shoe with a cushioning sole and good foot support. The popularity and success of this shoe established the new dominant design for the industry. In the 1970s, virtually every athletic shoe manufacturer in the world followed the trend that Nike had set with the Cortez, and soon there were hundreds of models of lightweight, technically innovative running shoes on the market. When physical fitness began to grow in popularity, the market for athletic shoes expanded dramatically from a small number of serious athletes to hundreds of thousands of joggers. Based on its technical edge, the boom in America's interest in running, and the emergence of jeans and sneakers as acceptable casual wear for adults, Nike's sales soared. In the early eighties Nike became the leading athletic shoe company in the

---

* Prepared by Alex Miller, University of Tennessee.

EXHIBIT 1
Athletic Footwear Sales outside the United States (in Millions of Dollars)

	1985	*1986*	*1987*
Adidas	$1,940	$2,040	$2,350
Asics Tiger	410	800	830
Puma	620	500	500
Nike	244	241	257
Reebok	24	92	200
Pony	71	45	45

Source: Courtesy of *SportStyle.*

United States, but in 1986 would be unseated from its number 1 position by Reebok. (Note that neither were top brands outside the United States—see Exhibit 1.)

THE MODERN ATHLETIC SHOE

Expanding on the breakthroughs at Nike, shoe manufacturers redesigned the standard for footwear in virtually every active sport. Athletic shoes were no longer all-purpose sneakers but highly technical sport-specific footwear. As interest in sports grew, sports medicine came to see how better equipment designs could improve athletic performance. For instance, studies revealed that running places loads of up to 350 percent of the runner's body weight on the foot with each stride. Over miles of training, feet without adequate padding and support could be beaten to a pulp. Such findings fueled a tremendous interest in technical shoe design, and leading innovators spent heavily on R&D. For instance, Nike reportedly had annual R&D budgets in the $5-million range.

By the mid-eighties, every major manufacturer had an extensive line of shoes blanketing numerous sports. Models retailed for $35 to $100, and top-of-the-line technical shoes from several companies were soon over $100. Even within individual sports categories, there were often levels of specialization. For instance, running shoes were designed for high-, medium-, and low-mileage runners, and addressed a host of biomechanical problems, like poor ankle alignment and other faulty running patterns. At the other end of the market, generic or unbranded shoes sold for less than $15 in discount outlets, while some stores maintained "sale-priced" low-end models of branded shoes retailing for $20 to $25. Exhibit 2 shows domestic sales data for 1984 to 1986, broken down by sport category. Additional categories are identified for the 1987 data in Exhibit 3.

Technical evaluations became the focus of an annual shoe ratings issue of *Runner's World.* These ratings carried tremendous influence in the retail demand for shoes, and are credited by some industry experts for both the rise and the fall of the Brooks company. Back-to-back years of good ratings created a level of demand for the shoes which the company was simply not capable of matching. Consequently, Brooks let lower-quality shoes through, its subsequent ratings plummeted, and eventually the bankrupt company was taken over.

EXHIBIT 2
U.S. Athletic Footwear Sales, 1984–1986 (in Millions)

	1986		1985		1984	
	Dollars	Units	Dollars	Units	Dollars	Units
Aerobics	$332.8	10.8	$177.5	5.8	$ 53.9	1.9
Basketball	186.8	5.4	185.4	5.6	158.5	5.0
Gym shoes	585.8	26.9	655.5	30.0	669.3	32.1
Running	545.2	17.1	572.0	17.6	590.8	19.4
Tennis	447.7	17.6	469.7	18.7	371.2	14.8
Walking	368.4	11.2	n/a	n/a	n/a	n/a
Fitness	150.7	4.7	n/a	n/a	n/a	n/a

Source: National Sporting Goods Association, Mt. Prospect, IL.

While research and development laboratories were vastly improving the technical features serious athletes required, a new and much larger market segment was emerging. This segment was composed of people who did not use the shoes for athletics, but because they were comfortable, or because they conveyed the image of an active and healthy lifestyle. As athletic shoes began to replace more traditional types of footwear, this segment accounted for nearly 80 percent of all athletic shoes sold. Exhibit 4 shows a breakdown of U.S. shoe sales by type of shoe and customer.

While this nonsport segment might never have tested the technical capabilities of their shoes, that did not mean shoe technology was unimportant to them. These consumers demanded visible technology, meaning a preference for complicated shoes that looked like the equipment demanding professionals would require. By the late eighties, there was a pronounced trend toward designing shoes "inside out" so customers could sport more of the technology for which they had paid a premium price. In this market segment, the distinction between performance technology and fashion technology became blurred. As one executive put it, "in this market, performance is fashion."

EXHIBIT 3
U.S. Athletic and Sport Footwear Sales, 1987 (in Millions of Dollars)

Gym shoes	$692.6
Walking shoes	511.5
Running shoes	475.0
Aerobic shoes	401.2
Tennis shoes	367.2
Fitness shoes	197.0
Basketball shoes	169.3
Hiking shoes	149.8
Golf shoes	130.2
Baseball shoes	94.5
Soccer shoes	72.7
Football shoes	50.2

Source: National Sporting Goods Association, Mt. Prospect, IL.

EXHIBIT 4
U.S. Footwear Sales by Type of Shoe, 1984 and 1987

	Total		Men's		Boys'		Women's		Girls'		Infants'	
Shoe Types	**1987**	**1984**	**1987**	**1984**	**1987**	**1984**	**1987**	**1984**	**1987**	**1984**	**1987**	**1984**
Total (million pairs)	955.5	734.2	252.9	192.2	70.0	52.5	522.6	402.5	57.5	48.6	52.6	38.3
Breakdown (%)												
Dress	31.6	35.6	25.8	30.9	12.1	13.6	38.9	41.4	26.6	22.9	21.2	24.6
Casual	19.7	24.5	11.4	13.7	6.4	8.5	26.1	32.3	19.2	26.9	15.5	16.0
Athletic/tennis	37.0	29.4	45.3	37.1	75.6	69.7	25.4	17.2	45.8	41.5	52.2	48.5
Work/duty	4.8	4.3	11.8	10.4	1.2	2.1	2.8	2.5	0.4	0.3	0	0
Western/casual boots	1.4	1.6	2.3	3.2	1.6	1.9	1.0	0.9	0.9	1.6	1.3	1.5
Other	8.5	4.6	5.7	4.7	5.8	5.7	5.8	5.7	7.1	6.8	9.8	9.4

Source: Footwear Market Insights.

MANUFACTURING

By the early 1980s, there were some thirty companies in the U.S. athletic shoe market. (Exhibit 5 identifies leading firms.) As a group, these companies were noted for their aggressive stances toward each other. One industry observer said, "They are all fighting for the dollars; they're countering each other. They're all awake, aware they have to constantly update their shoes, constantly promote their shoes."

Most of these companies designed the technical updates for their shoes and handled their marketing, but few actually manufactured shoes. In fact, the only leading athletic shoe companies that manufactured their own shoes in the United States were New Balance and Etonic. The other companies contracted for production abroad, primarily in southeast Asia.

Manufacturing athletic shoes was not technically difficult, and a number of countries had industries which specialized in producing shoes on contract. Most of these had factories that were either owned or heavily financed by the national government. Most of this production took place in the Pacific Rim, where labor rates compared favorably to the average U.S. shoe industry wage rate of \$6.50 to \$7.30 per hour. (Even with outsourcing, labor typically accounts for one-third of the total expense of making an athletic shoe.) Some of the most popular supplier nations were:

- South Korea and Taiwan, where workers earned a relatively high \$400 to \$430 per month, but language and material availability problems were minimal. Historically, these two countries had accounted for around 75 percent of all U.S. imports of athletic shoes.
- China offered the greatest supply of cheap labor (monthly wages were \$40), but political instability, lack of machinery, and quality control problems were offsetting considerations.

EXHIBIT 5
U.S. Athletic Footwear Sales by Brand (in Millions of Dollars)

	1985	*1986*	*1987*
Reebok	$299.0	$841.0	$991.0
Nike	625.0	557.0	597.0
Converse	180.0	205.0	263.0
Adidas	162.0	150.0	159.0
Avia	21.0	70.0	153.0
New Balance	101.0	90.0	100.0
Keds	40.0	65.0	100.0
Pony	147.0	85.0	75.0
Hyde	54.7	65.3	71.0
L.A. Gear	10.7	36.3	68.0
Puma	125.0	60.0	66.0
Fila	4.5	35.0	60.0
Asics Tiger	37.0	42.0	60.0
Kangaroos	42.0	47.3	45.0
K-Swiss	22.0	31.0	40.0
Autry	22.0	33.4	37.4
Brooks	29.0	33.0	37.0
Tretorn	20.0	23.9	36.6
Turntec	11.0	21.0	30.0
Lotto	14.0	19.6	26.5
Kaepa	30.0	22.4	25.6
Etonic	25.0	21.3	24.6
Foot-Joy	13.0	14.0	21.0
Spalding	15.0	17.0	17.0

Source: Courtesy of *SportStyle.*

- Thailand regularly offered underutilized production capacity and its $100 monthly wage rate was competitive. However, the experience of some of the first firms to contract with Thai companies led others to question how well they could adhere to a production schedule.
- Indonesia, with its huge labor force and wages of $60 per month, was attracting the attention of South Korean companies, some of whom shifted their operations to this country.

DISTRIBUTION

For years, all-purpose sneakers were generally sold through mass merchandisers, general sporting goods stores, or discount stores. However, more specialized shoes encouraged retailer specialization. This resulted in the creation of specialty athletic shoe stores. Exhibit 6 shows total U.S. retail unit and dollar sales by year and type of customer. Sales data by type of retail outlet are given in Exhibit 7. Leading brands, such as Reebok and Nike, were believed to be available at 7,000 to 10,000 retail outlets nationwide.

The leading brands sold more of their products through specialty shops than any other

EXHIBIT 6
U.S. Athletic Footwear Retail Market

	Pairs (In Millions)				Dollars (In Millions)			
	Total	Men	Women	Juvenile	Total	Men	Women	Juvenile
1982	184.7	61.2	58.7	64.8	$3,554.8	$1,451.2	$1,161.3	$ 942.4
1983	214.1	68.8	71.1	74.2	4,234.4	1,743.4	1,391.0	1,100.0
1984	234.6	77.8	75.3	81.6	4,527.6	1,956.0	1,447.4	1,124.1
1985	257.6	87.2	85.5	85.0	5,146.5	2,236.6	1,746.6	1,163.3
1986	308.3	103.3	104.5	99.6	6,758.1	2,932.1	2,368.7	1,347.3
1987	349.2	112.5	130.4	106.3	8,061.1	3,421.0	2,988.2	1,651.9
1988*	383.8	132.0	142.5	109.4	9,244.0	4,112.0	3,387.0	1,745.0

* Estimate for 1988.
Source: Footwear Market Insights.

outlet. Within the specialty retail sector, industry experts estimated there were some 200 "guru" shoe shops that had extremely knowledgeable sales people, and another 3,000 shops with sales staff offering less expertise, but still capable of advising shoppers. Most specialty shops carried a full line for four or five leading brands plus one or two models from other brands. Mass merchandisers often carried only two or three national brands and perhaps a store label. Discounters had, at most, one national brand (usually not one of the top brands), as well as unbranded shoes and sometimes a store label. Margins were highest in the specialty shops, often between 40 and 50 percent. Some retail experts estimated that only one of every five specialty retail stores had shoe sales margins of less than 36 percent, while one in twenty had margins above 50 percent, requiring a markup of more than 100 percent.

The largest single retail outlet was probably Mickey Finn, a 6,000-square-foot spe-

EXHIBIT 7
Retail Sales Categorized by Type of Outlet, 1986

	Aerobics	Basketball	Gym Shoes	Running	Tennis	Walking	Fitness
Specialty sporting goods	16.9%	26.9%	11.1%	21.6%	13.4%	9.1%	18.8%
Specialty athletic footwear	18.7	22.6	8.8	19.7	12.8	14.7	18.8
Specialty sport and pro shops	2.5	3.7	2.8	4.3	4.1	2.8	5.1
Discount stores	21.7	17.4	34.6	18.6	25.3	22.8	20.9
Department stores	28.3	14.1	23.8	22.6	28.5	27.3	23.8
Mail order	2.9	0.6	1.2	2.3	1.2	3.9	1.5
Catalog showrooms	0.3	0.0	0.1	0.3	0.1	0.5	0.3
Other (includes traditional shoe stores)	8.7	14.7	17.6	10.6	14.6	18.9	10.8

Source: National Sporting Goods Association, Mt. Prospect, IL.

cialty shop in downtown Boston. The store stocked 650 models, some of which it special ordered to its own specifications, including an occasional lizard skin or patent leather version of popular models. By 1987, the store emphasized basketball shoes rather than running shoes, because these had become the preference of its predominantly inner-city customer base. In a good year, the store could sell 35,000 pairs of basketball shoes alone. The three owners managed their own stocking decisions. Their attitude on adding new lines was "We don't need them, they need us." Some new brands were accepted only on a consignment basis: If the shoes did not sell in 30 days, the manufacturer retrieved them.

The most successful chain of specialty athletic shoe stores was Foot Locker, a division of Kinney shoes which was, in turn, a division of Woolworth, an international merchandising company. According to estimates, from 12 to 20 percent of all Reeboks, the leading brand in 1986, were sold through this particular chain. However, Foot Locker did not concentrate exclusively on the largest brands. The company was well known for testing products from new companies, and most experts agreed there were several brands that would not have lasted without the early exposure they got through this national chain. Every year, Foot Locker threw a party for its vendors; observers believe no other event drew as many leading management people together from throughout the industry.

MARKET SEGMENTS

The various retail outlets for athletic shoes served a large and diverse market. A Sporting Goods Manufacturers Association (SGMA) survey indicated that by the late 1980s, 93 percent of all U.S. citizens owned at least one pair of athletic shoes, and that 72 percent continued to buy a new pair each year. (Serious athletes, such as those who ran regularly, typically replaced worn-out shoes twice a year.) According to SGMA reports, customers could be divided into four primary market segments:

- *Pragmatic:* Shoppers concerned with economy, ease of care, comfort, wear, and so on (30 percent of the market)
- *Performance:* Mostly males, between the ages of 20 and 39 (30 percent of the market)
- *Fundamental fashion:* Customers concerned with style, color, and fitting the shoe to an overall wardrobe (less than 25 percent of the market)
- *Fashion forward:* Ethnic groups, teens, and others who establish, rather than follow, fashion trends (approximately 15 percent of the market)

Industry observers point out that within these segments, the market could be further subdivided by the consumer's age: adolescent, college, young professionals, and older actives. Though some sports were still male-dominated (only 27 percent of the 21 million regular participants in basketball were female), women were becoming more active in sports, and by the late eighties, several sports were clearly female-dominated (see Exhibit 8). Still others divided the market according to price. Shoes priced under $30 were considered the casual shoe market, while shoes retailing for more than $60 were purchased by serious athletes and fashion trend setters.

Across these various market segments, buying patterns differ markedly in terms of

EXHIBIT 8
Female-Dominated Sports

Sport	Total Participants (Millions)	Female, %
Aerobic exercising	23.1	85.5
Exercise walking	58.1	64.6
Roller skating	19.8	61.1
Ice/figure skating	6.4	61.0
Calisthenics	17.1	54.6
Swimming	66.1	52.7
Bicycling	53.2	51.4
Bowling	40.1	51.0
Volleyball	23.6	50.4
Cross country skiing	5.0	50.1

Source: National Sporting Goods Association, Mt. Prospect, IL.

price sensitivity and the number of shoes owned. Some segments, for instance, parents shopping for young children, were sometimes price-sensitive, but others were not. A survey conducted by *Apparel Merchandising* indicated that children in the 8- to 12-year-old category influenced their parents' purchasing decisions on the children's shoes (see Exhibit 9). Children were more concerned with brands than with prices. In fact, some retailers felt many high school adolescents actually preferred paying more for shoes. SGMA studies show that in the United States, 24 percent of the population owned one pair of athletic shoes, 50 percent owned two or three pairs, and 19 percent owned four or more pairs. These heavy owners accounted for 43 percent of all athletic shoe purchases. Retailers spoke of customers who stopped by weekly to appraise the latest models. Mickey Finn claimed that it had identified one set of customers who bought a new pair of athletic shoes at an average rate of once every 13 days. The store maintained a directory of beeper numbers for the most avid customers, so they could be paged immediately when a significant new release arrived.

Nationwide, the SGMA reported the heavy ownership segment to be equal portions of men and women. However, there were differences in heavy ownership by age and region.

EXHIBIT 9
Does Your Child's Opinion Influence Your Purchasing Decision?

	Parents of 8- to 12-Year-Old Boys, %	Parents of 8- to 12-Year Old Girls, %
Very much	53	61
Somewhat	30	33
Not too much	4	4
Not at all	13	2

Source: *Apparel Merchandising* (1989, January).

Twenty-one percent of all teenagers owned four-plus pairs, 27 percent of the 18 to 24 age group did, and so did 22 percent of the 25 to 34 age group. Geographically, the west had a high concentration of heavy ownership, 23 percent, while the northeast was a fairly light 17 percent.

Athletic shoes were such popular fashion items that even in the heavy ownership category, serious athletes were in the minority. Rather, most consumers wore the shoes as casual apparel. Many of the most active consumers were young people concerned about the personal statement their shoes made. Particularly in the inner city, adolescents were dedicated aficionados of athletic shoes, so much so that several observers commented that in this culture, "you are what you wear on your feet."

Linking shoes so strongly to personal image occasionally became grizzly. Within the intense, inner-city markets, young people were mugged for their flashy, top-of-the-line shoes, some of which carried suggested retail prices as high as $170. Law enforcement officials believed youths turned to small-time drug dealing because of pressure to wear the latest athletic footwear. Name-brand athletic shoes were cited as motives in violent deaths in many places, including Houston, Detroit, Philadelphia, and Los Angeles.

As a fashion statement, trends in sales could change suddenly and dramatically. For instance, British Knights, or BKs as they were more popularly known, almost instantaneously went from being a hit shoe with the gangs of Los Angeles to a serious social faux pas when, for reasons never understood, BK became the initials for "brother killer." Even without such unusual events, shoes were constantly undergoing changes on both the fashion and the technical front, and most models lasted but a single season.

MARKETING

Because such a large part of the total market bought shoes as much for fashion as for function, consumer marketing and promotion became a noted characteristic of the industry. By 1987, the top four or five firms in the market had combined promotional budgets well in excess of $100 million. This promotional effort had two primary components: advertising and endorsements.

The use of celebrity and athletic endorsements varied widely across the industry's history. The first endorsements were for Converse All Stars, sold during the great depression by professional basketball stars working out of their cars in the off season. Over time, the use of endorsements grew until on some professional basketball teams, every player received some sort of compensation for backing a particular brand. One star signaled that endorsements had gotten out of hand when he entered a game wearing competing brands he endorsed—one on each foot! As more and more competitors entered the market, bidding for endorsements made them prohibitively expensive. Because of the high cost, by 1985 only the top players in the various sports were being signed for endorsements. According to some observers, these endorsements actually had more impact on the markets as a result of the greater exclusivity.

Throughout the 1980s, advertising campaigns for the leading firms became bigger, splashier, and more expensive. Whereas advertising once consisted of a few pages in run-

EXHIBIT 10
Top Ten Brands in Media Advertising through Leading Outlets
(Athletic and Protective Footwear, in Millions of Dollars)

Brand	1987	1986	1985
Reebok	$12.1	$ 8.5	$ 3.8
Nike	10.7	6.4	2.4
Avia	3.6	1.5	--
Converse Sporting	2.8	1.6	1.6
Foot Joy	2.3	1.2	1.5
Timberland	1.5	--	--
Easy Spirit	1.4	--	--
Fila	1.3	--	--
Brooks	1.2	--	--
Keds	1.1	--	--
Adidas	--	1.4	--
Tretorn	--	1.5	--
Autry	--	2.4	1.4
Converse (other than Converse Sporting)	--	1.1	1.4
Sorel (boots)	--	1.0	0.9
Kaepa (boots)	--	--	1.6
Puma	--	--	0.9
Other	19.2	15.6	12.7
Total	$57.2	$42.2	$28.2

Source: LNA/Arbitron Multi-Media Service.

ning magazines, in 1987 the industry's advertising budget topped $31 million, about 42 percent of which was targeted to television. (Exhibit 10 shows data on 1987 media spending in this industry. Exhibit 11 shows historical data on media advertising for the overall apparel, footwear, and accessories category.) Firms regularly spent 6 to 8 percent of their revenues on advertising. Most observers agreed that consumers bought names—not shoes. Formal market research documented as much. One study showed that 38 percent of all mothers shopping for their child's back-to-school shoes were looking for only one brand.

EXHIBIT 11
Media Advertising* in Domestic Apparel, Footwear, and Accessories
(in Thousands of Dollars)

Year	Media Advertising
1987	$664,628
1986	613,833
1985	570,834
1984	638,901
1983	611,208

* Top seven media outlets.
Source: LNA/Arbitron Multi-Media Service.

EXHIBIT 12
Sportstyle 50
(U.S. Sales, in Millions of Dollars)

	1987	*1986*
Reebok (also Rockport, Frye, Avia)	$1,221.0	$903.0
Nike	727.0	702.0
Russell	480.0	397.0
Tultex	348.0	327.0
Spalding	345.0	312.0
Ocean Pacific	333.0	293.0
Coleman	314.0	293.0
Adidas	302.3	250.0
Bassett Walker	296.0	296.0
Converse	274.0	214.0
Pannill	259.0	245.0
Wilson	250.0	234.0
Acushnet (Foot-Joy, Titleist)	245.5	223.0
Jantzen	200.0	186.0
Stride Rite (Keds, Sperry, Herman's)	190.0	150.0
Fuqua	180.4	169.5
Champion	178.0	141.0
Woolrich	175.0	158.0
Catalina	110.0	102.0
Timberland	107.0	85.0
Puma	103.8	101.0
Izod/Lacoste	100.0	85.0
New Balance	100.0	90.0
MacGregor	98.0	85.0
Rawlings	90.0	104.0
Diversified Products	85.0	120.0
Weider	85.0	80.0
Etonic/Tretorn	83.1	61.3
Pacific Trail	82.0	78.0
Wolverine (also Brooks)	77.7	70.0
Fila	77.4	52.0
Pony	75.0	85.0
Northwestern	75.0	66.0
American Recreation	73.0	70.0
Hyde	71.0	65.3
Karsten	70.0	60.0
L.A. Gear	68.3	36.3
Salomon	67.2	63.0
Weslo	67.0	50.0
Asics Tiger	66.0	45.0
Gotcha	65.0	50.0
Hobie	62.0	62.0
Speedo	57.5	49.5
Prince	54.0	55.0
Raichle Molitor USA	52.6	50.0
Excel	49.8	36.2
Bike	49.0	59.0
Columbia	48.0	30.0
Head Sportswear	48.0	40.0

Source: Courtesy of *SportStyle*.

THE OUTLOOK FOR THE FUTURE

In 1987, the big question in the athletic shoe industry was whether or not the high historical growth rates would continue. The National Sporting Goods Association (NSGA) predicted that growth in wholesales revenues would rise only 4 percent in 1988. One poll showed that about 40 percent of all athletic shoe retailers expected 1988 sales to be no better, and possibly worse, than they were in 1987. Most believed that broad-based growth could not continue, but there was considerable disagreement within the industry about the possibility of opening up new niche market segments. Some contended that all potential niches had already been opened, but others remained optimistic.

Other industry developments included:

- The continued increase in the number of women employed
- Less leisure time, placing increased emphasis on quality nonworking activities
- An aging population shifting interests away from competitive team sports and toward individual activities
- A more fragmented population of customers
- New entrants building on brand names they have established in other sectors of the sports industry (see list of top fifty brand names in sports in Exhibit 12).

CASE 7

Nike and Reebok: One on One*

NIKE PIONEERS THE MODERN ATHLETIC SHOE

In the late 1950s, Bill Bowerman was coaching the track team at Oregon. One of his runners was an introverted 4:13 miler by the name of Philip Knight. After graduating from Oregon, Knight went on to get an M.B.A. at Stanford where he prepared a now-famous business plan for a small-business management class. The plan was to have Japanese manufacturers do to Europe's athletic shoe industry what they were already doing to its camera industry. Adidas and Puma were famous European brands of athletic shoes, but Knight felt that Europe was the wrong place to make shoes, arguing that the cost of production would be less in Japan. Upon graduation, he had an opportunity to travel to Japan where executives were quick to agree with his assessment.

Knight worked out a deal with the manufacturer of the ASICS brand in Japan, and the company agreed to manufacture Knight's shoes for sale in the United States. Upon returning home, Knight and his former coach, who had been working continuously on better shoe designs, invested $500 each to form Blue Ribbon Sports, a name selected to emphasize winning. Coach Bowerman and Mike Johnson, another former Oregon runner, worked on improving shoe designs while Knight was first a C.P.A. and then an assistant professor of business at Portland State. During this period, the company was characterized as a bunch of athletes selling shoes to another bunch of athletes. One group of runners/employees in Boston traveled to east coast races selling shoes out of their car trunks, while a similar group operated out of Portland along the west coast.

Working this closely with top athletes began to pay off in exciting new innovations at the fledgling company. The firm's reputation grew until, in 1969, Knight decided to devote full time to managing the company. By 1972, the firm was selling $2 million worth of shoes a year. The Japanese supplier insisted that Blue Ribbon sell it 51 percent of its stock at book value or lose it as a supplier. Knight and his team decided to sign with a new Japanese supplier, and start a new U.S. company. The new firm was named Nike after the Greek winged god of victory, an idea that came to Johnson in a dream. Its logo was a "swoosh" created for $35 by a graduate student in design. Nike imported the first of its new line of shoes in time for the 1972 Olympics trials. The new shoes finished well at the trials, and demand continued to grow. Knight and his coworkers began to speculate about someday reaching $10 million in annual revenues.

Nike's management continued to be dominated by athletes, and technical performance was a top priority. In 1975, Nike received worldwide attention by radically redesigning the soles of its running shoes. Bill Bowerman had been searching for a sole that was lightweight, absorbed energy, and gave good traction. One day over breakfast, he suddenly realized that a rubberized waffle would meet these requirements, and by the end of the day,

* Prepared by Alex Miller with assistance from Paula Smith, MBA student, both at University of Tennessee.

he had both ruined a waffle iron and produced the world's first prototype of a waffle sole. Nike introduced the new sole in 1975, and its success led virtually every competitor around the world to produce a similar design. Nike had established itself as a leader in the athletic shoe technology race.

In 1976, the company's sales surpassed Knight's earlier dreams, rocketing to $14 million. It was the beginning of an unprecedented growth period. For the next 5 years, sales grew by more than 75 percent every year, and from 1977 to 1983, profits grew at an annual compound rate of just over 100 percent. Domestically, the company quickly outsold Puma and Adidas, formerly the world's two leading brands. Tremendous profits and low investments combined to generate a return on equity of 60 percent in 1978 and 1979. Even after the company went public in 1980, raising $52 million in equity, Nike's return on equity (ROE) remained at 45 percent. By early 1983, only 3 years after going public, Nike's stock had already increased in value by more than 150 percent.

Much of Nike's success was the result of a change in casual fashions. Blue jeans and athletic shoes became the standard wardrobe of adolescents, college students, and a large part of the under-25-year-old population in general. When a 1980 transit strike in New York City put many commuters on foot, working men and women were seen sporting sneakers with business attire all over the city. After the strike ended, the habit of wearing athletic shoes to commute stuck, especially with women, whose dress shoes were generally less comfortable and durable. Eighty percent of all athletic shoes being purchased were used primarily for nonathletic purposes by the early 1980s.

By 1983, Nike was investing nearly $6 million a year in R&D and the company offered over 156 models of shoes covering six major categories:

Running: Nike was the dominant competitor in this market segment, holding a 50-percent share. The second closest competitor in the segment was New Balance with only a 15-percent share. By the end of 1982, every world record for distances between 800 meters and the marathon had been set by athletes wearing Nikes. At the top end of the market, Nike offered the Tailwind. This 1979 model utilized Nike's patented "air" technology, consisting of a small chamber of gas buried in the sole of the shoe to absorb shock.

Basketball: This market generated $144 million in sales for Nike. The company held a 20-percent share of the segment, third behind the market leaders, Converse (35 percent) and Puma (30 percent). By 1981, Nike executives admitted that their basketball shoes had been outdated, but they were excited about their new model. The Air Force I, introduced in 1982, utilized the same air technology which had been so successful in the Tailwind running shoe since 1979.

Children's: Nike felt that even though its sales of children's shoes had already passed the $100-million mark, they had only begun to scratch the surface of this market segment's potential. The Nike line of children's shoes was called Colors; these were basically scaled down versions of its adult shoes.

Racquet sports: With $60 million in sales from this segment, Nike held a 40-percent share, twice as high as Adidas, the former powerhouse in racquet sports.

Cleated shoes: These were football, field events, and baseball shoes, and as a segment, they accounted for only $15 million of Nike's 1982 sales. While the company was not a market leader here, executives thought continued emphasis on this market was essential. The college and professional athletes using these shoes were seen as trend-setters for the rest of the shoe-buying population.

Ath-leisure: These were shoes which the rest of the market called casual shoes. Nike was a small shareholder in this market, with sales of only $4 million. Its top-end shoe in this segment was the Air Casual, a 1980 shoe that incorporated the Tailwind's air technology. However, by 1982, managers admitted the shoe was a failure. It was considered technically superior but unsatisfactory from a fashion standpoint.

In addition to one of the largest lines of athletic shoes of any U.S. company, Nike had also entered the apparel market. The line had grown quickly, from 1979 sales of $2 million to 1983 sales of $100 million. The line had few high-tech products, but the power of the Nike brand generated impressive sales. Data on Nike's sales by product category as of 1986 and 1987 are provided in Exhibit 1.

As Nike's product line expanded, so did its organization, from a handful of athletes selling shoes part time to a full-time work force of 3,600. During this growth, managers at the company worked hard to maintain the climate and culture that originally attracted them. Even as a larger company, many of Nike's managers were former athletes. The organization was very decentralized and individuals were encouraged to be freethinkers—constantly on the lookout for ways to make Nike shoes of greater value to the market. Any sort of structure or control was met with considerable disfavor, as the team strived to

EXHIBIT 1
Nike Sales by Product Category
Years Ended May 31
(in Thousands of Dollars)

	1987	***1986***
Footwear (U.S.)		
Basketball	$132,500	$ 212,600
Running	115,500	150,000
Children's	75,600	115,400
Fitness	76,600	54,100
Racquet	36,200	68,500
Field sports	43,900	35,400
Other	29,700	13,500
Total footwear (U.S.)	$510,000	$ 649,500
Apparel (U.S.)	$130,700	$ 164,600
Athletic equipment (U.S.)	900	2,500
Total United States	$641,600	$ 816,600
Foreign		
Europe	$191,400	$ 166,300
Japan	--	42,400
Canada	20,300	22,900
Other	24,100	21,100
Total foreign	$235,800	$ 252,700
Total Nike	$877,400	$1,069,300

Source: Annual reports.

maintain its mixture of camaraderie and individualism. Many of the managers found similarities between working for Nike and being a member of an athletic team: Individuals were responsible for giving their all for the good of the whole. A strong esprit de corps reigned, and the obvious goal was to beat the competition.

By 1983, most industry observers believed the athletic shoe was reaching the mature stage of its market life cycle, and sales were widely expected to plateau. With a tremendous record of success in domestic sales, Nike began to look elsewhere for growth. In 1983, Knight handed responsibility for day-to-day domestic operations over to other managers, and began to focus on international competition, the segment of the market many expected to be the fastest growing, as the United States market became saturated.

REEBOK ENTERS THE UNITED STATES MARKET

In 1982, a tiny company by the name of Reebok was struggling to make a place in the United States athletic shoe market so thoroughly dominated by Nike. While the company had only recently come to the United States, it had as impressive a history as any athletic shoe manufacturer. In the early 1890s, Joseph William Foster of Bolton, England, made himself the first pair of track shoes with spikes. The idea was so popular that by 1895, Foster was in business, making shoes by hand for the best runners in England. In time, J. W. Foster & Sons developed a national reputation, supplying the shoes for the famous British track team at the 1924 Olympics, later immortalized in the film *Chariots of Fire.* In 1958, two of Foster's grandsons started a sister company they named Reebok, after the swift African antelope. That company eventually absorbed J. W. Foster & Sons, but until 1979, the Reebok name remained unknown except to a small group of world-class athletes.

In 1979, Paul Fireman, a college dropout from Boston University, was selling fishing tackle and outdoor gear in his family's business. He was at an international sports show looking for a new way to supplement his sales when he spotted a pair of Reebok shoes. He obtained the license to import Reebok into North America, and introduced three running shoes in the United States that same year. At $60 a pair, they were the most expensive production running shoes sold at that time.

By 1981, U.S. sales exceeded $1.5 million. But Fireman had grand aspirations that included turning the tiny Avon, Massachusetts, company into a $20-million corporation. This was an objective many, including Fireman, considered rather brash, given that in the early eighties the market was thought to be saturated with dedicated fans for the Adidas and Nike brands. In 1981, the company's president, Jim Barclay (formerly a salesman for General Foods) was traveling the country selling shoes out of the trunk of his car. In his travels he observed that women runners were buying attractive pastel-colored athletic clothing they wore with clunky-looking and garishly colored running shoes, like Reebok's own royal blue shoes with their canary yellow stripes. Mauve was one of the trendiest colors of the season, so Barclay ordered up a new model in mauve that he called the Orchid. It was soon the company's best seller.

In 1982, Barclay was on the road again looking for dealers to handle the Reebok line in California. He noticed dealers were besieged with requests for shoes to wear in aerobics classes. On his return, he explained to Fireman that aerobics was the current fad on the west coast, and that it might be a market worth pursuing. (Barclay had to explain to Fireman that aerobics was a form of exercise combining the elements of both dance and calisthenics.) Though their financial backers doubted the wisdom of trying to open a new market of athletic shoes for women, the two persisted, pushing designers to create two new models. The resulting Energizer was a nylon and suede shoe not much different from existing models. But its sister, the Freestyle, had an entirely different look and feel about it—all leather uppers made from garment leather as soft as ballet slippers, attached to a conventional sole and trimmed in soft pastels.

The Freestyle was introduced in late 1982, and initial sales were disappointing—for 3 months, virtually none of the new shoes were sold. Reebok lacked the resources to risk an expensive advertising campaign on something as unsure as a new-product concept targeting a new market. Consequently, there was virtually no traditional marketing associated with the new product's rollout. Rather than use the promotional efforts typical of the industry, Fireman and Barclay improvised, creating an energetic promotional effort narrowly targeted at a tiny market: aerobics instructors.

They coupled their promotional spending with the creation of the Reebok Professional Instructor Alliance, and underwrote the certification program for aerobics instructors the Alliance offered, the first of its kind. They also sponsored *Reebok Instructor News*, a bimonthly newsletter edited and produced by the Institute for Aerobics Research in Dallas, Texas. Angel Martinez, Reebok's product development director, traveled the California coast in her beatup Datsun imploring aerobics instructors to try the shoes she gave them. The healthy "all-American" instructors who accepted the Reebok shoes were apparently ideal models—sales jumped from $3.5 million in 1982 to $13 million in 1983. As sales grew, Reebok expanded the line of aerobic shoes to cover the $30 to $60 retail price range with five styles in six colors. Production demands quickly outstripped capacity back in England, and contracts were signed with factories in Korea. By now, managers at Reebok had set their sights on sales of "$1 more than $75 million"—just enough to edge out New Balance as the number 6 brand in the United States.

As more people became familiar with the shoes, the public discovered that the soft leather was comfortable right out of the box, and that they looked good with jeans, the staple fashion item at that time. Customers began wearing the shoes not just for aerobics, but as casual shoes replacing loafers. Several celebrities made public appearances in Reeboks, creating instant fashion news. On stage at the Emmys, Cybill Shepard wore a pair of tangerine-colored Reebok high-tops with her formal slit-to-the-thigh black gown. Mick Jagger and David Bowie wore black Freestyles in their rock video *Dancing in the Street* and Elton John had a pair of Reeboks personalized with white feathers and sequined piano keys. Meanwhile, Whoopi Goldberg wore a pair in the movie *Burglar*, and in *Back to the Future*, Michael J. Fox wore a scruffy pair so well-worn that keen fashion aficionados speculated they were his personal property.

As a result of such exposure, the power of the Reebok label as a fashion item reached unprecedented levels in the athletic shoe market. When a shipment of shoes with badly wrinkled leather came in from Korea, wrinkled leather became fashionable. When orders from suppliers ran late and the shoes were hard to find, it added to the air of exclusivity and further inflamed consumer demand.

While the shoe had tremendous fashion appeal with customers, sporting goods experts questioned how much support was provided by the soft leather Reebok used in its most popular shoes. Others criticized the shoes for not wearing well, complaining that with

EXHIBIT 2
Reebok Footwear Division: Sales by Product Lines (in Millions of Dollars)

Footwear	1984	1985	1986
Aerobic	$36.1	$130.4	$294.3
Tennis	17.3	88.4	174.7
Fitness	5.4	50.0	139.6
Children's	0.4	12.8	81.1
Basketball	--	0.7	72.0
Running	4.9	16.2	66.4
Other	--	0.7	12.9
Total	$64.1	$299.2	$841.0

Source: Annual reports.

serious use, the garment-type leather soon broke down. But such criticism did not deter the company, and it quickly introduced the Phase I, a lighter, more comfortable tennis shoe. Meanwhile, running for the Reebok Racing Club, Steve Jones won the America's Marathon in Chicago in a world record time wearing Reeboks.

To induce retailers to carry its running and tennis shoes along with its popular aerobics line, Reebok broke with the tradition of giving discounts on the basis of the number of pairs of shoes ordered. Instead, it based discounts on the number of different models stocked. It also opted to keep its price points reasonably high, which ruled out consideration by lower-end retail outlets. Despite these differences, retailers clambered for the shoes, many claiming an 80-percent conversion rate, meaning that an estimated 80 percent of their customers who tried on a pair of Reeboks eventually ended up buying a pair.

By the end of 1984, sales were an astounding $66 million, and Fireman organized a buyout from the British founder. In 1985, the company entered two new markets, children's athletic shoes and basketball shoes, and sales grew to $307 million. Soon, the company had a 50-percent share of the shoe market for racquet sports, 28 percent of the $700-million basketball market, and still held 75 percent of the aerobic and fitness markets. More recent data on sales by product category and year are given in Exhibit 2.

DIVERSIFICATION AT REEBOK

In 1986, sales reached $919 million. Reebok began to diversify. First, it introduced a line of full-support toddler shoes called Weeboks, and then it introduced a line of men's and women's performance active wear and sports apparel. In 1987, this internal diversification trend continued with the introduction of Metaphors, a new line of women's casual shoes combining nonsports fashion with athletic shoe technology. Internal developments were supplemented with external acquisitions:

- Rockport, purchased for $118 million, made a line of walking and casual dress shoes that borrowed heavily from running shoe technology. The company thoroughly dominated the walking market, where it was considered the leader in biomechanical design. The Rockport Walking Institute, established in 1985, was devoted to scientific research on the benefits of walking, and Rockport had sponsored three books and a movie in which experts promoted the health benefits of the activity. To capitalize on managerial strengths at Rockport, Fireman also bought Frye, a $20-million boot and loafer firm located nearby in Marlborough, Massachusetts. Frye became a subsidiary of Rockport.

- Avia, purchased for $180 million, was a designer and marketer of high-performance specialty sports shoes. The company placed considerable emphasis on technology, and offered a patented cantilever sole, a protruding midsole pad, and a pivoting flex joint, all designed to maximize the functionality of its footwear. The company conducted its R&D in its Portland, Oregon, laboratories. In addition to sneakers, Avia also marketed walking, casual, and hiking shoes from its Donner Mountain subsidiary. Avia's sales were expected to top $250 million in 1988.
- Late in 1987, Reebok was also thought to be negotiating with Ellesse International, an Italian maker of women's fashionable sportswear. Other deals rumored to be under development were for Stride-Rite (shoes), Esprit (casual apparel), Prince (tennis equipment), and perhaps a toy company.

Venturing into these new markets offered various managerial challenges at Reebok. For instance, Avia and Rockport were both very popular lines of shoes (see annual sales data by division in Exhibit 3), but their margins were not as good as those on Reebok's flagship line. Experts estimated that the corporation had to sell one and a half pairs of these shoes to generate the bottom-line effect of selling just one pair of Reeboks. The line of sports apparel had some rather serious quality problems, and many considered the company fortunate that its late delivery meant that defective products missed the Christmas market of 1987. On the other hand, moving the products in the off season required steep markdowns. Finally, shortages of leather and labor disputes in Korea (where 77 percent of Reebok's shoes were manufactured) had limited supplies at various times. To address such varied problems, Fireman began recruiting new managers.

In 1987, he surprised insiders at Reebok by breaking the firm's tradition of promotion from within and appointing Joseph LaBonte as the corporation's new chief operating officer. LaBonte had most recently been a venture capitalist heading the Vantage Group. Before that, he had established a reputation as a numbers man, managing mergers and

EXHIBIT 3
Reebok Sales by Division (in Millions of Dollars)

	1983	*1984*	*1985*	*1986*	*1987*
Reebok Footwear Division	$12.0	$64.0	$299.0	$ 841.0	$ 991.0
Avia	2.8	7.0	21.1	70.3	153.0
Rockport	26.0	38.4	64.5	92.9	152.0
Reebok Apparel Division	n/a	n/a	4.0	39.4	47.0
Reebok International Division	n/a	n/a	817.0	3,712.0	7,830.0

Source: Annual reports.

acquisitions at Twentieth Century Fox. (Coincidentally, at Fox, he had also been involved in the production of *Chariots of Fire.*) Many had considered Barclay to be a natural for the position, but Fireman argued that LaBonte was the better man, given Reebok's changing managerial needs. The day of the LaBonte announcement, Reebok's stock rose five points.

After his appointment, LaBonte worked with Fireman to recruit Mark Goldston, formerly president of Faberge, and Frank O'Connell, formerly CEO of HBO Video, to bolster Reebok's corporate management team. To manage the apparel division, Fireman hired Doug Arbetman, a former president at Calvin Klein. Fireman assigned the Rockport presidency to his longtime friend Stanley Kravetz, formerly president of Frye.

This new team of top managers oversaw increasingly decentralized operations at Reebok. Each business was given its own design and marketing functions, and LaBonte instructed each team to be aggressive in pushing their own products. His constant reminder was "If we are going to lose business, let's make sure we lose it to ourselves."

INSIDE REEBOK

By the end of 1987, Reebok's sales soared past the billion-dollar mark to hit $1.4 billion, representing an annual growth rate from 1981 of 155 percent per year. It now claimed 37 percent of the $3.5 billion wholesale athletic shoe market, and *Forbes* magazine had announced that it was the most profitable firm in the United States. Though it was rapidly passing the $1-billion sales mark, Reebok still had many of the entrepreneurial characteristics one would expect of an organization only 6 years old. Visitors almost never failed to note the spirit of enthusiasm, risk taking, and teamwork that pervaded the firm.

The typical Reebok employee (they called themselves Reebots) was notable for his or her vitality and seemingly endless energy. Most were between 25 and 35 years old, many had a background in sports, most were college educated, and apparently all were excited about working at Reebok. Many of the sales people serviced 150 to 200 accounts, making daily or nightly presentations on the Reebok line. They bragged about always being on the go, never being at home, living out of their cars, and thriving on the exciting pace. Morale was excellent, and most seemed to worship Fireman and the company he had built. For his part, Fireman encouraged them to speak out on what they felt the company should hear, and if they felt they were not heard, to come to him directly.

Such leadership encouraged Reebok employees to act as they thought best—even if it meant doing things which would normally be considered risky. For instance, halfway through the rollout of Weeboks, Betsy Richardson, one of four marketing directors under Reebok's decentralized corporate organization, decided "on a gut level" that the advertising campaign was wrong. Working outside official channels, she designed a new advertising approach with another ad agency, which she then took to management. They approved the expensive switch, which went on to be "a gorgeous campaign."

Teamwork was an important part of the corporate culture at Reebok. For example, product development at Reebok was described as a four-part relay team—the team members being (1) the consumer research staff, who turned data over to (2) marketing personnel, who created new images with (3) the product designers, who then worked with (4) the engineers to actually design and build prototypes.

The actual product design took place in a converted two-story warehouse Reebok rented. Four engineers, some of whom were serious runners themselves, occupied the first floor. There, the atmosphere was tense, professional, and scientific. Bookshelves were lined with texts on sports injuries, and life-size models and skeletons were scattered among treadmills, force plates, high-speed cameras, and computer equipment. Upstairs, four designers worked under skylights in a "funky" loft, amid drafting tables, potted plants, and loud music. The second-floor team consisted of a Vietnamese-born former Levi-Straus designer of sports apparel, a Spaniard with a background in European shoe design, an American engineer, and a former British footwear designer. The group joked that the only running they ever did was to a bar.

A good example of how all Reebok's entrepreneurial characteristics came together to make the company a market sensation is the fairy talelike story of the company's debut in golf shoes. Golf shoes represented a small segment of the overall athletic shoe industry, only about $180 million in annual sales. But, it was a market closely held by well-established names such as FootJoy, Etonic, and Dexter, popular with the pro shops that distribute about 80 percent of all golf shoes. The success of Reebok's aerobic shoes meant little in this market. The upper crust of the golfing community was known as being somewhat elitist in their thinking—they generally considered any sort of hard sell to be overzealous and inappropriate. Therefore, Reebok found a more subtle way of introducing itself to this market.

Every year, the 150 members of the pro-golf tour held the Tour Player's Championship at Sawgrass, Florida. In 1987, a group of the players' wives decided to host their own tournament—the first annual Tour Wives Championship. The proceeds were to be donated to then first lady Nancy Reagan's drug abuse center in Jacksonville, Florida. Plans called for the pro-golfer husbands to caddy, and Reebok had generously offered to be the event's corporate sponsor.

On the day of the championship, perky Reebok sales representatives arrived with gift packs (shoes, windbreakers, and visors in a Reebok tote bag) for all the wives, husbands, and children who would attend the event. After the tournament, the rain held off long enough for Mrs. Reagan to have her picture taken with golf legends Lee Trevino, who carried his box of Reeboks under his arm, and John Mahaffey, who wore his. As press cameras clicked and whirred, a light rain began, and everyone donned their Reebok windbreakers and adjourned to the Reebok tent for champagne. There, a company spokesman announced that Reebok had just signed a contract (later rumored to be a 5-year, $2.5-million deal) with Greg Norman, the 41-year-old golfing champion from Australia, who would design a new line of Reebok golfing shoes. As the party broke up, there were well wishes from all attendees, and the first lady returned to her limo to find an extra gift pack stashed there for her husband.

Most insiders attributed much of this sort of entrepreneurial pizzazz at Reebok to Paul Fireman. He refused most interviews, and worked especially hard at shielding his three children from the public. He drove his own Honda Accord between the office and his home where he maintained a modest life-style. On weekends, he played golf, his only sport, and on Mondays, he met with his high school pals for beer, pizza, and quarter-ante poker. On the other hand, he also traveled the world in the company's $10 million jet, and in 1987, in addition to his regular pay of $364,000 he received a bonus of $12.7 million in stock options, making him second only to Lee Iacocca in CEO pay for the year. His share of Reebok stock ensured that he was well on his way to making the *Forbes* 400, the annual list of the four

EXHIBIT 4
Reebok International, Ltd.: Income Statements
Years Ended December 31
(in Thousands of Dollars, Except per Share Data)

	1987	*1986*	*1985*	*1984*	*1983*
Net sales	$1,389,196	$919,401	$306,969	$66,022	$12,815
Other income	10,240	4,472	1,834	104	15
Total	$1,399,436	$923,873	$308,803	$66,126	$12,830
Cost and expenses:					
Cost of sales	$ 808,991	$521,978	$176,462	$39,144	$ 7,288
Selling expenses	164,896	83,294	31,846	9,383	2,978
General and administrative expenses	102,191	54,470	21,631	5,069	1,248
Amortization of intangibles	12,453	2,280	--	--	--
Interest expense	4,771	694	755	372	74
Total	$1,093,302	$662,716	$230,694	$53,968	$11,588
Income before income taxes	$306,134	$261,157	--	--	--
Income before income taxes and extraordinary credit	--	--	$78,109	$12,158	$1,242
Income taxes	140,934	129,023	39,147	6,013	606
Income before extraordinary credit	$165,200	$132,134	$38,962	$ 6,145	$ 636
Extraordinary credit	$ --	$ --	$ --	$ --	$ 31
Net income	$165,200	$132,134	$38,962	$ 6,145	$ 667
Net income per common share	$1.49	$1.27	$0.47	$0.08	$0.05
Average share price (adjusted for splits)	$17.58	$10.92	$4.23	--	--

Source: Annual reports.

hundred richest Americans. He explained to the press, in somewhat embarrassed tones, that his 1987 bonus was based on 5 percent of all pretax earnings greater than $20 million, a contract written when $20 million in *revenues*—let alone *earnings*—sounded rather far-fetched. In 1987, his goal was to turn Reebok into a $2 billion company by 1990. Reebok's financial statements for 1983 through 1987 are provided in Exhibits 4 and 5.

NIKE IN 1987

Reebok's success had taken its toll on Nike (see Nike's financial statements in Exhibits 6 and 7). No longer the market leader, Nike's share of the athletic footwear market had dropped to little more than 20 percent by 1987. The domestic work force had been reduced by 360 in an effort to lower costs 3 to 4 percent. To reduce inventory carrying costs (at one time, inventories had grown to an estimated 22 million pairs), the numbers of models and styles had also been reduced. In order to generate stronger demand for its shoes, Nike had greatly increased its use of advertising and promotion. By 1987, the firm was believed to be spending some $60 million annually on its total promotional and advertising efforts (see Exhibit 8 for a breakdown of industry spending on media advertising alone). Industry analysts estimated that Nike's stock traded at a discount to the market of about 40 percent, given their 1988 earnings estimates of around $2.10 per share.

Some observers thought that Nike was poised for a comeback in 1986 when its Air Jordan, a $65 shoe endorsed by Michael Jordan, the National Basketball Association's recent Rookie of the Year, was successful beyond all predictions. The initial estimates were that the shoe would generate retail sales of only about $5 million. Yet, sales in the first year (including sales from the line of apparel introduced along with the Air Jordan line) topped $100 million. Price-gouging retailers were selling out of the shoe at prices as high as $100 in some cities. The tremendous demand for the shoe was largely credited to a marketing campaign that linked the air technology, introduced in the 1979 Tailwind running shoe, with the famous hang time of Jordan's impressive leaps. However, in 1987, Jordan sat out the basketball season with a broken foot and demand for the shoes plummeted even faster than it had risen the previous year. Some retailers found themselves trying to sell the new model of the shoe, with a suggested retail price of nearly $100, while still holding the older model at a heavily discounted $20 retail price.

Meanwhile, a new entry to the market was generating tremendous consumer interest. L.A. Gear, a company which specialized in fashion-oriented athletic shoes, was now the most rapidly growing brand in the market. In 1986, the company had grown by 240 percent, and in 1987, it was expected to grow by perhaps another 100 percent. Industry analysts predicted that over the next 5 years, L.A. Gear's sales would continue to increase by at least 30 percent per year. This figure was three to five times the expected short-term growth rate for the industry as a whole. With developments like this taking place, it was not clear how Nike could fight its way back to its former dominance, nor was it clear that Reebok would be able to hold on to its newly acquired number 1 position.

EXHIBIT 5
Reebok International, Ltd.: Balance Sheets
Years Ended December 31
(in Thousands of Dollars)

	1987	1986	1985	1984
	Assets			
Current assets:				
Cash	$ 60,167	$ 66,077	$ 7,974	$ 998
Accounts receivable	204,676	120,075	73,737	15,781
Inventory	240,898	122,522	62,788	18,358
Refundable federal income taxes	--	--	--	954
Deferred income taxes	19,534	5,589	--	--
Prepaid expenses	10,821	2,324	278	178
Total current assets	$536,096	$316,587	$144,777	$36,269
Property and equipment	$ 73,447	$ 21,198	$ 4,134	$ 2,030
Less accumulated depreciation and amortization	8,968	1,980	821	306
Total property and equipment	$ 64,479	$ 19,218	$ 3,313	$ 1,724
Noncurrent assets:				
Intangibles, net of amortization	$251,490	$102,956	--	--
Cash, restricted	11,583	1,504	--	--
Other	4,688	115	--	--
Total noncurrent assets	$267,761	$104,575	--	--
Other assets	--	--	658	574
Total assets	$868,336	$440,380	$148,748	$38,567
	Liabilities and Stockholders' Equity			
Current liabilities:				
Notes payable	$ 54,626	$ 22,111	--	$ 9,688
Current portion of capital lease obligations	399	24	$ 23	21
Interest-bearing accounts payable	57,255	16,486	26,139	15,571
Accounts payable and accrued expenses	117,817	67,865	14,382	4,040
Income taxes payable	38,272	34,384	18,342	1,704
Dividends payable	--	--	--	--
Total current liabilities	$268,369	$140,870	$ 58,886	$31,024
Long-term debt	$ 10,570	--	--	--
Capital lease obligation, net of current portion	$ 2,042	$ 664	$ 687	$ 711
Deferred income taxes	$ 2,622	$ 1,245	$ 440	--
Stockholders' equity:				
Common stock	$ 1,125	$ 528	$ 160	$ 131
Additional paid-in capital	263,877	119,433	43,462	37
Retained earnings	320,886	177,844	45,710	6,748
Unearned compensation	(5,371)	(1,650)	(1,099)	--
Foreign currency translation adjustment	4,246	1,446	502	(84)
Total stockholders' equity	$584,763	$297,601	$ 88,735	$ 6,832
Total liabilities and stockholders' equity	$868,366	$440,380	$148,748	$38,567

Source: Annual reports.

EXHIBIT 6
Nike, Inc.: Income Statements
Years Ended May 31
(in Thousands of Dollars, Except per Share Data)

	_1987_	**_1986_**	**_1985_**	**_1984_**	**_1983_**	**_1982_**	**_1981_**	**_1980_**
Revenues	$877,357	$1,069,222	$946,371	$919,806	$867,212	$693,582	$457,742	$269,775
Costs and expenses:								
Cost of sales	$596,662	$ 722,923	$697,219	$658,549	$589,986	$473,885	$328,133	$196,683
Selling and administrative	204,742	209,219	204,834	163,414	132,400	94,919	60,953	39,810
Interest	8,475	15,820	21,933	19,597	25,646	24,538	17,859	9,144
Other (income) expense	(6,201)	11,243	(13)	(175)	1,057	435	92	107
Total costs and expenses	$803,678	$ 959,205	$923,973	$841,385	$749,089	$593,777	$407,037	$245,744
Income before income taxes and minority interest	$ 73,679	$ 110,017	$ 22,398	$ 78,421	$118,123	$ 99,805	$ 50,705	$ 24,031
Income taxes	37,800	57,760	15,630	37,567	60,922	50,589	24,750	11,526
Income before minority interest	$ 35,879	$ 52,257	$ 6,768	$ 40,854	$ 57,201	$ 49,216	$ 25,955	$12,505
Minority interest	- -	(6,954)	(3,502)	164	197	180	- -	- -
Net income	$ 35,879	$ 59,211	$ 10,270	$ 40,690	$ 57,004	$ 49,036	$ 25,955	$12,505
Net income per common share	$0.93	$1.55	$0.27	$1.07	$1.53	$1.37	$0.76	$0.77
Average share price (adjusted for splits)	$14.79	$14.11	$9.13	$14.98	$20.04	$12.88	$10.18	- -

Source: Annual reports.

EXHIBIT 7

Nike, Inc.: Balance Sheets, Years Ended May 31 (in Thousands of Dollars)

	1987	1986	1985	1984	1983	1982	1981	1980
Assets								
Current assets:								
Cash and equivalents	$126,867	$ 18,138	$ 7,017	$ 8,320	$ 13,038	$ 4,913	$ 1,792	$ 1,827
Accounts receivable	184,459	187,518	214,797	195,662	151,581	130,438	87,236	63,861
Inventory	120,663	180,205	186,285	280,630	283,788	202,817	120,229	55,941
Deferred income taxes	10,576	16,486	17,485	16,208	10,503	2,145	1,300	135
Prepaid expenses	6,717	9,163	11,739	8,039	6,625	5,198	2,487	2,151
Total current assets	$449,282	$411,510	$437,323	$508,859	$465,535	$345,511	$213,044	$123,915
Property and equipment	$ 96,988	$ 89,517	$ 90,832	$ 74,173	$ 61,359	$ 41,407	$ 23,845	$ 14,193
Less accumulated depreciation	48,508	39,834	40,084	31,293	21,628	12,485	7,673	4,027
Total property and equipment	$ 48,480	$ 49,683	$ 50,748	$ 42,880	$ 39,731	$ 28,922	$ 16,172	$10,166
Goodwill	$ 3,393	--	--	--	--	--	--	--
Other assets	$ 10,688	$ 15,645	$ 15,895	$ 7,420	$ 2,762	$ 1,040	$ 1,073	$ 534
Total assets	$511,843	$476,838	$503,966	$559,159	$508,028	$375,473	$230,289	$134,615
Liabilities and Shareholders' Equity								
Current liabilities:								
Current portion of long-term debt	$ 4,800	$ 3,417	$ 2,296	$ 2,560	$ 2,347	$ 3,936	$ 6,620	$ 3,876
Notes payable	43,145	61,634	117,573	143,532	132,092	112,673	61,190	36,500
Accounts payable	28,036	23,648	59,294	99,944	91,102	74,064	42,492	36,932
Accrued liabilities	39,792	44,027	37,644	28,476	19,021	22,894	15,401	10,299
Income taxes payable	8,309	--	2,667	--	11,102	19,774	12,654	6,693
Total current liabilities	$124,082	$132,726	$219,474	$274,512	$255,664	$233,341	$138,357	$ 94,300
Long-term debt	$ 35,202	$ 15,300	$ 7,573	$ 8,823	$ 10,503	$ 5,086	$ 8,611	$ 11,268
Deferred income taxes	$ 14,242	$ 11,666	$ 7,350	--	--	--	--	--
Minority interests in consolidated subsidiaries	--	--	$ (2,399)	$ 988	$ 948	$ 786	--	--
Redeemable preferred stock	$ 300	$ 300	$ 300	$ 300	$ 300	$ 300	$ 300	$ 300
Shareholders' equity:								
Common stock at stated value:								
Class A convertible	$ 174	$ 180	$ 199	$ 211	$ 225	$ 166	$ 194	--
Class B	2,705	2,697	2,673	2,660	2,646	1,414	1,386	--
Capital in excess of stated value	83,542	81,633	78,206	77,457	77,457	27,020	27,020	$ 71
Foreign currency translation adjustment	(1,938)	(507)	1,873	787	70	(67)	--	--
Retained earnings	253,534	232,843	188,717	193,421	160,215	103,427	54,421	28,496
Total shareholders' equity	$338,017	$316,846	$271,668	$274,536	$240,613	$131,960	$ 83,021	$ 28,567
Total liabilities and shareholders' equity	$511,843	$476,838	$503,966	$559,159	$508,028	$357,473	$230,289	$134,435

Source: Annual reports.

EXHIBIT 8

Top Ten Brands in Media Advertising through Leading Outlets
(Athletic and Protective Footwear, in Millions of Dollars)

Brand	*1987*	*1986*	*1985*
Reebok	$12.1	$ 8.5	$ 3.8
Nike	10.7	6.4	2.4
Avia	3.6	1.5	--
Converse Sporting	2.8	1.6	1.6
Foot Joy	2.3	1.2	1.5
Timberland	1.5	--	--
Easy Spirit	1.4	--	--
Fila	1.3	--	--
Brooks	1.2	--	--
Keds	1.1	--	--
Adidas	--	1.4	--
Tretorn	--	1.5	--
Autry	--	2.4	1.4
Converse (other than Converse Sporting)	--	1.1	1.4
Sorel (boots)	--	1.0	0.9
Kaepa (boots)	--	--	1.6
Puma	--	--	0.9
Other	19.2	15.6	12.7
Total	$57.2	$42.2	$28.2

Source: LNA/Arbitron Multi-Media Service.

CASE 8

The Sneaker Wars*

In 1987, Nike's share of the domestic athletic shoe market had dipped to nearly 20 percent, thanks to the good fortunes of Reebok, the upstart competitor who had replaced Nike as the number 1 athletic shoe company, grabbing nearly one-third of the market. (The market histories of the leading five brands as of 1989 are given in Exhibit 1.) Reebok had zoomed from $1.5 million in sales in 1981 to $1.4 *billion* just 6 years later by creating the first shoe for the aerobics market, focusing on the needs of women athletes, emphasizing fashion, and aggressively acquiring specialty shoe companies. In 1988, the counterattack that eventually put Nike back on top began to make progress, as the company bombarded the market with new models and unprecedented levels of advertising. These were the opening rounds of what would come to be called the "sneaker wars."

NIKE RECLAIMS THE NUMBER 1 SPOT

Technological Innovations

Nike's rebound to a dominant market position (financial statements are given in Exhibits 2 and 3) can be traced to its innovations on three simultaneous fronts: new shoe designs, increased promotional efforts, and improved customer service for its retailers. In creating its new shoe designs, Nike spent millions on an R&D effort widely considered to be the industry's best. In addition to its own staff of specialists in areas like biomechanics, exercise physiology, engineering, materials sciences, and industrial design, Nike utilized advisory research committees comprised of athletes, trainers, coaches, equipment managers, orthopedists, and other experts. A group of more than 100 volunteers across the United States provided further input as they monitored use of new prototypes in a wide variety of conditions. Product research and development cost the firm $5.5 million in 1987, $6.3 million in 1988, and was expected to grow another $1 million in 1989.

The centerpiece of Nike's design remained its air technology introduced in 1979. By the end of the 1980s, it had been through several generations of further development. The air technology employed the insertion of a gas-filled sack in the heel of Nike's shoes, the idea being that the air sack provided a lightweight shock absorber that protected the wearer's foot. By 1987, Nike had fifty models of shoes in its Air line; the 1.1 million pairs sold in that year generated $42 million in revenues. However, with the spirit captured in its corporate motto, "There is no finish line," Nike continued to enhance and refine its air products.

One of the most popular technological advances in air technology came when researchers devised a means for making the air sac visible through small windows on either side of the shoe's soles. Based on this breakthrough, Nike introduced the Air Max, the first shoe with visible air technology. In 1988, its first complete year of sales, more than 1 million

* Prepared by Alex Miller with assistance from Paula Smith, MBA student, both at University of Tennessee.

EXHIBIT 1
Historical Market Share Estimates for Five Leading Brands as of 1989

	1983	*1984*	*1985*	*1986*	*1987*	*1988*	*1989*
Nike	35.3	32.6	29.8	23.4	22.7	23.0	26.6
Reebok	0.07	3.3	14.3	30.3	32.8	27.0	24.0
Avia	0.02	0.4	1.0	2.7	5.0	4.2	4.5
Adidas	11.6	9.7	7.7	5.7	5.5	4.0	4.4
Converse	11.4	13.3	8.5	7.8	8.6	5.8	4.3
Other	40.6	40.5	38.7	29.9	25.0	36.0	36.2
Total U.S. branded athletic footwear wholesale market (in thousands of dollars)	$1,800	$1,900	$2,100	$2,600	$3,000	$3,900	$4,500

Source: Casewriter estimates.

pairs were sold, a $40 million business in itself. Based on that success, Nike hurried to introduce a complete line of ten visible air shoes covering sports from soccer to running with retail prices from $45 to $110. Still not satisfied, researchers at Nike developed a means of making a 180-degree view of the air sack—both sides and the bottom too.

A breakdown of Nike's sales by category is given in Exhibit 4. By 1989, Nike's product line covered much of the footwear spectrum:

EXHIBIT 2
Nike, Inc.: Income Statements
Years Ended May 31
(In Thousands of Dollars, Except per Share Data)

	1989	*1988*	*1987*	*1986*
Revenues	$1,710,803	$1,203,440	$877,357	$1,069,222
Costs and expenses:				
Cost of sales	$1,074,831	$ 803,380	$596,662	$ 722,923
Selling and administrative	354,825	246,583	204,742	209,219
Interest	13,949	8,004	8,475	15,820
Other (income) expense	(3,449)	(20,722)	(6,201)	11,243
Total costs and expenses	$1,440,156	$1,037,245	$803,678	$ 959,205
Income before income taxes and minority interest	$ 270,647	$ 166,195	$ 73,679	$ 110,017
Income taxes	103,600	64,500	37,800	57,760
Income before minority interest	$ 167,047	$ 101,695	$ 35,879	$ 52,257
Minority interest	--	--	--	(6,954)
Net income	$ 167,047	$ 101,695	$ 35,879	$ 59,211
Net income per common share	$4.45	$2.70	$0.93	$1.55
Average share price (adjusted for splits)	$29.82	$20.50	$14.79	$14.11

Source: Annual reports.

EXHIBIT 3
Nike, Inc.: Balance Sheets
Years Ended May 31
(in Thousands of Dollars)

	1989	1988	1987	1986
	Assets			
Current assets:				
Cash and equivalents	$ 85,749	$ 75,357	$126,867	$ 18,138
Accounts receivable	296,350	258,393	184,459	187,518
Inventory	222,924	198,470	120,663	180,205
Deferred income taxes	18,504	8,569	10,576	16,486
Prepaid expenses	14,854	12,793	6,717	9,163
Total current assets	$638,381	$553,582	$449,282	$411,510
Property and equipment:	$154,314	$112,022	$ 96,988	$ 89,517
Less accumulated depreciation	64,332	54,319	48,508	39,834
Total property and equipment	$ 89,982	$ 57,703	$ 48,480	$ 49,683
Goodwill	$ 81,899	$ 84,747	$ 3,393	--
Other assets	$ 15,148	$ 13,063	$ 10,688	$ 15,645
Total assets	$825,410	$709,095	$511,843	$476,838
	Liabilities and Shareholders' equity			
Current liabilities:				
Current portion of long-term debt	$ 1,884	$ 1,573	$ 4,800	$ 3,417
Notes payable	39,170	135,215	43,145	61,634
Accounts payable	71,105	50,288	28,036	23,648
Accrued liabilities	76,543	59,073	39,792	44,027
Income taxes payable	27,201	8,617	8,309	--
Total current liabilities	$215,903	$254,766	$124,082	$132,726
Long-term debt	$ 34,051	$ 30,306	$ 35,202	$ 15,300
Deferred income taxes	$ 13,352	$ 11,949	$ 14,242	$ 11,666
Redeemable preferred stock	$ 300	$ 300	$ 300	$ 300
Shareholders' equity:				
Common stock at stated value				
Class A convertible	$ 171	$ 173	$ 174	$ 180
Class B	2,700	2,696	2,705	2,697
Capital in excess of stated value	74,227	69,737	83,542	81,633
Foreign currency translation adjustment	(2,156)	(1,157)	(1,938)	(507)
Retained earnings	486,862	340,325	253,534	232,843
Total shareholders' equity	$561,804	$411,774	$338,017	$316,846
Total liabilities and shareholders' equity	$825,410	$709,095	$511,843	$476,838

Source: Annual reports.

Running: Sales of running shoes had declined from their 1983 high of $268 million, and were expected to be less than $200 million in 1989. This decline was attributed to the fact that running shoes had been replaced by basketball shoes as the most popular athletic shoe to wear for nonathletic purposes. Nike held an estimated 28 percent of this market.

EXHIBIT 4
Nike Sales by Product Category
Years Ended May 31
(In Thousands of Dollars)

	1989	*1988*
Footwear (U.S.)		
Basketball	$ 414,600	$ 287,300
Fitness	237,800	129,000
Running	202,600	177,900
Racquet	58,400	60,700
Other	153,200	102,600
Nonathletic	87,300	--
Total footwear (U.S.)	$1,153,900	$ 757,500
Apparel (U.S.)	$ 208,200	$ 142,900
Athletic equipment (U.S.)	--	--
Total United States	$1,362,100	$ 900,400
Foreign:		
Europe	$ 241,400	$ 233,400
Canada	52,200	31,500
Other	55,100	38,100
Total foreign	$ 348,700	$ 303,000
Total Nike	$1,710,800	$1,203,400

Source: Annual reports.

Basketball: This segment had grown to represent nearly one-third of all Nike's domestic athletic footwear revenue. Though sales of any one model were erratic from year to year, overall, Nike performance in this segment had been strong and its estimated sales in this category were $400 million, about 35 percent of the total market segment.

Fitness: Nike missed the initial rise of noncompetitive sports, especially the aerobics movement and the sharp rise in the numbers of women working out without participating in a competitive sport. But, in 1985, Nike introduced its line of cross trainers, shoes that supposedly combined the cushioning of a running shoe with the support of a court shoe. Cross training (participating in several activities, like running, court sports, aerobics, and weight lifting, as part of an overall fitness program) was seen as one of the market's most likely growth segments by 1989. In that year, Nike was expected to sell $240 million worth of cross trainers.

Racquet sports: This category was perhaps the most volatile of all sports categories for the shoe industry. Forecasts for 1989 called for Nike to generate revenues of only $70 million from this category, more than $10 million *less* than its 1984 sales in the same segment.

Other athletic footwear: In 1989, this segment was expected to be composed primarily of walking and golfing shoes, and Nike's expected sales were near $160 million.

Nonathletic shoes: Through a combination of internal development and acquisitions, Nike had moved aggressively to expand its participation in this segment. In May of 1988, Nike purchased Cole Hann, a maker of upscale traditional shoes, with annual sales near $90 million. Later that same year, the "i.e." line of sports-inspired younger women's shoes was introduced. The following year, Side 1, a line of women's casual shoes was launched. Nike's share of the overall nonathletic shoe market was negligible (1989 sales were less than $100 million), but the company was optimistic about the future.

Promotional Efforts

Nike's broad product line was backed up by what many considered to be the industry's most effective marketing effort. Breakthroughs in air technology were announced in an advertising campaign which featured the original version of the Beatles' hit, "Revolution." The song was used in the soundtrack to a series of black and white commercials shot on super-8 film, depicting professional athletes and amateurs of all ages involved in a variety of sports. These television ads were reinforced with horizontal format ads in *Glamour, Sports Illustrated, Rolling Stone, People,* and *GQ*, some appearing as eight-page inserts, explaining the entire Air line. Vertical format ads, featuring particular models, also ran in more focused sports magazines like *Runner's World.*

Paul McCartney, a member of the band who had originally produced the hit song "Revolution," sued Nike, complaining that he felt the commercials cheapened the Beatles' artistic accomplishments. (Nike had negotiated to use the song with Michael Jackson, another pop singer. Ironically, Jackson had bought the rights to much of the Beatles' library on earlier advice he received from McCartney.) The legal action and resulting hoopla was seen as beneficial publicity for the Air Revolution. The entire campaign cost an estimated $20 million dollars, excluding legal expenses.

Nike's next campaign featured a number of celebrity athletes telling viewers to "Just do it." The ads featured no-nonsense, get-tough messages evoking a mixture of get-tough machismo and can-do sentimentalism. One spot featured a female athlete who, along with urging the audience to get up and get active, also advised, "It might not hurt if you stopped eating like a pig." Nike capped off the Just Do It campaign by arranging to have the NCAA basketball champions from the University of Michigan all wear caps proclaiming "Just Did It" during their postgame interviews.

Following on the heels of the Just Do It campaign, Nike spent millions more on the "Bo Knows" campaign. These advertisements featured Bo Jackson, one of the few professional athletes to be a genuine star in both football and baseball. The ads with Jackson stressed his diverse sports interests and tied this to Nike's line of cross-training shoes. Again, they were among the most popular ads of their time.

Nike's total advertising and promotional budget was believed to have topped $70 million in 1988, and $100 million in 1989 (Exhibit 5 shows industry data on media advertising). Much of Nike's total marketing budget was spent on slick media advertising (see Exhibits 6 and 7) and expensive endorsement contracts, all aimed at consumers. But several million dollars were also targeted to the trade. *Sports Illustrated* estimated that Nike's expenses for the Sporting Goods Manufacturer's Association national trade convention in early 1989 were $4 million. This included a twelve-member dance group, a 120-screen

EXHIBIT 5
Top Ten Brands in Media Advertising through Leading Outlets (Athletic and Protective Footwear, in Millions of Dollars)

Brand	1989	1988	1987	1986	1985
Reebok	$ 33.0	$ 25.7	$12.1	$ 8.5	$ 3.8
Nike	30.8	30.8	10.7	6.4	2.4
L. A. Gear	15.1	9.7	--	--	--
Avia	7.9	10.1	3.6	1.5	--
Keds	5.6	3.5	1.1	--	--
Adidas	5.4	--	--	--	--
Easy Spirit	3.8	3.1	1.4	--	--
Converse Sporting	3.7	4.9	2.8	1.6	1.6
Etonic	2.3	--	--	--	--
Side 1 (Nike)	2.0	--	--	--	--
Foot Joy	--	1.9	2.3	1.2	1.5
New Balance	--	1.8	--	--	--
Tretorn	--	1.5	--	1.5	0.8
Timberland (boots)	--	--	1.5	--	--
Fila	--	--	1.3	--	--
Brooks	--	--	1.2	--	--
Autry (boots)	--	--	--	2.4	1.4
Converse (separate from Converse Sporting)	--	--	--	1.1	1.4
Sorel (boots)	--	--	--	1.0	0.9
Kaepa (boots)	--	--	--	--	1.6
Puma	--	--	--	--	0.9
Other	26.1	20.2	19.2	15.6	12.7
Total	$135.7	$113.2	$57.2	$40.8	$29.0

Source: LNA/Arbitron Multi-Media Service.

EXHIBIT 6
Nike and Reebok Advertising through Nine Leading Media Outlets (in Thousands of Dollars)

	1989		1988	
	Reebok	Nike	Reebok	Nike
Nine-media total	$45,027	$50,862	$41,376	$35,939
Magazines	13,302	18,932	11,369	16,659
Sunday magazines	107	2	148	9
Newspapers	419	330	383	277
Outdoor	526	292	469	77
Network TV	16,370	24,206	20,254	14,456
Spot TV	9,456	1,290	5,922	370
Syndicated TV	2,327	3,428	243	1,855
Cable TV	2,430	2,384	2,425	1,902
Network radio	--	--	166	335

Source: LNA/Arbitron Multi-Media Service.

EXHIBIT 7
Nike and Reebok Media Spending by Product Line (in Thousands of Dollars, across Eight Media Outlets)

	1989		1988	
	Reebok	Nike	Reebok	Nike
Aqua sock, men & women	--	233.6 m	--	180.2 m
Bodywear, men & women	--	676.6 m	--	367.9 m
Co GP	--	1.8 o	--	16.3 m
Golf shoes, men	--	607.2 m	--	758.1 m
Golf shoes, men & women	662.6 m	29.4 m	132.1 m	--
Sporting events	45.0 m	52.2 m	--	--
Spts. ftwr. & golf shoes (m. & w.)	--	1,586.0 m	--	--
Spts. footwear, children	--	296.7 m	--	440.0 m
Spts. footwear, men	2,991.6 m	5,490.6 monsy	1,852.5 m	3,688.8 mo
Spts. footwear, women	1,687.0 m	3,658.2 m	628.8 mo	3,958.1 mo
Spts. footwear, men & women	27,637.9 monsyc	18,864.1 mwonsyc	23,122.3 monsyor	21,782.4 mwonwcr
Sportswear & spts. ftwr., men	0.6 o	589.6 m	--	178.8 m
Sportswear & spts. ftwr. (m & w)	--	12,671.0 monsc	--	349.2 mosc
Sportswear & spts. ftwr., women	--	57.1 m	--	511.7 m
Sportswear, family	--	20.7 o	--	6.2 o
Sportswear, local dealers	114.6 o	--	116.1 o	42.2 o
Sportswear, men	--	458.6 m	--	558.6 m
Sportswear, women	--	316.2 m	--	610.7 m
Sportswear, men & women	327.9 wo	--	82.5 mwo	--

m = magazines; w = newspapers; o = outdoor; r = network radio; n = network TV; y = syndicated TV; c = cable TV; s = spot TV.
Source: LNA/Arbitron Multi-Media Service.

video display, and a party for several thousand trade customers, featuring entertainment by the Temptations.

Retailers responding to a *Sporting Goods Business* poll reported that Nike's promotional efforts apparently worked. The vast majority, 88.3 percent, of the 250 retailers surveyed in early 1989 reported that Nike's advertising campaign was the most effective in the industry. Three out of five retailers reported that Nike had been their best seller in 1988, and 89.1 percent predicted that Nike would be the hottest brand for 1989. Quotes collected as part of the survey included:

- "Nike has really got it together right now. Nike will be number one in 1989 because of strong advertising, the continued growth of cross training and the comfort and cushioning of the Air shoes, along with the fashionable looks."
- "There are too many people who will wear nothing but Nike. Other brands will have a lot of work to do to affect that."
- "Nike has a strong ethnic following, and its advertising seems to be the most effective. Its endorsements are highly effective."

Customer Service

Nike also redesigned several aspects of its dealer relations. This included a new electronic ordering service with 48-hour turnaround on in-stock items, a computerized product

EXHIBIT 8
Dealer Ratings of Sportswear Manufacturers

Category	No. 1	No. 2	No. 3
Product innovation	Nike	Tiger	Avia
Quality	Russell*	Nike	Tiger
Advertising	Nike	Reebok	Russell
Packaging	Nike	Wilson	Avia
Point-of-sale	Nike	Reebok	Russell
On-time delivery	Nike	Avia	Russell
Fill-ins	Nike	Avia	Russell
Return policies	Nike	Avia	Wilson
Responsiveness to complaints	Nike	Avia	Wilson

* Russell was primarily a sporting apparel manufacturer.
Source: *The Sporting Goods Dealer*, August 1989, Dealers Rate Manufacturers Survey.

substitution program to help retailers identify the best alternatives when a given order was not in stock, and increased use of bar coding to help retailers track their inventories. As a result of this improved service, retailers polled by *Sporting Goods Business* revealed their strong support for Nike:

- "On top of having the best styles all around, Nike has sent all others back to the Dark Ages when it comes to customer service. Nike has proven everyone wrong. You *can* have the fastest growing shoe and apparel line and give good service on the fill-ins and have knowledgeable people at the other end on the 800 number. No one is even close. This is the greatest event in sports shoe history."
- "Nike has on-time and accurate delivery; is not available in mail order; has excellent customer service 7 days a week, 12 hours a day, and excellent marketing."
- "No matter how good they get (i.e., shipping, customer service, and design), they keep getting better."
- "Finally a shoe manufacturer is looking out for the merchant with respect to special orders. Thanks Nike."

The Sporting Goods Dealer reported that Nike was ranked number 1 in eight out of nine categories by U.S. dealers polled (see Exhibit 8).

REEBOK IN THE LATE EIGHTIES

After such an explosive period of growth from 1980 until 1987, Reebok was faced with a changing set of managerial issues. (Exhibits 9 and 10 give financial statements.) The corporation had used its success in Reebok aerobic shoes to finance extensive internal and external diversification efforts. As a result, the company was now a diversified global competitor, designing, producing, and selling a wide range of footwear and sporting apparel around the world. In 1987 and 1988, Reebok had moved aggressively to acquire Rockport (casual and walking shoes), Frye (boots), Avia (technical athletic shoes), and

EXHIBIT 9
Reebok International, Ltd.: Income Statements
Years Ended December 31
(in Thousands of Dollars, Except per Share Data)

	1989	1988	1987	1986
Net sales	$1,822,092	$1,785,935	$1,389,196	$919,401
Other income	11,735	5,282	10,240	4,472
Total	$1,833,827	$1,791,217	$1,399,436	$923,873
Cost and expenses:				
Cost of sales	$1,071,751	$1,122,226	$ 808,991	$521,978
Selling expenses	278,939	260,891	164,896	83,294
General and administrative expenses	174,972	149,195	102,191	54,470
Amortization of intangibles	14,427	14,216	12,453	2,280
Interest expense	15,554	14,129	4,771	694
Total cost and expenses	$1,555,643	$1,560,657	$1,093,302	$662,716
Income before income taxes	$ 290,779	$ 230,560	$ 306,134	$261,157
Income taxes	115,781	93,558	140,934	129,023
Net income	$ 174,998	$ 137,002	$ 165,200	$132,134
Net income per common share	$1.53	$1.20	$1.49	$1.27
Average share price (adjusted for splits)	$14.69	$13.56	$17.58	$10.92

Source: Annual reports.

Ellesse (European sportswear). In 1989, Reebok diversified further when it acquired Boston Whaler, a 30-year-old recreational boat manufacturer, for $29 million. (Exhibit 11 gives data on Reebok sales by division.)

Given the complexity of the corporation, CEO Paul Fireman had felt it necessary to restructure the original Reebok organization so that the numerous divisions all reported to a corporate staff of executives. When Reebok was only a single-line shoe business, the corporate staff consisted of a handful of people who had been involved with Fireman during Reebok's creation. New corporate managers were recruited for their experience in managing diversified corporations rather than for knowledge of the shoe industry. While most of the new managers had extensive experience in consumer goods companies, virtually no new managers with experience in athletic shoes per se were hired at the corporate level. Fireman explained that this hiring pattern was necessary because the single largest challenge facing Reebok was managing its newfound size, and few other shoe companies could offer executives trained to deal with this challenge. A list identifying some of the new executives hired at the corporate level is given in Exhibit 12. Organization charts for 1986 (before diversification through acquisition began) and 1989 are given in Exhibits 13 and 14.

In addition to building a large staff inside Reebok, Fireman found it necessary to use more outside help in designing new products. In fact, the firm's greatest success of this period came from the design team at Design Continuum, a free-lance design firm that worked with a small team from within the larger design group at Reebok to develop the Pump. The Pump was a basketball shoe that used an inflation device to literally pump the shoe up around the wearer's foot, creating a snugger fit. The shoes, which retailed for up to

EXHIBIT 10
Reebok International, Ltd.: Balance Sheets
Years Ended December 31
(in Thousands of Dollars)

	1989	1988	1987	1986
	Assets			
Current assets:				
Cash	$ 171,424	$ 99,349	$ 60,167	$ 66,077
Accounts receivable	289,363	276,204	204,676	120,075
Inventory	276,911	301,920	240,898	122,522
Refundable federal income taxes	--	--	--	--
Deferred income taxes	34,845	26,293	19,534	5,589
Prepaid expenses	11,735	9,905	10,821	2,324
Total current assets	$ 784,278	$ 713,671	$536,096	$316,587
Property and equipment:	$ 136,776	$ 92,546	$ 73,447	$ 21,198
Less accumulated depreciation and amortization	30,542	18,419	8,968	1,980
Total property and equipment	$ 106,234	$ 74,127	$ 64,479	$ 19,218
Noncurrent assets:				
Intangibles, net of amortization	$ 261,398	$ 264,506	$251,490	$102,956
Cash, restricted	--	--	11,583	1,504
Other	14,457	11,145	4,688	115
Total noncurrent assets	$ 275,855	$ 275,651	$267,761	$104,575
Other assets	--	--	--	--
Total assets	$1,666,367	$1,063,449	$868,336	$440,380
	Liabilities and Stockholders' Equity			
Current liabilities:				
Notes payable	$ 1,651	$ 75,208	$ 54,626	$ 22,111
Current portion of capital lease obligations	598	404	399	24
Interest-bearing accounts payable	31,878	31,878	57,255	16,486
Accounts payable and accrued expenses	148,360	105,247	117,817	67,865
Income taxes payable	43,834	34,634	38,272	34,384
Dividends payable	8,538	8,490	--	--
Total current liabilities	$ 202,981	$ 255,861	$268,369	$140,870
Long-term debt	$ 110,302	$ 111,260	$ 10,570	--
Capital lease obligation, net of current portion		$ 1,402	$ 2,042	$ 664
Deferred income taxes	$ 8,788	$ 4,224	$ 2,622	$ 1,245
Stockholders' equity:				
Common stock	$ 1,139	$ 1,129	$ 1,125	$ 528
Additional paid-in capital	275,336	266,564	263,877	119,433
Retained earnings	564,987	424,002	320,886	177,844
Unearned compensation	(524)	(2,808)	(5,371)	(1,650)
Foreign currency translation adjustment	3,358	1,815	4,246	1,446
Total stockholders' equity	$ 844,296	$ 690,702	$584,763	$297,601
Total liabilities and stockholders' equity	$1,166,367	$1,063,449	$868,366	$440,380

Source: Annual reports.

EXHIBIT 11
Reebok Sales by Division (in Millions of Dollars)

	1983	1984	1985	1986	1987
Reebok Footwear Division	$12.0	$64.0	$299.0	$ 841.0	$ 991.0
Avia	2.8	7.0	21.1	70.3	153.0
Rockport	26.0	38.4	64.5	92.9	152.0
Reebok Apparel Division	n/a	n/a	4.0	39.4	47.0
Reebok International Division	n/a	n/a	817.0	3,712.0	7,830.0

Source: Annual reports.

$170, became a leading seller, outselling a similar Nike product 20 to 1. Nike's version had a detachable inflating device. Nike engineers argued that this allowed the shoe to be lighter, thereby improving performance. But retailers reported that consumers found the separate pump to be inconvenient. Others pointed out that the detachable device meant that part of the shoe's technology was no longer as visible as Reebok's pump technology. Eventually, Reebok's success with the Pump would lead designers to work similar technology into a broad range of shoes including cross-training and tennis models.

Another popular technological advance made at Reebok was its Energy Return System (ERS). This was meant to address the same biomechanical concerns as Nike's air technology. Athletic performance was said to be improved by an idea reminiscent of "flubber" or "superballs." Small tubes containing Hytrel, a resilient material made by Du Pont, were placed in the heel of the shoes. When compressed through running or jumping, the material within the tubes was said to store the energy, and then release it as the wearer's weight shifted, thereby returning some of the energy expended back to the wearer. Critics questioned Reebok's claims, pointing out that ERS returned only about 4 joules of energy, a negligible amount, given that something like 1,000 joules were required in the typical rebound jump in basketball. Nonetheless, the product was very popular in the market, and soon found its way into fourteen new styles.

In promoting its shoes, Reebok aggressively undertook several different advertising campaigns. (Exhibits 5, 6, and 7 give media advertising spending data.) For instance, in the

EXHIBIT 12
Samples of Reebok Corporate Staff Added in the Late Eighties

Name	Position	When Hired	Background
Joseph LaBonte	Chief Operating Officer	3/87	COO, Twentieth Century Fox
Douglas Arbetman	Head of Apparel Division	9/88	Divisional President, Calvin Klein
Mark Goldston	Chief Marketing Officer	9/88	President, Fabergé
Frank O'Connell	Vice President of Marketing	12/88	CEO, HBO Video
Marla Anderson	Head of Customer Service	1/89	Divisional Merchandise Manager, Kohl's Department Stores
John Duerden	President, Reebok Footwear Division	3/89	Marketing, Xerox Corporation

EXHIBIT 13
Reebok Organization, 1986

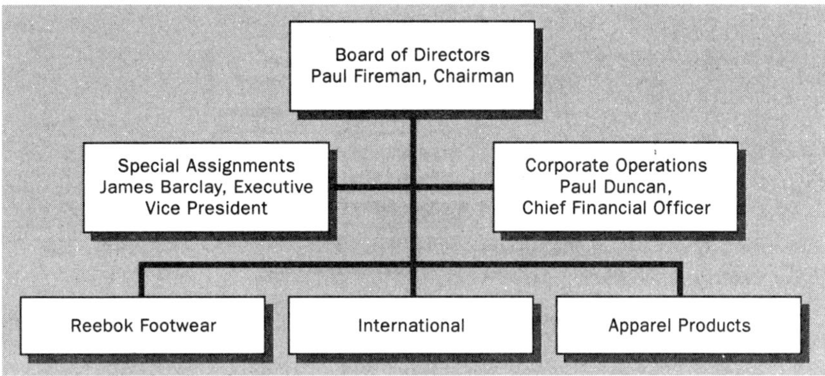

Source: Casewriter's reconstruction.

first quarter of selling the ERS shoes, Reebok spent $15 million introducing them. During the 1988 summer Olympics, the company spent $6 million on television advertising in just 2 weeks. While such focused campaigns were underway, the company continued its more general promotional efforts, pushing the entire line of Reebok products.

The most unusual of these campaigns was the "U.B.U." effort. The advertisements for this $35 million campaign are difficult to explain, and they were designed to be so. A reviewer in *Advertising Age* characterized them as involving "bizarre characters in garish outfits performing idiotically mundane tricks in out-of-context venues, all to the narrative background of nineteenth century pyschobabble and Hungarian folk music." Meanwhile, over the static of an old-fashioned carbon microphone, the narrator intoned Emerson's: "To believe in your own thought, to believe what is true in your private heart is true for all men—that is genius." (The reviewer gave it three and a half stars out of a possible four.)

Critics loved the ads, and department stores reported that they generated a lot of interest among those shoppers looking for trendiness. However, specialty athletic shoe and sporting goods stores were highly critical. They felt that by essentially ignoring the shoe and sports, Reebok had overlooked their customers' interests. Some Nike retailing specialists were delighted that Reebok seemed to have forgotten the athlete. A popular slogan around such stores was "Reebok, U.B.U. We be Nike!"

In the face of considerable criticism from its retailers, Reebok pulled the ad sooner than planned. Corporate executives, led by CEO Joseph LaBonte, argued that the ads had done what they were intended to do: they created interest in Reebok, stressed the Reebok value of self expression, and improved morale and restored the lost sense of excitement that had once prevailed at Reebok headquarters. For his part, Fireman took delight in pointing out that Nike would never have created such ads, much less have run them on national television.

To appease the specialty retailers who were displeased with the U.B.U. ads, Reebok replaced that campaign with one known within the industry as "Me Be Me." Officially, the campaign was entitled "The Physics Behind the Physiques," but as Goldston, head of

EXHIBIT 14
Reebok Organization, 1989

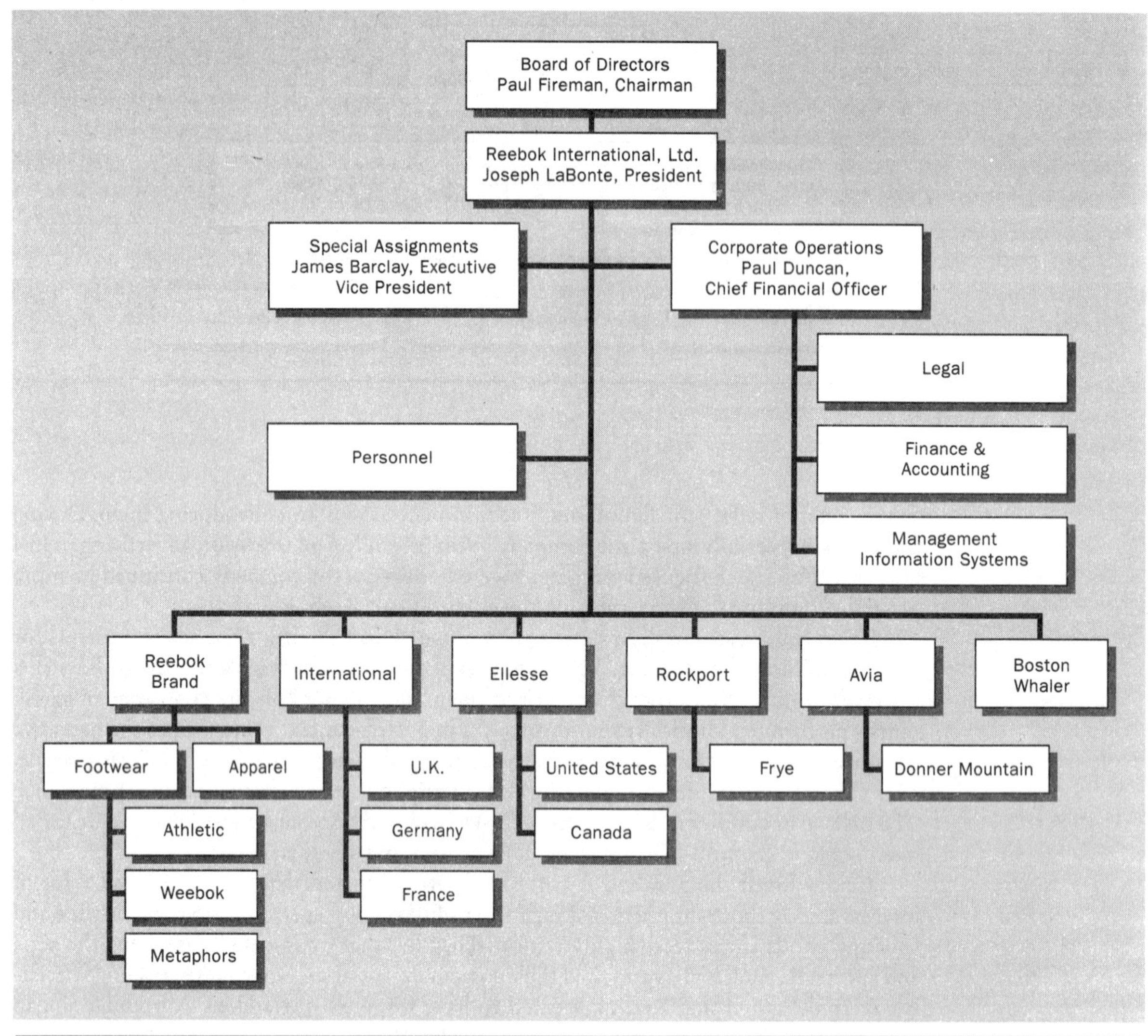

Source: Casewriter's reconstruction.

marketing, explained, the advertisements placed "emphasis on the self, as in narcissistic." He argued, "People don't exercise to lower their cholesterol levels and pulse rates anymore. That's out. They do it, let's face it, to look good."

The Me Be Me ads featured sweaty but beautiful young people, wearing revealing clothes and working out in steamy surroundings. Meanwhile, to emphasize the performance dimensions of Reebok shoes, physics equations flashed across the screen, accompanied by a sultry voice: "Power equals work divided by time. For every action, there is an equal and opposite reaction. Force equals mass times acceleration." The artsy ads reportedly cost $800,000 to produce, approximately four times the average for the athletic shoe industry.

Reebok spent $30 million during the Me Be Me campaign, which ran concurrently with a $10 million basketball campaign called "Legend" and the $20 million ERS promotion. While specialty retailers approved of Me Be Me, it was soon replaced by another campaign focusing on trendy fashions with pop singer Paula Abdul as the spokesperson. Some advertising experts speculated that these ads were meant to halt the inroads made by L.A. Gear, a young but rapidly growing west coast shoe company.

The Abdul spots were not the last round of Reebok's continually evolving advertising campaigns, and many of the ads that followed were quite controversial. One of the most controversial ads involved the sport of bungee jumping. In this ad, two young men attached bungees (elastic ropes) to their ankles before jumping from a bridge. The jumper wearing Reebok's Pumps bounced harmlessly at the end of his bungee, while the one wearing Nikes slipped out of his, with ramifications left to the viewer's imagination. The complaints of horrified parents resulted in removal from the air within its first week. Meanwhile, an Avia ad created strong reactions and resentment at Philip Morris, the giant cigarette manufacturer. Avia's campaign was entitled "For Athletic Use Only" and it ostensibly tried to persuade the 55 million Americans who were overweight, drinkers, or smokers, that they were not fit enough to wear Avias. One ad featured a burning cigarette in an ashtray with the tag line: "If this is the only thing that gives your lungs a work out, don't buy our shoes." After Philip Morris advised smokers reading its widely distributed *Smoker* newsletter to complain, Avia began getting eighty calls a day objecting to the ads.

Along with its "for jocks only" advertising, Avia began to run ads that were critical of other shoe companies, including its parent, Reebok. One six-page spread in *Sports Style* suggested that companies like Reebok and others made shoes for wimps. "The competition is scrambling to be all things to all feet," the copy explained. "While everyone else is zigging toward a multipurpose shoe, we intend to zag," it continued, in a remark obviously aimed at the cross trainers Nike had first created, and Reebok had later mimicked. The implication was clear: Serious athletes would insist upon Avia's specialized shoes.

Many observers found it surprising that Reebok's subsidiary would be so openly critical of the corporation's flagship line, but CEO LaBonte explained, "If we are going to lose sales, we'd rather it be to ourselves. Reebok didn't become the most profitable [athletic] shoe company by playing it safe." While LaBonte apparently approved of the Avia campaign after he saw it, he was not involved in its approval before it was launched. Reebok had each of its divisions operate separately and almost entirely independently of one another. For instance, they maintained separate design staffs, and they were careful not to share any market research that might give another business in the corporation a competitive advantage.

THE FUTURE AT REEBOK

As 1988 unfolded, it became apparent that Reebok was experiencing its first ever decline in earnings growth. Sales at both Rockport and Avia were lower than expected, though both businesses still had gains in sales. (Exhibit 8 gives sales by division.) As a result of the slowing sales growth, 100 employees at Rockport were dismissed, and Avia's management team was restructured.

By the year's end, Reebok was also proposing to alter the nature of its relationship with retailers. The company encouraged retailers to establish themselves as "brand franchisers." The concept called for retailers to set aside corners of their stores to be converted to boutiques containing a single brand of shoes. Fireman argued that the hundreds of millions invested in new-product development and advertising represented only about 60 percent of what was necessary to excite the public about buying new shoes. "The retailer can participate in the other 40 percent. The customer is inundated with millions of images on TV. When he comes into the retail store, that consumer wants to complete the fantasy. He wants to go from the TV to the store, and literally to the cash register." By creating the focus an exclusive boutique would offer, Fireman contended that the retailer would have the power to create such excitement. The media blitz would be designed to educate the consumer, and lure him into the boutique where the brand would "come alive," alleviating the need to promotionally price the shoes. In order to couple the power of media advertising with in-store promotion, Reebok offered to cover the cost of setting up the first 100 boutiques. Furthermore, Fireman suggested that if the franchising idea worked out as planned, Reebok would probably focus its efforts on working with a smaller number of retail outlets, perhaps 5,000 instead of the 7,500 or more currently supplied.

By the end of the year, Reebok was preparing to introduce new models of shoes that were intended to offer what Goldston, head of marketing, called "performance-panache." Goldston explained that while not forsaking "image driven" shoes, Reebok would pursue more aggressively the "performance driven" market which had accounted for much of the growth in the past 2 years. In a *Sporting Goods Business* survey, retailers made several predictions about the future at Reebok:

- "Look for Reebok to realize that function, not fashion, will create a core market that will allow a company to prosper even further."
- "Reebok's basics are still strong. It has name recognition with first-time sneaker customers (older people and foreigners)."
- "It will have continued success with classics, plus the introduction of new cross trainers and ERS models."
- "Reebok will come out with new products and change marketing directions to more functional products."

THE WAR OF WORDS

While their corporations fought each other in the marketplace, the press was happy to facilitate a war of words between Knight and Fireman. Below is a sampling of quotes from articles in *Fortune* and *Financial Network (FNM)* that included interviews of both CEOs:

On the Nature of Their Competition

Fireman: We're playing a game, okay. *I* know we're playing a game. I don't think he does. *(Fortune)*

Knight: It's more than a game. It's much more serious, because it's peoples lives. [As Reebok stormed the market, Nike had been forced to lay off about 10 percent of its work force.] It was terrible. It's the worse thing that could happen in business. *(Fortune)*

Fireman: He's been focused on Reebok as a thorn in his side since we passed in sales in 1986. *(Fortune)*

Fireman: Unfortunately, he has this idea that we took him off this number-1 perch, and he's driven, compelled. His driving goal is to get back there. *(FNM)*

On Each Other's Products

Knight: The Pump tends to put the foot to sleep. They'll get a short-term marketing punch from it. But we don't see it as a long-term threat. Basically, it's a long-term threat to people's feet. *(Fortune)*

About Personal Commitment

Knight: If Nike is going to fail, I want to be in it up to my eyeballs. I want to say I did everything I could to make it work. *(Fortune)*

Fireman: I am enjoying myself. . . . The industry has become my family and my life. So why would I want to retire or do something else? *(FNM)*

About Each Other as Competitors

Fireman: They are good competitors. They challenge us in the sense that they've gotten back on their feet and really do some good work. . . . I think they've done good and I think it has inspired us. *(FNM)*

Knight: I think one of my shortcomings as president of Reebok's competing company is that I simply don't understand them. And I don't say that with pride. I just don't get them. *(FNM)*

Fireman: I am positively, unequivocally not upset with Phil Knight. I personally would like to meet him and have lunch. . . . I think it's a pity he's driven by that need to have me on his wall on a dart board. *(FNM)*

On the Dimensions of Competition

Fireman: When pricing stops escalating, we're in dramatic problems; we've got ourselves an incredible headache. Stability [of prices] will only bring us stagnation. *(FNM)*

Fireman: Reebok has always, unequivocally put performance in every product it's ever made. We refuse not to do that. . . . We're going to have performance as the nucleus of everything we do, but bring it to life—make it entertaining and exciting and fashionable and fun. *(FNM)*

Knight: What we concluded is that it [the Nike brand] has always got to stand for sweat. But, there is also an athletics/fashion business. That's our reasoning behind Side 1. . . . We see the next billion dollar company being Side 1. *(FNM)*

On Each Other's Decisions

Knight: I would assume that it [advertising at Reebok] becomes more difficult after you reposition your brand four times in 2 years. They come up with fashion.

Then they did Reebok is performance. Then they came back with U.B.U. And now they are going back to ERS. *(FNM)*

Fireman: Cole-Hann's a nice company, but I think they overpaid considerably. . . . They had an urge to spend money. They wanted to buy a business to compete with Reebok rather than to build their own. If we go into the sewer business, they'll probably go into the toilet business. . . . They're definitely mimicking our actions. *(FNM)*

OTHER COMPETITORS

In addition to Nike and Reebok, several other companies were active contenders in the athletic shoe market. Technologically, many experts considered these firms to have products comparable to Nike's and Reebok's, although these firms were not as likely to be the sources of major new innovations. Many smaller-share firms were willing to imitate the market leaders. For instance, while Nike had introduced its air technology as early as 1979, and Reebok had answered with its ERS system in 1988, Puma had its X-Cell Power Core sole, a cellular honeycomb that reportedly both returned power and improved stability. And while they might not match the overall size of the industry leaders, firms like Adidas and L.A. Gear showed they were not afraid to develop new shoes—each of these companies offered over 500 styles. ASICS, the leading Japanese athletic footwear brand, was believed to be the leader of the industry in terms of overall R&D expenditures.

Similarly, the battle on the promotional front was far from simply a two-brand fight. The two market leaders expected to spend over $200 million in their combined promotional efforts in 1989, but this number included heavy fees for nonadvertising activities like endorsements, trade shows, and so forth. In terms of pure advertising, several other firms were also in the race. Adidas was planning on its largest U.S. advertising budget ever for 1989, an estimated $25 million, and L.A. Gear spent $13 million on advertising in 1988 and was expected to double that figure in 1989.

A *Sporting Goods Business* study of advertising expenditures (exclusive of cooperative advertising with retailers) for the top nine media outlets in the market concluded that advertising in these outlets alone had grown from $15.8 million in 1985, to $26.9 million in 1986, $39.8 million in 1987, and $34.4 million in just the first 6 months of 1988. This study predicted that Nike would spend $100 million on total advertising in 1989, while Reebok was expected to spend $60 million advertising its flagship line and another $35 million on Avia. (These estimates did not include promotional expenses other than advertising.) Though promotional efforts were rising rapidly in a number of companies, sales forecasts of the industry as a whole continued to call for slowing growth. The National Sporting Goods Association estimated that growth in dollar sales for athletic shoes would slow to only 6 percent by 1990. In light of such strong competition and such pessimistic forecasts, it was not clear what managers at Reebok or Nike should do.

CASE 9

L.A. Gear*

Robert Greenberg came to be CEO of L.A. Gear, the world's fastest-growing athletic shoe company during the late 1980s, in a roundabout fashion. After graduating from high school, he toured the United States from coast to coast. He liked Los Angeles so much that he stayed there for 3 months, before returning home to Boston. He then trained to become a hairdresser. At 21, he bought his first salon, and over the next 5 years, he expanded to five salons. Greenberg then decided that importing was more lucrative, sold the salons, and began importing wigs produced in South Korea to sell through salons back in Boston. As fashion changed, he switched to importing jeans for department stores, such as Filenes and Jordan Marsh. In 1979, he moved to Los Angeles. Noting that roller skating was so popular that rental lines were sometimes stretched around the block, Greenberg opened his own rental stand. When the popularity of the sport led to parts shortages, he began importing parts. With a foreign supplier of parts arranged, he began assembling his own line of skates through a company he called United Skates of America.

In 1982, Greenberg moved one step closer to L.A. Gear when he licensed the image of Steven Spielberg's E.T. character for use on children's shoe laces. Within 90 days, the business had grossed $3 million, and he decided to pursue other fashion items. In 1983, he started three businesses: one in retail, one in shoes, and a garment business making jeans-wear. The retail store, on Melrose Avenue, was called L.A. Gear. The 6,500-square-foot store sold its own line of apparel and casual footwear in addition to several brand names. Soon, the garment business was shut down, and the brand was licensed for a short time. The retail store was reasonably successful, but Greenberg attributed much of its success to its shoes. As he would explain later, "I found out that footwear is a great means of building a name brand. Just put the right shoes in the front window, and people will start to demand the brand."

Given the success of its shoe line, the company sold the retail store, and began to concentrate exclusively on footwear still sold under the L.A. Gear brand. For the first 2 years, the company avoided athletic shoes. It first sold canvas styles, then imported leather styles from Brazil, such as huaraches and sandals. Its first athletic shoe, a simple canvas workout shoe, was shipped in 1985, and the company managed to generate revenues of $10 million by year's end.

One day, when Greenberg was dropping his daughter (one of his six children) off at her junior high school, he noticed that many of the girls at the school were wearing boy's high-top basketball shoes. Soon, L.A. Gear had a line of women's and young girls' shoes on the market that looked like high-top basketball shoes, but had features Greenberg hoped would be popular with girls in the market he called "tweens," young people aged 9 to 16. He designed shoes that he called "ice cream for the feet": white leather shoes with pink, turquoise, and silver trim and accents made of sequins, rhinestones, and fringe. Some of the shoes featured palm trees or other symbols of the southern California life-style.

---

* Prepared by Alex Miller, University of Tennessee.

The tremendous success of the new line of shoes led to the decision to take the company public in July 1986. The stock was initially offered on the NASDAQ at $11.50, but by the end of the first day's trading, the price had soared to $24.75. In all, $16.5 million was raised in the initial placement offering, but nearly half of all the corporation's shares were still held by Greenberg and a handful of other managers and insiders. The money was used to greatly increase marketing efforts, and to expand the line of shoes into new markets.

PRODUCT LINES

A breakdown of sales by product lines is given in Exhibit 1. Exhibit 2 provides a breakdown of sales by major market segments. As these two exhibits indicate, L.A. Gear moved quickly to serve footwear needs in a wide range of sports (basketball, racquet sports,

EXHIBIT 1
L.A. Gear, Inc.: Product Mix by Year
(in Millions of Dollars)

	1989	*1988*	*1987*
Women's domestic footwear	$290.0	$134.2	$50.8
Men's domestic footwear	117.3	29.0	10.6
Children's domestic footwear	123.4	38.0	6.4
International footwear, apparel, and accessories	55.5	20.1	2.8
Domestic apparel and accessories	30.9	2.2	--
Total	$617.1	$223.5	$70.6

Source: Annual reports.

EXHIBIT 2
L.A. Gear, Inc.: Sales by Product Category
(in Thousands of Dollars)

	1988	*1987*	*1986*
Footwear:			
Basketball shoes	$108,947	$27,364	$ 327
Children's shoes	28,233	4,937	4,102
Aerobic shoes	25,001	12,412	16,552
Athletic-style leisure shoes			
Leather	13,161	8,040	10,745
Canvas	10,311	8,110	1,706
Court shoes	14,821	3,738	436
Infants' and toddlers' shoes	13,211	1,411	--
Cross-training shoes	3,462	--	--
Walking shoes	2,346	2,750	653
Fitness and running shoes	1,083	1,552	1,778
Apparel	2,761	211	--
Jeanswear	--	--	--
Watches	376	--	--
Total	$223,713	$70,525	$36,299

Source: 10-K.

aerobics, and cross training), as well as a broad range of customer types (infants, children, youth, men, and women). Additionally, the company made its products available on the international market.

In the fall of 1987, the company introduced a line of active apparel for young men and junior girls. The line consisted of 100 percent cotton T-shirts, cropped shirts, tank tops, sweat shirts, sweat pants, and shorts. Many of the garments featured splashy colors and graphics, often including the L.A. Gear name or company logo. In the following summer came a new line of moderately priced jeanswear for junior women. This line included twenty-two styles of pants, jackets, shorts, overalls, and skirts. But sales of these items were negligible in comparison to the continued growing demand for the firm's shoes. In the fall of 1988, the company added a line of quartz analog watches bearing the company's logo or name for teens and junior women. Though it expanded its line of products, L.A. Gear still imported virtually all its goods from manufacturers in southeast Asia, primarily South Korea.

ADVERTISING, PROMOTION, AND SALES

Advertising

Until 1984, L.A. Gear used the services of an outside agency for all its advertising. Greenberg then hired the president of this agency, Sandy Saemann, to become L.A. Gear's executive vice president. Saemann took charge of all advertising and promotion, with a budget that grew from $2.6 million in 1986, to $5.4 million in 1987, to $12.6 million in 1988. While this was impressive growth, the industry leaders, Nike and Reebok, were engaged in the much publicized sneaker wars; their advertising budgets were each expected to exceed $60 million in 1989, with total promotional budgets over $100 million each. L.A. Gear was expected to spend $25 million on promotion in 1989, almost all of it for advertising. (Exhibit 3 provides media advertising data for selected firms.)

L.A. Gear did not adopt its competitors' approach to advertising. Perhaps the most

EXHIBIT 3
Selected Media Advertising Data for the Shoe Industry (in Millions of Dollars)

		1989	***1988***	***1987***
Reebok	Revenues	$1,822.1	$1,785.9	$1,389.2
	Advertising	33.0	25.7	12.1
Nike	Revenues	1,710.8	1,203.4	877.4
	Advertising	30.8	30.8	10.7
L.A. Gear	Revenues	617.1	223.7	70.6
	Advertising	15.1	9.7	3.0*
Market totals	Revenues	4,500	3,900	3,000
	Advertising	135.6	113.1	57.2

* Casewriter estimate.
Sources: Annual reports, LNA/Arbitron Multi-Media Service.

obvious difference was that all work was done in-house by a staff reporting to Saemann. Saemann directed the advertising spots himself, and his permanent staff of fifteen was regularly supplemented with forty to fifty experts, many of whom were moonlighting employees from some of L.A.'s biggest agencies and Hollywood's leading studios. Using this team, Saemann claimed to save $125,000 each time he produced a 30-second spot.

L.A. Gear bucked another industry trend by contracting outside for the job of buying up media time for its ads. Many of its competitors, especially the larger ones, had in-house media buyers. Before outsourcing this work, L.A. Gear had concentrated its advertising on printed media, running two-thirds and full-page ads in magazines such as *Cosmopolitan, Vogue,* and *Glamour.* (Exhibit 4 provides information on advertising by product category.) The company hired Vitt Media International, a media-buying specialist in New York City. Vitt advised L.A. Gear to pursue higher profile advertising in more focused markets. Experience indicated that it would be difficult to reach L.A. Gear's primary target audience (girls 9 to 16 years old, and women up to 30 years old) using just network television, because network television attracted a more diverse, and somewhat older audience. Therefore, they began buying time on cable networks (MTV and Nickelodeon), reruns of *Fame* and *Saturday Night Live,* an occasional *David Letterman,* and some daytime soap operas. The ads first ran in the trend-setting Los Angeles market, spread to the twelve largest U.S. markets in 1987, and then on to the thirty-five largest U.S. markets in 1988. Vitt claimed they could buy advertising for 30 to 50 percent less than most media buyers; L.A. Gear estimated that if this were true, the savings on Vitt's commissions alone would be nearly $2 million per year.

A major difference between L.A. Gear's advertising and that of its competitors was its image and product positioning. An industry observer explained that while Nike sold performance, and Reebok sold fashion, L.A. Gear sold love. One early campaign, selling his and her basketball shoes, featured a handsomely tanned beach boy playing a game of one-on-one basketball with a stereotypically beautiful California blonde. As the voiceover purrs, "You've got the moves," the young girl steals the ball and darts inside for a lay-up. Her companion tries to block her shot, and as a result, they nearly embrace midair. The scene then cuts to a high school championship game, where the boy catches a glimpse of the

EXHIBIT 4
L.A. Gear: Media Advertising by Product Category (In Thousands of Dollars)

	1987	*1988*	*1989*
Aerobic gear	2,506 soc	438.6 c	--
Shoes, men and women	42 o	--	21.0 o
Sporting footwear, men and women	184 so	8,546.9 mosyc	13,032.0 monsyc
Sporting footwear, men	32 m	168.7 m	690.8 m
Sporting footwear, women	245 mo	958.7 mo	1228.6 mo
Sportswear, women	--	21.1 m	1403.5 m
Watches	--	80.6 m	281.7 m
Sporting footwear, children	--	--	51.8 m
Sporting footwear, family	--	--	114.4 mo
Sportswear and sporting footwear, men and women	--	--	6,747.2 onsyc

m = magazines; w = newspapers; o = outdoor; r = network radio; n = network TV; y = syndicated TV; c = cable TV; s = spot TV.
Source: LNA/Arbitron Multi-Media Service.

girl just as he sinks the game-winning shot. Finally, the scene cuts back to the beachside court, and the girl whispers to her hero, "It wasn't a fantasy." The blatant sex appeal of this new style of campaign seemed to take consumers by surprise.

Celebrity Endorsements

Promotional efforts featuring celebrities from sports and entertainment were arranged by Don Wasley, who had more than 15 years experience as a promoter, agent, and marketer in the entertainment industry. While L.A. Gear signed far fewer celebrities than Nike or Reebok, they had some impressive personalities endorsing their products. Athletes included Kareem Abdul-Jabbar, basketball legend, who endorsed L.A. Gear the last year of his twenty-season pro career; Michael Thompson, center for the Los Angeles Lakers; Akeem Olajuwan, National Basketball Association perennial All Star; and Joe Montana, star quarterback and three-time Super Bowl Most Valuable Player. Entertainment celebrities included Belinda Carlisle, pop singer; actress Priscilla Presley; Heather Locklear, also an actress; and pop music star Michael Jackson, who helped design the MJ line of footwear.

Promotions

In its earliest days, L.A. Gear linked many of its promotional activities to already established sites, products, or images of southern California. There were tie-ins to Universal Studios and local theme parks. Tourist-related promotions and giveaways helped spread the shoes eastward across the United States and around the world as travelers returned home with free shoes. There were also countless giveaways on local radio stations, a campaign with Hawaiian Punch fruit drink, another with the Suzuki Samurai sports jeep, and a series of skateboards, sun visors, and basketballs featuring the L.A. Gear logo. The company underwrote the twenty-city talent search for a girl to play a contemporary Cinderella to star in the film *Cinderella Rock.* An L.A. Gear sneaker was substituted for the glass slipper in the original fairy tale. The shoe was featured in the posters plastered throughout shopping malls across the United States. L.A. Gear's cost in underwriting the search was $25,000.

In 1988, L.A. Gear dazzled the 15,000 buyers attending the industry's two largest trade shows (New York and Atlanta). The company booths were 7,000-square-foot enclosures featuring a miniature version of Los Angeles that included a 25-foot-high replica of city hall and a Beverly Hills "hotel" complete with hospitality suite. On a stage, a cast of dancers and a Michael Jackson look-alike belted out four high-energy shows a day to guests with reserved seating. The booths cost $500,000 for theatrical designer James Dow (who also did the sets for *Close Encounters of the Third Kind*) to build and another $125,000 to transport and set up.

Wasley, vice president of promotions, explained to exhibit officials that the show booth was meant to let retailers know that L.A. Gear had arrived, and that it was capable of providing just as much excitement as Nike or Reebok. The idea must have worked. Eighteen order takers were scattered throughout the area, but they were still not enough to handle the volume of orders generated. More than 100 customers were turned away with promises that company sales staff would visit their stores as soon as possible. The following year, Nike spent $4 million on the Atlanta show alone; an effort observers thought was aimed primarily at outdoing L.A. Gear's 1988 show.

EXHIBIT 5
L.A. Gear: Income Statements
Years Ended November 30
(In Thousands of Dollars, Except per Share Dollar Amount)

	1989	1988	1987	1986	1985	1984
Net sales	$617,080	$223,713	$70,575	$36,299	$10,687	$9,007
Cost of sales	358,482	129,103	41,569	20,880	7,294	6,116
Gross profit	$258,598	$ 94,610	$29,006	$15,419	$ 3,393	$2,891
Selling, general and administrative expenses	154,449	53,168	19,955	9,053	2,437	2,620
Interest expense	12,304	4,102	1,110	686	526	368
Provision for loss from litigation	--	--	--	2,295	--	--
Earnings before income taxes, discontinued operations and extraordinary item	$ 91,845	$ 37,340	$ 7,941	$ 3,385	$ 430	$ (97)
Income tax expense (benefit)	(36,786)	(15,310)	(3,570)	(1,634)	199	(45)
Earnings before discontinued operations and extraordinary item	$ 55,059	$ 22,030	$ 4,371	$ 1,751	$ 231	$ (52)
(Loss) from discontinued operations, net of income taxes	--	--	--	(6)	(31)	(392)
Earnings before extraordinary item	$ 55,059	$ 22,030	$ 4,371	$ 1,745	$ 200	$ (444)
Extraordinary item—use of net operating loss carryforward	--	--	--	--	133	--
Net earnings	$ 55,059	$ 22,030	$ 4,371	$ 1,745	$ 333	$ (444)
Net earnings per common share	$3.01	$1.29	$0.27	$0.14	$0.03	(0.02)
Average share price (adjusted for splits)	$25.89	$6.58	$2.57	$3.49	--	--

Source: Annual reports.

Sales

The L.A. Gear sales force was organized into four distinct units: department stores, sporting goods stores, a men's division, and a children's division. Over 70 percent of the estimated 7,000 accounts were department stores or "ladies' shoe boxes." This was a considerable break from the market leaders, Nike and Reebok, who had specialty athletic shoe stores for more than 60 percent of their accounts.

Sales were not limited to the domestic market. Greenberg's plan was to establish name recognition and a strong identification with the southern California life-style, an image he believed was popular around the world. By the end of 1989, the company hoped to have thirty-five foreign distributors, and eventually ten licensees in each foreign country it entered. His philosophy on foreign licensing was that the L.A. Gear logo was versatile enough to "go on anything." In 1988, the company achieved considerable success in some foreign markets (500,000 pairs of women's and girls' shoes were sold in Japan alone), but licensing was still mostly limited to the domestic market. In the United States, the company licensed a broad range of products, ranging from doll clothes to sunglasses.

ORGANIZATION

Before it went public in 1986, L.A. Gear consisted of only fifty-one employees. By 1989, the company had grown to 448 full-time employees:

Warehousing	226
Corporate management	42
Sales and customer service	39
Administration	38
Overseas offices	36
Research and design	16
Technical representatives	14
Advertising and promotion	13
International operations	13
Apparel	7
Jeanswear	3
Watches	1

EXHIBIT 6

L.A. Gear, Inc. and Subsidiaries: Consolidated Balance Sheets
Years Ended November 30
(in Thousands of Dollars)

	1989	*1988*	*1987*	*1986*	*1985*
	Assets				
Current assets:					
Cash	$ 353	$ 4,205	$ 3,245	$ 3,509	$ 13
Marketable securities	--	--	12	7,611	15
Accounts receivable	100,749	49,526	15,148	2,738	665
Inventory	139,516	66,556	15,813	13,823	1,962
Prepaid expenses and other current assets	12,007	3,383	939	340	217
Total current assets	$252,625	$123,670	$35,157	$28,021	$2,872
Property and equipment	8,079	3,110	1,010	269	40
Receivables from shareholders, officers and directors	--	--	108	99	416
Deferred tax charges	4,589	1,034	14	79	15
Other assets	1,265	1,019	505	273	10
Total assets	$266,558	$128,833	$36,794	$28,741	$3,353
	Liabilities and Shareholders' Equity				
Current liabilities:					
Line of credit	$ 37,400	$ 57,230	$ 7,126	$ 2,500	$ 125
Accounts payable	25,619	7,748	3,886	2,230	596
Accrued loss from litigation	--	--	2,341	--	--
Accrued expenses and other current liabilities	17,627	12,402	999	4,675	2,268
Accrued compensation	16,906	5,927	--	--	--
Income taxes payable	783	4,217	323	1,588	169
Total current liabilities	$ 98,335	$ 87,524	$14,675	$10,993	$3,158
Shareholders' equity:					
Common stock	$ 84,863	$ 13,008	--	--	--
Preferred stock	--	--	--	--	--
Additional paid-in capital	--	--	$15,848	$15,848	$ 40
Retained earnings	83,360	28,301	6,271	1,900	155
Total shareholders' equity	$168,223	$ 41,309	$22,119	$17,748	$ 195
Total liabilities and shareholders' equity	$266,558	$128,833	$36,794	$28,741	$3,353

Source: Annual reports.

Robert Greenberg was the undisputed head and leader of the group. When reporters asked him to name his greatest skill, Greenberg explained simply, "I'm great at business." He was active in day-to-day operations, and believed in hands-on management. He saw his first responsibility as understanding where fashion trends were going. To stay abreast of the latest tastes, he read "every fashion magazine I can get my hands on." He spent 3 hours every Saturday disguised as a sales clerk in a valley shoe store to get fresh information on trends. He admitted that Nike and Reebok were good brands, but remained undeterred. A self-styled "predator" whose objective was to "replace the guy who is first," he remarked, "When I commit to something, I do it in a big way. I don't want to be a small fry, I want to be *the* business."

Observers noted that Greenberg appeared to be well on his way. The company made the *Business Week* list of the top 100 small firms in both 1987 and 1988. In the 1988 listing, L.A. Gear ranked third, with annual sales growth of 110 percent, annual profit growth of 335 percent, and return on capital of 45 percent over the preceding 3 years (see financial statements in Exhibits 5 and 6). By 1989, L.A. Gear had grown to $617 million in sales, too large to be eligible for the *Business Week* list. In 1989, the average annual share price leapt from $6.58 in 1988 to $25.89 and the *Wall Street Journal* identified the company's stock as the best performer on the New York Stock Exchange. Clearly, Wall Street felt L.A. Gear's good fortunes had only just begun.

CASE 10

Nike and the Inner-City Youth Market*

The athletic shoe market seemed to have matured by 1983, but later developments proved this assessment inaccurate. Between 1985 and 1989, domestic sales for athletic shoes more than doubled. Sneakers became a status symbol with an increasingly high price tag: high enough to trigger violent crimes in cities across the United States, as shoes were taken in muggings and even murders. The tremendous influence the top shoe companies wielded over some market segments, particularly inner-city adolescents, led critics to charge them with racial exploitation. As the market leader in 1989, Nike was the target for much criticism regarding mismanagement of the influential relationship sports business had with society.

NIKE AND THE ATHLETIC SHOE INDUSTRY

In 1989, the U.S. wholesale market for athletic shoes neared $5 billion. With domestic shoe revenues of $1.2 billion, Nike had the largest market share of any competitor, just over 25 percent. Nike was especially strong in basketball shoes, the single largest product category and the most popular sport (and athletic shoe) in the municipal market. (Nike was believed to hold nearly 55 percent of the basketball shoe market thanks to the tremendous success of its Air Jordan line.) In the market overall, Reebok ran a close second to Nike, holding just under 25 percent. Other major competitors were L.A. Gear, with 11 percent of the overall market, and Converse, Adidas, and Avia, with just under 5 percent each. A number of smaller firms held the remaining quarter of the market.

Industry experts credited the sneaker wars with creating the strong growth in demand for athletic shoes. The wars were waged through expensive promotional campaigns with industry advertising budgets topping $200 million a year. Nike reportedly spent $50 million, Reebok $45 million, and L.A. Gear $25 million on advertising in 1989. (These figures placed all three companies among the top 250 U.S. firms for total media advertising budgets.) Nike's most successful advertising was its "Just Do It" and "Bo Knows" campaigns. The ads were widely recognized as some of the best of their kind, featuring spectacular film footage, terse and exciting scripts, and striking portraits of athletic superstars in action. The ads focused attention on the image of the wearer rather than on the shoes.

Some industry critics argued that a disproportional part of promotional budgets was being directed to the inner-city adolescent market. This market was crucial to the shoe companies because it often served as a trendsetter. Today's fad in this small segment (e.g., leaving shoe strings untied) would be next year's fashion statement in the overall 15- to 22-year-old market, a segment that accounted for nearly a third of all athletic shoes sold. Just as fashion designers of haute couture often gave their new designs away to trendsetting celebrities, shoe designers worked to see their shoes on the streets of the inner-city, often using giveaways.

* Prepared by Alex Miller, University of Tennessee, and Greg Dess, University of Texas at Arlington.

But the industry's promotional efforts were by no means limited to such obvious tactics. For example, Reebok's sponsorship of the Human Rights Now! worldwide concert tour for Amnesty International was seen as an important soft-sell component of the corporation's overall promotional efforts. Reebok spent nearly $10 million to help finance the tour which featured rock stars such as Bruce Springsteen and Sting and included sixteen stops in major cities around the world. In return, Reebok got a "made possible by" credit in all the tour's advertising. A public relations firm made sure "roadies" and performers had all the Reebok sportswear they could wear on the tour. There were also links drawn between Amnesty International's Universal Declaration of Human Rights, and Reebok's "U.B.U." advertising campaign. Executives at Reebok explained to the press that Reebok was a company founded on the philosophy of freedom of expression and U.B.U. and Human Rights Now! were simply manifestations of this deeply held belief.

To further this theme, in 1989 Reebok established the Reebok Foundation. Its purpose, as stated in its annual report, was "expanding its involvement with organizations serving the needs of African-American, Hispanic, Asian, and Native American people." The annual report went on to explain that in the 1990s, Reebok would be actively involved with the National Urban League, the NAACP, and a special 3-year grant made to TransAfrica, a leading U.S. antiapartheid organization, among others. Additionally, Reebok planned to continue its community development efforts: improving urban playgrounds, running tennis clinics for inner-city youths, and sponsoring numerous citywide sports tournaments. Finally, after the successful Human Rights Now! concert tour, Reebok established the Reebok Human Rights Award to be granted each year to an individual under the age of 30 "who, against great odds and often at substantial personal risk, has advanced the cause of human rights around the world."

When combined with the hard-hitting media advertising campaign, such public awareness efforts helped keep athletic shoes constantly in the consumer's mind. In fact, the success of the industry's overall promotional efforts resulted in establishing shoes as status symbols. Retailers reported that some adolescents made a habit of purchasing new shoes on average once every 2 weeks to be sure they were seen only in the latest fashion. Avid customers even gave retailers beeper numbers to be paged whenever an especially exciting shoe arrived. Retailers noted some adolescents thought nothing of paying $125 or more for popular models. Suggested retail prices at the top end of Nike's and Reebok's line had gone as high as $170, but both companies later lowered their prices to $130. The price drop apparently was in response to social critics rather than to consumer price sensitivity. According to Tinker Hatfield, creative director at Nike, demand was such for the Air Jordans, retailing for $125, that some waiting lists were 3 months long. He speculated that with such strong demand, the products would sell well even priced as high as $200.

CELEBRITY PROMOTIONS

As the Nike advertisements described above suggest, the industry placed considerable emphasis on using celebrities to promote its products. For instance, Nike reportedly paid Michael Jordan, a black basketball star who was the sport's number 1 scorer, around $1 million per year to endorse its Air Jordan shoes. Bo Jackson, another black athlete and the star of the "Bo Knows" campaign, had successful careers in both baseball and football. The emphasis on black athletes in making such endorsements created what many saw as influence peddling and exploitation of ethnic minorities. Critics pointed out that white-dominated shoe companies were using black sports stars to attract more than $100 million annually from poor inner-city neighborhoods.

In response, shoe companies often made efforts to sign celebrities who portrayed a particularly wholesome image. For instance, when L.A. Gear signed Utah Jazz basketball star, Karl Malone, for $300,000 per year plus a commission from sales from all endorsed products, they emphasized his reputation as a hard-working, responsible individual as much as his number 2 scoring record. Malone's contract gave him the right to have some control over the nature of the advertisements in which he participated. Predicting the nature of promotions for the new "Mailman" line created for his endorsement, Malone stated that it would not be targeted to rich customers. Rather, it would be addressed to "kids in the projects." Malone felt confident that his voice would be heard and the new line would feature shoes priced $30 to $40; Malone thought these shoes should be of high quality, but affordable by young people in any community, and that quality and low prices was what L.A. Gear should stand for. He hoped the company would lead the industry toward more reasonably priced shoes.

Most basketball stars admitted that all major brands had good quality shoes, and endorsements hinged primarily on which companies offered the most compensation. (One basketball star made this point on national television when he played in shoes from the two competing brands he endorsed—one on each foot.) Some of the most successful stars earned greater fees from endorsing than from playing their sports, but the earnings from endorsements varied greatly. For instance, experts felt that Malone's earnings suffered because he played in Utah, a small market for sneakers compared to the favored markets: large cities with a heavy basketball-playing population. Contracts also were more lucrative for players with unusually high jumps because these were more often featured in slow-motion replays; the height of the jumps also put shoes in the picture more often. Some contracts also included publicity-related incentives, such as bonuses for making the cover of *Sports Illustrated.*

PUBLIC INTEREST GROUPS

Several social activist groups criticized the athletic shoe industry for turning the sneaker, once associated with youth and innocence, into a status symbol so compelling, and yet so expensive, adolescents were killing each other for them. Law enforcement officials confirmed that some of the most popular models had become the apparent target for numerous muggings and several murders. They also observed that these shoes had become part of the uniform for youth gangs, and wearing the wrong shoe in a gang's territory was often enough to elicit a beating. Finally, some young people had become small-time drug dealers in order to finance purchasing high-priced shoes.

At the Association of Black Journalists' annual convention in 1990, the group urged representatives from the shoe industry to address the inner-city situation on six fronts:

- Use black advertising agencies.
- Have celebrities advertise more affordable shoes.

- Work and exchange ideas with the black community.
- Create a specific commercial showing basketball players tossing off their sneakers and telling viewers that shoes were not worth young lives.
- Lobby the National Collegiate Athletic Association to route money from its televised basketball tournaments to inner-city communities.
- Air commercials showing black professionals in nonsport occupations like law and education.

People United to Serve Humanity (PUSH), a Chicago-based civil rights group once led by the Reverend Jesse Jackson, actively opposed the shoe companies; the group specifically targeted Nike because it was the industry leader. PUSH based its opposition on what it saw as imbalance between what companies like Nike gave to minority communities and what they received from these communities. They usually focused on industries where there was heavy consumption by minorities. PUSH leaders felt that these industries had a social responsibility to develop a reciprocal relationship in which industry would facilitate development of minority institutions. They looked at the banks, insurance companies, advertising agencies, and law firms of targeted companies to see how many were minority-owned. PUSH executive director, the Reverend Tyrone Crider, claimed that Nike received 30 percent of its revenues from blacks, but made minimal investments in developing the black community. PUSH called for Nike to name a black to its board of directors, and to use black advertising agencies and television and radio stations. In the meantime, the group was calling for a boycott of all Nike products.

Nike Responds

Nike officials responded to PUSH criticisms by countering that the company actually only received about 15 percent of its revenues from the black community. They also showed that, overall, black males from 13 to 24 years old accounted for only 9.8 percent of the sneaker industry's total sales. The company also pointed out that it directed most of its $10 million in annual charitable contributions to minority programs. Nike also discounted PUSH complaints by pointing out that the group had accepted money from Reebok for advertising in its publications. PUSH responded by accusing Nike of being on a smear campaign by, in effect, suggesting that PUSH was financed by Reebok, Nike's chief competitor.

As for its use of black sports celebrities, Nike pointed to its advertisements featuring David Robinson. These ads, a part of the larger Nike Air Force campaign, generally contained a public service message. For example, in one, Robinson equates drug dealers with garbage, and explains in ominous tones that "Mr. Robinson doesn't like garbage in his shoes." Nike could also point out its long history of working with college and professional athletes in providing a wide range of services that went far beyond the traditional endorser-endorsee relationship. For instance, Nike regularly held career-planning workshops for these athletes to help them think about their lives after sports.

While such actions were considered laudable, they did not alleviate all concerns about Nike's role in the inner-city problems. The success of the Nike ads was widely recognized by shoe retailers who pointed out that Nike was superb at targeting ethnic markets. They admitted the high demand from this marketing to be attractive from a business point of view, but many also indicated they were personally disturbed when they heard the shoes they sold were motives behind muggings or murders.

Employees at Nike expressed similar sentiments. For example, Hatfield, who was in charge of designing the Air Jordan shoes, admitted he was very disturbed when he watched a news report featuring the mother of a 16-year-old who was murdered when he refused to give up his Nikes. The mother held the pair of Air Jordans in her lap, and the camera closed in for a tight shot of the shoes Hatfield had spent 16 months designing. "That had an effect on me," he later told reporters. "We have, in a sense, created a problem. And, it is a toughie. You have to feel lousy. What can we do? We can't really sit and design less desirable shoes."

A Confrontation

In 1990, PUSH members interrupted Nike's annual stockholder meeting with thirty protesters chanting "Say No to Nike." The group marched to the front of the room where the Reverend Tyrone Crider began leading a prayer critical of Nike and its dealing with blacks. Nike CEO, Philip Knight, owner of Nike stock worth an estimated $1 billion, approached Crider and asked him to leave. After the group left, Knight downplayed the incident, and went on to report on the company's record earnings for the first quarter of fiscal 1990. Net income for the quarter as $99.6 million, an increase of 31 percent over the same quarter the previous fiscal year.

THE PC SOFTWARE INDUSTRY

CASE 11

A Brief History of the PC Software Industry*

ORIGINS AND GROWTH OF THE PC SOFTWARE INDUSTRY

A computer is of little use without a set of instructions to direct its operations. Software is the generic term for a series of these coded instructions written in many programming languages. As hardware prices have plummeted and computer usage has become almost universal, software has grown from an arcane art to a multibillion dollar industry.

The basic idea of the computer can be traced back to 1822 when Charles Babbage, an English mathematician, built a machine that combined the concepts of mechanized calculation and stored program control. However, it was not until the mid-1950s that advances in electronics made the commercial use of computers possible. Basically, a computer system consists of a microprocessor (semiconductor), computer (hardware), and programs (software). Over the last decade this triad has been developing in separate but interdependent ways. Advances in one are not normally sustainable without corresponding advances in the others.

One event that led to the emergence of a distinct software industry was IBM's 1969 announcement that it would price software separately. This unbundling of software and hardware gave independent software developers the impetus and opportunity to grow. In the same year, Bell Labs started developing a new operating system called UNIX, to be used primarily in minicomputers and personal computers, which won widespread acceptance at that time. By the late 1970s, companies such as Apple Computer, Tandy, and Commodore International started marketing relatively inexpensive personal computers. The development of operating systems such as CP/M and programming languages such as BASIC greatly helped the growth of the personal computer industry. The Apple II personal computer, introduced in 1978, further encouraged third-party software development. VisiCalc, introduced in May 1979, was the first electronic spreadsheet and instantly became a national bestseller, selling more than 100,000 copies in its first year. Many industry analysts credited VisiCalc as "the first software package to justify the purchase of a microcomputer."

When IBM entered the PC market in 1981, it became the de facto industry standard

* Prepared by Gregory G. Dess, University of Texas at Arlington; Paul Gerber, General Services Administration; and Abdul Rasheed, University of Texas at Arlington.

almost overnight. After adopting a new operating system called MS-DOS developed by Microsoft, the "IBM PC," as it is often called, won immediate acceptance among business users. This led manufacturers around the world to replicate (or clone) the IBM machines—referred to as IBM compatibles—resulting in greater availability and lower prices. The popularity of the MS-DOS–based machine and software remains strong, despite the development of more advanced operating systems. To exploit the capabilities of a new family of microprocessors introduced by Intel, Microsoft and IBM joined efforts again in 1987 to develop OS/2, a new operating system. While predictions that OS/2 would revolutionize the software industry have remained largely unfulfilled, many software companies have continued to develop applications using OS/2. Meanwhile, the relationship between Microsoft and IBM has become strained because of disagreements over the direction that operating systems development should take.

Apple Computer, often credited as the originator of the concept of personal computing, introduced the Macintosh in 1984. This extremely user-friendly machine with its intuitive graphic menus and commands has led to the development of a variety of easy-to-use software products. By choosing from an array of icons using a handheld device called a mouse, even novice users can use the machine easily. Microsoft and IBM have sought to match this with "Windows," a new graphical operating environment that can bestow the same graphic capabilities to IBM PCs. (IBM still favors OS/2. Microsoft presently favors Windows but would like to develop OS/2 3.0 or "NT" which would unite Windows and OS/2.[1])

The software industry has come a long way from its early days when it consisted mostly of expensive customized applications for large mainframe users. The 1990 worldwide software market is estimated to be approximately $43 billion.[2] An increasing percentage of this is software written for personal computers, a segment that barely existed a decade ago. This segment consists mostly of spreadsheet, word processing, and database management applications. They are generally priced under $1,000, easy to learn, and depend mostly on high-powered marketing and periodic updates of existing products to achieve sales growth.

Surprisingly, the old guard of the software industry (such as Computer Associates, Cullinet, and MSA) have made limited inroads in the fast-growing market for PC software. Instead, success has gone mostly to a small number of young technologists and entrepreneurs. The *Economist* magazine once pointed out, "never in the history of capitalism have so many become so rich so young."[3] Bill Gates, founder of Microsoft, and Mitch Kapor, founder of Lotus, are two good examples of this new breed of software developers. Bill Gates dropped out of Harvard at age 17 and went on to become the youngest self-made billionaire in history. Lotus 1-2-3, the brainchild of Mitch Kapor, an ex-psychology student and teacher of transcendental meditation, has sold more than 7 million copies since its introduction in 1983. The other two segments of the triad, computer hardware and semiconductors, also seem to be dominated by prodigies such as Steven Jobs of Next, Inc., and Andy Grove of Intel.

---

[1] Hooper, L. (1991, March 8). IBM is mustering its forces to save OS/2. *The Wall Street Journal,* p. B1.
[2] Computer equipment and software. (1991). *U.S. Industrial Outlook,* p. 28–15.
[3] Ibid.

PRODUCT SEGMENTS WITHIN THE PC SOFTWARE INDUSTRY

Competition in the PC software industry can be best understood by analyzing competition within each segment of this industry. Several different criteria can be used to classify the existing software products. Some of the more commonly used categories include operating systems versus applications, packaged versus customized, professional/business versus home educational/recreational, and computer size. The software world can be most broadly divided into two parts; operating systems and applications software.

Operating systems consist of very highly specialized programs that manage the flow of information between a system's components, schedule the commands of the applications software, allocate the computer memory, and control the system's hardware. It manages all the interactions between a computer and its peripheral devices. MS-DOS is the operating system used most by IBM PCs and compatibles. Early in 1990, DOS was challenged by OS/2, an operating system jointly promoted by Microsoft and IBM. However, the introduction of Windows, a graphical interface, has revived the popularity of DOS. Windows enables users to obtain the benefits of a graphical interface even with their older PCs on DOS. The Macintosh family of products uses a proprietary operating system. UNIX is the preferred operating system for workstations.

Applications software consists of programs written to allow a broad class of users to perform specific tasks. Applications software enables users with limited computer skills to perform a variety of tasks. The three major categories of applications software are spreadsheet, word processing, and database management.

Spreadsheets provide easy manipulation of quantitative business data with an electronic columnar pad. After overtaking VisiCalc in the early 1980s, Lotus has continued to dominate this segment with 1-2-3. Much of this dominance is due to its early penetration of the market for spreadsheets for IBM compatible PCs, enabling it to virtually set the industry standard.

Word processing programs allow the creation, editing, manipulation, storage, and retrieval of large amounts of text. The enormous popularity of word processing software can be attributed to its ability to make texts infinitely easier than when using a typewriter. Unlike the spreadsheet segment of the market, there is no clear industry standard in this segment. Wordstar was the early leader, but has since been overtaken by packages such as WordPerfect and Display Write. Microsoft Word and MacWrite dominate this segment for Macintosh users.

Database management systems (DBMS) store, edit, retrieve, and manipulate large amounts of data. They are also capable of generating reports from the data. For most of the 1980s, the clear leader in this segment was dBase, sold by Ashton-Tate. Wayne Ratliff, an engineer at the Jet Propulsion Laboratory in Pasadena, originally developed dBase to help with his football bets. Unfortunately, subsequent versions of dBase have been plagued by errors and the company is now facing stronger competition from rivals such as Microsoft and Oracle Corp. Database management programs are more complicated to use than spreadsheets or word processors, but efforts are underway to make them simpler.

EXHIBIT 1
Leading Competitors in Major Segments, 1989

Segment	*Product*	*Company*	*Market Share**
Word processing:			
1	WordPerfect	WordPerfect Corp.	58%
2	DisplayWrite	I.B.M.	13%
3	Microsoft Word	Microsoft	8%
Spreadsheet:			
1	1-2-3	Lotus	67%
2	Excel	Microsoft	13%
3	Supercalc	Computer Associates	4%
Database:			
1	dBase	Ashton-Tate	59%
2	Paradox	Borland International	10%
3	DataEase	DataEase International, Inc.	7%

* The figures for market share are *not* based on total sales for the year but rather are based on the "installed base," i.e., the total sales through 1989.

Source: Quinn, J. (1989, September 15). Getting with the program(s): Building a computer book collection. *Library Journal;* Day-Copeland, L. Word processors: Spreadsheets still top software purchases at big sites. (1989, June 12). *PC World,* p. 134.

Other growing segments of the industry include desktop publishing, business graphics, and communications. Demand is also growing for applications that allow specific users to perform very specific tasks, such as medical record keeping or oil and gas distribution systems. Software for computer games is a different industry by itself with a different set of players and different marketing techniques. Some small, but growing, product segments of applications software include more flexible database systems, client-server applications, network products, and imaging. Exhibit 1 provides market-share information for the word processing, spreadsheet, and database segments of the PC software industry.

Since 1989, there have been some rather dramatic changes in the market positions of the dominant firms in each segment. For example, in the spreadsheet segment, Lotus's share of annual unit sales dropped to 47 percent in 1990 from 54 percent in 1989. The share of Borland International's Quattro Pro has increased to 14 percent in 1990 from only 3 percent in 1989. Borland has replaced Supercalc, produced by Computer Associates, as the number 3 product in terms of installed units. The market share of Microsoft's Excel has remained almost constant, increasing to 14 percent in 1990 from 12.6 percent in 1989.[4]

KEY PLAYERS AND THE STRUCTURE OF THE SOFTWARE INDUSTRY

The microsoftware industry consists of thousands of small, independent developers and a few dominant, well-known firms. The three largest firms—Microsoft, Lotus Development, and Ashton-Tate—account for over 50 percent of the combined revenues of the 100

[4] Henricks, M. (1991, May). Spreadsheet clash improves user choices. *PC World,* p. 59.

EXHIBIT 2
Comparative Sales and Financial Data for Leading Competitors in the PC Software Industry
(In Millions of Dollars)

Company	*1986*	*1987*	*1988*	*1989*	*1990*
Ashton-Tate					
Net sales	$210.8	$267.3	$307.3	$265.3	$230.5
Net income	30.1	43.1	47.8	(28.6)	(18.1)
Lotus Development					
Net sales	282.9	395.6	468.5	556.0	684.5
Net income	48.3	72.0	58.9	68.0	23.3
Microsoft					
Net sales	197.5	345.9	590.8	803.5	1,183.4
Net income	39.3	71.9	123.9	170.5	279.2

largest independent firms. This gap will probably widen as the intensity of competition increases. Smaller firms will be less likely to flourish as the largest firms continue to grow, increasing industry entry barriers through aggressive acquisition strategies, broader and upgraded product lines, and increased hiring from the limited pool of talented programming personnel. As one industry analyst has stated, "The gap between professionally managed, well-financed operations and cottage-industry-type companies is widening."[5]

Despite intensified competitive forces, many smaller firms still continue to succeed by exploiting market niches. Such firms have developed software to perform any number of important functions, such as retrieving accidentally erased data, writing checks, drawing charts, sending memos, and calculating income taxes. When they are able to obtain shelf space at retail outlets, they are often able to enjoy pretax profits of 30 to 40 percent. Desktop publishing is an example of a niche that has evolved into an important market segment. Aldus Corporation, the pioneer of desktop publishing, posted sales of $87.9 million in 1989—up from $2.2 million in 1985. Overall, 90 percent of the independents are small firms with sales of less than $1 million, operating in very narrow market segments.

Ashton-Tate Corporation, Lotus Development Corporation, and Microsoft Corporation are the three largest microsoftware firms. Size provides these companies with the many competitive advantages, such as customer loyalty, well-developed distribution channels, established user bases, and costs, that are involved in switching to alternate products. Strong financial positions enable them to invest in research and development and acquire smaller, promising firms. Each of these three firms also has a strong foothold in one of the important market segments: Microsoft's niche is in operating systems, Lotus's main product is spreadsheet software, and Ashton-Tate's predominant software is database management software. However, the focus of competition is changing among the "big three" as they expand the base of their established products and diversify into new-product application areas. Exhibit 2 provides comparative sales and financial data for these three firms.

[5] Wiener, D. P. (1987, August 17). Closing down the garage of the little guy. *U.S. News and World Report*, p. 45.

Ashton-Tate

In 1979, Hal Lashlee and George Tate pooled $7,500 to start Software Plus, Inc., the first software distributorship in the United States. Shortly thereafter, they purchased an innovative software named Vulcan, and retitled it dBase II. As the company expanded, they decided to have a public stock offering and renamed the company Ashton-Tate. dBase II quickly became the industry standard for database management systems. In 1984, George Tate died of a sudden heart attack, and Edward Esber was named president. Esber, who stressed strategic and financial planning, quickly transformed the company from its start-up entrepreneurial style into one with a more formalized structure.

Under Esber's leadership, Ashton-Tate pursued an aggressive acquisitions strategy. The firm experienced rapid growth by acquiring many small software companies, such as Forefront Corporation and Multimate International Corp. (1985); Decision Resources (1986); Ann Arbor Software, Apex Software Corp., and Nippon-Ashton-Tate (1988). These acquisitions enabled Ashton-Tate to become one of the big-three competitors in the industry. In 1987, Ashton-Tate released dBaseMac, thereby attempting to become a major competitor for MacIntosh software products—a market dominated by Microsoft.

Recently, Ashton-Tate has diversified its product line outside of database systems. In 1988, for example, sales of dBase III accounted for 64 percent of total sales; down from 79 percent in 1986. While entering the word processing, integrated software, and business graphics markets, its overall market share in database systems has declined from 62.5 percent in 1985 to 43 percent in 1989. Some believe that a lack of focus on their core business may be at the root of the problems they have recently experienced. Delays associated with the upgrade of dBase IV have led to flat sales and excess inventory. Ashton-Tate's reputation was damaged further when an agreement with Microsoft to be the sole retail source of SQL did not materialize. (An SQL server permits PC users easier access to a mainframe database.) Because of problems associated with the dBase IV, Ashton-Tate failed to supply the front end to the SQL server in a timely fashion, and the agreement with Microsoft fell through.[6] Problems associated with product delays are a major threat facing the industry. Further delays of this type could seriously endanger Ashton-Tate's position of leadership in the database segment of the industry.

As Ashton-Tate continued to experience shrinking market share and declining revenues, Ed Esber came under increasing pressure. In April 1990, he was abruptly replaced by William Lyons, a 19-year IBM veteran who had been with Ashton-Tate only 18 months.

Lotus Development Corporation

In January 1983, Lotus Development, founded by Mitchell Kapor, shipped its first product, 1-2-3. 1-2-3 combines spreadsheet applications with database and graphics capabilities, and it quickly became the industry standard. Lotus shipped its second product, Symphony, in June 1984. Jim Manzi replaced Mitch Kapor as chairman in July, 1986. Under Manzi's leadership, the company developed a greater marketing orientation and a strategy of product diversification implemented primarily through a series of acquisitions. Lotus's product line now includes information management, data access, word and document processing,

[6] Lyons, D. (1988, August 15). Software firms notch record $1.8 B first-half sales. *PCWeek*, p. 112.

desktop management, graphics, and communication. Like all software firms, its future success depends on the viability of its new products.

In 1988 Lotus was plagued with development and shipment delays of its upgraded product, 1-2-3/3.0. Not only did this delay lead to a decline in Lotus's stock price, but it also provided spreadsheet competitors, Borland and Microsoft, with opportunities to erode Lotus's position. They were promoting their products, Quattro and Excel, respectively, with substantial discounts. By 1990, Lotus had adapted 1-2-3 to OS/2 and had begun work on a Windows version.

Microsoft

In June 1975, Bill Gates and Paul Allen established Microsoft to produce a software program for MITS, a manufacturer of rockets and electronic kits. Later, MITS ran into financial trouble and eventually went out of business. Microsoft went on to find other customers, and in January 1979, Gates and Allen moved their firm from Albuquerque to Seattle, Washington.

Microsoft's big break came in the form of a joint venture with IBM. IBM wanted a quick entry in the PC market and approached Microsoft about creating an operating system. Gates, in turn, bought an operating system from a small firm, Seattle Computer Products, and transformed it into the MS-DOS operating system—the basic software that runs millions of IBM personal computers and clones.

On March 14, 1986, Microsoft went public with one of the most successful stock issues ever made. With 1990 revenues of $1.18 billion, Microsoft has become the industry leader in the personal computer software industry. Microsoft's major competitive advantage is its ability to produce both operating systems and applications software, and software for IBM and Macintosh computers. Their strength in the area of operating systems gave them a head start in developing complementary applications software.

The systems software category consists of both operating systems and languages. Microsoft's operating systems include MS-DOS, MS OS/2, XENIX, and Windows. Introduced in 1981, MS-DOS became the first industry standard for personal computers. Microsoft also has developed interpreters and compilers for BASIC, FORTRAN, COBOL, Pascal, and Macro Assembler languages.

Applications software can be broken down into word processing, file management, spreadsheet, graphics, communications, and project management products. Microsoft's word processing programs include Microsoft Word products and Microsoft Write. Microsoft Word is compatible with MS-DOS, OS/2, XENIX, and Macintosh systems. (Microsoft Write is also compatible with Macintosh, but is simpler than Microsoft Word.)

Microsoft has developed the Multiplan spreadsheet for MS-DOS and OS/2 as well as Excel for the Macintosh. In addition, Microsoft Works, an integrated product with spreadsheet, database, word processor, and communications functions, is available for both MS-DOS and Macintosh.

COMPETITION IN THE SOFTWARE INDUSTRY

As the software industry matures there are many critical competencies that firms must possess in order to survive and prosper. These include the ability to hire and retain skilled technical employees, ensure customer loyalty, develop marketing prowess, and maintain a level of financial resources necessary for continuing investments in product development, acquisitions, and distribution channels.

Hiring and Retaining Skilled Programmers and Analysts

The software industry is very labor intensive and there is a growing shortage of skilled programmers and systems analysts. According to the Bureau of Labor Statistics projections, by 1995, the demand for computer programmers and systems analysts in the United States is expected to be nearly double the 1984 level, reaching 1.1 million professionals. However, recent studies have shown a declining enrollment in computer programming and related fields. Thus, programmers and analysts should be able to continue to command high salaries and software firms face the challenge of hiring and retaining them.

Firms that are effective in developing unique applications or systems software are able to acquire proprietary rights to their products. This often leads to a dominant position in their market segment. For example, Microsoft, the developer of the MS-DOS operating system for IBM, has—along with IBM—exclusive proprietary rights to its program. Similarly, Apple Computer, the developer of user-friendly graphics, has claimed exclusive rights to that feature. Apple has frequently filed lawsuits against competitors who have integrated similar features into their product offerings.

Customer Loyalty

Customer loyalty and brand name recognition are important attributes of successful firms in the PC software industry. High learning curves and high switching costs breed such loyalty. Users generally "hate to learn new software" because it can often be very frustrating and time-consuming. Changing brands of software or operating systems is very expensive. For example, to change from one database product to another requires that the user change the structure of the files and transfer all of the data in the files. New or additional hardware may often be required to accommodate new programs.

Strong user loyalty may often help a product become the industry standard. Products such as Lotus 1-2-3, dBase, and so forth, with huge user bases enjoy a captive market. Because users are reluctant to switch brands, they look for frequent upgrades and revisions. Competitors often scramble to imitate the standard and rush their own version of a product to the market. Product imitations often result in lawsuits alleging copyright violations. Interestingly, many software innovations result from the combination of two or more existing ideas or the modification of an existing product.

Technical support and service after the sale also serve to increase customer loyalty and heighten buyer switching costs. Software products with good documentation and the associated training manuals and seminars tend to be more in demand. The big-three firms offer such services as customer hotlines and newsletters as well as the deployment of support personnel who provide new product updates and briefings, applications design consultation, and problem solving. Users also often receive ". . . a warranty of perhaps 90 days; a guarantee that errors will be fixed or refunds will be given; a clear description of what features a PC needs to use the program; and a promise that the software meets a maker's ad claims and product description."[7]

---

[7] Kneale, D., & Malcolm, J. (1986, July 6). A new approach to software warranties. *The Wall Street Journal,* p. 27.

Distribution Channels and Marketing

The PC software industry relies on four major types of distribution channels: sales to dealers (retail), third-party distributors (mail order), international subsidiaries, and original equipment manufacturers.

Retail outlets for software include discount stores, department stores, book stores, and computer specialty stores. Mail order is not often used by the largest firms. However, because smaller firms are typically unable to obtain shelf space in retail outlets, they often must rely on mail order as a distribution channel. Although hardware manufacturers such as Apple Computer and Tandy's Radio Shack allow only exclusive franchise dealers to carry their hardware products, this is not the case with software products. Given the intensity of competition in the software industry, most firms must compete aggressively for shelf space.

Over the years, marketing has become increasingly complex and expensive in the software industry. In recent years, sales and marketing costs have averaged nearly 30 percent of the big-three's total revenues. Large firms typically enjoy the advantages of expert marketing groups, entrenched market positions, high brand name recognition, installed customer bases, established distribution channels, and corporate accounts. Marketing efforts also serve to differentiate one product from another and help to prevent one's product from being "out-marketed" by a competing product.

Financial Strength

Fast-paced changes and the need for constant innovation characterize the software industry. Firms must invest heavily in research and development in order to innovate successfully. A recent survey found that U.S. software firms spend an average of 10 percent of their total revenues on R&D. The industry ranked third out of twelve surveyed electronics industries.[8] Given their superior financial strength, the big three in the software industry have considerable advantages over the smaller firms. Thus, they are able to make the expensive investments in R&D necessary to create new products as well as commit sizable resources to strengthen distribution networks.

Once a software product is developed, it is relatively inexpensive to produce copies of it. Such operating leverage, combined with high unit volumes and additional sales from product upgrades, enable software firms to achieve relatively high profit margins. Thus, successful firms generally are cash rich, have strong balance sheets, little debt, and earn a high return on equity. In addition to investing their cash into product development and strengthening distribution channels, larger firms also aggressively acquire other promising software firms. Such acquisitions enable them to expand their product lines or market share and obtain new innovations.

MAJOR TRENDS IN THE SOFTWARE INDUSTRY

As the 1990s begin, the PC software industry is undergoing major changes that may have profound impact on the competitive nature of the industry. Such changes may also signifi-

[8] U.S. Department of Commerce, 1988.

cantly affect the way personal computers are used. Some of these important trends are reviewed in this section.

Industry Consolidation

For most of the early 1980s, software was a highly fragmented industry. However, toward the latter part of the decade, the industry was showing clear signs of consolidation. The larger software firms were acquiring smaller firms with promising products or capabilities. Acquisitions are often cheaper and faster than producing new products in-house. This has resulted in a steady increase in the market value of software firms. Most of these acquisitions tend to be cash transactions, and require prospective buyers to maintain large cash balances.

One of the major motivations driving the big three in the software industry is the need to have balanced product portfolios. The success of Microsoft, Lotus, and Ashton-Tate was founded on single products, a position difficult to sustain in a rapidly changing industry. However, as these firms are diversifying their products to enter newer market segments, they are stepping out of their well-protected niches and increasingly coming into direct competition with each other.

Even though the industry is clearly undergoing consolidation, many smaller firms continue to prosper by identifying and exploiting niches which the larger firms may have ignored. An example is Ken Skier, who, responding to the complaints of many laptop computer users that the cursors are difficult to see, wrote a program that makes laptop cursors larger and named it the No-Squint Laptop Cursor. As Mr. Skier puts it, "I am like little barberfish that go into the jaws of big fish and clean their teeth. I get morsels that are too little for the big fish."[9]

Legal Uncertainties and Piracy

Software firms in the United States are estimated to be losing hundreds of millions of dollars every year in revenue to piracy. There are between two and ten illegal copies available for every original sold in the United States and up to 250 illegal copies internationally.[10] Piracy is particularly a problem in countries with lenient or no copyright laws. In Taiwan and Singapore, for example, pirated copies of popular programs like Lotus 1-2-3 sell for less than $10 compared to original prices of about $500. Copy protection efforts have been inconvenient at best and ineffective at worst. To combat illegal copying, software firms have been resorting to aggressive prosecution of offenders, site licensing (where large corporate users pay a fee for permission to produce and use multiple copies), and developing services such as technical support and updates that promote purchasing over copying.

Another uncertainty software producers face is the recent spate of "look and feel" litigation among competitors. This type of litigation challenges the rights of software companies to develop products that have close resemblance to existing products. Lotus and Ashton-Tate have filed suits against smaller rivals, such as Paperback Software International and Queue Associates, Inc., for infringement of copyrights. Similarly, Apple has

---

[9] Ingrassia, L. (1988, October 11). Small software companies profit by exploiting niches. *The Wall Street Journal,* p. B1.

[10] *Standard and Poor's Industry Survey* (1986), p. C95.

EXHIBIT 3
Examples of Litigation Among Software Companies

Apple v. Microsoft

Apple contends that Microsoft's Windows 2.03 and Hewlett-Packard's New Wave misappropriated Apple's copyrights to the Macintosh computer screens. IBM and other computer companies are relying on the Window's operating program to compete against Apple.

Xerox v. Apple

Xerox claims it held the rights for the icons and other features that were later used in Macintosh. It claims that Apple founder, Steve Jobs, acquired the ideas while on a tour in Xerox labs.

Lotus, et al. v. Facts on File

A suit by Lotus, Ashton-Tate, Microsoft, Micropro, and WordPerfect against Facts on File, Inc., for unauthorized copies of software, was settled out of court for $100,000 per company. This is the *first* company to agree to pay piracy damages.

Lotus v. Paperback and Mosaic

Lotus brought suit against two small software firms for alleged copyright infringement involving keystroke-for-keystroke copies of 1-2-3's program. The 1-2-3 clones, VP Planner and Twin, sell for around $99 each, while the genuine article retails for $595 (Feb. 90). In June 1990, Lotus obtained a favorable ruling that "liability for infringement" of copyrights was established.

Lotus et al. v. Montedison S.p.A.

Lotus and Ashton-Tate brought suit in Italy against Montedison for copyright infringement. The Italian court ordered a surprise search of the company's headquarters and found 90% of the software in use were bootleg copies. Software companies sell 3.5 programs per 10 PCs in Italy, compared to 15 programs per 10 PCs in the United States. This extrapolates to be a $500 million loss of software sales in Italy annually.

SAPC v. Lotus

SAPC owns what remains of Software Arts, Inc. (bought by Lotus in 1985). The courts recently dismissed the suit that had alleged copyright infringement by Lotus and Mitchel Kapor, its founder, on VisiCalc, the first spread-sheet program.

Sources: Schmitt, R. B. (1989, April 7). The three computer industry leaders gird for battle over copyright infringement. *The Wall Street Journal*, p. B2; Carroll, P. B. (1989, May 24). Xerox seeking licensing fees for software. *The Wall Street Journal*, pp. B1, B13; Roberts, J. L. (1989, June 13). Software publishers win a big victory over illegal copies. *The Wall Street Journal*, p. C18; Colby L. (1989, April 10). Software firms sue Montedison over copyrights. *The Wall Street Journal*, pp. A9, C3; Barney D. (1987, April 13). Lotus sued for VisiCalc infringement. *ComputerWorld*, pp. 1, 8; Bulkeley, W. M. (1990, June 29). Lotus development wins suit charging Paperback Software violated copyright. *The Wall Street Journal*, p. A4.

sued both Microsoft and Hewlett-Packard, accusing that their operating systems, Windows and New Wave, have misappropriated the "look and feel" of Apple's popular Macintosh screens. While the legal outcome hangs in the balance, the fear of litigation has dampened the software development activities of firms, both large and small.[11] Current copyright law, originally written to protect literary works, appears to be inadequate for dealing with some of the unconventional aspects of software.

U.S. software producers have also been constrained by the various governmental

[11] Bulkeley, W. F. (1990, February 6). Lotus trial may clarify copyrights. *The Wall Street Journal*, pp. B1, B4.

regulations that restrict the export of hardware and software, especially to Eastern Bloc countries. In the past, these controls were so broad and sweeping, they often turned potential customers to other foreign sources. The changing relations with eastern Europe and the potentially vast size of foreign markets have led to some easing of these regulations in recent years. Exhibit 3 provides some representative examples of litigation in the PC software industry.

International Market Growth

International sales of U.S. software is expanding rapidly, more than offsetting the slowdown of the domestic market due to saturation of the PC market. According to an estimate by Dataquest, western Europe's annual sales could surpass America's in the mid-1990s.[12] It is important for U.S. software producers to get a firm foothold in western Europe prior to the economic integration of 1992, in order to establish their standards in Europe. There will also be significant opportunities in eastern Europe and the Soviet Union as they rush to modernize after four and a half decades of stagnation under nonmarket economic systems.

Lag between Development of New Technologies and Their Adoption

The progress of the software industry requires the rapid diffusion of newer technologies and their even faster adoption by users. In other words, PC makers must be able to use the latest advances in chip technology, operating and applications software must be available as soon as the computers reach the market, and the users must be willing to discard their existing hardware and software in favor of the new offerings. Currently, significant time lags exist between each of these stages. The extent of adoption of operating software such as OS/2, and computers and workstations produced by Next, Sun Microsystems, and so forth, have been well below expectations, mainly due to the lack of accompanying software. The industry is presently faced with a shortage of analysts and programmers. The number of programmers is growing at only 4 percent a year whereas average program size and overall demand for software are increasing at the rate of 25 percent and 12 percent, respectively, per year.

The process of creating software has not changed much over the past three decades. The output of code that comprises the programs is presently only in the region of one or two lines per programmer per hour. The solution lies in the adoption of advanced techniques for software development, such as computer-aided software engineering (CASE) that helps to automate the process of writing applications programs. By using pretested, error-free, common modules, programmer productivity can be greatly enhanced. Originally developed in France and Britain, CASE has been slow in gaining acceptance in the programmer community in the United States.[13]

Users have unexpectedly been reluctant to upgrade to newer generations of hardware and software. More than 22 million PCs with the now outdated 8086/8088 microprocessors are still in use and their owners are showing little eagerness to dump them in favor of the

---

[12] Kirkland, R. I. (1989, June 5). Europe goes wild for Yankee PCs. *Fortune,* pp. 257–260.

[13] Goldberg, R. (1988). Software engineering: An emerging discipline. *IBM Systems Journal, 5*(3/4), 336; The software trap: Automate . . . or else. (1988, May 9). *Business Week,* pp. 142–154.

new generation of machines using brawnier 80286 and 80386 microchips.[14] Most people, whose requirements seldom go beyond simple spreadsheet and word processing tasks, see little point in investing the money necessary to buy new software or upgrade their computers. Further, a whole variety of products are now available to reduce the need to switch. These are either hardware products that augment a low-end machine's memory and computing power or smarter programs that squeeze more performance from the old boxes. For example, DESQview, a program from Santa Monica–based Quarterdeck Office Systems enables a standard PC to have some of the features of OS/2.[15]

Competitive Tactics

As competition is intensifying in the software industry, new competitive tactics are emerging which are specific to the industry. Many companies resort to the practice of announcing yet to be developed applications in order to meet market pressures, or to dissuade users from switching to competitor's products. Sometimes, these announcements may even have the effect of deterring smaller rivals from developing similar applications. Such tactics are generally referred to as vaporware or foilware. In some cases at least, such premature announcements may be due to genuine underestimation of the complexities involved in completing, testing, and marketing new products or updates. One such example is the case of Release 3.0 of Lotus 1-2-3, the shipment of which was originally scheduled for April 1987, but was released in June 1989, after repeatedly missing several deadlines set by the company. An even more questionable practice that has emerged recently is the limited release of beta versions at deep discounts. These are often incomplete programs that require additional testing and evaluation before a full-fledged release. By doing so, software firms hope to preempt competition and satisfy market pressures generated by their hasty announcements of new products.

Most industry analysts and even many software companies believe that any competitive advantage gained from practices such as vaporware and beta versions is purely temporary and probably even counterproductive in the long run. Instead, success may go to the firms that can offer more connectivity and integration in their products. The personal computer and software industries are characterized by incompatibilities of languages, standards, and machines. This causes users considerable confusion and frustration. Compatibility between products and the ability to transport software across a variety of platforms are emerging as important selling points. Local area networks (LANs) which store data in file servers that link to more powerful computing units and allow access and data manipulation across the network is a hot growth area for the 1990s.[16] Steve Jobs, chairman of Next, Inc., sums it up: "While the eighties were the age of personal computing, the nineties will be the age of interpersonal computing."[17]

---

[14] Schwartz, J. (1989, August 28). A new life for old PCs. *Newsweek,* pp. 44–45.
[15] Ibid.
[16] LANs and client/server architecture. (1990, January). *Standard and Poor's Industry Survey,* p. C62.
[17] Schlender, B. R. (1990, February 12). Who's ahead in the computer wars. *Fortune,* pp. 59–61, 64.

CASE 12

Lotus Development Corporation*

LOTUS: THE EARLY YEARS

Mitch Kapor, founder and first president of Lotus, had a rather circuitous route to fame and fortune in the software industry. He took computer science courses while earning a degree at Yale in the early 1970s with a "hodgepodge major of psychology, linguistics, and computer sciences."[1] After college, he and his wife traveled to Boston and he took a job as an entry-level programmer.

> He dabbled in other things too: teaching transcendental meditation, reading Gregory Bateson and German philosophy and Freud, working as a disc jockey. He was a perpetual grad student who happened not to be in a degree program. He applied to several but never got around to attending any. His parents were in despair.[2]

Eventually, Kapor earned a masters in psychology and applied to numerous Ph.D. programs in psychology. But by the late 1970s he decided he wanted to work in the personal computer industry. During the early 1980s, he was a new-product manager for VisiCorp. At the same time, he was president of Micro Finance Systems, Inc.—a business applications firm that he founded. Micro Finance created Tiny Troll, a graphics and statistical package for use on the Apple II personal computer.[3] He received $500,000 in royalties before VisiCorp bought him out for an additional $1.2 million.[4] But VisiCorp rejected Kapor's idea for developing a software package which combined an electronics spreadsheet, a graphics package, and a report generator.[5] Micro Finance was then renamed the Lotus Development Corporation and, during 1982, developed this integrated package. 1-2-3 was first shipped in January 1983, and first year sales—expected to be $3 million—came to $53 million.[6] Lotus quickly established itself as a viable competitor in the personal computer software industry. Throughout its history, Lotus's mission has been to "provide innovative solutions to business problems through software and supporting services, and in the process, create a company that will become preeminent in the software industry."[7] This early success may be attributed to many factors. First, Lotus entered the market just as the PC industry was experiencing tremendous growth. In 1980 the market for PC software was $260 million, but by the first half of 1988, sales had reached $1.82 billion.[8] Second, Kapor

---

* Prepared by Paul Gerber, General Services Administration; Adbul Rasheed, University of Texas at Arlington; and Gregory G. Dess, University of Texas at Arlington.

1 Rose, R. (1984, December). Mitch Kapor and the Lotus factor. *Esquire,* p. 360.
2 Rose, R., op. cit., p. 358.
3 Lotus Development Corporation (1983). 10-K, p. 5.
4 Rose, R., op. cit., p. 360.
5 Ibid.
6 Ibid.
7 Lotus Development Corporation Annual Report (1983). p. 5.
8 Rose, R., loc. cit.; and *Computer Software and Services Industry* (1988, September 16).

decided to write 1-2-3 for the IBM PC, enabling Lotus to benefit from IBM's success. Finally, by identifying the critical success factors for growth, Lotus was able to quickly increase its market share.

Kapor's ability to create a user-friendly product and to understand customer needs was also vital to Lotus's rise to prominence. Although he cannot write sophisticated computer code and is not considered a good programmer, he has a very rare trait in the industry—user empathy.

> "He can sit in front of a half-finished program and weed out routines that seem obvious to the technically literate but would bewilder ordinary users. Of all the guys in the industry," says Bill Gates, chairman of rival Microsoft, "Mitch has the best feel for what users want next."[9]

Kapor also played the key role in establishing Lotus as the industry's marketing innovator.

> Kapor believed that if you wanted to sell a product to business people you ought to advertise in media that business people actually see. . . . He decided that the manual that accompanied a program ought to be clear and concise in its description of how the program works.[10]

Further, his knack for marketing and creativity have also spurred Lotus's success.

> He's a master showman, a charismatic figure with a flair for the theatrical. So closely have these qualities been identified with him that marketing, advertising, and showmanship are now known as the Lotus factor.[11]

As one might expect, during its early years, Lotus's culture was largely a reflection of Mitch Kapor's personality. "One of the perks of being founder," he says, "is that you get to build the company in your image."[12] The atmosphere was relaxed and casual; Kapor believed in loose control around creativity and innovation, with very tight control over finances.[13]

MAJOR PRODUCTS

The product for which Lotus is best known is 1-2-3. Soon after its introduction in January 1983, it became the personal computer software industry's best-selling business applications software product. Since its release in 1983, 1-2-3 has been updated several times and has sold over 7 million copies. Lotus introduced a second analytic product, Symphony, in July 1984. This is a multifunction, fully integrated software program that allows users to create turnkey applications that combine spreadsheet, database, word processing, graphics, and communications capabilities. Exhibit 1 provides shipment data for 1-2-3 and Symphony.

Though not as well known, the company offers a variety of software products in

[9] Petre, P. (1985, June 10). The man who keeps the bloom on Lotus. *Fortune,* p. 138.
[10] Rose, op. cit., p. 356.
[11] Lotus is diminished without Kapor (editorial). (1986, July 22). *PC Week,* p. 36.
[12] Petre, P., op. cit., p. 136.
[13] Rose, R., op. cit., p. 362.

EXHIBIT 1
Cumulative Shipments of 1-2-3 and Symphony

Year	*Cumulative Shipments (in Millions)*
1985	1.7
1986	2.0
1987	3.5
1988	4.8
1989	6.0
1990	8.0

Source: Lotus Development Corporation 10-K Reports.

graphics and information management, information services, and database management categories. Freelance Plus is a popular graphics package that provides a comprehensive set of graphics, including charting, diagrams, freehand drawing, and presentation management tools. In the information management category, major products are Agenda, Magellan, and Notes. In addition to applications software, Lotus markets a number of information services and related software under the name Lotus One Source. These enable personal computer users to access and manage data available from various external databases. The One Source product line consists of an expanding variety of offerings tailored for specific uses such as banking and mergers and acquisitions. A database management product is currently under development for the OS/2 environment. A summary of Lotus's major product offerings is provided in Exhibit 2.

In its early years, Lotus was virtually a one product (1-2-3), one environment (DOS) company. As recently as 1989, 72 percent of its revenues came from its spreadsheet product, 1-2-3. In recent years, Lotus has pursued a two-pronged strategy of protecting its dominance in the spreadsheet segment while reducing dependence on 1-2-3 by diversifying its product line.

Lotus has taken several steps to protect its dominance in the spreadsheet segment of the software industry. First, it has expanded into developing spreadsheet products for different operating environments and different platforms. The first move in this direction was Jazz. Introduced in 1985, Jazz was designed for Macintosh users, but the product was not successful: users found it sluggish and its capabilities were too limited.[14] The company announced plans to develop an enhanced version, Modern Jazz, but delays and development problems caused Lotus to abandon the idea in June 1988. This signaled a temporary withdrawal from the Macintosh segment.

Most of the development effort at Lotus between 1987 and 1989 focused on 1-2-3 Release 3.0. This was a major upgrade of the original 1-2-3 including many new features and improvements, such as a three-dimensional worksheet environment, enhanced support for databases inside the worksheet, file linking, and faster recalculation techniques. While aimed at the OS/2 environment, the product maintained compatibility with earlier versions of 1-2-3, and represented a major step toward the company's goal of developing a spread-

[14] Guterman, J. (1988, May 24). Lotus holds back on Modern Jazz, one more time. *PC Week*, p. 11.

EXHIBIT 2
Lotus Product Menu

	Decision Support Products
Lotus 1-2-3	The spreadsheet program that has been Lotus's flagship product. Release 3 has been completely rewritten in C programming language to allow 1-2-3 to run on several computers including the IBM PC. Major features include three-dimensional spreadsheets that work with multiple files simultaneously; direct access to external databases, direct printing of graphics, merged text, and graphics on one page; and support of more memory (above 640K). Release 2.2 is a major upgrade which can run on older-generation computers, incorporating better graphics and printer support.
Agenda	Lotus' personal information manager features artificial recognition capabilities, such as pattern matching, automatic recognition, and assignments of dates. Agenda is highly flexible but the startup cost in terms of time spent creating the database could be a barrier to wider acceptance.
	Word Processing/Integrated
Manuscript	A high-end word processor with desktop publishing capabilities, Manuscript's appeal has been largely in scientific and technical applications. It can combine text, graphics, and spreadsheets on the same page.
Symphony	Combines spreadsheet, word processing, database, graphics, and communications functions in one package. The growth of the integrated software market has been slower than projected, but Symphony has a large percentage of the total market.
	Graphics
Freelance +	Graphics software that works with or without Lotus 1-2-3 or Symphony. It combines charting and diagramming functions. Acquired by Lotus in 1986.
Graphwriter II	Production charting software. Links to spreadsheet for frequently updated charts; can put multiple charts on one page. Acquired by Lotus in 1986.
	Tools, Utility, and Communication Products
Magellan	A disk management system (indexing).
Data Lens	An application programming interface which provides bidirectional access to external databases.
Lotus Metro	Memory-resident desktop manager combining keystroke macro recording, phone book, calculator, list manager, ODS file manager, simple word processor, and clock.
Notes	A document-oriented database that enables work teams to maintain and access data. It includes built-in word processing and e. mail capabilities.
	Information Products
One Source Database	Financial database that imports Compustat and other data sources into Lotus 1-2-3.
CD/Networker	Combines the information available from One Source with local area network support. The Networker, a dedicated 386-based PC on a LAN, manages requests from the network users to multiple CD ROMs.

sheet product operable across a mix of platforms and environments. The development of 1-2-3/3.0 was plagued by repeated delays and many missed deadlines. Although product delays are common in the industry, the delay in shipping 1-2-3/3.0 shook Lotus's reputation for tight management.[15] Furthermore, the sales of 3.0 have lagged behind expectations.

[15] Bulkeley, W. M. (1988, August 30). Slowing down. *The Wall Street Journal,* pp. 1, 12.

This is mainly attributed to users continuing with earlier DOS versions. Still, Lotus continues to vigorously pursue a strategy of offering versions of 1-2-3 for different types of equipment and operating environments. 1-2-3/G is a new spreadsheet product designed for the OS/2 Presentation Manager operating system. 1-2-3/M is a version that works on IBM mainframes. Other versions so far developed include 1-2-3/Unix for Sun workstations as well as 1-2-3 for VAX/VMS and 1-2-3 for ALL-IN-1 for Digital Equipment Corporation's mainframe computers. A new version of 1-2-3, compatible with Windows, a graphical interface that is capable of running on older PCs, has also been under development. As Richard Shaffer, editor of the *Technologic Computer Letter* recently stated, "Lotus has moved in the last few years from a one-product company to a one-category company. Their multiplatform strategy is to dominate the spreadsheet category on every platform and to expand into other logical businesses including consulting services".[16]

Lotus has also offered their products in several different languages for overseas markets. Lotus products are currently available in French, German, Spanish, Italian, Swedish, Dutch, Portuguese, and Japanese. Within 2 months after its introduction in September 1986, the Japanese language version, which incorporated special features Japanese users wanted, became the best-selling software in Japan. In February 1987, 1-2-3/J received the prestigious Nikkei Award for Creative Excellence.

Lotus has also offered various add-on and add-in applications that supplement the basic spreadsheet in order to enhance 1-2-3's competitive position. Add-on packages, such as Freelance Plus, are loaded before entering 1-2-3 and remain in memory, ready to spring into action by special key strokes. Add-in packages such as HAL, on the other hand, share information and resources directly with 1-2-3 and are loaded into memory from within 1-2-3.[17]

Yet another element in Lotus's strategy of protecting its position in the spreadsheet market is providing various value-added services to high-volume users. Services such as the Corporate Accounts Program and the MultiValue Plan include support, training, and distribution. Support includes a telephone hotline and technical support to create spreadsheet "templates." The company organizes training centers and executive briefings and offers direct purchase agreements for large orders.

While trying to protect their position in the spreadsheet market, Lotus has also been simultaneously attempting to reduce their dependence on the 1-2-3 family of products by pursuing an aggressive strategy of product diversification. For example, Lotus has attempted an entry into the booming network software market with the introduction of Notes in late 1989. The company has introduced various information management and graphics products in recent years with mixed results.

Lotus uses internal development, strategic alliances, and acquisitions to implement its twin strategies of spreadsheet market domination and product diversification. Core products, such as various upgrades of 1-2-3, are developed almost entirely internally. In cases where internal development would be either too costly or would involve too much delay, the company prefers acquisitions. Lotus seeks young companies with promising products under development for acquisition. Recent major acquisitions include GNP, maker of HAL, Graphics Communication, maker of Freelance and Datext,

---

[16] Lyons, D. J. (1990, January 15). The new Lotus position: Consulting, direct sales. *PC Week*, pp. 1, 8.

[17] McLaughlin, H. S., & Sullivan, T. G. (1988, June). Integrating and processing with spreadsheets: Add-ons vs. add-ins. *Journal of Accountancy*, p. 124.

Inc., a provider of business reference information delivered on high-capacity optical disc (CD-ROM) media.

Lotus tried to establish a significant presence in the fast-growing network software market through a merger in 1989 with Novell, the Provo, Utah, based supplier of network operating software that had a 42 percent market share, but the merger never materialized. In November 1990, Lotus acquired Samna Corporation, a small maker of word processing software, for $65 million. Because the purchase price amounted to 5.9 times Samna's 1989 sales and 14 times its book value, many analysts feel that Lotus significantly overpaid for this acquisition. Lotus hopes that Samna, which specializes in word processing packages for Windows such as Ami and Ami Professional, may be able to exploit the increasing demand for software that supports Windows.[18]

Lotus has also entered into several strategic alliances to enhance their position in specific product market niches. An important alliance is the long-term deal with IBM. This involves Lotus and IBM jointly developing and marketing products for a full range of computers. IBM partially funds these projects, and retains exclusive distribution rights. Similar arrangements have been signed with Digital Equipment Corporation and Sun Microsystems. The agreement with DEC provides Lotus access to DEC's 9,000-member sales force.[19] In September 1989, Lotus entered into a strategic business alliance with Sybase, Inc., of Emeryville, California, a leader in relational database technology. This alliance included the acquisition of a 15 percent equity interest in Sybase and an agreement providing for joint development, marketing, and distribution of future products.

Another facet of Lotus's strategy is to be interoperable with other programs. Lotus and WordPerfect recently unveiled plans to develop a common interface that links applications under the OS/2 PM operation system. The association between the two companies will allow users of Lotus 1-2-3/G and WordPerfect 5.1 to share common commands and pull data from 1-2-3 spreadsheets into WordPerfect documents.[20] WordPerfect holds approximately 55 to 60 percent share of the word processing market, and 90 percent of WordPerfect users overlap to Lotus.[21] This alliance brings two market leaders together, a move that should further strengthen the dominance of the two companies. "We don't intend to be No. 1 in personal computer software," says Manzi, Lotus' CEO. "We intend to be No. 1 in software, period."[22]

MARKETING, OPERATIONS, AND FINANCIAL STRATEGIES

Initially, Lotus distributed its products through hardware manufacturers, operating systems suppliers, retailers, and a direct sales force. Lotus also used relatively new channels—

[18] Bulkeley, W. M. (1990, November 2). Lotus, hard-pressed by Microsoft, agrees to buy small software firm. *The Wall Street Journal*, p. B4.

[19] Martin, J. (1989, November 13). Lotus shows strategic targeting of mixed environments. *PC Week*, *6*(45), 116.

[20] Lewis, G. (1989, December 3). Two software leaders join forces. *The New York Times*, p. 14F.

[21] Giglio, L. (1990, January 12). 90% of WordPerfect users also use Lotus 1-2-3. *Investment Research*, p. 59.

[22] Field, A. R., & Bearn, A. (1987, May 25). Lotus's dream-come-true: A sweet deal with IBM. *Business Week*, p. 116.

corporate accounts and value-added resellers (VARs). (VARs add additional packages or support to a given product.) In mid-1984, Lotus announced it would no longer sell directly to corporate customers; instead it would depend on dealers and distributors.

In 1987, Lotus became the first major spreadsheet developer to issue its own catalog. The catalog, LotusSelects, includes add-on products for 1-2-3 and Symphony. To avoid competing with its own dealers it does not list either 1-2-3 or Symphony. In 1988, Lotus introduced the 1-2-3 Small Business Kit which includes, in addition to 1-2-3, financial management tools (templates for financial statements, financial ratios, and cash flows, for example) and 6 months of toll-free telephone support. Through this development, Lotus hopes to reach the small businesses that the firm's officials believe make up the bulk of future growth in sales of PC software and hardware.[23]

In January 1989, Lotus announced that it would raise the wholesale price of 1-2-3 and eliminate volume discounts for its dealers. Instead, Lotus provided rebates to dealers on the basis of the customer support they offered. This strategy was designed to give more power to the retailer who uses strong sales programs and training. This strategy also serves to decrease the influence of mail order and discount dealers.

EXHIBIT 3
Lotus Development, Inc.: Income Statements, 1985–1990
Years Ended December 31
(in Thousands of Dollars, Except per Share Data)

	1985	*1986*	*1987*	*1988*	*1989*	*1990*
Net sales	$225,526	$282,864	$395,595	$468,547	$556,033	$684,512
Cost of sales	43,706	54,724	68,676	$107,033	113,577	142,014
Gross margin	$181,820	$228,140	$326,919	$361,514	$442,456	$542,498
Costs and expenses:						
Research and development	$ 22,324	$ 39,167	$ 58,420	$ 67,629	$ 85,715	$102,650
Sales and marketing	76,376	87,455	126,848	170,750	221,745	275,874
General and administrative	22,189	37,662	46,546	54,124	61,078	62,497
Charge for purchased research and development	--	--	--	--	--	52,966
Total operating expenses	$120,889	$164,284	$231,814	$292,503	$368,538	$493,987
Operating income	$ 60,931	$ 63,856	$ 95,105	$ 69,011	$ 73,918	48,511
Interest income, net*	3,932	3,311	3,960	9,568	5,644	6,094
Other income	2,540	3,863	3,853	1,295	5,389	(1,779)
Income before provision for income taxes	$ 67,403	$ 71,030	$102,918	$ 79,874	$ 84,951	$ 52,826
Provision for income taxes*	29,253	22,730	30,875	20,949	16,990	29,572
Net income	$ 38,150	$ 48,300	$ 72,043	$ 58,925	$ 67,961	$ 23,254
Net income per share	$0.77	$1.03	$1.58	$1.29	$1.61	$0.54
Weighted average common shares and common share equivalents outstanding	49,596	46,752	45,720	45,551	42,301	43,100

* Net interest income and other income combined in 1989.
Source: 1985–1989 Lotus Development Corporation Annual Reports.

Continued

[23] Karon, P. (1988, July 11). After stormy spring, a more mature Lotus aims at $500M market. *PC Week*, pp. 127, 135.

EXHIBIT 3 (cont.)
Lotus Development, Inc.: Consolidated Balance Sheets (In Thousands of Dollars)

	1985	1986	1987	1988	1989	1990
Assets						
Current assets:						
Cash and temporary cash investments	$ 91,053	$ 93,157	$164,909	$192,433	$274,977	$245,386
Accounts receivable less doubtful allowance	36,433	37,844	45,541	92,035	97,712	120,346
Inventory	9,147	6,794	9,210	18,088	23,171	21,700
Prepaid expenses and other current assets	2,416	6,396	5,665	7,430	13,937	12,036
Total current assets	$139,049	$144,191	$225,325	$309,986	$409,797	$399,468
Property and equipment	$ 38,203	$ 40,964	$ 51,920	$ 86,953	$129,702	$147,758
Software and intangibles	$ 8,124	$ 23,270	$ 32,297	$ 16,026	$ 27,100	$ 62,074
Investments and other assets	$ 427	$ 584	$ 8,111	$ 9,157	$ 37,678	$ 47,507
Total assets	$185,803	$209,009	$317,653	$422,122	$604,277	$656,807
Liabilities and Stockholders' Equity						
Current liabilities:						
Notes payable	$ 3,514	$ 2,680	$ 7,736	$ 9,441	$ 2,975	$ 5,661
Accrued employment compensation	3,914	11,350	15,287	11,771	17,688	23,305
Accounts payable and accrued expenses	17,085	30,554	31,685	45,491	63,125	87,074
Deferred revenue	3,550	6,221	11,734	16,592	15,798	16,386
Income taxes payable	17,365	12,055	19,165	1,231	10,253	40,081
Total current liabilities	$ 45,428	$ 62,860	$ 85,607	$ 84,526	$109,839	$172,507
Deferred income taxes	$ 1,833	$ 1,556	--	$ 10,400	$ 13,693	$ 14,861
Long-term debt	--	$ 30,000	$ 30,000	$ 95,000	$202,440	$160,000
Commitments and contingencies	--	--	--	--	--	--
Total liabilities	$ 47,261	$ 94,416	$115,607	$189,926	$325,972	$347,368
Stockholders' equity:						
Preferred stock	--	--	--	--	--	--
Common stock	$ 171	$ 526	$ 546	$ 556	$ 579	$ 591
Additional paid-in capital	59,044	66,624	83,274	109,429	139,762	157,368
Retained earnings	87,368	135,317	207,360	266,285	334,246	357,500
Treasury stock	(3)	(83,135)	(87,743)	(144,030)	(194,937)	(206,587)
Translation adjustment	(247)	(776)	243	3	(1,345)	567
Deferred employee compensation	(7,791)	(3,963)	(1,634)	(47)	--	--
Total stockholders' equity	$138,542	$114,593	$202,046	$232,196	$278,305	$309,439
Total liabilities and stockholders' equity	$185,803	$209,009	$317,653	$422,122	$604,277	$656,807

Source: 1985–1989 Lotus Development Corporation Annual Reports.

The manufacturing operations of Lotus include duplicating diskettes, fabricating binders and slipcases, assembling purchased parts, and final packaging. The company has adopted alternate means to maintain low operating costs. First, Lotus uses its manufacturing plant in Ireland to supply most of the international market. Second, a facility in Puerto Rico produces most of 1-2-3 sold in North America. Third, only low-volume and new

EXHIBIT 4
Comparative Financial Information: Microsoft and Ashton-Tate

	Microsoft		*Ashton-Tate*	
	1989	*1990*	*1989*	*1990*
Net sales (in thousands of dollars)	$803,530	$1,183,446	$265,319	$230,537
Net income (in thousands of dollars)	$170,538	$ 279,186	($ 28,642)	($ 18,065)
Selected financial ratios:				
Quick ratio	2.59	3.37	2.25	1.96
Current ratio	2.95	3.85	3.00	2.41
Accounts receivable turnover	7.23	6.54	6.26	6.30
Net sales/employees	199,041	210,017	185,538	142,483
Total liability/total assets	0.22	0.17	0.26	0.31
Net income/sales	0.21	0.24	(0.11)	(0.08)
Net income/total assets	0.12	0.23	(0.11)	(0.07)

products are manufactured in its Massachusetts plant. The off-shore manufacturing facilities provide lower labor costs as well as tax benefits. The increased volume of sales has enabled Lotus to take advantage of economies of scale.

Lotus has traditionally pursued a conservative financial strategy and has always been in a strong financial position. The company raised $4.7 million in venture capital in 1982 on the strength of 1-2-3. Its strong financial performance in the first half of 1983 enabled it to raise $4 million through a public stock offering. In recent years, Lotus has increased its long-term debt from zero in 1985 to over $160 million in 1990. Most of this debt has been used for acquisitions and the repurchase of stock. As of 1990, Lotus had never paid cash dividends. Exhibit 3 provides balance sheet and income statement information. Exhibit 4 contains comparative financial information for two of the other leading firms in the PC software industry, Microsoft and Ashton-Tate.

LOTUS'S TOP MANAGEMENT, CULTURE, AND ORGANIZATION STRUCTURE

By 1990, the two key executives at Lotus were Jim Manzi and Frank King. Jim Manzi first became involved with Lotus in November 1982, as a consultant working for McKinsey and Company, a well-known international consulting firm. At Kapor's urging, he joined Lotus in May 1983 as director of corporate marketing. In September 1983, he was named vice president of marketing and sales. His strategy for marketing 1-2-3 was so successful that he was promoted to president in October 1984 and later named CEO in April 1986. Kapor and Manzi jointly led the company until July 1986 when Kapor decided to leave the company. His exit was viewed with considerable concern by many outsiders. For example, one industry analyst commented:

> With Kapor's departure from the chairmanship of the company, we imagine that Lotus will lower its research and development sights. We imagine it will strive—like

most other PC software companies—simply to produce a profitable product rather than try to invent a new class of tools.[24]

This prediction appeared to become true. Manzi turned Lotus into a market-driven company and relieved the firm of much of the risk associated with new-product development. He did this by purchasing most of Lotus's new products through the acquisitions of smaller companies. By contrast, Mitch Kapor went on to head a software company, ON Technology, devoted to developing new products.[25]

Many consider Manzi ruthless and arrogant. During the course of Lotus's expansion and continual reorganization, he fired between 50 and 100 people.[26] He replaced many of Kapor's executives, including six of seventeen vice presidents during a 5-month period in early 1988. The discipline brought by the new management team, most from larger companies, has changed the corporate culture; jeans and T-shirts have been replaced by suits and ties.[27] "Much has been made in the popular press about how Kapor's Hawaiian-shirt sushi-eating software developer's culture has been replaced by Manzi's business suits and tough attitudes."[28]

In March 1988, Manzi named Frank King as senior vice president of the Software Products Group. Mr. King, with 17 years of experience in IBM's Entry Systems Division, is generally viewed as a tough manager who could bring a needed element of discipline to the software group. Although he oversaw the RT PC, a slow-selling technical workstation that many felt was underpowered and overpriced, he was also responsible for the group that created the highly successful PS/2 computer line.[29] King provided a voice in upper management for the software group. Two of the changes brought about by King were putting an end to "vaporware" (announcing a product before it is in the final test stage) and abandoning Modern Jazz, an upgrade of Jazz, that was still in the developmental stage.[30] King also initiated the development of 1-2-3 version 2.2 which incorporated several new features but was still able to run on smaller and older machines.

During this period, Lotus underwent some major changes in its organization structure. In 1986, Lotus had a functional-type structure, including finance and operations, international and information services, sales and service, marketing and business development, and research and development. By 1990, however, Lotus had evolved into a divisional-type organization structure. This change in structure was attributed to expanded international operations and greater product-market diversity. (International sales were largely dependent on 1-2-3 spreadsheet software but the domestic sales were much more diverse.) This development led to the creation of four business groups, including a separate division for international operations. These groups operate in conjunction with two functional departments: (1) finance and operations and (2) corporate communications. Lotus's organizational structure is depicted in Exhibit 5.

---

[24] Lotus is diminished without Kapor, p. 36.

[25] Bulkeley, W. M., op. cit., pp. 1, 12.

[26] Nulty, P. (1989, February 29). America's toughest bosses. *Fortune*, p. 50.

[27] Hammonds, K. H., Brandt, R., & Field, A. R. (1987, November 16). The drill instructor who made Lotus snap to attention. *Business Week*, pp. 190–192.

[28] Wilder, C. (1988, September 12). The firm they love to hate. *Computerworld*, pp. 115, 118.

[29] Hammonds, K. H. (1988, July 4). Teaching discipline to six year olds. *Business Week*, p. 100.

[30] Ibid.

EXHIBIT 5
Lotus Development Corporation Organizational Structure, 1990

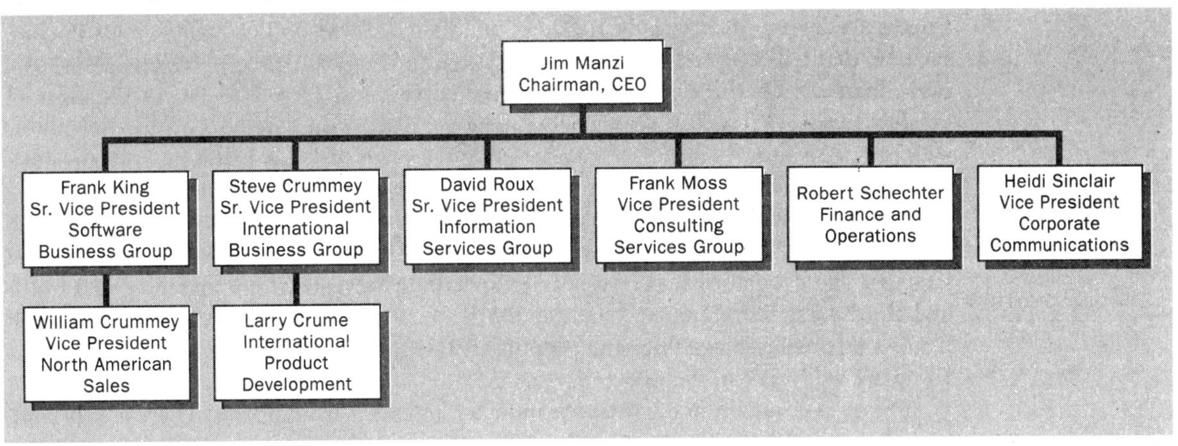

Sources: Harrington, M. J. (1990, March 26). Lotus juggles company structure. *Computerworld,* p. 6; Lotus set to become software consultant, revamp its business. *The Wall Street Journal* (1990, March 21), p. B4; and Lotus Development Corporation announces reorganization to decentralize company operations. *Business Wire* (1990, March 20), Cambridge, MA.

KEY ISSUES FACING LOTUS IN THE 1990s

After a decade of explosive growth, the PC software industry has entered a period of slowing growth rates. During most of the 1980s, first-time buyers, both business and individual, seemed to have an insatiable demand for personal computers and the software that runs on them. Currently, the growth rate of installed PCs has dropped while the survival rate of older PCs remains high. Competition among existing rivals for higher market shares has intensified. As the 1990s began, Lotus, like most software companies, faced many difficult decisions with very little margin for error.

A critical issue facing Lotus—or any organization in the computer hardware or software industry—is the rapid rate of change of technology. This forces firms within the industry to commit resources to specific courses of action with little certainty about the outcome. For example, prior to the release of OS/2, there was widespread expectation that it would become the operating system standard for newer and more powerful IBM-compatible PCs. However, a significant percentage of users have shown little hurry in abandoning MS-DOS, the previous standard. Meanwhile, Microsoft has also released a graphical interface called Windows which enhances DOS's capabilities. Most customers, unsure about which systems will eventually prevail, appear to have adopted a cautious wait and see strategy. Lotus, which enthusiastically embraced OS/2 in the development of 1-2-3 Release 3 suddenly found itself faced with a difficult decision about choosing an operating system.

Competition within the spreadsheet segment of the software industry is gradually undergoing a significant change. Ever since it replaced VisiCalc in the number 1 position in the spreadsheet segment in 1983, 1-2-3 has enjoyed unquestioned leadership within this niche. However, in recent years, Microsoft's Excel and Borland International's Quattro (priced well below 1-2-3) have been making steady inroads into 1-2-3's market share. Based on a survey of large companies, Computer Intelligence Corp., a market research firm, forecasts a drop in purchases of 1-2-3.[31] The 1990 *PC Week* poll of corporate satisfaction revealed that 1-2-3 ranked below Quattro, Excel, and SuperCalc 5 in overall reliability and performance.[32] Of the eight products in the survey, 1-2-3 came in last in the areas of product support access (on-screen help functions) and product support quality (telephone support). This indicated that the market no longer viewed 1-2-3 as the superior product. Lotus had to face the fact that their market leadership was possibly due to switching costs a user incurs in purchase price and training. Realizing the long-term consequences of this slip in performance, Lotus initiated a series of measures to improve the level of their product support. These included the creation of a Consulting Services Group that integrates Lotus and third-party software products for the company's clients. Jim Manzi believes that Lotus's expansion into service and support areas is the most important strategic move the company will make in the next few years.[33]

Piracy is common in the software industry and takes many forms. There is a thriving underground market in many Far Eastern countries for pirated software which sells at a fraction of the original price. Individual users often make copies of software they have and exchange it with fellow users. Yet another common form of piracy is corporate duplicating of a software program for multiple in-house use.[34] For a very long time, Lotus had refused to allow site licensing, common in the mainframe market, which allows regulated copying of software on a companywide basis.[35]

Regarded as a company quicker than most to sue, Lotus has initiated several lawsuits to protect what it considers its intellectual properties. In 1984, Lotus "stunned the industry by dragging a subsidiary of Schlumberger, the oil services firm, into court for software piracy."[36] Lotus finally dropped the copy protection code within 1-2-3 in May 1988. Lotus has taken heat from its customers for continuing copy protection long after most major software companies dropped it.[37] In June 1990, Lotus won a closely followed lawsuit against Paperback Software International for violating its copyright on 1-2-3. Emboldened by this victory, Lotus filed suits against Borland International and Santa Cruz Operations Incorporated for similar violations. Lotus's aggressive policy of suing rivals could potentially act as a powerful entry deterrent to many small firms who may be contemplating entry into the spreadsheet business.[38]

As the growth rate of the U.S. software market is slowing down, most software producers realize that a significant part of the future growth must come from international operations. Lotus has undertaken several steps to become a truly international company. The company currently has manufacturing facilities in Cambridge, Massachusetts, Caguas,

---

[31] Bulkeley, W. M., op. cit., pp. 1, 12.

[32] Quattro, Excel top Lotus releases in buyer survey. (1990, January 22). *PC Week*, pp. 87–89.

[33] Lyons, D. J. (1990, January 15). The new Lotus position: Consulting, direct sales. *PC Week*, pp. 1, 6.

[34] Tangorra, J. (1984, August 24). The fight against software piracy. *Publisher's Weekly*, pp. 34–40.

[35] Gillin, P. (1986, January 14). Site licensing gains favor: Lotus resists. *PC Week*, pp. 131–133.

[36] Petre, P., op. cit., p. 138.

[37] Freedman, B. (1988, May 17). Lotus to end copy protection of 1-2-3, plans utility-disk release. *PC Week*, p. 1.

[38] Bulkeley, W. M. (1990, July 29). Lotus development wins suit charging Paperback Software violated copyright. *The Wall Street Journal*, p. A4; and Suskind, R. (1990, July 3). Lotus takes hard line on software. *The Wall Street Journal*, pp. B1, B5.

EXHIBIT 6
Growth in International Sales, 1984–1990

Year	*Foreign Sales (In Millions of Dollars)**	*Percentage of Foreign Sales/Total Sales*
1985	$ 30.3	13%
1986	53.5	19
1987	97.6	25
1988	147.6	31
1989	204.5	37
1990	293.1	43

* Sales outside of North America.
Source: Lotus Development Corporation Annual Reports.

Puerto Rico, and Dublin, Ireland. In recent years, Lotus has also opened offices in many cities, including Milan and Sydney, to serve growing overseas markets. Great Britain and Japan are Lotus's strongest foreign markets. In Japan, considered the fastest growing regional market, Lotus has formed a wholly owned subsidiary. By 1990, international sales accounted for 43 percent of total revenues, a percentage that is expected to grow even further. Exhibit 6 indicates the increasing contribution of foreign sales to Lotus's total revenue.

In spite of these early successes in foreign markets, it might be premature to assume continued competitive success for Lotus or other U.S. software producers. Many foreign markets are much smaller than the American market and techniques developed for mass marketing in the United States may not be readily applicable in these countries. Some countries are multilingual, necessitating multiple versions of the same product. Many nations impose tariffs on U.S. software products, thereby reducing their price competitiveness. Other countries do not have well-developed copyright protection laws and many of those who have them are lax about enforcement. Bootlegged versions, easily available at a fraction of the original price, make it virtually impossible for companies like Lotus to operate profitably in many foreign markets. In some countries in the Far East it is even considered a compliment to copy another's product. Also, in some countries, trademarks can legally be taken preemptively by domestic firms that hope to exploit Lotus's reputation in the industry. In these countries Lotus is required to market their products under different names.

Although U.S. companies today enjoy near-complete domination of the world software industry, over the next few years competitors may emerge from other countries, as has been the case with so many mature industries, such as automobiles and consumer electronics. The increasing availability of personal computers and the diffusion of related knowledge all over the world could result in potential competitors emerging from a variety of other countries in the coming years. The low capital requirements and the very high knowledge intensity of the software industry means that a creative programmer anywhere in the world could produce a successful software product. The increasing availability of software programmers abroad, at what is often less than half the U.S. wages, provides several potential foreign competitors with a cost advantage. Thus, as Lotus enters the 1990s, it is clear that it has to come up with a strategy for long-term international competitiveness.

THE SOFT DRINK INDUSTRY

CASE 13

The Seven-Up Co., Division of Philip Morris Incorporated*

Philip Morris Incorporated was a leading international marketer of cigarettes and had increased its share of the U.S. cigarette market from 15 percent in 1970 to 35 percent in 1984. Philip Morris acquired the Miller Brewing Company in 1970 and engineered its growth from the seventh largest to the second largest U.S. brewery by 1977. In 1979 Philip Morris acquired the Seven-Up Co., the number three concentrate producer in the United States. After four years of losses, Seven-Up had registered an operating profit in 1984. Industry analysts were debating the role that Seven-Up would play in Philip Morris's future (see Exhibit 1).

HISTORY OF THE SEVEN-UP CO.

The Seven-Up Co. was founded in 1920 in St. Louis, Missouri, as the partnership of three men—C. L. Grigg, E. G. Ridgway, and F. Y. Gladney. Originally the company produced an orange drink, but in 1929 it introduced its "BIB Label Lithiated Lemon-Lime Soda." Renamed Seven-Up in 1937, the drink had to compete with over 600 lemon-lime drinks in the U.S. market. The company designed an attractive green bottle for Seven-Up, which was clear, unlike the caramel colored colas.

Seven-Up began to work to persuade bottlers of other soft drinks to market Seven-Up. Seven-Up managers took pride in the close, cooperative relations that they worked to establish with their bottlers. They always referred to their bottlers as "Developers" in order to demonstrate the importance that they placed on their bottlers' sales effort.

World War II sugar rationing helped to increase Seven-Up's U.S. sales because Seven-Up, using less sugar, was able to produce relatively more units than Coca-Cola and Pepsi-Cola were allowed during this period. After the war, Seven-Up emphasized its product's medicinal benefits, both for children (with such slogans as "Tune Tiny Tummies") and for adults (with such slogans as "Cure for Seven Hangovers"). The product was also widely used as a mixer for alcoholic beverages. Seven-Up plus Seagram's Seven Crown whiskey became a particularly popular drink.

By the 1950s Seven-Up had achieved national distribution through its franchise network. Seven-Up established and owned a small number of bottling operations. The vast

EXHIBIT 1

Financial Statistics on Philip Morris Incorporated

	1973	1974	1975	1976	1977	1978	1979	1980	1981	1982	1983	1984
Corporate:												
Total revenues	$2,603.0	$3,011.0	$3,642.0	$4,294.0	$5,202.0	$6,633.0	$8,149.0	$9,650.0	$10,722.0	$11,586.0	$12,976.0	$13,814.0
Net income	$ 149.0	$ 176.0	$ 212.0	$ 266.0	$ 335.0	$ 409.0	$ 507.0	$ 549.0	$ 660	$ 782.0	$ 904.0	$ 889.0
Net income/sales	5.7%	5.8%	5.8%	6.2%	6.4%	6.2%	6.2%	5.7%	6.2%	6.7%	7.0%	6.4%
Return on equity	18.3%	18.1%	17.3%	18.6%	19.8%	19.3%	20.5%	19.4%	20.4%	21.3%	22.4%	21.7%
Long-term debt/ total capital	41.3%	42.6%	44.5%	42.9%	1.7%	40.9%	42.1%	41.0%	40.9%	40.1%	36.8%	34.8%
Total operating income	$ 329.0	$ 404.0	$ 493.0	$ 635.0	$ 783.0	$ 968.0	$1,191.0	$1,273.0	$ 1,446.0	$ 1,716.0	$ 1,958.0	$ 2,346.0
Total capital expenditures	$ 174.7	$ 215.8	$ 244.5	$ 220.2	$ 279.8	$ 566.2	$ 629.4	$ 750.8	$ 1,018.5	$ 918.2	$ 566.2	$ 298.1
For tobacco	$ 105.2	$ 127.4	$ 149.9	$ 101.3	$ 143.2	$ 327.8	$ 321.7	$ 415.3	$ 633.5	$ 498.9	$ 319.9	$ 163.1
For beer	$ 59.6	$ 79.6	$ 88.9	$ 111.9	$ 126.3	$ 221.2	$ 259.3	$ 261.1	$ 328.9	$ 286.3	$ 174.6	$ 93.6
For 7UP	--	--	--	--	--	--	$ 29.1	$ 41.2	$ 35.2	$ 86.5	$ 49.9	$ 30.9
For industrial packaging	$ 9.9	$ 8.8	$ 5.7	$ 7.0	$ 10.3	$ 17.2	$ 19.3	$ 33.2	$ 20.9	$ 46.5	$ 21.8	$ 10.5

Source: Philip Morris annual reports.

majority of Seven-Up developers were bottlers for Coca-Cola, Pepsi-Cola, and RC Cola. Like Royal Crown, Seven-Up was particularly strong in the U.S. Midwest. Seven-Up sold its concentrate for approximately 15 percent more than Coca-Cola did because Seven-Up used less sugar, thus saving its bottlers some of the cost of sweetener. At retail, Seven-Up sold at prices comparable to Coca-Cola.

In the 1960s the company found through research that its consumption was significantly skewed toward older buyers and that the product was frequently viewed as an aid for indigestion or as a mixer but not as a soft drink. In 1968 Seven-Up launched its "Uncola" advertising campaign, designed to position Seven-Up as a soft-drink alternative to colas. The target market for the effort was the 16- to 24-year-old group. The campaign used Geoffrey Holder, a Jamaican actor with a distinctive sound and style, to convey the message. The television advertisements received high advertising recall ratings. Seven-Up became the dominant soft drink in the lemon-lime category, which comprised approximately 12 percent of the total soft drink market during the 1960s and the 1970s. The second best selling lemon-lime soft drink was Sprite, introduced by Coca-Cola in 1961. Seven-Up introduced a diet version of its product in 1970.

Seven-Up, like other concentrate producers, adopted many new packages during the 1960s and 1970s. In 1971 Seven-Up was the first company to use the plasti-shield glass bottle, introducing it in 12-ounce and 16-ounce sizes. In 1974 and 1975 Seven-Up could not obtain sufficient supplies of 32-ounce and 64-ounce plasti-shield glass bottles, which were the fastest growing package sizes.

Seven-Up did not enter the fountain market until 1960. However, by 1970, fountain sales represented 7 percent of Seven-Up unit sales, and by 1974 they were 12 percent. Seven-Up succeeded in convincing most of the major fast-food chains to direct their outlets to allocate one or two of their fountain dispensers (usually four or five per outlet) to Seven-Up products. In 1975 Seven-Up persuaded McDonald's to distribute sugar-free Seven-Up to all its outlets, the first time a major chain had taken on a diet drink. Seven-Up bottlers handled distribution of the product to individual fountain outlets. By 1976 Seven-Up had achieved the following distribution in the top 10 fast-food chains:

Seven-Up Distribution in Leading Fast-Food Chains, 1976

Chain	*Share of Fast-Food Market, %*	*Type of 7UP Sold*
1. McDonald's	20.0%	Sugar-free
2. Kentucky Fried Chicken	11.7	Regular
3. International Dairy Queen	6.0	Regular
4. Burger King	4.8	Both
5. Burger Chef	2.8	Sugar-free
6. A&W International	2.7	Both
7. Hardee's	2.6	Sugar-free
8. Denny's	2.6	Regular
9. Jack-in-the-Box	2.5	Not sold
10. Pizza Hut	2.5	Regular

Seven-Up also began to expand internationally during the 1960s and 1970s. It was sold in 89 countries by 1977, holding a minor share in each market, smaller than its share in the United States. As in the United States, Seven-Up was usually bottled internationally by bottlers of Coca-Cola or Pepsi-Cola.

In the late 1970s, the three founding families of the Seven-Up Co. still controlled 55 percent of the company. The other 45 percent had been sold in 1967 through a public stock offering. The company sold 9 of its 13 company-owned bottlers between 1975 and 1979. In 1979 Philip Morris bought the Seven-Up Co. for $520 million.

PHILIP MORRIS INCORPORATED

Philip Morris was founded before the turn of the century and held a minor share of the U.S. tobacco market before World War II. The industry was dominated by the American Tobacco Company, which held over 40 percent of the market. After decades of mediocre performance Philip Morris decided in 1953 to reposition its Marlboro brand, which had been introduced in 1924 and previously targeted toward women. The new positioning and advertising theme employed began to gain market share.

Cigarettes were highly subject to taxation. *Tobacco Industry,* a trade journal, estimated the following distribution of the end consumer dollar for cigarettes in 1981 and 1983:[1]

Percent of Each Consumer Dollar Spent for Cigarettes

Sector	*1981*	*1983*
Federal, state, and local taxes (excise, sales, and corporate income)	39%	44%
Wholesale and retail markups (excluding state and local taxes)	18	16
Product costs (leaf, labor, distribution, advertising, nontobacco materials, interest and general business overhead, net earnings, costs necessary to make and market the product)	43	40
Total	100%	100%

Tobacco leaf accounted for approximately 40 percent of the full production cost of cigarettes. Philip Morris engaged in extensive research and development regarding the growing, selection, curing, and blending of tobacco leaf. Tobacco leaf needed to be cured and dried for one year after it was purchased by the cigarette manufacturers before it could be used. At the end of 1984 Philip Morris had $2.2 billion in tobacco leaf inventory. The cigarette manufacturing process was capital-intensive and highly automated.

Manufacturers sold their cigarettes to independent wholesalers who in turn distributed the cigarettes along with hundreds of different products to many kinds of retail outlets and directly to major retail store chains. The companies employed sales forces who worked with wholesalers and retail chains to help gain fuller distribution for products and in particular to gain distribution for new brands.

In 1964 the U.S. Surgeon General announced findings that cigarette smoking was potentially hazardous to one's health, and by 1967 the Food and Drug Administration (FDA) ruled that cigarette packages sold in the United States would have to carry a health warning. In 1971 by act of Congress, cigarette advertising was banned from television.

[1] *Tobacco Industry,* February 22, 1985.

EXHIBIT 2
Diversification of U.S. Tobacco Companies in 1980

	Percentage of Total Sales*	Percentage of Total from Operations*
R. J. Reynolds Industries, Inc.:		
Domestic tobacco	34%	60%
International tobacco	20	13
Transportation (sea-land)	13	5
Energy operations (Aminoil)	9	14
Foods and beverages (Del Monte, etc.)	22	7
Packaging (RJR Archer)	2	1
Philip Morris Incorporated:		
Domestic and international tobacco	65	86
Beer (Miller)	26	11
Soft drinks (7UP)	4	(- -)
Paper and chemical products	3	1
Land development	2	2
B.A.T. Industries Ltd:		
Tobacco (Brown & Williamson)	57	72
Retail* (International Supermarkets, Koh, Gimbels Bros., Saks Fifth Avenue)†	23	9
Paper (Wiggins Tape)	9	11
Other (cosmetics, domestic products, investment, insurance)	5	4
American Brands, Inc.:		
Domestic tobacco	17	37
International tobacco (Gallaher)	47	22
Hardware (Master Lock)	3	5
Distilled beverages (James B. Beam)	3	4
Engineering	3	2
Food products (Duffy-Mott, Sunshine Biscuits‡)	8	4
Office services and supplies (Swingline)	2	3
Optical goods and services	1	1
Toiletries (Andrew Jergens)	1	1
Golf products (Achushnet)	1	1
Retail	7	1
Wholesale	5	3
Life insurance (Franklin Life)	- -	15
Other	2	2
Loews Corp.:		
Domestic tobacco (Lorillard)	23	36
Timing devices (Bulova)	4	1
Insurance (CNA Financial)	63	27
Hotels	5	18
Theaters	1	3
Consumer finance	3	11
Other (real estate)	1	4
Liggett Group:§		
Tobacco	32	38
Spirits and wines (J&B Scotch, Grand Marnier, etc.)	17	26
Pet foods (Alpo)	22	9
Soft drinks (bottling and distribution)	18	27
Other (sporting goods, food ingredients)	11	10

* Figures are approximate, derived from 1980 annual reports, Standard & Poor's, and Moody's *Industrial Manual.*
† Also acquired Marshall Field, March 1982.
‡ Sold to Cadbury Schweppes Ltd. for $60 million, March 1982.
§ Acquired by Grand Metropolitan Ltd. in 1980.
Source: HBS Case Services, "U.S. Tobacco Companies: Smoking and Health," case 382-155.

Throughout this growing controversy many large cigarette manufacturers began to diversify (see Exhibit 2).

After the ban on television and radio advertising Philip Morris and R. J. Reynolds were the only cigarette manufacturers to introduce entirely new cigarettes. Later in 1980 Brown & Williamson introduced Barclay, a brand that already was established in the United Kingdom. In the early 1970s Philip Morris and R. J. Reynolds began to fund extensive research concerning the question of smoking as a possible cause of cancer and lung and heart diseases. Both companies continued to assert that no scientific evidence existed to prove that smoking did cause health problems. R. J. Reynolds also increased its advertising expenditures to introduce new brands and support its best-selling established brands.

Philip Morris had grown in the 1960s under the leadership of Joseph Cullman, CEO from 1961 to 1978, and held 15 percent of the U.S. cigarette market in 1970. Philip Morris had also expanded its international cigarette business, fueled by the growth of the Marlboro brand, which grew by 1971 to become the largest selling brand in the world. Like Coca-Cola, Marlboro came to be one of the world's best-known brand names.

During the late 1960s and the 1970s Philip Morris set out to expand the number of brands and types of cigarettes that it sold in the United States. Its stated plan was to identify different segments of the cigarette market and to design and target new products to these segments. It introduced, among others, the following brands: Virginia Slims in 1967, a brand targeted toward women; Benson & Hedges in 1969, a 100-millimeter cigarette; and Merit in 1975, a low tar and nicotine cigarette (see Exhibit 3).

Philip Morris also developed new types of blends and packages for its best-selling brands. In particular Philip Morris expanded the breadth of offerings marketed under its Marlboro brand to include Marlboro Lights, a lower tar blend introduced in 1971, and three different kinds of packages. Each different tobacco blend and package was designed to fit a segment of the market that Philip Morris marketing research had identified as a discrete group. By 1984 the Marlboro brand in all its forms had become by far the leading U.S. cigarette brand, and Philip Morris had three of the top 10 selling brands (see Exhibit 4).

Philip Morris advertised heavily to build its Marlboro brand and to establish new brands (see Exhibit 5). Because television and radio advertising was banned Philip Morris made extensive use of magazine and billboard advertising and also began to sponsor sport-

EXHIBIT 3
Share of U.S. Cigarette Market
(In Units Sold of the Six Major Manufacturers)*

Company	*1963†*	*1970‡*	*1980‡*	*1983‡*
Philip Morris	9.4%	16.5%	30.9%	35.2%
R. J. Reynolds	34.3	31.7	32.6	34.1
Brown & Williamson	10.9	16.7	13.7	10.2
American Brands	24.8	19.6	10.8	8.8
Lorillard	10.9	8.7	9.7	10.2
Liggett Group	9.7	6.8	2.3	1.5
Total	100.0%	100.0%	100.0%	100.0%

* The six large U.S. cigarette manufacturers accounted for 98 percent of the U.S. market.
† *Printer's Ink*, February 14, 1968, p. 27.
‡ Lehman Brothers Kuhn Loeb Research.

EXHIBIT 4
Top Ten Brands in the U.S. Cigarette Market (Unit Share of Market)

	Percent	
	1983	*1984*
Philip Morris:		
Marlboro	20.1%	21.1%
Benson & Hedges	5.0	4.8
Merit	4.4	4.1
Total	29.5	30.0
R. J. Reynolds:		
Winston	11.9	12.0
Salem	8.1	8.1
Camel	4.6	4.5
Vantage	3.7	3.5
Total	28.3	28.1
Brown & Williamson:		
Kool	7.2	7.0
American Brands:		
Pall Mall	4.1	3.8
Lorillard:		
Kent*	3.9	3.3
Grand total	73.0%	72.2%

* Recalculated to include Golden Lights brand family.
Source: John C. Maxwell and Laidlow Ansbacher, published in *Tobacco International*, December 28, 1984.

ing events and concerts, even though these media were viewed as cost inefficient relative to television in introducing new cigarette brands. The cost of introducing advertising for a new cigarette brand had grown to the point that Brown & Williamson spent $150 million to launch the Barclay brand in the United States in the 1980s.

Throughout the 1970s and 1980s Philip Morris invested heavily to expand and modernize its cigarette manufacturing plants (see Exhibit 1). In 1984 Philip Morris, with cigarette revenue of $9.8 billion, carried on its books $2.5 billion in plant and equipment dedicated to cigarette manufacturing (see Exhibit 6).

THE MILLER BREWING COMPANY

In 1969 Philip Morris bought the Miller Brewing Company, the seventh largest U.S. beer manufacturer. This was the company's first investment outside the cigarette business except for a small industrial packaging company that had been purchased during the 1960s. The U.S. beer industry was populated by over 150 regional brewers. Most were family-owned operations that had been started before the turn of the century by emigrants from Europe.

Males accounted for 60 percent of all beer purchases and 80 percent of all beer consumption. Beer was sold in bottles and cans as well as in kegs. Beer consumption was

EXHIBIT 5

Major Media Advertising Expenditures of the Six Large Cigarette Manufacturers* (in Millions of Dollars)

	1974	1975	1976	1977	1978	1979	1980	1981	1982	1983	January–September, 1984
American Brand	$ 18.1	$ 18.6	$ 24.3	$ 31.2	$ 29.6	$ 31.6	$ 36.3	$ 37.8	$ 33.4	$ 39.4	$ 24.5
Brown & Williamson	45.2	34.2	39.6	49.1	48.8	41.7	67.2	115.9	135.1	78.3	37.8
Liggett Group	11.9	10.6	11.1	12.0	15.1	5.2	0.6	3.2	6.3	6.9	7.3
Lorillard	19.6	30.1	29.3	33.9	35.9	64.3	61.3	51.8	45.2	74.1	53.1
Philip Morris	58.7	65.9	69.7	89.2	85.1	119.0	126.0	156.1	205.6	215.2	143.5
R. J. Reynolds	68.6	82.2	95.0	111.7	135.8	182.2	167.2	141.9	159.7	243.3	218.2
Total six major media	$222.3	$237.6	$269.2	$327.1	$350.3	$444.0	$458.6	$506.7	$585.3	$657.2	$474.4

* The six media were estimated to account for 75–80 percent of all cigarette advertising. Other advertising expenditures included promotion through the sponsorship of sporting events and musical concerts.

Source: BAR/LNA (Leading National Advertisers) Multi-Media Service, 1974–1984.

EXHIBIT 6

Statistics on Phillip Morris Cigarette Operations (Revenues in Millions; Cigarette Units in Billions)

	1972	1973	1974	1975	1976	1977	1978	1979	1980	1981	1982	1983	1984
United States:													
U.S. cigarette industry unit sales	543	565	490	595	601	605	608	615	624	629	625	595	600
Philip Morris U.S.A.:													
Operating revenues	$1,165	$1,304	$1,501	$1,722	$1,963	$2,160	$2,737	$2,767	$3,272	$3,762	$4,330	$5,520	$6,133
Operating income	$ 194	$ 227	$ 295	$ 337	$ 401	$ 474	$ 568	$ 701	$ 786	$ 906	$1,012	$1,338	$1,745
Operating income/revenues	17%	17%	20%	20%	20%	22%	21%	25%	24%	24%	23%	24%	28%
Unit sales	81	103	124	142	152	163	170	180	197	201	206	202	212
Unit share of market	17%	18%	21%	24%	23%	27%	28%	29%	30%	32%	33%	34%	35%
International:													
Non-U.S. world cigarette industry unit sales	3,470	3,447	3,335	3,290	3,522	3,472	3,527	3,683	3,854	3,735	4,050	4,016	3,954
Philip Morris International													
Operating revenues	$ 624	$ 823	$ 860	$1,040	$1,084	$1,349	$1,811	$2,561	$3,205	$3,400	$3,564	$3,647	$3,741
Operating income	$ 84	$ 92	$ 96	$ 113	$ 130	$ 154	$ 189	$ 261	$ 318	$ 397	$ 446	$ 366	$ 421
Operating income/revenues	13%	11%	11%	11%	12%	11%	10%	10%	10%	12%	13%	10%	11%
Unit sales	125	131	140	148	169	184	201	221	239	249	243	245	253
Unit share of market	3.6%	3.8%	4.2%	4.5%	4.8%	5.3%	5.7%	6.0%	6.2%	6.7%	6.0%	6.1%	6.4%

Source: Philip Morris annual reports.

moving toward the take-home market and bottles and cans. Kegs, or draft beer, accounted for 14 percent of consumption in 1975 and 10 percent in 1983.

Brewers bottled and canned their own beer. Beer tended to be packaged in more expensive bottles and cans than were soft drinks, and packaging comprised the largest portion of a brewer's costs. The following estimates were made of a "typical"—or regional—brewer's cost structure in 1975:[2]

Typical Brewer's Cost Structure

Production costs:		90%
Agricultural inputs	17%	
Packaging	49	
Direct labor	13	
Depreciation and other	11	
Selling and administration:		10
Delivery	5	
Advertising	1.5	
Other	3.5	
Total		100%

Beer was distributed via independent regional beer distributors. The largest national brewers had exclusive distributorships, while small national brands used distributors that handled several brands at once. Regional brands usually distributed their own beer. Distributors sold to liquor stores, bars, restaurants, and other retail outlets.

Anheuser-Busch, with approximately 20 percent of the market, was the industry leader in every region of the United States. Majority ownership still belonged to descendants of the original Busch family. Anheuser-Busch sold three major brands: Budweiser, its flagship brand in the premium category, Michelob in the super-premium category, and Busch in the popular category. During the 1960s Anheuser-Busch invested in several new plants, increasing its total capacity by 50 percent during the decade. It incorporated the most modern, cost-efficient production techniques in its plants and also began to integrate backward into the production of aluminum cans in order to reduce costs (see Exhibits 7, 8, 9, and 10).

Miller Brewing Company's lead brand, Miller High Life, had carried the slogan, "The Champagne of Bottle Beer," since the early 1900s. The brand had held a constant share of approximately 4 percent throughout the 1960s. W. R. Grace, which had owned the brewery, had neither increased capacity nor advertised extensively. Chief Executive Officer W. R. Grace, Jr., stated that he did not want to play Anheuser-Busch's "capacity game." He initiated the sale to Philip Morris when he read that Joseph Cullman was considering buying the largest brewery in Canada.

In explaining the acquisition Philip Morris stated the following in its 1970 annual report:

> The product is a low-cost, mass-produced, disposable consumer good. It passes through many of the same outlets—supermarkets, convenience stores, even bars—and is enjoyed by many of the same customers (male, aged 18–44) and has good

[2] *The Wall Street Journal,* October 13, 1975.

EXHIBIT 7

Statistics on Miller Brewing Company Operations (Revenues in Millions of Dollars)

	1972	1973	1974	1975	1976	1977	1978	1979	1980	1981	1982	1983	1984
U.S. beer industry barrel shipments (in millions including imports)	131	137	147	151	154	161	167	194	177	180	181	183	181
Miller Brewing Company:													
Operating revenues	$276	$211	$404	$653	$983	$1,328	$1,835	$2,236	$2,542	$2,837	$2,929	$2,922	$2,928
Operating income	$ 0	$ (2)	$ 6	$ 29	$ 76	$ 106	$ 150	$ 181	$ 145	$ 116	$ 159	$ 227	$ 116
Operating income/revenues	0.0%	(0.9%)	1.5%	4.4%	7.7%	8.0%	8.2%	8.1%	4.6%	8.0%	5.4%	4.0%	5.0%
Millions of barrel shipments	5.8	6.9	9.3	13.0	18.8	24.5	31.6	36.5	37.3	41.2	40.0	38.2	38.2
Unit share of market	4.5%	5.0%	6.3%	8.6%	12.2%	15.2%	18.9%	21.0%	21.1%	22.2%	22.0%	20.9%	21.1%
Share rank	7th	6th	5th	4th	3rd	2nd	2nd	2nd	2nd	2nd	2nd	2nd	2nd

Sources: Philip Morris annual reports; *Beverage Industry* and John C. Maxwell.

EXHIBIT 8

Volume Share of U.S. Beer Market (Including Imports)

Company	1970	1971	1972	1973	1974	1975	1976	1977	1978	1979*	1980†	1981	1982	1983*
Anheuser-Busch	20.5%	19.2%	20.9%	21.6%	23.4%	23.7%	22.9%	23.3%	25.6%	26.8%	28.2%	30.0%	33.0%	33.5%
Miller	4.1	4.1	4.2	5.0	6.2	8.6	12.2	15.2	18.9	21.0	21.1	22.2	22.0	20.9
Stroh	4.1	4.2	4.3	4.4	4.3	4.4	4.5	4.3	4.1	5.4	4.8	4.2	5.3	13.4
Heileman	8.0	8.1	8.0	8.2	8.5	8.4	8.4	8.2	7.8	6.6	7.5	7.7	8.1	9.7
Coors	7.5	7.6	7.8	7.9	8.5	8.6	10.5	10.2	9.5	7.5	7.8	7.3	6.6	7.5
Pabst	8.5	8.7	8.8	9.5	9.8	10.6	11.3	10.0	11.1	8.8	11.9	10.5	9.8	7.3
Genesee	2.0	1.9	1.9	1.9	2.0	1.9	1.9	1.8	1.8	2.0	2.0	2.0	1.9	1.7
Schmidt	4.5	4.1	3.9	3.7	3.5	3.2	3.1	3.0	2.4	2.2	2.0	1.6	1.8	1.7
Pittsburgh	NA	NA	NA	NA	NA	NA	NA		NA	0.4	0.6	0.5	0.5	0.5
Schlitz	14.3	14.9	15.2	15.4	15.6	15.7	16.1	14.0	11.5	9.9	9.1	8.0	7.5	--
Others	26.5	27.2	25.0	22.4	18.2	14.9	9.1	10.0	7.3	9.4	5.0	5.3	3.5	3.8
Total	100.0%	100.0%	100.0%	100.0%	100.0%	100.0%	100.0%	100.0%	100.0%	100.0%	100.0%	100.0%	100.0%	100.0%

NA = not available.

* Stroh acquired the Schaefer Brewing Company in 1979 and the Schlitz Brewing Company in 1983.

† Pabst bought two regional brewers in 1980.

Sources: *Beverage Industry* and John C. Maxwell; annual reports of companies; *Modern Brewery Age;* U.S. Brewers Association.

EXHIBIT 9
U.S. Beer Industry Advertising Expenditures (in Millions of Dollars)

Company	1970	1973	1976	1977	1978	1979*	1980†	1981	1982	1983*
Anheuser-Busch	$10.1	$15.0	$ 25.7	$ 45.2	$ 63.1	$ 82.3	$111.4	$132.0	$155.4	$180.8
Miller	3.5	14.1	29.0	42.4	64.3	79.1	90.5	106.2	119.1	138.9
Stroh	2.2	3.3	5.0	7.2	9.0	20.9	25.1	29.4	32.0	54.4
Heileman	2.3	3.1	3.5	4.7	6.7	7.8	10.1	11.9	15.9	19.1
Coors	1.1	1.3	1.6	4.0	8.1	12.3	15.4	17.9	22.1	30.3
Pabst	8.1	8.9	9.1	10.9	18.1	20.2	23.1	25.1	26.0	26.2
Genesee	NA	NA	NA	2.8	3.0	4.5	4.7	5.1	5.4	7.5
Schmidt	NA	NA	NA	3.9	3.1	4.4	3.1	2.6	1.6	4.6
Others	25.3	29.4	65.1	75.4	79.7	50.1	41.5	37.9	28.5	32.9
Total	$52.6	$75.1	$139.0	$196.5	$255.1	$281.6	$324.9	$368.1	$406.5	$494.7

NA = not available.
* Stroh acquired the Schaefer Brewing Company in 1979 and the Schlitz Brewing Company in 1983.
† Pabst bought two regional brewers in 1980.
Sources: Leading National Advertisers, Inc.; LBKL Research. The six major media researched by LNA accounted for approximately 60–75 percent of total advertising expenditures for beer. Other expenditures included the sponsorship of sporting events and musical concerts.

margins. The technology, processing wet agricultural products as opposed to semi-dry as in the case of tobacco, is not foreign to us.

After the acquisition Philip Morris initially kept the existing Miller management. Philip Morris marketing executives, who were sent by Cullman to help Miller with its plans, suggested introducing a new 7-ounce pony bottle that would be sold in an eight-bottle "Pony Pack." Miller executives resisted, arguing that the bottle was too expensive on a per-ounce basis.

In 1971 Philip Morris installed a new president of Miller, John Murphy, who had been the executive vice president in charge of the Philip Morris International cigarette business. Murphy introduced the Pony Pack in 1973. Murphy also changed the slogan of Miller High Life to "Champagne of Beer." In 1974 Miller introduced a new advertising campaign around the theme, "Now, It's Miller Time." Murphy stated that Miller would reposition

EXHIBIT 10
1983 Profitability of Leading Brewers (Brewery Business Only) (in Millions of Dollars)

Brewer	Net Sales	Operating Income	Percent of Sales
Anheuser-Busch	$4,907.7	$649.9	13.24%
Miller	2,922.1	227.3	7.78
Pabst	799.9	13.7	1.70
Coors	1,110.4	154.3	13.90
Stroh	1,318.0	54.7	4.15
Heileman	870.8	82.9	9.50

Source: Company annual reports.

Miller's premier brand from the champagne bucket to the lunch bucket. The intent was to target working males and to use life-style advertisements emphasizing Miller High Life's role in the consumer's life after a successful day of work.

In 1975 Miller introduced Miller Lite, a beer with fewer carbohydrates. Lower carbohydrate beer had been introduced by some regional brewers in 1971 and promoted as containing fewer calories. Miller first introduced its Lite beer with little advertising. Through research and auditing, Miller executives discovered that the beer had become most popular not where it was viewed as a diet beer but rather in some working neighborhood bars where it was viewed as less filling. In 1976 Miller launched an extensive advertising campaign for Lite using well-known male sports stars endorsing the beer in witty commercials as good tasting and less filling. The execution proved highly memorable.

Miller invested heavily in new brewing capacity to meet the rapid growth of both Miller High Life and Miller Lite (see Exhibit 7). Miller designed larger plants than the industry to achieve economies of scale through new production techniques, involving a minimum-efficient scale of 4 million barrels annually. With high transportation costs for bottled beer, that capacity necessitated approximately a 10 percent share of a region's market. Miller could brew both Miller High Life and Miller Lite in its new plants. Despite these investments, Miller could not keep up with demand throughout the late 1970s. Miller also invested in aluminum can manufacturing and had become 50 percent backward integrated into aluminum canning by 1979.

Miller also purchased the rights to brew domestically a brand named Lowenbrau which had previously been imported from West Germany. The domestically brewed Lowenbrau was introduced nationally by Miller in late 1977, establishing Lowenbrau in the small but rapidly growing super-premium beer segment. By 1977 Miller had become the second largest brewer in the United States.

Murphy also moved to strengthen Miller's distribution. Miller had already achieved national distribution through a network of independent distributors dedicated to Miller. Murphy, however, increased the size of the Miller sales force that worked with the distributors to ensure that Miller products obtained extensive distribution in retail outlets in every region of the country. By 1979 Miller was the second largest brewer, behind Anheuser-Busch, in five of seven regions of the country and the third largest behind Anheuser-Busch and Coors in the Rocky Mountains and Pacific Coast regions.

In reviewing its performance in the cigarette and beer business Philip Morris made the following comments in its 1979 annual report:

> Ten years ago in this company's most profitable unit, Philip Morris U.S.A. held a 15 percent share. 1970 was the year all television and radio advertising of cigarettes was terminated. Philip Morris U.S.A. now holds approximately 29 percent of this market, with the total market itself in units almost 20 percent larger now than it was then.
>
> For Philip Morris International the 10-year story has been much the same. Revenues have increased at a compounded rate of 26 percent. Operating income has increased at 21 percent compounded, and market share has more than doubled.
>
> During 1970 Philip Morris acquired full control of the Miller Brewing Company. The next few years were a period of trial and preparation during which Miller revenues remained flat while operating income dropped steadily. But by then the early learning years had begun to produce results, and the second half of the decade

EXHIBIT 11
Top Ten Beer Brands
(By Unit Share of Market)

	1980		1981		1982		1983		1984	
	Share (Percent)	Rank	Share (Percent)	Rank	Share (Percent)	Rank	Share (Percent)	Rank	Share (Percent)	Rank
Budweiser	19.1%	1	20.6%	1	21.6%	1	22.8%	1	24.0%	1
Miller High Life	13.6	2	12.2	2	11.2	2	9.7	2	7.8	3
Miller Lite	7.5	3	9.0	3	9.5	3	9.5	3	10.0	2
Coors	6.5	4	6.1	4	4.9	4	5.2	4	5.0	4
Pabst Blue Ribbon	6.4	5	5.4	5	4.8	5	4.3	5	3.4	7
Michelob	4.9	6	4.6	6	4.6	6	3.9	6	3.8	6
Schlitz	4.3	7	3.1	7	2.3	10	--	--	--	--
Old Milwaukee	2.3	8	2.7	10	3.2	7	3.7	7	3.8	5
Busch	2.6	9	--	--	--	--	--	--	--	--
Michelob Light	1.5	10	--	--	--	--	--	--	--	--
Old Style	--	--	3.0	8	3.1	8	3.0	9	2.9	9
Stroh	--	--	3.0	9	2.9	9	3.1	8	3.2	8
Bud Light	--	--	--	--	--	--	2.1	10	2.3	10

Sources: *Beverage Industry* annual manuals; *Beverage World*, March 1985.

has been a period of spectacular success for Miller. In 1979 barrel shipments were more than seven times larger than 1970, and operating income was almost 16 times as great. Market share has quintupled to about 21 percent of the U.S. market, which itself grew more than 40 percent in units in the decade. In 1970 Miller ranked seventh among domestic brewers; today, it is a strong second.

During the early 1970s Anheuser-Busch continued its strategy of steady capacity expansion and cost reduction through modern plants and backward integration into can manufacturing. By 1975 Anheuser-Busch had achieved full backward integration into aluminum cans. It focused on the expansion of its Budweiser and Michelob brands, rather than on introducing any new brands, and increased advertising from $10 million in 1970 to $26 million in 1976.

In 1976 the Busch family recruited new marketing managers from General Mills and Procter & Gamble. The managers introduced a new advertising campaign in 1977 for the Budweiser brand with the theme, "This Bud's for You." The advertisements were designed to portray Budweiser as a reward for good, hard work and were targeted at the same consumer segment as Miller targeted in its "Miller Time" campaign. Anheuser-Busch increased advertising expenditures for this campaign. In 1982 Anheuser-Busch introduced Bud Light with an extensive advertising campaign saying that this was the first light beer worthy of the Budweiser name. This brand gained 2.1 percent and 2.3 percent of the U.S. market in 1983 and 1984, respectively (see Exhibit 11).

THE SEVEN-UP CO.

In 1979 Philip Morris completed the acquisition of the Seven-Up Co. for $520 million. In discussing the acquisition management stated the following in its 1978 annual report:

> Many of the characteristics of the soft drink industry are similar to those of our other businesses. Essentially, soft drinks—like cigarettes and beer—are reasonably priced, relatively low-cost consumer items that give pleasure to users, who repeat their purchases often when the quality of the product satisfies their expectations.
>
> Our major priority in soft drinks will be the Seven-Up brand in the United States. The first move to improve the position of the brand was the appointment by Seven-Up management of a new advertising agency and the creation of a new advertising campaign and marketing program for the Seven-Up brand. The campaign, introduced early in 1979, is designed to capitalize on the national trend to more active outdoor lifestyles. The theme, "America's Turning 7UP," is intended to develop a large and growing base of consumers whose primary soft drink is Seven-Up.

Following its first year of ownership Philip Morris described its moves at Seven-Up as follows:

- For the Seven-Up Co. 1979 was a significant year, principally characterized by a major restructuring program designed to position the Seven-Up organization for the future.
- Advertising was the principal component of Seven-Up's enlarged marketing program. The campaign—"America's Turning 7UP"— was intended not only to improve the awareness and product positioning of Seven-Up but also to assist our bottlers in improving distribution and retail availability of our products. The campaign, now featuring endorsements by such prominent athletes as Earvin "Magic" Johnson, Larry Bird, John McEnroe, and Earl Campbell, has created substantial consumer awareness. It has also helped to strengthen our relationship with our bottlers.
- In addition, Seven-Up has restructured and increased its staff—particularly its field sales force—and has substantially improved its product research activities.[3]
- In March William E. Winter, previously president, became chairman, and Edward W. Frantel, previously vice president-sales of Miller, was appointed president and chief executive officer of Seven-Up. During the remainder of the year a number of other organizational changes were made to establish the marketing, distribution, quality control, finance, and planning organizations needed for further growth consistent with Philip Morris' long-term objectives. To the extent that new senior positions could not be filled by existing Seven-Up personnel, they were largely filled by people from other divisions of Philip Morris.
- Also during the past year a sweeping graphics design program was begun, and the resulting new graphics will be introduced in the spring of 1980.
- For the Seven-Up Co. 1979 was a difficult year of transition. We restructured the Seven-Up organization adding new personnel to strengthen both our marketing and research capabilities and our relationships with bottlers in the United States, Canada, and Puerto Rico. In addition, Seven-Up International was integrated into Philip Morris International in order to take full advantage of the latter's long experience in the worldwide marketplace.

---

[3] The field sales staff were the people who worked with Seven-Up bottlers in developing and helping to improve the execution of advertising and promotion campaigns.

- As in the early stages of our Miller acquisition we do not expect Seven-Up to be a significant contributor to our profits for a few years. But we do not believe that this will adversely affect the trend lines of the corporation's overall performance.

In 1980 Seven-Up expanded the advertising for its "America's Turning 7UP" campaign. The company also initiated a $12 million investment in a new research and development facility that would focus on both product and packaging innovation.

In 1981 Seven-Up bought two of its franchise bottlers which had performed below sales projections. These investments began a series of other bottler acquisitions, resulting in a total of six by 1984. The Seven-Up bottler system had the following configurations in 1975, 1979, and 1984:

Seven-Up Bottler System

Bottlers	*1975*	*1979*	*1984*
7UP company-owned franchisees	13	4	10
7UP independent franchisees*	102	102	103
Coca-Cola and 7UP	97	99	84
Pepsi-Cola and 7UP	153	149	143
Royal Crown and 7UP	104	92	81
Total	482	446	421

* Some also bottle Dr. Pepper or smaller brands.

These acquisitions represented the vast majority of Philip Morris's investments in Seven-Up during these three years (see Exhibit 1).

In 1981 Ed Frantel, president of Seven-Up, announced a new advertising campaign that would emphasize the caffeine-free issue. The theme, "Never Had It, Never Will," was designed to emphasize that the major colas all contained caffeine and that Seven-Up did not. This campaign proved more effective than the "America's Turning 7UP" and helped to increase the share of the soft drink market accounted for by the lemon-lime flavor.

Each Flavor's Share (Percent) of Total U.S. Market by Year

	1977	*1978*	*1979*	*1980*	*1981*	*1982*	*1983*
Cola	62.4%	62.3%	62.3%	62.4%	62.6%	62.1%	63.6%
Lemon-lime	12.4	12.3	12.1	11.8	11.6	12.0	12.5
Pepper	7.2	7.5	7.5	7.5	7.4	7.0	6.8
Orange	7.4	7.4	7.3	7.4	7.4	7.6	7.4
Root beer	5.3	5.4	5.5	5.5	5.5	5.4	5.0
Others	5.3	5.1	5.3	5.4	5.5	5.9	4.7

Source: John C. Maxwell and *Beverage Industry.*

The Seven-Up brand's share also increased from 5.0 percent in 1981 to 5.4 percent in 1983.

In 1982 Seven-Up introduced Like, a caffeine-free cola. Seven-Up attempted to gain distribution through its franchised bottlers who also bottled other colas, contending that Like was not a regular cola. Upon a civil suit by Coca-Cola, a U.S. court determined that Like was a cola. Seven-Up spent $12.7 million in advertising for Like in 1982 and 1983. The product gained a 0.4 percent share of the market.

In 1983 Coca-Cola persuaded McDonald's to replace Diet Seven-Up on its list of

EXHIBIT 12

Financial Statistics on the Seven-Up Co. (Revenues in Millions of Dollars)

	1972	1973	1974	1975	1976	1977	1978*	1979	1980	1981	1982	1983	1984
Seven-Up sales	$133.0	$147.0	$191.0	$214.0	$233.0	$251.0	$186.0	$296.0	$353.0	$432.0	$531.0	$650.0	$734.0
Net income	$ 12.0	$ 14.1	$ 16.6	$ 10.3	$ 24.8	$ 25.8	--	--	--	--	--	--	--
Operating income	--	--	--	--	--	--	$ 2.6	$ 7.0	$ (7.1)	$ (1.7)	$ (1.2)	$ (10.8)	$ 5.3
Net income/sales	9.1%	9.6%	8.7%	9.5%	10.6%	10.3%	--	--	--	--	--	--	--
Operating income/sales	--	--	--	--	--	--	14.0%	2.4%	(2.0%)	(0.4%)	(0.2%)	(1.7%)	0.7%
Return on equity	23.7%	23.6%	23.9%	23.6%	24.0%	23.1%	--	--	--	--	--	--	--
Long-term debt/total capital	4.1%	4.5%	3.4%	2.3%	3.1%	4.2%	--	--	--	--	--	--	--

* Philip Morris bought the Seven-Up Co. in 1979 and consolidated earnings back to 1978.

Sources: Philip Morris annual reports; Seven-Up Co. annual reports.

required fountain soft drinks with Diet Sprite. The regular brand Seven-Up was placed on a list of authorized optional soft drinks.

In 1984 Seven-Up moved to adopt aspartame for its Diet Seven-Up soft drink. Ed Frantel stated that his decision was based on the need to remain competitive with Pepsi-Cola and Coca-Cola, which were also adopting 100 percent aspartame.

In March 1985 Ed Frantel reflected on the company's progress as follows:

> We had to take a few years to learn more about the business. When we came to Seven-Up, bottlers who believed Seven-Up had no share of voice in the media said to us, "You advertise, we'll promote." We're now doing both. Our marketing spending is at an all-time high. Bottlers have been very responsive to our marketing plans. They have noted the plans' flexibility for individual markets, and have increased their dollar participation as well. . . .
>
> The only constant is change. Anything is possible, because nobody is infallible. I just don't believe that Coca-Cola and Pepsi-Cola are incapable of mistakes. Executives make dumb decisions. There is always the challenge.
>
> We dare to be different. When you're not the leader, you have to be. To be different you have to do it with substance. Caffeine was an example of that; and Like was also a different approach to the cola business. When I went out personally and talked to some of the key retailers about Like cola, there was great interest in having another brand, someone else in that particular category that had some staying power to maintain the competitive position. I don't think that would change.[4]

RECENT DEVELOPMENTS

In 1984 Hamish Maxwell, who had headed the international cigarette unit, became chairman and chief executive of Philip Morris. He obtained the job over John Murphy, whose fortunes had apparently diminished with the problems of Miller High Life during the 1980s (see Exhibit 11). Some beer industry analysts believed that the "Miller Time" campaign had become ineffective and was relied upon for too long. In 1984, Philip Morris wrote down the asset value of a new $450 million Miller brewery that had never been used. Miller was operating at 83 percent capacity in 1984.

Maxwell stated in early 1985:

> I can say unequivocably that Seven-Up and Miller have never been for sale. And I promise you, we will keep Miller and Seven-Up for the foreseeable future.
>
> To protect our earnings growth we must use our resources to succeed in other businesses. It would be very shortsighted to get out of a business every time there is a downturn.[5]

[4] *Beverage World,* March 1985.

[5] *Fortune,* March 18, 1985.

CASE 14

New Coke: Coca-Cola's Response to the Pepsi Challenge*

THE ANNOUNCEMENT OF THE NEW TASTE—APRIL 23, 1985

> Shortly before 11:00 AM, the doors of the Vivian Beaumont Theater at Lincoln Center opened to two hundred newspaper, magazine, and TV reporters. The stage was aglow with red. Three huge screens, each solid red and inscribed with the company logo, rose behind the podium and a table draped in red. The lights were low; the music began. "We are. We will always be. Coca-Cola. All-American history." As the patriotic song filled the theater, slides of Americana flashed on the center screen—families and kids, Eisenhower and JFK, the Grand Canyon and wheat fields, the Beatles and Bruce Springsteen, cowboys, athletes, the Statue of Liberty—and interspersed throughout, old commercials for Coke. No political candidate would have gotten away with such patrioteering without howls of protest, and the members of the press weren't seduced by the hype.[1]

Chairman Roberto Goizueta came to the podium and boasted,

> The best has been made even better. Some may choose to call this the boldest single marketing move in the history of the packaged-goods business. We simply call it the surest move ever made because the taste of Coke was shaped by the taste of the consumer.[2]

New Coke was launched. The American people reacted immediately and violently. After three months of vigorous, unrelenting protest, stunned and humbled Coca-Cola executives called a second press conference to tell the American people that Coke was sorry. The corporate giant announced that it would reissue the original Coca-Cola formula as Coke Classic and asked the forgiveness of the American people.

How could a $7 billion corporation with a sterling track record commit such a blunder? How could this giant international company so totally misread consumers' feelings? How dare they tamper with an American institution? Or, did Coca-Cola orchestrate the entire affair as a huge publicity stunt to get millions of dollars of free advertising for its new Coke and boost the sales of the old one? How can Coca-Cola reestablish itself as the dominant force in the U.S. soft drink industry?

---

* Prepared by Patricia P. McDougall of Georgia State University; Manfred Hueber, District Manager for Coca-Cola USA; and Pat Tims and Jon Morris, both MBA students at Georgia State University. Distributed by the North American Case Research Association.

[1] Oliver, Thomas (1985). *The Real Coke, The Real Story.* New York: Random House, pp. 158–159.

[2] Ibid., p. 159.

UNITED STATES SOFT DRINK INDUSTRY ANALYSIS

The soft drink industry is dominated by two main competitors, the Coca-Cola Company and Pepsi-Cola. Both depend on a network of franchised bottling companies to distribute their bottled soft drinks. In the United States, Coca-Cola uses its own network of wholesalers for their fountain syrup distribution, while Pepsi distributes its fountain syrup through its bottlers.

A principal concern of the industry is long-term growth potential, and how this growth is affected by changing population demographics, per capita saturation, and changing consumer preferences. Changes in these variables have caused changes in the channels of distribution.

Industry Growth

Growth in the soft drink industry can be increased by consumption per individual and by population growth. Since the population of the United States is growing at only about 2 percent a year, the strongest potential for growth in the U.S. industry is through per capita growth. As reflected in Exhibit 1, per capita growth has risen steadily from about 19 gallons per year in 1966 to where average Americans drank almost 44 gallons of soft drinks in 1987. Industry analyst, Emmanuel Goldman, predicts that by the end of the decade, per capita consumption will be around 50 gallons. He notes that his 50 gallon estimate is not based on soft drinks in the conventional sense, as some soft drinks are becoming part juice.[3]

The 15 to 24 and 25 to 34 year old age groups have been the heaviest pop drinkers. Exhibit 2 graphs the age composition trends of the U.S. population. These heavy consumption groups are becoming a smaller percentage of the total population, while older groups which have historically consumed fewer soft drinks will grow rapidly. The real question is

EXHIBIT 1
Per Capita Consumption of Soft Drinks

Year	Gallons per Capita	Year	Gallons per Capita
1987	43.9	1976	28.6
1986	42.0	1975	26.3
1985	40.7	1974	26.4
1984	38.9	1973	26.6
1983	37.0	1972	25.3
1982	35.7	1971	24.0
1981	35.2	1970	22.7
1980	34.5	1969	21.5
1979	33.3	1968	21.4
1978	32.1	1967	19.9
1977	30.8	1966	19.1

Source: "Soft Drink Report," *Beverage Industry*, March 1988, p. 41.

[3] "Wall Street Wizards Conjure Up Soft Drink Visions of 1986," *Beverage World*, January 1986, pp. 28–34.

EXHIBIT 2
Projected Age Composition of U.S. Population

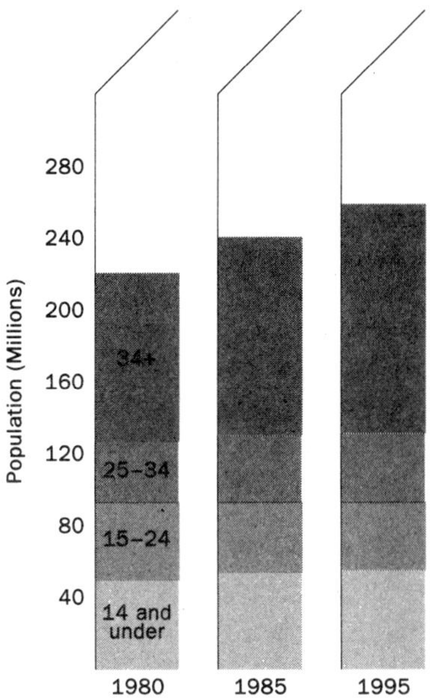

Source: Boston Consulting Group (1985). *The Future of the Soft Drink Industry, 1985–1990*, p. 2.

whether the present younger age, heavy consumption groups will retain their consumption patterns as they get older.

Optimistic analysts cite industry data such as Exhibit 3, which shows soft drink consumption for three sample periods. While the chart does show that older people drink less than younger people at any given time period, people are increasing their consumption even as they age. For example, today's 50 to 59 group consumed more in 1980 than when they were 40 to 49 years old in 1970, and ten years earlier when they were 30 to 39 years old in 1960.

Perhaps the more critical issue is the fear that the market may be approaching the point of saturation in per capita consumption. Just how many gallons of soft drinks can Americans drink per year? In a landmark study on the future of the soft drink industry which the Boston Consulting Group prepared for the National Soft Drink Association, it was reported that a tapering off of the growth rate in per capita consumption appears to have already started. The study notes that while still positive, these growth rates are slower than those to which the industry has become accustomed.[4]

Changing consumer preferences are expected to influence the sources of growth, as consumers switch to healthier products. Martin Romm, an industry analyst, credits the move away from alcoholic beverages in general, and the flatness in the beer industry, as

[4] Boston Consulting Group (1985). *The Future of the Soft Drink Industry, 1985–1990.* Prepared for the National Soft Drink Association.

EXHIBIT 3
Soft Drink per Capita by Age Group (8 Ounce Servings)

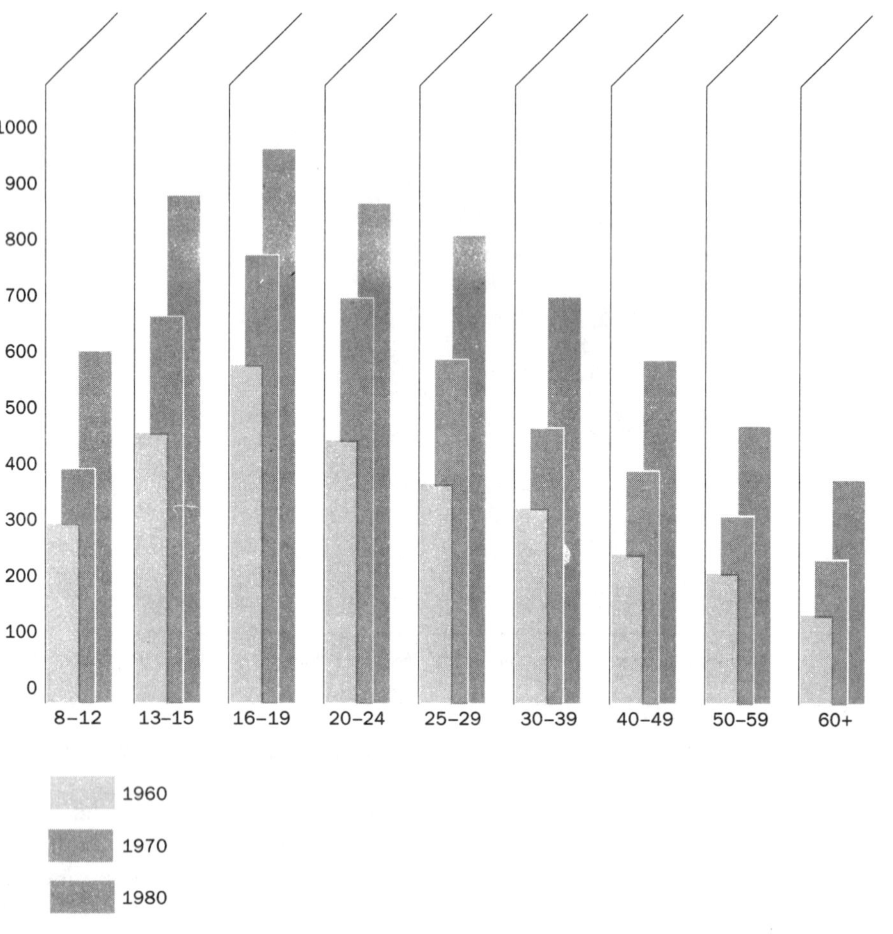

Source: Boston Consulting Group (1985). *The Future of the Soft Drink Industry, 1985–1990*, p. 3.

having helped the soft drink industry, and in particular the soft drink segment.[5] Exhibit 4 shows that market share in the diet segment has doubled since 1980. The Boston Consulting Group's research predicts that by 1990 this segment will account for about 40 percent of total soft drink consumption.

Channels of Distribution

More convenient availability has increased soft drink sales, as the beverages have become available in more and more outlets. The three most important channels are supermarkets,

[5] Op. cit., *Beverage World.*

EXHIBIT 4
Comparative Market Shares of Diet versus Naturally Sweetened Soft Drinks

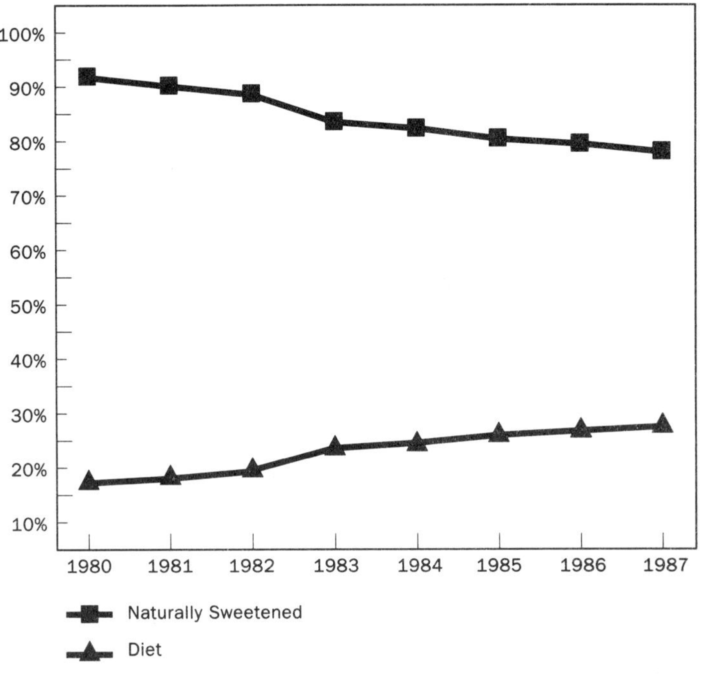

Source: Adapted from "Soft Drink Report," *Beverage Industry,* March 1988, p. 43.

fountain sales, and vending. In 1987, supermarkets accounted for about 40 percent of total U.S. soft drink industry sales, fountain sales represented about 25 percent, and vending accounted for approximately 13 percent. Other retailers represent the remaining percentage. While both Coca-Cola and Pepsi distribute their bottled soft drinks through a network of bottling companies, Coca-Cola uses its own network of wholesalers for their fountain syrup distribution, and Pepsi distributes its fountain syrup through its bottlers.

Bottler Structure

The bottling side of the business has undergone radical changes from the small plant in every town to the big consolidated production centers of today. Consolidation within the soft drink industry is not a new phenomenon. It started in the 1950s and continues to date. While 6,330 plants produced soft drinks in 1950, only 1,500 continued to operate by 1983. The Boston Consulting Group Industry predicts that by 1990, the number of plants will be between 1,200 and 1,250.[6]

This consolidation means bigger plants with lower production costs that can compete more aggressively in the marketplace. Substantial scale economies exist as both labor and

[6] Op. cit., Boston Consulting Group.

factory expenses decrease as size increases. Economies of scale are especially great in the small-plant range. Doubling volume from 500,000 to 1 million cases per year reduces the cost per case by as much as 25 cents; whereas, doubling the volume from 5 to 10 million cases reduces per case costs by only about 10 cents.[7] As future consolidations move plant size further down on the flatter portion of the cost curve, cost reductions will not be as significant as in the past.

Not only has the typical production center changed, but so has the typical franchise owner. When over 6,000 plants dotted the country in the early 1950s, the independent local franchise owner typically served a local community with one plant and several route trucks. Today, many of the franchises are owned by large bottling holding companies. These chains or headquarter companies reap scale economies by consolidating manufacturing plants, increased purchasing power, and lower distribution and selling costs. In 1987, the six largest headquarter companies, each with sales over $500 million, accounted for 31.9 percent of the wholesale soft drink dollar volume.[8]

Coca-Cola Enterprises (CCE), which is 49 percent owned by the Coca-Cola Company, acquired numerous franchises in 1986. Principal among these were the Louisiana Coca-Cola Bottling Company Limited ($151 million), the Barron Affiliated Coca-Cola Bottling Companies ($85 million), soft drink bottling operations of BCI Holdings Corporation (the successor of The Beatrice Companies, Inc.) ($1 billion), and bottling operations controlled by J. T. Lupton and his family ($1.4 billion).[9]

Near the end of 1987, Pepsi announced a joint venture with Pepsi-Cola General Bottlers, Inc., a subsidiary of IC Industries. The new venture, Pepsi-Cola General, gives IC Industries 80 percent ownership and Pepsi 20 percent ownership. Pepsi-Cola General is one of the six headquarters companies with soft drink sales volume over $500 million in 1987. Roger Enrico, president and CEO of PepsiCo Worldwide Beverages described the move as, "It's a strategic breakthrough in our relationship with key Pepsi bottlers. We're able to maintain all the benefits of the traditional franchise system and, at the same time, make that relationship even closer and more effective."[10]

According to *Beverage Industry,* operations worth under $100 million were the most attractive targets for takeovers in 1986. As evidence of this trend, in 1985 there were 198 companies under $100 million, but a year later the total number had dropped to 155 firms.[11]

Although most industry observers predict that the industry will continue to consolidate with the smaller independent franchise bottlers either aligning themselves with other independents or being purchased by large bottling operations, industry analyst George Haas does not see the issue as clearcut. Mr. Haas argues,

> You can't lay a number on it because it's not just a matter of economics. You talk to the bottler who says he's going to hang in there regardless because, for example, his sons are coming up in the business. If it were strictly an economic issue, every independent bottler would sell right now. But there is an emotional issue, and in many cases a family issue, involved in the decision.[12]

---

[7] Ibid., p. 12.
[8] "Just Who Owns Who These Days?" *Beverage Industry,* January 1985, pp. 1, 17.
[9] Form 10K, The Coca-Cola Company, 1987.
[10] Op. cit., *Beverage Industry,* p. 17.
[11] Op. cit., *Beverage Industry.*
[12] "The Deal-Makers," *Beverage World,* March 1988, pp. 30–33.

EXHIBIT 5
Major New Products Introduced in the 1980s

Company	*New Products*	*New Products, % of Total Company Sales*
Coca-Cola	Diet Coke New Coke Cherry Coke Regular Caffeine-Free Coke Diet Caffeine-Free Coke Minute Maid Caffeine-Free Tab	19.7
Pepsi-Cola	Regular Slice Diet Slice Regular Caffeine-Free Pepsi Diet Caffeine-Free Pepsi	13.4
Dr. Pepper	Regular Pepper Free Diet Pepper Free	2
Seven-Up	Cherry 7-Up Like New 7-Up Gold	15.7
A&W	Regular Creme Soda Diet Creme Soda	19
Royal Crown	RC100 Cherry RC Diet RC	10

Source: "Making a Splash," *Beverage Industry,* August 1988, pp. 1, 31.

Product Introductions

Starting in the 1980s there has been a barrage of new products or product reformulation changes. There have been few entrants into the sugared cola category, as most product introductions have principally occurred in such segments as diet colas, lemon-lime, and juice containing drinks. Major new products introduced since 1980 are presented in Exhibit 5. The importance of these products is evident from the share of total sales figures in column three. By 1987, the seven new products listed in column two of the exhibit accounted for 19.7 percent of total Coca Cola sales. Line extensions have also been important in gaining shelf space in supermarkets.

Competitors

The two major competitors—Coke and Pepsi—controlled 70.9 percent of the market in 1987 (see Exhibit 6). Most significant of the smaller competitors were Dr. Pepper, 7-Up, and Royal Crown. As evidenced in Exhibits 6 and 7, Coke and Pepsi dominate the top soft drink brands. One point of overall market share represents $250 million in sales at the retail level.

A comparison of the top soft drink brands (Exhibit 7) offers many insights into the nature of competition in the soft drink industry. While Coke ranked as number one in

EXHIBIT 6
Market Shares of Top Soft Drink Companies

	Market Shares, %				
	1983	1984	1985	1986	1987
Coca-Cola Co.	36.4	37.5	38.6	39.8	40.0
PepsiCo, Inc.	28.4	28.8	29.9	30.6	30.9
Dr. Pepper Group	4.9	4.9	4.9	4.8	5.0
Seven-Up Company	7.1	6.8	6.0	5.0	5.1
Royal Crown Company	3.5	3.1	3.1	3.0	2.9
Cadbury Schweppes	3.9	3.7	3.2	2.9	2.4
Shasta Beverages	1.8	1.8	1.8	1.7	1.6
A&W Brands	1.2	1.3	1.2	1.2	1.5
Crush International	1.4	1.4	1.4	1.4	1.3
Others	11.4	10.7	9.9	9.6	9.3
Total	100.0	100.0	100.0	100.0	100.0

Source: "Soft Drink Report," *Beverage Industry,* March 1988, pp. 39–40.

1984, the division of Coke sales between new Coke (Coca-Cola) and Coke Classic allowed Pepsi to capture the number one spot in 1985, although Pepsi's market share fell from 19.1 percent in 1984 to 18.9 percent in 1985. The 1985 combined market share of new Coke and Coke Classic was 21.0 percent. While Coke occupied only 2 of the top 5 spots in 1984, the introduction of new Coke allowed the company to seize 3 of the top 5 spots in 1985. By 1987, new Coke had fallen to ninth spot. The phenomenal growth rates of Diet Coke and Diet Pepsi should also be noted. Diet Coke appears well entrenched in third place. Eighth in 1983, Diet Pepsi moved into fourth place in 1987.

While Coke's earnings come primarily from soft drink operations, Pepsi's earnings are split among soft drinks, snack foods, and restaurants. In 1987, soft drink products accounted for 81 percent of Coke's net operating revenues and 96 percent of operating

EXHIBIT 7
Market Shares of Top Soft Drink Brands

	Market Shares, %				
	1983	1984	1985	1986	1987
Coke Classic	--	--	6.0	19.1	19.8
Pepsi-Cola	18.9	19.1	18.9	18.6	18.6
Diet Coke	3.3	5.2	6.6	7.2	7.7
Diet Pepsi	2.7	3.2	3.9	4.4	4.8
Dr. Pepper	3.6	3.8	3.9	3.9	4.0
Sprite	2.6	3.4	3.8	3.6	3.6
7-Up	4.9	4.6	4.0	3.5	3.4
Mountain Dew	3.0	3.0	3.0	3.0	3.3
Coca-Cola*	23.1	22.5	15.0	2.4	1.7
Royal Crown	2.0	1.8	1.7	1.6	1.7

* Approximately half this figure relates to old Coke in 1985.
Source: "Soft Drink Report," *Beverage Industry,* March 1988, pp. 39–40.

income. Soft drinks at more diversified Pepsi represented 32 percent, snack foods represented 41 percent, and restaurants contributed 27 percent of operating profits. Restaurants, the fastest growing division at Pepsi, represent the largest U.S. company-operated fast service restaurant system. Fast food restaurants owned by Pepsi include Pizza Hut, Kentucky Fried Chicken, and Taco Bell.

THE COCA-COLA COMPANY

As related by Thomas Oliver (1985) in *The Real Coke, The Real Story,** an Atlanta pharmacist registered a trademark for "French Wine Cola—Ideal Nerve and Tonic Stimulant" in 1885. The name for the brew was appropriate as it is said to have contained cocaine, along with wine and a few other ingredients. After about a year, the formula was changed and the name was changed to Coca-Cola because it was thought that the two C's, written in the Spencerian script that was popular at the time, would look good in advertising. Coke was sold by traveling salesmen as a cure for hangovers and headaches.

Asa Candler bought the rights to Coca-Cola in 1889 and expanded the business by selling syrup to wholesalers, who in turn sold to drugstores. The syrup was mixed with carbonated water and served at soda fountains.

Later that year, two Tennessee businessmen purchased for $1.00 the right to bottle throughout nearly all of the United States. Feeling that drugstore fountain sales would predominate, Candler wanted no part of the expensive bottling operation. The two men promptly sold regional bottling rights to other businessmen in the South, and later in the rest of the country. By 1930 there were approximately 1,000 independent bottlers.

Ernest Woodruff purchased the Coca-Cola company in 1919 for $25 million. Woodruff was president of what was later to be known as the Trust Company of Georgia, the bank whose vault still guards the secret recipe for Coke. The formula was so secret that no more than three people at any time ever knew the proper mixture of its ingredients.

By the 1920s the company was embroiled in legal battles against imitators and facing bankruptcy. Profits were falling, sugar prices were rapidly increasing, and because of the contract, syrup was sold to bottlers at the fixed cost set in 1899. Robert Woodruff, Ernest's son, was brought in as president in 1923 to restore morale and profits.

When Woodruff took control, Coke was sold in the U.S., Canada, Cuba, and Puerto Rico, but was otherwise unknown around the world. Woodruff outlined a plan to test Coke in Europe, and when the board refused to grant approval, he proceeded in secrecy to establish a foreign sales department. Within 3 years, the foreign department showed a profit.

During World War II, Coke became a morale booster to the overseas troops. Initially the drink was shipped from a base in Iceland, but this became impractical as demand increased. In 1943, General Dwight Eisenhower requested the War Department establish 10 bottling plants in North Africa and Italy. The War Department supplied the machinery and personnel, usually soldiers who had worked for Coca-Cola prior to the war. At the end

* Oliver's book *The Real Coke, The Real Story,* provided much of the background for this case. Although not authorized by the Coca-Cola Company, its management did cooperate in providing Oliver with extensive access to its executives and records.

of the war there were 64 worldwide plants which had been built at government expense. These were incorporated without cost into the company.

Coca-Cola has maintained a strong lead in the soft drink international arena with about 74 percent of its 1987 operating income attributable to overseas soft drink operations. By 1987, Coke was distributed to 155 countries and consumed more than 303 million times a day. The company is the largest manufacturer, marketer, and distributor of soft drink concentrates and syrups in the world. Coke is as much a symbol of the U.S. as the Statue of Liberty. It is so strongly identified with the U.S. that when an ambassador is expelled for political reasons, Coke is sometimes exiled as well.

Structure of the Coca-Cola Company

The company operates in three markets—soft drinks, foods, and entertainment. In 1984 the company had sold The Wine Spectrum, an operating unit which produced and marketed wines.

As the world's largest processor of packaged citrus products, Coca-Cola Foods manufactures and markets such brands as Minute Maid, Five Alive, Bright and Early, Hi-C, and Maryland Club. The primary business headquarters of Coca-Cola Foods is located in Houston, Texas.

Its entertainment sector, composed of Columbia Picture Industries, Inc., and its affiliates, produces and distributes theatrical motion pictures and television series and features, publishes and distributes sheet music and song books, and engages in other entertainment-related activities. Columbia Pictures was only recently acquired by the company in 1982. Columbia Pictures' executive offices are located in New York, but its movie and television businesses are conducted from Burbank Studios in California.

The company has always been and still is a soft drink company. The net operating revenues and operating income of soft drink products are presented in Exhibits 8 and 9. Syrups and concentrates are manufactured by the company and then sold to bottling and canning operations and to authorized fountain wholesalers. Syrups are composed of sweetener, water, and flavoring concentrate. Independent and company-owned bottling and canning operations combine the syrup with carbonated water or combine the concentrate with sweetener and carbonated water and then package the soft drink product in cans, plastic containers, and glass bottles for sale to retailers. Fountain wholesalers sell soft drink syrups to fountain retailers, who ultimately sell fountain soft drinks to consumers.

In support of its soft drinks business, the company also provides promotional and marketing services. In consultation with its bottlers and fountain customers, the company develops and introduces new products, packages, and equipment.

On September 12, 1986, the company transferred the operating assets and/or common

EXHIBIT 8
Soft Drink Products' Net Operating Revenues

1982	*1983*	*1984*	*1985*	*1986*	*1987*
73%	71%	67%	77%	81%	81%

Source: 1984–1987 Form 10Ks of The Coca-Cola Company.

EXHIBIT 9
Soft Drink Products' Operating Income

1982	*1983*	*1984*	*1985*	*1986*	*1987*
84%	81%	86%	88%	89%	96%

Source: 1984–1987 Form 10Ks of The Coca-Cola Company.

stock of substantially all previously owned and recently acquired U.S. soft drink bottling companies to Coca-Cola Enterprises, Inc. (CCE), then a wholly owned subsidiary of the company. A number of U.S. bottling company acquisitions were immediately made, such that by the end of September, CCE was the largest bottler of Coca-Cola soft drink products in the world. In November 1986, the company reduced its ownership interest to 49 percent. By the end of 1986, CCE estimated that the area in which it marketed soft drink products accounted for 38 percent of the U.S. population. Brian Dyson, president of Coca-Cola USA, was tapped to head CCE. CCE's executive offices are located within the Coca-Cola complex in the building which housed Coca-Cola USA before it moved into its larger headquarters building within the complex.

The soft drink business is divided into domestic and international operations. Domestic operations, referred to as Coca-Cola USA, are headquartered in a separate building within the company's Atlanta headquarters complex. In 1984 and 1985, it was reported in the company's Form 10K that the U.S. accounted for 38 percent of the company's unit sales of soft drink products. This dropped to 37 percent in 1986, and by 1987 domestic sales accounted for 35 percent and international sales accounted for 65 percent.

In support of the company's stated primary corporate objective of increasing shareholder value, the company's business level strategy focuses on maximizing unit volume growth and utilization of its distribution systems. In the U.S. division, the strategy seeks to achieve these objectives by expanding its product line, strengthening its bottler system, and aggressive marketing programs, thereby increasing unit volume at a rate in excess of the industry growth rate.

The Beginnings of Trouble

In spite of an outwardly healthy image, behind the scenes troubles began to plague Coke executives. Dissention began in 1971 when the FTC charged that the bottlers' contract restricted competition. This was followed by a fight with bottlers over the price of syrup, a dispute which eventually resulted in the chairman and the company's president not speaking with each other. Critics, such as Thomas Oliver, charged that Coke's personnel decisions began to reflect the good-old-boys' regime. One company executive was quoted as saying that compensation was awarded "not on performance, but perfect attendance."

Walls Down

In 1971, the FTC challenged Coke, charging that the bottlers' contracts granting territorial exclusivity violated antitrust laws by restricting competition. If the government prevailed, Coca-Cola bottlers were free to invade the territory of other bottlers. This concept was known as "walls down" at Coke headquarters. This would make a bottler's future uncertain, thus reducing the value of the franchise, with anarchy predicted to result. The bottlers' contract granted each bottler an exclusive right *in perpetuity* to bottle Coke in his area, and with the exception of soda fountains, no other Coca-Cola franchise could sell Coke in that market, and the company could not refuse to sell them syrup.

An administrative law judge ruled in October 1975 that the bottlers' territorial exclusivity was not a violation of federal trade regulations, but two and a half years later the ruling was reversed and the FTC reinstituted the complaint. By 1978 little else was discussed at company headquarters. Long range planning was prevented, as the system Coke knew might not exist. Donald Keough later complained that in 1974 after he assumed the office of president of Coca-Cola USA, the domestic soft drink arm of The Coca-Cola Company, the first 50 meetings he attended were legal briefings on the FTC battle. Admitting that he had made a mistake, Keough said, "I should have hired a roomful of lawyers and told them to deal with it and we could have gotten on with the business." [13] It was not until 1980 that the complaint was ruled in favor of Coca-Cola.

Escalating Syrup Costs

Dating back to 1899, the original bottlers' contract set syrup at a fixed price. In 1921, the contract was modified to fix the price of syrup at the 1921 current price, subject to quarterly adjustments based on the price of sugar. Only the rising cost of sugar could be passed on to the bottler. This agreement worked well for 50 years, until the seventies when the spiraling costs of the other syrup ingredients made it barely possible for the company to make a profit on Coke. So once again, Coke found itself in conflict with the bottlers over modifying the contract.

Even within the company there was disagreement as to how the contract should be amended. Lucian Smith, the president and COO of The Coca-Cola Company from 1976–1980, felt the outdated price was illogical and advocated a totally flexible price that would reflect future inflation, while others felt some accommodation to the bottlers was necessary and favored an annual cap on how much the company could raise the price of syrup.

Many bottlers put up a fierce resistance. Until bottlers representing 50 percent of the domestic volume agreed to the change, the amendment could not take effect. Keough described the fight as like trying to talk someone out of a birthright as "Every bottler on his dying bed calls his son to his side, and speaking his last words says, 'Don't you ever let them mess with that contract.' " [14]

In the end Keough went around Smith and convinced J. Paul Austin, chairman of the board, and Robert Woodruff to favor an annual cap. Although Woodruff had officially retired in 1954, many felt he effectively controlled the company until his death in 1985. The board of directors agreed soon after. As a result, Smith and Austin's relationship became so strained that the two highest ranking executives of the company didn't even speak to each other. Austin reduced Smith's power by his creation of an office of the chairman, in which seven executive vice presidents, in essence, assumed Smith's duties as COO. A slighted Smith resigned a year later.

---

[13] Op. cit., Oliver, p. 32.
[14] Op. cit., Oliver, p. 34.

Despite amendments to the contract, the contract is considered to still represent an obstacle to the company. In contrast, Pepsi has more flexibility in its pricing policies, since Pepsi has no fixed price contract with its bottlers.

Changes in Bottling-Franchise Ownerships

When Keough moved to the office of the chairman, he hired Brian Dyson from Dyson's native Argentina, where he was working for the international sector, to head up Coca-Cola USA. One of Dyson's first goals as the new head of Coca-Cola USA in 1978 was to alter the company's laissez-faire attitude toward changes in bottling-franchise ownerships. It had always been company policy not to get involved with franchise transfers. If a bottler decided to sell, Coca-Cola could not stop him from transferring the contract to a new owner, who had all rights in perpetuity. Thus, the company had no real control over who was selling its products or how well the products were being sold.

In comparison to Pepsi, Coca-Cola operated at a cost disadvantage in their bottling operations. Whereas Pepsi had strong concentrated bottlers, which, because of their large size, had substantial economies of scale, Coca-Cola had many small bottlers.

Dyson argued that rather than the laissez-faire attitude, the Coca-Cola Company should involve itself in franchise ownership since the owner's performance determined the company's performance. So in 1979, the Washington, D.C. franchise was purchased by the managers of the franchise through a leveraged buyout structured by Keough and Dyson. Dyson's strategy was that each time a franchise came up for sale, Coca-Cola would either find a friendly buyer or purchase and later resell it. This would allow Coke to organize regional companies into larger distributorships that made more sense geographically.

THE PEPSI CHALLENGE

In the 1960s Pepsi made a major change in their advertising strategy; they stopped talking about the product and started talking about the user. The 1963 "Pepsi Generation" advertising campaign captured the imagination of the baby-boomers. It enhanced the image of Pepsi Cola and anyone who chose to drink it.

Pepsi took the lead in 1975 supermarket sales and has led in every year since, except 1976. Supermarket sales are regarded as the freedom of choice segment, since in other segments the customer often has limited choice—he can buy only the brand that is offered. Supermarket sales are referred to as the take-home market as opposed to the on-premises market where the soft drink is consumed when it is purchased.

While Coca-Cola's corporate take-home share (all their soft drinks combined) grew from 1983 to 1985, their brand Coke lost share. Coke's corporate share gain came primarily from the successes of Diet Coke and Sprite. Take-home share of brand Coke and brand Pepsi and corporate Coke and corporate Pepsi for 1983 to 1987 are presented in Exhibits 6 and 7. Supermarket sales represent about a third of Coke's total market, with fountain sales accounting for another third and vending sales making up the other third. Fountain sales are estimated to account for about 19 percent of Pepsi's volume. Estimates indicate that Coke does about 60 percent of the industry's total fountain volume. Since contracts with major fountain clients, such as McDonald's, are based on Coke's status as the number one cola, Coke felt it imperative to lead in all categories; otherwise, fountain clients might switch to Pepsi.

The "Pepsi Challenge" started in 1975 when Pepsi's Larry Smith was sent to Dallas to crack the market in Coke's heartland, the South. Pepsi was number three in Dallas, lagging behind Coke and the home-brew Dr. Pepper. Smith could not even entice a major grocery chain with an offer to finance a Pepsi promotion. Pepsi would pay the chain money and sell them Pepsi at a discount in exchange for newspaper ad promotion and prominent in-store displays. The chain was not interested. They didn't need Pepsi.

Coke had a 35 share, Dr. Pepper had 25, and Pepsi had 6. The nationwide Pepsi Generation theme wasn't working in Texas. Convinced that people were drinking Coke for its name, not its taste, Smith requested a custom-made advertising campaign for his market. Alan Pottasch, the advertising mastermind of the Pepsi-Cola Company, was opposed to local campaigns because they were always product-oriented and would interfere with his carefully built emphasis on the user rather than the beverage. If it succeeded in one area, bottlers in other areas would hear of it and want it for their territories, and a campaign that works in one place might not in another.

Putting his job on the line, Smith hired the in-house advertising agency of the Southland Corporation's 7-11 convenience store chain to help him come up with a campaign. Field tests to determine how people felt about Pepsi gave consumers a choice between two unmarked colas and asked them which tasted better. Pepsi was chosen by most of the people. A couple hundred taste tests gave a slim advantage to Pepsi, 52 to 48. In comparative advertising a valid test that demonstrates a preference, however slim the margin, gives a company the legal right to claim superiority.

Pepsi ran its Dallas TV commercial showing loyal Coke drinkers selecting Pepsi as the better tasting drink of the two unmarked colas. Coke tried to disprove the claim, but found when they ran their own test that it wasn't false. Coke had never tested its soda against any competitive product. Coke's counter advertising was unsuccessful; in fact, they played into Pepsi's hands, mentioning Pepsi in an ad for the first time. Pepsi's share quickly went from 6 to 14. The Challenge extended to Houston and moved to Los Angeles, and by 1983 was spread across the country. Only Atlanta, Coke's headquarters, was spared the insult of the Challenge.

Wounded pride led to an obsession with Coke's image as number one. What concerned Coke the most was the loss in share in the food store segment of the business. Even when Coke out-spent Pepsi in advertising, Pepsi still maintained their share leadership in supermarket sales. Pepsi used its lead in supermarket sales to claim superiority over Coke.

Coke's Market Research and Project Kansas

In the mid-1950s Coke was outselling Pepsi by a 2 to 1 margin; however, this wide margin was gradually narrowed by Pepsi long before the introduction of new Coke. As early as 1976, Coke's marketing department compiled a top secret report that showed leadership over Pepsi was no longer a given.

A later report claimed that while in 1972, 18 percent of soft drink users were exclusive Coke drinkers and a mere 4 percent drank only Pepsi, 10 years later the tally was 12 percent to 11 percent in Coke's favor. One suggested reason for Coke's tenuous lead was Coke's greater availability. Even if someone wanted Pepsi, in some places, he or she might find only Coke.

Ray Stout, director of marketing research, developed a complicated formula to measure the effect of advertising on sales. Using an Advertising Pressure Index, based on a score computed by an outside research firm grading the quality of both Coke's and Pepsi's advertising, the index was multiplied by the dollar figure spent airing the ads, and then the promotional index. The promotional index was a complex formula weighing the influence of such devices as newspaper coupons. The results of the formula, although complicated to evaluate, indicated that despite the fact that Coke spent far more on advertising than Pepsi, Coke's advertising programs were not effective enough.[15] Pepsi, on the other hand, had very effective ad campaigns, most notably the "Pepsi Generation" and the Michael Jackson spots. Coke had earlier turned down Michael Jackson as a candidate for its advertising because he was considered too flashy and his appearance didn't agree with the company's image as the all-American boy.

Pepsi's attacks had narrowed Coke's once large lead down to a 3.4 percent lead by 1984. Even more disturbing to Coke executives was that Coke was trailing in the grocery store segment by 1.7 percent. Coke finally decided that the loss in its market share basically boiled down to one factor—taste.

In September 1983, Sergio Zyman, senior vice president of marketing for Coca-Cola USA, became manager of a special project, Project Kansas, so named after a newspaper article by William Allen White in the *Emporia (Kansas) Gazette:* "Coca-Cola is the sublimated essence of all that America stands for. A decent thing, honestly made, universally distributed and conscientiously improved with the years."[16] Mexican-born Zyman had defected from Pepsi-Cola in 1979. At Coca-Cola he had been vice president of bottler operations, director of fountain sales, and Keough's executive assistant. Perhaps because of his newness to headquarters or because of his foreign background, Zyman had little problem with the idea of changing the formula, and he was quick to accuse reluctant managers of an inability to act with the times.

Coke had previously begun to investigate the public's willingness to accept a different Coke, conducting 1000 interviews in 10 major markets to test the public's response. Two key findings were: (1) exclusive Pepsi drinkers would be interested in a new Coke, and (2) many people didn't think Coke should be tampered with.

A year after Project Kansas was born, the technical department finally felt they had developed the right formula, and Coke initiated blind taste tests between the new formula and Pepsi. According to *Beverage Digest,* Coke conducted 190,000 tests among the 13 to 59 year old group. The tests centered on two key questions: (1) how consumers responded to a new formula in taste tests versus old Coke, and (2) how new Coke fared versus Pepsi. New Coke beat Pepsi 47 to 43 percent with 10 percent expressing no preference, and new Coke outscored old Coke 55 to 45 percent.[17]

Throughout all of their studies, researchers never made it clear to the consumers they tested that old Coke could be taken off the shelves if the new Coke was introduced. No actual research was done as to whether Coke should merely introduce a line extension.

Top management reaction to the new formula was mixed. Some wanted to introduce a second Coke. Others pointed out that Coke's product line was already unwieldy and

---

[15] Op. cit., Oliver, pp. 117–118.

[16] Op. cit., Oliver, p. 122.

[17] *Beverage Digest,* April 19, 1985, pp. 1–2.

bottlers would not be happy about adding yet another. Concern over the fountain business raised questions as to which Coke companies like McDonald's would choose. If McDonald's chose the new taste over old Coke, executives felt it would damage the flagship brand. The obsession with being number one in all phases ruled out the idea of a second cola since two Cokes would most likely split Coke's market share, allowing Pepsi to become the number one soft drink.

Finally, Coke's market share decline, especially in supermarkets, and Stout's taste tests, which continued to show new Coke winning out over old Coke and Pepsi by staggering margins, forced Keough to ignore his gut reaction against changing Coca-Cola. Keough, Chairman Goizueta, Director of Corporate Marketing Herbert, and Dyson met and agreed to give Coke a new taste.

How to handle the introduction of new Coke was carefully considered. Since Coke's corporate culture wouldn't let the company admit in any way that Pepsi was superior, the introduction couldn't say that in taste tests new Coke beat Pepsi, because someone may then ask how old Coke did versus Pepsi. By not being more candid about taste, taste became the focal issue as the public judged new Coke against old Coke.

REACTION TO THE ANNOUNCEMENT AND THE RETURN OF OLD COKE

Pepsi Declares a Holiday

Pepsi placed full page ads of Pepsi's President Roger Enrico's congratulatory letter to Pepsi bottlers in the nation's major newspapers the same day as the Coke press conference. The letter read in part:

> It gives me great pleasure to offer each of you my heartiest congratulations. After seventeen years of going at it eyeball-to-eyeball, the other guy just blinked. Coca-Cola is withdrawing their product from the marketplace, and is reformulating brand Coke to be more like Pepsi. . . . Maybe they finally realized what most of us have known for years, Pepsi tastes better than Coke . . . we have earned a holiday. We're going to declare a holiday on Friday. Enjoy![18]

Public Reaction

Public reaction to the introduction of new Coke was swift, and for the most part, very negative. To many consumers, changing Coke's formula was like rewriting the Constitution. Many Americans, especially those who lived in the South, saw Coke as an institution, and a link to a simpler past. In short, these mainstream middle Americans felt betrayed by an old friend. Many frenzied consumers rushed to grocery stores and bought huge supplies of the soon to be scarce old Coke. Some people spent hundreds of dollars stockpiling old Coke.

Newspapers all over the country ran negative articles about the new product, adding more fuel to the fire. By the middle of May, over 5,000 calls per day were being received by

---

[18] Op. cit., Oliver, p. 155.

Coke's consumer affairs department. Coke answered over 40,000 letters in the spring of 1985. New workers were hired to augment the consumer-affairs department. A total of 158 workers—69 college students, 27 agency temporaries, 12 company retirees, 30 freelancers, and 20 permanent members of the staff—operated 83 WATS lines.[19]

The vast majority of the calls and letters were negative. Most people were more upset with the fact that the taste had been changed rather than the new taste per se. By the end of spring, Coke came to the painful realization that they had vastly underestimated the sentimental feelings millions of consumers had for Coke.

Bottler's Reaction

Initially, most of Coke's bottlers supported the introduction of new Coke. Even the southern bottlers were at least convinced of long-term gains. However, the short-term effects were not viewed with optimism. As one Coke bottler put it, "Getting from here to there could be a little rough." [20]

Some Coke bottlers reported immediate acceptance by their customers. Most of these bottlers were located in the northeastern part of the country. In these markets, the introduction of new Coke actually increased the bottler's market shares. However, in order to gain wide acceptance, new Coke was going to have to be welcomed by consumers in the South, as the South represented Coke's high per capita markets.

Those bottlers who feared negative short-term effects saw their fears realized when the full force of public resentment hit. Frank Barron, whose territory in Georgia led the world in per capita sales of Coke, saw his volume "go to hell in a handbasket" by mid-June. His experience was hardly unique. In mid-June 1985, Coca-Cola held a week-long conference in Monte Carlo with the largest bottlers in the world. The top Coca-Cola officials appeared collected and controlled. They never hinted to anyone the slightest intention of bringing back old Coke.

Upon returning from Monte Carlo, Marvin Griffin, a North Carolina bottler, was told that sales were not going well and employees were beginning to doubt new Coke. Griffin countered the saying "If it ain't broke, don't fix it" by calling the saying "a motto for losers." If the company operated under that motto, he said, there would have been no Diet Coke, no New Tab, and Sprite would not have been improved to become a close second to 7-Up. Griffin told his employees the real change had taken place a long time ago—the day Coca-Cola decided to use packages other than the six-and-a-half-ounce bottle.[21]

On July 3rd, several large bottlers met with Brian Dyson, president of Coca-Cola USA, to tell him that they had to come back with the old Coke. But the later reintroduction of Coke Classic did not offer the bottlers a panacea. A *Leisure Beverage Insider* article stated that the extension of brand Coke with Coke Classic meant an 18 percent increase in costs due to packaging, warehouse space, production capability, truck space, ingredients, labels, crowns, point of purchase materials, and labor. Despite this rather gloomy outlook, virtually all of Coke's bottlers hailed the reintroduction of the old Coke.[22]

---

[19] Op. cit., Oliver, p. 203.
[20] *Beverage Digest,* May 21, 1985, p. 2.
[21] Op. cit., Oliver, p. 206.
[22] "Brand Extensions: The Burden is Back on the Bottlers," *Leisure Beverage Insider,* July 29, 1985, p. 1.

Fountain Sales

McDonald's is Coke's number one customer, selling Coke as its only cola product. At Coke's request, McDonald's was the first major customer to run a promotion for Coke. McDonald's use of Coca-Cola brand identified cups in the promotion marked the first time McDonald's had ever used a supplier's package. The purpose behind the promotion was to get a quick trial run for the new formula. McDonald's, with over 7,200 restaurants in the U.S., was an obvious choice. It was never disclosed how much Coke paid for the promotion.

McDonald's stayed with new Coke for about a year, but in May 1986 they decided to go back to the old formula. The decision was made quietly as McDonald's issued a simple statement saying that their marketing research results indicated that Coke Classic was the choice of the majority of their customers, and based on that finding, McDonald's had no choice but to change. The option of carrying two colas was never considered. McDonald's felt it would be too confusing and expensive to carry both Coke and Coke Classic.

The key issue for food service restaurants was the limited number of fountain heads. Most dispensing units have only four heads, thus if a restaurant were to offer Coke Classic and new Coke, two of the four heads would be for a sugared cola product. This would likely mean dropping one flavored offering such as an orange or root beer. In essence, restaurants were forced to choose one brand of Coke over the other. At least in the fountain segment, the reintroduction of the old formula cannibalized new Coke's sales.

Wall Street

A breakdown by quarter of 1985 and 1986 stock prices of Coca-Cola and PepsiCo, Inc., is presented in Exhibit 10. Asked to summarize what happened in the soft drink industry in 1985 and to make predictions for 1986, three top analysts offered the following thoughts in a 1986 issue of *Beverage World*.

Emmanuel Goldman of Montgomery Securities:

1. New Coke can't just be yanked from the shelf. Some consumers actually liked it.

Martin Romm of Boston Corporation:

1. Given the current numbers, Coke seems to be showing reasonably good results with the two brands together. The sum of the parts is greater than the whole.
2. Pepsi-Cola has definitely benefitted from the current situation. In a sense, the new and the old versions of Coke are competing with one another.
3. Consumers have embraced the Pepsi brand while rejecting new Coke.

Allan Kaplan of Merrill Lynch:

1. Coke took a chance. What it refers to right now as its fighting brand (new Coke) is going to go head-to-head with Pepsi for the new generation of soft drink consumers who like sweeter drinks. The new Coke is as sweet, if not slightly sweeter, than Pepsi.
2. Coke feels it has retained the people who liked the old Coke with Coca-Cola

EXHIBIT 10
Coca-Cola and PepsiCo, Inc., 1984–1987
Common Stock Prices

	Coca-Cola	*PepsiCo*
1984:		
First quarter	54⅞	38⅝
Second quarter	57⅝	41¾
Third quarter	62⅝	43¾
Fourth quarter	62⅜	42⅞
1985:		
First quarter	70	54⅝
Second quarter	69⅜	60⅛
Third quarter	69¾	59⅞
Fourth quarter	84½	72¾
1986:		
First quarter	106	83⅞
Second quarter	125½	33¾†
Third quarter	33⅞*	26½
Fourth quarter	37¾	26
1987:		
First quarter	45¾	34¼
Second quarter	44½	36
Third quarter	48⅜	39¾
Fourth quarter	38⅛	33⅜

* A 3/1 stock split on 7/1/86.
† A 3/1 stock split on 5/29/86.
Source: Value Line.

Classic. It will use the new Coke to attack the new generation. New Coke will be around for a while.[23]

Two Cokes

When the return of old Coke as Coke Classic was announced at a news conference on July 11, 1985, the scene of this conference was entirely different. Goizueta told those present:

> Today, we have two messages to deliver to the American consumer. First, to those of you who are drinking Coca-Cola with its great new taste, our thanks. . . . But there is a second group of consumers to whom we want to speak today and our message to this group is simple, we have heard you.[24]

In the months following the decision to sell new Coke and Coke Classic, the company's marketing strategy shifted emphasis from specific brands to categories—the megabrand strategy was developed. All drinks with the name Coke were grouped together—Coke, Coke Classic, Cherry Coke, Diet Coke, Caffeine-Free Coke, Caffeine-Free Diet Coke, and later, Diet Cherry Coke—thus, providing a new way to read the numbers.

[23] *Beverage Digest,* July 19, 1985, p. 3.
[24] Op. cit., Oliver, p. 213.

By the end of 1985, Pepsi had become the number one soft drink, but Coke Classic was gaining rapidly. The switch of McDonald's and Hardee's back to Coke Classic presented a crippling blow to new Coke's projections of success. The following year Coke Classic returned to its number one spot, Pepsi followed in second place, and new Coke finished the year ranked as number nine with 2.4 percent of the overall market. The same relative positions held in 1987 (see Exhibit 7). Coke Classic's strong growth in 1987 may have come at the expense of new Coke. Coke Classic's gain of 0.7 was offset by new Coke's identical loss. With its 1.7 percent market share, new Coke barely squeaked into the top ten.

Commenting on Coca-Cola's decision to change the formula, Keough said, "Some critics will say Coca-Cola made a marketing mistake. Some cynics will say that we planned the whole thing. The truth is we are not that dumb and we are not that smart."[25]

[25] Op. cit., Oliver, p. 216.

CASE 15

The U.S. Pharmaceutical Industry*

The highly-fragmented U.S. pharmaceutical industry consists of over one-thousand firms. Over two-thirds of these firms manufacture primarily pharmaceutical products. Hundreds of these specialize in only one country or type of drug. Sixteen U.S. drug firms control two-thirds of domestic sales and twenty international drug firms control seventy percent of the worldwide market. However, no single firm accounts for more than seven percent of the total domestic and four percent of global sales. While such fragmentation seems to imply it is difficult to make money, the opposite is true. Through the 1980s, the pharmaceutical industry has been highly profitable, enjoying stability, high growth, and large cash flows. International sales of ethical pharmaceuticals are about $100 billion and should double by the mid-1990s. The industry's annual growth rate between 1970 and 1980 was ten to twelve percent, and profits—already the largest in manufacturing—continued to rise during the 1980s.

The stakes have always been high, however. The drug industry's above-average economic performance and its salient role in people's health and nations' economies have attracted public and governmental scrutiny. The result is heavy industry regulation. For instance, government agencies' price controls have become popular, especially in countries where the government, through a national health care system, is the direct purchaser of pharmaceuticals. Drug companies try to hold down their annual price increases to prevent government retaliation. Another burden is assuring the efficacy and safety of drugs before marketing them. Each country approves drugs differently, but the Food and Drug Administration's (FDA) drug approval process has grown in cost and complexity to the firms. U.S. companies often introduce products in their overseas markets where approvals are speedier before marketing them in the U.S.

Pharmaceutical companies depend heavily on new products because they must make major investments for a long time before they earn a reasonable profit. A major pharmaceutical company will have to spend at least $500 million a year for research and development (R&D) to carry out sophisticated technical innovations, the amount spent worldwide by all companies in 1964. Declines of the value of the dollar, even before the October 1987 stock market "crash," have made U.S.-based research and products less expensive for foreign acquirers. Growth and success of the larger pharmaceutical firms depend on the international distribution of their products. European firms are becoming more competi-

* Prepared by Paul Miesing, State University of New York at Albany, and Michael Lubatkin, University of Connecticut and Groupe ESC Lyon. We are grateful for the many useful suggestions made by an anonymous reviewer. This case is based on MBA student reports and published information and public documents.

tive and opportunities from licensing European drug products are declining. As a result of these conditions, U.S. pharmaceutical firms are vulnerable takeover targets from European and Japanese firms. Strategic alliances and joint ventures are also becoming common as giant U.S. companies are diversifying into pharmaceuticals and increased costs have forced smaller pharmaceutical producers to unite.

In summary, today's challenges come from increased competition, more regulation, declining numbers of new product introductions, lower profit margins, and uncertain growth rates. The changing health care environment is also exerting pressure on drug prices. Opportunities exist in this new environment, however. Drug firms are searching for a competitive advantage in their R&D, marketing, and global operations. In the face of the industry's changing structure and environment, many firms have hoarded considerable cash that is available to bolster their investments, buy other businesses, repurchase some of their common shares, or pass more cash to shareholders.

HISTORICAL PERSPECTIVE

The discovery of sulfonamides, antibiotics, and antihistamines in the first half of the twentieth century made possible the profit potentials of the industry. Public outrage caused by Upton Sinclair's *The Jungle,* describing filthy conditions in the meat-packing industry, led to the passage of the Pure Food and Drug Act of 1906. At first the law concentrated on food products and had very little impact on drugs. This was probably because codeine, digitalis, insulin, iron salts, morphine, quinine, and most of the other available medicines dated back to antiquity. There had only been a handful of significant discoveries and even those were the result of prolonged and tedious research. Innovation was infrequent without disease prevention or scientific methods of research.

The "therapeutic revolution" from 1930 to 1950 began to transform the pharmaceutical industry. Technological changes increased potential profit and encouraged the development of systematic research methods. Natural vitamins and hormones were discovered and antibiotic research began on a significant scale. Dramatically, the pharmaceutical industry entered an era of commercialization. With many medicines sold directly to customers without prescription, major revisions to the Pure Food and Drug Act increased requirements for marketing new products. When one-hundred people died after taking a new wonder drug, the Food, Drug, and Cosmetics Act of 1938 mandated government approval of all drugs and set *safety* standards. As a result, a manufacturer cannot distribute any drug until it provides convincing evidence of its safety to the FDA. The law also stiffened regulations against false and misleading advertisements, required warning labels, banned dangerous drugs, strengthened enforcement procedures, and increased penalties for violators. In 1948, streptomycin became the first drug to receive a U.S. patent.

The pharmaceutical industry began to emerge in its modern form during the 1950s when the number of U.S. firms proliferated. The Senate Subcommittee on Antitrust and Monopoly and the Federal Trade Commission investigated monopoly drug pricing. The 1961 thalidomide tragedy in Europe horrified the world as pregnant women who took the drug gave birth to deformed babies. The uproar kept thalidomide out of the U.S. and forced the industry and Congress to agree on legislation that would protect consumers. The result was the Pure Food and Drug Act amendments of 1962 which required pre-market approval of new drug *effectiveness.* There were also significant regulatory controls to monitor the testing, labeling, manufacturing, and marketing of all drugs. The pharmaceutical industry now faces a high degree of regulation, complete with continuous scrutiny, and must maintain the highest standards of quality, safety, and efficacy. The costs and the lead times for developing new drugs have greatly increased.

INTERNATIONAL COMPETITION

U.S. pharmaceutical firms have faced growing competition from foreign firms since World War II. Although dominated by twenty firms, the pharmaceuticals industry today is truly an international one (see Exhibit 1). Traditionally, drug firms (especially European ones) have looked abroad for growth. For the most part, however, the world pharmaceutical market consists of the U.S., Europe, and Japan. All companies of any size have foreign subsidiaries in these areas. This leads to a high degree of interdependence and intracorporate transfer sales. However, these firms differ in size and scope. For example, among the top firms, pharmaceutical sales account for between fifteen percent and ninety-five percent of their total sales.

U.S. pharmaceutical firms have maintained their ninety-five percent share of the domestic market over the last twenty years. They also have the largest dollar volume of

EXHIBIT 1
Top Worldwide Drug Firms, 1988

		Sales					
Company	Country	Rx (In Millions of Dollars)	Total (In Billions of Dollars)	Earnings (In Millions of Dollars)	R&D (In Millions of Dollars)	World Rx Share (%)	Assets (In Billions of Dollars)
Abbott Laboratories	USA	$1,450	$4.94	$752	$250	1.35	$4.83
American Cyanamid	USA	1,560	4.59	306	190	1.45	4.60
American Home Products	USA	2,420	5.50	932	250	2.25	4.61
Bayer	GER	2,370	23.65	954	480	2.20	n.a.
Bristol-Myers	USA	2,010	5.97	829	275	1.90	5.20
CIBA-Geigy	SWZ	3,020	12.73	865	440	2.80	n.a.
Glaxo Holdings	UK	3,160	3.52	976	405	3.00	n.a.
Hoffmann-La Roche	SWZ	1,940	5.79	427	470	1.85	n.a.
Hoechst	GER	2,700	23.53	973	330	2.50	n.a.
Johnson & Johnson	USA	2,350	9.00	974	385	2.20	6.55
Eli Lilly	USA	2,090	4.07	761	375	1.95	5.85
Merck & Co.	USA	4,240	5.94	1,207	615	3.95	6.13
Pfizer	USA	2,260	5.39	791	380	2.10	7.64
Sandoz-Wander	SWZ	2,230	7.26	493	390	2.10	n.a.
Schering-Plough	USA	1,670	2.97	390	300	1.55	3.43
SmithKline Beckman	USA	2,300	4.75	476	285	2.15	5.02
Squibb	USA	1,710	2.59	426	275	1.60	3.08
Takeda Chemical Inds.	JAP	1,480	5.06	304	n.a.	1.40	n.a.
Upjohn	USA	1,650	2.75	353	320	1.55	3.14
Warner-Lambert	USA	1,590	3.91	340	220	1.50	2.70

GER = Germany; JAP = Japan; SWZ = Switzerland; n.a. = not available.
Source: *Financial World* (1989, May 30). p. 77.

exports in the world. Although exporting only four percent of total production, U.S. pharmaceutical companies account for twenty percent of all exports by developed countries. Moreover, the U.S. has consistently been a leader in introducing drugs. The ability of pharmaceutical companies to compete successfully in the future will depend on how they exploit developments in the biological and chemical sciences, genetic engineering technology, and computer applications. Product positioning will also be critical to their success.

U.S. pharmaceutical firms have been particularly adept at gaining worldwide acceptance of their products, accounting for around forty percent of the world's major drugs. This successful global penetration is probably the reason for their good overall performance. Foreign exports account for anywhere from a fifth to one-half of total sales for the major firms. The U.S. is the world's largest exporter of legal drugs, having overtaken West Germany in 1982. Exports of U.S. pharmaceutical firms passed $3 billion in 1987, but this will drop as U.S. firms manufacture more drugs abroad. Imports of pharmaceuticals passed $3 billion in 1988 as foreign drug firms continued making inroads into the U.S. market and U.S. firms imported some of their drugs from overseas plants. Although the U.S. is the largest consumer, it has the smallest proportion of imports to consumption for Western nations. West Germany remains the world's largest importer of pharmaceuticals.

Industry analysts expect worldwide demand for pharmaceuticals to grow in the industrialized and developing countries. Developed nations spend six to eight percent of their gross national product on health care compared to the two to three percent spent by less-developed countries. However, the less-developed countries spend half of their health care dollars on pharmaceutical drugs. This is in contrast to the fifteen to twenty percent spent by industrialized countries. Nevertheless, the low per capita income of less-developed countries does not offer opportunities for significant increases in drug sales. Differences in medical, legal, and commercial environments also make marketing difficult in these countries.

The high performance of U.S. pharmaceutical companies will continue for several reasons. (See Exhibit 2 for a financial summary.) *First,* U.S. drugs have an excellent reputation overseas. Due to federal legislation and enforcement, U.S. drug firms have achieved a worldwide reputation for having the most stringent standards of safety and efficacy. The new drug approval process in the U.S. is second only to Sweden in the average length of time required to reach market. The agency's attitude has been that it is better to be safe than sorry. These regulations prohibit the export of U.S.-produced drugs that have not yet received approval from U.S. regulatory authorities. A U.S. firm producing a drug for export must first obtain approval for domestic production. Distribution rather than manufacturing is an inherent advantage because this long approval process assures foreign customers that the drugs meet the highest standards. Thus, U.S. drug companies have been able to turn a development liability into a marketing asset.

Second, the pharmaceutical industry has remained firmly committed to original research since the 1950s. This spending has provided the new products that spurred industry growth. U.S. pharmaceutical firms historically have spent two-and-one-half times more money on research than any other U.S. industry. Although this is impressive, R&D spending by foreign companies has been at a faster rate as worldwide expenditures hit $10 billion in 1988. Japan is the largest spender, followed by West Germany.

Third, U.S. companies have been able to maintain or even slightly increase the rate of new drug introductions since the 1960s. (A new drug is important if it reaches world sales of

EXHIBIT 2
U.S. Pharmaceutical Industry*
Aggregates and Averages

	1980	*1982*	*1984*	*1986*
Selected financial results (in millions of dollars):				
Sales (at retail)	23,757	24,695	25,796	26,681
Net profit	2,098	2,370	2,953	3,144
Working capital	5,680	6,521	7,105	n.a.
Long-term debt	1,958	2,850	3,037	n.a.
Net worth	10,810	13,750	15,003	n.a.
Selected financial ratios (%):				
Operating margin	22.2	20.8	22.0	n.a.
Net profit margin	11.7	12.1	13.8	12.8
Earnings/total capital	17.2	16.0	18.2	20.5
Earnings/net worth	19.4	17.2	19.7	16.9
Retained earnings/equity	11.3	10.0	11.0	n.a.
Average dividend yield	3.6	3.5	3.6	3.6
Average price/earnings	11.7	14.2	16.0	15.1
Consumer price index (1967 = 100)	246.8	289.1	311.1	328.4

* Includes biologicals, medicinals/botanicals, and pharmaceuticals.
Sources: *Drug Topics* (Oradel, NJ: Medical Economics); *Standard and Poor's Basic Statistics: Textile, Chemical, Paper* (New York: Standard & Poor's, 1986); U.S. Bureau of the Census, *Statistical Abstracts of the United States: 1983* (Washington, D.C.: Department of Commerce, December, 1982); U.S. Bureau of the Census, *Statistical Abstracts of the United States: 1987* (Washington, D.C.: Department of Commerce, December, 1986); and "U.S. Industrial Outlook," U.S. Department of Commerce (Washington, D.C.: 1987).

$20 million while a leading new drug achieves $100 million of worldwide sales.) U.S. companies accounted for sixty-two percent of all new drugs introduced in the U.S. between 1940 and 1983. In 1985, there were thirty new chemical entities (NCEs) approved for sale—more than in any year since 1961 (see Exhibit 3). Sixteen of the twenty-one new drugs the FDA approved in 1987 were of U.S. origin.

EXHIBIT 3
New Chemical Entities Produced

Nationality of Parent Company	***1981–1985***	***Percent of Total*** ***1981–1985***	***1961–1977***
United States	69	25	24
Japan	61	22	10
West Germany	45	16	13
Switzerland	23	8	8
Italy	20	7	7
France	19	7	20
United Kingdom	12	4	5
Scandinavia	7	2	3
Others	24	9	10
Total	280	100	100

Source: Heinz Redwood, cited in *Chemical & Engineering News* (August 29, 1988), p. 17.

Finally, U.S. pharmaceutical companies are far more productive than the rest of U.S. manufacturing. This fact placed U.S. drug manufacturers on equal terms with most of their international competitors with no real loss in cost position. While other U.S. industries suffer from high labor costs, the drug companies avoid becoming labor-intensive. Furthermore, their extensive international operations allow drug companies to draw on inexpensive labor pools.

INDUSTRY CLUSTERS AND MOBILITY BARRIERS

The U.S. pharmaceutical industry has been successful because of its research, unique products, marketing, and patents. However, the combination of these as well as profits vary depending on which of five broad clusters a competitor belongs to: the giants, imitators, specialty firms, generic, and over-the-counter (OTC) manufacturers. Exhibit 4 presents a breakdown of the three primary strategic clusters, which have considerable overlap with generic and OTC firms. (Total sales, earnings, and R&D expenditures for major firms were in Exhibit 1.) A hierarchy of mobility barriers act as hurdles separating these clusters (see Exhibit 5). About three quarters of the dollar value of all pharmaceuticals used in the U.S. are for tranquilizers, parasitic and infectious diseases drugs, cardiovascular drugs, respiratory drugs, and vitamins and nutrients (see Exhibit 6).

Almost one-fourth of all pharmaceutical sales are for *generic* brands that are copies or chemical "equivalents" of branded products. An estimated three-quarters of generics sales are from large pharmaceutical firms that have over $100 million in sales, including Bolar

EXHIBIT 4
Major Product Lines for Strategic Clusters, 1987

Company	***Top Two Product Categories***
Giant cluster:	
American Home Products	Health care products; food & household products
Bristol-Myers	Pharmaceutical/medical prods.; nonprescription health
Eli Lilly & Co.	Human health care; agricultural chemicals
Merck & Co. Inc.	Human/animal health prods.; environmental health
Pfizer Inc.	Health care; agricultural products
SmithKline Beckman	Therapeutics; diagnostic, analytical
Imitators cluster:	
Schering-Plough	Ethical pharmaceuticals; consumer products
Squibb Corp.	Pharmaceutical products; medical products
Sterling Drug*	Hshld. prods., cosmet., toilet.; proprietary prods.
Syntex Corp,	Human pharmaceuticals; dent., beauty care, diagn. prod.
Upjohn	Human health care; agricultural
Warner-Lambert	Ethical prods.; nonprescription prods.
Specialty cluster:	
ICI Pharm.	Pharmaceuticals; life sciences
Marion Labs.	Pharmaceuticals & hospitals
Rorer Group	Pharmaceuticals; surgical products

* Sterling Drug data for 1986.
Source: Company reports, cited in *Health Care Industry Surveys* (Standard & Poor's, June 9, 1988), p. H-18.

EXHIBIT 5
Mobility Barriers Separating Strategic Clusters

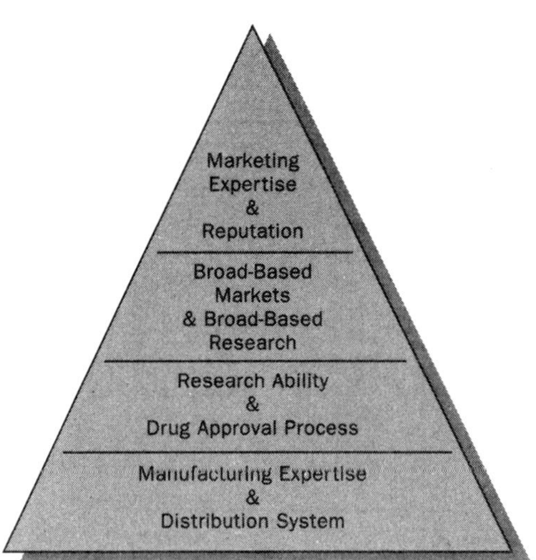

and Mylan. However, most of the two-hundred generic manufacturers are privately owned, limit their product lines and geographic scope, and have less than $1 million in sales. These small firms tend to manufacture private label drugs for the major distribution companies and pharmacies. The ones that are successful develop market niches and keep costs low. These companies enjoy higher pre-tax returns on sales than branded equivalents even though their products often sell for half as much. Experts estimate generic drug sales of $8.5 billion, or forty percent of the market, in 1990 as many patents for prescription drugs begin to expire (see Exhibit 7). About ten to twenty generics become available once a popular

EXHIBIT 6
Top Drugs (1987 Retail Market)

Product (Company)	*Function*	*Sales (In Millions of Dollars)*
Zantex (Glaxo)	Anti-ulcer	$542
Tagamet (SK&F*)	Anti-ulcer	423
Cardizem (Marion)	Cardiovascular	291
Naprosyn (Syntex)	Anti-arthritic	291
Tenormin (Stuart)	Cardiovascular	256
Dyazide (SK&F*)	Cardiovascular	252
Xanax (Upjohn)	Tranquilizer	249
Procardia (Pfizer)	Cardiovascular	234
Capoten (Squibb)	Cardiovascular	230
Ceclor (Lilly)	Antibiotic	220

* Smith Kline & French, a subsidiary of SmithKline Beckman.

Source: Pharmaceutical Data Services, cited in *Health Care Industry Surveys* (Standard & Poor's, June 9, 1988), p. H-21.

EXHIBIT 7
Expiring Ethical Drug Patents

Company	Drug Use	Expiration	1987 Sales (In Millions of Dollars)
CIBA-Geigy	Heart	1993	$169
Dow	Antihistamine	1992	118
Glaxo	Ulcer	1995	500
ICI	Heart	1991	250
Lilly	Antibiotic	1992	191
Marion	Heart	1992	300
Pfizer	Heart	1991	228
	Arthritis	1992	208
SmithKline	Ulcer	1994	523
Squibb	Heart	1993	115
	Heart	1995	207
Syntex	Arthritis	1993	275
Upjohn	Tranquilizer	1993	235

Source: Generic Pharmaceutical Industry Association, cited in *The Wall Street Journal* (February 20, 1990), p. B1.

drug loses its patent, requiring major firms to make defensive research investments. Moreover, recent U.S. legislation will permit firms to duplicate nearly all the top one-hundred patented prescription drugs. Finally, governments and third party payers (insurance companies, health maintenance organizations) will increase pressures for price reductions. For instance, the U.S. government—through Medicaid—is the largest single customer, and the Medicare Catastrophic Coverage Act of 1988 will require all U.S. pharmacies to dispense generic drugs to medicare patients beginning in 1991, unless a physician insists otherwise.

Proprietary (OTC) drugs make up nearly one-quarter of the total dollar value of U.S. pharmaceutical sales. Products such as analgesics (Tylenol, Anacin, and aspirin-based products), cough and cold items, vitamins, antacids, and laxatives are available without prescription, promoted directly to the public, and dispensed by physicians and pharmacists or through numerous retail outlets. There is a move toward making some anti-ulcer and anti-arthritic drugs available over the counter. There are 250 firms in this cluster, but ten account for half of all sales. These consumer drugs offer fifteen to twenty-five percent margins.

Drug manufacturers require *manufacturing expertise.* Because the pharmaceutical industry deals with sensitive areas of human life, all firms must maintain rigorous quality control to assure the highest standards of safety and efficacy. Not only are the companies responsible for any side effects of their drugs, but the doctors that prescribe them are also at risk. Another primary barrier into this industry is establishing a *distribution system.* Drug manufacturers market to two distinctly different types of customers: consumers and professionals. While most companies entering the drug business can effectively conduct consumer marketing, targeting professionals is a different matter. Successful marketing to this segment involves either company name recognition or wholesaler connections. Complicating matters, doctors are increasingly selling drugs directly to patients and cutting middlemen out of the distribution chain.

There are about 130 *specialty* companies that concentrate on only the pharmaceutical industry and support a small amount of R&D. It can take years before commercial *drug approval.* During this time companies must be able to pay out research money while receiving no return. Such projects require a financial stability not typically found in small companies. Giant companies often spend their development funds on projects yielding faster results. Although the members of this cluster have fairly narrow product lines, there is an extremely wide range of sizes. These firms are slowly expanding into international operations. Even though there are barriers to enter this cluster, they are not insurmountable. So it is not a surprise that many small manufacturers compete in this cluster causing intense competition and low profits. However, specialty firms that conduct their own R&D are successful because they develop *research capabilities* with financial and human resources.

The *imitators* are conservative followers that license or copy products. These companies have revenues ranging from $1 billion to $2 billion. This relatively small sales base makes it difficult to support R&D efforts. The firms in this cluster are too large to achieve a high degree of specialization and yet too small to achieve economies of scale. As niche players, they face intense competition from both the industry giants and specialized firms when they try to offer a full line of products. Nonetheless, their marketing has been successful in eroding competitors' first moves. In addition, some of the products are clever extensions of old products. A drug company wanting to enter the imitator cluster must be able to support a *broad-based research effort.* This means developing correspondingly *broad-based markets,* however. Some members of this cluster have depressed profits in spite of high entry barriers because they still compete directly with the giants.

The industry *giants* manufacture and distribute their products worldwide, receiving on average one-third of their revenues from foreign operations. They sell from $2 billion to $4 billion worth of branded products a year, placing them in the ranks of the largest multinationals. *Marketing and reputation* distinguish these firms from those in other clusters. All the giants conduct research in diverse areas and maintain broad product lines. They have marketing expertise and have built considerable consumer loyalty over the years. Although companies in the other clusters can develop consumer loyalty, they usually do not have the marketing capabilities. Spending the most on R&D and marketing allows them to reap the rewards of having many high-valued, patent-protected drug lines. American Home's acquisition of A. H. Robins demonstrates it is less expensive to acquire health care products than to develop brand names. The most regulated segment in the industry, they have succeeded by consistently turning out high-quality products that command high margins. Prices can reach 250 percent the level of generic drug equivalents. Although there is significant government pressure to use generic alternatives, many doctors and pharmacists are still reluctant to substitute generics. As a result, the giants continue to reap the benefits of extended sales of their branded drugs.

MARKETING

A large share of pharmaceutical costs goes toward marketing, often twice as much as for R&D. Drugs are unique in that the purchaser (doctor) is not the consumer (patient). Since drug firms' primary audience is practicing physicians, they advertise through medical representatives and medical media. A typical drug firm might spend one-half of its marketing budget for symposia, conferences, medical meetings, and special exhibits at scientific meetings. Another one-fourth might go for advertising in professional journals, one-fifth for staff, and the remaining for direct mail. Brand awareness and promotion is selective and occurs in medical radio and TV, direct mail, conferences, symposia, and free samples. Some analysts expect drug sales by mail to become a multi-billion dollar business in the 1990s.

Advertising, promotion, and other targeting strategies vary between the ethical, generic, and OTC drug groups. For instance, popular print and television media promote OTC drugs directly to consumers in an attempt to increase public awareness of the prescription products. However, advertising drugs competitively like other consumer products is in many instances illegal, controversial, and expensive. Recent legislation has mandated that warnings list various side effects of advertised drugs. The FDA placed a moratorium on advertisements in 1983 for specific drugs, exempting those based solely on price.

Nonetheless, marketing budgets continue to climb due to inflation, competition, product concentration, and increasing numbers of practicing physicians per capita. Marketing costs have also increased because promotional efforts to physicians require a well-educated and trained sales force. Drug companies also employ the services of agencies that prepare elaborate newsletters and periodicals for specialists. There are efforts to develop innovative approaches that will increase pharmaceutical advertising and marketing effectiveness. For instance, some firms are constructing statistical models to more accurately target physicians with the most desirable prescribing profile.

NEW DRUG DEVELOPMENT PROCESS

New drugs often sell for three to six times their costs. While the pharmaceutical industry has historically been productive in bringing new products to market, the rate of new product introductions slowed during the first half of the 1980s (see Exhibit 8). Such innovations are important because new products improve overall levels of sales and earnings. Firms that fail to market new drugs see their products' life cycles plateau. Other companies introduce superior drugs causing the decline of older products. The increased

EXHIBIT 8
Pharmaceutical Products Introduced in the U.S.

Year	Number of Firms	Total New Products	Newly Synthesized Drugs	Duplicate Single Products	Combination Products
1980	87	162	13	88	61
1981	100	120	18	57	45
1982	100	123	24	62	37
1983	102	123	22	60	41
1984	71	91	14	31	46
1985	56	83	23	13	47

Source: Paul de Haen International Inc, *S&P Industry Survey* (1987–1988), p. H-20.

time and cost of innovations result in a disproportionate amount of discoveries by larger firms and increased internationalization. Many U.S. companies are beginning to develop and manufacture drugs in their overseas subsidiaries as well.

Development, regulatory approval, and marketing of a new drug are lengthy and risky. Pharmaceutical companies may spend over $200 million to study ten thousand compounds over ten years and wind up with only one new drug for the consumer. To increase their chances of successful development, most firms conduct R&D on many drugs simultaneously. Drug firms spent a record $5.4 billion for R&D in 1987, a ten year annual compound rate of sixteen percent. The industry funds seventy percent, with twenty percent coming from government and the remaining ten percent from universities. About sixty percent of the R&D budget goes for testing safety and efficacy, and another twenty percent for clinical trials.

There are several distinct phases in research. *Pre-clinical* studies research a new product. A team analyzes a therapeutic problem, reviews the literature, and selects natural or man-made substances for further investigation. Using laboratory test tubes and animals determines the pathological and toxic effects of synthetic chemicals on biological functions and conditions. Only about two percent of the compounds are later tested in humans, and most of these substances will fail to show therapeutic advantages or will not be commercially promising.

After having spent an average of two years to complete the initial investigation, the new substance enters the human *clinical* trials. This is typically the most expensive part of development. The research design first undergoes regulatory review. In the U.S., clinical studies begin thirty days after the FDA accepts an Investigational New Drug (IND) application that details the completed research, including product formula and characteristics. These are typically lengthy documents of more than 50,000 pages each. Of the 2,000 INDs that the FDA receives each year, fewer than ten percent complete the required clinical studies. A limited number of healthy volunteers take the new drug to examine pharmacological effects and safety. Patients suffering from the condition the drug is intended to treat then take the drug to examine its efficacy in treating a specific illness. Extensive testing on a larger group of patients will confirm or reject the preliminary findings and uncover uncommon adverse reactions. After the clinical testing phase, the FDA receives the compound and decides whether or not to grant permission to *market* the drug. This review can take three years. Less than a fifth of drugs in clinical trials make it to the market. The FDA may require supplemental information after marketing has begun. It can also recall a drug if safety or efficacy is in question or for such other reasons as defective packaging, misleading labeling, insterility, or subpotency. Over 200 new drug applications were waiting review by the FDA at the end of 1987. The most promising included a cardiovascular agent, an anti-hypertensive drug, a cardioselective antagonist, a diabetes drug, an anti-depressant, interferons, and antibiotic agents.

Since a compound is patented before it is approved, the time from initiation of clinical studies to its sales reduces the seventeen year patent-protected marketing period for new drugs by about five years. It also increases the cost of new drugs and decreases the return on investment. To counter this, the Waxman-Hatch Drug Price Competition/Patent Term Restoration Act of 1984 extends a patent by the length of the regulatory review period. The Act also enables generic drugs to apply for an Abbreviated New Drug Application. In addition, recent FDA regulations will decrease the drug approval time to twenty-one months. The approval time will be less if a generic is chemically identical to the pioneer drug in composition, dosage form, strength, and conditions for recommended use.

The costly and lengthy process of drug development and approval has been a major barrier to entry in the industry. Such research has also become the foundation of competitive strength for pharmaceutical firms. There are unequal distributions of costs and benefits for innovation among drug firms, with extensive testing and years of delay increasing the costs and risks of innovation for small firms. Historically, in the pharmaceutical industry as in other sectors of the economy, the costs per innovation have not differed by firm size. Recent shifts in costs and risks have increased economies of scale in R&D and encouraged simultaneous testing of several new chemical entities. These higher costs increase the sales accounted for by the larger firms and the dependence of smaller firms on outside sources of innovation. Small firms license new products and split any profits with the innovator. They have also been relying on foreign firms for NCEs. This has been a convenient relationship since few foreign companies have subsidiaries in the U.S. However, this dependence also makes small- and medium-sized firms vulnerable. While the fees paid to outside innovators results in lower rates of return and less funding for internal R&D, a significant source of sales for domestic firms would disappear should these foreign firms establish their own subsidiaries in the U.S.

SCIENTIFIC INNOVATIONS

In spite of legal and financial obstacles, the U.S. continues to produce more innovative drugs than any other country. There are many opportunities for developing products and unique drug dosage forms. *Biotechnology* allows modifying and recombining human, animal, and plant life DNA. It might change medicine by the end of the century as antibiotics did in the middle of the century. The U.S. Patent & Trademark Office has issued thousands of biotechnology-related patents since the Supreme Court ruled in 1980 that genetically altered life forms are patentable. Recently approved drugs include those that will treat heart attacks, anemias, and cancer. Such genetic engineering has a promising future internationally, with markets predicted to reach as high as $100 billion by the year 2000. The Reagan Administration selected bioengineering (along with the computers, robotics, and semiconductors) as having the greatest potential for maintaining U.S. export leadership into the twenty-first century. As a result, investors and venture capitalists are providing funding to such leading firms as Amgen, Cetus, and Genentech. The U.S. dominates because of its basic research capabilities in biomedical sciences, strong industrial base, extensive research at major universities, and large pool of scientists and engineers involved in biotechnological R&D.

A revolution is also taking place in *drug delivery systems.* Dexedrine's "tiny time capsules" in the 1950s were the first controlled-release system. Today, new types of systems provide a steady dosage of medication which replaces the former "peak and trough" method (receiving high dosages right after taking the drug). Ideally, the new systems will provide the right dosage continually. For instance, polymer network systems mix the drug with a polymer that directs the active ingredient through a complex maze of pores. Transdermal patch delivery systems will permit drugs containing complex substances to penetrate the skin and enter the blood system. Respiratory delivery systems deliver drugs through sprays by taking advantage of the superior absorption properties of the respiratory tract. Enzyme-responsive release systems generate a minute pulse of electricity to open skin pores temporarily. Computer delivery systems release medication to the patient's diurnal rhythm. A plastic wafer carries powerful drugs to brain-cancer victims. An "intelligent" nasal spray releases the correct amount of insulin for diabetics.

The role of *computer applications* will continue to grow. Already the miniaturization of computer memory enables patients to carry their total medical history on a card. Computer networking systems connect hospitals, doctors, and pharmacists to more efficiently deliver products and services. Perhaps through home computers, artificial intelligence systems will diagnose a patient's illness. Drug research increasingly relies on "directed chemistry" for the identification and testing of new drugs. Therefore, the computer's ability to conduct a myriad of calculations and draw exact pictures of the results will become invaluable in drug design. This will save enormous amounts of time and effort by quickly revealing the appropriateness of a drug molecule. Furthermore, researchers knowing the molecular basis of a disease can deliberately design a suitable drug.

CASE 16

Eastman Kodak's Acquisition of Sterling Drug*

On Friday, January 22, 1988, Eastman Kodak Co. agreed to buy Sterling Drug Inc. for $5.1 billion or $89.50 per share. This was the largest non-oil acquisition in U.S. history. The announcement of the acquisition did not surprise some analysts. Kodak had shown an interest in the pharmaceutical industry after setting up a pharmaceutical division within its Life Science Group a few years before (see Exhibit 1 for Kodak's operating structure). "The company needed an acquisition to give us a worldwide infrastructure to register and market drugs," said Charles Smith, a spokesperson for the pharmaceutical division of Kodak. This acquisition permits Kodak to achieve its goal of $1 billion in sales by the early 1990s as well as providing products to complement its chemicals and diagnostic equipment as well as valuable experience in getting new drugs through the complicated federal regulatory process.

Kodak emerged as a "white knight" after F. Hoffmann-La Roche & Co., a Swiss pharmaceutical multinational, had bid $4.2 billion, or $72 a share, that escalated to $81. Sterling's all-time high stock price had been $69.25. Since Sterling insiders held only one percent of its stock, Hoffmann-La Roche's bid sent Sterling Chairman and CEO John Pietruski searching for a company with no pharmaceutical operations. Neil Sweig of Prudential-Bache Securities, Inc., said, "There is not much time or room to maneuver . . . this is a real bear hug." Other interested companies included American Home Products, Bristol-Myers, Johnson & Johnson, and Unilever, PLC. After losing the bid to Kodak, Hoffmann-La Roche Chairman and CEO Fritz Gerber stated, "We offered what we believe is a fair price." In justifying his company's bid, Kodak Chairman and CEO Colby H. Chandler said, "For us, the Sterling price was a good price . . . for IBM or GE it would be a bad price. But we have the synergies to justify it. We bring the scientific skills, Sterling brings the marketing strengths." Nevertheless, executives from both companies felt compelled to assure the financial community that the acquisition would start paying off in a year.

KODAK AT A TURNING POINT

Kodak has undergone extensive change since Mr. Chandler assumed its leadership in 1983. He trimmed costs, reorganized management, and exploited new market opportunities. Kodak's overall performance was impressive. Profits climbed to $1.2 billion in 1987 (triple 1986) on sales of $13.3 billion. (See Exhibit 2 for a financial summary.) Typical of the changes are the following comments made at a recent shareholders' meeting:

---

* Prepared by Michael Lubatkin, University of Connecticut and Groupe ESC Lyon, and Paul Miesing, State University of New York at Albany. We are grateful for the many useful suggestions made by an anonymous reviewer. This case is based on MBA student reports and published information and public documents.

EXHIBIT 1
Kodak's Operating Structure

Corporate staff:	Communications and public affairs Corporate commercial affairs Corporate planning Corporate relations Finance and administration Legal Research
Operating business groups:	Commercial and information systems (business imaging systems, graphics imaging systems, copy products) Diversified technologies (clinical products, health sciences, mass memory) Eastman chemicals division Life sciences Photographic products (consumer products, Kodak processing laboratories, motion picture and audiovisual products, photofinishing systems, professional photography, U.S. sales)
Operating support units:	Manufacturing Customer and marketing support operations International

Source: Annual reports.

"Commitment to a work force reduction . . ."

"Steps to operate more effectively . . ."

"Today's increasingly competitive environment calls for immediate action to bring our costs more into line . . ."

"The photographic Products Group will introduce more and improved products . . ."

"Stage is set for several years of solid gains in sales and earnings . . ."

Leadership, technological innovation, and quality built Kodak's reputation in photographic products. Its strong position in photographic films differentiated it from competitors who marketed only cameras. As a result, Kodak enjoyed hefty seventy percent margins in films and photographic paper in the 1970s. There was little interest in decreasing costs. "We'd choose suppliers because they were within 200 miles from Rochester, not because they were low bidders," said Robert Crandall, a manager of equipment design and manufacturing. Competition from low-cost producers eroded Kodak's huge market share by the early 1980s. Efficiency throughout the organization improved by redefining research and manufacturing goals and procedures, and eliminating operations that were inefficient and product lines that were unprofitable. There was a five percent decrease in divisional budgets and a ten percent reduction in the workforce (eliminating 12,765 positions) that saved over $500 million in 1987.

EXHIBIT 2
Kodak Financial Summary
(In Millions of Dollars)

	1980	*1982*	*1984*	*1986*	*1988 (Consolidated)*
Selected income data:					
Revenues	9,734	10,815	10,600	11,550	17,034
Operating income	2,296	2,435	2,305	2,200	n.a.
Capital expenditures	902	1,500	970	1,438	1,914
Total depreciation expense	399	575	758	956	1,057
Interest expense	46	89	114	255	697
Net before taxes	1,963	1,872	1,624	598	2,236
Net income	1,154	1,162	923	374	1,397
Selected balance sheet data:					
Cash	1,585	1,018	1,011	513	848
Current assets	5,246	5,289	5,131	5,811	8,684
Total assets	8,754	10,622	10,778	12,902	22,964
Total current liabilities	2,247	2,146	2,306	3,791	5,850
Long-term debt	79	350	409	911	7,779
Common equity	6,028	7,541	7,137	6,388	6,780
Total capitalization	6,378	8,337	8,269	8,508	n.a.

Source: Annual reports.

Kodak also restructured its rigid bureaucracy. Twenty-four new business units received profit, cost, and quality responsibilities, instilling a greater sense of competitiveness and a team spirit in the company's operations. "We must grow and our internal changes were necessary structural adjustments to assure that growth," said Mr. Chandler. As a result, new product introductions increased in 1987 (250 new or improved products in the two years prior to the acquisition). Pleased with such results, Mr. Chandler said, "We are a high margin company and it is new products that have the higher margins." William J. Janawitz, manager of manufacturing equipment, recently said, "Nowadays there is a sense of urgency. Everybody knows the future is not as certain as it once was."

However, that sense of urgency was not always part of Kodak's culture. "We used to brag about how long it took us to work on a product," an executive recalled. As a result, the company has often been on the defensive against more aggressive competitors. For instance, Kodak did not effectively challenge Xerox's entry into the dry copier market in the 1960s. Fuji's innovative marketing and Kodak's withdrawal from the 35mm camera market in the 1970s permitted Japanese dominance and a ten percent decline in Kodak's market share. Kodak underestimated the market potentials of instant photography until Polaroid dominated it.

In addition to photographic films and materials, Kodak markets a variety of chemicals, fibers, and plastics to industrial customers and audiovisual products to households. It also markets medical and industrial X-Ray films, equipment, and blood analyzers to hospitals and physicians. Although Kodak had been insular and averse to risk, a new attitude resulted in the following agreements, joint ventures, and acquisitions. On March 5, 1985, Kodak purchased a stake in Chinon Industries, a Japanese firm, to sell 35mm cameras under the Kodak name. On July 13, 1985, it acquired Verbatim, a maker of floppy disks for personal computers, for $175 million. On May 22, 1986, Kodak created a Lithium batteries business unit. On July 7, 1987, it entered into a joint venture with Imagica Corp., a Japanese photofinishing firm, to use Kodak's reagents and materials. On November 12, 1987, Kodak agreed with Digital Equipment to market Kodak's information system. On December 7, 1987, it agreed to merge with the U.S. photofinishing operations of Fuqua Industries that would result in the world's largest photofinishing operation. (The agreement was challenged in courts on antitrust grounds.)

Analysts viewed Kodak's diversification plans as an attempt to decrease its dependence on photographic films and papers. However, some of Kodak's new ventures in electronic publishing, batteries, optical memory, and floppy disks were performing below expectations. Some analysts doubted its ability to operate outside its core business. For example, Verbatim has barely been profitable. Its venture into videocassette recorders and cameras and the marketing of batteries did not result in a competitive advantage. "There is a difference between competing in a mature market [films], where you are dominant and in a leading-edge technology," said Scott C. McCready, an analyst at CAP International. The hefty profit margins provided by the mature products are expected to decline in the near future.

Kodak's Interests in Health Care

In 1974, Kodak formed a Life Science Group which holds the rights to a natural vitamin E patent. The group considered cancer, cardiovascular, and analgesic to be important therapeutic areas. In addition, a marketing agreement with Immunex showed an interest in immune deficiencies, specifically rheumatoid arthritis. Kodak also purchased a twenty percent interest in Neorx Corp. (a cancer research company) and a twenty percent interest in Enzon, Inc. (a developer of drug delivery systems). According to some estimates, Kodak spent over $100 million in its health-related investments. Executives from Kodak's photographic group were concerned about the possibility of classifying their group a "cash cow." They were also suspicious of their company's ventures into health care products, proud of their performance, and optimistic about the future. "Last year we had the largest percent growth in ten years in color negative exposure and that is the biggest barometer of photographic products health," said William Z. Prezzano, head of photographic products group. "That does not suggest this is an industry that is plateauing."

Kodak's health care ventures involved acquisitions, joint ventures, and internal developments. On December 18, 1985, Kodak agreed with Nova Pharmaceutical to have some of Kodak's 500,000 chemicals screened for possible therapeutic value. On February 27, 1986, it entered into a joint agreement with Amgen, a genetic engineering firm, for rights to manufacture and market specialty chemicals in the future. On May 15, 1986, Kodak agreed with Cytogen Corp. for joint development and marketing of products that diagnose cancer. On August 6, 1987, it acquired one-fourth of Genencor, a biotechnology firm. On January 22, 1988, Kodak announced the acquisition of Sterling Drug, Inc. Kodak expected Sterling to become a global pharmaceutical competitor, especially in OTC drugs and household products. By the year 2000, Kodak wanted Sterling to be among the top-twenty pharmaceutical companies.

Acquisition of Sterling Drug, Inc.

The $5.1 billion bid for Sterling was one of Kodak's boldest and speediest diversification moves. It even took some of its own executives by surprise. "We used to be so slow and ponderous, we'd still be talking about whether to buy it rather than discussing how to integrate it," said Kodak President Kay R. Whitmore. Wall Street did not respond well to the size of Sterling's price tag. Kodak's stock price dropped twenty percent following the announcement. "They overpaid," said John M. McCarthy of Lord Abbet & Co. "They collapsed the stock."[1]

There were concerns over Kodak's debt rising from thirty-five percent to fifty-seven percent of capital. "The acquisition dilutes their earnings and creates an extraordinary amount of leverage on their balance sheet," said Eugene Galser of Dean Witter Reynolds. On the other hand, analysts pointed out the valuable distribution network and some strong products that Sterling would bring Kodak. Mr. Chandler agreed: "Sterling makes Kodak a real drug industry player with greater certainty, sooner and at a better cost advantage . . . health care is the highest-margin business of the future with high cost of entry." However, Samuel D. Isaly of S. G. Warburg & Co. said, "they [Sterling] offer a worldwide network for prescription drugs but no record of doing well at it." However, as the January 9, 1988 issue of *The Economist* reported, the only affordable companies in the industry were small or middle size which "are not large because they backed the wrong horses."

STERLING DRUG, INC.

Like Kodak, Sterling Drug, Inc. had turned around during the 1980s. It slashed costs, expanded international operations, increased R&D expenditures, and bolstered advertising budgets. (See Exhibit 3 for a financial summary.) The company earned $197 million on $2.3 billion sales in 1987, a seventeen percent profit increase from 1986. The company's product segments include household and other consumer products, pharmaceutical specialties (prescription drugs and hospital products), and proprietary (OTC) products (see Exhibit 4).

Sterling's most successful pharmaceutical products are its OTC drugs, especially its analgesics.[2] Bayer Aspirin, Sterling's leading product with $100 million in annual sales, has recently gained market share as a result of its reported preventive effects on heart attacks and strokes as well as shrewd promotion ("The Wonder Drug That Works Wonders"). Other pharmaceutical products marketed to the consumer include decongestants and baby and skin care products. The only other product with around $100 million annual sales is Omnipaque. A leader in pharmaceutical specialties (prescription) products, it is a non-ionic radio-diagnostic agent used in medical diagnoses and visualization of organs, arteries, veins, and the spinal canal. Another recently introduced prescription drug, Inocor, is the company's first entry into the cardiovascular market. Sterling divested its subsidiary,

[1] Before the October 1987 market decline, the pharmaceutical industry commanded a purchase price that was over twenty-five times earnings.

[2] The over-the-counter (OTC) market is over $10 billion a year in the U.S. and is projected to grow further due to increased self-medication. There are 250 companies competing in this drug segment of lower profit margins (fifteen to twenty-five percent compared to over thirty-five percent for prescription drugs). Companies dominating this drug segment include Abbott Labs, American Home Products, Bristol-Myers, and Johnson & Johnson.

EXHIBIT 3
Sterling Financial Summary (in Millions of Dollars)

	1980	1982	1984	1986
Selected income data:				
Revenues	1,701	1,796	1,827	1,990
Operating income	256	287	290	343
Capital expenditures	70	80	73	68
Research and development	n.a.	68	85	103
Advertising and promotion	n.a.	286	335	413
Depreciation	31	34	37	44
Interest expense	15	17	43	46
Net before taxes	224	252	260	300
Net income	123	132	145	172
Selected balance sheet data:				
Cash	179	229	355	383
Current assets	873	916	1,029	1,099
Total assets	1,258	1,333	1,459	1,724
Current liabilities	342	326	390	476
Long-term debt	51	72	80	208
Common equity	797	861	924	974
Total capitalization	916	1,007	1,069	1,248

Source: Annual reports.

EXHIBIT 4
Major Product Segments for Sterling Drug, Inc., 1986*

Product Segment	Brand Name and Product Use
Household and other products (30% sales; 33% profits)	Lysol line of disinfectants and cleaners Love My Carpet, Mop & Glo, and Perk floor care products D-Con insecticides and rodenticides Minwax stains, finishes, and waxes Wet Ones moist towelettes
Pharmaceutical specialties (15% sales; 22% profits)	Amipaque, Hypaque, and Omnipaque radiodiagnostic agents Demerol, Talwin, and Marcaine analgesics Bronkosol and Tornalate bronchodilators Danocrine for endometriosis Inocor cardiovascular agent
Proprietary products (16% sales; 18% profits)	Bayer aspirin Panadol acetaminophen (non-aspirin pain reliever) Diaparene baby care products Neo-Synephrine nasal decongestants Stridex skin care items Midol analgesic Phillip's Milk of Magnesia laxative

* Does not include international business (39% sales, 27% profits).
Source: Annual reports.

Hilton-Davis Chemical Co., in 1986 to concentrate on its health care and consumer products.

Sterling also sought out two acquisitions to bolster its core business. In July 1986, it purchased Thomson & Formby, Inc., a producer of waterproofing and wood finishing products. This is an addition to its current line of "do-it-yourself" interior wood care products. In December 1986, it purchased Woodroof Labs., a producer of patented burn wound dressing. Wound care is a rapidly growing area.

Internationally, only in England was Sterling among the top ten drug companies in 1986. To make up lost ground, it bought several prescription pharmaceutical firms. One is from Schwarzhaupt GmbH, a German firm. Another is from two French companies with combined sales of about $30 million. Laboratoires Valda is an OTC drug producer with operations in Italy and Laboratoire du-Docteur Furt produces and markets fruit-extract laxatives. Sterling also entered into a joint agreement with Yamanouchi Pharmaceutical Co., the fifth largest ethical drug company in Japan. Japan, Germany, France, and Italy rank among the largest drug markets in the world.

In cutting its manufacturing costs in 1986, Sterling's cost of goods decreased from thirty-nine percent of sales to thirty-four percent. Sterling also reduced worldwide administrative costs. Outlays for R&D in 1987 increased to $119 million (five percent of its sales), a fifteen percent rise over the previous year. In addition, advertising and promotional budgets increased from $286 million to $413 million over the last four years. Sterling's developmental targets in health care included cardiovascular, antibacterial, and analgesics.

REFLECTIONS

Kodak's aggressive move into the pharmaceutical arena followed similar moves by companies with chemical operations, including Du Pont & Co. (marketing and development arrangement with Merck & Co.), Dow Chemical Co. (owns two-thirds of Marion Laboratories), and Monsanto (acquisition of G. D. Searle & Co.). Many analysts worried about the effect that Sterling's price tag would have on Kodak's plans and future earnings. Others, like David Presson from Edward D. Jones & Co., argued "Kodak is not so concerned about what its earnings will be this quarter, but is looking out into the 1990s." Furthermore, many believed that Kodak's pharmaceutical executives, including some recent recruits from Merck and CIBA-Geigy, increased Sterling's effectiveness. Mr. Whitmore, to whom Sterling reports, said, "We paid a handsome price for Sterling. We have to make sure we can get a return for it." However, as Norman C. Selby from McKinsey & Co. noted, "Research organizations have as much of an immune rejection system as the body."

The following occurred immediately after Kodak's acquisition of Sterling:

- Moody's Investors Service and Standard & Poor's Corp. lowered Kodak's debt ratings.
- On February 19, 1988, Polaroid Corp. announced that it would ask for $5.7 billion in damages after a court ruled Kodak infringed on its instant photography patent.
- On February 23, 1988, Kodak secured a $5 billion, thirty-year loan from an international group of banks to finance Sterling's acquisition. The short-term interest rates were around seven percent.

- In February 1988, Kodak offered \$1.1 billion of ten-year notes to be used for various corporate purposes, including Sterling's acquisition. Originally, it had planned to sell about \$750 million of notes. The notes, noncallable for seven years, are rated A2 by Moody's Investors Service and A− by Standard & Poor's Corporation.
- In August 1988, Leo J. Thomas, Sterling's chair, announced plans to consolidate Sterling's upstate New York facilities into Kodak's suburban Philadelphia operations.

As a result of these events, John Pietruski wondered if his successful pursuit of a buyer without pharmaceutical operations, like Kodak, would help preserve Sterling's independence. Kodak was uncertain if Sterling would increase its market value and power by making it a leading pharmaceutical company in an industry full of surprises, risks, and strong competitors.

THE PHOTOCOPIER INDUSTRY

CASE 17

Xerox Corporation: 1960 to 1980*

THE GENESIS OF THE PHOTOCOPIER INDUSTRY

From a user's standpoint, making photocopies of a document is a simple process, but the technology necessary to make a modern light lens copier utilizes many sciences, including chemistry, electrical engineering, optics, and mechanical engineering. A photocopying machine may contain ten or more microprocessors (small computers) that are controlled by a computer the user operates to control the machine. Development of these machines entails costs that are measured in the hundreds of millions of dollars; it involves thousands of technical personnel and often takes more than a decade to complete. For the sake of comparison, these figures are similar to those required in designing the jet fighters of the 1970s. And yet, unlike the jet fighter, the product must be easy enough to use that operators require little or no training.

The most successful copier ever designed was the Xerox 914, introduced in 1959. This was the model that launched Xerox and the entire photocopier industry. The 914 was the brainchild of Chester Carlson, a reserved visionary who made the first successful "xerographic" image in 1938. (The term combines the Greek words for "dry" and "writing.") Over the next several years, he offered his idea to more than twenty companies, including General Electric, IBM, and Kodak. They all turned him down, explaining that no one needed his machine as long as carbon paper existed. Even the most optimistic experts predicted that the worldwide market for copiers would never be more than 5,000 units.

Finally, in 1944, Batelle Memorial Institute signed a royalty-sharing agreement with Carlson and began supporting his research. In 1947, Joe Wilson, the president of Haloid, a struggling photographic paper company, heard about the research at Batelle, and agreed to fund and commercialize Carlson's technology. The result was the Model A copier. By following thirty-nine carefully prescribed steps, an expert operator could use the Model A to reproduce a single copy in 2 to 3 minutes. Carlson pressed on, supported by Wilson, who continually "bet his company" by investing more in Carlson's research than Haloid was making in profits. In the fall of 1959, 21 years after Carlson had made his first successful image, the 914 copier was announced. It was none too soon.

The massive development effort had left Haloid so poor it could not afford rent with

---

* Prepared by Alex Miller, University of Tennessee. In addition to interviews and materials provided by Xerox Corporation, *Xerox: American Samurai* (Gary Jacobson and John Hillkirk, 1986, Collier Books, a division of Macmillan Publishing Company) was an important source of information in preparing this case. Anyone who desires a more detailed look at Xerox through the mid-1980s is encouraged to consult this excellent example of business journalism.

round-the-clock heating. Yet, in order to refine the machine to make the spring shipping date Carlson had promised, engineers had to work 24 hours per day. Consequently, engineers at Xerox's Rochester, New York, plant spent much of the winter of 1959–1960 working in the cold. Because the machines themselves gave off some heat, the engineers, bundled in hunting jackets and insulated boots, huddled under blankets draped over their equipment to trap whatever warmth they could. As a group, they worked 7 days a week, 24 hours a day under these conditions to get the new product out on time.

THE ATOMIC DECADE

When the 914 was introduced, about thirty-five companies were making copying equipment using various technological processes for producing "wet" copies. (Wet technology resulted in damp copies, often smeared and usually having a noticeable smell.) Several could produce copies for as little as 4 to 9 cents each. Not only could these machines make inexpensive copies, the machines themselves were also inexpensive. For instance, Kodak offered Verifax machines for $350 each, and Minnesota Mining and Manufacturing (3M) sold a similarly priced machine called Thermofax. However, for a 914, the cost of material and labor alone were over $2,000 per machine. Obviously, a different marketing approach was required to surpass the lower cost alternatives already on the market. Wilson determined that the machines would not only be offered for sale, but they would also be leased. The lease would cost $95 per month, and would include 4 cents per copy for all copies over 2,000 per month. Additionally, leasing customers were given the right to cancel their contracts with only 15 days notice.

The combination of Carlson's technology and Wilson's leasing plan worked. The unprecedented success Xerox enjoyed in the 10 years after the 914 was introduced led those within the company to call the 1960s the "atomic decade." (Exhibit 1 gives operating data for this period.) Between 1960, when the first 914 was shipped, and 1970, when the last one was made, about 200,000 machines were put in service. Many were still in service 20 years later. To keep up with the seemingly universal demand, Xerox entered into 50/50 joint ventures with leading firms in Europe (Rank Xerox in the U.K.) and Asia (Fuji Xerox in Japan) to provide international marketing support and field service. These marketing and service organizations were meant to address details the fast-growing American company might overlook in shipping its products overseas. For instance, the first Xerox machines shipped into Japan were too high for most Japanese secretaries. Years later, many offices still kept a small box near their American copiers to serve as a booster platform.

The 914 moved Xerox to the billion-dollar sales level (and undreamed-of profits) faster than any company in history. *Fortune* ranked the 914 the most successful product ever marketed in the United States. In the 1980s, Apple Computer, Compaq Computers, and Reebok received much acclaim for reaching the billion-dollar mark still faster, but Xerox set its record at a time when the dollar was worth at least three times as much. Just 2 years after the 914 was introduced, Xerox made the *Fortune* 500, and 8 years after that, Xerox was ranked the 60th largest firm in the United States.

The marketing strategy Joe Wilson used to build Xerox was based on selling copies—not copiers. A research firm estimated that in 1967, the typical 914 brought in about $4,500 in annual revenue. (Later, in the seventies, as machines grew larger, a top-end Xerox

EXHIBIT 1
Xerox Corporation: Operational Data
(in Millions of Dollars, Except per Share Data and Ratios)

	1970	1969	1968	1967	1966	1965	1964	1963	1962	1961
Operations:										
Total operating revenues:	$1,636	$1,357	$1,125	$ 912	$698	$393	$282	$176	$115	$66
Rentals and services	1,324	1,073	877	659	469	268	184	114	66	31
Sales	312	284	248	253	229	124	97	62	49	35
Cost of rentals, services, and sales	398	417	376	294	224	--	--	--	--	--
Depreciation of rental equipment	192	174	165	122	83	58	37	20	12	6
Depreciation and amortization of buildings and equipment	32	27	25	22	18	9	6	4	3	12
Research and development expenses	87	101	75	65	73	--	--	--	--	--
Operating income	496	381	316	235	185	--	--	--	--	--
Interest expense	32	22	22	22	16	--	--	--	--	--
Income before taxes and extraordinary item	474	361	295	216	170	108	80	50	31	13
Net income	190	158	134	107	83	59	40	23	14	5
Net income per common share	$2.42	$2.04	$1.75	$1.43	$1.15	$2.78	$1.91	$1.17	$0.72	$0.28
Dividends declared per common share	0.65	0.58	0.50	0.40	0.30	--	--	--	--	--
Financial position:										
Current assets	$ 825	$ 649	$ 555	$ 461	$362	$179	$119	$ 81	$ 52	$38
Rental equipment and related inventories at cost	1,322	1,068	857	677	505	297	197	115	71	42
Accumulated depreciation of rental equipment	696	549	422	266	187	130	77	42	22	10
Land, buildings, and equipment at cost	432	353	281	245	202	101	73	48	36	26
Accumulated depreciation and amortization of buildings and equipment	144	116	90	68	49	26	18	11	8	6
Total assets	1,844	1,516	1,253	1,141	919	--	--	--	--	--
Current liabilities	492	419	387	301	209	83	57	42	29	25
Long-term debt	359	263	190	303	333	156	103	54	41	20
Shareholders' equity	883	726	592	461	312	192	133	85	49	35
Selected data and ratios:										
Employees at year end	55,367	49,335	41,142	37,039	30,645	15,758	11,981	7,918	5,297	3,778
Income before taxes to total operating revenues	29.0%	26.6%	26.2%	23.7%	24.4%	14.94%	14.16%	13.07%	12.06%	8.27%
Net income to average shareholders' equity	23.6%	24.0%	25.5%	27.7%	31.1%	30.57%	30.04%	26.99%	28.54%	15.83%
Long-term debt to total capitalization	27.0%	24.8%	22.5%	37.5%	48.7%	44.87%	43.58%	38.66%	45.69%	36.25%

Source: Annual reports.

machine could generate $20,000 in annual billings—sometimes more, depending upon the copying volume.) Most of this money flowed straight back to the manufacturer because there was no retail dealer network involved. That revenue stream was maintained for the entire life of the contract—generally 3 or 4 years. Even after that, the machine could usually be overhauled and made ready for several more years of use.

Some customers opted to buy rather than lease their machines, a source of revenue Xerox pursued much more heavily in the last part of the 1970s. In these cases, Xerox received a service contract that could eventually amount to thousands of dollars. Such arrangements meant the top end of the market was more lucrative than the lower end for companies like Xerox. By the end of the 1970s, prices had dropped so that low-end machines were cheaper to buy than to lease. But a low-end manufacturer might earn only $300 to $500 per unit sold and, of course, such sales included none of the additional revenues associated with leasing.

Initially, Wilson had hoped to make twenty-five of his machines a week—an outrageous forecast, given expert opinions about worldwide demand. But soon, Xerox was making twenty-five units per *day,* a figure that steadily climbed to ninety per day. Such growth often required Herculean commitment from the Xerox work force and management team. At one point, low supplies of a part made by a vendor in Chattanooga threatened to shut down production in Rochester. The director of manufacturing and a purchasing agent made an emergency trip to acquire the needed components. However, their plane was diverted to Washington, D.C., because of a snowstorm in Tennessee. The railroad from D.C. to Chattanooga would not accept their airline tickets as credit, so the pair tracked down a local Xerox employee to borrow money for tickets. When they finally reached Chattanooga, they had to drive the taxi from the station because the local drivers were unaccustomed to driving on ice. Once they got the parts, they split up and took alternate routes back to Rochester, in hopes of improving the chances of one person's getting through. In the end, the unshaven pair traveled 72 hours nonstop, living on peanut butter sandwiches and sleeping in their seats. The line never stopped.

With the success of the 914 came what a report from the Department of the Army called the "era of mass copying." In the fifties, before xerography was practical, approximately 20 *million* copies were made in the United States each year. In 1965, thanks to the success of the 914, that number had grown to nearly 10 *billion.* (Twenty years later, annual worldwide copier volume had grown to 700 billion.) The easy availability of high-quality copies fundamentally changed the way offices operated. At times, it seemed the world was not really sure how to deal with this newfound convenience. One study concluded that 29 percent of all the copies made in America were unnecessary, 130 billion wasted copies each year—enough to reach to the moon and back forty-seven times. Paul Allaire, the president of the document processing business within Xerox, explained why photocopying is fundamental: "The document is the currency of today's workplace and the window onto the enormous information and database that exists in the office. It is the medium by which work is exchanged, sales proposals are made, contracts are agreed upon, policies are recorded and communicated. In this sense, the document is much more than a static piece of paper. It is the dynamic organism that breathes life into the business process. It's the vehicle that organizes information into a format for human consumption."

The transformation in the way documents were processed made millionaires out of many people at Xerox, including some factory workers who had bought stock at the outset. Carlson himself never became an employee of Xerox; he preferred to work alone, and did much of his best research in his own basement. Still, his share of the business grew to be worth $200 million. A year before he unexpectedly died of a heart attack, his wife asked him if he had any unfulfilled dreams. "Just one," he said. "I would like to die a poor man." By the time of his death, the quiet visionary was well on his way to fulfilling that dream. He had given away more than $150 million to charitable social causes.

LEGAL ACTION AGAINST XEROX

As a result of the "atomic decade" of unparalleled growth, Xerox managers spent much of the following decade in court fighting a series of antitrust lawsuits. In 1972, the Federal Trade Commission accused Xerox of illegally monopolizing the photocopier industry. In

1973, SCM, another office equipment manufacturer, filed a $500-million lawsuit against Xerox for antitrust violations. Throughout the 1970s, there were numerous other antitrust suits including those by IBM, the Van Dyk Research Corporation, lesser-known manufacturers, copying centers, and even some Xerox customers.

These cases were typically lengthy affairs; the FTC case was not settled until 1975, and the IBM case went on until 1978. The SMC and Van Dyk cases went to trial in 1977 and 1978, but appeals lasted into the 1980s. The demand for testimonies and the evidence required was tremendous. In just one trial, Xerox and SCM introduced ninety-six volumes of documents, a stack 20 feet high, that included more than 60,000 exhibits. The official transcript of that trial was 45,000 pages long. Legal expenses to compensate the 35 lawyers and nearly 200 aides working both sides of the case were estimated to be $500,000 per month for SCM and $750,000 a month for Xerox. In just 1 year, Peter McColough, then CEO of Xerox, spent 40 days giving depositions, 30 days being briefed and advised by lawyers before taking the witness stand, and 10 days on the witness stand. Other trials were taking place concurrently, and each placed additional burdens on the company.

The stakes involved in the lawsuits were immense. In the FTC case, the government agency was suing to have Xerox make all of its patents available for royalty-free licensing, including any patents it might obtain over the next 20 years. Additionally, the FTC sought to have Xerox divest itself from its foreign joint ventures, Rank Xerox and Fuji Xerox. In the private lawsuits (from IBM, SMC, and others) Xerox faced the threat of trebled awards (punitive fines equaling three times the amount of found damages) if convicted of unfair competition.

Considering what the financial costs could have been, experts agree that Xerox fared well in all these trials. The FTC case was finally settled out of court; Xerox agreed to make 1,700 existing patents available to competitors, but retained its share in all foreign joint ventures. However, Xerox was forced to alter pricing arrangements found to protect its leasing contracts from competitors. The SCM and Van Dyk cases were settled for small fractions of the amounts originally sought. In the IBM case, Xerox was actually awarded $25 million because of patent infringements on the part of IBM.

REINFORCING THE ORGANIZATION

During much of the 1970s, managers devoted effort to strengthening the business foundation laid during the sixties. The great success of the 914 and the resulting explosive growth left many opportunities for managers to refine operations within Xerox. Hiring, particularly of management and staff, continued more or less unabated as the company recruited the expertise needed to address the many challenges of the copier business. These experts were positioned to ensure that Xerox made no mistakes that might jeopardize its position of market dominance. In fact, Xerox's organization was adapted from the matrix structure NASA used to perfect rocket development and ensure flawless space shots.

For instance, inside the engineering department, Xerox had several groups of specialists containing many of the nation's best talent in their particular discipline. Each specialty was organized into a functional department with its own hierarchy reaching to the level of vice president at the corporate headquarters in Stamford, Connecticut. Experts within these departments provided each other with a series of checks and balances to ensure that no one made any foolish mistakes. For example, the specialists in product design might create a new part they felt would enhance the performance of a particular copier model. After they designed the new part, they would pass it on to the drafting department where a drawing would be made. From there, the drawing would travel to a detailer who inserted the critical dimension. Then the service engineering department evaluated the design from a maintenance standpoint. Once they approved the plan, it was sent to production engineers to determine what would be needed to manufacture the part.

To eliminate any bad designs, each department had the authority to intercede in the process, insisting on changes, even if it meant returning the drawings to the original design engineers. The result of such a structure was heavy emphasis on painstakingly engineered products. It was not unusual for Xerox engineers to insist on something as mundane as a standard nut's replacement by a custom-designed alternative if they felt performance or reliability would improve. More substantial components, such as electric motors, were virtually always custom designed.

The marketing function also had a system of checks and balances. The marketing planners in the United States were supplemented with counterparts in the U.K., Latin America, Asia, and Canada. Each of these groups was responsible for getting as close to the customers in their region as possible. They brought market information back to a strategic planning staff in Rochester, New York (headquarters of the copier operation); from there it went to top managers at the Stamford headquarters. This system effectively identified thousands of details involved in conceptualizing new products or new marketing programs. Wayland Hicks, who oversaw much of the international operations, later recalled long and furious arguments over details such as the color customers preferred for a paper tray.

The marketing group faced difficult challenges in advertising and promoting technology as new and as complicated as photocopying. One of several advertisements stressing ease of use featured a monkey who successfully used a Xerox machine to make a number of copies. After the commercial aired on national television, calls from Xerox field personnel reported widespread incidences of operators being insulted by their coworkers. Bananas were left on copiers and signs were posted such as "If a monkey can do this, why are we paying you?" The spot was quickly pulled.

Within Xerox's matrix organization, functions like engineering and marketing were coordinated by program managers who had overall responsibility for ensuring each project's completion. These managers did not belong to any one function; instead, the personnel in the various functions reported to them as well as to their individual department heads. Because the program managers were separate from the strong functional orientation that dominated Xerox, they were in a more objective position to evaluate inevitable conflicts between functions. These managers had far-ranging responsibilities: making sure prototypes were available on time, ensuring that promotional material was timely and correct, seeing that service personnel had the materials and tools they required, and so on. Along with the department heads of the various key functions, they reported directly to headquarters, where a corporate staff of nearly 1,000 facilitated the coordination required to keep Xerox on the competitive forefront. At Stamford, Xerox presidents held authority over the various functions; any persistent integration problems were finally resolved at their level.

CONTINUED PRODUCT INNOVATION

Throughout the 1970s, Xerox invested heavily in R&D. (See Exhibit 2.) At the Palo Alto Research Center (PARC), 58 of the world's 100 best computer scientists worked at designing "the office of the future." Lured with unlimited budgets for whatever research they felt most promising, they shared a vision of a paperless world, and developed technology still considered modern today. Their Alto, a desktop computer with tremendous graphics capability, was controlled with a mouse using icons displayed in overlapping windows on a black and white screen. Apple later offered similar innovations in its MacIntosh, and, eventually, the technology would also find its way into high-end Xerox copiers. But in the

EXHIBIT 2
Xerox Corporation: Operational Data
(In Millions of Dollars, Except per Share Data and Ratios)

	1980	*1979*	*1978*	*1977*	*1976*	*1975*	*1974*	*1973*	*1972*	*1971*
Operations:										
Total operating revenues:	$8,197	$6,996	$6,018	$5,190	$4,515	$4,054	$3,505	$2,915	$2,338	$1,896
Rentals and services	5,152	4,606	4,131	3,821	3,592	3,243	2,800	2,384	1,904	1,541
Sales	3,045	2,390	1,887	1,369	923	811	705	531	434	355
Cost of rentals, services, and sales	3,543	2,928	2,462	2,110	1,852	1,072	870	677	558	459
Depreciation of rental equipment	602	562	512	486	504	460	391	325	291	321
Depreciation and amortization of buildings and equipment	201	191	163	156	150	102	82	61	46	35
Research and development expenses	434	376	311	369	226	199	179	154	117	96
Operating income	1,353	1,272	1,156	1,013	896	835	856	759	645	537
Interest expense	115	103	125	114	137	137	101	57	37	35
Income before taxes and extraordinary item	1,351	1,283	1,091	932	817	758	788	698	621	516
Net income	619	563	489	415	365	244	329	292	256	211
Net income per common share	$7.33	$6.69	$5.81	$4.95	$4.35	$3.07	$4.14	$3.68	$3.24	$2.67
Dividends declared per common share	2.80	2.40	2.00	1.50	1.10	1.00	1.00	0.90	0.84	0.80
Financial position:										
Current assets	$3,515	$3,104	$2,639	$2,338	$2,112	$1,687	$1,632	$1,276	$1,053	$ 918
Rental equipment and related inventories at cost	4,692	4,414	4,105	3,935	3,822	3,574	3,221	2,452	1,928	1,626
Accumulated depreciation of rental equipment	2,770	2,678	2,603	2,519	2,392	2,058	1,706	1,354	1,063	869
Land, buildings, and equipment at cost	2,403	2,103	1,879	1,769	1,692	1,245	1,090	853	668	542
Accumulated depreciation and amortization of buildings and equipment	1,033	880	768	660	569	400	337	268	215	172
Total assets	7,349	6,554	5,766	5,223	4,959	4,456	4,078	3,089	2,484	2,145
Current liabilities	1,984	1,679	1,401	1,205	1,127	1,115	1,037	840	659	556
Long-term debt	898	913	938	1,052	1,211	1,129	1,043	585	445	426
Shareholders' equity	3,625	3,221	2,854	2,520	2,224	1,907	1,741	1,484	1,249	1,041
Selected data and ratios:										
Employees at year end	120,480	115,705	107,679	106,677	100,458	93,532	97,399	90,200	72,237	62,638
Income before taxes to total operating revenues	16.5%	18.3%	18.1%	18.0%	18.1%	18.7%	22.5%	23.9%	26.6%	27.2%
Net income to average shareholders' equity	18.1%	18.5%	18.2%	17.5%	17.5%	13.4%	20.4%	21.4%	22.4%	21.9%
Long-term debt to total capitalization	17.9%	20.0%	22.7%	27.1%	32.4%	34.3%	34.7%	26.3%	24.6%	27.0%

Source: Annual reports.

1970s, scientists at PARC thought copiers would soon be obsolete and were uninterested in such old-fashioned technology.

Xerox also invested heavily in developing three new copiers. The 3100, introduced in 1973, was Xerox's successful entry into what it considered the low end of the market. At $12,200, it was known as the "Cadillac" of low-volume machines. The 9200, introduced in 1974, was the first machine producing such high-quality copies that photocopying could be viewed as a viable alternative to offset printing. Development of this machine cost $300 million, took 8 years, and involved thousands of engineers. Unlike the 3100 and the 9200, the 4000 was never a successful product. Its technical shortcomings were ironic given the careful attention that Xerox gave to the quality of all its products.

The R&D project named "Moses" was killed only 6 months before its introduction because managers were concerned about the machine's performance. Moses was to have been the first recirculating paper handler for Xerox. (These devices allow an operator to make multiple copies of a multipage document without having to collate it by hand.) Engineers at Xerox believed the worst possible failure would be for a machine to damage the customer's original document. This possibility was to be avoided at all costs. Shuffling pages through the recirculator was obviously the single greatest source of risk for the customer's original, so Xerox engineers spent $90 million and assigned over 1,000 employees to develop the recirculator. The result was a document handler that could accept any sort of paper—onion skin, carbon paper, card stock, and so forth—all in the same stack of originals. However, to accommodate this level of flexibility, the paper handler operated more slowly than components in the rest of the copier. Rather than limit performance by slowing down the entire machine, Xerox opted to keep Moses off the market until a faster paper recirculator could be developed.

This Xerox standard of bringing only the best technology to the marketplace encompassed both high- and low-end products. For example, SAM (Simply Amazing Machine), Mohawk, Elf, Yankee, Rebel, Gnome, and Nothing were all new low-end products pulled during the 1970s because of technical deficiencies that might have damaged the overall Xerox image of technological leadership and product quality.

THE MARKET AND THE COMPETITION

The unprecedented success of Xerox, especially in the 1960s, attracted numerous other firms to the copier market. At the beginning of the 1970s, Xerox was the only brand of copier available in the United States. By the end of the decade, there were thirty brands of copiers, spread across the three market segments identified in Exhibit 3. Between 1971 and

EXHIBIT 3
Market Segments

	Copies/Minute	*Cost*
Low-volume	Less than 25	Under $4,000
Mid-volume	25–90	$4,000–$60,000
High-volume	90 plus	$80,000–$130,000

1978, seventy-seven plain paper copiers were introduced in the United States, and between 1978 and 1980, another seventy models were introduced. As these new models flooded the market, the intensified competition drove prices down by an average of 10 percent per year.

In 1970, IBM introduced Copier I, a machine that Xerox engineers found to be "built like a tank" and capable of reliably making 50,000 copies a month. While reliable, the machine was not very sophisticated by the standards Xerox had set. It made only ten copies per minute, on paper rolls instead of precut sheets, and could not copy directly from books. By 1975, IBM had introduced Copier II, a successful, more up-market machine capable of making twenty-five copies per minute. 1976 brought the Copier III, a top-of-the-line model, designed to make seventy-five copies per minute. However, the product suffered from initial problems with paper jamming. The paper's path was so long that if a page jammed late in the process, three or four others behind it created a backup that often required a service technician to untangle. In 1978, after more than 10,000 Copier III's had been placed, IBM announced further shipments would be limited until a better design could be worked out. When the Copier III was reannounced later that year, many of the original machines already in the field were rebuilt to include the new design. This process required three on-site technicians for an entire week. Despite such problems, the machines in the Copier series sported the IBM brand, and that name, coupled with a sales force many considered to be the world's best, was highly valued. Throughout the 1970s, IBM presented formidable competition, especially in midpriced, midvolume copiers.

In 1975, Kodak introduced its Ektaprint copiers, technically sophisticated machines capable of doing all that the top-of-the-line Xerox machines could do—sometimes even better. For instance, Kodak had a successful document circulator. However, unlike Moses, it could not handle different thicknesses of paper. Customers were instead advised to make copies of any pages with odd thicknesses and to then feed the copies through as part of the stack of originals. Copy quality on the Ektaprint machines was good enough that the resulting copies of copies were usually indistinguishable from copies of the originals.

Kodak had been working on its photocopying technology for more than 20 years. The company actually had its first working high-speed copier in 1963, but engineers continued to work at refining this model until 1968, in hopes of producing a machine more reliable than the 914. Ironically, at that time Kodak decided that to have a machine superior to Xerox's, it must create the next generation of copiers. So in 1969, it scrapped its original model and began work on the Ektaprint model introduced 6 years later. Once the machine was introduced, Kodak moved cautiously into the market in order not to jeopardize its corporate reputation as a provider of quality goods and services. Leases were only permitted in regions with a complete sales and service staff. Because Kodak had never been in the business of leasing equipment before, this policy meant the product could be rolled out only as quickly as the sales and service network could be built from scratch. This careful progress made Kodak slow to open up new markets, but Ektaprint copiers were consistently the industry's top-rated in terms of the quality of the copies they produced and the service they provided.

IBM and Kodak were the competitors Xerox had long dreaded. These huge corporations had all the financial and technical skills needed to produce excellent products. Furthermore, they marketed their machines similarly to Xerox; they leased for a monthly charge, copies were sold for a few cents, and the contract included service by the manufacturer. But not all the firms to enter the industry were as similar to Xerox. Companies such as Minolta, Konishiroku, Toshiba, Matsushita, Sharp, Canon, and Ricoh (all Japanese) and Savin (a U.S. firm) entered the market offering much smaller machines sold through dealerships rather than leased like the mid-and high-priced American models. In 1972, Fuji Xerox introduced the 2200, its Japanese-designed and manufactured low-end machine.

Throughout the 1960s and much of the 1970s, this group of new entrants had to develop alternatives to the technology Xerox still protected by its hundreds of patents. Unlike IBM or Kodak, these companies generally lacked the technical and financial resources needed to carry out the necessary R&D. Initially, the products offered by these smaller newcomers generally had significant shortcomings. The first Savins made only wet copies and the company never sold more than 600 machines per month. The first Japanese copiers to be introduced in the United States were the Canon NP-1100 and the Konishiroku UBIX 480. The U.S. firm contracted to market the Canon copier went bankrupt, and the 480 kept catching fire! Xerox declined to import the 2200 from Fuji Xerox because Xerox engineers deemed it an inferior machine. The best of these various models never sold more than perhaps 8,000 or 9,000 units per month worldwide. At the low prices such machines carried, the manufacturer's revenues represented a very small portion of the worldwide market for copiers.

Initially, the single most successful model from these new entrants was a machine that

EXHIBIT 4
Xerox Corporation: Income Statements
(in Millions of Dollars, Except per Share Data)

	1980	*1979*	*1978*
Operating revenues:			
Rentals and services	$5,152	$4,606	$4,130
Sales	3,045	2,390	1,888
Total operating revenues	8,197	6,996	6,018
Costs and expenses:			
Cost of rentals and services	$2,118	$1,862	$1,692
Cost of sales	1,425	1,066	771
Research and development expenses	434	376	311
Selling, administrative, and general expenses	2,867	2,420	2,089
Total costs and expenses	$6,844	$5,724	$4,863
Operating income:	$1,353	$1,272	$1,556
Other income	(1)	11	(65)
Income before taxes	$1,352	$1,283	$1,091
Income taxes	605	592	528
Income before outside shareholders' interests	$ 747	$ 691	$ 563
Outside shareholders' interests	127	128	$ 87
Income before extraordinary items	$ 620	$ 563	$ 476
Extraordinary income	--	--	12
Net income	$ 620	$ 563	$ 488
Income per common share	$7.33	$6.69	$5.81

Source: Annual reports.

resulted from collaboration between Ricoh and Savin: the 750. Introduced in the United States in 1975, the 750 cost $500 to $600 for Ricoh to make. Ricoh then sold the machine to Savin for about $1,600 and Savin suggested their dealers retail the machine for just under $5,000. It made only twenty copies per minute, but it made the first copy in 4.6 seconds versus nearly 13 seconds for the typical Xerox machine. Compared to a conventional U.S.

EXHIBIT 5
Xerox Corporation: Balance Sheets (in Millions of Dollars)

	1980	1979
Assets		
Current assets:		
Cash	$ 89	$ 42
Bank time deposits	229	268
Marketable securities	207	448
Accounts receivable	1,164	1,120
Receivables from Xerox Credit Corporation	196	
Accrued revenues	377	259
Inventories	1,086	786
Other current assets	169	180
Total current assets	$3,517	$3,103
Long-term trade receivables	199	274
Rental equipment and related inventories	1,922	1,736
Land, buildings, and equipment	1,369	1,222
Investments, at equity	194	106
Other assets	149	111
Total assets	$7,350	$6,552
Liabilities and Shareholders' Equity		
Current liabilities:		
Notes payable	$ 208	$ 96
Payments due within 1 year on long-term debt	80	40
Accounts payable	316	325
Salaries, profit-sharing, and othér accruals	792	689
Income taxes	441	427
Other current liabilities	147	102
Total current liabilities	$1,984	$1,679
Long-term debt	$ 898	$ 913
Other noncurrent liabilities	133	127
Deferred income taxes	124	110
Deferred investment tax credits	86	70
Outside shareholders' interests	500	432
Shareholders' equity:		
Common stock	$ 84	$ 84
Class B stock	0.2	0.2
Additional paid in capital	305	289
Retained earnings	3,249	2,866
Total	$3,638	$3,239
Deduct Class B receivables and deferrals	14	16
Total shareholders' equity	$3,624	$3,223
Total liabilities and shareholders' equity	$7,350	$6,552

Source: Annual reports.

copier, the 750 was one-third the size, had one-third as many parts, and consumed one-third as much energy (a matter of no small importance after the energy crisis of 1974). The machine's simplicity provided better reliability; it averaged one problem in every 17,000 copies, versus one in every 6,000 for the more complicated U.S. machines.

While the accomplishments of their new competitors were impressive, Xerox continued to own most of the copier market for years after competitors began to enter. Until 1975, Xerox did not track the market shares of various competitors; its share was so large that tracking the fraction other firms held was simply not meaningful. Technical problems at IBM and the slow-growing marketing organization at Kodak severely limited their making inroads on Xerox; these companies were threats because of their potential more than their accomplishments. Other competitors lacked the resources to offer a real threat. Even Savin, one of the most successful of the low-end producers, was less than 5 percent the size of Xerox. In fact, sales at Xerox were *growing* each year by an amount greater than *total* sales at Savin.

Xerox did address these new entrants to the low end of the copier market by cutting the price on its 3100 to $4,400. In early 1976, Fuji Xerox began independent development of the 3500, a successful low-end copier that Xerox began importing in late 1977. And finally, in 1979, Xerox began importing the Fuji Xerox 2300, an improved version of the 2200 the Japanese venture had first introduced in 1972. That machine was so successful that a year later Xerox had to airlift 700 tons of the machines to the United States when the regular ocean deliveries could not keep pace with demand.

OUTLOOK FOR THE FUTURE

From 1960 to 1980, Xerox enjoyed an average compound growth rate of revenues of about 15 percent per year. Every year during this period, most of the managers at Xerox were managing a bigger operation than they had ever managed before. In 1980, revenues were a record $5.1 billion and profits were an all-time best at $619 million. (See Exhibits 4 and 5 for more complete financial data.) Even in the face of such hectic growth, the firm improved steadily in efficiency. Overall productivity at Xerox improved an average of 8 percent per year, considerably better than the U.S. industrial average. For instance, in the North American Manufacturing Division, productivity improvements had allowed for reductions in the work force from its peak of 12,500 down to 10,000 by 1980.

At the 1980 stockholder's meeting, officers announced that during the 1970s, Xerox had effectively met its competition head-on, "breaking new trails" in the top end of the market and "plugging the holes" in the lower end. "We can produce a copier today for the same amount it cost 5 years ago," they boasted. "It's like buying a 1980 car for 1976 prices." (Holding prices constant was especially noteworthy, given the near-record rates of inflation.) Executives felt the new efficiency and enhanced product line put Xerox in a position to outperform competitors in the coming decade.

CASE 18

Xerox Corporation: 1980 to 1983*

HERE COMES CANON

For Xerox, the 1980s began with a frightening message proclaimed in the headlines of *Forbes:* "Xerox, Here We Come." The "we" was Canon, the company that came out of nowhere to dominate the 35 mm camera market through new microprocessor technology and revolutionary marketing tactics. Experts predicted Canon would repeat this performance in the photocopier industry. Canon executives talked openly about "waging total war" on Xerox, and in 1980, Canon began introducing a nonstop parade of new, technologically advanced copiers. First came the NP-200, a tabletop, 20-cpm (copies per minute) model, retailing for $4,000. It featured fiber optics (an industry first) and the same sort of microprocessors that set Canon's cameras apart. In 1981 came the NP-120, a 12-cpm model that was the first successful application of cold-fusing copying, a breakthrough that reduced copier power consumption by 25 percent. Later that same year came the NP-400, a higher-speed, 40-cpm version of the NP-200.

Ironically, perhaps the most significant technological breakthroughs were at the very bottom of Canon's already low-end product line. These were on the NP-80, an 8-cpm machine designed for home use. The concept for a very compact, service-free copier that would retail for less than $1,000 originated with Canon dealers in the United States. They were confident they could sell such a machine, if the engineers in Japan could build it. Beginning in 1980, 140 Canon engineers spent 2½ years and the yen equivalent to $8 million to design the diminutive, but revolutionary copier dealers wanted.

The greatest single difference between the NP-80 and all other copiers was that all parts likely to need servicing were combined into one disposable cartridge. This included the copier drum, the charging device, the toner assembly—even a cleaning brush. At least some of the technology entailed in the cartridge came from Minolta, another Japanese company also trying to move from cameras into copiers. Minolta and Canon swapped rights to share in each other's patented technology, and this undoubtedly allowed Canon to develop the cartridge technology more quickly. When the NP-80 was introduced, the cartridge surprised the entire industry, including Fuji Xerox and Xerox. Xerox engineers had said at one time that such technology was not practically feasible. Later, research on Canon's copiers led Xerox engineers to predict that the machine would probably run on average for 5 years before breaking down. In the meantime, the NP-80 would produce higher-quality copies than several higher-priced U.S. machines.

The NP-80's other major technical breakthrough was the efficiency with which it

---

* Prepared by Alex Miller, University of Tennessee. In addition to interviews and materials provided by Xerox Corporation, *Xerox: American Samurai* (Gary Jacobson and John Hillkirk, 1986, Collier Books, a division of Macmillan Publishing Company) was an important source of information in preparing this case. Anyone who desires a more detailed look at Xerox through the mid-1980s is encouraged to consult this excellent example of business journalism.

could be built. In the United States, the NP-80 was called the PC-10 (PC standing for personal copier). Its suggested retail price was $995 but it could occasionally be bought at discount houses for less than half. For a unit to retail at such low prices and leave any margins for manufacturers, production costs had to be lower than ever before. With their PC line, Canon reached these new levels by emphasizing automation. The copier itself cost only $300 per unit to make, using eight subassemblies that were easily assembled using automatic equipment. The cartridge, which many had considered impossible to build, consisted of only 89 parts and was assembled using 146 robots on a production line that cost $4 million and employed almost no labor. The capacity on that line was for 5,000 units a day. The cartridges cost about $15 per unit to manufacture, and they typically retailed for $65. Quality, in terms of conformance to design, was very good, largely because of the extensive automation on both lines (yields were nearly 100 percent).

Even with such efficient plants, Canon headquarters in Japan decided to ship products to Canon USA at transfer prices that—initially, at least—were below their manufacturing costs. Competitors both in the United States and Japan accused Canon of predatory pricing and dumping. Canon executives denied the charges, countering that most corporations could not fathom the extensive cost-cutting measures taken throughout Canon in order to allow their entry into the copier market. Furthermore, they claimed the low prices were intended to generate the volume of sales required to make the machines profitable.

Canon also had one of the industry's strongest marketing efforts. In 1980 Canon USA received $10 million from its Japanese parent to introduce the NP-200. The campaign that resulted featured several splashy full back-page ads in *The Wall Street Journal.* However, two-thirds of the promotional budget was earmarked for television advertising, an unprecedented approach to selling copiers. NP-200 sales shot to 100,000 units per year worldwide. Industry experts speculated that Canon may have spent as much as $400 per unit sold in marketing the NP-200 in its early years.

The industry was shocked when Canon later topped these aggregate numbers in marketing its PC line. In rolling out the PC-10 and its slightly faster sister, the PC-12, Canon spent $15 million in advertising. Minolta executives said that this must have equaled nearly $200 per unit during the rollout. By the end of 1983, Canon USA was selling 10,000 personal copiers a month. It took Canon 10 years to sell its first half million machines. From 1980 to 1982, it sold its second half million.

APPRAISING JAPANESE COMPETITION

By the late seventies, the machines Xerox was importing from Fuji Xerox were among the most popular the company offered. The popularity of these machines and the threats posed by new machines from Canon convinced Charlie Christ, then vice president for copier manufacturing, that he should find out what the Japanese were doing differently. Christ sent a team to study manufacturing techniques using Fuji Xerox, as their Japanese host, to arrange visits with copier makers there. As a result of that visit, Christ wrote an internal report in early 1981 he called *Blueprint for Survival.* As he explained, "They were manufacturing copiers in Japan, shipping them to the United States, and selling them to distributors, who sold them to dealers, who marked up the cost to the final customer. Somehow, even after all this, the customer was only paying about what it cost us to build the machine in the first place!"

Before Christ's visit, the leading explanation within Xerox for the low Japanese prices was "They're dumping." But Christ's report indicated the real answer might not be so simple. He found the Japanese had beat Xerox's efficiency on a number of key measures. At that time, Xerox had about 1.3 workers in overhead for every 1 direct labor worker. The Japanese he studied had only 0.8 overhead to direct and he predicted they would eventually be at 0.6. The Japanese assembly line reject rates were ten times better than Xerox's. Their manufacturing defects per hundred machines made were seven times better. They carried 1 month of inventories, and Christ predicted they would soon reduce that to half a month, while Xerox kept 3.2 to 3.3 months of inventory on hand. Mysteriously, the Japanese saw better performance from their suppliers (more on-time deliveries, fewer rejected parts, etc.) even though Xerox had nine times as many suppliers competing for continued Xerox business.

Because the Japanese were able to sell products in the United States for retail prices comparable to Xerox's manufacturing costs, Xerox would have to fundamentally change their cost structure if they were to remain in the industry. Christ captured this idea graphically in a figure reproduced as Exhibit 1. Xerox productivity had been improving at 8 percent per year. As he explained in his report, even if the Japanese improved productivity just enough to offset inflation, and Xerox continued improving productivity at 8 percent, by 1985, the Japanese would still have a 21 percent cost advantage. Top management was not willing to accept that. To meet the Japanese costs by 1985, Xerox productivity gains had to rise to 18 percent per year, again assuming that the Japanese only improved at the rate of inflation. Christ felt the Japanese were actually a moving target, and to catch up with them the Xerox productivity rate had to triple, hitting 25 percent per year until 1985. Xerox had never before approached such levels of productivity gain; it was not at all clear to Christ that they ever could.

In 1981, the startling revelations in the Christ report led Xerox to send another group to Japan that focused on new-product development. Again, the findings were such that

EXHIBIT 1
Xerox's Need for Improvement

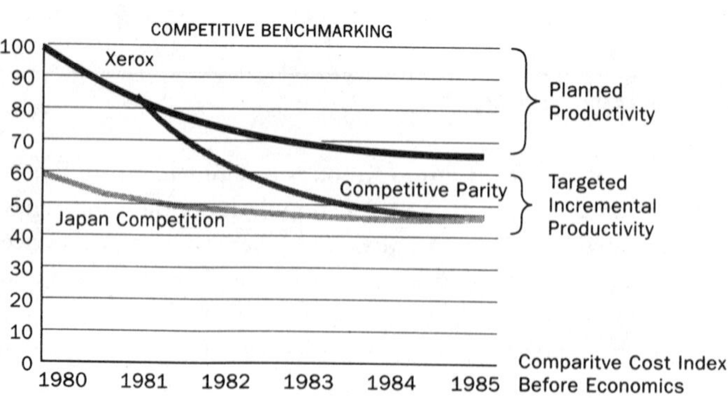

Source: Xerox Corporation.

many at Xerox denied they were even possible. The group found the Japanese able to produce new products in half the time and at half the cost of Xerox. The difference was not in what Xerox called the "burn rate," the dollars spent per day on the R&D project. The Japanese had about the same burn rate as Xerox, but because they only took half as long to complete a project, their costs were only half as much.

FUJI XEROX

Most of what Xerox discovered in its "benchmarking" trips to study Japanese competitors was comparable to what they found at Fuji Xerox. Fuji Xerox was originally founded to help Xerox market its U.S.-designed and U.S.-made copiers throughout Asia. However, when new products—especially markets for low-end products—were slow to come out of Xerox laboratories in the United States, Fuji Xerox began designing and making its own. Initially, Xerox managers in the United States did not support this decision, claiming the subsidiary it co-owned equally with the Fuji Film company lacked necessary technical and financial resources. However, managers at Fuji Xerox refused to stop their developmental work, and by the late 1970s, the most successful low-end machines Xerox was selling were imported from its subsidiary in Japan.

One reason Fuji Xerox machines were so successful was the "New Xerox" program started inside Fuji Xerox in 1976. New Xerox was a total quality control program implemented after the oil crisis of 1974. Japan imported virtually all its petroleum and the oil crisis made Japanese businesses more cost conscious. Suddenly, these businesses were not buying new copiers, and it looked as if predictions of failure from Xerox USA might be correct. As inflation soared after the oil crisis, Fuji Xerox tried to raise prices, taking a lead from successful Xerox practices in the United States. However, their competition in Japan did not follow with similar price increases, and as a result, Fuji Xerox revenues dropped further. Obviously, something different was required. This became the New Xerox total quality control program.

Fuji Film, Fuji Xerox's Japanese parent, had a long tradition of emphasizing quality control, and had won the coveted Deming Prize in 1956. (Edward Deming was the leading expert in statistical quality control sent from the United States to help rebuild Japan after World War II. His success led the Japanese government to create the Deming Prize for outstanding quality. While his work was largely ignored in the United States, in Japan Deming was said to be second only to George Washington as one of the most recognizable Americans.) With its heritage of quality control, Fuji Xerox embarked on its own total quality program. New Xerox built extensively upon the expertise in quality control brought to Fuji Xerox by former Fuji Film managers.

Historically, quality control in Japan first focused on applying statistical tools to improving the so-called quality of conformance. That is the degree to which products consistently conform to the specification set forth in its designs and blueprints. However, the Japanese working on total quality discovered early on that quality of conformance was only one part of the total quality equation. The other part was quality of design. Unless design engineers and manufacturing experts worked closely together, product designs might be impossible for manufacturers to replicate reliably and quality of conformance would be seriously limited. Furthermore, unless designers worked with marketing personnel who understood customer needs, the engineers might design new products which were technically superior, but only of limited interest to customers. Given the fundamental importance of quality of design, Fuji Xerox began their total quality movement by first rethinking the product design process.

Their goal was to reduce the time and expenses involved in designing a new product by 50 percent. This required a fundamentally different approach to managing product design. In 1976, Fuji Xerox began work on the 3500, a 60-cpm machine they hoped to design in only 2 years. In order to keep costs low, they assigned only fifty-two people to the project. In the United States, Xerox engineers wrote long reports explaining how the project was doomed to missed schedules, cost overruns, and poor design. In the end, the 3500 team took 26 weeks to design a 40-cpm machine, the entire design effort cost less than $8 million, and the resulting machine was amazingly successful. Almost immediately after its introduction in the United States, it became Xerox's best-selling low-end copier. As David Kearns, who would soon become the CEO of Xerox said, "The 3500 was a damn good machine. Fuji Xerox learned a great deal from doing that."

Emboldened by worldwide praise for the 3500, Fuji Xerox turned to the other part of the total quality formula, quality of conformance. Top managers challenged all employees to replicate the accomplishment of their ancestor, Fuji Film, by winning the Deming Prize. Pursuit of the national award became a rallying point for the entire organization. Winning the award was dependent upon besting all other Japanese manufacturers in an effort to reduce product rejects, raise yields, remove scrap, waste, and rework, and lower costs while raising quality.

Hourly employees were encouraged to become actively involved in the more than 1,500 quality circles at Fuji Xerox. These groups of hourly workers met after work to discuss new ways for making the factory more productive. Employee suggestion programs

---

EXHIBIT 2
Fuji Xerox Quality Circle Anthem

With beaming smiles exchanged
Friends gather with bright spirits
Ah, these friends talk about
New dreams of quality control
And strive with goals well in mind
QC Circle filled with light.

With morale constantly growing
The days assume the pure mission
Ah, these days are beautiful
Prosperous enterprises bloom as flowers
They strive for the ideal of tomorrow
QC Circle filled with aspiration.

By communicating well with each other
The path is chosen with proper measure
Ah, that path means happiness
Further growth of Japanese culture
Powerfully and affluently
QC Circle filled with future

Welcome to the Xerox Circle Convention.

---

were emphasized, and at some sites, the employees averaged more than 200 suggestions a year for making their work more efficient. Many were small improvements like altering workstations or changing handtools. The majority of these suggestions were implemented, and the cumulative effect was impressive.

A quality anthem was written (Exhibit 2) and learned by everyone in the organization from the board of directors down. It was sung, while standing at attention, by everyone attending any official Fuji Xerox meeting. As the desire to win the Deming Prize spread, some workers began punching out after their regular shifts and then returning to the factory floor to work—without pay—on their individual quality improvement projects. As 1980, the year managers hoped to win the Deming Prize, neared, wives began to write secretly to Tony Kobayashi, the vice president in charge of New Xerox, saying the ordeal was too much—children had not seen their fathers in 2 months. When Fuji Xerox actually won the Deming Prize in 1980, Kobayashi wrote back that because the prize had been won, the company must prove they deserved it. "The real work and sacrifice is only just beginning," his letter explained.

THE CHICAGO 7 AND EVERY MAN'S DREAM

Until Xerox began visiting Japan in the early 1980s, the more than 100,000 Xerox employees remained largely unaware of the very different approach the Japanese were taking to improve the product design process and manufacturing efficiency. One exception to this general lack of awareness was a tiny band of five engineers and a secretary under the direction of Jim Kearney. Kearney was an organizational maverick who sequestered his team, which he referred to as the Chicago 7, in rented Chicago office space known as EMD, for "Every Man's Dream."

Kearney's goal was to use his little group to beat IBM in the electric typewriter market. Many considered this to be foolish—IBM's line of "Selectric" typewriters was already firmly established as one of the most successful office equipment product lines of all time. The more optimistic of two studies within Xerox had concluded that the sophisticated machines required to compete against Selectrics would probably entail an unburdened manufacturing cost (UMC) of at least $900. But marketing studies indicated that a $1,200 retail price was the maximum feasible, and with a UMC of $900, the project looked incapable of producing the sort of return on investment Xerox held as a corporate goal. Cost accounting studies indicated that to make the return required, Xerox needed a UMC below $600.

Kearney, until then an independent designer, negotiated a contract with Xerox that compensated him based on how close he came to designing a competitive typewriter. The UMC had to be lower than $600 or he received no bonus; the lower it was, the greater his incentive pay. Kearney's engineers worked under a similar incentive plan.

Given the incentive based on manufacturing costs, the team designed their new typewriter with efficient production constantly in mind. They even helped design part of the production facility that would manufacture their new machine. Simplicity and speed were stressed above all else in the design process. Rather than use the existing Xerox prototype/model production group, Kearney hired a retired 71-year-old German toolmaker who brought in his own lathe to make prototypes of components. To simplify manufacturing, the number of parts was reduced to a bare minimum, and those were combined into easily assembled subcomponents. Six months after the work began, Kearney had a complete working model. Within a year, he had a prototype of a machine that would prove to have a UMC of only $364. Over the next 3 years, Kearney would collect $1 million in incentives, and his team of five engineers would collect another $1 million.

The Memorywriter Kearney's group designed was a tremendous success. The design greatly facilitated high-quality, low-cost production. It required only 200 workers, working two shifts, to produce more than 1,000 units a day, assembling modules into any of fifty to sixty different configurations according to market demands. Introduced in 1981, Memorywriters soon replaced Selectrics as the most popular typewriter on the market, and became the market leader with a 20 percent market share. By the mid 1980s, Xerox's typewriter business became a $500 million business—a *Fortune* 500 firm in its own right, had Xerox chosen to spin it off to stand alone.

DEVELOPMENTS IN THE XEROX COPIER BUSINESS

While the corporation had isolated pockets of success like the Memorywriter, the early 1980s were painful years for managers in Xerox's copier business. In 1981, profits were nearly $600 million. But in 1982, they fell to $424 million. A study by McKinsey & Company reported that the current organizational structure within Xerox was having a crippling effect. The monolithic organization was structured so that all functions reported through their individual departments up to the level of the president. To deal with the resulting flow of information at the corporate level, the staff at headquarters in Stamford, Connecticut, had grown to 1,000. Within this staff, there was a lack of direction, as each specialty argued for emphasis on its own pet projects and programs. Dwight Ryan returned from a posting at Rank Xerox in the U.K. to accept the position as vice president for marketing. In commenting on the corporate staff, he later recalled that "They were all at cross-purposes. While one faction argued for cutting prices and holding market share, another argued for maintaining high profit margins. No one got to the real problem of producing good, low-cost machines that could compete." From his hideaway in Chicago, Kearney assigned much of the blame for poor organizational performance to the matrix structure Xerox had adopted from NASA. He concluded that the many checks and balances in that matrix structure worked too well. Meant to prevent mistakes, they also prevented almost all innovation. Kearney complained that at Xerox, "you are promoted for not taking risks because the company is never exposed."

The McKinsey study concurred that part of the problem was structural, and part was also related to a certain lack of leadership. Eddie Miller, who headed the McKinsey study, later commented that Xerox suffered because of "an absence of strong management leadership. . . . Someone who would say, "Damn it, this is what we are going to do. Either follow it or get out of the way."

Faced with declining profits, costs that were not competitive, and the critical McKinsey report, top managers at Xerox began reducing its work force and restructuring. Worldwide, Xerox employment dropped by 2,000 in 1981, and by nearly 14,000 in 1982–1983. In United States manufacturing alone, the work force was reduced from 18,000 in 1980 to 12,000 in 1983. Virtually all of those 6,000 jobs came out of overhead, not direct labor.

Direct-labor reductions would have been greater, but the factory labor union took an active role in improving productivity.

Even before the hard times in the early 1980s, labor-management relations at Xerox were never particularly good. Strikes in the seventies involved baseball bats, suspected sabotage, and the state police. In 1980, when union leader Tony Costanza heard Xerox was planning layoffs, labor morale was at perhaps its all-time low, as massive dismissals were expected. (The mixture of fear and anger was captured in a poem from this era, widely circulated among labor, part of which is reprinted as Exhibit 3.) Some of the first layoffs would have resulted from management's plan to shut down a wire harness assembly line, layoff the 180 workers, buy the assembled wire harnesses from overseas, and reduce expenses by an anticipated $3.2 million. Costanza approached management with a coun-

EXHIBIT 3
Xerox Employee's Poem

There once was a man named C. Peter*
Who thought that he was a world-beater.
But his talents and brain
Sent his firm down the drain
And its stock prices started to teeter.

The shareholders truly were floored
By disasters that Peter had scored.
Before they could shout,
"Throw the bum out!"
He made himself head of the Board.

He said, "Here's my main man, Dave Kearns,
Who understands all my concerns.
I haven't a doubt
That he'll soon bail us out.
We've all seen how quickly he learns."

Dave said, "Just think of the challenge and fun
As lean and mean we start to run.
We can't be beat
Cause we're fast on our feet,
Treading water 'til OPD's† done.

In order to capture new highs,
The company we must resize.
I don't mean we'll fire,
We'll simply dehire—
The workforce we'll restrategize!"

As November's about to begin,
They've rented the Holiday Inn.
They'll first redeploy
And then deemploy—
While passing out Kool-Aid and gin.‡

* Peter McColough, Xerox CEO during the seventies.
† Office of Program Development.
‡ There was a note attached indicating that this was an "obscure reference to Guiana."
Source: Reprinted with permission of Macmillan Publishing Company from *Xerox: American Samurai* by Gary Jacobson and John Hillkirk. Copyright © 1986 by Gary Jacobson and John Hillkirk.

terproposal: "Give us a chance to compete, to go in and look at the budget: the cost of electricity, the space we rent, the overhead costs, our costs, the machinery, the process." In other words, the union asked for the right to "bid" on the wire harness work by offering to find cost savings equal to those available from offshore outsourcing. Management agreed, and the employees set to work in teams looking for ways to make the plant more efficient. One team found that by replacing light bulbs and by removing unnecessary ones, they could save $250,000 per year in one factory alone. By mid-1982, the employees had found $3.7 million in cost savings; in so doing, they saved their jobs.

Despite such efforts, Xerox products still were not competitive. Internal studies showed that the machines were overpriced, and external evaluations reported that Xerox did not have a machine rated top quality at any level or segment of the market. Meanwhile, the company's market share fell to 30 percent. (In the early 1970s, Xerox's share had been over 80 percent.) In 1982, profits slipped to $424 million, down from their record high of $619 million in 1980. Massive cost-cutting efforts in 1983 resulted in only a meager increase in net income, $466 million. (Exhibits 4, 5, and 6 give complete financial statements.) David Kearns, who had just been appointed CEO in 1982, knew that Xerox must either change radically, or concede defeat in the industry it had created some 20 years before.

EXHIBIT 4
Xerox Corporation: Income Statements
(in Millions of Dollars, Except per Share Data)

	1983	***1982***	***1981***	***1980***
Income:				
Rentals	$3,306	$3,974	$4,339	$5,152*
Services	1,274	1,001	761	--
Sales	3,884	3,481	3,410	3,045
Equity in net income of financial services	197	39	25	--
Business:				
Other income	141	162	142	--
Total income	$8,802	$8,657	$8,677	$8,197
Costs and other deductions:				
Cost of rentals	$1,634	$1,739	$1,822	$2,118*
Cost of services	592	476	356	--
Cost of sales	2,008	1,701	1,570	1,425
Research and development expenses	555	565	526	434
Selling, administrative, and general expenses	3,076	3,155	3,035	2,867
Interest expenses	190	153	129	--
Other net	77	270	106	--
Income taxes	136	153	434	605
Outside shareholders' interests	64	76	127	127
Total costs and expenses	$8,336	$8,288	$8,105	$7,576
Income from continuing operations	$ 466	$ 369	$ 572	$ 621
Other income	--	56	26	(1)
Net income	$ 466	$ 425	$ 598	$ 620
Income per common share	$4.42	$5.00	$7.08	$7.33

* Includes services.
Source: Annual reports.

EXHIBIT 5
Xerox Corporation: Balance Sheets (in Millions of Dollars)

	1983	1982	1981	1980
Assets				
Current assets:				
Cash	$ 326	$ 561	$ 45	$ 89
Bank time deposits	--	--	234	229
Marketable securities	45	54	148	207
Accounts receivable	1,368	1,246	1,245	1,164
Receivables from Xerox Credit Corporation	--	10	178	196
Accrued revenues	454	413	403	377
Inventories	1,285	1,286	1,132	1,086
Other current assets	177	242	230	169
Total current assets	$3,655	$3,812	$3,615	$3,517
Long-term trade receivables	275	235	246	199
Rental equipment and related inventories	1,529	1,641	1,905	1,922
Land, buildings, and equipment	1,470	1,440	1,434	1,369
Investments, at equity	2,220*	389	320	194
Other assets	149	148	149	149
Total assets	$9,297	$7,665	$7,669	$7,350
Liabilities and Shareholders' Equity				
Current liabilities:				
Notes payable	$ 543	$ 426	$ 224	$ 208
Payments due within 1 year on long-term debt	--	126	96	80
Accounts payable	309	281	340	316
Salaries, profit-sharing, and other accruals	960	951	910	792
Income taxes	209	234	347	441
Other current liabilities	285	185	163	147
Total current liabilities	$2,306	$2,172	$2,080	$1,984
Long-term debt	$1,461	$ 850	$ 870	$ 898
Other noncurrent liabilities	$ 204	$ 155	$ 145	$ 133
Deferred income taxes	$ 122	$ 212	$ 247	$ 124
Deferred investment tax credits	$ 101	$ 107	$ 104	$ 86
Outside shareholders' interests	$ 438	$ 445	$ 496	$ 500
Cumulative preferred stock	$ 442	--	--	--
Shareholders' equity:				
Common stock	$ 95	$ 85	$ 84	$ 84
Class B stock	--	0.2	0.2	0.2
Additional pain in capital	695	317	306	305
Retained earnings	3,804	3,670	3,500	3,249
Unrealized appreciation, equity investments	40	--	--	--
Cumulative translation adjustments	(402)	(335)	(150)	--
Total	$4,232	$3,737	$3,740	$3,638
Deduct Class B receivables and deferrals	9	12	13	14
Total shareholders' equity	$4,222	$3,725	$3,727	$3,624
Total liabilities and shareholders' equity	$9,297	$7,665	$7,669	$7,350

* Includes $2,017 investment in financial service businesses, at equity.
Source: Annual reports.

EXHIBIT 6

Xerox Corporation: Financial Summary (In Millions of Dollars, Except per Share Data)

	1983	1982	1981	1980
Per share data:				
Income (loss) per common share				
Continuing operations	$ 4.68	$ 4.21	$ 6.53	$ 6.45
Discontinued operations	(.26)	.79	.55	.24
Net income per common share	4.42	5.00	7.08	6.69
Dividends declared per common share	3.00	3.00	3.00	2.80
Operations:				
Income				
Sales, rentals, and service	$ 8,268	$ 8,258	$ 8,316	$ 7,886
Equity in net income of financial services businesses	197	39	25	3
Other income	142	162	142	143
Total	$ 8,607	$ 8,459	$ 8,483	$ 8,032
Research and development expenses	$ 536	$ 548	$ 511	$ 419
Income from continuing operations	491	357	551	545
Income (loss) from discontinued operations	(25)	67	47	20
Net income	$ 466	$ 424	$ 598	$ 565
Financial position:				
Current assets	$ 3,655	$ 3,814	$ 3,616	$ 3,560
Rental equipment and related inventories	3,987	4,196	4,621	4,845
Accumulated depreciation of rental equipment	2,458	2,555	2,715	2,879
Land, buildings, and equipment	2,778	2,641	2,565	2,460
Accumulated depreciation of buildings and equipment	1,308	1,201	1,127	1,050
Investment of financial services businesses, at equity	2,017	225	161	79
Total assets	$ 9,297	$ 7,668	$ 7,674	$ 7,514
Current liabilities	2,306	2,175	2,081	2,085
Long-term debt	1,461	850	870	898
Employees at year-end	101,178	106,833	114,733	114,172
Return on assets	5.4%	4.8%	7.6%	8.0%
Return on equity	10.7%	9.6%	15.0%	15.8%
Total debt to total capitalization	28.2%	25.2%	22.0%	22.2%

Source: Annual reports.

CASE 19

Xerox Corporation: 1983 to 1989*

In 1959, Xerox introduced the 914 copier, and created a new industry. The 914 is arguably the most successful product ever marketed in the United States. For years, Xerox dominated the market, placing four times as many copiers as the rest of the industry combined. But after some time, the Japanese began making inroads. Xerox did not respond to these developments and, as a result, its market share in the early 1980s had fallen to about only 20 percent. In response to this predicament, David Kearns, CEO, led the organization in the creation and pursuit of a new strategy that came to be called "Leadership Through Quality." Following is a description of the various elements of this strategy and its implementation.

BENCHMARKING

In 1980 and 1981, fact-finding trips to Japan had led to the discovery that Japanese copier manufacturers were able to design a new machine in half the time Xerox required. Furthermore, they could produce, ship, and sell units for about the same amount that it cost Xerox just to manufacture them. Initially, managers at Xerox went through a stage of denial, during which they argued that such performance was impossible, but eventual acceptance of their competitor's skill began to haunt Xerox managers, and pride drove them toward improvement.

This change in attitude had a significant effect on operating performance at Xerox. By the end of 1983, production yields had improved 70 percent, inventory levels had dropped by more than 50 percent, and overhead spending had been cut by $200 million per year. Product development times were reduced from 8 to 10 years to just 2 years for a low-end machine and 3½ years for a high-end machine. Variations on existing products were designed in less time. Based on such improvements, Xerox moved to make the "benchmarking" process an ongoing, pervasive part of its new strategy.

A small red booklet, defining benchmarking and explaining its implementation, was prepared and distributed to all managers. According to this manual, benchmarking was "The process of measuring our products, services, and practices against our toughest competitors, identifying the gaps and establishing goals. Our goal is always to achieve superiority in quality, product reliability, and cost." The manual's detailed instructions for this process are summarized by the flowchart reproduced as Exhibit 1.

Initially, managers focused on comparing Xerox to other copier manufacturers. Soon, however, managers found this too limiting. In some functions, the very best practices were not being developed by copier companies. So, a distinction was made between studying the best practices at copier companies, called *competitive benchmarking*, and studying the best practices of any given function, regardless of the industry, called *functional benchmarking*.

* Prepared by Alex Miller, University of Tennessee.

EXHIBIT 1
Benchmarking Process

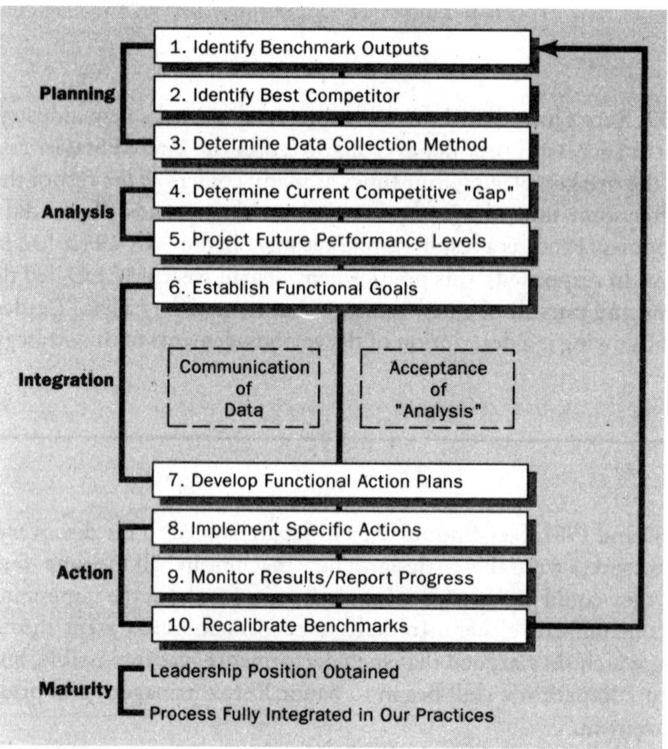

Source: Xerox Corporation.

One of the first examples of functional benchmarking was the study of how L. L. Bean managed its warehouses and inventories. Bean was a mail-order retailer of sporting goods and outdoor clothing. Filling an individual order consisted of gathering relatively small numbers of items from inventory. To make order filling more efficient, Bean had developed a computer program that actually arranged orders so that stock pickers would travel the shortest possible distance in gathering items from the warehouse. The resulting accuracy and speed of order filling convinced Xerox that they too could benefit from such software. A similar process was used to improve other functions.

As managers in these functions learned better ways of doing things and their performance improved, the use of benchmarking grew. Soon it was being used in hundreds of applications. The "Not Invented Here" attitude that had once characterized Xerox was replaced with a new attitude of attempting to learn from every situation. The new philosophy was rather irreverently dubbed "steal shamelessly," though, in fact, Xerox used only ideas that firms willingly gave away. In the spirit of information sharing, the rule at Xerox was to "ask no question of another firm that you would be unwilling to answer about your own." Using this as a guideline in the first several years of benchmarking, Xerox encountered only two firms which were unwilling to cooperate in the process.

MANUFACTURING STRATEGY

Many of the new ideas that grew out of the benchmarking process congealed to form a new manufacturing strategy. These new policies and practices actually affected a large number of functions. The unifying theme was that all functions were to stop looking inward to their own needs and start looking outward to see what their customers wanted. Each "family unit," a manager and his direct reports, was encouraged to identify both its *internal* customers and its *external* customers (see the training document reproduced as Exhibit 2). For instance, the group that built paper trays identified its external customer as the end user who would load the paper. Their internal customers were the assembly-line workers who would combine the paper tray with hundreds of other components to construct the finished copier. In function after function, this shift in emphasis toward internal and external customers resulted in important operational changes.

EXHIBIT 2
Customer Orientation

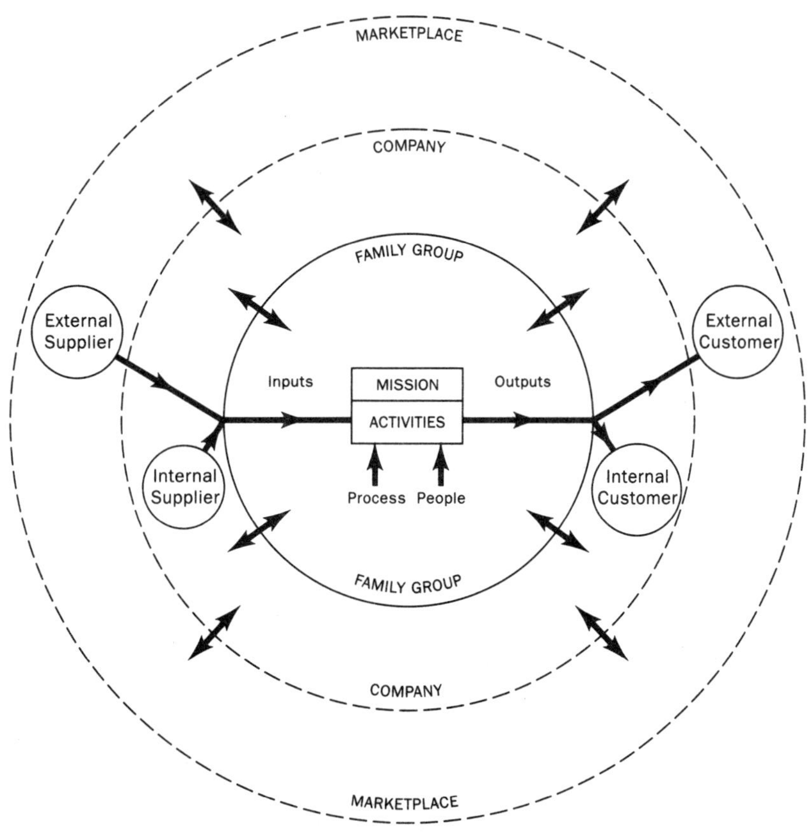

Source: Xerox Corporation.

EXHIBIT 3
Changing View of Quality

	Conventional View	*Leadership through Quality*
Definition	Goodness	Conformance to customer requirements
System	Inspection	Prevention
Performance standard	Allowable level of defects	Striving toward error-free output
Measure	Indices	Cost of lack of conformance

Source: Xerox Corporation.

Quality Control

Quality became a central concern in virtually all functions. Such change was encouraged by widespread top-management support for a newly drafted quality policy stating:

> Xerox is a quality company. Quality is the basic business principle for Xerox. Quality means providing our external and internal customers with the innovative products and service that fully satisfy their requirements. Quality improvement is the job of every Xerox employee.

Along with this policy statement came the new set of concepts reprinted in Exhibit 3. There was considerable debate within Xerox concerning the concept of the cost of quality. As portrayed in Exhibit 4, the cost of quality was broken down into three component parts. There was an opportunity cost associated with customers choosing higher-quality suppliers. There was a cost of nonconformance—the cost of reworking or scrapping poor output, for example. Finally, there was a cost of conformance, that is, the cost associated with steps taken to reduce nonconformance costs like scrap and rework. Over time, these costs were expected to fall, although not necessarily proportionally.

While the cost of quality was seen as a good concept for measuring improvement, there was some concern regarding the role that it would play in decision making—especially investment decisions made by upper managers. The compromise reached was that employees would calculate the impact of their efforts on cost of quality, but that top managers would not be asked to justify investments in quality improvements by predicting the impact of those investments on the cost of quality.

Marketing

The new emphasis on the customer placed new demands on marketing. Whereas previously, emphasis had been placed on selling, the new role for marketing became that of the voice of the customer. This came to entail market research on an unprecedented scale. Each month, 30,000 surveys would be collected, asking customers to evaluate the company's goods and services. At one point, the sales force was told not to seek any further business from their major accounts until each of these accounts had been visited three times to gather information on their concerns with Xerox. This emphasis on defining quality

EXHIBIT 4
The Cost of Quality

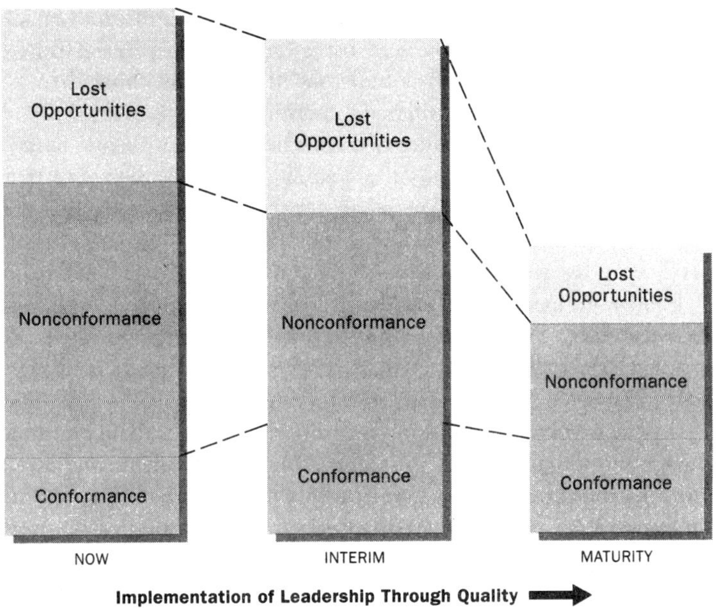

Source: Xerox Corporation.

from the customer's perspective reached the very top of the organization. The top twenty managers, led by CEO David Kearns, began rotating responsibility for manning a customer complaint phone, every manager serving 1 day a month. It was agreed that talking to customers took priority over all else: meetings, travel, and so on, for each manager when it was his or her turn.

Product Design

Xerox replaced the project management approach to research and development that had been a key component of matrix management throughout the 1970s. The fundamental problem with the matrix approach was that product development flowed sequentially through product planning, design engineering, manufacturing engineering, and then service engineering, and no one function was responsible for the end product. In the new system, product delivery teams were under the control of a single person, identified as the chief engineer. This manager was responsible for all quality, costs, and scheduling issues affecting his or her product. The chief engineer was also given complete authority to modify the design schedule and to make "go/no-go" decisions. To aid in the design of products that could be easily manufactured, all design teams had direct access to a model shop and a pilot plant. In the model shop, prototype parts or products could be cheaply and quickly produced; in the pilot plant, engineers could assess how easily various designs could be replicated in a production environment.

Supplier Management

Benchmarking from Japan in the early 1980s had shown that all the Japanese copier companies combined had only 1,000 suppliers, far fewer than Xerox's 5,000. To keep the number of suppliers low, the Japanese were using the same parts in each other's machines. It was not unusual for similar size and volume machines to have more than a 50 percent overlap in common parts. Because suppliers for common parts specialized, the suppliers increased the production volumes and lowered their costs. As one Xerox manager explained, "Canon will find a part that it likes on a Toshiba copier. Rather than trying to make the part themselves, they will go to Toshiba's supplier to cut a deal. They will offer to provide the supplier with 100,000 more orders, but in return, they expect some of the cost savings to be passed along by getting the part 10 percent cheaper than Toshiba got it."

Follow-up benchmark studies showed that by dealing with fewer vendors, the Japanese were able to maintain a very different relationship with them. Xerox and its suppliers had always interacted within the framework of a contract that kept relations formal and distant. However, the Japanese openly cooperated with their suppliers, often even sharing access to each other's accounting records. It was not at all uncommon for a Japanese firm to train a vendor's employees in quality control, manufacturing automation, and so forth. Coordination extended to just-in-time production scheduling, and suppliers were expected to deliver copier parts in small quantities on a schedule the customer set.

Adopting the Japanese practices at Xerox meant reducing the number of vendors for the copier business from 5,000 to only 400. Xerox also created a vendor certification process in which suppliers were either offered training or explicitly told what they needed to work on in order to continue as a Xerox vendor. In addition, vendors were consulted about their ideas on better designs and better customer service.

EMPLOYEE INVOLVEMENT

In 1982, Xerox executives had decided to shut down a wire harness assembly operation because their analysis showed how they could save $3.2 million annually by importing the harnesses. The 180 employees whose jobs were at stake responded by showing how, given a free hand, they could reduce the cost of their operation by $3.7 million and keep the jobs in the United States. This initiative convinced Xerox managers that by limiting employee involvement in analysis and cost-cutting measures, Xerox was missing an important source of expertise. However, to tap that expertise, several changes were needed.

Perhaps foremost among these was the role that managers would play. In the past, managers at Xerox emphasized what they grew to call one-on-one supervision: planning, telling, and controlling individuals in their work groups. To encourage initiative on the part of individual workers and groups, this style of oversight was replaced by something called team leadership—a style of management that emphasized teaching, coaching, and facilitating. In addition, this managerial style placed heavy emphasis on encouraging the work group to function as a team instead of a loose collection of individuals.

The shift to this new style of management was not always smooth. At first, employees complained that they had no spare time for taking on new responsibilities. They also questioned whether or not their suggestions would actually be implemented. Many asked how this new approach would benefit them. Some managers resisted because they felt the new approach shifted authority to workers while leaving responsibility with them. Managers also argued that it was unfair to ask more of employees than they were trained to provide. However, isolated successes encouraged further experimentation with the new approach, and eventually, it enjoyed widespread adoption. From 1986 to 1989, Xerox employees formed thousands of teams to work on many different problems. Typical teams included:

- Three secretaries at corporate headquarters who reduced the time they each required to duplicate and distribute internal documents by an average of 5 hours per week
- A group of Canadian service technicians who redefined the boundaries of their service territories, resulting in 30 percent faster average response time to customer calls
- A group of technical manual writers who reduced the number of pages in new service manuals by one-third without sacrificing any content

CULTURAL CHANGE

While benchmarking, the manufacturing strategy, and employee involvement were successful in making some changes at Xerox, top managers, led by David Kearns, wanted more. Specifically, they were interested in adapting the same ideas that were successful in manufacturing (such as benchmarking, customer orientation, employee involvement, etc.) to use throughout the organization. In other words, quality control would shift from an emphasis on production to concern for every aspect of what went on within Xerox. David Kearns argued that to accomplish this sort of change, Xerox would need to undergo the greatest series of cultural changes it had ever experienced.

Norm Rickards, head of quality at Xerox, identified six factors that he and others felt

EXHIBIT 5
Total Quality Transition

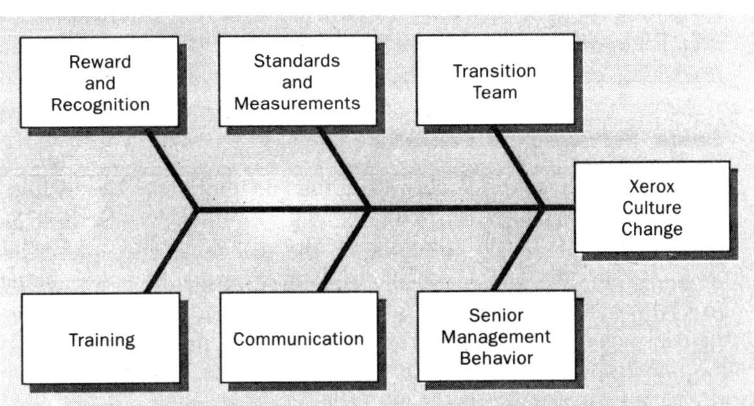

Source: Xerox Corporation.

contributed most to the cultural shift at Xerox. Typical of the Xerox management style, he and his staff presented these ideas using a fishbone diagram as in Exhibit 5. (A fishbone diagram is one of several popular quality improvement analysis techniques. It identifies the factors contributing to an outcome and relates these factors to each other. The one presented here is a summary chart. The more detailed versions typically used in problem solving at Xerox go several layers deep to get at root causes.) Following are the main factors identified in the chart.

Transition Team

While some of the elements identified in the fishbone chart evolved more or less on their own over time, others were the result of carefully considered planning on the part of two dozen high-ranking Xerox executives and managers. This group was originally assembled to participate in an executive retreat in Leesburg, Virginia, in February of 1983. There, along with consultants from McKinsey & Company, they began to map out a plan for building upon the strengths they felt the company had already developed in benchmarking, its manufacturing strategy, and the employee involvement process. Their intention was to encourage a cultural change that would spread total quality management throughout all of Xerox.

The transition team took action on two levels. First, they worked as missionaries to spread the word that Xerox was pursuing more widespread use of total quality management, TQM. Second, they identified and addressed the obstacles that were most likely to hinder the spread of TQM. These ranged from the corporation's function-dominated matrix structure to the need for new training programs. Many of the other factors identified in the fishbone diagram (Exhibit 5) were brought about as a result of the Leesburg Group's meeting in February and a subsequent meeting of the team in August of 1983.

Perhaps the greatest single change the transition team made was restructuring Xerox's organization from a single complex matrix to three simpler strategic business units (SBUs). These corresponded to the market segments Xerox had previously identified: the high-, medium-, and low-volume copier-market segments. Each of these SBUs would be more or less autonomous in terms of identifying the machines they needed. They also had authority for getting the parts (or even the entire machine if need be) from the best source of supply, even if it meant getting it from outside Xerox. The SBU would also control engineering, marketing, pricing—essentially all the functions necessary to run a copier business.

Senior Management Behavior

The Leesburg Group felt successful implementation of Leadership Through Quality required senior managers to "walk the talk." In other words, these managers must serve as role models, personally adhering to the guidelines they prescribed for the rest of the organization. This idea eventually led to the creation of a new set of management evaluation procedures. Subordinates were incorporated into the evaluation process, annually rating their managers on the twenty-seven items listed in Exhibit 6. These ratings were used in conjunction with other regular reviews to place managers in one of three categories: role model, competent, needs work. To be considered for further promotion, the top 200 managers in the business were required to maintain a rating of role model. Below this level, the minimum rating permissible for promotion was competent.

EXHIBIT 6
Annual Performance Appraisal Form

How frequently does your manager do each of the following? Please circle the response that best describes your manager's behavior.

My Manager:	*Very Infrequently*	*Infrequently*	*Sometimes*	*Frequently*	*Very Frequently*
1. Provides me with honest feedback on my performance.	1	2	3	4	5
2. Encourages me to monitor my own efforts.	1	2	3	4	5
3. Encourages me to make suggestions.	1	2	3	4	5
4. Provides me with an environment conducive to teamwork.	1	2	3	4	5
5. Gives me the information needed to do my job.	1	2	3	4	5
6. Clearly defines what he/she requires of me.	1	2	3	4	5
7. Acts as a positive role model for Leadership Through Quality.	1	2	3	4	5
8. Openly recognizes work well done.	1	2	3	4	5
9. Listens to me before making decisions affecting my area.	1	2	3	4	5
10. Makes an effort to solve my work-related problems.	1	2	3	4	5
11. Encourages all of us to work as a team.	1	2	3	4	5
12. Informs me regularly about the state of the business.	1	2	3	4	5
13. Displays an understanding of Xerox objectives and strategic directions.	1	2	3	4	5
14. Summarizes progress during meetings to seek understanding and agreement.	1	2	3	4	5
15. Encourages me to ask questions.	1	2	3	4	5
16. Asks questions to ensure understanding.	1	2	3	4	5
17. Encourages an environment of openness and trust.	1	2	3	4	5
18. Behaves in ways which demonstrate respect for others.	1	2	3	4	5
19. Makes an effort to locate and remove barriers that reduce efficiency.	1	2	3	4	5
20. Ensures regularly scheduled reviews of progress toward goals.	1	2	3	4	5
21. Monitors the Quality Improvement Process.	1	2	3	4	5
22. Monitors department progress through competitive benchmarks.	1	2	3	4	5
23. Rewards those who clearly use the Quality Improvement Process.	1	2	3	4	5
24. Sets objectives used on customer requirements.	1	2	3	4	5
25. Uses the Quality Improvement Process.	1	2	3	4	5
26. Uses the problem-solving process in order to solve problems.	1	2	3	4	5
27. Treats Leadership Through Quality as the basic Xerox business principle.	1	2	3	4	5

Source: Xerox Corporation.

Training

An extensive training program was devised to cover all 100,000 Xerox employees. The basic training was delivered in two parts. As seen in Exhibit 7, the first 2½ days of training were taken by individuals whenever they could arrange to enroll in the courses. (All new employees were required to enroll within the first 3 to 4 months of employment.) The remaining training was scheduled as a "training cascade" spreading from one "family group" (a manager and his or her direct reports) to another in a process known as LUTI. As

EXHIBIT 7
Training Sequence

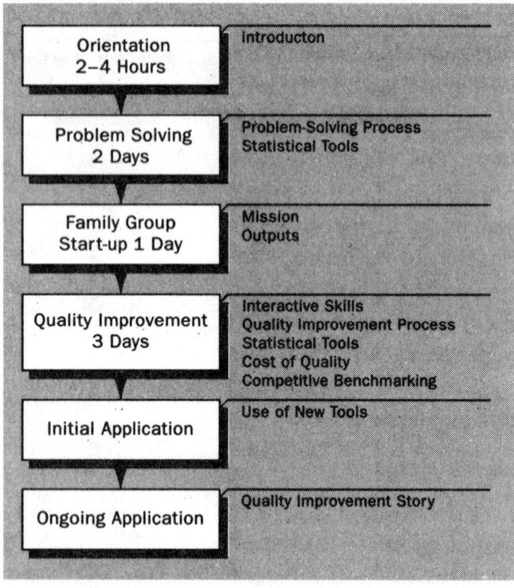

Source: Xerox Corporation.

described in Exhibit 8, LUTI stood for learn, use, train, and inspect. The first course in the cascade began in January of 1984, when David Kearns, with the help of outside specialists, taught a week-long course on total quality management to the half dozen top managers who were his direct reports. This was the *learning* phase of LUTI for those half dozen managers. They then moved to the *use* phase, in which they teamed up to carry out a

EXHIBIT 8
Training Cascade

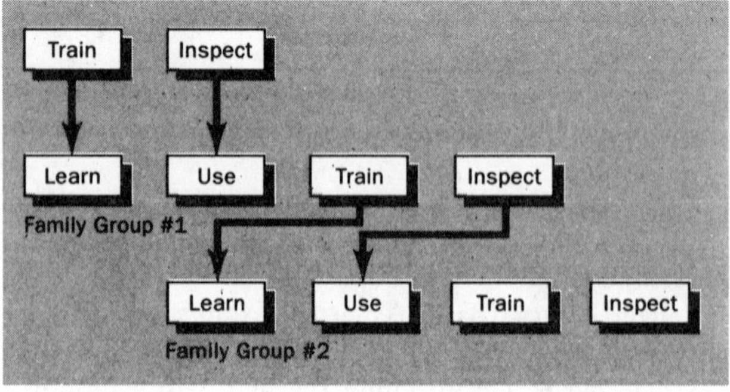

Source: Xerox Corporation.

project, applying the lessons they had been taught. After this hands-on experience, they were each required to *train* their own direct reports in the beginning of the second round of the cascade. During the projects that were entailed in this second round of training, the six managers would provide oversight for their direct reports, the *inspect* phase of the LUTI cycle. The cycle spread across and down the organization as one level trained and observed the next level. In early 1989, the last family group, a field unit in mainland China, had been through the core training. The total cost by that time was $125 million.

Standards and Measurements

This aspect of the cultural change encouraged what became known as "Managing by Facts." The movement began with narrowly defined applications of standard statistical process control: pareto analysis (histograms identifying the most common reasons for a given quality problem), control charts (plotting the ongoing performance of a machine), fishbone diagrams (charts that attempt to structure all the causes for a given problem), and so forth. These were the same tools that American statisticians had used to help rebuild Japan after World War II. These simple tools were widely used in Japan, where they were viewed as a key component to that nation's global success. But, in the western world, they had been largely discounted as being too "old fashioned."

In addition to these statistical tools, two generic managerial processes were developed. One of these was the problem-solving process portrayed in Exhibit 9. The other was the quality improvement process (QIP) flowcharted in Exhibit 10. The two were complementary and meant to be used together. When employees encountered a problem in the QIP,

EXHIBIT 9
The Problem-Solving Process

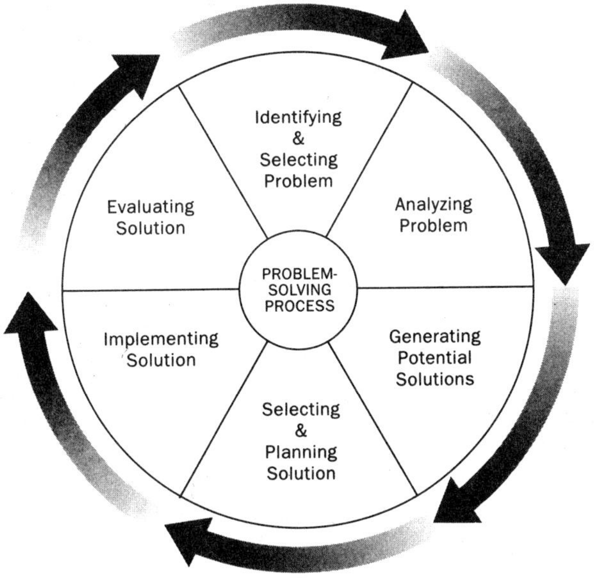

Source: Xerox Corporation.

EXHIBIT 10
Quality Improvement Process

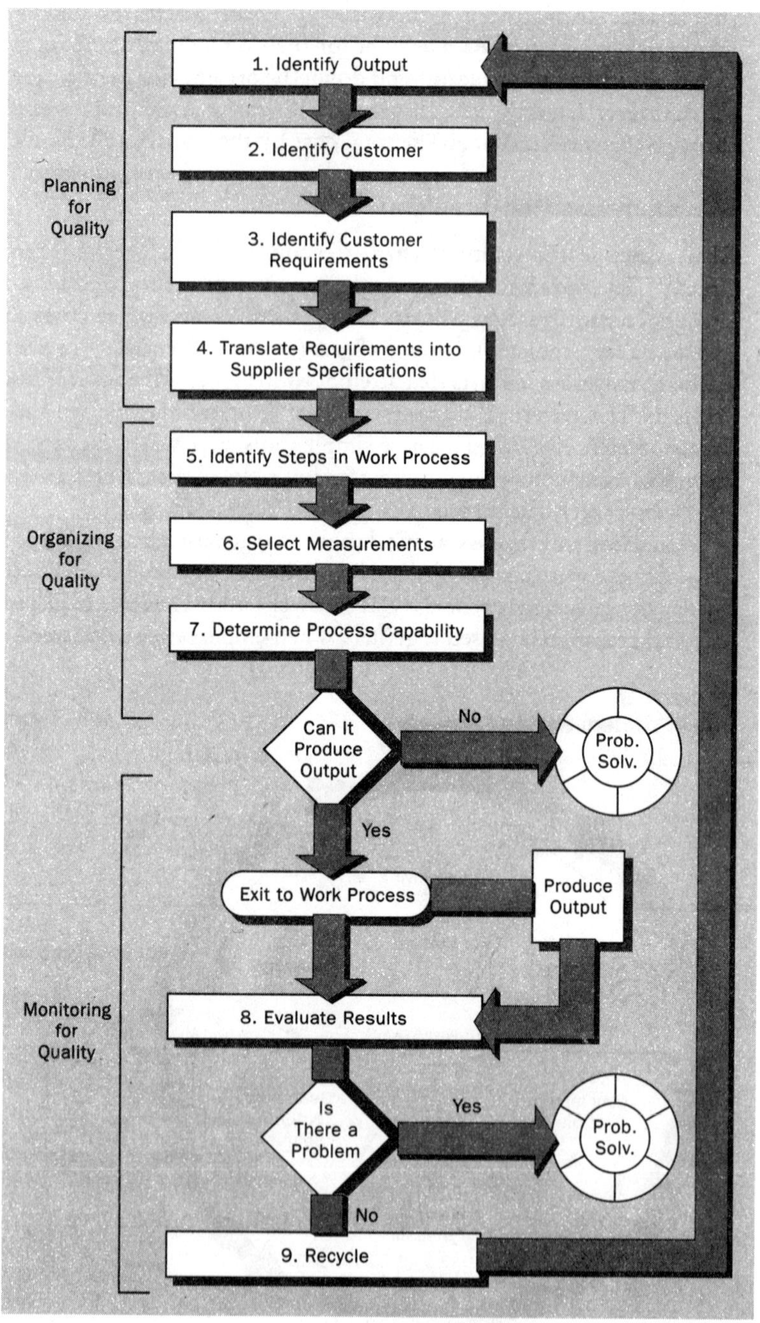

Source: Xerox Corporation.

they shifted to the problem-solving process until it was resolved, and then progressed further through the QIP. Training in these statistical tools and managerial processes formed a key component of the training program. In Xerox conference rooms from corporate headquarters to local field offices, diagrams for the problem-solving process and the quality improvement process were prominently displayed. In dozens of interviews, employees representing a wide range of organizational levels and functions spoke repeatedly and comfortably about the use of these processes.

Communication

A conscious effort was made to communicate quality as the overriding priority at Xerox. This communication effort had no apparent common theme other than that of all managers' being responsible for communicating the tenets of Leadership Through Quality. Based on that general guideline, managers responded with a variety of measures:

- Top managers let it be known that it was never appropriate to abbreviate Leadership Through Quality. It was not to be seen as just another set of acronyms like JIT, TQM, SPC, and so on. Instead, its use was to be "jealously guarded" as Xerox's own understanding of the critical importance of quality.
- Paul Allaire, president of the document processing business, established a habit of producing four videotapes a year on Leadership Through Quality. These were broadcast around the world through Xerox's own broadcasting unit, an arm of its corporate training office. In addition to these tapes, he began scheduling a 2-week, round-the-world, question and answer tour on the subject each February.
- A number of internal journals were published, each with its own target audience. These include *Quality Quarterly, Quality Update, Networking, Communique,* and *Xerox World.*
- In 1986, David Kearns decided to reorder the list of goals that Xerox considered its priorities. While the company literature would continue to refer to the three goals of return on assets, market share, and quality as being equally important, they would now be listed as quality, ROA, and market share.

Recognition and Reward

On a wide range of organizational levels, procedures were established for recognizing employee contribution to Leadership Through Quality. For example, quality was given significant weighting in individual executive bonus plans. Family groups were also recognized for their contributions through a corporate-wide competition that culminated in annual Teamwork Days. At these meetings, winning teams from each division and region were gathered at events that were half trade shows and half celebrations. These events began as fairly small affairs, but by 1989, they were so large that they had to be held at three locations scattered across the United States. At the Dallas site, more than 300 winning teams gathered to share their successes with one another. Each team had been evaluated on its overall effort in applying the tenets of Leadership Through Quality, starting with a problem statement and ending with careful documentation of what they had done to address the problem and what remained yet to be done.

These were teams like the Hi Rockers, the Xerox Service Work Group from Little Rock, Arkansas. As explained in their 75-page report, Hi Rockers' problem was that only 83 percent of their customers reported that they were satisfied with Xerox service in 1988. The team created a program they called "Spoil The Customer." This program was designed around a careful analysis of what the customers wanted, areas in which the team fell short, reasons for this failure, action plans for what could be done, the costs of quality, and control charts tracking customer complaints over the year. The report detailed what the team did to raise customer satisfaction levels to 98.7 by 1989. While the Hi Rockers' effort was impressive, it is described here merely as an example of the sort of work the family groups throughout Xerox undertook. (It is worth noting that while the Hi Rockers' impressive work won within their district, they did not place in the regional or national competition.)

LEADERSHIP FROM THE TOP

As the 1980s came to an end, the Leadership Through Quality strategy began to have an effect on Xerox's financial performance, as detailed in Exhibits 11, 12, 13 and 14. (Note that some of these financial statements reflect the consolidated operations of both the document processing and Xerox's financial services business. The corporation began moving into financial services in 1980 and expanded this business throughout the following decade.) A large portion of the credit for Leadership Through Quality success was given to a single person: David Kearns, CEO of Xerox. Upon meeting him, one would not suspect Kearns to be the sort of person to so thoroughly dominate an organization the size of Xerox. He is a father of six and remains dedicated to being home for family dinners. On the day he found out that he would be the next CEO of Xerox, he left on a previously planned family camping trip. Not a large man, he stays fit by running, including the occasional marathon. He is very approachable, very friendly, very human.

Yet, beneath this kind demeanor is a manager fiercely committed to leaving Xerox with a legacy of quality. When he first started traveling around the world telling Xerox employees about Leadership Through Quality, common reactions from company veterans were "Just another flavor of the month" and "This too shall pass." Many were surprised when he returned over and over again to deliver the same message. When they began to see that he was serious about quality, they began to challenge him on the wisdom of this emphasis. A

EXHIBIT 11
Xerox Corporation: Document Processing Operational Data, 1985–1989

	1989	*1988*	*1987*	*1986*	*1985*
Document processing revenue (dollars in billions)	12.4	11.7	10.8	9.7	9.1
Document processing income from continuing operations (dollars in millions)	488	392*	353	314	409
Research and development (dollars in millions)	809	794	722	650	597
Selling, administrative, and general expenses (% of revenue)	32.0	33.3	33.8	35.1	33.7
Return on assets (%)	12.4	11.0	9.9	7.8	10.9

* Before restructuring. Income after document processing restructuring was $148.
Source: Annual reports.

EXHIBIT 12
Xerox Corporation: Operational Data, 1980–1984
(In Millions of Dollars, Except per Share Data)

	1984	*1983*	*1982*	*1981*	*1980*
Per share data:					
Income (loss) per common share					
Continuing operations	$3.42	$4.68	$4.21	$6.53	$6.45
Discontinued operations	(.89)	(.26)	.79	.55	.24
Net income per common share	2.53	4.42	5.00	7.08	6.69
Dividends declared per common share	3.00	3.00	3.00	3.00	2.80
Operations:					
Income					
Sales, rentals, and service	$8,792	$8,268	$8,258	$8,316	$7,886
Equity in net income of financial services businesses	68	197	39	25	3
Other income	142	142	162	142	143
Total	$9,002	$8,607	$8,459	$8,483	$8,032
Research and development expenses	561	536	548	511	419
Income from continuing operations	376	491	357	551	545
Income (loss) from discontinued operations	(85)	(25)	67	47	20
Net income	291	466	424	598	565
Financial position:					
Current assets	$3,739	$3,655	$3,814	$3,616	$3,560
Rental equipment and related inventories	3,799	3,987	4,196	4,621	4,845
Accumulated depreciation of rental equipment	2,279	2,458	2,555	2,715	2,879
Land, buildings, and equipment	2,779	2,778	2,641	2,565	2,460
Accumulated depreciation of buildings and equipment	1,387	1,308	1,201	1,127	1,050
Investment of financial services businesses, at equity	2,175	2,017	225	161	79
Total assets	$9,537	$9,297	$7,668	$7,674	$7,514
Current liabilities	2,451	2,306	2,175	2,081	2,085
Long-term debt	1,614	1,461	850	870	898
Employees at year-end	103,457	101,178	106,833	114,733	114,172
Return on assets	4.0%	5.4%	4.8%	7.6%	8.0%
Return on equity	7.0%	10.7%	9.6%	15.0%	15.8%
Total debt to total capitalization	31.3%	28.2%	25.2%	22.0%	22.2%

Source: Annual reports.

common sort of question was "Won't this quality effort get in the way of what we're trying to do as a corporation?" His response to such questions was always direct: "Quality will not *get in* the way, quality *is* the way. Anyone who cannot understand this distinction would perhaps be better suited for work in another organization." Frank Pipp, formerly head of manufacturing, was one of the employees who had been with Xerox from its beginning. In reflecting on the various CEOs he had seen come and go, he commented that what made Kearns remarkable was that "he never blinked." Pipp explained that in countless meetings on endless tough issues, he had never once seen Kearns back away from quality or treat it as less important than some other consideration. Pipp says that when it comes to "walking the talk," no one is better than Kearns.

EXHIBIT 13
Xerox Corporation: Income Statement
(in Millions of Dollars, Except per Share Data)

	1989	1988	1987	1986	1985	1984	1983
	*Document Processing Business**						
Revenues:							
Sales	$6,696	$6,174	$5,702	$4,822	$4,318	$3,883	$3,392
Service and rentals	4,906	4,855	4,618	4,533	4,358	4,491	4,554
Finance income	689	531	366	100	106	116	116
Income from unconsolidated affiliates	140	128	148	326	116	103	224
Total revenues	$12,431	$11,688	$10,834	$9,781	$8,898	$8,593	$8,285
Costs and expenses:							
Cost of sales	$3,664	$3,281	$2,940	$2,412	$2,081	$1,949	$1,744
Cost of service and rentals	2,573	2,497	2,442	2,402	2,330	2,255	2,217
Research and development expenses	809	794	722	650	597	555	536
Selling, administration, and general expenses	3,929	3,847	3,614	3,370	3,011	2,977	2,849
Interest expense	465	329	264	212	230	261	190
Restructuring costs		275		65	(94)	71	1
Other, net	(27)	81	122	18	39	8	75
Total cost expenses	$11,413	$11,104	$10,104	$9,129	$8,194	$8,076	$7,612
Income before income taxes	$ 1,018	$ 584	$ 730	$ 652	$ 704	$ 517	$ 673
Income taxes	378	289	296	112	166	156	144
Income before minorities' interests	$ 640	$ 295	$ 434	$ 540	$ 538	$ 361	$ 529
Minorities' interests	152	147	81	75	63	70	64
Net income, document processing	$488	$148	$353				
Net income, Insurance, and Financial Services	$216	$240	$225				
Total net income	$704	$388	$578	$465	$475	$291	$465
Earnings per share	$6.56	$3.49	$5.30	$4.28	$4.44	$2.53	$4.42

* Please note: Before 1987, income statements were consolidated, as reflected in the above figures. But, beginning in 1987, Insurance and Financial Services are listed separately.
Source: Annual reports.

Kearns delivered a characteristically powerful speech on Teamwork '89 day, the celebration/trade show featuring the best of the hundreds of employee involvement projects scattered throughout Xerox. Teamwork Days were simultaneously scheduled at multiple sites across the United States, but Kearns was linked to the various sites by a video hookup. About midmorning, the booths were all closed at the conference center, and the crowd began to assemble in front of a wall-sized video projection. Music blasted out a beat reminiscent of a Rocky movie, while banks of lights flashed to the rhythm. The date was just 2 weeks before announcements were due for the winners of the Malcolm Baldridge National Quality award. Xerox was known to be one of the finalists, and everyone in the auditorium knew they had each done their part to help. Every face wore a proud grin as people shouted to one another over the music. Suddenly, everyone turned to the front, as the monitors displayed David Kearns bounding up through a crowd at the New York Teamwork Day site where the same music played and a similar crowd rose to give him a standing ovation. The crowd roared and Kearns waved enthusiastically, nodding to individuals he recognized. Eventually, the crowd quieted and he began to speak:

EXHIBIT 14
Xerox Corporation: Consolidated Balance Sheets (in Millions of Dollars)

	1989	1988
Assets:		
Cash	$ 142	$ 296
Accounts receivable, net:		
Trade	1,652	1,704
Premiums	750	752
Reinsurance recoverable and other	837	790
Finance receivables, net	8,572	6,657
Inventories	1,567	1,685
Investments	9,394	7,960
Equipment on operating leases, net	1,023	977
Land, buildings, and equipment, net	1,997	2,008
Investments and affiliates, at equity	1,048	962
Cost of acquired businesses in excess of net assets	1,123	1,089
Other assets	1,983	1,561
Total assets	$30,088	$26,441
Liabilities and equity:		
Accounts payable	$ 814	$ 878
Accrued compensation and benefit costs	922	811
Unearned income:		
Premiums	1,139	1,214
Other	418	418
Insurance reserves:		
Unpaid losses and loss expenses	6,220	5,685
Policy holders' funds on deposits	1,795	1,160
Other liabilities	1,980	1,928
Short-term debt	3,243	2,495
Long-term debt	7,511	5,379
Deferred ESOP benefits	(785)	--
Minorities' interests in equity of subsidiaries	715	806
Preferred stock	1,081	296
Common shareholders' equity	5,035	5,371
Total liabilities and equity	$30,088	$26,441

Source: Annual reports.

Let me first thank all of the people who worked so long and so hard to make this day possible. I think they deserve a big round of applause. Today has been a terrific success. You should all feel very good about it. . . .

Our two key weapons in our battle to become the premier document processing company are our people and our quality process. The combination is awesome! The evidence is all around us today. We are surrounded by outstanding examples of the way we are doing business at Xerox to better serve our customers.

The teams represented today—and literally thousands of others throughout the Xerox world—are producing hard, tangible results. We have reduced costs, become more productive, increased quality, and streamlined our business processes.

- Datapro research named our 1090 the best copier in the world—period!

- Dataquest found that customers rated Xerox number 1 in product reliability and service.
- In our survey of employees last year, 94 percent indicated that customer satisfaction was their top priority.
- Machine performance during the first 30 days has improved 40 percent in 4 years.

Perhaps most importantly, we have improved customer satisfaction. That's our top priority and the single most important measure of success. Since we began the quality journey, our attempts to improve customer satisfaction have been excellent. Let me give you just a few results:

- We have decreased our billing errors from 8.3 to 3.5 percent.
- In the high-volume copier-duplicator market segment, Kodak has been the industry leader in customer satisfaction for years. No more! Now we are the benchmark.
- In midvolume, we have improved customer satisfaction by 12 percent, and we continue to be the benchmark.
- In low volume—where the competition from Japan is the toughest—we have improved our customer satisfaction ratings by 33 percent and have cut the competitive lead in half.

I could go on, but I think you get the point. The quality process has enabled us to make quantum leaps in customer satisfaction.

There is no question about it. The pursuit of quality has made us a better and stronger company. We are now a recognized leader in total quality. The governments in England, Holland, France, and Japan have all given Xerox their highest quality award. And we are finalists this year for the national quality awards in both Canada and the United States.

Winning these awards would be the icing on the cake. But in a very real sense we have already won. We have proved to ourselves that we are among the very best. We have learned a great deal from the application process itself. And we have moved the quality ball forward.

There is a new sense of excitement and momentum around Leadership Through Quality. It is so real that you can almost reach out and touch it. It's in the air today. Our job now is to keep that momentum up. Our job now is to make sure there is no loss in momentum. Our job now is to intensify our efforts.

The longer I've been associated with quality, the more I understand that it is a continuous process. As good as we are today, we must be even better tomorrow. My entire management team understands this, and we are committed to intensifying our efforts to become a Total Quality Company.

We can't do it alone! We need your continued involvement. You are the true champions of Team Xerox. You are the leaders—the men and women who have learned the tools—who have used them—who have made them work for our customers.

But our task is not over! Don't be silent practitioners of the quality process.

Your outspoken support and enthusiasm for Leadership Through Quality is infectious. Spread the news—by your words, by your deeds, and by your behavior—that the quality strategy is a potent vehicle to improve results.

I urge all of you to look at Xerox through the only eyes that count—the eyes of our customers. Ask how you would expect to be treated by Xerox. Set your standards high. Raise your aspirations. And then use the quality process to reach your goals and to satisfy your customers—each time and every time.

Thank you for the opportunity to be with you today. It's been an invigorating experience. And thank you for your hard work. We appreciate it. Keep it up!

CASES EMPHASIZING STRATEGY FORMULATION

CASE 20

American Greetings Looks to the 90's*

As CEO Morry Weiss looked at the corporate rose logo of the world's largest publicly owned manufacturer of greeting cards and related social-expression merchandise, American Greetings (AG), he reflected upon the decade of the 1980's. In 1981, he had announced the formulation of a corporate growth objective to achieve $1 billion in annual sales by 1985, which would represent a 60 percent increase over 1982 sales of $623.6 million.

It was 1986 before AG reached that goal with sales of $1.035 billion. The profit margin, however, was 5.75, the lowest in five years and down from its high of 8.09 percent in 1984. In its fiscal year ending February 28, 1990, AG reported sales of $1.286 billion with a profit margin of 5.51 percent. He looked at the ten-year sales, net income and selling, distribution, and marketing costs summary prepared by his corporate staff (Exhibit 1). Weiss realized its increase in sales had come at a high price with an escalated and intensified battle for market share dominance among the three industry leaders, Hallmark, Gibson, and AG. In the final analysis, market shares had not really changed that much among the big three. Now each was determined to defend their respective market shares. The nature of the greeting card

EXHIBIT 1
American Greetings: Ten-Year Summary

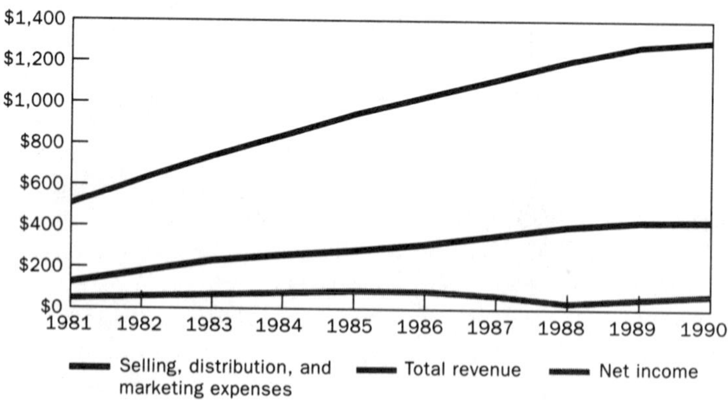

Source: American Greetings.

* Prepared by Dan Kopp and Lois Shufeldt, Southwest Missouri State University. The authors would like to acknowledge the cooperation and assistance of American Greetings. This case was presented at the 1990 North American Case Research Association's annual conference.

industry had changed dramatically. Previously, the two leading firms, Hallmark and AG, peacefully coexisted by having mutually exclusive niches. Hallmark offered higher priced, quality cards in department stores and card shops, and AG offered inexpensive cards in mass-merchandise outlets. However, AG's growth strategy to attack the industry leader and its niche followed by Gibson's growth strategy and Hallmark's defensive moves changed the industry. AG was now in the position of defending its competitive position.

THE GREETING CARD INDUSTRY

According to *GM News,* in 1988, Americans exchanged more than 7.1 billion cards—around 29 per person, which is down from the highest per capita card consumption of 30 in 1985. And with the average retail price per card of $1.10, that made "social expression" a $4 billion business. According to the Greeting Card Association, card senders sent the following cards:

Holiday	Number	Percent
Christmas	2.2 billion	30.99
Valentine's Day	850 million	11.97
Easter	180 million	2.54
Mother's Day	140 million	1.97
Father's Day	85 million	1.20
Graduation	80 million	1.13
Thanksgiving	40 million	.56
Halloween	25 million	.35
St. Patrick's Day	16 million	
Grandparent's Day	10 million	
Chanukah	9 million	
Other Seasons	5 million	

Half of the total greeting cards purchased in 1988 were seasonal cards. The remainder were in the category of everyday cards. Everyday cards, especially non-occasion cards or alternative cards, are on the increase. According to *Forbes* and *American Demographics,* the alternative card market is the fastest growing segment at 25 percent a year, while general card sales grew at only .6 percent a year, and the card industry as a whole grew at 5 percent a year. Alternative cards are not geared to any holiday, but can be inspirational, satirical, or ethnic in nature. This segment is directed toward the estimated 76 million baby boomers. Formerly, it was the focus strategy of the many small card makers who had 70 percent of the market. Now, however, the big three have captured 87 percent of the market.

Most industry analysts consider the greeting card industry to be in or near the maturity stage. According to Prudential-Bache, the industry unit growth rate was 2–4% from 1946–1985. The greeting card industry is comprised of from 500–900 firms, which range from 3 major corporations to many small family organizations. The industry is dominated by the big three: Hallmark, American Greetings, and Gibson. The estimated market shares are:

Company	1989	1985	1977
Hallmark	40–42%	42%	50%
AG	32–33%	33%	24%
Gibson	8–10%	9%	5%

Estimates vary according to the source.

During the 1980's the big three engaged in market share battles through intense price, product, promotion, and place competition. The primary price competition (through discounts to retailers) was during the period 1985 through 1987, although it still continues at a lesser rate today. According to *Value Line*, the end result was the reduction of profits with little change in market shares. In fact, retailer concessions made to gain accounts are difficult to remove; retailers are reluctant to give them up. However, according to Prudential-Bache, price competition may again emerge in the future due to the maturity of the industry, especially in selective target markets, such as large chains, as the card firms try to hold or steal accounts.

Market niches were also attacked. According to the *Insider's Chronicle*, the biggest battlefields were the gift and speciality card shops, which once were the exclusive domain of Hallmark and alternative cards. A 1989 comparison of the three firms reveals the following:

Firm	Sales (In Billions)	NI (In Millions)	Number of Employees	Number of Products	Number of Outlets
Hallmark	$2.0	NA	28,000	20,300	37,000
AG	$1.3	$44.2	29,000	20,000	90,000
Gibson	$0.4	$35.0	7,900	NA	50,000

Source: Form 10-K.

OBJECTIVES

When asked about AG's 1989 performance, Morry Weiss replied,

> Our goal was to improve competitiveness and enhance future earnings prospects in order to maximize shareholder value. AG refocused its world wide business operating strategies. While we have not reached the upper levels of that goal, substantial progress was made in 1989. We are especially pleased that significant improvement was made in reducing seasonal product returns, accounts receivable, and inventories. These are indicators of how well a business is being operated, and the results show that our people have made substantial progress. We are committed to making even further improvement in these areas (1989 Annual Report).

Weiss further explained,

> 1989 sales increased despite the loss of revenue caused by the divestiture during the year of the Company's AmToy and Plymouth divisions and several foreign subsidiaries.
>
> . . . net income was affected by restructuring costs which included the cost of relocating Carlton Cards/US to Cleveland, Ohio; consolidating certain manufacturing operations; and selling, consolidating or downsizing several unprofitable businesses (1989 Annual Report).

His assessment of AG's 1990 performance was:

> It was the kind of year you have to feel good about. Our performance demonstrated our ability to produce outstanding earnings, even in a year when the revenue gain was modest. To accomplish this required enormous effort in every department. It re-

quired a diligent watch over expenses while increasing productivity (1990 Annual Report).

Morry Weiss also commented about AG's growth:

> We are building a more synergistic relationship between our core business and our subsidiary operations in order to increase our value to our retailers.
>
> Our goal is to be a full-service provider to our retailer accounts. The more we represent a single source for a variety of consumer products, the more important a resource we become (1990 Annual Report).
>
> . . . growth is expected to continue as we accelerate new product development for the everyday cards (1989 Annual Report).

To reach this aim of providing retailers not only greeting cards, but complementary products, AG has made the following acquisitions:

Company	***Products***
Acme Frame Products	Picture frames
Wilhold Hair Care Products	Hair care products
Plus Mark	Promotional Christmas products
A.G. Industries	Greeting card cabinets/displays

MARKETING STRATEGIES

Product

AG produces a wide product line, including greeting cards, gift wrap, party goods, toys, and gift items. Greeting cards accounted for 65 percent of the company's 1990 fiscal sales. The breakdown of sales by major product categories follows:

Category	***1990***	***1986***	***1984***	***1980***
Everyday greeting cards	41%	37%	36%	34%
Holiday greeting cards	24%	29%	27%	27%
Gift wrap and party goods	17%	18%	21%	21%
Consumer products (toys, etc.)	9%	7%	7%	9%
Stationery	9%	9%	9%	9%

Source: AG's Annual Reports.

The essence of AG's product strategy is identifying consumer needs, creating responses that sell, and pre-testing to determine the winners. AG believes in identifying consumer needs and responding to them with creative products. Research is a key ingredient. Over 12,000 North American households are surveyed annually to obtain information about every greeting card purchased and received. AG utilizes focus group sessions, simulated shopping surveys, and shoppng mall interviews. Especially important is ongoing life-style research to identify changing tastes and consumer needs for product development.

Research efforts have resulted in new products. Couples, an everyday card line which answers the trend back to more sincere romantic relationships, and Kid Zone, which responds to the need for more effective communication with children, were introduced during fiscal 1990. 1960's popular Holly Hobbies designs were reintroduced when research indicated a trend toward more traditional values.

Morry Weiss commented on the Couples line:

> We've proven our ability to meet the challenge of the marketplace. Couples takes its place alongside a pantheon of our major greeting card innovations (1989 Annual Report).

AG has one of the largest creative staffs in the world, with over 550 artists, stylists, writers, designers, photographers, and planners. They create more than 20,000 new greeting card designs each year.

AG also engages in retail pre-testing to determine which product ideas have the greatest chance of sales. This is extremely important, due to the competitiveness of the market, and retailers' need to have fast turnover. A network of retail test stores is used. New cards are rated based upon actual sales performance, and those with the best sales ratings are distributed worldwide.

AG is trying to take advantage of the alternative card segment. Alternative cards now command 20 percent of the everyday greeting card market, and the double-digit annual growth rate is expected to continue. Carlton Cards is AG's speciality card subsidiary and has been recently moved from Dallas to AG's Cleveland headquarters. Carlton will concentrate on "swiftly developing products unique to the more avant-garde tastes of the speciality store consumer."

AG pioneered licensing and is an industry leader in character licensing. Their strategy has been to maximize the potential of their creative and marketing expertise. The following identifies some of AG's character licenses:

Character	***Year***
Holly Hobbie	1968/1989
Ziggy	1971
Strawberry Shortcake	1980
Care Bears	1983
Herself the Elf	1983
Popples	1983

Most of AG's licensed characters have been successful. Strawberry Shortcake has been one of the most popular licensed characters. According to *Forbes,* however, all of the AG licensed characters have not been successful. One flop, Herself the Elf, was perceived by retailers as being too much like Strawberry Shortcake; it also missed the Christmas season because of production problems. Another failure was Get Along Gang, which tried to appeal to both little girls and boys. AG's licensing income is shown below:

Year	***Income***
1984	$17.5
1985	$20.9
1986	$17.6
1988	$16.5
1989	$13.3
1990	$11.8

Source: AG's Annual Reports.

Distribution

AG distributes its products through 90,000 retail outlets throughout the world in 50 countries and 12 languages. AG's major channels of distribution, in order of importance, include drug stores, mass merchandisers, supermarkets, stationery and gift shops, combo stores (stores combining food, general merchandise, and drug items), variety stores, military post exchanges, and department stores (AG's 1989 10-K).

AG's primary channels of distribution (which include supermarkets, chain drug stores, and mass retail merchandisers) have experienced growth due to demographic and life-style changes. The increase of working women has caused consumers to purchase more cards in convenient locations. Today, 55 percent of all everyday greeting cards are purchased in convenient locations.

AG's five largest customers accounted for about 17.4 percent of net sales. These customers included mass merchandisers, major drug stores, and military post exchanges.

AG has 26 regional and 58 district sales offices in the U.S., Canada, United Kingdom, France, and Mexico.

Promotion

Service is a key value to AG's marketing effort, as reflected in the following:

> One of our cornerstone values is service to the customer. While we are a leader in marketing innovation, we earned our reputation for superior customer service by clinging to old-fashioned ideas. We get to know our customers—and their customers—and learn how their businesses operate (1990 Annual Report).

The services that AG provides its retailers are based upon three key ingredients: knowledgeable sales force, in-store service personnel, and quick response to needs. AG offers the following:

- Largest full-time sales force in the industry, which is composed of highly trained experts.
- National force of 12,000 part-time in-store merchandising representatives who visit mass retail stores to restock goods, realign products, set up new displays and point-of-purchase materials, generate reorders, and process returns.
- Provide computerized network that allows AG to more quickly and consistently ship complete and accurate orders to retailers (1990 Annual Report).

According to Weiss,

> AG is focusing on building a strong partnership with retailers and consumers. We will expand distribution of our products in the global marketplace. We will "partner" with retail accounts by making greeting card departments more profitable. And we will improve our response to consumers' needs for appropriate products and attractive, easy to shop departments (1990 Annual Report).

AG tries to achieve more sales and profits from the space allocated by retailers by making them more productive. This is accomplished by sophisticated merchandising that makes greeting card displays more "consumer friendly." Since women purchase approximately 90 percent of all greeting cards, AG has redesigned greeting card cabinets to respond to the fact that women spend less time in stores than previously. Redesigned greeting card cabinets display 40 percent more cards in the same amount of space. These include point of purchase signs and new caption locators ("Mother," "Stepdaughter," and the like).

Themes are becoming more important in merchandising. These are used for "particular seasons or occasions that project a strong message to consumers and evoke an immediate awareness of the occasion." Related to this is a new concept called "occasion merchandising," which groups various products for everyday occasions, such as cards, gift wrap, candles, invitations, party goods, and so on.

AG tries to design its marketing programs to increase customer traffic and profitability of the greeting card department. Realizing the need for retailers to differentiate themselves and their products, AG attempts to work on an individual basis to customize the greeting card department for each retailer. This is accomplished via market research and technology. This is especially important to large chains that must contend with regional differences. Greeting card departments can be customized to reflect a specific area's demographics. If, for example, the demographic profile is comprised of a large number of elderly or "yuppies," specific products would be featured to target that segment.

A summary of AG's selling, distribution, and marketing expenses is displayed below:

Year	*Percent*
1981	28.2
1982	28.7
1983	29.2
1984	29.3
1985	29.0
1986	29.8
1987	31.6
1988	33.4
1989	32.6
1990	32.9

Source: AG's Annual Report.

PRODUCTION STRATEGIES

AG has 34 plants and facilities in the United States, Canada, the United Kingdom, France, and Mexico. This is down from 49 plants and facilities in 1986. The company owns approximately 4.8 million square feet and leases 11.3 million square feet of plant, warehouse, store, and office space. It meets its space needs in the U.S. through long-term leases of properties constructed and financed by community development corporations and municipalities.

AG had taken steps in 1987 through 1990 to cut production costs. It has tried to improve its production efficiency by cutting costs and reducing work-in-process inventories. AG also invested heavily in automated production equipment to cut labor costs in 1988. AG has also benefited from lower cost for raw materials and fewer product returns because of better inventory control. AG's material, labor, and other production costs are as follows:

Year	Percent
1981	44.7
1982	44.3
1983	41.7
1984	40.5
1985	39.9
1986	40.2
1987	42.3
1988	45.1
1989	42.8
1990	41.5

PERSONNEL STRATEGIES

In 1989 American Greetings employed over 15,000 full-time and 14,000 part-time people in the United States, Canada, Mexico, and Europe. This equates to approximately 20,500 full-time employees.

Hourly plant employees at Cleveland, Ohio; Bardstown and Corbin, Kentucky; Greeneville, Tennessee; Chicago, Illinois; and in the United Kingdom and Canada are union. All other office and manufacturing employees are not union. Labor relations are considered to be satisfactory.

When asked about AG employees, Morry Weiss commented:

> But perhaps our greatest strength is the men and women who create, manufacture, distribute, sell, and support our products. They are committed to knowing our customers, meeting their needs with quality products, and providing service before and after the sale (1990 Annual Report).

AG has a non-contributing profit-sharing plan for most of its U.S. employees, as well as a retirement income guarantee plan. It also has several pension plans covering certain employees in foreign countries (1990 Annual Report).

FINANCE STRATEGIES

Exhibits 2–4 contain relevant financial information for American Greetings. The financial condition of AG has been fluctuating over the years. In the early to mid-1980's, AG profit margins increased from 5.42 percent in 1981 to its high of 8.09 percent in 1984. ROI was 6.14 percent in 1981; its high was 9.94 percent in 1985. However, AG's financial performance in the mid- to late 80's was disappointing, with the profit margin falling to 2.84 percent in 1988 with an ROI of 2.90 percent. In 1990, AG's profit margin had risen to 5.51 percent with an ROI of 6.33.

Irving Stone commented about AG's 1990 performance:

> Fiscal 1990 revenues were a record $1.31 billion. This marks the 84th consecutive year that revenues have increased since the Company's founding in 1906.
>
> And, . . . revenue was driven by higher sales of everyday greeting cards, our

EXHIBIT 2

Consolidated Statements of Financial Position, 1981–1990 (in Thousands of Dollars)

	1990	1989	1988	1987	1986	1985	1984	1983	1982	1981
				Assets						
Current assets:										
Cash and equivalents	$ 122,669	$ 94,292	$ 36,534	$ 17,225	$ 26,853	$ 66,363	$ 62,551	$ 19,950	$ 3,367	$ 2,522
Trade accounts receivable, less allowance for sales returns and doubtful accounts	254,285	242,582	278,559	284,135	240,471	173,637	146,896	148,018	131,996	114,051
Inventories:										
Raw material	51,075	48,478	56,122	56,057	59,343	59,197	48,738	47,636	53,515	39,329
Work in process	42,139	51,625	61,406	69,668	60,179	53,728	43,929	54,756	52,214	37,506
Finished products	208,918	197,618	245,801	202,412	181,237	152,543	139,275	122,167	97,221	88,759
	$ 302,132	$ 297,721	$ 363,329	$ 328,137	$300,759	$265,468	$231,942	$224,559	$202,950	$165,594
Less LIFO reserve	85,226	83,017	77,274	75,392	76,552	71,828	63,455	59,345	55,051	46,287
	$ 216,906	$ 214,704	$ 286,055	$ 252,745	$224,207	$193,640	$168,487	$165,214	$147,899	$119,307
Display material and factory supplies	25,408	25,192	30,299	29,770	26,826	20,809	11,531	12,245	11,724	14,529
Total inventories	$ 242,314	$ 239,896	$ 316,354	$ 282,515	$251,033	$214,449	$180,019	$177,459	$159,623	$133,536
Deferred income taxes	51,315	49,542	39,935	26,593	36,669	33,016	26,517	24,847	18,014	17,685
Prepaid expenses and other	10,362	11,020	8,672	9,679	6,228	4,795	4,187	3,524	2,057	1,985
Total current assets	$ 680,945	$ 637,332	$ 680,054	$ 620,147	$561,254	$492,260	$420,170	$373,798	$315,057	$270,079
Other assets	$ 107,788	$ 92,285	$ 95,752	$ 89,488	$ 47,085	$ 31,634	$ 34,820	$32,866	$ 22,063	$ 17,054
Property, plant, and equipment:										
Land	6,229	6,471	7,548	7,956	7,523	6,822	6,621	5,427	3,380	2,590
Buildings	215,458	216,545	223,491	183,481	165,241	143,671	133,868	118,598	110,479	101,781
Equipment and fixtures	354,979	340,233	319,353	269,644	222,718	182,101	158,507	133,731	115,927	108,463
	$ 576,666	$ 563,249	$ 550,392	$ 461,081	$395,482	$332,594	$298,996	$257,756	$229,786	$212,834
Less accumulated depreciation and amortization	224,383	205,246	175,917	148,097	130,519	108,591	95,092	83,745	75,052	66,763
Property, plant, and equipment, net	352,283	358,003	374,475	312,984	264,963	224,003	203,904	174,011	154,734	146,071
Total assets	$1,141,016	$1,087,620	$1,150,231	$1,022,619	$873,302	$747,897	$658,894	$580,675	$491,854	$433,204

	1990	1989	1988	1987	1986	1985	1984	1983	1982	1981
				Liabilities and Shareholders' Equity						
Current liabilities:										
Notes payable to banks	$ 36,524	$ 17,201	$ 13,956	$ 25,092	$ 15,921	$ 4,574	$ 4,647	$ 29,836	$ 4,564	$ 14,087
Accounts payable	75,146	79,591	98,270	69,175	66,685	56,840	52,302	40,568	39,016	34,479
Payrolls and payroll taxes	45,315	38,839	33,759	31,230	28,675	26,761	23,160	16,914	17,224	14,191
Retirement plans	10,878	8,573	4,148	10,966	11,697	12,612	10,362	7,405	5,696	4,990
State and local taxes				3,056	2,763	2,796	2,811	2,448	3,278	2,920
Dividends payable	5,281	5,311	5,338	5,343	5,317	4,622	3,304	2,641	1,918	1,776
Income taxes	6,430	6,693	13,782	--	18,988	27,465	23,672	8,841	12,177	12,079
Sales returns	21,182	24,543	28,273	29,964	23,889	21,822	17,795	16,423	9,241	10,752
Current maturities of long-term debt		3,740	54,150	10,894	4,786	4,359	6,432	6,998	6,531	7,033
Total current liabilities	$ 200,756	$ 184,491	$ 251,676	$ 185,720	$178,721	$161,851	$144,485	$132,074	$ 99,645	$102,307
Long-term debt	$ 235,497	$ 246,732	$ 273,492	$ 235,005	$147,592	$112,876	$119,941	$111,066	$148,895	$113,486
Deferred income taxes	$ 100,159	$ 91,409	$ 86,426	$ 77,451	$ 64,025	$ 47,422	$ 28,972	$ 21,167	$ 15,530	$ 11,861
Shareholders' equity:										
Common shares, par value $1:										
Class A	$ 29,946	$ 29,692	$ 29,628	$ 29,552	$ 29,203	$ 28,835	$ 28,397	$ 27,996	$ 12,293	$ 12,227
Class B	2,063	2,497	2,528	2,588	2,982	3,046	3,070	3,080	1,413	1,434
Capital in excess of par value	110,234	105,245	104,209	102,718	94,744	87,545	80,428	76,851	37,690	37,124
Shares held in Treasury	(26,692)	(14,767)	(14,199)	(15,409)	(1,689)					
Cumulative translation adjustment	(8,186)	(4,790)	(7,564)	(11,604)	(16,801)	(13,688)	(9,158)	(7,179)	(3,829)	
Retained earnings	497,239	447,111	424,085	416,598	374,525	320,010	262,759	215,620	180,217	154,765
Total shareholders' equity	604,604	564,988	538,687	524,443	482,964	425,748	365,496	316,368	227,784	205,550
Total liabilities and shareholders' equity	$1,141,016	$1,087,620	$1,150,281	$1,022,619	$873,302	$747,897	$658,894	$580,675	$491,854	$423,204

EXHIBIT 3

Consolidated Statements of Income, 1981–1990
(in Thousands of Dollars, Except per Share Amounts)

	1990	1989	1988	1987	1986	1985	1984	1983	1982	1981
Net sales	$1,286,853	$1,252,793	$1,174,817	$1,102,532	$1,012,451	$919,371	$817,329	$722,431	$605,970	$489,213
Other income	22,131	22,566	24,155	23,463	23,200	26,287	22,585	20,252	17,634	9,059
Total revenue	$1,308,984	$1,275,359	$1,198,972	$1,125,995	$1,035,651	$945,658	$839,914	$742,683	$623,604	$498,272
Costs and expenses:										
Material, labor, and other production costs	$ 543,602	$ 546,214	$ 540,143	$ 476,725	$ 416,322	$377,755	$339,988	$310,022	$276,071	$222,993
Selling, distribution, and marketing	431,254	415,597	400,033	355,363	308,745	274,095	246,456	217,022	179,021	140,733
Administrative and general	149,771	148,095	135,224	125,407	131,928	123,750	112,363	96,012	76,494	61,033
Depreciation and amortization	40,251	39,527	34,191	29,059	23,471	18,799	15,507	13,890	12,752	10,863
Interest	27,691	33,479	32,787	24,875	19,125	15,556	16,135	24,086	21,647	13,548
Restructuring charge	--	23,591	--	12,371	--	--	--	--	--	--
	$1,192,569	$1,206,503	$1,142,378	$1,023,800	$ 899,591	$809,955	$730,449	$661,032	$565,985	$449,170
Income before income taxes	$ 116,415	$ 68,856	$ 56,594	$ 102,195	$ 136,060	$135,703	$109,465	$ 81,651	$ 57,619	$ 49,102
Income taxes	44,238	24,582	23,203	38,834	61,635	61,338	49,807	37,069	24,776	22,587
Net income	$ 72,177	$ 44,274	$ 33,391	$ 63,361	$ 74,425	$ 74,365	$ 59,658	$ 44,582	$ 32,843	$ 26,515
Net income per share	$ 2.25	$ 1.38	$ 1.04	$ 1.97	$ 2.32	$ 2.35	$ 1.91	$ 1.54	$ 1.20	$ .97

EXHIBIT 4
Selected Financial Data
Years Ended February 28 or 29, 1986–1990
(in Thousands of Dollars, Except per Share Amounts)

		Summary of Operations			
	1990	**1989**	**1988**	**1987**	**1986**
Total revenue	$ 1,308,984	$ 1,275,359	$ 1,198,972	$ 1,125,995	$ 1,035,651
Materials, labor, & other production costs	543,602	546,214	540,143	476,725	420,747
Depreciation & amortization	40,251	39,527	34,191	20,059	23,471
Interest expense	27,691	33,479	32,787	24,875	19,125
Net income	72,177	44,274	33,391	63,361	74,425
Net income per share	2.25	1.38	1.04	1.97	2.32
Cash dividends per share	0.66	0.66	0.66	0.66	0.62
Fiscal year end market price per share	31.25	21.25	17.63	28.75	35.62
Average number shares	32,029,533	32,146,971	32,068,752	32,212,556	32,059,851
		Financial Position			
Accounts receivable	$ 254,285	$ 242,582	$ 278,559	$ 284,135	$ 240,471
Inventories	243,314	239,896	316,354	282,515	251,033
Working capital	480,189	452,841	428,378	434,427	382,533
Total assets	1,141,016	1,087,620	1,150,281	1,022,619	873,302
Capital additions	42,869	41,938	96,682	68,740	61,799
Long-term debt	235,497	246,732	273,492	235,005	147,592
Shareholders' equity	604,604	564,988	538,687	524,443	482,964
Shareholders' equity per share	18.89	17.55	16.75	16.32	15.01
Net return on average shareholders' equity	12.3%	8.0%	6.3%	12.7%	16.5%
Pre-tax return on total revenue	8.9%	5.4%	4.7%	9.1%	13.1%

low-cost high margin core products. Fourth quarter sales were particularly strong. We expect to continue reporting good sales results.

The market value of our common stock rose 47 percent, from $21.25 on February 28, 1989, to $31.25 at the fiscal year close on February 28, 1990. This compares favorably to 27 percent increases for both the Dow Jones Industrial Average and the Standard and Poor's 500 Stock Index. Total return to stockholders—share price appreciation plus dividends—was 50 percent in fiscal 1990 (1990 Annual Report).

AG's stock price has ranged from a low of 9½ in 1981 to a high of 37⅛ in 1990.

MANAGEMENT

AG is organized via a divisional profit center basis. Each division has its own budget committee, while an executive management committee comprised of five senior executives approves the strategic plans for all the divisions. Strategic plans are established in one, three, ten, and twenty year time frames. Corporate AG maintains strict budgetary and accounting controls.

The basic domestic greeting card business is placed under the U.S. Greeting Card Division. Domestic and International Subsidiary Operations, including the licensing division, are a second unit, with corporate management a third. AG decentralized its structure in 1983.

American Greetings is composed of the following divisions:

U.S. Greeting Card Division. Encompasses core business of greeting cards and related products, including manufacturing, sales, merchandising, research, and administrative services. Produces and distributes greeting cards and related products domestically. Same products are distributed throughout the world by international subsidiaries and licensees.

Domestic and International Subsidiaries. AG's domestic and international subsidiary operations include the following:

Domestic
Acme Frame Products
A.G. Industries, Inc.
Plus Mark, Inc.
Wilhold Hair Care Products
Summit Corporation/Summit Collection
Those Characters from Cleveland,Inc.
International
Carlton Cards, Ltd.—Canada
Rust Craft Canada
Carlton Cards, Ltd.—England
Carlton Cards France
Felicitaciones Nacionales S.A. de C.V.—Mexico

American Greetings had 6 domestic operations in 1990, down from 7 in 1986. Firms divested included AmToy, Inc., Drawing Board Greeting Cards, Inc., and Tower Products, Inc.

The number of international operations in 1986 was 13 versus 5 in 1990. Among the international operations consolidated included 1 in Canada, 4 in continental Europe, 1 in Monaco, and 4 in the United Kingdom.

Exhibit 5 provides a corporate directory of management personnel and their divisional assignments.

AG's domestic and international sales are listed below:

Year	*Domestic Sales*	*GPM**	*Foreign Sales*	*GPM**	*U.S. Sales (%)*	*Foreign Sales (%)*
1990	1,088,438	11.86	220,546	6.79	83.15	16.85
1989	1,039,464	7.75	235,895	9.22	81.50	18.50
1988	996,628	7.79	202,344	5.80	83.12	16.88
1987	940,565	13.28	185,430	1.19	83.53	16.47
1986	874,255	15.38	161,396	12.82	84.42	15.58
1985	799,805	16.51	145,853	13.18	84.58	15.42
1984	717,057	15.18	122,857	13.61	85.37	15.63
1983	631,143	14.29	111,549	13.94	85.00	15.00
1982	523,467	12.54	100,137	13.61	85.40	14.60
1981	440,516	12.27	57,756	14.87	88.41	11.59

* Gross profit margin.
Source: AG Annual Reports.

EXHIBIT 5
Corporate Directory

Board of Directors

Irving I. Stone*
Chairman

Morry Weiss*
President
Chief Executive Officer

Scott S. Cowen†
Dean, Weatherhead School of Management
Case Western Reserve University

Edward Fruchtenbaum*
President
U.S. Greeting Card Division

Herbert H. Jacobs
(personal investments and consultant)

Frank E. Joseph†
Retired Attorney

Millard B. Opper
Retired Chairman of Canadian Operations

Albert B. Ratner*
President and CEO
Forest City Enterprises, Inc.
(real estate development and operation)

Harry H. Stone†
President
The Courtland Group
(personal investments)

Milton A. Wolf†
Former United States Ambassador to Austria
(personal investments)

Morton Wyman*
Retired Executive Vice President

Abraham Zaleznik
Professor
Harvard Business School
(consultant to business and government)

Corporate Officers

Irving I. Stone
Chairman

Morry Weiss
President
Chief Executive Officer

Edward Fruchtenbaum
President
U.S. Greeting Card Division

Ronald E. Clouse
Senior Vice President

Rubin Feldman
Senior Vice President

Henry Lowenthal
Senior Vice President
Chief Financial Officer

Packy Nespeca
Senior Vice President
Corporate Trade Development

James R. Van Arsdale
Senior Vice President

John M. Klipfell
Senior Vice President

Harvey Levin
Senior Vice President
Human Resources

Jon Groetzinger, Jr.
General Counsel & Secretary

William S. Meyer
Controller

Eugene B. Scherry
Treasurer

U.S. Greeting Card Division

Edward Fruchtenbaum
President

Sales and Marketing:

Mary Ann Corrigan-Davis
Vice President
Product Management

Gary E. Johnston
Vice President
Creative

Raymond P. Kenny
Vice President
Planning & Research

William R. Mason
Vice President
General Sales Manager

Dan Moraczewski
Vice President, Sales
Zone I

William R. Parsons
Vice President, Sales
Zone II

Donovan R. McKee
Vice President, Sales
Carlton Cards

George Wenz
Vice President, Sales
National Accounts

Operations:

James R. Van Arsdale
Senior Vice President

James H. Edler
Vice President, Materials Management

Dean D. Trilling
Vice President, Information Services

John T. Fortner
Vice President, Manufacturing

Thomas O. Davis
Vice President, Manufacturing
Everyday Division

Robert C. Swilik
Vice President, Manufacturing
Seasonal Division

EXHIBIT 5 (cont.)
Corporate Directory

Domestic and International Subsidiary Operations

Ronald E. Clouse
Senior Vice President

Acme Frame Products, Inc.
Cleveland, Ohio
Howard Reese, President

A.G. Industries, Inc.
Cleveland, Ohio
Charles H. Nervig, President

Plus Mark, Inc.
Cleveland, Ohio
Erwin Weiss, President

Wilhold Hair Care Products
Cleveland, Ohio
Ronald J. Peer, President

Dale J. Beinker
Vice President, International

Carlton Cards, Ltd.
Dewsbury, England
Alistair Mackay, Chairman

Carlton Cards France
Paris, France
Raphael Barda, Managing Director

Felicitaciones Nacionales S.A. de C.V.
Mexico City, Mexico
Antonio Felix G., President

John M. Klipfell
Senior Vice President

Carlton Cards, Ltd.
Toronto, Ontario
James E. Semon, President

Rust Craft Canada
Brampton, Ontario
Mike Johnson, General Manager

The Summit Corporation
Cleveland, Ohio
Alan Vilensky, Vice President

Summit Collection
Cleveland, Ohio
Joy Sweeney, Vice President

Those Characters From Cleveland, Inc.
Cleveland, Ohio
Jack S. Chojnacki,
Ralph E. Shaffer,
Co-Presidents

* Member of Executive Committee.
† Member of Audit Committee.
Source: 1990 Annual Report.

FUTURE OF AG

When asked about the future of AG, Morry Weiss responded:

> We are poised for perhaps the most successful period in our history.
>
> We are prepared to strengthen our core business and improve our position in the greeting card industry; to provide a greater return to our shareholders; and to afford our employees even greater opportunities for growth and career advancement.
>
> The strategies we will employ to achieve our goals for the new year and beyond are clear. We have well defined corporate strengths which we will target to build even stronger partnerships with retailers and consumers (1990 Annual Report).

Irving Stone's view of the future included:

> We are optimistic about the future. We are confident that we can achieve even more exciting results . . . in the future.
>
> We face the future confident that our commitment to help people build and maintain relationships will produce even more innovative products like Couples (1989 Annual Report).

According to the *U.S. Industrial Outlook,* industry sales should grow between 3–4 percent annually through 1992. Moderate growth is predicted due to forecasted moderate growth in the GNP, real disposable personal income, and personal consumption expenditures. For continued growth and profitability, *U.S. Industrial Outlook* recommends diversification into related product lines, institution of more cost-cutting strategies, monitoring of demand for current lines, divesting of unprofitable lines, and better matching of demand with supply to avoid after-holiday returns.

The unit growth rate for the greeting card industry between 1987 and 2015 is estimated to be between 1–3%. Exhibit 6 provides the forecast according to Prudential-Bache Securities. The primary reason for the slowing of unit growth is due to the postwar baby boomers who have already entered their high card-consumption years. With the declining birth rate of the 1970's and 1980's, consumption of cards is expected to decline.

However, greeting card officials optimistically project that the rate of consumption will increase moderately from the current per-capita rate of 29 cards to 44 cards per-capita by 2015. Greeting card sources also report that consumers are upgrading their purchases to higher priced cards, thus generating more profits per sale. The aging population, those over 55, also tend to send more cards than do younger persons.

Prudential-Bache's expectations for the future of the greeting card industry include:

> Price competition will remain a concern because of the maturity of the industry and the limited number of large players.
>
> At least 5–10 percent of the industry's current sales are to retail outlets that the industry leaders will never serve due to the small size of these outlets, which makes it too expensive to reach.

EXHIBIT 6
The Greeting Card Industry: Consumption Forecast

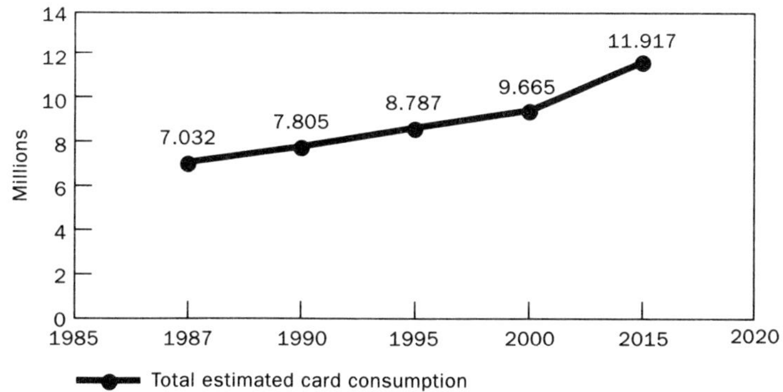

Source: Prudential-Bache Securities, Inc.

The greeting card industry is an area ripe for potential acquisition.

AG is and will continue to experience increased competition in its promotional gift-wrap area.

The big three can be challenged by any small well-run company.

It is unlikely that the big three with combined market share of 80–85 percent will continue to expand to "own the market." The dynamic competitive nature of the industry prohibits this.

There is not much room for the big three to grow by capturing more of the remaining market they are not reaching (Prudential-Bache, "Greeting Cards, Industry Update," August 9, 1989).

As CEO Morry Weiss thought about the future, he wondered what directions he would give his strategic planning committee as they formulated AG's strategies for the 1990's. Looking again at the ten-year summary, he pondered what changes AG should make in its competitive strategies.

Notes

American Greetings, Annual Reports, 1981–1990.

American Greetings, Form 10-K, 1988–1989.

"American Greetings," *Insider's Chronicle,* February 8, 1988, p. 3.

"American Greetings Corporation," *Moody's Industrial Manual,* 1989, p. 1428.

"American Greetings," *Value Line,* April 27, 1990.

"Flounder," *Forbes,* April 25, 1988, p. 352.

"Funny Valentines," *American Demographics,* February 1989, p. 7.

"Greeting Cards, Industry Update," Prudential-Bache Securities, December 30, 1988.

"Greeting Cards, Industry Update," Prudential-Bache Securities, August 9, 1989.

"Greeting Cards, Industry Update," Prudential-Bache Securities, September 27, 1989.

"Greeting Cards Departments . . . Mass Retail Outlets," *GM News,* 1989, pp. 10+.

U.S. Industrial Outlook, Department of Commerce, 1988, pp. 29-16 to 29-17.

CASE 21

Federal Express Corporation *

Federal Express proved the virtue of persistence with the right product in a growing market. In 1985 the company held a $1.2 billion share of the $3 billion overnight-delivery industry, which it had originally created. Most, if not all, of the credit went to the founder and Chairman of Federal Express, Frederick W. Smith.[1] He had taken an idea originally developed in a college term paper, for which he was awarded a "C," and gone on to change the way America did business. In the process he added a new cliché to the language: "when it absolutely, positively has to be there overnight."[2]

INDUSTRY

Within the aerospace and air transport industry, Federal Express became a leader in only a few short years.[3] While its main competitors had been around for two decades, satisfied with the traditional air-freight-forwarding market share they occupied, Federal took the market by storm and "changed the rules of the game."[4]

Federal Express laid claim to being the founder of the small package/document express market. Constantly expanding into areas of new services and extended service areas, this sector experienced phenomenal growth in the late 1970s and early 1980s.

Markets for all classes of cargo movement, from heavyweight to documents and letters, grew in 1984. Firms involved in cargo movement included all-cargo air carriers, traditional air-freight forwarders, passenger airlines, ground transportation companies, and air couriers. Although air-freight movement in general experienced a profitable year in 1984, the small-package express-shipping sector continued its five-year annual growth rate of 20%.[5]

Competitors that were directly involved in the small package/document express market included Federal Express, Emery Air Freight, Purolator, United Parcel Service (UPS), and the United States Postal Service. Through 1983 and 1984, price and service innovations abounded as participants struggled to gain a competitive edge.[6] This sector of the air-cargo industry was characterized by price wars, constant cost-cutting strategies, and innovative

* Prepared by R. J. Balhorn, Beverly Bowen, Jane Shouse, Steve Spencer, and Carey Spriggs under the supervision of Professor Sexton Adams, North Texas State University, and Professor Adelaide Griffin, Texas Woman's University. Reprinted with permission.

[1] Eugene Linden, "Frederick W. Smith of Federal Express: He Didn't Get There Over Night," *INC.* (April 1984), p. 89.

[2] Ibid., p. 89.

[3] *Standard & Poors Industry Surveys* (December 6, 1984), p. A36.

[4] Geoffrey Colvin, "Federal Express Dives into Air Mail," *Fortune* (June 15, 1981), p. 107.

[5] *Standard & Poors Industry Surveys*, p. A36.

[6] Ibid., p. A36.

marketing plans. To keep in the running for the growing market, most competitors felt an urgent need to earmark large capital investments for future expansion.[7]

Regulatory authority for participants in this industry was provided by the Federal Aviation Act of 1958, the Civil Aeronautics Board (CAB), and the Federal Aviation Administration (FAA). When the CAB was in existence, its authority related to the economic aspects of air transportation. The FAA's regulatory authority, however, related primarily to the safety aspects of air transportation, including aircraft standards and maintenance. Ground transportation services were exempt from regulation by the Interstate Commerce Commission; but because of the use of radio and communication equipment in ground and air units, Federal Express operations were subject to regulation by the Federal Communications Act of 1934. Finally, as of May 1984, Federal Express was in compliance with all regulations of the Environmental Protection Agency with regard to smoke emissions.[8]

HISTORY

Fred Smith was Chairman and Chief Executive Officer of the Memphis-based Federal Express Corporation, an air-cargo firm that specialized in door-to-door overnight delivery, using its own planes. Smith originated his revolutionary idea for his firm in the 1960s while majoring in economics and political science at Yale. He had a close acquaintance with aviation; he had earned a pilot's license at age fifteen and pursued his flying hobby while a student at Yale. During this same period, such companies as IBM and Xerox were already flying material out of airports not far from Yale's Connecticut campus.[9]

Smith spelled it all out in an overdue economics paper. To cut cost and time, packages from all over the country would be flown to a central point, there to be sorted, redistributed, and flown out again to their destinations. The flying would be done late at night when air lanes were comparatively empty. Airports used would be in sizable cities; and trucks would carry packages to their final destinations, whether in those cities or in smaller communities. Equipment and documents from anywhere in the United States could be delivered anywhere else in the United States the next day.[10]

Smith was thinking not only of parts and contracts, but also of canceled checks. His concept, he thought, could be sold to the Federal Reserve to cut down on the float, the period between receipt of a check and collection of funds. A general, commercial-delivery system could be built on that basis. When the time came to create his company years later, his ambition to serve the Federal Reserve and his desire for an impressive name with broad geographical connotation led him to the name "Federal Express." The Fed turned down his contract bid, but it now has its own check-delivery system, which Smith said was patterned after his operations.[11]

After college, Smith served two tours of duty in Vietnam, first as a platoon leader and then as a reconnaissance pilot. Upon returning home he decided to give his air express idea a try. Starting with $4 million that he had inherited, he chose Memphis as a home base. A

---

[7] Ibid., p. A36.

[8] *10K Report*, Federal Express Corporation, May 31, 1984.

[9] Henry Altman, "A Business Visionary Who Really Delivered," *Nation's Business* (November 1981), p. 50.

[10] Ibid., p. 50.

[11] Ibid., p. 50.

company study showed that Memphis was near the center of business shipping in the continental United States, and its airport was closed only an average of ten hours per year because of adverse weather conditions. The airport offered long runways, a large abandoned ramp, and a pair of inexpensive World War II hangars.[12]

Of course, $4 million was not much for starting a company that needed an entire fleet of planes. Smith had to have more funds. He went to New York and Chicago and brought Wall Streeters to Memphis. His knowledge of the air-freight field impressed investors; at the end of the year he had managed to raise a whopping $72 million in loans and equity investment.

Then Federal Express, which had been marking time operating a charter service, got down to its present business. Serving thirteen airports, it began transporting packages of under 70 pounds in April 1973. The first night's package total was eighteen. Volume picked up rapidly, and service was extended. Federal Express was an overnight success, but not for long. OPEC's inflation of fuel prices sent costs up faster than revenues were growing, and by mid-1974 the company was losing more than $1 million per month.[13]

Smith went back to his disappointed investors for more money to keep the company growing until revenues could catch up with expenses. Bankruptcy was a real possibility. After being turned down many times, Smith was able to raise $11 million, which was enough to get Federal Express over the hump. Federal Express, which lost $27 million in its first two years, went $3.6 million into the black in 1976 on $75 million in revenues. It has remained on the upswing ever since.[14]

Federal's short-term goals included increased surface productivity, telecommunications, and international expansion. Federal Express also considered the possibility of going into the passenger business. Chairman Smith considered this option "awfully tempting." All of Federal's big jets were easily convertible between freight-container pallets and passenger seats, and these jets were used an average of only 4.7 hours out of every 24. Nevertheless, the return on investment from carrying passengers would have been far below what it was from carrying small packages, and the chance of planes being delayed and out of position for the nightly race to deliver packages on schedule was too great. "Nothing," said Smith, "can be allowed to impair our primary business." [15]

MANAGEMENT/PERSONNEL

Fred Smith—Entrepreneur

Fred Smith was a man of integrity, whose charisma enabled him to motivate investors and employees to believe in his dream. His drive was mainly attributed to the scars that he carried from his military service, feelings so strong that Smith himself stated that Federal Express was a creature of Vietnam, and he would not have had the same perspective if not for his experiences there.[16]

[12] Colvin, pp. 106–108.
[13] Altman, p. 54.
[14] Ibid., p. 54.
[15] "Federal Express Rides the Small Package Boom," *Business Week* (March 31, 1980), p. 111.
[16] "Creativity with Bill Moyers: Fred Smith and the Federal Express," PBS *Video,* 1981.

As a true entrepreneur, Smith never threw in the towel. When the Arab embargo on oil in 1974 forced fuel costs sky high, Smith ran to investors, courting them for more money. When outdated CAB regulations made it impossible for Federal to expand into the larger aircraft it needed, Smith went to Washington and lobbied for deregulation of the airlines. When the U.S. Postal Service relaxed its regulations against private delivery of extremely urgent mail, Smith jumped at the opportunity and began testing the overnight letter service.[17]

And Smith did it with style. To win support from prominent Capitol Hill figures, he wined and dined them. To win the confidence of investors, he was always prepared with thorough market and economic analyses to support his ideas.[18] Unfortunately, by the late 1970s, Federal Express had grown too large for the wheeler-dealer, entrepreneurial approach to running an organization. But Smith believed that some principles remained the same in managing a $1.2 billion operation as in a $1.2 million operation:

> One of the biggest principles is that you've got to take action. Most large organizations reach a static point. They cannot take any action, because there are all types of barriers to doing so. There are institutionalized barriers that weren't there when the company was considerably smaller. What changes is your knowledge and your appreciation of how to deal with those institutional barriers, to eliminate them or use them to your advantage in achieving those changes. There are myriad number of changes that have to take place in the management style for the company to continue growing.[19]

Corporate Giants

Smith's colleagues also had the same "fighter pilot attitude" toward Federal Express. They were all former pilots and entrepreneurs; and although most thought his idea very strange, each one had the "right stuff" needed to make Federal Express fly.[20] From day one, the camaraderie and loyalty exhibited by employees of Federal Express was strong—strong enough to hold Federal together and transform it from an "entrepreneurial crusade" (us against them) to a respected corporate strength. (See Exhibit 1 for Federal's organizational chart.)

The year 1979, however, brought much change to Federal's ranks. President Art Bass, one of the initial crusaders, decided to leave and took five vice-presidents with him, all but one of whom had been with Federal from the start. The reason for their departure was shocking to some but easily understood by Smith. Federal had matured, and Bass and his colleagues felt they lacked the ability to adapt their entrepreneurial perspectives to management of a mature operation. Smith replaced his elite few with managers who were more comfortable with the traditional corporate organization, but he maintained associations with Bass and the others in a think-tank type of arrangement.[21] Their only responsibility, as far as Smith was concerned, was to think about the future of Federal.

---

[17] "The Memphis Connection," *Marketing & Media Decisions* (May 1982), p. 62.
[18] Ibid., p. 63.
[19] Katie Hafner, "Fred Smith: The Entrepreneur Redux," *INC.* (June 1984), p. 40.
[20] Ibid., p. 40.
[21] Colvin, p. 107.

EXHIBIT 1
Federal Express Organizational Chart

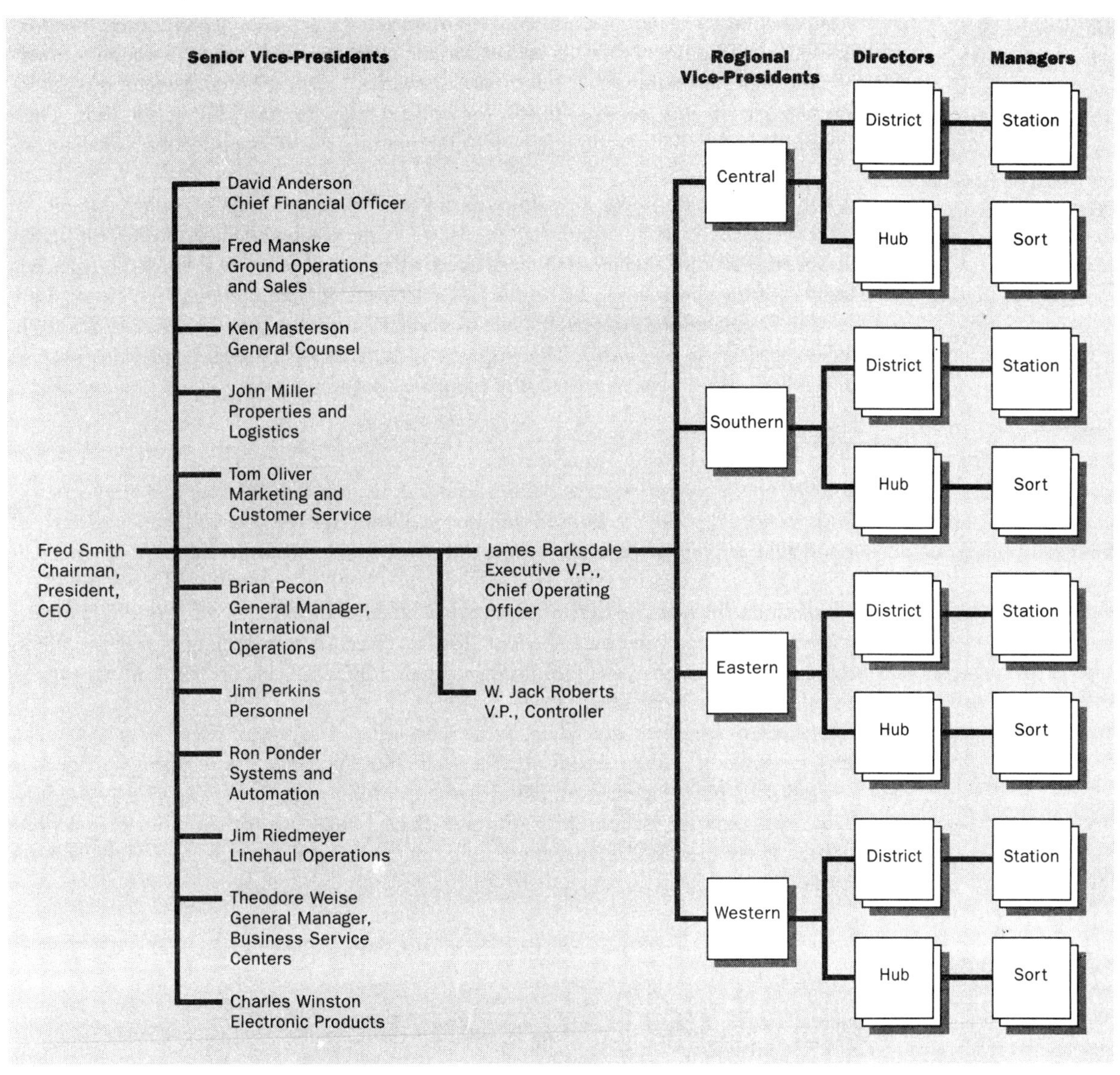

Source: Federal Express Corporation, *1984 Annual Report.*

Federal's Backbone

Dedication to professional, faultless service enabled Federal to "get it there overnight." From the beginning, Federal was a people organization. With an employee force of over 24,000, management felt a strong responsibility to provide an array of training programs, to support the image it wanted to portray.[22] For example, training for the ZapMail service, when it was first introduced, included courses for over 18,000 employees.[23] In addition to a thorough training program, Federal boasted of an active file of 45,000 applicants for positions ranging from pilot to courier and made the claim that this was an indication of the attractiveness of the company's policy and benefits.[24] One general benefit offered by Federal was paying full college tuition for college students working at the hub. These policies supported Federal's commitment to maintaining the image of professionalism and stability.

When the company hired an employee, it was viewed as a long-term investment. To minimize the necessity to furlough any employee, Federal scheduled part-time employees, so that operations could expand or contract according to traffic levels.[25] Smith, though, was exceedingly canny about labor. By employing part-time college students who would come and go as their education progressed, Federal set up a buffer between its operations and the entrance of unions to the hub.[26] This approach also allowed Federal Express to keep its labor costs low, lower than those of any company in the industry.[27]

Recruiting

Because of Federal's reputation of being a leader in its industry, it never had any difficulty in finding qualified people to uphold that image. Unfortunately, the old tactics used to fill Federal's ranks did not work when it came time for Federal to staff its ZapMail operation in 1984. The ZapMail operation required high-tech professionals who could go out to a client and sell them on the new, revolutionary service, but the ads Federal was running were not attracting this type of candidate. Federal had to target its advertising to a new, young professional crowd who were looking for career opportunities on the leading edge of technology.[28] And it worked.

Hundreds of qualified candidates were recruited, all because Federal targeted its advertising to a specific audience. But not only did Federal change its recruiting approach, it also restructured its compensation plan for the ZapMail sales force. ZapMail salespeople received low base salaries. Commissions were based solely on the number of machines installed in offices. Federal's management felt that this would help make ZapMail grow at a faster rate.[29]

OPERATIONS

Federal Express provided an overnight, door-to-door, express delivery service for high-priority packages and documents. In essence, two industries were merged to accomplish

[22] *1984 Annual Report,* Federal Express Corporation, p. 13.
[23] Ibid., p. 13.
[24] *1982 Annual Report,* Federal Express Corporation, p. 14.
[25] Ibid., p. 14.
[26] Colvin, p. 107.
[27] Ibid., p. 108.
[28] Rick Stoops, "How Federal Express Recruited for a New High-Tech Image," *Personnel Journal* (August 1984), p. 16.
[29] "Federal Express Readdresses ZapMail," *Sales and Marketing Management* (March 11, 1985), p. 26.

this: aviation and pickup/delivery trucking service. Federal Express services were available Monday through Saturday from 145 airports in the United States, Canada, Puerto Rico, Europe, and the Far East. Approximately 90% of the U.S. population was served through an intricate ground/air network—Smith's brainchild, the hub and spoke system.

Hub and Spoke

The service operation that made Federal Express unique in its field was its central sorting facility located in Memphis, Tennessee. The key factor was that every package and letter transmitted by Federal passed through the center in Memphis, where it was sorted and dispatched to the points of delivery across the country and internationally.

The operations at the hub had been fine-tuned for maximum efficiency. The central sorting process occurred in the middle of the night under "time bomb" pressure.[30] An executive gazing out over the bustling hub said, "If they decide to sit down for an hour, we're dead."[31] All during the day, packages had been collected in sorting facilities and local offices in 300 cities. Once transported to the local airports, the packages were flown to Memphis, where all planes arrived about midnight. The planes were directly unloaded into a giant warehouse of elaborate conveyor belts; there they were frantically sorted and loaded back into the planes headed for their intended destinations. By 3 A.M. the planes were ready to depart for sorting facilities located at the local airports, where couriers would then transport packages to local offices and then on to the receiver—and all of this happened overnight!

Contact with couriers was maintained through the use of Digitally Assisted Dispatch Systems (DADS). The system, installed in over 70% of Federal's vehicles, enabled the company to leave dispatch information in couriers' vans even when unoccupied. In late 1984, hand-held DADS units were introduced to help eliminate duplicated routes, retraced steps, and other inefficiencies.[32] This prototype microprocessor maintained constant data and voice contact between the courier and dispatcher even if the courier was on the upper floor of an office building, as foot couriers often were.

COSMOS, Federal Express's computer network for dispatch entry and tracking, used a satellite and telephone network to locate a customer's shipment at any time as it passed through six electronic gates during transit. Each parcel was bar-coded so that movement could be monitored and recorded at every step of the journey. Thus the whereabouts of a package, not just the paperwork, could be recalled in an instant.[33]

Facilities

Federal Express leased its facilities at the hub from the Memphis-Shelby County Airport Authority. These facilities consisted of a central sorting facility, aircraft hangars, flight training and fuel facilities, warehouse space, and a portion of the administrative offices.[34] Off-airport facilities in Memphis were also leased and consisted of Federal Express headquarters, PartsBank operations, and other administrative offices.[35]

---

[30] Ibid.
[31] Colvin, p. 107.
[32] Ibid., pp. 6–7.
[33] Ibid., p. 9.
[34] *10K Report,* Federal Express (May 31, 1984), p. 9.
[35] Ibid., p. 10.

City station operations were located in 300 cities throughout the United States, Canada, Puerto Rico, Europe, and the Far East. These stations were leased for 5- to 10-year periods. In 1984 a station and service-center expansion program was begun that included the construction of Business Service Centers and the installation of unmanned Overnight Delivery Counters, to supplement the city stations and to provide improved access to services in high-density areas.[36]

Equipment and Vehicles

Federal operated almost 10,000 delivery vehicles; approximately 2,000 of these were leased. Other vehicles owned by Federal included mainly ground support equipment, cargo loaders, transports, and aircraft tugs.[37] As of July 31, 1984, Federal owned fifty-eight aircraft and an inventory of spare engines and parts for each type. The company was committed to purchase eleven additional aircraft to be delivered in 1985–1987.[38] Deposits and payments to be made according to these agreements were:

$98,700,000 in 1985

$169,800,000 in 1986

$105,800,000 in 1987

PRODUCT LINES

On a domestic level, Federal Express offered three basic services: Priority One, ZapMail, and Standard Air, a 1- to 2-day package and document delivery service. Additionally, Federal provided special handling for dangerous goods and restricted articles, an air-cargo charter service, and an inventory-parts shipment service. Through the use of expanded direct service and exclusive agents, Federal Express could also deliver documents and custom-cleared packages internationally to areas in Canada, Puerto Rico, Western Europe, the Far East, and Australia.[39]

Priority One

Priority One, an overnight door-to-door delivery of business goods, absolutely, positively guaranteed a 10:30 A.M. next morning delivery. In either the sender's packaging or that of Federal Express, time-sensitive letters, boxes, and tubes up to 150 pounds in weight, 62″ in length or 120″ in length and girth combined could be shipped to almost any location in the contiguous states.[40] Couriers were used for pickup and delivery, or customers could bring packages and documents to self-service centers or Federal Express Business Service

[36] Ibid., p. 10.
[37] Ibid., p. 9.
[38] Ibid., p. 10.
[39] *1984 Annual Report,* Federal Express Corporation, p. 1.
[40] *Service Guide,* Federal Express Corporation (October 1, 1984), p. 19.

Centers. Permitting face-to-face customer contact, these staffed storefront facilities were located in high-traffic, high-density areas. Over 300 of the centers were planned to be in place by the end of fiscal 1985.[41]

Rates for overnight letters were $11.00 if delivered to a drop-off location by the sender and $14.00 if picked up by a courier. Courier-Pak boxes and tubes were subject to a five-pound or $34.00 minimum charge, while Courier-Pak envelopes were priced at a two-pound or $25.00 minimum. Schedules indicating price per pound then applied for parcels over the minimum weight. Up to 40% discounts were offered to qualified shippers.[42]

Standard Air

Standard Air gave the same array of service features offered under Priority One, except that packages were scheduled for delivery no later than the second business day after pickup. At approximately one-half the Priority One rates, Standard Air was promoted as, "when it has to be there, but doesn't have to be there overnight."[43] Many packages arrived the next business day, making this 1- to 2-day service an economical alternative for time-pressured shippers.

Charter/PartsBank

Beyond delivering packages, Federal offered two unique services to serve the larger distribution needs of U.S. business. The first, Air Cargo Charter, allowed the charter of McDonnell DC-10s, Boeing 727s, or Dassault Falcons on either a one-time or contractual basis. Subject to availability, aircraft could be chartered twenty-four hours per day, seven days per week. The second, PartsBank, arose from the need for the speedy handling of critical inventories. Combining a parts warehouse system with an overnight airline, PartsBank allowed companies to place time-sensitive inventory such as computer parts, medical supplies, and electronic components in Federal's Memphis PartsBank warehouse. A toll-free telephone call to PartsBank could have the item shipped immediately.[44]

ZapMail

An answer to electronic mail, ZapMail was conceived approximately seven years before its 1984 introduction, but it evolved into a major product because of indications of strong demand.[45] Users could call to request the service, and within an hour a courier arrived to pick up the document. Then the courier delivered the document to the nearest input station, where the document was inserted into a scanner, digitized, and sent over the Federal Express network to the receiving station. There it was printed and delivered to the recipient by courier. Total elapsed time from initial call to delivery time was two hours. If the sender took the document to a Federal Express Business Service Center, ZapMail

---

[41] *1984 Annual Report,* Federal Express Corporation, p. 10.
[42] *Service Guide,* p. 19.
[43] Ibid., p. 23.
[44] Ibid., p. 27.
[45] *Air Freight Progress Report* (New York: Morgan Stanley Investment Research, January 21, 1985), p. 1.

delivery was accomplished in one hour. In contrast to electronic mail, ZapMail was an electronically transmitted document rather than just a message. Therefore charts, contracts, invoices, artwork, etc., could be reproduced into high-resolution copies. Original documents would be either forwarded to the recipient or returned to the sender by 10:30 A.M. the next business day.[46]

ZapMail charges were $25 for the first twenty pages and $1 per page after twenty pages. If it was sent from a Service Center, the cost was reduced by $5.00.[47] For a leasing fee of approximately $200 per month, a frequent user could have a ZapMail terminal placed in his or her office with no installation or maintenance fees.[48]

Although much had been staked on the success of ZapMail, initial results were disappointing. Several marketing and operational problems had hindered the initial launch of the project, but optimism remained high for the long term.

From an operational standpoint, there had at first been a delay, later resolved, in the installation of dedicated long-distance lines by AT&T. More recently, in the second stage of the project—that of placing on-premises terminals (ZapMailers) with volume users—there was a one-month delay from installation of the software required for the simultaneous transmission of documents to multiple destinations. Thus the targeted goal of 3,000 ZapMailers in place by the end of May 1985 was in doubt. As of the end of January 1985, slightly over 700 orders for the machines had been placed.[49]

On the marketing front, management noted that it had been perhaps overly optimistic in relying on its market research indicating a pent-up need for the new service. ZapMail shipments were averaging about 3,200 per day, far below the 20,090–30,000 needed to reach the initial projected breakeven level twelve to eighteen months after startup.[50] It had become clear that the marketing approach that had been effective for small packages was not working in the same-day market. Part of the problem rested in consumer education. As with its overnight express service, Federal needed to get potential customers to understand exactly what was being offered and how to use it. The company had overestimated the ease with which its customer base could be educated about the benefits of ZapMail. It set about rectifying the problem.

Stressing how the new service should be used as a part of the business routine rather than merely in emergencies, Federal began pumping an additional $10 million into its planned advertising budget.[51] Anticipating difficulty in convincing prospects of the necessity for on-premise ZapMailers, Federal equipped its sales force with preprogrammed Radio Shack calculators. These were to be used to run a comparison of the prospect's current communications systems cost (based on estimated activity levels) with that of a comparable ZapMailer system.[52] Federal targeted the following industries as having the highest potential, at least initially, for ZapMailer installations:

---

[46] *Service Guide*, p. 17.
[47] *Air Freight Progress Report* (New York: Morgan Stanley Investment Research, November 19, 1984), p. 1.
[48] *Research, Federal Express*, Morgan Keegan & Company, Inc. (November 28, 1983), p. 4.
[49] *Air Freight* (January 21, 1985), p. 1.
[50] Ibid., p. 1.
[51] Ibid., p. 1.
[52] *Research, Federal Express*, Morgan Keegan & Company, Inc. (February 14, 1985), p. 4.

Legal	Banking
Accounting	Manufacturing
Consulting	Advertising
Retail	Commercial and Financial Printing
Insurance	Government[53]

In spite of its initial difficulties, ZapMail was highly regarded by analysts in the investment community, who believed that it would become an unqualified success once the glitches involved with any new product were resolved. Further, Federal's management indicated that possible future enhancements to ZapMailers might include the ability to communicate with word processors and personal computers.[54] Speculation was that Federal intended to be a major player in the "office of the future" through the use of ZapMailers. By connecting word processors and personal computers to the ZapMail network, Federal could leverage its ability to capture office-document traffic once the software was developed to do so.

International Operations

Federal Express also delivered Courier-Pak envelopes and packages up to seventy pounds to many international locations. Because of distance and time differences in the areas served, time of day and delivery varied. For the areas that they did not serve, Federal Express offered a Worldwide Referral Service that could arrange delivery to additional locations.[55]

In an effort to expand outside North America, in fiscal 1984, Federal acquired Gelco Express International, a world-wide, on-board courier service with offices in London, Amsterdam, Paris, Brussels, Hong Kong, Tokyo, and Singapore. In 1985 the Gelco operation was to be absorbed into the system with the Federal Express name and identity.[56]

Preparing at home for international service, Federal opened an international customer-service department with multilingual representatives. An added effort by Federal was made to give special attention to customs and cultures of the international markets.[57] But critics abroad said that running a domestic service in the United States was entirely different from operating an international one because it required a different expertise, and a common market approach could not be taken. Competition was growing in the international market as well as the U.S. market, so analysts felt that Federal could have problems promoting itself in Europe with only the experience of a small European courier for guidance.[58]

---

[53] Ibid., p. 4.
[54] Ibid., pp. 3–4.
[55] *Service Guide,* p. 162.
[56] *1984 Annual Report,* Federal Express Corporation, pp. 14–15.
[57] Ibid., p. 14.
[58] Sean Milmo, "British Air Couriers Welcome U.S. Entrant," *Business Marketing* (April 1984), p. 9.

MARKETING/ADVERTISING

The image of Federal Express was one of an innovator. Smith and his colleagues had created a demand for small-package express delivery and then cleverly set out to satisfy that demand. Smith, in analyzing Federal Express, stated that Federal was selling time, and people who save time in their daily routines and functions are more effective.[59] Once the message was heard, the public immediately altered their perspective from "get it there as soon as possible" to "get it there overnight."

Smith spared nothing to get the message across. Federal Express needed dramatic advertising to reach an indifferent world that needed to know about Federal Express.[60] Tom Oliver, Senior Vice-President of Marketing and Customer Service, said, "At the outset the advertising was oriented toward explaining the network system . . . focusing on the difference in Federal's system from their competitors." However, people could not understand how this strange combination of airplanes, hubs, and couriers could keep the boss from yelling.[61] The public just wanted to trust that Federal would do what it claimed to do, no matter how they did it.

After much effort, Federal did get the message across and won award after award for its clever spots. In the "motor-mouth" businessman; the pitch, "Federal Express. When it absolutely, positively has to be there overnight"; or the man uprooting a phone booth as the announcer says "Federal Express is so easy to use, all you have to do is pick up the phone," it was easy to appreciate the humor, and that was what Oliver wanted.[62]

But not everyone felt that Federal's humorous ads were of benefit to the company's objective. Competitors and advertisers alike felt that Federal ads often offended the little guy. Also, although attention-getters, the ads left no message as to what Federal really offered.[63] Unaffected by criticisms hurled at its campaigns, Federal believed that another factor—price—was not as important as dramatizing the problem people have in getting fast, sure, easy delivery. Cost of delivery was important to people only after they were sure it would get to the destination when they wanted it to.[64]

Federal's marketing plan for ZapMail also came under fire by industry analysts. The original ZapMail marketing plan was ill-conceived; no one really understood what ZapMail was.[65] But because of the newly recruited sales force for ZapMail and new leasing plans as an alternative to purchase of the machines, analysts believed that ZapMail would evolve into a tool necessary for business activities.

---

[59] Ibid.
[60] Ibid.
[61] "The Memphis Connection," p. 62.
[62] Ibid., p. 128.
[63] Hank Seiden, "The Delivery Doesn't Fly," *Advertising Age* (October 31, 1983), p. M66.
[64] "The Memphis Connection," p. 62.
[65] "Federal Express Readdresses ZapMail," p. 26.

COMPETITION

Federal Express Corporation was a major competitor in the time-sensitive package delivery or courier industry. It faced stiff competition from such firms as Purolator Courier Corporation, Emery Air Freight Corporation, UPS, and the U.S. Postal Service.

Purolator Courier Corporation

Purolator said that its packages were "overnight, not overpriced," and the company mandated that each package be delivered the next business day or on some other time-sensitive schedule. Most packages weighed less than five pounds and each was picked up and delivered door to door, either on call or on a scheduled basis.[66]

In 1984 Purolator had two major products that were designed to make its door-to-door courier services easy and economical. Customers could send two ounces (up to ten pages) of important documents anywhere in the continental United States at a very low price with the PuroLetter. The PuroPak could handle as much as two pounds of documents for delivery across town or across the country, and the customer was automatically billed at the lowest applicable rate. Very low rates applied up to 300 miles or between certain pairs of cities, and a competitive rate was applied for longer distances. A related product, called the PuroPak Box, offered a very low rate for one- to six-pound shipments.[67]

To enable the movement of shipments over long distances for next-day delivery, Purolator operated an air network with its central hub located in Columbus, Ohio. However, major volume constraints and operating inefficiencies were being experienced at the Columbus facility. To alleviate this problem and in anticipation of future growth needs, Purolator had a continuing program to upgrade terminal facilities. A major, new air-hub facility was under construction in Indianapolis, Indiana, that, upon its completion in 1986, would have a capacity of 125,000 packages per night.[68]

Purolator Courier, Ltd., the company's Canadian subsidiary, offered courier services to over 6,000 cities and towns in the ten provinces of Canada. Partly because of sluggish growth in the Canadian economy, operating results of this subsidiary had been mediocre. Management had concentrated on improving operating efficiency and modestly expanding terminal facilities.[69]

The management of Purolator Courier Corporation saw the company as "the most economical national supplier of overnight package delivery." To aggressively exploit this position, Purolator planned to capitalize on its large fleet of airplanes and ground delivery vehicles, all supported by an aggressive advertising campaign. As the U.S. and Canadian economies continued to improve, management expected Purolator to continue its record growth.[70]

For a comparison of Purolator and its competitors, see Exhibits 2 and 3.[71]

---

66 "Introduction," *1982 Annual Report,* Purolator Courier Corporation.
67 Ibid.
68 *Standard & Poors N.Y.S.E. Stock Reports,* p. 1885.
69 *1982 Annual Report,* Purolator Courier Corporation, p. 10.
70 Ibid., p. 8.
71 *Standard & Poors N.Y.S.E. Stock Reports,* p. 1885.

EXHIBIT 2

Sales Revenues of Federal Express and Selected Competitors, 1983 (In Thousands of Dollars)

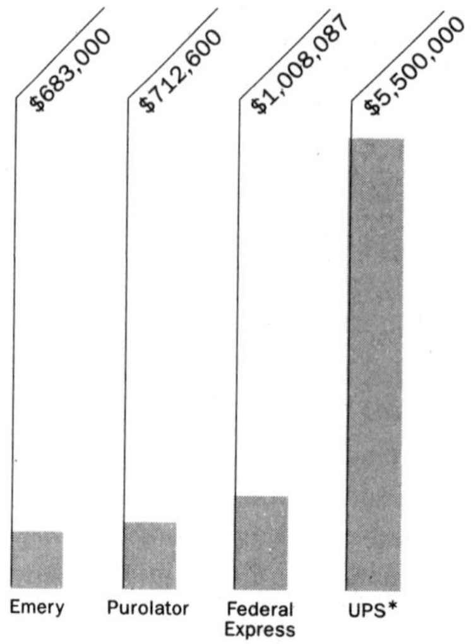

* Estimated sales revenue; no actual figure is available.

EXHIBIT 3

Numbers of In-Service Aircraft and Vehicles of Federal Express and Selected Competitors, 1983

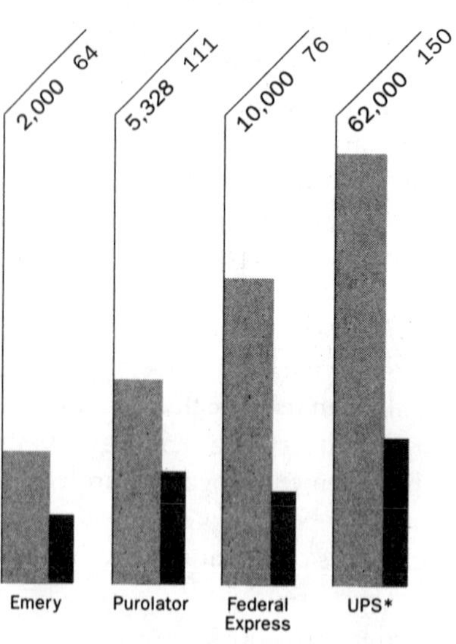

* UPS also makes extensive use of commercial airlines to ship its parcels.

Emery Air Freight

Emery was one of the largest domestic air-cargo carriers and was a major competitor in the international field as well. The company maintained 165 offices, fifty-three of which were outside the United States in twenty-seven different countries and territories. In another forty-two countries, agents acted on the company's behalf.[72]

Emery could provide overnight door-to-door delivery of any size, any weight package or shipment to over 56,000 cities and towns in North America. The company also had 24- to 72-hour door-to-door service to various cities around the world. Emery offered a variety of overnight delivery services including Same Day, A.M., P.M., Day 2, and the five-ounce Emery Urgent Letter.[73]

According to management, Emery's goal was to have "the lowest cost, highest quality, world-wide transportation system." To achieve this goal, Emery had spent large sums for expansion of existing facilities and the modernization of existing aircraft as well as the acquisition of new aircraft. In addition, the company had made major capital investments in state-of-the-art technology to foster its future business growth. For example, a $20 million expansion of its "superhub" terminal facility in Dayton, Ohio, was begun in March 1984 and was completed at year's end. This expansion increased the company's handling capacity to almost 2 million pounds per night, up from 1.7 million pounds. A major capital improvement at the Dayton facility in 1983 was the installation of an automated envelope-sorting system that was capable of handling 10,000 Emery Urgent letters or envelopes per hour.[74]

Emery had maintained a special "heavyweight" niche in the package delivery business. Its unique ability to deliver heavy air cargo the next day gave the company a competitive edge during the recent economic recovery. Approximately 45% of the company's seventy-pound traffic had a next-morning delivery requirement. This ability was particularly useful to large companies that often required cargo-transportation services for shipments of any size, weight, or shape. This "heavyweight" service was restricted to customers who purchased over $1 million of air cargo transportation services per year.[75]

Emery suffered a sharp drop in earnings per share in 1982, but made a strong recovery in 1983 and 1984. Historically, Emery had shown consistent growth in earnings per share, and dividends had been paid without interruption since 1952.[76]

United Parcel Service

United Parcel Service (UPS) was a giant in package delivery, its only competitor in terms of volume being the U.S. Postal Service. No other company could match its basic claim that it could deliver a package in two days anywhere in the continental United States if the customer was willing to pay the price. UPS had long had a reputation for dependability, productivity, and efficiency that was admired by customers and envied by competitors.

Building upon the success of its basic business, UPS entered the overnight package-

---

[72] Ibid., p. 827.
[73] "Introduction," *1983 Annual Report,* Emery Air Freight.
[74] Ibid., p. 3.
[75] Ibid., p. 13.
[76] *Standard & Poors N.Y.S.E. Stock Reports,* p. 827.

delivery market late in 1982. Any UPS customer that was currently served by daily pickups could make use of this overnight delivery service. Rates were usually 50% lower than those charged by Federal Express.[77]

UPS occupied a very strong position in the transportation industry. It was the largest single private shipper on most railroads, owned a large fleet of airplanes, and also shipped packages on other airlines. In addition, it owned a huge fleet of delivery trucks. (See Exhibit 3.) Its drivers were unionized and called on some 600,000 offices, factories, and stores each day.[78]

Financially, UPS was solid, with earnings that had more than quadrupled from $76.1 million in 1978 to $331.9 million in 1982. During this same period, revenues doubled, going from $2.8 billion in 1978 to $5.2 billion in 1982. Very few companies in any industry could match this earnings and productivity record.[79]

U.S. Postal Service

The U.S. Postal Service had been a competitor in the overnight-package delivery business for a number of years. With its Express Mail next-day service, the Postal Service could ship packages weighing up to seventy pounds and guarantee delivery to the addressee the next day. To make use of this service, customers simply took their packages and letters to the Express Mail window at the post office. Shipments were delivered to the addressee by 3:00 P.M. of the following day. The addressee also had the option of picking up the package personally as early as 10:00 A.M. of the next business day. All shipments were guaranteed to arrive on time; if they did not, the customer could obtain a full refund. According to Postal Service statistics, 95% of all shipments did arrive on time.[80]

The U.S. Postal Service also offered package pickup from the customer's place of business, but only on a planned, regularly scheduled basis. A single, flat charge was made per pickup, regardless of the number of packages or letters the customer might be sending.

The Express Mail Service could ship packages and letters to almost any major metropolitan area in the United States. Also available on an international basis, Express Mail Service served major cities in the United Kingdom, Australia, Brazil, Hong Kong, Japan, Belgium, France, and the Netherlands.[81]

FINANCIAL SITUATION

Federal Express did not become a financial success overnight. It took four years and $70 million in venture capital before the first profitable period in late 1975. The company nearly went bankrupt several times during that four-year drought because the venture-capital market was in a profound depression of its own.

In 1975, new capital was $10 million (versus $3 billion in 1983), and the initial offering in 1974–1975 raised only $32 million (against $5.5 billion in 1984). Federal Express was

[77] "Behind the UPS Mystique: Puritanism and Productivity," *Business Week* (June 6, 1983), p. 66.
[78] Ibid., p. 66.
[79] Ibid., p. 66.
[80] "Express Mail Next Day Service," *U.S. Postal Service Pamphlet Notice 43* (July 1977), p. 2.
[81] Ibid., p. 6.

EXHIBIT 4
Federal Express: Consolidated Financial Highlights
Years Ended May 31
(in Thousands of Dollars, Except per Share and Other Data)

	1982	***1983***	***1984***
Operating results:			
Express service revenues	$803,915	$1,008,087	$1,436,305
Operating income	119,466	150,737	165,208
Income before income taxes	131,080	150,216	152,260
Net income	78,385	88,933	115,430
Earnings per share	$ 1.85	$ 2.03	$ 2.52
Average shares outstanding	41,788	43,316	45,448
Financial position:			
Working capital	$ 79,669	$ 89,878	$ 72,226
Property and equipment, net	457,572	596,392	1,112,639
Long-term debt	223,856	247,424	435,158
Common stockholders' investment	350,319	503,794	717,721
Other operating data:			
Average daily package volume	125,881	166,428	263,385
Average pounds per package	6.5	5.8	5.5
Average revenue per pound	$ 3.81	$ 4.02	$ 3.80
Aircraft fleet at end of year:			
McDonnell DC-10-10s	4	6	6
McDonnel DC-10-30s	0	0	4
Boeing 727-100s	31	38	35
Boeing 727-200s	0	0	12
Dassault Falcons*	32	32	0
Average number of full-time equivalent employees during year	10,092	12,507	18,368

* As of May 31, 1984, the company removed its Dassault Falcons from scheduled operations. Ten of the aircraft had been disposed of at that date; and as of July 31, 1984, twelve were under contract for sale. The company was evaluating plans for the ultimate disposition of the remaining fleet.

constantly asking banks, corporations, and venture capitalists for new loans and equity participations. Ultimately, the company survived as over a dozen equity groups participated in three major rounds of financing. In his desperate search for money, Smith had to give up virtually all his equity in his company. (He eventually recaptured a substantial portion in later refinancings.)

Throughout the bad times, however, Smith earned the undying loyalty of the people who worked for him. "He was a fantastic motivator of people," said Charles Tucker Morse, the company's first General Counsel. "I have not worked since in a situation so intense and so free of politics." [82]

Financial results for fiscal 1984 were gratifying, despite the considerable expense incurred to improve existing service and to introduce a new electronic document-transmission product. Revenues increased by 42% to $1.4 billion. Net income totaled $115 million, or $2.52 per share; these were gains of 30% and 24%, respectively, over $89 million, or $2.03 per share, in fiscal 1983. (See Exhibits 4 and 5.)[83]

---

[82] *INC.*, Linden, p. 89.

[83] *1984 Annual Report,* Federal Express Corporation.

EXHIBIT 5
Federal Express: Consolidated Statement of Income (in Thousands of Dollars)

	1982	1983	1984
Express service revenues	$803,915	$1,008,087	$1,436,305
Operating expenses:			
Salaries and employee benefits	320,345	419,644	622,675
Depreciation and amortization	56,353	77,421	111,956
Fuel and oil	69,282	71,262	93,520
Equipment and facilities rental	46,116	59,115	89,775
Maintenance and repairs	38,795	44,083	59,482
Advertising	25,302	34,558	39,345
Other	128,256	151,267	254,344
Total expenses	684,449	857,350	1,271,097
Operating income	119,466	150,737	165,208
Other income (expense):			
Interest expense	(15,933)	(23,451)	(36,350)
Interest capitalized	2,852	5,831	11,851
Interest income	11,994	9,679	13,166
Gain on aircraft sales	7,318	4,224	2,463
Other	5,383	3,196	(4,078)
Total income (expense)	11,614	(521)	12,948
Income before income taxes	131,080	150,216	152,260
Provision for income taxes	52,695	61,283	36,830
Net income	$ 78,385	$ 88,933	$ 115,430
Earnings per share	$ 1.85	$ 2.03	$ 2.52
Average shares outstanding	41,788	43,316	45,448

Other extraordinary expenses incurred during 1984 were to expand the network geographically and to add Business Service Centers in high-density, downtown areas. Also, increasing customer use of volume discounts and the relatively rapid growth of the lower-priced Overnight Letter and Standard Air Services resulted in a decline in the yield, or average revenue, per package. This trend exceeded the impressive decrease in operating costs per package achieved during the fiscal year.

Management expected the trend in declining yields to reverse because of three policy changes, made during fiscal 1984, that produced higher than average yields. The first change was increasing the per package weight limit from 70 to 150 pounds. The second change was to introduce a Saturday pickup for Monday morning delivery service. The third and most important change was to charge by the pound rather than the package for multipackage shipments. Management hoped the third policy change would enable the company to enter the high-revenue air-freight market for the first time.[84]

Federal Express had a fiscal 1984 current ratio of 1.28 : 1, which had declined from 1.5 : 1 in fiscal 1983. One of the reasons for this decline was the 1984 implementation of ZapMail. To maintain its large credit agreements with banks and other lenders, the com-

[84] Ibid.

EXHIBIT 6
Federal Express: Consolidated Balance Sheet
Years Ended May 31
(in Thousands of Dollars)

	1983	1984
Assets		
Cash	$ 204	$ 2,190
Short-term investments	105,233	35,500
Net receivables	124,841	207,256
Inventories	16,203	39,725
Prepayments, etc.	18,690	43,465
Total current assets	265,171	328,136
Property, plant, and equipment	817,650	1,427,281
Accumulated depreciation and amortization	(221,258)	(314,642)
Net property, plant, and equipment	596,392	1,112,639
Construction funds in escrow	47,839	32,168
Equipment deposits and other	82,315	52,862
Total assets	$ 991,717	$1,525,805
Liabilities and Equity		
Current debt maturity	$ 12,171	$ 22,001
Notes payable	15,912	0
Accounts payable	59,047	129,960
Accrued liabilities	88,163	103,949
Total current liabilities	175,293	255,910
Long-term debt	247,424	435,158
Deferred income tax	59,094	112,439
Total liabilities	481,811	803,507
Preferred stock ($1 par)	6,112	4,577
Common stock ($.1 par)	2,197	4,639
Paid-in surplus	222,782	321,768
Retained earnings	278,815	391,314
Total equity	509,906	722,298
Total liabilities and equity	$ 991,717	$1,525,805

pany had been relatively conservative with its financial policies. It had not paid any dividends on common stock throughout its incorporated history and maintained minimum levels of working capital and certain financial ratios. The stock price showed consistent growth and split three times since the company went public in 1978. As of May 31, 1984, there were 46,386,287 shares of common stock. The 1983 and 1984 comparative balance sheets are shown in Exhibit 6.[85]

The company was determined to grow and expand its services geographically, as is shown by the large increases in capital expenditures during the three years prior to 1985 (see Exhibit 7). The bulk of these expenditures were for additional aircraft and additions and improvements to ZapMail equipment. Some of these capital funds had been internally generated; others were proceeds from loan agreements, tax-exempt bond issues and equity

[85] *Standard & Poors Industry Report,* p. 2551.

EXHIBIT 7
Federal Express: Capital Expenditures (in Thousands of Dollars)

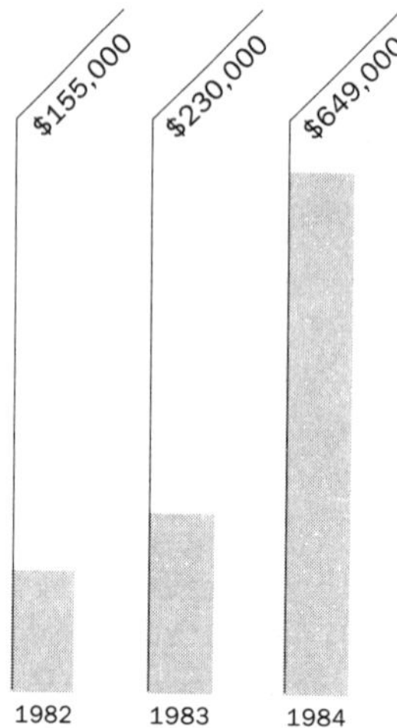

offerings. The commitment to growth had a significant effect on the company's cash and working capital. On May 31, 1984, both had suffered declines of 64% and 20%, respectively, from the previous year.

LEGAL SITUATION

Federal's only threat of liability due to litigation involved its ZapMail product. Federal was sued in November 1984 by Zap Legislative Courier Service of Albany, New York, for alleged trademark infringement over the use of the name ZapMail. A judge ruled that the company could seek unspecified monetary and punitive damages from Federal Express. As of May 1985 a trial date had not been set.[86]

OUTLOOK

Industry

Andrew B. Kim, a stock analyst for F. Eberstadt & Co., Inc., predicted that, from a stock market standpoint, investors perceived that the profit-margin squeeze would intensify as downward pressures on prices increased, especially if a downturn in the economy materialized. Kim also felt that the rapid increase in demand for the services of the air express and freight industry had been partly due to price reduction but, on the other hand, felt that

[86] *Wall Street Journal* (December 28, 1984), p. 33.

investors were asking why the companies were all cutting prices when demand was so strong.[87]

Large frequent shippers had become relatively more sensitive to pricing than before. But the quality of service was still the dominant variable for both frequent and infrequent shippers. Federal Express's 400,000 customer base at that time included many infrequent shippers.[88]

The industry's rapid consolidation had invited temporary pricing instability that resulted more from the service-mix change than actual price cutting. Once product lines were broadened, it was expected that future pricing would be essentially dictated by the differential in the cost structures of the six or seven major participants. The barrier to entry was expected to grow higher, not only in terms of capital requirements, but also in terms of service capability in the full range of markets being served. These markets included four-hour courier service, extended delivery, short-haul trucking, and international forwarding.

Federal Express

Looking at product differentiation, Fred Smith was worried about the startup difficulties of Federal Express's electronic mail service. He blamed these on the painfully slow process of educating the users, even the sophisticated customers.[89]

However, the possibility still remained that the predicted demand for ZapMail did not actually exist. Startup losses had already dramatically exceeded projections, and volume was significantly below expectations. Considering the enormous capital investment involved in the project, Federal was determined to make ZapMail a success and was placing a large stake of the company's future on the service. In view of the enormity of the challenge and the complexity of the logistical problems, historical experience suggested that such a revolutionary new service would need both time and effective marketing to generate volume.

---

[87] *Research Notes,* F. Eberstadt & Co., Inc. (May 3, 1984), p. 1.
[88] Ibid., p. 2.
[89] Ibid., p. 2.

CASE 22

The Swatch*

THE SWISS WATCH INDUSTRY IN THE LATE 1970s

In 1978 when Dr. Ernst Thomke became managing director of ETA after a 20-year leave of absence from the watch industry, the position of this Swiss flagship industry had changed dramatically. Just like other industries suffering from the competitive onslaught from the Far East, the Swiss watch industry faced the biggest challenge in its four hundred years of existence. Once the undisputed leaders in technology and market share—which the Swiss had gained thanks to breakthroughs in mechanizing the watch manufacturing process during the 19th century—the Swiss had fallen on hard times.

In 1980, Switzerland's share of the world market, which in 1952 stood at 56%, had fallen to a mere 20% of the finished watch segment while world production had grown from 61 million to 320 million pieces and movements annually. Even more troubling was the fact that the market share loss was more pronounced in finished watches compared to non-assembled movements (Exhibit 1). Measured in dollars the decline was not quite as evident, because the Swiss continued to dominate the luxury segment of the market while withdrawing from the budget price and middle segments.

The Swiss, once the industry's leaders in innovation, had fallen behind. Manufacturers in the United States, Japan and Hong Kong had started to gain share especially since the introduction of the electronic watch. Although in 1967 the Swiss were the first to introduce a model of an electronic wristwatch at the Concours de Chronometrie of the Neuchatel Observatory (Switzerland) smashing all accuracy records, they dismissed the new technol-

EXHIBIT 1
World Watch Production and Major Producing Countries, 1980

Country	Production (Million Pieces) Electronic	Mechanic	Total	Market Share, %
Switzerland: watches	10.4	52.6	63.0	20
incl. non-assembled movements	13.0	83.0	96.0	30
Japan: watches	50.4	17.1	67.5	21
incl. non-assembled movements	53.8	34.1	87.9	28
United States: watches & movements	2.0	10.1*	12.1*	
Rest of Europe: watches & movements	4.5	57.2*	67.7*	42†
Rest of Asia: watches & movements	76.0	31.3*	113.0*	
Latin America: watches & movements		2.7*	2.7*	

* Includes unassembled movements.
† Without unassembled movements.
Source: Swiss Watchmanufacturers Federation (FH).

* Prepared by Arieh A. Ullmann, State University of New York, Binghamton. Distributed by the North American Case Research Association.

EXHIBIT 2
Switzerland's 1975 Share of World Production by Type of Technology

Technology	*Year of Introduction*	*Stage of Product Life Cycle*	*Swiss Share, %*
Simple mechanical	Pre-WWII	Declining	35
Automatic	1948	Mature	24
Electric	1953	Declining	18
Quartz (high frequency)	1970	Growing	10
Quartz (solid state)	1972	Growing	3

Source: Swiss Watchmanufacturers Federation, Bulletin No. 13, Bienne, June 30, 1977.

ogy as a fad and continued to rely on their mechanical timepieces where most of their research efforts were concentrated. While the Swiss dominated the watch segments based on older technologies, their market shares were markedly lower for watches incorporating recently developed technologies (Exhibit 2). Thus, when electronic watches gained widespread acceptance the Swiss watch producers found themselves in a catch-up race against the Japanese who held the technological edge (Exhibit 3).

EXHIBIT 3
Share of Electronic Watches of Annual Output

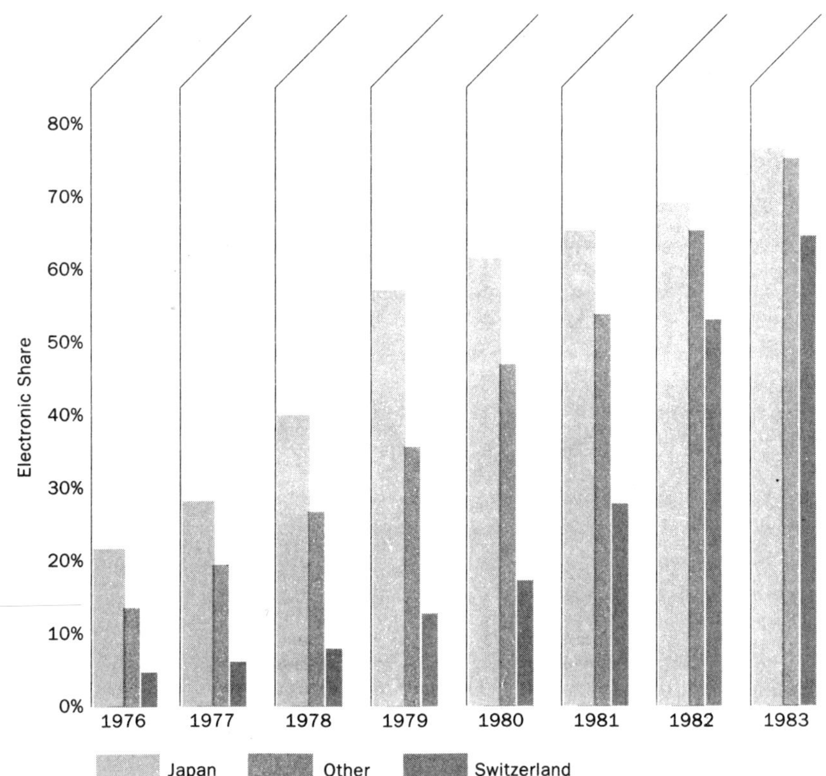

The situation of the industry which exported more than 90% of its production was aggravated by adverse exchange rate movements relative to the U.S. dollar making Swiss watches more expensive in the U.S.A.—then the most important export market. Until the early 1970s the exchange rate stood at US$1 = SFr. 4.30; by the end of the decade it had dropped to about US$1 = SFr. 1.90.

STRUCTURAL CHANGE IN THE INDUSTRY

Throughout its history the Swiss watch industry was characterized by an extreme degree of fragmentation. Until the end of the 1970s frequently up to thirty independent companies were involved in the production of a single watch. Skilled craftsmen called suppliers manufactured the many different parts of the watch in hundreds of tiny shops, each of them specializing on a few parts. The movements were either sold in loose parts ("ebauche") or assembled to "chablons" by "termineurs" which in turn supplied the etablisseurs, where the entire watch was put together. In 1975 63,000 employees in 12,000 workshops and plants were involved in the manufacture of watches and parts. Each etablisseur designed its own models and assembled the various pieces purchased from the many suppliers. Only a few vertically integrated manufacturers existed which performed most of the production stages in-house (Exhibit 4). The watches were either exported bearing the assembler's or manufacturer's brand name (factory label) via wholly owned distributors and independent importers, or sold under the name of the customer (private label). By the late 1970s private label sales comprised about 75% of Swiss exports of finished watches. In addition, the Swiss also exported movements and unassembled parts to foreign customers (Exhibit 5*a* & 5*b*).

EXHIBIT 4
Traditional Structure of the Swiss Watch Industry

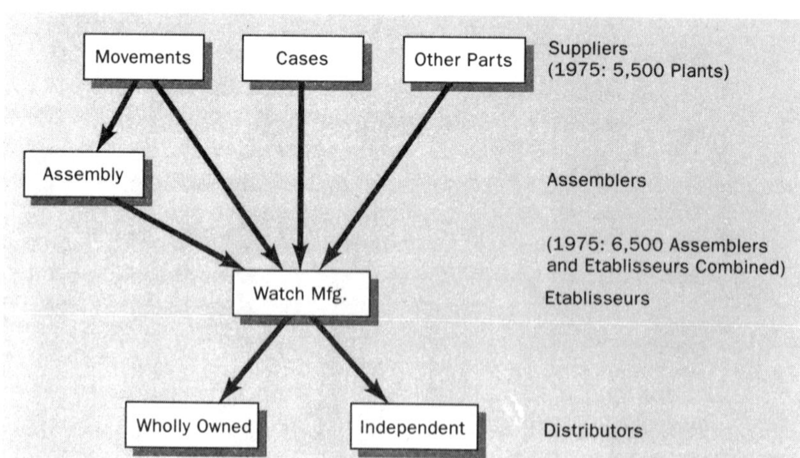

Source: Bernheim, 1981.

EXHIBIT 5a
Swiss Exports of Watches, Movements, and Parts, 1960–1980

	Finished Watches		Assembled Movements		Unassembled Movements	
Year	Pieces*	Francs†	Pieces*	Francs†	Pieces*	Francs†
1960	16.7	767.2	8.2	192.7	n.a.	n.a.
1965	38.4	1334.4	14.8	282.7	n.a.	n.a.
1970	52.6	2033.8	18.8	329.5	n.a.	n.a.
1975	47.2	2391.2	18.6	329.1	5.4	44.0
1976	42.0	2262.4	20.0	343.0	8.0	54.2
1977	44.1	2474.5	21.9	381.3	15.8	94.8
1978	39.7	2520.0	20.6	380.3	18.7	103.5
1979	30.3	2355.6	18.6	371.1	20.2	121.0
1980	28.5	2505.8	22.5	411.8	32.7	189.2

* In millions.
† In millions of current Swiss francs.
Source: Swiss Watchmanufacturers Federation.

EXHIBIT 5b
Swiss Exports of Watches, Movements, and Parts, 1981–1990

	Finished Watches		Assembled Movements		Unassembled Movements	
Year	Pieces*	Francs†	Pieces*	Francs†	Pieces*	Francs†
1981	25.2	2880.2	19.9	382.5	27.5	160.5
1982	18.5	2754.6	12.7	256.4	14.5	81.0
1983	15.7	2676.6	14.6	247.1	12.7	76.8
1984	17.8	3063.9	14.5	235.0	14.6	98.5
1985	25.1	3444.1	13.4	220.4	18.8	138.9
1986	28.1	3391.0	13.3	213.4	19.4	133.3
1987	27.6	3568.0	11.1	179.4	20.9	122.8
1988	28.0	4128.8	12.2	202.8	31.9	162.1
1989	29.9	5080.0	12.6	217.7	28.4	136.3

* In millions.
† In millions of current Swiss francs.
Source: Swiss Watchmanufacturers Federation.

This horizontally and vertically fragmented industry structure had developed over centuries around a locally concentrated infrastructure and depended entirely on highly skilled craftsmen. Watch making encompassed a large number of sophisticated techniques for producing the mechanical watches and this complexity was exacerbated by the extremely large number of watch models. The industry was highly specialized around highly qualified labor, requiring flexibility, quality, and first-class styling at low cost.

This structure was, however, poorly suited to absorb the new electronic technology. Not only did electronics render obsolete many of the watchmaker's skills that had been cultivated over centuries, it also required large production volumes to take advantage of the significant scale and potential experience effects. Whereas the traditional Swiss manufacturing methods provided few benefits from mass production, the extreme fragmentation from the suppliers to the distributors prevented even these. Furthermore, the critical stages in the value added chain of the watch shifted from parts and assembly—where the Swiss had their stronghold—to distribution where the Japanese concentrated their efforts. Encasement, marketing, wholesale and retail distribution which the Japanese producers emphasized represented over 80% of the value added.

Sales of mechanical watches in the budget and middle price segments dropped rapidly when electronic watches entered the market. Initially these were Instruments Inc., National Semiconductor Corp., Hughes Aircraft, Intel, and Time Computer. Due to rapidly rising production and sales volumes of electronic watches, prices dropped dramatically from $1,000 to $2,000 in 1970 to $40 in 1975 and less than $20 by the end of the 1970s. At this time most of the early American digital watch producers had started to withdraw from the watch business and it was the cheap digital watch from Hong Kong that flooded the market. As an indication of the eroded market power of the Swiss, the sale of assembled and unassembled movements had started to rise while exports of finished watches declined (Exhibit 5*a*)—a trend which negatively affected domestic employment.

The industry's misfortune caused large-scale layoffs, and bankruptcies started to increase steeply in the 1970s. Since the watch industry was concentrated around a few towns in the western part of Switzerland, the ensuing job losses led to regional unemployment rates unknown in Switzerland since the 1930s (Exhibit 6).

ETA, where Dr. Thomke became managing director, was a subsidiary of Ebauches SA which in turn was a subsidiary of ASUAG (General Corporation of Swiss Horological Industries Ltd.). ASUAG had been created in 1931 during the first consolidation period in the industry. It was Switzerland's largest watch corporation (total sales 1979: SFr. 1,212 million) and combined a multitude of companies under its holding structure including such famous brands as Certina, Eterna, Longines, and Rado. Ebauches, of which ETA was part,

EXHIBIT 6
Swiss Watch Industry: Companies and Employment

Year	*Number of Companies*	*Employment*
1960	2,167	65,127
1965	1,927	72,600
1970	1,618	76,045
1975	1,169	55,954
1976	1,083	49,991
1977	1,021	49,822
1978	979	48,305
1979	867	43,596
1980	861	44,173
1981	793	43,300
1982	727	36,808
1983	686	32,327
1984	634	30,978
1985	634	31,949
1986	592	32,688
1987	568	29,809
1988	562	30,122

Source: Swiss Watchmanufacturers Federation.

was the major producer of watch movements for ASUAG and most of the other Swiss etablisseurs. The other large Swiss manufacturer was SSIH (Swiss Watch Industry Corporation Ltd.) which also was a creation of the same 1931 consolidation and whose flagships were Omega and Tissot. During the second half of the 1970s ASUAG suffered from declining profitability and cash flow, poor liquidity, rising long-term debt, and dwindling financial reserves due to sluggish sales of outdated mechanical watches and movements which comprised about two thirds of ASUAG's watch sales. Diversified businesses outside the watch segment contributed less than 5% of total sales.

TURNAROUND AT ETA

Ernst Thomke grew up in Bienne, the Swiss capital of watch making. After an apprenticeship in watch making with ETA he enrolled in the University of Berne where he first studied physics and chemistry and later medicine. After his studies he joined Beechams, a large British pharmaceuticals and consumer products company as a pharmaceutical salesman. In 1978, when his old boss at ETA asked him to return to his first love, he was managing director of Beecham's Swiss subsidiary and had just been promoted to Brussels. However, his family did not wish to move and so, after 18 years, he was back in watches.

When he took over, morale at ETA was at an all-time low due to the prolonged period of market share losses and continued dismissals of personnel. ETA's engineers and managers no longer believed in their capabilities of beating the competition from Japan and Hong Kong. Although ETA as the prime supplier of watch movements did not consider itself directly responsible for the series of failures, it was equally affected by the weakened position of the Swiss watch manufacturers. When Thomke assumed his role as managing director of ETA he clearly understood that, for a successful turnaround, his subordinates needed a success story to regain their self-confidence. But first a painful shrinking process had to be undertaken in order to bring costs under control. Production which used to be distributed over a dozen factories was concentrated in three centers and the number of movement models reduced from over 1000 to about 250.

As a first step a project called "Delirium" was formulated with the objective to create the world's thinnest analogue quartz movement—a record which at that time was held by Seiko. When Thomke revealed his idea to ETA's engineers they were quick to nickname it "Delirium Tremens" because they considered it crazy. But Thomke insisted on the project despite his staff's doubts. To save even the tiniest fraction of a millimeter some watch parts were for the first time bonded to the case instead of being layered on top of the watch back. Also, a new extra thin battery was invented. In 1979 the first watch was launched with the Delirium movement and ETA had its first success in a long time. In that year, ASUAG sold more than 5,000 pieces at an average price of $4,700 with the top model retailing for $16,000.

The Delirium project not only helped to boost the morale of ETA's employees, it also led to a significant change in strategy and philosophy with ETA's parent, Ebauches SA. No longer was Ebauches content with its role as the supplier of movement parts. In order to fulfill its primary responsibility as the supplier of technologically advanced quality movements at competitive prices to Switzerland's etablisseurs, Ebauches argued, it was necessary to maintain a minimum sales volume that exceeded the reduced domestic demand. There-

EXHIBIT 7
World Watch Production by Price Category, 1970 vs. 1980

Price Category	*1970 Sales (Million Pieces)*	*1980 Sales (Million Pieces)*	*Growth, %*
Less than 100 SFr.	110	290	264
100–200 SFr.	33	50	52
200–500 SFr.	20	20	0
More than 500 SFr.	7	10	43

Source: Thomke (1985).

fore, in 1981 ETA expanded its movement sales beyond its then current customers in Switzerland, France and Germany. This expansion meant sales to Japan, Hong Kong and Brazil. Ebauches thus entered into direct international competition with Japanese, French, German and Soviet manufacturers. In short, ETA claimed more control over its distribution channels and increased authority in formulating its strategy.

As a second step, the organizational culture and structure were revamped to foster creativity and to encourage employees to express their ideas. Management layers were scrapped and red tape reduced to a minimum. Communication across departments and hierarchical levels was stressed, continued learning and long-term thinking encouraged, playful trial-and-error and risk taking reinforced. The intention was to boost morale and to create corporate heroes.

The third step consisted in defining a revolutionary product in the medium or low price category. By expanding even farther into the downstream activities, Thomke argued, ETA would control more than 50% instead of merely 10% of the total value added. Since 1970 the watch segments below SFr. 200 had experienced the highest growth rates (Exhibit 7). These were the segments the Swiss had ceded to the competitors from Japan and Hong Kong. As a consequence, the average price of Swiss watch exports had steadily risen, whereas the competitors exported at declining prices. Given the overall objective to reverse the long-term trend of segment retreat, it was crucial to reenter one or both of the formerly abandoned segments. Thomke decided to focus on the low price segment. "We thought we'd leave the middle market for Seiko and Citizen. We would go for the top and the bottom to squeeze the Japanese in the sandwich." [1] The new concept was summarized in four objectives:

1. *Price:* Quartz-analogue watch, retailing for no more than SFr. 50.
2. *Sales target:* 10 million pieces during the first three years.
3. *Manufacturing costs:* Initially SFr. 15—less than those of any competitor. At a cumulative volume of 5 million pieces, learning and scale economies would reduce costs to SFr.10 or less. Continued expansion would yield long term estimated costs per watch of less than SFr. 7.

[1] Moynahan, Brian, and Andreas Heumann, "The Man Who Made the Cuckoo Sing," *The Sunday Times Magazine,* August 18, 1985, p. 25.

4. *Quality:* High quality, waterproof, shock resistant, no repair possible, battery only replaceable element, all parts standardized, free choice of material, model variations only in dial and hands.

The objectives were deliberately set so high that it was impossible to reach them by improving existing technologies; instead, they required novel approaches. When confronted with these parameters for a new watch, ETA's engineers responded with "That's impossible," "Absurd," "You're crazy." Many considered it typical of Thomke's occasionally autocratic management style which had brought him the nickname "Ayatollah." After all, the unassembled parts of the cheapest existing Swiss watch at that time cost more than twice as much! Also, the largest Swiss watch assembler—ETA's parent ASUAG—sold 750,000 watches annually scattered over several hundred models. In an interview with the *Sunday Times Magazine* Thomke told the story: "A couple of kids, under 30, said they'd go away and look at the Delirium work and see if they could come up with anything. And they did. They mounted the moving parts directly on to a moulded case. It was very low cost. And it was new, and that is vital in marketing."[2] The concept was the brainchild of two engineers. Elmar Mock, a qualified plastics engineer, had recommended earlier that ETA acquire an injection moulding machine to investigate the possibilities of producing watch parts made of plastic. Jacques Muller was a horological engineer and specialist in watch movements. Their new idea was systematically evaluated and improved by interdisciplinary teams consisting of the inventors, product and manufacturing engineers, specialists from costing, marketing and accounting as well as outside members not involved in the watch industry.

The fourth step required that ETA develop its own marketing. In the 1970s and early 1980s it did not have a marketing department. Thomke turned to some independent consultants and people outside the watch industry with extensive marketing experience in apparel, shoes and sporting goods to bring creative marketing to the project. Later, as Swatch sales expanded worldwide, a new marketing team was built up to cover the growing marketing, communications and distribution activities.

PRODUCT AND PROCESS TECHNOLOGY

A conventionally designed analogue watch consisted of a case in which the movement was mounted. The case was closed with a glass or crystal. The movement included a frame onto which the wheels, the micromotor needed for analogue display, other mechanical parts as well as the electronic module were attached with screws. First the movement was assembled and then mechanically fixed in the case. Later the straps were attached to the case.

The Swatch differed both with regard to its construction as well as the manufacturing process.

Construction

First, the *case* was not only an outer shell, it also served as the mounting plate. The individual parts of the movement were mounted directly into the case—the Delirium

[2] Moynahan/Heumann, op. cit.

EXHIBIT 8
Swatch Components

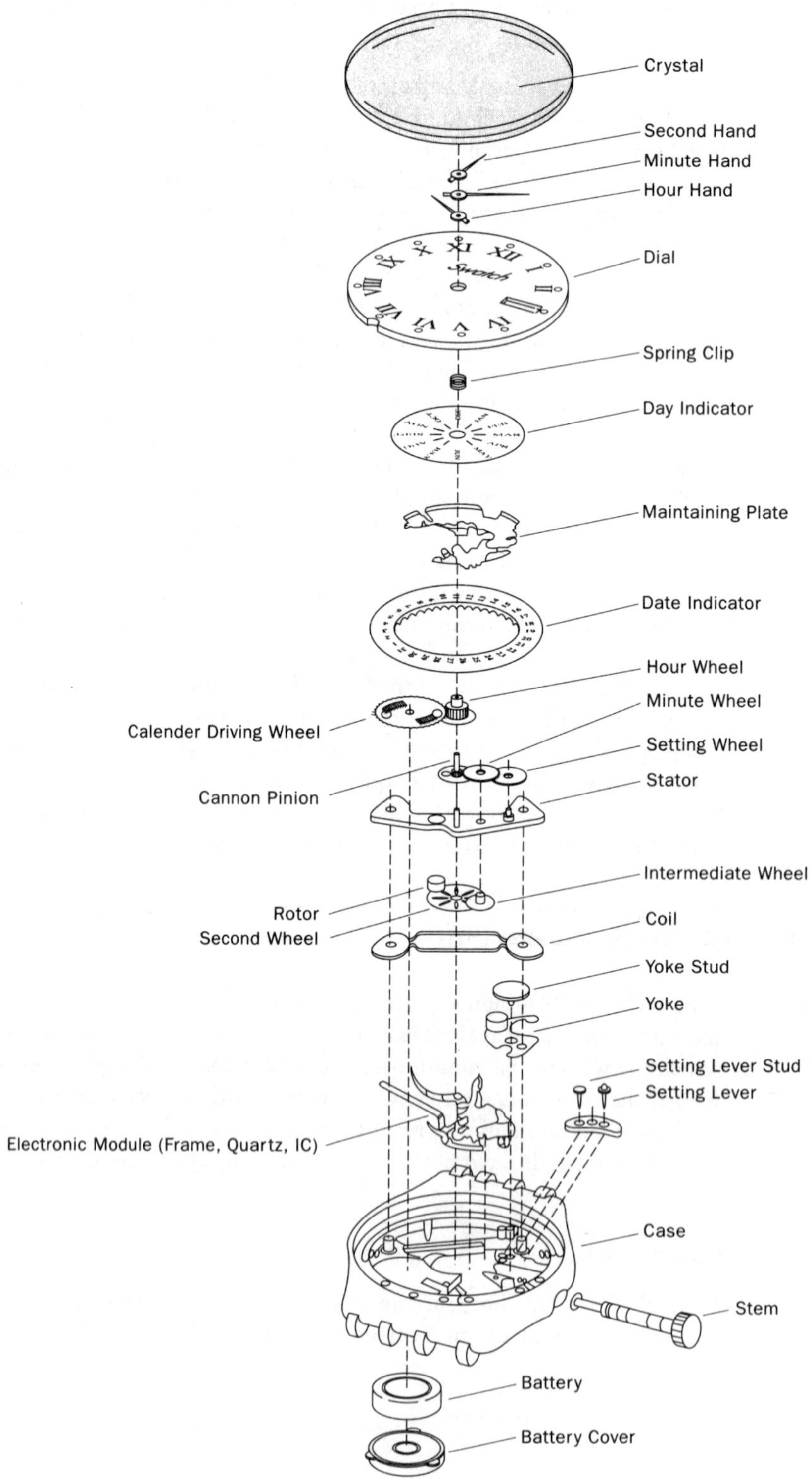

technology was perfected. The case itself was produced by a new very precise injection molding process which was specifically developed for this purpose. The case was made of extremely durable plastic which created a super-light watch.

Second, the number of *components* was reduced significantly from 91 parts for a conventional analogue quartz watch to 51 (Exhibit 8). Unlike in conventional watch assembly, the individual parts of the movement—the electronic module and the motor module—were first assembled in subgroups before mounting and then placed in the case like a system of building blocks.

Third, the *method of construction* differed in that the parts were no longer attached with screws. Components were riveted and welded together ultrasonically. This eliminated screws and threads and reduced the number of parts and made the product rugged and shock-resistant. As the crystal was also welded to the case, the watch was guaranteed water-resistant up to 100 feet.

Fourth, the tear-proof *strap* was integrated into the case with a new, patented hinge system which improved wearing comfort.

Fifth, the *battery*—the only part with a limited life expectancy of about three years—was inserted into the bottom of the case and closed with a cover.

Production

First, as a special advantage the Swatch could be assembled from one side only.

Second, because of this it was possible to fully automate the watch mounting process. Ordinary watches were assembled in two separate operations: the mounting of the movement and the finishing. The Swatch, however, was produced in one single operation (Exhibit 9). According to representatives of the Swiss watch manufacturers, this technology incorporated advanced CAD/CAM technology as well as extensive use of robotics and was the most advanced of its kind in the world.

Third, due to the new design, the number of elements needed for the Swatch could be significantly reduced and the assembly process simplified. As a prerequisite for incorporating this new product technology, new materials had to be developed for the case, the glass and the micro motor. Also, a new assembly technology was designed and the pressure diecasting process perfected.

Fourth, quality requirements had to be tightened, because the watch could not be reopened and therefore, except for the battery, not be repaired. Given these constraints, each step in the manufacturing process had to be carefully controlled including the parts, the pre-assembled modules, the assembly process itself as well as the final product. This was especially important because in the past high reject rates of parts and casings indicated that many Swiss manufacturers had difficulties with quality control which damaged their reputation.

Overall, the new product design and production technology reduced the costs significantly and raised product quality above watches in the same price category produced by conventional technology.

Marketing

The new marketing team came up with an approach that was unheard of in this industry dominated by engineers.

EXHIBIT 9
Swatch Assembly Process

1 A new kind of injection molding, employing high-strength plastic, produces the case and mounting plate in one piece, through a single molding step.

2 The electronic module is built in and riveted ultrasonically in place. It contains the quartz-integrated circuit, the coil connector and the battery contacts.

3 The hand-setting mechanism and coil are assembled.

4 The motor module is inserted. For the first time in the history of watchmaking, the second wheel is driven directly.

5 The train wheel and maintaining plate are riveted.

6 Assembly of the date indicator.

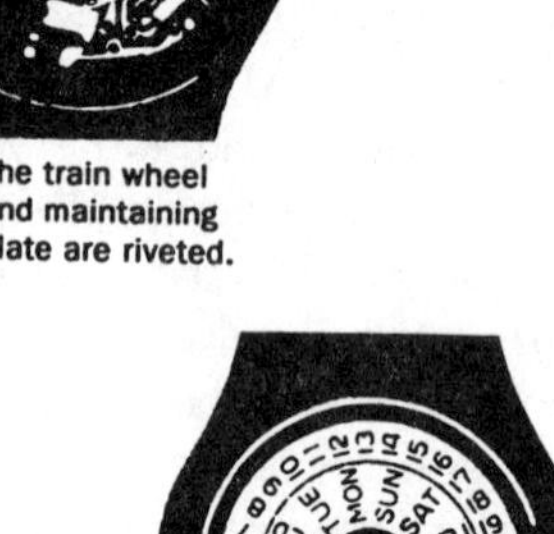

7 Mounting of the day indicator.

8 The dial and hands are put in place and the watch crystal is welded to the case to seal out water.

Product Positioning. Contrary to conventional wisdom in the industry it was not the product, its styling and technical value that were emphasized but its brand name. Quality attributes such as waterproofness, shock resistance, color, preciseness were less important than the association of the brand name with positive emotions such as "fun," "vacation," "joy of life." The watch was positioned as a high fashion accessory for fashion conscious people between 18 and 30. As it turned out many people outside this range started buying the Swatch. Jean Robert, a Zurich based designer, was responsible for Swatch's innovative designs.

Pricing. The price was set at a level that allowed for spontaneous purchases yet provided the high margins needed for massive advertising.

Distribution. As a high-fashion item competing in the same price range as some Timex and Casio models, the Swatch was not sold through drugstores and mass retailers. Instead, department stores, chic boutiques and jewelry shops were used as distribution channels. Attractive distributor margins and extensive training of the retailers' sales personnel combined with innovative advertising ensured the unique positioning of the product.

Brand Name. In 1982 20,000 prototypes of 25 Swatch models were pretested in the United States, which was viewed as the toughest market, setting the trend for the rest of the world. The unisex models only differed in color of the cases and straps and the dial designs. It was during these pretests that Franz Sprecher, one of the outside consultants of the marketing team, came up with the name "Swatch" (Swiss + Watch = Swatch) during a brainstorming session with the New York based advertising agency concerning the product's positioning and name. Up until then Sprecher's notes repeatedly mentioned the abbreviation S'Watch. During this meeting Sprecher took the abbreviation one step further and created the final name.

THE SWATCH TEAM

Besides Thomke, three individuals were crucial for the successful launching of the Swatch: Franz Sprecher, Max Imgrueth, and Jacques Irniger.

Franz Sprecher obtained a masters in economics and business from the University of Basle. Following one year as a research assistant and Ph.D. student he decided to abandon academia and to enter the international business world as a management trainee with Armour Foods in Chicago. After six months he returned to Switzerland and joined Nestle in international marketing. Two years later he became sales and marketing director of a small Swiss/Austrian food additives company. Later Sprecher moved to the positions of International Marketing Director of Rivella and then Account Group Manager at the Dr. Dieter Jaeggi Advertising Agency in Basle. Sprecher took a sabbatical at this point in his career and planned to return to the international business world as a consultant within a year. Towards the end of this period while thinking of accepting a position as a professor at the Hoehere Wirtschafts- und Verwaltungshochschule in Lucerne he received a phone call from Dr. Thomke concerning the new watch. Thomke told Sprecher: "You've got too much time and not enough money, so why don't you come and work for me." Sprecher then took over the marketing of the, as of yet unnamed, product as a freelance consultant.

Today, he continues to consult for Swatch as well as for other brands such as Tissot and Omega.

Another important person involved in the creation of the Swatch was Max Imgrueth. Max Imgrueth was born in Lucerne, Switzerland. Following graduation from high school in St. Maurice, a small town in the Valais surrounded by high mountains, he went to Italy and studied art history in Florence and fashion and leather design in Milan. After a brief stint in linguistics he enrolled in business courses at the Regency Polytechnic in England and New York University. In 1969 he left the United States because he had difficulties in obtaining a work permit and started to work in a women's specialty store in Zurich, Switzerland. Two years later he switched to apparel manufacturing and became manager for product development and marketing. In 1976 he was recruited by SSIH, owners of the Omega and Tissot brands. From 1976 to 1981 he was in charge of product development and design at Omega's headquarters in Bienne. Conflicts with the banks—which at that time de facto owned SSIH due to continued losses—over Omega's strategy led him to resign from his job and to start a consulting business. One of his first clients was ETA Industries which were just getting ready to test market the Swatch in San Antonio, Texas. He succeeded in convincing ETA that San Antonio was the wrong test market and that the Swatch as a new product required other than the traditional distributors. As a consequence New York and Dallas were chosen as primary test sites, and TV advertising and unconventional forms of public relations were tried out. While working on debugging the introduction of the Swatch, he was offered the position of President of Swatch USA, a job which initially consisted of an office on Manhattan's Fifth Avenue and a secretary.

The third individual involved in the early phase of the Swatch was Jacques Irniger who joined ETA in 1983 as Vice-President Marketing and Sales for both ETA and Swatch worldwide. In 1985 he was a board member of the Swatch SA, Vice-President Marketing-Sales of ETA SA Fabriques d'Ebauches and President of Omega Watch Corp., New York. Irniger received his doctorate in economics from the University of Fribourg, a small city located in the French-speaking part of Switzerland. After training positions in marketing research and management at Unilever and Nestle he became marketing manager at Colgate Palmolive in Germany. After Colgate, he moved on to Beecham Germany as Vice-President Marketing. Before joining ETA he was Vice-President Marketing and Sales for Bahksen International.

MARKET INTRODUCTION

The Swatch was officially introduced in Switzerland on March 1, 1983—the same year that ASUAG and SSIH merged after continued severe losses that necessitated a SFr. 1.2 billion bailout by the Swiss banks. During the first four months 25,000 Swatch pieces were sold—more than a third of the initial sales objective of 70,000 for the first 12 months. According to some distinguished jewelry stores located on Zurich's famous Bahnhofstrasse where Switzerland's most prestigious and expensive watches were purchased by an endless stream of tourists from all over the world, the Swatch did not compete with the traditional models. On the contrary, some jewelers reported that the Swatch stimulated sales of their more expensive models. The success of the Swatch encouraged other Swiss manufacturers to develop similar models which, however, incorporated conventional quartz technology.

Subsequent market introductions in other countries used high-powered promotion. In Germany, the launching of the Swatch was accompanied by a huge replica of a bright yellow Swatch that covered the entire facade of the black Commerzbank skyscraper in Frankfurt's business district. The same approach was used in Japan. On Christmas Eve 1985 the front of a tall building in Tokyo was decorated with a huge Swatch that was 11 yards long and weighed more than 14,000 pounds. Japan, however, turned out to be a difficult market for the Swatch. The 7,000 Yen Swatch competed with domestic plastic models half the price. Distribution was restricted to eleven department stores in Tokyo only and carried out without a Japanese partner. After six months it became obvious that the original sales target of SFr. 25 million for the first year could not be reached. The head of the Japanese Swatch operation, the American Harold Tune, resigned. His successor was a Japanese.

In the United States, initial sales profited from the fact that many American tourists coming home from their vacation in Switzerland helped in spreading the word about this fancy product which quickly became as popular a souvenir as Swiss army knives. U.S. sales of this $30 colorful watch grew from 100,000 pieces in 1983 to 3.5 million pieces in 1985—a sign that Swatch USA, ETA's American subsidiary, was successful in changing the way time pieces were sold and worn. No longer were watches precious pieces given as presents on special occasions such as confirmations, bar mitzvahs, and marriages, to be worn for a lifetime. "Swatch yourself," meant wearing two, three watches simultaneously like plastic bracelets. Swatch managers traveling back and forth between the United States and Switzerland wore two watches, one showing EST time, the other Swiss time.

The initial success prompted the company to introduce a ladies' line one year after the initial introduction, thus leading to 12 models. New Swatch varieties were created about twice a year. Also, special models were designed for the crucial Christmas season: In 1984 scented models were launched, a year later a limited edition watch called Limelight with diamonds sold at $100. The Swatch was a very advertising-intensive line of business. For 1985, the advertising budget of Swatch USA alone was $8 million, with U.S. sales estimated at $45 million (1984 sales: $18 million). In 1985, Swatch USA sponsored MTV's New Year's Eve show; the year before it had sponsored a breakdancing festival offering $25,000 in prizes, and the Fresh Festival '84 in Philadelphia.

Swatch managers were, however, careful not to flood the market. They claimed that in 1984 an additional 2 million watches could have been sold in the United States. In England, 600,000 watches were sold in the first year and the British distributor claimed he could have sold twice as many.

CONTINUED GROWTH

The marketing strategy called for complementing the $30 dollar time piece with a range of Swatch accessories. The idea behind this strategy was to associate the product with a lifestyle and thereby create brand identity and distinction from the range of look-alikes which had entered the market and were copying the Swatch models with a delay of about three months. In late 1985 Swatch USA introduced an active apparel line called Funwear. T-shirts, umbrellas, and sunglasses should follow in the hope of adding an extra $100 million in sales in 1986. Product introduction was accompanied by an expensive and elaborate publicity campaign including a four-month TV commercial series costing $2.5 million, an eight-page Swatch insert featuring a dozen Swatch accessories in *Glamour, GQ, Vogue,* and *Rolling Stone,* and a $2.25 million campaign on MTV. In January 1985 Swatch AG was spun off from ETA. The purpose of the new Swatch subsidiary was to design and distribute watches and related consumer goods such as shoes, leather and leather imitation accessories, clothes, jewelry and perfumes, toys, sports goods, glasses and accessories, pens, lighters and cigarettes. Swatch production, however, remained with ETA. Furthermore, licenses were being considered for the distribution of the products. All of these products as well as the watches were designed in the United States with subsequent adaptations for European markets.

This strategy of broadening the product line was, however, not without risks, because it could dilute the impact of the brand name. *Forbes* mentioned the examples of Nike which failed miserably when it tried to expand from runningwear to leisure wear, and so did Lewis when it attempted to attach its brand recognition to more formal apparel.[3] Yet Max Imgrueth was quick to point to other examples such as Terence Conran, a designer and furniture maker who succeeded in building a retail empire ranging from kitchen towels to desk lamps around his inexpensive, well-designed home furnishings aimed at the young.

ENSURING SUCCESS

At the end of 1985, 45,000 Swatch units were produced daily and annual sales were expected to reach 8 million pieces (1984: 3.7 million). The Swatch was so successful that by the end of 1984 Swatch profits above recovering all product related investments and expenditures contributed significantly towards ETA's overhead. The Swatch represented 75% of SMH's unit sales of finished watches and made it SMH's number one brand in terms of unit sales and the number two brand in terms of revenues, topping such prestige brands as Longines and Rado. SMH (Swiss Corporation for Microelectronics and Watchmaking Industries Ltd.) was the new name of the Swatch parent after the ASUAG-SSIH merger in 1983. Thanks to the Swatch SMH was able to increase its share of the world market (1985: 400 million units) from 1% to 3% within four years. The success also invigorated the Swiss industry at large (Exhibit 5*b*). Despite this success the managers at Swatch continued to perfect and expand the Swatch line.

In 1986 the Maxi-Swatch was introduced which was ten times the size of the regular Swatch. Before the start of the ski season during the same year the Pop-Swatch was launched which could be combined with different color wristbands. As a high-technology extravaganza the Pop-Swatch could also be worn in combination with a "Recco-Reflector" which had been developed by another SMH subsidiary. The Recco reflected radar waves emitted from a system and thus helped to locate skiers covered by avalanches.

In 1987 Swatch wall models were introduced, and the Swatch Twinphone. The latter was not just colorful. It had a memory to facilitate dialing and, true to its origin, provided an unconventional service in that it had a built-in "party line," so that two people could use it simultaneously.

---

[3] Heller, Matthew, "Swatch Switches," *Forbes,* January 1986, p. 87.

1988 saw the successful introduction of the Twinphone in the USA, Japan and the airport duty-free business as well as the expansion of the Pop-Swatch product line. The Swatch accessories line was discontinued due to unmet profit objectives and negative impact on the Swatch brand image.

In its 1989 annual report SMH reported cumulative sales of over 70 million Swatch pieces. Over 450 models of the original concept had been introduced during the first 7 years (Exhibit 10). The Swatch had also become a collector's item. Limited edition models designed by well-known artists brought auction prices of SFr. 1,600, SFr. 3,900 and SFr. 9,400—about 25 to 160 times the original price!

In 1990 the "Swatch-Chrono" was launched to take advantage of the chronometer fashion. Except for the basic concept—plastic encasement and battery as the only replaceable part—it had little in common with the original model and represented a much more complex instrument. It had four micromotors instead of only one due to the added functions and was somewhat larger in diameter. Despite the added complexity it claimed to be as exact and robust as the original Swatch. As a special attraction the watch which was available in six models retailed for only SFr. 100. The company was also experimenting

EXHIBIT 10
Swatch Sales (Millions of Units)

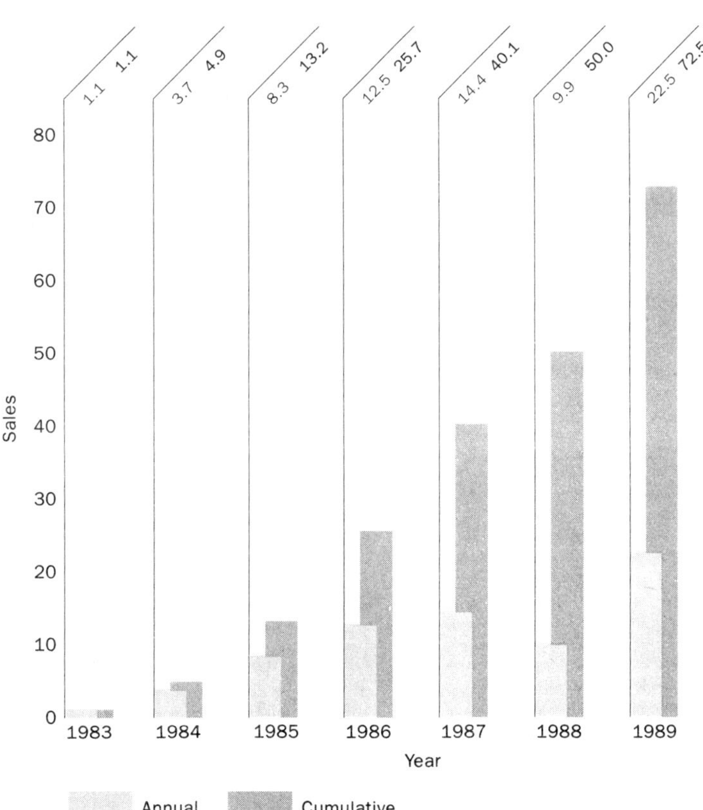

with a mechanical Swatch to be marketed in developing countries where battery replacement posed a problem. In this way the company hoped to boost sales in regions which represented only a minor export market for the Swiss.

The success of the Swatch at the market front was supported by a carefully structured organization. Just like the other major brands of SMH, the Swatch had its own organization in each major market responsible for marketing, sales and communication. These regional offices were supported by SMH country organizations which handled services common to all brands such as logistics, finance, controlling, administration, EDP and after-sales service.

The Swatch also meant a big boost for Dr. Thomke's career. He was appointed general

EXHIBIT 11
SMH: Financial Data
(All Monetary Values in Million SFr.)

	1989	1988	1987	1986	1985	1984
	Income Statement Data					
Sales revenues:						
Gross sales	2,146	1,847	1,787	1,895	1,896	1,665
Costs:						
Materials	793	681	670	759	812	714
Personnel	646	580	577	593	556	541
External services	346	331	335	356	360	286
Depreciation	80	71	73	68	61	60
Total operating costs	1,865	1,663	1,655	1,776	1,789	1,758
Operating profit (loss)	236	142	117	103	66	51
Income before taxes	209	126	90	82	72	38
Net income	175	105	77	70	60	26
	Balance Sheet Data					
Assets:						
Current assets	1,194	1,065	1,103	1,080	1,070	1,049
Inventories	602	562	528	568	513	524
Fixed assets	529	510	533	507	456	451
Total assets	1,723	1,575	1,636	1,587	1,526	1,500
Liabilities and stockholders' equity:						
Short-term debt	367	384	442	503	524	501
Long-term debt	295	302	798	801	862	898
Total liabilities	662	686	1,240	1,304	1,386	1,399
Total shareholders' equity	892	760	697	648	490	420
Total liabilities & shareholders' equity	1,723	1,575	1,636	1,587	1,526	1,500
	Other Data					
Personnel: in Switzerland	8,822	8,385	8,526	9,323	9,173	8,982
Personnel: abroad	2,963	2,893	2,597	2,611	2,353	2,311
Personnel: total	11,785	11,278	11,123	11,934	11,526	11,293
Stock price* high	560	395	490	700†	410	‡
Stock price* low	378	178	150	375†	127	

* Nominal value SFr./share.
† Trading moved from Basle to Zurich on 7/17/1986.
‡ No shares publicly traded.

manager of the entire watch business of the reorganized SMH and became one of the key decision makers of the new management team that took over in January 1985. The "Swatch Story" was instrumental in the turnaround of SMH which only six years after the merger of two moribund companies showed a very healthy bottom line (Exhibit 11).

FUTURE

Despite the smashing success of the Swatch and its contribution to the reinvigoration of the Swiss watch making industry, future success was by no means guaranteed.

First, competition remained as fierce as ever. The 1980s were characterized by an oversupply of cheap watches because many manufacturers had built capacity ahead of demand. Prices dropped, especially for the cheapest digital watches, a segment that the Swiss avoided. However, several competitors switched to the more sophisticated analogue models and thus created competition for the Swatch. Many look-alikes with names such as Action Watch, A-Watch, etc., flooded the market.

Second, the Swiss had to guard their brand recognition—not just because of the diversification of the Swatch line. It was not clear whether the Swatch brand name was strong enough to create a sustainable position against the imitations. Also, the quality advantage of the Swatch was neither evident to the consumer nor a top priority for the purchasing decision.

A third issue was for how long the Swatch could maintain its technological advantage. By the late 1980s all imitations were welded together. In addition, many competitors, especially the Japanese, were larger than SMH and therefore able to support larger R&D budgets.

A fourth threat was market saturation. While countries with a GDP per capita of over $5,000 comprised only 17% of the world's population, they absorbed 87% of Swiss watch exports. The changes in watch technology and pricing during the last 10 years had increased watch consumption. In England, consumption grew from 275 watches per 1,000 inhabitants in 1974 to 370 watches 10 years later. In the United States the respective figures were 240 and 425 units of which 90% was made up of low price electronic models. While the average life of a watch was much shorter today and consumers had started to own several watches, market saturation could not be ruled out. Also, given the trendy nature of the Swatch it could fall out of fashion as quickly as it had conquered the market. For this situation SMH was not as well prepared as, say, Seiko or Casio, whose non-watch businesses were much stronger and contributed more in terms of overall sales and profits.

A fifth threat was the continued rapid development of technology especially in the field of communications. Increasingly, time measurement was evolving into one of several features of an integrated communication system. Watches were already integrated in a wide variety of products including household durables, computers, telephones. Several SMH subsidiaries involved in microelectronics, electronic components and telecommunications were busy developing products in this area and searching for applications in other markets as well. In the late 1980s SMH started to test prototypes of a combined watch/pager. In late 1990 Motorola introduced a combined watch/pager. It was not clear how SMH and its Swatch subsidiary would fare in this evolving era despite its high-technology sector which, however, was smaller than that of its competitors (Exhibit 12).

EXHIBIT 12
SMH Subsidiaries, 1990

SMH Swiss Corporation for Microelectronics and Watchmaking Industries Ltd. Neuchâtel (Holding Company)

Company Name, Registered Offices	Field of Activity	Shareholding SMH Direct or Indirect, %
Omega SA, Bienne	Watches	100
Compagnie des montres Longines Francillon SA, Saint-Imier	Watches	100
SA Longines pour la vente en Suisse, Saint-Imier	Distribution	100
Columna SA, Lausanne	Distribution	100
Longines (Singapore) PTE Ltd, Singapore (SIN)	Distribution	100
Longines (Malaysia) Sdn, Kuala Lumpur (MAL)	Distribution	100
Montres Rado SA, Lengnau	Watches	100
Tissot SA, Le Locie	Watches	100
Certina, Kurth Freres SA, Grenchen	Watches	100
Mido G. Schaeren & Co SA, Bienne	Watches	100
Mido industria e Comercio de Relogios Ltda, Rio de Janeiro (BRA)	Distribution	100
Swatch SA, Bienne	Watches	100
ETA SA Fabriques d'Ebauches, Grenchen	Watches, movements, electronic components and systems	100
ETA (Thailand) Co Ltd, Bangkok (THA)	Watches and movements	100
Leader Watch Case Co. Ltd. Bangkok (THA)	Watch cases	100
Endura SA, Bienne	Watches	100
Lascor SpA, Sesto Calende (ITA)	Watch cases	100
Diantus Watch SA, Castel San Pietro	Watches and movements	100
Société Européenne de Fabrication d'Ebauches d'Annemasse (SEFEA) SA, Annemasse (FRA)	Watch components and electronic assembly	100
Ruedin Georges SA, Bassecourt	Watch cases	100
EM Microelectronic-Marin SA, Marin	Microelectronics	100
SMH Italia S.p.A. Rozzano (ITA)	Distribution (Omega, Rado, Tissot, Swatch, Flik Flak)	100
SMH (UK) Ltd, Eastleigh (GBR)	Distribution (Omega, Tissot)	100
SMH Australia Ltd, Prahran (AUS)	Distribution (Omega, Tissot, Swatch, Flik Flak)	100
SMH Belgium SA, Bruxelles (BEL)	Distribution (Omega, Tissot, Flik Flak)	100
SMH Ireland Ltd, Dublin (IRL)	Distribution (Omega)	100
SMH Sweden AB, Stockholm (SWE)	Distribution (Omega, Longines, Tissot, Certina, Swatch, Flik Flak)	100
SMH Uhren und Mikroelektronik GmbH, Bad Soden (RFA)	Distribution (Omega, Longines, Rado, Tissot, Certina, Swatch, Flik Flak)	100

EXHIBIT 12 (cont.)
SMH Subsidiaries, 1990

SMH Swiss Corporation for Microelectronics and Watchmaking Industries Ltd. Neuchâtel (Holding Company)

Company Name, Registered Offices	*Field of Activity*	*Shareholding SMH Direct or Indirect, %*
SMH France SA, Paris (FRA)	Distribution (Omega, Longines, Rado, Tissot, Certina, Swatch, Flik Flak)	100
SMH España SA, Madrid (ESP)	Distribution (Omega, Tissot, Swatch, Flik Flak)	100
SMH Japan KK, Tokyo (JPN)	Distribution (Longines, Tissot, Swatch)	100
SMH (HK) Ltd. Hong Kong (HKG)	Distribution (ETA, Longines, Swatch, Flik Flak)	100
SMH (US) Inc., Dover Del. (USA)	Holding company	100
Hamilton Watch Co Inc., Lancaster Pa. (USA)	Distribution	100
Omega Watch Corp., New York N.Y. (USA)	Distribution	100
Rado Watch Co Inc., New York N.Y. (USA)	Distribution	100
Swatch Watch U.S.A. Inc., New York N.Y. (USA)	Distribution (Swatch, Flik Flak)	100
ETA Industries Inc., New York N.Y. (USA)	Distribution	100
Unitime Industries Inc., Virgin Islands V.I. (USA)	Assembly	100
Movomatic USA, Inc., Lancaster Pa. (USA)	Distribution (Movomatic, Farco)	100
Tissot (US), Inc., New York N.Y. (USA)	Distribution	100
Omega Electronics Equipment (US), Inc., Lancaster Pa. (USA)	Distribution	100
SMH (US) Services, Inc., Lancaster Pa. (USA)	Service, watches	100
Technocorp Holding SA, Le Locle	Holding	100
Renata SA, Itingen	Miniature batteries	100
Oscilloquartz SA, Neuchâtel	High stability frequency sources	100
OSA-France Sarl, Boulogne-Billancourt (FRA)	Distribution	100
Omega Electronics SA, Bienne	Sports timing equipment, score-board information systems	100
Omega Electronics Ltd, Eastleigh (GBR)	Distribution	100
Lasag SA, Thun	Laser for industrial and medical application	100
Lasag USA, Inc., Arlington Heights Ill. (USA)	Distribution	100
Technica SA, Grenchen	Machine tools and tools	100
Meseitron SA, Corceiles	High precision length measurement (Cary) and automatic size control (Movomatic)	100
Farco SA, Le Locle	Bonding equipment	100
Comadur SA, La Chaux-de-Fonds	Products in hard materials	100
Nivarox-FAR SA, Le Locle	Watch components and thin wires	100
A. Michel SA, Grenchen	Industrial components and delay systems	100
Regis Mainier SA, Bonnetage (FRA)	Precision and watch components	97.5
Vuillemin Marc, Bonnetage (FRA)	Precision and watch components	70.1
Chronometrage Suisse SA (Swiss Timing), Bienne	Sports timing	100
Asulab SA, Bienne	Research and development	100
ICB Ingenieurs Conseils en Brevets SA, Bienne	Patents	100
SMH Marketing Services SA, Bienne	Services and licenses	100

Finally, despite the success of the Swatch and of several mid-priced models under other brand names such as Tissot, the Swiss continued to experience higher than average unit prices for their watches. This was partially due to the success of their luxury mechanical watch pieces which were frequently encased in precious metal and adorned with precious stones. However, executives of Swiss companies expressed concern about this trend.

References

Bernheim, Ronnie A., *Koordination in zersplitterten Maerkten.* Berne, 1981: Paul Haupt Publ.

ETA S.A., "SWATCH. The Revolutionary New Technology." Company brochure.

Federation de l'industrie horlogere Suisse (Swiss Watchmanufacturers Federation), *Annual Reports,* 1983–1989, Bienne.

Heller Matthew, "Swatch Switches," *Forbes,* January 27, 1986, pp. 86–87.

Hieronymi, O. et al., *La diffusion de nouvelles technologies en Suisse.* Saint-Saphorin, 1983: Georgi.

Hill, Wilhelm, *Die Wettbewerbsstellung der schweizerischen Uhrenindustrie.* Report for the Swiss Federal Department of Economics. mimeo., Basle 1977.

Ludwig, Benoit D., "Innovation ist mehr als neue Produkte," *io Management-Zeitschrift,* no. 2 (1985), pp. 54–59.

Moynahan, Brian and Andreas Heumann, "The Man Who Made the Cuckoo Sing," *The Sunday Times Magazine,* August 18, 1985, pp. 23–25.

Mueller, Jacques and Elmar Mock, "Swatch. Eine Revolution in der Uhrentechnik," *Neue Zuercher Zeitung,* Fernausgabe Nr. 50, March 2, 1983.

Neue Zuercher Zeitung, various issues 1980–1990.

SMH Swiss Corporation for Microelectronics and Watchmaking Industries Ltd., Annual Reports 1984–1989.

Swiss American Review, "Swatch-Chef in Japan hat den Hut genommen," July 2, 1986, p. 9.

Thomke, Ernst, "In der Umsetzung von der Produktidee zur Marktreife liegt ein entscheidender Erfolgsfaktor," *io Management-Zeitschrift,* no. 2 (1985), pp. 60–64.

Union Bank of Switzerland, *The Swiss Watchmaking Industry.* USB Publications on Business, Banking and Monetary Topics No. 100, Zurich, March 1986.

CASE 23

FoodsPlus*

Mr. Julius Mwanza, Managing Director of FoodsPlus, was considering a proposal to re-organize the company. FoodsPlus was an African holding company that managed investments in six operating companies. Three years ago FoodsPlus had decentralized much of the management responsibility and control to the operating companies in order to reduce the influence of headquarters executives and to develop the local managers in the operating companies.

Decentralization had served its purpose, but Mr. Mwanza now was not certain it still was appropriate. He felt that the operating companies were running away and that he no longer had sufficient control. Although his role now was more as a strategist, evaluator and coordinator, he did not seem to be getting the information he needed to accomplish these tasks.

There were no standardized operating reports coming to him, but that bothered him less than the inter-company coordination situation. No one seemed to have information on, or to be in control of, the numerous inter-company transfers of raw materials, by-products or other transactions. All the operating companies wanted more capital, but he could not tell to where it should be allocated. Mr. Mwanza now wondered whether or not these companies were being managed effectively. Maybe it was time to re-centralize the whole corporation.

BACKGROUND

Prior to the creation of FoodsPlus, there had been one large company known as Premier Brands. Premier had been founded early in the colonial period by European and Indian businessmen to provide basic dietary foodstuffs: wheat and maize meal. Twenty years ago, Premier came to the financial aid of another company, Ace Bakeries Ltd., and shortly assumed control as majority owner. The acquisition was Premier's first major expansion. Several years later, because of the imminent retirement of some of the founders, controlling interest in Premier was sold to FoodsPlus which had been incorporated by local African businessmen.

FoodsPlus and Ace Bakeries both traded on the national stock exchange. However, effective majority control of all operating companies was held by FoodsPlus (see Exhibit 1). Each company was a separate legal entity with separate management teams, and separate (although with some overlap) boards of directors. The operating companies were all in the agro-processing and food industries.

The FoodsPlus group of companies faced numerous challenges inherent in African food and agro-processing industries. Many of the company's products were staple food

* Prepared by Research Associate Steven Cox under the direction of Professors Harry Lane and Roderick White.

EXHIBIT 1
FoodsPlus

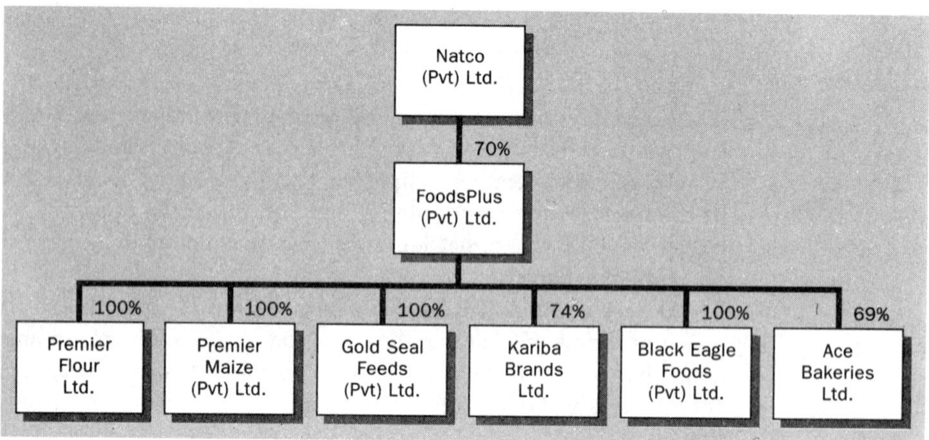

items and subject to rigorous government price control laws. Price controls were established on the raw materials, often its by-products, and the final product's selling price. These price control regulations affected the individual companies' costs and revenues, and were often cited by managers as the reasons for poor performance.

A continuing problem was shortages. Due to unpredictable weather, maize and wheat shortages occurred quite regularly. These commodities were controlled by the National Cereals Councils, which in turn sold them to processing companies. Many of FoodsPlus' products could become political in nature. When there were shortages, the politics became severe. Accusations of windfall profits and black marketing often were levelled at the companies. The government would step in with its own teams and closely supervise the allocation and distribution of cereals. One recent example highlights this problem. The government had purchased spoiled yellow maize. The maize contained a toxic fungus which if consumed could potentially harm humans. Very quickly, customers stopped buying maize as rumours circulated concerning its quality. One manager commented on the effect of shortages, "We lost good distributors. Some didn't come back to us." In times like these, Mr. Mwanza seemed to work continuously at managing relationships between FoodsPlus and organizations in its external environment—government, suppliers, and customers.

The Former System

Until recently FoodsPlus had expatriates in the top management positions and had operated with a centralized management system. FoodsPlus also had large investments in companies in neighboring countries but had lost most of these as a result of nationalization or during periods of social turmoil. Supervision of these companies across national borders had required the skills of an experienced executive group; and a centralized management system was needed to coordinate communication, co-operation, and resource sharing among the widely dispersed companies. The former Managing Director staffed the group office with other expatriates to oversee the operating companies. Mr. Mwanza commented:

> After independence most of the operating managers were new to their positions. Africans were finding their way into management jobs during the 1960s and 1970s, but because we lacked experience we required specialized assistance to perform effectively. The experienced advisors provided guidance and advice.

The centralized structure is shown in Exhibit 2. It had been set up so that the Group Managing Director headed an office of 14 senior executives. These 14 executives had functional responsibility for the operating companies, but only in an advisory capacity. Direct line responsibility was between the Group Managing Director, and the various General Managers of the operating companies. The centralized structure was designed to render assistance services, and FoodsPlus executive advisors had no power to implement policies, only to offer advice. FoodsPlus operated with its subsidiaries under revolving 10 year management agreements, whereby it earned a management fee of ½% of gross sales to cover its overhead.

This system began to fall apart. The nationalization of assets in neighboring countries took away much of the responsibility and work from the expatriate advisors. Although they supposedly had no implementation power, some tried to impose their authority. The Group Managing Director attempted to police this behavior and to minimize its occurrence. However, some operating company General Managers felt their authority was usurped by the advisory group. On occasion, an advisor would tell his counterpart in an operating company what to do without ever telling the General Manager. Conflict was common. One of the original advisors still working with one of the operating companies recalled the old system:

> We supervised the assets in four countries from headquarters. At times, it was frustrating. The turnover rate amongst government personnel in some of those countries

EXHIBIT 2
FoodsPlus, Centralized Management Structure, 1963–1983

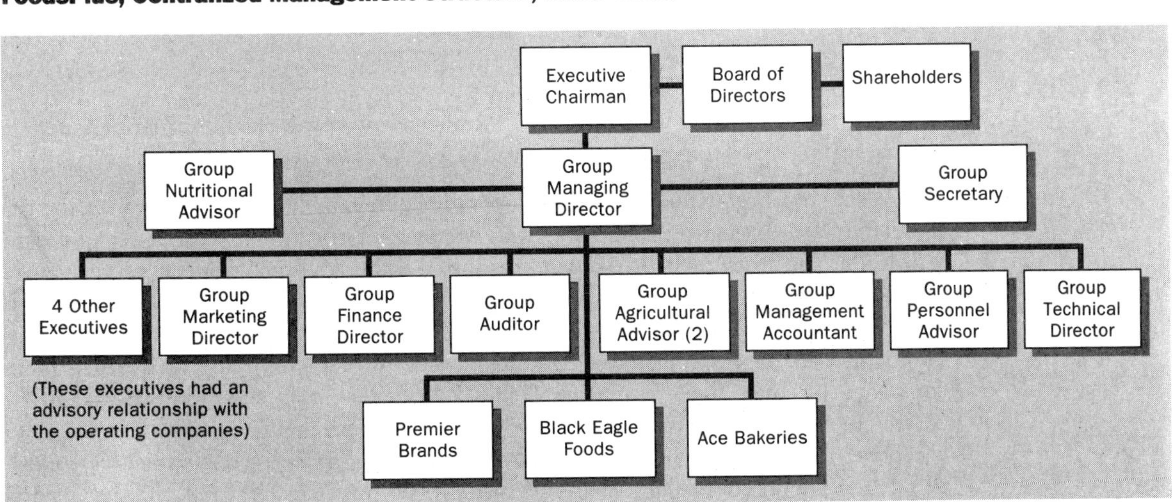

> was high—a Minister in the morning, a nobody after lunch. Also Group Advisors were expected to fill in for vacationing personnel at the subsidiary level in all the countries. There was frequent travel.
>
> In theory, we were supposed to communicate with our counterpart executives in the operating companies through the respective General Manager. In practice, this was difficult. We had to talk directly since the talk was often too technically detailed for the General Manager to understand. I suppose that is how a communications problem started.
>
> On routine technical and purchasing matters, our advice was usually taken. On controversial matters, that was another story. Controversy usually erupted over quality or pricing of by-products exchanged between the companies. In those days transfer prices were set at an agreed amount. Changes in these transfer prices were then related to the percentage change in the price of cereals. A 10% price increase in maize translated to a 10% increase in the maize by-product.

Under the centralized system, there were no formal performance evaluation systems in place, at either the holding company or operating company levels. Group Advisors and General Managers received their compensation increases from the Group Managing Director, and General Managers awarded increases to executives and staff at the operating company level.

Decentralization

Julius Mwanza began his career at Premier Brands and rose to the position of General Manager. He was the first Group Managing Director to be promoted to the holding company level from an operating company. Prior to his appointment, the group executives had been mostly expatriates. When Mr. Mwanza first took over, his impression was that there were roughly a dozen executives who did not have enough work and, who occupied themselves criticizing the existing system in place and causing unnecessary conflict. Since he had been General Manager of Premier Brands, and had experienced the problem first hand, he felt strongly that the system had to be changed in order to improve organizational effectiveness.

The Structure

> Under the old system we were over-centralized: too many chiefs, and not enough tribesmen. (Operating company executive)

This feeling had been widely held at the operating company level. Julius Mwanza and the FoodsPlus Board decided that a change was necessary. They announced a policy of decentralization, and disbanded the advisory group. All the advisory group executives were offered positions in the operating companies, and the practice of downward advice ended. They were promised that no one would lose their position or take a decrease in compensation as a result of the transition. Although, some former group advisors earned more compensation than their respective General Managers, this situation was gradually corrected. All of the secretarial staff also were moved with their respective former group executive. The management agreements in place with the operating companies were nullified. All of the Boards of the subsidiaries had outside Directors removed, and the General

Manager and Group Managing Director were installed together with an independent, outside Chairman. The operating companies were to be given independence and autonomy.

Prior to the decentralization, Premier Brands had become very large and was profitable. However, management did not know which of the 4 business areas profits were coming from (flour, maize, animal feeds, or food products); and whose performance was responsible for the profit. The company had grown too large and people did not have the time to pay attention to detailed operations. The solution was to split the company into 4 separate entities: Premier Flour, Premier Maize, Gold Seal Feeds (animal feeds), and Kariba Brands (consumer foodstuffs). Senior department managers at Premier were chosen to take charge of the new companies. The idea was to give these managers more responsibility and the time to manage smaller pieces of the company. The General Managers would now have increased operating responsibility and decision-making would be located closer to the action in operations. One of these individuals spoke of the change:

> My mandate was to make my division a viable entity. If it made money, FoodsPlus would keep it. Otherwise, they might sell it off. I was told to go in there and if I made the company lose less money I would be doing a good job. If I got it to break-even, that would be really good. If it made money, that would be outstanding. I was given the privilege of picking the ten best people from Premier to join my company with me.

For budgets and investment decisions, new executive committees (in operations, personnel, finance and marketing) were formed, composed of the functional executives from each of the companies. These committees were chaired by the Group Managing Director, and took over the functions formerly held by the advisory officers. Approval for capital decisions rested at the Board level of operating companies and then required ratification by the FoodsPlus Board. FoodsPlus' overhead was allocated approximately on the basis of company size and gross margins, not on the amount of FoodsPlus time or effort spent with the company.

Each company was responsible for preparing its own budgets for approval by FoodsPlus. General Managers forecast revenue and expenses, and set their profit budgets which went to the company board for initial approval.

The new decentralized organization was monitored through the following reporting systems:

1. All General Managers were required to submit a monthly written report to the Group Managing Director. This report presented an overall assessment on profitability, budget variances, and other company issues such as security. During the times of shortages, the General Managers reported once a week.

2. There was a monthly meeting of all General Managers with the Group Managing Director. The meeting discussed each of the subsidiaries and their current problems.

3. There was also a monthly meeting called the "finance and general purpose meeting." This was a meeting of the Group Managing Director and Group Financial Director with all of the senior executives of a subsidiary (General Manager, Production Manager, Finance Manager, Marketing Manager). These meetings discussed management

decisions specific to the subsidiary. Any capital asset that had to be bought, improved or demolished was discussed and decided upon and then referred to the Board of the subsidiary for approval.

Mr. Mwanza offered his views on the impact of change:

> The change was necessary and possible at that point because the subsidiary General Managers were experienced enough to operate on their own and their management teams didn't need advisors.
>
> However, 1983 was a very rough transitional year. The former Group Advisors still felt like group officers, and tried to behave the same way. They continued to take the major decisions to the Group Managing Director and "go over the head" of their respective General Managers. Although there were no serious power struggles, I had to bridge a lot of meetings. Most of the 14 former group executives quit soon after the decentralization was announced. As of now, only 4 former group executives remain within the organization, and all are at the operating company level. None have yet been promoted to the General Manager level.
>
> On intra-company pricing, my role is to act as the arbitrator to make sure the boys are not killing each other. If there is a dispute over pricing, we will hold a special meeting.

One of the original group advisors, now an executive at one of the operating subsidiaries, talked about the new system:

> When decentralization occurred, I was asked what position and title I wanted. My salary remained the same, and my salary and benefits were still paid by FoodsPlus, although this amount is crosscharged to the subsidiary company. I am classified as executive level. This distinction includes General Managers, Financial Managers, and some Marketing Managers.
>
> Now, in general terms, I report to the General Manager, since part of my function is to help the General Manager. I now have very limited contact with the Group Managing Director.

Performance Evaluation

There were two levels of management employees: the executive level and the graded management staff. Appraisals were only completed on a formal basis for the graded management staff in grades 4 (middle grade) through 8 (top grade). The appraisals were done by the Personnel Manager.

On the other hand, executive level employees (Production, Finance, Marketing, Personnel Managers) were responsible to the General Manager. One General Manager stated:

> I cannot evaluate them. All I can do is "devaluate" them. I can only say that a certain executive in the company is not doing his job. If I don't say anything, then they are assumed to be doing their job by the FoodsPlus Board.

Remuneration packages for executive level employees included a base salary, house, car, servants, security service, and substantial educational allowances for children.

Mr. Mwanza shared his perspective on performance evaluation in the new system.

> At present, there is no system for assessing the General Managers at the subsidiary company level. Basically, to date we have been surviving. It's very unfair to grade executives on corporate performance when most of the companies were just arbitrarily spun off from Premier Brands. They have no control over their raw material prices from the Cereal Councils.

A senior executive in one of the companies talked about his perception of performance evaluation.

> I am paid by FoodsPlus. The FoodsPlus Board determines my raises, but I have no idea how they are calculated. I don't even know that the increases have any relationship to performance. You just know if you are not performing—you'll be asked to leave.
>
> The most rewarding thing I get is when the auditors have signed the accounts and I have shown a contribution to FoodsPlus and the Board says thanks to us for getting their books done on time and operating within budget.

One former Group Advisor had not noticed a change in performance evaluation with the new system. "I have no idea how performance is assessed. My budgets are always approved without change. My annual salary review is signed by Julius Mwanza. I guess that means I am doing good work."

THE OPERATING COMPANIES

A brief description of each of the operating subsidiary companies' activities follows.

Premier Flour

Premier was the country's largest wheat milling company and had a 74% market share. Although market demand was relatively stable, wheat supply was unstable because of unpredictable drought and pestilence problems. Since bread was one of the country's major staple foods, it was strictly price controlled. Decisions on flour pricing, quality and distribution were very sensitive. Premier had rebounded from recent losses in a year of drought, and exhibited minor liquidity problems. Premier sold 54% of its annual flour production to a sister company, Ace Bakeries, at a small discount from "market price"[1] for bulk purchases. It also sold its entire by-product supply of wheat bran to another sister company, Gold Seal Feeds.

Premier Maize

Premier Maize was newly created from the breakup of Premier Brands. Its primary business was production of another staple food—maize meal, and it held a 60% market share. The maize was milled to produce maize meal (83%), maize bran (7%) and maize germ (9%). Maize meal was price controlled. Its production and prices were scrutinized closely

[1] Market price was defined as the price that a FoodsPlus subsidiary would receive from another non-related company, for both final products and by-products.

by politicians and the public, and this pressure had led to very small profit margins. Although profit margins were low, volumes were high. Premier Maize had just gone ten months without operating because of a drought and the resulting maize shortage, but still had managed to earn a profit. At full capacity, this company was expected to be very profitable. It sold maize bran to a sister company, Gold Seal Feeds, at roughly 65% below its market price. Another by-product, maize germ, was sold to Black Eagle Foods, for extraction of refined cooking oil.

Gold Seal Feeds

Gold Seal, founded two years ago, was the largest animal feeds company in the country. Its final products were not price controlled. In addition, Gold Seal produced animal veterinary products and mineral supplements. Most of its raw materials were by-products from sister companies' processes. These by-products were not price controlled. It purchased 100% of its wheat bran from Premier Flour at prices 16–18% below market price, 100% of its maize bran from Premier Maize at prices 65% below market price, and 100% of its maize cake from Black Eagle Foods. Gold Seal had the greatest return on capital largely because it benefited most from low intra-group prices. It also had a low equity base (mostly loans from other companies with low payback terms). In the view of FoodsPlus management, Gold Seal had outstanding long-term growth potential.

Kariba Brands

Kariba Brands started operations at the same time as Gold Seal, and was the smallest company in the group. It produced breakfast cereals, pet foods, animal feeds, sausage filler and other consumer food products. It also acted as distributor of Black Eagle oil, produced by its sister company. It purchased at a discount all of Ace Bakeries stale bread for use in its animal feeds. It also was viewed as having very good potential for growth and increased profits.

Black Eagle Foods

Originally a joint venture with a European businessman, Black Eagle was one of the older companies in the group. It produced spaghetti and other pastas, and edible corn oil products. Corn oil products were especially sensitive to price control and increases required approval. A recent price increase application had taken 4 years to get approved. Black Eagle purchased 100% of its maize germ needs from Premier Maize at prices 45% of market price, and sold all of its maize cake to Gold Seal Feeds at prices 52% less than market price.

Ace Bakeries

Ace was a long established company, acquired by Premier in 1960. It was the country's largest bakery. Although its market share hovered around 50%, there had been a steady decline over the decade. Ace produced only one product—a 500 gram loaf of bread. It had very small margins, and was closely price controlled. Its performance was highly dependent on selling large volumes of bread and operating economies of scale. Ace bought 100% of its wheat requirement from Premier Flour at bulk discount rates and sold all of its stale

EXHIBIT 3
FoodsPlus (Pvt.) Ltd., Flow of Products and By-Products

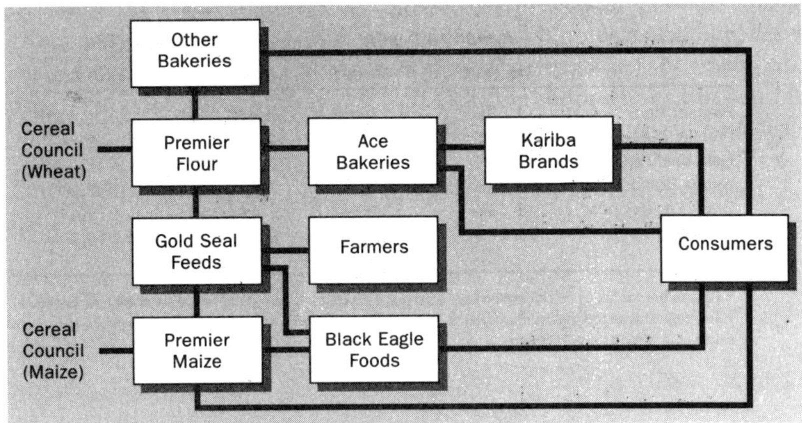

bread to Kariba at discounted rates. Ace's falling market share was a source of concern to the management of FoodsPlus.

Inter-Company Transfers

FoodsPlus operating companies sold numerous final products and by-products between themselves. A flow chart indicating the flow of products and by-products between subsidiary companies can be found in Exhibit 3, and a chart indicating which products were price controlled can be found in Exhibit 4. A summary of each company's financial performance is listed in Exhibit 5.

An important issue that FoodsPlus faced was intra-group pricing. The General Man-

EXHIBIT 4
FoodsPlus, Scope of Price Controls

	Price Controlled	Not Subject to Price Controls		
Company	**Final Products**	**Final Products**	**By-Products Sold**	**By-Products Purchased**
Premier Flour (PF)	Flour		Wheat bran to GSF	
Premier Maize (PM)	Maize meal		Maize bran to GSF Maize germ to BE	
Gold Seal Feeds (GSF)		Animal feeds Animal veterinary products Mineral supplements		Wheat bran from PF Maize bran from PM Maize cake from BE Stale bread from Ace
Kariba Brands (KB)	Black Eagle corn oil (distribution)	Breakfast cereals Pet foods Animal feeds Sausage filler Other consumer food products		
Black Eagle (BE)	Black Eagle corn oil	Spaghetti, pastas	Maize cake to GSF	Maize germ from PM
Ace Bakeries	Bread		Stale bread to KB	

EXHIBIT 5
FoodsPlus, Subsidiaries Performance

	Return on Capital		Profits after Tax		Gross Margin	Current Ratio
	This Year	Year Ago	This Year	Year Ago	This Year	Year Ago
Premier Flour	11.53%	– 1.24%*	25,372,440	(2,731,420)*	13.6%	0.73
Premier Maize	25.50%	n/a*	12,438,120	n/a*	8.9%	1.45
Gold Seal Feeds†	71.28%	17.86%*	3,777,860	946,320*	13.1%	1.00
Kariba Brands	1.85%	– 12.30%*	46,760	(309,840)*	16.6%	0.97
Black Eagle Foods	9.18%	11.90%	447,140	579,440	9.8%	1.32
Ace Bakeries	11.17%	45.30%	3,825,860	15,519,180	7.2%	1.00

* Figures are for seven month period only from the date of the breakup of Premier into the four separate entities.
† The capital invested in Gold Seal was low, and a long term loan, which was not being repaid, was regarded as quasi-equity. This inclusion would reduce the ROC figures.

agers were responsible for setting the price of their by-products. The operating companies sold significant products and by-products amongst each other, at prices that ranged from market value (commercial prices) to as little as 35% of market value (preferential prices). Given that most sales were at preferential prices, it was difficult for FoodsPlus to accurately assess financial performance of the various group companies. Intra-group pricing methods were based on the two following methods:

1. The negotiation method normally produced a contract between two companies. Some of these contracts had been in place for long periods of time. Prices were below market prices and were now in need of revision. These supply contracts set forth prices, quantities, mode of transportation and costs of transportation. If agreement could not be achieved then the directive method had to be used.

2. The group directive method was used in cases where an operating company requested a raw material pricing assistance. For instance, in a case where Premier Flour applied for a price increase from FoodsPlus for by-products sold to Gold Seal Feeds, Gold Seal might be able to persuade FoodsPlus not to approve the increase.

A NEW ORGANIZATIONAL STRUCTURE?

In assessing the decentralized system, Mr. Mwanza worried that the change had led to too much General Manager independence, and that maybe FoodsPlus was too removed from its investments. He was aware of the serious implications that yet another organizational change might have, but he wanted to come up with a structure that would operate smoothly, and yet still allow him to monitor the overall corporate performance on behalf of the FoodsPlus Board of Directors. He was having difficulty keeping track of all the company data that he was receiving and would probably need new staff to assist him. He wanted to improve communications and synergy across the various operating companies —in marketing, finance, production, and planning. Mr. Mwanza did not want to return to the bygone days of advisors; instead, co-ordinators or administrators might be a better head office group. But, what would ensure that a repetition of the earlier dissatisfaction with a centralized system would not occur again?

Mr. Mwanza also wanted to formulate a policy on price control management, intra-group pricing, budgeting, capital investment, and long-term planning. FoodsPlus had long desired to diversify into new business ventures, but lacked the organizational system to plan for them. A recent foray into real estate development had in Mr. Mwanza's words "taken a few years off my life." What industries should be investigated, and should the new business ventures be mergers, acquisitions, or new startups? Would it be better to shift emphasis out of price controlled foods, or was FoodsPlus management too specialized in food-related industries?

CASE 24

From Airline to Empire: United Airlines under Richard Ferris*

Richard Ferris, Chairman and Chief Executive Officer of Allegis Corporation, arrived in New York on June 9, 1987, to attend another in a series of meetings with the board of directors. This one had been hastily called by Charles Luce, the board's senior member. Ferris was prepared to discuss flaws that had appeared in Allegis' defenses against a hostile takeover. Several groups had emerged as threats to Allegis: the pilots of United Air Lines (Allegis' airline subsidiary), Coniston Partners (an investment firm that owned 13% of Allegis' stock), and a group of large institutional investors that were dissatisfied with the firm's stock price performance. Ferris planned to meet the next day with some of these investors to try to regain their support. He would never get the chance.

Less than two months previously, Luce had written the *Wall Street Journal*, pledging the board's support for Ferris' total travel company strategy. As this meeting started, Ferris realized that things had changed. Some of the directors openly criticized his strategy and takeover defenses. When Luce joined them, Ferris knew that his strategy was doomed.

The directors had a final offer for Ferris. If he would divest the non-airline divisions and concentrate on United's affairs, he could remain as Chairman and CEO. That was unacceptable. Rather than abandon the fly-drive-sleep concept that he believed would revolutionize the travel industry, Richard Ferris resigned.

THE AIRLINE INDUSTRY—DEREGULATION

The decade prior to 1987 had been one of significant change within the airline industry. Before 1978, the industry was tightly regulated by the Civil Aeronautics Board (CAB). CAB approval was required for any changes in routes or even significant adjustments in fares. The review process was a long and costly one for the applicants. However, the passage of the Airline Deregulation Act of 1978 was the first step in the process of deregulating the industry. This legislation was the federal government's first attempt in decades to deregulate an entire industry.[1] The target date for ending all regulation of carriers' route structures was 1981.

During the mid-1970s government regulation of industry had come under increasing criticism. Most airline executives, however, strongly opposed deregulation, even though the CAB sharply limited their flexibility.[2] Their rationale was simple—restricted competition on certain routes served to protect inefficient carriers. Deregulation would end monopolies, force increased price competition and lead to poorer financial performance.[3] One

---

* Prepared by Assistant Professor Gary E. Willard and Research Assistants David Krueger and Tim Schoenecker. Distributed by the North American Case Research Association.

[1] *Fortune,* November 20, 1978.

[2] *Forbes,* August 15, 1977.

[3] *Fortune,* November 20, 1978.

EXHIBIT 1
Routes Added by United Airlines, 1978–1979

Note: United flew into all cities shown in 1979. The arcs represent routes added after deregulation.

airline executive who favored deregulation was Richard Ferris. He told the *Wall Street Journal,* "Deregulation will be the greatest thing to happen to airlines since the jet engine."[4]

Response to deregulation by most of the major carriers was similar. Short, low profit routes to smaller cities were abandoned as the major airlines focused on longer routes between larger markets. United was a leader in this move toward consolidation, adding more flights from its "hubs" (airline terminology for a carrier's key airport in a geographic region) in Chicago and Denver while eliminating service to many smaller cities.[5] (See Exhibit 1 for new routes added by United Airlines in 1978 and 1979.) However, the major airlines found that an unexpected result of this tactic was that it "opened the door" to new airlines building their customer base from these smaller markets. It also put at risk the airlines' traditional "hub and spoke" strategy, since many of the discontinued routes had served to feed travelers into major hubs. By reducing their overall networks, the majors inadvertently gave passengers more freedom in choosing an airline.

Deregulation did have its intended effect on fares. Increased competition among the major carriers and the emergence of low-cost carriers like People Express and Britt led to

[4] *Wall Street Journal,* March 2, 1979.
[5] *Business Week,* August 18, 1980.

EXHIBIT 2
Airline Industry Performance

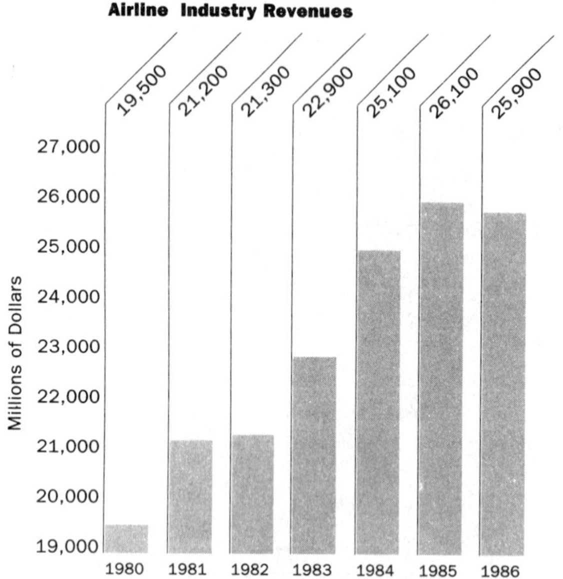

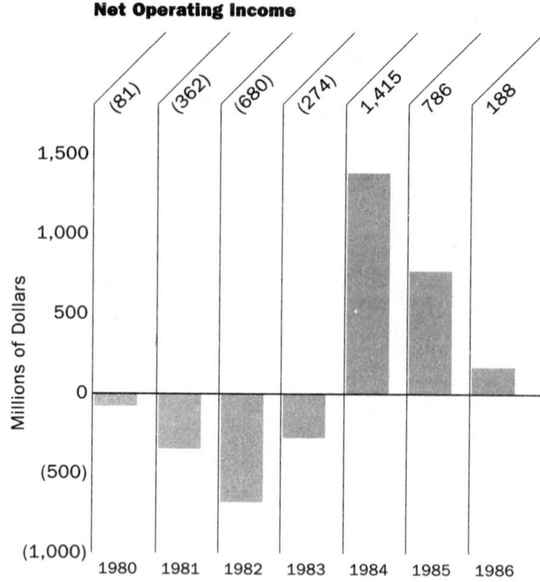

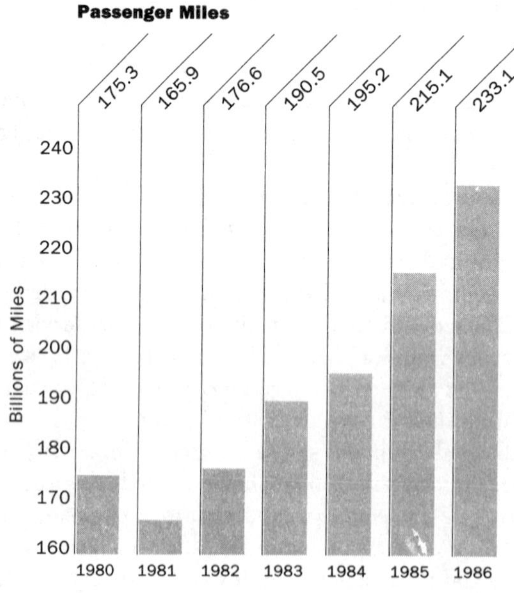

heavy discounting and price wars. This period saw the development of "super-saver" fares (discounts of up to 50%) as well as other pricing innovations. The airline industry changed from one that had competed primarily on service to one that competed on price.

The financial performance of the airlines in the years after deregulation made Ferris' rosy prediction seem foolish. In 1981, the industry registered a record $362 million in operating losses (see Exhibit 2). This was surpassed the following year when nearly $700 million in operating losses were recorded. Approximately 18,000 workers were laid off during these two years. It would be unfair to place the blame for all of this red ink on deregulation, however. Concurrent with the fare wars was a general slowdown in the nation's economy and a strike by the Professional Air Traffic Controllers Organization (PATCO). This and the subsequent firing of the PATCO strikers by President Reagan sharply reduced the capacity of the air traffic system. The airlines were forced to cancel many flights.

THE AIRLINE INDUSTRY—LATER DEVELOPMENTS

The airline industry's performance improved significantly after the hard times of those transition years. In 1984, the industry posted a record $1.4 billion in operating profits, although profits declined in 1985 and 1986. Revenue passenger miles grew throughout the mid-1980s with a 33% overall gain from 1980 to 1986. Passenger load factors (the percentage of seats filled), a key to profitability, climbed to 61% in 1986 from a low of 57% in 1981.[6] Finally, a decline of nearly 20% in fuel prices between 1981 and 1985 eased the upward pressure on a major component of operating costs.[7]

When deregulation was first instituted, some observers predicted consolidation to a maximum of seven primary carriers.[8] Consolidation became the trend as several carriers merged or were acquired by others. For example, Texas Air transformed itself from a regional carrier into a megacarrier by acquiring Continental, Eastern and People Express.

Throughout the 1980s, the development and use of computerized travel registration systems became increasingly important. Each of the five largest carriers had its own system (Northwest and TWA shared one) with American's Sabre and United's Apollo being the largest. These systems were not only marketing and distribution tools, they also generated revenue since airlines pay for tickets reserved on a competitor's system. This revenue could be significant. American's Sabre system produced revenues of over $400 million in 1986,[9] nearly 7% of parent AMR's total revenue.

The result of the changes in the market during the decade was the consolidation that the experts had predicted. Over 70% of the market was now concentrated among the top five carriers (see Exhibit 3). Brief sketches of United's top competitors follow:

Texas Air: Through aggressive acquisition tactics focused solely on the air transportation industry, Texas Air became the largest airline (in terms of revenue passenger

[6] Standard and Poor's, *Industry Surveys,* October 1987.

[7] UAL Annual Report, 1986.

[8] *Air Transport World,* July 1977.

[9] *Fortune,* May 11, 1987.

EXHIBIT 3
Airline Industry Competition, 1986
Selected Data on the Top 5 Domestic Carriers
(All Numbers in Millions)

Airline	Market Share*	Revenue Pass Miles	Passenger Revenues	Operating Income	Labor Costs As % of Rev.	Number of Employees	Major Hubs
Texas Air	20.0%	66,300	$4,030	$237	0.32	68,000†	Denver, Houston, Miami, Newark
United	17.9%	59,300	$5,960	$407	0.43	87,000†	Chicago, Denver, San Francisco, D.C.
American	14.7%	48,800	$4,960	$392	0.41	54,300	Dallas, Chicago, Nashville
Delta	9.6%	31,800	$4,200	$237	0.47	38,901	Atlanta, Dallas, Salt Lake City
Northwest	8.7%	28,800	$2,920	$167	0.35	33,427	Detroit, Memphis, Minneapolis

* Based on revenue passenger miles.
† Average number of employees for the year. All others are the number of employees at year end.

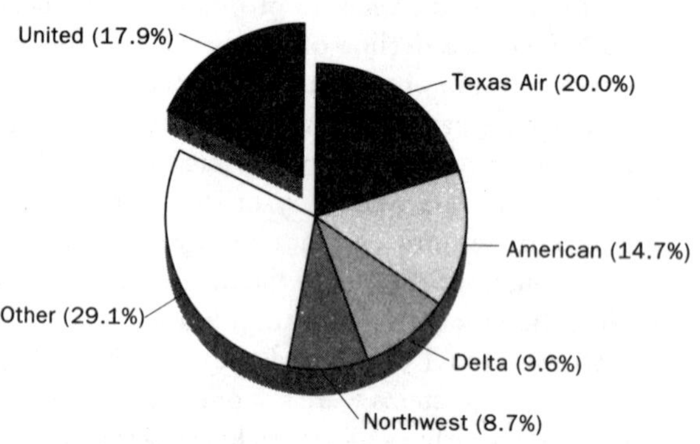

miles) in the United States. It was divided into two divisions—Continental (which included Frontier and People Express) and Eastern. The Continental division was non-union and noted for its low costs. Texas Air experienced problems integrating Eastern into its corporate structure, primarily because it was unionized.

American: American Airlines was known as an innovator in the industry. It pioneered the price war tactic of "super-saver" fares as well as the two-tiered wage scale (discussed later) as a way to control labor costs. American had the highest operating income of the top five, 7.9% of revenues. American relied on internal growth for expansion, acquiring only one regional carrier, Air Cal, during this period. American was the largest subsidiary of its parent corporation, AMR, accounting for approximately 88% of AMR's revenues in 1986.

Delta: Delta was traditionally strong in the southeast; it controlled a majority of the traffic at Atlanta's huge Hartsfield Airport. Its acquisition of Western Airlines gave Delta a new and strong presence in the west. This airline had a reputation for high quality service as well as high profits, however, in 1986 it had the lowest return on sales of the major carriers. Some thought that this was the result of its labor costs which were the industry's highest even though it was non-union. Delta was virtually undiversified in 1986; only 2% of its revenues were generated from non-airline business.

Northwest: From its hubs in Minneapolis, Detroit and Memphis, the Northwest/Republic team moved from a strong regional carrier to a major player in the industry with a 9% market share. Much of its strength lay in its Pacific routes and well integrated feeder network. Northwest also had moderate labor costs in comparison with its rivals. Northwest was the major subsidiary of NWA. Northwest's passenger revenues accounted for 81% and its freight revenues 14% of parent NWA's revenues in 1986.

UNITED AIRLINES—BEFORE DIVERSIFICATION

The idea of airlines owning hotel chains did not begin with UAL. In 1946, Pan American initiated the trend with its Intercontinental Hotel subsidiary. TWA followed by acquiring Hilton International in 1967, American Airlines had its Flagship Hotels, and Braniff owned a group of hotels in Latin America. This diversification was more than just a sideline. It was an important source of earnings intended to offset the cyclical nature of the airline industry.

United Airlines was the last major airline to follow suit with its 1970 acquisition of Western International, a hotel chain that outranked all but Sheraton and Hilton (U.S.) in the number of rooms available. For $82 million in stock, United acquired 71 major hotels in 13 countries, approximately one half in cities served by United. United also acquired two Western International executives, Edward Carlson and Richard Ferris, who would play significant roles in the operation of the airline.

However, 1970 was not a good year for United. The airline suffered a $46 million loss, its worst ever. A recession, new competition on its Hawaii and California routes and the cost of financing a large fleet of jumbo jets combined to squeeze United.

Shortly before the end of 1970, United's outside directors felt that CEO George Keck was not moving aggressively enough to solve the airline's problems. A bitter boardroom struggle ended when Keck, aloof and introverted, resigned and was replaced by Carlson. Carlson's lack of airline experience led United's employees to joke that he was going to ground all the 747s and make them into hotels.

Carlson promptly canceled all orders for jets, eliminated 300 of United's 1,800 daily flights, reorganized and decentralized the company's management, and cut the number of employees by 9%. These actions helped turn United around and the company suffered only a small loss in 1971 and was profitable again in 1972.

UAL's next diversification move was in 1975. Carlson acquired GAB Business Services, a small ($100 million) but profitable insurance business.

UNITED AIRLINES—RICHARD FERRIS

Richard Ferris traveled an unusual route to the helm of United Airlines and Allegis. After graduating from Cornell University's hotel management program in 1962, he went to work for Western International (later Westin) Hotels. Ferris quickly moved up the corporate ladder, managing hotels domestically and overseas. When Carlson was named CEO of Western's new parent, Ferris followed him to the airline and became the head of United's food service division. "Here was an industry being managed by the federal government through regulation," Ferris said, "I thought that it would be stifling."[10]

Ferris' next job at United was Vice President of Marketing. Then, in 1974, Carlson named Ferris president while he remained chairman and CEO. Industry observers were surprised at Ferris' selection, since he had never held an operating position in the airline before taking over.[11] This, plus his background in hotels made Ferris somewhat of an outsider in the close-knit airline industry. After two years as president, he became CEO of United and in 1979 he replaced Carlson as chairman of UAL, Inc., the holding company.

To overcome his lack of experience in the airline industry, Ferris placed heavy emphasis on employee relations during his early days as president. He traveled extensively to cities served by United, meeting with employees and discussing their problems. He was often a cockpit companion of the pilots during flights. He even obtained a pilot's license to increase his rapport with the pilots. But he would need more than just flying skills to guide United through the turbulent skies that lay ahead.

United under Ferris

United remained profitable for most of the decade, registering record operating earnings of $296 million in 1978. But, as Carlson stepped aside in 1979, Ferris faced a stormy introduction. Starting with an operating loss of $235 million that year, the airline lost half a billion dollars in Ferris' first three and one half years as Chairman of UAL, Inc. (see Exhibit 4).

The losses were the result of several factors:

1. Deregulation (discussed earlier).
2. A long strike by the International Association of Machinists; they rejected two pacts endorsed by their leaders before finally settling the strike.
3. A DC-10 flown by American Airlines crashed and all such aircraft were subsequently grounded. United, with 38 of these planes, was deprived of more than one-third of its long haul capacity.
4. The PATCO strike severely limited the capacity at Chicago's O'Hare Field. Since one-third of United's revenues flowed through this airport, the effect on United was severe.

Ferris responded by cutting costs. The number of employees dropped from 54,500 in 1979 to 42,500 by the summer of 1982. The company negotiated a new contract in 1982

[10] *Wall Street Journal,* March 2, 1979.
[11] *Wall Street Journal,* March 2, 1979.

EXHIBIT 4a
UAL, Inc.: Consolidated Balance Sheets
As of December 31
(in Thousands of Dollars)

	1979	1980	1981	1982	1983	1984	1985	1986	1987
Assets:									
Cash & cash equivalents	$355,121	$318,923	$194,621	$308,801	$292,146	$442,230	$750,511	$218,144	$2,208,016
Receivables	565,272	605,219	593,222	599,408	766,800	721,479	933,716	1,100,609	816,547
Prepaid expenses	232,606	285,832	180,787	165,928	194,835	262,502	307,652	390,171	402,455
Refundable taxes	11,051	2,556	0	0	0	0	78,163	61,118	0
Rental automobiles	0	0	0	0	0	0	1,019,418	1,378,468	0
Total current assets	1,164,050	1,212,530	968,630	1,074,137	1,253,781	1,426,211	3,089,460	3,148,510	3,427,018
Net assets of									
discontinued operations (A):									426,747
Owned equipment	4,017,495	4,085,781	4,453,980	5,120,131	5,718,546	5,891,084	6,829,915	7,672,264	7,214,028
Leased equipment	820,986	886,931	959,542	921,627	917,676	823,418	725,146	666,977	643,134
Accumulated depreciation	(2,258,137)	(2,300,283)	(2,581,767)	(2,785,527)	(2,983,258)	(3,171,040)	(3,439,077)	(3,650,639)	(3,851,278)
Net equipment	2,580,344	2,672,429	2,831,755	3,256,231	3,652,964	3,543,462	4,115,984	4,688,602	4,005,884
Other assets	118,055	156,499	175,392	248,526	226,898	189,369	668,775	879,405	366,620
Total assets	$3,862,449	$4,041,458	$3,975,777	$4,578,894	$5,133,643	$5,159,042	$7,874,219	$8,716,517	$8,226,269
Current liabilities:									
Short term borrowings	$	$152,192	$178,704	$75,985	$187,940	$297,518	$602,912	$987,819	$1,010,311
Current portion of LTD	102,114	105,247	116,406	84,672	130,585	81,525	409,164	146,938	47,198
Advance ticket sales	360,812	396,680	358,731	352,181	453,232	432,979	432,782	561,322	581,333
Accounts payable	699,690	752,832	813,989	945,267	1,152,024	1,059,241	1,451,411	1,857,303	496,216
Accrued/deferred taxes	13,840	23,409	22,005	8,482	10,455	80,390	76,951	207,285	1,274,803
Total current liabilities	1,176,456	1,430,360	1,489,835	1,466,587	1,934,236	1,951,653	2,973,220	3,760,667	3,409,861
Long term debt	1,234,291	1,176,086	1,181,346	1,794,899	1,311,267	986,803	2,642,234	2,066,008	1,427,295
Deferred taxes & other liabilities	294,219	264,737	204,131	196,452	290,795	326,373	465,552	593,734	464,005
Shareholders' equity:									
Preferred stock	9,532	8,850	8,441	8,038	200,737	251,296	234,345	3,498	3,021
Common stock	147,578	147,598	147,925	148,049	172,423	173,974	176,566	251,118	292,354
Paid in capital	419,290	419,507	420,677	421,100	555,427	560,456	578,258	1,260,595	1,678,306
Retained earnings	583,201	596,438	525,540	545,887	670,876	908,821	804,378	781,231	1,073,760
Treasury stock	(2,118)	(2,118)	(2,118)	(2,118)	(2,118)	(334)	(334)	(334)	(122,333)
Total equity	1,157,483	1,170,275	1,100,465	1,120,956	1,597,345	1,894,213	1,793,213	2,296,108	2,925,108
Total liabilities and shareholders' equity	$3,862,449	$4,041,458	$3,975,777	$4,578,894	$5,133,643	$5,159,042	$7,874,219	$8,716,517	$8,226,269

(A) Consists primarily of the Westin Hotels sold January 31, 1988 for $1,350.
Source: Company annual reports.

EXHIBIT 4b

UAL, Inc.: Consolidated Income Statements
Years Ended December 31
(In Thousands of Dollars)

	1979	*1980*	*1981*	*1982*	*1983*	*1984*	*1985*	*1986*	*1987*
Operating revenues	$3,831,523	$5,041,335	$5,141,174	$5,319,709	$6,021,840	$6,967,599	$6,383,405	$9,196,233	$11,013,028 (A)
Operating expenses:									
Aircraft fuel	804,380	1,342,529	1,346,205	1,289,577	1,266,700	1,368,099	1,143,568	1,099,441	(B)
Depreciation	283,061	305,102	315,509	368,124	411,324	445,623	540,648	781,938	
SG&A	609,769	740,347	851,371	956,332	1,082,922	1,224,598	1,247,342	1,853,350	
Other	2,295,094	2,635,448	2,706,100	2,715,064	3,044,577	3,285,953	3,555,270	5,054,305	
Total expenses	3,992,304	5,023,426	5,219,185	5,329,097	5,805,523	6,324,273	6,486,828	8,789,034	10,501,727
Operating income (loss)	(160,781)	17,909	(78,011)	(9,388)	216,317	643,326	(103,423)	407,199	511,301
Interest expense	79,725	105,746	116,218	168,766	171,401	142,620	213,793	318,968	
Other income/(expense)	54,792	92,045	46,699	187,916	202,729	2,382	222,133	2,069	(365,722)
Income before taxes	(185,714)	4,208	(147,530)	9,762	247,645	503,088	(95,083)	90,300	145,579
Income taxes	(112,900)	(16,800)	(77,000)	(21,000)	105,600	220,700	(46,400)	78,700	80,956
Gain on sale of discontinued operations, net of income taxes:									270,494
Net income (loss)	(72,814)	21,008	(70,530)	30,762	142,045	282,388	(48,683)	11,600	335,117

(A) Allegis changed the manner in which they reported in 1987. The information shown is the only comparable information publicly available.
(B) Aircraft fuel expense was $1,243,579 in 1987.
Source: Company annual reports.

EXHIBIT 4c
UAL, Inc.: Selected Segment Information
Years Ended December 31
(in Thousands of Dollars)

	1979	*1980*	*1981*	*1982*	*1983*	*1984*	*1985*	*1986*	*1987*
Airline:									
Revenues	$3,295,278	$4,458,832	$4,541,668	$4,695,294	$5,372,774	$6,218,720	$5,291,609	$7,105,141	$8,292,790
Operating profit	(235,390)	(65,558)	(148,819)	(66,748)	160,097	564,130	(242,656)	73,281	231,248
Hotels:									
Revenues	383,740	425,921	454,378	462,086	485,284	556,504	503,833	491,566	N/A
Operating profit	63,790	72,591	74,634	58,631	52,239	69,398	63,414	54,980	N/A
Hertz (A):									
Revenues							496,506	1,599,526	N/A
Operating profit							75,836	278,938	N/A
Business services (B):									
Revenues	152,505	145,128	156,582	162,329	163,782	192,375	91,457		
Operating profit	10,819	10,876	(3,826)	(1,271)	3,981	9,798	(17)		

(A) Four months in 1985.
(B) Six months in 1985.
Note: Hertz was sold December 30, 1987 for $1,300; Hilton International on October 14, 1987 for $1,070; Westin Hotels in January, 1988 for $1,300.
Source: Company annual reports.

with its 4,500 pilots, improving work rules in exchange for a no-layoff guarantee. For example, the new rules cut the cockpit costs of a Boeing 737 by 37%, from $430 to $270 per hour. Ferris also delayed shipment of twenty 767s on order. The situation began to turn around during the second half of 1982. After a disastrous first half, the consolidated operating loss for the full year was a modest $9 million.

By May of 1985, United's turnaround was complete and the picture so rosy that *Business Week* featured Ferris as the chief executive officer who returned shareholders the most for the pay received. In the same article, *Business Week* noted that UAL was the subject of leveraged buyout speculation. Fueling this speculation was the price of UAL's stock. It closed on May 1 nearly 15% below its book value of $47 per share.

In an attempt to enhance UAL's market value, Ferris sought additional productivity gains and wage concessions from the pilots' union. He felt that such concessions were necessary if the company was to compete with the new low cost, no frills airlines such as People Express. A two-tier pay proposal for pilots became the focal point of the negotiations.

United proposed hiring new pilots at a scale 40% below that of its 6,000 existing pilots. The lower scale would exist for the first 20 years of service by which time the pilots should have attained the rank of captain. New hires would also receive fewer fringe benefits, different work rules and smaller pensions. Worried about the effects that this proposal might have on other airlines, the ALPA (the pilots' union) called a strike in May 1987. The walkout was strongly supported by the union membership. Of approximately 6,000 pilots, only 250 plus a handful of trainees crossed the picket lines. United's flight schedule was reduced by more than 85%.

In an attempt to keep the airline going, United recruited pilots away from other airlines by offering comparatively high wages and flexible working hours. United also announced that all of the trainee pilots who supported the strike would not be reinstated. These actions quickly became the focus of the strike as an agreement was reached on the two-tier wage plan. The ALPA was adamant that the trainees be reinstated and that the recently recruited pilots be made subject to the new wage agreement. These were important to the ALPA since losing on these points would damage its ability to successfully organize strikes in the future. Ferris was unyielding on these issues as well. He stated "We would never forsake those who kept this airline going during the work stoppage. That is the word of this corporation and it is worth something." [12]

After 29 days the union agreed to end the strike. A modified two-tier wage system was instituted and the issues regarding the trainees and recently recruited pilots were to be taken to an arbitrator. While the airline was successful in obtaining the right to implement the new wage system, the strike cut deeply into operating revenues. It caused an estimated $92 million loss in the second quarter of 1985 and decreased revenues for the rest of the year as the company ran a series of promotions, such as half-fare coupons, doubling frequent flyer mileage credits, and reducing advance purchase requirements to regain lost market share.

---

[12] *Business Week,* June 10, 1985.

UNITED AIRLINES DIVERSIFICATION—HERTZ

The same day United was outlining these promotions to the press, UAL announced that it was acquiring Hertz from RCA for $587.5 million. Originally, RCA had asked $700 million but Ferris' team had negotiated a 16% reduction. Ferris claimed that Hertz was a natural addition to UAL's portfolio. He pointed out that 80% of all car rentals relate to an airline trip. Hertz was the undisputed leader in its industry with a 33% market share (although that was a decrease from its 42% share of 1975). The company, with 4,500 locations, rented a car every two minutes somewhere in the 122 countries in which it operated.

The business press raised questions regarding UAL's choice of industries in which to diversify. These concerns included:

1. The common cyclical swings of the two industries as the result of cars being rented in connection with air travel. In response to this criticism, UAL director Andrew Brimmer, a Washington-based economic consultant, said "Certainly the Hertz business will add some cyclical component to earnings, but this will be offset by added cash flow. We think the return on investment will justify the purchase." [13]
2. The car rental industry's overcapacity. The industry was in its second price war in three years. A senior vice president for marketing at Hertz stated "We are signing contracts at rates lower than we have since 1978." [14]
3. The policy of corporate discounting. Corporate discounting was the opposite of the airlines' philosophy where discounts to business travelers were discouraged.
4. Hertz had $1.1 billion of existing long term debt which would have to be assumed by UAL.
5. Hertz was a partner with other airlines in frequent flier programs and could not afford to lose their business.
6. In 1984, Hertz earned only $50 million in pretax earnings on revenues of $1.3 billion.

UNITED AIRLINES DIVERSIFICATION—PACIFIC ROUTES

In April of 1985, Ferris and UAL surprised the airline industry with the announcement that United was acquiring Pan American Airways' Pacific Division (excluding its Mainland-Hawaii routes) for $750 million plus the assumption of $136 million in lease obligations. United had long desired such Pacific routes and this would boost its share to 16.5% of the Pacific traffic (Northwest Airlines led with 19%). It would have taken United years to

[13] *Fortune,* September 30, 1985.
[14] *Business Week,* May 6, 1985.

establish a comparable presence since international airline routes require landing rights for each city served negotiated under near treaty conditions. National airlines would almost certainly have opposed such landing rights, adding years to the process, if not killing it. In this transaction, United purchased preexisting landing rights in 60 cities in 10 countries, in a region with enormous growth potential.

Pan Am had been having financial difficulties for several years, last reporting a profit in 1980. In view of Pan Am's financial condition and need for cash, some analysts felt that Ferris paid too much for what United received. Some felt that the price (22 times the pretax earnings of the division) was too high. Even Ferris conceded that the majority of the planes purchased might not be suitable for trans-Pacific flights because of their limited seating capacity.

United expected to benefit from these routes since many travelers bound for Asia prefer the same airline for flights from the interior of the country to a departure destination on the West Coast. Expansion into the Pacific seemed natural for United with its strength in the western part of the U.S. One competitor agreed when he said "With their very large domestic route system, the people at United will have an automatic control on the domestic scene. They could wind up with huge profits and a huge ability to control fares."[15]

In lengthy public hearings regarding the sale, United and Pan Am argued that the public would benefit because a relatively weak carrier was being replaced by a strong one. They saw it as a golden opportunity to break the Japanese stranglehold over trans-Pacific air routes. Ultimately the Department of Transportation approved the sale and it became the largest route exchange in the history of U.S. aviation.

In addition to the Pacific routes, United received 18 planes, $50 million worth of spare parts, and all Pan Am interests in Pacific ground facilities and equipment (except those in Hawaii). The planes had an average age of about 7 years (compared to an average age of 12 years for United's existing fleet). But they also agreed to hire 2,600 Pan Am employees.

In addition to this expansion, Ferris continued to search for other expansion opportunities. For example, UAL tried to acquire Frontier Airlines in 1986. The deal fell through when Frontier's pilots would not agree to concessions that Ferris felt were essential.

UNITED AIRLINES DIVERSIFICATION—HILTON INTERNATIONAL

In 1986, United acquired Hilton International, the hotel chain that Transworld (formerly TWA) first acquired in 1968. Transworld was selling its subsidiary in an effort to prevent a hostile takeover.

Hilton International (a separate entity from the domestic Hilton chain) operated 90 luxury hotels in 41 countries with 1985 revenues of $700 million. Transworld had originally signed an agreement to sell the unit to the Dutch Airline KLM for $975 million. When KLM backed out, UAL purchased the hotels for $980 million.

---

[15] *Business Week,* May 6, 1985.

UNITED AIRLINES DIVERSIFICATION—SYNERGIES

Ferris expressed enthusiasm for the acquisitions. (See Exhibit 5 for changes in revenues and assets as a result of diversification.) He stated that the operating synergies of the three divisions outweighed the cyclical risks. He recalled that after a family trip to Vail, he pulled his Hertz car into the return lot at Denver's Stapleton International Airport. There he paid for his car, deposited his luggage (including five sets of skis), and picked up his boarding passes for a United flight—all at an uncrowded Hertz counter. He argued that such travel experiences would be more pleasurable for the customer and create brand loyalty for UAL. Ferris expected to have such installations in other major cities by the end of 1986.

To the surprise of no one, UAL selected Hertz as its car rental firm in Hawaii for 1987, replacing Alamo. United flew 60,000 passengers to Hawaii in 1986 on package tours and expected to double that number in 1987. While all of these passengers would not rent cars, Hertz still expected a significant increase in rentals. This action generated a competitive

EXHIBIT 5
UAL, Inc.: Relative Segment Information Before and After Diversification

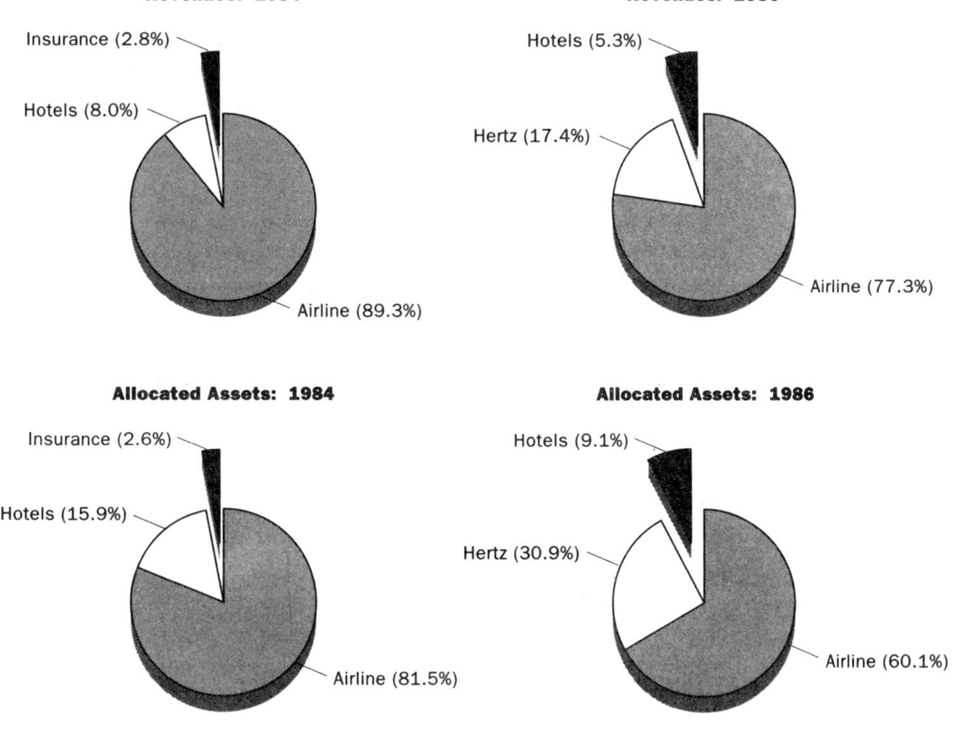

Source: Company annual reports.

reaction, however. Budget Rent-a-Car and Hyatt hotels canceled their participation in United's mileage plus program.

Among the reported synergistic results was the combined efforts of Hertz and United to reposition 600 cars from Denver to Phoenix in the fall of 1986. Hertz offered a midsize or larger car for one week, 1,500 free miles and two one-way airline coach tickets from Phoenix to Denver—all for $59. The airline tickets alone were regularly $89 each. Despite restricting the travel to a six-week period ending October 15, the offer sold out in three days. Without this combination, Hertz would have relied on its previous method of transferring the vehicles via truck or rail.

Critical to the attainment of these operating synergies would be the Apollo reservation system, now renamed Covia. Upgrading the system to include all travel related needs would allow for better customer service. Ferris expected to invest up to $1 billion in the reservation system over the next five years. This would help ensure that an adequate number of airplane seats, rental cars and hotel rooms would be available in the right place at the right time. Additionally, a database would be compiled that would keep a record of frequent travelers' preferences concerning travel related needs. This information would help Allegis implement the total travel strategy. Ferris felt that Allegis might eventually bypass travel agents and go directly to corporations with discounted full service travel packages that no competitor could match.[16]

UNITED AIRLINES—PROBLEMS BEGIN

UAL needed cash to pay for these acquisitions. Ferris also wanted to make the company less attractive to raiders, since some analysts insisted the stock, which closed at 57⅝ on August 1, 1985, was still undervalued. He began by pulling more than $500 million out of the company's overfunded pension plans. He sold GAB Business Services for a $28 million pretax gain, and announced that UAL would sell some Westin hotels. Merrill Lynch was retained to form partnership trusts containing two or more hotels. The trusts would then be sold to investors, netting UAL between $300 million and $500 million per trust. Westin was to be the general partner, would continue to manage the hotels, and would share in any appreciation of property values under this arrangement. Two hotels were packaged and sold in 1986 with UAL realizing net proceeds of $225.7 million.

Overall, 1986 proved to be a difficult year for Ferris and United. The Pacific route acquisition proved to be far more costly than anyone had estimated. Veteran Pan Am employees absorbed by United came in at the top of United's pay scales. A trans-Pacific captain, for example, received up to $170,000 per year. Maintenance, repair, and refitting of the aircraft acquired also proved to be more expensive than estimated. For the year, the Pacific Division's losses topped $100 million.

After losing $13 million in the fourth quarter in 1986, United laid off 1,016 white collar employees and placed a freeze on management salaries. UAL asserted that these actions would generate $100 million in savings. They also hoped the unionized employees would grant additional concessions.

The announcement of these cost cutting measures came only hours after Texas Air

[16] *Fortune,* September 30, 1985.

disclosed new discounted fares. These fares were up to 80% off full coach prices and 20% to 40% less than the previously low-priced super-saver fares. Industry executives, including those at United, were concerned that such discounts would spread to the business traveler, producing a free-for-all during the slack winter flying season. United, following its policy of matching price reductions, immediately matched the new fares where they competed directly with Texas Air's Eastern and Continental units.

THE BEGINNING OF THE END

Wall Street was unimpressed by Ferris' strategy. During a period when most airlines shared in a significant overall rise in stock prices, UAL's value rose less than 9%, from 49⅜ to 53¾, between the start of the diversification program (May 30, 1985) and the end of February 1987. In contrast, the value of AMR, the parent of American Airlines, increased nearly 24% during the same period. Further, a Solomon Brothers analyst was quoted as saying that UAL paid $1 billion above the fair market value for the businesses it had acquired.

On February 18, 1987, Ferris announced that UAL, Inc., would be renamed Allegis Corp. The new name, reported to cost UAL over $7.2 million to select and adopt, was to identify the company as being more than just an airline. Ferris expected this new awareness to help drive the company's stock price up. Perhaps the plan was working. On April 1, Allegis offered 5.5 million shares to the public at $56.50. The offering sold almost immediately.

On April 6, United's pilots made headlines by offering to purchase United Airlines from Allegis for $4.5 billion. This was nearly 50% more than the market value of the entire company. Outlining the proposal in a letter to management, the pilots cited concerns over the direction of the airline and the potential takeover threats to Allegis. The head of the union joked "It's our belief that they've been buying hotels so they can have more room for dissatisfied passengers."[17]

Allegis countered by claiming that the pilots' offer was an out-of-the-blue publicity stunt. The market took the pilots more seriously. The company's stock increased nearly 17% to $70 per share in the next week. There was no doubt that Ferris was concerned. He and seven others negotiated employment agreements. These "golden parachutes" assured these officers that they would receive their current compensation until April, 1992, or retirement, whichever was earlier. For Ferris that meant nearly $600,000 per year. Thirty-seven others were made eligible for severance pay of one to three times their base salary. In announcing the agreements, the company said that they would enable management ". . . to devote the necessary attention to the business of the corporation by giving them an objective, distraction free environment."[18] Ferris also hired Morgan Stanley & Co. to help ward off any takeover attempts.

Charles Luce, the senior member of Allegis' board, was appalled by a front page story in the *Wall Street Journal* on April 17 that said Ferris' job was on the line. In his letter published in *WSJ* on April 20, Luce stated that the directors fully supported Ferris, his management team, and his long-range strategy.

[17] *Wall Street Journal,* April 8, 1987.
[18] *Wall Street Journal,* April 21, 1987.

Three weeks after the pilots' offer, Allegis' board rejected the bid as grossly inadequate. Its advisors, Morgan Stanley & Co. and First Boston Corporation, concurred. The company asserted that the union proposal was subject to a number of conditions and uncertainties and was not in the best interests of shareholders.

The day after the rejection was announced, a minor shareholder filed suit against Allegis. The suit asked that the company be required to bargain with the pilots and requested that the employment contracts be enjoined. That same day, the pilots said they were reviewing their options, one of which was to buy the entire company and then sell the airline to themselves.

On May 1, less than a week after rejecting the pilots' bid, Allegis held its annual meeting. Ferris said that the pilots' offer would wreck the company's long-term growth prospects. In an effort to appease the pilots, he announced that the company was considering ways to offer its employees an ownership stake. After the meeting, Ferris answered questions from the stockholders for nearly four hours. Several stockholders wanted to know if the company was worth more if it were broken apart. There were also complaints about the employment contracts.

Less than two weeks later, Allegis made headlines again. The company signed a $1.5 billion order for 11 Boeing 747-400 jumbo jets, the largest order ever for such aircraft. Delivery was scheduled to begin in 1995; the planes would be used on the Pacific routes. While the size of the order was newsworthy, the contract details generated surprise among airline analysts. As part of the agreement, Boeing would be issued $700 million of notes, convertible to 16% of Allegis' stock. The stock, when issued, would contain special provisions requiring Boeing's approval of any takeover attempt. Boeing also agreed not to pursue a takeover bid of Allegis, the company that had once been Boeing's parent.

A Boeing spokesman indicated that the agreement was simply the result of fierce competition to sell aircraft. He said "We had to put together a deal that would win the business." [19] A United executive had a somewhat different view. The *Wall Street Journal* quoted him as saying "It's quite a coup for Ferris. He's improved the equity of the company and placed it in a better defensive posture with regard to takeovers." [20]

On May 27, the friendly skies hit new turbulence. Coniston Partners, an investment firm that had become known on Wall Street as an audacious and successful raider, announced it had acquired 13% of Allegis' stock and planned to seek control of Allegis' board. *Business Week*, in a December 1986 article, had portrayed Coniston as controlling only about $300 million, "hardly enough to do more than give a company a good scare." Success to Coniston, however, lay in convincing other shareholders that what they wanted to do made sense.

Coniston filed a plan with the SEC, outlining their belief that Allegis' three businesses would be stronger and significantly more valuable as independent companies. They also filed a lawsuit attacking the Boeing agreement, contending that the arrangement was for the purpose of entrenching management and that it gave Boeing control of Allegis.

Allegis considered others with more resources as bigger threats. A spokesman said "If Coniston bought 13%, we're assuming that's probably the maximum they could pull together at this time." [21] The company appeared to ". . . believe that the Coniston

---

[19] *Wall Street Journal*, May 13, 1987.
[20] *Wall Street Journal*, May 13, 1987.
[21] *Wall Street Journal*, May 27, 1987.

Partners simply want to be bought out at a premium to market price, a practice known as greenmail. Coniston denied it, saying they would not accept greenmail if it were offered."[22]

Ferris recognized, though, that his long-term strategy was in trouble. He asked Boeing to vote against Coniston, but Boeing was not yet ready to convert its notes to voting stock. Boeing may have faced a conflict of interest. How would other airlines, customers of Boeing, respond if Boeing took an equity position in one of their major competitors?

The same day, May 27, the company announced plans to pay a special dividend of $60 cash per share. But, Allegis did not have the $3 billion required for such a dividend. The company would have to borrow it, raising its long-term debt to more than $5 billion. If it completed such a deal, the company would be one of the most debt ridden companies in the airline industry. There was also the question as to whether the plan would violate the provisions of the Boeing agreement. In any case, it would require shareholder approval.

The stock price continued to climb, reaching $87 per share on May 28, a 22% jump in just one week. Ferris thought that Coniston would take their profits and run. Coniston, however, said Allegis was worth still more and that Coniston would continue to seek control of the company.

During this period, United was in the midst of negotiations with the International Association of Machinists. The machinists, who had spurned attempts by the pilots to involve them in the purchase of the company, were alarmed by the company's payout plan. They raised the possibility of a strike if Allegis went ahead with the recapitalization. At the height of the publicity and speculation surrounding Allegis, the company retained a proxy solicitor to informally poll the company's shareholders. Reportedly, institutional investors owned just under 75% of Allegis' outstanding stock, and a majority expressed support for the Coniston plan. They reported the company was likely to lose a shareholder vote.

On June 4, the pilots' sweetened their bid to buy the company, offering $70 per share plus stock in the airline. Their new strategy was similar to Coniston's plan—break up the company to generate cash for the proposed payout. They considered their offer to be competing with that of the company's $60 dividend and sought to have it submitted to the shareholders. Anticipating questions regarding the financing of such a payout, they obtained an opinion from the Salomon Brothers investment firm indicating that the proposed offer could be financed. The pilots also announced that they had a cash offer of $1 billion for the Hilton International hotels.

Allegis was having trouble raising the $3 billion needed for its recapitalization plan. Bankers were demanding an impossible guarantee that the company could win wage reductions from its increasingly antagonistic unions. Without such reductions, the banks contended that the company's cash flow would not justify the debt.

Ferris scheduled a trip to New York for June 10 and to Boston the following day to lobby institutional shareholders for support. The trips were canceled when Luce called a special board meeting for June 9th.

After meeting with the board for seven hours, Ferris resigned. He later confided to an associate that ". . . I thought Luce was in my corner but instead, he stabbed me in the back."[23] Reflecting on the turbulent events of the past two months, Richard Ferris wondered what he should have done differently.

---

[22] *Wall Street Journal,* May 27, 1987.

[23] *Wall Street Journal,* June 11, 1987.

CASE 25

Northrop Corporation: Dilemma of the Tigershark (Revised)*

> Los Angeles, May 15, 1985—Thomas V. Jones, chairman and chief executive of the Northrop Corporation, said that Tuesday's crash of an F-20 Tigershark jet fighter would not deter the company from promoting the plane to prospective buyers, including the Air Force. The crash, which killed the pilot, David Barnes, was the second of an F-20 in eight months and leaves only one Tigershark in operation. "Our belief in it [the F-20] has not changed," Mr. Jones said at a news conference after Northrop's annual shareholder's meeting in Hawthorne, California. Northrop has not received any orders for the plane, which has cost the company more than $800 million to produce. . . . *(New York Times)*

The second fatal crash of an F-20 fighter plane was unfortunate but such crashes were hardly unexpected. Test pilots often flew new planes to the limit of their capabilities and many times serious accidents were the result. Indeed, pilot error would be ruled as the cause of both Tigershark crashes rather than problems with the plane itself.

However, his confident comments to the stockholders aside, Northrop's CEO had reasons to worry. Northrop had developed the F-20 Tigershark for export to Third World and European allies. Despite high praise from the aviation press and pilots alike, not one had been sold. The plane was Thomas Jones' brainchild but the program's costs, which were approaching one billion dollars, were adversely affecting the company's financial performance (see Exhibits 1 and 2 for Northrop's consolidated financial statements).

Late in the 1970s the Carter Administration put out a call for an inexpensive, easy to maintain aircraft to be produced primarily for export and designed and built without Department of Defense (DOD) funding. The F-20 was Northrop's answer to that call. However, by 1985 the political sands had shifted and the F-20 was faced with competition from frontline U.S. fighters previously reserved for domestic use. It was becoming increasingly apparent that sales to foreign customers were going to be contingent upon either getting the Tigershark into the inventory of some branch of the U.S. military, a purpose for which it was not designed, or competing with some of the world's finest and best known fighter planes in the international marketplace. Mr. Jones had to decide if Northrop should continue the costly development of the potentially profitable F-20 program or close the project and divert the funds to other uses.

---

* Prepared by Thad Munnerlyn, Robert McNamara, and Frank Leibold, under the direction of James J. Chrisman, Louisiana State University. Distributed by the North American Case Research Association.

EXHIBIT 1
Northrop Corporation: Consolidated Statements of Income
Years Ended December 31
(in Millions of Dollars, Except per Share Data)

	1984	*1983*	*1982*	*1981*	*1980*
Net sales	$3,687.8	$3,260.6	$2,472.9	$1,990.7	$1,655.4
Cost of sales:	−3,444.4	−3,120.1	−2,539.5	−1,977.6	−1,548.3
Operating costs	−3,005.5	−2,725.0	−2,260.2		
Administrative & general expenses	−438.9	−395.1	−279.3		
Operating margin	243.4	140.5	−66.6	13.1	107.1
Other income & deductions	6.1	26.5	33.0	62.1	35.5
Interest expense	−7.5	−14.3	−3.1	−7.5	−2.9
Income before taxes	242.0	152.7	−36.7	67.7	139.7
Federal & foreign taxes (benefits)	−75.1	−52.0	42.1	−19.8	−53.6
Net income	$166.9	$100.7	$5.4	$47.9	$86.1
Per-share stock prices:					
High	$39.50	$32.75	$25.88	$21.00	$20.63
Low	$23.75	$21.88	$13.13	$11.00	$12.50
Book value per share	$15.72	$12.64	$10.87	$11.32	$11.27
Earnings per share	$ 3.63	$ 2.21	$ 0.12	$ 1.10	$ 2.01
Cash dividend per share	$ 0.90	$ 0.60	$ 0.60	$ 0.60	$ 0.60
Number of employees	41,500	37,200	35,500	31,400	30,200

Sources: Northrop Corporation, "Annual report," 1986; *Moody's industrial manual*, 1982; Standard & Poor's *NYSE reports*, 1985.

NORTHROP CORPORATION: COMPANY BACKGROUND

The Northrop Corporation was founded in 1939 by John K. Northrop. The new company manufactured aircraft, producing several lesser known and unexceptional designs prior to World War II. During World War II Northrop produced the P-61 Black Widow that appeared later in the Pacific theater. Northrop also produced one of the world's first production jet fighters, the F-89 Scorpion. It enjoyed moderate success in the Korean War era as an all-weather fighter.

Shortly after the end of World War II, Northrop commenced its innovative B-35 Flying Wing program. The company invested heavily in the boomerang-shaped plane only to have the program cancelled in favor of the B-36 developed by Convair, a forerunner of General Dynamics. The Air Force ordered all the remaining prototypes destroyed in what became a bitter loss for Northrop. The cancellation left the company near bankruptcy in 1953.

In 1953 Thomas V. Jones joined the company as a planner and assistant to the chief engineer. In 1960 he became Northrop's CEO, and in 1963 he was named Chairman of the Board. During his early tenure as CEO, Jones returned Northrop to profitability with the

EXHIBIT 2
Northrop Corporation: Consolidated Statements of Financial Position
As of December 31
(in Millions of Dollars)

	1984	*1983*	*1982*	*1981*	*1980*
Assets:					
Cash & cash items	$ 3.7	$ 60.2	$ 124.6	$ 194.3	$ 311.2
Accounts receivable	306.7	205.4	137.6	193.0	131.0
Inventoried costs	418.0	301.0	238.6	327.5	390.4
Prepaid expenses	15.0	10.7	10.8	11.4	9.0
Total current assets	$ 743.4	$ 577.3	$ 511.6	$ 726.2	$ 841.6
Land & land improvements	105.6	78.6	70.6		
Buildings	575.5	479.8	375.4		
Machinery & equipment	981.5	777.9	610.8		
Leasehold improvements	19.3	16.6	17.8		
Accumulated depreciation & amortization	-510.9	-379.5	-278.0		
Net property, plant, & equipment at cost	$1,171.0	$ 973.4	$ 796.6	$ 490.3	$ 343.5
Investments in & advances to affiliates	22.7	11.9	16.9		
Net investment in aircraft direct financing leases	17.1	19.2	17.9		
Notes & accounts receivable	2.3	14.2	9.5		
Total other assets	$ 42.1	$ 45.3	$ 44.3	$ 40.9	$ 48.6
Total Assets	$1,956.5	$1,596.0	$1,352.5	$1,257.4	$1,233.7
Liabilities:					
Notes payable	$ 43.4	$ 0.0	$ 0.0		
Trade accounts payable	233.7	214.1	177.3		
Accrued employees' compensation	149.9	133.1	114.4		
Advances on contracts	187.0	192.7	159.0		
Income taxes payable	25.3	26.7	16.9		
Deferred income taxes	331.5	255.1	224.2		
Other current liabilities	175.1	108.6	84.1		
Total current liabilities	$1,145.9	$ 930.3	$ 775.9	$ 666.8	$ 660.2
Long-term debt & capital leases	7.7	10.5	14.5	14.5	19.4
Long-term liabilities	31.7	29.1	32.0	40.5	43.6
Deferred income taxes	46.4	49.2	36.2	28.6	28.1
Total liabilities	$1,231.7	$1,019.1	$ 858.6	$ 750.4	$ 751.3
Shareholders' equity:					
Paid-in capital	$ 150.7	$ 133.3	$ 128.0	$ 116.2	$ 84.4
Retained earnings	596.7	471.1	397.9	419.7	398.0
Unvested employee restricted award shares	-22.6	-27.5	-32.0	-28.9	0.0
Total shareholders' equity	$ 724.8	$ 576.9	$ 493.9	$ 507.0	$ 482.4
Total liabilities & shareholders' equity	$1,956.5	$1,596.0	$1,352.5	$1,257.4	$1,233.7

Sources: Northrop Corporation, "Annual report," 1986; *Moody's industrial manual*, 1982; Standard & Poor's *NYSE reports*, 1985.

F-5 Tiger series, a relatively unsophisticated and inexpensive fighter plane that Jones correctly believed would fill a need for Third World countries. Dismissed by one critic as "toys for sheiks," the F-5 was nevertheless one of the premier success stories in aviation history. In the 1960s and 1970s the F-5 and its variations became the most widely used fighter plane in the world with more than 2,500 planes sold to nearly 30 countries. Its trainer derivative, the T-38 Talon, was the most widely used jet trainer, with 1,000 sold worldwide. After the B-35 cancellation, the F-5 program rallied the company and provided the funds for aerospace research and development and expansion into several new areas of military electronics.

Northrop made two attempts to build new military aircraft during the 1970s. Bidding against other companies for domestic business, it first lost out to Fairchild Aviation's A-10 Thunderbolt for a production contract for an anti-tank aircraft. Northrop then bid on contracts with the Air Force and Navy to produce a domestic fighter. Northrop asked McDonnell-Douglas to be the prime contractor on the Navy program and major subcontractor on the Air Force program. Northrop expected to be named the prime contractor for the Air Force project and thought the combined proposal would strengthen its overall bargaining position with DOD. Unfortunately, its F-17 prototype was rejected by the Air Force in favor of the F-16, designed by General Dynamics. The Navy, however, accepted the McDonnell-Douglas bid for the F-18 strike fighter. McDonnell-Douglas then subcontracted the F-18 fuselages to Northrop, leaving Jones' company without a prime contract on the plane that it had originally designed.

THE DEFENSE INDUSTRY

The defense industry consisted of thousands of companies that produced a wide variety of weapons and military products. The industry was dominated by two groups of firms: large diversified commercial companies, like General Electric, IBM, and Litton, and large aerospace companies such as General Dynamics, Boeing, McDonnell-Douglas, and Lockheed (see Exhibit 3). Like its competitors, Northrop competed for a limited number of large, long-term contracts as well as for numerous smaller, short-term contracts.

The industry supplied essentially one customer—the U.S. military, which consisted of the Army, Navy (including the Marines), and Air Force. The Department of Defense (DOD) managed the military and was responsible for preparing the national defense budget for the various military services, a complicated, consensus-building process that involved hundreds of agencies. About half of the military budget actually went towards weapons procurement; salaries and supplies represented the other half of the budget.

The funds available to the military each year were controlled by the Congress. The defense budget was determined both by the Administration's policy with regard to defense spending and by the funds required for other programs. Military policies changed from Administration to Administration. Thus the views of the President on defense and international politics were of critical importance. The interplay between Congress and the Administration in regard to the proposed defense budget obviously had a great impact on contractors. Under President Carter, defense spending sank to its lowest real levels since the end of World War II. In 1980 Ronald Reagan won a landslide victory over Jimmy Carter. Reagan planned to increase military spending by 9% per year (in real terms), nearly double the increases of the Carter years. The electronics component of the defense budget was expected to grow even faster.

Most defense contracts were for high technology items which required long development periods. It usually took from eight to nine years to develop a major defense item from the initial development stage to the start of full production. These costs were usually paid

EXHIBIT 3
Top Ten Defense Aerospace Companies, 1980 (in Millions of Dollars)

	Ranking in Value of Defense Contracts	*Value of Defense Contracts*	*Total Sales*	*Net Income*	*ROE*	*Assets*	*Major Defense Products*
General Dynamics	1	$3,518	$ 4,645	$195	21.0%	$2,242	F-16, Trident subs, SSN-668 submarines, Tomahawk missiles
McDonnell-Douglas	2	$3,247	$ 6,086	$145	9.9%	$3,900	F-18, F-15, & KC-10 planes, Trident II missiles
United Technologies	3	$3,109	$12,324	$393	17.5%	$7,326	UH-60 helicopters, jet fighter engines
Boeing	4	$2,386	$ 9,426	$601	28.8%	$5,931	AWACS, Stealth bomber, B-52 bomber
Lockheed	6	$2,037	$ 5,396	$ 28	7.5%	$2,443	C-5A & C-5B cargo planes, Trident II missiles
Hughes* Aircraft	7	$1,819	$ 2,610	NA	NA	NA	Defense electronics
Raytheon	8	$1,745	$ 5,002	$282	22.7%	$2,929	Hawk missiles, defense electronics
Grumman	10	$1,322	$ 1,729	$ 31	9.5%	$ 906	F-14 & A-6E planes, aircraft carriers
Northrop	11	$1,227	$ 1,655	$ 86	19.0%	$1,234	F-20 & F-5 planes, F-18 fuselage, Stealth bomber
Rockwell	14	$ 969	$ 6,907	$280	17.3%	$4,431	B-1 bomber

* Privately held.
Source: J. J. Chrisman, "Note on the defense electronics industry," 1982.

by the military under development contracts. Several companies were paid to develop designs for the item; the one with the best design was contracted to perform full scale engineering development (FSED). Once FSED was completed, the military asked for bids on the production contract. The company which carried out the FSED did not always get the production contract, which often led to inefficiencies in early production stages. The DOD had a tendency of awarding production contracts to manufacturers that had lost out on previous contracts.

Another source of inefficiency in this process was that at the time the initial production began, the final size of the production run could only be estimated. Therefore, contractors could never be certain if or when investments in plant and equipment would be recovered on a project because the size of the production run might change from year to year. The size of the total production run was an especially important concern for aerospace manufacturers whose profitability depended on experience-based cost reductions. Furthermore, the government did not allow the contractor to recover costs that were not directly tied to the particular program involved. Such conditions tended to discourage defense contractors from investing capital in new plant and equipment. Another problem inherent in the defense industry was the military's desire to compromise cost in favor of improved performance. The desire for better performance often led to product design changes halfway through the production run. These changes made it necessary for the contractor to "re-fit" all the previously produced items and increased costs. Disagreements between the contractor and the military over who should bear these costs often ensued.

THE FX ENVIRONMENT

Late in the 1970s, the Carter Administration became alarmed at the number of foreign requests for frontline military aircraft, particularly fighters. Nations with severe domestic problems were clamoring for planes that were costly and had capabilities that greatly exceeded their security needs. Sales to such countries were seen as politically and economically destabilizing. Thus, the Carter Administration approached the defense industry and asked for a privately-funded and developed aircraft specifically designed for foreign customers. The aircraft was to be simpler, less expensive, and less capable than frontline U.S. fighters. In return, the Administration promised not to license frontline planes for sales overseas, virtually forcing the potential buyers to purchase the foreign export fighter, or "FX" as it was known.

The program was put into place in late 1979. With a ready-made customer base of previous F-5 users and substantially improved performance, Northrop executives figured they had a "hot" aircraft in their new F-20 Tigershark. Less than a year later, however, Carter lost his reelection bid to Ronald Reagan. In 1982, the Reagan Administration, reacting to what it believed to be an increased threat from the Soviet military presence in Third World areas, overturned long-standing U.S. policy and began to sell U.S. inventory fighters to less-developed countries. The exports included some of McDonnell-Douglas's F-15s and F-18s, but consisted primarily of the General Dynamics F-16. An American fighter became a highly charged symbol of friendship and support. Nations with U.S. planes were dependent for parts and technical support. Also, the advisors, who necessarily accompanied the planes, provided an important American presence in these countries. Thus, the FX policy, for which the F-20 was built, was all but officially dead even though this policy change was reversed in December 1982.

Competition

Northrop initially believed its F-20 had few competitors in the export market, and was relatively free of political problems at home. However, along with the policy changes invoked by the Reagan Administration, significant competition from both domestic and foreign aerospace firms had developed.

Relative to the U.S. aerospace firms, foreign producers were not a major force in the export market. Dassault of France had made inroads into Third World markets with its Mirage 2000. However, it could not match the glamour or performance of American fighters. The Mirage was also more expensive to fly and lacked a large worldwide support network. Still, the French plane appealed to countries that wanted to avoid Soviet or American influence. For example, in 1983 the United Arab Emirates bought Mirage jets rather than F-20s or F-16s.

McDonnell-Douglas had two frontline domestic aircraft that were being exported, the Air Force's F-15, a sophisticated and expensive, air-superiority fighter, and the Navy's F-18 strike fighter, built with the assistance of Northrop. These planes were considered too sophisticated and expensive for all but the most affluent allies such as Canada, Australia, and Spain.

Northrop's main competitor in the export fighter market was General Dynamics Corporation, at that time the largest defense contractor in the U.S. The F-16 was General Dynamics' biggest aviation success; it had dominated the U.S. inventory in numbers since its introduction in the 1970s. In terms of performance, it was nearly equal to the F-15, but was priced considerably lower. However, at $14 million or more per plane, the F-16 was not inexpensive.

General Dynamics was well-suited to compete in the export market. It had developed an elaborate supply system for producing the F-16 that included both American and European subcontractors. It also had benefited from learning curves of about 80% for assembly and fabrication labor, and of 95% for materials and subcontracted items.

General Dynamics responded early to President Carter's FX request, but without much enthusiasm. In 1980, it offered a version of the F-16 known as the F-16/J79, so named because it had an older, less sophisticated engine, the J79, and fewer electronic refinements. The F-16/J79 suffered from comparisons with the more sophisticated U.S. Air Force version of the F-16. In 1984, General Dynamics made a request to designate its current series of F-16s as FX fighters and essentially abandoned the F-16/J79.

Comparison of the F-20 and F-16

While the F-16/J79 was an old plane with "detuned" technology, Northrop's export fighter was a completely new aircraft. Although initially built for the FX market, the F-20 was the first U.S. fighter plane to be designed with 1980s technology. Even the newer F-15s and F-16s were built with 1960s and 1970s hardware. Except for physical appearance, the F-20 bore little resemblance to its forerunner, the F-5, and was a legitimate rival to the top U.S. fighters. Despite costing at least $2.5 million less per plane, the F-20 was equal in most areas, and actually superior in some others, to the F-16 (see Exhibit 4).

Northrop had designed the new plane from the ground up starting with the engine. Its engineers used General Electric's new F404 engine, which sacrificed a small amount of power in exchange for increased reliability and repairability, as well as an uncanny ability to recover from stalls. The F-16 was powered by the Pratt and Whitney F100, a powerful but problematic and expensive-to-maintain engine. The F-20 engine held one more advantage over the engine used on the F-16: it could start in under 20 seconds, less than half the time of the F-16. The Tigershark also had the fastest scramble time (the time an aircraft needed to become airborne after an alert) of any fighter in the world. That was owed in large part to a new laser controlled inertial guidance system that replaced the traditional mechanical gyroscopes, as well as the faster starting engine.

In terms of electronics, the F-20 was, in many respects, superior to any other American fighter including the super-sophisticated F-15. Its radar was equal to the F-16's in performance, but was twice as reliable.

In other areas of performance the two planes were essentially equivalent. Maneuverability and weapons accuracy were approximately equal. The F-16 did hold a slight edge in sustained turns, although the F-20's smaller size could offset the advantage in aerial combat. The F-20 was designed primarily as a defensive aircraft and, as a consequence, did have less payload capacity (the amount of armaments—e.g., missiles and bombs—that a plane can carry aloft on one mission) than the F-16, which had been designed as an offensive fighter. The F-20 also had a shorter flight range than the F-16, a fact that prompted one

EXHIBIT 4
Specifications, Performance, Armaments, and Costs of the F-16 and F-20

	F-16	*F-20*
Specifications:		
1. Length	49ft 6in	47ft 3in
2. Height	16ft 9in	13ft 10in
3. Wing span with two AIM-9 missiles	31ft 0in	27ft 11in
4. Empty weight (lbs.)	18,496	12,049
5. Takeoff weight with two AIM-9 missiles (lbs.)	22,264	18,540
6. Combat weight—50% fuel, two AIM-9 missiles (lbs.)	18,348	16,015
7. Combat thrust/weight ratio	1.1 to 1	1.12 to 1
8. Maximum weight	33,000	28,000
9. Maximum external weapons carriage (lbs.)	12,000	10,000
9. Engine thrust (lbs.)	25,000	18,000
10. Number of weapon pylons	6	6
Performance estimates:		
11. Scramble time (seconds)	120	60
12. Sortie rate (in 12 hours)	Not available	12
13. Maximum speed at 40,000 feet	Mach 2 +	Mach 2 +
14. Sea level rate-of-climb (feet/minute)	72,834	53,800
15. Takeoff distance (feet)	1,200	1,475
16. Combat ceiling	50,000	55,000
17. Maneuverability	Essentially equivalent	
18. Weapons delivery accuracy	Essentially equivalent	
19. Range ratio F-16/F-20		
General Dynamics estimate	1.34–1.56/1.00	
Northrop estimate	1.12/1.00	
Costs (in millions):		
20. Annual operating & support costs (including fuel)	$ 12.2	$ 5.7
21. Procurement costs for 20 aircraft in flyaway condition		
Without spares	$280.0	$228.0
With spares	$420.0	$315.0
Armaments:		
22. Cannon	20mm	20mm
23. Ammunition per cannon	500 rounds	450 rounds

Sources: *Asian Defense Journal*, 1986; *International Defense Review*, 1985.

General Dynamics salesman to say, "[the F-20 is] a good plane if you want to bomb the end of your runway." Northrop countered by explaining that the F-20 was designed for Third World countries whose enemies were nearby, making range less critical and scramble time of far greater consequence. In test flights the F-20 set records for the number of missions that could be performed in a day, presumably an important attribute to nations with limited aircraft and manpower. However, Northrop decided to modify the plane to correct some minor design flaws and better differentiate the F-20 from the F-5, a decision that was soon leaked to the aerospace community. These modifications included increasing the F-20's wing area by 29% and modifying the plane to accommodate a larger engine.

Just as significant to Third World countries as performance, in the view of the F-20's designers, was the Tigershark's ease of maintenance and reliability. Air Force data suggested that the mean number of hours in the air between failures was 4.2 for the F-20 versus 3.2 for the F-16. The F-20 required slightly less than half the man hours of routine maintenance per hour of flight as the F-16. A squadron of 20 Tigersharks required a maintenance staff of only 180; the F-16 required a staff of 380. Northrop officials felt both these figures would take on added significance in Third World countries with limited numbers of trained personnel. According to company figures, lower fuel consumption and lower maintenance requirements reduced the cost per flight hour of the F-20 to $1,575 while the F-16 cost $3,497 per flight hour. The other savings in terms of support and maintenance were highly in favor of the F-20.

The lower price of the Tigershark also gave it a strategic advantage as well as an economic one since more planes could be bought for the same amount of money. During the Arab-Israeli wars the Israeli Air Force had found that a high density of aircraft offset performance differences between adversary aircraft during aerial combat.

MARKET FOR THE TIGERSHARK

Initially, the FX policy was not meant to apply to all overseas customers and the export market was divided into two segments. The first, or "high" segment included NATO allies and some other countries such as Israel and Japan. Countries in this group usually had State Department approval for frontline aircraft. The second, or "low," segment consisted of all remaining non-communist countries. It was this second group to which the FX program applied.

With the demise of the Carter policy, however, a third group of countries previously included in the FX group emerged. This "medium" segment included nations that wanted, and some that could afford, frontline fighters like the F-16, and were felt to have legitimate defense threats. Examples were Pakistan, Afghanistan's border neighbor and tacit ally to that country's anti-communist guerillas, and South Korea, whose border was with North Korea, a recent benefactor of Soviet air technology (see Exhibit 5).

The newly created medium segment of previously FX-only fighter buyers such as Venezuela, South Korea, and Pakistan represented a substantial number of potential orders, in part because the United States government helped finance their purchases through direct aid programs consisting of grants and long-term, low interest loans. Linked with other foreign aid packages, these arrangements greatly reduced initial costs. Essentially, the United States paid for the military aircraft of its less affluent allies. Over half of the $8.1 billion worth of F-16s sold to foreign countries through 1984 was paid for by grants from the U.S. government or by loans that were later forgiven.

In the three years after the FX policy went into effect, approximately 1,100 planes had been sold to foreign customers. Not one was an F-20. In fact, not one was an FX fighter. Those nations in the medium category which were seen as potential customers for the Tigershark opted for the Air Force issue F-16 after it became apparent that it would be made available to them. Pakistan, one of the poorest nations in the world, bought 40 F-16s at a cost of one billion dollars. Venezuela, another potential F-20 customer, purchased 24 F-16s. Turkey, viewed by the Reagan Administration as an important line of defense against a growing Warsaw Pact threat to NATO's southern flank, received special political consideration. A request on behalf of the Turkish government for $755 million in aid was

EXHIBIT 5
The Export Fighter Market

Country	*Market Segment*	*Remarks*
Australia	High	Never classified as FX country. Entitled to frontline equipment as major Pacific ally. Received F-16s and F-18s.
Austria	Medium	Neutrality stance led to purchase of French Mirages.
Canada	High	Traditional ally entitled to frontline planes such as F-15s and F-18s.
Egypt	Medium	Initially seen as big F-20 purchaser but was allowed F-16s by Reagan Administration. Sales possibilities for F-20 still existed.
European participating group	High	European allies entitled to frontline fighters. Involvement with successful coproduction agreement for previous F-16s made reorders likely.
Greece	Medium	Status as NATO ally allowed frontline aircraft purchases. Indicated interest in F-16s.
India	Medium	U.S. Government prohibited sales talks due to possibility of F-20 technology falling into the hands of Soviet military advisors. Bought Russian MIGs.
Indonesia	Low	Strong possibility for F-20 order but national economy delayed purchase plans.
Israel	High	Close relationship with U.S. allowed access to frontline fighters and substantial foreign aid. Ordered F-15s and F-16s.
Jordan	Medium	Sale of F-16s to other Middle-Eastern countries created pressure to sell to Jordan which was needed in Middle-Eastern peace talks. Purchase of F-20s still possible.
Malaysia	Low	Potential buyer of 50 planes. Would strongly consider F-20 but is very cautious and would not be a likely lead buyer in the region.
Pakistan	Medium	One of first FX countries to get approval to purchase F-16s. Proximity to Afghanistan figured in administration's decision.
Portugal	Medium	NATO ally, but favored French Mirage 2000.
Singapore	Low/medium	FX country considered F-20s and F-16/J79 but purchase of F-16s by Thailand caused reconsideration.
South Korea	Medium	Previously FX country. Seen as F-20 customer, but Reagan Administration allowed F-16 sales due to North Korean threat.
Spain	Medium/high	Potential member of NATO. Would probably seek F-16s for commonality with other NATO members.
Taiwan	Medium	Seen as first buyer for F-20 but potential sales of 150–200 planned stopped by Reagan Administration to avoid diplomatic problems with Red China.
Thailand	Low/medium	Previously FX country. Was given clearance to purchase F-16s due to threat from Vietnam. Important country in terms of setting precedent for region.
Turkey	Medium	NATO member. Receiving large amounts of military aid from U.S. Likely to include F-16s.
Venezuela	Medium	One of first FX countries to be allowed frontline fighters. Purchased F-16s.

Sources: Berstein & Company, 1981; *International Defense Review,* 1986.

put before the Congress for review in 1985. The aid was to be earmarked for military hardware and included specific mention of F-16s. Thailand was originally tagged as an FX country but the threat from Vietnam had it arguing for F-16s, with a large number of its regional neighbors anxiously awaiting the outcome before making their own decisions. Thailand had the potential to purchase up to 75 planes. Saudi Arabia, the best hope for a large order, was high on the F-20 but insisted that Northrop have the plane in production and that it be in the U.S. Armed Forces system before it would place an order. It already had some F-15s and F-16s in its inventory.

It was an all-too-familiar refrain for Northrop executives. Despite the high performance of the Tigershark, it had what one expert called a "training wheels" image. It was still associated with the concept of an underpowered FX fighter, lacking the aura of a U.S. Air Force or Navy plane. Technological glamour and the political prestige of owning a frontline U.S. fighter appeared to be paramount concerns for Third World countries despite the higher price and operating costs, as well as their inability to keep the planes in the air. As

California Congressman Mervyn Dymally noted, "They want the best. It doesn't matter if it works."

The countries that remained classified in the "lower" segment of the export market consisted of smaller, even less affluent nations that could afford only limited orders or whose needs dictated fewer planes. For example, the tiny kingdom of Bahrain wanted four Tigersharks but had to settle for F-5s because the F-20 was not yet in production. A significant problem now faced Northrop. The company had stated that it would have to have firm orders for 300 to 400 planes before the F-20 could be put into production. These smaller countries could not afford a frontline U.S. fighter but it was unclear whether or not this low segment of the FX market could collectively support the F-20 program. While some analysts believed that the lower segment might ultimately hold sales potential for 300 or more planes over a period of years, it remained to be seen whether enough of the countries in the lower category would place sufficient initial orders to justify the start-up of the F-20 production line. Most observers believed that obtaining orders for the F-20 from the middle segment, the one contested by General Dynamics, was the more likely route to success. Nearly all these nations, as well as some NATO countries, were considering the purchase of F-16s and some had already placed orders.

NORTHROP CORPORATION: CURRENT OPERATIONS

In 1985 Northrop was a diversified company with business units in the fields of aviation and aerospace, electronics, and technical and management support. The company was divided into three groups: Aircraft, Electronics, and Services. Exhibits 6 and 7 provide group sales and operating profits, respectively. Contract acquisitions, funded order backlogs, identifiable assets, capital expenditures, and depreciation and amortization for each group are shown in Exhibit 8.

Aircraft Group

Northrop's largest and most important business segment was the Aircraft Group which contributed over $2.5 billion of 1984 sales. The group consisted of three divisions: Aircraft, Advanced Systems, and Ventura.

Aircraft. The Aircraft Division handled production of the F-5s and the prototype F-20s. Sales of the F-5 were dwindling, notwithstanding a brief flurry of final orders. The final sales would have to be used to cover the costs of the write-down of inventory as the F-5 program came to an end. As for the F-20 program, one Prudential-Bache security analyst felt that it could "yield higher profits than any other major weapons production program in history," with pre-tax profit margins of 15 to 20%. Jones still believed a potential market of over 2,000 planes existed as numerous countries were going to have to replace their aging F-5s and other outmoded aircraft.

The division's F-18 subcontract with McDonnell-Douglas brought substantial cash flow to the company. Once thought politically vulnerable, the program had substantial backing in Congress and was far enough along in its production curve to survive. With approximately $623 million in 1984 sales and a backlog of over $1.1 billion, its future appeared secure. The division had also been involved with the assembly of the fuselage

EXHIBIT 6
Northrop Corporation: Group Sales
Years Ended December 31
(in Millions of Dollars)

	1984	*1983*	*1982*	*1981*
Aircraft:				
Net sales to customers	$2,563.9	$2,119.9	$1,452.5	$ 985.7
Intersegment sales	0.7	3.3	0.3	0.6
Other income (deductions)	−2.5	0.1	4.4	14.7
Total	$2,562.1	$2,123.3	$1,457.2	$1,001.0
Electronics:				
Net sales to customers	$ 702.4	$ 669.2	$ 525.0	$ 427.0
Intersegment sales	55.5	16.2	5.6	29.8
Other income (deductions)	0.6	−0.2	−0.6	2.6
Total	$ 758.5	$ 685.2	$ 530.0	$ 459.4
Services:				
Net sales to customers	$ 421.5	$ 457.7	$ 454.8	$ 519.6
Intersegment sales	0.3	0.1	0.2	0.0
Other income (deductions)	0.2	0.3	0.0	0.1
Total	$ 422.0	$ 458.1	$ 455.0	$ 519.7
Construction:				
Net sales to customers	--	13.8	40.6	58.4
Other income (deductions)	--	−6,7	0.0	0.3
Total	--	$ 7.1	$ 40.6	$ 58.7

Source: Northrop Corporation, "Annual reports," 1984–1987.

EXHIBIT 7
Northrop Corporation: Group Operating Profits
Years Ended December 31
(in Millions of Dollars)

	1984	*1983*	*1982*	*1981*
Aircraft	$203.3	$ 90.0	−$114.9	−$ 75.6
Electronics	81.7	77.3	54.1	51.8
Services	62.8	68.6	49.2	101.2
Construction	--	−22.7	−0.4	2.6
Total operating profit (loss)	$347.8	$213.2	−$ 12.0	$ 80.0
Less:				
Other income (deductions) included in total revenue	−1.7	−6.5	3.8	17.7
State and local income taxes	18.3	11.4	2.2	9.9
General corporate expenses	87.8	67.8	48.6	39.3
Operating margin (loss)	$243.4	$140.5	−$ 66.6	$ 13.1

Source: Northrop Corporation, "Annual reports," 1984–1987.

EXHIBIT 8
Northrop Corporation: R&D Expenditures and Group Operating Characteristics
Years Ended December 31
(in Millions of Dollars)

	1984	1983	1982	1981
R&D expenditures:				
Contract	$1,339.6	$ 858.5	$ 489.6	$ 289.5
Noncontract	238.6	266.0	312.9	192.2
Total R&D expenditures	$1,578.2	$1,124.5	$ 802.5	$ 481.7
Contract acquisitions:				
Aircraft	$2,903.6	$2,719.3	$1,513.9	$1,376.7
Electronics	1,335.7	715.9	591.1	402.8
Services	194.8	288.0	828.0	260.1
Construction	−2.8	3.0	8.7	28.3
Total acquisitions	$4,431.3	$3,726.2	$2,941.7	$2,067.9
Funded order backlog:				
Aircraft	$2,492.4	$2,152.7	$1,553.3	$1,491.9
Electronics	1,273.6	640.3	593.6	527.5
Services	218.3	445.0	614.7	241.5
Construction	0.0	2.8	13.6	45.5
Total backlog	$3,984.3	$3,240.8	$2,775.2	$2,306.4
Identifiable assets:				
Aircraft	$1,306.5	$1,001.9	$ 783.5	$ 693.6
Electronics	370.4	264.1	223.6	181.7
Services	49.6	41.6	31.9	43.4
Construction	0.0	8.7	7.5	20.1
General corporate	230.0	279.7	306.0	318.6
Total assets	$1,956.5	$1,596.0	$1,352.5	$1,257.4
Capital expenditures:				
Aircraft	$ 232.6	$ 201.2	$ 246.9	$ 103.2
Electronics	68.0	40.9	59.7	44.6
Services	3.5	2.3	1.9	4.5
Construction	0.0	0.0	0.1	0.8
General corporate	41.2	48.7	68.2	36.6
Total expenditures	$ 345.3	$ 293.1	$ 376.8	$ 189.7
Depreciation & amortization:				
Aircraft	$ 105.8	$ 75.2	$ 33.3	$ 21.5
Electronics	22.9	19.8	12.2	10.1
Services	2.3	1.6	1.6	1.9
Construction	0.0	0.0	0.2	0.2
General corporate	7.1	13.2	13.6	7.3
Total depreciation & amortization	$ 138.1	$ 109.8	$ 60.9	$ 41.0

Sources: Northrop Corporation, "Annual reports," 1984–1987.

midsection of Boeing's 747 airliner since the start of the plane's production in 1966. Sales from that product reached $125 million in 1984 and were expected to increase modestly into the 1990s.

Advanced Systems. In 1981, the Aircraft Group's Advanced Systems Division, along with team members Boeing, LTV/Vought, and the General Electric Aircraft Engine Group, was awarded the development contract for the Air Force's top secret Advanced Technology Bomber better known as the Stealth. The Stealth had been widely discussed in the media but little was actually known about the secret plane. A large strategic bomber with a radical shape and the technology to render it undetectable to radar, the Stealth was expected to cost nearly $500 million per plane. If it was put into production that price would make it the most expensive aircraft ever built. The Stealth was, as a consequence, politically vulnerable; its astounding price was a liability in Congress.

The development contract for the Stealth bomber had boosted company sales substantially. Although the exact figures were classified, analysts believed that the contribution to revenues from the development contract was near $1 billion in 1984 and would increase in 1985. While there was no assurance of Northrop being awarded the production contract, such a contract could produce sales of up to $35 billion over the next decade.

Perhaps as profitable would be the contract for the Air Force's Advanced Technology Fighter (ATF). Northrop's Advanced Systems Division had begun preliminary research and development on this project without the benefit of government funding. However, the ATF was as much of a gamble as the Stealth in some respects. Designed to be a "super-fighter" for the 21st century, the ATF was targeted to replace the F-15s and F-16s as America's top fighter. The competition for the contract, however, was expected to be long and costly. Teams consisting of a prime contractor and major subcontractor were required to put in bids to build the plane. The two winning teams would be selected in the early 1990s and each would then construct a prototype of their own design. One of these prototypes would be chosen for full-scale production by the team that created it. Northrop was the prime contractor on its team; McDonnell-Douglas was the major subcontractor. Vying with Northrop and McDonnell-Douglas for the contract were Lockheed, Rockwell Industries, and Boeing.

Although management at both companies believed they had an excellent chance of being one of the two winning teams, financial analysts saw such a possibility as a mixed blessing. Each winning team would receive $691 million from the Defense Department but would probably have to spend several times that amount again in order to complete a prototype. The stakes were high, however. The total production contract was expected to generate sales of $35 to $45 billion and extend into the next century.

Ventura. The Aircraft Group's Ventura Division had contributed sales of $350 million in 1984 and was the dominant producer of unmanned drones (self-propelled targets). Basically small monoplanes driven by turbojets, the drones were typically used to train pilots and anti-aircraft crews in the operation of various weapons systems. A derivative of these drones had also been used by the U.S. Navy as a remotely piloted reconnaissance vehicle. Northrop's UMVs (unmanned vehicle) and RPVs (remotely piloted vehicle) were being used by every branch of the U.S. Armed Forces and numerous NATO countries as well. The experience gained with unmanned flight vehicles helped land the Ventura Division a contract for a joint U.S. Air Force and Navy radar suppression missile system known as

Tacit Rainbow. Designed to seek out and attack enemy radar warning systems, it had the capability to loiter over an area until a transmitter activated and presented itself as a target.

Electronics Group

The Electronics Group consisted of four divisions: Defense Systems, Electro-Mechanical, Electronics, and Precision Products. Group sales were $750 million in 1984.

Defense Systems. By 1985 the Defense Systems Division of the Electronics Group was on its way to becoming the nation's largest producer of airborne jamming equipment. Broadly defined as electronic countermeasures (ECM), this equipment protected aircraft and crew by confusing and disrupting enemy radar-guided weapons systems. Enormously successful, Northrop's ECM equipment was installed on various aircraft such as the McDonnell-Douglas F-15 fighter and the Boeing B-52 bomber. In addition, Northrop was under contract with Denmark, Spain, and Canada to provide jamming systems for their armed forces. Britain had also purchased several ECM components for its Harrier aircraft.

Electro-Mechanical. The Electro-Mechanical Division had become an important producer of passive sensor devices. These devices used electro-optical television and infra-red technology to enable pilots and anti-aircraft crews to locate targets without the telltale emissions of radar. Both the U.S. Army and Navy had placed orders.

Electronics. The Electronics Division was involved in two major projects. The first was the development and manufacture of the navigation system for the Air Force's AWACS (early warning) plane. The other project involved a long-term contract to produce the Advanced Inertial Reference Sphere (AIRS), the primary element of the MX Peacekeeper missile's internal guidance system. The program had the potential to last into the early 1990s, and was expected to generate more than $1 billion in revenues. The MX was, however, a politically unstable program. Budget deficits and arms control talks made its future unclear.

Precision Products. Northrop's Precision Products Division pioneered the development of "strapdown" guidance and navigation systems. The name was derived from the method of bolting the systems' gyroscopes to a vehicle frame rather than mounting the devices in complex gimbals as was previously done. The design had applications in multiple areas including airplanes, helicopters, tactical missiles, spacecraft, and torpedoes. It was also used on the F-20. Northrop expected to receive a guidance system contract for the advanced medium range air-to-air missile from the U.S. Air Force and Navy, as well as the contracts for the Navy's Harpoon and Tomahawk anti-ship missiles.

Service Group

Service was the smallest group in terms of sales ($422 million in 1984). It was a no-growth business that lacked the excitement and glamour of Northrop's other groups. It consisted of one division, Aircraft Services, and two wholly owned subsidiaries, Northrop Services and Northrop Worldwide Aircraft Services.

Aircraft Services. The Aircraft Services Division provided on-the-job training in management and support for civil and military aviation personnel.

Northrop Services. This subsidiary provided environmental studies and general consulting to a number of Federal agencies such as NASA and the EPA.

Worldwide Aircraft Services. Northrop's Worldwide Aircraft Services subsidiary was the major revenue generator of the Service Group. It provided maintenance, support, and property management for military bases and for F-5s sold throughout the world. A large portion of the Group's operating profits came from this subsidiary's Peace Hawk/ATTS, a support services project for the Saudi Arabian Air Force. This project, however, was scheduled to end in 1986.

NORTHROP'S CORPORATE STRATEGY

With Thomas Jones leading the company, Northrop used a six-pronged strategy with aspects that distinguished it from many of its defense competitors. In the main, this strategy shaped the formulation of the F-20 program.

1. *High level of spending on research and development.* Research into radar avoidance won Northrop a profitable development contract for the Stealth bomber. Research in electronics, reinvestment, and the purchase of existing companies, such as the Hallicrafters Electronics Company, made Northrop the industry leader in ECM and other military electronics. The Tigershark became the first fighter with 1980s technology. By using avionics and electronics garnered from company research, the F-20 had some capabilities beyond those of its competitors.

2. *Use of company funds for plant and equipment.* Northrop owned 94% of its plants, putting it above the industry average in terms of capital spending as a percentage of sales. The DOD owned half of all other defense aerospace manufacturing facilities. Northrop's ownership of its plants allowed more flexibility and made the F-20 project possible without government funding.

3. *Conservative financial and accounting practices.* Northrop employed a financial policy described by one analyst as reactionary. The company chose to expense development costs as they occurred. For example, all of the costs of the Tigershark program, including fixtures and tools, were charged against earnings in the year incurred. So far the F-20 write-offs had amounted to $258.5 million in 1982, $168.1 million in 1983, and $148.5 million in 1984, with a like amount expected for 1985.

4. *Focus on defense aerospace and electronics.* Exclusive of its 747 subcontract, Northrop had no significant commercial business, a characteristic that it had in common with some of its competitors. Northrop's sales of F-5s to foreign governments, however, did give it a degree of protection from domestic budget cuts and political swings that might affect defense spending.

5. *Competing for major first-line contracts.* In 1985, Northrop competed for major domestic defense contracts and was building prototypes of the F-20.

6. *Willingness to take risks and reinvest cash flow.* Jones was adamant in his belief that private contractors should accept the risks inherent in developing new technology.

The F-20 was the only modern fighter ever developed solely from private funds without a government contract. Not everyone was comfortable with these policies, however. Wall Street analysts estimated that a decision to drop the F-20 program could add as much as $1.55 per share to the value of Northrop stock.

CONCLUSION

Northrop was clearly not prepared for the change in policy invoked by the Reagan Administration nor did it anticipate the political symbolism Third World countries would attach to having a top quality U.S. Air Force inventory plane. Relegating itself to the foreign market, Northrop had, in the past, managed to avoid most of the political infrastructure characteristic of the domestic defense market. It was unclear whether that approach would continue to be possible. Northrop's main competitor, General Dynamics, had the largest share of the industry, but many believed it also had an intangible advantage that went beyond its research and development prowess. General Dynamics built the F-16 in Texas, the home of Senate Armed Services Committee chairman John Tower (R) and within the district of Jim Wright (D), House majority leader. Both controlled key votes concerning foreign military aid packages. As one anonymous Air Force officer joked, "It rolls off the assembly line faster if it's built in Texas."

Another obstacle Northrop had to overcome was the Defense Department itself. The Pentagon acted as middleman for all export sales and disseminated information and performance data to interested parties. DOD officials had privately stated that both the Air Force and the Navy preferred to promote the sales of their own fighters overseas "to amortize costs and to keep production lines open." Other officials allowed that the Pentagon "procurement community" preferred planes it had ordered to privately designed aircraft like the F-20, regardless of capability. In addition, the Air Force received $745,000 for each F-16 sold to export to cover flight preparation and testing. Northrop officials had complained that data comparing the F-20 and F-16 had not been given to prospective buyers and that the State Department had done little to represent their fighter. In fact, Jones publicly asked that the Air Force be ordered to inform other governments of the low cost and high performance of the Tigershark.

The current success of Northrop was due in large part to the cash flows generated by the F-5 Tiger. For decades, it had bankrolled Northrop's entry and growth in military electronics and higher levels of research and development in aerospace. Now, American and foreign export fighters alike were outperforming the aging Tigers which were approaching obsolescence. To fail with the Tigershark would be tantamount to abandoning the market for export planes that Northrop had created and exploited for so long.

Ultimately, the future of Northrop's aircraft business rested on risky and uncertain programs: the Stealth (Advanced Technology Bomber), the Advanced Technical Fighter (ATF), and the F-20 Tigershark. The Stealth and ATF projects held great promise and Jones wondered if Northrop would be better served by writing off the F-20 program and diverting the funds to these new projects. On the other hand, he knew that a successful F-20 program could help fund these projects and more, as the F-5 had before it. In 1981, Jones had remarked that, "If we didn't make this investment [in the Tigershark], I would be telling you our future in fighter planes is less secure. It's riskier to do nothing." Four years later, with no orders in hand, Jones had to decide if that was still true.

References

Air Cal, "Northrop Corporation: The sky's the limit," May 1986.

Air Force Magazine, "Trials of the Tigershark," January 1985, pp. 72–77.

Asian Defence Journal, "Revving up for the big flyoff: F-20 vs. F-16," April 1986, pp. 1–7.

Atlantic Monthly, "The airplane that doesn't cost much," August 1984, pp. 46–55.

Aviation Week & Space Technology, "U.S. will assist Turkey in improving air defense," February 20, 1984, p. 68.

Berstein & Company, "General Dynamics," August 6, 1981.

Business Week, "Look who's heading for no. 1 in defense," April 19, 1982, pp. 70–75.

Business Week, "Northrop's campaign to get a new fighter flying in the Third World," June 18, 1984, pp. 74–75.

Chrisman, J. J., "Note on the defense electronics industry," University of Georgia, 1982.

Cunningham, R., Dampier, J. D., Fuqua, A., Gill, E., Pannell, D., & Turner, L., "General Dynamics Corporation: Defense electronics industry analysis," University of Georgia, 1984.

Dun's Business Month, "Northrop: The rewards of risk," December 1985, p. 36.

Electronic Industry Association, "Defense electronics market: Ten year forecast 1982–1991," October 1981.

Financial World, "A cloudy future for Northrop Corp.," February 20, 1985, pp. 38–39.

Flight International, "Tigershark tour raises sales hopes," October 6, 1984.

Flight International, "Stealth specialists win ATF contracts," November 8, 1986, p. 2.

Forbes, "High roller," March 2, 1981, pp. 38–39.

Fortune, "Northrop aims for a killing with the Tigershark," June 24, 1985.

Fox, J. R., with Field, J. L., *The defense management challenge: Weapons acquisition,* Cambridge, MA: Harvard Business School Press, 1988.

General Dynamics, "Annual reports," 1974–1984.

Insight, "Northrop uses spit and polish to keep an untarnished image," June 16, 1986.

Interavia, "The affordable fighter market," January 1985, pp. 23–26.

International Defense Review, "East Asian tactical fighter markets," December 1985.

Jurkus, A. F., "Requiem for a lightweight: The Northrop F-20 initiative," *Strategic Management Journal,* 1990, Vol. 11, pp. 59–68.

Leslie, J., "Northrop Corporation," University of South Carolina, 1988.

Moody's, *Moody's industrial manual,* 1980–1985.

Newsweek, "Northrop's F-20 goes begging," March 26, 1984, p. 71.

New York Times, "Dispute over fighter imports," April 5, 1985.

New York Times, "Northrop backs Tigershark jet," May 15, 1985.

Northrop Corporation, "Annual reports," 1982–1988.

Northrop Corporation Public Relations, "Northrop News," 1989.

Shearson/American Express, "Aerospace/defense outlook," March 17, 1983.

Standard & Poor's, *NYSE reports,* 1980–1985.

CASE 26

Maytag Corporation*

Maytag CEO Daniel Krumm was in his office when he received word that Salomon Brothers, a New York investment banking firm, had found a potential merger candidate that would provide Maytag an entry into the European appliance market before the European Economic Community pact took effect in 1992.

HISTORY OF MAYTAG

The Maytag company was founded by F. L. Maytag, with three other men in Newton, Iowa, in 1893. The company produced threshing-machine bandcutters and self-feeder attachments invented by one of the founders of the company. In the early 1900s the line was expanded to include a variety of farm products such as hay presses, hog waterers, and harvesting equipment. As a sideline to counteract the seasonal slump in the farm equipment line, the company produced a washing machine. About this time, F. L. Maytag became the sole owner of the firm.

Steady improvements were made in the next two decades which resulted in the company becoming a national leader in the new laundry appliance industry. The manufacture of farm implements was discontinued in the early 1920s and exclusive attention devoted to laundry and related products. The company went public in 1925. By 1927 Maytag produced its one millionth washer.

Despite the depression the Maytag company never experienced a loss. During World War II the company converted all its manufacturing to military purposes.

The production of clothes dryers was added in 1953 and 5 years later the company expanded into the commercial laundry field. Although Maytag marketed a line of ranges and refrigerators in 1946, manufactured under the Maytag name by other companies, they were discontinued respectively in 1955 and 1960.

The company reentered the kitchen appliance field in 1960 with a portable dishwasher and a food-waste disposer in 1968.

MANAGEMENT AT MAYTAG

In 1972 Daniel Krumm was appointed president and in 1974 chief executive officer. In 1986 he was also named chairman. Krumm, a Sioux City, Iowa, native, typifies Maytag's management, long on service and home bred. He has been with Maytag for 36 years; Sterling Swanger, senior vice president for manufacturing, 42 years (now retired); Robert Faust,

* Prepared by Peter P. Schoderbek, University of Iowa, and Satish P. Deshpande, Western Michigan University. Thanks to Maytag officials for their generous assistance. Distributed by the North American Case Research Association.

vice president, manufacturing, 34 years; Dean Ward, director of purchases, 35 years; Leonard Hadley, executive vice president and president of the Appliance Group, 30 years; Ray Dahlman, chief manufacturing engineer, 31 years; Doug Ringger, manager, product testing, 36 years; G. H. Weaver, manager, quality control, 20 years; Fred Swank, supervisor, manufacturing engineering, 41 years; Jesse White, who has played the role of Ol' Lonely, 23 years (now retired); Einar Larsen, director of advertising (now retired), 38 years.

Maytag prides itself on its conservatism which extends to most aspects of its business. Maytag stock is a favorite among widows, trust departments of banks, and pension funds. Although Wall Street does not tag Maytag as a glamour company it does respect it as a well-run firm that sticks to basic manufacturing and marketing.

It may be said that Maytag's executives are all cut out of the same solid mold. Not only do they work together, but they socialize together. The company strongly believes in promotion from within which fosters a fierce loyalty to the company; nearly all the top managers have started near the bottom of the organization. The company describes its employees, both management and the workers, as "down to earth with virtually no distance between the president and the assembly-line worker." Under Krumm, Maytag has pretty well maintained its image as a "comfortable, old shoes type of company, a builder of dependable products." Krumm admits that prior to their expansion in 1986 Maytag had a reputation of growing by "plodding along." Top officers state that Maytag is "no master of rapid change" but moves only if quality can be assured.

Wall Street thinks that their expansion in 1986 was necessary because of consolidation in the industry; however, one industry analyst at that time worried whether Krumm had done enough to lead Maytag into the future.

Krumm stated in early 1987 that Maytag was "dedicated to remaining independent. We have taken every protection for a company that we could take."[1] Although the company adopted a "poison-pill" antitakeover measure in the summer of 1986 rumors periodically circulate that the company is a target.

MAYTAG COMPANY'S CULTURE—QUALITY

Maytag managers and employees alike have the same commitment to quality. It has helped create a work force with a high degree of pride, says one Maytag manager. Another states:

> Quality is a religion here . . . we are brought up in an atmosphere of quality. Quality emanates from the top to the bottom and from the bottom to the top. Quality starts with design and doesn't end until the product is shipped out the door and even then it doesn't end because consumers must believe and know that they're getting a quality product. Our employees don't know anything other than quality since it's a philosophy here.[2]

The Maytag company has long practiced employee participation as a means of improving quality. Individual and team recognition and financial incentive programs are used

---

[1] *Des Moines Register.* (1987, January 25). p. 15W.

[2] Maytag manager, company interview, November 1, 1989.

extensively in improving productivity. An Employees' Idea Plan pays one-half of the net savings during a 6-month period up to a maximum of $7,500. In 1986, 95 percent of the production employees submitted suggestions to the plan which averaged out to cost savings of $375 per employee. The average submission rate was 3.2 per employee with an installation rate of 1.5 ideas per worker. The company's financial incentive systems cover 95 percent of the direct-labor operations.[3]

The Employees' Idea Plan is a consistent winner of the excellent performance award given by the National Association of Suggestions Systems. Teamwork pervades throughout the company and such things as quality circles aren't deemed necessary because employees constantly interact with their supervisors. Both new supervisors and new production employees go through a training program of work simplification aimed at cost-cutting measures.

Supervisors also participate in a cost-reduction program but receive no financial awards albeit they do receive recognition awards. In 1986, the submission rate resulted in an installation of 9.5 ideas per supervisor and a cost reduction of $24,835 per supervisor.[4]

Reliability testing is done based on market research which looks at average consumer usage. Test criteria are applied that are three times average consumer use. Many parts are tested for 20-year use equivalency.

PRICING STRATEGY OF THE MAYTAG COMPANY

Maytag Company's pricing strategy is one of charging for the quality that is built into the product. Maytag has chosen not to compete on price while other competitors have been known to cut prices in order to expand their markets. A cost leadership position dictates economies of scale and a large market share. Maytag has maintained its commitment to the high end of the market. Maytag has long recognized the importance of its brand name in developing and implementing its "pull" strategy, that is, the customer is committed to the Maytag brand before entering the store. Quality and dependability have been the cornerstone of its strategy.

In a "push" strategy manufacturers give retailers higher profit margins and advertising allowances in an effort to switch customers to higher-priced models. People are encouraged to enter the store by highly advertised low price models before they are moved up to higher-priced models. Store personnel are financially motivated to "trade-up" the customer.

Ol' Lonely, who personifies Maytag's commitment to quality, and is the cornerstone for advertising, has been around for over 20 years. His recognition, according to Maytag, is about 90 percent. The advertising strategy, according to Ol' Lonely, is "based on positioning the company as a supplier of superior products. . . . Dependability, which means 'Built better and built to last longer' to us, is not quite as easy to dramatize as performance. This is what the character of Ol' Lonely does so well for us. He dramatizes the benefits of long life and dependability."[5]

---

[3] Design for mechanization. (1987, November). *Appliance Manufacturer*, pp. 41, 44.

[4] Ibid.

[5] Ol' Lonely: Heart and soul of Maytag brand. (1987, November). *Appliance Manufacturer*, pp. 58, 60.

DISTRIBUTION AT MAYTAG

Until 1982 Maytag utilized independent dealers, some who carried only the Maytag line while others carried a variety of lines. Maytag bypassed independent distributors who were used by other manufacturers. Some of the old-line dealers had exclusive dealerships in some communities. In 1982 Montgomery Ward was franchised as a dealer for laundry equipment. Some viewed this as an opportunity to broaden Maytag's selling base and as a way to reach more consumers through a national chain store that offered revolving credit. A later survey showed that the availability of credit was the principal reason for purchasing a washer or dryer at Wards. In 1986 Montgomery Ward began selling Maytag dishwashers.

Because of the expanded line of products by 1985, Maytag established a financing plan for dealers (floor planning) to allow them to carry larger inventories. More recently, Maytag products have entered the discount trade in stores like Best Buy.

Because of their increased product line, Maytag, in 1986, initiated an aggressive program to market directly to the builder market. Up to this time Maytag concentrated on sales at the retail level since sales of laundry products were a small market to home builders. However, with the addition of kitchen appliances to their line, the builders market represented a new territory for Maytag that would not detract from existing retail business. Some believe that with the trend to two income families, consumers were becoming less price sensitive and more quality conscious. Builders were able to purchase Hardwick, Jenn-Air, or Maytag appliances directly from the company.

MARKETS

There are two major markets for appliances in the U.S.—retail and contract. Retailers include mass merchandisers such as Sears, appliance dealers who carry many brands, discount stores such as K-Mart or Best Buy, and department stores. Mass merchandisers such as Sears carry their own brands manufactured according to their specifications. In 1989 Sears made the decision to carry a variety of competitors' products. Department store sales have recently slipped and seem to have been taken up by regionals that specialize in appliances.

The contract market refers to builders and contractors who often make the decision as to what appliances to put into new housing. Builders are typically cost conscious and usually buy appliances at the middle or lower end of the line. Since they can save on transportation costs and can exact some price concessions because of quantity buying, all appliances are usually purchased from one manufacturer. General Electric has long dominated the new housing market because of their solid relations with builders and their strong brand image.

MAYTAG IN THE 1980s—A PERIOD OF GROWTH

Although Maytag expected to share in the expected growth of the appliance industry in the 1980s, the company felt that their participation was somewhat limited because of their

EXHIBIT 1
Selected Financial Data
(in Thousands of Dollars, Except per Share Data)

	*1989**	*1988*	*1987*	*1986*	*1985*
Net sales	$3,088,753	$1,885,641	$1,822,106	$1,632,924	$1,571,032
Cost of sales	2,312,645	1,413,627	1,318,122	1,183,377	1,141,119
Income taxes	75,500	79,700	105,300	97,500	99,300
Income from continuing operations	131,472	135,522	147,678	114,739	119,318
Percent of income from continuing operations of net sales	4.3%	7.2%	8.1%	7.0%	7.6%
Income from continuing operations per share	$1.27	$1.77	$1.84	$1.32	$1.38
Dividends paid per share	0.950	0.950	0.950	0.850	0.825
Average shares outstanding (in thousands)	103,694	76,563	80,151	86,619	86,502
Working capital	$650,905	$317,145	$286,124	$330,116	$393,967
Depreciation of property, plant, and equipment	68,077	34,454	35,277	32,659	33,765
Additions to property, plant, and equipment	127,838	101,756	42,564	45,619	41,066
Total assets	2,436,319	1,330,069	854,925	882,576	893,608
Long-term debt	876,836	518,165	140,765	46,189	98,570
Total debt to capitalization	50.6%	51.5%	28.1%	11.0%	16.9%
Shareowners' equity per share	$8.89	$6.55	$5.43	$6.53	$6.48

* These amounts reflect the acquisition of Hoover on January 26, 1989.

short line of products. At the same time the company had just completed a large modernization program. Capital needs were low and cash reserves were growing (see Exhibit 1). It was decided by company personnel to search out new opportunities and the best alternative was to purchase an existing product line rather than develop one of their own. The appliance industry at the time was consolidating partly because of the economies of scale that could be achieved with larger volume and partly because of pressure by dealers for full product lines. Because most dealers are members of groups which may order hundreds of millions of dollars of products a year, their desire for full product lines carries weight with manufacturers.

Maytag purchased Hardwick Stove in 1981 and Jenn-Air Corporation in 1982. Hardwick was a leading producer of gas and electric stoves whose history dated back 103 years. Hardwick was purchased for $4.5 million and 968,250 shares of Maytag stock having a value of $23.6 million.

Jenn-Air was acquired for $20.7 million cash and a promissory note of $30 million. Jenn-Air manufactures and markets a line of built-in and free-standing electric and gas ranges that utilize downdraft venting. The company sells to home construction and remodeling industries. Jenn Industries, which was a subsidiary of Jenn-Air and manufactured and marketed power ventilation equipment for institutional, commercial, and industrial buildings, was sold in 1988.

In the early 1980s Maytag decided to enter into the cooking appliance market with a complete line. New products included several versions of a microwave oven and new models of a free-standing stove with a variety of options such as continuous cleaning, gas, electric, attached microwave, and so forth. Wall ovens were also introduced as a companion feature to the Jenn-Air grill range and featured both conventional as well as convection cooking. In 1983, Maytag decided to suspend production of the wringer washer which was manufactured continuously for 76 years. Sales of this product totaled 11.7 million units.

In 1985 the company introduced a stacked pair of clothes dryers designed for use in commercial laundry stores or in coin-operated laundries in apartment buildings.

1986 was considered a banner year for Maytag. The company issued 16,072,000 shares of stock for the acquisition of all of the outstanding stock of Magic Chef, Inc., which produced a full range of appliances. Magic Chef brought to the merger the Admiral Company which makes refrigerators, freezers, and dehumidifiers. Magic Chef, Inc., also owned Norge which manufactures washing machines and dryers, and Warwick which produces compact refrigerators. CEO Dan Krumm stated that because of the consolidation in the appliance industry which has led to fewer, larger companies, there was increased concern about Maytag's long-range future in the industry. The purchase of Magic Chef tripled the number of employees from 5,000 to 15,000; sales increased from $700 million to about $1.8 billion; and factories from 6 to 21. Market share increased from 5 percent to 13 percent.

While Maytag and Jenn-Air have traditionally been positioned at the high end of the market, Magic Chef's target market is the broad middle range. Admiral and Norge, divisions of Magic Chef, also manufacture for the private label market. Maytag's officers felt that this merger allowed the company to serve more of the appliance market. As with Hardwick and Jenn-Air, each of the individual brands retain their own identity. As a full-line manufacturer, Maytag now ranks only behind GE, Whirlpool, and Electrolux. These companies dominate the American market.

In 1986 Jenn-Air introduced a line of refrigerators and freezers manufactured by Admiral. Admiral also introduced a forty-bottle Wine Cellar which is a temperature-controlled cooler. Toastmaster, a Magic Chef company, was sold because it did not strategically fit major appliances. Heatube, a division of Toastmaster, was not included in the sale; the company manufactures heating elements used by Magic Chef as well as other appliance manufacturers. Other companies included in the merger are Dixie-Narco which manufactures soft drink vending machines; Warwick, which manufactures compact refrigerators and freezers which are sold under a variety of labels including Magic Chef and Admiral; and Ardac, which manufactures electronic money changers. Magic Chef Air Conditioning (sold in 1988) produced a full line of residential and industrial heating and cooling equipment. Maycor is a new company formed to provide product service and repair parts distribution for all the appliances. Exhibit 2 depicts an organization chart for Maytag.

EXHIBIT 2
Organization Chart of the Maytag Corporation

Appliance Group	*Hoover Group*	*Diversified Products Group*
Admiral Company	Hoover North America	Dixie-Narco, Inc.
Heatube Company	Hoover United Kingdom	Warwick
Jenn-Air Company	Hoover Trading	
Maycor Appliance Parts & Service Co.	Hoover Australia	
Magic Chef Company	Domicor, Inc.	
Maytag Company		

THE ACQUISITION OF CHICAGO PACIFIC CORPORATION

On October 27, 1988, Maytag made a cash tender offer under which they bought 6.4 million shares, or about 49 percent of Chicago Pacific stock for $60 a share, or $384 million. The remainder of Chicago Pacific's shares were exchanged for Maytag stock at the rate of one share of Chicago Pacific for 2.72 shares of Maytag stock. Maytag Corporation issued 27.5 million new shares to complete the exchange. The total cost of the acquisition was in excess of $900 million. Maytag put more than $300 million of goodwill on its books.

Chicago Pacific Corporation, the successor of the Chicago, Rock Island, and Pacific Railroad, purchased the Hoover Company in 1985 for $534 million. The Hoover Company, which has product lines in vacuum cleaners and household appliances, has established bases in Britain and Australia. Its European operations include washers, dryers, dishwashers, refrigerators, and microwave ovens.

Hoover has fourteen manufacturing facilities in eight countries and approximately 15,100 employees. Net sales of Hoover in 1988 were $1.5 billion. The market for major appliances in Australia is $250 million.

With the acquisition of Chicago Pacific Corporation, Maytag also acquired six furniture businesses. These were sold a year later in late 1989.

At the time of the acquisition, Maytag, with its low debt and large asset base, was a prime target for a takeover, according to many Wall Street rumormongers. Analysts said that it was simply a question of "eat or be eaten."[6]

In the fall of 1988 Maytag's stock experienced a brief rise as a result of the rumors. This signaled officials of Maytag to firm up company strategy. Company officers claim to have already been committed to the globalization of Maytag because of (1) the changes that would be brought about by the European Economic Community in 1992, (2) market saturation in the United States, and (3) the trend toward other appliance firms internationalizing (see Exhibit 3).

EXHIBIT 3
Some Questions Directed to Maytag CEO Dan Krumm at the 1988 Annual Meeting

Q: What are the basic elements of Maytag's corporate strategy?

A: "Our business plan is to broaden market shares of premium-priced appliances, increase penetration with multiple brands in the midrange market and expand in the growing international markets. Implicit in this plan are our objectives of improving profitability and achieving long-term growth in both sales and earnings."

Q: Some people viewed the merger with Chicago Pacific as an antitakeover move on the part of Maytag. Was it?

A: "Clearly not. It was a strategic business move on our part to include international markets in Maytag's long-range plan for growth. Hoover's major appliance business is very strong in the United Kingdom and Australia, and it is growing on the European continent. This was just the type of entry into the overseas appliance market that we were looking for. Any defensive characteristics are incidental to our objective of providing long-term growth."

[6] Bremmer, Brian. (1989, January 30). Can Maytag clean up the world? *Business Week*, p. 86.

EUROPEAN ECONOMIC COMMUNITY

The European Economic Community pact that is expected to go into effect in 1992 will provide a market of 350 million people with a gross national product of about $4.5 trillion. This is a population of about 40 percent greater than the United States. In 1988 households numbered about 130 million in Europe versus about 91 million in the United States. Because of a rising standard of living, Europeans are enjoying a significant increase in purchasing power and are expected to have almost as much money as the consumers of the United States and Japan combined. Gross domestic product per capita in about half of the Western European countries exceeds that of the United States.

The potential of this tariff-free market is causing firms throughout the world to locate, merge, or acquire European firms to give them access to the market. Krumm feels "that it is absolutely essential that we have a presence established in Europe prior to 1992. . . . As an American company, if you're not there by 1992, you're not going to participate at all."[7]

MARKET SATURATION OF THE U.S.

Exhibit 4 shows the amount of saturation of the U.S. appliance market. Future sales are expected mainly from replacement demand and new housing. The saturation value, noted in column two of Exhibit 4, shows the percentage of households in the United States who own the corresponding appliance. The high values show that the American market is filled with 75 percent of sales going to replacement or upgrading. New housing starts account for most of the remaining appliance sales. For every new home built four new appliances are sold. The outlook for appliances shows a fairly steady demand over the next several years.

Although growth prospects for appliances in the U.S. market for the 1990s appear to be good, there is little doubt that the industry has taken on characteristics of maturity. The consolidation of firms, established market shares, and high levels of productivity all signal intense competition in the states. Several of the major participants feel that opportunities for increased market shares must come from overseas operations.

THE INTERNATIONALIZATION AND CONSOLIDATION OF APPLIANCE COMPANIES

Some appliance firms have already made a commitment to globalization. A.B. Electrolux, for example, recently acquired White Consolidated which already owned seven appliance companies including Westinghouse and Frigidaire. Electrolux also acquired appliance manufacturers in Italy and the United Kingdom. (See Exhibit 5 for recent consolidations in the appliance industry.)

Whirlpool established a joint venture with the Dutch giant N.V. Philips, in which it has a 53 percent stake. It also has joint ventures in India and Mexico. Whirlpool also owns 70

[7] Maytag: Pursuing a global market. (1989, February 12). *Cedar Rapids (Iowa) Gazette.*

EXHIBIT 4
Market Share—Major Appliance Manufacturers (1988)

Major Producers (Market Share)		Saturation
Refrigerators (7,227,000 unit sales)		99.9%
GE	34%	
Whirlpool	27%	
Electrolux/WCI	20%	
Maytag/Admiral	11%	
Raytheon/Amana	6%	
Others	2%	
Washers (6,190,400)		71.0%
Whirlpool	50%	
Maytag	18%	
GE	15%	
Electrolux/WCI	11%	
Raytheon/Speed Queen	4%	
Others	2%	
Dishwashers (3,907,400)		48.0%
GE	40%	
Whirlpool	29%	
Electrolux/WCI	21%	
Maytag	7%	
Thermador/Waste King	1%	
Others	2%	
Electric dryers (3,303,900)		51.4%
Whirlpool	50%	
GE	15%	
Maytag	15%	
Electrolux/WCI	13%	
Raytheon/Speed Queen	4%	
Others	2%	
Dryers (gas) (1,046,800)		na*
Whirlpool	50%	
Maytag	16%	
GE	15%	
Electrolux/WCI	13%	
Raytheon/Speed Queen	4%	
Others	2%	
Ranges (electric) (3,201,600)		62.0%
GE	41%	
Electrolux/WCI	21%	
Whirlpool	15%	
Maytag (Magic Chef, Hardwick, Jenn-Air)	11%	
Raytheon/Caloric	6%	
Thermador/Waste King	1%	
Others	5%	

Major Producers (Market Share)		Saturation
Ranges (gas) (2,167,300)		42.0%
Maytag/Magic Chef Hardwick	32%	
Electrolux/WCI	28%	
Raytheon/Caloric	18%	
GE/Roper	15%	
Brown	3%	
Others	4%	
Microwave ovens (10,810,000)		60.5%
Samsung	17%	
Goldstar	17%	
Sharp	15%	
Matsushita	12%	
Sanyo	12%	
Litton	6%	
Electrolux/Tappan	6%	
Raytheon/Amana	5%	
Maytag/Magic Chef	3%	
Toshiba	2%	
Whirlpool	1%	
Others	4%	
Freezers (1,348,800)		na
Whirlpool	33%	
Electrolux/WCI	33%	
Maytag/Admiral	23%	
Raytheon/Amana	6%	
Others	5%	
Disposers (3,907,400)		na
In-Sink Erator	60%	
Electrolux/Anaheim	30%	
Thermador/Waste King	5%	
Watertown/Metal Products	3%	
Maytag	1%	

* na = not available.
Adapted from Standard & Poor's Industry Surveys (1988); and *Appliance* (1989).

EXHIBIT 5
Consolidations in the Appliance Industry

1970	*1980*	*1988*	*1989*
GE	GE	GE	GE/GEC (England)
Roper	Roper		
Whirlpool	Whirlpool		
KitchenAid	Dart&Kraft		
Chambers		Whirlpool	Whirlpool/Philips
Roper	Roper		
Thermador/Waste King	Thermador/Waste King	Masco	Masco
Magic Chef			
Johnson Corp.			
Gaffers&Sattler	Magic Chef		
Admiral			
Norge		Maytag	Maytag/Hoover
Revco			
Warwick (Philco)	Warwick		
Maytag	Maytag		
Hardwick	Jenn-Air		
Amana			
Caloric			
Glenwood Range	Raytheon	Raytheon	Raytheon
Modern Maid			
Speed Queen			
Matsushita	Matsushita	Matsushita	Matsushita
AB Electrolux	AB Electrolux		
Arthur-Martin	Corpero		
Husqvarna	Zanussi		
Vest-Frost	Thorn		
Zanker	Domar		
Gibson			
Franklin			
Hamilton		AB Electrolux	AB Electrolux
Kelvinator	WCI		
Athens Stove			
Westinghouse			
Frigidaire			
D&M	D&M		
Tappan	ABE		
Eureka			
Philips	Philips		
Ignis	Baukecht	Philips	
Sanyo	Sanyo	Sanyo	Sanyo
	Samsung	Samsung	Samsung
Bosch	Bosch-Siemens		
Siemens	Constructa	Bosch-Siemens	Bosch-Siemens/Balay
	Neff		
Merioni	Merioni	Merioni/Indesit	Merioni
Candy	Candy	Candy Rosieres	Candy

percent of Inglis, Canada's second largest appliance company, and a 65 percent interest in an Italian company. It is the second largest appliance maker in Europe after Electrolux.

Recent consolidations in Europe have significantly altered market shares of both the major and minor players. Strong competition exists at both ends of the market. Firms like Bosch-Siemens, which dominates Germany, compete aggressively at the high-quality seg-

EXHIBIT 6
On Consolidation and Globalization

For a number of years, consolidation has been the dominant trend in the U.S. appliance industry, and 1988 was no exception. Whirlpool and General Electric each made a bid for Roper Corp., a manufacturer of gas and electric ranges and outdoor power equipment. Both firms sought Roper's gas range production capabilities plus the company's strong ties with Sears.

GE ended up acquiring Roper's factories and assets, but Whirlpool received the Roper brand name and an agreement from GE to supply Roper brand cooking appliances for 2 years. Whirlpool plans to market a full line of Roper brand major appliances in the low to middle price range. Meanwhile, GE announced it would activate the RCA brand name and use it on a complete line of major appliances.

In another move, Whirlpool's KitchenAid division acquired the dishwasher and trash compactor business of Emerson Electric Company.

Added to the continuing consolidation trend in 1988 was an increased interest in global appliance markets. In many parts of the world, the saturation levels of major appliances are much lower than they are in the mature U.S. market, so the potential for growth is greater.

Whirlpool implemented a joint venture by announcing its plans to acquire a 53 percent ownership in the major appliance division of N.V. Philips, which is based in the Netherlands. According to Whirlpool, the combination makes it the world's largest producer of major appliances, surpassing A.B. Electrolux of Sweden. At the end of 3 years, Whirlpool has the option to acquire the balance of Philips' appliance division.

A.B. Electrolux, which owns some ten companies in the United States including White Consolidated Industries, continued its long-running acquisition program in 1988 by buying Roper's outdoor power equipment division from GE. Electrolux now owns over 400 companies and has about 135,000 employees throughout the world.

Early in 1989, General Electric entered the overseas appliance business by teaming up with General Electric Company GEC, an unrelated British firm. In this joint venture, GE acquired 50 percent of GEC's European household appliance business.

Source: Maytag 1988 annual report.

ment of the market, and the Italian firms are strong competitors at the low-price end. Many of the large firms have a significant presence in Europe.

France is dominated by Thomson-Brandt which has a 40+ percent share of the refrigerator and washing machine market. The company markets a full price range of appliances.

Sweden and Holland, countries with well-developed markets, are dominated, respectively, by Electrolux and Philips.

Hoover, Maytag's recent acquisition, does not rank among the top ten producers in the United Kingdom although British consumers account for about 75 percent of Hoover's $600 million European market. Hoover is a very small player in the European market (see Exhibit 6).

THE TREND TOWARD STANDARDIZATION

Electrolux and Whirlpool believe that appliances worldwide will become standardized allowing for economies of scale and worldwide distribution. For example, custom tariffs have already been waived among most countries and an international agreement instituted for standardization of aperture size for built-in appliances.

Many industry observers maintain that even with differentiation in the various countries economies of scale persist because flexible factories allow for differentiated production batches. Some standardization of parts has already come about for individual companies. Most analysts agree that consolidation will occur as Europe moves toward becoming one market and those companies that will survive will be either the low-cost producers or niche marketers.

Krumm, CEO of Maytag, expressed confidence in this standardization as far back as 1982. He stated:

> Up until now many of the products we make have not been seriously challenged from abroad. Foreign makers have not been inclined to produce and export the full-size major appliances that the American market requires, without a viable domestic market of their own. But as we in the United States edge closer to what is being manufactured abroad, to perhaps produce a "world appliance"—one that can be sold throughout the United States, Europe, and Japan—the possibility of greater competition may grow. The potential would grow for vast new markets for U.S. manufacturers, but it also may well invite increased foreign competition within the United States.[8]

The benefits of standardization, however, may be some time in coming, some say. Loyalties die hard. For example, Frank Vaughn, head of Chicago Pacific's appliance group, states that while their front-loading washing machines are accepted in Britain, "you can't give them away in France. The French are a top-loading nation."[9]

THE DECISION TO COMPETE ABROAD

Although the European market is somewhat different because their appliances have fewer features and are somewhat smaller in size, Maytag officials feel that they definitely can compete overseas, not by producing for export but through an overseas acquisition. They expressed the thought that the overseas market would simply be a natural extension of their business. Albert Turner, an analyst with Duff & Phelps, Inc., doesn't think the task will be as easy as that. He states: "Maytag will essentially be introducing new products into new markets."[10] Others think that Maytag faces a real struggle since Europeans are fiercely loyal to domestic brands. Some European companies look to the United States as a potential source of sales.

An official of Thomson-Brandt, the French appliance producer, states:

> Our domestic market is Europe, and it is saturated; demand is on the decline. . . . Therefore, it is only logical that any company that can afford to invest in other markets should do so. . . . I believe the U.S., Canada, and Japan all offer an opportunity for our products. But at this stage, we are only evaluating the feasibility.[11]

The strategy of Maytag to penetrate the European market appears to be a turnaround position for the company that previously was on record as saying: ". . . there is little advantage in moving into international markets."[12] Times change and companies must

---

[8] AHAM (Associated Home Appliances Manufacturers): Execs wrestle with tough problem. (1982, June). *Mart.*

[9] *Business Week,* op. cit., p. 87.

[10] Ibid.

[11] Arbose, Jules. (1979, December). *International Management;* (1983, April). *Appliance Management.*

[12] Standard and Poor's Industry Surveys. (1988, September 8). 2, T100.

constantly review their markets, said one Maytag official. "While Krumm has admitted publicly that the deal is partly an exercise in raider-proofing, he has also said his overriding strategy is to grab some growth overseas."[13]

U.S. manufacturers who venture into Europe will find intense competition. Some skeptics flatly state that it may be the Maytag salesman rather than the repairman who gets lonely in Europe.[14] Maytag officials state that they have no intention to sell the Maytag brand in Europe but plan rather to throw their expertise behind the well-known Hoover name which is expected to contribute about one-third of Maytag's sales.

Maytag's entry into the European market is not its first. Krumm was sent to Belgium in 1962 to manage European distribution of coin-operated washers and dryers. When the president of a jointly owned facility in Germany died, Krumm was put in charge. After being clobbered in the marketplace by Italian-made appliances for 2 years, Krumm sold the plant and returned to Iowa.

Other U.S. appliance manufacturers, for the present, are content to stay at home in the belief that uniformity of appliances in Europe will not be achieved in the near future. Standardization which was tried in the past by European companies with both washers and stoves failed miserably. National preferences for certain features and cultural barriers have so far precluded the acceptance of uniform products. The exceptions to this appear to be room air conditioners and microwave ovens.

Bibliography

Company publications.

Elbert, David. (1989, March 26). Iowa firms await knock of opportunity in Europe in '92. *Des Moines Sunday Register,* pp. 1A, 5A.

Holders approve a merger with Chicago Pacific Corp. (1988, December 8). *The Wall Street Journal,* p. B10.

Home appliance industry. (1989, March 24). *Value Line Investment Survey,* p. 130.

Household goods. (1985, January 2). *Forbes.*

Low-key Krumm is key to Maytag success. (1987, January 25). *Des Moines Register.*

Maytag annual reports, 1985, 1986, 1987, 1988.

Maytag Corp. (1988, December 28). *The New York Times,* p. D4.

Maytag merger is completed. (1989, January 27). *The New York Times,* p. D4.

Maytag to spend millions. (1989, March 22). *Repository* (Canton, Ohio), p. B11.

Maytag's first step in Chicago Pacific takeover under way. (1988, December 8). *The Wall Street Journal,* p. C16.

Maytag's new girth will test its marketing muscle. (1987, January 16). *Business Week,* pp. 68–69.

---

[13] *Business Week,* op. cit., p. 86.
[14] Ibid.

Moody's Industrial Manual. (1988) (Vol. 1).

On the verge of a world war in white goods. (1987, November 2). *Business Week.*

Standard & Poor's Industry Surveys. (1988, September 8). 2, T98–T100.

Appendix to Case 26
European Market 1988*

Market Overview

In 1988, European appliance manufacturers sold approximately 50 million units of large kitchen appliances compared to approximately 40 million units sold in the United States. Table 1 provides a summary of European sales in the past five years.

European Saturation Rates of Appliances

Saturation rates in Europe are generally lower for all large kitchen appliances than in the United States except for washing machines; the saturation rate for freezers is the same in Europe as the United States. Table 2 displays the saturation rates of appliances in Europe and the United States.

European Appliance Sales by Country

Table 3 presents a summary of major appliance sales in Europe by country for the 1983 to 1988 period. The largest growth in appliances for all four countries is in microwave ovens where the Japanese manufacturers dominate. Of the eight firms that rule this market, six are

TABLE 1
Summary of Major Appliance Sales in Europe,* 1984–1988E

	Share of Total (Units in Thousands)					
Market	***1984***	***1985***	***1986***	***1987***	***1988***	
France	6,375	6,498	7,291	8,472	9,579E	18.8%
Germany	7,825	7,925	8,625	9,475	10,190	20.0%
Italy	4,769	5,333	5,698	5,811	6,350E	12.5%
United Kingdom	8,610	8,926	9,334	9,643	10,268E	20.2%
Big four total	27,579	29,682	30,948	33,401	36,387	71.6%
European total	38,038	39,673	42,582	46,405	50,825	100.0%
U.S. factory sales	33,216	35,718	39,178	40,814	39,511	

* Major appliances include refrigerators, freezers, ranges, microwave ovens, washers, dryers, and dishwashers.
E = estimate.
Source: Euromonitor Publications, Association of Appliance Manufacturers, Salomon Brothers, Inc.

* All of the information included in this section is drawn from Leavitt, Russell L., Knox, Peter, & Perla, Daniel. (1989, September). *Consumer Electrical Products: The White Goods Industry—Focus on Europe,* Stock Research Report, Salomon Brothers.

TABLE 2
Household Saturation Rates of Large Kitchen Appliances, 1987

	Washing Machines	*Tumble Dryers*	*Dishwashers*	*Refrigerators*	*Electric Freezers*	*Electric Ranges*	*Microwave Ovens*
Austria	89%	5%	28%	94%	57%	67%	8%
Belgium	83	28	21	98	58	34	6
Denmark	88	32	24	100	71	76	5
Finland	86	2	23	85	58	90	13
France	86	5	26	98	44	6	9
W Germany	91	17	32	96	56	74	11
Greece	69	na	3	73	24	74	na
Italy	96	na	22	99	22	4	3
Netherlands	95	15	9	98	42	16	3
Norway	92	na	25	96	na	95	na
Portugal	43	na	9	83	12	na	na
Spain	92	4	10	98	5	3	2
Sweden	93	28	38	96	73	na	12
Switzerland	96	19	36	99	63	na	10
United Kingdom	87	31	10	97	45	34	33
Europe	85%	15%	22%	95%	41%	50%	18%
United States	70%	42%	48%	100%	41%	59%	66%

na = not available.
Sources: Euromonitor Publications and Salomon Brothers, Inc.

Japanese (market shares not provided). Japanese manufacturers, however, have not been able to penetrate the other sectors of the European white goods market.

Growth of Appliance Sales in Europe

In the period from 1983 to 1988, average growth (excluding microwaves) has been 4.4 percent. Growth in appliance sales (excluding microwaves) in the major countries has been as follows:

United Kingdom	3.6%
West Germany	1.4%
France	4.9%
Italy	6.0%

Market Shares of European Major Countries

Table 4 depicts the ranking of market shares in Europe from 1980 to 1988; the large increases are accounted for mainly by acquisitions. As shown in the table, four firms have over 50 percent of the market and ten firms control 80 percent of the market.

Distribution in Europe

While the distribution of appliances in Europe varies significantly, the majority of them (52 percent) are sold through electrical chain stores; another 14 percent are sold through independent electrical retail outlets, and 12 percent through coop/department stores. Kitchen design specialists account for 5 percent and builders another 5 percent.

TABLE 3a
France—Unit Sales of Large Kitchen Appliances, 1983–1988E (Units in Thousands)

	1983	1984	1985	1986	1987	1988E	Growth Rate 1983–1988E
Refrigerators and refrigerators/freezers	1,735	1,545	1,530	1,600	1,800	1,895	1.8%
Freezers	665	660	670	730	740	715	1.5
Cookers/ovens	1,855	1,934	1,864	1,925	1,952	2,188	3.4
Microwave ovens	55	123	254	600	1,100	1,575	95.6
Washing machines	1,490	1,520	1,555	1,695	1,800	1,878	4.7
Dryers	60	90	130	180	470	612	59.1
Dishwashers	493	503	495	561	610	716	7.7
Total	6,353	6,375	6,498	7,291	8,472	9,579	8.6%
Total excluding microwave ovens	6,298	6,252	6,244	6,691	7,372	8,004	4.9%

E = estimate.
Source: Euromonitor Publications and Salomon Brothers, Inc.

TABLE 3b
The United Kingdom—Unit Sales of Large Kitchen Appliances, 1983–1988E (Units in Thousands)

	1983	1984	1985	1986	1987	1988E	Growth 1983–1988
Refrigerators and refrigerators/freezers	1,807	1,848	1,565	1,525	1,555	1,680	(1.4)%
Freezers	573	655	550	530	566	627	1.8
Cookers/ovens	2,022	2,297	2,328	2,545	2,558	2,700	6.0
Microwave ovens	700	1,100	1,380	1,720	1,800	1,834	21.2
Washing machines	1,730	1,753	2,050	1,875	1,924	1,990	2.8
Dryers	741	740	790	815	820	885	3.6
Dishwashers	190	217	283	324	420	552	23.8
Total	7,763	8,610	8,926	9,334	9,643	10,268	5.8%
Total excluding microwave ovens	7,063	7,510	7,546	7,614	7,843	8,343	3.6%

E = estimate.
Source: Euromonitor Publications and Salomon Brothers, Inc.

TABLE 3c
West Germany—Unit Sales of Large Kitchen Appliances, 1983–1988E
(Units in Thousands)

	1983	1984	1985	1986	1987	1988	Growth Rate 1983–1988
Refrigerators and refrigerators/freezers	2,050	1,990	1,950	2,000	2,000	2,000	(0.5)%
Freezers	935	855	830	850	870	880	(1.2)
Cookers/ovens	2,270	2,330	2,250	2,450	2,500	2,510	2.0
Microwave ovens	100	170	325	650	1,350	2,000	82.1
Washing machines	1,519	1,531	1,556	1,591	1,630	1,654	1.7
Dryers	311	359	414	449	460	466	8.4
Dishwashers	550	590	600	635	665	680	4.3
Total	7,735	7,825	7,925	8,625	9,475	10,190	5.7%
Total excluding microwave ovens	7,635	7,655	7,600	7,975	8,125	8,190	1.4%

E = estimate.
Source: Euromonitor Publications and Salomon Brothers, Inc.

TABLE 3d
Italy—Unit Sales of Large Kitchen Appliances, 1983–1988E
(Units in Thousands)

	1983	1984	1985	1986	1987	1988E	Growth Rate 1983–1988E
Refrigerators and refrigerator/freezers	1,379	1,242	1,331	1,524	1,520	1,608	3.1%
Freezers	367	299	322	359	345	363	(0.2)
Cookers/ovens	1,320	1,640	2,040	2,020	2,035	2,210	10.9
Microwave ovens	20	28	30	55	105	210	60.0
Washing machines	1,275	1,325	1,375	1,480	1,505	1,621	4.9
Dryers	50	40	35	30	25	25	(12.9)
Dishwashers	201	195	200	230	276	313	9.3
Total	4,612	4,769	5,333	5,698	5,811	6,350	6.6%
Total excluding microwave ovens	4,592	4,741	5,303	5,643	5,706	6,140	6.0%

E = estimate.
Source: Euromonitor Publications and Salomon Brothers, Inc.

TABLE 4
Major European Appliance Manufacturers and Respective Market Shares, 1980–1988

Company	*1980*	*1988*
Electrolux	8.0%	20.5%
Whirlpool International (Philips)	8.0	11.5
Bosch-Siemens	7.5	11.0
Merioni	2.0	10.0
Candy	2.5	5.5
Thomson	5.0	5.0
GEC Hotpoint	2.0	5.0
AEG	6.0	5.0
Miele	3.5	4.0
Ocean	0.5	2.5
Total	45.0%	80.0%

CASE 27

Procter & Gamble Europe: Vizir Launch*

Charlie Ferguson, Procter & Gamble's (P&G) European vice president, faced three critical decisions in June 1981 as he reviewed the German test-market results for Vizir, the company's new heavy-duty liquid (HDL) detergent.

- Should he follow the recommendation of Wolfgang Berndt, Germany's new advertising manager for laundry and cleaning products, and his German team and authorize a national launch on the basis of four months of test results? Or should Ferguson ask Berndt to wait until final test-market results were in, or perhaps even rethink the entire HDL product strategy?
- If and when the decision was made to launch Vizir, to what extent could this be considered a European rather than just a German product? If a coordinated European rollout was planned, to what degree should the company standardize its product formulation, packaging, advertising, and promotion?
- Finally, what organizational implications would these decisions have? For example, to what extent should the individual country subsidiary managers retain the responsibility to decide when and how this new product would be introduced in their national markets?

PROCTER & GAMBLE: COMPANY BACKGROUND

P&G's strong and long-established culture was reflected in its corporate values, policies, and practices, and the following paragraphs provide some background on each of these areas.

Corporate Values

Established in 1837 by two men of strong religious faith and moral conviction, P&G soon developed an explicit set of corporate standards and values. Prospective employees quickly learned of P&G's fundamental belief that the company's interests were inseparable from those of its employees. Over the years, this broad philosophy had been translated into various widely shared management norms such as the following:

- P&G should hire only good people of high character;
- P&G must treat them as individuals with individual talents and life goals;
- P&G should provide a work environment that encourages and rewards individual achievement.

* This case was prepared by Christopher A. Bartlett.

These shared beliefs soon became part of the company's formal management systems. General managers knew that they were evaluated on their achievements in three areas: volume, profit, and people. P&G also tried to attract people who were willing to spend their entire careers with the company. Promotions were made from within, and top management was chosen from career P&G people rather than from outside the company.

Management Policies

Over its almost 150-year history, P&G had also accumulated a broad base of industry experience and business knowledge. Within the company, this accumulated knowledge was recognized as an important asset and much of it had been formalized and institutionalized as management principles and policies. According to previous Chairman Ed Harness, "Though our greatest asset is our people, it is the consistency of principle and policy which gives us direction."

These operating principles and management policies were strategically important in the marketing area, for P&G had a reputation as a premier consumer marketer. A basic policy was that P&G's products should provide "superior total value" and should meet "basic consumer needs." This led to a strong commitment in research to create products that were demonstrably better than the competition when compared in blind tests. (One manager said, "Before you can launch a new brand, you must have a win in a white box.")

Furthermore, P&G highly valued market research. In a business where ill-conceived new product launches could be very expensive, and sometimes not very successful, continuous and detailed market research was seen as insurance against major mistakes. Harness described the market research objectives as being "to spot a new trend early, then lead it."

For similar reasons, P&G also believed in extensive product and market testing before making major brand decisions. Having spotted a trend through market research, the company typically spent two or three years testing the product and the marketing strategy it had developed before committing itself to a full-scale launch. One papergoods competitor said "P&G tests and tests and tests. They leave no stone unturned, no variable untested. You can see them coming for months and years, but you know when they get there, it is time for you to move."

Finally, P&G believed that, through continual product development and close tracking of consumer needs and preferences, brands could be managed so that they remained healthy and profitable in the long term. Their rejection of the conventional product-life-cycle mentality was demonstrated by Ivory soap, which was over 100 years old; Crisco shortening, which was over 70; and Tide detergent, which was over 35. Yet each product was still a leader in its field.

Organization Practices

Besides strong corporate values and clear management principles, P&G's culture was also characterized by well-established organization practices and processes. Its internal operations had been described as thorough, creative, and aggressive by some; and as slow, risk averse, and rigid by others.

Perhaps the most widely known of P&G's organizational characteristics was its brand manager structure. Created in 1931, the brand management system provided each brand with management focus, expertise, and drive at a low level in the organization. By legitimizing and even reinforcing the internal competition that had existed since Camay soap began to compete with Ivory in 1923, the brand manager system tended to restrict lateral communication. This fostered a norm among P&G management that information was shared on a need-to-know basis only.

Although the brand manager system impaired lateral communication, vertical communication within P&G was well established. Proposals on key issues were usually generated at the lower levels of management, with analysis and recommendations working their way up the organization for concurrence and approval. At P&G, top management was intimately involved in most large decisions (for example, all new brand launches; capital appropriations exceeding $100,000; and personnel appointment and promotion decisions three levels down). Although the approval system could be slow and, at times, bureaucratic (one manager claimed that a label change on Head and Shoulders shampoo had required 55 signatures), it was designed to minimize risk in the very risky and expensive consumer marketing business. When a project was approved, however, it would have the company's full commitment. As one manager said, "Once they sign off [on the new brand launch], they will bet the farm."

Another characteristic of the P&G management process was that proposals were committed to paper, usually as one- or two-page memos. This encouraged thoroughness and careful analysis from the proposal originators and objectivity and rationality from the managers who reviewed the document. Written documents could also easily circulate through the organization, either building support or eliciting comments and suggestions for improvement or rejection.

P&G INTERNATIONAL: EUROPEAN OPERATIONS

Expansion Principles

Although P&G acquired a small English soap company in 1926, it did not build a substantial European presence until the postwar years. In 1954, a French detergent company was acquired; two years later, a Belgian plant was opened; and by the end of the decade, P&G had established operations in Holland and Italy. A Swiss subsidiary served as a worldwide export center. In the 1960s, subsidiaries were opened in Germany, Austria, Greece, Spain, and the Scandinavian countries. The European Technical Center (ETC) was established in Brussels in 1963 to provide R&D facilities and a small regional management team.

By 1981, Europe represented about 15% of P&G's $11 billion worldwide sales, with almost all of that substantial volume having been built in the previous two and a half decades. The German and U.K. subsidiaries were the largest, each representing about one fifth of the company's European sales. France and Italy together accounted for another 30%, and Belgium, Holland, Spain, Austria, and Switzerland made up the balance.

As international operations grew, questions arose as to how the new foreign subsidiaries should be managed. As early as 1955, Walter Lingle, P&G's overseas vice president, laid down some important principles that guided the company's subsequent development abroad. Recognizing that consumer needs and preferences differed by country, Lingle emphasized the importance of acquiring the same intensive knowledge of local consumers as was required in the United States. Lingle said, "Washing habits . . . vary widely from country to country. We must tailor products to meet consumer demands in each nation. We cannot simply sell products with U.S. formulas. They won't work. They won't be accepted."

But Lingle insisted that the management policies and practices that had proven successful for P&G in the United States would be equally successful overseas. He declared, "The best way to succeed in other countries is to build in each one as exact a replica of the U.S. Procter & Gamble organization as it is possible to create."

European Industry and Competitive Structure

From their earliest exposure to the European market for laundry detergents, managers from the parent company realized how important the first of these principles would be. Washing habits and market structures not only differed from the familiar home country market but also varied from one country to another within Europe. Among the obvious differences in laundry characteristics were the following:

- Typical washing temperatures were much higher in Europe, and the "boil wash" (over 60°C) was the norm in most countries. However, lower washing temperatures were commonplace in some countries where washing machines did not heat water (for example, in the United Kingdom) or where hand washing was still an important segment (for example, in Spain and Italy).
- European washing machines were normally front loading with a horizontal rotating drum—very different from the U.S. norm of an agitator action in a top-loaded machine. The European machine also had a smaller water capacity (3 to 5 gallons versus 12 to 14 gallons in the United States) and used a much longer cycle (90 to 120 minutes versus 20 to 30 minutes in the United States).
- Europeans used more cottons and less synthetics than Americans and tended to wear clothes longer between washes. Average washing frequency was 2 to 3 times per week versus 4 to 5 times in the United States. Despite the lower penetration of washing machines, much higher detergent dosage per load resulted in the total European laundry detergent consumption being about 30% above the U.S. total.

Market structures and conditions were also quite different from the United States and also varied widely within Europe, as the following examples illustrate:

- In Germany, concentration ratios among grocery retailers were among the highest in the world. The five largest chains (including co-ops and associations) accounted for 65% of the retail volume, compared with about 15% in the United States. In contrast, the independent corner store in Italy was still very important, and hypermarkets had not made major inroads.
- Unlimited access to television, similar to the United States, was available only in the United Kingdom (and even there it was much more expensive). In Holland, each brand was allowed only 46 minutes of TV commercial time per annum; in Germany and Italy, companies had to apply for blocks of TV time once a year. Allocated slots were very limited.
- National legislation greatly affected product and market strategies. Legislation in Finland and Holland limited phosphate levels in detergent; German laws made cou-

pons, refunds, and premium offers all but impossible; elsewhere local laws regulated package weight, labeling, and trade discounts.

The competitive environment was also different from P&G's accustomed market leadership position in the United States. In Europe, P&G shared the first-tier position with two European companies, Unilever and Henkel. By the early 1970s, each company claimed between 20% and 25% of the European laundry detergent market. P&G's old domestic market rival, Colgate, had a 10% share and was in a second tier. Several national competitors fought it out for the remaining volume at a third level. Henkel competed in most European markets but was strongest in Germany, its home market. Unilever was also international, dominating in Holland and the United Kingdom. Colgate's presence in Europe was spottier, but it had built up a powerful position in France. Typically, national companies were strong at the lower-priced end of their local markets.

Each company had its own competitive characteristics. Unilever had long been a sleeping giant but was becoming much more aggressive in the late 1970s and early 1980s. Henkel was a fierce competitor and could be relied on to defend its home market position tenaciously. Colgate was trying to elbow its way in and tended to be impulsive and take bigger risks, often launching products with only minimal testing. As a result of this diverse activity, P&G's market share varied considerably by national market (see Table A).

By the mid-1970s, the rapid growth of the previous two decades dropped to a standstill. Not only did the oil crisis add dramatically to costs, but almost simultaneously, washing machines approached the 85% penetration rate that many observers regarded as the saturation point. In the late 1970s, volume was growing at only 2% per annum. As market growth slowed, competitive pressures increased.

P&G Europe's Strategy and Organization

These differences in consumer habits, market conditions, and competitive positions led to the development of strong national subsidiaries with the responsibility for developing products and marketing programs to match the local environment. Each subsidiary was a miniature P&G, with its own brand management structure, product development capability, advertising agencies, and typically, manufacturing capability. The subsidiary general manager directed the growth of the business and the organization (see Exhibit 1).

Each subsidiary attacked the task of establishing P&G in the basic detergent and soap business in its national market differently. The general manager tried to select the best volume and profit opportunity from over 200 products in the company's portfolio, then

TABLE A
Laundry Detergent Market (in Millions of Dollars)

	Total Market	*P&G Share*
Germany	$ 950	$200
United Kingdom	660	220
France	750	160
Italy	650	140
Spain	470	90
Total Europe	$3,750	$950

EXHIBIT 1
Abbreviated Organization Chart, P&G Europe

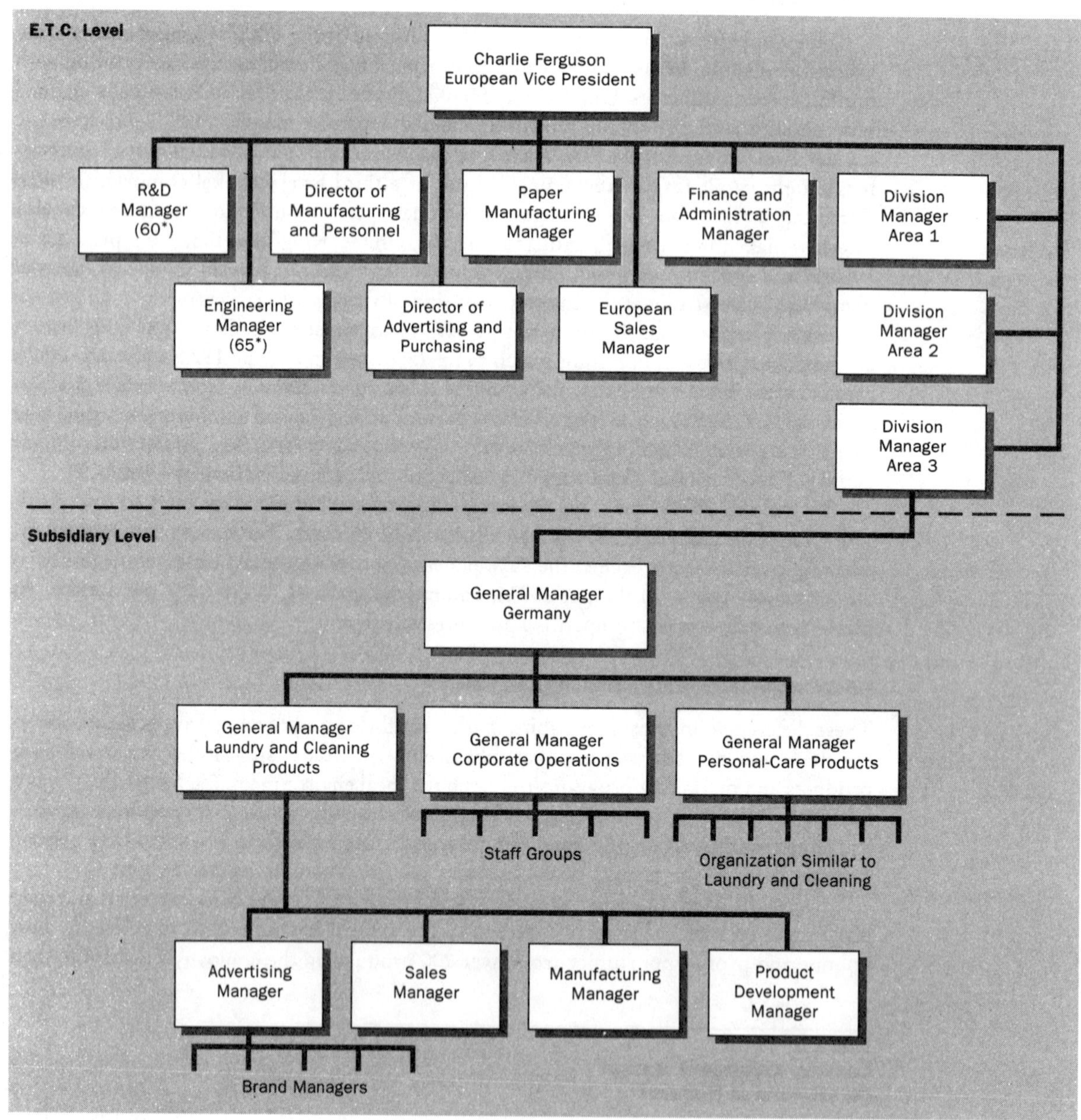

* Number of managerial and technical/professional staff. (Total number of managerial/technical/professional staff at ETC was 175.)

adapt them to the local situation. The general manager of the Italian subsidiary described the choices he faced when he took over in 1974:

> Given the limits of P&G Italy's existing brands [a laundry detergent, a bar soap, and a recently acquired coffee business], our priority was to build volume and profit and broaden our base. The choices we had were almost limitless. Pampers had been very successful in Germany and Belgium, but Italy couldn't afford such an expensive launch. Motiv, a new dishwashing liquid, was being launched in France and Germany, but we were unconvinced of its potential here. Mr. Propre [Mr. Clean in the United States] was successful in three European countries, but competition in Italy was strong. Finally, we decided to launch Monsavon, the French bar soap. It represented an affordable new product launch in a traditionally good profit line.

Since 1961, each of the country general managers had reported to Tom Bower, an Englishman who had headed up P&G's European operations. Bower had a reputation as an entrepreneur and an excellent motivator. He believed that by selecting creative and entrepreneurial country general managers and giving them the freedom to run their businesses, results would follow. Bower made sure that his small headquarters staff understood that they were not to interfere unduly in subsidiary decisions. Primarily, it was the subsidiary general manager's responsibility to call on ETC if a problem arose.

The strategy was most successful for P&G, and sales and profits grew rapidly throughout the 1960s and into the early 1970s. Growth was aided by P&G's entry into new national markets and additional product categories and by the rapid growth of the core detergent business with the penetration of washing machines into European homes.

When Bower retired in 1975, his successor, Ed Artzt, faced a situation different from the one that existed in the 1950s and 1960s. As growth slowed, competition intensified, prices weakened, and profits dipped. Artzt felt that if profit and sales growth were to be rekindled, the diverse country operations would have to be better coordinated.

Over the next five years, under his leadership, the role of ETC took on new importance. (Exhibit 1 shows an abbreviated organization chart.) As increased competition led to declining margins, Artzt moved to strengthen the ETC finance manager's role in controlling costs. The finance manager described the problems:

> Largely because of duplication of marketing and administrative groups in each subsidiary, our overhead expense per unit was almost 50% higher than in the U.S. parent. We needed to get it under control. Our problem was that we couldn't get meaningful or comparable costs by subsidiary. Our introduction of better cost and reporting systems helped put pressure on subsidiaries to control their costs. It had a very beneficial effect.

Artzt was also concerned about the slowing of innovation in P&G Europe. He felt that the scarcity of new product developments and their haphazard introductions contributed to the sales and profit problem. Under the able leadership of Wahib Zaki, Artzt's new R&D manager, ETC's role in product development shifted dramatically.

Previously each subsidiary initiated its own local product development. For example, the R&D group in the French subsidiary was around 30, while Germany's technical staff was perhaps twice that size. Responding to its own local market, the subsidiary defined and developed products with the appropriate characteristics, drawing on the parent company's basic technology and perhaps calling on ETC for specialized technical support or backup. Because subsidiaries were not required to use standard formulations or technology, products varied widely from country to country. As a result, Ariel detergent had nine different formulas throughout Europe. For example, it was positioned diversely as a low- and a high-suds powder and for low- and high-temperature usage, depending on the country.

Zaki concluded that developing products in this way provided insufficient focus, prioritization, or strategic direction for the work. Thus, the strong technical capabilities housed in the ETC, as well as in the United States, were not being fully or effectively utilized. Furthermore, local country management did not appreciate their efforts and tended to view the Technical Center as a high-cost, perfectionist group that did not respond rapidly enough to market needs.

Zaki aimed to change this by having ETC take a stronger leadership role in R&D and to assume responsibility for coordinating the new product development efforts among the subsidiaries. His analysis indicated that national differences in consumer practices and preferences were narrowing, and they no longer justified product differences that then existed from country to country. He wanted to establish priorities, to coordinate efforts, and as much as possible, to standardize products Europe-wide. To achieve these goals, he needed the involvement and cooperation of the subsidiaries.

In 1977, Zaki reorganized European R&D by creating European Technical Teams to work on products and technologies that had multiple market potential. In his vision, European products would be superior to existing local national products but without compromising performance or increasing cost. The objective was to focus the resources of the total European R&D community around key brands and to define a long-term European approach to product development.

As roles clarified, the ETC technical groups were seen as the developers of new technologies ("putting the molecules together," as one R&D manager described it), while the subsidiaries took responsibility for testing and refining the products in the field. After a couple of painful years, the new process seemed to be working. "Lead countries" were named for each of the key products, thereby giving more local subsidiary responsibility and ownership for the development process, and also ensuring ongoing coordination among subsidiaries. Transfer of technical staff between ETC and subsidiaries further encouraged interdependence and cooperation.

An experimental attempt at "Europeanization" in marketing, however, had been less successful. In a break from the philosophy of product adaptation, a group of managers in Cincinnati concluded that "a baby is a baby" worldwide and that the laborious market-by-market evaluations that had been assumed necessary for cleaning products would not be needed for disposable diapers. Therefore, it was decided to gain experience by managing key elements of Pampers (such as product and copy strategy) on a Europe-wide basis. A senior manager was transferred from the German subsidiary, where Pampers was launched in 1973, to ETC, where he was made responsible for leading key activities on Pampers in all subsidiaries.

The brand promotion manager, responsible for Pampers in France at the time, recalled the experiment:

> As soon as it was known I would be principally working with the European Pampers manager in ETC and not the subsidiary GM, my local support dried up. I couldn't get

> a brand manager or even an assistant to work with me. The French subsidiary manager was preoccupied with the Motiv [dishwashing liquid] launch and was trying to regain leadership with Ariel [laundry powder]. The Pampers situation was a disaster. Eventually Pampers was given back to the subsidiaries. It was the only way to get their support.

This experience conveyed an important lesson to P&G's top management. It appeared that although coordination and planning could be effectively centralized and implemented on a European basis, the day-to-day management of the business had to be executed at the local subsidiary level.

In 1980, Artzt was transferred back to Cincinnati as executive vice president of P&G, and Charlie Ferguson was named group vice president, Europe. Ferguson was an energetic, creative, and intelligent manager with a reputation for getting things done. Impressed by the effectiveness of the European approach to technical development, Ferguson was convinced that a similar approach could succeed in product marketing.

With the encouragement and support of his boss, Artzt, who remained a strong advocate of Europeanization, Ferguson began to test the feasibility of developing Europe-wide brand and marketing strategies. In pursuing the Eurobrand concept, as it was becoming known, Artzt and Ferguson saw Vizir, the new HDL being prepared for launch in Germany, as a good test case.

THE VIZIR PROJECT

Product Development

Following Lever's success in the United States with Wisk, P&G launched Era in 1974 as their entrant in the fast-growing HDL detergent segment. As a late entrant, however, it was unable to match Wisk's dominant share. P&G managers, watching developments from Europe, realized that if the HDL product concept was transferable to their market, the first company to stake out the territory would have an advantage. The success of liquids in other product categories (for example, household cleansers), the trend toward low-temperature washers, and the availability of liquid-product plant capacity all provided additional incentives to proceed with the project.

ETC initiated its HDL project in late 1974 by testing the U.S. product Era against European powders in a small-scale test panel. Given the differences in laundry habits on either side of the Atlantic, it was not surprising that Era was evaluated poorly. The panel reported problems not only with the product's washing performance (for example, whitening ability, suds level) but also with its form. European washing machines had drawers that allowed different powdered products (pretreatment, main wash detergent, fabric softener) to be activated at different times in the typical 90-minute cycle. To win acceptance of a laundry liquid would be difficult. Consumers would have to be convinced that this product would achieve similar results; then, their washing habits would have to be changed.

Undeterred, a group at ETC began to work on an HDL product that would be more suitable to European laundry practices. It was with high hopes and considerable corporate visibility that the modified European HDL product was placed in six full-scale blind tests in Germany, France, and the United Kingdom. The results were disastrous in all tests. Given the high expectations that had been created within P&G, many insiders felt that the product was dead because it would be impossible to rebuild internal support and credibility.

However, the scientists at ETC were convinced that they could capitalize on the intrinsic ability of a liquid detergent to incorporate three times the level of surfactants as compared to a powder. (The surfactant is the critical ingredient that removes greasy stains.) In addition to surfactants, laundry detergents contained builders (to prevent redisposition of dirt) and phosphates (to soften water). Unlike U.S. products, however, European powdered detergents also contained enzymes (to break down proteins) and bleach (to oxidize stains). Unfortunately, it was not then possible to incorporate enzymes and bleach into a liquid detergent, and this limited capability was behind the new product's blind-test failure against European powders.

Overcoming these deficiencies challenged P&G's scientists at ETC and in the United States. Eventually, they did patent a method to give enzymes stability in liquid form. Soon afterward, a bleach substitute that was effective at lower temperatures was developed. These product modifications led to improved consumer blind-test results. In late 1976, the new HDL product won a blind test against the leading French powder, Ariel; the following year, it won against Persil, the German market leader.

Although the project was still on shaky ground within P&G, these successes resulted in the establishment of an HDL brand group in Germany. The group reported to Germany's newly appointed advertising manager for laundry and cleaning products, Wolfgang Berndt, a 34-year-old Austrian, who was recognized as one of the promising young managers in Europe. He began his career 10 years earlier in the company's Austrian subsidiary. After gaining training and experience in brand management in Austria, the United Kingdom, and Germany, Berndt spent two years in Cincinnati as a brand manager in the parent company's Toilet Goods Division. He returned to Europe in 1973 as brand promotion manager at P&G Italy, before transferring to Germany a year later.

Soon after he was appointed advertising manager in 1977, Berndt was given responsibility to supervise this important, but delicate, new HDL responsibility. The main reason for the assignment, he believed, was that he and his German team had expressed their confidence in this new product's potential.

In early 1977, Colgate began test-marketing Axion, an HDL formula that was similar to its U.S. product, Dynamo. Axion showed excellent initial results, gaining an almost 4% share in three months. However, sales declined from this peak, and within 18 months, Colgate closed down the test market and withdrew Axion.

Meanwhile, P&G's research team had developed three important breakthroughs: a fatty acid that provided similar water-softening performance to phosphate, a suds suppressant so that the product would function in European drum washing machines, and a patented washing machine anticorrosion ingredient. By 1979, P&G's European development efforts had shifted to product aesthetics, and the search began for perfumes compatible with the newly formulated HDL-Formula SB, as it was known.

Henkel was also reformulating its leading powder and relaunched it as New Persil. Blind tests of Formula SB against New Persil in early 1980 broke even. Finally, in October 1980, with a new fragrance, Procter's Formula SB won a blind test against New Persil by 53 to 47. The product's superiority was confirmed in subsequent tests against the main competitive powders in France (a 58 to 42 win for Formula SB) and in the United Kingdom (a 61 to 39 win).

Berndt and his German brand group were ready to recommend a full-scale test market. During the previous 18 months, they had cleared the proposed brand name (Vizir), appointed an advertising agency (Grey), designed packaging (bottles and labels), and collected and analyzed the masses of consumer and market data that were necessary to justify any new product launched by P&G. Management, up to the highest level, was interested and involved. Although an initial capital approval had been received for $350,000, to buy molds and raw materials, the test-market plan for Berlin was expected to involve a further investment of $1.5 million plus $750,000, for original advertising production and research. A national launch would involve an additional $1.5 million in capital investment and $16 million in marketing costs. It would pay out in about three years if the product could gain a 4% market share. A Europe-wide launch would cost five or six times that amount.

Although Berndt and his team decided to proceed with the test market, uncertainty still surrounded Vizir. Some individuals in the company wondered whether it made sense to launch this product in Germany, particularly with the proposed marketing positioning and copy strategy. Other personnel were less concerned about the German launch but strongly opposed making Vizir a Eurobrand and launching it in all key European markets.

Vizir Launch Decision

Vizir's positioning in the detergent market concerned P&G's senior management. Vizir gave superior cleaning performance on greasy stains at low temperature and (following the product improvements) matched powder performance on enzymatic stains and whiteness. The problem was that P&G's Ariel, the leading low-temperature laundry powder in Germany, made similar performance claims, and management feared that Vizir would cannibalize Ariel's sales. These similarities were highlighted when two advertising agencies, operating independently, produced almost identical commercials for Vizir and Ariel in early 1981 (see Exhibit 2).

The German brand group favored this positioning for Vizir, because these characteristics had resulted in high trials during the Axion test. To position Vizir as a pretreatment product would severely limit its sales potential, and emphasizing its peripheral benefits, such as fabric care or softness, would not have broad appeal. They argued that Vizir had to be seen by consumers as a main wash product with superior cleaning performance at lower temperatures.

Some managers worried that P&G was creating a product segment that could result in new competitive entries and price erosion in the stagnant heavy-duty detergent market. Compared to powders, liquids were easier to make and required less capital investment. ("For powders, you need a detergent tower. Liquids can be made in a bath tub," according to one manager.) Although P&G had patented many of its technological breakthroughs, they were not effective barriers to entry. One product development manager explained:

> Our work on Vizir was very creative but not a very effective barrier to competition. Often, it's like trying to patent a recipe for an apple pie. We can specify ingredients and compositions in an ideal range or a preferred range, but competitors can copy the broad concepts and work around the patented ranges. And, believe me, they are all monitoring our patents! Even if they don't, or can't, copy our innovations, there are

EXHIBIT 2
Comparative Scripts: Vizir and Ariel Commercials

Vizir ("Peter's Pants") (Woman in laundry examining newly washed pants on her son)	***Ariel ("Helen Hedy") (Woman in laundry holding up daughter's blouse)***
Announcer: Hey, Peter's things look pretty nice.	**Announcer:** Looks beautifully clean again, doesn't it?
Woman: Thanks.	**Helen:** Yes, sure.
Announcer: Too bad they're not completely clean.	**Announcer:** Also close up?
Woman: What?	**Helen:** Well, no. When you really look up close—that's gravy. A stain like that never comes out completely.
Announcer: There's still oily dirt from his bicycle.	**Announcer:** Why is that?
Woman: I can't boil modern fabrics. And without boiling they don't get cleaner.	**Helen:** Because you just can't boil these modern things. I can't get Barbel's blouse really clean without boiling.
Announcer: Oh yes! Here is Vizir, the new liquid detergent Vizir, the liquid power that gets things cleaner. Without boiling!	**Announcer:** Then use Ariel. It can clean without boiling.
Woman: Bicycle oil will come out? Without boiling?	**Helen:** Without boiling? Even these stains? That I want to see.
Announcer: Yes, one cap of Vizir in the main wash and on tough soil pour a little Vizir on directly. Then wash. Let's test Vizir against boil wash powder. These make-up stains were washed in powder at 60°—not clean. On top we put this unwashed dirty towel, then pour on Vizir. Vizir's liquid power penetrates the soil and dissolves it, as well as the stain that boil wash powder left behind.	**Announcer:** The Test: With prewash and main wash at low temperature we are washing stubborn stains like egg and gravy. The towel on the right had Ariel's cleaning power.
Woman: Incredible. The bicycle oil—gone! Without boiling. Through and through cleaner.	**Helen:** Hey, it's really true. The gravy on Barbel's blouse is completely gone. Even against the light—deep down clean. All this without boiling.
Announcer: Vizir—liquid power to get things cleaner.	**Announcer:** Ariel—without boiling, still clean!

other ways to solve the problem. If enzymes are unstable in liquid form, you could solve that by dumping in lots of enzymes so that enough will still be active by the estimated usage date.

If capital costs were low and products could be imitated, then new entrants could open up a market for "white labels" (generic products). Without either the product or the market development costs of P&G, they probably could undercut P&G's prices. The Germans' proposed pricing strategy was to price at an equivalent "cost-per-job" as the leading powders. This pricing strategy afforded a slightly higher gross profit margin for Vizir compared to powders. A premium price was justified on two counts: it was consistent with the product's image, and it would avoid overall profit erosion, assuming that Vizir would cannibalize some sales of the company's low-temperature laundry detergent brands.

At this time, P&G held a strong number-two position in the German detergent market—the largest in Europe. Henkel's leading brand, Persil, was positioned as an all-temperature, all-purpose powder and held a 17% share.[1] P&G's entrant in the all-temperature segment was Dash, and this brand had a 5½% share. However, the company's low-temperature brand, Ariel, had an 11% share and was a leader in its fast-growing segment, far ahead of Lever's Omo (4½%) and Henkel's new entrant, Mustang (2½%).

The opponents' final argument was that even if these risks were ignored, there were serious doubts that Vizir represented a real market opportunity. P&G's marketing of its HDL in the United States had not been an outstanding success. Furthermore, Colgate's experience with their European test market had been disappointing.

In early 1981, Berndt's attention was drawn to an article that had been presented to an industry association congress in September 1980 by Henkel's director of product development and two other scientists. They concluded that HDLs would continue to expand their penetration of the U.S. market, due to the less-demanding comparison standard of American powder detergents and also to the compatibility of HDLs with American washing practices. The paper claimed that in Europe, however, liquids were likely to remain specialty products with a small market share (1% compared with 20% in the United States). This limited HDL market potential was due to the superiority of European powder detergents and the different European washing habits (higher temperatures, washing machine characteristics, and so forth).

While managers in Brussels and Cincinnati wrestled with these strategic issues, Berndt's nervousness increased. He and his Vizir brand group were excited by the product and committed to its success. Initial test-market readings from Berlin were encouraging (see Exhibit 3), but Berndt and his associates were certain that Henkel was also monitoring the test-market results. Vizir had been in development and testing for seven years. The German group believed that Henkel knew of their intentions and that it would counterattack to protect its dominant position in its home market. By the early summer of 1981, rumors began to spread in the trade that Henkel was planning an important new product. Henkel salespeople were recalled from vacation, and retailers were being sounded out for support on promotional programs.

On three occasions, Berndt or an associate presented the group's analysis of the test market and their concerns about a preemptive strike, but on each occasion, approval for a national launch was delayed. Senior management, on both sides of the Atlantic, explained that it was too risky to invest in a major launch, based on only three or four months of test results. Experience had shown that a one-year reading was necessary before deciding to act.

Eurobrand Decision

Another critical decision concerned the scope of the product launch. Within P&G's European organization, the budding Eurobrand concept was controversial. Although it fostered coordination of marketing strategies of brands in Europe, some managers thought that it conflicted with the existing philosophy that allowed country subsidiary managers to decide what products were most likely to succeed in their local markets, in what form, and when.

Artzt, Ferguson, and other managers countered by arguing that the time was ripe for a common European laundry detergent. Although widely differing washing practices among

[1] These share data represented the total detergent market (including dishwashing liquid). The heavy-duty segment (that is, laundry detergent) represented about two thirds of this total.

EXHIBIT 3
Selected Test-Market Results: Vizir Berlin Test Market

A. Total Shipments and Share

	Shipments: MSU (Volume Index)		Share (Percent)	
Month	Actual	Target	Actual	Target
February	4.6	1.8		
March	5.2	2.5	2.2	1.8
April	9.6	4.5	5.2	2.7
May	3.1	3.1	3.4	3.4

B. Consumer Research Results

	Use and Awareness (At 3 Months; Percent of 293 Responses)			Attitude Data (At 3 Months; Including Free-Sampling-Only Users)	
	Vizir	Mustang*		Vizir	Mustang*
Ever used†	28%	22%	Unduplicated comments on:		
Past 4 weeks	15	9	Whiteness, brightness, cleaning, or stain removal	65/11‡	58/8‡
Ever purchased†	13	15	Cleaning or stain removal	49/8	52/4
Past 4 weeks	8	6	Cleaning	12/2	17/n.a.
Twice or more	4	n.a.	Stain removal	37/6	35/n.a.
Brand on hand	15	11	Odor	30/4	15/3
Large sizes	3	5	Effect on clothes	7/—	13/6
Advertising awareness	47	89	Form (liquid)	23/11	n.a.
Brand awareness	68	95			

n.a. = not available.

* Mustang was a recently launched Henkel low-temperature powder on which comparable consumer data were available. It was judged to have been only moderately successful, capturing 2½% market share compared with Ariel's 11% share as low-temperature segment leader.

† Difference between use and purchase data due to introductory free-sample program.

‡ Number of unduplicated comments, favorable/unfavorable, about the product in user interviews. (For example, among Vizir users interviewed, 65 commented favorably about whiteness, brightness, cleaning, or stain removal, while 11 commented negatively about one or more of those attributes.)

countries had justified national products tailored to local habits, the market data indicated a converging trend in consumer laundry habits (see Exhibit 4).

Opponents quickly pointed out that, despite the trends, the differences in washing habits still outweighed the similarities. For example, Spain and Italy still had large hand-wash segments; in the United Kingdom and Belgium, top-loading washers were still important; and in Southern Europe, natural-fiber clothing still predominated. Besides, the raw statistical trends could be misleading. Despite the trend to lower-temperature washing, even in Germany, over 80% of the households still used the boilwash (over 60°C) for some loads. In general, the boilwash was the standard by which consumers judged washing cleanliness.

Some subsidiary managers also emphasized differences other than consumer preferences. Their individual market structures would prevent any uniform marketing strategy from succeeding. They cited data on differences in television cost and access, national legislation on product characteristics and promotion-tool usage, and distribution structure

EXHIBIT 4
Selected Market Research Data

A. Selected Washing Practices

	Germany		United Kingdom		France		Italy		Spain	
	1973	1978	1973	1978	1973	1978	1973	1978	1973	1978
Washing-machine penetration										
Households with drum machines (percent)	76	83	10	26	59	70	70	79	24	50
Washing temperature										
To 60° (including handwash)	51	67	71	82	48	68	31	49	63	85
Over 60°	49	33	29	18	52	32	69	51	37	15
Fabric-softener use										
Loads with fabric softener (percent)	68	69	36	47	52	57	21	35	18	37

B. Selected Consumer Attitude Data (German Survey Only)

	Laundry Cleaning Problems (Percent Respondents Claim)*		
	Grease-Based	Bleach-Sensitive	Enzyme-Sensitive
Most frequent stains	61	53	34
Desired improvement	65	57	33
In washes to 60°	78	53	25
In washes above 60°	7	36	65

* Does not add to 100% because multiple responses allowed.

and competitive behavior. All these structural factors would impede standardization of brands and marketing strategies across Europe.

The second point raised by Artzt and Ferguson was that greater coordination was needed to protect subsidiaries' profit opportunities. (However, they emphasized that subsidiary managers should retain ultimate profit responsibility and at least a concurrence role in all decisions affecting their operations.) Increasingly, competitors imitated P&G's new and innovative products and marketing strategies, and preempted them in national markets, where the local subsidiary was constrained by budget, organization, or simple poor judgment from developing the new-product category or market segment. For example, Pampers was introduced in Germany in 1973 but was not launched in France until 1978. Meanwhile, in 1976, Colgate launched a product named Calline (a literal French translation of Pampers). Its package color, product position, and marketing strategy were similar to Pampers, and it quickly won dominant market share. Late introduction also cost Pampers market leadership in Italy. The product was not introduced in the United Kingdom until 1981. Lenor provided an equally striking example. Similar to Downy in the United States, this new brand was launched in 1963 in Germany and created the fabric-softener product category. It quickly became an outstanding market success. Nineteen years later, Lenor debuted in France as the number-three entrant in the fabric-softener category and consequently faced a much more difficult marketing task.

Determined to prevent similar recurrences, particularly for new brands, Artzt and Ferguson wanted to ensure that product development and introduction were coordinated with a consistent Pan-European approach. Furthermore, they wanted marketing strategies to be thought through from a European perspective. This meant a thorough analysis of the possibility of simultaneous or closely sequenced European product introductions.

At the country level, many managers quickly pointed out that because the company wanted to keep the subsidiary as a profit center, this concept was not feasible. To establish a new brand—or even more so, to create a new product category such as disposable diapers—was incredibly expensive and highly risky. Many country general managers questioned whether they should gamble their subsidiary's profitability on such costly, chancy launches, especially if they were not at all convinced that their local markets were mature enough to accept the product. In many markets, subsidiary managers felt that their organizations should not be diverted from the primary goal of building a sound base in heavy- and light-duty detergents and personal products.

The third set of arguments put forward by the advocates of the Eurobrand concept was related to economics. They cited numerous examples: there were nine different Dash formulas in Europe; Mr. Clean (known as Mr. Propre, Meister Proper, and so forth) was sold in nine sizes throughout Europe. To go to a single formula, standard-size packs, and multilingual labels could save the company millions of dollars in mold costs, line downtime for changeovers, sourcing flexibility, and reduced inventory levels.

Other managers pointed out that the savings could easily be offset by the problems that standardization would create. The following comments were made at a country general managers' meeting when Ferguson raised the Eurobrand issue for discussion:

> We have to listen to the consumer. In blind tests in my market that perfume cannot even achieve break even.
>
> The whole detergent market is in 2 kilo packs in Holland. To go to a European standard of 3 kg and 5 kg sizes would be a disaster for us.
>
> We have low phosphate laws in Italy that constrain our product formula. And we just don't have hypermarkets, like France and Germany, where you can drop off pallet loads.

One general manager put it most forcefully in a memo to ETC management:

> There is no such thing as a Eurocustomer, so it makes no sense to talk about Eurobrands. We have an English housewife whose needs are different from a German hausfrau. If we move to a system that allows us to blur our thinking, we will have big problems.
>
> Product standardization sets up pressures to try to meet everybody's needs (in which case you build a Rolls Royce that nobody can afford) and countervailing pressures to find the lowest-common-denominator product (in which case you make a product that satisfies nobody and which cannot compete in any market). These pressures probably result in the foul middle compromise that is so often the outcome of committee decision.

Organization Decision

The strategic questions of whether to launch Vizir and, if so, on what scale, also raised some difficult questions about the existing organization structure and internal decision-making processes. If product market decisions were to be made in relation to Europe-wide strategic assessments and less in response to locally perceived opportunities, what implications did that have for the traditional role and responsibility of the country general manager? And if the Eurobrand concept was accepted, what organizational means were necessary to coordinate activities among the various country subsidiaries?

By the time Ferguson became vice president of P&G Europe, the nontechnical staff in ETC had grown substantially from the 20 or so people that worked with Bower in the early 1970s. Ferguson was convinced that his predecessor, Artzt, had been moving in the right direction by trying to inject a Pan-European perspective into decisions and by aiming to coordinate more activities among subsidiaries. Ferguson wanted to reinforce the more integrated perspective by changing the responsibilities of the three geographic division managers that reported to him.

Besides their existing responsibilities for several subsidiaries, Ferguson gave each of these managers Europe-wide responsibility for one or more lines of business. For example, the division manager responsible for the British, French, Belgian, and Dutch subsidiaries was also given responsibility for packaged soaps and detergents for Europe as a whole. Although the new roles were clearly coordinative, the status and experience of these managers meant that their advice and recommendations would carry significant weight, particularly on strategic and product planning issues.

For the first time, this change permitted clear Europe-wide objectives and priorities to be set by line of business, product group, or brand. Some country subsidiary managers naturally wondered whether their authority and autonomy were being eroded. Partly to deal with this problem and partly because the division managers had neither the time nor the resources to adequately manage their product responsibilities, Ferguson created an organizational forum that he termed the Euro Brand Team.

Borrowing from the successful technical team concept, Ferguson would assign each key brand a team headed by a "lead country." Typically, the country subsidiary with the most resources, the leading market positions, or the most commitment to a product would be given the lead role so that it could spread its knowledge, expertise, and commitment. The charter of the lead country would be to coordinate the analysis of opportunities for the standardization of the product formula, its promotion, and its packaging. The team concept also aimed at coordinating activities across subsidiaries and eliminating needless duplication of the brand's management.

The main forum for achieving this responsibility would be the Euro Brand Team meetings. Various managers from the regional office and the subsidiaries would be invited to these meetings. From ETC, the appropriate European division manager and European functional managers (for example, technical, manufacturing, purchasing, advertising, and so forth) would be invited. Advertising and brand managers from all the countries that sold the product would also be invited. It was proposed that the meeting would be chaired by the brand manager from the lead country. Thus, a typical team might have 20 or more invited participants.

At the subsidiary level, the idea received mixed reviews. Some saw an opportunity for increased local-management participation in Eurobrand decisions. These individuals viewed the European technical teams as evidence that such an approach could work and felt that this was a better solution than having such decisions dominated by an enlarged staff group at ETC. Other individuals felt that the Euro Brand Teams posed a further risk to the autonomy of the country manager. They also saw it as a threat, rather than an aid, to intersubsidiary relations. One general manager from a smaller country subsidiary explained:

> When a big, resource-rich subsidiary like Germany is anointed with the title of Lead Country, as it probably will be for a large number of brands, I am concerned that they will use their position and expertise to dominate the teams. The rich will become more powerful, and the small subs will wither. I believe this concept will generate further hostility between subsidiaries. Pricing and volume are the only tools we have left. The general manager's role will be compromised if our means to control these are dissipated in team discussions.

Another concern was that team meetings would not be an effective decision-making forum. With individual subsidiaries still responsible for and measured by their local profitability, it was felt that participants would go in with parochial views that they would not be willing to compromise. Some managers claimed that, because the teams' roles and responsibilities were not clear, it would become another time-consuming block to decision making rather than a means to achieve progress on Eurobrands. A subsidiary general manager commented:

> The agenda for the Euro Brand Teams is huge, but its responsibilities and powers are unclear. For such a huge and emotionally charged task, it is unrealistic to expect the "brand manager of the day" to run things. The teams will bog down, and decisions will take forever. How many of these meetings can we attend without tying up our top management? Our system is all checks and no balances. We are reinforcing an organization in which no one can say yes—they can only veto. With all the controls on approvals, we've lost the knack to experiment.

At least one manager at ETC voiced frustration, "If we were serious [about standardization], we would stop paying lip service, and tell everyone 'Like it or not, we're going to do it.'"

Ferguson remained convinced that the concept made sense and felt that *if* Vizir was launched and *if* it was considered a Eurobrand, it might provide an early test for his Euro Brand Team concept.

CASES EMPHASIZING IMPLEMENTATION ISSUES

CASE 28

The Lincoln Electric Company*

> People are our most valuable asset. They must feel secure, important, challenged, in control of their destiny, confident in their leadership, be responsive to common goals, believe they are being treated fairly, have easy access to authority and open lines of communication in all possible directions. Perhaps the most important task Lincoln employees face today is that of establishing an example for others in the Lincoln organization in other parts of the world. We need to maximize the benefits of cooperation and teamwork, fusing high technology with human talent, so that we here in the USA and all of our subsidiary and joint venture operations will be in a position to realize our full potential. *(George Willis, CEO, The Lincoln Electric Company)*

The Lincoln Electric Company is the world's largest manufacturer of arc welding products and a leading producer of industrial electric motors. The firm employs 2,400 workers in two U.S. factories near Cleveland and an equal number in eleven factories located in other countries. This does not include the field sales force of more than 200. The company's U.S. market share (for arc-welding products) is estimated at more than 40 percent.

The Lincoln incentive management plan has been well known for many years. Many college management texts make reference to the Lincoln plan as a model for achieving higher worker productivity. Certainly, the firm has been successful according to the usual measures.

James F. Lincoln died in 1965 and there was some concern, even among employees, that the management system would fall into disarray, that profits would decline, and that year-end bonuses might be discontinued. Quite the contrary, twenty-four years after Lincoln's death, the company appears as strong as ever. Each year, except the recession years 1982 and 1983, has seen high profits and bonuses. Employee morale and productivity remain very good. Employee turnover is almost nonexistent except for retirements. Lincoln's market share is stable. The historically high stock dividends continue.

A HISTORICAL SKETCH

In 1895, after being "frozen out" of the depression-ravaged Elliott-Lincoln Company, a maker of Lincoln-designed electric motors, John C. Lincoln took out his second patent and began to manufacture his improved motor. He opened his new business, unincorporated,

* Prepared by Arthur Sharplin, McNeese State University.

with $200 he had earned redesigning a motor for young Herbert Henry Dow, who later founded the Dow Chemical Company.

Started during an economic depression and cursed by a major fire after only 1 year in business, the company grew, but hardly prospered, through its first quarter century. In 1906, John C. Lincoln incorporated the business and moved from his one-room, fourth-floor factory to a new three-story building he erected in east Cleveland. He expanded his work force to thirty and sales grew to over $50,000 a year. John preferred being an engineer and inventor rather than a manager, though, and it was to be left to another Lincoln to manage the company through its years of success.

In 1907, after a bout with typhoid fever forced him from Ohio State University in his senior year, James F. Lincoln, John's younger brother, joined the fledgling company. In 1914 he became active head of the firm, with the titles of general manager and vice president. John remained president of the company for some years but became more involved in other business ventures and in his work as an inventor.

One of James Lincoln's early actions was to ask the employees to elect representatives to a committee which would advise him on company operations. This "advisory board" has met with the chief executive officer every 2 weeks since that time. This was only the first of a series of innovative personnel policies which have, over the years, distinguished Lincoln Electric from its contemporaries.

The first year the advisory board was in existence, working hours were reduced from 55 per week, then standard, to 50 hours a week. In 1915, the company gave each employee a paid-up life insurance policy. A welding school, which continues today, was begun in 1917. In 1918, an employee bonus plan was attempted. It was not continued, but the idea was to resurface later.

The Lincoln Electric Employees' Association was formed in 1919 to provide health benefits and social activities. This organization continues today and has assumed several additional functions over the years. In 1923, a piecework pay system was in effect, employees got 2 weeks paid vacation each year, and wages were adjusted for changes in the Consumer Price Index. Approximately 30 percent of the common stock was set aside for key employees in 1914. A stock purchase plan for all employees was begun in 1925.

The board of directors voted to start a suggestion system in 1929. The program is still in effect, but cash awards, a part of the early program, were discontinued several years ago. Now, suggestions are rewarded by additional "points," which affect year-end bonuses.

The legendary Lincoln bonus plan was proposed by the advisory board and accepted on a trial basis in 1934. The first annual bonus amounted to about 25 percent of wages. There has been a bonus every year since then. The bonus plan has been a cornerstone of the Lincoln management system and recent bonuses have approximated annual wages.

By 1944, Lincoln employees enjoyed a pension plan, a policy of promotion from within, and continuous employment. Base pay rates were determined by formal job evaluation and a merit rating system was in effect.

In the prologue of James F. Lincoln's last book, Charles G. Herbruck writes regarding the foregoing personnel innovations:

> They were not to buy good behavior. They were not efforts to increase profits. They were not antidotes to labor difficulties. They did not constitute a "do-gooder" program. They were expression of mutual respect for each person's importance to

the job to be done. All of them reflect the leadership of James Lincoln, under whom they were nurtured and propagated.

During World War II, Lincoln prospered as never before. By the start of the war, the company was the world's largest manufacturer of arc-welding products. Sales of about $4 million in 1934 grew to $24 million by 1941. Productivity per employee more than doubled during the same period. The Navy's Price Review Board challenged the high profits. And the Internal Revenue Service questioned the tax deductibility of employee bonuses, arguing they were not "ordinary and necessary" costs of doing business. But the forceful and articulate James Lincoln was able to overcome the objections.

Certainly since 1935 and probably for several years before that, Lincoln productivity has been well above the average for similar companies. The company claims levels of productivity more than twice those for other manufacturers from 1945 onward. Information available from outside sources tends to support these claims.

COMPANY PHILOSOPHY

James F. Lincoln was the son of a Congregational minister, and Christian principles were at the center of his business philosophy. The confidence that he had in the efficacy of Christ's teachings is illustrated by the following remark taken from one of his books:

> The Christian ethic should control our acts. If it did control our acts, the savings in cost of distribution would be tremendous. Advertising would be a contact of the expert consultant with the customer, in order to give the customer the best product available when all of the customer's needs are considered. Competition then would be in improving the quality of products and increasing efficiency in producing and distributing them; not in deception, as is now too customary. Pricing would reflect efficiency of production; it would not be a selling dodge that the customer may well be sorry he accepted. It would be proper for all concerned and rewarding for the ability used in producing the product.

There is no indication that Lincoln attempted to evangelize his employees or customers—or the general public for that matter. Neither the chairman of the board and chief executive, George Willis, nor the president, Donald F. Hastings, mention the Christian gospel in their recent speeches and interviews. The company motto, "The actual is limited, the possible is immense," is prominently displayed, but there is no display of religious slogans, and there is no company chapel.

Attitude toward the Customer

James Lincoln saw the customer's needs as the *raison d'etre* for every company. "When any company has achieved success so that it is attractive as an investment," he wrote, "all money usually needed for expansion is supplied by the customer in retained earnings. It is obvious that the customer's interests, not the stockholder's, should come first." In 1947 he said, "Care should be taken . . . not to rivet attention on profit. Between 'How much do I get?' and 'How do I make this better, cheaper, more useful?' the difference is fundamental and decisive." Willis, too, ranks the customer as management's most important constituency. This is reflected in Lincoln's policy to "at all times price on the basis of cost and at all times keep pressure on our cost. . . ." Lincoln's goal, often stated, is "to build a better and better product at a lower and lower price." "It is obvious," James Lincoln said, "that the customer's interests should be the first goal of industry."

Attitude toward Stockholders

Stockholders are given last priority at Lincoln. This is a continuation of James Lincoln's philosophy: "The last group to be considered is the stockholders who own stock because they think it will be more profitable than investing money in any other way." Concerning division of the largess produced by incentive management, he wrote, "The absentee stockholder also will get his share, even if undeserved, out of the greatly increased profit that the efficiency produces."

Attitude toward Unionism

There has never been a serious effort to organize Lincoln employees. While James Lincoln criticized the labor movement for "selfishly attempting to better its position at the expense of the people it must serve," he still had kind words for union members. He excused abuses of union power as "the natural reactions of human beings to the abuses to which management has subjected them." Lincoln's idea of the correct relationship between workers and managers is shown by this comment: "Labor and management are properly not warring camps; they are parts of one organization in which they must and should cooperate fully and happily."

Beliefs and Assumptions about Employees

If fulfilling customer needs is the desired goal of business, then employee performance and productivity are the means by which this goal can best be achieved. It is the Lincoln attitude toward employees, reflected in the following comments by James Lincoln, which is credited by many with creating the success the company has experienced:

> The greatest fear of the worker, which is the same as the greatest fear of the industrialist in operating a company, is the lack of income. . . . The industrial manager is very conscious of his company's need of uninterrupted income. He is completely oblivious, evidently, of the fact that the worker has the same need.
>
> He is just as eager as any manager is to be part of a team that is properly organized and working for the advancement of our economy. . . . He has no desire to make profits for those who do not hold up their end in production, as is true of absentee stockholders and inactive people in the company.
>
> If money is to be used as an incentive, the program must provide that what is paid to the worker is what he has earned. The earnings of each must be in accordance with accomplishment.
>
> Status is of great importance in all human relationships. The greatest incentive that money has, usually, is that it is a symbol of success. . . . The resulting status is the real incentive. . . . Money alone can be an incentive to the miser only.

There must be complete honesty and understanding between the hourly worker and management if high efficiency is to be obtained.

LINCOLN'S BUSINESS

Arc welding has been the standard joining method in shipbuilding for decades. It is the predominant way of connecting steel in the construction industry. Most industrial plants have their own welding shops for maintenance and construction. Manufacturers of tractors and all kinds of heavy equipment use arc welding extensively in the manufacturing process. Many hobbyists have their own welding machines and use them for making metal items such as patio furniture and barbecue pits. The popularity of welded sculpture as an art form is growing.

While advances in welding technology have been frequent, arc welding products, in the main, have hardly changed. Lincoln's Innershield process is a notable exception. This process, described later, lowers welding cost and improves quality and speed in many applications. The most widely used Lincoln electrode, the Fleetweld 5P, has been virtually the same since the 1930s. The most popular engine-driven welder in the world, the Lincoln SA-200, has been a gray-colored assembly including a four-cylinder continental "Red Seal" engine and a 200 ampere direct-current generator with two current-control knobs for at least four decades. A 1989 model SA-200 even weighs almost the same as the 1950 model, and it certainly is little changed in appearance.

The company's share of the U.S. arc-welding products market appears to have been about 40 percent for many years. The welding products market has grown somewhat faster than the level of industry in general. The market is highly price-competitive, with variations in prices of standard items normally amounting to only a percent or two. Lincoln's products are sold directly by its engineering-oriented sales force and indirectly through its distributor organization. Advertising expenditures amount to less than three-fourths of a percent of sales. Research and development expenditures typically range from $10 million to $12 million, considerably more than competitors.

The other major welding process, flame welding, has not been competitive with arc welding since the 1930s. However, plasma arc welding, a relatively new process which uses a conducting stream of super heated gas (plasma) to confine the welding current to a small area, has made some inroads, especially in metal tubing manufacturing, in recent years. Major advances in technology which will produce an alternative superior to arc welding within the next decade or so appear unlikely. Also, it seems likely that changes in the machines and techniques used in arc welding will be evolutionary rather than revolutionary.

Products

The company is primarily engaged in the manufacture and sale of arc welding products—electric welding machines and metal electrodes. Lincoln also produces electric motors ranging from one-half horsepower to 200 horsepower. Motors constitute about 8 to 10 percent of total sales. Several million dollars has recently been invested in automated equipment that will double Lincoln's manufacturing capacity for ½ to 20 horsepower electric motors.

The electric welding machines, some consisting of a transformer or motor and generator arrangement powered by commercial electricity and others consisting of an internal combustion engine and generator, are designed to produce 30 to 1,500 amperes of electrical power. This electrical current is used to melt a consumable metal electrode with the molten metal being transferred in super hot spray to the metal joint being welded. Very high temperatures and hot sparks are produced, and operators usually must wear special eye and face protection and leather gloves, often along with leather aprons and sleeves.

Lincoln and its competitors now market a wide range of general purpose and specialty electrodes for welding mild steel, aluminum, cast iron, and stainless and special steels. Most of these electrodes are designed to meet the standards of the American Welding Society, a trade association. They are thus essentially the same as to size and composition from one manufacturer to another. Every electrode manufacturer has a limited number of unique products, but these typically constitute only a small percentage of total sales.

Welding electrodes are of two basic types: (1) Coated "stick" electrodes, usually 14 inches long and smaller than a pencil in diameter, which are held in a special insulated holder by the operator, who must manipulate the electrode in order to maintain a proper arc width and pattern of deposition of the metal being transferred. Stick electrodes are packaged in 6- to 50-pound boxes. (2) Coiled wire, ranging in diameter from 0.035 to 0.219 inch, which is designed to be fed continuously to the welding arc through a "gun" held by the operator or positioned by automatic positioning equipment. The wire is packaged in coils, reels, and drums weighing from 14 to 1,000 pounds and may be solid or flux-cored.

Manufacturing Processes

The main plant is in Euclid, Ohio, a suburb on Cleveland's east side. The layout of this plant is shown in Exhibit 1. There are no warehouses. Materials flow from the half-mile-long dock on the north side of the plant through the production lines to a very limited storage and loading area on the south side. Materials used on each work station are stored as close as

EXHIBIT 1
Main Factory Layout

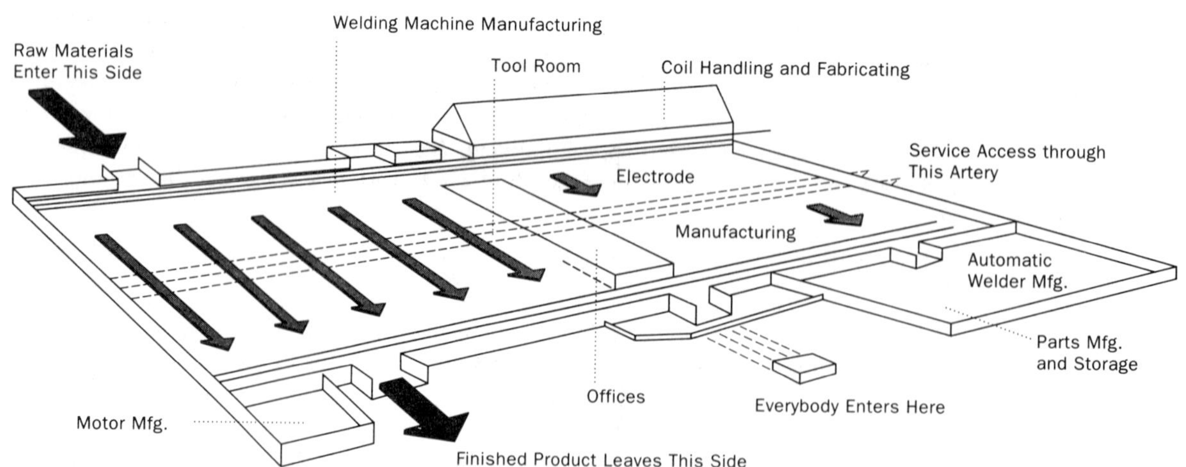

possible to the work station. The administrative offices, near the center of the factory, are entirely functional. A corridor below the main level provides access to the factory floor from the main entrance near the center of the plan. *Fortune* magazine recently declared the Euclid facility one of America's ten best-managed factories, and compared it with a General Electric plant also on the list:

> Stepping into GE's spanking new dishwasher plant, an awed supplier said, is like stepping "into the Hyatt Regency." By comparison, stepping into Lincoln Electric's 33-year-old, cavernous, dimly lit factory is like stumbling into a dingy big-city YMCA. It's only when one starts looking at how these factories do things that similarities become apparent. They have found ways to merge design with manufacturing, build in quality, make wise choices about automation, get close to customers, and handle their work forces.

A new Lincoln plant, in Mentor, Ohio, houses some of the electrode production operations, which were moved from the main plant.

Electrode manufacturing is highly capital intensive. Metal rods purchased from steel producers are drawn down to smaller diameters, cut to length and coated with pressed-powder "flux" for stick electrodes, or plated with copper (for conductivity) and put into coils or spools for wire. Lincoln's Innershield wire is hollow and filled with a material similar to that used to coat stick electrodes. As mentioned earlier, this represented a major innovation in welding technology when it was introduced. The company is highly secretive about its electrode production processes, and outsiders are not given access to the details of those processes.

Lincoln welding machines and electric motors are made on a series of assembly lines. Gasoline and diesel engines are purchased partially assembled but practically all other components are made from basic industrial products, for example, steel bars and sheets and bar copper conductor wire.

Individual components, such as gasoline tanks for engine-driven welders and steel shafts for motors and generators, are made by numerous small "factories within a factory." The shaft for a certain generator, for example, is made from raw steel bar by one operator who uses five large machines, all running continuously. A saw cuts the bar to length, a digital lathe machines different sections to varying diameters, a special milling machine cuts a slot for the keyway, and so forth, until a finished shaft is produced. The operator moves the shafts from machine to machine and makes necessary adjustments.

Another operator punches, shapes, and paints sheet metal cowling parts. One assembles steel laminations onto a rotor shaft, then winds, insulates, and tests the rotors. Finished components are moved by crane operators to the nearby assembly lines.

Worker Performance and Attitudes

Exceptional worker performance at Lincoln is a matter of record. The typical Lincoln employee earns about twice as much as other factory workers in the Cleveland area. Yet the company's labor cost per sales dollar in 1989, 26 cents, is well below industry averages. Worker turnover is practically nonexistent except for retirements and departures by new employees.

Sales per Lincoln factory employee currently exceed $150,000. An observer at the factory quickly sees why this figure is so high. Each worker is proceeding busily and thoughtfully about the task at hand. There is no idle chatter. Most workers take no coffee breaks. Many operate several machines and make a substantial component unaided. The supervisors are busy with planning and record-keeping duties and hardly glance at the people they "supervise." The manufacturing procedures appear efficient—no unnecessary steps, no wasted motions, no wasted materials. Finished components move smoothly to subsequent work stations.

The appendix includes summaries of interviews with employees.

ORGANIZATION STRUCTURE

Lincoln has never allowed development of a formal organization chart. The objective of this policy is to ensure maximum flexibility. An open-door policy is practiced throughout the company, and personnel are encouraged to take problems to the persons most capable of resolving them. Once, Harvard Business School researchers prepared an organization chart reflecting the implied relationships at Lincoln. The chart became available within the company, and present management feels that it had a disruptive effect. Therefore, no organizational chart appears in this report.

Perhaps because of the quality and enthusiasm of the Lincoln work force, routine supervision is almost nonexistent. A typical production foreman, for example, supervises as many as 100 workers, a span of control which does not allow more than infrequent worker-supervisor interaction.

Position titles and traditional flows of authority do imply something of an organizational structure, however. For example, the vice-president, Sales, and the vice-president, Electrode Division, report to the president, as do various staff assistants such as the personnel director and the director of purchasing. Using such implied relationships, it has been determined that production workers have two or, at most, three levels of supervision between themselves and the president.

PERSONNEL POLICIES

As mentioned earlier, it is Lincoln's remarkable personnel practices which are credited by many with the company's success.

Recruitment and Selection

Every job opening is advertised internally on company bulletin boards and any employee can apply for any job so advertised. External hiring is permitted only for entry-level positions. Selection for these jobs is done on the basis of personal interviews—there is no aptitude or psychological testing. Not even a high school diploma is required—except for engineering and sales positions, which are filled by graduate engineers. A committee consisting of vice presidents and supervisors interviews candidates initially cleared by the Personnel Department. Final selection is made by the supervisor who has a job opening. Out of over 3,500 applicants interviewed by the Personnel Department during a recent period fewer than 300 were hired.

Job Security

In 1958 Lincoln formalized its guaranteed continuous employment policy, which had already been in effect for many years. There have been no layoffs since World War II. Since 1958, every worker with over 2 year's longevity has been guaranteed at least 30 hours per week, 49 weeks per year.

The policy has never been so severely tested as during the 1981–1983 recession. As a manufacturer of capital goods, Lincoln's business is highly cyclical. In previous recessions the company was able to avoid major sales declines. However, sales plummeted 32 percent in 1982 and another 16 percent the next year. Few companies could withstand such a revenue collapse and remain profitable. Yet, Lincoln not only earned profits, but no employee was laid off and year-end incentive bonuses continued. To weather the storm, management cut most of the nonsalaried workers back to 30 hours a week for varying periods of time. Many employees were reassigned and the total work force was slightly reduced through normal attrition and restricted hiring. Many employees grumbled at their unexpected misfortune, probably to the surprise and dismay of some Lincoln managers. However, sales and profits—and employee bonuses—soon rebounded and all was well again.

Performance Evaluations

Each supervisor formally evaluates subordinates twice a year using the cards shown in Exhibit 2. The employee performance criteria, "quality," "dependability," "ideas and cooperation," and "output," are considered to be independent of each other. Marks on the cards are converted to numerical scores which are forced to average 100 for each evaluating supervisor. Individual merit rating scores normally range from 80 to 110. Any score over 110 requires a special letter to top management. These scores (over 110) are not considered in computing the required 100-point average for each evaluating supervisor. Suggestions for improvements often result in recommendations for exceptionally high-performance scores. Supervisors discuss individual performance marks with the employees concerned. Each warranty claim is traced to the individual employee whose work caused the defect. The employee's performance score may be reduced, or the worker may be required to repay the cost of servicing the warranty claim by working without pay.

Compensation

Basic wage levels for jobs at Lincoln are determined by a wage survey of similar jobs in the Cleveland area. These rates are adjusted quarterly in accordance with changes in the Cleveland area wage index. Insofar as possible, base wage rates are translated into piece rates. Practically all production workers and many others—for example, some forklift operators—are paid by piece rate. Once established, piece rates are never changed unless a substantive change in the way a job is done results from a source other than the worker doing the job.

In December of each year, a portion of annual profits is distributed to employees as bonuses. Incentive bonuses since 1934 have averaged about 90 percent of annual wages and somewhat more than after-tax profits. The average bonus for 1988 was $21,258. Even for the recession years 1982 and 1983, bonuses had averaged $13,998 and $8,557, respectively. Individual bonuses are proportional to merit-rating scores. For example, assume the

EXHIBIT 2
Merit Rating Cards

QUALITY

This rating has been done jointly by your department head and the Inspection Department in the shop and with other department heads in the office and engineering.

⇨ Increasing Quality ⇨

This card rates the QUALITY of work you do.

It also reflects your success in eliminating errors and in reducing scrap and waste.

DEPENDABILITY

This rating has been done by your department head.

⇨ Increasing Dependability ⇨

This card rates how well your supervisors have been able to depend upon you to do those things that have been expected of you without supervision.

It also reflects your ability to supervise yourself including your work safety performance, your orderliness, care of equipment, and the effective use you make of your skills.

IDEAS & COOPERATION

⇨ Increasing Ideas & Cooperation ⇨

This card rates your Cooperation, Ideas and Initiative.

OUTPUT

This rating has been done jointly by your department head and the Production Control Department in the shop and with other department heads in the office and engineering.

⇨ Increasing Output ⇨ Days Absent

This card rates HOW MUCH PRODUCTIVE WORK you actually turn out.
It also reflects your willingness not to hold back and recognizes your attendance record.
New ideas and new methods are important to your company in our continuing effect to reduce costs, increase output, improve quality, work safety and improve our relationship with our customers. This card credits you for your ideas and initiative used to help in this direction.
It also rates your cooperation—how you work with others as a team. Such factors as your attitude towards supervision, co-workers and the company, your efforts to share knowledge with others, and your cooperation in installing new methods smoothly, are considered here.

amount set aside for bonuses is 80 percent of total wages paid to eligible employees. A person whose performance score is 95 will receive a bonus of 76 percent (0.80 × 0.95) of annual wages.

Vacations

The company is shut down for 2 weeks in August and 2 weeks during the Christmas season. Vacations are taken during these periods. For employees with over 25 years of service, a fifth week of vacation may be taken at a time acceptable to superiors.

Work Assignment

Management has authority to transfer workers and to switch between overtime and short time as required. Supervisors have undisputed authority to assign specific parts to individual workmen, who may have their own preferences due to variations in piece rates. During the 1982–1983 recession, fifty factory workers volunteered to join sales teams and fanned out across the country to sell a new welder designed for automobile body shops and small machine shops. The result—$10 million in sales and a hot new product.

Employee Participation in Decision Making

Thinking of participative management usually evokes a vision of a relaxed, nonauthoritarian atmosphere. This is not the case at Lincoln. Formal authority is quite strong. "We're very authoritarian around here," says Willis. James F. Lincoln placed a good deal of stress on protecting management's authority. "Management in all successful departments of industry must have complete power," he said. "Management is the coach who must be obeyed. The men, however, are the players who alone can win the game." Despite this attitude, there are several ways in which employees participate in management at Lincoln.

Richard Sabo, assistant to the chief executive officer, relates job enlargement/enrichment to participation. He said, "The most important participative technique that we use is giving more responsibility to employees. We give a high school graduate more responsibility than other companies give their foremen." Management puts limits on the degree of participation which is allowed, however. In Sabo's words:

> When you use "participation," put quotes around it, because we believe that each person should participate only in those decisions he is most knowledgeable about. I don't think production employees should control the decisions of the chairman. They don't know as much as he does about the decisions he is involved in.

The advisory board, elected by the workers, meets with the chairman and the president every 2 weeks to discuss ways of improving operations. As noted earlier, this board has been in existence since 1914 and has contributed to many innovations. The incentive bonuses, for example, were first recommended by this committee. Every employee has access to advisory board members, and answers to all advisory board suggestions are promised by the following meeting. Both Willis and Hastings are quick to point out, though, that the advisory board only recommends actions. "They do not have direct authority," Willis says, "and when they bring up something that management thinks is not to the benefit of the company, it will be rejected."

Under the early suggestion program, employees were awarded one-half of the first year's savings attributable to their suggestions. Now, however, the value of suggestions is reflected in performance evaluation scores, which determine individual incentive bonus amounts.

Training and Education

Production workers are given a short period of on-the-job training and then placed on a piecework pay system. Lincoln does not pay for off-site education, unless very specific company needs are identified. The idea behind this latter policy, according to Sabo, is that everyone cannot take advantage of such a program, and it is unfair to expend company funds for an advantage to which there is unequal access. Recruits for sales jobs, already college graduates, are given on-the-job training in the plant followed by a period of work and training at one of the regional sales offices.

Fringe Benefits and Executive Perquisites

A medical plan and a company-paid retirement program have been in effect for many years. A plant cafeteria, operated on a break-even basis, serves meals at about 60 percent of usual costs. The Employee Association, to which the company does not contribute, provides disability insurance and social and athletic activities. The employee stock ownership program has resulted in employee ownership of about 50 percent of the common stock. Under this program, each employee with more than 2 years of service may purchase stock in the corporation. The price of these shares is established at book value. Stock purchased through this plan may be held by employees only. Dividends and voting rights are the same as for stock which is owned outside the plan. Approximately 75 percent of the employees own Lincoln stock.

As to executive perquisites, there are none—crowded, austere offices, no executive washrooms or lunchrooms, and no reserved parking spaces. Even the top executives pay for their own meals and eat in the employee cafeteria. On one recent day, Willis arrived at work late due to a breakfast speaking engagement and had to park far away from the factory entrance.

FINANCIAL POLICIES

James F. Lincoln felt strongly that financing for company growth should come from within the company—through initial cash investment by the founders, through retention of earnings, and through stock purchases by those who work in the business. He saw the following advantages of this approach:

1. Ownership of stock by employees strengthens team spirit. "If they are mutually anxious to make it succeed, the future of the company is bright."
2. Ownership of stock provides individual incentive because employees feel that they will benefit from company profitability.

EXHIBIT 3
Condensed Comparative Financial Statements (in Millions of Dollars)*

	1979	*1980*	*1981*	*1982*	*1983*	*1984*	*1985*	*1986*	*1987*
				Balance Sheets					
Assets:									
Cash	2	1	4	1	2	4	2	1	7
Bonds & CDs	38	47	63	72	78	57	55	45	41
N/R & A/R	42	42	42	26	31	34	38	36	43
Inventories	38	36	46	38	31	37	34	26	40
Prepayments	1	3	4	5	5	5	7	8	7
Total CA	121	129	157	143	146	138	135	116	137
Other assets†	24	24	26	30	30	29	29	33	40
Land	1	1	1	1	1	1	1	1	1
Net buildings	22	23	25	23	22	21	20	18	17
Net M&E	21	25	27	27	27	28	27	29	33
Total FA	44	49	53	51	50	50	48	48	50
Total assets	189	202	236	224	227	217	213	197	227
Claims:									
A/P	17	16	15	12	16	15	13	11	20
Accrued wages	1	2	5	4	3	4	5	5	4
Accrued taxes	10	6	15	5	7	4	6	5	9
Accrued div.	6	6	7	7	7	6	7	6	7
Total CL	33	29	42	28	33	30	31	27	40
LT debt	—	4	5	6	8	10	11	8	8
Total debt	33	33	47	34	41	40	42	35	48
Common stock	4	3	1	2	0	0	0	0	2
Ret. earnings	152	167	189	188	186	176	171	161	177
Total SH equity	156	170	190	190	186	176	171	161	179
Total claims	189	202	236	224	227	217	213	197	227
				Income Statements					
Net sales	374	387	450	311	263	322	333	318	368
Other income	11	14	18	18	13	12	11	8	9
Income	385	401	469	329	277	334	344	326	377
CGS	244	261	293	213	180	223	221	216	239
Selling, G&A‡	41	46	51	45	45	47	48	49	51
Incentive bonus	44	43	56	37	22	33	38	33	39
IBT	56	51	69	35	30	31	36	27	48
Income taxes	26	23	31	16	13	14	16	12	21
Net income	30	28	37	19	17	17	20	15	27

* Column totals may not check and amounts less than $500,000 (0.5) are shown as zero, due to rounding.
† Includes investment in foreign subsidiaries, $29 million in 1987.
‡ Includes pension expense and payroll taxes on incentive bonus.

3. "Ownership is educational." Owners-employees "will know how profits are made and lost; how success is won and lost. . . . There are few socialists in the list of stockholders of the nation's industries."
4. "Capital available from within controls expansion." Unwarranted expansion would not occur, Lincoln believed, under his financing plan.
5. "The greatest advantage would be the development of the individual worker. Under the incentive of ownership, he would become a greater man."
6. "Stock ownership is one of the steps that can be taken that will make the worker feel that there is less of a gulf between him and the boss. . . . Stock ownership will help the worker to recognize his responsibility in the game and the importance of victory."

Until 1980, Lincoln Electric borrowed no money. Even now, the company's liabilities consist mainly of accounts payable and short-term accruals.

The unusual pricing policy at Lincoln is succinctly stated by Willis: "At all times price on the basis of cost and at all times keep pressure on our cost." This policy resulted in the price for the most popular welding electrode then in use going from 16 cents a pound in 1929 to 4.7 cents in 1938. More recently, the SA-200 welder, Lincoln's largest-selling portable machine, decreased in price from 1958 through 1965. According to Dr. C. Jackson Grayson of the American Productivity Center in Houston, Texas, Lincoln's prices increased only one-fifth as fast as the Consumer Price Index from 1934 to about 1970. This resulted in a welding products market in which Lincoln became the undisputed price leader for the products it manufactures. Not even the major Japanese manufacturers, such as Nippon Steel for welding electrodes and Osaka Transformer for welding machines, were able to penetrate this market.

EXHIBIT 4
Revenue Distribution

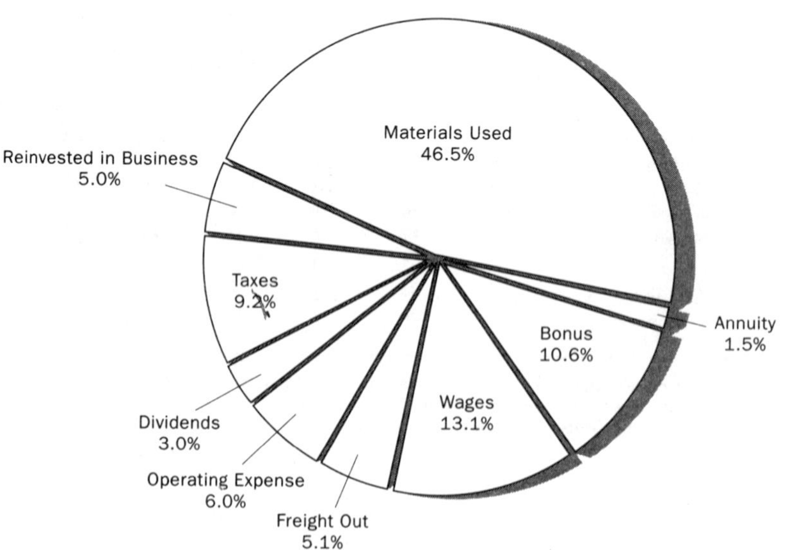

Substantial cash balances are accumulated each year preparatory to paying the year-end bonuses. The bonuses totaled $54 million for 1988. The money is invested in short-term U.S. government securities and certificates of deposit until needed. Financial statements are shown in Exhibit 3. Exhibit 4 shows how company revenue was distributed in the late 1980s.

HOW WELL DOES LINCOLN SERVE ITS STAKEHOLDERS?

Lincoln Electric differs from most other companies in the importance it assigns to each of the groups it serves. Willis identifies these groups, in the order of priority ascribed to them, as (1) customers, (2) employees, and (3) stockholders.

Certainly the firm's customers have fared well over the years. Lincoln prices for welding machines and welding electrodes are acknowledged to be the lowest in the marketplace. Quality has consistently been high. The cost of field failures for Lincoln products was recently determined to be a remarkable 0.04 percent of revenues. The "Fleetweld" electrodes and SA-200 welders have been the standard in the pipeline and refinery construction industry, where price is hardly a criterion, for decades. A Lincoln distributor in Monroe, Louisiana, says that he has sold several hundred of the popular AC-225 welders, which are warranted for 1 year, but has never handled a warranty claim.

Perhaps best served of all management constituencies have been the employees. Not the least of their benefits, of course, are the year-end bonuses, which effectively double an already average compensation level. The foregoing description of the personnel program and the comments in the appendix further illustrate the desirability of a Lincoln job.

While stockholders were relegated to an inferior status by James F. Lincoln, they have done very well indeed. Recent dividends have exceeded $11 a share and earnings per share have approached $30. In January 1980, the price of restricted stock, committed to employees, was $117 a share. By 1989, the stated value, at which the company will repurchase the stock if tendered, was $201. A check with the New York office of Merrill Lynch, Pierce, Fenner, and Smith at that time revealed an estimated price on Lincoln stock of $270 a share, with none being offered for sale. Technically, this price applies only to the unrestricted stock owned by the Lincoln family, a few other major holders, and employees who have purchased it on the open market. Risk associated with Lincoln stock, a major determinant of stock value, is minimal because of the small amount of debt in the capital structure, because of an extremely stable earnings record, and because of Lincoln's practice of purchasing the restricted stock whenever employees offer it for sale.

A CONCLUDING COMMENT

It is easy to believe that the reason for Lincoln's success is the excellent attitude of the employees and their willingness to work harder, faster, and more intelligently than other industrial workers. However, Sabo suggests that appropriate credit be given to Lincoln executives, whom he credits with carrying out the following policies:

1. Management has limited research, development, and manufacturing to a standard product line designed to meet the major needs of the welding industry.

2. New products must be reviewed by manufacturing and all producing costs verified before being approved by management.
3. Purchasing is challenged to not only procure materials at the lowest cost, but also to work closely with engineering and manufacturing to assure that the latest innovations are implemented.
4. Manufacturing supervision and all personnel are held accountable for reduction of scrap, energy conservation, and maintenance of product quality.
5. Production control, material handling, and methods engineering are closely supervised by top management.
6. Management has made cost reduction a way of life at Lincoln, and definite programs are established in many areas, including traffic and shipping, where tremendous savings can result.
7. Management has established a sales department that is technically trained to reduce customer welding costs. This sales approach and other real customer services have eliminated nonessential frills and resulted in long-term benefits to all concerned.
8. Management has encouraged education, technical publishing, and long-range programs that have resulted in industry growth, thereby assuring market potential for the Lincoln Electric Company.

Sabo writes, "It is in a very real sense a personal and group experience in faith—a belief that together we can achieve results which alone would not be possible. It is not a perfect system and it is not easy. It requires tremendous dedication and hard work. However, it does work and the results are worth the effort."

Appendix to Case 28
Employee Interviews

Typical questions and answers from employee interviews are presented below. In order to maintain each employee's personal privacy, fictitious names are given to the interviewees.

Interview 1

Betty Stewart, a 52-year-old high school graduate who had been with Lincoln 13 years and who was working as a cost accounting clerk at the time of the interview.

Q: What jobs have you held here besides the one you have now?
A: I worked in payroll for a while, and then this job came open and I took it.
Q: How much money did you make last year, including your bonus?
A: I would say roughly around $25,000, but I was off for back surgery for a while.
Q: You weren't paid while you were off for back surgery?
A: No.
Q: Did the Employees Association help out?
A: Yes. The company doesn't furnish that, though. We pay $8 a month into the Employee Association. I think my check from them was $130.00 a week.
Q: How was your performance rating last year?

A: It was around 100 points, but I lost some points for attendance for my back problem.
Q: How did you get your job at Lincoln?
A: I was bored silly where I was working, and I had heard that Lincoln kept their people busy. So I applied and got the job the next day.
Q: Do you think you make more money than similar workers in Cleveland?
A: I know I do.
Q: What have you done with your money?
A: We have purchased a better home. Also, my son is going to the University of Chicago, which costs $13,000 a year. I buy the Lincoln stock which is offered each year, and I have a little bit of gold.
Q: Have you ever visited with any of the senior executives, like Mr. Willis or Mr. Hastings?
A: I have known Mr. Willis for a long time.
Q: Does he call you by name?
A: Yes. In fact he was very instrumental in my going to the doctor that I am going to with my back. He knows the director of the clinic.
Q: Do you know Mr. Hastings?
A: I know him to speak to him, and he always speaks, always. But I have known Mr. Willis for a good many years. When I did Plant Two accounting I did not understand how the plant operated. Of course you are not allowed in Plant Two, because that's the Electrode Division. I told my boss about the problem one day and the next thing I knew Mr. Willis came by and said, "Come on, Betty, we're going to Plant Two." He spent an hour and a half showing me the plant.
Q: Do you think Lincoln employees produce more than those in other companies?
A: I think with the incentive program the way that it is, if you want to work and achieve, then you will do it. If you don't want to work and achieve, you will not do it no matter where you are. Just because you are merit rated and have a bonus, if you really don't want to work hard, then you're not going to. You will accept your ninety points or ninety-two or eighty-five because, even with that you make more money than people on the outside.
Q: Do you think Lincoln employees will ever join a union?
A: I don't know why they would.
Q: So you say that money is a very major advantage?
A: Money is a major advantage, but it's not just the money. It's the fact that having the incentive, you do wish to work a little harder. I'm sure that there are a lot of men here who, if they worked some other place, would not work as hard as they do here. Not that they are overworked—I don't mean that—but I'm sure they wouldn't push.
Q: Is there anything that you would like to add?
A: I do like working here. I am better off being pushed mentally. In another company if you pushed too hard you would feel a little bit of pressure, and someone might say, "Hey, slow down; don't try so hard." But here you are encouraged, not discouraged.

Interview 2

Ed Sanderson, a 23-year-old high school graduate who had been with Lincoln 4 years and who was a machine operator in the Electrode Division at the time of the interview.

Q: How did you happen to get this job?
A: My wife was pregnant, and I was making three bucks an hour and one day I came here and applied. That was it. I kept calling to let them know I was still interested.
Q: Roughly what were your earnings last year including your bonus?
A: $45,000.00
Q: What have you done with your money since you have been here?
A: Well, we've lived pretty well and we bought a condominium.
Q: Have you paid for the condominium?
A: No, but I could.
Q: Have you bought your Lincoln stock this year?
A: No, I haven't bought any Lincoln stock yet.
Q: Do you get the feeling that the executives here are pretty well thought of?
A: I think they are. To get where they are today, they had to really work.
Q: Wouldn't that be true anywhere?
A: I think more so here because seniority really doesn't mean anything. If you work with a guy who has 20 years here, and you have 2 months and you're doing a better job, you will get advanced before he will.
Q: Are you paid on a piece rate basis?
A: My gang does. There are nine of us who make the bare electrode, and the whole group gets paid based on how much electrode we make.
Q: Do you think you work harder than workers in other factories in the Cleveland area?
A: Yes, I would say I probably work harder.
Q: Do you think it hurts anybody?
A: No, a little hard work never hurts anybody.
Q: If you could choose, do you think you would be as happy earning a little less money and being able to slow down a little?
A: No, it doesn't bother me. If it bothered me, I wouldn't do it.
Q: Why do you think Lincoln employees produce more than workers in other plants?
A: That's the way the company is set up. The more you put out, the more you're going to make.
Q: Do you think it's the piece rate and bonus together?
A: I don't think people would work here if they didn't know that they would be rewarded at the end of the year.
Q: Do you think Lincoln employees will ever join a union?
A: No.
Q: What are the major advantages of working for Lincoln?
A: Money.
Q: Are there any other advantages?
A: Yes, we don't have a union shop. I don't think I could work in a union shop.
Q: Do you think you are a career man with Lincoln at this time?
A: Yes.

Interview 3

Roger Lewis, a 23-year-old Purdue graduate in mechanical engineering who had been in the Lincoln sales program for 15 months and who was working in the Cleveland sales office at the time of the interview.

Q: How did you get your job at Lincoln?
A: I saw that Lincoln was interviewing on campus at Purdue, and I went by. I later came to Cleveland for a plant tour and was offered a job.
Q: Do you know any of the senior executives? Would they know you by name?
A: Yes, I know all of them—Mr. Hastings, Mr. Willis, Mr. Sabo.
Q: Do you think Lincoln salesmen work harder than those in other companies?
A: Yes. I don't think there are many salesmen for other companies who are putting in 50- to 60-hour weeks. Everybody here works harder. You can go out in the plant, or you can go upstairs, and there's nobody sitting around.
Q: Do you see any real disadvantage of working at Lincoln?
A: I don't know if it's a disadvantage but Lincoln is a spartan company, a very thrifty company. I like that. The sales offices are functional, not fancy.
Q: Why do you think Lincoln employees have such high productivity?
A: Piecework has a lot to do with it. Lincoln is smaller than many plants, too; you can stand in one place and see the materials come in one side and the product go out the other. You feel a part of the company. The chance to get ahead is important, too. They have a strict policy of promoting from within, so you know you have a chance. I think in a lot of other places you may not get as fair a shake as you do here. The sales offices are on a smaller scale, too. I like that. I tell someone that we have two people in the Baltimore office, and they say "You've got to be kidding." It's smaller and more personal. Pay is the most important thing. I have heard that this is the highest paying factory in the world.

Interview 4

Jimmy Roberts, a 47-year-old high school graduate, who had been with Lincoln 17 years and who was working as a multiple-drill press operator at the time of the interview.

Q: What jobs have you had at Lincoln?
A: I started out cleaning the men's locker room in 1967. After about a year I got a job in the flux department, where we make the coating for welding rods. I worked there for 7 or 8 years and then got my present job.
Q: Do you make one particular part?
A: No, there are a variety of parts I make—at least twenty-five.
Q: Each one has a different piece rate attached to it?
A: Yes.
Q: Are some piece rates better than others?
A: Yes.
Q: How do you determine which ones you are going to do?
A: You don't. Your supervisor assigns them.
Q: How much money did you make last year?
A: $53,000.
Q: Have you ever received any kind of award or citation?
A: No.
Q: Was your rating ever over 110?
A: Yes. For the past 5 years, probably, I made over 110 points.
Q: Is there any attempt to let the others know . . .?
A: The kind of points I get? No.

Q: Do you know what they are making?
A: No. There are some who might not be too happy with their points and they might make it known. The majority, though, do not make it a point of telling other employees.
Q: Would you be just as happy earning a little less money and working a little slower?
A: I don't think I would—not at this point. I have done piecework all these years, and the fast pace doesn't really bother me.
Q: Why do you think Lincoln productivity is so high?
A: The incentive thing—the bonus distribution. I think that would be the main reason. The paycheck you get every 2 weeks is important too.
Q: Do you think Lincoln employees would ever join a union?
A: I don't think so. I have never heard anyone mention it.
Q: What is the most important advantage of working here?
A: Amount of money you make. I don't think I could make this type of money anywhere else, especially with only a high school education.
Q: As a black person, do you feel that Lincoln discriminates in any way against blacks?
A: No. I don't think any more so than any other job. Naturally, there is a certain amount of discrimination, regardless of where you are.

Interview 5

Joe Trahan, 58-year-old high school graduate who had been with Lincoln 39 years and who was employed as a working supervisor in the tool room at the time of the interview.

Q: Roughly what was your pay last year?
A: Over $56,000; salary, bonus, stock dividends.
Q: How much was your bonus?
A: About $26,000.
Q: Have you ever gotten a special award of any kind?
A: Not really.
Q: What have you done with your money?
A: My house is paid for—and my two cars. I also have some bonds and the Lincoln stock.
Q: What do you think of the executives at Lincoln?
A: They're really top notch.
Q: What is the major disadvantage of working at Lincoln Electric?
A: I don't know of any disadvantage at all.
Q: Do you think you produce more than most people in similar jobs with other companies?
A: I do believe that.
Q: Why is that? Why do you believe that?
A: We are on the incentive system. Everything we do, we try to improve to make a better product with a minimum of outlay. We try to improve the bonus.
Q: Would you be just as happy making a little less money and not working quite so hard?
A: I don't think so.
Q: Do you think Lincoln employees would ever join a union?
A: I don't think they would ever consider it.
Q: What is the most important advantage of working at Lincoln?
A: Compensation.

Q: Tell me something about Mr. James Lincoln, who died in 1965.
A: You are talking about Jimmy, Sr. He always strolled through the shop in his shirt sleeves. Big fellow. Always looked distinguished. Gray hair. Friendly sort of guy. I was a member of the advisory board one year. He was there each time.
Q: Did he strike you as really caring?
A: I think he always cared for people.
Q: Did you get any sensation of a religious nature from him?
A: No, not really.
Q: And religion is not part of the program now?
A: No.
Q: Do you think Mr. Lincoln was a very intelligent man, or was he just a nice guy?
A: I would say he was pretty well-educated. A great talker—always right off the top of his head. He knew what he was talking about all the time.
Q: When were bonuses for beneficial suggestions done away with?
A: About 18 years ago.
Q: Did that hurt very much?
A: I don't think so, because suggestions are still rewarded through the merit rating system.
Q: Is there anything you would like to add?
A: It's a good place to work. The union kind of ties other places down. At other places, electricians only do electrical work, carpenters only do carpenter work. At Lincoln Electric we all pitch in and do whatever needs to be done.
Q: So a major advantage is not having a union?
A: That's right.

CASE 29

Nucor*

INTRODUCTION

Nuclear Corporation of America had been near bankruptcy in 1965, when a fourth reorganization put a 39-year-old division manager, Ken Iverson, into the president's role. Iverson began a process which resulted in Nucor, a steel mini-mill and joist manufacturer which rated national attention and reaped high praise.

In a 1981 article subtitled "Lean living and mini-mill technology have led a one-time loser to steel's promised land," *Fortune* stated:

> Although Nucor didn't build its first mill until 1969, it turned out 1.1 million tons of steel last year, enough to rank among the top 20 U.S. producers. Not only has Nucor been making a lot of steel, it's been making money making steel—and a lot of that as well. Since 1969, earnings have grown 31% a year, compounded, reaching $45 million in 1980 on sales of $482 million. Return on average equity in recent years has consistently exceeded 28%, excellent even by Silicon Valley's standards and almost unheard of in steel. The nine-fold increase in the value of Nucor's stock over the last five years—it was selling recently at about $70 a share—has given shareholders plenty of cause for thanksgiving.

The Wall Street Journal commented, "The ways in which management style combines with technology to benefit the mini-mill industry is obvious at Nucor Corp., one of the most successful of the 40 or more mini-mill operators." Ken Iverson was featured in an NBC special, "If Japan Can, Why Can't We?" for his management approach. As *The Wall Street Journal* commented, "You thought steel companies are only a bunch of losers, with stodgy management, outmoded plants and poor profits?" Well, Nucor and Iverson were different.

However, the challenges hadn't stopped. The economy made the 1980's a horrible time for the steel industry. All companies reported sales declines, most lost profitability and some, in both major and mini-mill operations, closed or restructured. Nucor's 30% plus return on equity hit 9%. Iverson, however, was one of 52 recipients of the bronze medal from *Financial World* in 1983 for holding on to profitability; they kept costs down but not at the expense of laying off their people—a near-religious commitment at Nucor.

By 1989 Nucor was the ninth largest steel producer in the U.S. and number 323 on the Fortune 500 list. But the easy gains scored by the new mini-mill operations over the integrated mills were over. The historical steel companies were arousing from their twenty-year slumber, adding modern technology, renegotiating with their equally aged unions, and closing some mills. They were determined to fight back. Mini-mill was fighting mini-mill, as well as imports, and a number had closed. Thus the industry faced a picture of excess

* Prepared by Frank C. Barnes, University of North Carolina–Charlotte.

capacity which would be the backdrop in the battle for survival and success over the next years.

Iverson and Nucor knew how to fight the battle. They invested $325 million in new processes in 1988. They went from $185 million in idle cash in 1986 to $180 million in debt by 1988. They had opened the first new fastener plant in the U.S. in decades, completed a joint venture with the Japanese to build a plant to make structural steel products, were the first mini-mill in the world to enter the flat-rolled market, the largest market and major business of the integrated producers, and had announced plans to build a second plant. Iverson believed with their new products they should double sales, and probably earnings, by 1991. Analysts predicted a jump to 7th largest among mills and doubling or tripling share price in the immediate future.

BACKGROUND

Nucor was the descendant of a company that manufactured the first Oldsmobile in 1897. After seven years of success, R. E. Olds sold his first company and founded a new one to manufacture the Reo. Reo ran into difficulties and filed for voluntary reorganization in 1938. Sales grew 50 times over the next ten years, based on defense business, but declined steadily after World War II. The motor division was sold and then resold in 1957 to the White Motor Corporation, where it operates as the Diamond Reo Division. Reo Motors' management planned to liquidate the firm, but before it could do so, a new company gained control through a proxy fight. A merger was arranged with Nuclear Consultants, Inc., and the stock of Nuclear Corporation of America was first traded in 1955. Nuclear acquired a number of companies in high-tech fields but continued to lose money until 1960, when an investment banker in New York acquired control. New management proceeded with a series of acquisitions and dispositions: they purchased U.S. Semi-Conductor Products, Inc.; Valley Sheet Metal Company, an air conditioner contractor in Arizona; and Vulcraft Corporation, a Florence, South Carolina, steel joist manufacturer. Over the next four years, sales increased five times, but losses increased seven times. In 1965 a New York investor purchased a controlling interest and installed the fourth management team. The new president was Ken Iverson, who had been in charge of the Vulcraft division.

Ken Iverson had joined the Navy upon graduation from a Chicago-area high school in 1943. The Navy first sent him to Northwestern University for an officer training program but then decided it needed aeronautical engineers and transferred him to Cornell. This had been "fine" with Iverson, because he enjoyed engineering. Upon receiving his bachelor's degree in 1945 at age 20, he served in the Navy for six months, completing his four-year tour.

He wasn't too excited about an A.E. career because of the eight years of drafting required for success. At Purdue he had worked with the new electron microscope. International Harvester's research physics department had just acquired one and hired Iverson as assistant to the chief research physicist. Iverson stayed there five years and felt he was set for life. He had great respect for his boss, who would discuss with him the directions businesses took and their opportunities. One day the chief physicist asked if that job was what he really wanted to do all his life. There was only one job ahead for Iverson at

International Harvester and he was too ambitious to end his career in that position. At his boss's urging, he considered smaller companies.

Iverson joined Illium Corporation, 120 miles from Chicago, as chief engineer (metallurgist). Illium was a 60-person division of a major company but functioned like an independent company. Iverson was close to the young president and was impressed by his good business skill; this man knew how to manage and had the discipline to run a tight ship, to go in the right direction with no excess manpower. The two of them proposed a new foundry which was necessary for them to become competitive. When the parent company insisted they delay three to four years until they could handle it without going into debt, Iverson began looking at new jobs.

After two years at Illium, Iverson joined Indiana Steel Products as assistant to the vice-president of manufacturing, for the sole purpose of setting up a spectrographic lab. After completing this job within one year, he could see no other opportunity for himself in the company, because it was small and he could get no real responsibility. A year and a half later, Iverson left to join Cannon Muskegon as chief metallurgist.

The next seven years were "fascinating." This small ($5–6 million in sales and 60–70 people) family company made castings from special metals that were used in every aircraft made in the United States. The company was one of the first to get into "vacuum melting," and Iverson, because of his technical ability, was put in charge of this activity. Iverson then asked for and got responsibility for all company sales. He wasn't dissatisfied but realized that if he was to be really successful he needed broader managerial experience.

Cannon Muskegon sold materials to Coast Metals, a small, private company in New Jersey which cast and machined special alloys for the aircraft industry. The president of Coast got to know Iverson and realized his technical expertise would be an asset. In 1960 he joined Coast as executive vice-president, with responsibility for running the whole company.

Nuclear Corporation of America wished to buy Coast; however, Coast wasn't interested. Nuclear's president then asked Iverson to act as a consultant to find metal businesses Nuclear could buy. Over the next year, mostly on weekends, he looked at potential acquisitions. He recommended buying a joist business in South Carolina. Nuclear said it would, if he would run it. Coast was having disputes among its owners and Iverson's future there was clouded. He ended his two years there and joined Nuclear in 1962 as a vice-president, Nuclear's usual title, in charge of a 200-person joist division.

By late 1963 he had built a second plant in Nebraska and was running the only division making a profit. The president asked him to become a group vice-president, adding the research chemicals (metals) and contracting businesses, and to move to the home office in Phoenix. In mid-1965 the company defaulted on two loans and the president resigned. During that summer Nuclear sought some direction out of its difficulty. Iverson knew what could be done, put together a pro-forma statement, and pushed for these actions. It was not a unanimous decision when he was made president in September 1965.

The new management immediately abolished some divisions and went to work building Nucor. According to Iverson, the vice-presidents of the divisions designed Nucor in hard-working, almost T-group-type meetings. Iverson was only another participant and took charge only when the group couldn't settle an issue. This process identified Nucor's strengths and set the path for Nucor.

By 1966 Nucor consisted of the two joist plants, the Research Chemicals division, and the Nuclear division. During 1967 a building in Fort Payne, Alabama, was purchased for conversion into another joist plant. "We got into the steel business because we wanted to be able to build a mill that could make steel as cheaply as we were buying it from foreign importers or from offshore mills." In 1968 Nucor opened a steel mill in Darlington, South Carolina, and a joist plant in Texas. Another joist plant was added in Indiana in 1972. Steel plant openings followed in Nebraska in 1977 and in Texas in 1975. The Nuclear division was divested in 1976. A 4th steel plant was opened in Utah in 1981 and a joist plant was opened in Utah in 1982. By 1984 Nucor consisted of six joist plants, four steel mills, and a Research Chemicals division.

In 1983, in testimony before the Congress, Iverson warned of the hazards of trade barriers, that they would cause steel to cost more and that manufacturers would move overseas to use the cheaper steel and ship back into this country. He commented, "We have seen serious problems in the wire industry and the fastener industry." *Link* magazine reported that in the last four years, 40 domestic fastener plants had closed and that imports had over 90% of the market.

In a dramatic move, Nucor began construction in 1986 of a $25 million plant in Indiana to manufacture steel fasteners. Iverson told the *Atlanta Journal,* "We are going to bring that business back." He told *Inc.* magazine, "We've studied for a year now, and we decided that we can make bolts as cheaply as foreign producers and make a profit at it." He explained that in the old operation two people, one simply required by the union, made one hundred bolts a minute. "But at Nucor, we'll have an automated machine which will manufacture 400 bolts a minute. The automation will allow an operator to manage four machines." Hans Mueller, a steel industry consultant at East Tennessee State University, told the *Journal,* "I must confess that I was surprised that Iverson would be willing to dive into that snake pit. But he must believe that he can do it because he is not reckless."

Before making the decision, a Nucor task force of four people traveled the world to examine the latest technology. The management group was headed by a plant manager who joined Nucor after several years experience as general manager of a bolt company in Toronto. The manager of manufacturing was previously plant manager of a 40,000-ton melt-shop for Ervin Industries. The sales manager was a veteran of sales, distribution, and manufacturing in the fastener industry. The plant's engineering manager transferred from Nucor R&D in Nebraska. The Touche-Ross accountant who worked on the Nucor account joined the company as controller. The first crew of production employees received three months of in-depth training on the bolt-making machines, with extensive cross-training in tool making, maintenance, and other operations. By 1988, the new plant was operating close to its capacity of 45,000 tons.

In what *The New York Times* called their "most ambitious project yet," Nucor signed an agreement in January 1987 to form a joint venture with Yamato Kogyo, Ltd., a small Japanese steelmaker, to build a steel mill on the Mississippi River with a 600,000 ton per year capacity. The two hundred million dollar plant would make very large structural products, up to 24 inches. Structural steel products are those used in large buildings and bridges. Iverson noted, "These are now only made by the Big Three integrated steel companies." The Japanese company, which would own 49% of the stock, had expertise in continuous-casting in which Nucor was interested. Their 1985 sales totaled $400 million, with approximately 900 workers. They would provide the continuous casting technology while Nucor would provide the melting technology and management style. The mill was

EXHIBIT 1
Nucor Corporation: Balance Sheet Data, 1980–1990

	1980	1981	1982	1983
Assets				
Current assets:				
Cash and short-term investments	21,753,068	8,704,859	44,892,546	79,054,410
Accounts receivable	35,537,959	42,983,058	34,685,498	51,110,372
Inventories	57,585,250	78,715,785	52,488,077	63,613,905
Other current assets	489,450	978,590	476,527	110,475
Total current assets	115,365,727	131,382,292	132,542,648	193,889,162
Property, plant and equipment:				
Land and improvements	5,806,711	12,142,613	12,215,375	12,577,104
Buildings and improvements	34,853,546	53,037,722	53,668,523	55,971,208
Plant machinery and equipment	139,182,579	245,037,510	244,143,769	258,305,715
Office and transportation equipment	5,711,199	6,868,069	9,565,667	9,736,448
Construction in process and equipment deposits	36,323,686	2,559,867	3,279,232	2,444,220
	221,877,721	319,645,781	322,872,566	339,034,695
Less accumulated depreciation	46,021,581	66,245,946	83,782,273	107,356,805
Total property, plant, and equipment	175,856,140	253,399,835	239,090,293	231,677,890
Total assets	291,221,867	384,782,127	371,632,941	425,567,052
Liabilities and Stockholders' Equity				
Current liabilities:				
Long-term debt due within one year	1,696,815	1,654,784	1,603,462	2,402,462
Accounts payable	36,640,991	32,237,889	22,948,867	37,135,084
Federal income taxes	4,362,619	10,733,627	12,535,096	14,813,909
Accrued expenses and other current liabilities	23,793,020	28,406,013	29,015,281	34,135,340
Total current liabilities	66,493,445	73,032,313	66,102,706	88,486,795
Long-term debt due after one year	39,605,169	83,754,231	48,229,615	45,731,000
Deferred federal income taxes	7,519,563	15,619,563	25,019,563	33,219,563
Minority interest	--	--	--	--
Stockholders' equity:				
Common stock	2,758,713	2,797,948	2,802,796	5,642,727
Additional paid-in capital	13,353,856	16,531,759	17,696,568	17,022,043
Retained earnings	161,952,033	193,355,403	211,921,654	235,569,108
Treasury stock	(460,912)	(309,090)	(139,961)	(104,184)
Total stockholders' equity	177,603,690	212,376,020	232,281,057	258,129,694
Total liabilities and stockholders' equity	291,221,867	384,782,127	371,632,941	425,567,052

completed in 1988 at a cost of $220 million for 650,000 tons of capacity. By the end of 1988, the plant was operating at 50% of capacity and at capacity in 1990.

Nucor's innovation was not limited to manufacturing. In the steel industry, it was normal to price an order based on the quantity ordered. In 1984, Nucor broke that pattern. As Iverson stated, "Some time ago we began to realize that with computer order entry and billing, the extra charge for smaller orders was not cost justified. We found the cost of servicing a 20 ton order compared with a 60 ton order was about 35 cents a ton and most of

1984	1985	1986	1987	1988	1989	1990
112,710,490	185,144,473	128,736,584	72,779,584	26,380,115	32,553,520	51,648,627
58,408,244	60,390,448	61,268,892	80,080,553	97,427,217	106,950,620	126,745,998
82,260,117	89,120,101	105,594,811	81,497,469	123,215,022	139,449,786	136,643,745
74,522	114,125	137,968	359,631	736,262	1,080,008	89,116
253,453,373	334,769,147	295,738,255	234,717,237	247,758,616	280,033,934	315,127,486
12,918,519	12,818,723	15,041,782	23,143,374	30,309,295	29,829,310	30,642,736
58,909,921	61,709,286	75,217,588	87,690,196	113,985,857	118,362,171	125,917,477
277,553,868	279,579,407	331,945,921	375,446,242	604,990,695	866,721,302	905,687,289
8,643,752	14,883,272	16,358,988	15,080,397	14,416,129	13,318,378	14,961,929
2,576,972	7,505,692	18,736,585	117,174,597	178,569,987	19,781,432	9,154,660
360,603,032	376,496,380	457,300,864	618,534,806	942,271,963	1,048,012,593	1,086,364,091
131,867,940	150,954,339	181,431,475	199,161,904	240,368,869	294,215,015	363,115,517
228,735,092	225,542,041	275,869,389	419,372,902	701,903,094	753,797,578	723,248,574
482,188,465	560,311,188	571,607,644	654,090,139	949,661,710	1,033,831,512	1,038,376,060
2,402,462	2,402,462	3,052,462	2,210,154	2,214,000	2,267,000	2,204,500
32,691,249	35,473,011	53,165,551	68,459,917	93,171,767	89,746,212	78,721,596
23,705,195	27,597,464	14,309,565	24,343,944	35,803,552	13,203,371	10,650,895
41,734,778	55,782,891	47,913,395	52,459,255	84,917,983	88,343,962	134,004,239
100,533,684	121,255,828	118,440,973	147,473,270	216,107,302	193,560,545	225,581,230
43,232,384	40,233,769	42,147,654	35,462,500	113,248,500	155,981,500	28,777,000
38,819,563	41,319,563	27,319,563	19,319,563	15,319,563	18,819,563	25,819,563
--	--	--	23,825,439	72,704,896	81,024,425	105,441,051
5,669,757	5,732,382	8,665,397	8,701,944	8,737,064	8,781,534	8,815,775
18,991,334	24,299,195	25,191,988	27,379,060	30,542,937	34,226,463	37,669,232
275,035,788	327,816,850	367,575,659	410,510,347	511,456,991	559,895,248	624,662,995
(94,045)	(346,399)	(17,733,590)	(18,581,984)	(18,455,543)	(18,457,766)	(18,390,786)
299,602,834	357,502,028	383,699,454	428,009,367	532,281,449	584,445,479	652,757,216
482,188,465	560,311,188	571,607,644	654,090,139	949,661,710	1,033,831,512	1,038,376,060

that was related to credit and collection. We did agonize over the decision, but over the long run we are confident that the best competitive position is one that has a strong price to cost relationship." He noted that this policy would give Nucor another advantage over foreign suppliers in that users could maintain lower inventories and order more often. "If we are going to successfully compete against foreign suppliers, we must use the most economical methods for both manufacturing and distribution."

In August 1986, Iverson told Cable News Network, "We are talking about within the

EXHIBIT 2
Nucor Corporation: Sales, Earnings, and Statistical Data, 1980–1990

	1980	*1981*	*1982*	*1983*
For the Year				
Sales, costs and earnings:				
Net sales	482,420,363	544,820,621	486,018,162	542,531,431
Costs and expenses:				
Cost of products sold	369,415,571	456,210,289	408,606,641	461,727,688
Marketing and administrative expenses	38,164,559	33,524,820	31,720,377	33,988,054
Interest expense (income)	(1,219,965)	10,256,546	7,899,110	(748,619)
Total cost and expenses	406,360,165	499,991,655	448,226,128	494,967,123
Earnings from operations before federal income taxes	76,060,198	44,828,966	37,792,034	47,564,308
Federal income taxes	31,000,000	10,100,000	15,600,000	19,700,000
Earnings from operations	45,060,198	34,728,966	22,192,034	27,864,308
Gain on sale of research chemicals	--	--	--	--
Net earnings	45,060,198	34,728,966	22,192,034	27,864,308
Earnings per share:				
Earnings per share from operations	2.21	1.67	1.06	1.32
Gain per share on sale of research chemicals	--	--	--	--
Net earnings per share	2.21	1.67	1.06	1.32
Dividends declared per share	.15	.16	.17	.20
Percentage of earnings from operations to sales	9.3%	6.4%	4.6%	5.1%
Percentage of earnings from operations to average equity	29.0%	17.8%	10.0%	11.4%
Average shares outstanding	20,414,109	20,756,583	20,912,577	21,066,448
Sales per employee	150,756	155,663	133,156	148,639
At Year End				
Working capital	48,872,282	58,349,979	66,439,942	105,402,367
Current ratio	1.7	1.8	2.0	2.2
Stockholders' equity per share	8.64	10.17	11.07	12.21
Shares outstanding	20,549,991	20,890,521	20,987,823	21,135,272
Stockholders	22,000	22,000	22,000	21,000
Employees	3,300	3,700	3,600	3,700

next two years perhaps building a steel mill to make flat roll products, that would be the first time a mini-mill has been in this area." It was expected that approximately $10 million would be needed to develop this process. The thin-slab would also produce feed stock for Vulcraft's 250,000 tons per year steel deck operation.

Flat rolled steel was the largest market for steel products at 40 million tons in 1988 and 52% of the U.S. market. This is the thin sheet steel used in car bodies, refrigerators and countless products. Making flat rolled steel required casting a slab rather than a billet and had not been achieved in the mini-mill. Nucor had invested several million in research on a process but in 1986 chose to go with a technology developed by SMS, a West German company. SMS had a small pilot plant using the new technology and Nucor would be the first mini-mill in the world to manufacture flat rolled steel commercially.

1984	1985	1986	1987	1988	1989	1990
660,259,922	758,495,374	755,228,939	851,022,039	1,061,364,009	1,269,007,472	1,481,630,011
539,731,252	600,797,865	610,378,369	713,346,451	889,140,323	1,105,248,906	1,293,082,950
45,939,311	59,079,802	65,900,653	55,405,961	62,083,752	66,990,065	70,461,830
(3,959,092)	(7,560,645)	(5,288,971)	(964,823)	2,558,914	11,132,657	6,869,970
581,711,471	652,317,022	670,990,051	767,787,589	953,782,989	1,183,371,628	1,370,414,750
78,548,451	106,178,352	84,238,888	83,234,450	107,581,020	85,635,844	111,215,261
34,000,000	47,700,000	37,800,000	32,700,000	36,700,000	27,800,000	36,150,000
44,548,451	58,478,352	46,438,888	50,534,450	70,881,020	57,835,844	75,065,261
--	--	--	--	38,558,822	--	--
44,548,451	58,478,352	46,438,888	50,534,450	109,439,842	57,835,844	75,065,261
2.10	2.74	2.17	2.39	3.34	2.71	3.50
--	--	--	--	1.82	--	--
2.10	2.74	2.17	2.39	5.16	2.71	3.50
.24	.27	.31	.36	.40	.44	.48
6.7%	7.7%	6.1%	5.9%	6.7%	4.6%	5.1%
16.0%	17.8%	12.5%	12.5%	15.4%	10.4%	12.1%
21,169,492	21,345,852	21,405,440	21,153,584	21,224,217	21,342,888	21,441,079
176,069	197,011	181,983	189,116	218,838	241,716	271,859
152,919,689	213,513,319	177,297,282	87,243,967	31,651,314	86,473,389	89,546,256
2.5	2.8	2.5	1.6	1.1	1.4	1.4
14.10	16.65	18.16	20.19	25.00	27.31	30.38
21,241,618	21,472,508	21,131,298	21,196,088	21,287,691	21,399,620	21,487,674
22,000	22,000	22,000	27,000	28,000	25,000	27,000
3,800	3,900	4,400	4,600	5,100	5,400	5,500

In January 1987, Nucor announced an 800,000 ton, $265 million flat roll plant would be built in Crawfordsville, Indiana, with an April 1988 startup. It was expected that labor hours per ton would be half the integrated manufacturer's 3.0, yielding a savings of $50 to $75 on a $400 a ton selling price. If the project were completed successfully, Nucor planned to have three plants in operation before others could build. Investment advisors anticipated Nucor's stock could increase to double or triple by the mid 1990's. However, it would not be as easy as earlier ventures. In April 1989 *Forbes* commented, "If any mini-mill can meet the challenge, it's Nucor. But expect the going to be tougher this time around." The flat-rolled market was the last bastion of the integrated manufacturers and they had been seriously modernizing their plants throughout the '80's. In July 1989, when Nucor announced a 14% drop in 2nd quarter earnings due to startup costs, its stock went up $1.62 to

$63. The startup had gone just about as they had planned. The plant was breaking even in 1990 as they announced plans to build a second plant. Iverson stated, "We hope this will map out the future of the company for the next decade."

In December 1986 Nucor announced its first major acquisition, Genbearco, a steel bearings manufacturer. At a cost of more than $10 million, it would add $25 million in sales and 250 employees. Iverson called it "a good fit with our business, our policies and our people." It was without a union and tied pay to performance. In October 1988, Nucor agreed to sell its Chemicals Division to a New York Company for a $38 million gain.

THE STEEL INDUSTRY

The steel industry was one of those industries in the U.S. facing major problems. The early 1980's had been the worst years in decades for the steel industry. Data from the American Iron and Steel Institute showed shipments falling from 100.2 million tons in 1979 to the mid-80 levels in 1980 and 1981. Slackening in the economy, particularly in auto sales, led the decline. In 1986, when industry capacity was at 130 million tons, the outlook was for a continued decline in per-capita consumption and movement toward capacity in the 90–100 million ton range. The chairman of Armco saw "millions of tons chasing a market that's not there; excess capacity that must be eliminated."

The large, integrated steel firms, such as U.S. Steel and Armco, which made up the major part of the industry, were the hardest hit. *The Wall Street Journal* stated, "The decline has resulted from such problems as high labor and energy costs in mining and processing iron ore, a lack of profits and capital to modernize plants, and conservative management that has hesitated to take risks."

These companies produced a wide range of steels, primarily from ore processed in blast furnaces. They had found it difficult to compete with imports, usually from Japan, and had given up market share to imports. They sought the protection of import quotas. Imported steel accounted for 20% of the U.S. steel consumption, up from 12% in the early 1970's. The U.S. share of world production of raw steel declined from 19% to 11% over the period. The product lines of the steel industry were composed of wire rod, structurals, plate, bar, pipe and sheet. Imports of bar products accounted for 10% of U.S. consumption of those products in 1989, according to the U.S. Commerce Department, while imports of wire rod totaled 23% of U.S. consumption. "Wire rod is a very competitive product in the world market because it's very easy to make," Ralph Thompson, the Commerce Department's steel analyst, told the *Charlotte Observer.*

Iron Age stated that exports, as a percent of shipments in 1985, were 34% for Nippon, 26% for British Steel, 30% for Krupp, 49% for USINOR of France, and less than 1% for every American producer on the list. The consensus of steel experts was that imports would average 23% of the market in the last half of the 1980's.

Iverson was one of very few in the steel industry to oppose import restrictions. He saw an outdated U.S. steel industry which had to change. In 1987, he testified:

> About 12% of the steel in the U.S. is still produced by the old open hearth furnace. The Japanese shut down their last open hearth furnace about five years ago. . . . The U.S. produces about 16% of its steel by the continuous casting process. In Japan over

> 50% of the steel is continuously cast. . . . We Americans have been conditioned to believe in our technical superiority. For many generations a continuing stream of new inventions and manufacturing techniques allowed us to far outpace the rest of the world in both volume and efficiency of production. In many areas this is no longer true and particularly in the steel industry. In the last three decades, almost all the major developments in steel making were made outside the U.S. There were 18 continuous casting units in the world before there was one in this country. I would be negligent if I did not recognize the significant contribution that the government has made toward the technological deterioration of the steel industry. Unrealistic depreciation schedules, high corporate taxes, excessive regulation and jaw-boning for lower steel prices have made it difficult for the steel industry to borrow or generate the huge quantities of capital required for modernization.

By the mid-1980's the integrated mills were moving fast to get back into the game; they were restructuring, cutting capacity, dropping unprofitable lines, focusing products, and trying to become responsive to the market. The president of USX explained: "Steel executives, in trying to act as prudent businessmen, are seeking the lowest-cost solutions to provide what the market wants." Karlis Kirsis, director of World Steel Dynamics at Paine-Webber, told *Purchasing Magazine,* "The industry as we knew it five years ago is no more; the industry as we knew it a year ago is gone."

Purchasing believed that buyers would be seeing a pronounced industry segmentation. There would be integrated producers making mostly flat rolled and structural grades, reorganized steel companies making a limited range of products, mini-mills dominating the bar and light structural product areas, specialty steel firms seeking niches, and foreign producers. There would be accelerated shutdowns of older plants, elimination of products by some firms, and the installation of new product lines with new technologies by others. There would also be corporate facelifts as executives diversified from steel to generate profits and entice investment dollars. They saw the high-tonnage mills restructuring to handle sheets, plates, structurals, high quality bars, and large pipe and tubular products which would allow for a resurgence of specialized mills: cold-finished bar manufacturers, independent strip mills and mini-mills.

Wheeling-Pittsburgh illustrated the change underway in the industry. Through Chapter 11 reorganization in the late 1980's, it had cut costs by more than $85/ton. They divided into profit centers, negotiated the lowest hourly wage rate ($18/hour) among unionized integrated steel plants, renegotiated supply contracts, closed pipe and tube mills, and shut 1.6 million tons of blast furnace capacity in favor of an electric furnace with continuous casting.

Paine Webber pointed out the importance of "reconstituted mills," which they called the "People Express" of the industry. These were companies which had reorganized and refocused their resources, usually under Chapter 11. These include Kaiser Steel, The Weirton Works, Jones and Laughlin, Republic, Youngstown, Wheeling, LTV, and others.

Joint ventures had arisen to produce steel for a specific market or region. The chairman of USX called them "an important new wrinkle in steel's fight for survival" and stated, "If there had been more joint ventures like these two decades ago, the U.S. steel industry might have built only half of the dozen or so hot-strip mills it put up in that time and avoided today's overcapacity." *Purchasing* observed, "The fact is that these combined operations are the result of a laissez faire attitude within the Justice Department under the Reagan administration following the furor when government restrictions killed the planned USS takeover of National Steel (which later sold 50% interest to a Japanese steelmaker)."

However, the road ahead for the integrated mills would not be easy. While it was estimated they would need $10 billion to improve their facilities, the industry had lost over $7 billion since 1982. *Purchasing* pointed out that tax laws and accounting rules are slowing the closing of inefficient plants. Shutting a 10,000-person plant could require a firm to hold a cash reserve of $100 million to fund health, pension and insurance liabilities. The chairman of Armco commented: "Liabilities associated with a plant shutdown are so large that they can quickly devastate a company's balance sheet."

The American Iron and Steel Institute (AISI) reported steel production in 1989 of 97.9 million tons, down from 99.9 in '88. As a result of modernization programs, 65% of production was from continuous casters. Japan and the ECC achieved 90%. Exports of steel were increasing, 2 million tons in 1988 and 4.5 in 1989, and imports were falling, 18% in 1989. Some steel experts believed the U.S. was now cost competitive with Japan. Because of strong worldwide demand, several countries did not fill their quotas (19.1%) allowed under the five year old voluntary restraint agreement, which was extended three years to March 1992. The role of service centers in the distribution of steel continued with its fifth consecutive record year in 1988 of 23.4 million tons.

"If 1988 is remembered as the year of steel prosperity despite economic uncertainties, then 1989 is just as likely to go down as the year of 'waiting for the other shoe to drop,'" according to *Metal Center News* in January 1989. The fears and the expectation of a somewhat weaker year arose from concerns of a recession, expirations of the voluntary import restraints, and labor negotiations schedules in several companies. Declines in car production and consumer goods were expected to hit flat-rolled hard. Service centers were also expected to be cutting back on inventories. AUJ Consultants told *MCN*, "The U.S. steel market has peaked. Steel consumption is trending down. By the early 1990's, we expect total domestic demand to dip under 90 million tons."

THE MINI-MILL

A new type of mill, the "mini-mill," emerged in the U.S. during the 1970's to compete with the integrated mill. The mini-mill used electric arc furnaces to manufacture a narrow product line from scrap steel. In 1981 *The New York Times* reported:

> The truncated steel mill is to the integrated steel mill what the Volkswagen was to the American auto industry in the 1960's: smaller, cheaper, less complex and more efficient. Although mini-mills cannot produce such products as sheet steel [flat rolled] and heavy construction items, some industry analysts say it is only a matter of time before technological breakthroughs make this possible.

Since mini-mills came into being in the 1970's, the integrated mills' market share has fallen from about 90% to about 60%, with the loss equally divided between mini-mills and foreign imports. While the integrated steel companies averaged a 7% return on equity, the mini-mills averaged 14%, and some, such as Nucor, achieved about 25%.

The leading mini-mills were Nucor, Florida Steel, Georgetown Steel (Korf Industries),

North Star Steel, and Chaparral. Nucor produced "light bar" products: bars, angles, channels, flats, smooth round, and forging billets. It was beginning to make more alloy steels. Florida Steel made mostly reinforcing bar for construction (rebar) and dominated the Florida market. Korf Industries had two mini-mill subsidiaries which used modern equipment to manufacture wire rod.

The mini-mills were not immune to the economic slump in the early eighties. Korf Industries, which owned Georgetown Steel, found its interest charges too large a burden and sought reorganization in 1983. In March of 1983 Georgetown followed the historic wage cutting contract between the United Steel Workers of America and the major steel companies and asked its union to accept reductions and to defer automatic wage increases. In 1982 Nucor froze wages and executives took a 5% pay cut. Plants went to a four-day schedule in which workers would receive only base rate if they chose to work a fifth day doing clean-up.

Florida Steel, with two-thirds of its sales in Florida, also felt the impact. At its headquarters in Tampa, a staff of over 100 handled accounting, payroll, sales entry, and almost all other services for all its facilities. Their division managers did not have sales responsibilities. Florida Steel experienced a sales decline for 1982 of 22% and an earnings drop from $3.37 per share to a loss of $1.40. The next year was also a year of losses.

Florida Steel employees had faced periodic layoffs during the recession. The firm was non-union (although the Charlotte plant lost an election in 1973) and pay was based on productivity. A small facility at Indian Town, near West Palm Beach, never became productive, even with personnel changes, and had to be closed. A new mini-mill in Tennessee was completed in late 1983.

Mini-mills had tripled their output in the last decade to capture 17% of domestic shipments. Paine Webber predicted the big integrated mills' share of the market would fall to 40%, the mini-mills share would rise to 23%, "reconstituted" mills would increase from 11% to 28%, and specialized mills would increase their share from 1% to 7%. Iverson stated mini-mills could not go beyond a 35% to 40% share due to technical limitations; mini-mills could not produce the flat-rolled sheet steel used in cars and appliances.

Iverson told *Metal Center News* in 1983: "We are very interested in the development of a thin slab, which would then allow mini-mills to produce plate and other flat rolled products . . . actually, the thinnest slab that can now be produced is about 6 inches thick. . . . (That results in a plant that is too large.) There are a number of people working to develop the process. . . . We have done some work, but our primary efforts at the moment are in connection with other people who are working on it. . . . The likelihood is it would be developed by a foreign company. There are more efforts by foreign steel companies in that direction than in the United States. . . . I'd say probably a minimum of three to five years, or it could take as much as 10 to achieve this."

In 1983 Iverson described the new generation of mini-mills he foresaw: "If you go way back, mini-mills got started by rolling reinforcing bar. With the advent of continuous casting and improvements in rolling mills, mini-mills gradually got into shapes. Now they have moved in two other directions: one being to larger sizes, and the other being a growing metallurgical expertise for improved product quality and production of special bar quality in alloys. Both of these represent expansion of markets for mini-mills."

By 1986 the new competitive environment was apparent. Four mini-mills had closed their doors within the year and Iverson saw that more shutdowns were ahead. The overcapacity of steel bar products and the stagnant market had made it difficult for some companies to generate the cash needed to modernize and expand their product lines. "The mini-mills are going through the same kind of restructuring and rethinking as the integrated mill. They know the problem of overcapacity isn't going to go away quickly. And, for some of the remaining firms to survive, they will have to move into more sophisticated products like special quality and clean-steel bars and heavier structurals and, once the technology is perfected, flat-rolled products. You won't see the market growth by the mini-mills the way it was in the past until the overcapacity issue is resolved and the mills begin entering new product areas."

ORGANIZATION

Nucor, with its 18-person corporate office located in Charlotte, North Carolina, had divisions spread across the United States. The 15 divisions, one for every plant, each had a general manager, who was also a vice-president of the corporation, directly responsible to Iverson and Aycock (see Exhibit 3). The divisions were of two basic types, joist plants and steel mills. The corporate staff consisted of single specialists in personnel and planning and a four-person financial function under Mr. Sam Siegel. Iverson, in the beginning, had chosen Charlotte "as the new home base for what he had envisioned as a small cadre of executives who would guide a decentralized operation with liberal authority delegated to managers in the field," according to *South* magazine.

Iverson gave his views on organization:

> You can tell a lot about a company by looking at its organization chart. . . . If you see a lot of staff, you can bet it is not a very efficient organization. . . . Secondly, don't have assistants. We do not have that title and prohibit it in our company. . . . In this organization nobody reports to the corporate office, the division managers report directly to me. . . . And one of the most important things is to resist as much as possible the number of management layers. . . . I've often thought that when a company builds a fancy corporate office, it's on its way down.
>
> Each division is a profit center and the division manager has control over the day-to-day decisions that make that particular division profitable or not profitable. We expect the division to provide contribution, which is earnings before corporate expenses. We do not allocate our corporate expenses, because we do not think there is any way to do this reasonably and fairly. We do focus on earnings. And we expect a division to earn 25 percent return on total assets employed, before corporate expenses, taxes, interest or profit sharing. And we have a saying in the company—if a manager doesn't provide that for a number of years, we are either going to get rid of the division or get rid of the division manager, and it's generally the division manager.

A joist division manager commented:

> I've been a division manager four years now and at times I'm still awed by it: the opportunity I was given to be a Fortune 500 vice-president. . . . I think we are successful because it is our style to pay more attention to our business than our competitors. . . . We are kind of a "no nonsense" company. That is not to say we

EXHIBIT 3
Nucor Organization Chart

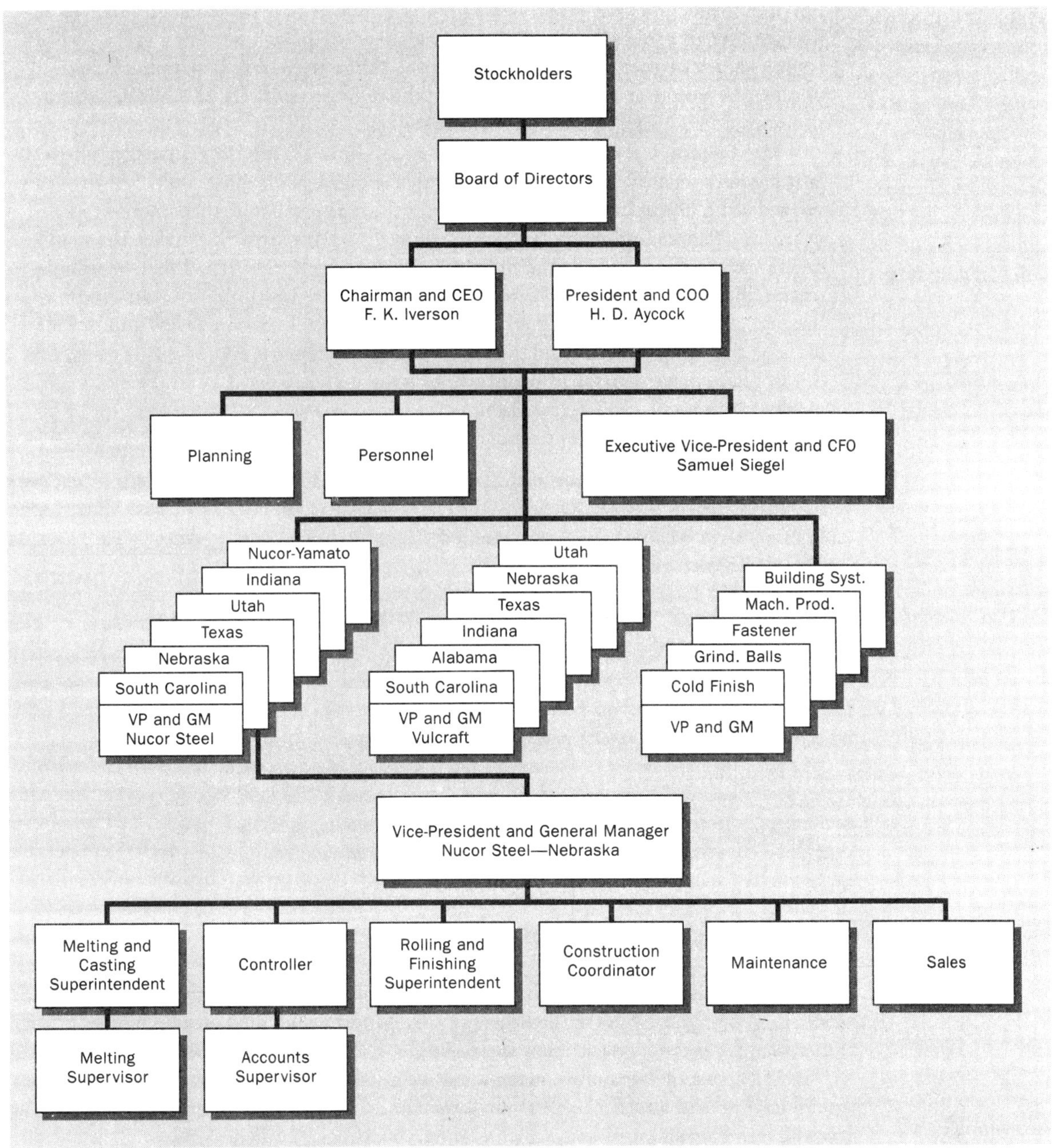

> don't have time for play, but we work hard when we work and the company is first and foremost in our minds. . . . I think another one of the successes of our company has been the fact that we have a very minimum number of management levels. We've been careful to avoid getting top-heavy and so consequently we put a great deal of responsibility on each individual at each level. It has often been said, jokingly, that if you are the janitor at Vulcraft and you get the right promotions, about four promotions would take you to the top of the company.
>
> Mr. Iverson's style of management is to allow the division manager all the latitude in the world. His involvement with the managers is quite limited. As we've grown, he no longer has the time to visit with the managers more than once or twice a year. . . . Whereas in many large companies the corporate office makes the major decisions and the people at the operating level sit back to wait for their marching orders, that's not the case at Nucor. . . . In a way I feel like I run my own company because I really don't get any marching orders from Mr. Iverson. He lets you run the division the way you see fit and the only way he will step in is if he sees something he doesn't like, particularly bad profits, high costs or whatever. But in the years I've worked with him I don't believe he has ever issued one single instruction to me to do something differently. I can't recall a single instance.

The divisions did their own manufacturing, selling, accounting, engineering, and personnel management. A steel division manager, when questioned about Florida Steel, which had a large plant 90 miles away, commented, "I really don't know anything about Florida Steel. . . . I expect they do have more of the hierarchy. I think they have central purchasing, centralized sales, centralized credit collections, centralized engineering, and most of the major functions." He didn't feel greater centralization would be good for Nucor. "The purchasing activity, for example, removed from the field tends to become rather insensitive to the needs of the field and does not feel the pressures of responsibility. And the division they are buying for has no control over what they pay. . . . Likewise centralized sales would not be sensitive to the needs of their divisions."

South magazine observed that Iverson had established a characteristic organizational style described as "stripped down" and "no nonsense." "Jack Benny would like this company," observed Roland Underhill, an analyst with Crowell, Weedon and Co. of Los Angeles, "so would Peter Drucker." Underhill pointed out that Nucor's thriftiness doesn't end with its "spartan" office staff or modest offices. "There are no corporate perquisites," he recited. "No company planes. No country club memberships. No company cars."

Fortune reported, "Iverson takes the subway when he is in New York, a Wall Street analyst reports in a voice that suggests both admiration and amazement." The general managers reflected this style in the operation of their individual divisions. Their offices were more like plant offices or the offices of private companies built around manufacturing rather than for public appeal. They were simple, routine, and businesslike.

In 1983, one of Iverson's concerns had been that as Nucor continued to grow they would have to add another layer of management to their lean structure. In June 1984 he named Dave Aycock president and chief operating officer, while he became chairman and chief executive officer—they would share one management level. Aycock had most recently been division manager of the steel mill at Darlington. But he had been with the company longer than Iverson, having joined Vulcraft in 1955, and had long been recognized as a particularly valued and close advisor to Iverson.

Iverson explained: "The company got to the size that I just wasn't doing the job that I thought should be done by this office. I couldn't talk to the analysts and everyone else I have to talk to, put the efforts into research and development I wanted to, and get to all the units as frequently as I should. That's why I brought Dave in. And, of course, he has been with the company forever." In a February 1985 letter he told stockholders: "These changes are to provide additional emphasis on the expansion of the company's businesses." "Dave is a very analytical person and very thorough in his thought process," another division manager told *33 Metal Producing*, an industry publication. "And Ken, to use an overworked word, is an entrepreneurial type. So, they complement each other. They're both very aggressive men, and make one hell of a good team." Aycock stated: "I am responsible for the operations of all our divisions. To decide where we are going, with what technologies; what our purposes are. And what is our thrust. I help Ken shape where we are going and with what technologies. . . . I've been quite aggressive my whole career at updating, adapting, and developing new technology and new ideas in production and marketing." "Dave's the fellow who now handles most of the day-to-day operations," Iverson commented. "And he handles most of the employees who write to us,"—about 10–15% of his time.

DIVISION MANAGERS

The general managers met three times a year. In late October they presented preliminary budgets and capital requests. In late February they met to finalize budgets and treat miscellaneous matters. Then, at a meeting in May, they handled personnel matters, such as wage increases and changes of policies or benefits. The general managers as a group considered the raises for the department heads, the next lower level of management. As one of the managers described it:

> In May of each year, all the general managers get together and review all the department heads throughout the company. We have kind of an informal evaluation process. It's an intangible thing, a judgment as to how dedicated an individual is and how well he performs compared to the same position at another plant. Sometimes the numbers don't come out the way a general manager wants to see them, but it's a fair evaluation. The final number is picked by Mr. Iverson. Occasionally there are some additional discussions with Mr. Iverson. He always has an open mind and might be willing to consider a little more for one individual. We consider the group of, say, joist production managers at one time. The six managers are rated for performance. We assign a number, such as +3 to a real crackerjack performer or a −2 to someone who needs improvement. These ratings become a part of the final pay increase granted.

The corporate personnel manager described management relations as informal, trusting, and not "bureaucratic." He felt there was a minimum of paperwork, that a phone call was more common and that no confirming memo was thought to be necessary. Iverson himself stated:

> Management is not a popularity contest. If everybody agrees with the organization, something is wrong with the organization. You don't expect people in the company

to put their arms around each other, and you don't interfere with every conflict. Out of conflict often comes the best answer to a particular problem. So don't worry about it. You are always going to have some conflict in an organization. You will always have differences of opinion, and that's healthy. Don't create problems where there are none.

A Vulcraft manager commented: "We have what I would call a very friendly spirit of competition from one plant to the next. And of course all of the vice-presidents and general managers share the same bonus systems so we are in this together as a team even though we operate our divisions individually." The general managers are paid a bonus based on a total corporate profit rather than their own divisions' profits. A steel mill manager explained:

I think it's very important for the general managers to be concerned with contributing to the overall accomplishment of the company. There is a lot of interplay between the divisions with a flow of services, products, and ideas between divisions. Even though we are reasonably autonomous, we are not isolated. . . . We don't like the division managers to make decisions that would take that division away from where we want the whole company to go. But we certainly want the divisions to try new things. We are good copiers; if one division finds something that works, then we will all try it. I think that's one of our strengths. We have a lot of diverse people looking at ways to do things better.

Iverson revealed his view of management in his disdain for consultants:

They must have a specific job to do because they can't make your decisions. . . . The fellow on the line has to make decisions. . . . First he has to communicate and then he has to have the intestinal fortitude and the personal strength to make decisions, sometimes under very difficult conditions. . . . A good manager is adaptable and he is sensitive to cultural, geographical, environmental, and business climates. Most important of all, he communicates. . . . You never know if someone is a good manager until he manages. And that's why we take people as young as we possibly can, throw responsibility at them, and they either work or they don't. In a sense it's survival of the fittest. But don't kid yourself; that's what industry is all about.

A steel division manager commented in comparing the Nucor manager to the typical manager of a large corporation:

We would probably tend to have managers who have confidence in their abilities and, very importantly, have confidence in other people in their division. And people who are very sensitive to the employees of their division. . . . But I think if you saw four or five different division managers, you'd have four or five different decision-making styles.

A Vulcraft general manager in his early 40's who had been promoted to the division manager level nine years earlier said:

The step from department manager to division manager is a big one. I can't think of an instance when a general manager job has been offered to an individual that it has been passed up. Often it means moving from one part of the country to another. There are five department heads in six joist plants, which means there are 30 people who are considered for division manager slots at a joist plant. Mr. Iverson selects the division managers.

His own experience was enlightening:

> When I came to this plant four years ago, we had too many people, too much overhead. We had 410 people at the plant and I could see, because I knew how many people we had in the Nebraska plant, we had many more than we needed. That was my yardstick and we set about to reduce those numbers by attrition. . . . We have made a few equipment changes that made it easier for the men, giving them an opportunity to make better bonuses. Of course the changes were very subtle in any given case but overall in four years we have probably helped the men tremendously. With 55 fewer men, perhaps 40 to 45 fewer in the production area, we are still capable of producing the same number of tons as four years ago.

The divisions managed their activities with a minimum of contact with the corporate staff. Each day disbursements were reported to Siegel's office. Payments flowed into regional lock-boxes. On a weekly basis, joist divisions reported total quotes, sales cancellations, backlog, and production. Steel mills reported tons-rolled, outside shipments, orders, cancellations, and backlog. Mr. Iverson graphed the data. He might talk to the division about every two weeks. On the other hand Iverson was known to bounce ideas off the steel division manager in Darlington with whom he had worked since joining the company.

The Vulcraft manager commented on the communications with the corporate office: "It's kind of a steady pipeline. I might talk to the corporate office once a day or it might be once a week. But it generally involves, I would not say trivial information, just mundane things. Occasionally I hear from Sam or Ken about serious matters."

Each month the divisions completed a two-page (11″ × 17″) "Operations Analysis" which was sent to all the managers. Its three main purposes were (1) financial consolidation, (2) sharing information among the divisions, and (3) Iverson's examination. The summarized information and the performance statistics for all the divisions were then returned to the managers.

VULCRAFT—THE JOIST DIVISIONS

Half of Nucor's business was the manufacture and sale of open web steel joists and joist girders at six Vulcraft divisions located in Florence, South Carolina; Norfolk, Nebraska; Ft. Payne, Alabama; Grapeland, Texas; St. Joe, Indiana; and Brigham City, Utah. Open web joists, in contrast to solid joists, were made of steel angle iron separated by round bars or smaller angle iron. These joists cost less and were of greater strength for many applications and were used primarily as the roof support systems in larger buildings, such as warehouses and stores.

The joist industry was characterized by high competition among many manufacturers for many small customers. The Vulcraft divisions had over 3,000 customers, none of whom dominated the business. With an estimated 25% of the market, Nucor was the largest supplier in the U.S. It utilized national advertising campaigns and prepared competitive bids on 80% to 90% of buildings using joists. Competition was based on price and delivery performance. Nucor had developed computer programs to prepare designs for customers and to compute bids based on current prices and labor standards. In addition, each Vulcraft plant maintained its own Engineering Department to help customers with design problems or specifications. The Florence manager commented, "Here on the East Coast we have six or seven major competitors; of course none of them are as large as we are. The competition for any order will be heavy, and we will see six or seven different prices." He added, "I think we have a strong selling force in the marketplace. It has been said to us by some of our competitors that in this particular industry we have the finest selling organization in the country."

Nucor aggressively sought to be the lowest-cost producer in the industry. Materials and freight were two important elements of cost. Nucor maintained its own fleet of almost 100 trucks to ensure on-time delivery to all of the states, although most business was regional because of transportation costs. Plants were located in rural areas near the markets they served.

The Florence manager stated:

> I don't feel there's a joist producer in the country that can match our cost. . . . We are sticklers about cutting out unnecessary overhead. Because we put so much responsibility on our people and because we have what I think is an excellent incentive program, our people are willing to work harder to accomplish these profitable goals.

JOIST PRODUCTION

On the basic assembly line used at Nucor, three or four of which might make up any one plant, about six tons per hour would be assembled. In the first stage eight people cut the angles to the right lengths or bent the round bars to the desired form. These were moved on a roller conveyer to six-man assembly stations, where the component parts would be tacked together for the next stage, welding. Drilling and miscellaneous work were done by three people between the lines. The nine-man welding station completed the welds before passing the joists on roller conveyers to two-man inspection teams. The last step before shipment was the painting.

The workers had control over and responsibility for quality. There was an independent quality control inspector who had the authority to reject the run of joists and cause them to be reworked. The quality control people were not under the incentive system and reported to the Engineering Department.

Daily production might vary widely, since each joist was made for a specific job. The wide range of joists made control of the workload at each station difficult; bottlenecks might arise anywhere along the line. Each work station was responsible for identifying such bottlenecks so that the foreman could reassign people promptly to maintain productivity. Since workers knew most of the jobs on the line, including the more skilled welding job, they could be shifted as needed. Work on the line was described by one general manager as "not machine type but mostly physical labor." He said the important thing was to avoid bottlenecks.

There were four lines of about 28 people each on two shifts at the Florence division.

EXHIBIT 4
Tons per Manhour, 52-Week Moving Average

1977	1978	1979	1980	1981	1982	1983	1984	1985	1986	1987
.163	.179	.192	.195	.194	.208	.215	.214	.228	.225	.218

The jobs on the line were rated on responsibility and assigned a base wage, from $6 to $8 per hour. In addition, a weekly bonus was paid on the total output of each line. Each worker received the same percent bonus on his base wage.

The amount of time required to make a joist had been established as a result of experience; the general manager had seen no time studies in his fifteen years with the company. As a job was bid, the cost of each joist was determined through the computer program. The time required depended on the length, number of panels, and depth of the joist.

At the time of production, the labor value of production, the standard, was determined in a similar manner. The general manager stated, "In the last nine or ten years we have not changed a standard." The standards list in use was over ten years old. Previously, they adjusted the standard if the bonus was too high. He said the technological improvements over the last few years had been small. The general manager reported that the bonus had increased from about 60% nine years earlier to about 100% in 1982 and had stabilized at that point. Exhibits 4 and 5 show data typically computed on performance and used by the manager. He said the difference in performance on the line resulted from the different abilities of the crews.

> We don't have an industrial engineering staff. Our Engineering Department's work is limited to the design and the preparation of the paperwork prior to the actual fabrication process. Now, that is not to say they don't have any involvement in fabrication. But the efficiency of the plant is entirely up to the Manufacturing Department. . . . When we had our first group in a joist plant, we produced 3½ tons an hour. We thought that if we ever got to 4 tons, that would be the Millennium. Well, today we don't have anybody who produces less than 6½ tons an hour. This is largely due to improvements that the groups have suggested.

EXHIBIT 5
A Sample of Percentage Performance, July 1982

	Shift	
Line	1st	2nd
1	117	98
2	97	102
3	82	94
4	89	107

JOIST PLANT MANAGEMENT

In discussing his philosophy for dealing with the workforce, the Florence manager stated:

> I believe very strongly in the incentive system we have. We are a non-union shop and we all feel that the way to stay so is to take care of our people and show them we care. I think that's easily done because of our fewer layers of management. . . . I spend a good part of my time in the plant, maybe an hour or so a day. If a man wants to know anything, for example an insurance question, I'm there and they walk right up to me and ask me questions which I'll answer the best I know how. . . . You can always tell when people are basically happy. If they haven't called for a meeting themselves or they are not hostile in any way, you can take it they understand the company's situation and accept it. . . . We do listen to our people. . . . For instance last fall I got a call from a couple of workers saying that the people in our Shipping and Receiving area felt they were not being paid properly in relation to production people. So we met with them, discussed the situation and committed ourselves to reviewing the rates of other plants. We assured them that we would get back to them with an answer by the first of the year. Which we did. And there were a few minor changes.

The manager reported none of the plants had any particular labor problems, although there had been some in the past.

> In 1976, two years before I came here, there was a union election at this plant which arose out of racial problems. The company actually lost the election to the U.S. Steelworkers. When it came time to begin negotiating the contract, the workers felt, or came to see, that they had little to gain from being in the union. The union was not going to be able to do anything more for them than they were already getting. So slowly the union activity died out and the union quietly withdrew.

He discussed formal systems for consulting with the workers before changes were made:

> Of course we're cautioned by our labor counsel to maintain an open pipeline to our employees. We post all changes, company earnings, changes in the medical plan, anything that might affect an employee's job. Mr. Iverson has another philosophy, which is, "Either tell your people everything or tell them nothing." We choose to tell them everything. We don't have any regularly scheduled meetings. We meet whenever there's a need. The most recent examples were a meeting last month to discuss the results of an employee survey and three months before was held our annual dinner meetings off site.
>
> We don't lay our people off and we make a point of telling our people this.
>
> In the economic slump of 1982, we scheduled our line for four days, but the men were allowed to come in the 5th day for maintenance work at base pay. The men in the plant on an average running bonus might make $13 an hour. If their base pay is half that, on Friday they would only get $6–7 an hour. Surprisingly, many of the men

> did not want to come in on Friday. They felt comfortable with just working four days a week. They are happy to have that extra day off.

Recently the economic trouble in Texas had hurt business considerably. Both plants had been on decreased schedules for several months. About 20% of the people took the 5th day at base rate, but still no one had been laid off.

In April 1982 the executive committee decided, in view of economic conditions, that a pay freeze was necessary. The employees normally received an increase in their base pay the 1st of June. The decision was made at that time to freeze wages. The officers of the company, as a show of good faith, accepted a 5% pay cut. In addition to announcing this to the workers with a stuffer in their pay envelopes, meetings were held. Each production line, or incentive group of workers, met in the plant conference room with all supervision—foreman, plant production manager, and division manager. The economic crisis was explained to the employees by the production manager and all questions were answered.

STEEL DIVISIONS

Nucor had six steel mills in five locations: Indiana, Nebraska, South Carolina, Texas, and Utah. The mills were modern "mini-mills," all built within the last 20 years to convert scrap steel into standard angles, flats, rounds, and channels using the latest technology. Sales in 1990 were 2.8 million tons. This figure represented about 80% of the mills' output, the remainder (.6 million) being used by other Nucor divisions. In recent years, Nucor had broadened its product line to include a wider range of steel chemistries, sizes, and special shapes. The total capacity of the mills had risen from 120,000 tons in 1970 to about 4,000,000 tons in 1990.

A casewriter from Harvard recounted the development of the steel divisions:

> By 1967 about 60% of each Vulcraft sales dollar was spent on materials, primarily steel. Thus, the goal of keeping costs low made it imperative to obtain steel economically. In addition, in 1967 Vulcraft bought about 60% of its steel from foreign sources. As the Vulcraft Division grew, Nucor became concerned about its ability to obtain an adequate economical supply of steel and in 1968 began construction of its first steel mill in Darlington, South Carolina. By 1972 the Florence, South Carolina, joist plant was purchasing over 90% of its steel from this mill. The Fort Payne plant bought about 50% of its steel from Florence. The other joist plants in Nebraska, Indiana and Texas found transportation costs prohibitive and continued to buy their steel from other steel companies, both foreign and domestic. Since the mill had excess capacity, Nucor began to market its steel products to outside customers. In 1972, 75% of the shipments of Nucor steel was to Vulcraft and 25% was to other customers.

Iverson explained in 1984:

> In constructing these mills we have experimented with new processes and new manufacturing techniques. We serve as our own general contractor and design and build much of our own equipment. In one or more of our mills we have built our own continuous casting unit, reheat furnaces, cooling beds and in Utah even our own mill

> stands. All of these to date have cost under $125 per ton of annual capacity—compared with projected costs for large integrated mills of $1,200–$1,500 per ton of annual capacity, ten times our cost. Our mills have high productivity. We currently use less than four manhours to produce a ton of steel. This includes everyone in the operation: maintenance, clerical, accounting, and sales and management. On the basis of our production workers alone, it is less than three manhours per ton. Our total employment costs are less than $60 per ton compared with the average employment costs of the seven largest U.S. steel companies of close to $130 per ton. Our total labor costs are less than 20% of our sales price.

In contrast to Nucor's less than four manhours, similar Japanese mills were said to require more than five hours and comparable U.S. mills over six hours. Nucor's average yield from molten metal to finished products was over 90%, compared with an average U.S. steel industry yield of about 74%, giving energy costs of about $39 per ton compared with their $75 a ton. Nucor ranked 46th on *Iron Age*'s annual survey of world steel producers. They were second on the list of top ten producers of steel worldwide based on tons per employee, at 981 tons. The head of the list was Tokyo Steel at 1,485. U.S. Steel was 7th at 479. Some other results were: Nippon Steel, 453; British Steel, 213; Bethlehem Steel, 329; Kruppstahl, 195; Weirton Steel, 317; and Northstar Steel, 936. Nucor also ranked 7th on the list ranking growth of raw steel production. U.S. Steel was 5th on the same list. U.S. Steel topped the list based on improvement in tons-per-employee, at 56%; Nucor was 7th with a 12% improvement.

THE STEELMAKING PROCESS

A steel mill's work is divided into two phases, preparation of steel of the proper "chemistry" and the forming of the steel into the desired products. The typical mini-mill utilized scrap steel, such as junk auto parts, instead of the iron ore which would be used in larger, integrated steel mills. The typical mini-mill had an annual capacity of 200,000 to 600,000 tons, compared with the 7 million tons of Bethlehem Steel's Sparrow's Point, Maryland, integrated plant.

A charging bucket fed loads of scrap steel into electric arc furnaces. The melted load, called a heat, was poured into a ladle to be carried by overhead crane to the casting machine. In the casting machine the liquid steel was extruded as a continuous red-hot solid bar of steel and cut into lengths weighing some 900 pounds called "billets." In the typical plant the billet, about 4 inches in cross section and about 20 feet long, was held temporarily in a pit where it cooled to normal temperatures. Periodically billets were carried to the rolling mill and placed in a reheat oven to bring them up to 2000°F at which temperature they would be malleable. In the rolling mill, presses and dies progressively converted the billet into the desired round bars, angles, channels, flats, and other products. After cutting to standard lengths, they were moved to the warehouse.

Nucor's first steel mill, employing more than 500 people, was located in Darlington, South Carolina. The mill, with its three electric arc furnaces, operated 24 hours per day, 5½ days per week. Nucor had made a number of improvements in the melting and casting operations. The former general manager of the Darlington plant had developed a system which involved preheating the ladles, allowing for the faster flow of steel into the caster and resulting in better control of the steel characteristics. Less time and lower capital investment were required. The casting machines were "continuous casters," as opposed to the old batch method. The objective in the "front" of the mill was to keep the casters working. At the time of the Harvard study at Nucor each strand was in operation 90% of the time, while a competitor had announced a "record rate" of 75% which it had been able to sustain for a week.

Nucor was also perhaps the only mill in the country which regularly avoided the reheating of billets. This saved $10–12 per ton in fuel usage and losses due to oxidation of the steel. The cost of developing this process had been $12 million. Not all research projects had been successful. The company spent approximately $2,000,000 in an unsuccessful effort to utilize resistance-heating. They lost even more on an effort at induction melting. As Iverson told *Metal Producing,* "That costs us a lot of money. Timewise it was very expensive. But you have got to make mistakes and we've had lots of failures." In the rolling mill, the first machine was a roughing mill by Morgarshammar, the first of its kind in the Western Hemisphere. This Swedish machine had been chosen because of its lower cost, higher productivity, and the flexibility. Passing through another five to nine finishing mills converted the billet into the desired finished product. The yield from the billet to finished product was about 93%.

The Darlington design became the basis for plants in Nebraska, Texas, and Utah. The Texas plant had cost under $80 per ton of annual capacity. Whereas the typical mini-mill cost approximately $250 per ton, the average cost of all four of Nucor's mills was under $135.

The Darlington plant was organized into 12 natural groups for the purpose of incentive pay: two mills, each had two shifts with three groups—melting and casting, rolling mill, and finishing. In melting and casting there were three or four different standards, depending on the material, established by the department manager years ago based on historical performance. The general manager stated, "We don't change the standards." The caster, the key to the operation, was used at a 92% level—greater than the capacity claimed by the manufacturer. For every good ton of billet above the standard hourly rate for the week, workers in the group received a 4% bonus. For example, with a common standard of 10 tons per run hour and an actual rate for the week of 28 tons per hour, the workers would receive a bonus of 72% [(28 − 10) × 4] of their base rate in the week's paycheck.

In the rolling mill there were more than 100 products, each with a different historical standard. Workers received a 4% to 6% bonus for every good ton sheared per hour for the week over the computed standard. The Darlington general manager said the standard would be changed only if there was a major machinery change and that a standard had not been changed since the initial development period for the plant. He commented that, in exceeding the standard the worker wouldn't work harder but would cooperate to avoid problems and moved more quickly if a problem developed: "If there is a way to improve output, they will tell us." Another manager added: "Meltshop employees don't ask me how much it costs Chaparral or LTV to make a billet. They want to know what it costs Darlington, Norfolk, Jewitt to put a billet on the ground—scrap costs, alloy costs, electrical costs, refactory, gas, etc. Everybody from Charlotte to Plymouth watches the nickels and dimes."

The Darlington manager, who became COO in 1984, stated:

The key to making a profit when selling a product with no aesthetic value, or a product that you really can't differentiate from your competitors, is cost. I don't look at us as a fantastic marketing organization, even though I think we are pretty good; but we don't try to overcome unreasonable costs by mass marketing. We maintain low costs by keeping the employee force at the level it should be, not doing things that aren't necessary to achieve our goals, and allowing people to function on their own and by judging them on their results.

To keep a cooperative and productive workforce you need, number one, to be completely honest about everything; number two, to allow each employee as much as possible to make decisions about that employee's work, to find easier and more productive ways to perform duties; and number three, to be as fair as possible to all employees. Most of the changes we make in work procedures and in equipment come from the employees. They really know the problems of their jobs better than anyone else. We don't have any industrial engineers, nor do we ever intend to, because that's a type of specialist who tends to take responsibility off the top division management and give them a crutch.

To communicate with my employees, I try to spend time in the plant and at intervals have meetings with the employees. Usually if they have a question they just visit me. Recently a small group visited me in my office to discuss our vacation policy. They had some suggestions and, after listening to them, I had to agree that the ideas were good.

NUCOR'S PERSONNEL SYSTEM

The foremost characteristic of Nucor's personnel system was its incentive plan. Another major personnel policy was providing job security. Also all employees at Nucor received the same fringe benefits. There was only one group insurance plan. Holidays and vacations did not differ by job. The company had no executive dining rooms or restrooms, no fishing lodges, company cars, or reserved parking places.

Absenteeism and tardiness were not problems at Nucor. Each employee had four days of absence before pay was reduced. In addition to these, missing work was allowed for jury duty, military leave, or the death of close relatives. After this, a day's absence cost them bonus pay for that week and lateness of more than a half hour meant the loss of bonus for that day.

Employees were kept informed about the company. Charts showing the division's results in return-on-assets and bonus payoff were posted in prominent places in the plant. The personnel manager commented that as he traveled around to all the plants, he found everyone in the company could tell him the level of profits in their division. The general managers held dinners at least twice a year with their employees. The dinners were held with 50 or 60 employees at a time. After introductory remarks the floor was open for discussion of any work related problems. The company also had a formal grievance procedure. The Darlington manager couldn't recall the last grievance he had processed.

There was a new employee orientation program and an employee handbook which contained personnel policies and rules. The corporate office sent all news releases to each division where they were posted on bulletin boards. Each employee in the company also received a copy of the Annual Report. For the last several years the cover of the Annual Report had contained the names of all Nucor employees. Every child of every Nucor employee received up to $1,200 a year for four years if they chose to go on to higher education, including technical schools.

The average hourly worker's pay was $31,000, compared with the average earnings in manufacturing in that state of slightly more than $13,000. The personnel manager believed that pay was not the only thing the workers liked about Nucor. He said that an NBC interviewer, working on the documentary "If Japan Can, Why Can't We," often heard, "I enjoy working for Nucor because Nucor is the best, the most productive, and the most profitable company that I know of."

"I honestly feel that if someone performs well, they should share in the company and if they are going to share in the success, they should also share in the failures," Iverson stated. There were four incentive programs at Nucor, one each for production workers, department heads, staff people such as accountants, secretaries, or engineers, and senior management, which included the division managers. All of these programs were on a group basis.

Within the production program, groups ranged in size from 25 to 30 people and had definable and measurable operations. The company believed that a program should be simple and that bonuses should be paid promptly. "We don't have any discretionary bonuses—zero. It is all based on performance. Now we don't want anyone to sit in judgment, because it never is fair . . . ," said Iverson. The personnel manager stated: "Their bonus is based on roughly 90% of historical time it takes to make a particular joist. If during a week they make joists at 60% less than the standard time, they receive a 60% bonus." This was paid with the regular pay the following week. The complete paycheck amount, including overtime, was multiplied by the bonus factor. Bonus was not paid when equipment was not operating: "We have the philosophy that when equipment is not operating everybody suffers and the bonus for downtime is zero." The foremen are also part of the group and received the same bonus as the employees they supervised.

The second incentive program was for department heads in the various divisions. The incentive pay here was based on division contribution, defined as the division earnings before corporate expenses and profit sharing are determined. Bonuses were reported to run as high as 51% of a person's base salary in the divisions and 30% for corporate positions.

There was a third plan for people who were neither production workers nor department managers. Their bonus was based on either the division return-on-assets or the corporate return-on-assets.

The fourth program was for the senior officers. The senior officers had no employment contracts, pension or retirement plans, or other normal perquisites. Their base salaries were set at about 70% of what an individual doing similar work in other companies would receive. Once return-on-equity reached 9%, slightly below the average for manufacturing firms, 5% of net earnings before taxes went into a pool, that was divided among the officers based on their salaries. "Now if return-on-equity for the company reaches, say 20%, which it has, then we can wind up with as much as 190% of our base salaries and 115% on top of that in stock. We get both." In 1982 the return was 8% and the executives received no bonus. His pay in 1981 was approximately $300,000 but dropped the next year to $110,000. "I think that ranked by total compensation I was the lowest paid CEO in the Fortune 500. I was kind of proud of that, too." In 1986, Iverson's stock was worth over $10 million. The young Vulcraft manager was likewise a millionaire. Half the bonus was paid in cash and half was deferred.

In lieu of a retirement plan, the company had a profit sharing plan with a deferred trust. Each year 10% of pretax earnings was put into profit sharing. Fifteen percent of this was set aside to be paid to employees in the following March as a cash bonus and the remainder was put into trust for each employee on the basis of percent of their earnings as a percent of total wages paid within the corporation. The employee was vested 20% after the first year and gained an additional 10% vesting each year thereafter. Employees received a quarterly statement of their balance in profit sharing.

The company had an Employer Monthly Stock Investment Plan to which Nucor added 10% to the amount the employee contributed and paid the commission on the purchase of any Nucor stock. After each five years of service with the company, the employee received a service award consisting of five shares of Nucor stock. Additionally, if profits were good, extraordinary bonus payments would be made to the employees. In December 1988, each employee received a $500 payment.

According to Iverson:

> I think the first obligation of the company is to the stockholder and to its employees. I find in this country too many cases where employees are underpaid and corporate management is making huge social donations for self-fulfillment. We regularly give donations, but we have a very interesting corporate policy. First, we give donations where our employees are. Second, we give donations which will benefit our employees, such as to the YMCA. It is a difficult area and it requires a lot of thought. There is certainly a strong social responsibility for a company, but it cannot be at the expense of the employees or the stockholders.

Nucor had no trouble finding people to staff its plants. When the mill in Jewett, Texas, was built in 1975, there were over 5,000 applications for the 400 jobs—many coming from people in Houston and Dallas. Yet not everyone found work at Nucor they wanted. In 1975, a Harvard team found high turnover among new production workers after startup. The cause appeared to be pressure from fellow workers in the group incentive situation. A survival-of-the-fittest situation was found in which those who didn't like to work seldom stuck around. "Productivity increased and turnover declined dramatically once these people left," the Harvard team concluded. Iverson commented: "A lot of people aren't goal-oriented. A lot of them don't want to work that hard, so initially we have a lot of turnover in a plant but then it's so low we don't even measure after that."

The Wall Street Journal reported in 1981:

> Harry Pigg, a sub-district director for the USW in South Carolina, sees a darker side in Nucor's incentive plan. He contends that Nucor unfairly penalizes workers by taking away big bonus payments for absence or tardiness, regardless of the reason. Workers who are ill, he says, try to work because they can't afford to give up the bonus payment. "Nucor whips them into line," he adds. He acknowledges, though, that high salaries are the major barrier to unionizing the company.

Having welcomed a parade of visitors from other companies over the years, Iverson had become concerned with the pattern: "They only do one or two of the things we do. It's not just incentives or the scholarship program; its all those things put together that result in a unified philosophy for the company."

AS 1990 CLOSED

Looking ahead in 1984, Iverson had said: "The next decade will be an exciting one for steel producers. It will tax our abilities to keep pace with technological changes we can see now on the horizon." Imports didn't have to dominate the U.S. economy. He believed the steel industry would continue to play a pivotal role in the growth of American industry. He pointed out comparative advantages of the U.S. steel industry: an abundance of resources, relatively low energy costs, lower transportation costs, and the change in the government's attitude toward business.

The "excitement" he had predicted had occurred. Imports were a challenge for steel, just as for textiles, shoes, machine tools, and computers. The old steel companies were flexing their muscle and getting back into the game. Overcapacity hadn't left the mini-mill immune; there was no safe haven for anyone. Nucor was no longer a small company, David, with free shots at Goliath.

The honeymoon appeared over. Wall Street worried about what Nucor should do. Cable News Network posed the position of some on Wall Street: "They say basically you guys are selling to the construction companies, you are selling to some fairly depressed industries. They also say, Nucor, they were a specialized little niche company. They did what they did very well; but now all of a sudden, they are going out, building these big mills to make huge pieces of steel and they are talking casted cold, all that stuff. They're worried that you may be getting into deals that are a little too complicated from what they perceive you as being able to do well."

The New York Times pointed out that expansion would certainly hurt earnings for the next several years. They quoted a steel consultant. "It is hard to do all that they are trying to do and keep profits up. With the industry in the shape it's in, this is not the time to expand beyond the niche they've established."

When they were sitting with $185 million in cash, Iverson told *Inc:* "It (going private) has been mentioned to us by a number of brokerage firms and investment houses, but we wouldn't even consider it. It wouldn't be fair to employees, and I don't know whether it would be fair to the stockholders. . . . You're going to restrict the growth opportunities. . . . You either grow or die. . . . Opportunities wouldn't be created for people within the company."

Iverson told CNN: "We've decided that really we want to stay in that niche (steel). We don't want to buy any banks. . . . All of the growth of the company has been internally generated. We think there are opportunities in the steel industry today. . . . There are ample opportunities, although they are somewhat harder to find than they used to be.

"Another of my strengths is the ability to stick to my knitting. The reason executives make a lot of mistakes is that sometimes they get bored—they think the grass is greener on the other side so they go out and buy a bank or an oil company or they go into businesses where they have no expertise. . . . I have never gotten bored with this company. I've done this job so long that I think I have some insight into the needs and the capabilities of the company. I'm not misled into thinking we can do something that we can't."

An economics professor and steel consultant at Middle Tennessee State University told the *Times*, "You're not going to see any growth in the steel market, so the only way to make money is to reduce costs and have new technology to penetrate other companies' business."

The New York Times stated: "Critics question whether it is wise to continue expanding production capabilities, as Nucor is doing, when there is already overcapacity in the steel industry and intense competition already exists between the mini-mills." Iverson insisted the strategy would pay off in the long-term. He told the *Times*, "The company's strategy makes sense for us. To gain a larger share in an ever-shrinking market, you've got to take something from someone else."

They had sold the Chemicals Division, gotten into the structural steel components business, into the fastener industry, and were now ready to go head-to-head with the major integrated producers for the lucrative flat-rolled market. Sales and earnings were projected to double in the next two years, as the stock price doubled or tripled.

Iverson's position was clear: "We're going to stay in steel and steel products. The way we look at it, this company does only two things well, builds plants economically and runs them efficiently. That is the whole company. We don't have any financial expertise, we're not entrepreneurs, we're not into acquisitions. Steel may not be the best business in the world, but it's what we know how to do and we do it well."

CASE 30

J & M Airframes, Ltd.*

HISTORY

The present company is the result of a merger in 1958 between two aircraft manufacturers, Javelin and Morton-Harman, both based in Yorkshire. Prior to the merger Javelin tended to concentrate on military transport aircraft, whereas Morton-Harman were essentially light aircraft specialists who had particular success with crop spraying planes.

The merger was seen at the time as a defensive measure. These two were almost the last remaining independent aircraft manufacturers in the UK. Due to the increasing complexity of aircraft design and the rapidly escalating costs of developing new aircraft, fewer and fewer firms had the resources to "go it alone." The industry had seen specialisation occurring in the 1920s and 1930s, with the emergence of airframe manufacturers and aero-engine firms. And in the fifties a spate of merger activity had reduced the number of firms in the industry dramatically.

The merger was a gentlemanly affair; a process that was considerably assisted by the retirement of the founder of Javelin. Following the merger there was some rationalisation of production facilities. This process has continued over the years and now all manufacturing is concentrated on one site on the outskirts of York.

The most urgent task facing the combined companies in the late fifties was to design and develop a new aircraft to replace their ageing range of models. J & M responded by successfully launching a low-level heavy bomber (the "Tempest") which proved to be the mainstay of the company throughout the 1960s and 1970s. The Tempest took the industry by surprise, outperforming competing models from more established suppliers of military aircraft, and securing as a result a large long term contract with the RAF.

This major contract tended to eclipse J & M's previous areas of specialism, so that by the end of the 1970s they could be regarded as a "one product" firm. However, although there were disadvantages in being dependent on the single product, there have been major compensations. The original contract for 80 aircraft has expanded to the point where there are now over 400 Tempests in service with air forces around the world. Specialisation has enabled them to keep production costs down through the development of better methods, and through design improvements. Although production of new aircraft has been winding down since 1975, there is still a large volume of work to be done re-fitting older models with, for example, more modern avionics and weapon systems.

* Prepared by Cliff Bowman, Cranfield School of Management, C.I.T., Cranfield, Beds., England.

J & M IN 1980

There are 4500 people working on the York site; 2800 are in production, the remainder being split between technical, commercial and support activities. Since the decline in demand for new Tempests the company has tried to utilize its capacity in other ways. (Tempest related work now only accounts for about 30% of the firm's activity.) Since 1975 the firm has begun to take on sub-contracted work from other major aerospace manufacturers based in the UK, Europe, and the USA.

This work is extremely variable in the size of the unit to be manufactured (from a complete wing to a minor sub-assembly), and the number of units in any one order (from one-offs, to large batches.)

NEW CHALLENGES FACING J & M

This shift from a one-product firm selling to only a handful of customers, to a multiple product operation dealing with many diverse customers has created many strains on the management, the workforce and the organization structure.

Quotes from management indicate some of the problems:

Tony Fuller, Production Planning Manager:

> From our point of view in production planning the problems have escalated with every new job we take on. When we were churning out Tempests we could see bottlenecks, shortages, and delays quite easily. Now, we have eight major programmes on the factory floor requiring upwards of 30,000 separate components. To be frank, we often have little idea what is actually going on on the shop floor. Part of the problem is that with Tempest we never really had to develop sophisticated production planning and control systems. I wouldn't say it was anarchy out there, but it seemed to work OK. Consequently, even when we have tried to put in systems, there isn't the discipline on the shop floor to maintain them; often they can't see the point of logging "waiting time," for instance, but this is vital information for us.

Brian Simons, Foreman, Conventional Machining:

> It's difficult to motivate the shop floor now. In the old days they saw a Tempest fly out of here nearly every week. I know that gave everyone a tremendous thrill; knowing that they had contributed to that aircraft. Now all the guy sees is a truck loaded with sub-assemblies leaving the site.

Sarah George, Personnel Manager:

> We suspect that efficiency has declined dramatically over the last two years. You can put this down to the running down of the Tempest programme, but we also made some decisions which, although they seemed right at the time, they have since exacerbated our problems. To try to cut costs we offered an attractive early retirement deal to 150 of our supervisors and foremen. Unfortunately, the supervisors we wanted to leave stayed, and our best people took the money; I know that a lot of them

had already lined up good jobs in other firms. I think we lost an awful lot of experience as a result. The other decision was the scrapping of the Payment by Results system. This had to go; it was so corrupt it was a joke. Rate fixers were intimidated, absurd times were not amended, and in many respects the system was running the factory, rather than the management.

Rowly France, Head of Production Engineering:

For most of my department the shift of work away from the Tempest has meant a more varied job. We need to be much more flexible now, because we don't know what the next job will involve. Some of the younger graduates like the challenge of new jobs, but I know that a lot of the older hands preferred the way it used to be. In the old days you could be working on a problem for months, especially when we were trying to lower the production costs of Tempest in the late sixties and early seventies. In those days we used to work very closely with the production people, working as a team to solve the problems. But now I would say most of the department don't like going down to the shop floor. The atmosphere has changed; there's a lot of cynicism down there.

ORGANIZATION STRUCTURE

The firm is organized functionally (see Exhibit 1). This structure has remained essentially the same since the merger. Although over time departments have grown and new ones have been set up, the basic functional arrangement has been maintained. Management generally

EXHIBIT 1
J & M Airframes, Ltd., 1980

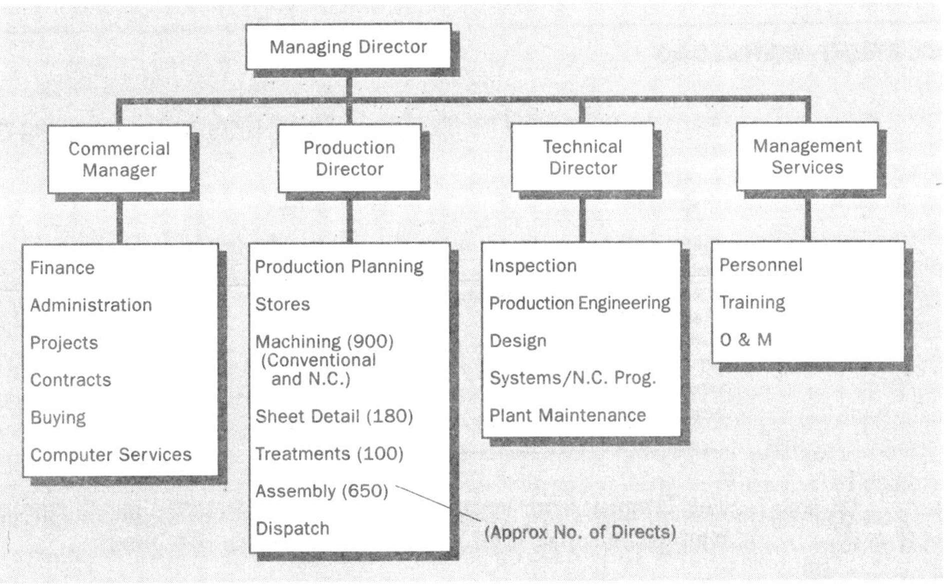

accept that this organization served them well over the life of the Tempest. When everyone was working on the same programme there was not much need for communication across the organization. Over the years each function had got on with its own job, and the long term nature of the project provided the stability needed to refine the procedures and systems in the factory.

But the sheer size of the firm has caused some problems. Communication from the top downwards is reasonably effective (although the shop floor don't think they get anywhere near enough information), but upward communication is almost nonexistent. The few individuals that have moved functions (e.g., from the Technical Department to Production) reflect on the differences between departments. These differences cause particular problems in the areas of discipline, standards of behaviour and management style.

Longer serving production foremen complain that their powers have been eroded over the years:

> I used to be able to hire and fire, set quality standards, load the jobs into the shop, discipline a lad that had got out of line. Now my hands are tied. If I so much as raise my voice to an apprentice I have to give him a written apology copied to half the factory. (Anonymous foreman)

Although this is a somewhat jaundiced view, there has been a large increase in the number of staff positions over the years. Now there are separate departments dealing with work study, production control, quality assurance, value engineering, training, costing, production scheduling, procurement, etc.

Along with the growth of the firm there has been an increase in the number of management levels. There are chargehands, supervisors, senior supervisors, foremen, superintendents, production managers, and manufacturing managers, who report to the production director.

CURRENT WORKLOAD

Apart from the refits on existing Tempests, there are the following major programmes on the site:

Programme	*% of Workload*
Firefly Tailplane	15
Panther Flaptracks	12
Scanscope (for aerial photography)	10
Otter fuselage	9
Galaxy Winglets	8
ARV Cockpit Mods	6
A350 Ribs	6
Miscellaneous	4

The Tempest refits account for the remainder (30%) but this programme is forecast to represent less than 10% of the workload within two years.

THE EXECUTIVE COMMITTEE

J & M's executive committee is the most powerful senior management group. It is made up of the managing director, the production director, the commercial manager, the technical director, and the head of management services. At a recent meeting the commercial manager had some disturbing news to impart:

> I heard a whisper at the Paris show that Lockheed were getting much tougher with their suppliers. Apparently, they pulled out of a long term deal with Hughes following an unannounced QA audit. I dread to think how we would shape up to a really thorough examination of our quality systems. As I see it, we might not only lose the Galaxy work; bad news travels fast. Our other customers might start wondering whether they should keep dealing with us.

The technical director responded:

> Come on, Frank, we've heard all this before. This is just another scare story put around to keep us on our toes. Our quality is OK. I know we've had some problems with the ARV Cockpit Mods, but that was down to a lack of communication between the design office and the machine shop. Anyway, we are still approved by the MoD, so what's the problem?

At this point the production director intervened:

> I can't believe I'm hearing this! How can you say we don't have a problem with quality when our scrap and rework costs are going through the roof! I'm convinced that most of your inspectors enjoy rejecting jobs. I sometimes think they are secretly paid by our competitors.

The technical director reacts forcefully:

> It's a good job somebody takes quality seriously here. If it was left to your supervisors we'd be letting all sorts of crap leave the factory.

Then the managing director took control:

> Look, there's little point in having a slanging match. We know we've got problems, so let's look for some solutions rather than blaming each other. We have got a problem with quality. We've also got problems with delivery, and costs. It seems that nobody can tell me precisely where we are on any of our contracts. Far too often we only know we have a problem when it's too late to do anything about it. To be honest, sometimes I feel this place is running out of control.

Frank agrees, adding:

> Yesterday I had a most embarrassing phone call from Panavia. They wanted to know why they had not received the last batch of sub-assemblies yet. Well, I said I'd get right back to them with an explanation. I spent the next two hours trying to track down somebody who could give me a straight answer. It seems to me that nobody is

taking responsibility for the customer anymore. Everyone passes the buck. Assembly blamed treatments, treatments criticized the NC Machining. NC Machining said the delays were caused by poor NC Programming. And when I eventually spoke to Alan Gough in NC Programming he said that design kept changing the drawings.

If we're looking for solutions, I think we need to organize the factory differently. There needs to be a focus on the customer's requirements. I can't see, in principle, why we shouldn't split up the site into lots of mini-factories, each one concentrating on one project.

The production director responds:

> Good grief, Frank, have you any idea what's involved in this kind of change? I admit you've got a good point, but it would mean a lot of changes for everybody, and some activities, like treatments, couldn't be split up between different projects.

Then the technical director intervened:

> Well, what you do in production is your business, but I would be very unhappy about splitting up my designers, production engineers and, particularly, the inspectors. To be honest, I think this would be a big mistake, and I'm sure quality would suffer if we moved inspection staff to be under the control of production. Anyway this sounds like a matrix organization, and I've never seen one that worked!

Then the managing director commented:

> Ok, well we haven't time at this meeting to go into something as big as this. I suggest we get somebody to look into what options are available to us. Maybe he could take a look at what other firms have done; or should we bring in consultants? Anyway, Frank, could you get something moving on this?

CASE 31

Management Wins a Round Against Wall Street? The Santa Fe Southern Pacific Case*

HISTORICAL DEVELOPMENT

The beginnings of the Santa Fe Southern Pacific Co. date back to 1859, when a lawyer, Cyrus Kurtz Holliday, obtained a state charter for the Atchison & Topeka Railroad. Holliday had founded the town of Topeka and lobbied the Kansas State constitutional convention to make it the capital. Now it needed a railroad. Not much happened for a while until he got a land grant bill through the U.S. Congress. The bill granted 3 million acres in alternate sections in Kansas to the firm on the condition that the railroad reach the Colorado border in 10 years. By 1872 this was completed and the Atchison & Topeka railway had agents as far away as Russia distributing pamphlets and trying to lure farmers into the area. Vigorous expansion, acquisitions, and legal and paramilitary action expanded the line to 9,000 miles by the 1890's. At the time it was the longest in the world.

In the Panic of 1883, it, like many of the railroads of the day, lost a considerable amount of mileage in reorganization. The line was down but not out and between then and the 1970's the Atchison, Topeka & Santa Fe Railroad Co. acquired approximately 25 more railroad holdings and their related land, mining, and timber properties.

Early in the 1970's a number of major changes occurred. The Company was reorganized under the Santa Fe Industries name. Its passenger business was sold off to Amtrak. There was a major effort to simplify the corporate structure and rationalize the distribution of assets and subsidiaries along the lines of their predominant economic activities.

THE CURRENT COMPANY

The Santa Fe Southern Pacific Corporation (SFSP) was formed in 1982 as a merger of Santa Fe Industries and The Southern Pacific Company. See Exhibit 1 for a time line of these events. The outstanding shares of the Southern Pacific Transportation Co., the wholly owned subsidiary conducting all of Southern Pacific's rail and truck business, was placed in an independent voting trust pending the approval by the Interstate Commerce Commission (ICC) of the merger. Approval by the ICC was widely expected. In the past decade the commission had approved a series of western mergers which had diverted $250 million in traffic from the SFSP. Also, the merger economics were not based on traffic diversion. Of the $287 million benefit that was expected to be realized, three-fourths were from operating

* Prepared by Mark Smith and Dorothy Griest, University of Southwestern Louisiana. Distributed by the North American Case Research Association.

EXHIBIT 1
Santa Fe Southern Pacific Corporation
Chronological List of Events and Happenings Ending January 27, 1988

1983

I. Santa Fe Railroad and Southern Pacific merge to form Santa Fe Southern Pacific (SFSP)
By merging, it was thought the following would occur.
1. SFSP would save $650 million in capital expenditures and $145 million in operating expenses.
2. SFSP would lure business since they could now provide the market with shorter routes.
3. SFSP would be able to generate $260 million more in revenue in the first year alone.
4. SFSP would now have $11 billion in assets, 38,000 miles in rail track, and would become the largest real estate owner and railroad company in the country.

II. The Interstate Commerce Commission (ICC) received a formal application for a merger and took thirty-one (31) months to rule on the application.

III. John Schmidt, past Chief Executive Officer (CEO) of Santa Fe, became CEO of SFSP. From past history, the ICC was expected to give approval to the merger.

1986

I. In July, the ICC, in an unprecedented move, denied the merger of SFSP. The ICC stated that the merger would create a geographic monopoly.

II. SFSP immediately filled to reopen the case.

III. Schmidt was forced to resign by the Board of Directors, for the following reasons:
1. He was granted competing railroads concessions. For instance, Schmidt would give competing railroad companies the right to use the Santa Fe railroads if they would not oppose the merger.
2. The Board of Directors did not like Schmidt's confrontational style.

IV. John Reed, a former CEO of Santa Fe, became the new CEO of SFSP on a temporary basis. SFSP believed that his low-key style could bring about a reversal of the ICC's decision.

1987

I. The ICC once again denied the merger of SFSP and ordered CEO Reed to divest the existing company within 90 days.

II. In July, Robert Krebs, past CEO of Southern Pacific, became CEO of SFSP.

III. In October, Michael Dingman of the Henley Group attempted a hostile takeover of Southern Pacific. Krebs, calling Dingman's bluff, made an offer to sell Southern Pacific for $63 per share. The offer was refused.

IV. When it was apparent that Dingman still wanted to take over Southern Pacific, Krebs ordered a $30 dividend to be paid to stockholders. Thus, Dingman sold his shares.

1988

I. By January, in order to divest portions of SFSP as ordered by the ICC, and to raise dollars to pay off the debt used to defend the company from takeover, Krebs chose to sell the following:
1. Robert E. McKee, a general building contractor.
2. Bankers Leasing and Financial Corporation
3. Two pipelines to Koch Industries, Inc.

II. In addition, there was an agreement to sell Santa Fe Pacific Timber Co. to Sierra Pacific Industries and another agreement to sell Southern Pacific Railroad to Rio Grande Industries.

efficiencies. Although the combination would control 80% of the rail traffic originating or terminating in California, 95% of all California freight is carried by truck.

EVENTS WHICH PRECIPITATED THE STOCKHOLDER LETTER OF JAN. 27, 1988

It was John Schmidt who engineered the attempted merger of the Santa Fe and Southern Pacific in 1983. Schmidt, 56, joined Santa Fe right out of law school. Schmidt was described as the bulldog-grim chairman of Santa Fe Southern Pacific Corp.

For three years or more Schmidt was obsessed with one objective—the merger of the two railroads and what he saw as an enormous potential. Even after the 4–1 majority rejection of the merger by ICC in July of 1986 Schmidt continued to be determined that the merger could be consummated. The ICC said they saw no way of solving this issue and ordered the divestiture of the other railroad (see Exhibit 2). The SFSP immediately filed to

EXHIBIT 2
When Is a Monopoly Not a Monopoly?

In October the Interstate Commerce Commission officially rejected the proposed merger of the Santa Fe and the Southern Pacific railroads on the grounds that it would create rail monopolies in California and in the southern corridor between California and Texas and the Gulf Coast. The merged company would handle nearly 80% of the rail traffic originating or terminating in California and over 90% of the rail traffic moving between California and such cities as Houston, Dallas and New Orleans. Trouble is, trucks handle 95% of all traffic within California and 42% of the freight traffic in the southern corridor. Some monopoly.

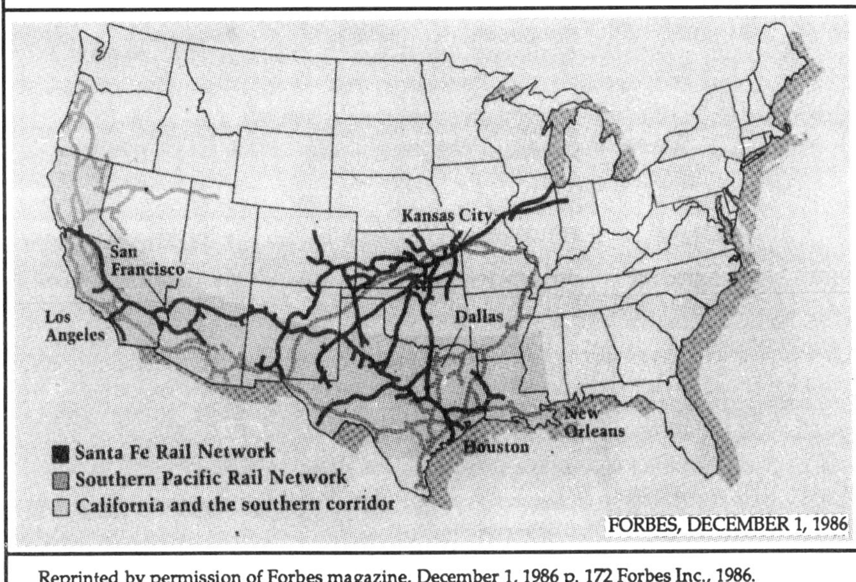

Reprinted by permission of Forbes magazine, December 1, 1986 p. 172 Forbes Inc., 1986.

reopen the case and began negotiations with other railroads to address the ICC's concerns. In February of 1987 the ICC responded with a request for more information.

Wall Street analysts and investors had been watching events closely. Railroad assets had been selling well even in bankruptcy. SFSP was estimated to be worth $2 billion or $12/share on its rail assets alone. First Boston thought that adding in the natural resource, real estate, and pipeline assets the stock could be worth $45 a share. Bear Stearns thought the stock was worth up to $60 and possibly $90 a share. The stock had a book value of $34, but had been rising slowly from a low of 20¼ in 1984 to the mid 30's at the end of 1986. These same analysts felt that there was also some danger Schmidt would give away more than the stockholders would get by the merger. He proposed many alternatives to meet the ICC objection that the merger was not in the public interest, such as selling off all of one line and/or parts of both, dividing them back to stockholders and many other schemes. He was accused of moving too slowly and then began moving more quickly selling oil and gas reserves into a limited partnership, with part being sold to the public. He also sold Kirby forest products to Louisiana-Pacific. His purpose was to use the money to shrink Santa Fe's equity and ratchet up its per share earnings. All the while these sales and proposed sales were going on Schmidt insisted there was no fire sale. He finally irritated directors by granting competing railroads costly concessions—including the right to use Santa Fe track. He did this in an effort to win ICC support and to make the merger appear less of a monopolistic threat.

Schmidt was ousted in the spring of 1987 by the Santa Fe board who chose John Reed, former head of Santa Fe Industries, as acting CEO to run the company. Reed, 60, is said to cloak an iron will beneath a courtly, gracious manner. Reed rose from track maintenance supervisor to Santa Fe board chairman. The industry felt that unless Reed could move quickly after being named CEO, that Henley Group or some other interested party would likely attempt a buyout.

Robert D. Krebs, 45, a 21-year industry veteran who was running Southern Pacific before the 1983 merger, took over as the permanent president and chief executive officer on July 28, 1987. Krebs is viewed by competitors as a bright young man which the industry needs. One of Krebs's favorite phrases is, "give us a little time and we'll do more for the value of your stock than any raider could."

This was important because the rising market for railroad assets and the ICC's actions stimulated a great deal of interest in the stock by investment groups. By 1987 SFSP had entered into talks with two such groups. The Henley Group and Olympia & York Developments Ltd. were both offering around $63 a share. The investment groups were negotiating both with the company and with each other. It was in this climate that the following letter was sent to the shareholders:

January 27, 1988

Dear Shareholder:

I am pleased to report to you in full detail recent actions of your Board of Directors and management that are designed to expedite the realization of values inherent in the Company's assets for your benefit.

On January 26 your Board of Directors declared a dividend distribution of $25 in cash plus $5 principal amount of new senior subordinated debentures for each outstanding share. This distribution will be funded by cash received from the sale of Southern Pacific Transportation Company, our non-core businesses, certain real estate and additional debt. After this dividend is paid, you will retain the same number of shares and proportional equity in the Company that you now own, although the stock will then undoubtedly trade at a lower price.

Your Board believes that the plan represents a balance between short-term and long-term investment goals, as it provides significant up-front value now in the form of a $30 dividend, while allowing shareholders to benefit from continued ownership in what we believe will be a company with good potential for future growth.

We plan to pay this dividend to holders of record on February 5, 1988, with the cash portion to be paid February 16 and the debenture portion March 1. Payment of the cash portion of the dividend is subject to receipt by the Company of $3.8 billion from lending institutions. A bank group headed by Morgan Guaranty Trust Company of New York and Security Pacific National Bank has agreed to lend the Company the necessary funds, subject to certain conditions.

Payment of the debenture portion of the dividend is subject to the following conditions:

1. Payment of the cash portion of the dividend.
2. Approval for listing the debentures on the New York Stock Exchange.
3. Registration of the debentures under the Securities Exchange Act.
4. Qualification of the indenture related to the debentures under the Trust Indenture Act of 1939.

Although these conditions, including those regarding borrowings, are not totally in the control of the Company, we anticipate that they will be satisfied in time to meet the indicated payment schedule. If a delay should arise, your Board of Directors presently intends to adjust the record and payment date so that the dividend distribution may be paid as promptly as practicable.

Background and Reasons for the Special Dividend

Payment of this dividend is an important step in our restructuring program, the strategy for which originated in the Spring of 1987. At that time our proposal to reopen our pending railroad merger case was under consideration by the Interstate Commerce Commission (ICC), and it appeared likely to us that the ICC could reject our petition to reopen. In addition, the combination of Santa Fe Industries and Southern Pacific Company at the end of 1983 had created a large and diverse company with a significant portion of its assets in undeveloped real estate and natural resources. In our opinion the true value of these assets was not fully reflected in the stock price. We therefore began a review of the Company's strategy and operations, assisted by our investment bankers, to identify the structural changes that could enhance shareholder value. Our objective was to create added value for you in the short term, and restructure the Company so that it would be well-positioned to develop its core assets in the future.

During this review, we considered what our individual businesses would bring up front if we concluded to sell them, compared with their value in terms of earnings and cash flow if we concluded to retain them. Our investment bankers provided a substantial amount of information regarding values we might receive through outright sales or public offerings. Based on this information and our analysis, we decided to sell a number of our companies.

Companies Already Sold or Being Sold

The first company we elected to sell was Robert E. McKee, a general building contractor. McKee contributed little in terms of earnings or cash flow, nor did it provide any material synergism with our real estate business. We saw little potential in retaining McKee, and sold it to Jacobs Engineering in September 1987.

Our leasing company, Bankers Leasing and Financial Corp., had a good track record and was well-respected. However, large financial institutions were moving into Bankers' traditional leasing areas as a result of changes in the tax laws, and it appeared that it would become increasingly difficult for Bankers to remain competitive. We concluded that Bankers would fit better within a financial services company able to provide it with greater financial support. We closed the sale of Bankers to Citicorp on January 15, 1988, at an attractive price.

Previous plans to improve the return from timber operations had succeeded in increasing operating income from these assets to the range of $20 million a year. Cash flow was approximately half that amount. From our analysis it became clear that the sale value of the timber assets was higher than the value we could recognize from continued ownership. On that basis we determined that the sale would be in your best interests, and a definitive agreement for the sale of Santa Fe Pacific Timber Co. to Sierra Pacific Industries was reached in October 1987. We expect to close the sale shortly.

A review of our pipeline assets indicated that our core refined petroleum products systems have good potential for growth and should be retained. Three other pipeline systems appeared mature, based upon our projections. We signed a definitive agreement for the sale of two of those systems to Koch Industries, Inc., in January 1988. One small system is still earmarked for sale.

Review of Railroad Assets

Our analysis of railroad assets was more complex. As we awaited the ICC's decision on reopening the merger case, we investigated alternative strategies in the event the decision was negative. It was important to determine whether to remain in the railroad business with only one railroad. At first glance it might have appeared that the best choice would have been to get out of the railroad business. The Santa Fe Railway is profitable, has an excellent reputation, and probably could have been sold quickly through an initial public offering or distributed to shareholders through a "spin-off." It might also have appeared to anyone not doing a thorough review that liquidating Southern Pacific Transportation Company (SPT) would be the way to get the best value from it, as SPT owns valuable non-operating real estate. A closer look, however, revealed several good reasons for not adopting that strategy.

It is critically important to realize that restructuring of regulated companies must go forward under the scrutiny and review of regulatory bodies, because their approval is essential if any change is to take place. The more we explored SPT's future with the relevant constituencies, including the ICC, U.S. Department of Justice, U.S. Department of Transportation, state regulatory bodies, various railroads, rail labor and shippers, the more we became convinced that it would be difficult to gain the consensus necessary to convince the ICC that breaking up the SPT was in the public interest. There was a widespread view that continuing SPT as an intact, viable transportation company was important, in view of the interests of its shippers and employees. There was also a widely-held opinion that the divestiture should be handled promptly, because of the demoralizing effect that would be involved with more long delay. Even if such a breakup were ultimately possible, it became clear to us that the amount of time and risk involved outweighed any possible increase in the proceeds we might recognize from such a breakup.

It thus became evident that the sale of SPT intact in the range of $1 billion net would be the best alternative for you. In December we completed a binding agreement to sell SPT to Rio Grande Industries for $1.8 billion gross, including $1.02 billion in cash and the assumption of outstanding SPT debt.

We also reviewed The Atchison, Topeka and Santa Fe Railway (ATSF) very closely. We were concerned about its size in relation to competitors such as Union Pacific and Burlington Northern, which is what prompted our efforts to merge the ATSF and SPT originally. We were also concerned about the railroad industry in general, as there is no question that it is a mature industry. On the other hand, results from some railroads suggest that improvement in returns should be possible. There are some very powerful positive factors related to ATSF and its position within the parent company.

Over the last five years the ATSF's rail operations have provided the Company with approximately $10.5 billion of revenue, and about $900 million of operating income. In 1987 it was the single largest contributor to SFSP's operating income, considering its earnings from railroad operations plus its other income of approximately $35 million. Most of that "other" income is shown on the real estate line in our earnings report. ATSF's total contribution was greater than that provided by Santa Fe Pacific Realty Corp., and more than all three of our natural resources companies combined, energy, mining and timber.

As we reviewed ATSF's potential from a competitive standpoint, we recognized that its routes from Chicago to Los Angeles and Northern California provide superior service; it is a well-maintained property; and it has an excellent reputation with shippers for quality service. It is the nation's number one intermodal carrier, and intermodal business is the fastest-growing part of the railroad industry. ATSF serves an area of the nation with a strong economy, with opportunity for growth in volume. After examining these factors, it was evident to us that the potential for improvements in ATSF's operating income dwarfed the gains possible from even the most aggressive efforts feasible in our other operating areas.

For all these reasons keeping the ATSF and trying to improve its results made more sense to your Board of Directors and management than selling both railroads. Appropriate changes designed to improve the ATSF's results are under way, and the positive results are reflected in improved performances in both 1986 and 1987. The railroad has moved aggressively to reduce costs, and is being restructured to make its operations more efficient and effective. Although volume has increased, approximately 3,400 permanent positions have been phased out in the last two years, including 750 non-union personnel. We expect to work closely with labor unions to develop programs that will further increase productivity and improve the ATSF's competitive position.

The financial aspects of the decision to stay in the railroad business and build on the strength of the ATSF were independently confirmed as a valid approach to the Company's future success by two investment banking firms. We are firmly convinced that this decision is prudent and that the course we have set is in your best interest.

Review of Real Estate Operations

As we conducted a very careful review of the Company's considerable real estate holdings, our goal was to develop a strategy that would maximize the value of those holdings. Real estate companies in the development business generally concentrate on cash flow, not earnings. There are often long lead times between the time plans for development are announced, local approvals are received, actual development occurs and, ultimately, the property is sold. It is difficult to predict the length of time required to carry such projects through to the point of sale and, for the most part, earnings are not recognized until that occurs. For that reason, difficulty may arise in having the ultimate value of the real estate reflected in the Company's current stock price.

As we analyzed incremental changes in the value of real estate through these various steps, it became clear that the greatest share of the increase is realized in the process of upgrading the property by achieving zoning changes, installing infrastructure, and securing development agreements, rather than in the construction itself. Ultimately we reached the conclusion that, rather than continuing to enlarge our portfolio of buildings through construction or acquisition, it was more desirable to sell those properties on which the major portion of the incremental increase in value has already been realized, and concentrate on bringing our other properties to that stage. Last Fall we announced that a Real Estate Investment Trust to be comprised of a significant portion of our developed properties was under consideration, but after analysis of recent market conditions with our investment bankers we concluded that an outright sale of these properties would be more advantageous.

We now plan to sell buildings totalling approximately 8 million square feet, including research and development projects, warehouses, office buildings and neighborhood shopping centers. Most of these buildings were constructed over the past four or five years on land owned by the Company, and others were acquired. We also plan to sell 4,500 acres of industrial and commercial land which has been developed to the point where we will realize appropriate values. As previously announced, we have also started disposing of our agricultural holdings in the San Joaquin Valley of California, and expect to complete that process by the end of 1990. The proceeds from the sale of all these real estate assets should approximate $1 billion.

Utilization of Proceeds from Sales of Assets

The proceeds from our various divestitures will be received at different times. As indicated, we have already closed the sales of Robert E. McKee and Bankers Leasing, and we anticipate closing the sale of our pipeline and timber assets shortly. Proceeds from the sale of SPT will not become available until the ICC approves the transaction. The ICC is planning an expedited hearing in this case, which could result in a decision in late summer of this year. Cash from the real estate sales will be received throughout the year.

Combining all these proceeds, we expect to realize about $2.75 billion on a pretax basis, or approximately $2.25 billion after taxes. At that point we will have a focused company concentrating on transportation, including Santa Fe Railway and our refined products pipeline system; natural resources, including petroleum and hard minerals; and real estate at a somewhat reduced level. We believe that this will be a strong, viable company with a good future.

Your Board of Directors and management believe that the best use of those proceeds is to pass them on to the shareholders. The conservative financial policies of the past now provide large unused debt capacity. We believe that borrowing additional funds for use in this distribution is prudent fiscal policy and will permit you to realize on a more current basis the value of the remaining assets in the Company, which we expect to grow over time. For that reason we have entered into an arrangement with a group of banks to borrow $4.05 billion. These borrowings will take the form of a divestiture loan of some $1.9 billion which we expect to repay from the cash we expect to receive from the divestitures and real estate sales described above, a six year loan of $1.9 billion which we expect to repay from cash flow and additional real estate sales, and a revolving credit facility of $250 million for working capital purposes.

Consistent with this program, the focus of the Company will be to concentrate on earnings improvement and increased cash flow in order to pay down the debt. In order to make those payments, we will have to reduce our dividend. It is the Board's present intention to pay a dividend of 10¢ annually, instead of the previous annual return of $1.00. We hope to increase the dividend in future years.

Description of Debentures

The debentures you will receive as part of the distribution will bear interest at the rate of 16 percent. If you elect to retain the debentures, in the first year that will amount to 80¢ paid in kind for each share of common stock you now own. Because of working capital needs, it is expected that interest will be paid in the form of additional debentures rather than cash until 1994, and those additional debentures will also earn interest at the rate of 16 percent. From 1994 to 2003 when the debentures are due all interest will be paid in cash. Application will be made to list the debentures in principal amounts of $1,000 or multiples thereof on the New York Stock Exchange. The Company intends to use its best efforts to cause a trading market to develop in the over-the-counter market for those debentures in principal amounts of less than $1,000.

This Distribution Is Prudent and Treats All Shareholders Equally

Your Board of Directors and management feel confident that this restructuring and dividend distribution are prudent steps to take. The plan represents a balance between short-term and long-term investment goals, as it provides significant up-front value now in the form of a $30 dividend, while allowing shareholders to benefit from continued ownership in what we believe will be a company with good potential for future growth. The plan treats all shareholders equally, both those with major holdings and those with small holdings. Each of you will retain exactly the same proportion of ownership in the Company as you held before the dividend. If you retain the debentures you receive, the 80¢ paid in kind interest in the first year of the debenture plus the expected 10¢ cash dividend will combine to create value that nearly equals the former dividend.

We have covered the basic facts relating to the plan in this letter, but the enclosed information has much more detail (including certain federal income tax

EXHIBIT 3
Santa Fe Southern Pacific Corporation and Subsidiary Companies: Statement of Income Twelve Months Ended December 31 (in Millions of Dollars)

	1988	***1987***	***1986***
Revenues:			
Natural resources	$ 396.6	$ 416.8	$ 326.5
Real estate	429.9	307.8	296.2
Transportation	2,317.1	2,113.7	2,118.6
Total revenues	3,143.6	2,838.3	2,741.3
Operating expenses:			
Natural resources	367.5	335.7	457.0
Real estate	136.4	102.9	93.0
Transportation	2,008.8	1,876.3	1,861.1
Rail restructuring costs	--	--	312.8
Total operating expenses	2,512.7	2,314.9	2,723.9
Operating income	630.9	523.4	17.4
Other income-net	118.1	(11.0)	(7.2)
Interest expense	487.3	72.2	47.4
Income (loss) from continuing operations before income taxes	261.7	440.2	(37.2)
Federal income tax:			
Currently payable	(2.1)	77.7	22.1
Deferred	87.1	77.8	(35.4)
State income tax	30.0	44.8	.3
Total income taxes (benefit)	115.0	200.3	(13.0)
Income (loss) from continuing operations	146.7	239.9	(24.2)
Discontinued operations, net of income taxes	(193.2)	133.6	(113.7)
Net income (loss)	$ (46.5)	$ 373.5	(137.9)
Net income (loss) per share of common stock			
Continuing operations	$ .93	$ 1.52	$ (.15)
Discontinued operations	(1.23)	.85	(.69)
Total	$ (.30)	$ 2.37	$ (.84)
Average number of common and common equivalent shares	157.0	157.9	165.0

consequences of the dividend distribution) and I urge you to read it. We plan to keep you informed as we continue to implement the strategy we have set forth for managing your assets. We appreciate your interest in the Company, and if you have questions please feel free to write or call us as at (312) 786-6210.

Sincerely,

Robert D. Krebs
President and Chief Executive Officer

EXHIBIT 4
Santa Fe Southern Pacific Corporation and Subsidiary Companies: Balance Sheet
Years Ended December 31
(in Millions of Dollars)

	1988	*1987*
Assets		
Current assets:		
Cash and cash equivalents, at cost which approximates market	$ 356.6	$ 59.3
Short term investments	4.9	19.5
Accounts receivable, less allowances	479.4	404.3
Inventories	91.5	105.6
Other	28.5	20.2
Total current assets	960.9	608.9
Net assets of discontinued operations	--	2,058.4
Other assets	647.5	570.4
Properties, plant, and equipment:	7,972.6	8,184.1
Less-accumulated depreciation, depletion and amortization	2,756.7	2,692.2
Net properties	5,215.9	5,491.9
Total assets	$6,824.3	$8,729.6
Liabilities and Stockholders' Equity		
Current liabilities:		
Accounts payable and accrued liabilities	$ 686.6	$ 634.2
Long term debt due within one year	341.7	90.3
Total current liabilities	1,028.3	724.5
Long term debt due after one year	3,405.4	986.7
Other liabilities	203.8	201.3
Deferred income taxes	1,703.9	1,609.2
Stockholders' equity:		
Common stock	190.0	190.0
Paid-in capital	673.3	686.2
Retained income	616.2	5,368.2
Unamortized value of restricted stock	(6.7)	(2.9)
Treasury stock, at cost	(989.9)	(1,033.6)
Total stockholders' equity	482.9	5,207.9
Total liabilities and stockholders' equity	$6,824.3	$8,729.6

CASE 32

Oklahoma Meets Wall Street*

"We're still in business," said spokesman Steve Milburn. He said despite the fact that the company has shut down its famous oil well on the state capital grounds in Oklahoma City, along with its historic Burbank Field wells in Osage county, Phillips still has 8,000 producing wells in the U.S.[1]

Phillips Petroleum was on the ropes. The giant oil company dropped nearly 10,000 people between 1985 and 1987, close to 25 percent of its work force worldwide. Bartlesville, Oklahoma, its affluent, largely white-collar headquarters city of 38,000, was especially hard hit.

"Anyone with the brains God gave a grasshopper is not buying a house in Bartlesville," said one Phillips manager in summer 1986.[2] Two of the only retailers with something to smile about were the local U-Haul and Ryder truck renters, whose volume always goes up "as people pack up to move on. . . . 'If you wanted a truck today, you couldn't get one,'" said Gordon Brown, owner of Bartlesville Auto Supply.[3] Social workers noticed a different kind of increase—in the amount of anxiety and tension among Phillips employees as they saw their job prospects dwindling. Even before the waves of layoffs and early retirements, Jerry Poppenhouse, art director at Phillips, told a reporter, "The mood now is, 'Who's going to be next?'"[4] Another manager and Bartlesville resident added, "Outsiders don't understand that even if you aren't laid off, or your co-workers aren't, you still go to church or scouts or soccer with someone who is."[5]

Phillips Petroleum, the nation's seventeenth largest industrial corporation and eighth biggest oil producer, was cash poor. Deeply in debt, it had to raise vast sums of money very quickly. Asked which of the company's far-flung operations might be for sale in 1985, Chairman and Chief Executive Officer William Douce said, "All of them—and that's no joke."[6] This included oil fields in Africa, Alaska, the Gulf of Mexico, and the North Sea around Holland—where Phillips had been the first to discover oil that helped Europe become less dependent on supplies from the Middle East. All or parts of these were soon

---

* Paul Hirsch, *Pack Your Own Parachute*, © 1987, Addison-Wesley Publishing Co., Inc., Reading, Massachusetts. Pages 1–13. Reprinted with permission.

Note: All unattributed quotes in this case come from interviews arranged and conducted by Dr. Dennis Wheaton, a native of Whizbang, Oklahoma, an abandoned boomtown located fifty miles west of Bartlesville in the Burbank Field of Osage County.

[1] "Wells in the U.S." Tim Hartley, "Conflicting Signals: Phillips Reductions Complete but Home Sales Continue Strong," *Bartlesville Examiner–Enterprise* (8/4/86), p. 2.

[2] "House in Bartlesville." Personal interview (7/86).

[3] "Couldn't Get One." Tim Hartley, op. cit., p. 1.

[4] "To Be Next?" David Clark Scott, "Although Raid at Phillips Is Over, the Company Is the Poorer," *Christian Science Monitor* (3/12/85), p. 21.

[5] "Someone Who Is." In Sallie Turcott, "Phillips Workers Wait for Bad News," *Tulsa World* (4/4/86), p. D-1.

[6] "That's No Joke." John Williams and Charles McCoy, "Phillips, Icahn Set Pact to Halt Takeover Effort," *The Wall Street Journal* (3/5/85), p. 20.

sold, along with coal and geothermal facilities in Texas, Utah, Nevada, and California. In addition to selling off petroleum reserves and other properties, Phillips axed or delayed some big research and exploration projects.

Cutting back its work force and payroll was another policy Phillips adopted to raise cash. Nearly every employee was offered incentives to quit voluntarily before the company moved on to layoffs and terminations. People fifty-five or older were promised a larger pension if they signed up for early retirement immediately. A majority of long-service managers at all levels took the offer. Some were ready and welcomed the opportunity. But others felt rejected, helpless, and all alone.

"Some simply have resigned themselves to resigning," said one. "I mean to retiring without knowing if they would be able to get another job and if they will need one. . . . Many would rather still be working, and not only just for the money."[7] Another recent retiree added:

> The ones I feel sorry for are those still in their middle fifties. Fifty-five is early to retire. There's no other work here right now, though if you want to go to California or New York you can probably start over. But it's not just a matter of getting in your car and going. Say you're a homeowner. If you were transferred the company would take it off your hands. But you're retired now. You have this real estate you can't dispose of. Right now I don't think you can even rent out many of the houses for sale. It's a tough situation.[8]

In spite of these hardships, Phillips employees and Bartlesville residents still considered themselves "lucky." Only seventeen months earlier, Phillips had won a crucial victory for them. It succeeded, against strong odds, in keeping the company independent and in Oklahoma. In an extraordinary four-month period etched in the memory of Bartlesville's small population, corporate raiders T. Boone Pickens and Carl Icahn each attempted to purchase Phillips Petroleum from its shareholders. "How would you feel," asked one Bartlesville citizen, "if Godzilla and Frankenstein both stomped through your town?"[9]

To beat them back, Phillips had repurchased much of its own stock and taken on billions of dollars in new debt to pay for it. Both current and former employees knew why the company had to raise so much cash. They knew their pain stemmed from the bills falling due for this victory. If employment was down here, many said, look at what happened to people at the other companies that tangled with T. Boone Pickens or blew themselves up to avoid him.

"Look at Gulf and its white knight, Chevron," exclaimed one Phillips staffer. "I have a good friend at Chevron. In another year or two they'll be operating both companies with the same number of employees Chevron had when they took Gulf over. That's 50 percent fewer people working than when the two companies were running separately."[10] Before driving Gulf into Chevron's embrace, Pickens had made profitable runs on Cities Service (in neighboring Tulsa), Superior Oil, Supron Energy, and General American Oil (which chose to be acquired by Phillips in 1983, rather than be taken over by Pickens's Mesa

---

[7] "For the Money." Personal interview (7/86).
[8] "A Tough Situation." Personal interview (7/86).
[9] "Through Your Town?" Personal interview (7/86).
[10] "Were Running Separately." Personal interview (10/86).

Petroleum Company). None of these companies exists independently any longer. "The other companies all lost their identities, and we feared that," commented another Phillips veteran. "Everybody's pleased Phillips was able to retain it. We're grateful the company is still intact." [11]

Soon after Phillips repulsed its invaders, one of its computer engineers, A. J. Lafaro, received an unusual request from Los Angeles, home of Unocal ("76") Oil. Pickens had selected Unocal as his next takeover target, and some of its employees remembered a "Boonebuster" T-shirt worn all over Bartlesville during the time Phillips was fighting the same battle. Lafaro had designed it at about the same time that the movie *Ghostbusters* was a big success. He superimposed the international symbol for "No" over a picture of Mr. Pickens, who also purchased some to give as Christmas presents. Unocal employees now wanted them for their impending struggle. Said one Phillips official, "Believe me, if they're going through anything like what we went through, they could use [them]!" [12]

The "Boonebuster" shirt is only one example of the enthusiasm and commitment Bartlesville citizens showed for Phillips during its bitter fights to stay independent. The community was shocked, angered, and scared at the possibility of losing any or all of the company to a corporate takeover. Here was the largest employer in the state brought to its knees, with its fate hinging on maneuvers in far-away boardrooms on Wall Street. "I get the feeling that a bunch of strangers are out there playing Russian roulette with the future of this community—this state, really—and I don't like it," said Josef Derryberry, a jeweler in Bartlesville.[13]

At a crisis forum of 8,000 residents, speakers discussing what the loss of Phillips would mean to the community and nation included the area's school superintendent, the director of the National Institute for Petroleum and Energy Research, the Sears manager at a newly built shopping mall, a former vice president of what had been the Cities Service Oil Company, student officers from the local high school, and the Osage Indian chief on whose nearby land Frank Phillips had originally struck oil. Rudy Taylor, a newspaper publisher in neighboring Caney, Kansas, received a standing ovation when he said:

> Without Phillips, we'd just be Mayberry R.F.D., and with Phillips we have a lot of confidence in our future and we have a world of ideas on how we can improve our little corner of the world. . . . Our chief industry in Caney, Kansas, is Phillips Petroleum Company; it's been that way for over a half century and . . . because of their influence our community is a progressive one. We feel the Phillips influence in our schools, and in our places of business and in our churches and our lodges. . . . We're in this fight with you and we're in it to win. Let's do it! [14]

Looking back on the community's outpouring of support, a Phillips manager later commented:

> Farming and oil are the lifeblood of this part of the country. And farming was already in bad shape. Bartlesville has no other appreciable industry that I am aware of. It's

---

[11] "Is Still Intact." Personal interview (10/86).

[12] "Could Use [Them!]." "Odds & Ends," *The Wall Street Journal* (4/11/85), Section 2, p. 1.

[13] "Don't Like It." "Bartlesville Is Wary," *The New York Times* (2/6/85), p. 29.

[14] "Let's Do It!" *Bartlesville Constitution: Extra* (12/14/84), p. 3.

> pretty much Phillips, and if Phillips goes or starts trimming down, everything turns down. The impact on the community if Phillips were to go is that others would just vanish. Bartlesville would be a ghost town. But as long as there is some nucleus of Phillips here, there will be the Phillips people and there will be these other people from the supporting communities in surrounding areas who will come to Bartlesville.[15]

Christmas in Bartlesville, 1984, turned out to be a happy one. On Christmas eve, just three weeks after Pickens launched his takeover bid, he and Phillips announced a settlement. "We were very pleased Phillips maintained its identity," recalls one retiree, "but at the same time I think people resented Mr. Pickens making the profit he did." [16] In financial terms, Phillips agreed to repurchase the 8.9 million shares in the company Pickens had accumulated, for $10 a share more than they had cost him. This yielded a gross profit of $89 million for Pickens on shares he had held for roughly six weeks. Phillips would also pay Pickens and his group $25 million more to cover expenses they ran up in making their run on the company.

But this was only the beginning. The settlement also required Phillips to present an expensive plan at its next annual meeting designed to raise its shares' value for other investors as well. The company would propose to buy back 38 percent of all its stock. (Pickens had only owned about 6 percent, or less than one-sixth of the additional amount the company agreed to repurchase.) To remove Pickens's takeover threat and satisfy his demands, Phillips had spent $57 million in three weeks and was now committed to borrowing nearly $3 *billion* to cover its proposed stock buyback program.

As the dust settled from one battle and the new year got under way, Phillips next heard from Carl Icahn, perhaps Wall Street's most feared financier and corporate raider. Icahn was buying big blocks of the company's stock and demanding Phillips pay more for the shares it proposed to buy back. He had substantial support from what *New York Times* writer Daniel Cuff called "those cold and distant institutions that own 47 percent of Phillips [stock] and hold the key to its future." [17] On February 5, 1985, Icahn offered to buy Phillips from its shareholders for a higher price. Now in its second battle in two months, there was little doubt at Phillips or in Bartlesville this time about the company's fate if it lost this ownership contest. Pickens at least said he would move to Bartlesville and run the company if he gained control. Financial analyst George Sneed's chilling interpretation of Icahn's intentions made Pickens sound like a long-lost friend:

> Icahn and his backers have no interest in buying Phillips Petroleum Company to operate it. They would liquidate the company if they get control of it. They are trying to force the price up and if they can get Phillips merged or bought out at a higher price, that is what they want. . . . There is an awful lot of stock in the hands of short-term speculators and they absolutely do not care what happens to Bartlesville.[18]

---

[15] "Come to Bartlesville." Personal interview (10/86).

[16] "Profit He Did." Personal interview (10/86).

[17] "To Its Future." Daniel Cuff, "Hometown Fights for Phillips," *The New York Times* (2/11/85), p. D1.

[18] "Happens to Bartlesville." In "Icahn Moves to Block Phillips Plan," *Bartlesville Constitution* (2/6/85), p. 1.

While local residents disliked both corporate raiders, Icahn was generally deemed even less trustworthy and more dangerous than Pickens. Jeweler Josef Derryberry again spoke for many when he said he could not trust Icahn's remarks about his plans for Phillips: "One moment you'll keep Phillips in Bartlesville and the next moment you say you'll sell it to the highest bidder. There's only one business I know of that you can sell and keep it too," he said.[19] Asked to compare people's reactions to Icahn and Pickens, a Phillips manager recalled:

> Pickens wasn't too well liked, but Icahn, well we really had to campaign against him. . . . Pickens was a petroleum man. But Icahn, and there were several with him, had made quite a reputation and a lot of money just moving parts of companies around. They were both looked at in a different way. I think in Bartlesville they both were considered SOB's, but Boone at least was Mr. SOB.[20]

Not everyone agrees. As one retail merchant, whoşe business has still not recovered, sees it, "We put Icahn and Pickens in the same classification. One was an easterner, one a southwesterner. You know, it doesn't make any difference whether you got shit on your boots or wear a bow tie. If you're a corporate raider looking for a quick profit, who cares who he is?"[21]

On March 5, 1985, Phillips assured its independence for the foreseeable future by meeting Icahn's terms. It "sharply improved the terms" of its offer to repurchase much of the company's stock from its shareholders.[22] To pay for it, the company took on more debt. Published estimates of Mr. Icahn's gross profit from his roughly six-week investment in Phillips stock range from $30 million to $75 million. The company also paid an additional $25 million of Icahn's expenses from their takeover fight. These included payments to "a consortium of private and institutional investors, including such active raiders as the Canadian Belzberg family, Saul Steinberg, and the Leucadia National Corporation, [which, for holding aside] $1.5 billion for about two weeks [to loan Icahn if he had needed it], received $5,625,000 in fees and never had to put up a nickel."[23] In return, Phillips got agreements from Carl Icahn and his main Wall Street backer, Drexel Burnham Lambert, Inc., to stop trying to buy the company. Phillips' outlay, for the three months of legal and financial services it bought itself and its raiders, exceeded $200 million. Irwin Jacobs, one of Icahn's best-known allies in the just-finished battle, summed it up very well: "Phillips has bought its independence, and the town of Bartlesville can rest easy tonight."[24]

Once again, Phillips employees and Bartlesville were relieved the company stayed independent and intact. The city had recently been in the news for mailing heart-shaped Valentine's Day cookies with the Phillips 66 shield on them to Icahn and large shareholders during the latest battle. But the mood was less joyful and more subdued than when the

---

[19] "Too,' He Said." Scott Andrews, "Douce: Phillips Has Other Options," *Bartlesville Examiner–Enterprise* (2/28/85), p. 1.

[20] "Was Mr. SOB." Personal interview (7/86).

[21] "Who He Is?" Personal interview (7/86).

[22] "Improved the Terms." Robert J. Cole, "Icahn Ends Offer for Phillips; All Shareholders to Get More," *The New York Times* (3/5/85), p. 1.

[23] "Put Up a Nickel." Moira Johnston, *Takeover: The New Wall Street Warriors.* New York: Arbor House (1986), p. 151.

[24] "Rest Easy Tonight." Robert J. Cole, op. cit., p. D9.

contest with Pickens ended. Now, Bartlesville heaved "a collective sigh of relief. 'Conservative optimism' is how the editor of the local paper describes the mood," reported the *Christian Science Monitor.*[25] A Phillips manager recalls:

> After a while people had just sort of gotten used to it. A little jaded, probably more fatalistic. Yeah, we might be taken over. Another one just showed up with more threats, so they'll fight it out. Much of the outrage and shock was probably used up in the struggle with Pickens. Everyone was still upset, but people just got on with other things as the fights dragged on.[26]

Six weeks after Phillips settled with Icahn, David Oakley, owner of the city's Pontiac-Buick dealership, reported that car sales were improving. "People are convinced now that there is going to be a community, although they're not sure if they're going to have a job," he said.[27]

To remain independent and keep raiders at bay, Phillips had taken a very high stakes gamble. This was that its oil and gas, combined with the sale of assets, would keep generating enough cash to cover payments due on the billions it borrowed to buy back 50 percent of its stock.

In less than a year, the company's debt had tripled from $2.8 to $8.6 billion. Its credit rating had been lowered. Phillips's interest payments for 1985 zoomed to $846 million, more than double its earnings. Company officials, and some oil industry experts, downplayed the seriousness of the situation. Phillips planned to reduce its debt quickly by selling at least $2 billion in assets. "They've got salable stuff coming out their ears . . . [and] could get rid of $2 billion without blinking," said one industry analyst.[28] Company Chairman William Douce acknowledged that "it's a pretty good debt load for a while, but we have a strong cash flow and that's really the name of the game."[29] After leading his company through the two brutal takeover wars, Douce referred to himself as a "born-again debtor."[30] "We can remain strong and vital, no question," he said.[31]

Others were less optimistic about the firm's chances for a quick comeback. "Phillips has mortgaged its future. The price of independence is a mountain of debt," said Sanford Margoshes, senior oil analyst at Shearson/American Express.[32] He believed that "this is a company where some of the glow has been extinguished."[33] Many observers called Phillips's debt, now between 75 and 80 percent of its total capital, "staggering." They predicted management's energy would be absorbed more by cutting debt and expenses than by

---

[25] "Describes the Mood." David Clark Scott, op. cit.

[26] "Fights Dragged On." Personal interview (7/86).

[27] "Have a Job." David Clark Scott, "How Citizens and Businesses Rally Round When a Takeover Threat Strides into Town," *Christian Science Monitor* (4/22/85), p. 14.

[28] "$2 Billion Without Blinking." John Williams and Charles McCoy, "Phillips Is Expected to Retain Its Current Shape Even After Planned Sale of $2 Billion in Assets," *The Wall Street Journal* (3/6/85), p. 2.

[29] "Name of the Game." Daniel Cuff, "Phillips Sees Benefits in Fight; Others Unsure," *The New York Times* (3/6/85), p. D1.

[30] "Born-Again Debtor." Mark Potts, "Phillips Offers Blueprint for Industry Change," *Washington Post* (3/17/85), p. D8.

[31] "Vital, No Question." John Williams and Charles McCoy, op. cit.

[32] "Mountain of Debt." David Clark Scott, op. cit.

[33] "Glow Has Been Extinguished." Daniel Cuff, op. cit.

competing hard for new oil fields and customers. Phillips is "definitely a weaker competitor," said Lawrence Funkhauser, Chevron's vice president for exploration and production.

"They've got a period of four or five years to get back to where they were before Pickens attacked them."[34] Amoco's chief economist, Ted Eck, also commented, "It's hard to see how you could be a superaggressive exploration company when you've got 75 percent debt."[35]

The most critical wild card in Phillips's high-stakes gamble would be the price of oil. The cash flow it needed to pay off its huge debt required a minimum price of $20 per barrel. After the big stock buyback, the *Washington Post* reported:

> About the only thing analysts believe could put Phillips' rebuilding efforts out of kilter would be an unexpected drop in the price of oil. In setting up its restructuring, Phillips has assumed an average oil price for the next few years of about $27 a barrel, and a worst-case scenario of about $20 a barrel.[36]

"If the price of oil goes down, Phillips is going to be in trouble," said oil analyst Fred Leuffer.[37] Another analyst, who asked not to be identified, added, "If oil prices went down to $20 a barrel, Phillips faced financial peril."[38] The experts' consensus tied Phillips's recovery to these magic numbers. If they fell below $20, that would mean lower prices for the assets Phillips needed to sell, and less cash from the sale of its own oil and gasoline. Since the company had to repay its steep loans, no matter what, the missing balance would have to come from elsewhere if oil prices did drop.

Within five months of Phillips's successful fights to stay independent, oil prices started a plunge toward $10 a barrel. The company's strategy of "borrow now, pay later" began to unravel. Its high debt and cash-poor position left it without any of the "rainy day" money companies need to tide themselves over during hard times. Phillips was more vulnerable to falling prices than any other oil company (except Unocal, which had followed Phillips's example by also going into deep debt to fight off another bid by T. Boone Pickens). Two *Wall Street Journal** reports show how precarious the company's financial position became by the summers of 1985 and 1986:

> Bob Crawford raises his voice to be heard over a thumping oil pump he has just lubricated in the Phillips Petroleum Co. oil field here [in Shidler, Oklahoma]. "If oil prices drop farther, Phillips will have to liquidate this field and me with it," he says. For Phillips and several other major oil companies, "the crunch" came mainly from taking on massive increases in debt at a time when oil prices were slumping. The result is a double-edged sword that threatens to seriously reduce both revenue and profit in the industry.

---

[34] "Pickens Attacked Them." In "Shifting Strategies: Surge in Restructuring is Profoundly Altering Much of U.S. Industry" (Special Report), *The Wall Street Journal* (8/12/85), p. 12.

[35] "75 Percent Debt." Mark Potts, "Does Another Oil Shock Lie Ahead?" *Washington Post* (5/5/85), p. F20.

[36] "$20 a Barrel." Mark Potts, "Phillips Offers Blueprint For Industry Change," *Washington Post*, op. cit., p. D1.

[37] "Be in Trouble." David C. Scott, op. cit.

[38] "Faced Financial Peril." Daniel Cuff, "Phillips Sees Benefits in Fight; Others Unsure," op. cit.

> The heavy debt, low-price bug has made no big oil company sicker than Phillips. Just last year, Phillips was weathering the energy slump quite nicely. Its profit rose 12%, and its debt load was one of the lightest around. But the company's bitter takeover battles with Messrs. Pickens and Icahn earlier this year changed all that. To fend them off, Phillips borrowed $4.5 billion, raising its debt-to-equity ratio to a staggering 80%. That's easily the highest among the majors, and analysts are worried, particularly in light of falling prices.
>
> "They're over my danger line," says Kurt Wulff, a Donaldson, Lufkin & Jenrette analyst. . . . Living on the edge is proving painful for the nation's eighth biggest oil company.[39]

> Most energy-related companies have been forced to cut costs sharply because of the oil price plunge, but Unocal and Phillips are in especially difficult positions . . . "they're hanging on with bloody fingers at this point," says [analyst] Alan Edgar. . . .
>
> For its part, Phillips has taken drastic steps in light of lower oil prices. Its work force has been cut by 3,400 employees, to 21,900, since the first of the year.[40]

In Bartlesville, Phillips acknowledged that by summer 1985, it was using up oil reserves faster than it was replacing them. "If we continued that way, it would make us self-liquidating," said Bill Thompson, vice president for planning and development. "It's like having a house that takes four gallons of paint and you've got only three—the house will look like hell."[41] A common feeling managers expressed was that budget reductions were cutting into the bone of their operations. For example:

> Staffing and operations have been cut back to a point where I can no longer function smoothly. This happened just as markets became chaotic because of falling oil prices. So now we are missing business we should be getting because we just can't handle it. And it's not because people are lazy or stupid, people are working very hard at nights and on weekends. I work feverishly all day and then bring a briefcase full of work home and work until 10:30 or so every night, and still can't keep up. If things stay like this, Phillips has a serious problem, because we can't continue as we are.[42]

Referring back to the takeover battles, the same manager says, "We've done the equivalent of somebody who was threatened by a mugger, sitting there slashing your wrist so you scare them off with all the blood. We don't have the strength to go out and lift weights anymore. We've had to pull back our operations and try to conserve cash as much as possible."[43]

Mr. Pickens was not convinced the company's operations had been streamlined far enough. His recommendations in both summer 1985 and 1986 reportedly suggested that

---

[39] "Biggest Oil Company." Laurie Cohen and Johnathan Dahl, "Phillips Is Pressured by Debt, Oil-Pride Slide," *The Wall Street Journal* (8/9/85), p. 6.

[40] "First of the Year." Frederick Rose and Karen Blumenthal, "Heavy Debts Weigh on Unocal, Phillips," *The Wall Street Journal* (7/28/86), p. 6.

[41] "Look Like Hell." Laurie Cohen and Johnathan Dahl, op. cit.

[42] "Continue As We Are." Personal interview (10/86).

[43] "Much as Possible." Personal interview (7/86).

Phillips should continue "slimming the . . . payroll"[44] and "cut their costs and trim exploration budgets before cutting dividends further."[45]

Phillips Petroleum has retained its independence, but the price of victory was very high for the company, its employees, and the people of Bartlesville. Many jobs were lost, and for those remaining the company is a much leaner "home away from home." The takeover battles also left scars on the community at large. One of the city's leading retailers believes the experience "destroyed a part of" its spirit.[46] John Norell, president of a Phillips research subsidiary, wrote in a letter to the U.S. House Energy and Commerce Committee, "There is something fundamentally wrong in America that a $16 billion company who is financially strong and interested in long-range developments for itself, the country, and humanity on one day can then on the next day, after a run on it by Mr. T. Boone Pickens, be reduced to a debt-ridden, short term, and cost-cutting entity."[47]

Oil industry analyst Sanford Margoshes spoke for many when he said, "As a member of the planet I would say one should not be pleased with a proliferation of this type of development."[48]

[44] "Slimming the . . . Payroll." In "Shifting Strategies: Surge in Restructuring . . . ," op. cit.
[45] "Cutting Dividends Further." Frederick Rose and Karen Blumenthal, op. cit.
[46] "Destroyed a Part of." Personal interview (10/86).
[47] "Cutting Entity." David Clark Scott, "How Citizens and Businesses Rally Round When Takeover Threat Strides into Town," op. cit.
[48] "Type of Development." Daniel Cuff, "Phillips Sees Benefits in Fight; Others Unsure," op. cit.

CASE 33

The Fallon McElligott Advertising Agency: Image Making by Image Makers*

In the fall of 1987 Dr. Neala Schleuning, director of the Woman's Center at Mankato State University in Minnesota, attended a statewide conference on marketing higher-education services. One of the most striking sessions she attended was presented by Mr. Charles Anderson of the Duffy Design Group—a part of the highly regarded Fallon McElligott advertising agency.

In just two and a half years after Fallon McElligott was started with a $200,000 personal investment by its partners, the advertising agency was named 1983 Agency of the Year by *Advertising Age.* At the time of the award, the editors of *Advertising Age* noted that, "Messrs. Fallon and McElligott say they want to break the industry norm of compromise, and maintain idealistic standards of arresting, witty advertising that sells the product."[1] Since 1984, the agency has continued to dominate national award shows. By 1987, the company's billings totalled $130 million and major clients included Porsche USA, Lee Jeans, First Tennessee Corp., Continental Illinois National Bank and Trust Company of Chicago, and *The Wall Street Journal.*[2]

A noted woman's magazine described the agency's reputation as being:

> . . . an enviable place for educated, talented, ambitious professionals of both sexes to work. Its staff of 124 consists of 71 women and 53 men. A little over half the managerial and professional positions are filled by women. Women head several departments, two management supervisors are female, and 31 of 37 people promoted to professional positions have been women. From all accounts the company that Fallon and McElligott head appears to be a model of equal employment and tolerant accommodation to individuals' family and flextime needs. In addition the agency cultivated a high community profile by doing pro bono advertising campaigns for a number of organizations—among them the Minnesota Women's Fund and the Children's Defense Fund.[3]

At Mr. Anderson's presentation Dr. Schleuning heard how it "takes balls" to design an aggressive marketing program and how one shouldn't "prostitute" oneself for customers. At one time in the presentation, a slide of an advertisement for the TV show *Dynasty* showed pictures of three actresses with the heading "Bitch, Bitch, Bitch."

Offended by the language and what she considered negative stereotyping of the presentation, Dr. Schleuning wrote a letter to the presenter. Her letter stated:

---

* Prepared by Patricia P. McDougall of Georgia Institute of Technology. Distributed by the North American Case Research Association.

[1] "Agency of the Year: Fallon McElligott Rice," *Advertising Age,* 55:1, March 28, 1984, p. 1.

[2] "Fallon McElligott Loses a Major Client Over 'Stupid' Reply to Sexist Ad Charge," *The Wall Street Journal,* January 14, 1988, p. 10.

[3] "The $10 Million Blunder," *Working Woman,* May 1988, p. 95.

October 29, 1987

Dear Mr. Anderson:

I had the opportunity of sitting in on your presentation at the Minnesota State University System conference on marketing, "Telling Our Story Better."

While I was generally impressed with the creative level and quality of the work of your organization, I would like you to know that I was both annoyed and offended by the persistence of negative stereotypes of women in your AV presentation. I appreciate your personal apologies and discomfort with that material, but it somehow didn't make up for the references to "bitches," "whores," and, in particular, your company's interest in perpetuating what I will forevermore think of as the male gonad style of doing business.

While you may dismiss my complaints as those of a "feminist," I would also like to point out to you the irony that a company which prides itself on new images and creativity must continue, for some strange reason, to perpetuate such base and offensive stereotypes in its promotional literature. It's a shame that you have to resort to such shop-worn ideas to convince us of your creativity.

Sincerely yours,

Neala Schleuning, Ph.D.
Director

Mr. Anderson responded to Dr. Schleuning as follows:

November 6, 1987

Dear Dr. Schleuning:

Thank you for your deeply thoughtful and perceptive letter. All of us here at The Duffy Group feel embarrassed and properly chastened for our behavior. Based on your insightful comments, we are currently re-examining not only our approach to design, but to life as well.

At the same time, Doctor, something else has come to our attention. Something we all find extremely disturbing on many levels.

As the enclosed photo clearly illustrates, the Dinka Tribe of East Africa has a rather barbaric ritual that has apparently been going on for centuries. I know

> you'll find it as deeply troubling as we do, but I pass it along to you believing that you will be able to deal with these people in the same firm, yet even-handed manner in which you dealt with us. Won't you please write them (or better yet, *visit* them), and put an end to this horrible practice, Doctor?
>
> Again, thank you for your letter. We will eagerly await to hear your response to the Dinka problem.
>
> Best regards,
>
> Charles S. Anderson

The 8 × 11 photo which Mr. Anderson enclosed was of a naked East African boy whose mouth appears to be pressed to the anus of a cow. Dr. Schleuning mailed a copy of the correspondence to Gloria Griffin, coordinator of the Minnesota Women's Consortium, with the following comments:

> Thought you would be interested in the attached exchange of correspondence. Women thinking about doing business with advertising agencies might want to take this into account. I would be curious as to whether this is their stock response to criticism about sexist stereotypes.

The Minnesota Women's Consortium has a paid staff of experienced business and political specialists and has over 150 established organizations as members. Many of the state's women professionals, politicians, lobbyists, civic and church leaders, and communications specialists belong, each sharing the organization's concern with women's rights. Upon receiving Dr. Schleuning's letter, Ms. Griffin wrote to the agency's founding partners—Mr. Patrick R. Fallon and Mr. Thomas McElligott.

Question 1: You are Neala Schleuning. What do you think of Charles Anderson's response?

Question 2: You are Patrick Fallon. Should you respond, and if so, how?

CASE 34

ARCO Solar, Inc.*

In early 1988, the top management of Atlantic Richfield (ARCO) had an important decision to make concerning the future of the company's solar energy division. The wholly owned subsidiary, ARCO Solar, Inc., was a world leader in photovoltaic cell production (photovoltaics are semiconductors that produce electricity directly from sunlight), yet in the eleven years since ARCO had purchased the company, it had never shown a profit. ARCO had instituted a restructuring plan in 1985 that called for the company to divest itself of operations not related to its core oil, gas, chemical, and coal businesses; yet, the solar technologies being developed by ARCO Solar seemed finally within a few years of being profitable. In addition, ARCO enjoyed a reputation as a model of good corporate citizenship for continuing to support photovoltaic research and development for so long.

ARCO

Atlantic Richfield was originally incorporated in 1870 as the Atlantic Refining Company and, until the 1960s, was exclusively an oil and gas business. The company was renamed when it merged with the Richfield Oil Corporation in 1966. In 1961, ARCO expanded into the chemical and plastics business, and by 1977 was well established in the coal business. By 1988, ARCO was one of the largest integrated petroleum enterprises in the industry. ARCO subsidiaries conducted oil and gas exploration, production, refining, transportation, and marketing. The chemical, plastics, and coal operations along with the oil and gas businesses constituted the core of ARCO's business.

ARCO had expanded into non-petroleum-oriented businesses with limited success. In 1967, ARCO bought the Nuclear Materials & Equipment Company, a producer of uranium- and plutonium-bearing fuels, which it sold in 1971. ARCO also, at one time or another, owned a newspaper, an air-conditioning company, a plant cell research institute, and a building products operation. All were eventually sold.

The 1970s were a turbulent time for the petroleum industry. The energy crises of 1973–74 and 1979 precipitated a national search for energy alternatives to petroleum. One of the most attractive alternatives was solar energy. It was clean and the supply was not controlled by foreign countries. It was also abundant: the sunlight striking the earth in a year contains about 1,000 times the energy in the fossil fuels extracted in the same period. With gasoline and heating oil prices rising beyond anything the public had experienced before, there was a great deal of enthusiasm for solar power.

The enthusiasm seemed justified. Photovoltaic (PV) cells, which produce electricity directly from sunlight (see appendix), were invented in 1954, and were first used to power U.S. satellites at a cost of over $1,000 per peak watt (a measure of a cell's output at maximum

* Prepared by Mark C. Jankus with the editorial assistance of Dr. Alfred Marcus and Gordon Rands, both of the Curtis L. Carlson School of Management, University of Minnesota.

sunlight). By 1974, the price had dropped to $50 per peak watt; by 1977 it was $17 and was continuing to decline as the cells were improved.

ARCO initiated a study of the potential of the solar energy field in 1972. By 1976, with oil apparently on the way out and solar energy a promising energy source for the future, the company's studies had culminated in a decision to enter the field. ARCO did so in 1977 with the purchase of Solar Technology International, Inc., a tiny Chatsworth, California, operation with eight employees. Solar Technology was renamed ARCO Solar, Inc.

ARCO SOLAR, INC.

Solar Technology International was founded in 1975 by an engineer, J. W. (Bill) Yerkes, with $80,000 he scraped together by mortgaging his home and obtaining loans from relatives. The company produced PV panels that powered microwave repeater stations, corrosion-prevention systems in pipelines, navigational aids, irrigation pumps, electrified livestock fences, and trickle chargers for batteries on boats and recreational vehicles. When Yerkes sold the company to ARCO in 1977 for $300,000, he stayed on as ARCO Solar's first president.

In 1979, the company bought a 90,000-sq.-ft. building in Camarillo, California, north of Los Angeles, and built the world's first fully-automated production line for PV cells and panels. By 1980, the company was the first to produce more than a megawatt of panels in a year. Sales had more than doubled from the previous year.

In order to interest electric utilities in photoelectric power generation, the company decided to construct demonstration projects where PV's potential for supplying large amounts of energy could be proven. Toward that end, the company installed a prototype power generation facility on the Navajo reservation in Arizona and New Mexico in 1981 that was large enough to power 200 homes. The project was judged a success, and the company moved from a largely research mode into a marketing stage.

An even larger demonstration project was conceived, and by the end of 1982 the company had constructed a PV power facility three times larger than the biggest such plant then in existence. The $15 million, one megawatt plant near Hesperia, California, large enough to power 400 homes, was constructed on 200 acres of Southern California high desert 75 miles northwest of Los Angeles, an area with no strong winds that might blow sand on the panels, blocking sunlight and wearing down the mechanisms.

The power at Hesperia was generated by 108 "trackers," double-axis computer-controlled structures that turn to follow the sun. Each tracker had 265 1′ × 4′ 40 watt PV modules, which were in turn made of 35 individual single-crystal silicon cells. The trackers' ability to follow the sun boosted their power output by 40 percent over what a stationary panel could generate. The electricity generated by the plant fed into the Southern California Edison grid and was purchased by the utility.

The plant was constructed in six months from construction start-up to completion in December 1982, a record for a power plant. Even more impressive, the plant was completed under budget, an uncommon occurrence for a new power generating facility.

Encouraged by the success of the Hesperia project, the company began construction of a 16 megawatt plant on the Carissa Plain, near Bakersfield, California. The six megawatt first phase of the project, completed in early 1984, occupied 640 acres and utilized several technical improvements in the PV module and tracker construction that increased each tracker's peak power output by 50 percent, reducing the number of trackers needed. As at Hesperia, a utility bought the power generated by the plant at the avoided cost of generating power from its most expensive fuel, gas or oil. This rate (around 6 cents/kWh) was less than what it cost ARCO Solar to generate the power, but a 37 percent federal and state tax credit for the solar installation brought the cost down enough to justify it as a demonstration of PV's potential.

Meanwhile, in 1983, ARCO Solar took the industry by surprise by announcing that it would begin selling thin-film amorphous silicon products the next year, much earlier than industry analysts had thought possible. "Genesis," a one-square-foot amorphous silicon cell, was the first use of thin-film technology beyond the tiny cells used in calculators and watches. Developed by a 100-person ARCO Solar research team whose existence had been kept secret, the five-watt module had a 6 percent conversion efficiency, a 20-year design life, and sold to distributors for about $45. It generated enough electricity to maintain batteries in recreational vehicles, cars and boats, or to power security systems or other low-power remote applications.

"Genesis" made ARCO Solar the world leader in the race to commercialize thin-film technology. The company's sales doubled again in 1984, and its international network of distributors continued to expand. By 1986, the company was selling 400 Genesis modules per month.

ARCO Solar increasingly turned its attention to thin-film technology. The efficiencies of the thin-film cells steadily improved: by 1985 the company's researchers had a thin-film cell with a record 13.1 percent efficiency, and were predicting 20 percent efficiencies by 1990. Sales volume continued to climb, thanks to the success of the Genesis modules.

In 1986, the company entered into joint ventures with a Japanese company, Showa Shell Sekiyu K.K., and a German firm, Siemens A.G., to manufacture and market ARCO Solar products in the Pacific and Europe. ARCO Solar was by now the largest manufacturer of PV products in the world.

But even though sales continued to climb, the company still had never made a profit. Research and development continued to require a large commitment (35–40 percent of sales revenues), and though ARCO Solar's products had improved greatly, the market for PVs, thanks to the oil glut, was not growing as the company had hoped.

THE PV INDUSTRY

When ARCO entered the industry in 1977, it was only one of a number of oil industry giants investing in the infant industry. Exxon had become involved in 1969, Shell in 1973, Mobil in 1974, and Amoco in 1979. Chevron, Union Oil of California, Occidental Petroleum, Phillips, Sohio, Gulf, Sun, and Texaco were also funding PV research.

All of these oil companies, flush with profits from the rising price of oil, were interested in expanding into new businesses that showed promise. And in the late 1970s, solar energy seemed to be the energy source of the future.

As an energy source, PVs competed directly with the fossil fuels. With oil prices rising and the equivalent price of PV electricity dropping, the new technology's future looked promising. Worldwide sales of PV products rose rapidly, from around $11 million in 1978

EXHIBIT 1
U.S. Photovoltaic Shipments, in Megawatts

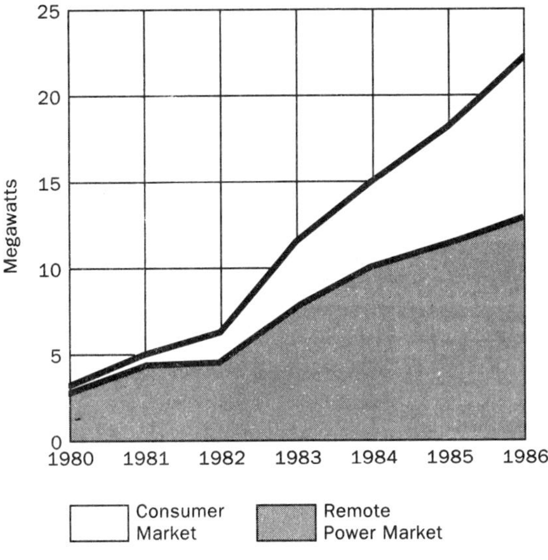

Source: U.S. Dept. of Energy, "National Photovoltaic Program: 1987 Program Review."

to an estimated $150 million in 1983. Industry analysts forecasted a billion-dollar PV industry by 1990 and PV electricity at half the equivalent price of oil. The government's 1976 Project Independence goal of PV electricity at 50 cents per peak watt seemed achievable in the not-too-distant future. See Exhibit 1.

However, things began to sour for the industry in the early 1980s. By 1982, the price of oil had begun to fall (see Exhibit 2). As the nation learned to conserve energy, the demand for electricity fell below projections in many areas, and utilities, not needing new capacity, lost interest in PV demonstration projects. The oil glut that developed as the decade wore on made fossil fuels plentiful once again and renewables like PVs appear unnecessary. The utilities that did need to expand wanted an established, uninterruptible source of power, and were unwilling to invest in an unproven technology.

Another threat to PVs arose in the early 1980s: a severe cutback in the federal government's commitment to solar energy research and development. Ronald Reagan, elected by a landslide and committed to slashing federal non-military spending, cut heavily into the funding that facilitated much of the progress in PV technologies. Federal funding for solar energy (including research, business and residential tax credits, guaranteed loans for solar installations, energy conservation programs, and demonstration programs), which had risen from $2 million in 1972 to $2 billion in 1978, was cut by more than half in 1982 from its 1981 levels. With two exceptions, federal funding continued to drop every year for the rest of the decade (see Exhibit 3). In 1987, the imposition of the Gramm-Rudman deficit reduction cuts in the federal budget reduced the PV research budget to the lowest level ever. The burden of financing solar energy research, of which the government had shouldered 75 percent in 1980, fell increasingly on industry alone.

EXHIBIT 2
World Crude Oil Prices, 1977–1987

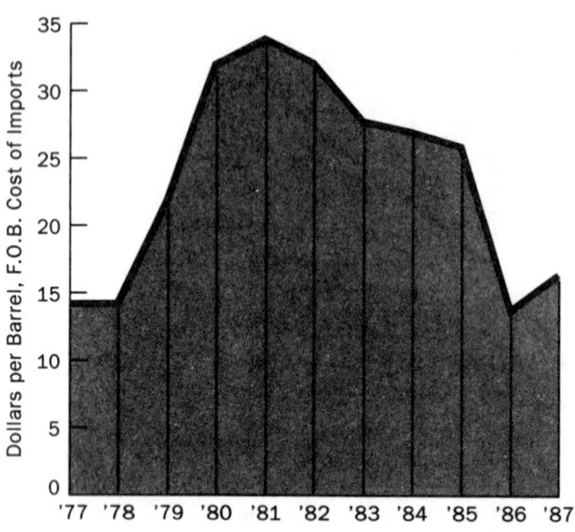

Source: Solar Energy Industries Association.

Besides cuts in research funding, the federal tax credits that encouraged consumers and business to invest in solar technologies expired in 1985. The 40 percent residential tax credit and 15 percent tax credit for industrial, commercial, and agricultural installations had helped the solar industry's sales to rise rapidly. While the commercial tax credits were extended in 1986 after an intensive lobbying effort by the solar energy industry, the residential credits were not renewed when they expired in 1985.

By the mid-1980s, the decline in crude oil prices was forcing the oil industry to slash capital spending and lay off employees. Oil companies which were forced to sell service stations and refineries took a hard look at their portfolios, and some decided to get out of the solar energy business. Exxon's Solar Power Company ceased operations in 1983; Standard Oil wrote-off the $85 million it had invested in a solar energy joint partnership and quit in 1986. By 1988, ARCO and Amoco were the only major U.S. oil companies that still played a significant role in the PV industry.

Foreign competition grew tougher throughout the decade. While U.S. government R&D funding fell throughout the 1980s, this was not true of the funding commitment of some foreign governments. By 1985, the Japanese government was spending 19 percent more on PV R&D than the U.S. government. In 1988, for the first time, both the West German and Japanese governments spent more on PV research than the United States. Their investments seemed to be paying off as well; the U.S. companies' share of the world PV market fell from 80 percent in 1981 to 60 percent in 1983 to about 35 percent in 1987. In 1985, only five of the top 20 PV firms in the world were located in the United States, though ARCO Solar was number one worldwide. At the same time, the market itself seemed to be stagnant. After growing rapidly in the late 1970s and early 1980s, world PV sales stalled at the $125–150 million level in the mid-1980s. With all its promise, solar power still only accounted for 0.1 percent of the electricity generated each year.

EXHIBIT 3
Federal Appropriations for Photovoltaic Research and Development, 1977–1987

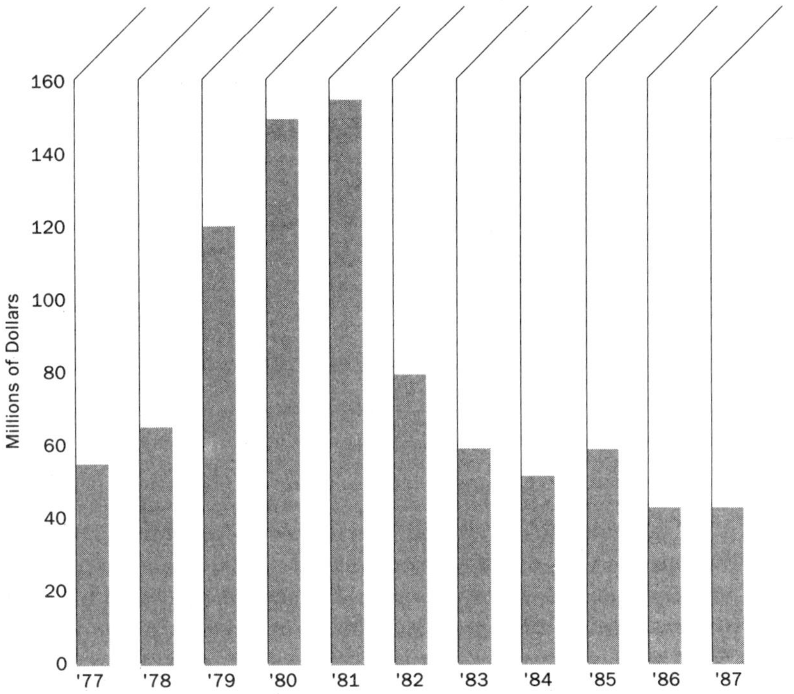

Source: Solar Energy Industries Association information pamphlet, "Fifteen Years in Business With the Sun," 1989.

Competition in the PV Market

As they had in other industries, the Japanese showed their expertise in taking an existing technology and commercializing it. In the late 1970s, most attention in the PV industry was directed toward developing cheaper, more efficient single-crystal cells. These cells had the highest conversion efficiencies of any of the PV technologies, but they were also very expensive.

The Japanese, however, used a new type of cell (amorphous silicon) which was much less efficient than the single-crystal cells (3–5 percent efficiency vs. 15–20+ percent efficiency) but much cheaper to produce. They used amorphous silicon cells to power small consumer electronic products like calculators. By 1985, the Japanese were selling 100 million amorphous-silicon-powered calculators and other small electronic products per year. Their experience in amorphous silicon cell production gave them the early lead in PV manufacturing technology, along with economies of scale and lower production costs. In 1985, the Japanese manufacturers shipped seven megawatts of amorphous silicon, almost all of it in consumer products, compared to 0.5 megawatts by U.S. producers.

The most lucrative market for PVs, though, was utility or grid power generation. In 1987, PVs were economical in grid systems only for what is known in the utility industry as "peaking power": more costly power sources that are only used during peak load periods.

EXHIBIT 4
Cost of a Solar Cell per Peak Watt of Electricity Generated

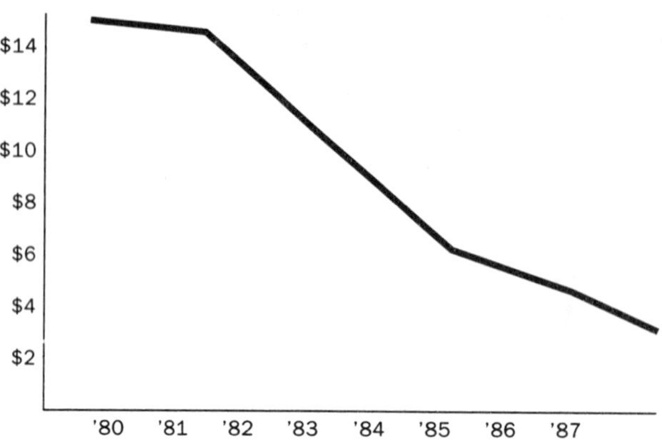

Source: Solar Energy Industries Association.

The other major potential market was in providing power for areas without grid systems. Three-quarters of the world's population do not have grid electricity, yet many people live in areas where sunlight is abundant and intense. Thousands of small solar power systems were already operating in these areas and the potential market seemed huge. The Department of Energy estimated that the potential market was 10 to 20 times the current sales level.

Most of the U.S. producers' attention was directed toward developing a cell that could generate electricity at a price competitive with fossil fuels. The price of PV electricity was falling, but whereas electricity from coal cost about 4–8 cents per kilowatt-hour (kWh) and

EXHIBIT 5
Efficiencies of Experimental Amorphous Silicon Cells

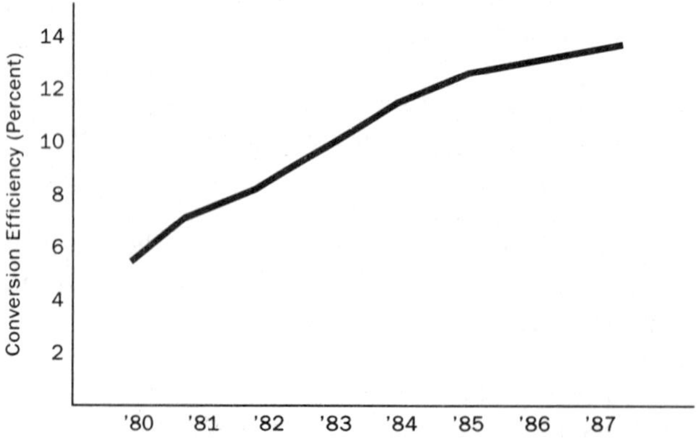

Source: National Photovoltaics Program 1987 Review, U.S. Dept. of Energy.

EXHIBIT 6
Estimates of PV Module Selling Prices Required to Meet Different Levelized Costs of Electricity for Central Station PV Plants*

Required PV Module Price of Modules (Cents/kWh)	*Required Selling Efficiency*	*Levelized Cost Price Modules ($/Peak Watt)†*
6	10	0
6	15	0.30
6	20	0.39
9	10	0.51
9	15	0.69
9	20	0.81
12	10	0.90
12	15	1.09
12	20	1.29

* Based on fixed, flat-plate PV array.
† This represents the price for a PV module at which a generator of electricity would be indifferent between PV-generated electricity and other sources of electricity. For example, at a levelized cost of electricity of 6 cents/kWh, an electric utility would not be interested in 10% efficient PV modules at any price. However, assuming the same levelized price of electricity, the utility would be willing to pay up to $0.30/peak watt hour for 15% efficient panels.
Source: Carlson, David E. (1989). Low cost power from thin-film photovoltaics. In T. B. Johansson (Ed.), *Electricity: Efficient end-use and new generation techologies and their planning implications*. Washington, DC: American Council for an Energy Efficient Economy.

oil or natural gas 5–10 cents/kWh, PV electricity cost about 25–30 cents/kWh. (See Exhibits 4, 5, and 6.)

By the mid-1980s, "thin-film" technologies, like amorphous silicon, seemed to hold the most promise. These technologies, which used a fraction of the material required to produce single-crystal cells and less labor, were continually being refined to yield more and more efficient cells. By 1986, thin-film technologies had been developed to the point where they seemed to be within a few years of reaching 7–8 cents/kWh that would make PVs competitive with fossil fuels and nuclear power.

Besides the emergence of thin-film technologies, there was another reason for optimism. By 1988, the search for new energy sources began to regain the momentum it had in the 1970s, though for a different reason. The threat posed by global warming was beginning to draw attention. Experts warned that consumption of fossil fuels had to be reduced significantly to address the problem. The Three Mile Island and Chernobyl nuclear accidents had severely damaged the nuclear power industry's credibility and chances for a large role in the future of electricity generation. Hydroelectric power, while clean and safe, had limited expansion potential. Solar energy's potential was once again becoming apparent.

ARCO Solar, Inc., in 1988

By 1988, ARCO Solar was the undisputed world leader in the PV industry, with 20 percent of the $150 million market. The company was leaner than it had been, with 350 employees, half the number it had in 1983, and the sales forecasts were optimistic; the company had a growing backlog of orders. The company's research labs had made advances in a new type of thin-film material, copper indium diselenide (CIS), which promised non-degradability and had even better efficiencies than amorphous silicon. The company was four to five years ahead of the competition in CIS technology, and a line of CIS cells was planned.

Though ARCO Solar was the world's leading producer of PV cells, it still had never made a profit. Its $30 million in revenue was matched every 15 hours by its parent company. Analysts estimated the company lost $15 million annually. Though ARCO Solar's president was confident the company could stand on its own feet within two or three years, some analysts believed that the $200 million ARCO had invested in its solar subsidiary had hurt the parent company's standing.

Other criticisms began to surface in the press. J. W. Yerkes, the founder and first president of the company, told the *Los Angeles Times* that, "the company was screwed up two years after [ARCO] bought it. We went from making cells for $10 a watt and selling them for $15 to making cells for $32 a watt and selling them for $5."[1] Other former employees cited other examples of instability: the company's headquarters had shifted five times, and six men had been president in twelve years (three presidents in the first three years alone). One former employee recalled how a colleague had more than a dozen different job titles during this tenure.

What Should ARCO Do?

Meanwhile, in 1985, ARCO had undergone a restructuring that signaled a shift in corporate strategy. Anticipating continued low oil prices, the company cut costs by $500 million, repurchased 24 percent of its outstanding common stock, and wrote off $1.5 billion for losses on the sale of assets and expenses due to personnel reductions. The Chairman of the Board retired and the CEO stepped down.

On the other hand, the new CIS thin-film technology showed promise of being the basis of a line of PV cells that would be truly competitive with fossil fuels for utility-scale power generation in the next few years. Given the rising concern over global warming, an economically competitive PV cell for large-scale power generation could be a bonanza.

Finally, ARCO enjoyed a reputation as a socially responsible corporation for continuing to support its solar subsidiary when so many oil companies had dropped out of the solar energy field. Whereas in the late 1970s critics had claimed that the oil companies were buying up the solar technology in order to suppress it, it was generally acknowledged now that "Big Oil," with its deep pockets, was good for the PV industry. ARCO was a hero of sorts in the renewable-energy community.

Should ARCO sell ARCO Solar? Top management had a difficult decision to make.

Appendix to Case 34

How Photovoltaic Cells Work

A photovoltaic cell produces electricity directly from sunlight. When the sunlight strikes the surface of the semiconductor material of which the cell is made, it energizes some of the semiconductor's electrons enough to break them loose. The loose electrons are channeled

[1] *Los Angeles Times,* March 7, 1989, p. IV-11.

through a metallic grid on the cell's surface to junctions where they are combined with electrons from other cells to form an electric current.

Different semiconductor materials' electrons are broken loose by different wavelengths of light, and some wavelengths of sunlight reach the earth's surface with more intensity than others. Consequently, much of the effort of photovoltaic research has been to find semiconductor materials that are energized by the light wavelengths that are most intense and thus have the potential to provide the most energy.

Single-crystal silicon cells were the first type widely used, powering satellite radios as early as 1958. These cells are energized by some of the most intense sunlight wavelengths, and have achieved conversion efficiencies (percentage of light energy converted to electricity) over 20 percent. Other, non-silicon, single-crystal cells have achieved efficiencies over 27 percent.

While efficient, these single-crystal cells are also expensive to produce and the crystals are difficult to grow. Much of the crystal is wasted when it is sawed into pieces for individual photovoltaic cells. Because they cost so much, their use has been limited mainly to applications where electricity is necessary and there are no other alternatives, such as in the space program.

In order to reduce production costs, researchers began to search for ways to fabricate silicon into cells that did not require the expensive and wasteful single-crystal techniques. One result of their efforts are *polycrystalline silicon cells,* which sacrifice some efficiency in return for cheaper manufacturing methods. The most efficient polycrystalline cells to date achieve better than 15 percent efficiencies. Together, single-crystal and polycrystalline cells account for two-thirds of those sold.

Perhaps the most promising PV technologies are the "thin-film" techniques, in which cells as large as four square feet—as opposed to crystalline cells which are in the neighborhood of ¼ inch in diameter—are produced by depositing a film of PV material less than one-hundredth the thickness of a crystalline cell on a suitable base, or substrate. These cells are only about half as efficient as single-crystal cells, but because they can be produced for about one-fourth the cost or less, they offer the greatest potential for large-scale use.

Thin-film silicon cells (called *amorphous silicon*) accounted for 37 percent of the world market for photovoltaics in 1987. One drawback to amorphous silicon cells, however, is that they typically lose about one-sixth of their power output in the first few months of use. There are other thin-film materials that do not suffer from this light-induced degradation. Two of the most promising are copper indium diselenide (CIS) and cadmium telluride (CdTe).

The world leader in CIS technology is ARCO Solar. The company has developed a four-square-foot CIS cell with a 9 percent conversion efficiency, demonstrating that large-scale applications of thin-film technology are feasible.

A Texas company, Photon Energy, Inc., has developed an inexpensive, simple process for applying CdTe to panels as large as ARCO's, achieving 7 percent efficiency. The company has managed better than 12 percent efficiencies in the laboratory and expects to do even better in the near future.

Besides improving conversion efficiencies by developing new photovoltaic compounds, researchers have been breaking efficiency records by "stacking" cells. These "mechanically stacked multijunction" (MSMJ) cells are actually two cells pasted together. The top cell extracts the energy from one part of the light spectrum, and the lower cell uses the energy from a different part. A MSMJ cell composed of a single-crystal gallium arsenide cell and a single-crystal silicon cell achieved a better than 30 percent efficiency last year, and researchers believe that a three-layer cell with a 38 percent efficiency is possible. Efficiency improvements via stacking of more economical thin-film cells are also being investigated.

The continuing improvements in conversion efficiencies are especially remarkable considering that as recently as 1982, theoretical physicists believed that the maximum achievable efficiency of a solar cell was 22 percent. The highest efficiency achieved at that point was 16 percent. Now, theoreticians estimate that 38–40 percent is the limit, although the physics of thin-film technology is not completely understood.

Other Sun-Powered Energy Sources

Photovoltaics are not the only way of utilizing the sun's energy. In fact, PVs are not even the major producer of electricity from sunlight. That distinction belongs to solar thermal technologies. Solar thermal systems work by using the heating rays of the sun to warm air, water, or oil for space heating or thermal power generation. Luz International of Los Angeles is the world's largest producer of solar thermal electric plants. The company's seven plants in California's Mojave Desert produce 90 percent of all solar-generated power in the world. Company officials estimate that solar thermal plants occupying just 1 percent of the Mojave could supply all of Southern California Edison's peak power requirements. Solar thermal facilities, which on sunny days can achieve conversion efficiencies twice that of some PVs, generate power at a cost equal to late-generation nuclear plants, and the cost is dropping.

Biomass technologies focus on developing quick-growing plants that can be burned to extract the solar energy the plants store. A promising biomass technique involves growing certain types of algae in shallow ponds located in the desert. The algae produce an oil which can be extracted and used as fuel.

Ninety percent of the wind-generated electricity in the United States is produced by wind turbines located in three mountain passes in California. These three passes have been credited with having 80 percent of the world's usable wind supply, though experts estimate that under the right conditions, wind power could generate up to 5 percent of the nation's electricity. The California turbines accounted for 1 percent of California's electrical production in 1989. Production of new wind-powered facilities has been sluggish since tax credits for such construction ended in 1985, and also because at current prices, wind power is not quite competitive with fossil fuels.

Hydro power, which is the cheapest power source, is the largest generator of electricity among the renewables. It has limited potential for further expansion, though, since all the most convenient rivers have already been dammed.

Altogether, renewables (hydro, wind, solar, biomass, and geothermal) account for about 9 percent of the electric power generated in the United States.

EXHIBIT 7

Atlantic Richfield: Consolidated Statement of Income and Retained Earnings (in Millions of Dollars, Except per Share Amounts)

	1987	*1986*	*1985*
Revenues:			
Sales and other operating revenues, including excise taxes	$16,829	$14,993	$22,492
Interest	308	283	176
Other revenues	471	498	412
Total revenues	17,608	15,774	23,080
Expenses:			
Costs and other operating expenses	10,760	9,495	14,770
Selling, general, and administrative expenses	1,107	1,223	1,295
Taxes other than excise and income taxes	702	629	1,114
Excise taxes	547	506	769
Depreciation, depletion, and amortization	1,661	1,646	1,762
Interest	985	972	622
Unusual items	0	0	2,303
Total expenses	15,762	14,471	22,635
Income from continuing operations before gain on issuance of stock by subsidiary	1,846	1,303	445
Gain from issuance of stock by subsidiary	322	0	0
Income before income taxes, minority interest, and discontinued operations	2,168	1,303	445
Provision for taxes on income	932	688	112
Minority interest in earnings of subsidiary	12	0	0
Income from continuing operations	1,224	615	333
Discontinued operations, net of income taxes:			
Loss from operations	0	0	(21)
Loss on disposal	0	0	(514)
Net income (loss)	1,224	615	(202)
Earned per share:			
Continuing operations	6.68	3.38	1.55
Net income (loss)	6.68	3.38	(0.97)
Retained earnings:			
Balance, January 1	6,173	6,264	8,782
Net income (loss)	1,224	615	(202)
Cash dividends:			
Preference stocks	(4)	(5)	(8)
Common stock	(710)	(701)	(766)
Cancellation of treasury stock	0	0	(1,542)
Balance, December 31	$ 6,683	$ 6,173	$ 6,264

EXHIBIT 8
Atlantic Richfield: Consolidated Balance Sheet
Years Ended December 31
(in Millions of Dollars)

	1987	1986
Assets		
Current assets:		
Cash	$ 174	$ 122
Short-term investments	3,761	2,275
Marketable equity securities	758	0
Accounts receivable	709	348
Notes receivable	57	246
Refundable income taxes	0	764
Inventories	801	779
Prepaid expenses and other current assets	204	209
Total current assets	6,464	4,743
Investments and long-term receivables:		
Affiliated companies accounted for on the equity method	898	920
Other investments and long-term receivables	289	338
	1,187	1,258
Fixed assets:		
Property, plant, and equipment, including capitalized leases	26,663	26,175
Less accumulated depreciation, depletion, and amortization	12,258	11,325
	14,405	14,850
Deferred charges and other assets	614	753
Total assets	$22,670	$21,604
Liabilities and Stockholders' Equity		
Current liabilities:		
Notes payable	$ 1,373	$ 872
Amounts payable for securities purchased	626	0
Accounts payable	1,147	957
Taxes payable, including excise taxes	243	225
Long-term debt and other obligations due within one year	422	874
Accrued interest	229	356
Other	427	466
Total current liabilities	4,467	3,750
Long-term debt	6,028	6,661
Capital lease obligations	286	307
Deferred income taxes	3,641	3,562
Other deferred liabilities and credits	2,154	2,065
Minority interest	216	0
Stockholders' equity:		
Preference stocks	2	2
Common stock ($2.50 par value: shares issued—1987: 217,484,404; 1986: 217,279,037; shares outstanding—1987: 177,686,928; 1986: 177,510,339)	544	543
Capital in excess of par value of stock	1,034	1,073
Retained earnings	6,683	6,173
Treasury stock, at cost	(2,438)	(2,445)
Foreign currency translation	53	(87)
Total stockholders' equity	5,878	5,259
Total liabilities and stockholders' equity	$22,670	$21,604

CASE 35

Arthur D. Little, Inc., and the Toxic Alert*

> We who are associated with Arthur D. Little, Inc., are indeed fortunate in that, in the course of serving our personal, professional, and corporate interests, we serve society as well. Our central function, that of bridging the gap between the development of new knowledge and its practical application by business and government, has never been more important. We do this by developing new products and processes based on emerging technologies, like genetic engineering or artificial intelligence, and other consulting assignments; we also transfer know-how to developing economies through the ADL Management Education Institute programs. In pursuing our professional work for our clients, the relationship of our activities to the societies in which we operate is a matter of daily, overriding concern. (John Magee, President, 1984)

Arthur D. Little, Inc. (ADL), an internationally known consulting firm, was founded in Boston in 1886 and moved to neighboring Cambridge in 1917, a year after MIT made the same move. The company thus became the first research-oriented commercial organization in a city which later would be home to hundreds of high-tech firms. By 1984 ADL employed over 2,600 people and had offices in 14 countries. Sales volume for 1984 exceeded $200 million.

More than 1,400 ADL employees worked in the extensive network of laboratories and office buildings at Acorn Park, the company's 40-acre headquarters campus in North Cambridge. The research, engineering, and management consulting services offered by ADL involved disciplines ranging from strategic management to hazardous waste management to forensic economics. Thirty-seven corporate vice presidents served as "professional services officers," in charge of various technical specialties. Twenty-nine more vice presidents and senior vice presidents oversaw geographic offices or administrative functions. Ten independently-organized "complementary business units," each with its own president and staff, offered a wide range of services such as systems management, opinion research, and property valuation. Five of these units were headquartered at Acorn Park; two more were located in nearby Lowell.

Arthur D. Little had experienced consistent growth in revenues for the past decade, from $81 million in sales in 1975 to $213 million in 1984. Net income had grown from $3.1 million in 1975 to $6.1 million in 1983, but fell to $3.6 million in 1984. Disappointing results in three of the complementary business units accounted for the drop, according to the 1984 annual report. (See Exhibit 1 for a 10-year summary of the firm's financial highlights. Exhibits 2 and 3 summarize 1984 financial results.)

Until 1969, ADL was wholly owned by the Memorial Drive Trust, a deferred compensation profit-sharing plan whose beneficiaries were past and present employees of the firm. Thirty percent of ADL's stock was sold to the public in 1969, but two-thirds of that

---

* Prepared by John A. Seeger, Bentley College. Distributed by the North American Case Research Association.

EXHIBIT 1

Arthur D. Little, Inc.: Ten-Year Summary of Financial Highlights (Dollars and Shares in Thousands, Except per Share Data)

	Operating Results for the Year									
	1984	***1983***	***1982***	***1981***	***1980***	***1979***	***1978***	***1977***	***1976***	***1975***
New contracts, net	$174,420	$158,268	$132,972	$144,755	$136,911	$116,063	$129,963	$ 96,566	$75,777	$67,353
Index	259	235	197	215	203	172	193	143	113	100
Professional service income, net	$161,097	$147,580	$141,174	$137,119	$127,463	116,099	$ 99,098	$ 87,585	$70,908	$64,621
Index	249	228	218	212	197	180	153	136	110	100
Royalties and venture income	$ 1,421	$ 1,619	$ 1,344	$ 3,104	$ 3,434	$ 2,340	$ 1,772	$ 3,113	$ 2,038	$ 1,595
Index	89	102	84	195	215	147	111	195	128	100
Revenues	$213,363	$192,478	$181,398	$175,600	$163,215	$141,036	$120,879	$106,619	$86,221	$80,827
Index	264	238	224	217	202	174	150	132	107	100
Salaries, wages, and other employment costs	$112,999	$102,598	$ 97,483	$ 94,298	$ 86,900	$ 79,922	$67,419	$60,189	$49,753	$45,016
Index	251	228	217	209	193	178	150	134	111	100
Income from operations	$ 9,063	$ 10,724	$ 11,086	$ 12,651	$ 10,826	$ 11,080	$ 10,344	$ 11,082	$ 6,529	$ 6,080
Index	149	176	182	208	178	182	170	182	107	100
Income before taxes on income	$ 7,456	$ 11,088	$ 10,496	$ 12,800	$ 10,975	$ 10,984	$ 10,545	$ 10,834	$ 6,971	$ 6,257
Index	119	177	168	205	175	176	169	173	111	100
Net income	$ 3,611	$ 6,070	$ 5,510	$ 6,740	$ 5,793	$ 5,777	$ 5,300	$ 5,578	$ 3,574	$ 3,142
Index	115	193	175	215	184	184	169	178	114	100
Cash flow from operations	$ 8,728	$ 10,988	$ 9,976	$ 10,257	$ 8,832	$ 8,388	$ 7,460	$ 7,226	$ 4,628	$ 4,217
Index	207	261	237	243	209	199	177	171	110	100
Revenues per share	$ 84.47	$ 76.57	$ 72.17	$ 69.86	$ 64.93	$ 56.11	$ 48.09	$ 42.42	$ 34.30	$ 31.91
Income before taxes on income per share	$ 2.95	$ 4.41	$ 4.18	$ 5.09	$ 4.37	$ 4.37	$ 4.20	$ 4.31	$ 2.77	$ 2.47
Earnings per share	$ 1.43	$ 2.41	$ 2.19	$ 2.68	$ 2.30	$ 2.30	$ 2.11	$ 2.22	$ 1.42	$ 1.24
Dividends declared per share	$ .70	$ .70	$ .70	$ .60	$ .50	$ .48½	$ .44	$ .37	$ .23	$ .17

Financial Position at Year End										
Cash and cash equivalents	$ 10,301	$ 14,337	$ 8,380	$ 14,554	$ 12,550	$ 11,841	$ 12,912	$ 17,622	$11,945	$ 4,993
Index	206	287	168	291	251	237	259	353	239	100
Accounts receivable and unbilled services	$ 56,209	$ 49,707	$ 45,414	$ 38,487	$ 36,823	$ 31,328	$ 27,633	$ 24,589	$20,448	$22,744
Index	247	219	200	169	162	138	121	108	90	100
Working capital	$ 27,761	$ 28,001	$ 24,906	$ 24,226	$ 24,353	$ 21,677	$ 19,521	$ 22,888	$19,077	$17,237
Index	161	162	144	141	141	126	113	133	111	100
Total assets	$107,520	$102,575	$ 91,442	$ 87,142	$ 79,333	$ 71,321	$ 65,860	$ 60,119	$49,904	$37,784
Index	285	271	242	231	210	189	174	159	132	100
Long-term debt and capital lease obligations	$ 3,617	$ 3,488	$ 3,830	$ 4,212	$ 4,624	$ 4,972	$ 5,212	$ 6,952	$ 7,944	$ 1,220
Index	296	286	314	345	379	408	427	570	651	100
Stockholders' equity	$ 61,197	$ 5,865	$ 54,555	$ 50,805	$ 45,573	$ 41,037	$ 36,479	$ 32,291	$27,634	$24,647
Stockholders' equity per share	$ 24.16	$ 23.42	$ 21.70	$ 20.21	$ 18.13	$ 16.33	$ 14.51	$ 12.85	$ 10.99	$ 9.81
Other Data										
Return on average stockholders' equity	6.0%	10.7%	10.5%	14.0%	13.4%	14.9%	15.4%	18.6%	13.7%	13.4%
Net income as percent of revenue	1.7%	3.2%	3.0%	3.8%	3.6%	4.1%	4.4%	5.2%	4.1%	3.9%
Average number of shares outstanding	2,526	2,514	2,514	2,514	2,514	2,514	2,514	2,514	2,514	2,534
Number of employees at year end	2,606	2,424	2,330	2,340	2,394	2,529	2,308	2,078	1,821	1,798
Index	145	135	130	130	133	141	128	116	101	100

EXHIBIT 2
Arthur D. Little, Inc.: Consolidated Balance Sheets at December 31 (Dollar Amounts in Thousands)

	1984	1983	1982
	Assets		
Cash and cash equivalents	$ 10,301	$ 14,337	$ 8,380
Receivables and unbilled services	56,209	49,707	45,414
Prepaid and other current assets	3,957	4,179	4,169
Total current assets	70,467	68,223	57,963
Land	2,301	2,241	2,241
Buildings and leasehold improvements	33,002	30,591	29,428
Equipment, furniture, and fixtures	31,447	27,498	23,369
Less accumulated depreciation	(33,840)	(28,834)	(24,442)
Total net fixed assets	32,910	31,496	30,596
Investments and other assets	4,143	2,856	2,883
Total assets	$107,520	$102,575	$91,442
	Liabilities and Equity		
Accounts payable	$ 4,145	$ 6,446	$ 4,304
Accrued expenses	24,850	19,835	16,350
Accrued income taxes	3,398	4,471	2,860
Advance payments from clients	10,313	9,470	9,543
Total current liabilities	42,706	40,222	33,057
Long-term debt	1,487	1,199	1,394
Capital lease obligations	2,130	2,289	2,436
Total liabilities	46,323	43,710	36,887
Common stock and paid-in capital	4,908	4,427	4,427
Retained earnings	56,289	54,438	50,128
Total stockholders' equity	61,197	58,865	54,555
Total liabilities and equity	$107,520	$102,575	$91,442

had been reacquired by individual employees or by the Employee Investment Plan. In 1985 about 10 percent of ADL's stock was held by the public, while 78 percent was controlled by the trustees of the Trust and the Plan. The company had contributed to these plans (and charged to operations) about $9 million in each of the past three years.

CONSULTING OPERATIONS

ADL dealt with an average of 1,000 clients and undertook about 4,000 to 5,000 individual assignments annually, according to Senior Vice President and General Manager of Profes-

EXHIBIT 3
Arthur D. Little, Inc.: Consolidated Income Statements
Years Ended December 31
(Dollar Amounts in Thousands)

	1984	1983	1982
Revenues	$213,363	$192,478	$181,398
Employment costs	112,999	102,598	97,483
Other operating expenses	40,456	35,877	33,949
Client reimbursable costs	50,845	43,279	38,880
	204,300	181,754	170,312
Income from operations	9,063	10,724	11,086
Income from short-term investments	884	1,038	1,902
Other income (charges)	(2,491)	(674)	(2,492)
Income before taxes	7,456	11,088	10,496
Provision for income taxes	3,845	5,018	4,986
Net income	$ 3,611	$ 6,070	$ 5,510

sional Operations Alfred E. Wechsler. Some three-quarters of ADL's clients were repeat customers.

New projects and activities at ADL went through a formal acceptance procedure, usually beginning with a prospective client contacting a professional staff member, who would draft a proposal for the work. The proposal was submitted to a 10-member management group composed of five permanent members of the senior staff and five junior ADL professionals who rotated every three months. The management group met every morning to evaluate all potential assignments according to a four-question formula.

The four questions, said Wechsler, were:

- Is the work something that ADL would be happy to do?
- Will the work create a conflict of interest with other work ADL is doing?
- Can the client pay the bill?
- Does ADL have the staff on hand to do the job?

Upon acceptance of the project, a budget was established and an ADL professional was given the task of assembling a team to do the job, drawing from whatever disciplines were needed. The team leader did not have to get approval from department managers for the use of their people.

A 10-year graph in ADL's 1983 annual report showed billings to U.S. federal government sponsored projects ranging between $25 million and $27 million per year from 1979 to 1983, while U.S. state and local government revenues were $10 million to $13 million per year. No similar graph was included in the 1984 annual report, but tabulated results showed federal billings rose by $3.2 million in 1984, while state and local government business dropped by $3 million.

COMPANY POLICIES

The founder of ADL, Dr. Arthur Dehon Little, was deeply committed to the idea that science and technology were the keys to progress. He felt that positive thinking and a "can-do" attitude could successfully apply new ideas to the problems of industry and government. In 1921, the thirty-fifth anniversary of ADL's founding, Dr. Little found a symbolic representation of his credo and a lasting beacon for his firm: he decided not only that it *should* be possible to make a "silk purse from a sow's ear," but that his people *would* do it. Starting with 1,000 ears, his staff boiled up a gelatinous goo, spun a thread from it, and produced a purse which is now on display at the Smithsonian Institution.

The same sense of irreverence for dogma was shown again fifty-six years later, when the firm set out to debunk another platitude of impossibility, the old cliché, "It went over like a lead balloon." Anthony Baldo, writing in the *Cambridge Chronicle,* reported, "for ADL staffers, this provided a weighty challenge . . . in fact, three very differently designed lead balloons were created. Curiously, the winning entry was so buoyant that it tore away from where it was tied. 'It was last seen going over the Atlantic,' said Alma Triner, ADL's Vice President for Public Relations."

ADL attempted to provide its staff with an intellectual climate to encourage free thinking as well as bottom line results, wrote Baldo. Staff members were not required to work on a specific quota of projects. Staff members set their own goals. Nobody was required to work on a project found personally objectionable. No dress code existed, and personnel were free to decorate their offices any way they liked. "I think we have a lot of respect for each other as individuals," the *Chronicle* quoted ADL President John F. Magee. "We have a respect for individual tastes and idiosyncracies."

"Humor, too, has a place within ADL's corporate structure," continued the *Chronicle.* "It starts at the top with the firm's chairman of the board, Robert K. Mueller, who has written a book called 'Behind the Boardroom Door.' While the book is about corporate rivalries and politics, Mueller, according to an ADL release, mostly concludes that 'too few businessmen, and hardly any directors, have the ability to laugh at themselves.' "

At the corporate level, a set of governing policies reinforced the firm's fundamental regard for people and the communities within which it operated. For example, ADL supported the "Sullivan Principles" [1] and conducted evaluations of the equal rights provisions of those principles for corporations maintaining offices in South Africa. As a corporate policy, ADL donated 2.5 percent of its pretax income to projects and institutions "designed to improve the quality of life in our communities throughout the world." Corporate policy also prohibited development work on weapons systems.

Additionally, company-paid staff time was contributed to a variety of public interest programs, and staff members were encouraged to contribute their own personal time to education, social programs, and political service. Senior Vice President D. Reid Weedon,

[1] In 1978, the Reverend Leon Sullivan proposed a list of voluntary guidelines which have become the accepted standard of ethical and moral behavior for American employers in South Africa. These principles seek improvement in the economic, educational, and social life of South African workers, through full integration, equal benefits, fair and equal pay at the workplace, and through employee assistance outside of work as well.

Jr., was a prime example of the kind of community involvement found in the ADL staff; he served as a Life Member of the M.I.T. Corporation, a Life Trustee of the Boston Museum of Science, and Board Chairman of the Winchester Hospital.

The company also carefully preserved its links with the university community. In 1984, the presidents of M.I.T., Smith College, and the Woods Hole Oceanographic Institution—Paul E. Gray, Jill Ker Conway, and Paul M. Frye—were members of the Arthur D. Little Board of Directors. So was C. Roland Christensen, University Professor at Harvard University and one of the country's leading authorities in the field of Business Policy.

In the spring of 1984, Arthur D. Little, Inc., was justifiably proud of its standing as a socially involved and concerned pillar of the community.

By the spring of 1985, however, some residents of Cambridge, Arlington, and Belmont were referring to Arthur D. Little and its officers as arrogant, hypocritical, lying, avaricious outlaws—unwelcome intruders in the community and threats to the safety and security of all. The President's letter to the stockholders in the annual report published in March, 1985, noted

> Over the years we have taken considerable pride in the manner in which our pursuit of our professional and corporate objectives serves the interest of society as well.
>
> Ironically, during the past year the Company has been plagued by activist community opposition to certain research that we consider of vital importance to the defense of the United States, its military personnel and civilian population against chemical warfare agents. The purpose of the research, performed in a safe, secure laboratory built in our Cambridge, Massachusetts, headquarters, is to develop better protective materials and methods of detecting and detoxifying chemical agents. This work is important, and the chemicals are handled in a manner that assures the safety of our staff and our neighbors. It is worth noting that, although safety is the expressed concern, opponents of our research for the U.S. Department of Defense appear to be unconcerned about nondefense-related research with substances of comparable hazard. I am saddened, however, by the strain in the fine relations we have enjoyed with Cambridge since the early days of this century.

THE TOXIC ALERT

Chief among ADL's critics was a loosely-knit community organization called the North Cambridge Toxic Alert Coalition (later shortened to "Toxic Alert"). Key members of the organization as of August 1985, are described in Exhibit 4. Charlie Rose, a professional organizer and one of Toxic Alert's founders, described the conditions which led to its formation:

> People in North Cambridge already had a strong feeling they were being dumped on. For years, W. R. Grace and the Dewey and Almy chemical company had left chemical wastes standing in ponds. They often spilled naphthalene, and left whole neighborhoods smelling like mothballs; that frightened people, and when the managers denied spilling anything it made people mad. The old city dump caught fire occasionally. The subway construction over the past five years threatened a lot of changes.

EXHIBIT 4
Key Members of the Toxic Alert Coalition

Ed Cyr Age 28. Native of North Cambridge. Studied economics at University of Massachusetts, now studying planning at U. Mass. Boston. Former organizer for Cambridge Economic Opportunity Commission and North Cambridge Planning Team. Executive Director, Cambridge Committee of Elders.

John O'Connor Age 31. Professional organizer. Coordinator of the National Campaign Against Toxic Hazards, an umbrella organization with affiliates in 28 states. Travels and speaks extensively, concentrating in 1985 on the superfund law. Studied sociology and journalism at Clark University.

Charlie Rose Age 27. New England Co-Director of the Clean Water Action Project. Professional organizer, beginning in 1977 as a Volunteer in Service to America (VISTA). The only Toxic Alert worker not resident in Cambridge.

Sharon Moran Age 27, 3 years resident. Involved with Toxic Alert from its founding. B.A. in Chemistry, Boston University. Para-legal worker with an environmental law firm.

Wendy Baruch Pretzel salesperson at public events, known near Fenway Park for her singing pretzel call. Teaches home construction skills. With Dan Grossman, led the ADL balloon release project and was interviewed on "20/20" and other programs. Major interest: waste cleanup at W. R. Grace.

Hillary Frank On leave from studies at Harvard University. Employed by CWAP, on loan to Toxic Alert. Ran first canvas for TA. Keeps member records, does the telephone and mail work to encourage meeting attendance and committee work.

Dan Grossman Age 27. MIT Ph.D. candidate, Political Science. Cambridge resident since 1977. Toxic Alert representative to the Health Care task force of the Massachusetts legislature.

Michael Kanter Owner/manager of Cambridge Natural Foods store. 12 years in Cambridge. B.A. in History, University of Buffalo.

Steve Schnapp Age 39, 8 years resident. Professional organizer on Boston's North Shore. Studied organization at Boston University. Chairperson, Cambridge Peace Commission.

Richard Durling-Shyduroff Director, Cambridge Institute of the Arts and Sciences. Provided sound systems and space for membership meetings and fund-raising events in his headquarters building.

> There was a growing awareness. John O'Connor and I had seen the changes. We had scoped out an organizing plan for W. R. Grace a year earlier.
>
> Then the discovery that ADL was testing nerve gas came as the last straw. Things crystalized. We sat down and planned it. There were already good people in the neighborhood. We brought in skilled, professional, paid organizers beginning in the summer of 84.

As New England co-director of the Clean Water Action Project, Charlie Rose had resources available. CWAP employed door-to-door canvassers who spent half their time soliciting funds (on commission). Their remaining time was spent studying and applying community skills in Rose's "Organizing School." "Canvassers should get people involved," said Rose. "It's not enough just to let people pitch money into the hat." One CWAP canvasser, Hillary Frank, became a mainstay of Toxic Alert.

Toxic Alert operated through meetings of sub-committees, a steering committee, the membership at large, and meetings planned as media events for the whole population. The group had a volunteer treasurer, but no other officers. There were no elections; anyone with the initiative to find the steering committee meetings could attend. Members of the steering committee took turns chairing the larger membership meetings, which might see 25 to 40 attendees.

Originally the steering committee was made up of representatives of other neighborhood organizations, who generally listened to and agreed with the ideas of the professional organizers. By August of 1985 many of its members were local residents who took initiative and carried out programs without the organizers' involvement.

Between meetings, organizers and volunteers knocked on doors and made telephone calls, sought business support, wrote and distributed newsletters and publicity flyers, met with government officials, and maintained liaison with the press.

Ed Cyr, another Toxic Alert founder and a professional organizer, reported spending one hour per week at the *Cambridge TAB* and two hours at the *Cambridge Chronicle* (both weekly newspapers). "The *Boston Globe* never did catch on with the story," Cyr said. "It was really a television type story." Cyr succeeded in bringing ABC's "20/20" to one community-wide meeting. "It's not hard to get coverage when you have a sexy issue," he said. "You just find an assignment editor four days ahead of the event, and then visit with them every day." Contacts with local radio and television stations were handled by Charlie Rose.

A CHRONOLOGY OF CONTROVERSY

Before a partisan audience and a battery of cameras at a community meeting sponsored by Toxic Alert in March of 1985, Reid Weedon reviewed the events of the previous two years.

In January of 1983, he said, Arthur D. Little informed the Cambridge police and fire departments that work in a planned new laboratory facility "would involve highly toxic materials of particular interest to the Department of Defense." Specific information on chemical names, structures, and toxicities was not requested by the city officials, Weedon said. In a series of meetings, Cambridge police and fire officials reviewed the design. Several modifications were made at their suggestion.

Construction proceeded with an investment of approximately $800,000. In September of 1983 the building was ready for operation and ADL again met with Cambridge fire and police officials, this time with instructions on handling public safety in the event of fire or intrusion into the facility.

In the event of fire, the laboratory should be allowed to burn to the ground. In the event of unauthorized entry into the laboratory, police should surround it and allow nobody to leave, but under no circumstances should they attempt to enter it themselves. The laboratory, it was explained, was engaged in testing highly toxic materials including Department of Defense "surety agents." ADL technical people would respond to any alarm; nobody should enter without their assessment of the hazards involved. Furthermore, it was requested in the interests of security that the city authorities make no public announcements that would call attention to the laboratory.

TA: See there? "Surety agents," they call them. That's nerve gas and blister agents—the most deadly stuff ever invented for killing people. And ADL wanted the city authorities to lie about it for them.[2]

ADL: We didn't want or ask anyone to lie about anything. It was in the best interests of the public and our employees not to advertise that we had chemical warfare materials here. It was in the interest of maximizing safety.

Cambridge officials, under reciprocal public safety agreements with neighboring towns, asked ADL to inform the authorities in Arlington and Belmont. After touring the laboratory, the town manager of Arlington informed ADL that he could not, in good conscience, comply with the request for confidentiality; he would raise the issue at the next meeting of the selectmen, October 17.

"On that same day," wrote Sheldon Krimsky later,[3] "ADL issued a news release announcing the opening of a high security laboratory for the testing and analysis of toxic materials. The news release was skillfully written and avoided any mention that the facility would be handling chemical warfare agents or that the research undertaken there would be defense-related."

ADL: There was nothing secret about the work. We sent memos to literally hundreds of staff members, because we were concerned about staff reaction. We held a reception for the lab's dedication; that's what the press release was for. It just never occurred to us that this would be a safety concern to the community. We made the assumption, perhaps naively, that since it *was* safe, people would recognize that.

A *Boston Globe* story on the Arlington selectmen's meeting was noticed by Nancy Cyr in Cambridge; her calls to Cambridge city hall resulted in the issue's appearance on the City Council agenda that same night. The Council asked the city's Commissioner of Health and Hospitals, Dr. Melvin Chalfen, to inspect the new laboratory. He did so on October 19th.

The Council also asked for a hearing with Arthur D. Little's officers, who appeared on October 24th. They reported that the Levins Laboratory (it was named to honor Dr. Philip L. Levins, the senior ADL officer who had advocated the facility's construction, who had died in a swimming accident before its completion) was the safest conceivable facility for its purpose, and that its purpose was in the public interest. ADL's contracts with the Department of Defense dealt with detecting chemical nerve agents, with neutralizing them, and with developing improved protective clothing.

TA: All very well, but it doesn't explain why we should welcome nerve gas in one of the most densely populated cities in the country. Put the laboratory in the desert

---

[2] Throughout this case, inserts like this are used to interject points of view of the Toxic Alert ("TA") or Arthur D. Little managers ("ADL").

[3] Sheldon Krimsky, "Local Control of Research Involving Chemical Warfare Agents," in Malcolm L. Goggin, ed., *Science and Technology in a Democracy: Who Should Govern?*, University of Tennessee Press.

or on some military post where it can be properly guarded, and those arguments make sense. Not here.

ADL: The words, "nerve gas," have a frightening connotation. They show a deliberate attempt to mis-describe the situation. We don't receive gas. We don't store gas. We use these agents in liquid form, in minute quantities. It's not easy to disperse these materials. Even when it's used on the battlefield, this material isn't a gas, by and large. It's an aerosol. This talk about "gas" is designed purely to heighten people's anxieties.

The Cambridge City Council had faced a similar issue before. In 1976 a substantial public debate erupted over the dangers and propriety of genetic research, in which DNA molecules might be modified to create new life forms—in the worst case scenario to create an "Andromeda strain" of lethal bacteria. After a great deal of political gesturing and scientific consideration, Cambridge became the first city in the country to regulate genetic research. Its new ordinance, based on federal guidelines developed by the National Institutes of Health, became a model for other cities facing the same problem.

Following its meeting with Arthur D. Little management, the Cambridge City Council called for creation of a Scientific Advisory Committee "to advise the City Council and the Commissioner of Health and Hospitals on issues of public health and safety related to the environmental hazards of ADL's research with chemical warfare agents." Arthur D. Little had already received its first consignment of nerve agents and begun testing.

In the fall of 1983 and winter of 1984 several individual city councillors attempted to stop the ADL work or to gain a moratorium while the Scientific Advisory Committee (SAC) was organized and deliberating. ADL officials responded that the terms of their contracts with the Department of Defense imposed a schedule which could not be interrupted. ADL offered a 30-day moratorium on initiation of new contracts and offered to cooperate with any committee, but would not interrupt work already begun. Finally, on March 13, 1984, Dr. Chalfen issued an emergency order barring the testing of five specified nerve and blister agents until the SAC rendered its report.

ADL: A moratorium would have removed any incentive for the Council to appoint the Committee or for the Committee to act. Dr. Chalfen had previously told us he considered the laboratory to be safe. He issued his order under pressure from the City Council, not on the basis of his professional judgment.

On March 16, Arthur D. Little went to court, claiming that no city action could legally infringe on Department of Defense work, since federal regulation (in this case, by DOD) took precedence over regulation by local authorities. Superior Court Judge Robert Hallisey granted an injunction to restrain the city from enforcing the Commissioner's order. Tests continued at the Levins Laboratory.

On April 12, 1984, the Scientific Advisory Committee held its first meeting. Dr. Sheldon Krimsky, a former member of the panel which had drawn up the city's regulations on DNA research, served as chairman. The names, occupations, and institutional affiliations of the SAC members are shown in Exhibit 5.

In May, the city's legal department attempted to end the temporary restraining order on the basis of a technical consulting report. The court ruled for ADL and continued the

EXHIBIT 5

Membership of the Cambridge Scientific Advisory Committee

Sheldon Krimsky (Chair) Assoc. Prof. of Urban and Environmental Policy, Tufts University. Ph.D. in Philosophy of Science.

Ann Hochberg (Vice-Chair) Fisheries Specialist, New England Fishery Management Council. B.A. in Biology, M.S. in Oceanography.

Frederick Centanni, Jr. Cambridge resident. Business Element Manager, EG&G Wakefield.

Edmund Crouch Research Fellow in Energy and the Environment, Harvard University. Ph.D. in high-energy physics.

Edward Cyr Cambridge resident. Executive Director, Cambridge Committee of Elders.

Lou DiBerardinis Industrial Hygienist, Department of Environmental Health and Safety, Harvard. B.S. in Chemical Engineering, M.S. in Industrial Hygiene.

Joseph Fantasia Cambridge resident and restaurant owner, active in Chamber of Commerce affairs. Cornell University.

Paul Fennelly Arlington resident. Group Scientist and Manager, Environmental Measurements Department, GCA Technology Division, GCA Corp. Ph.D. in Physical Chemistry.

Richard Goldstein, M.D. Department of Microbiology and Molecular Genetics, Harvard Medical School. Ph.D. in Biology.

Jack Martinelli Cambridge resident and Volkswagen mechanic. Ph.D. in Chemistry. Former student of Judith Harris.

Henry Mautner Chairman, Dept. of Biochemistry & Pharmacology, Tufts University School of Medicine. Ph.D. in Medicinal Chemistry.

John O'Connor Cambridge resident. Coordinator, National Campaign Against Toxic Hazards.

David Ozonoff, M.D. Chief, Environmental Health Section, Boston University School of Medicine; former President, Massachusetts Public Health Association.

Placido John Paula Radiation Technologist, Office of Environmental Health and Safety, Harvard University.

John J. Malone Belmont resident. Director, Belmont Dept. of Public Health, and member, Governor's Hazardous Waste Council.

Ralph Wolfe Cambridge resident. Technical coordinator, Skidmore, Owings & Merrill. M. Arch. degree. Son of a chemist.

preliminary injunction barring enforcement of the city's health regulation. Cambridge retained a prominent Boston law firm, Palmer and Dodge, to continue the case.

For the next five months, the Scientific Advisory Committee worked to define and resolve the complex issues of technology and values which underlay the risk and benefit arguments of ADL and the city. Subcommittees were set up to investigate the physical and chemical properties of nerve agents, the various scenarios which could result from releases at ADL, and comparable risks presented by other chemicals in general use. (Exhibit 6 shows one of many graphic representations presented in the SAC report. It is a "ground zero" map of the ADL area, showing the "zone of lethality" for the plume of gas emanating from a postulated half-liter spill of the agent "VX," with a southwesterly wind.)

In September, 1984, the Committee issued its final report. The risks involved in transporting and processing chemical warfare agents in densely populated areas were not justified, the SAC concluded. Even though the risk might be very small, as ADL contended, the

EXHIBIT 6
"Ground Zero" Map of the ADL Area

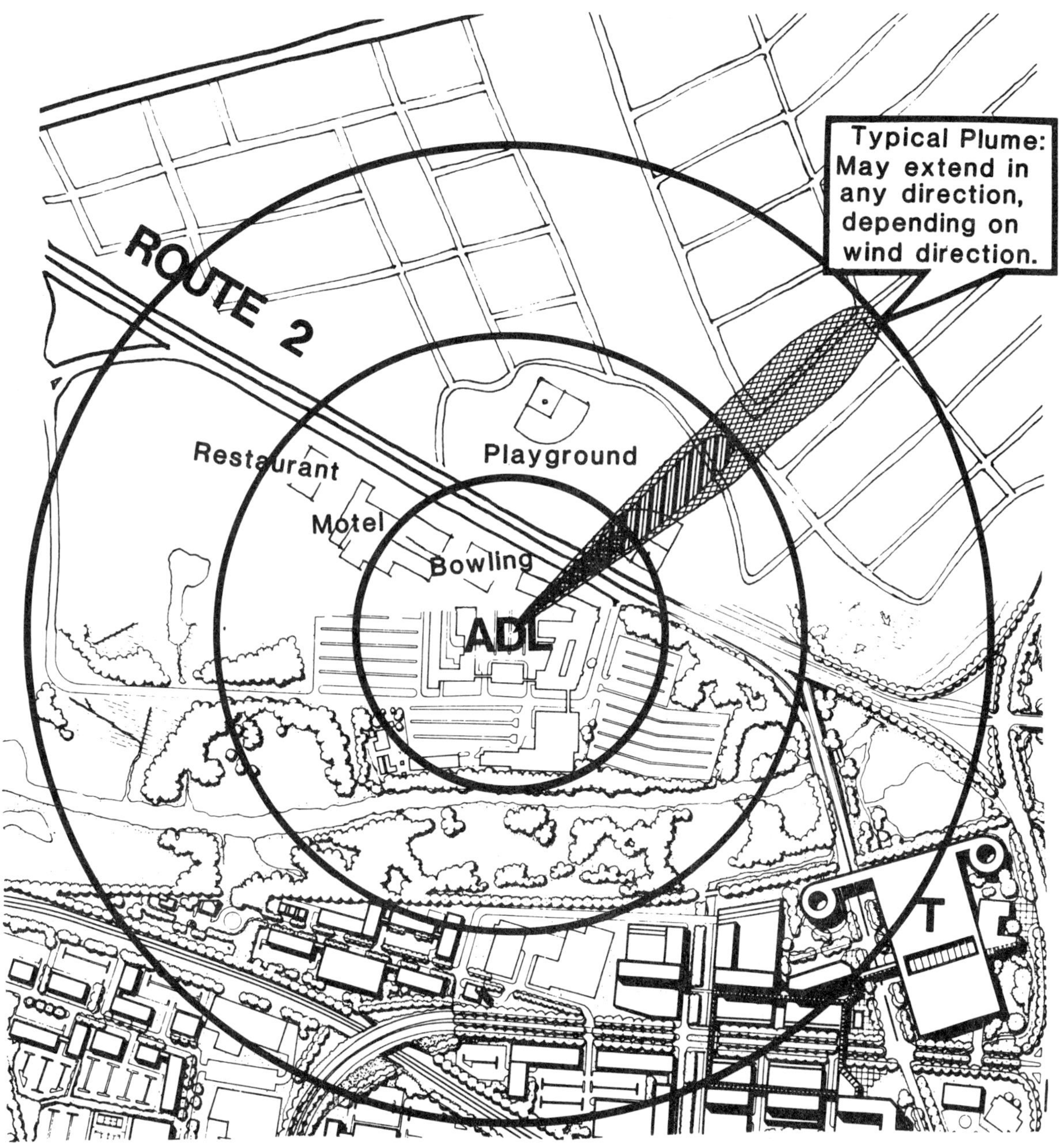

Figure 2: Distances Associated with Various Inhalation Levels

VX, 500 ml. Release

LD50 Adult	164m (538')
LD01 Adult	314m (1030')
LD01 Children	510m (1673')

consequences if an accident did occur were such that the ADL work should not continue. The SAC found no discernible benefit to the city from the work's location in Cambridge; a majority of members saw no benefit in the work regardless of its location.

ADL: That report is incompetent. It was not written by a group of scientists. To call that a "Scientific" Advisory Committee was absurd! The representation on that committee of anyone who knew anything about risk analysis and these materials was essentially nil. There were some scientists, but what kind? There was one man, from MIT, who had direct working experience with this kind of issue. But he was the only one, and he quit the Committee—in disgust.[4]

Judge Hallisey called a meeting to hear attorneys' arguments on the federal "supremacy" issue. He would rule separately on the reasonableness of Cambridge's action, if the local regulation were found to be valid. Pending those decisions, the court continued its restraining order against Dr. Chalfen's regulation. The testing continued.

TA: And it's *still* going on. ADL still says it's their own job to decide whether it's safe enough, and nobody else's opinion counts for beans. They'll appeal this forever, and the courts will always give them another restraining order. We thought the SAC decision would *decide* something. Are we going to stand for this?

Impatient residents of the North Cambridge area were already concerned over another environmental issue—the location and disposal of chemical wastes on a 17-acre W. R. Grace site scheduled for industrial development. This was fertile ground for dissent, and the "nerve gas" issue was both threatening and compelling. SAC members Ed Cyr, John O'Connor, and Ralph Wolfe decided to organize, and O'Connor asked Charlie Rose for help. The North Cambridge Toxic Alert Coalition took shape with a community meeting in October 1984.

"We were surprised at the turnout," Ed Cyr said later. "It showed again the basic law of organizing: the number of bodies at a meeting depends on the hours of dirty work done before." Toxic Alert workers had blanketed North Cambridge with three different flyers, had knocked on doors and rung telephones to build grass roots communications. "After the October meeting, it was like a tidal wave," Cyr continued. "People signed up. We had 40 or 45 people helping plan the next steps."

Loudly, NCTAC challenged both W. R. Grace and Arthur D. Little to appear at a public meeting on November 29, 1984. W. R. Grace countered by holding a series of small neighborhood meetings of its own, announcing it would not attend the NCTAC affair. ADL made no comment on the NCTAC challenge and was not expected to attend either.

"We saw no benefit in appearing at a meeting where we had no idea of the agenda, the structure, the process," said ADL's John Magee later. "There was no assurance of an opportunity to do anything but be pilloried."

Television crews did attend the November meeting, and so did the managers of the

[4] Members of the Scientific Advisory Committee expressed substantial surprise at this comment by a high ADL official. They reported that the chairman of MIT's Department of Nutrition and Food Sciences, Dr. Gerald N. Wogan, had contributed greatly to the subcommittee on toxicity before international commitments forced his resignation from the SAC for lack of time. When asked for clarification, Dr. Wogan commented, "In disgust? That certainly is not the case."

W. R. Grace division concerned with the real estate development. Patently obvious to viewers of the evening news was the empty chair labelled "Arthur D. Little." Speakers included Ed Cyr and John O'Connor, Dr. Sheldon Krimsky, Cambridge City Manager Robert Healy, a city councillor, and two technical consultants on environmental pollution. At the close of the meeting an angry Ed Cyr called for the city to retaliate against the absent Arthur D. Little by freezing building permits, refusing permission to park on public land, or shutting off water and sewer connections until the firm agreed to talk. The following day at three p.m., he announced, the Toxic Alert would meet on the highway outside ADL to release a cloud of black balloons, demonstrating how the wind could carry particles from Acorn Park to the neighboring blocks of densely-packed two- and three-family houses. Television crews were invited to the demonstration; an ABC News "20/20" crew working on the story filmed the launching the next day. Cameras in pursuit, the Toxic Alert balloon people then strode into the Arthur D. Little reception area, demanding a meeting with President John Magee. The negotiation process for defining a forum for public debate began.

TA: So we win a round. But we still don't have Weedon and Magee out where people can see them. People have to hear ADL's arguments first hand, to recognize how blind these guys are. They're still testing nerve gas next door. We have to get them out in the open.

Four days after the NCTAC meeting, on December 3, 1984, the Bhopal tragedy in India made poison gas a common topic and a more credible threat. ABC television, which had filmed the Cambridge meeting without a specific production schedule, aired the ADL segment on "20/20" the following week. Toxic Alert members continued to organize.

On December 14, 1984, Superior Court Judge Robert Hallisey ruled in favor of the City of Cambridge on the "supremacy" question, establishing the right of the local government to regulate activities on DOD work at Arthur D. Little. ADL requested reconsideration of the issue. On January 14th, Judge Hallisey issued a Supplemental Decision reconfirming his stand. Still to be heard were arguments over whether Cambridge's actions were reasonable. In the meantime, the testing continued.

Negotiations also continued between Toxic Alert leaders and ADL management about the timing and format of a public meeting in which each side could present its views. On several occasions, steering committee members visited ADL to demand that a date be set. After each meeting, local TV crews with "minicameras" were waiting to interview participants, often for the live 5:30 news. Finally, March 7th was selected.

At the end of January 1985, 61,000 residents in North Cambridge, Arlington, and Belmont received by first class mail a package of materials including a three-page letter from ADL President John Magee, a four-page specification on the Levins Laboratory, and a four-page reproduction of a *Cambridge Chronicle* story describing Arthur D. Little's history, strengths, and virtues. Exhibit 7 contains excerpts from this letter and enclosures.

TA: Will you look at this! We've been trying to smoke him out and here he comes, all by himself! Comparing nerve gas to water, for God's sake! Valuing our good opinion! So sorry they had to turn down this work before! And so very, very safe! That lab has enough nerve gas on hand to kill 300,000 people but we should all have confidence because it's so very safe. This letter is a Christmas present from Magee to the Toxic Alert!

EXHIBIT 7
Excerpts from John Magee's Letter of January 28, 1985

Dear Neighbor,

You probably have heard about some research being conducted in one of our analytical chemistry laboratories on highly toxic substances, referred to in the press as "nerve gases." . . . Although as liquids these agents are no more volatile than water, we realize the term "nerve gas" causes reasonable people to wonder whether the existence of such substances in the neighborhood should be cause for concern.

Because we value your good opinion and the friendship of our community, I would like to share with you the reasons we consider this research so important and why we are doing it here in Cambridge rather than in some isolated area. . . . We believe something must be done to reduce the threat of uncontrolled toxic chemicals in the environment. . . . Before our Levins Laboratory was constructed, we had to turn down community requests, including one from the Commonwealth of Massachusetts, for work involving dioxins and other contaminants. We did not like having to refuse to help our home state.

The research . . . is for defensive and protective purposes only . . . to develop better methods of detecting minute quantities . . . and safer, more effective means of destroying them on a large scale. We also are working to develop better protection, including clothing, for people who might be exposed to these substances.

We are doing the work here in Cambridge because this kind of chemical analysis cannot be performed in isolation. . . . Moving the laboratory to a remote location would mean moving much of our technical work out of Cambridge. This we do not want to do. . . . We have a record as good citizens of the community and a major investment here.

We invested nearly a million dollars . . . worked closely with the Cambridge City Manager and the relevant public safety officials. . . . The result, experts concur, is a laboratory that advances the state of the art for the safe handling of hazardous substances.

If you have any comments or questions . . . I would appreciate your sending those to: Mr. D. Reid Weedon, Jr., Senior Vice President. We are interested in your views.

Sincerely,

/s/ John F Magee, President and Chief Executive Officer

Reaction to ADL's communication was not limited to NCTAC activists. Weekly newspapers in all three affected communities took note of the mailing, and their readers responded with a barrage of letters to the editors, printed in mid-February. Three of those letters are excerpted in Exhibit 8. Exhibit 9 shows segments of a *Cambridge Chronicle* editorial of March 14.

"Public reaction was either moderately supportive or 'ho-hum'," said John Magee later. "There are a lot of people in those communities and very few letters in the newspapers. A substantial number of people called or wrote in support, and of course those people don't write to the papers. When you look at the demonstrations and think of the numbers of people involved—why, I've almost gotten to know them on a first-name basis, because it's always the same small group."

On February 26, 1985, Superior Court Judge Hallisey ruled that the Cambridge regulation prohibiting chemical warfare agent work was valid and enforceable under the law. In an addendum to the decision, called "remarkable" by both parties and the press, the judge expressed reservations about his decision, thinking it unfair but unavoidable under the law. The next day he removed the restraining order which prevented the regulation's enforcement. The testing stopped.

In preparation for the March 7th public meeting, Toxic Alert wrote to the Directors of ADL, inviting them to attend the meeting in order to inform themselves, independently of

EXHIBIT 8
Excerpts from Letters to the Editors, *Cambridge Chronicle* and *Arlington Advocate*, March 7 and 21, 1985 (Ellipses Omitted)

Do you know what "the arrogance of power" is? It's a large corporation deciding to do something extremely dangerous to others and using its money and influence to steamroll over the local opposition. It's writing a patronizing letter to the locals afterwards saying, essentially, "If you only knew the facts you'd understand," as if we're too ignorant or misguided to realize what's really in our best interest. It's writing us a letter and saying, at the end, that if we have a reply, we should send it to someone else. Who is D. Reid Weedon, Jr., and why do I care whether he reads my reply to your letter?

Anyone who would build a lab for testing nerve gas in one of the most heavily populated urban areas in the United States is clearly beyond the reach of rational protest.

As ADL's neighbors we cannot accept this risk. Magee never wanted to know whether his neighbors feel safe. He never wanted us to know the lab exists. His new found concern is insulting and absurd.

This is one resident who doesn't give a hoot about how many safety precautions they've taken. That just proves how lethal the stuff is. Testing those chemicals in our highly populated area is damn poor policy from a company that I've come to expect good judgment from.

management, on the issues and the potential impact on the company's good name. The letter also appealed for formation of a Board-level Committee on Social Responsiveness. It noted that ADL's relationships with its neighbors had always been so positive that Board inputs to management had not been necessary. Now the inputs were needed, the letter said, but "it seems unlikely such a committee would be organized at Mr. Magee's own request, given his level of commitment to continued testing." One director responded to the Toxic Alert letter; none attended the March 7th meeting.

"Some directors asked my advice—what would management prefer they do about the invitation," John Magee recalled. "My reaction was, 'do what you please.' In their view, it wouldn't have been appropriate to attend as Board members."

EXHIBIT 9
Excerpts from a *Cambridge Chronicle* Editorial, March 14, 1985 (Ellipses Omitted)

There are times when it is prudent to recognize that most lead balloons do not, in fact, fly. Now is the proper time for the Arthur D. Little Co. to recognize that the best way to remain [a] "good neighbor" is to give up its quixotic battle against the city's ban on nerve agent testing.

ADL has handled the nerve agent issue with rather surprising stupidity, first attempting to stonewall its residential neighbors and City Hall, then, belatedly, attempting to patch things up with a deceptively reassuring mass mailing. (Which included, for the record, a reprint from the "Chronicle." It is not likely the firm will ask for reprint permission on this editorial.)

ADL has not come up with any particularly convincing arguments on its own behalf. Above all, company officials have stressed that the facilities where the nerve agents are stored and tested are "state of the art" safe.

The one fact which inevitably weakens any defense of ADL's position is that what's at issue here is a substance to which exposure can mean instant death, pure and simple. The city's ban is not an effort to restrict research and it is not yet another attempt to over-regulate business. Instead, the ban is the proper execution of the city's responsibility to its people.

MARCH 1985: THE PUBLIC FORUM

Television crews, reporters, and some 300 citizens attended the March 7th meeting in the auditorium of the Fitzgerald School in Cambridge. Moderator Anthony Cortese gave a brief chronology of events, noting that testing operations were now stopped due to the recent court decision, and outlined the rules of the program: each side would have 30 minutes, 45 minutes would be allowed for questions from the floor, and each side would have five minutes for summarizing. Cortese introduced D. Reid Weedon, Jr., John Magee, ADL Vice President for Chemical and Food Sciences Judith Harris, and Safety Officer R. Scott Stricoff. Weedon presented the ADL case.

The Arthur D. Little Position

Arthur D. Little, he said, had two concerns—one with the hazards of their work and another with the hazards of banning research. Safety for ADL staff and the community had always been uppermost in their minds, in all their work on pesticide wastes, PCBs, dioxin, and chemical warfare agents such as nerve gas, "or, really, nerve agents, since they're not gasses." All authorities who had seen the Levins Laboratory had praised it as representing the state of the art in safety. Indeed, ADL was now doing design work for the U.S. Centers for Disease Control. Weedon quoted expert authorities to vouch for the lab's safety and noted the Health and Hospitals Commissioner had delayed five months between inspecting the lab and issuing his regulation—hardly the behavior of someone concerned about public health perils.

Weedon described the precautions taken in transporting nerve agents under armed escort and showed the audience a gray steel cannister called a "pig," which had withstood drops from an army helicopter onto concrete without damage to the flame-sealed glass vials packed inside it. A pig could carry five, 20-milliliter vials of liquid. On arrival at the laboratory, each vial was opened and its contents transferred to 1-ml vials. Since most experiments required less than one milliliter, any risk of spilling was minimized by working with the smaller standard quantity.

Near the end of the SAC deliberations, ADL had announced it would limit its inventory to a maximum of 40 ml of any of the three most hazardous nerve agent concentrates: Sarin (GB), Soman (GD), and VX. Additionally the combined inventory of all three would not exceed 100 ml, although larger quantities of Mustard (HD) and Lewisite (L), up to a combined inventory of 500 ml, might be on hand at one time. Weedon referred to ADL's self-imposed limit of 1/10 of a liter as a primary safeguard against the kind of accidental spills postulated in the SAC report.

Further, said Weedon, ADL used mostly dilute concentrations and would never leave a spill to evaporate. Household bleach was an effective decontaminating agent. The SAC report scenario showing a "puff" of gas, as from an explosion, could not happen because the agents decomposed in temperatures over 500 degrees. Besides, the injury and fatality counts deemed possible by the SAC assumed none of the injured received medical treatment—again, an assumption without credibility. Any accidents in any of the 14 laboratories doing this kind of work in America had resulted in injuries successfully treated; no testing-related fatalities had ever been reported. The assumptions used in the SAC report, Weedon said, were totally unrealistic. It was not fair to postulate impossible risks.

Weedon went on to describe the need for knowledge about chemical warfare agents, which were in current use in the Iran-Iraq war and might pose a threat to American military forces at any time. There was need, too, for research using these agents for medical applications. Hodgkin's disease had been found by an Army lab to respond to a nerve agent, and Alzheimer's disease was thought to be a prospective target. But if there could be no research, he said, there might be no cures.

"We're often asked, 'Why locate chemical warfare work in Cambridge?'" Weedon said. "The appropriate answer is, 'Because it is safe, and Arthur D. Little is here.' Usually the larger part of the work in an assignment does not use toxic materials, and therefore is done outside the toxic materials laboratory. The next question is, 'Why not locate just the toxic materials laboratory elsewhere?' We do not have, nor do we expect, sufficient volume of work on chemical warfare agents to justify full-time staff in such a laboratory.

"Furthermore, a separate location would require medical personnel whenever people were in the laboratory, full-time guard service, and immediate-response technical and maintenance support services. All of these services are in place at our Acorn Park facility, and duplication, while possible, would price us out of the competition," Weedon said.

He went on to enumerate a list of toxic chemicals, many similar to the nerve agents, which were widely used in medical schools and were available from lab supply houses with no regulation at all. "A typical hardware store or garden center will have on its shelves a quantity equivalent to more than 100 lethal doses of the pesticide Malathion in concentrated form, in totally unventilated spaces. This pesticide acts on the human nervous system by exactly the same biochemical mechanisms as do the DOD chemicals GD, GB, and VX. . . . True, ounce-for-ounce, Malathion is less toxic than the chemical warfare agents. But because use and storage of Malathion is totally uncontrolled and the available quantities are so large, I submit that the risk of exposure to this nerve agent is much greater than the risk of exposure to similar chemicals safely stored within the Levins Laboratory."

Weedon concluded the ADL presentation with an appeal for the city to establish standards and regulations for *all* toxic agents, rather than banning a certain class of them based on their purpose as weapons of war. Arthur D. Little, he volunteered, stood ready to use its substantial talents to help the city in this effort.

"Arthur D. Little has been a part of Cambridge since the early days of this century," Weedon concluded. "We love this city. We're proud of it. The city we love is a world-class city, which provides an environment that encourages and supports scientific talent in a spirit of research and investigation. We trust you also wish, as we do, to protect that very special environment that is Cambridge."

The Toxic Alert Presentation

Five speakers shared the presentation and summary of the Toxic Alert position. The moderator introduced Ed Cyr, Sharon Moran, John O'Connor, and Steve Schnapp, all of the Toxic Alert, and David Ozonoff, M.D., a Cambridge resident and SAC member. Steve Schnapp began the presentation:

Responding to ADL's many assurances of safety, Schnapp said, "It seems to me we've heard this kind of corporate reassurance before." As the house lights dimmed and a slide of a bushy-whiskered sea-captain appeared on the screen, Schnapp continued:

> Captain Edward J. Smith said, "I cannot conceive of any kind of vital disaster happening to this vessel. Modern shipbuilding has gone beyond that." On April 12,

> 1912, Captain Smith's ship, the *Titanic*, struck an iceberg and sank with a loss of 1,500 lives. *John Magee says there is no credible danger in nerve gas testing at ADL. The risk is vanishingly small.*

The Captain's picture changed to a slide showing a newsboy hawking papers with the headline, "Titanic Lost!", and then to a handful of capsules. Schnapp continued,

> "We have firmly established the safety, dosage, and usefulness of Kevidon," said Frank Gettman, the president of William S. Merrill Company in 1960. "There is still no positive proof of a causal relationship between the use of thalidomide during pregnancy and malfunctions in the newborn." But in 1962 the drug was pulled off the market. More than 8,000 children suffered grave birth defects. *John Magee says, "There are more risks in the kitchens of Cambridge than in the laboratories of Arthur D. Little."*

The slide switched to a view of Niagara Falls.

> "When you come right down to it," said an ad of Hooker Chemical Company in the 1940s, "you would be hard pressed to find any group of people who care as much about the environmental well-being of Niagara Falls as the people at Hooker." In 1979, 239 families were evacuated from the Love Canal neighborhood. *Arthur D. Little cares just as much for Cambridge.*

The slide showed a refugee family leaving Love Canal, and then the ominous cooling towers of a nuclear power plant.

> "Do you think I'd work here if it was dangerous?" said William Metzger, a Three Mile Island employee, shortly before the catastrophic near-meltdown of March 29, 1979. *"If this lab weren't safe," said Alma Triner, Vice President for Public Relations at Arthur D. Little, "I wouldn't be working here."*

The slide changed again, to show a chemical plant and then a *Newsweek* photograph of the Bhopal disaster.

> "A factory is not a small stone that can be shifted elsewhere," State Labor Minister Tarasingh Viyogi told the provincial assembly of Madhya Pradesh in India. "There is no danger to Bhopal, nor will there be." *Arthur D. Little, working with compounds 50 to 100 times more toxic than methyl isocyanate, is just as certain of their safety.*

All of those assurances came from highly trained, competent people who most probably believed what they were saying, Schnapp said. "Will Cambridge be next on the 11 o'clock news?"

Sharon Moran told of attending the first Cambridge City Council meeting on the topic, in October of 1983. She described how Mr. Weedon "spent 10 minutes telling the council there wasn't any nerve gas at ADL. There were chemical surety agents, he said. It came out later these were liquids, which would explode into a shower of tiny droplets called an aerosol when a chemical warfare shell detonated. *That* was nerve gas, and ADL didn't have any. Later the SAC received a letter saying ADL would vaporize the liquid agents. Tonight again they say they don't."

Moran told of hearing "evasive answers" on what agents were at the laboratory and what tests and end results were expected. "What can you believe?" she asked. "What disturbs me is that, in spite of all their professional expertise, they couldn't—or maybe they didn't want to—be clear and coherent and forthcoming about what substances they were using. Confusing us with technical jargon is too often the trick of the arrogant scientist—not the kind of behavior I expect from a company with a commitment to be a good neighbor, as ADL has told us they have."

Left out of tonight's presentation, said Moran, was information about the agents themselves. They were invented with one purpose, she said: "killing people. One one-hundredth of a drop of Agent VX will kill you, if it touches your skin or if you inhale it. These chemicals affect the nervous system, causing all bodily processes to go haywire. The victim sweats intensely, and vomits and defecates uncontrollably. Finally, the person becomes completely paralyzed and unable to take a breath; death follows by asphyxiation. Nerve agents are awesomely lethal, compared to compounds like Malathion. That is why I find it disturbing when Mr. Magee minimizes their danger by telling us that greater danger exists in the average kitchen."

"Also disturbing," said Moran, "was ADL's discounting of the SAC's findings. This was a group of professionals, not a bunch of radicals, and they found that an accidental release *could* happen. It is not impossible. Further, however small the risk, it was unacceptable in so densely populated an area. The only group that likes the idea of ADL's work is ADL. This kind of work should be done in remote military installations," Moran concluded. "Commercial companies have too much at stake to be the sole judges of whether their work is acceptable."

David Ozonoff introduced himself as a physician with a bias in favor of public health. "The issue here," he said, "is not freedom of inquiry as Mr. Weedon would have the audience believe. The testing of nerve gas has about the same relationship to science as pornography has to photojournalism. Nor is the issue about trading one risk for another. There is a perfect way to have no risk at all from nerve gas in the City of Cambridge, and that is not to do this work in the city. Nor is the issue about regulation; Cambridge can and should regulate ADL, because otherwise they would be regulated only by the Department of Defense—reputed to be the worst polluter in the country.

"In fact," Ozonoff said, "everybody knows what the issue is about: it's the Willie Sutton principle. You may remember that, when somebody asked the late bank robber Willie Sutton why he robbed banks, he said, 'Because that's where the money is.' EPA money has dried up and consultants are turning to where the money is—the Department of Defense."

Ozonoff concluded, "This controversy is about risk and the notion of what is acceptable. Some risks are unacceptable even though their numeric measurements are very, very small; examples are the presence of dangerous chemicals in drinking water, asbestos in schools, and cyanide in Tylenol capsules. The Levins Laboratory risks are also very small, but they are real and they have been judged unacceptable by everyone in the community except ADL."

Ed Cyr took the platform next to argue that this was not a question for scientists or managers to answer. "This is too important to be left to experts, businessmen, or scientists because they are unable to deal with being wrong, and that makes them dangerous," Cyr said. "Informed citizens," he went on, "have a basic right to full information about all the risks they are exposed to. More importantly, they have a right to decide for themselves what risks they will take.

"I will not fall into the scientists' trap of trying to prove how an accident could happen," Cyr said. "Instead, I look at why I am afraid in this case the stage has been set for one." Claiming that public officials and businesses normally keep accidents secret until they get out of hand, Cyr said, "we must judge the people who would run the facility as well as the facility itself. ADL planned the lab in secret, with no public consideration in siting, design tradeoffs, or security considerations. ADL went to great lengths to make sure we were *not* informed until contracts were in hand; they asked our police and firefighters to lie for them.

"It would be good if I could tell you that, when the story broke, ADL saw the folly in their approach and came clean. At least then we would know they were capable of admitting a mistake. But no. At every meeting, ADL has downplayed the danger and played us for fools. They paint themselves as victims, even after 16 weeks of hearings at the SAC. No Cambridge project has ever been looked at as thoroughly as this one.

"Can you trust ADL to safely manage this lab, when they worked so very hard to avoid telling you about it in the first place? . . . Can you trust a company that regularly, in forum after forum, compares these incredibly deadly chemicals to *water*? To *backyard pesticides*? And to things that are commonly found in your *kitchen*?

"Do *you* believe the Department of Defense intends to kill a million Russians with two gallons of liquid plumber?"

Discussion and Summaries

John O'Connor summarized for Toxic Alert, calling the ADL public relations campaign a "snow job" to cover the main reason for ADL's involvement—to make money. "The community has the right to say 'no' to nerve gas testing," he said, demanding that ADL drop its appeal, renounce nerve gas forever, and move present stocks out of Cambridge. "The one person with power to do that is Mr. Magee," O'Connor continued. "We are angry, frightened—and also on the move to ensure that not one dime of taxpayer money will be used to support a corporation that is chemically trespassing on our city. If need be, we will take to the streets like the founders of our country, to demand that our rights as citizens to be free from toxic hazards be recognized."

Mr. Magee summarized for Arthur D. Little, voicing appreciation for the audience's courtesy. He held up a quarter-teaspoon to demonstrate how small the quantity involved at any one time was, and how hard it would be to make that quantity reach beyond ADL's property. He quoted a recent visitor as saying the facility was "superb." Cambridge officials had been kept informed from the beginning, he said, adding, "We've continued to stay in touch with the city, and *not once* have city officials, even yet, expressed concern to us about the safety of our laboratory!"

"That's not true," said a voice from the back of the hall.

"That is true," Magee replied.

"I was in the laboratory, and I told Mr. Weedon at the time I examined it that I wasn't impressed with . . . "

Magee interrupted, "Who are you?"

"My name is Tom Danehy and I'm a City Councillor, and I live in Cambridge, not in Wellesley."

"I must admit I was speaking specifically of the fire, police, and public health officials," said Magee.

"Those aren't the ones we elect," Danehy concluded.

Magee resumed his talk with an attack on what he called the bias of Dr. Ozonoff. Magee said Ozonoff, as director of a group called the Committee for Responsible Genetics, had taken a position against *any* defensive research on chemical or biological warfare agents. "That political stand has nothing to do with neighborhood safety," Magee said, "and we shouldn't let that point of view be imposed on the community under the disguise of a concern for neighborhood safety." He urged all who were "really concerned with safety" to join with ADL to help the city develop comprehensive regulations for all toxic substances, wherever they were used.

As the crowd left the auditorium, members of Toxic Alert took an "exit poll," asking whether nerve gas work should be done in Cambridge. Four people said it should; 127 said no. Recognizing the possible bias in the population, the poll-takers also asked whether respondents were members of Toxic Alert or employees of ADL. Seven were ADL workers, while 39 were Alert members.

TA: See that? Seven employees here, but only four votes for the testing. Do you suppose three-sevenths of ADL's own people are on our side? Think what we could do with that!

ADL: We got a stronger reaction from staff members to raising the price of tuna sandwiches in the cafeteria than to this issue.

SPRING AND SUMMER, 1985: THE DEBATE CONTINUES

Commenting in the *Cambridge Chronicle* on the impact of the interruption in testing, Laboratory Manager Dr. Judith Harris said that ADL was currently committed to several DOD contracts and had "several million dollars" in proposed contracts under consideration. "If we are forced to close down for some time, I think there's going to be a serious problem," she said, noting that if the ban on research held, ADL would have to subcontract its work to another of the nation's 14 high-security laboratories. "We'd have to send this to some other downtown area," she said, noting that most of the other labs were in densely populated areas like Birmingham, Alabama, or Columbus, Ohio.

In the weeks after the public forum, the *Cambridge Chronicle* took a strong editorial stand against nerve agent testing, and other local groups also took public positions on the issue. In a March 20 letter to ADL, the presidents of the Cambridge, Arlington, and Belmont Leagues of Women Voters supported the ban on testing. Alma Triner, ADL's Vice President for Public Relations, told the *Chronicle* that the Leagues' position was "very disappointing" to the Company, which had contributed funds to League projects in the past. The League "has lost credibility in the eyes of ADL" as a result of its stand, Triner said.

While gaining local support, however, the movement lost ground in the courts. On March 12, ADL asked the State Appeals Court for a stay of Judge Hallisey's order; three days later Judge John Greaney complied, reinstating the injunction against enforcing Dr. Chalfen's regulation. Cambridge attorneys at once asked State Supreme Judicial Court Justice Paul Liacos to remove the case from the Appeals Court and hear it directly at the supreme court level, short-cutting one step of the appeals process. The case was heard by the Supreme Judicial Court on April 4th, but no immediate finding was expected. Although no formal announcements were made, it was assumed by Toxic Alert members that testing had resumed in the Levins Laboratory.

On March 30, 1985, the new Boston subway station next door to ADL was opened. Toxic Alert members took advantage of the large crowds to picket with the message that the entire station was inside the "zone of lethality." On April 5, a group called the Boston Committee for No Business as Usual held a "twitch-in" rally in front of ADL's offices. On April 12, at the annual meeting of Arthur D. Little stockholders, pickets walked the sidewalks in front of the Harvard Club in Boston, passing out leaflets questioning the ability of management to view the situation objectively.

ADL: The "twitch-in" was a demonstration by about six people who called themselves the "Revolutionary Communist Youth Brigade" and operate out of an office at M.I.T. The *Globe* covered the annual meeting but didn't do a story because the demonstration was a non-event involving the usual 8–10 people.

On April 19, State Rep. Thomas Gallagher introduced a bill which would ban the testing of chemical warfare agents within a mile of any home, business, or public road. For the next two months the scope of possible regulations was debated in the Joint Legislative Committee on Health Care, whose chairman toured the ADL laboratory and said he was much impressed. On June 12, ADL's Dr. William Augerson testified to the committee on the need for regulating *all* highly toxic chemicals, not just those designed as weapons. He named 16 "relatively common chemicals" whose toxicity, he said, equalled that of the agents prohibited in Cambridge. The list included strychnine, parathion, phosgene, arsine, and methyl isocyanate. A special Task Force was eventually set up by the legislature, to report back in the fall. At the same time, Cambridge's Scientific Advisory Committee continued to work on drafting an ordinance to control toxic substances in general.

On May 28, 1985, the Army's undersecretary of Research and Development, Amaretta Hoeber, met with ADL and Toxic Alert representatives in the offices of Senator Edward Kennedy to reiterate the nation's needs for this research and the Army's confidence in its safe conduct at Acorn Park. On June 3, the Cambridge City Council okayed a referendum question for the November ballot, asking voter opinion on the ADL testing work.

As the summer passed, both sides awaited the ruling of the Supreme Judicial Court. The Supreme Court of the United States would be the next legal step if the Massachusetts loser decided to appeal further. Toxic Alert members wondered about their own next steps, and expected Arthur D. Little again to avoid complying with the Health and Hospitals regulation. How, they pondered, could they most effectively raise the cost to ADL to the point where testing would be abandoned? In the meantime, testing continued at the Levins Laboratory.

Publisher Russel Pergament of the *Cambridge Tab* summarized the situation on July 23rd:

> The story is simple. ADL says they don't plan to manufacture these deadly nerve gases, a thimbleful of which can kill thousands. No sir. They plan to study ways of making these gases inert. That reminds me of the guy who was arrested for stealing hubcaps. When the police collared him he said, "But, officer, I wasn't stealing them, I was putting them back on." And so it is with ADL, who have double talked, double

dealed and deceived the city's health department since day one about their plans here. They never played straight with the city and so they rate no special considerations, especially in view of the great danger their work puts local families in.

ADL: Quoting a Russ Pergament editorial from *The Tab* as a voice of local opinion is like quoting *The National Enquirer* as an authority on national mores.

John Magee was unaware of the Pergament column and did not recall the local editorials. "Those things have no impact, really," he said. "Oh, we receive the papers, and of course we have a clipping service. And we recognize they have an impact on other people. But do they cause us to stop and ask ourselves whether we're doing the right thing? No."

Most ADL people, Magee said, believed the company's standing in the community had not been damaged by the controversy. "There may be some circles where our standing is diminished," he said, "and that may be true with some of our staff as well. But in other circles we've received sympathy—where people say, 'They got to you, just like they've gotten to Harvard or MIT or Polaroid in the past.' Still other circles have expressed substantial admiration for our willingness to stand up and fight."

Magee speculated on how he and his managers formed their impressions of the people arrayed against them. "When it becomes difficult to engage these people in a discussion of the technical issues," he said, "then you begin to consider the question, are there other issues that are driving them? We look for what brings them together. We know Ozonoff and Krimsky are very active in anti-military political activity.

"Ozonoff has been quoted as making some outlandish statements concerning the level of risk involved. The idea that one drop of this stuff could kill 10,000 people or whatever . . . that we have enough to kill . . . I don't know. . . . Anybody who is a serious student of the risks involved with toxic materials and dispersal issues *has* to see that as not being a factual estimate. It assumes people line up to get precisely the right dose. So there's got to be some kind of motivation here, to put out that kind of number. It's not put out as a factual analysis.

"We don't use gas at all. *We're* not the ones who are using misnomers or clouding the issue with semantics." Reminded that ADL's contracts included work on detection of gas, which seemed to imply the presence of gas, Magee paused. "I don't think we're generating any aerosols," he said. "I'd have to check."

Had the testing been pursued up to now as a matter of principle? "Well, there are principles and principles," said Magee. "If the principle is one of essential ethics, then you press it. But if it's a matter of being allowed to do something we think we ought to be allowed to do, then there is a practical limit to how far you want to press it, because there are alternatives. For example, if this is saying to us that Cambridge is no longer a healthy community for an organization like ours, then we have options. We have to address the issue of principle in that context."

CASE 36

The GM Acquisition of EDS: A Clash of Organizational Cultures*

In June, 1986, Bill Engelke, then of Electronic Data Systems (EDS), General Motors' data processing division, pondered his future. He had spent the past eleven years in data processing for GM, starting long before EDS was acquired to upgrade the GM facilities. Shortly after the acquisition, the acquired company was running the show in data processing for GM and had taken in the GM data processing personnel. EDS had methods, policies, and procedures that were very different from those previously employed at GM. While Bill saw benefits to GM in making some data processing changes, he didn't feel comfortable with the radical shifts that were occurring. He had been offered a lucrative severance package if he wanted to leave the organization. What was best for his career—stay with GM-EDS, or take the severance package and get out of the high-pressure environment that was consuming his vitality?

GM ACQUIRES EDS

In 1986, the General Motors Corporation was the world's largest manufacturing company with almost 900,000 employees and sales in excess of $100 billion (see Exhibit 1). The corporation had enjoyed a history of excellent leadership and ability to adapt to changes in the environment. In recent years, however, General Motors became a sluggish giant, overbureaucratic in decision making and unable to react effectively to environmental threats. Chairman and CEO Roger B. Smith attempted to streamline operations in the 1980s with a reorganization and refocus on the market. These changes had not yet improved the company's performance by 1990.

General Motors' share of the domestic car and truck market which had been above 50 percent fell to 40.3 percent in 1985 and further to 38.5 percent in 1986. Unofficial figures for 1987 showed that GM sold one million fewer vehicles than in the previous year and its share of the domestic market fell to about 33 percent. In 1986, the profits earned from operations fell behind those of Ford for the first time since 1924. Some of the decrease in earnings resulted from a $750 million buyout of the stock held by the Chairman of a GM subsidiary, H. Ross Perot of Electronic Data Systems (EDS).

EDS was purchased by GM in 1984 to consolidate GM's data processing operations. The purchase arrangement left EDS with a considerable amount of autonomy and the right to take on non-GM contracts. EDS Chairman Ross Perot was made a member of the GM Board of Directors. Conflicts in managerial style between Perot and GM executives caused

---

* Prepared by James K. McCollum and William D. Engelke, University of Alabama in Huntsville. Distributed by the North American Case Research Association.

EXHIBIT 1
General Motors Corporation and Consolidated Subsidiaries
Statement of Consolidated Income
Years Ended December 31, 1986, 1985, and 1984
(in Millions of Dollars)

	1986	*1985*	*1984**
Net sales and revenues:			
Manufactured products	$101,506.9	$95,268.4	$83,699.7
Computer systems services	1,306.8	1,103.3	190.2
Total net sales and revenues	102,813.7	96,371.7	83,889.9
Costs and expenses:			
Cost of sales and other operating charges, exclusive of items listed below	88,298.0	81,654.6	70,217.9
Selling, general, and administrative expenses	5,203.5	4,294.2	4,003.0
Depreciation of real estate, plants, and equipment	3,499.6	2,777.9	2,663.2
Amortization of special tools	2,596.1	3,083.3	2,236.7
Amortization of intangible assets	498.0	347.3	69.1
Special provision for scheduled plant closings and other restructurings	1,287.6	--	--
Total costs and expenses	101,382.8	92,157.3	79,189.9
Operating income	1,430.9	4,214.4	4,700.0
Other income less income deductions, net	983.1	1,299.2	1,713.5
Interest expense	(953.7)	(892.3)	(909.2)
Income before income taxes	1,460.3	4,621.3	5,504.3
United States, foreign, and other income taxes (credit)	(300.3)	1,630.3	1,805.1
Income after income taxes	1,760.6	2,991.0	3,699.2
Equity in earnings of nonconsolidated subsidiaries and associates (dividends received amounted to $1.7 in 1986, $100.5 in 1985 and $706.1 in 1984)	1,184.1	1,008.0	817.3
Net income	2,944.7	3,999.0	4,516.5
Dividends on preferred stocks	10.8	11.6	12.5
Earnings on common stocks	$ 2,933.9	$ 3,987.4	$ 4,504.0

* Certain amounts for 1984 have been reclassified to conform with 1985 classifications.
Source: General Motors Corporation Form 10-K for year ended December 31, 1986, page 22.

continual friction in the organization and the solution chosen by GM top management was to pay Perot twice the worth of his GM holdings to get him off the GM Board of Directors.

The previous initiatives by Roger Smith were hailed by observers such as Kanter (1983) and Naisbitt and Aburdene (1985) as farsighted and necessary for the corporation's entry into the 21st century. More recently, other observers such as Frons, Hampton, Mason (1986) and Todd (1987) faulted Smith for his handling of the conflict with Perot and for GM's failing profits and inability to compete successfully.

What was the state of the General Motors Corporation under Roger Smith's tutelage? Was it a strong, but sluggish giant that was gradually adapting to needed changes in its organizational structure and was in process of regaining predominance over the automotive industry? Was it a hopeless bureaucratic monster that will continue to sink under its own weight?

GENERAL MOTORS

Begun in 1908 by William C. Durant, the General Motors Corporation grew from a single company making the Buick automobile to become the world's largest automobile manufacturing organization with five automobile companies and a truck company in U.S. operations plus several overseas manufacturing companies. Durant brought the five car companies together by 1920 but was ousted by the Board of Directors because of his inability to control expenditures. The directors then turned to Alfred P. Sloan, Jr., who had a reorganization plan that corrected the corporation's problems and set it on the road to dominance in the U.S. automobile industry. The plan gave operational autonomy to the automobile companies while centralizing overall planning and financial operations at the corporate level. Under this plan the corporation became the industry leader in profitability as well as volume from the years 1928 until 1986. In 1986, the number of units sold in domestic operations still exceeded that of the other companies, but the corporation's profits fell behind those of Ford.

General Motors in the 1980s

When Roger Smith became GM's Chairman in 1981, the corporation was beginning to come back from the slump of the late 1970s. In an insightful book, John DeLorean (1979) severely criticized the corporation for its "management by committee" methods that caused slow reaction to environmental threats and opportunities. Smith also perceived too

EXHIBIT 2
General Motors Corporation and Consolidated Subsidiaries
Statement of Consolidated Income
Years Ended December 31, 1986, 1985, and 1984
(in Millions of Dollars, Except per Share Amounts)

	1986	*1985*	*1984*
Earnings attributable to:*			
$1—2/3 par value common stock	$2,607.7	$3,883.6	$4,498.3
Class E common stock (issued in 1984)	$ 136.2	$ 103.8	$ 5.7
Class H common stock (issued in December 1985)	$ 190.0	--	--
Average number of shares of common stocks outstanding (in millions):			
$1—2/3 par value common	317.6	316.3	315.3
Class E common (issued in 1984)	63.8	66.5	36.3†
Class H common (issued in December 1985)	63.9	--	--
Earnings per share attributable to (Note 10):*			
$1—2/3 par value common stock	$8.21	$12.28	$14.27
Class E common stock (issued in 1984)	$2.13	$1.57	$0.16†
Class H common stock (issued in December 1985)	$2.97	--	--

* Earnings and earnings per share attributable to common stocks in 1985 and 1984 have been restated to reflect the Class E common stock amendment approved by the stockholders in December 1985.

† Adjusted to reflect the two-for-one stock split in the form of a 100% stock dividend distributed on June 10, 1985.

Source: General Motors Corporation Form 10-K for year ended December 31, 1986, page 23.

much duplication of effort in the autonomy of the car companies and he devised a reorganization to streamline the company. Chevrolet, Pontiac, and Canadian operations were combined into a CPC division while Buick, Oldsmobile, and Cadillac were combined into a BOC division. These divisions were to combine the research and design functions of their subordinate companies in the interest of economy and rapid decision making. Even after the reorganization, however, there were as many as 14 layers of management from top to bottom compared to five layers in the Toyota Corporation. This excessive management overhead contributed to costs of $250 more per car than that spent by Ford or Chrysler.

Despite the excessive overhead, GM's earnings soared to record highs in 1984 and 1985. With the money in hand, Smith spent more than $45 billion to modernize factories, revitalize car lines and improve internal functioning.

Chairman Smith also saw the need for a single data processing unit that would standardize the computerized record keeping in all divisions. To accomplish this purpose, he arranged for the purchase of EDS, the largest data processing firm in the U.S.

Another acquisition made by Smith was intended to give GM greater diversification to cushion the impact of economic cycles and to assist in the development of a worldwide satellite communications network. This was the acquisition of Hughes Aircraft in 1985. Separate classes of GM stock were issued for both the EDS and Hughes acquisitions: Class E for EDS and Class H for Hughes. Stock dividends of one Class E share for each 20 shares of GM common in 1985 and one Class H share for each 20 shares of GM common in 1986 were distributed to GM's common stock owners (see Exhibit 2).

ELECTRONIC DATA SYSTEMS

EDS is a computer services company founded by H. Ross Perot in 1962. With $1,000 and a secretary, Perot went forth to sell data processing services complete with personnel and hardware. His first contract was with Frito-Lay and by Spring 1963 EDS had grown to seven employees working 18 hour days. Perot, a graduate of the U.S. Naval Academy, had made his start as a salesman for IBM. At IBM he set sales records and when his commission was capped and his suggestions for new IBM ventures were ignored, he left to form EDS. Perot required great dedication, high ethical and moral standards, and a stringent dress code for his employees. In return, he rewarded them well and was heavily committed to their well-being.

The company developed an entrepreneurial "can do" culture which stimulated growth and innovative software solutions for customer demands. Unlike GM which proceeded methodically in its committee-approved changes, EDS had a reputation for "ferocious internal debate." The entrepreneurial spirit brought about a huge expansion to the point where EDS had annual revenues in excess of $786 million by 1984 (EDS Annual Report, 1984). Some of its large customers in addition to GM include the U.S. Navy, U.S. Postal Service, General Mills, and Blue Cross/Blue Shield.

EDS offered services to its customers in the following ways:

Facilities management: EDS assumed virtually all of the data processing requirements for the customer.

Systems integration: EDS designed, implemented, and installed the appropriate combination of hardware and software, including telecommunications equipment, integrated into a total system to fulfill customer requirements.

Communications service: EDS designed complete communications systems for customers and overseas installations, managed the systems, and kept them updated with advancements in the state of the art.

Fiscal agent: EDS processed and paid claims and coordinated benefits for customers.

Other professional services: EDS also provided consulting, engineering, education, clerical, and training services related to data processing.

The company directed its business through five operating groups:

1. *Insurance:* Providing service to health and commercial insurance companies, universities, state and local governments, and companies and governmental agencies responsible for Medicare Programs.
2. *Finance and industrial:* Providing services to companies that had significant data processing requirements related to financial, inventory, and/or production controls.
3. *Government:* Handling contracts with federal, state, and local governmental agencies.
4. *Health services:* Servicing health care institutions.
5. *International:* Operating and maintaining data processing activities in a number of foreign companies.

In 1984, these five groups contributed revenues as follows: Insurance, 23 percent; finance and industrial, 30 percent; governmental, 41 percent; health services, 4 percent; international, 2 percent.

GM ACQUISITION OF EDS

In the early 1980s, GM had amassed huge profits and was cash rich. With the cash, Roger Smith sought acquisitions that would support his grand strategy of modernization that would prepare the company for the 21st century. Thus on October 18, 1984, GM purchased EDS with its 15,000 employees for $2.5 billion. The purchase price was 35 times EDS's expected earnings for 1984. At the time, Reilly (1984) noted that "it would take GM 17 years to recoup its investment if EDS maintains the 23% annual compound growth rate of the past five years." Under terms of the acquisition, GM data processing personnel were transferred into EDS.

It was envisioned that EDS would initially get 75 percent of its revenues and business from GM. Additionally, Smith hoped that the entrepreneurial spirit of EDS would invigorate his stagnating organization. To perpetuate EDS stock's image as a high-tech, high-growth offering, performance of Class E stock, EDS was linked to EDS's profit rather than GM's. GM's financial planners believed that this would keep the stock's multiple high and maintain investor interest.

Perot entered into the new relationship with enthusiasm. He retained his position as chairman of EDS and was put on the GM Board of Directors. At that time, he stated, "This is truly a new beginning and the greatest day in EDS's history." Roger Smith stated, "Together, GM and EDS will create the largest and most technologically advanced computer services company in the world."

With more than one hundred IBM mainframe computers scattered through its facilities, GM was the single largest computer user outside of the U.S. government. However, its computer operations were haphazard and duplicative, each computer represented a different fiefdom, and few could communicate with others. EDS thrust itself on this highly differentiated group of data processing facilities and attempted to integrate them using common software, thus reducing software maintenance costs. The 16,000 former GM data processing employees were brought with reluctance into the EDS organization. At many facilities, the GM data processing personnel didn't know they had been subsumed by the EDS organization in advance of the arrival of EDS managers who came on the scene saying, "You take orders from us now."

By 1986, EDS had combined more than 50 of GM's data processing facilities into a linked network of 14 information processing centers nationwide. With its ability to process claims for insurance carriers, EDS streamlined GM's benefit claims and insurance information to employees. In 1984, GM's medical costs ran to approximately $2.2 billion or $450 per car. Soon after the merger, EDS created a database to capture all health claims and get a start on controlling these costs.

In most of its previous (non-GM) contracts, EDS provided all its services under fixed-price agreements. This allowed EDS's customers to accurately forecast their costs for data processing and EDS to reap the benefits of its own increases in efficiency. EDS proposed that this method also be used to encompass the costs of its services to GM. GM agreed to negotiate fixed-price agreements for the bulk of EDS's services, seeing this as an additional cost saving measure.

But all was not sweetness and light in the new GM-EDS organization. Several lawsuits were initiated by GM data processing personnel due to the change in their employment status. Disgruntled GM personnel drafted a petition to request affiliation with the United Autoworkers Union (UAW), an eventuality that horrified EDS's managers. The EDS hierarchy believed that there was no place for a union in the organization. The attempt at union affiliation was quashed.

About 600 GM data processing personnel left the organization when offered a severance package. They left behind an organization that was severely divided—the GM data processors and the EDS personnel. The two groups were integrated into a single organization with great difficulty. Bill Engelke stayed with the company for several more months. Then he resigned citing continuing high stress.

The Perot Buyout

Early in the relationship, conflicts emerged between Perot's entrepreneurial style and the GM style. Perot accused GM of moving too slowly in its efforts to revitalize itself and felt that the company had lost customer contact. The excessive use of committees and task forces earlier decried by DeLorean were still much in evidence and a stumbling block to progress, in Perot's opinion. He once related how GM studies problems to death. "The first EDS'er that sees a snake kills it. At GM, the first thing you do is form a committee on snakes, then you bring in a consultant who knows a lot about snakes. Third thing you do is talk about it for a year."

Additionally, Perot criticized GM's poor use of people. As he saw it, no matter how much was invested in new technology, the company would never be competitive until it began to make better use of its greatest resource, the 800,000 employees. He criticized GM for taking five years from go-ahead decision to actual production on the Saturn automobile. His caustic comment on the long time to create a single auto was "It only took us four years to win World War II."

And at a time when GM was facing its earnings slump of the mid-1980s, Perot criticized GM constantly. He criticized GM's bureaucracy, its inability to act swiftly, and its preferential treatment of upper management. He also opposed GM's decision to close nine plants and he opposed the 1985 acquisition of Hughes Aircraft.

Insisting upon a high degree of independence for himself and for EDS, he refused to allow the parent company to audit EDS and he insisted on a separate pay structure from that of GM for EDS employees. EDS had pioneered in fixed-price contracts pegged to a client's unit volume of data processing. When EDS reduced its costs and still gave the client the agreed upon level of service, it made a bigger profit and EDS executives responsible for the efficiencies were given bonuses. GM managers, however, approached the pricing question from a strict cost point of view. They balked at signing contracts that would enrich EDS managers and not benefit themselves. Interestingly, in 1987, GM changed its salary compensation and bonus plan to a "pay for performance" incentive system similar to the incentive system for EDS managers.

In June 1986, Perot wrote a letter to Smith stating that he either wanted to run EDS his way or be bought out. Smith started looking for a way to separate Perot from GM and negotiated with AT&T to try to sell part of EDS in November 1986. These negotiations were not successful, so Smith made an offer to buy Perot and other top EDS executives out of the company.

The total payment to Perot was $742.8 million. GM paid Perot $396 million for the Class E shares he held and $346.8 million for contingent notes and tax liabilities Perot sustained.

In the buyout agreement, Perot was prevented from making an attempt to take over EDS for five years, from criticizing Smith and other GM managers, and from starting a computer services operation that would compete with EDS for three years. True to form, Perot expressed distaste for the buyout noting that the money paid to him could have been better used to save assembly lines from being shut down and jobs being lost.

Assessment

Despite the problems incurred, GM's acquisition of EDS has, however, accomplished some positive actions. The standardization of health claims saved the company $200 million per year. The networking of worldwide communications allowed for better decisions, and the combining of logistical computer nets saved inventory costs. Automation played a greater role as shown by the GM-EDS new pickup truck development program that included a revolutionary approach to plant floor information networks.

Those benefits were not, however, reflected in GM profit and loss statements. The corporation's profits were going downward as shown in the accompanying financial statements. Meanwhile, EDS's fortunes were soaring. Since GM gives EDS nearly 100 percent of its data processing business, much of GM was losing ground while the EDS subsidiary profited. EDS's Class E stock dividend increased 31 percent in fourth quarter, 1987, to reflect the strong earnings of the subsidiary.

Was this a point for concern? EDS's profitability ultimately comes back to GM. As the largest stockholder of EDS (GM Class E stock), GM could use those profits as it saw fit.

And was GM supposed to turn itself around in a year after going downward for three years? Probably not. GM's goals in modernizing its factories, setting up the Saturn Corporation, and acquiring EDS and Hughes aircraft were to take the corporation into the 21st century. The moves made by Smith brought about a short-term loss, but have the potential to bring about huge benefits in the future, if top-level decision making is improved.

Roger Smith was described as a man America needs, who "in an era of managers obsessed with quarterly results . . . dared to dream vast dreams and plan decades into the future" (Moore, 1988). But he may have ignored the quarterly results too much—quality suffered, styling stagnated, and profits and market share fell. Smith confidently predicted that GM will again capture 49 percent of the market and that Ford and Chrysler will also have to engage in a modernization campaign like that at GM, but at greater cost. Will they, like GM, spend an exorbitant amount of money buying out a board member who was taken on as the result of an acquisition?

Another possible outcome for EDS is that Perot would form another computer services company after the three years in which he is banned from doing so and the key people of EDS would leave the GM subsidiary and join Perot. This would be another blow to EDS's spirit and culture and GM would be left with a hollow shell if enough of the key people leave.

The money GM paid for EDS and then paid to get rid of Perot could have been spent on improving manufacturing and information processing facilities and staff. However, the EDS, GM affair may be restating some old lessons that corporate America is relearning. The *Economist* (December 1986) claims it is better to hire new skills and buy innovative components than to acquire the companies that provide them. The clash of organizational cultures can be disruptive.

The organizational cultures of the parent and its subsidiary in this case were greatly divergent. GM needed the entrepreneurial EDS organization, yet it could not ingest the EDS founder and many of the EDS methods. Although Perot was the companies' largest stockholder, he was unable to move the giant in ways he perceived to be right and instead, he was moved. Meanwhile, plants were closed and market share was lost to overseas and domestic competitors. Profitability of the parent organization decreased. Six years after the merger the issue is not resolved. The pluses provided by EDS do not outweigh the minuses caused by this culture clash.

References

Barker, R. and Weiss, G. (1984). "The Odd Couple: Will GM and EDS find Happiness Together?" *Barrons* (July 9), 6.

Buss, D. D. and Guiles, M. G. (1986). "GM-Perot Split is the Talk of the Town," *The Wall Street Journal* (December 3), 3.

Chandler, A. D. (1962). *Strategy and Structure: Chapters in the History of the American Industrial Enterprise,* Cambridge, Massachusetts: MIT Press.

Cook, W. J. (1986). "Perot's War with GM Ends in $743 Million Goodbye," *U.S. News and World Report* (December 15), 52.

DeLorean, J. A. (1979). *On a Clear Day You Can See General Motors.* New York: Avon Books.

Frons, M., Hampton, W. D., and Mason, T. (1986). "Ross Perot's Crusade," *Business Week* (October 6), 6.

Glassman, J. M. (1986). "The Wreck of General Motors," *New Republic* (December 29), 22.

"GM Boots Perot." (1986). *Newsweek* (December 15), 56–8.

Gray, B. J. (1988). "Top 50," *Human Resource Management Executive* 2 (January), 11.

Hampton, J. and Norman, J. R. (1987). "General Motors: What Went Wrong," *Business Week* (March 16), 106.

Kanter, R. M. (1983). *The Change Masters.* New York: Simon and Schuster.

Keller, M. (1989). *Rude Awakening: The Rise, Fall and Struggle for Recovery of General Motors.* William Morrow.

Lener, U. C. and Cohen, L. P. (1984). "GM to Acquire EDS in Transaction Valued at as Much as $2.55 Billion," *The Wall Street Journal* (June 29), 1.

Levin, Doron P. (1989). *Irreconcilable Differences: Ross Perot versus General Motors.* Boston: Little, Brown and Company.

Lienert, P. (1987). "Letter from Detroit," *Road and Track* (March), 110–11.

Moore, T. (1988). "Make or Break Time for General Motors," *Fortune* 117 (February 15), 32–42.

Naisbitt, J. and Aburdene, P. (1985). *Reinventing the Corporation.* New York: Warner Books, Inc.

"Punctured by Perot." (1986). *The Economist* (December), 15.

Reilley, B. (1984). "Is Perot Good for General Motors?" *Fortune* (August 6), 124.

Schlesinger, J. M. (1988). "GM New Compensation Plan Reflects General Trend Tying Pay to Performance," *The Wall Street Journal* (January 26), 37.

Sloan, A. P. (1964). *My Years with General Motors.* Garden City, New York: Doubleday and Company.

NAME INDEX

SUBJECT INDEX

ABOUT THE AUTHORS

Gregory Dess is a professor of strategic management at the University of Texas at Arlington. He received his Ph.D. from the University of Washington. Prior to entering academia, he worked as an industrial engineer at the Western Electric Company in Atlanta, Georgia, and Charlotte, North Carolina. Professor Dess has been active in several professional organizations, and he recently served on the executive committee of the Business Policy and Strategy Division of the Academy of Management. He is currently a member of the editorial boards of the *Academy of Management Journal*, *Journal of Management*, and *Journal of Business Research*. He has presented papers at several professional meetings, and his work has appeared in such journals as the *Administrative Science Quarterly*, *Academy of Management Journal*, *Academy of Management Review*, *Strategic Management Journal*, and *Journal of Management*. He is co-author of an article, "Nurturing Strategic Coherency," that won first place in the 1991 Planning Forum Competition and was published in *Planning Review*.

Alex Miller is an associate professor of management at the University of Tennessee at Knoxville. He earned an M.B.A. from Amos Tuck School of Business, where he was a Tuck Scholar, and a Ph.D. from the University of Washington. In 1989 he was a visiting research scholar at the Cranfield Institute of Technology in England. He is on the editorial board of the *Journal for Business Venturing*, and his research has been published in such journals as the *Academy of Management Journal*, *Strategic Management Journal*, *Journal for Business Venturing*, and *Journal for High Technology Management Research*. Professor Miller is an active consultant whose clients have included Procter & Gamble, Rockwell International, Martin Marietta, Eastman Kodak, Freddie Mac, and the Internal Revenue Service, as well as a number of smaller firms. He is a member of the twelve-person team responsible for designing and team-teaching the innovative integrated course that forms the first-year core of Tennessee's unique M.B.A. program. He is also the only two-time winner of the Faculty Accomplishment Award from students in the Tennessee Organization of M.B.A.s.